V&R

Novum Testamentum et Orbis Antiquus/ Studien zur Umwelt des Neuen Testaments

Volume 127

Alan H. Cadwallader

Colossae, Colossians, Philemon

The Interface

Vandenhoeck & Ruprecht

Bibliographic information published by the Deutsche Nationalbibliothek:
The Deutsche Nationalbibliothek lists this publication in the Deutsche Nationalbibliographie; detailed bibliographic data available online: https://dnb.de.

Typesetting by SchwabScantechnik, Göttingen
Printed and bound by ® Hubert & Co, Göttingen
Printed in the EU

Vandenhoeck & Ruprecht Verlage | www.vandenhoeck-ruprecht-verlage.com

ISSN 1420-4592
ISBN 978-3-525-50002-6

To colleagues and friends in the
Colloquium on Material Culture and Ancient Religion

To its leaders, Steven J. Friesen, Daniel Schowalter,
Christine Thomas and James Walters

And in memory of Dennis E. Smith

Table of Contents

Acknowledgements

Colossae has been a research focus for me since 1998. The inquiry into its history and remains has uncovered clues from across the world, from The Hermitage in St Petersburg to the Special Libraries at the University of Aberdeen to the British Institute in Ankara, and so many more collections that occasionally will be glimpsed in these pages. Museoarcheology has been a critical component of the investigation, built on the slightest hint and clue coming from individuals or submerged in a footnote in an outlier text. The expanding digitalization of materials — coins, inscriptions, papyri and artifacts — has released an invaluable volume of evidence, some of which has proven intricately relevant to the study of the site but most providing a rich store-house of *comparanda* that has helped to elucidate the jewels of the site itself. Most valuable of all have been the feet on the ground and, occasionally, eyes in the heights. My primary purpose herein, an objective that has driven me for more than two decades, is to provide as complete a coverage as possible of the material evidence of Colossae as can be recovered to date. I am under no illusion that this accumulation will not be supplemented in coming years; indeed, my hope is that herein will be found as complete a gathering as currently possible that will enable progress in the research on Colossae to be untrammeled by the need to repeat the foundational aggregation that has pre-occupied me these years past. My secondary purpose has been to establish that textual materials, most fulsomely two books of the Christian Testament, can fruitfully be brought into dialogue with the material resources that have been mustered. In that sense, this is a hybrid work, neither occupying the sometimes hermetic bubble of Christian commentary nor acquiescing in the sometimes justifiable suspicion of Christian texts for historical enquiry.

Inevitably, and thankfully, this work has been fostered, encouraged, supported (sometimes with good Turkish coffee) and critiqued (sometimes with fine wine in disparate locales). Those who have been almost constant companions and those who have simply dropped in with serendipitous offerings are manifold. There is always the danger in surveying such a span of time, that the memory of names and faces will suffer a glitch, much like the random fortunes of inscriptions, one passing to lime manufacture, another preserved in a museum. So it is with some trepidation that I make an attempt to recall those whose contributions have been essential to the shaping of this work.

From germinating days at Flinders University in South Australia, Michael Trainor and Claire Smith held out the hopes and vision of research into Colossae. Their expertise conjoined the two poles of the spectrum mentioned previously; their congeniality demonstrated that a hybrid enterprise was possible, indeed desirable. The enthusiasm of post-graduate students in the Flinders Greek Reading Group ensured that I was constantly fired to draw in material and textual evidence for study and was made accountable for premature interpretations and challenged to consider alternatives. The membership of course changed over the years; a number have articulated into their own fields of excellence. Nonetheless, the names of Rosemary Canavan, Julie Hooke (†), Joan Riley, Emily Harding, Christine Lawrance (†), Jutta Jokiranta, Cameron Doody, Shelly Li are inscribed as honorands of the early years.

Librarians can be gate-keepers to a world of discovery; they can also energize that role with their welcome, their suggestions and their introductions to other scholars. The list is long and some have since moved on to other ventures: Beth Prior at Flinders not only ensured that ways were found for materials but even took time out of her own sabbatical to dig out manuscripts at the British Library; Kimberley Stansfield at the London Library; Sue Hemmens at the Archbishop Marsh Library; Ciara Stewart at the National Library of Ireland; Paul Jackson at the Joint Library of the Hellenic and Roman Societies at the University of London; Patsy Williams and Louisa Yates at Gladstone Library; Michelle Gait at the Special Libraries at Aberdeen; Dimitrios Chronis at the Halki Theological Library at Heybeliada; Fr Nicodemos at the Leimonos Monastery on Lesbos; and the numerous staff at the British Library and at Dumbarton Oaks Library — all these went out of their way to hunt down rare books and manuscripts to assist my research.

Archive and museum directors have been similarly generous in their accommodation of my often very particular requests, at times supplementing the provision of access with a well-timed tea, coffee or meal. Special thanks to Ian Jenkins (†) of the Greek and Roman Antiquities Department at the British Museum, and at the same institution, Andrew Meadows in Numismatics and Sheila O'Connell in Prints; to Hilary Chambers of the Warrington Record Office; to Georgios Matzelos, Nikos Giannaros and Anna Lyssikatou who opened for me the treasures of the Patriarchal Institute of Patristic Studies in Thessalonike; to Peter Catt for permission to view the substantial coin collection at St John's Anglican Cathedral in Brisbane; to Svetlana Adaxina, Zhanna Etsina and Olga Gorskaya for uncovering an exquisite intaglio-ring held in The Hermitage Museum at St Petersburg; to Hugh Elton, Lutgarde Vandeput, Gülgün Erdivan and Yaprak Eran at the British Institute in Ankara; to Jonathan Shea curator of lead seals at Dumbarton Oaks; to Maurice Tucker, Master of University College Durham; to Karsten Darmen at the Münzkabinett of the

Staatliche Museum in Berlin; to James G. Crow at the Gertrude Bell Archives at the University of Newcastle-on-Tyne; and to Eugene Rae at the Royal Geographic Society in London.

No attempt to promote scholarly research can succeed without the learned contributions of colleagues. It will be clear from the Dedication how important the leadership and membership of the *Colloquium on Material Culture and Ancient Religion* has been in my formation. They too belong among the following. Sometimes a snatch of conversation, sometimes an extended discussion, sometimes a harsh reminder of either methodology or missing reference, sometimes the digging out of a buried source, have made an inestimable impact on my thinking and writing. Of course, being academics, they are still likely to dispute some of the results presented here, whether lingering mistakes or determined lines of interpretation. That is as it should be. Nonetheless, for their timely, even if, at times, intemperate remarks, I remain deeply grateful. So manifold thanks (in no particular order) to Marie Turner, Michael Theophilos, Elizabeth Minchin, John Chryssavgis, Müjgan Koç, Greg Horsley, Flora Karagianni, David Sim, Endor Varinlioğlu, Thomas Corsten, Felicity Harley, David Laiteo, Ali Ceylan, Paul Foster, Charlotte Roueché, Erim Konakçi, James McLaren, Cédric Brélaz, Ekatarini Tsalampouni, Bilal Sögüt, Daryn Lehoux, Cristian Tomas, Stephan Heilen, Angela Standhartinger, Larry Welborn, Christina Kokkinia, Valeriy Alikin, Katharina Martin, Bahadır Duman, Ros Kearsley, Patrick Armstrong, Pauline Allen, Chris de Wet, Ismail Albayrak, Wolfgang Hübner, Lukas Bormann, Celal Şimşek, Bronwen Neil, Haşim Yıldız, Wendy Mayer, Ulrich Huttner, Tina Shepardson, Andrew Burnett, Geoff Dunn, Hatice Erdemir, Peter Arzt-Grabner, Kosta Simic, Mike White, Peter Lewis, Halvor Moxnes and by no means least, Jim Harrison.

But the collegiate of learning and research is not the complete picture. Numerous people have been incredibly generous in time, interest and in contributing their knowledge and abilities for my research. More than that, they have offered hospitality, even, in some cases, without any introduction to me. I have learned that, at least at ground level, the fundamental convention of Turkish life is hospitality. Particular thanks must be extended to Deniz Canpolat and his wider family, especially his uncle, the novelist Kemal Yaçsin, to a succession of Governors of Denizli, Yusuf Ziya Goksü, Gazi Şimşek and Abdülkadir Demir, and mayors of Honaz, Melüt Tüfekçi and Turgut Devecioğlu and their staff, to the Denizli Rotary and Rotoract Clubs who invited updates on research, to local media professionals, Hakan Kurt and Irfan Çam, and most especially to the Iyilikçi and Bayrak families whose kindness and assistance were boundless.

A particular debt needs to be acknowledged for the support and professionalism of the Vandenhoeck & Ruprecht publishers who committed to bringing this book into the light of day, most especially Jörg Persch, Izaak de Hulster and the editors of the series, with a special thanks to the ever-patient and helpful Miriam Lux and Renate Rehkopf.

Finally, a special thanks is due to my son Daniel, whose architectural design expertise was in constant demand for the presentation of photographs and diagrams herein, and to my partner, the novelist Robyn Cadwallader, who has managed to combine a keen interest in my work with a healthy sense of humor through the long months of pandemic lockdown.

August 2021

Abbreviations

The abbreviations followed are those recommended by:
- the *Association Internationale d'Épigraphie Grecque et Latine* (for epigraphical sources)
- the *Checklist of Greek, Latin, Demotic and Coptic Papyri, Ostraca and Tablets* (for papyri)
- the *Society of Biblical Literature Handbook of Style*[2] (for classical and biblical texts)
- *L'année philologique* (for journals).

Where additional abbreviations are given, they are clarified in the text.

All photographs are by the author unless otherwise specified.

Introduction: Colossae and a material life

The revival of interest in artifacts and spatial arrangements of the ancient Greek, Roman and Phrygian worlds has led to the "material turn" in recent classical and New Testament scholarship.[1] This has had enormous benefits in re-situating New Testament writings as participants in the ancient world rather than as reinforcements of ecclesial positions. The approaches are generally less interested in archaeology as biblical proofs. Rather material culture reconnects biblical texts with the visual, spatial and societal locale from which they emerged, to which they contributed and within which they competed. Helmut Koester was adamant that "To understand the history of religions, it is necessary to study all materials relating to the life of a society, including nonliterary data — not as the 'background' of early Christianity but as the world of the early Christians."[2] The appreciation of the past, interpreted through various disciplines and theoretical constructs, enables contemporary Pauline readers to gain a more nuanced understanding of the meaning of texts and of the demand for hermeneutical sophistication in appropriating the past.

1 See, for example, L. Mitchell and L. Rubinstein (eds.), *Greek History and Epigraphy: Essays in honour of P. J. Rhodes* (Swansea: Classical Press of Wales, 2009); N. P. DesRosiers and L. C. Vuong (eds.), *Religious Competition in the Greco-Roman World* (Atlanta, GA: SBL, 2016); M. Arnhold, H. O. Maier, and J. Rüpke (eds.), *Seeing the God: Image, Space, Performance and Vision in the Religion of the Roman Empire* (Tübingen: Mohr Siebeck, 2018); D. C. Burnett, *Studying the New Testament through Inscriptions: An Introduction* (Peabody, MA: Hendrickson Academic, 2019); M. Kotrosits, *The Lives of Objects: Material Culture, Experience and the Real in the History of Early Christianity* (Chicago: University of Chicago Press, 2020). Note also the Harvard Theological Studies monographs edited by S. J. Friesen, D. N. Schowalter *et al.* and *The First Urban Churches* series, edited by J. R. Harrison and L. L. Welborn.

2 H. Koester, "Epilogue: Current Issues in New Testament Scholarship," in *The Future of Early Christianity: Essays in Honor of Helmut Koester* edited by B. A. Pearson (Minneapolis: Fortress Press, 1991), 473.

This remembering is nothing new. It was played out in the dynamics of urban and rural life in the ancient world.[3] For a center with Colossae's immense chronological span, the memory of past ages was etched into the topography of settlement, the negotiations of the flux and continuity of change in material expressions and even into the name that governed the identity of its inhabitants. That memory was fluid, as much constructed by the inherited material and narrative traces as construed by the demands and conceptual frameworks that each passing "present" brought to bear in the handling of the bequest. Occasional stations of memories occurred, but, if nothing else, the renowned ethnic mix in ancient Anatolia testifies to the fragility of the stationary. In this sense, the modern search for ancient Colossae is a participant in memory-making, albeit harnessed to different epistemological tools and interests, themselves also as subject to change as the remembrance(s) they construct.

But what is clear is that no longer are texts either privileged or sealed from their participation in materialist contexts, contexts replete with actors expressing a variety of responses. Even the texts themselves have been recognized as material artifacts that have their own material artifice contributing to a wider engagement than simply with the written documentation they house. In this sense, like an inscription, their construction occurs amongst a relative minority of human (and sometimes animal) contributors, but their impulse, performance, perception, appreciation and sheer survival encompasses a far wider audience, frequently consumerist if not illiterate (in the ancient world). It is worth recalling that, in spite of the mantra of the poverty of inscriptions from ancient Colossae to date, many of the epitaphs that have survived have done so *in situ*, that is, in the recognized city necropolis. These known epitaphs span almost three hundred years of the life of the necropolis (according to paleographical and internal dating methods). The analysis of anepigraphic, visible graves extends this period to half a millennium; the borrowed Phrygian typologies of graves or parts of graves touch a millennium of appropriated and transformed remembrance (see chapter 12). This most primal expression of memory — the management of the memory of the dead — demonstrates the ongoing contribution of material remains and textual testimony (in epigraphy and, less securely, archival record) to generations of Colossians and even now to contemporary historical researchers who, like me, are driven to relinquish the ephemeral world of the text and return the text to the world. Textuality, as Andrej Petrovic argues, is predicated on materiality,[4] but not merely on the material on which a text is cast but the sweep of materiality in which such a text gains a meaningful life.

3 See F. Rojas, *The Pasts of Roman Anatolia: Interpreters, Traces, Horizons* (Cambridge: Cambridge University Press, 2019).

4 A. Petrovic, "The Materiality of Text: An Introduction," in *The Materiality of Text — Placement, Perception, and Presence of Inscribed Texts in Classical Antiquity* edited by A. Petrovic, I. Petrovic and E. Thomas (Leiden: Brill, 2019), 4.

The beginnings of modern material awareness of Colossae

In the sixteenth century, a relatively large number of European powers began to negotiate mercantile openings with the Ottoman sultans resplendent at "Le Porte", that is, old Constantinople, modern Istanbul. Trade was displacing military encounters as the preferred means of accumulating wealth and influence. At this stage, this was not a colonizing venture, though the attitudes that shaped that later development were already apparent. John Speed's popular map of "The Turkish Empire" provided a reader's hermeneutic in its margin, "The Turk is admired for nothing more than his sudden advancement to so great an Empire."[5] That Empire embraced huge tracts of land and peoples and provided access to spices, silk and other desirable goods, and created a demand for wool and mechanical "toys".

By the seventeenth century, France, Germany, Venice and England had a significant business presence in Constantinople/Istanbul, Smyrna and Aleppo further east. The Dutch, Swedish and other smaller European countries were also carving an active trading mission across the Ottoman Empire. Frequently, these mercantile companies were headed by a consul, who had much of the authority of a government diplomat, as well as responsibilities for the owners of "factories" (that is businesses) who ventured under license from the same country as the diplomat. But the larger companies also maintained chaplains whose primary charge was the spiritual care of the members and associates of the respective companies. These chaplains were also expected to promote learning and culture so that European identity would not be lost in the East, indeed would be demonstrated to be superior.

The opportunity to visit sites on the ground that had previously, for two hundred years or more, been substantially confined to a textual memorialization (for Europeans), brought a fundamental and radical change to interpretive method. The geographically blessed Smyrna, whose commerce and trade — the filthy lucre of material reality — had managed to shield the city's fortunes from Byzantine into Ottoman times, was a fitting capital from which to launch coastal and inland explorations. More importantly perhaps, cultured gatherings and the maintenance of loose records of findings established a reservoir of base knowledge. This in turn encouraged a gradual increase in understanding,[6] as well as a measure of competition to outdo one another's "finds".[7] Charles Perry could barely contain his sarcasm after Richard Pococke

5 J. Speed, *A Prospect of the Most Famous Parts of the World* (London: George Humble, 1626/7), sv.

6 F. Hasselquist, *Voyages and travels in the Levant: in the years 1749, 50, 51, 52. Containing observations in natural history etc, particularly on the Holy Land and the natural history of the Scriptures* (London: printed for L. Davis and C. Reymers, 1766), 22, 51.

7 This competition nudges into view with the occasional sharp barb of rebuke from one writer about another, often accusing of plagiarism or at least unacknowledged or distorted contributions. Jacob Spon's friendship with George Wheler evaporated when the former mis-appro-

passed off as his own labor sketches in his own book published in 1745.[8] He wrote, "This we presume is what our Betters have sometimes done before us; and that, perhaps, with less Candour and Ingenuousness, not acknowledging that they borrowed them, but given them to the World as the genuine Fruits of their own Pains and Dexterity."[9]

Evidently, there were gains, such as ecclesial and educational preferment, to be made from publishing as well as collecting artifacts and accounts of exploring Asia Minor.[10] The seven churches of Revelation, and, in Laodikeia's case, the bordering cities of Hierapolis and Colossae, were especially targeted for these cultural forays. But they were made possible by the extensive provision of economic and administrative supports by the Levant companies. Needless to say they provided important returns — confirmations of attitudes of Europeans about "Mahometan" Turks and "decadent" Greeks; a material support for the Renaissance knowledge project; and a fairly constant supply of artifacts, from coins to pottery, sculptures to inscriptions. One only has to peruse the eighteenth century auction catalogues of estate sales of deceased European aristocrats to gain some idea of how much additional material, besides the formal business goods, had been shipped from Ottoman ports. Laura Nasrallah's recent sketch of the "material turn" has focused on the nineteenth and early twentieth century.[11] This enabled North American involvement to be factored. But in reality the foundation goes back two centuries earlier and beyond.[12]

Two early chaplains of the English Levant Company stand out — the Reverend Doctor John Luke (1635?–1702) and the Reverend Thomas Smith (1638–1701) — the former helping the other to be awarded his position.[13] Luke

---

priated significant parts of the latter's work: G. Wheler, *A Journey to Greece* (London: Cademan, Kettlewell and Churchill, 1682), preface. Paul Rycaut seems to have considered that his position as consul authorized him to "borrow" and not return notes and journals made by the Rev'd John Luke and William Trumbull; see S. Anderson, *An English Consul in Turkey: Paul Rycaut at Smyrna 1667–1668* (Oxford: Clarendon Press, 1989), 282. So concerned was Thomas Smith that his Latin books were going to be translated into English by another (Wheler? Without acknowledgement?) that this became a spur to doing the work himself: *Remarks upon the Manners, Religion and Government of the Turks together with a Survey of the Seven Churches of Asia, as They Now Lye in Their Ruines* (London: Moses Pitt, 1678), preface.

8 R. Pococke, *Description of the East and Some Other Countries* (London: W. Bowyer, 2 vols, 1745).

9 C. Perry, *A View of the Levant particularly of Syria, Egypt and Greece, In which their Antiquities, Government, Politics, Maxims, Manners and Customs (with many other Circumstances and Contingencies) are attempted to be Described and Treated on* (London: T. Woodward, C. Davis & J. Shuckburgh, 1743), xv. Perry was not the only one whose work was appropriated by Pococke; see R. Finnegan (ed.), *Letters from Abroad: the Grand Tour Correspondence of Richard Pococke and Jeremiah Milles* (Piltown: Pococke Press, vol 3, 2019), 8–12. He lifted entire sections from the volumes of Spon and Wheler as well!

10 N. Glaisyer, *The Culture of Commerce in England 1660–1720* (Suffolk: Boydell, 2006), 80.

11 L. S. Nasrallah, *Archaeology and the Letters of Paul* (Oxford: Oxford University Press, 2019).

12 See T. M. P. Duggan, "On early antiquarians in Asia Minor to the start of the 19th century," *Gephyra* 17 (2019): 115–67.

13 Glaisyer, *Culture of Commerce*, 72.

was chaplain at Smyrna 1664–1669; Smith was chaplain at Constantinople 1668–1670. These two Church of England clergymen, as almost all who were appointed for the consolation of the Levant Company personnel, were required, in their application for the position, to deliver a sermon attended by up to a hundred people. This extravagant employment panel would then vote on whether the audition had gained the applicant the desired appointment.

John Luke's sermon provides a revelatory window into the change that was occurring in biblical scholarship. His was not the typical sermon, either in length (it was nearly twice as long as most) or content. The usual application sermon extolled business as a key means of demonstrating piety. Such an exponent was Edmund Chishull (chaplain 1702–1710). He draped his sermon about his assigned text, Psalm 107: "those that go down to the sea in ships to do business on the great waters". He argued from the general piety — that one should "prove the glory of God as the principal Aim of our Undertakings" — to the specific application that one should "show that the glory of God may more especially be promoted by Travel and Foreign Commerce". He unabashedly applied the epithet "the great Proprietor" to God.[14]

John Luke's performance, however, neither had as easy a text (he was assigned 1 Cor 15:29 that speaks of baptism of the dead)[15] nor delivered a saccharine blend of morality and commerce.[16] Rather, Luke repeatedly trumpets the "plain" reading of Scripture, one of the hallmarks of protestant exegetical method. It is clear that for Luke, history, along with the views and opinions of the ancient church — those closest to the text's writing — were critical components in the establishment of this "plain" reading. No longer was "plainness" to be established by traditional reiterations repeated over time or overweaning attention to grammatical and philological dissection. Striking in his survey of the various opinions about the Pauline verse was his assertion that the text ought not to be taken to establish the history, given the difficulty of interpretation. Rather history ought to be taken to deliver the meaning of the text.[17] This was a massive shift in method and governing assumptions. Moreover, that history was more likely, he argued, to be found by reference to those authors who wrote nearest the time. But again,

14 E. Chishull, *Sermon preached before the honourable company of merchants trading to the Levant-seas at St Hellen's, January 16 being Sunday 1697/8* (London: S. Manship, 1698), 1, 4.

15 For recent treatments, see J. R. White, "'Baptized on Account of the Dead': The Meaning of 1 Corinthians 15:29 in its Context," *JBL* 116 (1997): 487–99; N. H. Taylor, "Baptism for the dead (1 Cor 15:29)?" *Neotestamentica* 36 (2002): 111–20; M. F. Hull, *Baptism on account of the Dead (1 Cor 15:29): An Act of Faith in the Resurrection* (Leiden: Brill, 2005); R. D. Aus, *Two Puzzling Baptisms: First Corinthians 10:1–5 and 15:29: Studies in their Judaic Background* (Lanham: Hamilton, 2017).

16 Luke's sermon receives a short coverage in A. Ganes, *The Web of Empire: English Cosmopolitans in an Age of Expansion, 1560–1660* (Oxford: Oxford University Press, 2008), 225. She does not appear to note the importance of the accent on history and "plain reading."

17 J. Luke, *Sermon Preached before the Right Worshipfull Company of the Levant Merchants at St Olav's Hart-Street, Thursday Dec 15, 1664.* (London: R. Daniell, 1698), 14.

this informative history was not confined to Christian sources. The ritual in the Christian text, he argued, might be able to be elucidated by practices that were evident in Greek and Roman culture, such as lustrations for the dead practiced at the calends of February by the Romans.[18] The "history-of-religions" school might wait until the end of the nineteenth century for formal conceptualization,[19] but the roots are clearly evident here two centuries before.

Of particular importance is a rhetorical aside that Luke makes when he refers to an ancient notice of the church of Smyrna. It is worth quoting:

> concerning the martyrdom of the famous S. Polycarp, … the Christians used to assemble at his tomb for performing festival celebrations in honour to his memory, and for exercising, preparing and confirming others to the same conflict for the holy Faith; a custom well known to many here present to be in some part continued by the poor reliques of that once famous and flourishing Church to this very day.[20]

Here is an acknowledgement that the presence of English people focused on commercial ventures in Türkiye was also prizing open other, less-obviously mercantile opportunities. The appeal to "many here present" was a critical confirmatory witness to archaeological remains and observance of then-current Greek customs ("the poor reliques"!).[21] The rhetorical flourish nevertheless indicates that the gaining of this knowledge was already becoming a well-known practice amongst the European nationals gathered at Smyrna (and Constantinople). There was genuine excitement in re-establishing physical contact with a site mentioned in "the holy scriptures".

Attachment to Asian topography was retained, in microcosm, by the expropriation of *in situ* material artifacts that testified to the site. Both the making of a tour and the continued reflection on (retrieved) artifacts were seen as pious acts. A contemporary, George Wheler, credited the chaplain John Luke for improving the "Devotions" of Smyrna "factors" (that is, businessmen). This was demonstrated in the increased numbers of merchants (and occasionally the consul) joining Luke on his expeditions to the cities of the Book of Revelation's seven churches.[22] Pack animals returned with carry-pouches laden with items collected along the journey.[23] Wheler again mused without any trou-

18 Luke, *Sermon*, 24.

19 See Nasrallah, *Archaeology and the Letters of Paul*, 22.

20 Luke, *Sermon*, 15.

21 The visit to Polycarp's tomb is mentioned by travellers before John Luke in their, then-unpublished journals. See, for example, R. C. Anderson (ed.), *The Journals of Sir Thomas Allin* (London: Navy Records Society, 2 vols, 1939–40), vol 1, 14 (an entry dated 19th December 1660).

22 Wheler, *A Journey to Greece*, 230.

23 This appropriation accelerated in the nineteenth century as the Ottoman empire was encouraged to modernize. Western powers were eager to assist in the laying of railway lines across the country — which, inter alia, facilitated the removal of artifacts. See M. Greenhalgh, *From the Romans to the Railways: The Fate of Antiquities in Asia Minor* (Leiden: Brill, 2013).

bling of the order of things, that "no place has contributed more than Smyrna to enrich the collections and cabinets of the curious in Europe."[24] The buzz of interest in what were called "medals" (a fateful designation of the bronze coins essential to the Roman economy),[25] developed into a justifying construction of numismatic meditation as an act of piety. Early in the nineteenth century, William Till repeated Renaissance ideas,[26] arguing that the sheer gazing on coins would bequeath moral advancement (usually along the lines of adherence to an injunction to pay government taxes!).[27] Whatever the rationale for ethical curation, collecting such treasures was certainly a means of guaranteeing a retirement nest-egg or a testamentary legacy for the end of a person's life, when the artifacts were sold off,[28] or, occasionally, bequeathed to a museum.

Even with the moral overlays, the contact with sites began a remarkable process of reconfiguring the attitude toward the past and the material referent of texts, both scriptural and classical. History was in the process of being turned from a providential periodisation of time directed toward an eschatological *telos* into a material testimonial to the truth of ancient texts. There was no diminution at this stage in the instruction about the providential meaning and intent of history, no question that history would do anything other than prove the truth of the literary text. Indeed such history could prove particularly advantageous in repudiating certain methods and results of exegesis. Two targets especially came into view: the allegorization of the churches of the Apocalypse as a gradated ascent in spirituality; and the construction of prophetic ages of the Church built on the same magnificent seven. But materiality had entered the arena of text to yield a construction of history and biblical inter-

---

24 Wheler, *Journey*, 72.

25 On the critical importance of bronze currency, see C. Katsari, *The Roman Monetary System: The Eastern Provinces from the First to the Third Century AD* (Cambridge: Cambridge University Press, 2011), 136–154. The old notion that these bronzes were commemorative "medallions" or occasional largesse needs to be dismissed, unless compelling evidence suggests otherwise. For this obsolete interpretation see B. V. M. Head, *A Catalogue of the Greek Coins in the British Museum* (London: British Museum, 1906), li; C. Babington, "On Two unedited Autonomous Coins of Colossae in Phrygia," *NC* (ns) 3 (1863): 2.

26 See J. Cunnally, *Images of the Illustrious: The Numismatic Presence in the Renaissance* (Princeton: Princeton University Press, 1999).

27 W. Till, *An Essay on the Roman Denarius and English Silver Penny …* (London: Longman, Brown, Green and Longmans, 1838), 31–32. See A. H. Cadwallader, "In Go(l)d we Trust: Literary and Economic Exchange in the Debate over Caesar's Coin (Mk 12:13–17)," *BibInterp* 14.5 (2006): 486–91.

28 See, for example, the substantial array of Richard Pococke's collection: *A Catalogue of a Large and Curious Collection of Ancient Statues, Urns, Mummies, Fossils, Shells and Other Curiosities, of the Right Reverend Dr. Pococke, Lord Bishop of Meath, Deceased; Collected by his Lordship, during his Travels. Which (by order of the Administrator) will be sold by Auction, Bt Mr. Langford and Son, At their House in the Great Piazza, Covent Garden, on Thursday the 5th, and Friday the 6th of this instant June 1766*. It took three days to clear the bidding on items. Other famous explorers or residents in Asia Minor are regularly named in auctions of their coins and artifacts — such as William Hamilton, Henry Borrell, James Whittal among many others.

pretation. This materiality was only possible because of the actual tours to the sites that had long been lost to European visitors.

Reports of the dramatic architecture found at the sites, even in ruinous states, had profound reverberations in European architecture. Bolstered by the Renaissance conceit that the rediscovery of Greek and Roman cultural texts had anointed Europeans as successors to those ancient civilizations, a demonstration of that divine right of succession was to be made in buildings and statuary modeled on the discoveries in "the East". The English *Society of Dilettanti* provided the necessary backing for Richard Chandler to visit Asia Minor (in 1740) and return with accurate sketches and measurements so that the refined taste expressed through the material aesthetics of buildings, constructed spaces and sculptures might be replicated in the homeland.[29] French and German imitators were also commissioned. The results are readily seen in the entrance to the British Museum, the current building in "Greek Revival style" begun in 1823, completed in 1852. But Europe and America are replete with similar inspiration. The "Oriental" fascination captured not only the material objects as a new, rich field for understanding the history expressed in texts; it also asserted European (and later American) rightful inheritance of the riches of the past. This past was to be emulated in a solipsistic confirmation of divine — but historical — election, and now restored to its proper expression and ownership, whether that be the transportation of numerous obelisks to various modern western cities or the recapitulation of architectural forms and constructions of space within those cities.

Material culture is never divorced from frameworks of assumptions about what they (can) mean, who is authorized to handle them (and how), and what political advantage might be gained from their appropriation. A Letter of Lord Aberdeen of the British Foreign Affairs office in 1829 to William Leake, a British military adviser to the Ottoman sultan and coincidentally (?) an avid collector of antiquities, is a salutary reminder of the wide dimensions of interests in material culture. He expressed grave concern, and a measure of righteous indignation that the French Government might be turning foreign debt repayment from the newly rehabilitated Greek nation into a bargaining tool for antiquities:

> This however is not so easy; for as we give the Greeks no pecuniary assistance we are scarcely entitled to interfere in a matter of this nature. If the French, for their subsidy of four hundred thousand francs a month think proper to take payment in antiquities, it would not be very gracious in us to oppose the bargain.

29 R. Chandler, *Travels in Asia Minor and Greece or An Account of a Tour made at the Expense of the Society of Dilettanti* (London: J. Booker, 1775). There were a number of French equivalents. See, for example, C. Texier and R. Popplewell Pullan *The Principal Ruins of Asia Minor Illustrated and Described* (London: Day & Son, 1865).

> Perhaps the best chance of preventing any spoliation of this kind, will be found in the extreme jealousy of the Greek government on the subject. They are perfectly aware of the value which belongs to these monuments of antiquity; and know that they form a chief part of the national wealth, for which it would be difficult for money to repay them.
>
> It is also possible that the French who exhibited so much virtuous indignation at what they called the spoliation of Athens by the English, may feel some shame at the thoughts of imitating the proceeding upon a greater scale.[30]

The competition between European countries for prizes from Asia Minor and the Aegean was intense.[31] They were laying claim to the past as warrant for their present, and frequently over against each other. Recognized here also is the Greeks' own claim on their heritage. This may explain that even as self-assured Europeans were wont to denigrate Turkish life and thought, their treatment of the Greeks was not far removed. They effectively asserted that contemporary Greeks were no longer qualified to handle the sophistication of their own historical forebears. This gained a particular fallacy in regards to Colossae. Thomas Smith's excuse for a failure to explore Colossae, was that the inhabitants of "Chonas" were "a vile sort of people; so that we doubted our safety among them." The Greeks there had "forgot their own tongue."[32] The "material turn" had become embroiled in the politics of identity and the self-definition of nation-states, precisely because they had invested so heavily in a Greco-Roman supersessionist paradigm.

So a succession of chaplains became leaders and educators in arranging expeditions along the coastline of western Turkey and into the hinterland, primarily intent on reconnecting with sites known from scriptural and classical sources. Thomas Smith, a Levant Company chaplain at Constantinople (1668–1670),[33] inserted a marginal note in his own copy of a book by Paul Rycaut, consul at Constantinople. He wrote that, in the second half of the seventeenth century, hundreds of people were making the two-to-three week round trip tracking and traipsing the seven churches of Asia Minor.[34] He could

30 Lord Aberdeen to William Leake 14/2/1829 (*BL* Add Ms 43233, f.44).

31 See W. Wittman *Travels in Turkey, Asia Minor, Syria and across the desert into Egypt during the years 1799, 1800 and 1801 in company with the Turkish army and the British MM mission to which are annexed observations on the plaque and on the diseases prevalent in Turkey and a meteorological journal* (London: 1803), 66.

32 Smith, *Remarks*, 249. See N. Matar, "Britons and Muslims in the early modern period: from prejudice to (a theory of) toleration," in *Anti-Muslim Prejudice in the West, Past and Present: an introduction* edited by M. Malik (Oxford: Routledge, 2010), 23.

33 See C. Bennett, "Thomas Smith," in *Christian-Muslim Relations: A Bibliographical History Volume 13, Western Europe (1700–1800)* edited by D. Thomas and J. Chesworth *et al.* (Leiden: Brill, 2019), 58–67.

34 Smith's annotation here is to page 31 of P. Rycaut, *The Present State of the Greek and Armenian Churches, anno Christi 1678* (London: John Starkey, 1679), the copy held by the London Library; see also Anderson, *English Consul*, 221. It seems that Luke and Smith were repeating

not restrain an added barb that they had done so "with greater care and better observation" than the royal appointee, the author of the work receiving Smith's scribbles.[35] Smith himself is credited with the first published book on the seven churches of Asia in the early modern period,[36] as well as returning to Oxford with a number of priceless manuscripts, coins and sculptures, now treasures securely held by the university authorities.[37]

But along with Smith's annotations about and harvestings from the seven churches, were his perspectives on the country and its current peoples. A topographical confusion between Colossae and Honaz, a foundational trope of the inferiority of Turks and Greeks especially at Honaz, and an enforced collation of the three (biblically-named) cities of the Lycus Valley were all laid for Colossae. These were to govern the interpretation of the site for the next three hundred and fifty years. For all the interest in material culture that marked Smith's work and those adventurers and more circumspect scholars who followed, and for all the impact that such interest had on the reconstruction of ancient (especially Greco-Roman) history and on the interpretation of the Second Testament, it was clear that less admitted interests and values also attached to the objects and the way they were interpreted. When, however, such barnacles were confronted, some acknowledgement did occur. Sir Charles Fellows, for example, admitted that his assessment of the Mohametan Turks was not initially favorable, an assessment into which European opinion had socialized him. Experience of the people however had completely transformed his own prejudices.[38] The Anglican clergyman-become-epigrapher, Edward T. Daniell,

the seven churches tour begun some decades earlier. Robert Bargrave, a young Levant merchant clerk, reported shortly into his arrival at Smyrna that "From Smirna in a Forth-nights travel, may be conveniently seen all the Seaven holy Churches of Asia". M. G. Brennan (ed.), *The Travel Diary of Robert Bargrave, Levant merchant 1637–1656* (London: Hakluyt Society, 1999), 72 (diary spelling).

35 Smith seemed to have been particularly upset that Rycaut had taken material that Smith had supplied and had given him no credit. Worse still, Rycaut had proceeded to bowdlerize the contents. See Smith's marginalia to the London Library copy of Rycaut, *Present State*, 85, 152.

36 T. Smith *Epistolae duae, quarum altera de moribus ac institutis Turcarum agit, altera septem Asiae ecclesiarum notitiam continent* (Oxford: H. Hall, 1672). A second Latin edition followed in 1674: *Epistolae quatuor, quarum duae de moribus ac institutis Turcarum agunt, duae septem Asiae ecclesiarum et Constantinopoleos notitiam continent* (London: H. Hall, 1674). This was more of an addendum as it omitted the "letter" on the seven churches in the earlier edition. The combined work was published in English by Smith "with some enlargements" in 1678. William Leake provides an early testimonial to Smith's initiating work: W. M. Leake, *Journal of a Tour in Asia Minor with Comparative Remarks on the Ancient and Modern Geography of that Country Accompanied by a Map* (London: 1824), 254.

37 Compare the notice of one consul, William Ray, presenting 2000 coins and medals to the Bodleian Library, collected during his time in Smyrna. See R. Walsh, *Account of the Levant Company; with some notices of the benefits conferred upon society by its officers, in promoting the cause of humanity, literature and the fine arts* (London: J. and A. Arch, 1825), 14.

38 C. Fellows, *A Journal Written During an Excursion in Asia Minor* (London: John Murray, 1838), v.

concurred.[39] It is a salutary reminder that the interpretation of material objects is inevitably invested with contemporary values and (con)formations, some of which, hopefully, can be admitted, even revised, at least after confrontation.[40]

Colossae in the ancient material world

In spite of the reiterations of Smith's negative adjudication on the peoples of Honaz across two centuries, there were some who ventured to explore the area. Initially there was a narrow ambition simply to find the place for which there was an untethered name (see chapter 1). However much reliance was placed on brief references in the texts of Herodotos and Xenophon, there was nonetheless a deep drive to find material confirmation of the assumed accuracy of the texts. European explorers went out armed with the compasses of the *Histories* and the *Anabasis* as their primary cartographical resources, supplemented by more immediate predecessors whose own additions to and sometimes tremulous corrections of the classical writers were at times a welcome guide or occasionally a further confounding — as happened with Colossae. It didn't help that Colossae's re-naming as Chonos drew explorers to the small Ottoman village of Honaz (see chapter 2), replete with Turkish and Greek quarters, some, like Francis Arundell, with the intent of declaring Honaz to be "ancient Colossae".[41] Others were enamored of discovering a disappearing river, the fantasy of Herodotos that was fixed as the topographical identifier for the ancient city.

It was assumed that if an inscribed stone could be found that preserved the name of the city, then this would locate what otherwise was confined to literary texts. In the course of the Spratt-Forbes' expedition in Lycia and Caria in 1842, the Reverend Edward T. Daniell wrote excitedly to *The Athenaeum*, the magazine preferred by English gentlemen. He announced that eighteen ancient sites had been "unquestionably ascertained by inscriptions."[42] The problem was that when he found a mention of a Colossian near the village of Trimile (modern Altınyayla), the classical texts had Colossae to the north of the Taurus mountain range, a geological edifice he was yet to cross. So the inscription

39 T. A. B. Spratt and E. Forbes, *Travels in Lycia, Milyas and the Cibyratis in Company with the late Rev. E. T. Daniell* (London: John van Voorst, 2 vols, 1847), vol 2, 5–6.

40 Compare M. Kotrosits, *The Lives of Objects: Material Culture, Experience and the Real in the History of Early Christianity.* Chicago: University of Chicago Press, 2020), 8–10.

41 F. V. J. Arundell, *Discoveries in Asia Minor* (2 vols; London: R. Bentley, 1834) vol 2, 164.

42 *The Athenaeum*, 23rd July, 1842 (p. 675). He rattled off the cities, adding brief descriptions: 1. Araxa; 2. Phellus; 3. Candyba; 4. Cyaneae; 5. Sura; 6. Corydalla; 7. Rhodiapolis; 8. Idebessus, 9. Acalissus; 10. Gagae; 11. Lagon; 12. Termessus Major; 13. Lagbe; 14. Cibyra; 15. Bubon; 16. Balbura; 17. Penanoanda; 18. Arsa.

became, for him, a mention of a small town called "Colossa."[43] Daniell died from malaria during the course of the expedition so did not live to learn the cautionary lesson that the naming of a city did not necessarily map a location — quite apart from the notorious movement of stones (*pierres errantes*) across Asia in the course of their historical survival.[44] But his instinct, perhaps cultivated by his training and practice as an artist (which drove him in Daniel Roberts' wake to explore the light of "the East"), was correct. The natural environment and millennia-old human interactions with it provided an access and stimulant that no text read in isolation in Oxford, Paris or Berlin could deliver. As Walter Scheidel and Steven Friesen have observed, paucity in the evidence of *realia* and their interpretation is no more limited than seeking to construct a world out of the confines of literary texts such as the Bible,[45] certainly when the Bible is privileged as a sacred text somehow divorced in imaginative appropriation from its own materialistic indebtedness and embeddedness. Daniell was in no way inclined to allow the evidence he discovered to question either classical or biblical texts, at least as they had been interpreted up until his time. That heuristic shift came later in the nineteenth century, not least with the recognition that the hunt for a disappearing river Lycus was a futile enterprise and that another explanation beside historical realism must frame Herodotos' text.[46]

Material culture never provides an encyclopedic coverage of a city or region even when excavations have been in full swing for a century or more (as at Ephesos). Moreover, artifacts and remains nevertheless join with ancient texts and documents not to confirm but to inform, building a composite picture that will necessarily contain gaps and inconsistencies in what Scheidel and Friesen called "controlled conjecture". As Michael Wise has astutely recognized,

> As usual with the study of ancient history, we have to make do with snippets, individual frames lifted here and there from within a moving picture. They stand before us isolated and stationary. Yet, if the frames are sufficiently and fortunately distributed, one may hope to recover and extrapolate a fair idea of the plot. Notable gaps will persist, but restrained imagination can accomplish much.[47]

---

43 The inscription was printed in *CIG* 4380 k^3 corrected to identifying the woman Aphias as from Colossae. The reading was further corrected by Christina Kokkinia in *I.Boubon* 102. See chapter 9.

44 See L. Robert, "Pierres errantes, muséographie et onomastique," *Berytus* 16 (1966): 5–40.

45 W. Scheidel and S. Friesen, "The Size of the Economy and the Distribution of Income in the Roman Empire," *JRS* 99 (2009): 63.

46 See G. Weber, "Der unterirdische Lauf des Lykos bei Kolossai," *Ath. Mitt.* 16 (1891): 194–99.

47 M. O. Wise, *Language and Literacy in Roman Judaea: A Study of the Bar Kokhba Documents* (New Haven: Yale University Press, 2015), 40.

The elision of Colossae from materialist investigation

The irony in the litany of the cry for Colossae to be excavated,[48] was how little attention has actually been given to the remains that had survived at the site and the artifacts that have been recorded or secreted into museum depots or private collections over the last four hundred years. Only with the "materialist turn" in classical and biblical studies has there been some initial steps into what can be learned of Colossae beyond the sometimes-fanciful deductions from classical and biblical texts. This genesis has focused primarily on inscriptions, with, more recently, the addition of numismatic considerations.[49]

But even here, the examination has too often been diverted and supplanted by concentrations on *comparanda*, that is, material evidence that has come from other sites, usually more plentiful and in receipt of considerable debates in its analysis. Here the long-held assumption, fostered by ecclesial construction that goes back to Eusebius that Colossae, Laodikeia and Hierapolis are to be equated in interpretative approaches, still exerts a powerful hold.[50] The repeated ecclesial affirmation of "neighbors" and "brotherliness" amongst the Lycus Valley trio takes no account of the tensions and disputes that existed between these three and with other cities in the region (chapters 3 and 4). No doubt the recent intensive excavations and reconstructions at Laodikeia and the longer-term measured appraisals at Hierapolis have cultivated the willingness to give continued life to the assumption. There is so much more evidence to access from these sites that there is almost a willingness to by-pass Colossae's impoverished trove of evidence for the lavish banks of material from its neighboring cities and make deductions about Colossae from those resources, not least in the unwarranted assertion about a significant Jewish population residing at Colossae. This pushes demographic and material corroboration of apparent Jewish allusions in the epistle to the Colossians in an undifferentiated attestation of the presence of

---

48 N. T. Wright, *Judas and the Gospel of Jesus* (Grand Rapids, MN: Baker, 2006), 1; B. Witherington, *The Letters to Philemon, the Colossians and the Ephesians: a socio-rhetorical commentary on the captivity Epistles* (Grand Rapids, MN: Eerdmans, 2007); M. R. Cosby, *Apostle on the Edge: An Inductive Approach to Paul* (Louisville, KY: Westminster John Knox Press, 2009), 238.

49 See A. Standhartinger, *Studien zur Entstehungsgeschichte und Intention des Kolosserbriefs* (Leiden: Brill, 1999); L. Bormann, *Der Brief des Paulus an der Kolosser* (Leipzig: Evangelische Verlagsanstalt, 2012); U. Huttner, *Early Christianity in the Lycus Valley* (Leiden: Brill, 2013); P. Foster, *Colossians* (London: T & T Clark, 2015); see generally, J. Verheyden, M. Öhler, and T. Corsten (eds.), *Epigraphical Evidence Illustrating Paul's Letter to the Colossians* (Tüboingen: Mohr Siebeck, 2018). For an overview see A. H. Cadwallader and J. R. Harrison. "Perspectives on the Lycus Valley: An Inscriptional, Archaeological, Numismatic, and Iconographic Approach," in *The First Urban Churches 5: Colossae, Hierapolis, and Laodicea* edited by J. R. Harrison and L. L. Welborn. Atlanta, GA: SBL Press, 2019), 3–70.

50 See L. Bormann, "Early Christians in the Lycus Valley," in *Early Christian Encounters with Town and Countryside: Essays on the Urban and Rural Worlds of Early Christianity* edited by M. Tiwald and J. K. Zangenberg (Göttingen: Vandenhoeck & Ruprecht, 2021), 213–19.

Jews at Laodikeia and Hierapolis (chapter 3).[51] Laura Nasrallah spreads her net even further, drawing in material from Ephesos and Philippi to interpret parts of letters traditionally provenanced to Colossae,[52] without ever sifting through material that Colossae itself has yielded, nor allowing that material to prompt the direction of research into comparative material.

There is undoubtedly a line of interconnection, if not influence, from Ephesos to Colossae, but the warrant for this exchange needs to be anchored in evidence from Colossae, if at all possible. In any case, the claim on relationships between Colossae and other cities in the province (and beyond) ought to be tested as well — for Smyrna, Sardis, Keretapa, Tripolis, Eukarpeia, Eumeneia, Attouda, Apameia and others whose silhouette can sometimes be discerned in the background to Colossae (chapters 6, 10). Similarly, the use of papyrological material from Egypt to paint the picture of slavery in Colossae in hues reminiscent of Roman law, as Peter Arzt-Grabner has done,[53] is important for insights into the variegated experiences of slaves but has to confront the critical presence of Greek patterns of legal jurisdiction that continued to operate, albeit in negotiation with Roman juridical interventions. Traces of the operations of a system of a plurality of laws can be found in Colossae's own evidence, but these have rarely been granted any impact, even when multiple legal jurisdictions are acknowledged (chapter 11).

It needs to be strongly affirmed that *comparanda* are crucial as a means of providing controls and restraints (as well as encouragements) for the conjectural and imaginative reconstruction of the lives of an ancient settlement. The invaluable contribution that on-line catalogues have provided (sometimes with analyses) cannot be underestimated nor avoided. As John Davies recognizes,

> No-one who browses the annual harvest as reported in *Supplementum Epigraphicum Graecum*, *L'année épigraphique*, or *Kadmos*, or as summarized periodically in successive editions of the *Guide de l'épigraphique*, can fail to be intoxicated, indeed overwhelmed, by the ever-growing wealth of available material.[54]

Davies was deliberately selective in his examples of invaluable resources, even a decade ago. Not only will it be evident in what follows, the array of critical

---

51 See A. H. Cadwallader, "On the Question of Comparative Method in Historical Research: Colossai and Chonai in Larger Frame," in *The First Urban Churches 5: Colossae, Hierapolis, and Laodicea* edited by J. R. Harrison and L. L. Welborn. (Atlanta, GA: SBL, 2019), 105–51.

52 Nasrallah, *Archaeology and the Letters of Paul*, 42, 44–5.

53 P. Arzt-Grabner, *Philemon* (Göttingen: Vandenhoeck & Ruprecht, 2003); "How to Deal with Onesimus? Paul's Solution within the Framework of Ancient Legal and Documentary Sources," in *Philemon in Perspective: Interpreting a Pauline Letter* edited by D. F. Tolmie. Berlin: de Gruyter, 2010), 113–42; "'Neither a Truant nor a Fugitive': Some Remarks on the Sale of Slaves in Egypt and Other Provinces," in *Proceedings of the 25th International Congress of Papyrology* edited by T. Gagos (Ann Arbor: Scholarly Publishing Office, 2010), 21–32.

54 J. K. Davies, "Rhodes Forward: Meditations on the Progress of a Discipline," in *Greek History and Epigraphy*, 265–6.

collations that are available in the field of epigraphy that have made the search for comparative material so much the easier.[55] But Davies omitted any reference to papyrology and the increasing contribution being made to historical research from the field of numismatics.[56] For the former, the *Papyri.info* site has become the standard resource, closely followed by *Trismegistos*. The online *Roman Provincial Coinage* has opened treasures in comparative analysis that have underscored Colossae's effort to carve an identity that was distinct from its near neighbors, as well as witness surreptitiously to tensions that found expression in iconographic and epigraphic assertions on its coins (chapters 2, 3, 4).[57] Similarly the *Lexicon of Greek Personal Names*, resplendent in multiple volumes covering a geographical spread across the empire eastwards from Rome, has been mirrored by an online search engine. This has fostered a greater understanding of ethnic origins and cultural affiliations — not least with significant results for confirming that the Letter to the Colossians and that to Philemon are most likely to have Colossian or at least Phrygian Christ-followers as their audience (chapter 9). For Second Testament manuscripts, there are two voluminous digital reservoirs, the Münster *Institut für neutestamentliche Textforschung* and the *Center for the Study of New Testament Manuscripts*.

Some justification for by-passing evidence from Colossae and hastening a direct advance to *comparanda*, at least among those seeking to engage material remains for Second Testament interpretation, has leaked from the debates over authorship, provenance and destination of the Letters to the Colossians and Philemon.[58] Even should the advanced arguments over pseudepigraphy be accepted, the avoidance of investigation of the material evidence of Colossae and its immediate surrounds confines the interpretation to a shifting store where any number of scholastic if not fantastical polemics can be resourced. The evidence that Colossae has already released is sufficient in my view to support the balance of probabilities in favor of Colossae as the destination of both letters, albeit written by different authors (see especially chapters 6 and 9). Where the balance of probabilities leaves an ante-chamber for doubt (as

---

55 Note especially Philip Harland's *Associations in the Greco-Roman World*, the *Packard Humanities Institute Epigraphy* site, the *Clauss-Salby Epigraphik-Datenbank*, the *Collection of Greek Ritual Norms*, and the *Thesaurus Graecae Linguae*. These have often been supplemented by more specialist sites, such as the *Inscriptions of Aphrodisias*.

56 For papyrology as providing the bridge between history and the New Testament, see the *Papyrologische Kommentare zum Neuen Testament* series edited by Peter Arzt-Grabner. For the value of numismatics for historical research (including lexicography) see M. Theophilos, *Numismatics, Greek Lexicography and the New Testament* (London: T & T Clark, 2019) and the various essays by Ulrich Huttner.

57 For Roman Imperial Coins, see the *Online Coins of the Roman Empire* (OCRE) at http://numismatics.org/ocre/; for Seleucid coins, see http://numismatics.org/sco/.

58 See especially, V. Balabanski, "Where is Philemon? The Case for a Logical Fallacy in the Correlation of the Data in Philemon and Colossians 1.1–2; 4.7–18," *JSNT* 38 (2015): 131–50; D. Lincicum, "Mirror-Reading a Pseudepigraphal Letter," *NovT* 59 (2017): 171–93.

inevitably it must), the evidence assembled and dissected here provides ample material for adjudging how the letters known as "to the Colossians" and "to Philemon" might have been read, heard and engaged *by* those at Colossae. Aural reception is always the critical test of a letter given that, as much as an author might be assumed to be aware of at least the broad sweeps of a cultural context, authorial intent is a figment of later interpreters' imagination, frequently informed by un-interrogated assumptions.

Restoring Colossae to material existence

The primary yield of artifactual material from Colossae is summarized in the four appendices at the conclusion of the book, along with a fuller sweep of testimonia than has previously been assembled. The profuse instances of *comparanda*, some of which are given detailed treatment, are listed in full indices. Nonetheless, the emphasis is on the Colossian material as the primary store of evidence. Much of it has never been critically analyzed since its initial publication. In some cases (the Dionysos altar in chapter 7, the Tyche Protogeneia ring in chapter 5, the *defixio* in chapter 8), the material is almost completely new, having previously been confined to remote, obscure or old publications and, in the latter two instances, thought lost. In the case of coins, many of the new additions to Colossae's cabinet have only been published on the websites of auction houses, sometimes incorrectly described; nonetheless, proprietors and sometimes private collectors have been hearteningly generous in granting me permission to incorporate photographs of relevant items. In a number of cases, these new coins have lead to a major re-assessment of Colossae's life — the role of elite women as benefactors, the appropriation of the heliotic Colossus of Rhodes to redefine the meaning of its toponym, the re-drawing of Colossae's territorial boundaries. In the chapters that follow, I have pursued, as uncompromisingly as I can, the agenda of foregrounding the material evidence of Colossae that we currently have and to press it, in dialogue with resonating comparative evidence, to yield a glimpse of the life of an ancient city, or better, glimpses of the lives of an ancient city as it passed through a succession of hegemonic influences that left traces on memories as much as on landscapes. Occasionally also, we snatch a view of those well outside the political controllers of succeeding eras who react to and reshape such influence in their own negotiations for advantage in their own day (chapter 8). Almost all the known inscriptions of Colossae have been re-assessed, frequently given new reconstructions and interpretations. In four cases, inscriptions that have previously been claimed for Laodikeia have been re-assigned to Colossae,[59]

59 *I.Laodikeia Lykos* 1, 61, 114, 118.

and their significance for the latter city re-appraised. In addition, engagement with the topography, visual displays and surface remains, from tombs in the necropolis to ceramic remains strewn across and around the höyük (artificial mound) have gained the attention that no attempt at material analysis can avoid. Even though it is now likely that the coming years will reveal more of Colossae's lives, the failure thoroughly to investigate the evidence already available has robbed Colossae of its material foundation on which subsequent discoveries can build.

Restoring Second Testament Letters to a material context

It is here, especially, that the Second Testament Letters to the Colossians and to Philemon become so valuable. They are, in their writing and especially in their immediate reception, reflections of small, fledgling religious groups attempting to compete (albeit in different ways) in a locality saturated with religious expressions, especially expressions that are politically and economically infused or initiated.

In the detailed analyses in the book the primary accent has been on the ancient material as the evidentiary store for understanding Colossae, its territory and inhabitants and its religious groups, including the Christ-followers. I have no interest in burning the fossil fuel of material evidence to prove or demonstrate sacred texts, especially as that would construct texts as a world apart from the material realm. Whilst there are occasional, loud reverberations that occur in the incorporation of the Second Testament Letters into the material mix, these are few — the exemplars of purity injunctions of Col 2:21, the primacy of "Greek" in the "race-code" of Col 3:11, the significance of the name Apphia in Phmn 1, the explanation of a succession of metaphors from the gymnasium and from foundation narratives, spring to mind.

I am nervous even at the use of "illustrations" as the primary motivation for a search of the material evidence. This seems to me only a relatively small departure from the older drive of biblical archaeology that operated from the nineteenth century assumption that such material would prove the truth of some scripture or other, such "truth" already understood in a pre-determined interpretation. Here John Luke's sense that history was critical for the determination of a "plain" reading of scripture has lost none of its potential, even if the yield of insight needs redirection. Accordingly, the close reading is directed primarily to what can be learned about Colossae, the city and territory and only secondarily, though importantly, to interactions with the texts of the Second Testament that are identified as bearing on the discussion. Occasionally the texts raise the driving questions, as in the governance of slavery at Colossae. Very occasionally, the texts contribute to the wider discussion, being themselves participants in the world of values and conventions that circulated in ancient cities. More often they provide examples of how fledgling religious groups negotiated their immediate surrounds, as revealed through a close reading.

The relevant letters, now incorporated into one or other confessional canons called "the New Testament", are understood here as material players in the life of Colossae, as texts within themselves and in the handling of their contents by composers, bearers, readers, and auditors/recipients. Sometimes they yield insight into the populace, or into groups among the inhabitants and even into relationships with neighbors, whether Christ-followers or not. Consequently, there is no full-blown commentary on even substantial parts of the Letters to the Colossians and to Philemon, although virtually the entirety of both letters gains mention. My hope is that the model and the results contingently offered here will promote a greater awareness of how text and material reality might be conjoined to yield greater insight into the lives of first and second century peoples in inland Asia, including the lives of the Christ-followers. So the concentration has been on select verses, sections, and occasional pericopes that are drawn into the analysis of some aspect of Colossian life in the hope that they will further illuminate that life even as the texts and the immediate players in their conception and appropriation are illuminated in and through the engagement. Consequently, it will be clear that I am impatient at the dismissal of these texts somehow to be excluded from such investigations,[60] and I have attempted to give them due weight in themselves and in the interpretations that scholars have devoted to them. The Italian epigraphy specialist, Tullia Ritti, has recognized how important early Christian texts are to painting as fully as possible the canvas of the early centuries of the Common Era in Hierapolis, and she has done so with the same critical acumen that she has applied to epigraphical texts in their expanding ripples of contexts.[61] My compass-bearing swings to Colossae and to a goal of bringing the relevant texts into a closer exchange with the topographical and material environment of that city and its territory.

A skeletal overview

Each of the chapters herein seeks to bring the wider historical and material evidence into exchange and dialogue with, primarily, the Second Testament Letters to the Colossians and to Philemon, occasionally with sections of the Book of Revelation. Sometimes the Second Testament texts provide the prompt

60 This has sometimes been the adverse judgment passed on the early collection of essays I edited with Michael Trainor, *Colossae in Space and Time* (2011), even though there was a deliberate conjunction of historical (4), epigraphical (2), archaeological (2), New Testament (3) and Byzantine essays with appendices (2) along with full indices. Contrà F. d'Andria, "Saints and Pilgrims in the Lykos Valley (Asia Minor)," *Deltion* 38 (2017): 37.

61 T. Ritti, *Hierapolis di Frigia IX: Storia e Istituzioni di Hierapolis* (Istanbul: Ege, 2017), 190–209.

to investigation, sometimes they accompany the analysis, sometimes they are drawn in as recipients of the benefaction granted by the archaeological and historical investigation.

The multiple problems associated with the name Colossae/Colossians are explored in the first two chapters, problems that infect ancient texts and their scribal transmission whether classical or scriptural. Not only has this muddied the philological and etymological understanding of the toponym itself but it also affected the efforts to locate accurately the city within the geographical expanse of Asia Minor and its related islands (notably Rhodes). However, the city itself seems to have unwittingly exacerbated the problems for later scholarship by its redefining of an ancient Hittite identity and name by siphoning another memory, the heliotic Colossus that confronted ancient mariners and later memorialists. Here numismatic witness to a particular aspiration for divine governance at Colossae sets the city's identity apart from other cities of the Lycus Valley and its immediate surrounds. This discovery of a probable appropriation of Greek meaning into a pre-Greek toponym becomes a critical counterpoint to the singular address that opens the Letter to the Colossians and pulses through the letter, including the vice-lists of Colossians 3.

Chapter 3 pursues the recent re-orientation of classical and Christian studies to broaden the accent on urban life to take account of the territory within which a city was set and over which it had, or asserted, control. There has been little effort to divine the territorial limits of the cities of and around the Lycus Valley. But the provocation to do so has increased as dispute resolution (such as between Laodikeia and Hierapolis, and in the recently published water regulations of Laodikeia) frequently refers to the territory within which rights and privileges could be exercised. Ulrich Huttner's insightful handling of numismatic evidence to discern the marking of Laodikeia's boundaries, at least in terms of rivers, provides the warrant for a similar examination of Colossae's evidence. The refinement of the boundaries between *poleis* allows some dramatic reassignment of at least four inscriptions to the Colossian inventory, including notice of at least two rural villages. The recognition of the importance of the countryside to the life of the city is felt in the agricultural metaphors present in the Letter to the Colossians and presses the issue of the ideological mechanisms deployed to enable city and country to coexist with a semblance of mutual benefit. Here the prevalence of foundation stories in Asia directs attention to the role of founder-figures in the nexus of country and city, with the possibility raised of one of Colossae's foundation stories being hidden in a later popular Christian hagiography — the *Story of St Michael the Archangel of Chonai*. An examination of these narratives and their elements becomes helpful in explaining a conjunction of metaphors in Colossians 1 and 2 that follow a processional, ritualised movement from city to country and back, this time with Christ borne aloft as the new founder figure — at least for the Christ-followers at Colossae.

The fourth chapter forces a reconsideration of the relationship between the cities of the Lycus Valley. Ecclesial tradition has accented the friendship and neighborliness of the big three, largely ignoring other settlements that dot the upland rim surrounding the valley. However, there are a number of indications that there were numerous tensions operating between the cities, some sparked by economic competition, some given the added accelerant of attempts at status accumulation that inevitably, on the one hand, relied on an economic store-house to finance the ambitions and, on the other, constantly had an eye to Rome as the arbiter and standard by which the measurement of success might be made. The discovery that the cities of the Lycus were no different from other cities of the eastern provinces, especially those in close proximity to one another, in experiencing and sometimes promoting the currents of conflict raises the *prima facie* question of whether such tensions filtered into relationships between groups of Christ-followers in the different cities. The seemingly innocuous greetings list is unraveled to suggest that the crucial ministry of Archippos underscored in Col 4:17 has conflict resolution as its prime function. It is further suggested that the diverse demographic of the groups of Christ-followers in the cities of Colossae and Laodikeia has the issues of Jewish membership in the latter as an ingredient in that conflict, and that this provides a reasonable explanation for the Jewish allusions in the Letter to the Colossians. That is, they are references designed for the secondary readership and hearing of the letter — at Laodikeia.

Chapter 5 seeks to extract the full significance of a ring with a double-faced intaglio gem-stone that was long thought lost. The trail has led from eighteenth century French collections through to the purchase by Catherine the Great at a fire-sale to repay a French nobleman's gambling debts and thence to the rediscovery of the ring in the vast stores of The Hermitage Museum in St Petersburg. The elaborately carved ring carries the inscription naming "Tyche Protogeneia of the Colossians", a unique affirmation in Asia Minor. The carved symbolism on both sides of the gem, including a zodiac, a winged figure with a cornucopia and a hebdomadic complex, extend the privileged position of Tyche in universal terms. The Christological affirmations in the Colossians hymn and the affirmation of the constancy and stability for those hidden with Christ in God become a powerful alternative to the sometimes capricious Tyche on whom the universe was asserted to depend and yet who could unleash seismic disaster without warning. The notorious worship of angels that has preoccupied commentators on the letter may well have found its most immediate, local exemplar, or at least a highly visual option of a Colossian religious expression that letter recipients could readily imagine.

One forgotten inscription that mentions a young Colossian prompts the detailed explorations in chapter 6. As frequently occurred in the first and second centuries, young scholars departed their home city seeking further education at leading intellectual centers of the empire, in this case at Smyrna. At the very least, it demonstrates that philosophy or perhaps another discipline was a magnet for some Colossians. The Smyrna connection is sifted for its particular reputation that attracted young men from other less-credentialed centers.

The Middle Platonic master, Theon of Smyrna, known from epigraphical and visual evidence as well as literature, is coterminous with the approximate date of the short epitaph for the Colossian *philologos*, Diodotos. Without forging a necessary connection between the teacher and this student, Theon's philosophy is examined both in terms of its content and its structure to test why some accents are found in the letter, such as the Christological hymn and its connection with the household code (further developed in chapter 12). Here the Platonic emphasis on cosmic harmony is explored in terms of the consequences for mundane life — of city and its microcosmic training ground, the family. Critically, the importance of hymns as educational and socializing agents is examined, with the consequence that even though no genealogical link can be made between Theon and the Letter to the Colossians, not only are some of the ideas held in common even with different accents. More significantly, hymns are recognized as one of the pre-eminent defining instruments of common life for groups in a city — from the leadership cartel to small associations. The writer of the letter has carved distinctive Christian emphases but has done so according to templates readily available in the cities of Asia.

Chapter 7 takes its inspiration from the purity regulations dismissively rattled off in Colossians 2. A perspective from the commentary on the letter by Theodore of Mopsuestia interprets the list of purity regulations as a sample grab evoking a wider host of regulations governing religious activity at Colossae (and elsewhere). Often forgotten in the chase for religious analogues however is that members of religious associations were governed as much in their personal behavior as in their economic contribution — not least from behavioral infractions. These frequently spilled into civic reflections, both as to moral rectitude and to its economic reinforcement, such that one is symbiotically embroiled in the other. This connection between religiosity and economics, commerce and the sacred, is explored in terms of the debt structures of the ancient world, a perspective that adds a razor-sharp edge to the material dimensions of release from debt in Col 2:14. The minutiae of execution of debt procedures and their release provide a critical insight into the imagery employed in the integrated section running from Col 2:8 to 23. Here is one of the critical challenges that Christ-followers at Colossae made to the social cohesion of the Colossian *polis*, at least in the conceptual perspective encouraged by the writer. It will be a challenge that will find mollification of potential confrontation in other sections of the letter, in the delicate balancing act between what James Harrison calls "collisions and convergences."[62] But the rider on this dichotomy is that the choice of the constituents of those two poles lies in the hands of the epistolary author and then in the levels of consent gained in the reception of the composition.

---

62 J. R. Harrison, *Paul and the Ancient Celebrity Circuit: The Cross and Moral Transformation* (WUNT 430; Tübingen: Mohr Siebeck, 2019), 146.

In chapter 8 we turn from the highly regulated sphere of temples and associations to the occult. A forgotten *defixio* or curse-tablet is restored in chapter 8 to its central importance for understanding Colossae as a *polis* (city-state) defined by its overall territory rather than its prominent architectural imprint on the landscape. The inscribed lead diptych was thought not to have survived its initial publication and subsequent replication and incorporation into a generic collection at the turn of the twentieth century. In fact, it was bequeathed to the British Museum. A re-examination of the engraved metal pieces has enabled a new reading to be made and a more detailed examination of its significance for understanding the tensions that existed between differently situated persons in Colossian life. That significance has a topographical and a contextual edge. It was found in what was probably a village grave distant from the city. Here the conflicts between persons not usually surfacing in the epigraphic register allow us to catch a glimpse of how ordinary folk, with little access to institutional means of resolving disputes, might find an instrument to secure, at least in their own minds, a measure of justice. However, the general conventions that condemned such actions as disturbing a grave to activate a curse through dark arts, provides an imaginative construction of what might qualify as reprehensible behavior, such as is named in general terms of the former lives of the Christ-followers at Colossae in Col 1:20–23. In the ancient Greco-Roman world, evil deeds are those which destabilize society, not least by a failure to accept and defer to its institutions, values and leadership. This conjunction of the *defixio* with the letter does not assert the explicit target of the epistolographer but it does allow that at least one material witness to the under-belly of life at Colossae could readily fire an imaginative application among some of the aural recipients. However appropriated, the writer underscores that Christ is the circuit-breaker of the alienation that ferments such antagonistic responses and abject states.

In chapter 9 comes the focus on names. The onomastic sweep for Colossae and its territory is now more extensive than usually admitted. Names gathered from the ancient world number in their hundreds of thousands and provide a concentration of information on demographics, ethnicities and relationships. Beginning with one of the traditional store-houses of names and groups — the theater — we confront the denuded state of Colossae's entertainment and civic center. However, other sources of names have yielded about 167 names of Colossae's personnel. The number is small, especially when reckoned according to their chronological spread, but is sizeable enough to elicit some deductions about population changes, ethnic origins, religious and virtue aspirations and gendered recognition. Colossae is confirmed as a cosmopolitan city whose population was willingly involved in cultivating a Greek identity, albeit with an acceptance of a variety of ethnic pasts, notably Phrygian, and a desire among the elite for the naming additions of Roman citizenship. The onomastic survey is then brought to bear on a peculiar verse, frequently ignored as to its profound significance for the cultural commitment of Colossians and the pseudepigraphy of the Second Testament Letter, namely Col 3:11. The conjunction of the store of Colossae's names with the relatively long list of names given in the Letters to the Colossians and to Philemon, then allows some critical issues of Second Testament scholarship to be addressed, not least as to authenticity of authorship and its implications for audience and provenance. A crucial name for determining or at least clarifying these issues takes center stage: Apphia.

Chapter 10 returns us to one of the key institutions of a city's life — the gymnasium. Two Colossian inscriptions in particular demonstrate that Colossae cultivated the appearance of a typical Greek *polis*, with the paired accents of learning and physical prowess. New readings and interpretations reveal something of the complexities of intra- and inter-polis education and training located in the gymnasium and baths. But a fragmentary relief witnesses to the disruption and re-visioning of the athletic and educational ideal. The rapid expansion of the Roman spectacles of gladiatorial and venatorial combats became complicated in the eastern provinces by the expropriation of gymnasial ideals into their own advertisement and memorialization. As much as the spectacles were a frequent accompaniment of the local expressions of the imperial cult, a soft-war entertainment package harnessing popular adherence to Roman governance, Greek values attached to the displays and adapted their appreciation so that a measure of distinctive Greek identity was maintained. Metaphorical use of the spectacles was ubiquitous, from rhetorical flourishes to literary competitions. The Letter to the Colossians is not isolated from this multi-faceted cultural panorama. Accordingly, the metaphors in the letter are revisited to test whether the athletic, gladiatorial or other fields of human endeavor have prompted their use and to what extent any challenge is mounted even in the utilization of dominant cultural values and expressions.

One of the peculiar exposures of the Letters to the Colossians and to Philemon is the window onto slavery. Onomastic study has probably revealed some of the slaves in Colossae's population but explicit mention of the servile engine of the Colossian economy and society is absent apart from these letters. Chapter 11 therefore seeks to discern how slavery in Colossae was managed, at least at a juridical level. Here the developing contribution of the study of plurality of laws is brought to bear on Colossae. Initially, the search is directed towards whatever hints of multiple legal jurisdictions can be discovered — in memorials, epitaphs and in one recently published inscription honoring the chief interpreter and translator of the Colossians. The confirmation of a diversity of legal operations, both Roman and Greek, at Colossae raises a crucial question in application to slavery, namely, which system of law is the most likely to have lain in the background as a potential resource determining the various actions by and in relation to Onesimos. Many of the considerable assumptions governing previous assessments become untenable once it is admitted that Colossae's local Greek constitution and decision-making are critical to the assessment, including the current, vexed question of manumission.

The final chapter, chapter 12, attempts to discern how households and family structures are to be recognized. A number of methodological conundrums beset the exploration once it is acknowledged that literary texts are of limited use — the gap between rhetorical presentation and actual practice is too great. Recent efforts to garner insights from funerary inscriptions — the most voluminous of epigraphical testimonies in the ancient world — are examined both as to their methodological issues and their evidentiary results. With tentative advances, the epitaphs and memorials of Colossae, the most numerous of the small trove of Colossian inscriptions, are closely examined against the backdrop of what can be affirmed from the anepigraphic remains in the northern necropolis — the variety of grave styles, their arrangement and functioning in relation to the living population of the city and villages of its territory. The results have points of contact with similar studies of other cities and villages in Asia, notably Aphrodisias and the Upper Tembris Valley. But these same studies, including that of Colossae, bear little more than occasional if not accidental relation to the assumed family and household structure of the so-called household code in the Letter to the Colossians and the obscure glimpses of actual households in both Colossian Letters. The fulcrum of interrogation therefore becomes directed towards the function of the household code in the letter and what the first recipients might have heard and appropriated.

My hope is that Colossae, the Colossians (in city and territory) and the various alliances and groupings among that populace will become a little clearer in their own right rather than by being subsumed to general historical or confessional configurations or pursuits. Colossae was a proud city, striving to give its citizens a distinctive identity amidst an ongoing drive for prosperity (even if unevenly distributed and experienced). Groups within the city, whether religious, occupational, gymnastic or other, all played their role in the dynamism and competition of a city's life. From the late second century BCE, this inevitably meant negotiating the reality of the Roman empire, just as such negotiations were locked into competition with other cities similarly positioning themselves to best advantage in that reality. But this was not a new skill being tested. Colossae's history had supplied a succession of governments and falls of governments, that demanded a flexible resilience if the city was to survive. Survive it did, long after many have declared its demise both in the far and recent past. In that sense, Colossae needs to be appreciated as much as possible on its own terms, even if interrogated as much as to what it currently offers as to the absences that continue to haunt any narrative of its life. Subsequent discoveries will bring revisions and re-directions. But that is the excitement and joy of scholarship. What follows is the fruit of two decades of research, substantially a detailed re-drawing and re-visioning of the known foundations which previous scholars have, in their day, sought to provide.

Chapter One
Colossae, a name in search of a city

For centuries, Colossae existed as no more than a name on vellum and paper, at least in the European mind. The two main research pursuits were the late history of the Achaemenid empire and the Second Testament, with an occasional but fateful glimpse of bishop lists for eastern synods. Here a bishop of Colossae is occasionally included, a diocese that was formally recognized as Chonai in 787 CE (with a retention of Colossae as its former toponym).[1] The methodology for harnessing and assessing information about Colossae was textually based. Philological and grammatical concerns dominated to construct a largely literature-supplied edifice that masqueraded as history. The fatal flaw in this approach was that when the testimonia were lacking — notably in the Roman imperial period — that edifice could no longer be allowed to stand. Colossae was collapsed at the hands of an earthquake — a frequently appropriated solution for a literary conundrum. Consequently, the search for Colossae "on the ground" rather than "on the page" was given a trigonometric bearing of a literature-supplied disappearing river, a literature-vacuum deduction of manifest signs of ruin and the confusion caused by two names (further examined in chapter 2). This chapter opens our investigation of Colossae with the search for the ancient city, the presumptions that governed that search and the results that, for a time, were deemed to corroborate those presumptions. Finally, we turn to the weight of material finds that has finally overcome the demise conjured by the mis-interpretation and misplaced valorization of literature. This not only "discovers" the ancient city but sets in train a new path for assessing the city and its resilience.

1 W. M. Ramsay, *The Cities and Bishoprics of Phrygia* (Oxford: Clarendon, 2 vols, 1895, 1897), 1.213. A substantial list of testimonia is found in Appendix 1.

The testimonia

Herodotos and Xenophon provide the main sources naming Colossae in the Persian period, with a small vignette added by the first century (BCE) encyclopaedic historian, Diodorus Siculus and embellished by the second century (CE) rhetorician and pedagogue, Polyaenus of Bithynia. The references are brief and frequently have not been examined in their rhetorical and literary context.[2] I seek to overcome this myopia in part in chapter 3 for Herodotos. The brief references were nonetheless crucial in the long-term self-perception of Colossae through to the time when it was known predominantly as Chonai, as shown in the overt and covert citations by the twelfth century Choniates brothers, Michael and Nicetas. But this small collection of early witnesses also became key to the cartographical resources relied upon centuries later in the quest for the site of Colossae.

Most of these witnesses, excepting the saints' lives (though these sometimes surfaced in the well-known menologia), were familiar to the early travellers and explorers.[3] They frequently carried works such as Xenophon's *Anabasis* in small pocket editions effectively relying upon them as travellers' guides. Some, like the Reverend Edward T. Daniell, a willingly press-ganged participant in the Spratt and Forbes expedition of 1841–2, took the time spent in quarantine on the island of Rhodes and in preparations at Smyrna to ransack the available libraries to compile the necessary notes for a picture of the Turkish hinterland.[4]

The key elements extracted from these literary texts were a disappearing river, evidence of earthquakes, the shepherding of glistening black sheep (whether on the crimson or purple spectrum!), the conjunction of river and city with the necessary provisions such as might supply a large army for several days, a city that betrayed a past that was large and prosperous, a city whose name might have left a legacy in an Ottoman toponym (Chonos, later Honaz), and finally, a conjunction with two other cities in the Lycus Valley, Laodikeia and Hierapolis. Sometimes, these literary harvests were converted into carto-

2 For criticism of the limited methodology of testimonia citation and usage, see A. H. Cadwallader, "The Historical Sweep of the Life of Kolossai," in *Epigraphical Evidence Illustrating Paul's Letter to the Colossians* edited by J. Verheyden, M Öhler and T. Corsten (Tübingen: Mohr Siebeck, 2018), 27–9.

3 See, for example, the list of testimonia (not always accurate) in W. F. Ainsworth, *Travels in the Track of the Ten Thousand Greeks: being a Geographical and Descriptive Account of the Expedition of Cyrus and of the Retreat of the Ten Thousand Greeks as related by Xenophon* (London: John W. Parker, 1844), 241.

4 T. A. B. Spratt and E. Forbes, *Travels in Lycia, Milyas and the Cibyratis in Company with the late Rev. E. T. Daniell* (London: John van Voorst, 2 vols, 1847), 1.viii, 2.8, 9, 23.

graphical representation, maps bearing the full authority of the classical and, occasionally, scriptural writers upon which they relied.[5]

But, as has been writ large into contemporary scholarly inquiry, map is not territory.[6] However much sanctity attached to the classical and scriptural texts and the itineraries that could be deduced from them, adventurers and explorers were frequently at a loss once on the ground. Sometimes they turned to the journal descriptions of immediately prior travellers, blaming them for misrepresentation or failure to properly negotiate the text's directions.[7] Sometimes, travellers "saw" what they expected to see. Richard Pococke, for example, claimed to have seen black sheep throughout the region in his travels in the late 1730s.[8] But two decades later, Richard Chandler reckoned that, of sheep corralled at the Laodikeian ruins for night-time protection, "only one or two which were very black and glossy." Rather than impugn the ancient author, he judged that "The breed, perhaps, has been neglected."[9] Both authors did not visit Honaz or Colossae; both authors assumed that their general observations based on Laodikeia and Hierapolis were transferrable to the as-yet unconfirmed site of Colossae; both authors assumed Strabo was accurate, either confirmed in the present or confined in his authenticity to his own time. The maps, whether in the imagined deductions from texts by the travellers or the sketches provided by their immediate predecessors, were proving somewhat fluid.

More than that, any map is built on certain assumptions; in this case, the European conceit that they (that is, the competing countries of Europe) were the inheritor and enhancer of Greco-Roman civilization. That is, they sought texts, interpreted them and imagined the territory with a western eye, even when, as is clear from the references of Herodotos and Xenophon, Colossae's anchor of cultural and political deference was the east.[10] In simple terms, European adventurers set their compasses for the discovery of Colossae from Smyrna, then Laodikeia and Hierapolis (the constructed ecclesiastical neighbors) rather than from Persepolis, then Apameia. And one fundamental problem underlay their sources and jaundiced their assumptions, namely, that the literary testimonia measured

---

5 See A. H. Cadwallader and M. Trainor, "Colossae in Space and Time: Overcoming Dislocation, Dismemberment and Anachronicity," in *Colossae in Space and Time: Linking to an Ancient City* edited by A. H. Cadwallader and M. Trainor (Göttingen: Vandenhoek and Ruprecht, 2011), 20–2.

6 See J. Z. Smith, *Map is not Territory: Studies in the History of Religions* (Chicago: University of Chicago Press, 1978).

7 R. Chandler, *Travels in Asia Minor and Greece or An Account of a Tour made at the Expense of the Society of Dilettanti* (London: J. Booker, 1775), 239, 241. He tartly criticized the directions given by Richard Pocock "by whom its antient geography is greatly mistaken."

8 R. Pococke, *Description of the East and Some Other Countries* (London: W. Bowyer, 2 vols, 1745), vol 2, part ii, 74.

9 Chandler, *Travels in Asia Minor*, 228.

10 See H. Sancisi-Weerdenburg, "The Fifth Oriental Monarchy and Hellenocentrism," in *Achaemenid History II: The Greek Sources* edited by A. Kuhrt and H. Sancisi-Weerdenburg (Leiden: Netherlands Institute for the Near East, 1987), 117–31.

the significance of Colossae, particularly fateful when the testimonia dried up between the early Roman imperial and the middle to late Byzantine periods.

Toponymy and other confusions

The fundamental confusion came in the assumption that Honaz, spelled in a variety of forms by early European writers, was the ancient site of Colossae, a name that had shifted to the progenitor of Honaz — Chonai. The Byzantine testimony to the name-change and its spelling was considered to have yielded more modern variations in form. More importantly, the assumption, driven by Byzantine authors, was that Chonai, taken as the village or small town of Honaz, *was* Colossae. The tenth century work ascribed to Constantine Porphyrogenitos, *On the Themes*, added a notation to Colossae, beyond the rendition of the previous eleven cities and the nine following. That is, Colossae was highlighted: "Colossae, the place now called Chonai, where there is a famous shrine of the archangel Michael."[11] The Choniates brothers, Michael and Nicetas, less than two centuries later repeated the equation of Colossae as Chonai, with Nicetas supplementing Xenophon's description about its grandeur. Reiteration made the collation more convincing. This became the explicit supporting reference for the equation of Colossae and Chonai/Chone in the famous sixteenth century atlas, the *Theatrum Orbis Terrarum*, of Abraham Ortelius.[12]

A Levant Company merchant, Jeremy Salter, participated in a seven churches tour in 1668. His diary account is truncated for Colossae, merely mentioning what he took as the site's Turkish name, "Chonos" and though Greeks were among the inhabitants, he reckoned there was neither church, nor surviving Greek language, nor favorable welcome. Nothing more was recorded and even what found its way into his journal was frequently inaccurate.[13] Nonetheless, the more learned chaplain of the Levant Company in Constantinople, Thomas Smith, in his 1678 publication of a 1671 tour,[14] basically reiterated Slater's observations to such a close extent that one wonders whether Smith ever made a visit to Colossae/Chonos at all. The French explorer, Pitton de Tourne-

11 Κολοσσαὶ αἱ νῦν λεγόμεναι Χῶναι, οὗ ἐστι ναὸς διαβόητος τοῦ ἀρχαγγέλου Μιχαήλ. *Them.* 1.3. Glenn Peers rightly identifies a toponymic aetiology at work here, even though he dates the popular story (wrongly in my estimation) to the iconoclast crisis of the eighth century. See G. Peers, *Subtle Bodies: Representing Angels in Byzantium* (Berkeley: University of California Press, 2001), 163–5.

12 *Cartographica Neerlandica Map*, text for Ortelius Map nr. 216 (1584).

13 J. Salter, "A Brief Relation of the Travels of Jerom Salter [1668]," Bodleian Library, Eng. Msc. e. 218, p. 67.

14 T. Smith, *Remarks upon manners, religion and government of the Turks. Together with a survey of the seven churches of Asia as they now lye in their ruines and a brief description of Constantinople* (London: Moses Pitt, 1678), 249. Smith recorded that he wrote up his diary in Smyrna

fort, early in the eighteenth century, provided a sketch of a then extensive and relatively intact fortress complex on the slopes of Mt Cadmos (Honazdağ) and labeled it "Chonae or Couleisar" (the latter meaning Colossae).[15] A little over a century later, Francis Arundel, an English chaplain at the Levant Company in Smyrna (İzmir), pulled down the identification of ancient Colossae to the small township below the fortress (Pl. 1.1), repeating Pococke, who had made the same identification, but who called the village Konous.[16]

Plate 1.1: An etching designating the village of "Khonos" as the ancient Colossae. It was drawn by W. Brockedon from a sketch of the Rev'd F. V. J. Arundel who visited both the mound and the village in 1826. A correlation with Col.1:2 is added below the title.[17]

(preface), so he had ample occasion to peruse the materials that had been written and collected by others among the European merchant inhabitants. He admits that others (unnamed) had written their own journals (before his own tour).

15 P. de Tournefort, *Relation d'un Voyage du Levant* (Paris: L'imprimerie Royale, 2 vols, 1717), sketch facing vol 1, 320.

16 Pococke, *Description of the East*, 2.ii, 78.

17 See F. V. J. Arundell, *Discoveries in Asia Minor* (2 vols; London: R. Bentley, 1834), vol 2, 164. The two-stage progression to published form should prompt reserve about its accuracy. Nevertheless, the elaborate building complex (the fortress) on the mountain should be noted.

The equation of Colossae with the village of Honaz via the ancient re-naming of the city as Chonai was a commonplace and continued well beyond the discovery that the site of Colossae was about 2 to 3 miles north of Honaz.[18] Joseph Conder, for example, in 1824 made the same collation, though spelling the village variously as Konous, Khonas or Chonas.[19] He repeated the observation of the Italian explorer Antonio Picenini, included in Chandler's book,[20] that a church resembling a wine-vault was located in the "castle" above the village and this was taken as some corroboration that here was the city of the New Testament epistle.[21] The presence of a church at the fortress above Honaz (possibly St. Panteleimon's)[22] was the implicit successor to the Christ-followers of the Letters to the Colossians and to Philemon (Pl. 1.2).

Conder relied on Eusebius's connection of the three cities of the Lycus to affirm that Colossae was "destroyed" along with Laodikeia and Hierapolis,[23] but, unlike later commentators' over-reading of Tacitus' observation that only mentioned Laodikeia as rebuilding, he affirmed that "Colosse doubtless rose again, like her sister cities, from its ruins."[24] The surmise later proved the more accurate assessment than that of William Mitchell Ramsay or Joseph Barber

18 See H. Christmas, *The Shores and Islands of the Mediterranean, including a visit to the Seven Churches of Asia* (London: R. Bentley, 3 vols, 1851), vol 3, 300; J. Farrar, *A Biblical and Theological Dictionary* (London: John Mason, 1852), 145; L. Schmitz, *A Manual of Ancient Geography: with Map Showing the Retreat of the 10,000 Greeks under Xenophon* (Philadelphia: Blanchard and Lea, 1857), 428; J. Eadie, *A Biblical Cyclopaedia* (London: Charles Griffin, 20th ed., 1878), sv Colossae.

19 There is even one European effort at transliteration that emerged as Canessi; see T. H. Horne, *Landscape Illustrations of the Bible, consisting of views of the most remarkable places mentioned in the Old and New Testaments from original sketches taken on the spot* (London: John Murray, 2 vols 1836), sv. Colossae. J. A. Cramer varied this to "Kanassi": *A Geographical and Historical Description of Asia Minor* (Oxford: Oxford University Press, 2 vols, 1832), vol 2, 45; this was repeated in A. Charles, *A Classical Dictionary, containing an account of the principal proper names mentioned in Ancient Authors* (New York: Harper, 1841), 365. Another early, unpublished traveller, heard the village's name as Khonasis: F. C. Brooke, "Travel Journals, Vol III: Asia Minor," *BL* Add Ms 62144, fol. 299b.

20 The materials had been found by Chandler among the papers of Edmund Chishull and dated to 1705; see Chandler, *Travels in Asia Minor*, 113. Picenini's diary (in Latin) still exists; see Picenini, "Travel Diary, Asia Minor [1841]," *BL* Add Ms 6269.

21 Chandler, *Travels in Asia Minor*, 240.

22 See F. J. A. Arundel, *A Visit to the Seven Churches of Asia: with an excursion into Pisidia, etc* (London: John Rodwell, 1828), 318–9 (Letter from a Greek correspondent).

23 The summary notice was repeated by George Syncellus with an adjustment from dating by Olympiad to that from the creation of the world and from the incarnation of the Lord. See Appendix 1.

24 J. Conder, *The Modern Traveller: A Description, Geographical, Historical and Topographical, of the Various Countries of the Globe* (London, James Duncan, 2 vols, 1824), vol 1, 152–4. See also L. A. O. de Corancez, *Itineraire d'une partie peu connu de l'Asie Mineure* (Paris: 1816), 418–34.

Plate 1.2: Remains of a long, narrow, vaulted structure on the heights of Honazdağ, Mt Cadmus, adjoining the remains of the medieval fortress above the modern Turkish town of Honaz. Some of the materials used in the construction appear to have been removed from the site of Colossae, 2 to 3 miles to the north. Some plaster survives on the walls but whether this was the water-proofing of a cistern or the finish of a room is not yet known.

Lightfoot.[25] The Herodotos' reference found its way into Conder's text but it was clear that the twofold Byzantine affirmations — that Colossae was to be numbered with Hierapolis and Laodikeia (a triadic cultivation of Eusebius promoted by Col 2:1–2, 4:13) and that Colossae and Chonai were to be equated — dominated this line of interpretation. The latter equation is frequently found in Byzantine texts (see Appendix 1) but a sleight of hand was missed.

Instead of recognizing that Byzantine connections were unqualified in tying Chonai to the ancient city of Colossae simply as a renaming, the later linguistic tie of Honaz to Chonai provided the geographical anchorage for Colossae, even though the spelling of the toponym by Europeans remained highly unsettled. It generated two developments once the actual site of Colossae was located. Firstly, it resulted in Colossae and Chonai being separated as settlements, against the Byzantine affirmations. Secondly, the separation was extrapolated to form a chronological succession, reinforcing the supposition that Colossae had become terminal following the earthquake of 60 CE, with Chonai (appearing as Honaz

25 See A. H. Cadwallader, "Refuting an Axiom of Scholarship on Colossae: fresh insights from new and old inscriptions," in *Colossae in Space and Time*, 152–9, 162–6.

in the Ottoman period)[26] replacing Colossae as the settlement center in the area. Both deductions are flawed.[27] There are compelling reasons, as Colossae became a Christian city, for a name-change *for the same settlement* to have occurred. It drew on its burgeoning fame as a Christian pilgrimage site and loosened its association with a key emblem of its idolatrous past — the heliotic Colossus (sequestered from the history of Rhodes — see chapter 2). Moreover, with the site of a sacred spring confirmed most probably at the western edge of Honaz, it is likely that the Christianized site of St Michael's hagiasma (with a story punning on the name Chonai), was interpreted as belonging to the city of Colossae just over two miles to the north, perhaps linked by a sacred way. On this understanding, Chonai was a name associated with the spring and its hagiographical origins. It was counted as part of Colossae's civic neighborhood (not just territory) and over time attracted further inhabitants. Subsequently in the early Ottoman period, it emerged as the main town center while the old center's buildings became a quarry for alternate constructions in the district (such as the Ak Khan between "old" Colossae and Denizli). It is no coincidence that the Greek quarter of Honaz, whenever it was noted by travellers, was located at the western edge of the village, close to the spring (now the Göz Picnic Ground).[28] But this inheritance, forged from a scriptural and Byzantine amalgam, did not deliver a satisfactory site for the ancient city of Colossae.

Topography and other confusions

The second effort to locate the ancient site was constructed on the more ancient testimonia, most especially that of Herodotos. In 1829, John Williams repeated the scholarly assumption of the day: "… perhaps it may be said, that in the subterranean current and re-appearance of the Lycus, we have a certain guide for the discovery of the site of Colossae."[29] But Williams went on to refute the notion that a disappearing-reappearing stream was of itself sufficient to locate

26 Another Levant company chaplain, the Rev'd Dr John Luke, recorded in 1669 two related Arabic names for the village, *Haunah* and *Hunaz*, from which Honaz is most directly derived. Nonetheless he took them as the then-contemporary names for "Colosso". See A. H. Cadwallader, "The Reverend Dr. John Luke and the Churches of Chonai," *GBRS* 48 (2008): 331.

27 A third speculative explanation was that the actual ruins of Colossae were themselves called Khonas; H. I. Smith, *The Course of Ancient Geography* (New York: D. Appleton, 1861), 239. He may have abbreviated his expression overmuch for the suggestion that Honaz was built from stones from Colossae. See, more accurately, W. F. Somerville, *The Churches in Asia: Extracts from the Home Letters of Rev. A. N. Somerville DD from the Region of the Seven Churches* (Paisley: J & R Parlane, 1885), 78.

28 We return to this issue more fully below.

29 J. Williams, *Two Essays on the Geography of Ancient Asia: intended partly to illustrate the campaigns of Alexander and the Anabasis of Xenophon* (London: John Murray, 1829), 85.

Colossae. He knew from a number of references in other ancient literary texts (especially Strabo) that the phenomenon was a relative commonplace in a countryside so filled with "numerous perforations" which he tied to the frequent seismic events it experienced.[30] In fact, earthquake was the reason, he suggested,[31] for the disappearance of Colossae from the literary record — a deduction which would become axiomatic in the assessment of Colossae for the next one hundred and fifty years.[32] Williams did not dispute Herodotos's landmark for Colossae; he simply pointed to the need to locate the city by other means, for which Herodotos's text would become corroboration. Significantly, he argued that texts would not be the determinant. Indeed, he was not persuaded even that the discovery of the site of Chonai would immediately determine the position of Colossae. Rather, feet on the ground, diligent inquiry of locals and a search for inscriptions were his proposed methodological principles. One and a half centuries earlier, Thomas Smith had argued that the "marbles" (by which he meant inscribed stones) that had been brought to England had given invaluable aid to the resolution of "many difficulties in History and Chronology."[33] Williams' simple methodology reveals that a material approach to history was attracting scholarly endeavor.

William Hamilton largely followed Williams' proposal. He eventually nailed (with help from local directions) the city of Colossae at the so-called biconical mound two-and-a-half miles to the north of the village of Honaz. This no doubt housed the central civic and religious precincts from Hittite through to Byzantine times, but, as we will see, "Colossae", like most ancient sites, governed a more expansive area than an urban heart. However, Hamilton made the identification by having to construct an apologetic for the main tour guide at the time — the ancient historian, Herodotos.

Herodotos had written of Colossae being positioned near the Lycus River right at the point where the river disappeared beneath the ground only to re-appear five stadia further on.[34] Herodotos became the compass for European searches for the site. The problem was that the general indicators from Laodikeia in combination with the river, formed from the few other classical testimonia,[35] hit a very large artificial mound (a "höyük") but no disappearing water channel. Herodotos' corroboration could not be applied. Here arose a key issue, and a key debate, in the turn to material evidence. Sometimes, it appeared that the available realia and topographical information challenged the text, whether classical or biblical. The reliance on history as derived from material artifact was coming up against an assumption that classical accounts

30 Williams, *Two Essays*, 86.
31 Williams, *Two Essays*, 87.
32 See Cadwallader "Refuting an Axiom," 151–66.
33 Smith, *Seven Churches*, preface.
34 Herodotos *Hist* 7.30.
35 Xenophon *Anab* 1.2.6; Polyaenus *Strat.* 7.16.1. See Appendix 1.

and biblical narratives could be relied upon for the provision of secure, historical data. Hamilton delivered a response that has been repeated many times since, that is, to deny that there was any fault in the text and to attempt a concordance between text and artifact. He pointed to large travertine formations arching over the river at a gorge to the west of the höyük and suggested that an earthquake had destroyed Herodotos's evidence,[36] leaving only a broken witness to corroborate the ancient anchor (Pl. 1.3).

Plate 1.3: Travertine formations overhanging the Lycus River (Ak Su) west of the höyük of Colossae.

It was not the first nor would it be the last time that an earthquake was summonsed to fill a vacuum in evidence or critical analysis. It wasn't until the end of the nineteenth century that it was finally admitted that Herodotos was wrong;[37] even then Herodotos continued to curry support.[38] The material environment provided the evidence for that repudiation and had risen in value for the construction of historical narrative.

Before Hamilton made his announcement however, the French explorer, Alexandre de Laborde, with his son, Léon, had in 1826 found a disappearing and emerging river, replete with its own white travertine encrustation. Unfor-

36 W. J. Hamilton, "Extracts from Notes made on a Journey in Asia Minor in 1836," *JRGS* 7 (1837): 56, substantially repeated in his *Researches in Asia Minor, Pontus and Armenia* (2 vols; London: J. Murray, 1842), vol 1, 508 and Lightfoot, *Colossians and Philemon*, 14.

37 Georg Weber, "Der unterirdische Lauf des Lykos bei Kolossai," *Ath. Mitt.* 16 (1891): 194–99.

38 See, for example, S. Ximinez, *Asia Minor in Ruins* translated by A. Chambers (London: Hutchinson, 1925), 158.

tunately for him, the publication of his work came later.[39] He claimed this was the long-sought indicator for the city of Colossae. The only problem was that this striking geological feature was nowhere near any remains indicating an ancient population center. As it turned out, later discoveries would point to the presence of an ancient quarry and a village possibly associated with it, so the area was not devoid of settlement. But no evidence of a city was found, even though, as I argue in chapters 3 and 4, the signs of slight human habitation nevertheless belonged to the territory of Colossae.

Plate 1.4a and b: The disappearing river at Kaklık Mağarasi as sketched by Léon de Laborde from his 1826 discovery, which he took as vindication of Herodotos. A photograph of the same phenomenon from approximately the same position as that giving the sketch is at the right.

The place now called Kaklık Mağarasi (Kaklık Cave), where Laborde's find lies, is approximately ten miles north-east from the equally striking höyük of Colossae. Herodotos's subterranean flow had been confirmed. But its failure to corroborate the site of an ancient city did not stop some French writers extolling their compatriot,[40] just as English commentators were ready to spoil the celebrations. Joseph Barber Lightfoot, the foremost nineteenth century commentator on the Letter to the Colossians, summarily dismissed Laborde's

39 A. Laborde, *Voyage de l'Asie Mineure* (Paris: Firmin Didot, 1838). A brief report had been made to the Royal Academy of France but it asserted no more than having successfully plotted the source and course of the Maeander, Lycus and Marysas rivers; A. L. J. de Laborde, *Extrait d'un rapport fait à l'Académie royale des Inscriptions et Belles-Lettres* (Paris: L'Institut Royal de France, 1828), 44. The delay in publication caused "palpable distress" for a number of reasons; see S. Mitchell and M. Waelkens, *Pisidian Antioch: The Site and its Monuments* (London: Duckworth, 1998), 22–3.

40 E. Renan, *Histoire des origins du Christianisme* (Paris: Michel Lèvy Frères, 6 vols, 1863–79), vol 3, 357.

claims: "Obviously no great reliance can be placed on the accuracy of a writer who treats his authorities thus."[41] Again, beneath the espousal of intellectual rigor, lay a competition over who was best qualified, even amongst the Europeans, to deal with material remains and the assessment of the provenance of an ancient site.

The confusion had spread to the river itself. The ancient Lycus River that meanders through the plain of the valley between Laodikeia and Hierapolis on its course to the Maeander River just below the ancient city of Tripolis has two main tributaries, the Çürüksu, the river where Laborde secured his prize, and the Ak Su where Hamilton pinned his identification. Laborde had taken the Çürüksu at the travertine cave as the Lycus River, understandable given that the ancient epithet "Laodikeia ad Lycum" is today Laodikeia near the Çürüksu. But the ancient naming of the Lycus attached to the river tributary flowing past Colossae, the Ak Su. The two water courses conjoin just east of Laodikeia, and the Lycus that meanders through the plain anciently gave its name to both tributaries.

The confusion doesn't end there. George Lampakis, a Greek nationalist and archaeologist, visited western Türkiye at the beginning of the twentieth century. He was eager to report on the survival of "the seven churches of Asia". Inspired in part by the eighteenth century labors of Bishop Meletios of Ioannina,[42] Lampakis was striving to establish points of continuity between the past and present as a bolster to national pride and stimulant to new intellectual life.[43] Laodikeia and Hierapolis were disappointments as to churches though not as regards inscriptions.[44] Lampakis was also watchful for inscriptions near Colossae, but he especially celebrated the resilience of the Greek community (understood as synonymous with the Christian church) at Honaz.[45] The crucial narrative that dramatically portrayed survival was *The Story of St Michael the Archistrategos of Chonai*. Lampakis tagged one of his photographs with what was, to him, the important part of the story, the striking of the rock to allow threatening flood waters to pour into an abyss but yet supply, under the patronage of Michael the archistrategos, a powerful healing spring of water.[46]

---

41 J. B. Lightfoot, *Saint Paul's Epistles to the Colossians and to Philemon: a revised text with introductions, notes and dissertations* (London, Macmillan, 1880), 15 n3.

42 Lampakis refers a number of times to Meletios's major work, Γεωγραφία παλαιὰ καὶ νέα [*Ancient and New Geography*] (Venice: 1728; new edition in 4 vols, 1807).

43 See R. S. Peckham, *National Histories, Natural States: Nationalism and the Politics of Place in Greece* (London: I. B. Tauris, 2001), 10.

44 See G. Lampakis, Οἱ ἑπτὰ ἀστέρες τῆς Ἀποκαλύψεως (Athens: 1909), 415–39 (Laodikeia), 439–47 (Hierapolis).

45 Lampakis, Οἱ ἑπτὰ ἀστέρες, 448–61.

46 Lampakis, Οἱ ἑπτὰ ἀστέρες, 451, pl. 247. The photograph is labelled Ἡ θέσις τοῦ ποταμοῦ Λύκου, ἐν ᾗ τὸ πλῆγμα τῆς πέτρας ὑπὸ τοῦ Ἀρχιστρατήγου Μιχαήλ, κατὰ τὸ Συναξάριον τῆς 6 Σεπτεμβρίου. "The site of the river Lycus, at which occurred the shafting of the rock by Michael the archistrategos, as given in the Synaxarion for September 6th."

He named this water flow as "the Lycus" and tied it to the marvel provided by Herodotos, further asserting that here was the origin of a name-change to Chonai/Chone.[47] He was clearly driven by wanting the location of the Honaz Greek quarter, the Synaxarion account of the archistrategos Michael and the evidence "on the ground" to twine together as a threefold cord — a nationalist Orthodox equivalent to a biblical archaeology perspective. Even though Lampakis knew that the mound of Colossae was at some remove,[48] a measure of coherence and continuity with the past had, in his view, been established.

Plate 1.5: The spring of St. Michael emerging from the ground but named as the River Lycus by the photographer George Lampakis.

The photograph above (taken in 1906) is not as sharp in its contrast as we might desire. However, the figure of Lampakis's local Greek guide showing the place (center-left border),[49] the rock construction passing behind the guide and over the mouth of the flow, and the volume of water, almost certainly indicates the stream bubbling from the ground that is located at what is now called the Göz Picnic Ground. This area, approximately two and one-half miles to the sou' south-west of the höyük, adjoined the designated "Greek quarter" of Honaz before the repatriation of Greeks and Turks to their respective "homelands" in 1923.

47 Lampakis, Οἱ ἑπτὰ ἀστέρες, 450.

48 Lampakis, Οἱ ἑπτὰ ἀστέρες, 448.

49 John Hartley reported that the site was readily pointed out by the local Greeks from Honaz as the location of St. Michael's descent and salvific opening of a chasm for the floodwaters to be swallowed; *Researches in Greece and the Levant* (London: Seeley, 1833), 53.

Plate 1.6a and b: The "St Michael Spring" outlet today with the modern pool construction for leisure-seekers.

Inscriptions and a possible material mooring for Colossae

In the eighteenth and early nineteenth centuries, inscriptions were frequently valued simply for the written information they conveyed. Consequently, we often lack other crucial material evidence — the lithic typology, its design, reliefs, letter shapes and most of all, the context of its discovery. There was one notable exception to this last element however. When a stone mentioned the name of a place, this was taken as proof that the ancient city had been "discovered". The excitement was tangible when the Reverend Edward T. Daniell, an artist-become-epigrapher for the 1842 Spratt-Forbes expedition,[50] wrote to the gentlemen of the Athenaeum Club. He claimed to have found eighteen ancient sites "unquestionably ascertained by inscriptions."[51] Daniell died from malaria in Türkiye. Samuel Birch, later Keeper of Oriental Antiquities at the British Musem (1865–85) was charged with editing the inscriptions in Daniell's notebooks. He selected only thirty-nine from the more than two hundred that Daniell had copied, the criterion governing selection being the ones that "throw new light on the geography of ancient Lycia and the other provinces visited during our jour-

50 Lieutenant Thomas A. B. Spratt of the Royal Navy and the naturalist Edward Forbes, a Fellow of the Royal Society, had been sent out to assist in the removal of "marbles" from Xanthus in southern Türkiye. Their vessel was quickly recognized as inadequate for the purpose, so their time was spent on a research and discovery expedition, picking up Daniell at the port in Rhodes. The Xanthus marbles did eventually arrive in England and were proudly displayed at the British Library-Museum. For the Spratt-Forbes expedition see Spratt and Forbes, *Travels in Lycia, loc. cit.*

51 *The Athenaeum* 7/23/1842 (p. 675).

ney. They are mostly such as fix the names of ancient sites, hitherto unvisited or not satisfactorily determined."[52] Clearly at this time, inscriptions were being prized in circles of learning for the confirmation of toponyms known from the classical and biblical texts on which scholars had been raised.[53]

Daniell's clerical education was assumed by his colleagues to have fitted him perfectly for the role of the expedition's epigraphist. After all, Latin and Greek were the foundation of a clergyman's training. Arabic, that had gained considerable attention from John Luke and Thomas Smith over a century before, no longer merited any priority. However, the limits of his own learning about epigraphy and that of even more specialized practitioners of the discipline, were exposed when he discovered the epitaph of a woman named Aphias.[54] Of particular interest was that the epitaph was concerned to detail that she was γένει Κολοσσηνῇ "by birth, a Colossian."[55] The problem was that he knew that he was in the region of Lycia not Phrygia when the inscription was discovered. He concluded that there must be a small town called Colossa nearby. The ethnic had been confused with a toponym, driven by the demand that inscriptions declare place-names and thereby enable scholarship to corroborate inherited texts by evidence on the ground.

The compulsion to pin down the site of Colossae by reference to an inscription achieved a reconstruction in the third volume of the great compendium of Greek inscriptions initiated by August Boeckh in 1828.[56] Frances Arundell had found a fragment of an inscription near "Khonos", the village previously mentioned. It ended in … ΗΝΩΝ.[57] Unable to resist the tantalizing invitation, the then editor, Johannes Franz, decided that it must be the termination for ΚΟΛΟΣΣΗΝΩΝ, completely ignoring an earlier part of the published inscription. He opted for a reconstruction of ὁ δῆμος ὁ Κολοσσ]ηνῶν, "the citizens' assembly of the Colossians."[58] The default mechanism to pin down Colossae's location had determined the result.[59] Lightfoot was not convinced,[60] but the

52 Spratt-Forbes, *Travels in Lycia*, vol 2, 266.

53 See L. Pollard, "'Every stone tells a story': the uses of classical texts by seventeenth-century English visitors to Greece and Asia Minor," *Classical Receptions Journal* 4 (2012): 48–65.

54 Spratt and Forbes, *Travels in Lycia*, vol 2, 289 (= *CIG* 3.4380k³).

55 The inscription was reported again in 1880 (Louis Robert, "Documents d'Asie Mineure: XXVII. Reliefs Votifs" *BCH* 107 (1983): 555 n9). Thomas Corsten photographed it in 1997, which enabled a slightly different reading of the woman's name (Daniell: Arphias; Corsten: Aphias). See C. Kokkinia (ed.), *Boubon: The Inscription and Archaeological Remains, A Survey 2004–2006* (Athens: de Boccard, 2008), 126, nr. 102. See chapter 9, Plate 9.8.

56 A. Boeckh, *Corpus Inscriptionum Graecarum* (Berlin: G. Reimer, 4 vols, 1828–1877).

57 Arundell, *Seven Churches of Asia*, 98.

58 *CIG* 3956.

59 In fact, the inscription probably was on a bomos (a large upright stone, shaped at its peak in the fashion of a temple pediment) from the necropolis of Colossae and provided a name, likely Zenon. See A. H. Cadwallader, "A New Inscription [=Two New Inscriptions], a Correction and a Confirmed Sighting from Colossae," *EA* 40 (2007): 114–15.

60 Lightfoot, *Colossians and Philemon*, 14 n1.

fact that he had referred to the inscription at all was indicative of the change in biblical commentary. No longer was Second Testament interpretation reliant solely on classical texts and ecclesial traditions. The "material turn" in Second Testament interpretation had gained traction.

The undervalued potential of numismatics

Lightfoot preferred to rely on the (few) coins that had surfaced that bore the ethnic that had been found wanting, to that date, in inscriptions. That ethnic was ΚΟΛΟϹ(Ϲ)ΗΝΩΝ — a lunate sigma being the only orthographical form on Colossian coin legends then known. Coins had been prized for illustrative purposes for the seven churches of Asia,[61] but again, they were relied upon only for the information conveyed through iconography and legend — nothing was relayed about the context in which the coins were found. So, even with the few coins bearing witness to a place called Colossae, the existence rather than the location was the dividend from the acquisition of these artifacts.[62] And its precarious state was, in Lightfoot's view, indicated by the switch between double and single sigmas in the legends of the few, extant coins.[63] The coins, even in suggesting the city's existence, were constructed as pointing to its lack.

Colossae was proving difficult to pin down, even when Hamilton secured a consensus as to its location. No *in situ* inscription providing a toponym was found (even though that has since been remedied);[64] coins were consistently described as, in the words of Churchill Babington in 1863, "without exception rare"[65] and, perhaps most telling of all, the monumental remains that Europe so desired to collect and imitate, were absent. The "material turn" was frustrated when it came to Colossae, so different from the lavish larder available at Ephesos, Hierapolis, Laodikeia and other places on the seven churches tour. The failure to deliver led to a fateful judgement, expressed most authoritatively by Lightfoot, "Its comparative insignificance is still attested by its ruins, which are few and meager, while the vast remains of temples, baths, theaters, aqueducts, gymnasia and sepulchers, strewing the extensive sites of its more fortunate neighbours, still bear witness to their ancient prosperity and magnificence." Its strength was drained, it disappeared "wholly from the pages of history", its

61 See J. Spon and G. Wheler, *Voyage d'Italie, de Dalmatie, de, Grece et du Levant* (Lyon: Antoine Cellier, 3 vols, 1678), vol 3, 161–86.

62 For the importance of coins for another issue related to Colossae, see the next chapter.

63 Lightfoot, *Colossians and Philemon*, 16.

64 See Cadwallader, "A New Inscription," 113–14; "Honouring the Repairer of the Baths: A New Inscription from Kolossai," *Antichthon* 46 (2012): 151, 158–9.

65 C. Babington, "On Two unedited Autonomous Coins of Colossae in Phrygia," *NC* (ns) 3 (1863): 2.

coins witnessing its "comparative obscurity and its early extinction".[66] And, in a remarkable collation that always seemed to lock Colossae onto Laodikeia and Hierapolis as the impoverished member of the Lycus Valley triumvirate of cities, some early European biblical commentators interpreted the obvious ruinous state of the churches in their equally ruinous cities as an indication that the threatened judgment in the Book of Revelation was fulfilled — "candlesticks" had been removed (Rev 1:20, 2:1, 5, AV, RV). If this was the case for, say, Laodikeia, then the manifest absence of remains at Colossae, implied an even more profound punishment for her.[67] Colossae and "punishment" even became an etymological exercise (see chapter 2).

Destruction as an explanation

Two factors were held responsible for the difficulties in the discovery of Colossae: the displacement of Colossae's importance in the Lycus Valley by the foundation of the Seleucid city of Laodikeia and yet another earthquake, the devastation of 60 CE. Here the tension between text and artifact was revealed again, this time with a certain reading of Tacitus' report of the seismic destruction further darkening Colossae's future. Tacitus had noted that Laodikeia recovered from the seismic demolition of 60 CE, rebuilding its civic credentials from its own resources (*Ann.* 14.27). Because Colossae was not mentioned, the assumption from silence was that Colossae did not revive. This interpretation has been reiterated into the late twentieth-early twenty-first centuries in Second Testament and historical studies.[68] Tacitus's text was exempted from scrutiny — his view from Rome uncritically replayed by modern interpreters as if that view was the determinant of reality, his privileging of a Roman assize district headquarters (of most interest to Romans), his ignoring of Hierapolis and other sites impacted by the confluent shifting of the Eurasian, African and Arabian Plates.[69] No alternate explanation was sought, such as the use of materials from an ancient site as a quarry for new projects (such as the Ak

66 Lightfoot, *Colossians and Philemon*, 14, 16. For a full coverage of the demise of Colossae at the hands of scholars, see Cadwallader "Refuting an Axiom," 151–66.

67 Lightfoot, *Colossians and Philemon*, 41, 60.

68 See P. Pokorný, *Colossians: A Commentary* (trans. S. S. Schatzmann; Peabody, MA: Hendrickson, 1991), 19; M. Y. MacDonald, *Colossians and Philemon* (Sacra Pagina; Minneapolis: Liturgical Press, 2008), 9 (with reservations); P. O'Brien, *Colossians and Philemon* (WBC; Waco, TX: Word, 1982), xxvi–xxvii; R. McL. Wilson, *A Critical and Exegetical Commentary on Colossians and Philemon* (ICC; Edinburgh: T & T Clark, 2005), 4, 18, 19, 34.

69 Tullia Ritti notes "the historical sources often report only information concerning Laodikeia and its politics, while nothing is said of the position taken by Hierapolis." *Storia e Istituzioni di Hierapolis* (Istanbul: Ege, 2017), 277.

Khan, a caravanserai between Colossae and Denizli).[70] The bare mound and surrounds of Colossae may in fact be a witness to continued settlement, albeit differently configured and differently housed.

For Second Testament commentators wedded to the penning of the Letter to the Colossians by Paul the apostle, a further problem was generated. Given that there appeared to be no reference to the earthquake in the letter,[71] it was argued that the letter must have been written beforehand. It helped that Eusebius had dated the earthquake to 64 CE, tying it to a divine judgment upon Nero's collapsing reign,[72] but the resigned admission that Eusebius had, again, manipulated chronology to suit his theology, pulled the date back to 60 CE.[73] Consequently, the letter had little time to have any effect in re-directing Colossian Christian practice.[74] It didn't matter that Colossae in the first century "was the least important church to which any epistle of St Paul was addressed".[75] It was, effectively, extinct within a few years. The one piece of saving grace was that the letter survived and carried an acorn of the oak of being a "circular letter" (Col 4:16). Little wonder that Lightfoot extended his disconnection of the letter from the city by claiming, "Colossae was from the very first a cipher."[76]

In recent days, the pseudonymity of Paul's Letter to the Colossians has been used to carry such disconnect further, with the claim that pseudepigraphy requires that no elements of onomastics or toponym of the letter can have any sure or even probable relationship with Colossae or any other city. Pseudepigraphy has been harnessed to seal not only the demise of Colossae (by rendering it irrelevant for consideration) but also the irrelevance of material evidence from that city (alive or dead) for considering the context within

---

70 See A. H. Cadwallader, *Fragments of Colossae: Sifting through the Traces* (Adelaide: ATF Press, 2015), 45. Some stones incorporated into the walls of the caravanserai bear fragments of Greek inscriptions; see "One Grave, Two Women, One Man: Complicating Family Life at Colossae," in *Stones, Bones, and the Sacred: Essays on Material Culture and Ancient Religion in Honor of Dennis E. Smith* edited by A. H. Cadwallader (Atlanta, GA: SBL Press, 2016), 165 n36.

71 Marcus Öhler however has argued that the references to the elemental forces of the universe in Col 2:8, 20 may refer to seismic upheavals. See "Earthquakes and the Elements of the World in the Letter to the Colossians," in *New Documents Illustrating the History of Early Christianity Vol 12: The Lycus Valley*, edited by J. R. Harrison, *et al.* (Grand Rapids, Mich: Eerdmans, 2024), forthcoming.

72 Ben Witherington wants an earthquake in both years! See his *The Letters to Philemon, the Colossians, and the Ephesians: a Socio-Rhetorical Commentary on the Captivity Epistles* (Grand Rapids, MN: Eerdmans, 2007), 19, 34.

73 This lead to quite elastic contortions by Bo Reicke in the effort to retain the historicity of an authentic Pauline text: "The Historical Setting of Colossians," *RevExp* 70 (1973): 429–38.

74 So C. J. Hemer, *The Book of Acts in the Setting of Hellenistic History* (Winona Lakes, IN: Eisenbrauns, 1990), 275.

75 Lightfoot, *Colossians and Philemon*, 16.

76 Lightfoot, *Colossians and Philemon*, 68.

which the Letter to the Colossians and those to whom it is addressed might be active participants.[77]

This has not necessarily returned the Letter to the Colossians or to Philemon to a metaphysical garrison with no particular terrestrial focus. The "material turn" has not been forgotten. It simply means that almost any site can be raided for its potential to offer a perspective on the letters named "to the Colossians" and "to Philemon." Thus one can assert that the letter is actually intended for the Laodikeians, effectively supplanting Col 1:2 with Col 4:16 — hence is unlocked the plethora of Laodikeian materiality.[78] Or, by claiming that we know nothing about the location of the writing of Philemon or the location of its recipients, one can substitute Ephesos as the fitting contributor of a context.[79] The "material turn" here reaches one of its fundamental constraints — the need to handle carefully what might be asserted from *comparanda*, the bearing of material from other sites for the interpretation of one's specific concentration. The sharpening of the contribution of materiality must always be mindful of the local, rather than assume that empire-wide generalizations apply equally in every place.[80] Nowhere is this more pertinent than in understanding the plurality of laws in the early Roman imperial period that governed slavery.[81] But it also pertains to the question of the provenance of a pseudepigraphal writing — never disinterested in a local response, never forged from a-contextual influences.

Rethinking Chonai and Colossae

There was a supplementary topographical issue. There is relatively plentiful textual evidence that a place called Chonai was situated in the area. Once the last rites were pronounced over the body of Colossae, an explanation had to be made for some sort of continuation of a Christian community in the area. For Lampakis, it wasn't an issue. Following the lead of Meletios of Ioannina, the name Chonai, he argued,[82] was simply the name change that followed the

77 See D. Lincicum, "Mirror Reading a Pseudepigraphical Letter," *NovT* 59.2 (2017): 171–93.

78 See A. Lindemann, "Die Gemeinde von 'Kolossä': Erwägungen zum 'Sitz im Leben' eines pseudopaulinischen Briefes," *WuD* 16 (1981): 111–34; W. T. Wilson, *The Hope of Glory: Education and Exhortation in the Epistle to the Colossians* (Leiden: Brill, 1997), 82–3; A. K. Peterson, "Colossians's Grounding Traditionalization of Paul," in *The Early Reception of Paul the Second Temple Jew: Text, Narrative and Reception History* edited by I. W. Oliver and G. Boccaccini (London: T & T Clark, 2018), 65–6.

79 Nasrallah, *Archaeology and the Letters of Paul*, 42. Even so, Nasrallah feels that it is legitimate to build a substantial part of her case on an inscription from the region of Philippi in Macedonia (44–5).

80 In this, I fundamentally agree with Nasrallah, *Archaeology and the Letters of Paul*, 34.

81 See chapter 11.

82 Lampakis, Οἱ ἑπτὰ ἀστέρες, 450, relying substantially on Meletios, Γεωγραφία (1st Ed.), 457.

miracle of St Michael the archangel in funneling a death-dealing flood into a subterranean cavern from which it emerged in controlled measure as a healing spring. "Chonai" means "funnels". It is the word that is repeatedly punned at the end of the thrilling narrative that became part of the Synaxarion for remembrance on September 6th.[83] Chonai was a direct continuation of the city of Colossae. The textual references to "Colossae, now called Chonai" and "Chonai, known of old as Colossae" are harnessed as support.[84] The full justification came at the end of the summation of the story for September 6th in the Menologion of Basil (dated to the turn of the eleventh century): καὶ ἐκλήθη ὁ τόπος ἐκ τότε Χῶναι. "And the place was, from that time, called Chonai."[85]

The converse is argued by those who factor Colossae's demise. Chonai became the alternate site of settlement, moved, for some inexplicable reason, *closer* to the fault-line that runs the course of the Taurus mountains and that unleashes periodic seismic activity. For those who slowed the pace of Colossae's decline until the advent of Arab and then Seljuk incursions, Chonai became a retreat site claiming the Taurus mountains (and eventually a fortress built on the slopes of Mt Cadmus/Honazdağ) as some kind of protection.[86] Chonai was thus a settlement from the rump of Colossae after the latter's destruction. The fundamental difficulty here is that the ceramic survey on the höyük and on its north and eastern perimeters shows no sign of an interruption in occupation of the area, except perhaps in 1200 BCE, coinciding with the collapse of the Hittite kingdom.[87]

A third option is that Chonai was one place, perhaps a rural sanctuary with supporting settlement,[88] within the wider administrative reach of the civic center of Colossae, located at a sacred spring known from time immemorial. There is a hint of this in the varied introduction for the miracle of the archan-

---

83 M. Bonnet, *Narratio de Miraculo Michaele Archangelo Chonis Patrato* (Paris: Hachette, 1890) 19.5–6 (citation refers to page and line number in Bonnet's edition). A synaxarion is a collection of hagiographic stories ordered according to the liturgical calendar. See, for one example, H. Delehaye, *Synaxarium ecclesiae Constantinopolitanae (e codice Sirmondiano nunc Berolinensi)* (Brussels: Society of Bollandists, 1985 [1902]).

84 Constantine Porphyrogenitos *Them.* 1.3 (ed. Bekker) = 3.24 (ed. Pertusi); Nicetas Choniates *Chron.* 178.19.

85 The Menologion of St Basil has enjoyed a number of printed facsimiles and reproductions (most recently in 2005), mirroring its more ancient popularity. Evangelos Chrysos dubs it a "best seller" of the Byzantine era. See "El Reinardo de Basilio II: El Marco Histórico," in *El 'Menologio de Basilio II': Città de estudios con ocasión de la edición facsimil* edited by F. D'Aiuto (Vatican: Biblioteca Apostolica Vaticana, 2008), 6.

86 Significantly a post-Byzantine text (by Damascene the Studite, dated about 1570 CE) calls Chonai a κάστρον, a "garrison". See Appendix 1.

87 B. Duman and E. Konakçı, "The Silent Witness of the Mound of Colossae: Pottery Remains," in *Colossae in Space and Time: Linking to an Ancient City* edited by A. H. Cadwallader and M. Trainor (Göttingen: Vandenhoek & Ruprecht, 2011), 272. On the collapse of the Hittite empire, see G. Beckman, "Hittite Chronology," *Akkadica* 119–20 (2000): 23, A. Sagona and P. Zimansky, *Ancient Turkey* (London/New York: Routledge, 2009), 291–8.

88 Compare Malay-Petzl, *Lydia* 4 (second/third century CE) where a village adjoining a sanctuary secured funding from a nearby city (Magnesia ad Sipylum) for the functioning of the center.

gel Michael in one late retelling — it occurred ἐν ταῖς Χώναις ἐν Κολασσαῖς τῆς Φρυγίας.[89] The hagiasma was central to the life of the city (probably even from Hittite times), at a relatively short distance from the höyük and possibly connected by a sacred way not unlike that connecting the administrative centre of Ephesos with the Temple of Artemis. It is suggested in the next chapter that the shift of nomenclature from Colossae to Chonai occurred in the aftermath of the tenure of the emperor Julian ("the Apostate") when idolatry received a frenzy of forensic attack by church leaders. The toponym Colossae had become tied, sometimes inaccurately in later Byzantine fantasy, sometimes intentionally in earlier civic "re-branding", with the Colossus of Rhodes, the god Helios. "Chonai" as the replacement name of the city alleviated the unwanted, accusing glare of bounty hunters tracking idolatry.

Confirmation of location and continuing life from material witness

Lightfoot had harnessed to his niggardly conclusion the few remains on the surface of the site, long a disappointment to travellers (unlike Ephesos for example).[90] When to this was added the accent on "few coins", "coins very rare", the picture was being built that Colossae had no effective life beyond the first century. The irony was that Lightfoot had relied on coins from the second and third century to decide a first century toponym. It seems that Colossae's punishment, even though the etymological derivation of a mis-applied place-name had been disproved, was revived under a broader, dismissive assessment.[91]

In more recent times, we have witnessed a historical reconstruction of Colossae as a thriving city in the second century and beyond.[92] The ethnic has

89 See Appendix 1.

90 One early tourist handbook canned a visit to Colossae with the abrupt "nothing much to see"; see MacMillan & Co, *Guide to Greece, the Archipelago, Constantinople, the Coasts of Asia Minor, Crete and Cyprus* (London: Macmillan, 1908), 195. Although Ephesos at this time had received none of the reconstruction familiar today (such as Celsus's library), the vast quantities of surface artifacts had curried British Museum backing for J. T. Woods' expeditions in search of the temple of Artemis. See his *Discoveries at Ephesus*.

91 See Cadwallader, "Refuting an Axiom," 151–66. For an alternate explanation of the meager finds at Colossae, that accents continued habitation across the centuries, see Cadwallader, *Fragments of Colossae*, 5–27. For the etymology tying Colossae to punishment, see chapter 2.

92 Lukas Bormann, *Der Brief des Paulus an die Kolosser*, ThHK X/1 (Leipzig: Evangelische Verlagsanstalt, 2012); Paul Foster, *Colossians* (BNTC; London: Bloomsbury 2016); Paul McKechnie, *Christianizing Asia Minor: Conversion, Communities and Social Change in the Pre-Constantinian Era* (Cambridge: Cambridge University Press, 2019); Rosemary Canavan, "A Woman, a Coin and the Prosperity of Colossae," *ABR* 67 (2019): 1–16.

been unequivocally visible on two recently discovered inscriptions, one found *in situ*, a second confirmed as removed from the site. The first inscription honors Markos, the chief translator and interpreter of the Colossians;[93] the second honors the benefactor Korymbos who provided for the reconstruction of the city baths and the extensive renovation of the water infrastructure.[94]

Its coins have become a key witness to its prosperity and civic self-confidence, though still substantially lacking the context of discovery. When Hans von Aulock provided the great service of pulling together a catalogue of the coins of Colossae (and other cities), there were 153 in total, spanning 56 types.[95] Only four coins, of a single type, were dated to the Attalid monarchy, the barest glimpse of Colossae's significance in the late Hellenistic period.[96] The total was not exorbitant but compared to some other cities in or bordering the Lycus Valley — Attouda and Trapezopolis for example — it was sizeable.[97] Since von Aulock's catalogue was published in 1987, not only have further examples of known Colossian coins come to light, but also numerous coin types previously unknown have surfaced. There are now three known coin types from the Attalid period (one with an additional variation — see i) in Pl. 1.7 following), with a total of 25 examples. From the imperial Roman period (that is, for Colossae's mint, from the time of Hadrian to that of Gallienus), there are now 82 or 83 known types represented by over 300 examples.

The eagerness of benefactors to become involved in the re-foundation of the Colossian mint during the reign of Hadrian, suggests that there was a renaissance of sorts occurring in the city — three sponsors, led by a woman (Claudia Eugenetoriane), struck in total 22 different coin types in the twenty-one year reign of Hadrian (117–138). A number of these coin types are attested by examples from different dies, indicating that the coins necessary for the local economy numbered far more than the 20,000 to 30,000 estimated to be produced by a single die mold before replacement was required.[98] Just from the current crop of known coins, Colossae's bronze coin circulation in this period would,

93 A. H. Cadwallader, "A New Inscription [=Two New Inscriptions], a Correction and a Confirmed Sighting from Colossae." *EA* 40 (2007): 109–18. See chapter 11.

94 A. H. Cadwallader, "Honouring the Repairer of the Baths: A New Inscription from Kolossai." *Antichthon* 46 (2012): 150–83. See chapter 9.

95 Von Aulock included a coin featuring Caligula (*MSPhryg* 2.545) which has since been rejected as a forgery: A. Burnett, M. Amandry and P. Ripollès, *Roman Provincial Coinage: Supplement 1* (London: British Museum/Paris: Bibliothèque nationale de France, 1998), 35, no. 2891; M. Amandry and A. Burnett, *Roman Provincial Coinage, Volume III: Nerva, Trajan and Hadrian (AD 96–138), Part I: Catalogue* (London: British Museum/Paris: Bibliothèque nationale de France, 2015), 286.

96 von Aulock, *Münzen und Stadte Phrygiens*, vol 2, 83–94.

97 According to *RPC online*, Attouda boasts 76 coins of 30 types; Trapezopolis has 104 coins of 31 types. For the sake of balance in statistics, *RPC online* grants Colossae 218 coins of 59 types (as at June 2021). For the location of these cities, see the Map of the Lycus Valley and environs.

98 See F. de Callataÿ, "Calculating Ancient Coin Production: Seeking a Balance," *NC* 155 (1995): 289–312.

conservatively, have been well over half a million pieces.[99] This correlates well with John Casey's estimate that today we possess 0.003% of Roman coinage.[100] It means the volume of output from the Colossian mint can be accepted as demonstrating anything but the demise of this Phrygian city.

I table here the twenty-six types of Colossian coins unknown to von Aulock.[101] Some will be explored in closer detail in the course of this book.

Plate 1.7: Coins of Colossae not included in von Aulock's catalogue.

99 For a detailed analysis of coins from this period, see Cadwallader, "Wealthy, widowed, astute and beneficent: Claudia Eugenetoriane and the Second Century Revival of the Colossian mint," in *New Documents illustrating the History of Early Christianity,.volume 12: The Lycus Valley* edited by J. R. Harrison *et al.* (Grand Rapids: Eerdmans, 2024), forthcoming.

100 P. J. Casey, *Understanding Ancient Coins: an Introduction for Archaeologists and Historians* (London: Batsford, 1986), 84.

101 For the complete list, see Appendix 2.

Key:[102]

i) Obverse: radiate head of Apollo, facing right; reverse: kithara of three/four strings flanked by the city's citizenry identification, ΚΟΛΟΣ|ΣΗΝΩΝ. 13–15 mm, 3.18 g (av.)

ii) Obverse: the head of Artemis with stephane, facing right, with quiver, arrows and bow at shoulder; reverse: lion pelt and club, flanked either side by the sectioned legend, ΚΟΛΟΣ|ΣΗΝΩΝ. 13 mm, 2.66 g (av.).

iii) Obverse: radiate and draped bust of Helios facing right: ΚΟΛΟCCH | ΝΩΝ; reverse: Demeter facing left, sceptre in left hand and a sheaf in right hand: ΚΛ•ΕΥΓΕΝΕΤΟ | ΡΙΑΝΗ•ΧΗΡ | Η. 17–18 mm, 3.17 g (av.). *RPC online* 3.2307A.

iv) Obverse: radiate and draped bust of Helios facing right: ΚΟΛΟCCH | ΝΩΝ; reverse: Demeter facing left, sceptre in left hand and a sheaf in right hand: ΚΛ•ΕΥΓΕΝΕΤΟ | ΡΙΑΝΗ•ΑΝΕ | ΘΗ. 18 mm, 3.22 g (av.). *RPC online* 3.2307E.

v) Obverse: radiate and draped bust of Helios facing right: ΚΟΛΟCCH | ΝΩΝ; reverse: Demeter facing left, sceptre in her left hand and a sheaf in her right hand: ΚΛ•ΕΥΓΕΝΕΤΟΡΙ | ΑΝΗ•ΚΟΛΟC | CHNOIC. 18 mm, 3.44 g. *RPC online* 3.2307C.

vi) Obverse: draped, youthful personification of Senate, facing left: ΙΕΡΑ CYN | ΚΛΗΤΟC; reverse: Artemis, with leaping hound, advancing right, holding bow in left hand and drawing arrow from quiver with her right hand: ΚΛ•ΕΥΓΕΝΕΤΟΡΙ | ΑΝΗ•ΚΟΛΟCCHNOIC | ΑΝΕΘΗΚΕΝ. 29 mm, 11.39 g. *RPC online* 3.2307D.

vii) Obverse: youthful, beardless, bare head of personified *Dêmos*, facing right: ΔΗΜΟC | ΚΟΛΟCCHNΩΝ; reverse: left-reclining, himation-draped river-god, long reed in right hand, left arm resting on water-urn from which waters flow: ΚΛ•ΕΥΓΕΝΕΤΟ | ΡΙΑΝΗ | ΑΝΕΘΗ. 22.5 mm, 7.70 g. *RPC online* 3.2307B.

viii) Obverse: draped bust of Herakles, facing right, club behind neck: ΚΟΛΟC | CHNΩ | Ν; reverse: bucranium surmounted by crescent above which are two eight-pointed stars all joined by a thin line: ΚΛ•ΕΥΓΕΝΕΤΟ | ΡΙΑΝΗ•ΑΝΕ. 14 mm, 2.21g (av.). *RPC online* 3.2307F.[103]

---

102 When the coin has been entered into *RPC online*, this is noted, without prejudice to the primary publication or collection. Weights give the average (av.) when there is more than one example, diameter gives the average of the known range in extant examples. Photograph of coin iv) from the CGT collection by permission; coin vi) by permission of Roma Numismatics; coin vii) by permission of St Paul Antiques; coins x) and xviii) from the Dunning collection by permission; coin xi) by permission of Savoca Numismatics; coin xvii) by permission of CNG coins; coin xix) by courtesy of Numismatik Lanz; coin xx) by permission of Leu Numismatik; coin xxi) by permission of SNG Turkey Erdem collection; coin xxiv) by permission of St John's Cathedral (Brisbane) collection; coin xxv) from the C. Piras collection by permission. All other coin images (except coin xii — see the following note)) are from a private collection, by permission.

103 An almost identical design of both faces occurs in a coin of Eukarpeia minted by Pedia Sekunda (*RPC* 3.2593; see also *RPC online* 4.2.1985 temp.). See A. H. Cadwallader, "Moneyed Women in Phrygia," *NC* (2023) forthcoming.

ix) Obverse: radiate, draped bust of Helios facing left (contrast *RPC* 3.2313): ΚΟΛΟC | CΗΝΩΝ; reverse: left-reclining river-god, reed in right hand, left arm resting on water-urn from which waters flow: ΙΕΡΩΝΥΜΟC | (in exergue) ΑΝΕΘΗ. 17 mm, 4.06 g. *RPC online* 3.2313A.

x) Obverse: draped bust, laureate head of youthful, personified *Dêmos*, facing right: ΔΗΜΟC | ΚΟΛΟCCΗΝΩΝ; reverse: standing Tyche, head turned left, holding rudder in right hand and cornucopia in left: ΙΕΡΩΝΥΜΟC ΑΝΕΘΗΚΕΝ 24 mm, 8.30 g. *RPC online* 3.2312A.

xi) Obverse: bare-headed bust of Hadrian, facing left, paludamentum: ΑΔΡΙΑΝΟC | ΟΛΥΜΠΙΟC; reverse: draped standing Zeus Aetophoros, holding eagle in right hand, left hand resting on scepter: ΟΚΤ • ΑΠΟΛΛΩΝΙΟC • ΟΥΑ •ΑΝΕΘΗΚΕ | ΚΟΛΟC | CΗΝΩΝ. 26 mm, 9.63 g (av.) *RPC online* 3.2310A.

xii) Obverse: bust of Mên facing right, wearing Phrygian cap and crescent at shoulders: ΚΟΛΟC | CΗΝΩΝ; reverse: standing stag, facing left: ΟΚΤ | ΑΠΟΛΩΝ | ΙΟC.?mm, 2.34 g. Lindgren collection.[104]

xiii) Obverse: head of Silenus facing right: ΚΟΛΟCC | ΗΝΩΝ; reverse: boar facing right: C | ΑΚΕΡΔΩC. 14–15 mm, 2.29 g (av.). *RPC online* 4.2.11890 temp.

xiv) Obverse: laureate head of Antoninus Pius facing right: ΑΥ•ΚΑΙCΑΡ•Τ•ΑΙΛΙΟC | ΑΝΤΩΝΕΙΝΟC; reverse: nude, standing, radiate Helios with chlamys draped across left arm, torch in right hand, globe in left: ΚΛ CΑΚΕΡΔΩC ΑΡ | ΧΩΝ ΚΟΛΟCCΗΝΩΝ C. 27–31 mm, 15.42 g (av.). *RPC online* 4.2.11597 temp.

xv) Obverse: draped bust of radiate Helios facing right: ΚΟΛΟCC | ΗΝΩΝ; reverse: hind standing, facing right: ΚΛ CΑΚΕΡΔΩC. 19 mm, 4.27 g.[105]

xvi) Obverse: laureate, draped bust of Commodus, facing right: ΑΥΓ ΚΑΙ Λ ΑΥ | ΡΗ ΚΟΜΜΟΔΟC with countermark Η in circular incuse; reverse: standing Tyche holding rudder in right hand and cornucopia in left: ΑΠΟΛΛΩΝΙΟC Β ΖΩCΙΜΟΥ | ΔΙΟΚΡΑΤΟΥC ΑΝΕΘΗΚΕ | Ν, in field: ΚΟΛΟC | CΗΝΩΝ. 35 mm, 24.08 g.[106]

xvii) Obverse: laureate headed bust of Commodus, with cuirass and paludamentum, facing right: ΑΥΤ ΚΑΙ Λ ΑΡ | ΚΟΜΜΟΔΟC CΕ; reverse: standing Tyche Poliade of Colossae and of Aphrodisias, facing and clasping hands, each holding a sceptre: ΚΟΛΟCCΗΝΩΝ Α | ΦΡΟΔΕΙCΙΕΩΝ ΟΜΟΝΟΙΑ (in exergue) | ΕΠΙ ΚΛ | Π | ΡΕΙCΚΟΥ. 34 mm, 25.46 g (av.). *RPC online* 4.2.2446 temp.

104 This coin has not been noted by von Aulock or *RPC online*, but was published by H. C. Lindgren and F. L. Kovacs, *Ancient Bronze Coins of Asia Minor and the Levant from the Lindgren Collection* [vol. 1] (San Francisco: Chrysopylon Publications, 1985), 48, nr. 929A. I am very grateful to Professor David Leitao of San Francisco State University for tracking down the (rare) volume for me and supplying the relevant text and plate of the coin. The text does not record the diameter and my reading of the plate indicates a single lambda in the sponsor's name in the reverse legend.

105 This is listed in *RPC online* 4.2.1895 temp. without distinguishing the reverse legend: ΚΛ CΑΚΕΡΔΩC rather than simply CΑΚΕΡΔΩC. This may explain not only the different die but the increase in weight (from 3.22 g av.).

106 Part of lot 883, Obolos Web Auction 24, 21st August 2022, unpublished.

xviii) Obverse: Geta, draped and bare-headed; Λ CΕΠ ΓΕΤΑC ΚΑΙ (here with countermark CAPB); reverse: Artemis Ephesiaca poliadic holding poles, flanked by hinds; ΚΟΛΟC | CΗΝΩΝ; 25 mm, 7.23 g (av.).

xix) Obverse: Laureate, draped and cuirassed bust of Septimius Severus: ΑΥ•ΚΑΙ•Λ• CΕΠ•C | ΕΟΥΗΡΟC•ΠΕΡ; reverse: standing Artemis, facing right, with left hand holding antlers of stag and right hand holding branch: ΜΕΝΕΚΛΗC•Β•CΤ | ΕΦΑΝΗΦΟΡΟC•ΑΝΕ | Θ | Η (in field) ΚΟΛΟCCΗΝ | ΩΝ (in exergue); 36 mm, 25.19 g.

xx) Obverse: Laureate bust of Elagabalus, cuirass and paludamentum: ΑΥΤ•ΚΑΙ Μ•ΑΥΡ• ΑΝΤΩΝЄΙΝΟC•CЄ; reverse: seated Tyche, facing left, supporting in right hand Artemis Ephesiaca holding a pole in each hand, and a cornucopia in her left, with facing (named) river-gods below, reclining on waters containing fish: Κ | ΟΛ | ΟC | CΗΝΩΝ | ΛΥΚΟC | Ο ✝ Θ | ΚΑΠΡΟC. 37 mm, 22.66 g (av.) *RPC online* 6.10900 temp.

xxi) Obverse: Laureate bust of Elagabalus facing right, draped and cuirassed: ΑΥΤ ΚΑΙ Μ ΑΥ ΑΝΤΩΝΕΙΝΟC CΕΒ; reverse: two Nemeseis each wearing long peplos, each plucking at fabric at shoulder, the Nemesis at left holding a bridle (?), that at right holding a cubit: ΚΟΛΟCCΗΝΩΝ Θ Ο. 35 mm, 17.85 g. *RPC online* 6.10829 temp.

xxii) Obverse: Laureate and draped bust of *Dêmos*: ΔΗΜΟC | ΚΟΛΟCCΗΝΩΝ; reverse: radiate and caped standing Helios with torch in right hand and globe in left; ΚΟΛ | ΟC | CΗ | ΝΩΝ; beneath cape: ΟΤ | Θ (hence, time of Elagabalus) 30 mm, 15.3 g.[107]

xxiii) Obverse: head of Sarapis wearing corona and modius, facing right; reverse: Isis standing on platform (feet covered), facing left, holding sistrum in right hand and situla in her left: ΚΟΛΟC | CΗΝΩΝ, possibly small ΟΤΘ below platform (hence, with style of lettering generally, time of Elagabalus). 19.4 mm, 4.7 g.

xxiv) Obverse: Volusian, laureate, draped and cuirassed, facing right; Γ Ο Α Γ Ο ΟΥΟΛ | ΟΥCCΙΑΝΟ | C here with countermark Δ; reverse: Artemis Ephesiaca poliadic holding poles, flanked by stags; ΑΥ ΜΑΡΚΙΑΝΟC ΕΠΑΦΡΑ CΤΕΦΑΝ | ΗΦΟ | ΡΟC | ΚΟΛΟCCΗ | ΝΩΝ (in exergue). 29 mm, 9.18 g (av.).

xxv) Obverse: Volusian, laureate, draped and cuirassed, facing right; Γ Ο Α Γ Ο ΟΥΟ | ΛΟΥCCΙΑΝΟ | C (in field); reverse: radiate, caped, standing, naked, facing Helios with torch in right hand and globe in left; ΚΟΛΟCCΗΝ | Ω | Ν Α ΜΑΡΚΙΑΝΟC C | ΤΕΦΑΝ | Η | ΦΟΡ Τ^{Ο} Ρ | ΙΑ. 31 mm, 11 g. *RPC online* 9.789A.

xxvi) Obverse: Personification of youthful Senate, draped, facing right: ΙΕΡΑ | CΥΝΚΛΗ | ΤΟC; reverse: semi-nude, front-standing Dionysos, face turned left, kantharos in right hand, staff in left hand: ΚΟΛΟCCΗ | ΝΩΝ. 18 mm, 4.79 g.

107 This coin is included as example 6 in *RPC* 4.2.1896 temp., a coin type minted by Publius Ailius Ktesikles under the reign of Commodus as Caesar. *RPC online* simply adopted the mistaken reading of Naumann Numismatik auction 94, lot 384 (October 2020) which omitted the abbreviated letters and assumed that Ktesikles's name was included in the legend, as in the examples of the second century coin. (It is not, though the diameter and weight are similar [31 mm av., 16.34 g av.].)

When these "new" coins are drawn together, it is amply demonstrated that Colossae, far from looking terminal in the second century, was in fact booming. Not only is it clear that the rejuvenation of the Colossian mint during the reign of Hadrian was manifest in a wide array of coin types, but the coins, in their size and weight fall into the range of values required for small, daily transactions, from a quarter of an assarion through to three assaria — that is, precisely the "coin" needed to purchase wine at a tavern or fish at a market. This plenitude of production continued through the reigns of succeeding emperors in the second century. Even the third century is marked by stylistically complex artistry in coin design, at least in the first fifty years or so.

Colossae's agricultural and commercial life appears to have been thriving in this period. Quite apart from the epigraphical and numismatic evidence, which contributes the substance of the arguments in the chapters that follow,[108] there are snatches of artifactual, architectural, visual and funerary evidence that point to a vibrant center. Colossae produced its own pottery, assuredly in late republican and early imperial Roman times and probably in other periods as well.[109] It had fine leather workers,[110] a fishing industry,[111] and a variety of agricultural goods besides wool and its value-enhanced textile products — grapes and wine, olives and oil, fish, grain, pork and fruit.[112] And it undergirded the city infrastructure with manufacturing production lines in stone, metal and timber.[113] It is clear from the literary evidence that Colossae's textile industry contributed to an export trade but, at least in the funerary industry, imported elaborate marble tombs also figured in commercial transactions. Fine, expensive jewelry was also present, not least in its expansive religious life.[114]

Until the last two hundred years, Colossae had skated precariously at the edges of the literary rink, frequently falling into unknown or misnomered territory, sometimes blighted with premature oblivion. The actual site was only confirmed for European observers in the 1840s and even then the privileging of literary sources and the mishandling of material remains not only jaundiced the assessment of the life of the city; it also prejudiced the way in which the two Second Testament Letters associated with the city — Colossians and Philemon — were interpreted. More recent attention to the material remains, especially numismatic and epigraphical evidence, has demanded a complete review of how Colossae and the two Second Testament Letters associated with the ancient city are to be understood. The remaining chapters seek to overcome the handicaps that have burdened Colossae and its prized witnesses, as the name has become a place.

---

108 For the list of coins and inscriptions, see Appendices 2 and 4.

109 See the graphs of instances matched to eras in Duman and Konakçi, "Silent Witness," 272–5.

110 *MAMA* 6.44. See chapter 12.

111 See coin xx) above and chapter 3.

112 See Alcaeus of Messene *apud Gk Anthol* 16.8; Leo of Synnada *Ep.* 43; see also chapters 3, 12.

113 See chapters 8, 12.

114 See chapter 5.

Chapter Two
Colossae, a city in search of a name

We have seen that the site of Colossae evaded discovery until two centuries ago. The difficulty was exacerbated by the variety of spellings, etymologies and geographical options on offer. Even when the site was confidently located in the European mind, the classical and Christian drive for precision had to confront the obscurity that attached to the toponym. Was Chonai simply Colossae by another name or an alternate location? How was one to understand the variety of spellings that denoted both Chonai and Colossae? What meaning, etymological or otherwise, explained the names? These questions arose from manuscripts of both classical and Christian texts where no stability was to be found, and in the oscillations of interpretations offered by the learned. This chapter explores these questions of the name(s) of Colossae and allows the witness of material culture, from Colossae and elsewhere, to sketch a pathway through the complexity of three millennia towards a resolution. That resolution owes much to what appears to be the city's own efforts (evident especially in its coins) in re-shaping its identity by privileging (fictively) a Greek etymology for its name.

The punishment of Colossae

"Colossae" means "punishment". That, at least, was the authoritative pronouncement of Edward Wells at the turn of the nineteenth century.[1] Given the time and his audience, he defaulted to the spelling of the KJV, Colosse,

1 E. Wells, *Sacred Geography or A Companion to the Holy Bible being a Geographical and Historical Account of Places mentioned in the Holy Scriptures* … (Charlestown: Samuel Etheridge, 1817), 326. The emphasis on punishment was a stock element of later apocalypses (such as the *Apocalypse of Paul* and the *Apocalypse of Mary*). Whether Wells had been influenced by an ἀποκάλυψις … περὶ τῶν κολάσσων (the opening of the Apocalypse of Mary in *BL* Add Ms 25881 fol 229r) is unknown.

but he seems to have based his judgment on the spelling of the place-name as "Colassae". The etymology was tracked from Κολασσαί to κολάζω, meaning "I punish, chasten, reprove", compelling κολόσσος now read as κολάσσος to conform to the meaning. Wells' book became the fifth volume of the famous *Dictionary of the Holy Bible* by Augustin Calmet, which had passed through numerous editions and expansions from a century earlier,[2] though Calmet had made no mention of this derivation. Wells' pronouncement instigated a series of reiterations from William Flemings' *Gazetteer* to the entry in James Orr's *Bible Encyclopedia* a century later.[3] It survives closer to present time in entries about the Christian East by Robert Taft, who notes various spellings are used of the same location.[4]

The tracking of the meaning of the place-name through this invented etymology was perhaps understandable. The developing transmission of the Greek Second Testament incorporated Colassae/Colassians into titles for the Second Testament Letter (*tituli* and superscripts), into chapter headings (*kephalaia*) and subscripts and, if they extended further beyond the text itself, the prologues (or *hypotheses*) that are frequently found in later Byzantine manuscripts. And all this before even looking at the text itself, which read at Col 1:2, "to the saints in Colassae" (τοῖς ἐν Κολασσαῖς ἁγίοις). Consistency however was not manifest in the manuscripts themselves. Occasional justifications in favor of Colassae over Colossae were felt necessary. Calmet believed that Colassae was the better reading but acknowledged that some preferred Colossae. However, he thought this was tied to the confusion with the Colossus of Rhodes that had led some Byzantine writers to consider "in Colossae" a colloquial or popular name for the destination of the letter: "to the Rhodians" was thereby adjudged as the intent, based on this collation.[5]

---

2 A. Calmet, *Dictionnaire historique, critique, chronologoque, geographique et litteral de la Bible* (Geneva: Marc-Michel Bousquet, 2nd ed., 1730 [1722]), vol 2, 125. The Calmet dictionary was incorporated into the monumental series *Encyclopédie théologique* under the general editorship of Jacques-Paul Migné.

3 W. Fleming, *A Gazetteer of the Old and New Testaments: to which is added the Natural History of the Bible* (Edinburgh: Edinburgh Printing and Publishing, 2 vols, 1838), vol 1, 365; E. J. Banks "Colossae" in *The International Standard Bible Encyclopaedia* edited by James Orr *et al* (Grand Rapids, MI: Eerdmans, 5 volumes, 1939), vol 2, 676.

4 R. F. Taft, *The Christian East, its institutions and its thought* (OCA 251; Rome: Pontificio Istituto orientale, 1996), 487, 491.

5 Calmet, *Dictionnaire historique*, vol 2, 125.

A colossal segue

There was a decided advantage in reading Colassae. The visual evocation of colossus in the name Colossae had generated an errant geographical connection in mid- to late-Byzantine speculation. Three examples, drawn from different texts, demonstrate how widespread such an association had become.

Manuel Philes (1280–1330) was a court poet in the reign of the infamous Byzantine emperor Michael Paleologos. His work is replete with appropriations of earlier classical learning. One of his epigrams was written to extol Paul and the power of his Letter to the Colossians. The consummation of Paul's victory rested in setting him against the Colossus of Rhodes. Here is my translation:

> The golden Paul conquered the bronze Colossos
> Having been taken from earth to the third heaven
> And he shatters the monstrous by the sling-shot of his words
> Setting the foundation stone in their midst.[6]

Whatever poetic license might excuse Philes for the Rhodian allusion, many Byzantines had already begun to literalize the connection. Metropolitan Eustathius of Thessalonica (1115–1195) put it more prosaically, "Because a great colossus was raised on high, the Rhodians, as from a great sham, were called Colossians."[7] It probably helped that, in Philes' time, the Seljuks had taken control of Colossae in the Lycus Valley. The actual site and church of Colossae, even when known under its actual contemporary and popular name, Chonai, had effectively been lost to Byzantine Christianity.[8]

But this is not the case for what seems (as far as I have found) to be the earliest double-naming/equation of the Colossians and the Rhodians, that is, in the fragments of the seventh century historian, John of Antioch. He wrote, "the Rhodians, having asserted their dominance over the sea, set in place a stele, which because of its gigantuan proportions, they called 'the Colossus', and because of this the people are dubbed 'the Colossians'."[9] George Monachus, "the monk" but self-described as "the Sinner" delivered little more than a tentative modulation.[10] His work was compiled during the

6 See Appendix 1.

7 Διὰ δὲ τὸν ἀνωτέρω ῥηθέντα μέγαν κολοσσὸν καὶ Κολοσσαεῖς ὡς ἐκ μεγάλου παρασήμου ἐκαλοῦντο οἱ Ῥόδιοι. Eustathius *Comm. Dion.* 504.30–32 (ed. Müller).

8 For further analysis of the Colossae-Rhodes equation, see A. H. Cadwallader and M. Trainor, "Colossae in Space and Time: Overcoming Dislocation, Dismemberment and Anachronicity," in *Colossae in Space and Time: Linking to an Ancient City* edited by A. H. Cadwallader and M. Trainor (NTOA 94; Göttingen: Vandenhoek and Ruprecht, 2011), 11, 18–21.

9 Οἱ Ῥόδιοι θαλασσοκρατήσαντες στήλην ἔστησαν, ἣν διὰ τὸ μέγεθος Κολοσσὸν ἔλεγον. καὶ διὰ τοῦτο ὠνομάσθησαν Κολοσσαεῖς. Fr. 30 (ed. Müller).

10 "The Rhodians, having asserted their dominance over the sea, raised a bronze statue of Helios, which because of its gigantuan proportions, they called 'the Colossus', from which connection the people are dubbed 'the Colossians'." Ῥόδιοι θαλασσοκρατήσαντες ἀνέστησαν ἐν

ninth century, when the Byzantine empire, though having been challenged by Arab incursions in the previous two centuries, was still relatively intact, certainly as regards the city of Colossae (by then known as Chonai) in the province of Asia or, as it became under the Byzantines, in the theme (administrative-military district) of Thrakesion. This would suggest that the Rhodians were already nick-named "the Colossians" prior to the seventh century, without any reference to the city of Colossae or, as it was then spelt in texts, Colassae.

Alternately (though less likely), George himself was displaying the Byzantine literary method of inventive embellishment on the legacy of his predecessors such as gained fulsome performance in the poet Manuel Philes. In any case, there is no hint of drawing the Letter to the Colossians into this collation. Accordingly, John of Antioch unwittingly laid the foundation for the contraction of "Colossians/Colassians" to a single entity — not the inhabitants of a mainland city but those of an island power that later resisted the overpowering influence of the Seljuks, and to some extent, the Turks.[11] The Letter to the Colossians therefore, just as Philes intimated, came to find an ongoing ecclesial embedding, albeit in another place.

The unembellished assertion of the Rhodian connection came in the encyclopedic Byzantine lexicon of the tenth century, the Suda. The tome flatly stated that the singular Κολασσαεύς was a toponymic derivation and identified that place, through its plural, Κολασσαεῖς, as Rhodes/the Rhodians. This spelling, with the alpha, is found repeatedly in Second Testament manuscripts as well. But the conflation of the two spellings is evident from the Suda's affirmation that Rhodes was the place where the Colossians were the inhabitants, adding that it was a derivation from the Colossus (Ῥόδος: … καὶ Κολοσσαεῖς οἱ οἰκήτορες, διὰ τὸν Κολοσσόν).[12] So, for the compiler, there was no difference in the meaning and derivation of Colassae/Colassians and Colossae/Colossians. Both belonged to Rhodes, both derived their name from the gleaming bronze Colossus. An earlier lexicographer, Hesychius readily allowed that the substantive of κολάζω, that is κόλασις, meant "vengeance", "retribution" (τιμωρία was the synonym offered as explanation) but distinguished it from κολασσία which, he suggested, was the shadow thrown by a (presumably large) statue or other protrusion.[13] He is generally dated to the fifth or sixth century so the Rhodian dalliance is clearly a later development. More pertinently for our inquiry he shows that the doubling of the sigma cannot be tied to κολάζω.

τῇ νήσῳ χαλκοῦν ἀνδριάντα τοῦ Ἡλίου, ὃν διὰ τὸ μέγεθος ἐκάλεσαν Κολοσσόν, ἀφ' οὗ καὶ αὐτοὶ Κολασσαεῖς ὠνομάσθησαν. George Monachus, *Chron.* 285.20–22 (ed. de Boor, volume 1). This is virtually copied in the work credited to George Cedrenus, *Comp. Hist.* 1.755.15 (ed. Bekker), dated to the eleventh-twelfth century, and the thirteenth century Joel the Chronographer, *Chron. Comp.* 23.15–18 (ed. Bekker).

11 The Seljuks were a powerful people that expanded through Anatolia in the eleventh and twelfth centuries, in a sense preparing the way for a second wave of Moslem advances with the Turks, who centred the Ottoman Empire on Constantinople after conquering it in 1453.

12 The Suda K.1931, 1932; R.205 (ed. Adler).

13 Hesychius K.3313, 3314 (ed. Latte).

A third permutation of evidence for the Rhodes connection comes in some Second Testament manuscripts themselves. At this time, the actual text of the Second Testament was cushioned within many reading aids — headings, "chapter" breakdowns, prologues, and commentary. The last — commentary — varied in its visual placement in the layout of the manuscript. Sometimes the commentary followed after the writing of a sentence of text that was frequently in a highlighted color (red, for example) to set it off from the "exegesis". At other times, comments were placed in the margins, that is, in the empty space around the perimeter of the page, frequently with small marks or signs connecting one comment with its hook word or phrase within the biblical text itself. The eleventh or twelfth century minuscule Second Testament manuscript, 1360, belongs to this latter type.[14] It has a titulus, πρὸς Κολασσαεῖς, "to the Colassians" and a series of ten kephalaia, the first of which, numbered "one" with the letter *alpha* and matched to the relevant section of text, reads εὐχαριστία ὑπερ κολοσσαέων οἰκειωθέντων θῶι ἐπ' ἐλπίδι, that is "thanksgiving for those Colossians dwelling with God in hope." Already we can see how the spelling of the identification of the addressees of the letter is not fixed, swinging between an *alpha* and an *omicron* for Colo/assae and the Colo/assians. Notably verse two of the text of the letter in this manuscript opts for Κολασσαῖς, as if the distinction between the letter *alpha* and *omicron* was no longer significant for the spelling of the toponym. Like the Suda mentioned previously, the marginal comment equates the Colossians (regardless of the spelling) with the Rhodians, and repeats that the reason for the name sprang from the huge, bronze statue, called the "Colossus".

The commentator adds a further intriguing remark that the Colossus was erected in the time of Manasseh, king of the Jews. For this insight, and indeed some of the wording, there seems to be reliance on the sixth century chronicler, John Malalas.[15] Given that Manasseh died around 643 BCE, and the Colossus of Rhodes was completed in 280 BCE, this seems to be a wild conjecture,[16] only compounding the fictional complexity of the whole notion. But this scribe does recall the builder of the wonder of the ancient world — Chares of Lindos — referred to by Pliny the Elder,[17] a reference not found in John Malalas. Malalas had not drawn the circle to include the Letter to the Colossians. Six hundred years later, the Second Testament copyist and commentator was not troubled by such niceties.

14 Here I am reliant on the digitalized reproduction at the *Centre for the Study of New Testament Manuscripts*: http://www.csntm.org/manuscript/View/GA_1360?filter=2. The codex has been paginated at a later date with Arabic numerals, here p. 511.

15 John Malalas *Chron.* 5.73. (ed. Roberto).

16 Another Manasseh, a high priest of the Jews, would be closer in date. See Josephus *Ant.* 11.301–305.

17 Pliny *NH* 34.9.18.

Relocating Colossae again

The retrieval of the Letter to the Colossians from across the Carpathian Sea back to mainland Türkiye, involved a two-pronged repudiation, chronologically sequential. Firstly, there was a Renaissance return to the references ("testimonia") to Colossae in classical authors. Secondly, the advent of European mercantile interests in Türkiye ushered in a reconnection with material culture.

The first charge was lead by Desiderius Erasmus (1466–1536). Erasmus had constructed a critical edition of the Greek Second Testament, albeit favoring Colassians as the Greek addressees of the Pauline Letter but Colossians for the Latin addressees in his bilingual interface! He also provided a quite erudite series of annotations on the Greek text, following the rough model yielded to him from a study of such manuscripts as he accessed.[18] He demolished the Rhodian connection by reviewing the references to Colossae in classical and, significantly, early Christian sources. The familiar testimonia were paraded and he added a reference to Ptolemy's *Geography* (second century CE) as well. Even though Ptolemy doesn't mention Colossae (an omission that fostered the arguments of some that Colossae had already become a basket-case),[19] Erasmus was interested in Ptolemy's inclusion of Hierapolis and Laodikeia, precisely because they figured in the text of the letter (Col 2:1, 4:13, 15–16). He reasoned that the passing of greetings and other contact between Colossae, Hierapolis and Laodikeia implied a proximity that an island in the Mediterranean couldn't muster.

More pointedly for Erasmus's array of evidence, the Phrygian connection was expressly named by Theophylact (1050–1107): "Colassae is a city in Phrygia now called Chonai. And, as is clear, Laodikeia was a neighbor to it."[20] The Byzantine commentator's first affirmation is little more than a reiteration of the mention of Colossae in Constantine Porphyrogenitos's work on the administrative districts of the Byzantine Empire in the tenth century.[21] It crops up in other places as well. Nicetas Choniates (c. 1155–1217), as the name suggests, would certainly have known where Colossae was, having grown up there. He adopted the same phrasing.[22] One of the manuscripts of the legendary *Life of Titus* has both Timothy and Titus visiting, "in Colassae, a Phrygian city now called Chonai" (ἐν Κολασσαῖς πόλιν τῆς φρυγίας τὴν νῦν Χώνας λεγομένην)

---

18 M. L. van Poll-van de Lisdonk, *VI–9 Ordinis sexti tomus nonus: Annotationes in novum testamentum (pars quinta)* (Opera Omnia Desiderii Erasmi; Leiden: Brill, 2009), 332–4.

19 See J. B. Lightfoot, *Colossians and Philemon* (London: Macmillan, 9th ed., 1890^9), 16.

20 Πόλις Φρυγίας αἱ Κολοσσαὶ αἱ νῦν λεγόμεναι Χῶναι. Καὶ δῆλον ἐκ τοῦ τὴν Λαοδίκειαν εἶναι πλησίον (*PG* 124.1208B).

21 Constantine Porphyrogenitos *de Them.* 1.3 (ed. Bekker) = 3.24 (ed. Pertusi).

22 Nicetas Choniates, *Chron.* 178.19 (ed. van Dieten).

before they went their separate ways, Timothy to Ephesos, Titus to Crete.[23] Here the city is of old recorded as Colassae, but has given way to a replacement new name, but not new settlement, it being "now called Chonai". If the text's editor, François Halkin, is correct in dating the *Vita* to the eight or ninth century then the phrasing, "Colassae, a city of Phrygia, now called Chonai" seems to have already become locked in as the formula for describing the city. This analysis has demonstrated that, from about the eighth century at least, there were two strands of thought competing for ascendancy, that is, ascribing the Colossians/Colassians and the Second Testament Letter to Rhodes or supporting the Phrygian connection for a city that had begun to be called Chonai.

The second sentence in Theophylact's brief description, that is, that Laodikeia was a neighbor, may be little more than a statement of the obvious. But I suspect the accent on neighborliness was designed to direct the interpretation of Col 4:16 along irenic lines.[24] That verse refers to an exchange of letters written to Colossae and Laodikeia respectively,[25] and has been cited in support of the characterization of the Letter to the Colossians as a "circular letter",[26] though we shall have reason to investigate the nature, purpose and limitations of this circularity in a later chapter. Theodoret's commentary on Colossians avoided the word πλησίον (neighbor), preferring the word ὅμορος — sharing a common boundary.[27] For him, the so-called worship of angels was a point of antagonism between Laodikeia (and its fourth century synod) and Colossae, a tension that guided his choice of word.[28] His interpretation, which implicitly aligned Paul with the Synod of Laodikeia, demonstrates that Col 4:16 does not necessarily require a congenial relationship between the cities.

Certainly Erasmus picked up on a networking connection. Some minuscule manuscripts likewise seem to have adopted Theophylact's two-fold affirmation (though often without accreditation).[29] It is clear that the Rhodian explanation for the provenance of the addressees was not universally adopted by late Byzantine copyists and commentators. Erasmus's corrective quickly gained sway

23 The reading is found in Codex Vindobonensis 45, § 6, as designated by the editor, François Halkin. See his "La Légende crétoise de Saint Tite," *Anal.Boll.* 24 (1905): 254. See Appendix 1.

24 See chapter 4.

25 I argue in chapter 4 that the so-called Letter to the Laodikeians of Col 4:16 is rather the Letter from the Laodikeians, and probably a response to the Letter to the Colossians read to the Christ-followers of Laodikeia. See also my "Greetings in stone: shifting the accent from papyri to epigraphy in Col 4:15–17," in *God's Grace Inscribed on the Human Heart: Festschrift for James R. Harrison* edited by P. Bolt and S. Kim (Sydney: SCD Press, 2022), 441–65.

26 See V. Balabanski, *Colossians: An Eco-Stoic Reading* (EBC; London: T & T Clark, 2019), 11, 163.

27 See Appendix 1.

28 See Demosthenes *Or.* 18.241.

29 See manuscript 254. This manuscript uses red ink for the text of the Second Testament and black ink for the commentary written below each section of text within the same margins. The manuscript has been paginated with Arabic numerals; the specific page here is p. 582.

amongst interpreters.[30] It did not resolve the problem of spelling however. That awaited the second prong of attack — the contribution of material culture.

The name in material culture

The collecting of coins and artifacts was a favorite pastime of the Europeans at the various Levant business companies in the eastern Mediterranean. One Aleppo chaplain to the "factors", Robert Huntington (chaplain 1671–1681), was described by his friend, Thomas Smith, as "always possessed by a searching indefatigable curiosity of seeing rarities."[31] In the mid-eighteenth century, Robert Pococke, an ardent traveller around the Levant before becoming Bishop of Meath in Ireland, published a collection of inscriptions. In his Latin preface, he allowed that there was a certain aesthetic pleasure in contemplating the items, but also that they were important for insights into history and language.[32]

It was precisely the provision of insights from artifacts that settled the question of the spelling of Colossae, although the first publication of coins from Colossae might be excused for compounding the spelling problem. Joseph Pellerin was at the vanguard of publishing a coin catalogue that included coins from Colossae,[33] though the fashion of granting viewings of private collections meant that some additional coins were known.[34] Three observations were made. Firstly, the coins of Colossae were said to be few. Even in 1863, Churchill Babington asserted that they were "without exception

30 See, for example G. Calixtus, *In epistolam Sancti apostoli Pauli ad Colossenses* (Braunschweig: A. Duncker, 1654), 1; J. Davenant, *Expositio Epistolae D. Pauli ad Colossenses* (Geneva: Samuel Chouët, 9th edition, 1655 [1625]), iv. Davenant confirmed his assessment by an aside about the perfidious Muslims who had overrun this part of the world (comment on v.2).

31 T. Smith, "The Life and Travels of the Right Rev. and Learned Dr. Robert Huntington," *Gentleman's Magazine* 95 (1825): 11–12. This was a considerably later translation of Smith's *Admodum reverend & doctissimi viri, D. Roberti Huntingtoni, S. theologiae doctoris et episcopi rapotensis, epistolae* (London: 1704).

32 *Neque enim est cur contemnatur hoc studiorum genus, unde fructus aliquis redundare possit, sive in proprium Literarum oblectamentum, sive ad Historiarum et Linguarum illustrationem*; R. Pococke, *Inscriptionum antiquarum Graec. Et Latin liber: Accedit, numismatum Ptolemaeorum, imperatorum, Augustarum, et Caesarum, in Ægypto cusorum, e scriniis Britannicis, catalogus* (London: 1752), i.

33 J. Pellerin, *Recueil de Médailles de Peuples et de Villes qui n'ont point encore été publiées* (Paris: H. L. Guerin and L. F. Delatour, 1762), Vol 2, 40 and pl. 45. Jacob Spon and George Wheler had published sketches of coins minted by each of the seven churches of Asia, but did not include any from Colossae. These may have been from their own collections or from that held in the Vatican or the "cabinet" of the Cardinal de Medicis, both of which are cited; see J. Spon and G. Wheler, *Voyage d'Italie, de Dalmatie, de Grece, et du Levant* (Lyon: Antoine Cellier, 1678), vol 3, 166–86, 358.

34 Augustin Belley claimed to know of five Colossian coins: *Histoire des Ouvrages de l'Academie Royale des Inscriptions et Belles-Lettres* (Paris: Panckoucke, 1780), 13. Frederic Hasselquist, who died during a stay in the east in 1752, knew of Colossian medals struck in honor of Ask-

rare".[35] Such an assessment was curried by auction houses, no doubt anticipating thereby a higher return on their sales.[36] As we have seen from the full title of Thomas Smith's 1678 book, there was a certain *frisson* attached to the term, especially when it came to artifacts in collections or renditions of remote oriental travels. This assessment of rarity would come to bedevil the significance of Colossae's coins, and the city itself, for over a century. This was compounded by calling these bronze coins "medals", as if they were merely a commemorative device rather than a crucial part of the city's economy. Henry Borrell, who had lived in the Levant, based at Smyrna, for more than thirty years collecting all the while and writing occasional notes for the *Numismatic Chronicle*, expressed surprise: "The coins of Colossae are much scarcer than might be expected from its importance."[37] This quickly was flipped in its logic, namely, that because the coins were scarce, Colossae's importance had disappeared.

Secondly, coins were asserted to be autonomous if a person's name were given in the legend (often labeled a "magistrate", a high-ranking official within Colossae's governing structures). This ascription of autonomy was reinforced by the naming of the *Dêmos*, a representative body of the citizens of Colossae, on two of the coins.

Thirdly, there did not appear to be a settled spelling of the ethnonym. Pellerin listed and provided engravings of three coins, and, he claimed, each had a different spelling: ΚΟΛΟCΗΝΩΝ, ΚΟΛΟCCΗΝΩΝ and ΚΩΛΟCCΗΝΩΝ.[38] There was not, however, a Colassae or a Colassian to be seen. Pellerin was the source for repetitions of this three-fold option in spelling, such as by Edward Wells whom we have already encountered, and subsequent numismatic catalogues.[39] However, just as coin interpretation was in its infancy (and still to shake off the use of the word "medal"), so Pellerin's eye was not as sharp as it might have been. He correctly identified one magistrate (his nr. 55) as Apollonios Val(erian?) but a second (his nr. 56) he named as Ti(berius) Apeireidos, a substantial distance from the actual magistrate's name on the legend of the

lepios, the god of medicine: *Voyages and travels in the Levant: in the years 1749, 50, 51, 52. Containing observations in natural history etc, particularly on the Holy Land and the natural history of the Scriptures.* (London: L. Davis and C. Reymers, 1766), 20.

35 C. Babington, "On Two unedited Autonomous Coins of Colossae in Phrygia," *NC* (ns) 3 (1863): 2.

36 See, from one auction of Leigh Sotheby and John Wilkinson, *Catalogue of the Important Collection of Ancient Greek Coins … by The Chevalier N. Ivanoff, Consul General for Russia at Smyrna* [29/6/1863], § 582 of Sarapis and Isis "of great rarity and in very fine condition" — see *RPC online* 4.2.1903 temp. for which there are now at least 31 examples known and § 583 Helios in a quadriga, "very rare" — see *RPC online* 4.2.1899 temp. for which more than 22 examples are known.

37 H. P. Borrell, "Unedited Autonomous and imperial Greek Coins," *NC* 8 (1845–6): 23.

38 The spelling with an *omega* (but with a single *sigma*) also occurs in the *Menologion of Basil* in the opening of its entry for Sept 6th, the story of the miracle of St Michael. See Appendix 1.

39 See, for example, J. H. von Eckhel, *Doctrina numorum veterum* … (Vienna: J. Camesina, 8 vols, 1792–1798), vol 3, 147.

coin: Ti(berius) Cl(audius) Sakerdos. Here are Pellerin's coins (Pl. 2.1a (from *Bibliothèque nationale de France*, probably his exemplars), b, c) with contemporary photographs demonstrating what he was seeking to reproduce.

Obverse: Draped bust of personified *Dêmos*, facing right; ΔΗΜΟC ΚΟΛΟCΗΝΩΝ "The people's assembly for/of the Colossians".
Reverse: Radiate Helios riding a quadriga, holding torch in his right hand and globe in his left; ΑΠΟΛΛΩΝΙΟC Β ΖΩCΙΜΟΥ ΔΙΟΚΡΑΤΟΥC ΑΝΕΘΗΚΕΝ "Apollonios, son of Apollonios, grandson of Zosimos, great grandson of Diokrates, authorized this."[40]

Obverse: Draped bust of personified *Dêmos*, facing right; ΔΜΗΟC ΚΟΛΟCCΗΝΩΝ "The people's assembly for/of the Colossians".
Reverse: Demeter standing, facing left, holding ears of wheat (not patera) in right hand, with left hand resting on staff; ΟΚΤ ΑΠΟΛΛΩΝΙΟC ΟΥΑ ΑΝΕΘΗΚΕΝ "Octavius Apollonios Val(erian?), authorized this".[41]

Obverse: Draped bust of Sarapis with kalathos on his head, facing right; ΚΟΛΟCCΗΝΩΝ "For/of the Colossians".
Reverse: Zeus Aetophoros standing, facing left, holding eagle in his right hand and holding a staff in his left; ΤΙ ΚΛ CΑΚΕΡΔΩC ΑΡΧΩΝ "Tiberius Claudius Sakerdos, governor".[42]

Plate 2.1a, b and c: The Colossian coins published by Joseph Pellerin in 1762.

40 *RPC online* 4.2.1897 temp; H. von Aulock, *Münzen und Stadte Phrygiens* (Tübingen: Ernst Wasmuth, 2 vols, 1980, 1987), vol 2, nrs 487–93 (hereinafter cited as *MSPhryg* 2).

41 *RPC* 3.2316; von Aulock *MSPhryg* 2.447. Some doubt must attach to the equation between Pellerin's very clear sketch and the single known coin (pictured) that we have which is quite worn. Certainly Joseph von Eckhel corrected Pellerin's reading of the legend so as to include OKT(avius).

42 *RPC online* 4.2.1894 temp.; von Aulock *MSPhryg* 2.471–482.

Pellerin's mistake was reiterated, though as one can see from the plate of the actual coin he most likely sketched, the *omicron* is damaged and thereby might readily conjure an *omega*.[43]

One of the finest commentators in nineteenth century Second Testament scholarship was Joseph Barber Lightfoot. His commentary on Colossians (and Philemon) continues to provide considerable insight for recycling in contemporary work. The material witness from the legends of the coins was precisely the evidence he needed to dismiss Colassae and Colassians as claimants to the city name or its inhabitants, at least at the time of the writing of the Pauline Letter. The witness of the coins to the spelling of the city name remained constant through to the end of provincial coinage under the emperor Gallienus around 268 CE,[44] with Colossae vastly outshining Colosae. Both Lightfoot and Babington before him ignored the confusion of *omicron* and *omega*,[45] perhaps recognizing from the study of Second Testament manuscripts, and in Lightfoot's case, of epigraphy,[46] how easily optical slippage might occur. Classical references to Colossae, even though occasionally infected in transmission by the *alpha* spelling, were now confirmed by material witness.[47] At the time Light-

43 The use of the *omega* for an *omicron* in the opening syllable in the name Colossae, was repeated by von Eckhel and T. E. Mionnet, *Description de médailles antiques, Grecques et Romaines …* (Paris: vol 4, 1809), 267–268, nr. 420. Other examples of the type held by the *Bibliothèque nationale de France* acquired late in the nineteenth century quite clearly show an *omicron* — knowledge of this may have filtered through scholarly circles even without any publication, perhaps even as known from the immense collection of William-Henri Waddington. Certainly when Ernest Babelon published an inventory of Waddington's coins recently acquired by the *Bibliothèque nationale de France*, this coin type was listed with the ethnic spelled correctly viz. ΚΟΛΟCCΗΝΩΝ. See E. Babelon, *Inventaire Sommaire de la Collection Waddington acquise par l'État en 1897* (Paris: Rollin & Feuardent, 1898), 346 nr. 5857.

44 Barclay Head tentatively assigned two Colossian coins featuring the "Sacred Senate" (ΙΕΡΑ CΥΝΚΛΗΤΟC) on one and the "Sacred Council" (ΙΕΡΑ ΒΟΥΛΗ) on another coin to the time of Gallienus (*BMC Phrygia*, Colossae 10, 11). Von Aulock removed the hesitation for the former and migrated the latter to the time of Severus: *MSPhryg* 2.537–9 (Boule), 543–4 (Senate).

45 The narrowing of options seems to have occurred relatively early. Thomas Horne used the coins to address the correct spelling of the city ethnic by reference to ΚΟΛΟΣΣΗΝΟΙ and ΔΗΜΟΣ ΚΟΛΟΣΣΗΝΩΝ alone: *An Introduction to the Critical Study and Knowledge of the Holy Scriptures Volume 4* (The Strand: T. Cadell, 1828[6]), 389 n1. His reference to the nominative ΚΟΛΟΣΣΗΝΟΙ is curious however, as no coin of Colossae has this legend; it may be a mistake for ΚΟΛΟCCΗΝΟΙC "for the Colossians" in which case, Horne has had access to a coin not found in earlier catalogues. He seems to have been followed by S. F. W. Hoffmann, *Griechenland und Die Griechen im Althethum* (Leipzig: Vol 6, 1841), 1798, who nevertheless cites Eckhel in support (without warrant for the first option).

46 Lightfoot, along with his Cambridge colleague, F. J. A. Hort, was one of sixteen consultants for deciphering inscriptions for J. T. Wood's study of Ephesos: *Discoveries at Ephesus: including the Site and Remains of the Great Temple of Diana* (Boston: Osgood, 1877), xix (to which the name of William-Henri Waddington is to be added — see p. ix).

47 Lightfoot, *Colossians and Philemon*, 17.

foot wrote his commentary, he relied on numismatic evidence.[48] The default approach for early European efforts to lock in a city's location was to find an inscription (*in situ*) that contained the city's name or ethnic.[49] Here epigraphy might have corroborated the witness of the coins as to spelling. We have seen already (chapter 1) how one early inscription was forced into demonstrating the ethnic; but it failed to gain Lightfoot's approval.

However, Lightfoot missed one inscription that had already been published. Even though it did not serve the purpose of locating the site of Colossae, it would have bolstered his case as to its spelling. We have seen already (in chapter 1) the inscription recorded by the Rev. Edward T. Daniell in the course of the Spratt and Forbes expedition in Lycia. The inscription was re-published in volume 3 of Boeckh's corpus, in 1853,[50] when Lightfoot was still a student at Trinity College, Cambridge. So, he might have adduced further support for a double *sigma* spelling.[51] It would also have confirmed that the preferred suffix for adjectival self-identification was –ηνός not –αεύς, the latter becoming almost universal in Byzantine texts and copies of manuscripts of "to the Colossians".[52]

However, a caveat on the *sigma* spelling comes from another reference to a Colossian, this time a male student of philosophy who had travelled to Smyrna at the beginning of the second century. He was named on his epitaph as Διόδοτος Κολοσηνός, "Diodotos the Colosian", spelled with one *sigma*. It was first cited in publication in 1899,[53] so falls outside of Lightfoot's range (d. 1889).[54] There are now a further two inscriptions that include the ethnic — Colossians. The first is an inscription honouring Markos, "the chief interpreter and translator of the Colossians", dated to the late first to early second century CE.[55] A second, similarly dated, honours Korymbos for repairing the baths and water-infrastructure and so restoring security(?) for "the Dêmos of the Colossians".[56] Both use the double *sigma*.

---

48 The witness of the coins to the spelling Colossae was first made by Joseph von Eckhel, *Doctrina numorum* vol 3, 147–8.

49 Lightfoot, *Colossians and Philemon*, 13–14.

50 *CIG* 4380k^3. For an engagement with the photographed inscription, see chapter 9.

51 Lightfoot made a number of references to Boeckh's complete corpus in *Colossians and Philemon*; see for example, p. 19, n.1. The inscription in Boeckh is also overlooked by Babington, "Coins of Colossae", 6 n9.

52 Lightfoot briefly explored the two adjectival endings — not restricted to Colossae; *Colossians and Philemon*, 18 n4 (continuation). On the shift to –αεύς see further below.

53 A. Héron de Villefosse and E. Michon, "Erwerbungen des Louvre im Jahre 1899," *Archäologischer Anzeiger* 15 (1900): 156, nr. 24; see now *I.Smyrna* 440. See chapter 6.

54 See chapter 5.

55 Μάρκωι Μάρκου | Κολοσσηνῶν | ἀρχερμηνεῖ | καὶ ἐξηγητῆ[ι]; see Cadwallader, "New Inscription", 113–14. See chapter 11.

56 τοῦ δήμου Κολοσσηνῶν. The preceding word is fragmentary on the inscription. It may be "stability of supply" (διάρ]κειαν), which would make sense in the context, but other possibilities would fit the space. See Cadwallader, "Honouring the Repairer of the Baths: A New Inscription from Kolossai," *Antichthon* 46 (2012): 151, 158–9; see also chapter 9.

There was however a further inscription of sorts that had been mentioned in von Eckhel's coin catalogue that Lightfoot had raided for some of his key historical notes. Von Eckhel had added a reference to a carved gem, sourced in an earlier journal,[57] in illustration of the importance of the representation of Helios/Sol on a coin of Colossae, previously noted.[58] He took the radiate head on one side of the coin as indicating the sun-god.[59] We shall have occasion to look more closely at this two-sided intaglio gem in chapter 5. But for now the inscription on one of its sides is significant as confirmation of Lightfoot's adjudication about the spelling of Colossae: Τύχη Πρωτογ[ένεια] Κολοσσαί[ων], "Tyche Protogeneia of the Colossians".

The gain from archaeological reference may appear small, even if the sheer incorporation of artifacts into biblical interpretation marked a seismic shift in method. However, having consistency across three different types of artifact — coins, inscriptions and a gem — is particularly significant as "multiple attestation" for the double *omicron* and an occasional variation of a single or double *sigma* in the place-name/ethnic. The chronological span on this material spelling with omicron was probably from about 80 to about 260 CE, although some suggest an earlier date for the gem.

Confronting a toponym with different spellings

Lightfoot held the opinion that the lack of consistency in the spelling of the name (even when reduced from three numismatic options to two) indicated the city's "comparative obscurity and its early extinction."[60] As we have seen however, he did not avail himself of all the material evidence to hand. Furthermore, his "comparative" had not yet rigorously extended to *comparanda*, for, if consistent spelling were the key determinant of a city's prosperity, then few cities in Asia Minor would be left standing![61] Almost all other cities with a

57 Von Eckhel's abbreviated reference was to A. Belley, "Observations sur une Cornaline Antique du Cabinet de Mgr le Duc D'Orléans," *Mémoires de Littérature, tires des registres de l'Académie royale des inscriptions et Belles-Lettres* 36 (1784): 11–17.

58 von Eckhel, *Doctrina numorum veterum*, vol 3, 147.

59 That adjudication has been rightly challenged. See J. Champeaux, *Fortuna: Recherches sur le culte de la Fortune à Rome et dans le monde romain des origins à la mort de César. I. Fortuna dans la Religion archaïque* (Rome: École Française, 1982), 120 fn 529.

60 Lightfoot, *Colossians and Philemon*, 16.

61 As random examples, see Termessos *RPC online* 4.3.8647 temp. (TEPMEIZO[N]) cf *RPC online* 4.3.8648 temp. (TEPMHCCEΩN); Smyrna *RPC* 2.999 (ZMYPNAIΩN) cf *RPC online* 4.2.238, temp. (CMYPNAIΩN); Nicopolis ad Istrum *RPC online* 4.1.11112 temp. (NEIKOΠOΛEITΩN) cf *RPC online* 4.1.10210 (NIKOΠOΛEITΩN); Hierapolis *RPC* 3.2343 (IEPAΠOΛEITΩN) cf *RPC* 1.2932 (IEPOΠOΛEITΩN). Note that lunate sigmas (C) replaced the four-bar sigma (Σ) in the second half of the first century on most provincial Greek coins.

geminated *sigma* in their name (such as Halicarnassos, Ariassos, Prymnessos) have numismatic examples where a single *sigma* is used.[62] Toponyms were not the only words to find their syllabic separation lost through the elision of a *sigma*. Θάλασσα ("sea"), for example, occasionally occurs with a single *sigma* in inscriptions across the eastern Mediterranean.[63]

The question remains, however, as to how to understand the shift to Colassae and Colassians in the sources. The occurrence of the form in Clement of Alexander or Origen,[64] even in some manuscripts of classical writers (such as Herodotos and Xenophon), can be put down to Byzantine copyists.[65] The evidence of the early Second Testament manuscripts, potentially at least, does offer us a hold on a time frame. 𝔓[46] is the earliest extensive Pauline corpus that we have. The manuscript is dated, on the most contained paleographical grounds to a fifty-year span — 175–225 CE, 200–250 CE, or 250–300 CE, with a weight of textual critics favoring the first. The relevant folio for our purposes is folio 90r (Pl. 2.3).[66]

The problem immediately confronting us when we pore over this piece of papyrus is that the damage to the margins is most pronounced right at the point where we would hope to find the text of verse 2. We have the opening identification, "Paul an apostle of Christ Jesus by the will ..." on the third last line of the extant sheet. It breaks off on the right hand margin leaving only the first three letters of "of the will", namely θελήματος. Six letters have been lost from the worn text. But "of God" opens the next line in the abbreviated form ΘΥ with overbar — a so-called *nomen sacrum* — a way of designating a sacred word in Christian textual practice. Then follows "and Timothy" (spelled *Teimotheos* in this manuscript) and "the brother" with the final *sigma* of ὁ ἀδελφός

62 Halicarnassos — double sigma: *RPC* 1.2721, 3.2153, *RPC online* 4.2.890 temp.; single: *RPC* 3.2149; *RPC online* 4.2.896 temp., 4.2.9720 temp.; Ariassos — double: *RPC online* 4.3.7294 temp.; single: *RPC online* 4.3.7293 temp; Prymnessos — double: *RPC* 1.3196; *RPC online* 4.2.1914 temp.; single: *RPC* 2.1396, *RPC online* 4.2.1920 temp. The same holds for Edessa, Coropissos, Odessos, Termessos in Pisidia, and even Sagalassos (an instance on *Asia Minor Coins* online, not yet entered into *RPC*). Even Colbasa, spelt usually with a single sigma (eg *RPC online* 4.3.7322 temp.) can find its name geminated (*RPC online* 6.6104 temp.). Only a few cities, and these with no substantial range of coin types, are consistent in their double sigma: Cidyessos, Colybrassos, Pednelissos, Tityassos.

63 *IG* IV,1 96 (Epidauros, 4th–3rd century BCE), *IG* II 13222 (Athens, 3rd century BCE), *IG* II 13336 (Athens, 5th–6th century CE), *MAMA* 10.177 (Appia, 250–300 CE), *IGR* 3.478 (Kibyra, 3rd century CE).

64 Clement of Alexandria *Strom.* 1.1.15.5; Origen *Comm. Jn.* 10.14.84, *Philok.* 1.13.

65 See for example the appearance of Κολασέων for Κολοσσέων in Herodotos *Hist.* 7.30 in *BnF* ms 1643. Friedrich Blass mentions a similar orthographical shift in a manuscript variant of Xenophon *Anab.* 1.2.6; see his *Grammar of New Testament Greek* (trans. H StJ. Thackeray; London: Macmillan, 2nd ed., 1911), 21.

66 I have relied here on the facsimile edition of Frederic Kenyon, *The Chester Beatty Biblical Papyri: Descriptions and Texts of Twelve Manuscripts on Papyrus of the Greek Bible Fasciculus III, Part 2* (London: Emery Walker, 1937), now in the public domain.

Plate 2.2: Folio 90r of the Second Testament manuscript of the Pauline epistles numbered $\mathfrak{P}^{46}$, showing a page number, the end of Philippians (Phil 4:14–23, with the addition of an "Amen"), the stichoi numbering, a titulus (heading) for "Colassians" and the opening two verses (fragmentary) of the letter.

leaving barely a trace of the top part of the pen stroke, followed by a similar trace of the horizontal stroke of the *tau* letter of the definite article τοῖς. Counting these two traces as lost, there appear to be fourteen letters missing — if we take the size of the letters to match those of the line above. The beginning of the last extant line on the sheet is the letter *alpha*, then a substantial lacuna follows before πιστοῖς can be seen. This indicates that the alpha begins the word ἁγίοις, "to [the] saints" rather than being a part of the word Κολοσσαῖς/

Κολασσαῖς. This returns us to the second last line having to admit that the lacuna cannot be reconstructed, except to suggest that the sixteen letters in [ς τοῖς ἐν Κολοσσαῖς/Κολασσαῖς probably ran a little longer than the previous line, longer still if the ethnic was spelt Κολασσαεῖς. Codex Alexandrinus (G-A 02) suffers from a similar lacuna. It has a titulus reading Πρὸς Κολασσαεῖς (which is likely a later addition); the subscript (also by a later hand) repeats the spelling of the titulus, though with a curious gap between sections of the ethnic (a feature found in other subscripts in the manuscript): πρὸς Κολασ … σαεῖς ἀπὸ Ῥώμης "To the Colassians, from Rome".[67]

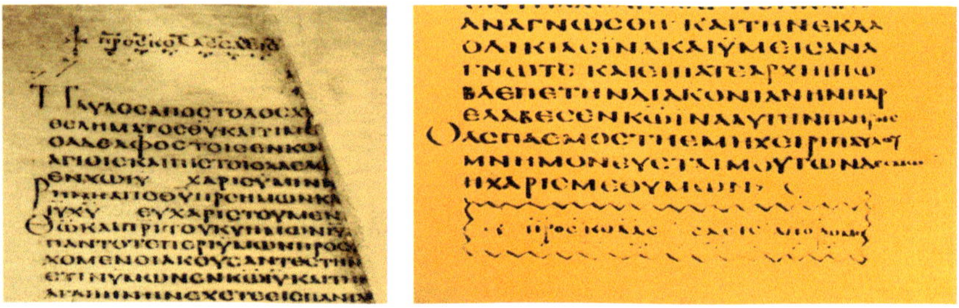

Plate 2.3a and b: The beginning and end of Colossians as it appears in Codex Alexandrinus, folio 108v and 110r, respectively, as re-numbered.

The late fourth-early fifth century Codex Vaticanus (03), reads ἐν Κολ^{οσ}σαῖς in verse 2 (without an epsilon) but in a book title raised considerably above the third column (and not placed between the end of Philippians and beginning of Colossians). It reads Πρὸς Κολασσαεῖς, only to have the offending first *alpha* given an omicron directly above it, by way of "correction". The fourth century Codex Sinaiticus (01), reads ἐν Κολοσσαῖς in verse two and, in a considerably later addition of a title, Πρὸς Κολοσσαεῖς. However a subscript has also been added to the end of the letter by another hand. It reads Πρὸς Κολασσαεῖς. Variation seems the norm.

Some Second Testament textual apparatuses have taken $\mathfrak{P}^{46}$ as a witness to the form Colassians. However this cannot be proven from the text because of its lacuna. And as we have seen already, manuscripts were quite capable of reading one form in the text and a different form in a titulus, prologue or marginal comment. In miniscule G-A 312 from the eleventh or twelfth century, the

67 The reproduction (public domain) of the relevant parts of Codex Alexandrinus (fols 134v, 136r) pictured here comes from *The Codex Alexandrinus (Royal MS. 1 D v–viii) in Reduced Photographic Facsimile* (London: British Museum, 1909). It has been checked against the online digitized manuscript of the British Library (re-numbered as fols 108v, 110r). The only difference is that the red ink of the first two lines of Colossians comes out clearly in the digitized version.

prologue, chapter/section heading and verse 2 all use the form "Colossians" but the titulus reads Πρὸς Κολασσαεῖς ἐπιστολή. The ninth century Codex Boernerianus (Codex G, G-A 012) defies any consistency in its headings. It uses ἀρχέται πρὸς Κολοσσαῖς, "Here begins [the letter] to the Colossians" on folio 73r (followed in its spelling in verse 2). But thereafter, dividing the heading across pairs of facing pages, it has Πρὸς | Κολοσσαεῖς (ff. 73v–74r), Πρὸς | Κολασσαεῖς (ff. 74v–75r), Πρὸς | Κολοσσαῖς (ff. 75v–76r), Πρὸς | Κολοσσαεῖς (ff. 76v–77r), Πρὸς | Κολασσαεῖς (ff. 77v–78r) before the finale of ἐτελέσθη πρὸς Κολοσσαεῖς for the subscript's departure from the form in the superscript!

This is where the titulus of 𝔓[46], Πρὸς Κολασσαεῖς, becomes critical, because of the date of the manuscript. The papyrus has been recognised as being worked on by more than one hand, with some scribes adding material at a later date. In the photograph above there are two clear examples of such activity: the addition of a page number at the top of the page — ρο. with a third number likely following the omicron, making one hundred, seventy-something; and the abbreviation for "stichoi" (στιχ) followed by a number (σκε = 225)[68] a line below the end of the Letter to the Philippians (Phil 4:23, with an added "Amen"). It is the third "addition" to the text on this page — designed to help the reading task to be sure — that is problematic, that is, the titulus. These titles are extant for most of the Pauline Letters in 𝔓[46].

Edgar Ebojo has made a thorough study of manuscript 𝔓[46]. Taking into account palaeography, comparative consistency among the titles and ink color, he concluded that "these book titles are part of the main hand's original work and not added later."[69] Regardless of the missing text for verse 2, it confirms that the spelling Colassae – Colassians was being used around the turn of the third century, although the form with the letter "a" (*alpha*) probably did not enter the biblical text proper until some centuries later.

Thus, we have a papyrus manuscript from Egypt with the spelling Colassae. But we have no mirroring of that spelling in coins and inscriptions from Colossae for the same period. The coin featuring the Roman emperor Volusian (see the table in chapter 1, nr. xxiv) can be dated somewhere in his reign, 251–253 CE, that is, at the outer extreme of one of the date ranges given for 𝔓[46]. If von Aulock is correct in assigning to the reign of Gallienus (253–268 CE)[70] those Senate coins of Colossae without a named sponsor in the legend, then the locally-manufactured items self-identified through an ethnic, still use "Colossians" with the *omicron* in the second half of the third century.

68 Scribes frequently kept some control on their own accuracy of transcription by counting the number of "stichoi" that is lines of about sixteen syllables. Inevitably some variation occurs especially in earlier manuscripts, even though, as time went on, scribes were expected to keep to a standard number of stichoi.

69 E. B. Ebojo, "A Scribe and his Manuscript: An Investigation into the Scribal Habits of Papyrus 46 (P. Chester Beatty II – P. Mich. Inv. 6238)," PhD, University of Birmingham, 2014, 179.

70 *MSPhryg* 2.543–544.

The evidence that has survived to us breeds a certain tension. On the one hand, the artifacts from Colossae or manufactured by/for Colossians consistently read Colossae/Colossian (with a small incidence of a single rather than a double *sigma*). Only in texts, albeit from a relatively early period, does the spelling Colassae/Colassians occur. Further, the texts from that early time are not produced in Phrygia but elsewhere — Alexandria, Antioch, Beirut for example (albeit acknowledging the better chances of survival in the climates of these centers).

Here I want to make a suggestion, no more. It relates to the very period when we witness the rise of the name Colassai. In about 365 CE there was a church council, a synod, held at Laodikeia. The bishop of Colossae was not listed as present. The decisions, called canons, are registered in simple form, almost like a codified epitome. One of the decisions is familiar in Second Testament commentary because it is often cited as a relevant element in the interpretation of Col 2:8, a reference to the worship of angels. Indeed, one of the earliest commentators on this verse, Theodoret of Cyrrhus, expressly saw the canon as rebuking the practice of angel veneration there mentioned — specifically, the honoring of the archangel Michael. The canon is worth quoting in full, in both Greek text and English translation.

> Ὅτι οὐ δεῖ Χριστιανοὺς ἐγκαταλείπειν τὴν ἐκκλησίαν τοῦ θεοῦ καὶ ἀπιέναι καὶ ἀγγέλους ὀνομάζειν καὶ συνάξεις ποιεῖν, ἅπερ ἀπηγόρευται. Εἴ τις οὖν εὑρεθῇ ταύτῃ τῇ κεκρυμμένῃ εἰδωλολατρίᾳ σχολάζων, ἔστω ἀνάθεμα, ὅτι ἐγκατέλιπε τὸν κύριον ἡμῶν Ἰησοῦν Χριστὸν, τὸν υἱὸν τοῦ θεοῦ καὶ εἰδωλολατρείᾳ προσῆλθεν.
> Christians shall not forsake the Church of God and turn to the worship of angels, thus having gatherings in their honor. This is forbidden. Those who devote themselves to this hidden idolatry, let them be anathema, because they have forsaken our Lord Jesus Christ, the Son of God, and gone over to idolatry.[71]

It seems that the period between the writing of Colossians and the gathering of a relatively small number of bishops at Laodikeia had not witnessed any decline in "the worship of angels". There will be cause to refer to this canon again later. For now, I simply want to underscore the peculiar word choice σχολάζων, "giving one's leisure over to." We know from the story of St Michael of Chonai that deliberate punning on city names occured relatively frequently. There, in reaction to the forces gathered at Laodikeia who are opposed to the veneration of Michael and his healing spring (much like the gathering of bishops in 365 CE),

71 An expanded text, (ms. Vindobonensis) is reproduced by P-P. Joannou, (ed.), *Discipline générale antique (IIe–IXe s.)*, I.2, *Les canons des synodes particuliers (IVe–IXe s.)*, (Pontificia commissione per la redazione de le codice di diritto canonico orientale. Fonti. ser. 1 fasc. 9; Rome–Grottaferrata: Tipografia Italo-Orientale "S. Nilo", 1962), 144–45. The inclusive translation is by L. Johnson, *Worship in the Early Church: An Anthology of Historical Sources* (Collegeville, MN: Liturgical Press, 4 vols, 2009), 2.302; cf C-J. Héfélé, *A History of the Councils of the Church* (translated by W. R. Clark and H. N. Oxenham; Edinburgh: T & T Clark, 1876), 317.

the popular story slams Laodikeia as "the people of unrighteousness", "the lawless mob", a deliberate false etymologizing of the city ethnic. There are other indications that the popular story is consciously targeting the adverse Synod canon and its formulators.[72] This reaction may be directed not merely to the content of the canon and its perpetrators, but also against one of the rhetorical techniques perceived in the language of the canonical attack — that is, an oblique but misdirecting pun on the name of Colossae in the word σχολάζων. This emphatic *alpha* in the key word of the charge of idolatry may have given additional weight, and not necessarily positive, to the spelling Colassae. The blatant attribution of idolatry to the city's life was countered in the popular story by a counter-allegation of idolatry on the part of Laodikeia (then tainted with the stain of Arianism). But it may also have fostered the need for a name change for the city, also punned into the Michael of Chonai account by the repeated "funnel" (ἐν τῇ χώνῃ … χωνευόμενοι) terminology at the climax of the story of the archangel's salvific action.[73]

Consequently, based on this conjecture, the toponym Colossae gained an unwanted support for the spelling Colassae (already in existence) through the charge of idolatry and became Chonai in order to avoid any association with that charge (especially important, as I argue below, given the city's earlier cultivation of a Helios approbation of its identity). Chonai became a place-name marking its authentic Christian identity as a careful obscuring of its pagan past and heterodox reputation. Even so, this suggestion can be no more than a conjectural explanation that attempts to connect the pieces of evidence in their historical setting.

A Phrygian explanation?

Lightfoot had tethered the double and single *sigma* versions of the toponym to Colossae's terminal trajectory. He implied that Phrygian origins and multiple ethno-linguistic interference were to blame "for the spelling variations", though he shied away from being too definitive about what language "Colossae" stemmed from.[74] Slightly earlier, Christopher Wordsworth had been less restrained, suggesting that Colassae was "probably a Phrygian accommodation

---

72 See A. H. Cadwallader, "Inter-city Conflict in the Story of St Michael of Chonai," in *Religious Conflict from Early Christianity to the Rise of Islam* edited by W. Mayer and B. Neil (Arbeiten zur Kirchengeschichte 121; Tübingen: de Gruyter, 2013), 109–28.

73 *S. Mich. Chon.* 19.5–6 (ed. Bonnet).

74 "in a Phrygian city over which so many Eastern nations swept in succession, who shall say to what language the name belonged, or what are its affinities." Lightfoot, *Colossians and Philemon*, 17.

of the Greek word Colossae."[75] Their assessments (especially that of Lightfoot) reverberated into twentieth century scholarship.[76] F. F. Bruce, for example, extended the claim. Not only might "Kolassai … [reflect] an earlier possibly Phrygian, pronunciation," but the spelling Kolossai might "represent an attempt to provide the place-name with an artificial etymology", namely κολοσσός.[77] Other recent commentators ignore the issue altogether.

Since the nineteenth century, scholarship into ancient languages of Asia Minor has largely dismissed this claim of Phrygian interference, as more headway has been made into an understanding of the language.[78] Again, material artifacts have driven the new insights, most particularly inscriptions. As Claude Brixhe, the leading analyst of Phrygian and Greek linguistic exchange, points out, koine Greek too easily is spoken of as an undifferentiated development in the language. Rather koine is a spectrum. Its Attic origins continued to manifest as the written standard, represented in literary prose, diplomatic documents and municipal decrees. At the opposite pole, there is the "natural" spoken koine, polymorphous because of the wide range of heterogenous regions where Greek had taken hold, to which we do not have access. But we gain glimpses in inscriptions, graffiti and dipinti. Here, in spite of a constant if inconsistent reference back to literary texts and school training, close analysis gives us a sense of how the language gained regional forms in its interaction with indigenous tongues, especially those feeding in from the countryside for markets.[79] Living pronunciation inevitably delivered an impact into written, if unrefined, expression.[80]

Here a fundamental qualification on comparison of Phrygian-influenced Greek with our concerns is delivered. The manuscript copies of Colossians that have been noted, even, or perhaps clearly, 𝔓[46], come from the hands of those trained in the schools, in both Greek and scribal practice. As Brixhe has noted many times, "Public documents demonstrate that the written version of this standard tongue remained close to the language of [the fourth century BCE

75 C. Wordsworth, *New Testament of our Lord and Saviour Jesus Christ, Volume II, St Paul's Epistles* (London: Rivingtons, 1870 [1859]), 316.

76 See J. H. Moulton and W. F. Howard, *A Grammar of New Testament Greek Vol. II Accidence and Word Formation* (Edinburgh: T & T Clark, 1939), 73 (citing Lightfoot in support); R. McL. Wilson, *Colossians and Philemon* (ICC; London/New York: T & T Clark, 2005), 3 n1 (following Lightfoot).

77 F. F. Bruce, *The Epistles to the Colossians, to Philemon, and to the Ephesians* (NICNT; Grand Rapids, MI; Eerdmans, 1984), 4.

78 See generally, R. Woodhouse, "An Overview of Research on Phrygian from the Nineteenth Century to the Present," *Studia Linguistica* 126 (2009): 166–88.

79 Neophrygian inscriptions are predominantly from rural locations.

80 C. Brixhe, "Linguistic Diversity in Asia Minor during the Empire: *Koine* and Non-Greek Languages," in *A Companion to the Ancient Greek Language* edited by E. J. Bakker (Oxford: Blackwell, 2010), 229–31, 251.

Attic orator] Demosthenes."[81] Even though one might argue that some if not most of the Second Testament documents reflect a more popular Greek idiom, in the hands of later copyists both the text and its accouterments became refined upwards in register. They do not come from the world that produces small epitaphs and other popularly-produced inscriptions where we gain a small hold on the Phrygian impact on Greek or which have bequeathed us a little more than one hundred actual Phrygian inscriptions from the Roman period.[82] Names especially, such as Apphia in Phmn 2, tend to survive longer than the grasp of its originating language, especially when, as in this example, it had become a name of affection, a *Lallname* that migrated across ethnic backgrounds.[83]

At Colossae and the surrounding region, we gain a few clues of the impact of local pronunciation on Greek forms. The epitaph of Dion the son of Appas, still extant in the northern necropolis (in 2013), describes his occupation as a "leather-worker".[84] The word is carved as διφθεροπύς rather than the morphologically "correct" διφθεροποιός. This orthography is a widespread phenomenon in Greek inscriptions in Phrygia,[85] reflecting a pronunciation that displaces the diphthongs -οι- and -ου- and/or the *omicron* with an *upsilon*.[86] A certain dedicant near Ankara, one Cleopatra, became Κλευπάτρα.[87] Laodikeia (whether on the Lycus or one of the number of other places bearing the name) was in danger of losing the omicron altogether, very occasionally becoming Λαδικεία,[88] and sometimes Λαυδικεία.[89] Although this is an irregular example, because it touches the first syllable, grammarians from the second century CE on, simply explained the loss of the *omicron* from the combination with *alpha* as an example of crasis, so that the resultant *alpha* was regarded as "long" (μακρόν).[90]

---

81 Brixhe, "Interactions between Greek and Phrygian under the Roman Empire," in *Bilingualism in Ancient Society: Language Contact and the Written Text* edited by J. N. Adams, M. Janse and S. Swain (Oxford: Oxford University Press, 2002), 266.

82 Brixhe puts the figure at 114 — 63, possibly 64 of which are bilingual: "Interactions," 248.

83 Brixhe, "Linguistic Diversity," 250. Ladislav Zgusta, *Kleinasiatische Personennamen* (Prague: Czechoslovakian Academy, 1964), 83.

84 *MAMA* 6.44.

85 Brixhe, "Interactions," 260, 263–4.

86 See as but a few examples, *MAMA* 4.33, 5.29, 6.73, 274.

87 T. Drew-Bear, C. M. Thomas and M. Yıldızturan, *Phrygian Votive Steles* (Turkey: Museum of Anatolian Civilizations, 1999), 63, nr. 22.

88 *I.Ephesos* 1615 (probably meaning Laodikeia-on-Lycus) cf *MAMA* 1.86 (Laodikeia Combusta). It must be admitted that the loss of the omicron (Ladike, Ladikos etc) had become widespread in onomastics.

89 *MAMA* 8.423 (Aphrodisias, "Imperial"); G. Petzl and E. Schwertheim, *Hadrian und die dionysischen Künstler: drei in Alexandria Troas neugefundene Briefe des kaisers an die Künster-Vereinigung* (AMS 58; Bonn: Habelt, 2006), 8/16 (Alexandria Troas, 133–134 CE).

90 Apollonios Dyscolos, *Adv.* 2.1/1.174 (ed. Schneider); Aelius Herodianus *Onom.* 3/2.649 (ed. Lentz); Heraclides *Fr* 3 (ed. Cohn).

Plate 2.4: The *bomos* (here with the meaning "sacred tombstone")[91] is for Karpon, his wife Euthenia and son Artemidoros, dated to the second century CE.[92]

This is but one example of orthographical shifts in Greek at a more popular level, influenced by Phrygian and other languages.[93] But, among all the shifts that Brixhe and others have isolated from mainly material sources, the shift from *omicron* to *alpha* is *not* apparent. There has been one example that has persuaded some scholars that a (reverse) move from *alpha* to *omicron* may have happened in Greek rubbing against Phrygian. ακκαλος, known from neo-Phrygian (or part-Phrygian) inscriptions,[94] has been thought to transform into ἄκολος meaning "morsel, bit".[95] But, given the early appearance of ἄκολος (for example in Homer's *Odyssey* 17.222) the exchange, if such it be, must come from centuries before, probably in pre-paleo-Phrygian times before the col-

91 βομός is capable of broad nuances in meaning (and architectural reference). See J. J. Coulton, "Pedestals as 'Altars' in Roman Asia Minor," *AS* 55 (2005): 127–57.

92 We return to this funerary bomos again, along with others, in chapter 12.

93 See Brixhe, "Linguistic Diversity," 232–3; Orsat Ligorio and Alexander Lubotsky, "Languages of Fragmentary Attestation: Phrygian," in *Handbook of Comparative and Historical Indo-European Linguistics* edited by J. Klein, B. Joseph and M. Fritz (HSK 41.3; Boston: de Gruyter Mouron, 2017), 1818–21. See also Brixhe, "La Langue comme critere d'acculturation: l'exemple du Grec d'un district Phrygien," *Hethitica* 8 (1987): 45–80; *Essai sur le grec anatolien au début de notre ère* (Nancy: Presses universitaires, 1987).

94 See *MAMA* 7.313, 454, all part of a standard curse formula against desecration of a tomb.

95 Shane Hawkins, "Greek and the Languages of Asia Minor," in *Companion to the Ancient Greek Language*, 225. *LSJ* sv. is more reserved.

lapse of the Hittite kingdom and its remnants (from 1200–800 BCE) allowed Phrygians to become more entrenched and self-contained in Asia Minor from the end of the ninth century BCE. Significantly, ἄκολος was not affected by the survival of ακκαλος in neo-Phrygian, that is, in Roman imperial times — the very period when Colossae is apparently under threat from Colassae.[96] Indeed, the connection may prove to be little more than visual impressionism, given that ακκαλος probably means "water" not "morsel of bread" and likely related to a Greek hydronym, the river Acheloos (Ἀχελῷος). Fred Woudhuizen's list of lexical correspondences between Phrygian and Greek, allows no example that might suggest a propensity for Phrygian *alpha* to replace Greek *omicron*.[97]

There are a couple of examples where *alpha* does replace *omicron* in Greek words but these have explanations other than Phrygian interference. At least one of them may be relevant for our search for an explanation of the advent of "Colassae". The first comes in the number of examples where γενάμενος has displaced γενόμενος.[98] This is nothing more than another example of the *sigma* (or *alpha*)-aorist forms displacing (or sometimes co-existing with) thematic/root forms.[99] In fact, in one papyrus fragment of a biography of Thucydides dated to the end of the second century (*P.Oxy.* 1800), the scribe wrote γενάμενος and then corrected him/herself by adding an *omicron* above the *alpha* (l. 71).[100] This is precisely what occurred in the titulus to Colossians in Codex Vaticanus, mentioned previously. Clearly, the training of the schools was intruding on the respective scribes' natural acceptance of an evolved/evolving usage. As Fenton Hort long ago observed, "all our MSS have to a greater or less extent suffered from the effacement of unclassical forms of words."[101] Such training did not however bother writers and copyists of popular literature such as the *Acts of the Pagan Martyrs* or the *Protoevangelium of James*.[102] The Thomas *Gospel of the Infancy of Jesus* happily deploys both forms within a few lines of each other![103] There is a curious instance of γενάμενος in Codex Alexandrinus. Although in the vast number of cases where the aorist of γίνομαι is used in the

96 It needs also to be recalled that Phrygians derived their alphabet from the Greeks not vice-versa. See Woodhouse, "Overview of Research," 170.
97 F. C. Woudhuizen, "Phrygian & Greek," *Talanta* 40–41 (2008–2009): 183–91.
98 See, for example, *MAMA* 6.225 (Apameia, 3rd century CE); Louis and Jeanne Robert, *La Carie: Histoire et géographie historique avec le recueil des inscriptions antiques. Le Plateau de Tabai et ses environs II* (Paris: Adrien-Maisonneuve, 1954), nr. 168 (Sebastopolis, 116/117 CE). In the papyri, see *PSI* 12.241 (Alexandria, 159 CE); *P.Oxy*. 2419 (6th century CE).
99 See B. F. Westcott and F. J. A. Hort, *The New Testament in the Original Greek: Introduction, Appendix* (London: Macmillan, 1881), Appendix, 164–66.
100 See T. Mészáros, "Two Critical Notes on the Ancient Biographical Tradition of Thucydides," in *Investigatio Fontium. Griechiche und lateinische Quellen mit Erläuterungen* edited by H. László (Budapest: Eötvös-József, 2014), 57–8.
101 Westcott and Hort, *Appendix*, 141.
102 *Acta Alex.* 11a.2.28 (ed. Musurillo); *Protoev. Iac.* 33.16 (ed. de Strycker).
103 *GInf.* 16.2.1–2 (first recension; ed. Burke).

Greek of the First Testament, the thematic usage holds,[104] there is one striking exception. In eight of eleven cases where a pseudo-title is given to an oracle of Jeremiah, the form in Codex A is ὁ λόγος ὁ γενάμενος παρὰ κυρίου πρὸς Ἰερεμιαν "The word of the Lord that came to Jeremiah". No correction is made to the form γενάμενος. Moreover, the phrasing is incorporated into an indented and colorized section of text, supplementing the titular language into a titular format. It is as if the evolving form is permitted for such "titles", at least to the copyist(s) working on this prophetic book. Over time in general usage, coexistence was achieved such as to earn a sanguine mention from late Byzantine grammarians.[105] But, for all this, the shift *cannot* be ascribed to Phrygian influence, just as the change from Hieropolis to Hierapolis as the toponym of Colossae's neighbour in the Lycus Valley is nothing other than an alternate Atticizing correction.[106]

The second recognizes that different etymologies (and hence meanings) can be ascribed to words, sometimes leading to a subtle change in spelling, sometimes trying to justify one. These can be caused by "code-switching", that is, in drawing on a similar sounding word in another language to forge a new direction of meaning. Or they can be simple inventions drawing upon word-plays which become literalised into designated etymologies. Sometimes, the sheer overlap of meaning might propose a forced etymology. Thus Plutarch speculated that the word ἄψ (an adverb meaning returning, back again) came from the word ὀπίσω (meaning before), with the *omicron* turning into an *alpha* and the *pi* into *psi*.[107] Such highly inventive manipulation — "more creative than plausible" at times[108] — is particularly apparent in Greek tragedy. But the benchmark for later etymological wizardry and lexical collections was Plato's *Cratylus*. One example will suffice. In line with his teaching about the soul, Plato invented an etymology for the body (τὸ σῶμα) that was built solely on assonance: καὶ γὰρ σῆμά τινές φασιν αὐτὸ εἶναι τῆς ψυχῆς "for, as they say, it [the body] is the tomb of the soul."[109] Part of

---

104 There is a thimble-full of occasions where the *alpha*-usage slips into the text: see Jer 2:31[A] (ἐγενάμην), Jer 51:17[A] (ἐγενάμεθα), Is 63:19[ℵ] (ἐγενάμεθα).

105 Zonaras *Lex.* sv. *gamma* 439.8–16 (ed. Tittmann); Symeon *Etym.* 97.1–14 (ed. Baldi).

106 Paul McKechnie notes that the spelling distinction between Hieropolis and Hierapolis was not observed closely among the ancients: *Christianizing Asia Minor: Conversion, Communities and Social Change in the Pre-Constantinian Era* (Cambridge: Cambridge University Press, 2019), 45. In part this is so, although the shift in spelling on coins is marked. Some lexicographers tried to find an explanation elsewhere. The sixth century Stephanus for example (*Ethn. epit.* 327.9–10 ed. Meineke) credited the name to the number of temples at the site, seemingly taking ἱερά as a neuter plural, an expansion on a single focus at, probably, the temple and precincts of Apollo. This hardly coincides with the change on the coins. Hierapolis is not found with this spelling prior to the time of Augustus and dominates thereafter with only a rare reversion to the form Hieropolis: see *BMC Phrygia* Hierapolis, lxvi, 234 nr. 41; *SNG Cop.* 477. For interpretations of the difference in spelling, crediting Hieropolis to a native development accenting a sacred site and Hierapolis to a Hellenistic (and Roman) accent on the polis, see T. Ritti, *Hierapolis di Frigia IX: Storia e Istituzioni di Hierapolis* (Istanbul: Ege, 2017), 278–9.

107 Πλούταρχος δὲ ἀπὸ τοῦ ὀπίσω τὸ ἄψ λέγει εἶναι, τοῦ ο εἰς α τραπέντος καὶ τοῦ π εἰς ψ. *Fr* 183 (ed. Sandbach).

108 So C. C. de Jonge and J. M. van Ophuijsen, "Greek Philosophers on Language," in *Companion to the Ancient Greek Language*, 490.

109 Plato *Crat.* 400c.

the strengthening of such an etymological connection (here between σῶμα and σῆμα) is its repetition in subsequent writings.[110] Reiteration naturalizes the etymology, even when alternate etymologies might be proposed by the ancients. And Byzantine literati were masters of both — etymologies and variation. As such, these changes are literary artifices rather than morphology trailing pronunciation.[111]

This therefore leaves open the question of whether the shift from Colossae to Colassae was the result of a variant-constructed etymology that moved from a pre-occupation with κολοσσός to something else. Here we are returned to the effort to use κολάζω, "I punish" as the explanation for the name Colassae. But the arbitrary aspect of such speculation, as much an ancient characteristic as a modern one, can be seen in Leonhard Bertholdt's 1820 suggestion that Colassae was derived from κολλᾶν "to mix, mingle".[112] The note from Herodotos about Colossae (*Hist.* 7.30) that its river Lycus fed into the Maeander probably prompted the suggestion. One glimpse of early explorers' notes should have been enough to dispatch this topographical implausibility. Colossae, even when confused with the town of Honaz, lies about 27 miles to the east of the point where the Lycus feeds into the Maeander river, with Laodikeia and Hierapolis lying between. We shall return to the question of word-plays on toponyms in chapter 3.

A colossal explanation

In spite of F. F. Bruce's dismissal of the κολοσσός etymology behind the name of Colossae, that connection has held considerable influence over the efforts to plumb an understanding of the toponym. The Rhodian colossus was only ever an instance of the application of the term, even if a grandiose example — a benchmark for other colossi. Thus when Pausanias, the "lonely planet guide" for the second century Aegean, reports the Athenian provision of a colossus of Hadrian in his honour,[113] the colossi of Rhodes and Rome were his points of

110 See S. Valente, "From Plato to the Byzantine Etymologica: The etymologies of 'ἥρωες' in the *Etymologicum Gudianum*," in *Studies in Greek Lexicography* edited by G. K. Giannakis *et al.* (Berlin: de Gruyter, 2019), 79–91, from whom this example has been drawn.

111 Hence the ascription of Colassae to pronunciation, given that it occurs only as a textual shift as far as the evidence will allow us to decide, is probably inaccurate. See, for example, G. B. Winer, *A Treatise on the Grammar of New Testament Greek* (trans. W. F. Moulton; Edinburgh: T & T Clark, 1870), 47–8.

112 L. Bertholdt, *Historische-Kritische Einleitung in Schriften des Alten und Neuen Testaments* (Erlangen: Palmschen, 6 vols, 1812–1819), vol 6, 3443.

113 Compare the honouring of Antoninus Pius with a colossal statue by the city of Hyrkanis (*IGR* 4.1354).

comparison.[114] The Rhodians had been happy to cultivate the vanity.[115] Churchill Babington, who was convinced of the etymology for Colossae being Κολοσσός, speculated that the city had its own statuesque Helios in its precincts — the heliotic coins from Colossae that he had seen no doubt encouraged this line of thought.[116]

Temples throughout the Mediterranean frequently housed as their dominant focus a colossus of the particular god central to the cult, and coins eagerly advertise these.[117] There are good reasons for thinking that Zeus, not (Apollo-) Helios, was Colossae's patron deity,[118] but perhaps significantly, the giant statue located in a temple has yet to appear as part of Colossae's numismatic repertoire. The twelfth century *Etymologicum Magnum* considered that οἱ ὑπερμεγέθεις ἀνδριάντες "stupendously-big statues" were called "colossi" in the ancient world,[119] and the term was readily enough applied to large statues erected in various cities in the eastern Mediterranean, whether of gods or men (as they invariably were). One can understand how the word might (very occasionally) become a person's name, whether a nickname capturing a person's size, or an ambition imposed on a child by its parents.[120] The fifth century bishop of Caesarea in Cappadocia named Firmus wrote one of his Letters to a certain Kolosianos,[121] a name which probably means "son of colossus," unless the single sigma intentionally differed from the geminate form, in which case it would mean "son of stubby"![122] As we have seen, the single *sigma* could survive, meaning nothing other than Colossae or a colossus; such variation between -σσ- and -σ- continued into late Byzantine times.[123] Similar to onomastic appropriation, the term could become a metaphor as when extolling a deceased person's quality of life, "honoured above golden colossi".[124]

---

114 Pausanias 1.18.6. Pausanias probably had in mind the massive statue of Nero which went through at least two modulations, into Sol (Helios) by Vespasian and into Heracles by Commodus.

115 See Richard Ashton, "Rhodian Coinage and the Colossus," *RN* (ser. 6) 30 (1988): 75–90.

116 Babington, "Coins of Colossae," 3. von Eckhel had earlier expressed his opinion that Sol/Helios was the titular god of the Colossians: *Doctrina numorum veterum*, vol 3, 147.

117 See, for one example, P. J. Riss, "A Colossal Athenian Pan," *Acta Archaeologica* 45 (1974): 124–33. Coins regularly deployed the motif of the giant deity standing in a temple. See, for example, *RPC online* 4.2.9773 temp. (Maionia, time of Antoninus Pius).

118 See chapter 3.

119 *Etymologicum magnum* 525.5 (ed. Gaisford).

120 *I.Priene* 147 (on a list of ephebes). In Soknopaiu Nesos in the Arsinoites in Egypt, one witness to a document is recorded as Anoubios, also called the Colossos (Ἀνουβί(ων) ὁ καὶ Κολοσσί(ων)): *P.Gen.* 2.1.36, ll. 27–8 (170 CE).

121 Firmus *Ep.* 18.1 (ed. Calvet-Sebasti and Gatier).

122 The *-ianos/-iana* ending originally did communicate "son/daughter of x". By the second century it had lost this express denotative force. See T. Corsten, "Names in -ιανός in Asia Minor: A Preliminary Study," in *Onomatologos: Studies in Greek Personal Names presented to Elaine Matthews* edited by R. W. V. Catling and F. Marchand (Oxford: Oxbow, 2010), 456–63.

123 See for example Theodore Lascaris *Or.* 7.49 (ed. Tartaglia); Manuel Chrysoloras *Comp. vet. nov.* 3.1 (ed. Billò).

124 *Milet* VI,2 735 (Miletos, 2nd to 1st century BCE).

Plate 2.5: Surviving fragments from Ephesos of a colossus of the emperor Domitian.

A number of writers have made a detailed historical study of the use of the term κολοσσός and recognize in some the earliest statues — the huge passive *korai* and *kouroi* for example — an artistic mirroring of massive natural features in a landscape.[125]

In this interface, the colossus was marked by coldness, fixity, immobility — all those facets that accent impressive substantiality and profound stability in the midst of life's uncertainty. Little wonder that emperor after emperor wanted their own colossal statue to fix their place in the world's gaze. They were, like the gods, the anchor points of the universe; they were, like the gigantuan, aniconic monuments geologically formed in the environment, emblems of the gods, the products of their fashioning and testimony to their power.

The link between a colossus and a toponym has been explored through the repetition of the prefix *kol-* in toponyms — Colossae, Colophon and Coloura. Jean-Pierre Vernant argues that this prefix indicates something extraordinarily large.[126] But this is unlikely to refer to a human construction. Rather it applies to some natural feature. The colossus as a statue was a derivative not a foundation. Accordingly, we need to move beyond speculations about what kind of megalithic statue stood directing traffic and devotion at Colossae. Babington as we have seen, opted for Helios; Alfred Heubeck saw the suffix -αι as a feminine plural (much like other place-names Ἀθῆναι, Κελαιναί, Ἐρυθραί), a Greek addition to a pre-Greek stem indicating that Kolossai had been filled with female cult images. The key contender was the Anatolian mother goddess, Kybele/Kybebe,[127] sometimes

125 See J. Ducat, "Fonctions de la statue dans la Grèce archaïque: Kouros et Kolossos," *BCH* 101 (1976): 246–51; M. W. Dickie, "What is a *Kolossos* and How Were *Kolossoi* Made in the Hellenistic Period?" *GRBS* 37 (1996): 237–57.

126 J. P. Vernant, *Myth and Thought among the Greeks* translated by J. Lloyd and J. Fort (London: Routledge, 1983), 305.

127 A. Heubeck, "Zu einigen kleinasiatischen Ortsnamen," *Glotta* 63 (1985): 124–26.

simply known as "the great mother".[128] Although little survives in Colossae's coinage that might build some buttress to the suggestion (unlike Eukarpeia), "the great mother" does appear as a prominent deity contending with Christianity in the late-fourth/early-fifth century popular narrative of St Michael the Archangel of Colossae/Chonai.[129] But the plural remained a problem. Theodoret of Cyrrhus provided the feminine plural article αἱ, obviously persuaded (if efficiently pragmatic) by the termination of the city name, Κολοσσαί.[130] But this was extremely rare. Less rare but consistent with this, was the use of the feminine plural with Athens (αἱ Ἀθῆναι) and Kelainai (αἱ Κελαιναί).[131] Ecclesiastical commentators were far happier deploying Κολοσσαεῖς/Κολασσαεῖς when writing of the Colossians — it was, after all, reassuringly masculine![132] Athens was simpler (οἱ Ἀθηναῖοι),[133] though the constructed ending to Κολοσσαί on the intaglio gem previously mentioned, suggests that a similar suffix for the ethnic might have been in use as well. Kelainai (Apameia) boasted two possibilities, Κελαινίτης and Κελαινεύς,[134] though this may have been borrowed from Ἀπαμεύς, Apameia being the alternate city name.[135] The irony is that, if the name Κολοσσαί derives from a Hittite/Luwian toponym, then the ending -αι could be a neuter plural.[136]

The Hittite/Luwian option

There are two issues that touch upon such a pressing for the origins of the name Colossae. The first is implied in Heubeck's tacit acknowledgment that the stem of the name was not Greek. The second is the almost complete absence of any search for an aniconic megalith that might have attracted reverence, an

128 C. Thomas, "The 'Mountain Mother': The Other Anatolian Goddess at Ephesos," in *Les cultes Locaux dans les mondes grec et romain: actes du colloque, de Lyon 7–8 Juin 2001* (Lyon/Paris: Université Lumière-Lyon, 2004), 249–62.

129 M. Bonnet, *Narratio de Miraculo a Michele Archangelo Chonis Patrato* (Paris: Librairie Hachette, 1890), 2.8 (citations by page and line number of Bonnet's edition).

130 Theodoret of Cyrrhus, *Comm. Phmn* (*PG* 82.871A). The exegetical comments attached to the text in miniscule GA 254 (p. 582 in the Arabic numbering) also uses the feminine definite article αἱ Κολασσαί when explaining the city of Phrygia.

131 Thucydides *Hist.* 2.8.1, 4.5.2, 4.27.1; Arrian *Anab.* 1.29.1, Strabo *Geog.* 13.1.70.

132 So Clement of Alexandria *Strom.* 5.10.60 πρὸς τοὺς Κολοσσαεῖς γράφων "writing to the Colossians"; Gregory of Nyssa *Ill.* 18.23 καθώς φησι πρὸς τοὺς Κολοσσαεῖς ὁ ἀπόστολος "just as the apostle says to the Colossians"; John Chrysostom *Hom. in Phlmn.* Οἱ γὰρ Κολοσσαεῖς τῆς Φρυγίας εἰσί "For the Colossians are from Phrygia" (*PG* 62.708).

133 Thucydides *Hist.* 1.18.2, 1.45.1.

134 Stephanus *Ethn.* 1.351 (ed. Billerbeck).

135 Stephanus *Ethn. Epit.* 103.11 (ed. Meineke).

136 A. M. Davies, "The Linguistic Evidence: Is there any?" in *The End of the Early Bronze Age in the Aegean* edited by G. Cadogan (Leiden: Brill, 1986), 114.

association through the name, and mimesis in architecture and sculpture. We turn to these in turn.

Heubeck was, like a number of commentators, struck by the use of -ss- as a formative suffix, strongly apparent in Hittite toponyms, a number of which survived into Greek: Mylassa, Telmessos, Halikarnassos. The names of known Hittite cities, most notably *Ḫulašša*, *Tarhuntašša* and *Šariššа* provide support for the suggestion that Colossae's name was not Greek in origin. Indeed, it has been suggested that *Ḫulašša* (or perhaps *Ḫuwalušša*) is the Hittite name from which the Greek form Colossae derived homonymically.[137] These cities could demonstrate Bronze Age foundation (or earlier). Certainly, for Hittite and Luwian scholars, Colossae stood as one of many Hittite cities that were part of the Hittite empire networked into the capital *Hattuša*, near modern Boğasköy in eastern Anatolia, from 1800 to 1200 BCE.[138] It seems that a variety of hegemonic techniques were used by the Hittite central rulers to expand and maintain their authority. In western Anatolia, Luwian kingdoms governed by "small kings", retained some measure of distinctiveness but were subject to the Hittite "great king".[139]

Hittite inscriptions from the capital, and from a handful of other excavated sites,[140] indicate that key accents of imperial policy were building, fortification and hydraulic engineering (often associated with religious sanctuaries),[141] along with a deliberate admixture of peoples as part of population transfer. It was precisely these accents that enabled individual cities to survive the collapse of the Empire. Some have claimed the designation "Neo-Hittite" for the minor kingdoms of the next five hundred years (into the Iron Age). Others are now privileging the description "Luwian", noting especially the ascendancy of the

137 See A. Scherer, "Paphlagonische Namenstudien," in *Studien zur Sprachwissenschaft und Kulturkunde, Gedenkschrift für W. Brandenstein* edited by M. Mayrhofer (IBK 14; Innsbruck: Amoe, 1968), 383; F. Cornelius, *Geschichte der Hethiter: Mit besonderer Berücksichtigung der geographischen Verhältnisse und der Rechtsgeschichte* (Darmstadt: Wissenschaftliche Buchgesellschaft, 1973), 208 n27; J. Freu, "Les débuts du nouvel Empire Hittite et les origins de l'expansion Mycénienne. A propos d'une nouvelle datation des textes des rois Tuthaliya et Arnuwanda," *Annales de la Faculté des Lettres et Sciences humaines de Nice* 35 (1979): 27.

138 For Colossae as a Hittite listed site, see https://oi.uchicago.edu/research/camel/anatolian-atlas-bibliography-and-list-sites and https://luwianstudies.org/site/kolossai-honaz-hoyuk/.

139 Alvise Matessi, "The Making of Hittite Imperial Landscapes: Territoriality and Balance of Power in South-Central Anatolia during the Late Bronze Age," *JANEH* 3.2 (2016): 119.

140 See D. P. Mielke, "Key Sites of the Hittite Empire" in *The Oxford Handbook of Ancient Anatolia* edited by G. McMahon and S. Steadman (Oxford: Oxford University Press, 2011), 1031–54.

141 D. P. Mielke, "Hittite Settlement Policy," in *Places and Spaces in Hittite Anatolia I: Hatti and the East* edited by M. Alparslan (Istanbul: Türk Eskiçağ Bilimleri Enstitüsü, 2017), 14; Andreas Müller-Karpe "Planning a Sacred Landscape: Examples from Sarissa and Ḫattusa," in *Sacred Landscapes of Luwians and Hittites: Proceedings of the International Conference* edited by A. D'Agostino, V. Orsi and G. Torri (Studia Asiana 9; Florence: Firenze University Press, 2015), 83–6.

kingdom/region of Arzawa,[142] within which Colossae continued a critical position because of its location and fortification at the eastern end of the Lycus Valley. Here are witnessed continuing Hittite elements in language and hieroglyphics (notably the distinctive Luwian script in the west and south), religious and political expressions, art and culture. The gradual arrival of Phrygians and other peoples brought changes but Hittite-Luwian influence endured.[143]

Plate 2.6a and b: A Neo-Hittite tombstone (8th century BCE) remembers Tarhuwaris son of Tarhuzarmas. It was re-used in the Byzantine period as a Christian tombstone, leaving the Luwian hieroglyphic script intact at the base,[144] and without change to its overall shape,[145] but recasting the symbols. Funerary values of virtue, provision by oneself, or by one's family in the event of premature death, the importance of ancestors and genealogy are already paramount. Similar values passed into the Roman imperial period.[146]

We have already explored the archaeological basis for affirming the Hittite/Luwian contribution to the life of Colossae, limited though it may be. For all this fertile Hittite-Luwian *prima facie* case for an exploration of Hittite and/or Luwian origins for the name Colossae, Zgusta was content to leave the name grasping at the etymology of κολοσσός, even while recognising the similarity with Hittite and Luwian forms. It should be remembered that Greeks and Romans had no mortgage on the sculpting of colossi. The Hittites were also

142 See E. Zangger, *The Luwian Civilization: The Missing Link in the Aegean Bronze Age* (Istanbul: Ege, 2016); F. Woudhuizen, *The Luwians of Western Anatolia: Their Neighbours and Predecessors* (Oxford: Archaeopress, 2018).

143 R. L. Alexander, "The Storm-God at 'Ain Dara," in *Recent Developments in Hittite Archaeology and History: Papers in Honor of Hans Gustav Güterbock* edited by K. A. Yener and H. A. Hoffner (Winona Lake, IN: Eisenbraun, 2002), 11.

144 J. D. Hawkins, *Corpus of Hieroglyphic Luwian Inscriptions* (Berlin: de Gruyter, 2 vols, 2000), vol 1.2, 492, nr. X.23 (Istanbul Archaeological Museum inv. 7766). The stone was found at the village of Eğrek about 220 miles ESE of Ankara.

145 G. W. Elderkin, "A Christian Stele from Cappadocia," *AJA* 41 (1937): 97–9.

146 See chapter 12.

famous, even into Greco-Roman times, for their massive statues.[147] Zgusta allowed that both the Greek and Luwian languages might depend on an earlier epichoric foundation. But he emphasized that, as we have seen with many Greek constructions of etymologies, the Greeks *claimed* the connection.[148] He was nevertheless persuaded that a natural feature stood behind the name.[149]

However, no-one has suggested that such a natural feature might be in the vicinity of Colossae. The textual hold of Herodotos's disappearing river has dominated the investigation of topography, even when it is repudiated. The exploration we have traced of the tie between the mound and a sacred spring, invites us to lift up our eyes to the hills … or mountains to be more exact. The sacred spring lies at the foot of Honazdağ, or, as classically named, Mt Cadmus. And protruding out from the side of the mountain, as a sentinel over the site of Colossae is a huge megalith, easily seen from the mound.

The immense monolith is not named or represented to date on coins or reliefs. However, in the late fourth-to-early-fifth century popular story of *St Michael the Archangel of Chonai* (a name that is a later toponym of Colossae) the rock is renowned. It became one of the key identifying landmarks of the story: "an impregnable monolith of massive breadth".[150] The power of the archangel is manifest in the story's action by the sheering of the side of the monolith, a geological feature still apparent today. In this location, the Hittite-favored combination of a settlement with natural features occurs — mountains and springs. The reverence extended to the features seems to have continued through different permutations, laden with different values and explanations, for more than a thousand years. So Colossae could indeed draw on a colossus of immense, natural, visual confrontation. But this did not necessarily make its name a Greek derivation. It simply confirmed

Plate 2.7: The towering, sheered monolith rises out of the slopes of Mt. Cadmus in the Taurus Mountains to the south of Colossae and above a prolific natural spring.

147 See F. Rojas and V. Sergueenkova, "Traces of Tarhuntas: Greek, Roman, and Byzantine Interaction with Hittite Monuments," *JMA* 27.2 (2014): 135–60; Alexander "Storm-God," 11–12.

148 Zgusta, *Kleinasiatischen Ortsnamen*, 278.

149 Zgusta, *Kleinasiatischen Ortsnamen*, 30, 34, 278–9.

150 πέτρα στερεὰ ἔχουσα πλάτος καὶ μῆκος πολύ. *S. Mich. Chon.* 12.5–6 (ed. Bonnet). My English translation of the story is found in *Colossae in Space and Time*, 323–30.

that the Greeks inherited both a name and a natural justification for making an etymological connection.[151]

The appropriation of a colossal etymology

However, the hellenization of Colossae following the sweep of Alexander the Great from the south and onto the Persian and Bactrian east left in its wake, not only a rule that promoted the adoption of Greek cultural conceptions of city life. There are hints also that Colossae was pragmatically attentive to the need to adapt to the new realities. It is clear that its name remained, whatever its form and spelling in the previous flow from Hittite to Persian hegemony. But now, its name, as Zgusta recognized, had to become Greek in spelling and, I would suggest, in its "meaning". It was motivated by two highly significant developments in the third century BCE. The first was the oft-noted foundation of Laodikeia about 11 miles to the city's west. Pliny the Elder gives the succession of Diospolis and Rhoas as earlier names for Laodikeia,[152] though it is more likely that these were descriptors or epithets rather than indicating a prior settlement history.[153] Its foundation as "Laodikeia", by the Seleucid king, Antiochus II in circa 255 BCE in honor of his wife Laodike, was accompanied by a significant input of resources and Hellenistic cultural markings. Whatever losses to Colossae in terms of prestige and territory may have resulted,[154] it was clear that Greek signification was to be the dominant expression and status. Hierapolis, "sacred city",[155] similarly displayed, in its very name, the character of a Greek *polis*.[156] The city names were likewise given elaborate foundation narratives, cultivated and celebrated to underscore the divine approbation of the settlement. These foundation myths were not necessarily singular, consistent or uncontested, but they were designed to fill the city's self-identity with a powerful authorization of its existence. Hierapolis' sacrality lay in the divine beneficence of Apollo.[157] Indeed, on a number of its coin types, the coin legends remind the populace and visitors, that Apollo was the inspiration behind

151 See further Cadwallader, "Historical Sweep," 60–6.

152 Pliny *NH* 5.29.105.

153 See chapter 3.

154 This is a common trope explaining Colossae's supposed decline.

155 The name is sometimes explained as initially the city of a sanctuary (hence, spelled Hieropolis) which, as the sanctuary curried a fully-functioning city, became the sacred city (Hierapolis) of Apollo.

156 On the foundation of Hierapolis, see Huttner, *Lycus Valley*, 36–7.

157 Another foundation story, built on a retelling of the Endymion myth by the third century poet, Quintus of Smyrna, reflects a later time but is still accenting mythic origins. See P. Thonemann, *The Maeander Valley: A Historical Geography from Antiquity to Byzantium* (Cambridge: Cambridge University Press, 2011), 75–6.

its pioneering colonization. Three bronze coin types of the Hierapolitan mint, probably from the time of Trajan, feature the bust of Apollo. He is easily recognized from his trademark kithara (if not his redolent coiffure), but, strikingly, he is named as ἀρχηγέτης, "founder/pioneer/colonizer."[158] A cognate of the word occurs in the Second Testament (ἀρχηγός), not as an epithet of Apollo (though this form is found elsewhere for Apollo),[159] but of Jesus Christ (Acts 3:15, 5:31; Heb 2:10, 12:2).

The second development is, ironically, a collapse. An earthquake in 228/227 BCE brought to a sudden end a 32 meter-high structure at Lindos on the island of Rhodes. The giant bronze statue of Helios was so impressive, especially when the bronze was struck by the sun's beams, that its rays were cast to sea vessels tens of miles away. Even when fractured from its exalted height, Pliny the Elder held that "even thrown down it is a marvel (*miraculo est*)."[160] The memory and the surviving artifacts combined to foster its renown as *the* colossus above all others.[161] Even in its own century, it began to be acclaimed as one of the wonders of the world, a reputation that seems to have grown more secure in the coming centuries.[162] The tenth century Byzantine Emperor Constantine Porphyrogenitos in an attempt to extol the "Theodosius obelisk" in the hippodrome at Constantinople, described it as comparable to the Colossus of Rhodes.[163] As one nineteenth-century traveller deftly put it, "The fame of this colossal bronze statue of the sun is disproportioned to its period of existence."[164] Rhodes basked in this reputation and gained control of mainland territory in the second century BCE (largely due to an Attalid power vacuum and Roman indifference) at least to the southern edge of the Taurus range, in what is more familiarly known as the region of Caria — the neighboring region to Phrygia.[165]

158 *RPC online* 3.2351, 2352; 4.2.2061 (temp). The iconography of the reverse of these coins features, respectively, Artemis Ephesiaca, Cybele and (possibly) Hygieia. A further type bearing the legend (on the obverse) with a radiate Apollo, has a standing Apollo carrying a bipennis (*RPC online* 3.2358G). See further chapter 3.

159 See *OGIS* 212.

160 Pliny *NH* 34.18.41.

161 *ante omnes autem in admiration* Pliny *NH* 34.18.41.

162 See its inclusion in Antipater of Sidon's seven wonders in *Anth. Pal.* 9.58; compare Diodorus Siculus 1.63.

163 *CIG* 8703 as corrected by A. H. M. Jones, "The Inscriptions," in *Preliminary Report upon the Excavations carried out in the Hippodrome of Constantinople in 1927* edited by S. Casson (London: British Academy, 1928), 44–5.

164 C. D. Weaver, *In the Levant* (Boston: Houghton, Mifflin and Co, 1894), 246.

165 See J. Labuff, *Polis Expansion and Elite Power in Hellenistic Karia* (Lanham: Lexington, 2016), 40–2. This Rhodian expansionism brought the financial and visual impact of Rhodian currency. Imitation of Rhodian coins is clearly attested; see R. Ashton and G. Reger, "The Pseudo-Rhodian Drachms of Mylasa Revisited," in *Agoranomia: Studies in Money and Exchange presented to John H. Kroll* edited by P. G. van Alfen (New York: American Numismatic Society, 2006), 128–31.

Its coins regularly featured the radiate head of the sun-god Helios and gained widespread imitation.[166]

One of Colossae's coins struck before the Attalid kingdom was bequeathed to the Romans, similarly featured a radiate head. It has regularly been described as a radiate Apollo or Apollo-Helios because the reverse of the coin carries Apollo's instrument of prophecy, the kithara.[167] One type has a kithara of three strings, a second bears four strings (a feature to which we return in chapter 6).

In the second century BCE, a blend of the two gods had occasionally begun to happen. The Roman writer on agriculture, Columella, (using the alternate name of Apollo, that is, Phoebus) waxed lyrical "When Phoebus' rays are gentle and invite one to lie on gentle grass."[168] But the conjunction was not a mere literary device. At a religious sanctuary claimed by Hierapolis as part of its territory (at least in the first centuries of the Common Era) — the sanctuary of Apollo Lairbenos — inscriptions regularly fold the terms Apollo Helios Lairbenos into one deity.[169] Thus, Olympias, a resident of the village of Motella and the small city of Blaundos, "dedicates" her son Nikon Ἡλίῳ Ἀπόλλωνι Λαιρμηνῷ, "to Helios Apollo Lairbenos."[170] The last name, Lairbenos, occurs in one of a dozen or more known spellings.[171] The lack of exactitude is attributed to an indigenous origin to the name. This may invite a parallel for the various spellings of Colossae. It is considered that an old indigenous god had been blended to the patron god of Hierapolis, Apollo, retaining the name but in this and a number of inscriptions given a "heliotic" confluence.

It is encapsulated in a range of Hierapolitan coins having a radiate head on the obverse with the simple legend ΛΑΙΡΒΗΝΟϹ (Lairbenos).[172] Apollo was not named explicitly but was understood from the iconography and the epithet. So important was Apollo to the city and its territory that there were a number of Apollo sanctuaries that were threaded (possibly by a pilgrim way) from the central city temple near the theater up to the plateau to the north,

166 A. Bresson, "Drachmes rhodiennes et imitations," *REA* 98 (1996): 65–77.

167 See further chapter 3 (with photograph).

168 Columella, *Rust.*, pref. 283–4.

169 A number of inscriptions use the singular "god" to convey this unity, for example τῷ θεῷ Ἡλίῳ Ἀπόλλωνι "to the god Helios Apollo" (*MAMA* 4.279 ll. 17–18); τῷ θεῷ Λαιρμηνῷ Ἀπόλλωνι "to the god Lairbenos Apollo" — T. Ritti, C. Şimşek and H. Yıldız, "Dediche e καταγραφαί dal santuario frigio di Apollo Lairbenos," *EA* 32 (2000): 29, nr. K31. In one unpublished fragmentary inscription lying at the site, the god is addressed as κύριος "lord".

170 *MAMA* 4.275 B1. See K. M. Miller, "Apollo Lairbenos," *Numen* 32 (1985): 46–70; M. Ricl, "Les ΚΑΤΑΓΡΑΦΑΙ di sanctuaire d'Apollon Lairbenos," *Arkeoloji Dergisi* 3 (1995): 167–95.

171 See I. Moga, *Religious Excitement in Ancient Anatolia: Cult and Devotional Forms for Solar and Lunar Gods* (Leuven: Peeters, 2019), 85.

172 On the range of Apollo coins minted at Hierapolis, see S. Kerschbaum, "Die Apollines von Hierapolis in Phrygien," *JNG* 64 (2014): 15–42.

culminating in the sanctuary of Apollo Lairbenos on the remote spur overlooking the upper Maeander valley.[173]

Plate 2.8a, b and c: The remains of the sanctuary of Apollo Lairbenos looking southwest down the Maeander Valley (a). The peak of the temple pedestal (now at Denizli Museum) featuring Apollo Lairbenos with bipennis (double-ax), branch and grapevine (b). The obverse of the coin (c) has the head of Apollo Lairbenos with radiate crown (almost in the form of a city head-dress), with the simple legend ΛΑΙΡ | ΒΗΝΟϹ but the reverse has a wreath surrounding the inscription ΠΥΘΙΑ that captures not only the main epithet of Apollo ("Pythian Apollo") — the source of oracles — but, with the wreath, indicating games held in his honor. The surrounding legend is ΙΕΡΑΠΟΛΕΙΤΩΝ ΝΕΩΚΟΡΩΝ "for/of the Hierapolitans, guardians of the imperial cult."[174]

173 See A. H. Cadwallader, "Bodily Display and Epigraphical Confession at the Sanctuary of Apollo Lairbenos: an examination of emotional responses," *JES* 1 (2018): 183–201.

174 *RPC online* 6.5471 temp. (The example in Pl. 2.8c has a countermark on the obverse.) Photograph from a private collection by permission (24 mm, 5.53 g). The coin is dated to the time of the emperor Elagabalus (218–22 CE). See A. Johnston, "Hierapolis Revisited," *NC* 144 (1984: 52–80.

Hierapolis only once produced alliance (homonoia) coins with her neighbor Laodikeia — highly unusual given the number of repeated homonoia coins Hierapolis struck with other cities (especially Ephesos).[175] Tullia Ritti, the Italian epigrapher, has suggested this was a (grudging) minting following a dispute over fishing rights with Laodikeia that required the intervention of the emperor Hadrian. His decision included a none-too-subtle hint that the two cities mend their relationship and foster the concord that was touted as a mark of Roman rule.[176] The iconography of such homonoia coins is dominated by three styles, although there are occasional departures: the city patron gods of the two cities are featured on the reverse often facing or with hands held, the city Tyche goddesses might sometimes be the deities represented, or, thirdly, a grasping of hands alone is given. The homonoia coin between Hierapolis and Laodikeia is quite clear. Laodikeia's patron god is Zeus Aetophoros (eagle-bearer); Hierapolis's god is Apollo, clearly marked by the kithara (and plectrum) that he holds.[177]

Plate 2.9: Relief of Apollo, the patron-god of Hierapolis (in Denizli Museum), robed as a citharoedus (kithara-player), holding a plectrum in his right hand, and lyre, resting on a tripod, in his left hand.

175 *RPC online* 4.2.2015 temp. (reign of Marcus Aurelius), 2017 (reign of Commodus); 6.5494 temp. (reign of Elagabalus); 8. ID20744 (reign of Philip I).

176 T. Ritti, E. Miranda and F. Guizzi, "La ricerca epigrafica: risultati dell'ultimo quadrennio e prospettive future," in *Hierapolis di Frigia I: Le attività delle campagne di scavo e restauro 2000–2003*, edited by F. D'Andria and M. Piera Caggia (Istanbul: Ege, 2007), 583–618 at 589; T. Ritti, *Hierapolis di Frigia IX: Storia e istituzioni di Hierapolis* (Istanbul: Ege, 2017), 395; see also A. H. Cadwallader, "The Battle over Lake Lycus: Inter-city Conflict in the Lycus Valley," in *New Documents vol. 12*, forthcoming.

177 *RPC* 3.2356, 2357; 3.2340 (reign of Hadrian). See P. R. Franke and M. K. Nollé, *Die Homonoia-Münzen Kleinasiens und der thrakischen Randgebeite* (Saarbrücken: Saarbrücken Verlag, 1997), 67, 80–1.

Colossae was not party to this conflict with Laodikeia (though other disputes beset relationships between these two cities). But each of these Lycus Valley centers was determined to carve its own distinct identity. A crucial component of this curating of identity was in religious accent. Johannes Nollé emphasizes that it is a mistake to speak of "Greek religion"; rather one should speak of the "religion of Greek cities".[178] That is, each city carved their own accents even for gods that were found elsewhere in multiple centers. In this sense, it is a mistake to assume that the blend of Apollo with Helios that is demonstrated at Hierapolis (especially as focused on the sanctuary of Apollo Lairbenos) is a universal collation, even though the amalgam seems to have been encouraged by the late Seleucid king, Antiochus I.[179] Helios retained an identity distinct from Apollo in numerous places,[180] or might be blended with another god, such as Sarapis.[181] Apollo confers his share of theophoric names on Colossae's inhabitants,[182] as does Helios,[183] though, to this date in the epigraphical finds, less than the son of Zeus. So, there seems no question that both Apollo and Helios figure significantly, and separately, in the panorama of deities configuring religious life at Colossae.

178 J. Nollé, "Vielerorts war Bethlehem — Göttergeburten im kaiserzeitlichen Kleinasien," *AW* 34.6 (2003), 638. See also the important methodological considerations regarding "the variety which may exist between different local expressions" of the same cult: *New Doc. Early Christ.* 3, p. 22.

179 See C. C. Lorber and P. Iossif, "The Cult of Helios in the Seleucid East," *Topoi* 16.1 (2009): 19–42.

180 For example, Helios is a distinct god, along with Apollo, Zeus, Gaia, Herakles, Hermes in the Beroian gymnasium regulations (*SEG* 43.381, 2nd century BCE); Ptolemaus VII Euergetes II similarly lists a range of gods as his divine witnesses — Zeus, the "Great Gods", Helios, Apollo Archegetes (*SEG* 9.7, 155 BCE). The city of Rhodes, as might be expected, attests a temple of Helios, as well as separate temples to Aphrodite, Apollo, Zeus, Athena and Asclepius. A manumission at Gorgippia on the north coast of the Black Sea, protective witness to the release of a θρεπτή (house-bred slave) is sought from Zeus, Gê and Helios (*CIRB* 1123, 41 CE). No mention is made of Apollo, even though the god is found in inscriptions from neighboring cities, such as Olbia (*I.Olbia* 95). In a first/second century funerary stele from Thessalonike, a woman "bears witness" (μαρτύρεται) to Helios, the children of Helios (that is, the Ὧραι, the Hours, goddesses presiding over the change of seasons), the Χάριτες, the [three] Graces, goddesses of beauty, favor and elegance, Selene, the moon goddess, and Ἠώς, the goddess of the dawn) — and finally to the paired gods Hosios (purity) and Dikaios (justice) (*IG* XII, 2, 1 Supp. 1362). These examples are not exclusive and demonstrate that different cities accented, combined, embellished or even ignored the repertoire of gods and heroes in the Greco-Roman entourage of deities.

181 See, for example, *SEG* 54.1501 (Epiphaneia, 1st to 2nd century CE).

182 *MAMA* 6.46 — the brothers Apollonios and Apollonides (as reconstructed); *SEG* 51.1160 (four examples of Apollonios); *RPC* 3.2311; *RPC online* 4.2.1882 temp.; 4.2.1898 temp.; A. Audollent, *Defixionum Tabellae quotquot innotuerunt tam in graecis Orientis quam in totius Occidentis partibus praeter Attica in Corpore Inscriptionum Atticarum editas* (Paris: Fontemoing, 1904), 19, nr. 14A.

183 *IGR* 4.870 (Heliodoros).

But, at Colossae, Helios (not Apollo) figures prominently on its imperial coins. A small but significant piece of evidence prompts a consideration of what Colossians (or the ruling class directing Colossian values) actually presented about their own city name. The coins of Colossae are completely devoid of any representation of Apollo, except on a single type, where he is one of the two children carried by their mother Leto.[184] That this is a conscious and deliberate erasure is suggested by the fact that the second child, Apollo's sister Artemis, gains a ubiquitous iconographic presence on Colossae's coins. The reason seems to be directly related to the converse accent at Hierapolis, where Apollo is the city's patron god. Colossae avoided any suggestion that it was a Hierapolitan satellite or groupie.

It is helpful to see just how distinctive Colossae's accent on Helios is by comparison to the cities of the Lycus Valley and its immediately surrounding regions. In the following table, the statistics for obverses and reverses of coins with iconography of Apollo and Helios are provided. For further comparison, the coins of the seven cities mentioned in the letters to the seven churches in the Book of Revelation are added in the text's order. (Laodikeia is included twice for this exercise.) The table is drawn from the immensely helpful resource of *Roman Provincial Coinage online*.[185] Even though there are some coins that have surfaced in archaeological catalogues and numismatic auctions that are yet to be added to the collation, it provides the most complete foundation for meaningful comparison. The number in brackets following the city name gives the total number of coin types (in *RPC online*) identified for that city in the Roman imperial period (that is, from Augustus to Gallienus in the mid-third century). Occasional brief explanations are given in the final column to demonstrate, *inter alia*, the validity of Nollé's observation. Colossae is given first. Rhodes is added for reasons that will become clear in the analysis.

184 *RPC online* 4.2.1878 temp. = *MSPhryg* 2.564. Note that the name of the sponsoring magistrate should be corrected to Ἐκλέγων (so *LGPN* V.C).

185 *Roman Provincial Coinage* online is updated regularly. The latest update of figures given here was collated in February 2023.

City	Apollo		Helios		Notes
	Obv	Rev	Obv	Rev	
Colossae (59)[186]	0	1	11	$7_{corr.}$	Apollo & Artemis in Leto's arms; Helios head (11×), standing (5×), Helios in quadriga (2×).
Aphrodisias (145)	0	2	3	0	Apollo + branch, bow, tripod, lyre, serpent; Helios radiate profile.
Attouda (32)	0	1	0	0	Apollo + branch, bow;
Blaundos (78)	0	30	0	0	Apollo + lyre, plectrum; on horse (Apollo-Mên), bipennis, tetrastyle temple
Ceretapa (20)	0	0	0	0	
Dionysopolis (30)	0	0	0	0	
Eucarpeia (34)	0	0	0	0	
Eumeneia (66)	0	14	0	0	Apollo + bipennis, raven, horse (Apollo-Mên); + Dionysos
Heracleia Sal. (47)	0	3	0	0	Apollo + Nike, bipennis; stdg triad: Leto+Apollo+Artemis
Hierapolis (338)	35	84	0	0	Apollo-Archegetes, -Lairbenos; branch, lyre, radiate (when Lairbenos), phiale, bipennis; horse, bow, serpent, tetrastyle/hexastyle temple, tripod; tree; (includes homonoia coins; no Leto)
Laodicea (280)	3	2	2	0	Apollo + laureate, lyre (incl. homonoia with Hierapolis); Helios radiate
Tabae (47)	0	0	0	0	
Trapezopolis (33)	1	4	0	0	Apollo + lyre, branch, bow
Tripolis (141)	1	19	3	4	Apollo with Leto 11×; with Artemis alone 4×; Helios radiate; standing with globe, torch (1×)
Rhodes (73)	0	0	23	6	Helios radiate (facing 1×) + star, crescent; + female "Rhodes", trophy.

186 Alert readers will observe that the number of types in *RPC online* is almost the same figure as that given previously for von Aulock's catalogue. However, the identity is misleading. *RPC online* includes 13 types that are not found in von Aulock, combines (wrongly in my view) two types that von Aulock had given separately and omits 11 types included by von Aulock. See Appendix 1.

City	Apollo		Helios		Notes
	Obv	Rev	Obv	Rev	
Ephesus (825)	0	12	0	3	Apollo + Leto, Artemis, kithara, bow, branch, lyre, plectrum, stag; Helios as Elagabal? + emperor.
Pergamum (323)	0	5	0	2	Apollo + branch, patera, branch, altar, + Asclepius; Helios + biga, + Zeus, Selene
Philadelphia (187)	0	6	0	7	Apollo + lyre, plectrum, omphalos, branch, bow, Artemis; Helios, radiate + duostyle/ tetrastyle temple; scepter, torch, bow, whip, thyrsus
Sardis (241)	0	3	0	5	Apollo + raven, branch, lyre; Helios radiate as Elagabal? + quadriga, globe, raised hand
Smyrna (316)	0	0	0	1	Helios radiate + Selene
Thyatira (319)	0	47	0	3	Apollo + bipennis, branch, serpent, (incl homonoia), quadriga, column, bucranium, radiate, tetrastyle temp-le, agonistic crown, horse + river-god, Asclepius, Tyche, Amazon and Nemeseis, emperor (Elagabalus)
Laodicea (278)	3	2	2	0	Apollo + laureate, lyre (incl. ho-monoia with Hierapolis); Helios radiate

The table confirms that Helios secured a particular accent in the coin iconography of Colossae. The radiate Apollo coin of its earlier Attalid coinage disappeared. The famous Sestos inscription that mentions the rationales behind the city seeking to establish a mint, named the desire that the image of the city should be current.[187] For Colossae, the move to Helios was a conscious choice. It is a distinctive that no other city in the region matches. And it is a distinctive that defines Colossae against all other cities in the region, competing for attention and laying claim to an ancient pedigree. Most cities in the region ignored Helios for their coins; only Tripolis and Aphrodisias show

187 *OGIS* 339. See C. Howgego, "Why did Ancient States strike Coins?" *NC* 150 (1990): 20.

any interest but neither of these rival Colossae's concentration.[188] Significantly, Hierapolis turned all her attention to an expansive rendition of Apollo; Laodikeia's coins show little evidence for either god. Indeed, as I suggest in chapter 3, Laodikeia changed its predominant coin iconography: its initial accent, under Seleucid and Attalid rule, was on Laodike/Aphrodite and a caduceus with cornucopia, reflecting its first "foundation" story. This shifted to that of Zeus Aetophoros as Laodikeia saw its fortunes increasingly harnessed to the juggernaut of Rome, with a new foundation story as its concomitant rationale. Given that Colossae, as a Greek city, originally claimed Zeus as its patron god, Laodikeia's shift in accent to Zeus gave an added impulse for Colossae to develop an emphasis on the heliotic colossus, even if Zeus remained, nominally, the prime civic god (crucial for Colossae's hopes for a pan-hellenic *adventus* of the emperor Hadrian in 129 CE).

When attention is turned to the cities accommodating the seven churches of Asia, the poverty of Helios iconography is underscored by the considerably larger volume of coin types. In two cases (Ephesos and Thyateira), the brief appearance of Helios can be tied directly to imperial politics. The Emperor Elagabalus earned his remembered name as a tag from his self-designation as imperial priest of Elagabal, the Syrian sun-god. This may also explain the raised hand in the Elagabalus-Helios coins from Sardis.[189] These cities (at least) were concerned to follow the fashion that the Emperor had instigated — the Greek equivalent to the Syrian deity was Helios who became the obvious bearer of this diplomatic sycophancy. Significantly, Colossae flagged that its numismatic and cultural veneration of Helios was of considerably longer standing, predating Elagabalus. During the reign of Elagabalus, the city revived the same design that had been minted in the period of Commodus as Caesar thereby staking a claim for imperial recognition that no other city in the region could match.

188 Barbara Zając has drawn attention to a number of cities with Helios iconography on their coins (including Amastris, Apollonia Salbake, Tripolis and Colossae) but does not recognize how much of an accent is found at Colossae. The only city approaching Colossae's volume is Aradus in Phoenicia, a phenomenon readily explained by the prominence of the Syrian sun-god Elagabal. See "Who, why and when? Pseudo-autonomous coins of Bithynia and Pontus dated to the beginning of the second century AD" in *Pecunia Omnes Vincit: Coin as a Medium of Exchange throughout Centuries* edited by B. Zając, P. Koczwara and S. Jellonek (Kraków: Jagiellonian University, 2018), 82. Her instances are drawn from the printed *Roman Provincial Coinage* volumes and should be supplemented by the online edition.

189 *RPC online* 6.4489–4492 temp.

Plate 2.10a and b: Coins featuring the laureate head of the *Dėmos* of Colossae on the obverse and a standing, caped but naked, radiate Helios holding a torch and globe on the reverse. The first coin is dated to the time of Commodus (178–180 CE), allocated on the basis of the sponsor's name in the reverse legend: Publius Ailius Ktesikles.[190] The second coin, previously unpublished, dates to the time of Elagabalus (218–222 CE). Although the second coin lacks a sponsor's name, it can be confidently assigned to the time of Elagabalus on the basis of the abbreviation O-T-Θ beneath the cape — lettering only found on other Colossian coins belonging to the reign of Elagabalus.

One can readily see the later coin's replication of the earlier minting. The coins were also roughly identical in size (and, presumably, value: 3 assaria). The Commodus coin averages 16.55 g with a 31 mm diameter with small variations that can be attributed to different dies; the Elagabalus coin, so far known only by this worn example, weighs 15.28 g with a 30 mm diameter. The elements on the reverse are common to both — radiate head, naked, but caped body, with a torch held in the right hand and a globe in the left. However, the differences, apart from the legends, are also noteworthy — the posture, trunk and leg proportions are different and the cape is longer on the second example, perhaps intimating the known propensity of the emperor for lavish clothing. Here was a potent display of Colossae's enduring heliotic commitment, now gaining more prominent attention because of the Roman empire's "new" religious emphasis on the Syrian sun-god, Sol Elagabal.[191]

In its other coins from Elagabalus's reign, the city found another means of falling in with imperial propaganda, by adding a cryptic anagram to the Elagabalus coins — the letters O-T-Θ. They may refer either to a homonoia above all others, namely the homonoia of the gods (ὁμονοία τῶν θεῶν); or to a touted prophecy that saw the seventieth year as the culmination of the Antonine dynasty, with Elagabalus (by imaginative conjuring of the reigns of previous emperors) as the ninth Antonine emperor — the capstone of the suc-

190 Π. ΑΙΛ. ΚΤΗϹ | Ι | ΚΛΗϹ ΑΝΕΘΗΚ | ΕΝ (in exergue); *MSPhryg* 2.484–6 = *RPC online* 4.2.1896 temp. (here following von Aulock's assignment of the coin to Commodus as vice-regent). Photography of Pl. 10a courtesy of St John's Anglican Cathedral, Brisbane, by permission; photograph of Pl. 10b from a private collection by permission.

191 *AE* 1962.229: *Deo p[atrio] Soli Ela[gabalo]*

cession;[192] or have some other explanation.[193] Colossae's numismatic emphasis on Helios goes back to the beginnings of its imperial mint under the beneficent widow, Claudia Eugenetoriane, probably in 117 or 118 CE and can now be tracked through to its pinnacle under the priest of the sun-god, Elagabalus, and continuing into the opening of the brief reign of Volusian, co-regent with his father Trebonianus Gallus (251–253 CE).[194] Even with the assassination of Elagabalus, Colossae did not relinquish its identity-forming commitment to (the colossus) Helios.

The issue therefore goes to the rationale behind this distinctive emphasis. There can be no doubt that it was a deliberate commitment driven by the leaders of Colossian society. As Christopher Howgego puts it, "The imagery on the coinage is that of '*polis*-religion', in other words it represents the view of those who controlled the *polis*."[195] It is here that Rhodian coinage becomes crucial and trains back to the discussion of the massive Colossus of Rhodes. Richard Ashton has argued persuasively that there was a special minting of coins to coincide with the construction of the monumental, statuesque domination of the eastern Mediterranean in the third century BCE. Two particular elements stand out — the special minting featured a profile-right die, a complement to the more ubiquitous, continuing presentation of a three-quarters right-facing head of Helios; secondly, the head is radiate, a feature which Ashton takes as an imitation of the actual head of the colossus.[196] The two representations of the colossal Helios, the profile and the three-quarter face, remained the common feature in Rhodian coinage into Roman imperial times, along with, on the reverse, a single rose (to which we return below).

At one stage (especially 188–167 BCE) Rhodes was the leading force in the region of Caria, the southern border of Phrygia. Indeed one of its coins, bearing the sponsor's name, Erasikles, featured a Phrygian helmet (Pl. 2.11b) as an accompaniment to the dominant rose of the reverse.

192 See *RPC online* 6.5521 temp., 10900 temp., 10829 temp.

193 See further chapter 4.

194 *RPC online* 9.789A. See chapter 1, Pl. 1.7 and key.

195 C. Howgego, "Coinage and Identity in the Roman Provinces," in *Coinage and Identity in the Roman Provinces* edited by C. Howgego, V. Heuchert and A. Burnett (Oxford: Oxford University Press, 2005), 2.

196 Ashton, "The Colossus," 86. Some corroboration might come from Rhodian amphora stamps (dated to 235–198 BCE) which similarly feature a radiate head; see N. Badoud, "Les colosses de Rhodes," *CRAI* (2011): 140–4.

Plate 2.11a and b: The radiate profile and three-quarter minting from Rhodes, from the time of the Colossus. The second coin, on its reverse, has a Phrygian helmet to the lower left of the rose.[197]

The connections, in trade, cultural exchange and military manoeuvres, were strong. The early imperial coinage continued the emphasis in iconography just as the reputation of Rhodes, as we have seen, preserved the memory of the mighty colossus, long since fallen. While the three-quarter facing head is known, by far the most common was the profile radiate head of Helios.[198] This is the same iconographic style repeatedly adopted by the Colossian mint; the Rhodian examples also include the variation of the head turned left and a consistency in showing clothing draped around the neck.[199]

Two coin types of Colossae present not the head of Helios, but the full heliotic colossus, with radiate head, holding a flaming torch in one hand and a globe in the other. One bears the image of the Emperor (Antoninus Pius) on the obverse (Pl. 2.12);[200] the second has the personified head of the youthful, laureate *Dêmos*, the representative assembly of citizens of Colossae.[201]

Plate 2.12: One of the known Colossian coin types of the standing, radiate Helios, here featuring the Emperor Antoninus Pius (138–161) on the obverse. The reverse legend tells us that the coin was minted by Claudius Sakerdos for the Colossians (31 mm, 15.05 g).

197 Ashton 18 = *SNG von Aulock* 2770 (dated 295–280 BCE); Ashton 207 (dated 250–230 BCE). Photographs courtesy of CNG coins (18 mm, 6.62 g) and Leu Numismatik (14 mm, 3.20 g) respectively.

198 See R. Ashton, "Rhodian Coinage in the Early Imperial Period," in *Recent Turkish Coin Hoards and Numismatic Studies* edited by C. S. Lightfoot (Oxford: Oxbow, 1991), 71–90.

199 Ashton, "Rhodian Coinage", 86 pl. 4.2, nrs 55–65. Compare, for Colossae, *RPC online* 3.2317, *RPC online* 3.2313A.

200 *RPC online* 4.2.11595 temp.

201 *RPC online* 4.2.1896 temp. Photograph from a private collection, by permission.

Here the emphasis is not on the movement of the sun-god in his quadriga across the sky, that is found, with a high level of artistry, on a number of Colossian coins,[202] and, less aesthetically, on coins of other city mints.[203] Rather the evocation is of the heliotic colossus. But there was another imaginary description of the Colossus of Rhodes that supports the quadriga rendition. A second-century Latin epitomist, almost forgotten, one Lucius Ampelius, conceived of the Rhodian statue as a solar quadriga.[204] Both images — the standing colossus and the quadriga driver — could, therefore, lay claim to a Rhodian inspiration. The more common stand-alone presentation is very close to the evocation of Helios, "the Lord of heaven and earth" found in the magical papyri: "... you will see a youthful god, beautiful in appearance, with fiery hair and in a white tunic and a scarlet cloak and wearing a fiery crown."[205] The description neatly combines the presentation of Helios on the two Colossian coin reverses (one naked with cloak, one with tunic). The text vividly captures the way in which the coin iconography would be understood. The imperial head conjoined with the colossal Helios that we see in the two types signals the authorization given and sought for this Colossian emphasis.

It seems therefore that at some stage between the cessation of Colossae's Attalid period minting (probably around 133–129 BCE) and the revival of its mint under Hadrian, the Colossian political leadership had begun to cultivate the association of its city name with the massive colossus of Rhodes. Colossae had, as we have seen, a huge natural colossus — the monolith on the southern mountain range — but the homonymic similarity of the Greek phonology of the city name, Kolossai, to a familiar Greek word (κολοσσός) invited the harnessing of the earlier Hittite toponym (*Ḫulašša* or *Ḫuwalušša* or similar) to a contemporary cultural icon. The Colossians wanted to portray themselves, and be esteemed by others, as marked by that wonder of the ancient world. Rhodes itself had used an image of the rose (ῥόδος) on the reverse of its coins, punning its own name. It was not the only city to engage in such "canting".[206] Colossae simply joined the ranks of those using a symbol to pun its own name in a language and literary commonplace with which the people of the day were readily

202 *RPC online* 4.2.1897 temp., 1899 temp.

203 *RPC online* 6.4504 temp. (Sardis); 6.4376 temp. (Thyateira).

204 Lucius Ampelius, *Liber Memorialis* 8.

205 *PGM* 4.635–41 (translation by Hans Dieter Betz). The difference lies in the conjunction in the magical papyrus between Helios and Mithras, who follows in the further ascent of the visionary. See J. B. Pettis, "Seeing the God in the Greco-Roman World," in *Seeing the God: Ways of Envisioning the Divine in Ancient Mediterranean Religion* edited by J. B. Pettis (Piscataway, NJ: Gorgias, 2013), 27–8.

206 So for example, a number of Hellenistic coins of Aspendos, bear the iconography of a slinger (σφενδόνη, "sling"). See A. Baldwin, "Symbolism on Greek Coins," *AJN* 49 (1915): 167. Compare the anchor (ἄγκυρα) used on some coins of Ankyra in Galatia: *RPC online* 4.3.971 temp., 4.3.4034 temp.

familiar. This "canting" was already deployed in the Lykos Valley.[207] Laodikeia had, in the Republican period, used visual puns for its two main rivers, the Lykos and the Kapros. So, even without a legend explicitly identifying the rivers, the visual cues of the wolf (λύκος) and the boar (κάπρος) provided the signifying symbols.[208] Colossae did the same, at least for the Lykos river (Pl. 2.13).[209]

Plate 2.13: A small coin of Colossae (15 mm, 2.3 g) minted by the grammateus (city clerk) Tiberius Asinios Philopappos (time of Antoninus Pius), featuring a helmeted head of Athena on the obverse and the wolf on the reverse indicating the Lykos River, with the legend "of/for the Colossians.[210]

The interpretation here seeks to make sense of the weight of numismatic witness. It would be bolstered if other evidence came to light. The thesis helps to explain two later developments that attach to the city name. Firstly, there is an ease with which Byzantine interpreters made the mistaken re-location of Colossae to the island of Rhodes. The ubiquitous word-plays engaged by Byzantine writers are more easily explained if they felt they had some warrant from the old cultural values of the city itself, for making that association of the city named Colossae with the Rhodian colossus. Secondly, when the (colossal) Helios began to be tarnished with the accusation of idolatry as Christianity increased its legal tethering in the empire, the name "Colossae/Colossians" could not help but collapse under the derogatory charge given that, for possibly three centuries or more, the city had promoted itself as a heliotic colossus among Asian cities. The polis was nothing more than an extension of the god, both captured in the name. This may even have ushered in a name-change (to Chonai) as a means of obviating the now-odious stain of idolatry. The use of the term εἰδωλολατρία twice in Canon 35 of the Council of Laodikeia (c. 365 CE) in anathematizing the worship of angels was a blatant castigation of practices at Colossae.[211] The word itself, charged with political and ecclesial sensitivities

207 Such practices were not confined to coins; see E. S. McCartney, "Canting Puns on Ancient Monuments," *AJA* 23.1 (1919): 59–64; Thonemann, *Maeander Valley*, 31–49.

208 See further chapter 3.

209 Colossae did have the boar on a number of its coins but it is not obvious that any of these is a visual pun on the river Kapros.

210 *RPC online* 4.2.1891 temp. = *MSPhryg* 2.465–468. Photograph from a private collection by permission.

211 See above.

in the period after the death of Julian "the Idolian" (εἰδωλιανός),[212] was found in the Letter to the Colossians itself.

Colossians 3:5 contains a short list of vices to be eschewed:

> Νεκρώσατε οὖν τὰ μέλη τὰ ἐπὶ τῆς γῆς, πορνείαν ἀκαθαρσίαν πάθος ἐπιθυμίαν κακήν, καὶ τὴν πλεονεξίαν ἥτις ἐστὶν εἰδωλατρία …
>
> Put to death those parts of you belonging to the earth — fornication, uncleanness, passion, evil desire and gluttony (which is idolatry) …

Another vice-list follows in verse 8.

> νυνὶ δὲ ἀπόθεσθε καὶ ὑμεῖς τὰ πάντα ὀργήν, θυμόν, κακίαν, βλασφημίαν, αἰσχρολογίαν ἐκ τοῦ στόματος ὑμῶν …
>
> now you are to remove all these things — anger, rage, malice, blasphemy, your foul-mouthings …

Such vice lists are common in the Second Testament and in philosophical texts throughout the ancient world. They serve a rhetorical function, designed to multiply the sense of behaviors to be avoided (or those people who follow such practices). Rarely are they to be taken as providing a rap sheet of morality crimes that an individual or group have actually committed. Rather they generate an ambience of those elements that an author used to color a general picture of an unsavory lifestyle or to impugn an individual or group without too much regard for accuracy (cf Col 1:21).[213] Here the function is to create distance between pagan life and the new pattern of life as a Christ follower, without necessarily accusing every member of the plural category "you" (as in "you walked" v.6) of committing each particular vice.

A number of the elements in this list in Colossians occur in other lists, including the fifth-century story of St Michael of Chonai. There we find impurity (ἀκαθαρσία) and evil desire (ἐπιθυμία κακή) again, but the whole list is anchored to gluttony (παμφάγος γαστριμαργία) and the occult (as if these are connected).[214] This assembly of elements was probably cultivated by a vilification of several features of Julian's reign — he was nick-named in some quarters as "the butcher" because of the inflation of the number of sacrifices for religious feasts, and he was instrumental in the cultivation of theurgic interests. Whereas many Western commentators seem preoccupied with the sex-

---

212 Gregory Nazianzus, *Or.* 4.77. See A. H. Cadwallader, "Inter-City Conflict in the Story of St Michael of Chonai," in *Religious Conflict from Early Christianity to the Rise of Islam* edited by W. Mayer and B. Neil (Berlin/Boston: de Gruyter, 2013), 109–27.

213 See A. H. Cadwallader, "Keeping Lists or Embracing Freedom: 1 Corinthians 6:9–10 in Context," in N. McI. Wright (ed.), *Five Uneasy Pieces: Essays on Scripture and Sexuality* (Adelaide: ATF Press, 2011), 47–67.

214 *Michael of Chonai* 7.16–18.

ual dimension of the terms in the Pauline Letter's list,[215] the later Colossian text about the archangel Michael clearly sees insatiability as the overarching issue. Given that an epexegetical comment is delivered only for the last term in Col 3:5 (πλεονεξία ἥτις ἐστὶν εἰδωλατρία), this may in fact be the capstone of the list (rather than the first item mentioned). While there is no sense that the fifth century text provides the general meaning for the first century writing, and while there is no need for each item to have a specific instance of offense behind it, it does seem clear that some pertinent historical and cultural context spawns this list as a response.

Colossae had, for perhaps two centuries, been overshadowed by the rise of Laodikeia's fortunes. The fall from its eminence as the leading and controlling city in the Achaemenid satrapy of the fifth and fourth centuries BCE — second only to Kelainai-Apameia[216] — seems to have festered in the concerns of the Colossian *polis* (see further, chapters 3 and 4). Xenophon's description of the Colossae of his day as "a large, prosperous and established city" (πόλις οἰκουμένη καὶ εὐδαίμων καὶ μεγάλη)[217] was adopted as *the* descriptive mark of Colossae for almost a millennium and a half.[218] The reality was often divergent but as raw as the disjunction was at times, the aspiration to augment Colossae's reputation and fortunes remained. We see it in the story of St Michael of Chonai, where the grandiose claim is broadcast in the pronouncement of the archangel that "the glory of this site will go everywhere".[219] Competition for advancement was part of the DNA of a Greek *polis* and it remained a vibrant, functioning drive long into Byzantine Christendom. The Romans skillfully exploited this preoccupation to their own advantage.

For a number of emperors, a heliotic and colossal self-conception was nothing other than an imitation of their own conceits. Nero had commissioned a colossus — of himself of course.[220] At least one of the cities of the Lycus Val-

215 "In the sexual context of the Roman Empire …" (!): Scot McKnight, *The Letter to the Colossians* (NICNT; Grand Rapids, MI: Eerdmans, 2018), 303. See also Jerry L. Sumney, *Colossians: A Commentary* (Louisville/London: WJKP, 2008), 189–91, Christopher R. Seitz, *Colossians* (Grand Rapids, MI: Brazos, 2014), 155–6. Paul Foster is a little more restrained, *Colossians*, 322–3. Compare also B. J. Walsh and S. C. Keesmart, *Colossians Remixed: Subverting the Empire* (Downers Grove, IL: IVP, 2004), 160–4.

216 N. Sekunda, "Changing Patterns of Land-Holding in the South-Western Border Lands of Greater Phrygia in the Achaemenid and Hellenistic Periods," in *Colossae in Space and Time*, 48–76 at 72.

217 Xenophon *Anab.* 1.2.6.

218 Nicetas Choniates *Chron.* 178.19.

219 *S. Mich. Chon.* 19.7–8.

220 Pliny *NH* 34.18.45–6. It seems that Nero deliberately sought to surpass the Helios of Rhodes in height. The Rhodian colossus extended 70 cubits (105 feet) to its apex; that of Nero, 106½ feet (Pliny *NH* 34.18.41, 45 — different manuscripts have other measurements for Nero's colossus but they all surpass the Helios of Rhodes).

ley, Tripolis, may have mirrored the adulation, if not the size.[221] Vespasian, with his more subtle sophistication, refashioned the same statue as the god Sol (the Roman formulation of Helios), but nevertheless thereby marked the god's favor upon his earthly representative and dedicant.[222] Raw power and religious sanction were two sides of the same coin in the *oikonomia* of Rome, though the seeds were certainly laid in late Hellenistic ideology.[223]

With the erection of the colossus and costs associated with it, came regular worship. One papyrus from Arsinoe in Egypt lists the costs associated with the imperial cult. Quite apart from the mounting of "the divine colossal statue of our lord, the Emperor Severus Antoninus" (θείου κολοσσιαίου ἀνδριάντος τοῦ κυρίου ἡμῶν Αὐτοκράτορος Σεουήρου Ἀντωνίνου) there were the costs of the annual sacred celebrations: crowning the temple's monuments, oil-provision, pinecones, spices, the cost of the hire of donkeys for carrying tree and palm branches, polishing and other upkeep, the wages of officials ... and on it goes to the final combined expenditure of 2424 drachmas or 2141 denarii[224] — more than enough to feed 5000 men (and the women and children) for ten picnics (see Mk 6:37)[225] or meet the annual salary of two legionary soldiers or ten prison guards![226] A huge colossus of Domitian (81–96 CE) was erected in the temple of the imperial cult in Ephesos, a visual confrontation that Stephen Moore considers was the inspiration behind the Christ-colossus in the Book of Revelation (1:13–16).[227] It seems that the erection of colossi had become something of a rage.[228]

Colossae's colossal aspirations appear to have been part of its efforts to re-establish its standing in the polity of the Lycus Valley, if not beyond. This was doubtless important for local inhabitants' pride in their own city — a cru-

---

221 See C. Zoroğlu, "Tripolis'ten Kolossal Zırhlı Heykel Ayağı," in *Tripolis Araştırmaları* edited by B. Duman (Istanbul: Ege, 2017), 83–90. Zoroğlu assigns the 7 meter colossus to Hadrian but there is nothing certain about the ascription (or mine). What is certain is that colossi were part of Roman imperial symbolism related to the immensity of the emperor through into late antiquity. The aspiration to divinity was blatant; see S. Price, *Rituals and Power: The Roman Imperial Cult in Asia Minor* (Cambridge: Cambridge University Press, 1984), 187–8.

222 Suetonius *Vesp.* 18. One tradition had the face of Nero's colossus refashioned as Titus, perhaps thereby eliciting a divinely-approved dynastic succession; see Dio Cassius 66.15.1.

223 See, for example, *I.Pergamon* 246 = *OGIS* 332 (138–133 BCE) where a five-cubit (7½ feet) high statue of Attalos III was to be erected in the temple of Asklepios (ll. 7–8).

224 *BGU* 2.362 (215–216 CE).

225 On the rough calculation of a denarius being the equal of 16 assaria (*IGR* 4.352, time of Hadrian) and one assarion having the purchasing power of one loaf of barley bread (compare Jn 6:9), this would yield over 34,000 loaves of barley bread (less if the more costly, fine flour bread was purchased). The abacus might not come to ten picnics, admittedly; this may be why Philip in Jn 6:7 adjusts the hyperbole of Mk 6:37 against literalist scrutiny.

226 *New Doc. Early Christ.* 6.21.

227 S. D. Moore, "The Beatific Vision as a Posing Exhibition: Revelation's Hypermasculine Deity," *JSNT* 60 (1996): 27–55.

228 See Phlegon *FGrH* 257 Fr 36.xiii on the intent of a number of Asian cities to mount a colossus of Tiberius in the forum in Rome.

cial instrument of social cohesion. As Humphrey Sutherland long ago wrote in a sustained defense of the value of coins for historical analysis, "the ceaseless propagation of those types was intended to conciliate opinion … their choice directly reflects official mentality."[229] He had imperial coinage in view, but the propaganda mimesis by local cities, with their mints sponsored by local dignitaries, stands equally under his judgment.

The emphatic brandishing of Helios in local Colossian coinage readily demonstrates how greed and idolatry could be easily equated. Temples, after all, were the banks of the ancient world.[230] The sculpted colossi of that world demanded massive appropriations of resources — Rhodes' colossus cost a staggering 300 talents, according to an amazed Pliny.[231] At coastal Tlos (or perhaps Xanthos) in Lycia, just across the Carpathian Sea from Rhodes, one voluntary association of coppersmiths seem to have claimed Helios as their patron (*SEG* 58.1640, A, 150–100 BCE) — certainly offences against the regulations of the association were to be punished by a fine of 1000 drachmas to the god (that is, the temple treasury).

The opening of the Letter to the Colossians and heliotic Colossae

The writer of the Letter to the Colossians preceded the revival of the Colossian mint at the onset of Hadrian's reign by half a century, but the iconographic emphases on Colossae's coins were not new, even if the mint was. They reflect developments that had been unfolding for some decades. Prosperity was attached to and demonstrated by religious devotion (a commonly reiterated deception, even today). Somewhere in that conjunction stood Helios, emblematic of the Colossians' colossal ambition. Seeded also in that conjunction lay a critique, characterizing greed or gluttony as idolatry (Col 3:5). The potency of the contrast for the Christ-followers who received the letter was more telling because not a city nor its symbol of aspiration was to be preeminent but

229 C. H. V. Sutherland, "The Intelligibility of Roman Imperial Coin Types," *JRS* 49 (1959): 55.

230 See A. H. Cadwallader, "In Go(l)d we Trust: Literary and Economic Exchange in the Debate over Caesar's Coin (Mk 12:13–17)" *BibInterp* 14.5 (2006): 486–507. Penelope Glare points out that the temple of the imperial cult at Arsinoe in Egypt, drawing as it did substantial levies and rentals from surrounding villages, provided low-interest loans to the very elite charged with maintaining the cult. The interest on the loans was used to finance much of the temple's operations but also to channel investment opportunities to the elite. The religious center was therefore little more than a conduit of resources from peasant stock to the elite, who all the while maintained lucrative deference to their imperial masters. See "The Temple of Jupiter Capitolinus at Arsinoe and the Imperial Cult," in *Proceedings of the 20th International Congress of Papyrologists, Copenhagen, 23–29 August, 1992* edited by A. Bülow-Jacobsen (Copenhagen: Museum Tusculan Press, 1994), 550–1.

231 Pliny *NH* 34.18.41.

rather the Christ who had abrogated so many of the superlative attributes previously dispersed among the religious and political terminology of the *polis* state (Col 1:15–20). The writer of the letter may have drawn on the resources of a Jewish polemic that collated greed and idolatry, as is distilled, for example, in the Testament of Judah's castigation of the fetish of money: "The love of money beats a path to idolatry because, by the deception of coin, people come to worship (ὀνομάζουσιν) those without substance as gods."[232]

But more patent is the south-western Phrygian city context that shapes and colors the content of his critique, and, most importantly, the letter's initial reception.[233] Andrej Petrovic has demonstrated that the opening ἅγιοι of Col 1:2 is far from unusual in a Hellenistic environment. Devotees approaching a god's temple were greeted by the same designation, which was followed by a list of practical and moral regulations that unfolded the meaning to be attached to such an honorific epithet.[234] The god was holy;[235] any audience had to display the same quality.[236] Whilst the Colossian description of devotees is more fulsome, tying together ἅγιος and πιστός, such extensions were becoming familiar in late hellenistic and early Roman sacred contexts. Thus a first century requirement for entry into the precincts of an Asklepeion on the island of Lesbos, called for purity and holy thoughts (ἁγνὸν πρὸς τέμενος στεόιχειν ὅσια φρονέοντα),[237] almost as if one is defined by the other. These might be funneled into individual accolades: a woman from Smyrna is applauded on her epitaph as "most faithful and pure" (Τατίαν … πιστοτάτην καὶ ἁγνοτάτην);[238] similar plaudits are given to a civic leader and his family at Claudioupolis (τοῖς ἁγνοτάτοις καὶ θεῷ πιστεύσασιν Μαρ. [Αὐ.] Δημητριανῷ).[239] There is implied

232 *Test12Patr*, *Judah* 19:1. I have translated ὀνομάζω as "worship" not only because this is the implication of Ps 115:4–8, 135:15–18 (idols are silver and gold) but this is the clear meaning of the term in Canon 35 of the Synod of Laodikeia that denounces the worship (ὀνομάζειν) of angels.

233 See A. Petrovic, "Do Seize, Do Eat, Do Touch — But Mind Your Thoughts: Colossians and Greek Purity Regulations," in *Epigraphical Evidence Illustrating Paul's Letter to the Colossians* edited by J. Verheyden, M. Öhler and T. Corsten (WUNT 411; Tübingen: Mohr Siebeck, 2018), 151–60.

234 Petrovic, "Colossians and Greek Purity Regulations," 149–51. He follows in large measure, T. B. Slater, "Translating Ἅγιος in Col 1,2 and Eph 1,1," *Biblica* 87 (2006): 52–4.

235 One rectangular amulet gem distills the sanctity of the god and the reason for approach. On black amber is engraved Ζεῦ ἅγιε, ἀποστρεψίκακε, "O holy Zeus, averter of evil"; *Campbell Bonner Magical Gems Database*, CBd-1262 (http://www2.szepmuveszeti.hu/talismans/visitatori_salutem).

236 Compare Aristonoos *Paian to Apollo* 26 Athenaios(?) *Paian and Prosodion to Apollo* 9–10 (ed. Furley and Bremer).

237 *IG* XII, Supp. 23.

238 *I.Smyrna* 429 (1st century CE).

239 *I.Klaudiu polis* 44 (3rd century CE). The deceased and/or his family may have been Christian, Jewish or "pagan". Markus Öhler opts for the first: "Graeco-Roman Associations, Judean Synagogues and Early Christianity in Bithynia-Pontus," in *Authority and Identity in Emerging Christianities in Asia Minor and Greece* edited by C. Breytenbach and J. Ogereau (Leiden:

that what follows in the Colossians Letter is the distinctive brand of holiness/purity in the midst of a competitive religious market-place, an emporium that had a major saturation of Helios enthusiasm, actively encouraged by civic authorities. It is clear from the often curious differences in purity requirements and moral aptitudes between temples and associations (even of the same general devotion or rationale) that the regulations were driven by factors pertaining to self-definition and extra-distinction as much as by religiosity. The influence of a powerful personality might also contribute to the local characteristic expression of a group.[240]

Here we are returned to the critical importance of the material locality within which the people of Colossae lived out their lives and to which they made contributions for its shaping. More particularly for those who are keen to factor in the presence of Christ-followers in that urban and rural environment, it is crucial to allow them to be real actors in a geographical, social and historical, often agonistic setting. As Jack Livingstone reiterated, "The realm of religious self-definition in the late Roman world usually presupposed the significant, close-at-hand "other" in a complex, multi-facetted social landscape …"[241] This demands a recognition that texts belonging in or contributing to that context be allowed to be players, themselves "artifacts", within the mesh of insights that various disciplines are able to supply.

This is why statements such as that of Eduard Lohse lack any particularity of application and turn into bland, confessional affirmations. He commented on the introduction of the letter as addressed to "the people of his own possession in the midst of a world that is given to another faith", adding that the mention of location (Col 1:2) was "almost incidental."[242] Not only does "a world given to another faith" fly in the face of the weight of evidence that we have already noticed that shows plainly that Greek and Roman religious practices varied considerably in their accents and applications across the various cities of Asia Minor. (The same is true of the systems of jurisprudence which survived in substantial, if constrained, measure at least until the *Constitutio Antoniniana*

Brill, 2018), 87–88. However, his argument that the offices held by Demetrianos (pre-eminently, "first *archon*") would have been "quite unusual for a Judean" (87 n61) fails to account for the greater longevity of Jews in Asia and for the evidence for Jews holding civic offices elsewhere: see A. R. R. Sheppard, "R.E.C.A.M. Notes and Studies No. 6: Jews, Christians and Heretics in Acmonia and Eumeneia," *AS* 29 (1979): 169–80. For the early combination in a "pagan" testimonial, see *IG* IX,1.270 (post-229 BCE).

240 See Greg Horsley's comments on a religious association of the god Mên in *New Doc. Early Christ.* 3.6 at p. 22.

241 J. N. Livingstone, "Urbanization in the Roman East and the Inter-Religious Struggle for Success," in *Religious Rivalries and the Struggle for Success in Sardis and Smyrna* edited by R. S. Ascough (Waterloo, Ont: Wilfred Laurier University Press, 2005), 211.

242 E. Lohse, *Colossians and Philemon* translated by W. R. Poehlmann and R. J. Karris (Hermeneia; Philadelphia: Fortress, 1971), 8. See also P. Müller, *Kolosserbrief* (KEK 9/2; Göttingen: Vandenhoeck & Ruprecht, 2022), 56, 120–1.

in 212 CE.)[243] It also dehistoricizes and dislocates the letter from any accents (religious or otherwise) that we might discover for Colossae — and this has enormous implications cultivating the dematerialization of human life and inconsequentiality of ecological sanctity. A critical dialogue between material remains and the Letters to the Colossians and to Philemon assists in the construction of the immediate reception of the writings by affirming probabilities of understanding (if not implementation) and removes other theories as unlikely — not least, as we shall see, the presence of a significant Jewish population in the city.

Lohse's generalizing summation has lead to a substantial blending of the introduction to this letter with epistolary openings in the Pauline Letter corpus. Although it has been clear that the formal characteristics and often much of the content of Pauline Letters differ little from the thousands of letters found in the papyri,[244] there has been a desire, at the same time, to seal the distinctives of Paul's Letters from those emanating from non-Christian sources. But the forensic hunt for uniqueness evaporates when the letters themselves are compared with one another.[245] Governed by the commitment, the Colossians opening becomes merely a modulation on what is found in the rest of the Pauline corpus. The "church" (ἐκκλησία) is absent, but this is true in Rom 1:7 and Phil 1:1 (cf Eph 1:1). In any case, the reference to ἅγιοι seals the homogeneity because both terms are found in 1 Cor 1:2 with slight variation in 2 Cor 1:1, essentially meaning the same thing. Thus a bridge is made to those letters where ἐκκλησία is the characterisation of the Christ-followers (Gal 1:2 [plural], 1 Thess 1:1, 2 Thess 1:1); but such apologetic only seems to underscore the absence of the term in Col 1:2.

The sticky issue is that the addition of "faithful companions" (πιστοὶ ἀδελφοί) is unique among Pauline addresses, though closely followed by that in Eph 1:1. The commitment signaled in πιστ- cognates is found in a number of cultic, holiness regulations;[246] it is one of the acclaimed personified attributes adorning the funerary monument of Zoilos, the famous son of Aphrodisias.[247] So here in the letter is not a *sui generis* collation. The syntax disrupts the ease

243 See chapter 11.

244 See Peter Arzt-Grabner, "How to Deal with Onesimus? Paul's Solution within the Frame of Ancient Legal and Documentary Sources," in *Philemon in Perspective: Interpreting a Pauline Letter* edited by D. F. Tolmie (BZBW 169; Göttingen: de Gruyter, 2010), 113–42 at 114.

245 See J. D. G. Dunn, *The Epistles to the Colossians and to Philemon* (NIGTC; Grand Rapids, MI: Eerdmans, 1996), 48–9. Dunn recognizes "faithful brothers" as "without parallel in Paul's greetings" but by retaining ἅγιοι as a substantive he can readily blend all the elements into a standard paradigm of Paul's (even with Timothy as the proposed author of Colossians). He is substantially influenced by his forebear at Durham, J. B. Lightfoot; see *Colossians and Philemon*, 130.

246 See *TAM* V,3 1539 ll. 55–7 (Philadelphia, late 2nd to early 1st century BCE).

247 *I.Aphrodisias 2007* 11.212 (late 1st century CE).

with which ἅγιοι is understood as a substantive, that is "saints",[248] because the normal understanding derived from the use of the definite article before "holy" but not before "faithful" (τοῖς ἐν Κολοσσαῖς ἁγίοις καὶ πιστοῖς ἀδελφοῖς ἐν Χριστῷ) is that both are to be understood as qualifying descriptors of "companions",[249] that is, as "holy and faithful companions". I am not interested here in trying to hang Pauline pseudepigraphy on this unique peg — a far stronger hook is found in Col 3:11 (see chapter 9). Rather I am arguing that those addressed *are addressed in their context* — ἐν Κολοσσαῖς. That context includes, as I have suggested above, an identification that serviced a grandiose (if pretentious) self-inflation — a colossus of heliotic proportions. The argument for a heliotic colossus provides a plausible reconstruction of the extant material, though the case needs further evidence. That is admitted, but the evidence we do have provides an insight into at least one prism of the variegated context that is to be found at Colossae, within which and perhaps against which, Christ-followers were encouraged to define themselves.

The "faith" of the Christ-followers was no general commitment devoid of content, but was a "faithfulness" to be worked out in a setting where a colossal, heliotic, civic identity was in the process of being fashioned. "Faithfulness" (and for that matter, "holiness") was not merely an identity defined in relation *to* "Christ"; it was defined *against* the demands and impositions of the context in which the Christ-followers of Colossae found themselves, a context that bore the marks of greed and idolatry. The carefully-constructed syntax in the opening underscores the polar definitions of identity: ἐν Κολοσσαῖς or ἐν Χριστῷ. Here Colossae is more than a location.

There is no οὖσιν to flag mere topography such as we find in 1 Cor 1:1, 2 Cor 1:1 (τῇ οὔσῃ ἐν Κορίνθῳ; cf Eph 1:1).[250] This latter is the usual locative expression found in Egyptian papyri. From priests to ordinary members of households, the standard formula of ὁ ὢν ἐν/οἱ οὖσιν ἐν is applied.[251] A commonly-cited papyrus dated to 182 BCE

248 See C. R. Campbell, *Colossians and Philemon: A Handbook on the Greek Text* (Waco, TX: Baylor, 2013), 2; Foster, *Colossians*, 129–31.

249 Literally, the word is to be translated "brothers", but it is to be understood as a generic expression of the Christ-followers in their relationships with one another and, significantly, with the author of the letter. Contemporary bible translations opt for "brothers and sisters".

250 Petr Pokorný takes the locative participle as implied in Colossians on the basis of Ephesians as a commentary: *Colossians: A Commentary* translated by S. S. Schatzmann (Peabody, MA: Hendrickson, 1991), 33. By doing so, he can combine Colossians as consistent with the thrust of the Pauline corpus (even though admitting Colossian's pseudepigraphy). But commentaries can direct, mis-direct or correct the work on which they are based. The singular thrust of the Colossians' opening (admitted as directed towards the specifics of the church's life at Colossae by Lightfoot and Dunn amongst others) is thereby lost in what is basically a textual amalgamation operating canonically with little reference to the historical circumstances.

251 See P. Arzt-Grabner *et al*, *1. Korinther* (PKNT 2; Göttingen: Vandenhoeck & Ruprecht, 2006), 41.

lists a number of priests and priestesses, designated by location as in Alexandria: ἱερείας Ἀρσινόης Φιλοπάτ[ο]ρος τῆς οὔσης ἐν Ἀλεξανδρείαι ("of the priestess in Alexandria for Arsinoe Philopator"). The papyrus registers a mortgage and designates the security for the loan, also using the same locative formula: ἐπὶ ὑποθήκηι τῆι ὑπαρχούσηι αὐτῶι οἰκίαι καὶ αὐλῆι καὶ τοῖς συγκυροῦσι πᾶσι τοῖς οὖσιν ἐν Ἀπιάδι τῆς Θεμίστου μερίδος ("on the security of the house belonging to him, its courtyard and all the fittings that are at Apias in the regional district of Themistes").[252] The phrasing remained constant into the common era.[253] It is no peculiar Hellenistic Egyptian expression. The same model is demonstrated in inscriptions across Asia Minor. So, in an honorific inscription for Dionysios son of Nikophoros, the *Boulê* and *Dêmos* of the city of Ephesos, recite his praiseworthy deeds which included the provision of oil ἐν τοῖς βαλανείοις τοῖς οὖσιν ἐν Ἐφέσῳ ("in all the baths in Ephesos").[254] So the appearance of this locative formula in some of the Pauline Letters is nothing unusual.

The use of the participial copula, ὤν/οὖσιν and so on, is far from required. So, for example, the farmers of estates in Tapteia in Egypt are simply located: τοὺς γεωργοὺς τοὺς ἐν Ταπτεια.[255] So also the letter-carriers at Oxyrhynchus: τοῖς ἐν τῶι Ὀξυρυγχίτηι βυβλιαφόροις.[256] Personal letters can use the same simplicity when sending greetings "to all those in the house" (τοῖς ἐν οἴκωι πᾶσι χαίρειν).[257] In fact, this form served also as an "address" on the outside of the letter (the verso). One letter opens with "Platon to the priests in Pathyris and to the others who dwell (there), greetings." (Πλάτων τοῖς ἐν Παθύρει ἱερεῦσι καὶ τοῖς ἄλλοις τοῖς κατοικοῦσι, χαίρειν). But the verso is identical, now functioning as the address for the letter: τοῖς ἐν Παθύρει ἱερεῦσι καὶ τοῖς ἄλλοις τοῖς κατοικοῦσι.[258] The same mode of identification of location can occur in inscriptions.[259]

If the letter opened briefly with τοῖς ἐν Κολοσσαῖς ἁγίοις "to the saints in Colossae" there would be nothing more than a locative situating of the saints, of a piece with Rom 1:7, 1 Cor 1:2 and 2 Cor 1:1 (overlooking the ellipse of the copula). It would be parallel to numerous other texts such as Plutarch's τοῖς ἐν

252 *P.Tebt.* 3.1.817, ll. 6–7, ll. 12–14. The document deals with a mortgage loan between two Jews, Apollonios and Sostratos, "the best known specimen of a typical Hellenistic contract where both the contracting parties are Jews." Victor R. Tcherikover and Alexander Fuks, *Corpus Papyrorum Judaicarum* (Cambridge MA: Harvard University Press, 3 vols, 1957), vol 1, 612 nr. 23.

253 See *BGU* 14.2376 (36–35 BCE), l. 2, *P.Oxy.* 3271, l. 6 (47–75 CE).

254 *I.Ephesos* 661, l l. 23–24 (140–150 CE); see also *MAMA* 8.413C, ll. 13–14, 20–21 (Aphrodisias 117–138 CE).

255 *P.Cair. Zen.* 1.59130, ll. 17–19 (Memphis, 256–254 BCE).

256 *BGU* 6.1232, ll. 7–8 (Oxyrhynchus, 111–110 BCE).

257 *P.Tebt.* 3.2.848, l. 2 (Tebtynis, 3rd–2nd century BCE); *UPZ* 1.74, ll. 6–7 (Memphis, after 161 BCE). A different form of expression is used in Phmn 1 (τῇ κατ᾽οἰκόν σου ἐκκλησίᾳ), an expression that implies more than simple location.

258 *P.Bour.* 12, ll. 1–4 and verso (88 BCE); see also *P.Bad.* 2.16, verso (Pathyris, 88 BCE).

259 See for example *SGDI* 2.2506, ll. 26–7 (Delphi, 277 BCE); *IGR* 4.1524, ll. 9–10 (Sardis, early 2nd century).

Ἀσίᾳ φίλοις "to the friends in Asia",[260] or even within the letter itself: τοὺς ἐν Λαοδικείᾳ ἀδελφούς (Col 4:15 cf Col 4:13). But that is not what we have. The expression in Col 1:2 is closer to that in Phil 1:1, though the latter phrasing is fuller: πᾶσιν τοῖς ἁγίοις ἐν Χριστῷ Ἰησοῦ τοῖς οὖσιν ἐν Φιλίπποις. Philippians not only uses the copula οὖσιν but it duplicates the definite article, setting off the repetition of the preposition ἐν with the statement of affiliation first and that of location second. And that affiliation is "Christ Jesus". None of these elements is found in Colossians. Not only is Colossians' opening phrase of address more compact, not only is there no mention of "church" even though the earlier Colossian text, Philemon, admits of at least one *ekklêsia* in the city (Phmn 2), but the order is reversed and "Jesus" is omitted. (So concerned were some scribes about the omission, unique in Pauline Letter openings, that the name was restored.)[261]

The phrasing could be suggested to be related to the double use of ἐν in some documents that indicate a progressive narrowing of location. When Thucydides related the opening of an engagement in the course of the Peloponnesian War, he had Demosthenes send two ships to seek help from the Athenian fleet at Eurymedon. His phrase provides a double locative τοῖς ἐν ναυσὶν ἐν Ζακύνθῳ Ἀθηναίοις, literally "to the Athenians in ships in Zacynthos."[262] The sophist Athenaeus relates the story of the minor king Harpalus sending for a renowned courtesan (as Athenaeus tells the tale) to come οἰκεῖν ἐν τοῖς βασιλείοις τοῖς ἐν Ταρσῷ "to live in the palaces in Tarsus".[263] The narrowing of reference by repetition of ἐν is known in inscriptions and the papyri.[264]

However, this is not quite what we have in the Colossians opening. One would expect a repetition of the definite article before "in Christ", namely … τοῖς ἐν Χριστῷ, if it was simply intended to convey a more precise narrowing of the designated group. But as we have seen the single τοῖς ties both the "holy" and "the faithful companions" to Christ. The formal structural identity ἐν Κολοσσαῖς … ἐν Χριστῷ with the specific syntactical linkage of the "holy and faithful companions" to the latter, sets up a tension between the two locations. The letter is not to those in Colossae, as if the expression is nothing more than a topographical locator, such as we find in numerous inscriptions. The addressees are a much-narrowed group, yet with a vastly larger scale of reference. It is no surprise then to find that the secure *location* for the Christ-followers is "with Christ in God" (σὺν τῷ Χριστῷ ἐν τῷ θεῷ Col 3:3), not as a future anticipation but as a present reality. Their primary *civic* identity is not defined by Colossae but by Christ. The "in Christ" is no mere sub-group of those "in Colossae". Rather the "in Christ" group is defined over against the

260 See, for example, Plutarch *Ages.* 6.2 τοῖς ἐν Ἀσίᾳ φίλοις.
261 Mss A D* F G 33 as weighty examples amongst a small number of witnesses.
262 Thucydides *Hist.* 4.8.
263 Athenaeus *Deip.* 13.586c.
264 *IG* XII,9 207; *IG* IX,2 508; *I.Eleusis* 175; Boesch, Theoros 28; *P.Iand. Zen.* 2.

larger "in Colossae" population. Peter Müller is right in seeing the phrase "in Christ" as the "horizon of reality within which the believers are to understand their life;"[265] but this needs to be understood as operating in contra-distinction from the horizon of reality "in Colossae."

It will mean that the eminence of Christ will need to be demonstrated so that those living in the socio-political ambit of Colossae can yet go about their lives confident that the foundation of their identity is more secure than either a colossus or the natural elements that brought down the most famous colossus in history. The writer does not construct Christ as an alternate colossus. The elaborate imagery of that comparative path was adopted by "John of Patmos" (Rev 1:12–20). Even though Patmos John did not leave the massive metaphorical model unscathed in his Christian refashioning,[266] his imagery demonstrates that "the colossus" did capture some Christian attention for the development of Christological reflection. The Colossian author however ignored that option as vapid, a civic ambition, anything but "humble",[267] a construct building a new Greek imagery for the toponym and city, Colossae. For the Colossians author, that civic sensibility was deceptive and ultimately futile. After all, as the anti-idolatry psalms succinctly put the question of identity, "those who make them shall be like them" (Pss 115:8, 135:18) — not merely blind, dumb and deaf, but subject to the primal *stoicheia* of the universe (cf Col 2:8, 20). This is not to deny that the author will borrow from the resources that constrain all writers of a particular time and place. However, the choice of the resources to harness for his purpose was different from that of the writer of the Apocalypse. It is already flagged by the "re-location" of Colossae's Christ-followers just mentioned (Col 3:3). It will be given its symphonic rendition in a hymn that owes much of its genre, imagery and content to the cosmological speculations of the time (chapter 6) and it will include a new foundation narrative for this new settlement of people (chapter 3). Only in this cosmic Christ, so the author argues, can the Christ-followers' identity be securely grounded and steadfast (Col 1:23), a stability that no colossus, natural or constructed, could guarantee. Significantly, given the epexegetical addition to the vice of greed (Col 3:5), only in Christ will be found riches (πλοῦτος) and treasures (οἱ θησαυροί; Col 2:2–3). The contrast, according to the author, could not be greater.

It is attention to the material background that helps to deliver a sense of how that contrast is to be understood. We have moved considerably from the conundrums associated with the different spellings of the city name(s) and plumbed the etymological options to discover a new possibility, namely that

265 Müller, *Kolosserbrief*, 121.

266 See the partial modulation of Stephen Moore's interpretation in A. H. Cadwallader, "'Bad to the Bone': Reading Revelation Rooned," *ABR* 66 (2018): 13–29 at 23, 25–27.

267 McKnight, *The Letter to the Colossians*, 85. McKnight uses the descriptor in the sense of the inconsequentiality of Colossae at this time. But neither the city nor its pretensions warrant such a term.

an original Hittite name was not only transliterated into Greek but, at a later time and under threats to its regional standing, was given an ambitious Greek etymology. At a later date, under attack from the idolatry straiteners of ecclesial decision-makers, Colossae was to yield to an alternate name, Chonai, itself with an etymology claiming a different divine authority. At least given the concentration we have observed in the coins of the city, the contrast sharply given in the letter's vice-lists but subtly presaged in the very opening of the letter is with the religious focus (with all its economic and political embroilment) of those who ruled Colossian society in the late Republic to the early Roman imperial period. The text thereby became a player in the life of the city at least among the letter recipients (to a greater or lesser extent). The letter writer used the city to think with; its cultural resources were appropriated in the interests of a new religious group, setting or confirming the Colossian Christ-followers on a delicate agonistic course with civic values and practices. How far that competition extended and whether it transformed into visible confrontation or was tempered by accommodation to its environment will occupy considerable attention in subsequent chapters.

Chapter Three
Holding together city and country

The urban lens through which early Christianity has been viewed has distorted the way in which the *poleis* of the Lycus Valley (and elsewhere) have been understood.[1] Our easy translation of *polis* as "city" reflects this jaundiced view. In part, it gains some ancient warrant. The second-century travel writer, Pausanias, understood city in terms of its conveniences — fountains, gymnasium, baths — that is, those elements that bore the stamp of human architectural intervention.[2] He was not alone. But a *polis* was a small, semi-autonomous state albeit, in Asia from 129 BCE, under Rome's overarching authority. Indeed, a city simply could not exist unless it was serviced by the fundamentals of human existence: food, water, wood, beasts of burden, raw materials such as stone, fleeces, clay and so on. For these supplies, territory was required. The editors of the last volume of the *Lexicon of Greek Personal Names* make the important observation that for some cities, "the proportion of people ascribed to their territories can greatly exceed those known from the urban centre."[3] Significantly, they include Colossae as an example, even if their vision tends to be constrained by the size of the höyük. Conversely, they consider Laodikeia, one of the largest cities, to have had "a much smaller territory than many of its smaller counterparts."[4]

In this chapter, I gauge something of the territory of Colossae, while admitting that borders were subject to change implemented by succeeding regimes.

---

1 See M. Tiwald and J. K. Zangenberg (eds.), *Early Christian Encounters with Town and Countryside: Essays on the Urban and Rural Worlds of Early Christianity* (Göttingen: Vandenhoeck & Ruprecht, 2021).

2 Pausanias 10.4.1.

3 See also T. Drew-Bear, "Map 62 Phrygia," in *Barrington Atlas of the Greek and Roman World: Map-by-Map Directory* edited by R. J. A. Talbert (Princeton, NJ: Princeton University Press, 2 vols 2000), vol 2, 957.

4 J.-S. Balzat, R. W. V. Catling, É. Chiricat and T. Corsten, "Introduction," to *Lexicon of Greek Personal Names Volume V.C, Inland Asia Minor* (Oxford: Clarendon Press, 2018), xxi.

Precision of a city's territorial boundaries, whilst jealously guarded in their own day, remain considerably ill-defined for us — coins, inscriptions (especially the rare but invaluable boundary stones) and a knowledge of the topography are all crucial snatches of material evidence contributing to the discussion. But even when the results are somewhat indeterminate, that Colossae and other cities controlled and relied upon territory is indisputable. The question then becomes a matter of how a city, often substantially outsized by the population of the surrounding countryside, held the territory together and ensured it was responsive to its requirements. Here, commercial, administrative and ideological instruments — what Ernest Gellner calls production, coercion and cognition[5] — combine to facilitate cohesion of operation. This is a critical framework by which to understand "the Letter to the Colossians" (and "to Philemon") and we can rightly expect to find hints, perhaps even an address of that framework of city and its territory, within its text.

Herodotos and the first literary glimpse of Colossae

The earliest literary witness to Colossae from Greek sources is that of Herodotos. It comes in the context of the narrative about the Achaemenid leader, Xerxes, who, under the impulse of a forceful series of dreams advising conquest of Greece, led his army west. The initial destination was Kelainai (Apameia) in Phrygia and from there the soldiers marched for Sardis. They were buoyed by a lavish offering of support from a Lydian aristocrat named Pythios. His holdings of slaves and landed estates were more than able to accommodate his gift.[6] No doubt his avowed hatred of the Greeks was undergirded by strategic diplomacy in securing Xerxes' favor — at least that appears to be what he hoped when he later tried to call in the king's debt.

The advance from Kelainai brought them into the length of the Lycus Valley, a relatively short span of about fifty miles from the shallow pass in the east to the course of the Maeander River in the west. The Maeander traditionally demarcated Phrygian-Lydian territory. Surprisingly perhaps, only three toponyms are mentioned in Herodotos's briefly covered itinerary:

---

5 E. Gellner, *Plough, Sword and Book: The Structure of Human History* (Chicago: University of Chicago Press, 1988), 19–20.

6 Herodotos 7.13–29. The story of Pythes/Pythios' wealth and/or generosity is embellished by a series of authors: Plutarch *Mulier. virt.* 262A–263A, Polyaenus *Strat.* 8.42, Stephanus the Byzantine lexicographer sv. Πυθόπολις. See N. Sekunda, "Changing Patterns of Land-Holding in the South-Western Border Lands of Greater Phrygia in the Achaemenid and Hellenistic Periods," in *Colossae in Space and Time: Linking to an Ancient City* edited by A. H. Cadwallader and M. Trainor (Göttingen: Vandenhoeck & Ruprecht, 2011), 49–51.

> Passing by the Phrygian city [Φρυγῶν πόλιν] called Anaua, and the lake from which salt is obtained, he (Xerxes) came into Colossae, a great city in Phrygia [πόλιν μεγάλην Φρυγίης]; there the river Lycus empties into a chasm in the land and disappears, until it reappears about five stadia away; this river issues into the Maeander. From Colossae the army held its course for the borders of Phrygia and Lydia [τοὺς οὔρους τῶν Φρυφῶν καὶ Λυδῶν], and came to the city of Kydrara [Κύδραρα πόλιν], where there stands a stone pillar firmly set in the ground [ἔνθα στήλη καταπεπηγυῖα] set up by Croesus which registers the boundary with an inscription [καταμηνύει διὰ γραμμάτων τοὺς οὔρους].[7]

The usual attention to this passage — the vanishing and re-appearing water-course of the Lycus — is of little interest here, even though it preoccupied European explorers for over two hundred years as they, in vain, used Herodotos's penchant for the fantastic as a compass to find the ancient site of Colossae.[8] Rather, several other points of interest need to be noted.

Firstly, the route to Sardis is not the only possible one — later roads were constructed from Apameia north-west to Peltae and Motella, following the upper Maeander through the Çal plateau and then striking onwards to Philadelphia at a junction north of Tripolis and thence to Sardis. However, many of these cities were non-existent at the time. The tried and refreshing road through the Lycus was much to be preferred both for its agreeable gradient and for the supplies of food, wood and water which every army required as supports to its movements and stations.[9]

Plate 3.1: The slight gradient of the lower Lycus plain encourages gentle meanders in the Lycus River as it moves through fertile agricultural land to the Maeander River. The course of the Lycus has changed through the centuries, in part because of flooding,[10] but it remains an elemental contributor to the region's prosperity.

7 Herodotos 7.30.

8 See chapter 1.

9 H. Elton, "Military Supply on the South Coast of Anatolia in the 3rd century AD," in *Patterns in the Economy of Roman Asia Minor*, edited by S. Mitchell and C. Katsari (Swansea: Classical Press of Wales, 2005), 289–304.

10 Georg Weber reported to John Anderson that the remains of a Roman bridge on the Lycus Valley plain no longer spanned any waterway: J. G. C. Anderson, "A Summer in Phrygia, II," *JHS* 18 (1898): 89–90.

Secondly, only three cities are named in the text, possibly one too few to cover an army march from Anaua (probably Sanaos) to the Maeander crossing somewhere near a city called Kydrara. These centers are placed in a hierarchy: Anaua and Kydrara both named as cities, Colossae as a "great city" defined not by the Lycus Valley but by reference to the entire region of Phrygia.[11] There is no necessity for armies to have an overnight station at a city, much as soldiers may have looked for urban distractions. Indeed, at this time (481 BCE), it seems that the bulk of Asian territory in the Achaemenid empire was divided into large estates, such as that controlled by Pythios. One inscription from the early third century BCE from Apollonia in Lydia (by the time of Augustus called Tripolis)[12] honors a certain Mardonios son of Aristomachos. Even though he had not been a citizen of the new city, he had proved a critical support in assisting a synoikism of four settlements to establish a civic foundation, with the support of the Seleucid regime.[13] A number of commentators underscore that the name Mardonios reflects a Persian descent, even though his father's name, Aristomachos, was Greek. This is attributed to a "political" decision by Aristomachos's own father (probably also named Mardonios given the frequency with which grandfathers' names are given to the third generation at this time).[14] The benefaction (εὐεργέτης) and apparent political clout of Mardonios suggests that he was a member of a family with considerable estate holdings (perhaps including lands at Hypaipa, near the Cayster River beneath Mt Aipos). It earned him and his descendants the award of citizenship in the new city and an honorific stele. Crucial here is that this is the territory through which Xerxes travelled in his journey to Sardis. Apollonia was non-existent as a city at the time (though human settlement in the area dates back to Late Neolithic or Early Chalcolithic times).[15] However, Mardonios' ancestors likely did own estates (or later were assigned them from previous owners who fell out of favour) that would have yielded the space and provisions (and possibly some extra troops) for the itinerant army. The frequency of highway usage through the Lycus Valley reinforces the suggestion that, even with few cities, the rich, fertile valley —"the fat fields and hills of Asia"

11 This perception was accented by Michael Choniates *Or.* 2.39. See Appendix 1.

12 For a brief history of Tripolis, see B. Duman, "Location, Importance and Short History of Tripolis," in *Tripolis Araştırmaları* edited by B. Duman (Istanbul: Ege, 2017), 17–22. The name "Tripolis" may reflect its origins as a proposed four-settlement confederation, with one settlement declining the amalgamation or forming an independent entity (Apollonos Hieron?).

13 The text is to be found in L. Robert, "Documents d'Asie Mineure XXIII–XXVIII," *BCH* 107 (1983): 500; see also L. Moretti, "Epigraphica 18: A proposito di Apollonia al Meandro," *Riv. Fil,* 107 (1979): 295–300.

14 Sekunda, "Changing Patterns," 66–7; P. Thonemann, "Hellenistic Inscriptions from Lydia," *EA* 36 (2003): 100–1.

15 E. Konakçi, "Prehistorik Tripolis: Akkaya (Yenice) ve Hamambükü Höyük," in *Tripolis Araştırmaları*, 23–46.

(Horace)[16] — had been divided among loyal supporters, satraps and "friends" (ξεῖνοι) of the Persian king.[17] These included, in 395 BCE, probably Ariaios and possibly Tithraustres,[18] who became critical conspirators in the assassination of Tissaphernes at a bath-house at Colossae. As a reward for executing the desire of the king (Artaxerxes II) and his ambitious, if ultimately unfortunate general, Tissaphernes, Ariaios and Tithraustes were granted satrapies in Caria and Lydia respectively.[19] Such assignment was a strategic dispensation, a privilege of power, used by subsequent regimes as well.

Thirdly, the city Kydrara is not known. The toponym, given the ending -*dra*, is probably Phrygian in origin and hence stemming from the ninth or eighth century.[20] Various equivalences have been sought in the territory — the sanctuary of Mên Karou (or Karura) at the edge of the Taurus mountain range near the Maeander; Hierapolis; Hydrela; and Tripolis itself. None have attracted wide support.[21] Whether or not Kydrara is to be connected with one of these cities or not, what is important to recognize is that cities were not sacrosanct in their names, their allocated territory or even their existence. That Colossae was known, exalted in the hierarchy of cities and a crucial station on an army's journey is significant. That its name withstood the changes that regularly attached to other cities in the Greco-Roman period in the Lycus Valley — Laodikeia from Rhoas and Diospolis (possibly),[22] Hierapolis from Hieropolis, Tripolis from Apollonia — is testament to its ancient foundation and proud heritage. Even when it sought, for similarly "political" reasons as choices governing the naming of an individual,[23] to re-orient the etymology of the name (from a Hittite foundation to a Greek *colossus*) and eventually to change it to Chonai,[24] the name was tenaciously remembered.

Fourthly, Herodotos confirms that territory at this time is known to have been demarcated, at least in regional terms. The attribution of the bound-

16 *pingues Asiae campi collesque*: Horace *Ep.* 1.3.5.

17 For this technical use of the term, see Herodotos 7.29 (of an award to Pythios). For hints of other Persian estate-owners, surviving in the onomastics of the Lycus Valley see *IG* II^2 9180; *SEG* 35.1395.

18 Sekunda, "Changing Patterns," 54–5.

19 See Diodorus Siculus 14.80.6–8; 16.22.1–2; Polyaenus *Strat.* 7.16.1. For an analysis of the narrative of the assassination, see A. H. Cadwallader, *Fragments of Colossae: Sifting through the traces* (Adelaide: ATF Press, 2015), 32–4.

20 O. Haas, *Die phrygischen Sprachdenkmäler* (Sofia: Académie bulgare des sciences, 1966), 21, 70.

21 See, for example, C. J. Hemer, *The Letters to the Seven Churches of Asia in their Local Setting* (JSNTs 11; Sheffield JSOT Press, 1986), 179–80, 272–3; J. Z. van Rookhuizen, *Herodotus and the Topography of Xerxes' Invasion: Place and Memory in Greece* (Berlin: de Gruyter, 2019), 49 n39.

22 Pliny *NH* 5.29.105. Pliny takes the names as successive toponyms. As argued below this may be a misreading of epithets sometimes applied to Laodikeia.

23 Compare the homonym "Jesus also called Justus" in Col 4:11.

24 See chapter 2.

ary stone to King Croesus of Lydia is not antiquarian erudition, but signals a highly-charged political moment to come.[25] Pythios, mentioned above, was Croesus's grandson. Croesus had engineered as part of the post-war settlement with the then Persian-king Cyrus, that the loss of his crown would not be accompanied by the loss of his own estates.[26] Pythios was the beneficiary, including, it seems, of estates around Kelainai.[27] Pythios's own later efforts to secure the exclusion of his son from Xerxes' Greek campaign, had a similar intent in mind as that of his grandfather but his strategy of lavish financial backing (purchasing power?) for Xerxes massively imploded — his eldest son was gruesomely dissected and paraded as a concourse for the army to march through to their anticipated confrontation with the Greeks. That army included Pythios' remaining four sons who had already been conscripted for service.[28] And, in spite of the intimation from Herodotos that Pythios managed to salvage his holdings, this is not a guaranteed deduction — there is some evidence that Xerxes confiscated his estates.[29] Croesus's inscription therefore served as Herodotos's reminder that kings felt little compunction to emulate their ancestors when either mood or advantage seized them. Alexander the Great's edict "I have decided that the land of the x, the Myrseloi and the P– will be my land"[30] is characteristic of regime behavior before, after and since, even if flowered with softer expressions. Taxation, just as characteristically, followed,[31] as the means by which the land worked (and previously owned) by others would yield its return to the new owner. Here is glimpsed one of the prime motivations of authorities for the delineation and assignment of land.

The use of stones to divide territory and imply ownership is ancient, attested in the Hebrew Scriptures (Deut 19:14, 27:17, Prov 22:28, 23:10 Hos 5:10) and earlier, as we find, for example, in Hittite law codes.[32] These references however go to individual property rights or allocations. Croesus's inscription demarcates a region or even a kingdom — that it still was standing probably indicates the former option, though identifying it as set up by Croesus allows for some

25 See E. Bagwanath, *Motivation and Narrative in Herodotus* (Oxford: Oxford University Press, 2008), 269–75.

26 Sekunda, "Changing Landscapes," 49.

27 On Croesus and his kingdom, see C. H. Greenewalt, "Croesus of Sardis and the Lydian Kingdom," in *Civilizations of the Ancient Near East* edited by J. M. Sasson *et al.* (New York: Scribner, 2 vols, 1995), 1173–83.

28 Herodotos 7.38–40.

29 See Sekunda, "Changing Landscapes," 55.

30 *I.Priene* 1, ll. 9–11 (as reconstructed). See P. Thonemann, "Alexander, Priene, and Naulochon," in *Epigraphical Approaches to the Post-Classical Polis — Fourth Century BC to Second Century AD* edited by P. Martzavou and N. Papazarkadas (Oxford: Oxford University Press, 2013), 33–36.

31 ll. 12–13.

32 H. A. Hoffner, *Laws of the Hittites: A Critical Edition* (Leiden: Brill, 1997), 135–6, nrs 168–9.

doubt. Treaties frequently defined boundaries between kingdom territories,[33] and these were then tiered down in divisions to small partitions, whether for agriculture or building. Almost all the larger boundary markings claim, if they were inscribed, some form of divine sanction.[34]

Here it seems clear that the inscription on the stone identified Croesus and the respective territories formed not by the stone itself but by the stone naming the natural defining feature — the Maeander River — as the boundary line between Lydia and Phrygia.[35] Lydian was probably the language used on the inscription, though it may have been bilingual or even trilingual,[36] given that Greek had begun to expand in usage under Croesus.[37] In any case, the Lydian language shares substantial letter forms with Greek and may have been readable to some.

The regional boundary marker in the context of the cities of Colossae and Kydrara identifies the Maeander as the western-most line of their territory. Given that Kydrara held a lower status, the question then becomes one of the extent of Colossae's territory. That is, did Colossae's territory stretch as far as the Maeander? Depending on where Kydrara is to be located (that is, north or south of the Lycus River as it enters the Maeander), Colossae might have controlled some territory as far west as the Maeander, additional to the administrative governance it probably held at some level of hierarchical oversight. Certainly the Byzantine metropolitan of Athens, Michael Choniates, in the twelfth century read Herodotos and Xenophon with pride as indicating that Colossae had no neighbor (οὐ γείτων) up to the Maeander River.[38] This was his birth-city. It must be remembered that the valley's heavy urbanization came later; local estates owned by those with some relationship to the king carried considerable responsibilities and autonomy.

---

33 See A. Matessi, "The Making of Hittite Imperial Landscapes: Territoriality and Balance of power in South-Central Anatolia during the Late Bronze Age," *JANEH* 3 (2016): 117–62.

34 See G. H. R. Horsley and R. A. Kearsley, "Another Boundary Stone between Tymbrianassos and Sagalassos in Pisidia," *ZPE* 121 (1998): 123–9.

35 The Maeander River became the formal boundary between Attalid and Rhodian territory under the Roman settlement in the Treaty of Apameia of 188 BCE: Polybius 21.46.8. Compare the Hybandos River as the boundary between Magnesia-on-Maeander and Miletus (*I.Milet* 1.3.148 (196/175 BCE).

36 Compare the bilingual and trilingual inscriptions from Xanthus: *TAM* I 44 (440–410 BCE) and *SEG* 27.942 (337 BCE).

37 M. Mellink, "Anatolia," in *The Cambridge Ancient History: IV, Persia, Greece and the Western Mediterranean c. 525–479 B. C.* edited by J. Boardman, *et al.* (Cambridge: Cambridge University Press, 1988), 213.

38 Michael Choniates *Or.* 2 (*Encom. Nic.*) 35.28–9 (ed. Lampros; see Appendix 1).

An early inscription from Colossae's territory

There is one surviving Greek inscription that pre-dates the foundation of the city of Laodikeia and offers some clues to movements in Colossae's territorial control.[39] Because of the arguments that follow, I give the inscription here in full:[40]

Βασιλευόντων Ἀντιόχου καὶ [Σ]-
ελεύκου πέμτου καὶ τεσαρακο-
στοῦ ἔτους, μηνὸς Περιτίου, ἐ-
π᾽Ἐλένου ἐπιμελητοῦ <τοῦ> τό[πο]υ· ἐκκλησί-
ας γενομένης ἔδοξε Νεοτειχείταις
καὶ Κι<δ>διοκωμίταις· ἐπειδὴ Βανά-
βηλος ὁ τὰ Ἀχαιοῦ οἰκονομῶν καὶ Λα-
χάρης Πάπου ἐγλογιστὴς τῶν
Ἀχαιοῦ εὐεργέται αὐτῶν γεγένηντ-
αι κατὰ πάντα καὶ κοινῆι καὶ ἰδίαι ἑκάσ-
του ἀντειλημμένοι εἰσὶν κατὰ τ[ὸ]-
μ πόλεμον τὸν Γαλατικὸν καὶ πολ-
λῶν αὐτῶν γενομένων αἰχ[μ]α-
λώτων ὑπὸ τῶν Γαλατῶν ἐμφα-
νίσαντες Ἀχαι[ω[ι] ἐ[λυτ]ρώ[σα]ντο,
ἐπαινέσαι τε αὐτοὺς καὶ ἀ<να>γράψαι
τὴν εὐεργεσίαν αὐτῶν εἰς στή-
λην λιθίνην καὶ στῆσαι ἐν τῶι
τοῦ Διὸς ἱ<ε>ρῶι ἐμ Βάβα κώμηι καὶ
ἐν τῶι τοῦ Ἀπόλωνος ἐν Κιδδίου
<κώμηι>, δεδόσθαι δὲ αὐτοῖς καὶ ἐγγόνοις
εἰς πάντα τὸν χρόνον προεδρίαν
ἐν ταῖς δημοτελέσιν ἑορταῖς,
θύειν δὲ καὶ Ἀχαιῶι κυρίωι τοῦ τό-
που καὶ σωτῆρι κατ᾽ ἐνιαυτὸν
ἐμ μὲν τῶι τοῦ Διὸς ἱερῶι βοῦν,
Λαχάρηι καὶ Βαναβήλωι εὐεργέται[ς]
κριοὺς δύο ἐν τῶι τοῦ Ἀπόλλωνος
ἱερῶι τῶι ἐγ Κιδδίου κώμηι, ἱερεῖα τρία·

---

39 *I.Laodikeia Lykos* 1 = *I.Mus. Denizli* 2 = *CGRN* 143.

40 Greek text from *I.Laodikeia Lykos* 1 (Corsten). to be preferred to that of Francesco Guizzi, "Iscrizioni ellenistiche," in *Museo Archeologico di Denizli-Hierapolis: Catalogo delle iscrizioni greche e latine* edited by T. Ritti [Naples: Liguori, 2008], 39–40 nr. 2. For a detailed analysis, see my "Village Life in the Lycus Valley," in *The Village in Antiquity and the Rise of Early Christianity* edited by A. H. Cadwallader *et al.* (London: T & T Clark, 2023), forthcoming.

ὅπως εἰδ[ῶ]σι καὶ οἱ ἄλλοι, ὅτι Νεοτ[ει]-
χεῖται καὶ Κι[δ]διοκωμῖται, ὑφ’ ὧ[ν]
ἄν τι πάθωσι ἀγαθ[ό]ν, ἐπίσταν-
ται τιμὰς ἀντιδιδόναι.

In the 45th year of kings Antiochos (I) and Seleukos, in the month Peritios, when Elenos was commander of the place; in the assembly, (5) it was decided by the Neoteichitai and the Kiddiokomitai: since Banabelos the administrator of the properties of Achaios and Lachares son of Papos the accountant of the affairs of Achaios have in everything been benefactors (10) and they both publicly and privately provided for each one during the Galatian war, and when many of their own had been captured by the Galatians, after informing (15) Achaios (of this) they managed to ransom them, (it is necessary) to praise them and to record their beneficence on a stone stele and to set it up in the sanctuary of Zeus in Babakome, and another (20) in the sanctuary of Apollo in Kiddioukome; and to give them and their descendants in perpetuity the right to a front seat in all public festivals; and to sacrifice each year for Achaios, master (25) of this place and savior, an ox in the sanctuary of Zeus, for the benefactors Lachares and Banabelos two rams in the sanctuary of Apollo in Kiddioukome, three sacrificial animals (in total); (30) so that others may also witness that the Neoteichitai and the Kiddioukomitai, when they experience some benefit, instituted that honors would be reciprocated.[41]

Three settlements are mentioned — Neon Teichos, Kiddioukome and Babakome. These all seem to be located within a larger estate, owned by a certain Achaios, a member of the elite with familial ties to the Seleucid dynasty. The settlements and the estate appear to be under the wider oversight of a certain Helenos who contributes part of the eponymous dating formula opening the inscription (ἐπ᾽ Ἑλένου ἐπιμελητοῦ τοῦ τόπου, "when Helenos was overseer of the place" ll. 3–4). Achaios, nonetheless, has direct control, being called "master of the place" (κύριος τοῦ τόπου, l. 24). On the basis of the dating schema, the inscription can be assigned to 267 BCE.

The two villages, Kiddioukome and Babakome, seem to have a significant history:

i) they have sanctuaries, respectively to Apollo and Zeus, whereas the garrison, Neon Teichos,[42] does not, even though representatives of Neon Teichos were involved in the assembly of Kiddioukome (ἡ ἐκκλησία) that voted for honors of sacrifices and priority seating for Achaios, his estate manager

41 Translation adapted from *CGRN* 143 (J-M. Carbon and S. Peels) and T. Corsten, "The Foundation of Laodikeia on the Lykos: An Example of Hellenistic City Foundations in Asia Minor," in *Regionalism in Hellenistic and Roman Asia Minor* edited by H. Elton and G. Reger (Bordeaux: Ausonius, 2005), 132.

42 One wonders where the παλαιὸν τεῖχος was located. "Old forts" are occasionally found in the sources (*I.Priene* 414, l. 5 [mid 4th century BCE]; Stephanus sv Γάγαι).

(ὁ οἰκονομῶν) Banabelos (a semitic name meaning "created by Bel," or "Bel creates")[43] and his accountant (ὁ ἐγλογιστής), Lachares. Kiddioukome, therefore, had its own decision-making body, and probably also Babakome;

ii) the village names may reflect an origin in a leading man, that is, Κιδδίου κώμη "the village of Kiddios" and Βάβα κώμη "the village of Babas"; in the latter case, the name might even be indigenous for a god that was integrated with Zeus under the new realities of religious observance brought by the Macedonians;[44]

iii) the villages have regular festivals where priority seating can be allocated — in this inscription, to the three honorands;[45]

iv) and the villages have the organizational infrastructure (ἐκκλησία, ll. 4–5; δημοτελής, l. 23) to decree, finance, and execute such honors in annual commemoration and record them on a stele.

Corsten finds such honors to "provincials" remarkable (such usually flowing to royalty, generals and deity),[46] but this may be little more than village imitation of elite practice that has survived with more evidence, much as towns in Australia have their small shrines of remembrance, imitating those in capital cities, listing the names of local "fallen heroes" from the country's military conflicts.

The hierarchy in relationships is indicated by Achaios receiving, in his honor, the sacrifice of a bull to Zeus and the epithet σωτήρ, "savior"; Banabelos and Lachares each were to be honored with the sacrifice of a ram to Apollo at Kiddioukome. There may be an elevated status given to the settlement Neon Teichos, given that it is, on both occasions of naming, placed before Kiddioukome. This is no more than a possibility. The "newness" of the settlement is probably related to the reason stated for the honors for the three men. They had been instrumental in fighting off the marauding Galatians from the territory (ὁ πόλεμος ὁ Γαλατικός, ll. 11–12), and in redeeming (λυτρόω, l. 15) some of their own who had been taken as prisoners of war by the Galatians. Given the Galatians' reputation for wealth accumulation[47] and the use of the term εὐεργετής in the honors, this is likely to have meant significant outlays of money or valuable goods. The garrison seems to have been

43 Cf. *SEG* 7.401 (Dura Europos, 23–40 CE).

44 This is built on a possible phonological similarity between Παπας, which is known as a collation with Zeus, and Βαβας. See T. Corsten, *Die Inschriften von Laodikeia am Lykos* [I.Laodikeia Lykos] (IGSK 49; Bonn: Habelt, 1997), 16–17; compare, however, J. Curbera, "Simple Names in Ionia," in *Personal Names in Ancient Anatolia* edited by R. Parker (Oxford: Oxford University Press, 2013), 118.

45 Priority seating at festivals was an ancient form of honor: see Plato *Leg.* 12.947a.

46 Corsten, *Laodikeia*, 15.

47 S. Mitchell, *Anatolia: Land, Men and Gods in Asia Minor* (Oxford: Clarendon Press, 2 vols, 1993), vol 1, 17.

hastily established as a direct result of the Celtic incursions, not as a separate colony.[48] Accordingly it was, initially, simply part of the estate(s) of Achaios.[49]

All commentators on the inscription acknowledge that it pre-dates the royal foundation of Laodikeia (c.255 BCE) but proceed to suggest the way in which the settlements mentioned became part of the new city.[50] The garrison is likely to have been on raised ground and probably became the city's nucleus with the villages drawn into its direct ambit of control or even embraced within the formal civic walls. This is a surmise. However, direct ties are drawn between the gods mentioned in the inscription and those of Laodikeia. Zeus, regardless of whatever indigenous coloring he received, was adopted by Laodikeia, to the point where many speak of Zeus Laodicensis (a misnomer in my opinion for Zeus Aetophoros).[51] Indeed, one fragment sometimes credited to the second century (CE) Greek historian Phlegon of Tralles relates the story of Antiochos II receiving an oracle from Zeus instructing the king to found Laodikeia with Hermes as the guide.[52] The prime operational god in the story is Hermes. The narratival epitome is one of more than a hundred foundation stories proliferating through Asia Minor designed somehow to authenticate and elevate the stature of cities, and provide an ideological cohesion and identity to the territories under their control. Apollo does rank in Laodikeia's pantheon but apparently not high enough to secure a place on

48 G. M. Cohen, *The Seleucid Colonies: Studies in Founding, Administration and Organization* (Vienna: Franz Steiner, 1978), 26–8.

49 F. Guizzi, "Iscrizioni ellenistiche," in *Museo Archeologico di Denizli-Hierapolis: Catalogo delle iscrizioni greche e latine* edited by T. Ritti (Naples: Liguori, 2008), 42.

50 Pierre Debord even suggests that an inscription from Stratonikeia (*I.Stratonikeia* 1402) that mentions Laodikeians might point to Laodikeia being at least at some early stage (under brief Rhodian hegemony from 188 BCE) reduced to a *koinon* (confederacy of settlements) rather than a polis. See "Questions stratonicéennes," in *Les cités d'Asie Mineure occidentale au IIe siècle a.C.* edited by A. Bresson and R. Descat (Bordeaux: Ausonius, 2001), 167–70. It is more likely that there was a substantial community of Laodikeians at Stratonikeia; see J. Labuff, *Polis Expansion and Elite Power in Hellenistic Karia* (Lanham, MD: Lexington, 2016), 136–7.

51 So W. E. Metcalfe, *The Cistophori of Hadrian* (New York: American Numismatic Society, 1980), 70. It should be noted that some cities and regions did claim a civic epithet for Zeus; see, for example, Zeus Keleneus from Apameia-Kelainai: *SNG Copen* 198. No such creditation is found at Laodikeia.

52 Stephanus *Ethn.* 11.37. A German translation is given by Margarethe Billerbeck *Stephani Byzantii Ethnica: K-O* (Berlin: de Gruyter, 2006), 199. The oracle itself is translated in Parker, *Greek Gods Abroad*, 217. The sixth century citation by the lexicographer Stephanus was credited (potentially) to Phlegon by August Meineke, *Stephan von Byzanz. Ethnika* (Berlin: Reimer, 1849), 411, an assignment adopted by Peter Fraser, *Greek Ethnic Terminology* (Oxford: Oxford University Press, 2009), 356 citing *FGrH* 257 F41 but there is no certainty of attribution, unlike the dating of the tradition to early in the Common Era. See A. H. Cadwallader, "The Lust for Recognition and Influence: Laodikeia and the Quest for Neokorate Status," in *Revelation, the Aegean and Material Culture: Festschrift in Honor of Steven J. Friesen* edited by A. Keddie, D. Smith and N. Leach (London: Routledge, 2023), forthcoming.

its coinage.[53] The name does occur for one of the formal groupings (*phylai*) of citizens.[54] Pliny the Elder is often cited for his reference to earlier names for Laodikeia, that is Diospolis and then Rhoas.[55] The first, city of Zeus, is patent enough; Rhoas, if it is to be associated with the poppy, might indicate characteristic local flora.[56] William Ramsay however, already conscious of the problems these prior city names generated for comprehending the chronological development of the city, suggested that Pliny might be adding little more than epithets that were applied to the name Laodikeia — the city of Zeus, the place of poppies.[57] Zeus is ubiquitous on Laodikeia's imperial coinage but poppies also feature.[58]

Forgotten in the analyses is that when Laodikeia did not exist, Colossae *did*. Ramsay recognized this, though he could not know this inscription. It raises the question of the relationship of Achaios' estate(s) and the named villages to Colossae. Christopher Tuplin considered that Colossae was not a garrison-city because it was, in his view, the capital of the satrapy immediately west of Kelainai.[59] This would explain the formation of Neon Teichos, especially after the Galatian incursions, but it too would have fallen under Colossae's general oversight for a time.

There is little question that Colossae's foremost gods of this time were Zeus and Apollo, albeit the evidence comes from civic coins of the second century BCE (Pl. 3.2).

53 There is however one coin-type from the Attalid period featuring on the reverse a tripod with the city ethnic: *SNG von Aulock* 3805. The obverse nonetheless retains Queen Laodike/Aphrodite.

54 *I.Laodikeia Lykos* 84, l. 8 (1st to 2nd century), 108, ll. 5–7 (2nd to 3rd century). There was such a designated *phylê* at Hierapolis also, though there it received the added eminence of being called the πρώτη φυλή; see F. Kolb, "Zur Geschichte der Stadt Hierapolis in Phrygien: Die Phyleninschriften im Theater," *ZPE* 15 (1975): 261–4.

55 *NH* 5.29.105.

56 Alternately Pliny may have excised the name from Hierapolis' main river, the Chrysorhoas, though this, I think, is remote.

57 W. M. Ramsay, *The Cities and Bishoprics of Phrygia* (Oxford: Clarendon Press, 2 vols, 1895, 1897), vol 1, 35. Ramsay speculates that Rhoas may have been a village. Poppies are one of the more ubiquitous plants in the Denizli region today and have been found on some ornamental relief decoration from the ancient city; see O. Düşen, *et al.*, "Laodikeia Antik Kenti'nin Floristik Yapısı," in *10. Yalındı Laodikeia (2003-2013 Yılları)* edited by C. Şimşek (Istanbul: Ege, 2014), 370, 383.

58 *RPC* 3.2337; *RPC online* 4.2.2088 temp., 4.2.2138 temp. — all held by Tyche along with her cornucopia.

59 C. Tuplin, "Xenophon and the Garrisons of the Achaemenid Empire," *Archäologische Mitteilungen aus Iran* 20 (1987): 183, 236.

Plate 3.2a and b: Two of the three known coin types of Colossae from Attalid times. The larger coin (18 mm, 6.80 g) features the laureate head of Zeus, facing right, on the obverse, and a winged thunderbolt on the reverse, flanked by the city ethnic ΚΟΛΟΣ | ΣΗΝΩΝ. The second coin (13 mm, 3.74 g) features the radiate head of Apollo, facing right, with, on the reverse, a four-stringed kithara, flanked by the city ethnic (here partially lost because both faces have been struck off-center).[60]

Corsten had relied on second and third century (CE) coins of Laodikeia (especially homonoia coins) to provide confirmation of Laodikeia's patron deity.[61] However, it is far from obvious that Laodikeia's Attalid-period coins privilege Zeus (and certainly not Apollo).[62] Laodikeia was one of six cities given the privilege of minting cistophoric coins for the Attalid kingdom,[63] but none that the city struck carries an indication of Zeus or Apollo. Rather they accent the wolf (symbol of the Lycus River) and the caduceus of Hermes (perhaps an early strand of the legend mentioned previously).

Plate 3.3: A cistophorus coin (25 mm, 12.06 g) minted at Laodikeia, that features on the obverse the ubiquitous snake-emerging-from-a-basket and on the reverse, the minting city (in abbreviated form: ΛΑΟ), the coin benefactor (Apollonios son of Euarchos), snakes, bow-case, grain ears and, hugging the right perimeter, the caduceus of Hermes.[64]

60 For a discussion of this Attalid coin from Colossae, see A. H. Cadwallader, "On the Question of Comparative Method in Historical Research: Colossae and Chonai in Larger Frame," in *The First Urban Churches 5: Colossae, Hierapolis, and Laodicea* edited by J. R. Harrison and L. L. Welborn (Atlanta, GA: SBL, 2019), 109–13. This photograph from a private collection by permission.

61 Corsten, *Laodikeia*, 16. Compare T. Ritti, *Storia e Istituzioni di Hierapolis* (Istanbul: Ege, 2017), 277.

62 I am primarily reliant here on Barclay Head's *A Catalogue of the Greek Coins in the British Museum: Catalogue of the Greek Coins of Phrygia* (London: British Museum, 1906) supplemented by more recent but limited online and individual catalogues.

63 The cities were Pergamon, Sardis, Ephesos, Tralles, Apameia and Laodikeia. See P. Thonemann, *The Hellenistic World: Using Coins as Sources* (Cambridge: Cambridge University Press, 2015), 77–80; compare C. Michels, "Unlike any Other: The Attalid Kingdom after Apameia," in *Rome and the Seleukid East* edited by A. Coşkun and D. Engels (Brussels: Latomus, 2019), 338–42.

64 See G. R. Stumpf, *Numismatische Studien zur Chronologie der römischen Statthalter in Kleinasien (122 v. Chr. – 163 n. Chr.)* (Saarbrücken: Saarbrücken Druckerei und Verlag, 1991), 52 nrs 85–7. This photograph from a private collection by permission.

Laodikeia's bronzes from this period rarely include Zeus, and then, only his head.[65] The dominant iconography is Queen Laodike (after whom the city was named), who was frequently portrayed as Aphrodite (Pl. 3.4).[66]

Plate 3.4: An Attalid-period bronze (17 mm, 5.11 g) from Laodikeia, featuring, on the obverse, the head of Queen Laodike facing right and, on the reverse, a cornucopia bound with a trailing fillet, and a caduceus, flanked by the city ethnic ΛΑΟΔΙ | ΚΕΩΝ.[67]

This dominant style at Laodikeia does not appear to have been supplanted by the Attalid partiality for Zeus, Apollo and Herakles (all mimicked in the coins of Colossae at that time), nor by the Attalid imitation of coinage of the Achaean League (which, understandably, proliferated Zeus iconography).[68] Only in the second half of the first century BCE, does Zeus begin to predominate on Laodikeia's coinage, almost certainly a reflection of the city's rising position in the Roman political schema for the province. By contrast, Hierapolis coins display Apollo as a predominant iconographic feature from the beginning of the mint's operation in the second century BCE.[69]

Colossae's role in the Galatian War (278–276 BCE) can only be hypothesized, but her military force must have been required and perhaps, like the city of Kyzikos, received royal support for the φυλακὴ τῆς χώρας, the "defence of the region".[70] This stele of Kiddioukome imitates the honors given to the nobility elsewhere. Indeed the two specified gods and festivals are precisely those widely acclaimed for salvation from the Galatian menace.[71] It may well be that local

65 *BMC Phryg* Laodikeia 24, 48–9; there is no standing Zeus holding an eagle in this period.

66 This seeming deification of the (estranged) wife of Antiochos II would be unusual, but the encouragement for cultic honoring was made by Antiochos III in 193 BCE for his own sister-wife, also called Laodike (*OGIS* 224). This may have assisted the tenacity of this obverse iconography into Attalid times.

67 *BMC Phryg* Laodikeia 40, cf 22–3, 25–39, 41–7. This photograph from a private collection by permission.

68 See P. Thonemann, "The Attalid State, 188–133 BC," in *Attalid Asia Minor: Money, International Relations, and the State* edited by P. Thonemann (Oxford: Oxford University Press, 2013), 33–4.

69 See *BMC Phryg* Laodikeia 1–7; A. Travaglini and V. G. Camilleri, *Hierapolis di Frigia: Le Monete, Campagne di Scavo 1957–2004* (Istanbul: Ege, 2010), 72 nrs 201, 202.

70 *OGIS* 748, ll. 6, 13 (probably 276–275 BCE).

71 See R. Strootman, "Kings against Celts: Deliverance from Barbarians as a Theme in Hellenistic Royal Propaganda," in *The Manipulative Mode: Political Propaganda in Antiquity: A Collection of Case Studies* edited by K. A. E. Enenkel and I. L. Pfeijffer (Leiden: Brill, 2005), 110. R. E. Allen argues that "traditions developed on the theme of resistance to the Galatians": *The Attalid Kingdom: A Constitutional History* (Oxford: Oxford University Press, 1983), 140.

mimesis had a template to follow close by at Colossae. Corsten considers that the eponymous dating mentioning Helenos in addition to naming Antiochos I (in his 45th year) and Seleukos (his son), gave a local reference.[72] It might be possible that Helenos was commander of the Neon Teichos garrison, but the lack of a religious center in the fortification, the garrison's joining the assembly of the Kiddioukomitai and Helenos's description as ἐπιμελητής τοῦ τόπου suggests otherwise. Neon Teichos was *within* the area falling under Achaios as κύριος τοῦ τόπου. τόπος is an encompassing reference but Achaios' "place" was certainly smaller than the region over which Helenos exercised "satrapic" supervision. An inversion of position, that is, with Helenos as overseer of the region commanding a place falling under Achaios "lordship", is extremely unlikely. It seems reasonable therefore to conclude that Helenos was based at Colossae.[73]

The foundation of Laodikeia and the reduction of Colossae's territory

Colossae's territorial hold was substantially reduced when Laodikeia was founded about twelve years later in c.255 BCE by the Seleucid king Antiochus II. It is likely that the three settlements and probably the estate(s) of Achaios named in this inscription were excised from Colossae's general authority. This probably meant the end for the city of any territory to the west of the new foundation. However, the means of demarcating territory probably did not change. That is, mountain ranges, rivers and other permanent topographical features contributed to the mapping out of territorial holdings and responsibilities.[74] This inevitably meant a certain deference to past decisions about boundaries — antiquity held considerable sway in these matters, interrupted as it may have been by invasions (such as that of the Galatians in 278–6 BCE, possibly the Galatians again in 168 BCE and Mithridates in 89 BCE).[75] New settlements doubtless required mediation of

72 Corsten, *Laodikeia*, 13.

73 Curiously, none of the names from this inscription are included in *LGPN V.C*, viz. Ἀχαιός, Βανάβηλος,Ἕλενος, Λαχάρης, Πάπας, as well as Κιδδιος/ας and Βαβας (epichoric names) if the villages are named by reference to earlier key men. All the names are attested elsewhere except for Βανάβηλος.

74 See *CIL* 3.586 where a resolution of a boundary dispute between Lamia and Hypata in Macedonia during the time of Hadrian, makes the decision by reference to a spring, a river, and cultivated land, as well as human constructions such as a shrine, tomb and monument, all named. See B. Campbell, *The Writings of the Roman Land Surveyors* (London: Society for the Promotion of Roman Studies, 2000), 468–71.

75 For a general overview of these military encroachments on territory in the Lycus Valley, see A. N. Sherwin-White, "Roman Involvement in Anatolia, 167–88 B. C.," *JRS* 67 (1977): 62–75; Mitchell, *Anatolia* 1.13–19, 21–26; C. Marek, *In the Land of a Thousand Gods: A His-*

claims and counter-claims by an overarching authority. Colossae was compelled to negotiate a succession of governments, Seleucid, Attalid and Roman, within a two hundred year period. The city's borders were subject to the decisions of these authorities, all of which had their own interests to impose.

For all the Roman posturing about honoring past boundaries, it was frequently their tampering with both tradition and geography that impacted on the boundaries of cities. The carving up of the province of Asia into a series of assize districts (*conventus*)[76] saw the Lycus Valley collated under the Kibyran district, that is, with a Carian metropolis on the southern side of the Taurus mountain range. For a brief period in the 50s BCE, the entire Kibyran *conventus* was shifted into the province of Cilicia. The massive Taurus range that fences the Lycus Valley on its the southern boundary acted as a natural territorial division between the region of Caria and Phrygia. The Kibyran conventus initially compelled those in the valley to negotiate the steep pass from Laodikeia between Mount Cadmos (Honazdağ) and Mount Salbake (Babadağ) through Themisonion and on to Kibyra for commercial and juridical interests and delegations to the provincial governor. When the metropolis was moved to Laodikeia, the situation was reversed.

There is some evidence for Colossae's contact with the south: a woman named Aphias is specifically remembered as a Colossian, even though she married, lived and died near Boubon, a town to the south of the Taurus.[77] However, prestige and convenience saw the assize metropolis shift to Laodikeia, now firmly back in the province of Asia, relatively soon after the initial cartography was drawn. Colossae, as part of that *conventus,* necessarily had to take account of Laodikeia's rank in the Roman administrative network.

The formal boundaries of *poleis* territories are however generally opaque to us, with only occasional indications of connections providing clues. One such clue comes in a recently published inscription from the time of Hadrian; a newly recovered Colossian coin from the time of Elagabalus provides some extra precision.

---

tory of Asia Minor in the Ancient World (Princeton, NJ: Princeton University Press, 2016), 265–89.

76 The date of this administrative imposition is debated; the choice is between the foundation of the province in 129 BCE or the 90s BCE or even as a consequence of Sulla's restoration of order after the conclusion of the Mithridatic War in 84 BCE. See C. Habicht, "New Evidence on the Province of Asia," *JRS* 65 (1975): 68.

77 *I.Boubon* 102:῾Ερμᾶς Ἀφιάδι | τῇ ἰδίᾳ γυναικὶ | τῇ Τρυφίωνος | θυγατρί | γένει | Κολοσσηνῇ | μνήμης ἕνεκα "Hermas (set up this epitaph) for his own wife Aphias, the daughter of Tryphion, by birth a Kolossian, for the sake of her memory." The round funerary stele was first seen by the Rev'd Edward T. Daniell on the Spratt-Forbes expedition in May 1842 and published in the expedition record: T. A. B. Spratt and E. Forbes, *Travels in Lycia, Milyas and the Cibyratis in Company with the late Rev. E. T. Daniell* (London: John van Voorst, 2 vols, 1847), vol 2, 289 (=*CIG* 3.4380k[3]). Daniell's copy read Ἀρφιάδι for the woman's name and Τρυφώνος for the father's. Thomas Corsten saw and photographed the inscription in 1997 (see chapter 9). *LGPN V.C* has duplicated the stone, adopting both *CIG* 4380k[3] and *I.Boubon* 102; only the latter should be retained.

A dispute over fishing rights

It seems that in the Greco-Roman period the Lycus River flowed into a small lake between Laodikeia and Hierapolis before continuing its course west to the Maeander.[78] The expanse of water may well have been an incentive for the foundation of Laodikeia. By the beginning of the second century CE, the lake was sponsoring a significant fishing industry and, probably, a harbor for punts and small barges for the transport of goods (textiles, for example) to cities along the Maeander and onwards to the Mediterranean coast for export.[79]

The industry was productive enough to attract commercial operations from three cities, Laodikeia, Hierapolis and Tripolis, but disputes over fishing and access rights erupted. Phrygia had become renowned (or slandered) for disputes over territory.[80] But this aggravation became so severely entrenched that one or all city authorities referred the matter to the Roman emperor Hadrian for decision.[81] The only record of his judgement (dated 130 or 131 CE) comes from Hierapolis,[82] but it is clear that rescripts were sent to all three cities.

78 Swamps and small bodies of water were frequently commented upon by European travellers in the eighteenth and nineteenth centuries; so, for example, J. Hartley, *Researches in Greece and the Levant* (London: Seeley, 1833), 253; J. G. C. Anderson, "Summer in Phrygia: I," *JHS* 17 (1897): 413. The geologist Alfred Philipson even included a small lake between Laodikea and Hierapolis in his early twentieth century map: "Geologische Karte des westlichen Kleinasien Blatt 4," in his *Reisen und Forschungen im westlichen Kleinasien IV: Das östliche Lydien und südwestliche Phrygien* (Gotha: Perthes, 1914). Modern archaeological investigation, using thermal remote sensing has confirmed a sub-surface humidity area consistent with an ancient lake; see G. Scardozzi, "Remote sensing and archaeological survey in the Hierapolis of Phrygia territory, Turkey," in *Remote Sensing for Environmental Monitoring, GIS Applications, and Geology VII*, edited by M. Ehlers and U. Michel (SPIE Proceedings 6749; Washington: SPIE, 2007), 674904-1-12.

79 A Laodicean merchant is attested as far west as Gaul: J. Rougé, "Un negotiator Laudecenarius à Lyon," *ZPE* 27 (1977): 263–9.

80 *Corpus Agrimensorum Romanorum* (Hyginus 2), T. 169.3. The Phrygians received a number of such denigrations in Roman literature — their propensity to being slaves, their propensity to being bad slaves, their embellished if not lurid mode of music, their "softness" fostered by the climate — all having a deleterious impact on Roman hardness (Sallust *Cat.* 11.5–6; Livy 39.6). None of these have any objective worth, even if sometimes taken as disinterested assessments by modern commentators. James Dunn asserts without any circumspection about a consensual adoption of Roman attitudes (Cicero *Quint. Frat.* 1.1.16), "We know that Phrygian slaves were notoriously unsatisfactory." J. D. G. Dunn, *The Epistles to the Colossians and to Philemon* (NIGTC; Grand Rapids, MN: 1996), 302.

81 There is a hint in the rescript that other conflicts had occurred as well; the incomplete lines 14–15 read …]τα ἄλλα παύσασθαί ποτε ἤδη καὶ ὑμ[ᾶς] | [καὶ τοὺς Ἱ]εραπολείτας διαφερομένους which I read as enjoining that the parties "cease whatever other disputes, both you and the Hierapolitans have been quarreling about" [that is, with the Laodikeians].

82 The *editio princeps* is found in T. Ritti, *Hierapolis di Frigia IX: Storia e istituzioni di Hierapolis* (Istanbul: Ege, 2017), 388–95.

I have given a critical reconstruction, detailed analysis and interpretation of the inscription elsewhere.[83] Here the interest lies in the means by which Hadrian negotiated a settlement. The rescript identifies the disputed territory as the lake "lying in the farmland" and states that "the lake both historically and also across three successive assessments, has been credited as yours [ie the Laodikeians-on-Lycus]."[84] Here antiquity is garnered as the principle for the decision: anciently and through three assessments (or censuses), control of the entire lake had been Laodikeia's and presumably the plain in which it occured, *on both sides of the water*. Laodikeia's early coins, even before Roman control in 129 BCE, feature the wolf as a symbol of the Lycus,[85] and its citizens were frequently pinpointed as Laodikeian ἀπὸ Λύκου.[86] The most famous early indication that Laodikeia was defined by the Lycus river is a bilingual inscription that Hadrian probably would have known, since it labeled a statue of the "People of Rome", set up on the Capitoline Hill in Rome. The date is disputed. Some argue that the inscription was erected by the Laodikeians when Asia became an official senatorial province in 129 BCE and then renewed following the end of the Mithridatic War, in 83 BCE, when Laodikeia's stocks were tarnished for relinquishing the Roman general Quintus Oppius shortly after the city was besieged by Mithridates.[87] Certainly it does appear to have been renewed early in the imperial period — a clear signal of Laodikeia's determination to retain, if not advance Roman support. The Latin opens with *Populus Laodicensis a f(lumine) Lyco* "The Laodikeian people from the river Lycus …"; the Greek reads "ὁ δῆμος ὁ Λαοδικέων τῶν πρὸς τῶι Λύκωι, "The Laodikeian people, those near the Lycus … "[88]

83 A. H. Cadwallader, "The Battle over Lake Lycus: Inter-city Conflict in the Lycus Valley," in *New Doc. Early Christ 12* forthcoming.

84 ἡ ἐν χώρᾳ κ]έκλιται (as my reconstruction option for l. 11) and ἡ λίμνη καὶ τῶι χρόνωι | [καὶ ἐπι το]ῖς τρισὶν ἑξῆς ἀποτειμήσεσιν ὑμετέρα (ll. 9–10).

85 *BMC Phryg* Laodikeia 1–2, 2–32 (to be interpreted as a wolf not a lion). See U. Huttner, "Wolf und Eber: die Flüsse von Laodikeia in Phrygien," in *Internationales Kolloquium zur kaiserseitlichen Münzprägung Kleinasiens* edited by J. Nollé, B. Overbeck and P. Weiss (Nomismata 1; Milan: Ennerre, 1997), 93–108 and 109, nrs 3, 4, 14.

86 See *IG* XII 4,2.454 of a competitor from Laodikeia in the Asclepian games held at Kos, perhaps 173 BCE; see also Diogenes Laertius 9.12.116 (Timon).

87 See F. Santangelo, *Sulla, the Elites and the Empire: A Study of Roman Policies in Italy and the Greek East* (Leiden/Boston: Brill, 2007), 53.

88 *CIL* 1^2 728 = *IGUR* 1.6 = *CIG* 5881. The inscription has received extensive commentary; see A. H. Cadwallader, "The Historical Sweep of the Life of Kolossai," in *Epigraphical Evidence Illustrating Paul's Letter to the Colossians* edited by J. Verheyden, M Öhler and T. Corsten (WUNT 411; Tübingen: Mohr Siebeck, 2018), 50–1 and the bibliography there cited.

Plate 3.5: Chrysorhoas is the only river-god found on coins of Hierapolis. This civic bronze features Sarapis, facing right. His beard signals age, wisdom and experience; the modius, a container for grain, on his head communicates fecundity. The reverse provides the name of the river in the exergue beneath a rivergod who reclines on a water-urn and holds poppies in his right hand and ears of wheat draped across his left arm.[89]

By contrast, the Lycus never features on the coins of Hierapolis. Laodikeia's geographical identity marker had become its title of ownership. Hierapolis's extolled river is the Chrysorhoas (see Pl. 3.5), although one Hierapolitan citizen in Rome identified himself by reference to the Maeander,[90] perhaps an indication of a western boundary of the city territory. The Chrysorhoas never fed into the Lycus. It barely extended a mile onto the plain, falling short of the Lycus by at least two miles.[91]

The evidence that we have supports the claim in Hadrian's rescript that recourse to archival material provided the means of adjudication.[92] He was not averse to material that dated from Attalid and Seleucid times.[93] As it turned out, Hierapolis and Tripolis were granted access to the fishing product but not to the fishing grounds. It seems clear that the Lycus was *not* the boundary between Laodikeia and Hierapolis. Rather some line was drawn further north of the river — perhaps applied at the point of disappearance of the Chrysorhoas. Little wonder that Hierapolis sought to extend its territorial holding further up

---

89 *RPC online* 4.2.2972 temp. (dated to second century CE). This coin's value is thought to be two assaria. It weighs 6.62 g, with a diameter of 21 mm. Photograph by courtesy of Leu Numismatik.

90 Μένανδρος Ἱεραπολείτης πρὸς Μέανδρον ποταμόν: *IG* XIV 1848 = *IGUR* 2.784 (nd).

91 Erhan Altunel and Francesco D'Andria, "Pamukkale Travertines: A Natural and Cultural Monument in the World Heritage List," in *Landscapes and Landforms of Turkey*, edited by C. Kuzucuoğlu, A. Çiner, and N. Kazankı (Switzerland: Springer, 2019), 224–5. Significantly, at the end of the nineteenth century, John Anderson, confirming an anecdotal account of William Ramsay, observed that the Chrysorhoas disappeared into a "hole in the ground" a short distance south of the travertine cliffs: "Summer in Phrygia: I," 413. The story of St Michael of Chonai mentions a river Chryses (*S. Mich. Chon.* 9.13 [see infra for the edition]). The loose pinpointing of the river as flowing from the west and remaining "at the right" (north?) of the sacred spring of St Michael, divided in two, suggests that in earlier times the river flowed further east along the base of the northern plateau without ever breaching the Lycus.

92 See the reliance on "earlier times" ([ἤδη ἐπὶ τῶν προτέρ]ων χρόνων) in a series of instructions about the Epicurean School at Athens; S. Follet, "Lettres d'Hadrien aux Épicuriens d'Athènes," *REG* 107 (1994): 162, l. 8 (= *SEG* 43.24).

93 See G. Burton, "The Resolution of Territorial Disputes in the Provinces of the Roman Empire," *Chiron* 30 (2000): 195–215.

Plate 3.6: The ancient city of Hierapolis featuring the baths (now museum) down the line of Frontinus Street (right of center), in a north-westerly direction towards Tripolis. To the left are the famous white travertine cliffs, falling into the northern edge of the Lycus Valley.

the plateau to the north, probably as far as the sanctuary of Apollo Lairbenos as its many coins featuring Lairbenos suggest.[94]

This of course leaves open the question of Laodikeia's eastern border, given that Colossae clearly was tied to the Lycus River further upstream from Laodikeia (and, it seems on both sides, like Laodikeia). To this we turn.

The twin rivers on the coins of two cities

In his catalogue of the British Museum coins for Phrygia, Barclay Head used a Laodikeian coin to map some of the boundaries of that *polis*'s territory. The coin shown here (Pl. 3.7) carries two animals, the wolf and the wild boar, a visual "canting" symbol. The symbols are for Laodikeia's two main rivers, the Lycus and the Kapros, claimed as the boundaries of Laodikeia's geographical polity.[95]

94 *RPC online* 4.2.9993 temp. 8.ID20729–32, ID20756 temp.
95 Head, *Phrygia*, 287 n1.

Plate 3.7: A small bronze (14 mm; 2.75 g) generally dated to the final half-century of the Roman republic, shows a wild boar (κάπρος) on the obverse. Beneath it is the monogram of the minting benefactor EKT.[96] The reverse has a wolf (λύκος) flanked above and below by the city ethnic ΛΑΟΔΙ | ΚΕΩΝ.

This pairing of the wolf and the wild boar made regular appearances on Laodikeia's coins for three centuries.[97]

Plate 3.8: A coin of Laodikeia probably to be dated to 217 CE from the † ΠΗ in the exergue of the reverse (indicated by arrow).[98] On the obverse is the emperor Caracalla. The reverse has the two river gods, the Lykos and the Kapros, portrayed through their symbols, without legend (17 mm, 10.30 g).[99]

---

96 The monogram appears on a number of different coin-types from Laodikeia but the official has yet to be identified — perhaps Ἑκαταῖος or Ἑκατᾶς or similar theonym. Photograph from a private collection, by permission.

97 *RPC online* 4.2.2101 temp., 8.ID20771, 20777, 20778, 71427 temp. Rarely, the boar appears alone: *BMCPhryg* 296 nr. 111. See generally, F. Imhoof-Blumer, "Fluss- und Meergötter auf griechischen und römischen Münzen (Personifikationen der Gewässer)," *RN* 23 (1924): 324–7 nrs 376–85.

98 The year occurs frequently at this period on the Laodikeian coins featuring Julia Domna (widow of Septimus Severus) and occasionally those with Caracalla. The allocation to 216/217 CE is argued by W. Leschhorn, *Antike Ären. Zeitrechnung, Politik, und Geschichte im Schwarzmeerraum und in Kleinasien nördlich des Tauros* (Stuttgart: Steiner, 1993), 382–5 and followed by Thonemann, *Maeander Valley*, 214 (contra Head, *BMC Phrygia*, lxxx). However, Thonemann's suggestion that this is a Caracallan invention, throwing back to Hadrian's Olympian visit in 129 CE, is to be modulated in light of the recent publication of an honorific inscription (and statue) for Hadrian where Laodikeia is described as *neokoros* and Hadrian bears the title Olympios. See F. Guizzi, "Greek and Latin Inscriptions of Laodikeia on the Lykos 2003–2018," in *15. Yılında Laodikeia*, 175. It should be noted that there is no mention of a senatorial award of *neokoros* status. It would appear that Laodikeia had a somewhat "checkered career" when it came to its neokorate status, only finally sealed by the Senate (the proper authorizing body) in the reign of Elagabalus (so A. Johnston, "Caracalla or Elagabalus? A Case of Unnecessarily Mistaken Identity," *ANS* 27 (1982): 115). However, Laodikeia retained the memory of Hadrian's award by recalibrating its calendar according to his visit in 129 CE. It should be noted that Laodikeia never claimed a "Twice Neokoros" status, unlike other leading cities. See chapter 11.

99 *SNG Copen* 591, *KM* 273 nr. 48. Photograph courtesy of Zeus Numismatics.

Two coin types, one from the time of Antoninus Pius (Pl. 3.9), one from that of Marcus Aurelius, feature on the reverse, a seated, poliadic Tyche holding a statue of Zeus Aetophoros in her right hand and a long scepter in her left. Below her curia recline two facing river-gods who are named in a field legend as the Lycus and the Kapros respectively.

Plate 3.9: Laodikeian coin featuring, on the obverse, the head (and identifying legend) of Antoninus Pius and, on the reverse, the iconic rivers of Laodikeia, the Lycus and the Kapros, identified by the legend above them in the field of the coin (35 mm, 17.88 g).[100]

Head was probably influenced by William Ramsay when imagining the Kapros. Ramsay had identified a small river flowing into the Lycus near the modern Turkish town of Sarayköy, fifteen miles to the west of Laodikeia, as the Kapros.[101] He named the Kapros and the Lycus as the boundaries of Laodikeia's territory. The influence can be traced through to recent descriptions. Celal Şimşek even extended Ramsay's territory border of Laodikeia to an imagined eastern boundary, which he held was Colossae, adding that "Overall, the Lykos plain was mainly within the territory of Laodikeia."[102] Ramsay himself in corrections to his own work, had submitted to the description of the rivers *around* Laodikeia given by Pliny the Elder, naming them as the Asopos and the Kapros,[103] and confessing that his familiarity with the topography of the Lycus Valley was inferior to his knowledge of other districts.[104]

Ramsay's authority was conclusively overturned by John Anderson in 1897 and Georg Weber in 1898.[105] The Kapros was confirmed as flowing past the *eastern* edge of Laodikeia, relatively close to the settlement. However, of the two options raised for the Kapros — a small stream close to the Syrian gate (the Gökpınar) or a small river a mile or so further east towards Colossae (the Başlıcay) — it seems clear that the latter is the most likely. This is

100 Photograph courtesy of *Biblioteque nationale de France*, public domain.

101 Ramsay, *Cities and Bishoprics*, 1.34 with map.

102 C. Şimşek, "Urban Planning of Laodikeia on the Lykos in the Light of New Evidence," in *Landscape and History in the Lykos Valley: Laodikeia and Hierapolis in Phrygia* edited by C. Şimşek and F. D'Andria (Cambridge: Cambridge Scholars Publishing, 2016), 2.

103 Pliny *NH* 5.29.105.

104 Ramsay, *Cities and Bishoprics*, 2.785–6.

105 Anderson, "Summer in Phrygia I," 404–7; G. Weber, "Die Flüsse von Laodicea: Lykos, Kadmos, Kapros, Eleinos und Asopos," *MDAI(A)* 23 (1898): 178–95; see also Huttner, "Wolf und Eber," 94–5.

now the accepted assignment by Celal Şimşek, the director of the Laodikeian excavations.[106]

The rescript addressing the fishing dispute confirmed that Laodikeia's territory extended across the Lycus,[107] probably to some surveyed boundary just south of where the Chrysorhoas ceased its flow, dispersed into irrigation channels and, if Anderson be correct, disappearing underground.[108] Hence the question arises as to whether the Kapros also is the natural boundary or is within an as-yet-unknown boundary of Laodikeia drawn further east (as Şimşek asserted).

The issue becomes heightened by a recently published coin of the Colossian mint that has two river-gods in its iconography, named as the Lycus and the Kapros.[109] The coin type is the second minted of a series of twin deities from the time of Elagabalus.[110] But this one has a particular potency for Colossae's assertions of its identity "on the ground". By the addition of a second river (the Kapros), the Lycus is transformed from a river known by its direct association with, indeed incorporation into, the city precincts, to one claimed as a territorial marker. Both ties to the city, that is, as a natural feature defining the city and as a landmark marking that city's geographical governance, ensure that topographical place is converted into controlled space; but the second delivers a far more expansive territory.[111]

---

106 See C. Şimşek, *Laodikeia (Laodikeia ad Lycum)* (Istanbul: Ege, 2007), 54.

107 Guizzi Scardozzi, in his important work on the hinterland of Hierapolis, hesitates, thinking that the Lycus River formed the boundary between Hierapolis and Laodikeia (and Trapezopolis): *The Territory of Hierapolis in Phrygia* (Istanbul: Ege, 2020), 24. This underestimates the rationale for Hadrian's decision, the clearer if my reconstruction ([κ]έκλιται, l. 11) yielding "of the lake lying in the farmland" is accepted; see my "Battle over Lake Lycus", *supra*. The milestone marking the first mile on the road from Hierapolis to Laodikeia (Scardozzi, *Territory of Hierapolis*, 120, fig. 86) from the time of Gordian III, may therefore have a horological as well as hodological significance.

108 Anderson, "Summer in Phrygia I," 413.

109 Curiously Joachim Silwa refers to the Lykos and Kapros appearing on coins of "the Phrygian cities of Kolossai and Laodicea"; *Egyptian Scarabs and Magical Gems from the Collection of Constantine Schmidt-Ciazynski* (Cracow: Jagiellonian University Press, 1989), 27 n4. Whether he had seen this or another Colossian coin-type prior to its recent publication or was offering a generalized sweep of the occurrence of two rivers in iconography, I do not know.

110 See chapter 4.

111 See V. Sauer, "Urban Space: The Evidence of Coins," in *Space, Place and Identity in Northern Anatolia* edited by T. Bekker-Nielsen (Stuttgart: Franz Steiner, 2014), 111–4.

Plate 3.10: A Colossian civic minting from the time of Elagabalus, repeated here for convenience. The large coin (37 mm, 22.66 g av.) features, on the obverse, the laureate, cuirassed (with paludamentum) bust of Elagabalus facing right. On the reverse, a seated, poliadic Tyche holds a statuette of Artemis Ephesiaca in her right hand and a cornucopia in her left. Below the central figure recline two river-gods; at the left, though with worn lettering, is identified the Lycus river; at the right is identified the Kapros, holding a cornucopia in his right hand. Both waters contain fish.[112]

The elaborate design imitates the coins of Laodikeia that celebrate the same two rivers (see Pls. 3.7–9 above). Ulrich Huttner's detailed study of the wolf and wild-boar coins of Laodikeia held, firstly, that "The meaning of these coin images is always the same: the polis and the rivers comprise a unit; the rivers are part of it."[113] Secondly, the cornucopia held by the Kapros river-god somehow privileged that water-course with its benefits for agricultural production to the south and east of the city proper as well as for its aqueduct supply.[114] Thirdly, from a heavily worn coin (time of Caracalla), Huttner built an elaborate foundation story of Laodikeia with its main rivers, the Lycus and the Kapros, as the birthplace and nursing support for the infant Zeus.[115]

One can immediately see how the Colossian coin problematizes this reading. At the very least, using Huttner's approach, it asserts that Colossae's western boundary is the Kapros. That is, the Kapros has become a *shared* natural territorial division. Presumably then, Colossae held the rights to the Lycus river east of where the Kapros joined it. The statuette of Artemis Ephesiaca in Tyche's right hand may strongly imply that Colossae, holding the source of the Lycus in her territory, has a particular affinity with (and supply to) the leading city of the province (even though the Maeander entered the Mediterranean at Priene). The recently published proconsular water regulations at Laodikeia does not name Colossae, but it does underscore arrangements for the security of the water-supply for Laodikeia and for its countryside (ὑδάτων τηρήσει τῶν γὲ ἐπὶ τῆς πόλεως καὶ τῶν ἐπὶ τῆς χώρας l. 24).[116] The inscription, dated about

112 The coin is listed in *RPC online* 6.10900 temp. with two examples. Photograph courtesy of Leu Numismatik.

113 *Der Sinngehalt dieser Münzbilder ist immer der gleiche: Polis und Flüsse bilden ein Einheit, die Flüsse gehören dazu*; Huttner, "Wolf und Eber," 100.

114 Huttner, "Wolf und Eber," 101.

115 Huttner, "Wolf und Eber," 101–2; coin reference: *SNG Copen* nr. 589; see further F. Imhoof-Blumer, "Antike Münzbilder," *JDAI* 3 (1888): 290 nr. 2.

116 F. Guizzi, "An Edict of a Proconsul of Asia on the Aqueduct of Laodikeia (114/115 CE?)," in *15. Yalındı Laodikeia (2003–2018)* edited by C. Şimşek (Istanbul: Ege, 2019), 149.

114 CE, charges that it is unjust that those who have access to the water before it reaches Laodikeia diminish its common and necessary use (l. 8) —hence the heavy fines, strict regulations and policing that the inscription details. While a number of the instances imply individual theft of water or damage to the water infrastructure, one wonders whether the proconsular rescript applied to those with estates on the *eastern* side of the Kapros, that is, in Colossae's territory. Francesco Guizzi, the editor of the inscription, considers it likely "that the imperial intervention was a response to the need of using water from springs *belonging to other cities*."[117] Here was a ready-made aggravation to the already sensitive if not troubled relations between Colossae and Laodikeia.[118]

Plate 3.11: A postcard of Laodicea affixed into the travel diary of the Reverend William John Beamont,[119] showing remarkably intact sections of (two?) aqueduct lines, with one straddling a small river (the Kapros?). The more distant aqueduct is presented as climbing into the mountains. Beamont, from Warrington near Liverpool in England, made his "Seven Churches Tour" in 1855.

It may be that the symbolic association of the boar with the Kapros is found in another recently surfaced coin. In chapter 5 we explore the importance of the cult of Dionysos at Colossae. Another recently recovered coin featuring Silenus on one side and a boar

117 Guizzi, "Edict on the Aqueduct," 154 (my emphasis).
118 See chaper 4.
119 Beamont 1855 Diary, Warrington Library, Ms 706 f.2a. There may well be some artistic license in the portrayal but large stretches of the aqueduct also appear in Alexandre de Laborde's 1838 sketch of Laodikeia: *Voyage de l'Asie Mineure* (Paris: Firmin Didot, 1838), 86, pl. 39.

on the other confirms that assessment (Pl. 3.12). Silenus was the nurse for the infant Dionysos according to myth.

Plate 3.12: The small coin (14–15 mm; 2.29 g average) was part of the currency range minted by Tiberius Claudius Sakerdos in the time of the emperor Antoninus Pius, now, with this coin, including a quarter or third assarion value. The obverse has the head of the satyr Silenus with the city ethnic ΚΟΛΟCC | ΗΝΩΝ. The reverse shows a wild boar with the legend CΑΚΕΡΔΩC.[120]

It is difficult to judge whether the boar is meant to indicate the Kapros or not. Silenus is found on the coins of several cities, often paired with other symbols of the Dionysiac cult, such as the panther, grapes or dancing satyr.[121] Others repeat the main accents of his care for the infant Dionysos,[122] or his drunkenness.[123] On other coins, the connections are more difficult to fathom, such as that between Silenus and the ploughing of a field for example.[124] The city of Silandos (possibly intending a verbal pun on its own city name: Σιληνώδης — like Silenus) seems to have been quite fond of representing Silenus on its coins — one combining the head crowned with an ivy wreath on the obverse with his famous drunken riding of a donkey on the reverse.[125]

The question therefore is whether the wild boar is a familiar association with Silenus's Phrygian country wanderings. There is little in the textual evidence to warrant that connection. Boars frequently appear in coin iconography, often alone,[126] sometimes in a hunting scene (including two coin types from Colossae),[127] sometimes capturing the fourth labor of Herakles.[128] But any direct connection seems to be confined to a rare numismatic inclusion of a gryllos — a combination of heads, in this case Silenus, a boar and Pan/a goat.[129] A similar form also occurs on gems.[130] One fine bronze figurine, provenanced to Central Europe, features Silenus riding a wild boar rather than a donkey (Pl. 3.13).

---

120 *RPC online* 4.2.11890 temp. Photograph from a private collection by permission.

121 See *RPC online* 4.2.2405 temp. (Teos), 4.2.8491 temp. (Silandos), 4.2.1746 temp. (Hyrkanis).

122 *RPC* 3.2407, 2408, *RPC online* 3.2408A (Sardis); *RPC online* 4.2.1589 temp. (Tmolus), 4.2.1324 temp. (Maionia).

123 *RPC* 3.190, 203 (Corinth); *RPC online* 4.1.9311 temp. (Bizya).

124 *RPC* 1.11 (Emerita).

125 *RPC online* 4.2.1508 temp.

126 *RPC* 1.2063 (Nikomedia); *RPC online* 1.4443A (Laodikeia ad Mare)

127 *RPC online* 4.1.4826 (Prusa ad Olympum); *RPC* 9.789, *MSPhryg* 2.586, 587 (Colossae).

128 *RPC online* 4.1.11777 temp. (Nicaea); 4.4.15597 (Alexandria).

129 *Historia Numorum* Italy 343.

130 See for example, M. H. Story-Maskelyne, *The Marlborough Gems: Being a Collection of Works in Cameo and Intaglio ...* (London: 1870), 110 nr. 666, 111 nr. 684. For the artistic phenomena of hybridization, see K. Lapatin, "Grylloi," in *Gems of Heaven: Recent Research on Engraved Gemstones in Late Antiquity, c. AD 200–600* edited by C. Entwistle and N. Adams (London: British Museum, 2011), 88–98.

Plate 3.13: The satyr Silenus, clasping a bunch of grapes in his left hand, while precariously balanced on a wild boar.[131]

None of these really satisfy the search for understanding the relationship between the obverse and reverse of the small Colossian coin. We are left wondering whether the boar on the coin is an emblem of the hunt, a representation of a companion of Silenus in a now-lost tale, a symbol of the river Kapros, or some other association.

It may be difficult to imagine that the western boundary of Colossae's territory extended to the Kapros River. However, this may be little more than the socialization of scholarship into accepting that Colossae was so heavily overshadowed by Laodikeia that she lost any ability (and territory) to exert influence or retain civic pride. The Elagabalus coin counters this, and the apparent imitation of Laodikeia's coins of the two rivers (Pl. 3.9) suggests there was either a reinforcement of the anciently-drawn boundaries executed at the foundation of Laodikeia or even a challenge being mounted by Colossae. My suspicion is the former, probably agitated into action by the characteristic privileging of Laodikeia that we see in the proconsular water edict. Significantly, the later popular story of St Michael the archangel has little doubt that the Kapros is tied in some measure to the territory of Colossae/Chonai. It blends the Lycus and Kapros into one name, speaking of the "Lycokapros" as beginning its course in the mountain, "near that holy place', that is, the sacred spring and sanctuary under the patronage of Michael.[132] There can be little doubt that the Kapros is known here as a tributary of the Lycus and that it was seen as a part of Colossae's territory. Consequently, whilst re-affirming the poverty of evidence for territorial demarcation, the witness we do have points to the Kapros as the likely western boundary of the city of Colossae.

131 Photograph courtesy of Barakat Gallery Museum, Beverly Hills, California.

132 *S. Mich. Chon.* 10.7. The Greek edition of the popular story is found in M. Bonnet, *Narratio de Miraculo a Michaele Archangelo Chonis Patrato* (Paris: Hachette, 1890) and is cited here by page and line number. A new edition is in preparation.

Exploring Colossae's territory

These detailed inquiries into the boundaries between some of the cities of the Lycus Valley have brought a modicum of clarity. But what has become obvious is that walls of cities (or what remains of them) ought not to be equated with the boundaries of the city's jurisdiction. The very existence of "boundary-riders" (ὁροφύλακες) in ancient Hellenistic cities (though not attested at Colossae as yet) is a strong indication that cities understood themselves in terms of territory under their control, not merely their cityscape.[133] If the provisional conclusion from analysis of the Elagabalus coin from Colossae is accepted, it means that some inscriptions assigned to Laodikeia whose provenance is either dubious or which have been found east of the Kapros,[134] may need to be re-allocated. Also emerging is the recognition that territorial boundaries were critical for the determination of the application of various taxes and, sometimes more importantly, the reach of a city's legal jurisdiction. Juridical reach is determined by territory and (delegated) power to operate. Often forgotten in the debates over Onesimos, for example, is that Roman law was most unlikely to have any application in Colossae's territory over matters that had little concern to the Roman *imperium*. The debates over whether Onesimos was a slave runaway or a slave vagrant simply evaporate once Onesimos stepped outside Colossae's territorial boundaries; from that moment he is a fugitive, unless he holds specific (usually written) authorization.[135]

The proconsular water regulation edict that has been briefly mentioned, points to how important were areas outside city walls for the continued functioning of cities. The edict mentions "royal estates and other holdings

133 The office seems to be subject to the oversight of a *paraphylax* at Apollonia Salbake (Robert, *Carie* 162) which strongly suggests "border guard". However, in some cases, such surveillance seems to have encompassed mountainous terrain, hence ὀροφύλαξ with a different aspiration of the *omicron*. Such officials seem to have been involved in the pursuit of runaway slaves within their territorial parameters as well as the collection of pasturing and customs dues. See A. Chaniotis, "The Impact of War on the Economy of Hellenistic Poleis: demand creation, short-term influences, long-term impacts," in *The Economies of Hellenistic Societies, Third to First Centuries BC* edited by Z. Archibald, J. K. Davies and V. Gabrielsen (Oxford: Oxford University Press, 2011), 140. The Roman empire changed the taxation regime in the office but the functions seem to have continued in some reduced form. See *I.Sultan Dağı* 230 (Hadrianopolis, last 2nd to early 3rd century CE, an epitaph for a ὁροφύλαξ who paid for his pursuit of bandits [λῃσταῖ, l. 6] with his life). His jurisdiction however may have been confined to an estate; cf *IGR* 4.897 (Pisidia, 255 CE).

134 See, for example, H. Malay, "New Inscriptions from Phrygia (in the Denizli Museum," *AD* 2 (1994): 173–83.

135 See A. H. Cadwallader, "Complicating Class in the Letter to Philemon: a prolegomenon," in *The Struggle over Class: Socioeconomic Analysis of Ancient Jewish and Christian Texts* edited by G. A. Keddie, M. Flexsenhar and S. J. Friesen (Atlanta, GA: SBL, 2020), 95–122. See also chapter 11.

above (the city)" (κατὰ τὰς βασιλικὰς δωρεᾶς καὶ τῶν λοιπῶν τῶν ἄνωθεν, l. 3),[136] and also "private landed holdings" (τὰ ἴδια χωρία, l. 27). There is a recognition that irrigation is practiced (μετοχετεύσῃ ἀρδείας, ll. 9–10), though if this interrupts or diminishes the flow to the city, large fines were to be slapped on offenders (5000 denarii for water diversion or damage to the infrastructure, l.10, payable to the imperial *fiscus*). Irrigation was apparently part of agricultural practice on the higher slopes of the valley as well as on the plain.[137] There is reference also to houses, groves, baths and suburban pastures (ἤτοι ἐν οἰκίας, ἢ κήποις ἢ βαλανείοις ἢ προαστίοις, l. 13).[138] These are all presumably closer to the city than the previously mentioned group but still sufficiently distant to be inconvenienced from gaining water allocations supplied by the city infrastructure — which is specified in line 24 as servicing both city and countryside (ὑδάτων ... τῶν γὲ ἐπὶ τῆς πόλεως καὶ τῶν ἐπὶ τῆς χώρας). This breakdown of the areas of territory is, in the main, devolved by loose geographical anchorage to the city itself: royal estates, "upland" holdings, private estates, suburban houses, parks, baths, and pastures — all generically grouped as "countryside", χώρα, which both services the city and, in turn, is serviced by the city (in the main). The countryside in general is, of course, crucial to the primary source of the valley's famous production of textiles — sheep (though flax was also grown to service this industry). Shepherds in the ancient world were notoriously "unbounded", that is, they were not hemmed by divisions of landed holdings; this sometimes spawned fractious debates with those whose agriculture was dependent on the observance of borders — such as viticulturalists — and required the decision of the local city council and the execution of that decision by

---

136 My translation varies from that given by Guizzi, who takes ἄνωθεν as a temporal indicator (cf *I.Ephesos* 26, l. 2, 180 or 192 CE). I interpret it as a spatial reference ("Edict on the Aqueduct," 149); compare *IGBulg* 3,1.947, *IG* II^2 1343, l. 11 (Attica, 37/6 BCE) *I.Crete* 1. 19, l. 12 (Malla, 2nd century BCE), *I.Stratonikeia* 7, l. 5 (Panamara, 300 or 166 BCE). The inscription lacks an additional extrapolation of ancient times but does refer to inspections that expressly include a "going up" (ἀνιοῦσαι) to carry out duties (l. 23). Second Testament commentators will be thoroughly aware of this dichotomy of interpretation of the word ἄνωθεν from Jn 3:3, 7.

137 Justinian's Law Digest contains the interesting aside that "It is a fact that the Hierapolitans in Asia irrigate their fields with warm water" (*constat enim apud hierapolitanos in asia agrum aqua calida rigari. Dig.* 43.20.1.13 Ulpian); compare also Vitruvius 8.3.14.

138 I am hesitant about the translation of κῆπος here; it is frequently equated with garden (Latin: *hortus*) but can expand to mean vineyard, perhaps even orchard: see Thonemann, *Maeander Valley*, 193. The Persian inheritance, especially with its accent on recreating the beauty of Babylon in its parks, is likely to have still held some significant cultural capital: hence "groves." The second century (CE) re-inscription in Greek of the Letter of Darius I to his satrap Gadatas (*I. Magnesia* 115) shows the value that one city, Magnesia-on-Maeander, put on its Achaemenid inheritance in this regard.

the city's *paraphylakes*.[139] There is no reason to think that the territory held by the *polis*-state of Colossae was any different.

Moreover the edict also indicates that cities ensured that they had the formal mechanisms to enforce the flow of critical resources into their markets — everything from the bureaucracy of management and property administration to the effective policing of desired (city) objectives. The water regulation mentions a *curator aquarum* (ἐπιμελητὴς τῶν ὑδάτων, l. 4) and numerous other officials (including three public slaves, τρεῖς δημοσίους, l. 23) to ensure compliance. In effect, the city had priority use (l. 8) and it had the surveillance and the muscle to enforce it. The elaborate patrolling of the countryside (at least as it concerns the water-supply) is very much a city matter reinforced by fines payable to the imperial treasury office in Laodikeia.

At Colossae, we know of similar arrangements, if less elaborately drawn. In the inscription honoring the brother(?) of Heliodoros,[140] to which we shall return,[141] a number of the sixteen positions held by the honorand at various times includes considerable demonstration of the city's control of the countryside within its borders. He is "a warden of the interior" (παραφυλάξας, l. 5), "an overseer of the city's estates" (ἐπιμεληθεὶς χωρίων δημοσίων, l. 7),[142] and, it seems, also of the grain supply, implying control of agriculture and the storage of grain (ll. 8–9),[143] all these in addition to the offices that saw his leadership connected with institutions functioning in the city.

We know that the first position, "warden of the interior" was a powerful one, granting him oversight of all the villages and holdings within the city's reach. To date these villages remain unknown (but see below), though two settlements, Graos Gala ("Crone's Curd") and Charax were known in middle-to-late Byzantine times.[144] At Hierapolis, for example, a specific decree was passed by the city *Boulê* to prevent a *paraphylax* from exacting work from the residents of villages (presumably for his own ends).[145] The second position, "overseer

139 *MAMA* 4.297 (from a village near Apollo Lairbenos) and the same Hierapolitan decree from another area (near Thiounta) in *I.Mus. Denizli* 15 (mid-3rd century CE). I had earlier accepted the preference of Buckler-Calder-Guthrie for a proconsular edict, even though they had allowed it might be a local Hierapolitan decree. See the correcting discussion in Thonemann, *Maeander Valley*, 193–5. For the prevalence of *paraphylakes* in the valley and plateaus, see Scardozzi, *Territory of Hierapolis*, 26, fig. 9.

140 *IGR* 4.870 = *I.Laodicée Lycos nymphée*, 277–8.

141 See chapter 5.

142 The same office is known at Laodikeia (*CIG* 3945).

143 The word σεῖτος is used in the inscription (in simplex and compound form) but it tended to be a generic term for grain produce, whether wheat or barley (or the misleading term, "corn").

144 Nicetas Choniates *Chron.* 195. See chapter 8. Ramsay, in an early article, added the names Panasios, Lakerios, Karia (not the region), and Tantalos as somehow connected with Kolossai. He relied on his own expansive reading of Nicetas Choniates for these additions (*Chron.* 195, 494). See W. M. Ramsay, "Antiquities of Southern Phrygia and the Borderlands (I)," *AJA* 3 (1887): 346.

145 *OGIS* 527.

of the city's estates" demonstrates that the city institutions were considerably endowed and provided significant income for city projects and the payment of officials. Presumably, these estates were worked by appointed managers (οἰκονομοί), such as the man named Banabelos of four centuries earlier on the large estate(s) owned by Achaios mentioned previously, and squads of public slaves. The third position mentioned here "manager of the grain allocation" points to one small part of the administrative governance a city organized to ensure that civic demands were met.

A view from the village

Archaeological testimony to the existence of villages is extremely thin, though more evident in inland Asia Minor.[146] The sheer materiality of human settlement, animal husbandry and plant cultivation can be transient. Literary testimonia rarely offer more than an occasional reference usually associated with steps from one city to another, as in the Acts of the Apostles. Where cities were lacking, the importance of larger villages (the *komopoleis*) as stations for the military increased, leading to toponymic notice, as in the so-called *Parthian Stations* by the Augustan geographer, Isidore of Charax.[147]

However, the sacrality of death sometimes bequeaths evidence for the historian to probe, both in the tombs that survive, simple as they may be, and in the epitaphs that even villagers desired as a grasp after immortality (of mem-

146 Note especially the *Xenoi Tekmoreioi* inscriptions near Pisidian Antioch: W. M. Ramsay, *Studies in the History and Art of the Eastern Provinces of the Roman Empire* (Aberdeen: University of Aberdeen Press, 1906), 316–77. In the sixteenth century, Honaz is reported in Ottoman records as being the administrative hub for at least 30 villages: M. A. Ünal, "Yüzyılda Honaz Kazâsı," in *Uluslararası Denizli ve Çevresi Tarih ve Kültür Semposyumu Bildiriler* (*International Symposium on the History and Culture of Denizli and its Surroundings*) edited by A. Özçelik *et al.* (Denizli: Pamukkale University, 2 vols, 2007), vol 1, 104–10. Of course, this cannot be transferred uncritically to the first and second centuries, but it is a powerful indication of the dominance of village settlements in the region, many of which are only known from taxation records. The research combining archaeological field surveys with epigraphical studies of Frank Kolb, Martin Zimmerman, Christof Schuler and Rinse Willet that speak of *ländlicher Unterzentren*/secondary agglomerations are critical for a new appreciation of village settlements in Asia Minor. See the bibliography; see also A. H. Cadwallader, "Methodological Issues in the Study of Ancient Villages," in *The Village in Antiquity and the Rise of Early Christianity* edited by A. H. Cadwallader *et al.* (London: T & T Clark, 2023), forthcoming. The recent work of Guiseppe Scardozzi has begun to apply their techniques to the hinterland of Hierapolis; see his *The Territory of Hierapolis in Phrygia* (Istanbul: Ege, 2020).

147 On Isidore's surviving work and its insight into types of settlements, see A. H. Cadwallader, "Sometimes one word makes a world of difference: rethinking the origins of Mark's Gospel," in *The Impact of Jesus of Nazareth: Historical, Theological and Pastoral Perspectives* edited by J. R. Harrison and P. Bolt (Sydney: SCD Press, 2020), 247–51. The Charax here refers to the harbor town on the Persian gulf, not the small settlement within Colossae's territory of a later time.

ory at least) and a warning to others of the sacredness of the final resting place. Occasionally, as in the case of Babakome and Kiddioukome we find something more. Sometimes city interests are piqued by village and estate issues and, as a consequence, we learn of the existence of villages, their religious life, social organization and concerns. Finally, one of the more ubiquitous features of non-urban life in Asia Minor is the presence of "rural sanctuaries," the most famous in literature being that of Mên Karou,[148] and, in archaeological and epigraphical remains, that of Apollo Lairbenos.[149] Rinse Willet lists 320 named "secondary agglomerations" in the imperial Roman province of Asia compared to 226 "self-governing cities".[150] The number of "secondary agglomerations" is vastly more given that anepigraphical evidence (such as tombs, quarries, housing, farms, ceramic intensity) is abundant, including in the Lycus Valley.[151] Where intensive surveys have been conducted, such as in the Kaystros Valley and the hinterlands of Pergamon and Kyaneai, evidence of settlements in fertile territory indicates that villages were frequently of no greater distance apart than about 3 hours' walk — an essential density for agricultural husbandry and markets.[152] Larger villages sometimes acted as surrogate centres for commercial purposes (*komopoleis*), surrogate in the sense that the controlling hub for villages were cities, even if substantial initiative in local matters remained with village leaders. This strongly implies that Colossae, as other cities in and around the Lycus, were surrounded by many more villages than have left epigraphic record. The proliferation of sherds and occasional carved stone fragments in the field west of the Çinaraltı Restaurant, barely 2 kilometers from the Colossae höyük, and the number of small artificial mounds rising from the plain are an impressionistic reflection of the more detailed analyses previously mentioned — an invitation for future archaeological study.

One inscription from a village called Eleinokapria was attributed to the territory of Colossae by a number of early scholars, from the time it was discovered by Francis Arundell.[153] Ramsay had seen in the name of the village a toponym formed from the names of two rivers, the Eleinos and the Kapros.

148 Strabo 12.8.20; some coins of Attouda feature Mên without legend (*RPC online* 4.2.598, 861 temp.), a general depiction found from a number of mints, but also some with a legend MHN KAPOY (*SNG Munich, Caria* nr. 185; and some with Mên and a garlanded altar (*BMC Caria* 65 nrs 16, 17; 68 nrs 39, 40).

149 See A. H. Cadwallader, "Bodily Display and Epigraphical Confession at the Sanctuary of Apollo Lairbenos: an examination of emotional responses," *JES* 1 (2018): 183–201.

150 R. Willet, *The Geography of Urbanism in Roman Asia Minor* (Sheffield: Equinox, 2020), 317–43.

151 See generally, T. Ismaelli and G. Scardozzi (eds), *Ancient Quarries and Building Sites in Asia Minor: Research on Hierapolisin Phrygia and other cities in south-western Anatolia: archaeology, archaeometry, conservation* (Bari: Edipuglia, 2016); Scardozzi, *Territory of Hierapolis, passim.*

152 Willet, *Geography of Urbanism*, 115–34.

153 F. V. J. Arundel, *A Visit to the Seven Churches of Asia Minor with an excursion into Pisidia* (London: John Rodwell, 1828), 157 nr. 26 = *CIG* 3954 "at Bonjalee near Denizli" = Ramsay, "Southern Phrygia," [infra] 394 = Ramsay, *Phrygia* 1.77 nr. 11 = *MAMA* 6.19 = *I.Laodikeia*

But because he had assessed Colossae as terminal and because he had located both the Kapros and Eleinos rivers near Sarayköy far to the west of Laodikeia, he assigned the village, its chora-territory and the epitaph to that city. He explained the find of the stone at the village of Böçeli as yet another example of *pierres errantes*, archaeological stone artifacts (especially inscriptions) that are transported elsewhere for re-use or decoration or both.[154] He may have been corrected on the location of the rivers, but the re-allocation of the inscribed stone to Laodikeia has not been adjusted. It is another example of scholarly exacerbation of Colossae's decline at the hands of Laodikeia pre-empting a decision about provenance.

The efforts of John Anderson and Georg Weber to pin down the various rivers were supported towards the end of the nineteenth century by the meticulous survey of the British Company responsible for the extension of the Ottoman Railway through to Dinar.[155] Anderson relied on one of the company maps to illustrate the position he had reached,[156] which was substantially endorsed by Weber.[157]

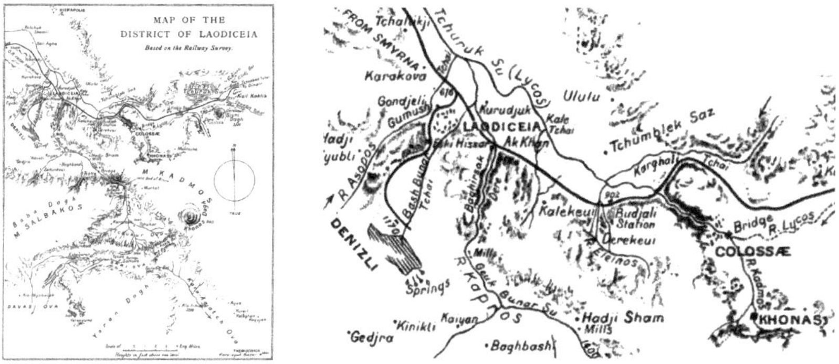

Plate 3.14: The Ottoman Railway Map of 1897, showing the main rivers of the territories of Laodikeia and Colossae (enlarged inset); from the left: the Asopos River, running along the western line of the city of Laodikeia past the village-railway station of Goncalı (Gonjeli), the Kapros River coursing from the mountain range between Babadağ (Mount Salbakos) and Honazdağ (Mount Kadmos), the Eleinos River running past the village-railway station of Böçeli (Budjali) and the Kadmos River flowing to the east of the Colossae höyük. All four rivers flow into the Lycus River.

Lykos 114. The last catalogue provides the necessary data and apparatus for the inscription, plus a valuable commentary. A squeeze of the stone is held at the British Institute, Ankara (Denizli 09 = DM 933).

154 Ramsay, "Antiquities of Southern Phrygia," 345. He proved to be prophetic however. I consider the find at Böçeli to be closest to its original location; from there it went to the front of a mosque at Denizli, and thence to the Denizli Museum depot.

155 See Cadwallader, "Gertrude Bell's Resolution," 1–3.

156 Anderson, "Summer in Phrygia I," 424, pl. XII.

157 Weber, "Die Flüsse von Laodikeia," 192.

Given the emphasis that scholars have placed on the Lycus-Kapros coins of Laodikeia to help plot the territory of the city, a consistent weight ought similarly to be applied to the coin of Colossae featuring the same two rivers. This pulls the Eleinos "River" (the brook, Dere-Köy) into the territory of Colossae, at least in the early third century CE and probably to be applied retrospectively. The description of the river given by Anderson and Weber accented that it flowed from the southern highlands above the Ak-han (a caravanserai completed in 1245, using stones "quarried" from surrounding sites, especially Colossae). It is precisely at this point that the tumultuous flow of the Lycus settles into a more sedate journey into the meanders of the Lycus plain, there being a substantial fall in elevation and leveling of gradient in the landscape. Therefore, the village and its territory must be located in the land bounded by these rivers, not, as Corsten suggests, north-east of Laodikeia.[158]

Not noticed by commentators is that the Greek name, *Eleinos*, is almost identical to the name of the Seleucid commander of the region (*Helenos*) briefly but importantly provided in the inscription (*I.Laodikeia Lykos* 1) that mentions the third-century (BCE) villages of Babakome and Kiddioukome.[159] It is a familiar itacistic phenomenon in Asian inscriptions for the vowel –ι– to become a formal diphthong or the reverse (which can be seen in line 10 of the inscription following — τῷ πατρεί).[160] Given the date of that inscription (267 BCE), that is, less than a century after the defeat of the Persians and the break-up of Alexander's brief empire, it would not surprise to find a satrapic local governor authorizing his own toponymic memorial — after all that was precisely what Antiochus II did in the naming of Laodikeia a decade or so later.[161] So, toponomy, topography and numismatics combine to make a strong argument for considering the epitaph as part of Colossian territory. Regardless of whether this argument is accepted, it makes an important contribution to the relationship between villages and cities in the Lycus Valley. Accordingly, it is worth providing the inscription in full.[162]

158 Corsten, *Laodikeia*, 197. The site is described as "near Bucalı" by Thomas Drew-Bear's entry in the *Barrington Atlas of the Greek and Roman World: Map by Map Directory Volume II* edited by R. J. A. Talbert (Princeton: Princeton University Press, 2000), 999.

159 *I.Laodikeia Lykos* 1, l. 4.

160 See G. H. R. Horsley, *The Greek and Latin Inscriptions in the Burdur Archaeological Museum* (RECAM V; London: British Institute at Ankara, 2007), 303–4.

161 See J. B. Campbell, *Rivers and the Power of Ancient Rome* (Chapel Hill: University of North Carolina Press, 2012), 67–9.

162 I have minimized the epigraphical construction marks found in *I.Laodikeia Lykos* 114 and allowed Tatarin in l. 6 to be read as an epichoric name (hence, no accent and not as Τατάριον), following *LGPN V.C* sv. (and, as an alternative, by W. H. Buckler and W. M. Calder, *Monumenta Asiae Minoris Antiqua Vol. VI: Monuments and Documents from Phrygia and Caria* (Manchester: Manchester University Press, 1939), 157. Ramsay, who was concerned to provide an accurate transcription of the stone, had found no lacuna or doubtful letters. Buckler and Calder however (*MAMA* 6.19) seem to have had more trouble than Corsten in reading

Plate 3.15: The bomos-shaped epitaph of Tatia and Moscha from the village of Eleino-kapria, likely within the territory of Colossae. It is housed in the Denizli Museum. Thomas Corsten assigns it to the "imperial period"; the size of the fine for infraction of the tomb, by comparison with other epitaphs, suggests second to third century, probably late second to early third given the letter shapes.

Τοῦτο τὸ θέ-	This platform
μα καὶ ⟨ὁ⟩ ἐπ' αὐτῷ βωμός	and the *bomos* on it
ἐστιν Τατιας καὶ τοῦ ἀν-	belong to Tatia and
4 δρὸς αὐτῆς Μοσχᾶ, ἐν ᾧ	her husband Moschas, in which
κεκήδευται ἡμῶν	is buried our
ἡ θυγάτρην Ταταριν·	daughter Tatarin.
οὐδενὶ δ' ἐξέσται {ΑΛ}	It is not permitted for any
8 ἄλλῳ κηδευθῆναι	other person to be buried (here)
εἰ μὴ τῇ μητρὶ αὐτῆς	except for her mother
καὶ τῷ πατρεί. Εἰ δὲ	and father. And if anyone
μετὰ τὴν ἡμετέραν	after our
12 τελευτὴν ἀπ⟨ε⟩ιθή-	death should not obey
σει τις τῶν προγε-	(our) directives
γραμμένων, δώσι	above, he will pay
τῷ χώρῳ τῷ Ἐλεινοκα-	to the village of the
16 vacat πριτῶν Χ φ´.	Eleinokaprians 500 denarii.

---

the inscription! However, I follow their reading of ἐπιθή- in line 12, after close inspection of the (magnified) photograph and the squeeze nr. Denizli 09 (= DM 933 probably executed in 1976) held at the British Institute in Ankara.

This platform and the bomos on it belongs to Tatia and her husband Moschas, in which is buried our daughter Tatarin. It is not permitted for any other person to be buried (here), except for her mother and father. And if anyone after our death should not obey (our) directives above, he will pay to the village of the Eleinokaprians 500 denarii.

The inscription and the stone on which it is carved provide some important insights into territory life away from the city controlling that territory (whether Colossae or Laodikeia).

Firstly, the bomos-shaped epitaphal stone is identical to those that predominate at the northern necropolis of the city of Colossae.[163] The pediment and acroteria design, deliberately evocative of a temple, and designated a *bomos* (sometimes within inscriptions, as here, l. 2) is an indication of its sacrality (*bomos* = altar) and is known elsewhere in the region (at Eumeneia and Laodikeia for example).[164] The reference to the θέμα (l. 1), translated here as "platform", seems to be quite specific in the context of this type of burial construction: two large stone slabs with a jointed edge ("shiplap") locked in and over the pit tomb,[165] an in-ground sepulcher, the slabs further secured by the weight of the funerary bomos set on top of them.[166]

It shows that at least these villagers were influenced by urban trends in the internment and marking of the burial, and in displaying their conventional values of care for the deceased, here with the added notice that they had prepared for their own demise as well.[167]

163 It measures 1.37 m in height, the approximate height for the smaller variety of *bomoi* at Colossae.

164 See Cadwallader, *Fragments of Colossae*, 155–75. Nonetheless, the *bomoi* of Eumeneia are not identical.

165 The mechanics explain the use of the plural (βωμὸν σὺν τοῖς θέμασιν) in one inscription (*I.Hierapolis Judeich* 158, l. 2) from Hierapolis, that puzzled Jadwiga Kubínska, *Les monuments funéraires dans les inscriptions Grecques de l'Asie Mineure* (Warsaw: PWN, 1968), 86–7. The Hierapolitan construction is much more elaborate but multiple stones or slabs acting as a single cover are intended; see T. Ritti, "Alcune figure femminili nelle Iscrizioni di Hierapolis di Frigia," *Med.Ant.* 16 (2013): 163. The term does not refer to the plinth of the *bomos*. The *bomos* was carved as one solid stone to fulfill its pragmatic purpose of a heavy seal. Elsewhere, such as at Nikomedia in Bithynia, the word can become a term generally encompassing "grave" (*TAM* IV,1.140). Its mundane use can be for anything "laid down" whether materially (a "deposit") or figuratively (a "proposition").

166 See also chapter 12.

167 The expression ζωσ{ε}ῖν on some funerary bomoi is the common succinct statement: "while living" (see *MAMA* 6.43 = *I.Laodikeia Lykos* 104 (Denizli 67 = DM 944) — another inscription disputed between Colossae and Laodikeia); cf *MAMA* 5.23, 6.322, *I.Smyrna* 314. See C. M. Thomas and C. Içten, "The Ostothekai of Ephesos and the Rise of Sarcophagus Inhumation: Death, Conspicuous Consumption, and Roman Freedmen," in *Akten des Symposiums des Sarkophag-Corpus 2001* edited by G. Koch (Mainz am Rhein: Philipp von Zabern, 2007), 342.

Secondly, there is the possibility that these villagers were able to afford this expensive part of the tomb because the stone was flawed in execution from the outset, and hence, likely, cheaper. Buckler and Calder noted that the letters Π Ι Θ in line 12 were spaced to avoid a defect in the stone.[168] Even so, the fine for grave disturbance (500 denarii) is the same as specified in other epitaphs from Colossae's northern necropolis.[169] Whether this penalty is mimetic or realistic is difficult to plumb. But it also shows that such grave structures were above the financial reach of many, both in villages and cities, so much so that at least some were tempted to give their own dead a reasonable burial by adding their remains to those in a previously constructed and occupied tomb.[170] Given the ubiquity of epitaphal injunctions against the addition of a dead stranger to the tomb, this seems to have been a common, if uncountenanced, occurence — even, perhaps, in burial grounds adjoining villages.

Thirdly, it seems that Tatia, the wife and mother, took responsibility for the burial arrangements for the daughter Tatarin and for herself and her husband. She is consistently named first in the inscription (ll. 3–4, 9–10). One can only speculate about the reasons for this (literacy, financial resources, incapacitated husband?) but that it was an acceptable role and one which could be broadcast publicly seems clear.[171] It coheres with other evidence of a more public role/visibility of women in the Lycus Valley and Phrygia generally.[172]

Fourthly, the names on the epitaph show Greek and epichoric backgrounds. It is common to find the male with the Greek name, here Moschas, while the females carry the names with a longer reach of tradition behind them, even though this does not necessarily equate to ethnic background. Tatia is a Phrygian *lallname*,[173] but is also a Latin name.[174] The former is the case in this instance because of the cognate name, also Phrygian in origin, given to the daughter —

168 Buckler and Calder, *Monumenta Asiae*, 11.

169 *MAMA* 6.43, *IGR* 4.871, *AS* (2006): 108.

170 Johannes Strubbe judges poverty to have been a strong motivator to the encroaching into the grave set up by an unrelated party; see "Curses against Violation of the Grave in Jewish Epitaphs of Asia Minor," in *Studies in Early Jewish Epigraphy* edited by J. W. van Henten and P. W. van der Horst (Leiden: Brill, 1994), 71.

171 Compare *MAMA* 6.42 (3rd century CE) where the mother, Aurelia Ammiane, arranges with the *Boulê* (city council) for an annual remembrance of her deceased son with monies advanced from her (deceased?) husband's resources.

172 See Balzat *et al*, "Introduction" to *LGPN V.C*, xxv; Ritti, "Alcune figure femminili," *passim*; Cadwallader, "Claudia Eugenetoriane," and "Moneyed Women in Phrygia," *NC* forthcoming *passim*.

173 L. Robert, *Noms indigènes dans L'Asie Mineure gréco-romaine* (Paris: Hakkert, 1991 [1967]), 348; T. Drew-Bear, C. Thomas and M. Yıldızturan, *Phrygian Votive Steles* (Turkey: Ministry of Culture, 1999), 380.

174 L. Zgusta, *Kleinasiatische Personnenamen* (Prague: Czechoslovakian Academy, 1964), 502.

Tatarin.[175] The husband's name may simply be the adopted "Greekness" needed for public advancement (anticipated by his parents), even in a village.

Fifthly, the village is known by a term, χῶρος, that is given a technical application beyond the general sense of "country". It probably means the Eleinokaprian territory but this would be generally limited to the travel-reach of villagers pursuing agricultural labor, given the general location of fertile land well serviced by water supply. But there is also a sense of surveyed allotment. Ramsay suggested that the city-state territory was divided into formal *Choroi*, sub-divisions of the overall territory.[176] (He meant Laodikeia, but the point is nonetheless valid.) The village has sufficient bureaucratic infrastructure to police the sanctity of the village burial ground or at least to receive (exact?) a penalty. It may be significant that Weber reported that when the Ottoman Railway line was laid down just past the Ak Khan, the engineering preparations uncovered small remains of an ancient temple, though with no inscriptions reported so it is not possible to tie the village and the temple together.[177]

However, this raises an important issue. At Apollo Lairbenos, penalties for infractions of the manumission of slaves are to be paid usually to the god and/or the general treasury (either of the sanctuary or perhaps of the city or village from which the dedicant-manumitter came); sometimes specific city institutions are named,[178] or even the formally named imperial treasury (εἰς τὸν τοῦ κυρίου/τῶν κυρίων/δεσποτῶν φίσκον).[179] Sometimes the ταμεῖον or φίσκος is left unspecified, which may mean that the dedicant-manumitter looked to her/his own settlement (occasionally a specified village). It seems that some villages could have corporate or communal "treasuries" and the means to conduct their operations.[180]

It seems, albeit from only one inscription for this otherwise unknown village, that Colossae, perhaps 6 to 8 miles away, was not relied upon for policing nor was the beneficiary of any penalties. If the village was within an imperial, public or private estate, one might expect some recourse to the owners/managers for enforcement, on the presumption that their position and standing would carry more clout. So the village probably relied on what autonomy it could muster. Whether this simply reflects the standing of Tatia (and Moschas) for jurisdictional intervention or their own preference cannot be decided. At the very least, however, it flags a separateness in this village's life at least in the perspective of some villagers. This had already been hinted at in the Hierapoli-

175 Corsten suggests a correction to Τατάριον (*Laodikeia*, 197), but the phonology in Phrygian-influenced pronunciation is probably reflected in the spelling.

176 Ramsay, *Cities and Bishoprics*, 1.36.

177 Weber, "Die Flüsse von Laodikeia," 191.

178 T. Ritti, C. Şimşek and H. Yıldız, "Dediche e Καταγραφαι dal Santuario Frigio di Apollo Lairbenos," *EA* 21 (2000), nrs K43, K51.

179 Ritti- Şimşek-Yıldız, "Dediche e Καταγραφαι," nrs K6, K29, K37.

180 Compare Ricl, *Kaystros* 23.

tan decree threatening penalties on shepherds and herders whose animals ventured onto vineyards causing damage, and on those who permitted them to do so (masters or villagers) and who, presumably, sheltered them.[181] The tension over land use and jurisdiction lies in the background of the Hierapolitan decree. It was no doubt exacerbated by the Roman predilection (read "incentivization") for intensification of certain cropping, viticultural and orchardist land uses,[182] along with the promotion of pig husbandry.[183] Cities, in this period, were the operational centers of control over how land was utilized. In this funerary inscription then, we witness the tension in an adoption of urban funerary memorialization qualified by the desire to retain the village as one's primary point of reference and support.

If my arguments hold that Eleinokapria lay in Colossae's territory, two further inscriptions come into play for consideration. The find spot for both inscriptions was given by Ramsay as Hacıeyüplü (to the east of Denizli);[184] Corsten agreed that the find spot was probably close to the original location of the stones,[185] which places this particular village, Kilaraza, *to the east* of Eleinokapria.[186] Corsten held it to be a village of Laodikeia but my arguments would require it to be even more firmly in Colossian territory than Eleinokapria. The inscription names the village in the course of a brief epitaph, an indication that, even in a compact remembrance, the connection to a community was important. The stone is not a bomos but a stele (fixed in place by a tendon at its foot, probably marking the entrance to a tomb) familiar in style to another

---

181 *MAMA* 4.297 (Kagyetteia); *I.Mus. Denizli* 15 (Thiounta, 54–5 CE); see M. Trainor, "Rome's Market Economy in the Lycus Valley: Soundings from Laodicea and Colossae," in *First Urban Churches* 5, 300–3. I am less inclined to see a market economy at work here — a potentially loaded, anachronistic category that sidelines slavery as the underpinning labor-force and thus replicates the divorce of economy from the means of production that dominated free Roman conceptions of ownership and wealth accumulation. Nevertheless, I agree with the agonistic perspective on this decree.

182 For an example of Roman intensification practices that accented the harvesting and controlled dispersal of water, see B. Lucke, M. Schmidt, Z. Al-Saad and R. Bäumler, "Water Systems of the Decapolis (Northern Jordan) and their Relation to the Landscape During the Hellenistic and Roman Periods," in *L'Eau comme patrimoine: De la Méditerranée à l'Amérique du Nord* edited by E. Hermon (Quebec: PUL, 2008), 226–7. On the use of terraces to push agriculture to higher elevations, see B. Golomb and Y. Kedar, "Ancient Agriculture in the Galilee Mountains," *IEJ* 21 (1971): 136–40.

183 The prosperity of one pig farmer from Colossae is evident on one fragmentary funerary stele, unfortunately with the inscription missing (*MAMA* 6.50). It depicts the stereotypical banquet-of-the-dead but has three pigs in line carved under the stock scene. See chapter 12.

184 Ramsay, "Antiquities of Southern Phrygia," 345–6 nr. 2, Ramsay, *Phrygia*, 1.77 nr. 12.

185 Corsten, *Laodikeia*, 200 (nr. 118).

186 I am at a loss as to why the *Barrington Atlas of the Greek and Roman World*, Map 65, 2B places the village to the west of the Asopos River, which would, of course, situate it squarely under Laodikeia's authority.

design found at Colossae (and elsewhere), that is, a pediment with acroteria in which is carved a boss/rosette/star.[187] The simple funerary inscription reads:[188]

(on the architrave of the pediment)
Ζωσᾶδι Μολοσσῷ ὁ χῶρος
ὁ Κιλαραζέων μνίας χάριν·
(along the arch below the pediment)
Ἐλπὶς παροδίταις χέριν.

The village of Kilaraza (set up this epitaph) for Zosas, son of Molos(s)os, in his memory.
Elpis offers greetings to the passers-by.

Here the responsibility for commemoration is taken by the village (identified by the use of χῶρος, l. 1, again a synonym of κώμη),[189] suggesting that Zosas may have held some stature in the settlement and perhaps died without issue. Elpis is likely a relative — a wife or sister — a deduction based on Sterrett's description of the stele relief having two figures beneath the gable. Again we are reliant on an epitaph for the identification of a village, an indication of the value placed on burial and the public display of such virtue before inhabitants and travellers. The names are Greek although Ramsay wondered whether Molossos had a Thracian origin. It has long been recognized that the name while only attested here for Phrygia is common at Aphrodisias in Caria, and marginally less so in Ionia.[190] However, the name has early attestation in Magna Graecia and Greece,[191] notably Sparta where an ethnic group from Epiros are so designated. This seems to lie behind its appearance in Ephesos, perhaps derived from Spartan mercenaries of the fourth century BCE.[192] Angelos Chaniotis noted that the name at Aphrodisias frequently occurs as a "second name," and wondered whether it indicated an ancestral tradition.[193] Whatever circuitous history might lie behind the conferring of the ethnically-derived name on Zosas's father, the Hellenistic flavor of these names is plain, even if there is some speculation that the village ethnic -αζο/υ- reflects Phrygian influence.[194]

187 The description of the stele is reliant on J. R. S. Sterrett, *An Epigraphical Journey in Asia Minor during the Summer of 1884* (Boston: Damrell & Upham, 1888), 14–15, nr. 12. He described the feature in the pediment as a "sun" but this is probably infelicitous.

188 The reading follows *I.Laodikeia Lykos* 118 (Corsten), who, with Sterrett (*Epigraphical Journey*, nr. 12) and Robert ("Inscriptions," 352 n12) correcting Ramsay, saw Ἐλπίς as a woman's name.

189 So Corsten, *Laodikeia*, 201.

190 See *LGPN V.A, V.B* s.v.

191 *LGPN III.A*, s.v.

192 R. W. V. Catling, "Sparta's Friends at Ephesos: the Onomastic Evidence," in *Onomatologos: Studies in Greek personal Names presented to Elaine Matthews* edited by R. W. V. Catling and F. Marchand (Oxford: Oxbow, 2010), 211–2.

193 A. Chaniotis, "Second Thoughts on Second Names in Aphrodisias," in *Personal Names in Ancient Anatolia* edited by R. Parker (Oxford: British Academy, 2013), 221–2.

194 Ramsay, *Phrygia* 1.77, nr. 12 (commentary).

A further inscription is probably to be included though there is no mention of a village name. It is a fragment found in the same location as the previous instance (Hacıeyüplü) and likely to have travelled but a short distance from its original location. Weber's notice of a small temple/shrine, noted above, is evocative of religious sensibilities even if the following inscription cannot be assigned to it. The fragment reads:[195]

- - - - - (name and patronymic?)[196]
ς Θεῷ Ὑψέσ-
τῳ εὐχήν.
(N. son/daughter of NN. offered this) as a prayer to Theos Hypsistos.

This is not the place to enter the lengthy discussions over the cult of Theos Hypsistos (the most high god),[197] but it is now generally accepted that this was a pagan deity not derived from nor an expression of Jewish commitments, even if elsewere capable of sharing terminology. Two points can be made however. First, this is a rare attestation of the cult in the Lycus Valley and region. The only other instance is similarly non-civic, being found in a highly damaged fragment from the rural sanctuary of Apollo Lairbenos, possibly as a hyperelative addition to Apollo Lairbenos or, less likely, a joint dedication.[198] Ties with agriculture are likely.[199] Second, the phraseology is stereotypical suggesting that this dedication is not novel even if similar forms of expression are directed towards other gods.

Although the evidence for villages under the sway of Colossae's authority is slight, what can be discerned enables considerable insight into village life:

i) there was a level of mimesis of civic practices and offices,
ii) villages frequently possessed the mechanics of administrative organization reflecting an autonomy over local issues though under the oversight of civic officials,
iii) villagers placed a high esteem on respect for the dead,
iv) exchanges of honor were a typical pattern of behavior among inhabitants,

195 *I.Laodikeia Lykos* 61 = Ramsay, *Phrygia* 1.78, nr. 14 = Mitchell, "Theos Hypsistos" 142, nr. 217 (assigned to Laodikeia).

196 Compare *I.Perge* 231; *MAMA* 10.427 (Synaos), *SEG* 44.1058 (Dorylaion), 59.743 (Mesambria).

197 See S. Mitchell, "The Cult of Theos Hypsistos," in *Pagan Monotheism in Late Antiquity* edited by P. Athanassiadi and M. Frede (Oxford: Clarendon, 1999), 81–148, "Further Thoughts on the Cult of Theos Hypsistos," in *One God: Pagan monotheism in the Roman Empire* edited by S. Mitchell and P. van Nuffelen (Cambridge: Cambridge University Press, 2010), 167–208; J. Riley, "Beyond the Mainstream: The Cultural Environment of Asia Minor as a Matrix for Expressions of a Highest God," PhD Thesis, Flinders University, 2018.

198 Ramsay, *Phrygia*, 1.154 nr. 55. Compare *I.Pergamon* 330. The inscription is not included in the extensive collection of T. Ritti, C. Şimşek and H. Yıldız. "Dediche e Καταγράφαι dal Santuario frigio di Apollo Lairbenos." *EA* 32 (2000): 1–88, nor in Mitchell's two catalogues.

199 Corsten, *Laodikeia*, 124; Mitchell, "Cult of Theos Hypsistos," 106.

v) village demography often sprung from mixed origins,
vi) families were esteemed although with no regular/regulated pattern of structure or internal lines of authority,[200]
vii) religious sensibilities were highly practiced if not developed,
viii) literacy was recognized and deemed as having an important function in village life regardless of low levels of skilled literacy among inhabitants,
ix) proximity to other settlements was a frequent feature, cultivating commercial and other contacts, and
x) agriculture was a predominant if not the only pursuit forging the establishment and maintenance of a settlement.

Foundation myths, festival markets and territory cohesion

When Dio Chrysostom delivered an oration to the people of Tarsus, he identified the expectations of the assembled listeners to hear recounted the foundation myth of the city replete with heroes, demigods, even Titans, all designed to display the city's Greek credentials.[201] It is a telling recognition of how important foundation stories were to a city's identity and self-esteem. We have had cause to mention some foundation myths already. Laodikeia seems to have had at least two foundation myths at different times, a phenomenon not confined to that city.[202] One, perhaps attributable to Phlegon of Tralles, tied Queen Laodike to an oracle from Zeus delivered to her (estranged) husband Antiochos II that privileged the guiding role of Hermes in marking out the new city foundation. The second, if Ulrich Huttner's reading of a Laodikeian coin from the time of Caracalla is accurate, reconfigured the focus of Laodikeia's foundation to the birth-place/nursery for the infant Zeus, an accent that probably owes much to the city's growing engagement with and importance to Rome. It may be that the shift in foundation stories occurred as part of Laodikeia's scramble to reassure Rome of its fidelity after the city's surrender of the Roman general Oppius early in the Mithridatic War (89–85 BCE). Laodikeia's bilingual monument honoring the Senate and People of Rome erected on the Capitoline Hill signaled the city's devotion.[203] Her Roman credentials were swiftly established — including a rapid adoption of gladiator spectacles[204] — and the inscription and mon-

200 For the development of this particular aspect, see chapter 12, and A. H. Cadwallader, "Family Life in Asia Minor," in *Ancient Literature for New Testament Studies 10: Inscriptions, Graffiti, Documentary Papyri* edited by R. Richards and J. R. Harrison (Grand Rapids: Zondervan, 2023), forthcoming.

201 Dio Chrysostom *Or.* 33.1.

202 Marek, *Land of a Thousand Gods*, 474–6.

203 *CIL* 1^2 728.

204 Cicero *Att.* 6.3.9.

ument were renovated over the following two centuries. This recovery from an embarrassing failure would have provided a strong incentive to adjust its foundation story and mark that repair with a change in its pervasive mint stylistics reminiscent of Zeus-Jupiter's religious and political dominance on the Capitoline Hill in Rome.

Hierapolis's foundation myths laid powerful claim to the involvement of Apollo. Apollo was *the* deity of ancient Greek foundation myths. The consultation at his sanctuary at Delphi was essential to gain a favourable blessing and directions for the establishment of a colony. Hierapolis had cultivated a long tradition of an Asian home for Apollo, merged with the indigenous god or place-name, Lairbenos.[205] In the second century, the city minted coins that attracted one of the key epithets of Apollo in his guidance for the foundation of a city — ἀρχηγέτης.[206] Pythian games were a feature of the cultic remembrance of the city's foundation, as other Hierapolitan coins also celebrated.[207]

Plate 3.16: Hierapolitan coin (16 mm, 1.97 g) with the head of radiate Apollo bearing the legend of ΑΡΧΗΓΕ | ΤΗC on the obverse and standing Apollo carrying the bipennis — the double-bladed axe — on the reverse. The legend reads ΙΕΡΑΠ | ΟΛΕΙΤ | ΩΝ.[208]

Historical realities often belie the claim of the foundation story, whatever the narrative details were. But history is not the point of a foundation narrative. It serves rather to confer a coherent identity for the city and its territory. In the case of Hierapolis this had particular numismatic accentuation with the head of Apollo being alternately given the legend of ΛΑΙΡΒΗΝΟC thereby asserting that the territory between the formal city and the rural sanctuary belonged to Hierapolis and was allocated and accessed centrally.

An inscription from Ephesos helps to demonstrate this clearly. It is an honorific dedication to the city's legendary founder, Androklos, a foundation that occurred, as the narrative goes, with the guidance and support not of Apollo but his sister Artemis. The naturalistic feature of the narrative, the slaying of a wild boar as the marker for

205 See C. Brixhe, "La langue comme critère d'acculturation: l'exemple du Grec d'un district phrygien," *Hethitica* 8 (1987): 51.
206 *RPC* 3.2351, 2352 (time of Trajan)
207 *RPC online* 6.5437 temp. (time of Elagabalus).
208 *RPC online* 3.2358G. Photograph from the CGT collection by permission.

the surveying and settling of a city, has an ancient pedigree, going back to the sixth century (BCE) chronicler, Creophylos.[209]

But the second century CE dedication at Ephesos witnesses to how long the founder's story continued, albeit with some significant changes. In fact, Ephesos's coins retain the founder's iconography through to the mid-third century, almost to the end of the provincial mints, featuring Androklos hunting down a wild boar.[210]

Plate 3.17: The second century inscription honoring the founder of Ephesos, Androklos, located in Curetes Street. The stone-cutter has used three sizes of lettering to convey the hierarchical importance of the elements: the honorand, his "office", and the dedicators.[211]

The inscription reads Ἄνδροκλον | τὸν τῆς πόλεως | κτίστην | οἱ περὶ Αὐρ(ήλιον) Νεικόστρατον τὸν | καὶ Εὐπάλιν Εὐπαλίου φιλο-|σέβαστον παραφύλακες | ἀνενεώσαντο,[212] that is, "The wardens of the interior under the supervision of Aurelius Nikostratos also known as Eupalis, son of Eupalis, devotee of the Emperor, set up this new monument (in honor of) Androklos, the founder of the city." Two matters are important for our purposes.

Firstly, the "wardens of the interior", the *paraphylakes*, erect the monument in the heart of the city. Their responsibilities might cover the sweep of Ephesos's territory but their focus is the center. In the background, lies the role of a founder — the κτίστης — that is, he was understood not only to have laid the foundations of the city but to have mapped out the territory that fed, and fed into, the city. Allotments of land and the legal administration necessary to maintain the organization of that territory were all credited to his purview. In this sense, the *paraphylakes* are laying claim to be the lawful successors and protectors of the city's foundation.

Secondly, their manager/supervisor, their *archiparaphylax*,[213] is described as a devotee of the Emperor. The foundation of the city and the maintenance of order in its territory are now dovetailed into the Roman imperial administration. This is blatantly

209 Athenaeus *Deip.* 8.361d–e. The fragment of Creophylos does not mention Androklos, but rather "founders" in the plural (οἱ … κτίζοντες). Strabo 14.1.3–21 and Pherecydes *FGrHist* 3 F155 provide the name; another turn to the story is given in Pausanias 7.2.8.

210 *RPC* 9.610, 611.

211 Compare Gal 6:11, Plutarch *Mor* 663C, *HA* 24.4–5.

212 *I.Ephesos* 1094.

213 See *IGR* 4.524 (Dorylaion, 71/72 CE).

demonstrated in one coin minted at Ephesos during the reign of Hadrian, when Hadrian's lover, Antinoos, became the model for Androklos, walking with the sacrificial boar at his feet, the reverse to the portrait of Antinoos on the obverse.[214]

These foundation stories were pronounced on the Mediterranean seaboard where the Ionian *duodecapoleis* were established, Ephesos being one of them. Even when the Greek colonies were, in fact, takeovers of existing or abandoned settlements, the foundation stories were concerned to present a new human civilization on a wild natural realm (not unlike the British colonial declaration that Australia was *terra nullius*). The standard formal elements of these older narratives was a crisis motivating the search for a resolution (natural disaster, a family contest over succession, overpopulation); a request for guidance from a deity (most usually Delphic Apollo); directions to a new land and the organization of settlement, both in terms of a *polis* center and the ordering of the surrounding territory.[215] The death of the founder ushered in a succession built on hallowing the memory of the founder, celebrated in a sanctified tomb usually situated in close connection with the agora (rather than the usual extra-mural cemetery), in annual sacrifices and games in his honor and in a festival procession that retold, even re-enacted, the story of the city-state's identity built on the glorified past. The beneficial return for the inhabitants of the wider territory came in the extended markets that were integral to the cultic celebrations, even as villages were often sequestered into the provision of animals and other goods for sacrifice and cult.[216] These provided the financial incentive (sometimes through inflated prices)[217] that curried a willingness to comply with the *polis* identity being forged through the foundation story and its annual cultic iterations. Thus, foundation stories bound together *polis* and *chora*.

Over time, not only did stories adjust, they multiplied. Naoíse Mac Sweeney has built a catalogue of Greek foundation stories; it seems to be expanding towards 150 examples.[218] There were sometimes rival stories, especially in the context of competition between city-states and the need to accommodate new socio-political realities. Moreover, where cities of pre-Greek origins existed, such as Colossae, these foundation stories expanded the mythological origins even as they adjusted the cultural realities within which they were framed, especially when multiple ethnicities were part of the demographic fabric.[219] Foundation stories were not an invention of the Greeks. The city-gate inscriptions of

214 *RPC* 3.2084. On Roman reshaping of the content and practice of the foundation myths of Ephesos, see G. Rogers, *The Sacred Identity of Ephesus: Foundation Legends of a Roman City* (London: Routledge, 1991).

215 See C. Dougherty, *The Poetics of Colonization: From City to Text in Archaic Greece* (Oxford: Oxford University Press, 1993), 15–29.

216 See, especially, *SEG* 38.1462, ll. 113–29 (Oinoanda, 124–125/6 CE).

217 See Oliver, *Greek Constitutions* 77.

218 See N. M. Sweeney, *Foundation Myths and Politics in Ancient Ionia* (Cambridge: Cambridge University Press, 2013) and "The Deviant Daughters of Miletus: Foundation Traditions in Ionia" Brown University lecture 2016: https://www.youtube.com/watch?v=RCjWvcPlB4o.

219 See S. Kerschbaum, "Die Apollines von Hierapolis in Phrygien," *JNG* 64 (2014): 15–29, 33.

Hittite rulers were substantially the same in intent and function, even if their reference to the past was framed in terms of surpassing whatever had been.

But there was a further development in the use of the technical language of foundation and the matters to which they were applied, especially in late Hellenistic and Roman Republic times. Foundation language was used sometimes of contemporary benefactors whose munificence enabled endowments, innovations or restorations judged to be beneficial to a city's prosperity and advancement.[220] They too might be honored as κτισταί or οἰκισταί, "founders".[221] But foundation narratives might also have a strong aetiological function, that is, to explain a natural wonder. Hierapolis, for example, with its luminescent white cliffs, attracted such stories.[222] They might also, as we shall see, provide warrant for the establishment of a cultic center associated with a wonder, such as a healing spring.

Foundation stories were not locked into a transtemporal content but changed when the circumstances of the city were fundamentally altered. However, crucial to every foundation myth is the avowal of cornucopian fecundity. In the ancient world, this was always factored in terms of harnessing agricultural produce for the city's needs. But under Rome, the intensification of urban life and symbiotically of agriculture combined to strengthen the ties between city and country.[223] The hinterland of a city — its territory — was therefore a crucial component of a foundation story, sometimes obliquely represented, but more often given a critical place in the narrative movement of a foundation story: the provision of water, the slaying of an animal as a marking of a site and a witness to nature's provision. This movement was almost always centripetal, that is, the country was harnessed as a critical part of the story of a city — it was its life-blood. But the city was the protector and civilizer of that life-giving flow. The only exceptions arise in heavily contested distantiations from the encroachments of city authorities. The multiplicity of foundation stories shows the impact of changing circumstances, which, for a time, may lead to polemical engagements over what is to be *the* foundation narrative.[224] But, as Stephen Mitchell saw clearly, "This invention of the past provided the cities with a much firmer sense of their own identity than the creation of workaday administrative structures and institutions."[225]

220 See, for example, A. H. M. Jones, "A Deed of Foundation from the Territory of Ephesos," *JRS* 73 (1983): 116–25.

221 See C. S. Lane, "Archegetes, Oikistes, and New-oikistes: the Cults of Founders in Greek Southern Italy and Sicily," Ph.D thesis, University of British Columbia, 2009.

222 See Thonemann, *Maeander Valley*, 75–7.

223 See A. D. Rizakis, "Town and Country in Early Imperial Greece," *Pharos* 20 (2014): 241–67.

224 J. C. Hanges, *Paul, Founder of Churches: A Study in Light of the Evidence of the Role of "Founder-Figures" in the Hellenistic-Roman Period* (WUNT 292; Tübingen: Mohr Siebeck, 2012), 82.

225 Mitchell, *Anatolia*, 1.208.

A Colossian foundation narrative

We don't know of the emergence of a foundation myth for Colossae in Hellenistic times from literary sources. One or more would certainly have developed in the aftermath of the foundation of Laodikeia; the crisis for civic identity would have demanded a new narrative that sought to instill cohesion and pride in "being Colossian". Some hints of a story are probably to be discerned in the emphasis on the heliotic colossus that we have seen accented in the coins of Colossae. But these mintings belong to the second and third centuries of the Common Era, three centuries or more after the foundation of Laodikeia. It is the time of the Second Sophistic, when the fervor for recovery and reinvention of Greek origins was in full swing.[226]

There is a trace of an earlier foundation story worked into the popular Christian story of the archangel Michael of Chonai. There is usually no mention of Colossae written into the title given to it in manuscripts. However, both Hierapolis and Laodikeia are mentioned as neighbors — the former good, the latter far from it.[227] We can be confident that the popular story in its developed narrative was connected with the life of the church at Colossae and probably the city in the late fourth to early fifth century. It continued to serve its identity-defence (especially against those who impugned its veneration of the archangel Michael) even as it allowed a significant degree of flexibility in re-tellings of the story to serve unfolding needs in subsequent centuries. This flexibility is seen in substantial variations in the text in manuscript transmission,[228] and in at least three recensions of the story received in later times, as the tenacity of the city and church's adherence finally proved to be of benefit to the wider church.[229]

In brief, the story begins with the apostolic prophecy of a sacred, healing spring, the establishment of a sanctuary at the site and appointment of its custodian named (in a significant echo of Col 4:17, Phmn 2), Archippos. The bulk of the narrative unfolds a lengthy defence of the site, the sanctuary and its custodian by the archistrategos Michael against a succession of attacks.[230] The second element — the establishment of a sanctuary at the site — contains strong

226 See A. M. Kemezis, "Greek Ethnicity and the Second Sophistic," in *A Companion to Ethnicity in the Ancient Mediterranean* edited by J. McInerney (Malden, MA: Wiley, 2014), 390–404.

227 *S. Mich. Chon.* 1.10, 5.7 (Hierapolis); 3.15, 11.10 (Laodikeia).

228 See A. H. Cadwallader, "The Devil as an Agent of Diplomacy: variations in the transmission of the story of St Michael of Chonai," in *Dealing with Difference: Patterns of Response to Religious Rivalry in Late Antiquity* edited by G. Dunn and C. Shepardson (Göttingen: Mohr Siebeck, 2021), 217–36.

229 See A. H. Cadwallader, "A Stratigraphy of an ancient city through its key story: the archistrategos of Chonai," in *Colossae in Space and Time*, 282–95.

230 For a summary of the story see A. H. Cadwallader, "Epiphanies and religious conflict: the contests over the hagiasma of Chonai," in *Reconceiving Religious Conflict: New Views from the Formative Centuries of Christianity* edited by C. de Wet and W. Mayer (London: Routledge,

indicators that the source of this part of the narrative lies in a pre-Christian foundation story for the site of a cult center at a sacred spring. The Christianization of the foundation story is a fairly thin veneer and can be peeled away relatively simply.[231] The full Christian defence of the site (and of devotion to the archangel who delivers it) comes in the bulk of the narrative. But the initial foundation story is loosely dovetailed into the longer drama as a second, non-apostolic introduction. This foundation story, with the Christian elements removed, probably reads close to the following:

> A man from Laodikeia with a daughter who was dumb from birth came to the healing spring in obedience to a dream of an eagle-winged divine being. He was unimpressed with the accounts of healing at the site, but when the waters were fed into her mouth, she cried out, 'Great is Zeus; great is the power of his angel.' The father confessed his ignorance and dedicated this building in thanksgiving for the healing of his daughter.

When I first pruned away the Christian version of the foundation story found in the story of St Michael of Chonai, I was hesitant about the mention of Laodikeia and the specific naming of the acclaimed god as Zeus.[232] Now I am more confident of the importance of these two names to the original story. Not only do accounts of healing frequently mention the provenance of the suppliant,[233] but here, the motivation to include the suppliant's origin is strong. Laodikeia never had its own site for a healing center — it had to stake a claim on the sanctuary of Mên Karou and syphon fame for its medical school.[234] Colossae could claim an ancient foundation that pre-dated the establishment of Laodikeia and continued to draw its residents out of that city to seek benefit elsewhere. We have seen already that Zeus was a prominent god in the Lycus Valley from before Laodikeia's settlement. But we have also seen in the earlier Laodikeian foundation story found in Stephanus and occasionally attributed to Phlegon of Tralles that a messenger of Zeus — his angel — was crucial. The role of an angelic being

2018), 122–3; for an English translation, see Cadwallader, "The Story of the Archistrategos, St Michael of Chonai," in *Colossae in Space and Time*, 323–30; for a re-telling and partial analysis, see Thonemann, *Maeander Valley*, 77–83.

231 See A. H. Cadwallader, "'As if in a Vision of the Night …' Authorising the Healing Spring of Chonai," in *Dreams, Memory and Imagination in Byzantium* edited by B. Neil and E. Anagnostou-Laoutides (Leiden: Brill, 2018), 265–92.

232 Cadwallader, "Vision of the Night," 278–9.

233 See, for example, L. R. LiDonnici, *The Epidaurian Miracle Inscriptions: Text, Translation and Commentary* (Atlanta, GA: Scholars, 1995), 86–7 nr. A2; 88–9 nr. A4.

234 The sanctuary of Men Karou/Karura was probably within the territory of the small mountain city of Attouda. Laodikeia cultivated the munificence (and ambition) of one of the sanctuary's famous practitioners, Zeuxis Philalethes, as part of its Augustan bronze coinage: *RPC* 1.2893–2895. Laodikeia did develop a medical school (as distinct from a healing sanctuary); it gained a reputation for the treatment of eye complaints. See Huttner, *Early Christianity*, 171–7.

was well-established. The form might vary — from winged Hermes to a particular manifestation of winged Zeus. The presentation of Michael in the Christian story retains a number of key markers indicative of Zeus in the description of the archangel.[235] I have already noted in the Hellenistic bronze coins of Colossae that Zeus (with a winged thunderbolt) seems to have held the exalted position in the pantheon of gods in the Colossian religious landscape. The foundation story, probably inscribed on a wall or free-standing stele at the healing spring, consequently proclaimed for the Colossian territory that the Zeus of Colossae delivers benefits not to be found at Laodikeia, just as the later story of St Michael recounted the fame of the site as spreading across the whole land.[236]

An alternate foundation story for the Christ-followers at Colossae

Commentators on the Letter to the Colossians have sometimes noted the agricultural metaphors found especially in the first two chapters. The husbandry of grain, fruit trees and vines is clearly behind Col 1:6, 10 where "bearing fruit and growing" καρποφορούμενον/καρποφοροῦντες καὶ αὐξανόμενον/αὐξανόμενοι are alternately applied to the global spread of the gospel and to the Christ-followers at Colossae in their works and knowledge that reflect the gospel focus on Christ and God. There is nothing necessarily related to a city's foundation narrative here (cf Mk 4:8, 20, 28), except that fecundity is generally understood from an urban perspective at least to be dependent on properly demarcated and husbanded land.

The remarkable pre-Qumran discovery of parchment documents in a sealed ceramic jar in a cave on Kūh-e Sālān in Iran is particularly revealing. One document, dated to 88/87 BCE, executed in the reign of the "king of kings" Arsace (βασιλεύοντος βασιλέων), is a contract of sale of a section of land containing a vineyard. The land is precisely delineated by a name, a proximate settlement (a village called Kopanis), a probably natural feature (a water-supply) and rights of access. It included in the sale a reference to planted vine-stock, both fruitbearing and without fruit. The vendors were co-possessors, but are precisely defined in terms of the overall land parcels. The purchase was of a part of the land bounded by neighbouring plots. The relevant section of the document for our purposes reads … τειμὴν ἀμπέλου τῆς οὔσης ἐν κώμῃ Κωπάνει

235 See A. H. Cadwallader, "St Michael of Chonai and the Tenacity of Paganism," in *Intercultural Transmission throughout the Medieval Mediterranean: 100–1600 CE* edited by D. Kim and S. Hathaway (London/NY: Continuum, 2012), 37–59.

236 ἐγένετο εἰς πᾶσαν τὴν γῆν; *S. Mich. Chon.* 3.11, cf 19.8.

τὴν ἐπονομαζομένην Δαδβρακανδράς, τὸ ἴδιον μέρος, τὸ ἐπιβάλλον αὐτῷ μέρος παρὰ τῶν συνκλήρων μετὰ ὕδατος καὶ ἀκροδρύοις καρποφόροις τε καὶ ἀκάρποις καὶ εἰσόδῳ καὶ ἐξόδῳ … "the price of a vineyard located in the village of Kopanis called Dadbrakandras, his own share due to him being his part of the joint-ownership (of the *kleroi* land divisions), including the water supply and the vine-stock both fruit-bearing and without fruit, as well as rights of ingress and egress …" (Document 1A, ll. 10–13).[237]

The mention of fruit-bearing, a part-possession and allotments is redolent of the language of Col 1:10, 12. One might also note the guarantee of ingress and egress in terms of the walking metaphor that opens verse 10 (περιπατῆσαι). Verses 12–14 of the epistle form the proemic rationale for the famous hymn of 1:15–20; that is, the hymnic accolade of the Son gains its warrant from thanksgiving for the share of the allotment (or share which is the allotment) of the saints in the light: εὐχαριστοῦντες τῷ πατρὶ τῷ ἱκανώσαντι ὑμᾶς εἰς τὴν μερίδα τοῦ κλήρου τῶν ἁγίων ἐν τῷ φωτί (v.12). Of course, in the craft of the letter writer the metaphors are directed towards spiritual development in light of a heavenly inheritance. However, metaphors only arrest attention when some material grounding in the experience of the hearer can be relied upon.

This is where commentators have again been caught as they seek to appropriate the biblical traditions of the division of the land of Canaan as the tribal inheritance of the people of Israel,[238] along with the heavily spiritualized rendition of these traditions in writings from the Dead Sea Scrolls. So the imagery becomes Jewish and κλῆρος is given a narrowed meaning, suffused into a spiritualized jacket of κληρόνομος, with the added weight of Romans 8 and Galatians 4 thrown in. For those who accept a Jewish constituency in the Colossian Christ-followers, or even, as I have suggested, a Jewish constituency in the second aural reception of the letter, that is, in the assembly at Laodikeia, the problem of discerning the background feeding the metaphors might seem to be obviated. But this hardly renders the metaphors sharp and confronting for the non-Jewish hearers, far and away the majority of the Christ-followers in both cities. They have their own ready-to-hand knowledge of agricultural allotments (called *kleroi*), the commonality of joint-ownership, the issues (sometimes disputes) over inheritance, and the recognition of access (especially in territory which, among small farmers, was not fenced).

The Kūh-e Sālān document is a strong reminder that the terminology of the Colossians Letter here is drawn from the surveyed and business dealings of the countryside. Here is a portion, a *meros*/*meris*, of a *klêros*, defined by reference to

237 E. H. Minns, "Parchments of the Parthian Period from Avromanin Kurdistan," *JHS* 35 (1915): 28, translation adapted from Minns (p. 31).

238 So, for example, P. Pokorný, *Colossians: A Commentary* (Peabody, MA: Hendricksen, 1991), 51–2, M. M. Thompson, *Colossians & Philemon* (Grand Rapids, MN: Eerdmans, 2005), 25–6, P. Foster, *Colossians* (BNTC; London: T & T Clark, 2016), 164–6; P. Müller, *Kolosserbrief* (KEK 9/2; Göttingen: Vandenhoeck & Ruprecht, 2022), 142.

a settlement (note the parallel between ἐν κώμῃ of the parchment and the ἐν τῷ φωτί of Col 1:12, the latter labelled by Lohse as "the domain in which God has placed his own").[239] The allotment fosters both fruit-bearing and growing stock.

Some might consider that a cave in a mountain above a village in Kurdistan is far removed from Colossae of Phrygia. Crucial is the recognition that both settlements were transferred from the kingdom of the Persians to that of the Seleucids. We do not have extensive Greek manuals on land surveying and division parallel to those that have survived from Latin writers.[240] However, inscriptions that have survived, especially from Mylasa in Caria, Magnesia-on-Maeander in Ionia, and Sardis in Lydia indicate that the Hellenistic land surveys and divisions were grounded in the parcel of land designated the *klêros*. They were meticulously marked out by boundary stones, natural or permanent features, or rupestral engravings,[241] often specifically named or numbered and located in relation to an estate or settlement,[242] recorded in a centralized registry,[243] and were the foundation for ownership transfers and taxation purposes.[244] These *klêroi* came to include the "improvements" made to them, from housing to crops to gardens.[245]

With the advent of Rome, the aggregation of *klêroi* into large estates that had begun in later Seleucid and Attalid times, accelerated as more land was subjected to intensified agricultural pursuits.[246] The letters between Pliny and Trajan demonstrate that land surveys and divisions not only increased but the tasks were largely met by *local* officials: "dependable surveyors can be found in every province" assured the emperor.[247] The Hellenised cities of Asia, even with the increase in imperial, public and private estates, nevertheless retained much of the terminology of Greek land surveys and divisions.

We sometimes see the term arising in legacies left for the maintenance of honors or the provision of resources for civic improvements. Here the boundary between *klêros*

---

239 E. Lohse, *Colossians and Philemon* (Hermeneia; Philadelphia: Fortress, 1971), 36.

240 The *Corpus Agrimensorum Romanorum*. See Campbell, *Roman Land Surveyors*, xxvii–xliv.

241 See *I.Mylasa* 257, 584 (nd); Ricl, *Kaystros* 42 A–F.

242 *I.Ephesos* 4 (298/297 BCE); *I.Sardis* 7,1.1 (200 BCE).

243 See A. V. Walser, *Bauern und Zinsnehmer: Politik, Recht und Wirtschaft im frühhellenistichen Ephesos* (Vestigia 59; Munich: CH Beck, 2008), 226, commenting on a particular accent of *I.Ephesos* 4, ll. 19–22.

244 *I.Iasos* 1 (367/354 BCE); *I.Sardis* 7,1.1; *I.Mylasa* 810, 821 (150–100 BCE). The "Diataxis of Epikrates" formulated to establish a funerary cult centred on his deceased, heroized son, Diaphantos, followed the pattern of land surveying of territory allocated to support the cult — boundaries marked out by landscape features, toponyms, lands of named neighbours and the laying down of boundary stones (*horoi*). See Sara Campanelli, "Family Cult Foundations in the Hellenistic Age: Family and Sacred Space in a Private Religious Context," in *Understanding Material Text Culture: A Multidisciplinary View* edited by M. Hilgert (Berlin: de Gruyter, 2016), 165.

245 See I. Pernin, *Les baux ruraux en Grèce ancienne: corpus épigraphique et etude* (Lyon: Maison de l'Orient et de la Méditerranée, 2014), 296–445; C. H. Roosevelt, "The Inhabited Landscapes of Lydia," in *Spear-won Land: Sardis from the King's Peace to the Peace of Apamea* edited by A. M. Berlin and P. J. Kosmin (Madison, WN: University of Wisconsin Press, 2019), 150–2.

246 See Thonemann, *Maeander Valley*, 242–51.

247 *Mensores … in omni provincial inveniuntur, quibus credi possit*; Pliny *Ep.* 10.18.

and *klêronomos* blurs. At Aphrodisias, the foundation document for a dedication to Thea Aphrodite and the building of a *thyepoleion deipnisterion* (a dining hall for ritual banquets) clearly understands that part of the support for the benefaction would be derived from revenue received from a number of sown allotments (ἐπὶ ὑποθήκαις κλήροις τρισὶν σπόρου κύπρων).[248] Another dedication by a certain Marcus Aurelius Hermes provided a large sum of money for "perpetual allocations among the most powerful *Boulê*" (εἰς αἰωνίους κλήρους τῇ κρατίστῃ βουλῇ).[249]

Two general observations can be made. Firstly, the use of *klêros* in Asia fundamentally is to be understood in terms of land survey/division and land development (its "fruitfulness and growth") and only, secondarily, as a testamentary disposition that lies behind its meaning as "inheritance/bequest". It is not to be understood in terms of judgment by lot,[250] even though this is a further derivative meaning elsewhere. Secondly, land survey was centrally organized, administered and enforced. The "walk" in the metaphorical accumulation in Col 1:10–12 has the countryside in view — a going out — but it is a countryside that remains controlled by the city.

This leads us to the second "walk" in the letter (Col 2:6–7).[251] This time it is a return walk — a coming in — with the city as its focus.[252] It points to the ideological buttress by which the countryside was won to an acceptance of the centralized authority exerted by the city, that is, the foundation story. Commentators have noted that there is a succession of metaphors in Col 2:7 following the instruction to "walk" in/among Christ Jesus the Lord (Col 2:6). These have been noted as an agricultural metaphor (ἐρριζωμένοι, "being rooted"), an architectural metaphor (ἐποικοδομούμενοι "being established/built on") and an authority metaphor (βεβαιούμενοι "being confirmed").[253] These are to find their meaningful compass "in him" (ἐν αὐτῷ) and "by loyalty" (τῇ πίστει).

The problem that besets commentators is that the succession of metaphors have appeared difficult to combine. Margaret MacDonald suggests there may be a mixed metaphor (often an offence to English linguistic puritans) or, more

---

248 *MAMA* 8.413c, l. 12–13 (117/138 CE).

249 *I.Aphrodisias and Rome* 43, ll. 15–17 (time of Severus).

250 Contra, S. McKnight, *The Letter to the Colossians* (NICNT; Grand Rapids, MN: Eerdmans, 2018), 120.

251 There are two other "walks" in the letter. One belongs to the former pattern of life (Col 3:7); the other is quite contemporary but pertains to the interaction with Colossians who are not Christ-followers (Col 4:5).

252 I am not persuaded that the participles governed by the first and second "walks" are closely paralleled as Wilson and McKnight postulate: R. McL. Wilson, *A Critical and Exegetical Commentary on Colossians and Philemon* (ICC; London: T & T Clark, 2014), 241–2; McKnight, *Colossians*, 220. However, I do think a case can be made for an "egress" and "ingress" as directional indicators for the two walks.

253 L. Bormann, *Der Brief des Paulus an die Kolosser* (ThHK10/1; Leipzig: Evangelische Verlagsanstalt, 2012), 64.

simply, a combination of agricultural and architectural elements. This hardly advances our understanding.[254] Scot McKnight tries, on the other hand, to resolve the clash by offering an urban resolution, namely, that both are architectural images.[255] Wilson suggests, if not two, then the three, are architectural.[256] It is clear that whatever agreement might in general be harnessed as to the metaphors individually, it is the succession that is problematic.

However, in the light of the foundation myths and legends that are so crucial to the life of a city and its territory — the walk from the countryside into the heart of the city, to its agora and central civic temple with its inscriptions memorializing founder and foundation in the letter's succession of metaphors — this succession fits the annual processional celebration aptly. The procession of commemoration of the founder ends with the seal placed on the validity of the foundational narrative for the participants in the celebration. The verb βεβαιόω has a similar sense of authoritative pronouncement in the rescript of Hadrian to the rulers, council and popular assembly of Hierapolis in 117 CE. Hierapolis had sent congratulations to the new emperor and, along with the gifts and greetings, had sought his confirmation of their ancient privileges (including the previously unknown right of provision of asylum). Hadrian's reply confirmed all this: ἐγὼ βεβαιῶ.[257] This language is familiar in imperial edicts and rescripts related to the identity and standing of cities.[258] It secures the city populace in the identity markers which they have held (rights, privileges, festivals, even territory and so on). Similarly in Col 2:7, the verb secures the adherents of this new founder in that loyalty/faith that expresses the foundation (both in content and in ritual iteration).

If the sacred healing spring was a major emblem of Colossian distinction, then it is likely that the 2.5 mile distance from the spring to the city agora was a sacred way, passing through rich agricultural land, for such foundation celebrations. The Colossians Letter has taken the critical importance attached to city foundation myths and their commemorating processions, and applied it to Christ. Here is being portrayed in the combination of rural fecundity, urban structures and regulating authority the key elements of a foundation myth now anchored to Christ. We know that other early Christian writers applied the metaphor of founder to Christ — in the Letter to the Hebrews (Heb 2:10, 12:2

254 M. MacDonald, *Colossians and Ephesians* (Sacra Pagina; Minnesota: Liturgical Press, 2000), 88; similarly J. L. Sumney, *Colossians, A Commentary* (Louisville: WJKP, 2008), 128.

255 McKnight, *Colossians*, 221. Insofar as elements of nature were incorporated into reliefs adorning city buildings, there is some material basis for the suggestion, but it is derivative. See, for example, C. Şimşek and B. Yılmaz Kolancı, "Laodikeia, Mimari Bloklarında yer Alan Balık Kabartmaları aları Üzerine Gözlemler (Observations on Fish Reliefs on Laodikeia Architectural Blocks)," in *15. Yılında Laodikeia (2003–2018)* (Laodikeia Çalısmaları 5) edited by C. Şimşek (Istanbul: Ege, 2019), 273–86.

256 Wilson, *Colossians and Philemon*, 192–3.

257 *SEG* 55.1415, l. 12 as reconstructed by Tullia Ritti.

258 See, for example, *TAM* V,2.1396, l. 2; Oliver, *Greek Constitutions*, 20, ll. 13–14; 44, l.4.

cf Acts 3:15 and especially 5:31) for example, Christ is dubbed the ἀρχηγός, a standard substitute for the ἀρχηγέτης connected with Apollo, the inspirer of new foundations.[259] The use of (καινὴ) κτίσις in 2 Cor 5:7, has recently been convincingly interpreted as a reference to a new foundation not a new creation.[260] For the writer, this is a received tradition, which is the very sense conveyed by the term παραλαμβάνω at the beginning of Col 2:6. Whether or not the notion of Christ as "founder" was an actual received tradition for the letter-writer or was part of his own overall appropriation of the imagery of a foundation narrative is moot.

The usually-annual celebration of the foundation and the founder was full of festivities, markets, games (both athletic and artistic) and sacrifices. This giving of thanks for the city's life is precisely the sort of activity envisaged in the call for lavish thanksgiving at the end of Col 2:7 (περισσεύοντες ἐν εὐχαριστίᾳ). Presumably some of the elements of the Christ-followers' celebration of their founder are glimpsed in the letter — the christological hymn, associated acts of praise (Col 3:16–17 where thanksgiving is a constant repetition). Occasionally, elsewhere, we catch glimpses of how foundation celebrations were to be organized and executed.[261] Not the details but the emphasis on celebration, festivity and thanksgiving in the letter corroborates the suggestion here that the explanation for the succession of metaphors in Col 2:6–7, usually seen as "mixed", in fact belong to the metaphorical appropriation of a processional celebration of a foundation myth, this time for Christ. A foundation myth or legend was so familiar in virtually every *polis* of the province of Asia that the metaphors and their sequence would have resonated with the letter's audience, furnishing a means to comprehend and reiterate the Christ story. After all, the movement from country to city is one of the fundamental threads of the synoptic gospels. Perhaps significantly, the Letter to the Colossians does not advocate the return to the country that we find in Mark (16:7). The foundation narrative has been harnessed to the Christ-story but the fundamental privileging of the city as the meaning and focus of the territory (of Colossae) remains unchallenged, even as the Christ-followers at Colossae are being drawn away from being "of Colossae".

We have traversed the territory of the Lycus Valley searching for clues that might alert us to the boundaries between the major cities. It has become clear that to speak of cities must include cognisance of the territories that they controlled, even though today those territory boundaries remain somewhat oblique to us, except in broad terms usually defined by natural features. The

---

259 See *F.Delphes* III,2.48, l. 13 (97 BCE).

260 See D. Kurek-Chomycz and R. Beringer, "The Corinthian ΚΑΙΝΑΙ ΚΤΙΣΕΙΣ? Second Corinthians 5:17 and the Roman Refoundation of Corinth," in *Stones, Bones and the Sacred: Essays on Material Culture and Ancient Religion in Honor of Dennis E. Smith* edited by A. H. Cadwallader (Atlanta, GA: SBL, 2016), 195–220.

261 See *I.Priene* 399 on the Panionian festivities.

fundamental buttress to the formal administrative control of city over countryside was ideological — the elevation of a foundation story by ritual observance that explained/provided the city-state's identity and tied the countryside into the city's values, conventions and ways of life. These foundation stories could change and be replaced should the experience of the city undergo significant crisis. The Letter to the Colossians provides a glimpse into how an alternate foundation story might be engineered to provide Christ-followers in the city (and its countryside) a narrative reconfiguration of their identity, one which retained sufficient familiar items as to not appear totally idiosyncratic. Of course, city territories (and their justifying foundation stories) inevitably bumped against neighbouring cities with their territories and their competing interests. To this we turn.

Chapter Four
Rivals and Neighbors: competing cities in the Lycus Valley

After the first century CE, the dominant Christian portrayal of the cities of the Lycus Valley was of a cohesive relationship between Hierapolis, Laodikeia and Colossae, the three cities mentioned in the Letter to the Colossians (Col 1:2, 2:1, 4:13, 15). Other settlements and networks are largely ignored as are the tensions that sprang from the supplanting of Colossae's eminence by the Seleucid foundation of Laodikeia in approximately 255/256 BCE.[1] Competition and conflict are constants in relationships between Greek cities. This re-sets how Colossians and Philemon might be interpreted.

We begin the exploration with a simple question and move to a transaction conjured in Paul's Letter to Philemon that unwittingly adds a conundrum to the discussion. This becomes the means to open up the agonistic element in the civic consciousness of Colossae, that was played out in relation to other cities in the Lycus Valley, most especially Laodikeia. It then suggests that the agonistic element also impacted on the relationships between the Laodikeian and Colossian Christ-followers.

Bronze coins and the costs of civic life

And so to the simple question that often passes unnoticed in discussions of minted coins in the ancient world — why did cities mint bronze coins? In the Second Testament, coins figure often enough but they are almost always silver denarii (for example, Mk 12:15–16) or even higher value exchange metal (gold or silver) perhaps to be measured in weights, such as the talents or minas —

1 See chapter 3.

the illustrative, inflated currency in parables (for example, Matt 25:14–30; Lk 19:11–27). The search for a bronze coin proves unrewarding: one, a grand total of the cost of a poor person's sacrifice (of variable price in different markets: Matt 10:29; Lk 12:6), and, two, the token called a *quadrans* (Mk 12:42).[2] One gets the impression from the hyperbole of Paul's comparison of Onesimos's financial damage (whatever it was) with Philemon's life (Phmn 18–19), that the imagined sum was unlikely to be calculated in the bronze in his money belt (cf Mk 6:8)!

The cost of slaves was measured in denarii or equivalent, not in assaria.[3] The purchase price varied considerably, but appears to have depended on age, gender, training and, occasionally, even ethnic background.[4] Thus one contract from Egypt (129 CE) records the sale of a young (unnamed) female slave for "the price of 1200 silver drachmae" (τειμῆς ἀργυρίου δραχμῶν χειλίων διακοσίων).[5] Significantly, the amount was only refundable if she was found to have epilepsy or had been illegally on-sold. Wrongful dealing (even by the slave illicitly expropriating himself from another's ownership — as by flight, for example) lies behind Paul's use of ἠδίκησεν in Phmn 18: εἰ δὲ τι ἠδίκησέν σε ἢ ὀφείλει, τοῦτο ἐμοὶ ἐλλόγα "If he has brought you loss or owes you anything, bill me." The term ἀδικέω in the papyri rests on juridical infraction,[6] and came also to designate damage to a grave.[7] Similarly ὀφείλω occurs frequently in legal documents.[8] If we take Paul's use of ὀφείλει in the same verse as referring to the financial disadvantage (or equivalent) that Philemon has nominally incurred from the loss of Onesimos's servile labour (and excluding costs involved in Philemon's efforts to find him) rather than the market

2 A quadrans was about one-sixteenth the value of a sestertius under the Roman currency system. A denarius was worth three to four sestertii. Hence a quadrans was between one-forty-eighth and one-sixty-fourth of a denarius. No wonder that the first-century Roman satirical poet, Martial, dismissed the coin as little more than a nominal entrance fee to the baths: Martial *Ep.* 3.30, 8.42. Was this the comparison behind Mark's rendition of the widow's performantial denunciation of the temple (Mk 12:41–4)?

3 See Hans-Joachim Drexhage, *Preise, Mieten/Pachten, Kosten und Löhne im Römischen Ägypten bis zum Regierungsantritt Diokletians* (St Katherinen: Scripta Mercaturae, 1991), 249–79; Walter Scheidel, "Real Slave Prices and the Relative Cost of Slave Labor in the Greco-Roman World," *AncSoc* 35 (2005): 1–17.

4 See Peter Arzt-Grabner, "How to Deal with Onesimus? Paul's Solution within the Frame of Ancient Legal and Documentary Sources," in *Philemon in Perspective: Interpreting a Pauline Letter* edited by D. F. Tolmie (Berlin/New York: de Gruyter, 2010), 116.

5 *P.Oxy.* 95 (ll. 20–21). The amount is approximately equal to 1060 denarii or about three years' earnings for an unskilled, rural labourer; see Walter Scheidel, "Slavery" in *The Cambridge Companion to the Roman Economy* edited by W. Scheidel (Cambridge: Cambridge University Press, 2012), 99.

6 See Peter Arzt-Grabner, *Philemon* (PKNT 1; Göttingen: Vandenhoeck & Ruprecht, 2003), 235–6.

7 *I.North Galatia* 246; *I.Mus. Palermo* 18. It should be noted that Roman law expressly outlawed and severely punished tomb violation (*Dig.* 47.12), but the examples here rely on punishment from a higher power.

8 Arzt-Grabner, *Philemon*, 237–8.

value of the slave body,[9] then, perhaps in realistic terms, such labor might be monetized in bronze coin, rather than the silver or gold measuring the value of a life.

On the Aegean island of Kalymnos for example, a first-century inscription records the amount that a recently freed woman, Monarchia, would owe her master should she rescind from her on-going service in or for the household (even though she possessed a different status from prior to her manumission). The amount is given as four assaria per day (ἀποδώσει ἑκάστης ἡμέρας ἀσσάρια Δ), that is, about a quarter of a denarius.[10] Four assaria was the going rate for recompense to an owner for the commandeering of a pack animal to carry goods over a distance of 60 stadia (6½ miles).[11] This is close to what seems to be the occasional honorarium made to some slaves that is called a *peculium*. However, the *peculium* was a particular Roman practice of inducement to efficient servile labor that irregularly filtered into local jurisdictions through the Mediterranean world.[12] At the elite Terraced House 2 at Ephesos, a graffito in the kitchen scribbles various account items for foodstuff (mainly seafood) but includes a payment of 6 assaria to a slave. It is likely that this refers to a slave's *peculium*.[13] In second-century (CE) Egypt, it is suggested that a slave's *peculium* was one *chalkine* or about 12 assaria, though because the document seems to indicate the hire of slaves, some or all of this might simply be recompense to the actual slave-owner for a day's work.[14]

If Paul was imprisoned in Ephesos, the closest of the three incarceration options usually entertained by commentators (Ephesos, Caesarea Maritima, Rome),[15] this was six days' walk from Colossae on the most direct roadway. A runaway, if that is how to cast Onesimos (see chapter 11), would hardly have followed such a route. But even at this minimal travel time, the absence of Onesimos

9 There is no need to postulate Onesimos as stealing anything other than himself from Philemon, even though a frequent stereotype of slaves was that they were thieves (Terence *Eun.* 776 *cf* Martial *Ep.* 11.54). It should also be admitted however that runaways are frequently recorded in the papyri as absconding with some of their masters' possessions (see, for example, *SB* 24.16257; *P.Cair. Preis.* 1).

10 *Tit. Calymnii* 176.

11 *I.Mus. Burdur* 335 ll. 10, 33 (bilingual regulation dated to 14–19 CE).

12 See generally Morris Silver, "At the Base of Rome's *Peculium* Economy," *Fundamina* 22 (2016): 67–93. The *peculium* features discretely in Roman law but other, less-preserved codes are, by comparison, limited. There is no specific amount (or requirement) for a *peculium*.

13 Hans Taeuber, "Graffiti und Inschriften," in *Hanghaus 2 in Ephesos: Die Wohneinheit 7* edited by E. Rathmayr (FIE 8.10; Vienna: Österreichische Akademia der Wissenschaften, 2016), 246.

14 See *P.Scholl* 9 (Memnoneia in western Thebes) and the comments by Peter Arzt-Grabner, "Everyday Life in a Roman Town like Colossae: The Papyrological Evidence," in *The First Urban Churches 5* edited by J. R. Harrison and L. L. Welborn (Atlanta, GA: SBL, 2019), 225 n121.

15 See Scot McKnight, *Philemon* (Grand Rapids, MI: Eerdmans, 2017), 21, 37. Other options have been entertained, such as Apameia — closer to Colossae but a less likely option. The Ephesos option is not without its detractors. See Ben Witherington, "The Case of the Imprisonment that did not happen: Paul at Ephesus," *JETS* 60 (2017): 525–32.

from Philemon's work-place and/or household would alone have racked up a sizeable deficit. To this calculation would be added the time taken for the various events intimated in the letter to have occurred — gaining access to Paul, conversion, some form of service to Paul and negotiating a return. At a bare minimum, the amount owing for Onesimos's unauthorized "absence" would come to 10 to 12 denarii (for a six week furlough). However, if Onesimos's name has any intentionality behind Philemon's probable naming of him, that is "profitable", then his productive/occupational worth to his master in this nominal period was likely far more than this amount. This seems to lie behind the pun on Onesimos's name in Paul's use of ὀναίμην in verse 20.[16] It is a monetized half-jest that reinforces the proprietorial and financial purpose of slavery, even as it humorously turns that to the free-born (and perhaps business) relationship "in the Lord" between Philemon and Paul. In any case, for our purposes, the visualization of the minimal level of loss is readily cast in terms of bronze coins.

Slaves, apprentices and returns

Peter Arzt-Grabner has noted that in Phmn 13, Paul used phrasing that is reminiscent of apprentice contracts found in the papyri: ὃν ἐγὼ ἐβουλόμην πρὶς ἐμαυτὸν κατέχειν, ἵνα ὑπὲρ σοῦ μοι διακονῇ ἐν τοῖς δεσμοῖς τοῦ εὐαγγελίου. "I indeed wanted to retain him, so that he, according to your release, might be of service to me in the indenture of the gospel."[17] Arzt-Grabner suggests that Paul is deliberately using terminology (especially the accent on service) with which Philemon would himself be familiar, though now directed towards their partnership in gospel matters not textiles (note κοινωνία/κοινωνός in Phmn 6, 17). His papyrological examples are drawn largely from family businesses seeking to extend their expertise through contracting out the training of a family member, not a slave.[18] However, such contracts are also known to have been negotiated for slaves. We know of one, named Apollophanes, described as a weaver (γέρδιος), whose master filed to have his name removed from the tax register, because he had died.[19] Presumably at some stage he had been trained

16 This is the pun on the name in the letter, rather than the stereotypical antithesis χρῆστος/ἄχρηστος. See A. H. Cadwallader, "Name Punning and Social Stereotyping: Re-inscribing Slavery in the Letter to Philemon," *ABR* 61 (2013): 18–31.

17 I have slightly paraphrased the translation to bring out the commercial dimensions of the language.

18 Arzt-Grabner, *Philemon*, 66–8. His examples are *SB* 10.10236; *P.Oxy.* 275, *P.Wisc.* 1.4, *P.Mich.* 3.171–3; *SB* 24.16253 all from Oxyrhynchus and the Arsonite nome in the first century CE: "Everyday Life," 226–9. Examples are not confined to Oxyrhynchus; see *PSI* 8.902 (Tebtynis, 48–56 CE).

19 *P.Oxy.* 262 (61 CE). It seems that taxes were due not only on the production of goods but also on the exercise of the trade itself, even for apprentices; see *P.Tebt.* 2.385 (117 CE).

in the craft. A substantial navvy of slaves engaged in contracted weaving seems to be referred to in one letter in the "Sarapion archive".[20]

An actual contract however has survived for a young slave woman (παιδίσκη) named Helene, whose master, Herakleon negotiated with a master weaver for a two and a half year apprenticeship.[21] Another master, Ision, contracted with a woman weaver, Aurelia Libouke, for the training, in a year, of a slave girl he had probably fathered (name missing because of a lacuna).[22] Of course, we have no papyrological records from Asia, apart from the few examples of documents written in Asia but dispatched to Egypt where the climate was more conducive to preservation.[23] However, inscriptions have survived that confirm the involvement of slaves in the textile industry, sometimes with elevated authority.[24]

I am interested here in the payments that are mentioned in the second document between Ision and Libouke. Should the slave-apprentice be unavailable due to sickness or other absence,[25] the same number of days are to be added to the period of service laid down in the apprenticeship. In some other but similar instances, an alternative to supplementing the length of contracted service is given — one silver drachma per day (*P.Oxy.* 275; *P.Wisc.* 1.4). Further, a failure by either party in fulfilling the stipulations of the slave weaver's contract was to result in a penalty of 200 silver drachmas.[26] However, if the contract period passed without hitch, there was still to be a payment of 60 drachmas. This is very particularly expressed as "received by the girl slave ... to the account of

20 *P.Sarap.* 80, ll. 12–13 (90–133 CE). There is some dispute over the reading (a place, Hyphanton or the older word for weavers in the genitive, ὑφαντῶν). However, another letter in the archive (*P.Sarap.* 92, l. 15 with plate), I think is decisive. See J. L. White, *Light from Ancient Letters* (Philadelphia: Fortress, 1986), 168–9.

21 *P.Mich.* 5.346a (Tebtynis, 13 CE).

22 *SB* 18.13305 (Karanis, 271 CE).

23 Such as *P.Turner* 22 (from Side, 142 CE). A number of such documents concern sales of slaves, indicating that Asia was either a continued source of slaves or had established slave markets for channeling those sold. That papyrus was the common medium for written records, public and private, is evidenced from the tiny fragments of papyri that have survived by being stuck to seals affixed to documents, such as in the hoard found at Zeugma. See Mehmet Önal, "Deities and Cultures Meet on the Seal Impressions in Zeugma," *Bollettino di Archeologia* (Special Volume) online (2010): 25–53.

24 See, for example, *I.Milet* 6.2.666 (an imperial slave, supervisor of the purple trade, 50–68 CE); *SEG* 46.737 (Beroia, late 2nd century CE) which lists the members of a cult association, some with their genealogy, some only by reference to their occupation and, hence, probably slaves — including one Hilarus, a fuller. One slightly damaged inscription from Apollo Lairbenos records the manumission of a house-born slave who may have been well-trained in textiles; see E. Akıncı Öztürk and C. Tanrıver, "New Katagraphai and Dedications from the Sanctuary of Apollon Lairbenos," *EA* 41 (2008): 92–3, nr. 2.

25 Sometimes these conditions in a contract are more specific, mentioning truancy, insubordination "or any other reason"; see *P.Oxy.* 275 (66 CE), 725 (183 CE).

26 The same penalty is prescribed in *P.Oxy.* 275 but divided between the offended party and the public treasury.

Ision" (λαμβανούσης τῆς παιδὸς … εἰς λόγον Ἰσίωνος, ll. 41–2). This appears to be a crucial difference from apprentice contracts with fathers or mothers on behalf of their own family members. Under these contracts, the apprentice usually (especially if the period runs beyond a year) gains some wages on the basis that they contribute to the profitability of the business as they are learning.[27] Contracted slaves' earnings, by contrast, go to the account of the master, *just as Paul prescribes* in Phmn 18 (ἐλλόγα).[28]

Two insights can be gained for our purpose. Firstly, if Arzt-Grabner is correct in discerning weaver's contract terminology in Phmn 13 and in suggesting that Philemon, thereby, was engaged in the textile industry for which Colossae and the Lycus Valley was famed, then it is reasonable to hypothesize that Onesimos was (being?) trained in this lucrative business (in one or other of the specialized skills, whether spinning, weaving, fulling, dyeing, embroidery or transport and sales).[29] If Philemon was in a position to secure control of a weaving monopoly in one of the villages within Colossae's territory, Onesimos conceivably might have been charged with the oversight.[30] But if a slave apprentice, his truancy could bring a penalty that returns us to the approximate worth of servile labour per day that we have plotted already, namely 4 to 12 assaria, whether any of this was factored as a *peculium*. Sizeable penalties were involved to breaking a weaver's apprenticeship contract. 200 drachmas amounts to about 150 denarii, which if crudely apportioned across the two year period, comes very close to the 12 denarii previously calculated for a postulated six week "absence" by Onesimos. However, his position in the household and/or in Philemon's business generally could well inflate this figure. We need to be aware that levels of specialization and intensification had extended textile production from house-based enterprises to include dedicated shops and small factories.[31]

Secondly, the weaving apprentice contracts for slaves stipulate a return *to* the slave-owner from the master-weaver. This is phrased as a payment to the

27 See, for example, *P.Oxy.* 725, *P.Tebt.* 2.385.

28 For a detailed analysis, see my "Value-adding a slave, or, how much is an Onesimus worth?" 2023 forthcoming.

29 In fact, the segmented specializations might be multiplied further. See G. Labarre and M.-Th. Le Dinahet, "Les Metiers du textile en Asie Mineure: de l'époque hellénistique à l'époque imperial," in *Aspects de l'artisanat du textile dans le monde méditerranéen (Égypte, Grèce, monde romain)* (Lyon: Université Lumière, 2 vols, 1996), 2.56–9.

30 On the control of a village weaving industry by a textile merchant, see *P.Ryl.* 2.98 (Krokodilopolis, 172 CE). The annual rent was assessed at 300 silver drachmas (about 225 denarii), an indication of the value of the monopoly. Monopolization of the produce of various regions seems to have become a reasonably common practice — it forms part of Cicero's attack on Verres for his efforts to garner control of the Miletian wool trade (*Verr.* 2.1.86).

31 Labarre – Le Dinahet, "Metiers du textile," 54; for an archaeological example of a major textile factory, see Celal Şimşek, "Laodikeia 'da Tekstil ve Üretim Atölyeleri (Textile and Manufacturing Ateliers at Laodikeia)," *Home Textile* 86 (2015): 138–44 cf *SEG* 57.1101, l. 10 (Mylasa, c.200–150 BCE); *pace* Michael Trainor, "Rome's Market Economy in the Lycus Valley: Soundings from Laodicea and Colossae," in *First Urban Churches* 5, 293–324.

account of the slave-owner. The terminology, "to the account (εἰς λογόν) of N." (the named owner) is common in business and taxation accounts in the papyri. In one document, a son, Dionysios, agrees to act as guarantor for his father, Dioskoros "for what he owes you in the account of taxes" (ὀφείλοντά σοι εἰς λόγον τελεσμάτων), remarkably similar to the language of Phmn 18, where the less common verbal form ἐλλογάω/-έω is used.[32] Although the end of the papyrus is lost, it is clear that Dionysios stipulates what liabilities he will discharge should his father default.[33] If we recall the above-mentioned contract of Ision and Libouke regarding the female slave, she is to receive, at the end of the contracted period of training, payment for the work she contributed to the business while being skilled. However, this money is to go to her master, even though formally registered as her earnings. This suggests that Paul's reference to what Onesimos might *owe* Philemon (as distinct from any damage/illicit loss caused — ἀδικέω) is somehow configured on the basis of his time away from Philemon, that is, on the basis of what Philemon might reasonably have expected as a return from Onesimos in the period of his absence. Paul has strategically, if fictively, recast Onesimos's absence into a familiar slave apprenticeship model, using the terminology of the contract to color both Onesimos's relocation and Paul's acknowledgment of payment for service.

Monetary exchange in first century Colossae

But here we are returned to what coin Paul would have relied upon — silver, gold, bronze and from which mint — if he were to make good on his rhetorical flourish of recompensing Philemon for a legal infraction or for repaying a debt (Phmn 20). Of course, the question is impossible to answer. Given that payment in kind had become quite rare by this time,[34] it is almost certain that Paul conceived of a monetary amount, even if he had no intention of implementing his grandiose declaration.

This leads us to ask what coins were available in Colossae in the first century CE, and about the larger issue of Colossae's civic mint. Silver denarii would be less a concern, as these were almost totally official imperial currency. Cis-

32 On the variation in the form of the verb, see J. B. Lightfoot, *Saint Paul's Epistles to the Colossians and to Philemon* (London: Macmillan, 1890⁹), 341–2. For the synonymity in usage, see J. H. Moulton and G. Milligan, *The Vocabulary of the Greek Testament* (London: Hodder & Stoughton, 1952), 204, where they highlight the use of ἐν λόγῳ rather than εἰς. Arzt-Grabner finds the use of the verb rare although the meaning is clear: *Philemon*, 238–40.

33 *P.Batav.* 9 (Arsinoite nome, 128 CE).

34 See C. Katsari, *The Roman Monetary System: The Eastern Provinces from the First to the Third Century AD* (Cambridge: Cambridge University Press, 2011), 223. Compare however, S. Mitchell, *Anatolia: Land, Men and Gods in Asia Minor* (Oxford: Clarendon Press, 2 vols, 1993), vol 1, 248–50 on some coin shortages that provoked payment of taxes in kind.

tophoric silver coins (each worth about three denarii), a peculiarity of Asian currency in the Roman imperial period, might have been an alternative. These had a long-standing circulation prior to the advent of Roman control (from 181 BCE at least),[35] and continued in use through the late Republic, though there was a certain elite Roman snobbery that favored the denarius.[36] Augustus had harnessed the cistophors to his own use, a partial trade-off for the continued existence of local civic mints. Rather than Greek, Latin was used in the legend and the emperor's head guarded virtually the entire series, with reverses that carefully registered Roman values (monumentality and beneficence, a Zeus-controlled pantheon, civic stability and loyalty) even though there were subtle indications of the mint honored with the task. Subsequent emperors reiterated these marks of imperial presence in Asia. In the second century, Hadrian had authorized the nearby mints at Laodikeia, Hierapolis, Eumeneia and Aphrodisias (among more than 20 in the province) to overstrike the coins produced under Augustus in order to prolong circulation.[37]

Plate 4.1a and b: At the left is a cistophoric coin (*RPC* 1.2203, 27 mm av., 11.60 g av.) minted early in the reign of Augustus (Ephesos mint, 28 BCE), highlighting both the Roman Pax and the continuation with the past shown by the snake emerging from a basket, the cista mystica — the standard Hellenistic representation of the cistophoros, "the basket-bearer". At right is a re-strike (*RPC* 3.1359, 25 mm av., 10.58 g av.) during Hadrian's reign of the same coin type, with the head of the emperor superimposed on the wreathed reverse of the Augustan coin. The seated Zeus, along with the COS III legend on the reverse of the re-minted coin, points to a date after 128 CE at the launch of Hadrian's pan-Hellenic tour.[38]

35 The advent of locally-struck coins was an innovation of the Attalid kingdom. See Peter Thonemann, *The Maeander Valley: An Historical Geography from Antiquity to Byzantium* (Cambridge: Cambridge University Press, 2011), 170.

36 Cicero, *Att.* 26.2, 36.4. The cistophori were generally thought to be overvalued; hence exchanges of denarii into cistophori inevitably incurred some loss.

37 W. E. Metcalfe, *The Cistophori of Hadrian* (NS 15; New York: American Numismatic Society, 1980). Metcalfe considers that these coins (mainly Augustan) were old, worn cistophoric coins, re-struck as an economic measure to ensure both continuing acceptance and regularity in the exchange rate (pp. 119–20).

38 Photographs by permission of Leu Numismatik.

This suggests that cistophoric coins were a familiar sound in a well-traveled scrip along the Lycus Valley. But it also suggests advantages beyond mere monetization were discerned and cultivated. It served Augustus and subsequent emperors to stamp these coins with visual and inscriptional reinforcement of their programs.[39] *Pax* and *Fortuna* register the Roman impress unequivocally.[40] To an extent, the mere handling of these coins flagged some measure of acceptance, even allegiance (cf Mk 12:16–17, noting the Markan Jesus's emphasis on a coin's image and legend, ἡ εἰκὼν αὕτη καὶ ἡ ἐπιγραφή).[41] As Andrew Burnett observed, "it was common ground that people looked at coins, attaching moral values to them."[42]

We can affirm that Colossae had not minted any bronzes for its own mundane exchanges since, probably, the Mithridatic War of 89–84 BCE. The single coin ostensibly from the time of Caligula included in von Aulock's catalogue and initially in *Roman Provincial Coinage* has been demonstrated to be a re-tooled coin from another city.[43] Accordingly, with confidence limited to available evidence, no Colossian bronzes were available in the first century. Colossae was far from alone in this dearth. Two options were available. Colossae may have come to an arrangement with a minting city for the supply of bronze coins — and suffered the indignity of having its base currency marked with the legend of an apparently more illustrious neighbor — Laodikeia or Apameia for example. Or Colossae may have relied on the good graces of a wealthy benefactor to arrange for a supply of Roman bronzes, imported either from Rome or Lugdunum. This in fact was probably the provision made for the cities of Lycia. One of the most famous benefactors of Asia was a certain Opramoas, whose elaborate mausoleum (?) provides a detailed inscription relating his manifold acts of euergetism.[44] Constantina Katsari considers that one of these proclaimed provisions named the meeting of costs for the importation of Roman bronzes into Lycia.[45] Beyond the bronzes, the alternatives were basi-

39 See A. Burnett, *Coinage in the Roman World* (London: Spink, 1987), 66–85, M. P. Theophilos, "Employing Numismatic Evidence in Discussions of Early Christianity in the Lycus Valley: A Case Study from Laodicea," in *First Urban Churches* 5, 260–6.

40 *Pax* occurs frequently. The portrayal of Hadrian as *Fortuna* is singular, and all the more striking because of that. See Metcalfe, *Cistaphori*, 78–9.

41 See Alan H. Cadwallader, "In Go(l)d we trust: Literary and Economic Currency Exchange in the Debate over Caesar's Coin (Mark 12:13–17)," *BibInterp* 14 (2006): 501–4.

42 Burnett, *Coinage in the Roman World*, 67, citing Arrian *Epict. diss.* 3.3.3.

43 *MSPhryg* 2.545; A. Burnett, M. Amandry and P. Ripollès, *Roman Provincial Coinage: Supplement 1* (London: British Museum/Paris: Bibliothèque nationale de France, 1998), 35, no. 2891; M. Amandry and A. Burnett, *Roman Provincial Coinage, Volume III: Nerva, Trajan and Hadrian (AD 96–138), Part I: Catalogue* (London: British Museum/Paris: Bibliothèque nationale de France, 2015), 286.

44 *TAM* II 905. See C. Kokkinia, *Die Opramoas-Inschrift von Rhodiapolis. Euergetismus und soziale Elite in Lykien* (Bonn: Habelt, 2000).

45 C. Katsari, "Opramoas and the importation of bronze coins into Roman Lycia," *EA* 35 (2003): 141–5.

cally two, both silver — the imperial cistophori or the empire-wide denarii — and both firmly under the direct control of Rome.

Coinage and contest in civic life

This leads us to the issue that exposes the agonistic element in the life and decision-making of Greek cities under Rome. The very public presence and place that coins, especially bronzes, proclaim for a city concern us here. During Paul's time, Colossae had no easy broadcast of its commercial presence. It might have been able to rely on its long-standing fame for certain textile products, an iteration that modern commentators are content to replicate with little interest in using it as a prod to interpretation.[46] After all, Strabo had carved the city's significance by mutating the city name into a color of wool. The citizens and the color were collapsed into the term *Colosseni*, Κολοσσηνοί, the very ethnic identifier that marked their Attalid and, later, Roman provincial bronzes.[47] Whether Strabo was signaling a difference from Laodikeia's "raven-black" (ἡ κοραξὴ χρόα) colored wool is unknown.[48] The wool of Miletus is proffered for comparison. It seems a reasonable inference from Colossae's coins (which nowhere parade its textile industry) that Colossae did not seek fame for a wool-color or its textiles, or at least not only or predominantly so. In fact, Strabo's brief reference is little more than an aside in a larger exposition of the greatness, prosperity and famous sons of Laodikeia, an understandable concentration given Laodikeia's position as head of the Roman assize district. But by the

46 The two notable exceptions are Rosemary Canavan (*Clothing the Body of Christ at Colossae: A Visual Construction of Identity* [WUNT 334; Tübingen: Mohr Siebeck, 2012]) and Peter Arzt-Grabner, *op. cit.* Ulrich Huttner draws some interpretive connections for the Apocalypse: *Early Christianity in the Lycus Valley* (Leiden: Brill, 2013), 166–170.

47 Strabo 12.8.16. See Appendix 1.

48 Some have suggested that Colossae's famed wool was dyed a deep purplish-red; see N. Lewis and R. Meyer, *Roman Civilisation: The Empire (Selected Readings)* (New York: Columbia University Press, 2 vols, 1990), 2.82. This notion can be credited to Pliny the Elder who described the flower of the cyclamen as *colossinus* in color (*NH* 21.27.51). The evidence for such dyed color is far stronger for Hierapolis: Strabo 13.4.14; Labarre-Le Dinahet, "Metiers du textile" nrs 57, 59, 61, 62, 63, 65, 66. The large northern theater of Laodikeia has an inscription on one of its benches reserving its patronage for the association of purple dyers (πορφυραβάφοι). This may indicate Laodikeia's own guild or it may be an honorific reservation for the esteemed association of Hierapolis (the same theater has seat reservations, *inter alia*, for the Trapezopolitai, that is, leading citizens of the city of Trapezopolis). See C. Şimşek and M. Ayşem Sezgin, "Laodikeia Kuzey Tiyatrosu (Laodikeia's North Theater)," *Olba* 19 (2011): 173–201. For an analysis of the different types, costs and manufacturing processes of purple-dyeing, see G. Steigerwald, "Die Purpursortenim Preisedikt Diokletians vom Jahre 301," *ByzF* 15 (1990): 219–76; I. Bogensperger, "Purple and its Various Kinds in Documentary Papyri," in *Textile Terminologies from the Orient to the Mediterranean and Europe, 1000 BC to 1000 AD* edited by S. Gaspa, C. Michel and M.-L. Nosch (Lincoln, NE: Zea, 2017), 235–49.

time of Diocletian's *Price Edict* (301 CE)[49] — the well-circulated and ill-fated effort to freeze prices as a check on inflation — the textile production of the entire region was classified as "Laodikeian" (*Laodicenus*),[50] including linen along with wool.[51] Various styles were so labeled, including one tunic with a purple border.[52] Miletian products were similarly recognised,[53] but "Colossian" was no longer apparent; nor for that matter was "Hierapolitan".

Plate 4.2a and b: Fragments of the Diocletian Price Edict in Latin or Greek have been found in approximately 30 locations from Asia Minor to North Africa. This example is in situ on the north external wall of the bouleterion at Stratonikeia. The detail (section 2.1 of the edict) gives the regulated prices for beer and wine — for example, two denarii for a pint *(sextarius)* of beer brewed from barley, twenty-four denarii for a pint of golden Attic wine!

We have already noted that Colossae seems to have been intent on carving a connection with the Helios-Colossus of Rhodes, emulating the fashion (especially among emperors) for building self-adulating colossi.[54] This was certainly an emphasis on its coins and I have postulated that this iconography was a development from earlier reconfigurations of the meaning and impression to be conveyed by its city name. But the evidence at present comes, singularly, from the coins.

The return of Colossae's mint at the beginning of Hadrian's reign deserves further consideration. City mints were an important cog in Roman monetary policy but they were also a critical statement of a city's place in the region

49 For the edict, see S. Lauffer, *Diokletians Preisedikt* (Berlin: de Gruyter, 1971); M. Giacchero, *Edictum Diocletiani et collegarum de pretiis rerum venalium in integrum fere restitutum e Latinis Graecisque fragmentis* (Genoa: Istituto di storia antica e scienze ausiliarie, 2 vols, 1974).

50 So Thonemann, *Maeander Valley*, 188.

51 *Ed. pret.* sections 25, 26.

52 *Ed. pret.* sections 19, 22.

53 *Ed. pret.* section 24.

54 The fact that Pliny the Elder devotes considerable time to recounting the colossi indicates the prevailing fashion and interest: see his *Natural History* Book 34, sections 20–29.

and the empire. Katharina Martin has concluded after a massive study of the bronzes of Asia, "the cities utilized the mass-circulation medium — coins ... to propagate not only their religious and cultural but also their (Greek) political identity."[55] This was directed as much to a home audience as to the neighboring cities and regions. During Hadrian's reign alone, Colossae launched twenty-one different coin types, one of only four new civic mints in Phrygia and by far the most prolific.[56] Colossae had embarked on a concerted program of self-promotion, whatever the purely economic drivers may have been.

Tom Jones estimated that civic bronzes had a circulation range of 50 to 100 miles from the minting city.[57] This is borne out by the evidence. The imperial-period coins of Colossae have been found in Tripolis, Aphrodisias and Sardis. These provenances are confirmed in the first two places by controlled excavations on the sites,[58] in the last by a Sardis countermark on a Colossian coin.

Plate 4.3: A rare surviving coin of L(ucius) Sept(imius) Geta, minted in Colossae, probably on or just after the occasion (197 CE) when he was declared Cae(sar). On the reverse, Artemis Ephesiaca wears a mural headpiece and holds poles in each hand, flanked by hinds. The obverse has a vertical running countermark: CAPB which indicates Sar(dis) and an assigned value of B = two assaria (25 mm, 7.07 g).[59]

The difficulty that besets the myriads of extant Asian bronze coins is that very few have had their provenance recorded, even those coins of Colossae that have been displayed in Turkish museums, such as at Manisa, Afyon and Denizli. But of particular note is that Laodikeia and Hierapolis have yet to record any coins of Colossae in finds on site. This lacuna needs to be handled cautiously since the multiple volumes on the Laodikeia excavations since 2003 have yet to include a dedicated numismatic section; only the occasional finds, mainly asso-

55 K. Martin, *Demos•Boule•Gerousia: Personifikationen städtischer institutionen auf kaiserzeitlichen Münzen aus Kleinasien* (Bonn: Habelt, 2 vols, 2013), vol 1, 245.

56 For details, see Alan H. Cadwallader, "Wealthy, widowed, astute and beneficent: Claudia Eugenetoriane and the second century revival of the Colossian mint," in *New Documents Illustrating the History of Early Christianity* edited by J. R. Harrison *et al.* (Grand Rapids, MI: Eerdmans, 2023), forthcoming.

57 T. B. Jones, "A Numismatic Riddle: The So-Called Greek Imperials," *PAPS* 107 (1963): 318. Katsari extends this a little to 100–200 kilometers: *Roman Monetary System*, 28.

58 See D. MacDonald, *The Coinage of Aphrodisias* (London: Royal Numismatic Society, 1992), 15–16; for Tripolis, see B. Duman, "Tripolis'in Yeri, Önemi ve Kısa Tarihi/Location, Importance and Short History of Tripolis," in *Tripolis Araştırmaları* edited by B. Duman (Istanbul: Ege, 2017), 7–9 (fig. 15).

59 See chapter 1, new coins, nr. xviii and key. Photograph courtesy of Mark Dunning.

ciated with graves, have been published.[60] Celal Şimşek, the director of the Laodikeia excavations, has published a chronological chart of imperial-byzantine period coins recovered during the excavations and reconstruction of the city centre, which includes the volume of coins.[61] So, one can expect the lacuna to be remedied soon. Hierapolis boasts a more substantial publication from 2010.[62]

Civic mints and competition in the Lycus Valley

Nevertheless, a caveat is placed on the ease with which commentators reiterate early Christian collations of Hierapolis, Laodikeia and Colossae into a collegial triad of cities of the Lycus Valley.[63] Eusebius almost certainly relied simply on the appearance of the three names in the Letter to the Colossians (Col 2:1, 4:13, 15–16) to construct a seemingly agreed network,[64] alike in experiencing an earthquake and in receiving Paul's gospel. The irenic literary construction of neighborliness is then assumed to be historical. But this triangulation of cities nowhere occurs outside these later Christian collations.

Laodikeia and Hierapolis *are* paired, however. Both were permitted to re-strike cistophoric coins with Hadrian's image and credentials, a considerable and rare honor among the cities of Asia.[65] Both cities received valuable benefactions early in the third century from a Roman senator from Xanthos, a city to the south.[66] Both cities boasted leading officers of the guild of Dionysiac artists in the reign of Hadrian, the emperor himself sometimes designated the "new Dionysios".[67] But not Colossae.

---

60 See C. Şimşek, *Laodikeia (Laodikeia ad Lycum)* (Istanbul: Ege, 2007), 367–9; C. Şimşek, H. Baysal and M. Ohunak, "Korucuk Kurtama Kazısında Açiğa Cıkartılan Mezarlar (The Tombs unearthed in the Korucuk Rescue Excavation)," in *10. Yılında Laodikeia (2003–2013 Yılları)* edited by C. Şimşek (Istanbul: Ege, 2014), 251–2, 270–1; C. Şimşek (ed.), *Laodikeia Nekropolü (2004–2010 Yılları) (Katalog)* (Istanbul: Ege, 2011), nrs 45, 46, 172–5, 390, 643–4, 926–30, 1303, 1351, 1413–4, 1546–8, 1555, 1574.

61 C. Şimşek, "Lykos Vadisi Içinde yer Alan Laodikeia (Laodikeia in the Lycos Valley)," in *10. Yılında Laodikeia*, 46–7. The volume is low for the first two centuries but this sits curiously with the volume for the same period recorded in museum and other catalogues. The chart should be compared with that in Katsari, *Roman Monetary System*, 115.

62 A. Travaglini and V. G. Camilleri, *Hierapolis di Frigia: Le Monete, Campagne di Scavo* 1957–2004 (Istanbul: Ege, 2010).

63 So, especially, B. Reicke, "The Historical Setting of Colossians," *RevExp* 70 (1973): 429–38; L. Bormann, "Early Christians in the Lycus Valley," in *Early Christian Encounters with Town and Countryside: Essays on the Urban and Rural Worlds of Early Christianity* edited by M. Tiwald and J. K. Zangenberg (Göttingen: Vandenhoeck & Ruprecht, 2021), 213–19.

64 Eusebius *Chron.* 183.21; so also Orosios 7.7.12.

65 Metcalfe, *Cistophori*, 64–71.

66 M. Christol and T. Drew-Bear, "Un senateur de Xanthos," *Journal des Savants* 3 (1991): 213. See also *TAM* II 194.

67 *I.Aphrodisias 2007* 12.27 (127 CE).

The familiar trope of the demise of Colossae surfaces here in an endeavor to explain the imbalance of notice about the three cities. But this defeats any attempt to triangulate them in the first place. Moreover, it flies in the face of the evidence of Colossae's efforts to revive its fortunes and assert its place in the region and perhaps the province.[68] A key indicator of Colossae laying claim to its ancient prominence and its contemporary ambitions lies in the revival of its civic mint.

One inscription has become replayed for the insight it provides into a city's self-understanding when faced with the question of establishing its own mint.

Comparative insights from Sestos

The honorific inscription, from late Hellenistic times at the city of Sestos in Thrace, relates the various achievements of one of the city's own, a certain Menas. Among the highlights of his illustrious career, one benefaction was his support for the foundation of the city's mint.[69] A number of reasons are given for the mint. First, it was a decision of the *Dêmos*, the council of the citizens of the city (τοῦ τε δήμου προελομένου, l. 43). It is crucial to recognize that the move for minting civic coinage comes formally from one leading organ of a city's governance — the *Dêmos*. This recognition of the *Dêmos* is manifest in Colossae's coins.[70]

Plate 4.4: One of ten examples of a coin of Colossae featuring the head of a personified youthful *Dêmos*, facing right. The legend is simple, *Dêmos* of (or for) the Colossians (ΔΗΜΟC ΚΟΛΟCCΗΝΩΝ).[71] The reverse of this coin type features Artemis Ephesiaca, presented in a fashion similar to the Geta coin above, but with a fulsome legend identifying the sponsor, Apollonios II, grandson of Zosimos, great grandson of Diokrates, as the one who authorized the minting (ΑΠΟΛΛΩΝΙΟC Β ΖΩCΙΜΟΥ ΔΙΟΚΡΑΤΟΥC ΑΝΕΘΗΚΕ).[72]

68 See generally, Alan H. Cadwallader, "Refuting an Axiom of Scholarship on Colossae: fresh insights from new and old inscriptions," in *Colossae in Space and Time: Linking to an Ancient City* edited by A. H. Cadwallader and M. Trainor (Göttingen: Vandenhoeck & Ruprecht, 2011), 151–79.

69 *I.Sestos* 1 = *OGIS* 339, ll. 43–51.

70 *RPC online* lists 9 coin types, eight with the legend ΔΗΜΟC, one which relies completely on the iconography for identification (*RPC online* 4.2.1888 temp).

71 The legend is omitted in one coin type that nevertheless bears the *Dêmos* iconography. It also reads simply ΚΟΛΟCCΗΝΟΙC; on the obverse it carries the name of Philopappos the *grammateus* of the Colossians (*RPC online* 4.2.1888 temp.). Photograph from a private collection, by permission.

72 *MSPhryg* 2.494, 495 = *RPC online* 4.2.1898 temp. This example is 31 mm diameter, 17.23 g. A further eight examples of a similar coin exist, but without the named sponsor: *RPC online* 4.2.1900 temp.

Secondly, the decision is specific that the city should "use" its own coins (νομίσματι χαλκίνωι χρῆσθαι ἰδίωι, l. 44). "Use" is the common translation of χρῆσθαι here but the middle infinitive conveys more than a pragmatic utility. It carries with it a declarative sense, even of "supply". There is something noticeable in whatever transaction is intended.

This becomes more specific in the explanation that follows — the third reason — namely "for the sake of the stamp of the city being promulgated" (χάριν τοῦ νομειτεύεσθαι μὲν τὸν πόλεως χαρακτῆρα, ll. 44–5). Second Testament readers are familiar with the word *charaktêr*, as it is turned to render the precision of Jesus' communication of the nature (ὑπόστασις) of God (Heb 1:3).[73] Here it refers to a coin capturing a city's style and life, or at least what is officially set down (νομειτεύεσθαι) as the expression/nature of the city. Christopher Howgego captured the dynamic here: "A competitive desire for self-advertisement by both cities and individuals is a fundamental factor in the typology of the civic coinages of the Roman East and it is hard to believe that it was not at times also a motivation for the coinage."[74] In chapter 7, we will see the flip-side, where the city of Tralles embarked on a moral improvement drive in part to avoid its stature being tarnished (τὸ σεμνὸν ἐνοχλῆται τῆς πόλεως).[75]

A further Colossian example of the Sestos rationale: Artemis

Previously, we saw the particular emphasis that Colossae cultivated with its Helios coins, beyond anything in the Lycus Valley and the region. This was not the only distinctive style found on Colossae's coins. Artemis, of course, is found in many permutations throughout Asia, but dominated by the Ephesian wonder of the world, the temple of Artemis. The cult figure moved considerably beyond the large port city.

Plate 4.5: Torso marble fragment of Artemis Ephesiaca (slightly less than life-size) from Gadara in the Decapolis dated to the second century CE.

73 See especially, M. Theophilos, *Numismatics and Greek Lexicography* (London: T & T Clark, 2020), 165–73.

74 C. Howgego, "Why did Ancient States Strike Coins?," *NC* 150 (1990): 20–1. See also Katsari, *Roman Monetary System*, 212–3.

75 H. Malay, M. Ricl and D. Amendola, "The City of Tralleis combats Immorality: Measures taken against οἱ ἐν κιναιδείᾳ βιοῦντες in a new civic decree," *EA* 51 (2018): 91, l. 22 (2nd century CE).

Artemis Ephesiaca is known on many cities' coins, including those of Colossae (see Pl. 4.4 above). However, the highly dynamic, hunting Artemis is absent from the coinage of Colossae's immediate neighbors, Laodikeia and Hierapolis, and rarely found in the wider region. Conversely, Colossae's coins regularly feature Artemis the hunter in various postures. Colossae even places the head of Artemis (with bow and quiver at her shoulder) on the obverse of some coins — a reiteration of one of her Attalid coins — only paralleled at Hierapolis and Tripolis.[76]

Plate 4.6: One of the most dramatic portrayals of Artemis the hunter on a Colossian coin. The obverse presents the stately bust of Commodus, a marked contrast to the dynamism of Artemis the hunter in full flight, reaching for an arrow in her right hand and holding her bow in her left, all while in a biga drawn by two galloping stags. The sponsor, Zosimos IV, has pushed himself fully into the picture with a long legend that occupies the perimeter and crowds into the field. The legend reads: Στρατη(γὸν) τῶν περὶ Ζώσιμον Δ Φιλοπάτορα Κολοσσηνῶν "For the Colossians led by Zosimos IV, Strategos and Philopator."[77] The form of expressing his relationship to the Colossians is unique among Colossian coins.[78]

Colossae's emphasis on Artemis is only paralleled (but to a more limited extent) at Tripolis and Tabae, though these two cities have their own distinctive emphases as well, the former accenting Artemis and Apollo as Leto's children,[79] the latter situating the hunting goddess in a temple.[80] If we return to the same minting cities surveyed in relation to the Apollo and Helios coin types in chapter 2, we again see (below) Colossae's prominence in minting types featuring Artemis, strikingly contrasted from Blaundos which shows no Artemis iconography in its 78 coin types (that include 30 of Apollo). The creativity and diversity of rep-

76 Colossae: *MSPhryg* 2.513–514 = *RPC online* 4.2.1901 temp; Hierapolis: *RPC online* 4.2.2057 temp (head only); Tripolis: *RPC* 3.2565, 2566, 2567; *RPC online* 4.2.1642 temp.

77 *MSPhryg* 2.566–574; *RPC online* 4.2.1880 temp. (31 mm, 25.76 g). Photograph courtesy of the Bode Münzkabinett, Staatliche Museen, Berlin.

78 This variation is missed by R. Bennett, *Local Elites and Local Coinage. Elite Self-Representation on the Provincial Coinage of Asia, 31 BC to AD 275* (London: RNS, 2014), 24, who accents that Colossae's pervasive use of the nominative of the names of coin sponsors stood apart from the general trend of using ἐπί with the genitive of the name. The use of περί with the accusative of the sponsor's name is found on the coins of very few other cities. Wolfgang Leschhorn and Peter Franke list only Adramytion, Aphrodisias, Stratonikeia and Tralles: *Lexikon der Aufschriften auf griechischen Münzen Band I* (Vienna, OAW, 2009), 241. To this should probably be added Germe (*RPC online* 3.1766B).

79 *RPC online* 4.2.9726 temp., 4.2.1644 temp., 6.5551 temp., 8.ID71181; *RPC* 9.791.

80 *RPC online* 4.2.11542 temp., 4.2.2665 temp., 6.5383 temp., 4.2.933 (the temple alternates between tetrastyle and sextastyle).

resentation is noteworthy — the first eleven entries are all attested at Colossae, but there are a further seven examples from the review. I have included coins which feature only a stag or hind on the reverse, since this is one of the animals especially connected with Artemis. In the table following, the variety of styles is listed first, with those cities that feature the style in the iconography of their coins in the next column (with occasional brief notes of explanation). In order to avoid congestion I have not included the *Roman Provincial Coinage online* coin-type numbers for each style, though this is the basis on which the table is conceived. There will be, of course, additions that could be made that might qualify the results marginally,[81] but *RPC online* is the most extensive catalogue available. Homonoia coins, where the alliance with another city is frequently signaled by that city's patron god, are indicated by (H) if that is the only coin-type registering the style or (+H) if the homonoia coin is an additional witness to the style.

Artemis style	Cities
Artemis Ephesiaca holding poles, flanked by stags	Colossae, Attouda (Artemis Anaitis), Dionysopolis, Eumeneia, Heracleia Salbace, Hierapolis (+H), Laodicea (+H), Tripolis
Artemis Ephesiaca with Tyche poliadic	Colossae, Eucarpeia (H)
Artemis Ephesiaca as cult statuette	Colossae, Eucarpeia, H
Artemis Hunter standing, drawing arrow	Colossae, Tripolis
Artemis Hunter advancing, drawing arrow	Colossae, Tripolis, Tabae
Artemis Hunter in biga	Colossae
Artemis Hunter in biga, shooting boar	Colossae
Artemis Hunter with dog	Colossae, Aphrodisias
Artemis Hunter with stag	Colossae, Eumeneia
Artemis Hunter head, with quiver, bow	Colossae, Hierapolis(head only), Tripolis
Stag/hind	Colossae, Laodicea, Tabae
Leto carrying Artemis and Apollo	Colossae, Tripolis (+Zeus)
Artemis Ephesiaca in temple	Eumeneia, Heracleia Salbace

81 For example, Aphrodisias struck homonoia coins with Ephesos that are yet to be entered into *RPC online*. These have Artemis Ephesiaca in the iconography; see P. R. Franke and M. K. Nollé, *Die Homonoia-Münzen Kleinasiens under der thraksichen Randgebeite: I Katalog* (Saarbrücken: Saarbrücker Verlag, 1997), nrs 66–69. For relevant Colossian coins not yet included in *RPC online*, see chapter 1.

Artemis style	Cities
Artemis Hunter in temple	Tripolis
Artemis paired with Apollo	Tripolis
Artemis in long chiton, stag	Eucarpeia
ditto + cult statue/priestess	Eucarpeia
Artemis with Demeter and Amazon	Heracleia Salbace
Artemis and Mên	Tabae

Of the nineteen general iconographic presentations, Colossae boasts eleven, with more coin types of Artemis than any other city in the region. Notably, of the thirteen cities selected for comparison, Blaundos, Keretapa and Trapezopolis register no coin types of Artemis (in the *RPC online* catalogue). So, again, we are confronted with a deliberate commitment by Colossian authorities to carve a distinct stylistic in the city's coins. There can be little doubt that Colossae is presenting itself with committed Artemisian values (alongside its Heliotic advertising), with a particular accent on Artemis the hunter.[82] It is also clear that the city has chosen to carve a distinction from its nearest neighbor, Laodikeia, which is notably absent from the table above, apart from Artemis Ephesiaca and the solitary stag or hind. One earlier interpreter had even suggested that we were warranted in seeing an Artemis Colossensis here.[83] This is probably as misleading as calling Zeus Aetophoros, Zeus Laodicensis.[84] But because Laodikeia made such a pronounced display of Zeus Aetophoros as its city patron, Colossae's own claim upon Zeus as its city god (probably Zeus Bronton/Katabeites)[85] had to accentuate some complementary embellishments from the pantheon. The city did not drop its claim on Zeus, as had happened with Apollo. The visit from Hadrian on his 129 CE pan-hellenic tour confirms Colossae's

82 This has implications for the foundation myth of the city, as explored in chapter 3.

83 Stanley A. Cook, "A Lydian-Aramaic Bilingual II," *JHS* 37 (1917): 224, 231 n38.

84 Zeus Aetophoros is common in iconography in a range of cities, just as is Artemis the hunter (including at Ephesos); see R. Lesser, "The Nature of Artemis Ephesia," *Hirundo* 4 (2005–2006): 43–54. Note the objection to the attribution by Christopher Howgego, "There was no such title as Zeus Laodikeus …" *Greek Imperial Countermarks: Studies in the Provincial Coinage of the Roman Empire* (London: Royal Numismatic Society, 1985), 157; *pace* T. Corsten, *Die Inschriften von Laodkeia am Lykos* (IK49; Bonn: Habelt, 1997), 126. Recent published inscriptions from Laodikeia record Zeus Sotêr and Zeus Ktesios connected with the Emperor gods. See F. Guizzi, "Greek and Latin Inscriptions of Laodikeia on the Lykos 2003–2018," in *15. Yılında Laodikeia (2003–2018)* edited by C. Şimşek (Istanbul: Ege, 2019), 176–7. These confirm some previously-known epithets — Zeus Katachthonios and Zeus Patrios (*I.Laodikeia Lykos* 26, 69).

85 See A. H. Cadwallader, *Fragments of Colossae: Sifting through the Traces* (Adelaide: ATF Press, 2015), 65–8; "St Michael of Chonai and the Tenacity of Paganism", in *Intercultural Transmission throughout the Medieval Mediterranean: 100–1600 CE* edited by D. Kim and S. Hathaway (London/NY: Continuum, 2012), 37–59.

credentials as "a Zeus-city".[86] But Colossae supplemented that long-standing allegiance with a number of other pronounced commitments that said, very clearly, "we are not Laodikeia" (and to a lesser extent, Hierapolis) as much as it proclaimed "we are Colossae". The cities may have been neighbors, but they were also competitors concerned, at least for home consumption, to exalt their distinctive attributes, values and expressions.

City pride and prosperity

We return to the Sestos inscription to explore a fourth reason for a city to cultivate the minting of its own coins — that is, the gaining of revenue: "and (so that) the *Dêmos* might receive the profit gained from such a financial venture" (τὸ δὲ λυσιτελὲς τὸ περιγεινόμενον ἐκ τῆς τοιαύτης προσόδου λαμβάνειν τὸν δῆμον, ll. 45–6).[87] There is no metaphor intended here. Raw cash-flow was often in the mind of city authorities.[88] Prosperity was yoked to publicity and civic pride in any case. Howgego lists the way in which the city might gain profit from its own mint — an overvaluation of its coinage, selling its monopoly on exchange or from charging a fee for using its mint to strike coins for other cities.[89] The first does not seem to be the case for Colossae at least in the beginning, though such problems bedeviled the variety of currencies (not least the cistophori). The range of Colossae's coins minted during Hadrian's reign cover the requirements of its daily individual transactions — from one-quarter assarion to three assaria. This coinage variety largely conformed to the weights and diameters of bronze coins from other cities in Asia.

Howgego's third option — renting its minting facilities — similarly does not seem to apply for Colossae, at least at the outset. It is clear from an edict of Hadrian that city authorities expected to turn a profit from the regulated exchange of "foreign" coins (that is, coins minted in other *poleis*) to the local currency, and especially in the conversion of silver denarii or cistophori into the

86 *IGR* 4.869; *RPC* 3.2309; *RPC online* 2310A (Colossian coins featuring Hadrian Olympios). See Helmut Halfmann, *Itinera principium: Geschichte und Typologie der Kaiserreisen im Römischen Reich* (Stuttgart: Franz Steiner, 1986), 206.

87 *I.Sestos* 1. I have translated πρόσοδος more generally here; usually when "revenue" is meant, the word occurs in the plural. See Guizzi, "Greek and Latin Inscriptions," 167 (late 1st or early 2nd century CE). Here it is almost a synonym for λυσιτελές — an apparent tautology (if revenue is meant) says Andrew Meadows, "The Spread of Coins in the Hellenistic World," in *Explaining Monetary and Financial Innovation: A Historical Analysis* edited by P. Bernholz and R. Vaubel (Cham: Springer, 2014), 190. I have also retained "the Dêmos" even though "the people" would be acceptable. It is clear that the decision-making body lies behind the honorific inscription as well as being a major beneficiary of Menas' munificence.

88 Compare *I.Laodikeia Lykos* 2.

89 Howgego, "Why did Ancient States Strike Coins?" 18.

smaller-value bronzes. The bronze coins were crucial to the ease of daily transactions — "of the shopkeepers and retailers and the salt fish dealers accustomed to do business for small bronze" (τῶν ἐργαστῶν καὶ καπήλων καὶ τῶν ὀψαριοπωλῶν εἰς τὸν λεπτὸν ἐμπολᾶν εἰωθότων), as the edict runs.[90] Irregularities in the exchange market had disrupted currency movements in Pergamon. Hadrian, probably in 129 during his tour of Asia, confirmed that the usual rate was one denarius for 18 assaria when sold and 17 assaria for purchasing. The official exchange rate had, from the time of Augustus, been 16 assaria to the denarius. This meant that the city pocketed one assarion, and the contracted exchangers the same, for each denarius exchange. Illicit commissions and, probably, illicit enforced discounts on worn coins (such as the Augustan cistophori) were accordingly outlawed.[91] Colossae thereby gained confirmation of this additional injection into city finances, doubtless enforcing the use of its sparkling new bronzes throughout its territory among villages and small markets (one responsibility of Heliodoros' "brother" in second century Colossae)[92] and amongst the visiting traders and soldiers. It meant also that the outlays the city (or a lavish benefactor) had made for bronzes from elsewhere (whether provincial or Roman) were expunged, which had been a dent to civic pride, if not to civic finances.

The role and returns for benefaction of provincial mints

Fifthly and finally, the Sestos inscription speaks of the role of benefactors in ensuring the smooth establishment and operations of the mint. The terminology is replete with laudatory, euergetical sentiments — "The *Dêmos,* because of the just dealings, on top of the liberality, of these men [especially Menas], was able to enjoy its own coinage" (ὁ δῆμος διὰ τὴν τῶν ἀνδρῶν δικαιοσύνην τε καὶ φιλοτιμίαν χρῆται τῶι ἰδίωι νομίσματι, ll. 48–9); "(the *Dêmos*) handpicked those who would secure the trust faithfully as well as honestly" (προχειρισαμένου τοὺς τὴν πίστιν εὐσεβῶς τε καὶ δικαίως τηρήσαντας, ll. 46–7). Menas gained the honorific returns for his euergetism of time and money by this stele. Coins at this time had made the significant shift to parading the minting community in their legends.[93] But Sestos was rewarded for its long-lasting commitment to

90 *OGIS* 484 = Oliver, *Greek Constitutions* 84, ll. 8–9 (Oliver's translation).

91 See the discussion in Oliver, *Greek Constitutions*, pp. 213–5, Katsari, *Roman Monetary System*, 140. Hadrian's re-striking of Augustan cistophori was a further instrument of regulating the monetary (and exchange) system.

92 One of his offices, besides also being named as *strategos*, was that of *paraphylax*, to be understood as a superintendent of regulations applicable to the countryside (*IGR* 4.870, l. 5). See chapter 3. The designation of Heliodoros as the unknown honorand's brother is an epigrapher's reconstruction that has no basis in the published transcription.

93 For Sestos, see, for example, *BMC Thrace* 11, 12.

its civic coinage, continuing to mint regularly once the small province of Chersonessus became Augustus' personal possession in 12 BCE.[94] Interestingly, it never moved into coins being a bearer of a legend proclaiming the euergetism of some leading, wealthy benefactor.

Not so Colossae. Its coins regularly feature the names of its eminent men, and, significantly, one woman, Claudia Eugenetoriane. On one coin, she names herself "widow" and, in my reckoning, is the benefactor responsible for reviving the Colossian mint. In the third century, Menander the Rhetor of Laodikeia, emphasized that one of the means of asserting a city's greatness was to recount its famous citizens.[95] So there was a symbiosis of celebration when a coin's legend named both the city and the coin's benefactor, all the while exercising due diligence in recognizing imperial realities. Colossae displays a succession of minting benefactors from the second to the third centuries, who frequently ensured that the stability of a long genealogy was recorded in the legends, sometimes with public magistracies held as well.[96] So, in Pl. 4.6 above, the benefactor who interwove his credentials into the celebration of city and Artemisian values (of animals, the hunt, rural life, the control of nature, divine authorisation and so on), records that he is the fourth in a line of those named Zosimos and that he was governor (*strategos*) of the city and a "patriot" (*philopator*), a term that had also entered a benefactor's virtue-record.[97]

Colossae's coins became a witness to the rise in Colossae's confidence, its self-promotion, and efforts to carve a renewed, distinct identity, one that drew on the distant past but also took into account those aspects of the environment against which to build that self-definition, all wrapped into a religious framework. As Jaś Elsner has noted, "The specific space created for local self-assertion lies above all in religion."[98] I have suggested that the construction of Heliotic and Artemisian features of Colossae's values and characteristics was as much about carving a separation from Laodikeia and Hierapolis as affirming its own traditions. The natural environment certainly lent its full weight to these emphases — the geological colossus protruding from Mount Cadmus above a healing

94 *RPC* 1.1739 (Augustus), 1742 (Caligula), 1744 (Claudius); 2.358 (Vespasian), 3.575 (Hadrian); *RPC online* 4.1.7815 temp (Commodus?), 8.ID68408 (Philip I).

95 *Treatise* 1.3.364. It is disputed whether this treatise is actually composed by Menander, even if attributed to him; but the sentiments certainly are authentic.

96 The coin sponsors at Colossae, as currently known, were Claudia Eugenetoriane, Hieronymos, Octavius Apollonios Valerian (or Valerios), Tiberius Asinius Philopappos, Tiberius Claudius Sakerdos, Eklegon, Claudius Priscus, Ktesikles, Apollonios II (grandson of Zosimos), Menekles, Nigros, Aurelius Markianos Epaphras. See Appendix 2. The city authorities also, on occasion, assumed direct financial responsibility for minting.

97 A. Zuiderhoek, *The Politics of Munificence in the Roman Empire: Citizens, Elites and Benefactors in Asia Minor* (Cambridge: Cambridge University Press, 2009), 73, 111.

98 J. Elsner, "Describing self in the language of Other: Pseudo(?) Lucian at the temple of Hierapolis," in *Being Greek under Rome: Cultural Identity, the Second Sophistic, and the Development of Empire* edited by S. Goldhill (Cambridge: Cambridge University Press, 2001), 151.

spring was testimony to the colossus of the Colossians, a high country reflection of the Helios of Rhodes. Its pine forests supporting all manner of wild and husbanded life, was tailor-made for visions of the hunting Artemis.[99] After all, few as the early literary testimonia to Colossae may be,[100] they consistently point to the fertility of the region — one filled with parks, pleasurable satrapic estates and the necessary supports of food, wood and water for stationing armies.[101] This is borne out not only in the continued agricultural prosperity of the region today, but in symbols of that prosperity from the late first or early second century — the hunting dog and the fruiting tree — carved alongside the list of names honoring Korymbos for the repair of Colossae's baths (Pl. 4.7).

Plate 4.7: Carved alongside the list of names of those honoring Korymbos for his euergetism at Colossae are a leaping dog and a fruiting branch.[102]

Three coin-types flag an agonistic contradistinction from Laodikeia: one a homonoia coin, a second, probably a pseudo-homonoia coin and a third, a bold affirmation of territorial boundaries.

Colossae's coins and the city's distinction from Laodikeia

Firstly, the homonoia coin. Homonoia coins are a particular feature of the provincial coinage of Asia and Thrace in the first three hundred years of the Roman empire.[103] Those cities that struck the coins were seen as significant in provincial political relations such that the minting fulfills some agenda in those rela-

99 On the natural environment of Colossae, see Cadwallader, *Fragments of Colossae*, 47–52, 135–41.

100 See Appendix 1.

101 Xenophon, *Anab.* 1.2.6 (allusively repeated by Nicetas Choniates, *Chron.* 178.19 a millennium and a half later), Herodotos 7.30, Diodorus Siculus 14.80.5; Polyaenus *Strat.* 7.16.1.

102 See A. H. Cadwallader, "Honouring the Repairer of the Baths: A New Inscription from Kolossai," *Antichthon* 46 (2012): 150–83.

103 The curious exception to this eastern feature is Corinth, which although re-founded as a Roman colony, yet became incorporated into Hadrian's panhellenion and minted an alliance coin with Patrae (*CONCORD CORINT ET PATR*). Mary Walbank describes it as "a Roman version of the well-known *Homonoia* coins struck by the Greek cities of Asia Minor"; see her

tionships.[104] Commercial privileges remain one of the contenders on the agenda of inter-city relations, though these may be generated by intermittent crises as much as fostering longer-term economic advantages.[105] But trade has been seen as far from the only, or predominant factor, behind the negotiation of alliances that are reflected in the coins. Crucial here is the larger Roman setting that cultivated competition for imperial favor *within* the ideology and enforcement of *concordia*.[106] Concord was privileged as one of the cardinal virtues of empire.

Plate 4.8: Denarius (18 mm, 3.18 g) featuring SABINA AUGUSTA, Hadrian's wife on the obverse, paired with CONCORDIA AUG(usta) on the reverse, personified as a standing woman, resting on a column, holding a patera of pious sacrifice in her right hand and double cornucopia in her left.[107] Here monumentality, religious reverence and overflowing prosperity are woven together with familial serenity, all as the mark of empire.

Along with extolling the benefits of *concordia* (*homonoia*, the Greek equivalent), came the enforcement. As we have noted in the previous chapter, in late 130, a long-running dispute between Hierapolis and Tripolis with Laodikeia, reached an intensity that demanded the intervention of the emperor.[108] Part of the arrangement laid out by Hadrian to the Hierapolitans for resolving the dispute, was that the quarreling was to cease and the parties were responsible for "implementing Concord among you" (πρυτανεύοντος ὑμῖν ὁμόνοιαν, l. 19). The editor of the inscription, Tullia Ritti, considers that the relatively early homonoia coins (Pl. 4.9) between Laodikeia and Hierapolis were a tan-

"Aspects of Corinthian Coinage in the Late 1st and early 2nd Centuries A. C." in *Corinth: The Centenary 1896–1996* edited by C. K. Williams II and N. Bookidis (Corinth Vol XX; Princeton: American School of Classical Studies at Athens, 2003), 342.

104 On the variety of reasons behind homonoia coins, see Ursula Kampmann, "*Homonoia* Politics in Asia Minor: The Example of Pergamon," in *Pergamon: Citadel of the Gods: Archaeological Record, Literary Description, and Religious Development* edited by H. Koester (Harvard Theological Studies: Harrisburg, PA: Trinity Press International, 1998), 373–93; Dietmar Kienast, "Die Homonoiaverträge in der römischen Kaiserzeit," *JNG* 14 (1964): 51–64.

105 See Francois Kirbihler "Les émissions de monnaies d'homonoia et les crises alimentaires en asie sous marc-aurèle," *REA* 108 (2006): 613–40.

106 See especially J. A. Lobur, *Consensus and Concordia and the Formation of Roman Imperial Ideology* (London/NY: Routledge, 2008).

107 *RIC* 2 Hadrian 390. Photograph from a private collection by permission.

108 See Tullia Ritti, *Hierapolis di Frigia IX: Storia e istituzioni di Hierapolis* (Istanbul: Ege, 2017), 388–95; Alan H. Cadwallader, "The Battle over Lake Lycus: Inter-city Conflict in the Lycus Valley," in *New Documents 12*, forthcoming.

gible expression and symbol of both parties abiding by the edict.[109] She is particularly taken by the fact that these two cities never entered into homonoia arrangements again, even though both were to receive subsequent neokorate status (which frequently lead to a flurry of homonoia mintings among cities).

Plate 4.9: One of the four varieties of homonoia coins struck between Laodikeia and Hierapolis (36 mm, 29.13 g) around 131 CE.[110] The reverse shows Zeus Aetophoros (eagle-bearer) on the left turned towards Apollo Kitharoidos (kithara player) on the right, the respective patron deities of the cities. Another type reverses the two gods, suggesting that both cities, through their mints, took responsibility for registering their concord. The perimeter legend on the reverse reads "Concord (homonoia) of the Hierapolitans and the Laodikeians."

Even though Laodikeia and Hierapolis were often collated in the Roman mind (as seen in the Xanthos' senator inscription mentioned above), this often concealed tensions in their relationship. The eruption here must have been substantial to warrant Hadrian's intervention. We need to keep this in mind for the "neighborly" triangulation of three Lycus Valley cities so constructed by early and contemporary interpreters of the Letter to the Colossians. Proximity did not always promote neighborliness.

Consequently, when we approach Colossae's homonoia coin, we need to bear in mind that there may be tension in the air, though not necessarily of the same kind as that between Hierapolis and Laodikeia. There are two known specimens of the coin, (probably) of the same die.[111]

Plate 4.10: Homonoia coin between Colossae and Aphrodisias from the early sole rule of Commodus. The sponsor of the coin, probably minted at Colossae, was Claudius Priscus, whose name appears in the interior field of the reverse. Here the clasping of hands by the two city Tyches (a common alternative to the patron deities of the cities) is patent, quite different from the gesture in Pl. 4.9 above.[112]

109 T. Ritti, E. Miranda and F. Guizzi, "La ricerca epigrafica: risultati dell'ultimo quadrennio e prospettive future," in *Hierapolis di Frigia I: Le attività delle campagne di scavo e restauro 2000–2003*, edited by F. D'Andria and M. Piera Caggia (Istanbul: Ege, 2007), 589; Ritti, *Storia e istituzione*, 395.

110 Franke–Nollé, *Die Homonoia-Münzen Kleinasiens*, 799–801, 1148–51; *BMC Phrygia*, Hierapolis 162 = Laodikeia 270; see also *RPC* 3.2356, 2357, 2358. Photograph courtesy of *CNG coins*.

111 *RPC online* 4.2.2446 temp. The diameter is identical for both coins (34 mm), the weight 28.49 g and 22.43 g respectively.

112 Photograph from the H. I. Collection by permission.

One of the specimens was published by David MacDonald, from a private collection, in 1983.[113] He dated it, on the basis of stylistic features of the laureate bust of Commodus, to 180/181 CE.[114] Nomenclature enables greater precision. Commodus' titular formality from 176 to 180 was Caesar Lucius Aurelius Commodus Augustus. In October of 180 "Lucius" was replaced by Marcus.[115] The use of Σεβαστός with "Lucius" for Commodus pictured alone on coins therefore has a narrow time-frame: between March (the death of Marcus Aurelius) and October of 180 CE.

The key question is to discern the reason for this alliance. No single rationale covers every homonoia arrangement just as no single rationale usually explains any individual instance completely. However, some cities appear to have negotiated homonoia relationships less for the connection with a particular city as for the cultivation of recognition at a wider level: regional, provincial even imperial. Ursula Kampmann has argued that the reason Laodikeia sought to establish repeated homonoia relationships with Pergamon, Smyrna and Ephesos was initially to siphon prestige for its own ambitions from their neokorate status.[116] As willing as these big three were to receive Laodikeia's initiative, they did not respond in kind with their own mintings advertising the homonoia arrangements. Laodikeia had quickly been dismissed from neokorate contention in the first century, when Smyrna's claim on longevity, beauty and prestige secured the prize. However, Laodikeia's political elite worked assiduously to attract recognition from the leading neokorate cities secured through negotiated homonoia relationships (and their numismatic advertisement) along with associated festivals and games,[117] to assemble its own position of claim. That honor has recently been adjudged to have arrived with the visit of Hadrian in 129 CE, earlier than has hitherto been thought. The newly-recovered statue base inscription is succinct but revealing: "The city of the Laodikeians,

113 D. J. MacDonald, "The *Homonoia* of Colossae and Aphrodisias," *JNG* 33 (1983): 25–27 and plate 9.2, repeated in his *The Coinage of Aphrodisias* (London: Royal Numismatic Society, 1992), 155. This was reproduced by Franke and Nollé, *Die Homonoia-Münzen Kleinasien*, 993 (with plate) but with a "correction" of the obverse legend to read AYT KAI Λ AY instead of AYT KAI Λ AP. The latter is correct.

114 Sideburns but no beard mark the stylistics of Commodus in 180 CE.

115 It seems that the close observance of his titles reached across the empire. This particular title is not evidenced in inscriptions from Aphrodisias or Colossae. It is rare on provincial coins (see *RPC online* 4.2.2109 temp. [homonoia between Laodikeia and Nikomedia]; *RPC online* 4.2.292, 293, 294, 295, 296 temp. [Smyrna; the last a homonoia coin with Nikomedia], but all without the CE(βαστός) (Augustus).

116 U. Kampmann, *Die Homonoia-Verbindungen der Stadt Pergamon, oder, Der Versuch einer kleinasiatischen Stadt unter römischer Herrschaft eigenständige Politik zu betreiben* (Saarbrücken: Saarbrücker Druckerei, 1996), 58.

117 Luigi Moretti, *Iscrizioni Agonistiche Greche* (Rome: Signorelli, 1953), 174–79, nr. 65 (inscription in Rome recording games at Laodikeia, dated c. 60 CE).

guardian of the temple (*neokoros*) (set this up for) the Emperor Caesar Trajan Hadrian Augustus Olympios, benefactor and savior of the world (*kosmos*)."[118]

At this time, Colossae's mint was just underway and requiring concerted attention and munificence to ensure that the city's emerging self-confidence would not take another dent, especially if, as the inscription's editor, Francesco Guizzi, suggests, the announcement of *neokoros* was made at Laodikeia as part of Hadrian's pan-hellenic tour. However, there is no mention in the inscription of the proper authority for the award of neokorate status, namely, the Senate. This appears to have sullied Laodikeia's claim; the city never proclaimed a "twice neokoros" status.[119] I have argued elsewhere, that it is more likely that Laodikeia was proclaiming its *local* neokorate of the Zeus temple, perhaps in the context of joining Olympian Hadrian syntheotically with its own patron god.[120]

Laodikeia's second bite at the neokoros cherry, early in the reign of Commodus,[121] was more regular in its process and it seems to have brought on one of the familiar responses to the award of "guardian of the imperial cult". Cities that either were part of the bidding war for the honor, or, more usually, simply reacting to the swell of attention (games, festivals, lavish delegations, building projects) that heralded the award, sought to reaffirm both to its own citizens and to others peeved at the glory lavished on the honorand, that they too had a claim on dignity, honor and status. This time, in 180 CE, the award for Laodikeia was senatorial and Colossae, along with a number of cities, reacted. In other words, the award of neokorate status ushered in a period of culture wars where cities worked to reaffirm their own standing. Homonoia coins were an instrument used to achieve this,[122] and they were supported by a marked artistic advance. In Colossae's case, we see this especially with the coins minted in Commodus' reign. The Artemis-in-a-biga coin noted previously (Pl. 4.6) is but one of several coins of exquisite artisan's skill.[123]

118 Αὐτοκράτορα Καί- | σαρα Τραιανὸν Ἁ- | δριανὸν Σεβασ- | τὸν Ὀλύνπιον ἡ νεω- | κόρος Λαοδικέων | πόλις τὸν εὐεργέτην | καὶ σωτῆρα τοῦ κόσ- | μου. Francesco Guizzi, "Greek and Latin Inscriptions," 175.

119 See further chapter 11.

120 See my "The Lust for Recognition and Influence: Laodikeia and the Quest for Neokorate Status," in *Revelation, the Aegean and Material Culture* edited by A. Keddie, D. Smith and N. Leach (London: Routledge, 2023), forthcoming.

121 Barbara Burrell makes a strong case for the grant of the neokorate to Laodikeia early in the reign of Commodus, at the same time as the neokorate granted to Nikomedia in the province of Bithynia: B. Burrell, *Neokoroi: Greek Cities and Roman Emperors* (Leiden: Brill, 2004), 119–20.

122 C. Howgego, "Coinage and Identity in the Roman Provinces," in *Coinage and Identity in the Roman Provinces* edited by C Howgego, V. Heuchert and A. Burnett (Oxford: Oxford University Press, 2005), 2.

123 See also chapter 1, Plate 1.7, item xvi).

Claude Vermeule described the Colossian coin featuring the full frontal display of Helios riding in a quadriga (chapter 2, Pl. 2.1a) as "one of the most startling compositions of all Greek numismatics".[124] Two general minted types of the iconography are known, one by an individual benefactor,[125] the other apparently by the city authorities (possibly the *Dêmos* itself).[126] At the very least, the Colossian leadership was reassuring its own citizens that Colossae's cultural and regional heritage stood proud and significant even in the shadow of strutting Laodikeia.[127] The obverse of both coins has the head of the personified, youthful *Dêmos* — a signal of who took responsibility for the creation of the coin (albeit one financed by a certain Apollonios II). It probably explains why Colossae did not resort to its patron god, Zeus, in the iconography of the *homonoia* coin, but turned to its city Tyche. Any hint of Zeus with Laodikeian features would have severely undermined the program of civic reassurance.

Multiple homonoia-types from the time of Elagabalus

The pseudo-homonoia coins minted during the reign of Elagabalus seem to address similar concerns, even if no actual city alliance was arranged. The exact impact of the award of a second neokorate to Laodikeia is difficult to plot. The *damnatio memoriae* imposed on Commodus seems to have tarnished the first honor, however stringently Laodikeia had, this time, followed the proper procedure for its conferral. It appears that a renewal of that award occurred late in the reign of Caracalla, perhaps on the occasion of his visit to Laodikeia in 215–216 CE. However, the formalities do not seem to have been sealed until Elagabalus succeeded as emperor in 216.[128] Laodikeia (on the evidence to date), did not proclaim a "twice neokoros", unlike Ephesos. Even the homonoia coins

---

124 C. C. Vermeule, *Roman Imperial Art in Greece and Asia Minor* (Cambridge, MA: Belknap Press, 1968), 164. Its artistry is certainly superior to similar designs on other civic coinage of the time: see, for example, *RPC online* 4.2.2832 temp. (Mytilene), 4.2.1547 temp. (Thyateira), 4.2.1342 temp. (Mostene).

125 *RPC online* 4.2.1897 temp.

126 *RPC online* 4.2.1899 temp. The minting of this iconography seems to have been quite prolific, as indicated by the various placements of the ethnic ΚΟΛΟCCΗΝΩΝ on the obverse: for the civic type, below the forelegs of the horses, around the perimeter; for the sponsor in a variety of arrangements, with the ΑΝΕΘΗΚΕ(Ν) sometimes intruding into the field.

127 So too Aphrodisias: three of Aphrodisias's seven or eight alliances fall in the reign of Commodus, probably as a direct consequence of Laodikeia's receipt of the neokorate. There is a later indication of the rivalry between Laodikeia and Aphrodisias, when provincial boundaries were reorganized: *I.Laodikeia Lykos* 10. Similarly Hierapolis had a small surge in its alliance coins at this time, striking them with three cities.

128 So Burrell, *Neokoroi*, 123.

between Laodikeia and Ephesos allow the latter's "thrice neokoros" at the time when Laodikeia supposedly gained the "second" award.[129]

There are three coins with twin facing temples in the iconography of Laodikeia's neokorate coins;[130] the use of visual communication may have been a classic visual misdirection, a substitute for the absence of epigraphical or legislative testimony. These coins mainly come from the time of Elagabalus but Laodikeia retained ΝΕΩΚΟΡΟϹ in coin legends through to the time of Philip 1 (244–249 CE).[131] But the city mint never added the "B". It did add ΔΟΓΜΑΤΙ ϹΥΝΚΛΗΤΟΥ "by the decree of the Senate" repeatedly. This addition is known only on one other civic coin, a single issue from the Ephesian mint on the occasion of the award of its fourth neokorate, a coin that squeezes four temple facades onto the reverse field.[132] Given that no coin of Laodikeia prior to the reign of Elagabalus, adds *neokoros* to the legend, one is strengthened in the suspicion that there was something irregular about the award in the time of Hadrian (if that is what it was). Perhaps Hadrian had breached the formal allocation boundaries — Asia, after all, was a senatorial province, and the Senate held the authority (even if formal) for making the award. More likely it was merely a local affair. But once able to add, without qualification, the esteemed *neokoros* to its titulature, Laodikeia threw itself into associated parades of its eminence — the holder of the Koinon of Asia games, the Asklepeion festival, the "Sacred World games" — and dared to portray itself as the metropolis not only for Phrygia, but also of Caria,[133] well before a new province of Phrygia Pacatiana was created by Diocletian around 295 CE.

Other cities, faced with this promethean display, were compelled to match their requisite imperial acknowledgement with assertions of their own value and honor. Colossae at this time had a singular advantage. Because the conferring/confirming emperor, Elagabalus, was a devotee and self-proclaimed high-priest of the sun god Elagabal, Colossae's long-standing Heliotic self-portrayal wedded neatly with the latest imperial fashion. Other cities, as we have seen, scrambled to appropriate the radiate sun-god for their coins, Ephesos among them.[134] Colossae harvested this sycophantic flattery with what appears to be a pseudo-homonoia coin. All the formal visual signals of a homonoia coin are present in one issue during the time of Elagabalus.

129 *RPC online* 6.5520 temp.
130 *RPC online* 6.5502, 5503 temp., 8.ID20763.
131 *RPC online* 8.ID20763 temp.
132 *RPC online* 6.4867 temp.
133 R*PC online* 6.5519, 8.ID20766, 8.ID58864.
134 See *RPC online* 6.4884 temp., 4898 temp., 4906 temp. These are the only coins of Ephesos featuring Helios — all from the time of Elagabalus.

Plate 4.11: Colossian coin (41 mm, 33.90 g) with Elagabalus on the obverse and a homonoia display on the reverse, featuring Artemis Ephesiaca with mural head-piece (a kalathos) and veil, and holding staves with stags beside her feet and, at the right, Tyche Poliadic, that is with mural head-piece, rudder in her right hand and cornucopia in her left, and resting on a pedestal. The perimeter legend simply reads KO | ΛO | C | CHN | ΩN but in the upper field are the letters OT | Θ.[135]

The absence of the ethnic ΕΦΕCΙΩΝ indicates that this coin was not inscribing a formal homonoia arrangement even though, as we have seen with Laodikeia's twin temple coins, the visual may be deliberately designed to evoke what cannot be named in the legend, the moreso given that Artemis is on the left, the usual (though not ubiquitous) position of the minting authority in official alliance coins. In this sense, it appears that the Colossian authorities are fostering a calculated public exercise for local consumption. This is compounded by the letters OTΘ. Hans von Aulock suggested (but no more) that the letters might stand for ὁμονοία τῶν θέων, the "alliance of the gods."[136] The appeal to the concord of the gods taps into one of the major planks of imperial ideology, namely that the homonoia of the Caesars, the *concordia augustorum*, mirrored the homonoia of the gods, the *concordia deorum*.[137]

It would be quite a claim by Colossae, even with its privileged environment beneath the towering Mount Cadmus, (another) home of Zeus and the gods. Imperial sensitivities are not completely absent however, not simply because of the emperor's portrait on the obverse. An Antonine emperor had apparently delivered a rescript, preserved in Justinian's *Digest*, that a proconsul should travel to the province of Asia by sea and arrive at Ephesos, dubbed "the first of all the metropolitan centers" (καὶ τῶν μητροπόλεων ἔφεσον *primam*).[138] Paul Trebilco thinks it a rescript of Antoninus Pius, but Barbara

135 *SNG von Aulock* 3771; *MSPhryg* 2.592, 593 = *RPC online* 6.5521 temp. Photograph from the H. I. collection, by permission.

136 von Aulock, *Münzen und Städte Phrygiens*, 93, notes to nrs 592, 593.

137 L. de Blois, *The Policy of the Emperor Gallienus* (Leiden: Brill, 1976), 110; S. Williams, *Diocletian and the Roman Recovery* (London: Routledge, 2000 [1985]), 58. Note also Lobur, *Consensus and Concordia* loc. cit.

138 *Dig.* 1.16.4.5 (Ulpian; a rare example of Greek being used in the *Digest*, strongly indicative of the language Antoninus Pius used for the rescript). The *Digest* claims the rescript was a response to the petition of "the Asians" (*ad desideria Asianorum*). One can only speculate as to how agreement for such an honor was reached. More likely, the rivalry between Smyrna, Pergamon and Ephesos could not be decided by the koinon of Asia and the emperor's decision was elicited.

Burrell brings it considerably later to the time of Caracalla.[139] This section of the *Digest*, on the duties of a proconsul, is excerpted from Ulpian, who writes that it was a decision of "our Emperor Antoninus Augustus" (*imperator noster Antoninus Augustus*). Ulpian was secretary to Caracalla, an Antonine emperor, and wrote most of his works during his reign; so, Burrell is likely correct, especially given that Elagabalus, also a (manufactured) Antonine emperor, banished Ulpian. Accordingly, Colossae's choice of the imperially backed Ephesos for the coin is aligning its loyalties profoundly to a city (and through it to an emperor) that carried a status beyond that banked (and bank-rolled) by Colossae's more immediate neighbor, Laodikeia. It is no surprise then to find that Artemis the hunter is replaced by Artemis Ephesiaca on this coin (and on another of the Elagabalus series at Colossae — see below). However, Artemis the hunter returned under the sponsorship of the Colossian *stephanephoros*, Aurelius Markianos son of Epaphras, in the reign of Trebonianus Gallus, but contemporaneous with a coin of Gallus's co-emperor, his son Volusian (251–253 CE) with Artemis Ephesiaca on the reverse.[140]

Since the publication of this singular coin type, two smaller coin types from the time of Elagabalus have surfaced that carry variations of the seeming-acronym. One bears only ΘO (Pl. 4.12), which might be a retrograde legend for ὁμονοία θέων but doubt must attend this.[141] However, the coin also pairs deities, with two female gods facing one another as in a homonoia pose, both with trailing braided locks of hair in archaic style — a deliberate evocation of ancient standing.

Plate 4.12: The coin (35 mm, 17.85 g) of Colossae featuring Elagabalus on the obverse and the two Nemeseis on the reverse with the simply perimeter legend KOΛOC | CH | N | Ω | N with ΘO in the exergue.[142]

139 P. Trebilco "Asia" in *The Book of Acts in its First Century Setting. Vol 2 Graeco-Roman Setting* edited by D. W. J. Gill and C. Gempf (Grand Rapids, MI: Eerdmans, 1994), 305 n56; Burrell, *Neokoroi*, 289.

140 *RPC online* 9.789. For the coin of Volusian, see chapter 1.

141 *RPC online* 6.10829 temp.

142 Photograph from the Erdem collection by permission.

The publishing editors called them "two Nemesis",[143] while the editors of *RPC online* settle for "two female figures ... placing hand next to their mouth".[144] In fact, the design is modeled on one of the repeated issues of the city of Smyrna that incorporate the ancient tradition of twin Nemeseis as foundational for the city's life. These feature as the city's patron(s) on homonoia coins.[145] The posture of both women has their right hand touching their chiton at the shoulder. The figure on the right holds what is probably a cubit (possibly a short scepter) and the figure on the left holds what is probably a bridle.[146] The clinching of the identification comes in the faint remains of a wheel at the right foot of the figure on the right, identifiable from a magnified photograph. It is the unmistakable symbol of Nemesis, known at Colossae from a gladiator fragment which has an honorific herm with a wheel at its base — Nemesis was the favored deity governing the fortunes of the combative arena.[147] So Nemesis's presence in the Colossian panorama of religious devotion is confirmed. However, the pairing, whilst known on some coins outside Smyrna in a similar wingless iconography,[148] remained unequivocally the symbol of Smyrna. The homonoia posture thus attracts a larger signification for the Colossian leadership. It is designed for local consumption, that is, evoking a relationship of concord with Smyrna, however unofficial it may have been.

Colossae's numismatic territorial claim

The next Elagabalus coin from Colossae is perhaps the most arresting of all and takes us into our third example of numismatic witness to tensions between Colossae and Laodikeia.[149] Again it features a pair of deities, in fact two pairs, and raises enormous questions not merely of concerns about local

143 O. Tekin and A. Yacı, *SNG: Turkey 11, The Çetin Erdem Collection* (Istanbul: TEBE, 2019), nr. 498. They record the letters as TO Θ but I cannot see the *tau*.

144 The same comment is made for a similar coin from Temnus: *RPC online* 6.4617 temp.

145 For example, *RPC* 2.1079, 1081 (Ephesos and Smyrna, time of Domitian); *RPC online* 4.2.2909 temp. (Cyzicus and Smyrna, time of Commodus); 4.2.1068 temp. (Miletus and Smyrna, time of Antoninus Pius); 4.2.2107 temp. (Laodikeia and Smyrna, time of Marcus Aurelius). A later homonoia coin between Philadelphia and Smyrna, from the time of Trajan Decius has a single large Tyche holding in her hand cult statues of the two Nemeseis.

146 Compare *RPC* 3.1966 (Smyrna).

147 See chapter 10.

148 *RPC online* 4.2.11524 temp. (Philadelphia); 6.4620 temp. (Temnus, time of Elagabalus); 4.4.15261 temp. (with Apollo; Alexandria time of Antoninus Pius); 6.5646 temp. (Dionysopolis).

149 A second example was identified by Dario Calomino of the *RPC online* project. It was a retooled coin to show falsely Neapolis in Samaria, held at the Bibliothèque de France: https://gallica.bnf.fr/ark:/12148/btv1b8498117n.

civic self-confidence but also of Colossae's ambition in mounting at least a symbolic challenge to its larger neighbor.[150]

Plate 4.13: Colossian coin (37 mm, 24.18 g) featuring Elagabalus on the obverse and on the reverse, a seated Tyche holding a cult statue of Artemis Ephesiaca in her right hand and a cornucopia in her left. Two river gods recline beneath, the named Lycus (albeit worn) on the left and named Kapros on the right. Fish swim in the waters. The letters ΟΤΘ or Ο ☥ Θ are placed in the field below the chair, depending on how the circle is interpreted.[151]

Again homonoia relationships are visually presented, with the poliadic Tyche of Colossae holding the cult statue of the Ephesian Artemis, and two river gods, the Lycus and the Kapros, facing one another. So, as part of a competitive self-definition from neokorate Laodikeia, the three known Elagabalus coins from Colossae all accent homonoia relationships, even if no formal homonoia-alliance is named in the legend. Concord may not have been high on Colossae's list of priorities in the relationship with Laodikeia, but its adherence to the key Roman imperial value is manifest. Because the three Elagabalus coins are quite large,[152] other lower-value coins can be expected. Two have surfaced thus far.[153]

It is the consistent visual aesthetics proclaiming concord that adds weight to von Aulock's speculation that the homonoia of the gods may be proclaimed (with Colossae as a, if not, *the* civic focus!). But the presence of ☥ in this coin raises some difficulties. A number of possibilities arise, not all as compelling:

i) The small circle may be a roller for movement of Tyche's chair (as in a procession) and thus of no letter significance;
ii) It may be an unprecedented Egyptian ankh sign (meaning "life") similar to its use by some Christian scribes' transformation of the letter *tau* especially when writing C☥ΑΥΡΟC ("cross");[154]

---

150 See chapter 3.

151 *RPC online* 6.10900 temp. Photograph courtesy of Leu Numismatik. The *RPC* editors have not noted the faint letters of ΛΥΚΟC. However, above the head of the left rivergod can be seen a faint ΛΥ then a fragment (= K) then faint OC, the lunate sigma touching the right knee of Tyche. There has to be something interrupting the flow of K to ΟΛΟC | CΗΝΩΝ in the civic identifier, and this confirms the reading. So both rivers are named.

152 Artemis Ephesiaca and Colossian Tyche 41 mm av, 30.54 g. av.; river gods 37 mm av., 22.66 g av.; Nemeseis 35 mm, 17.85 g.

153 See chapter 1, Plate 1.7, items xxii), xxiii).

154 See Lk 9:23 𝔓[75] where a ligature of the *tau* and *rho* is thought to deliberately evoke the ankh sign — also found in Sahidic manuscripts of the Second Testament and the "Gospel of Truth" in the Jung Codex. J. B. Lightfoot was so taken by the evocative symbolism that he used it as

iii) The TO, especially in this ankh-style ligature, may be intended as an abbreviation,[155] such as τόπος ὁμονοίας θέων, a writ-large conception familiar from the inscribed place markers given to recognized associations in civic or religious functions,[156] and/or the location given to a sanctuary of a god.[157]

Plate 4.14: At Magnesia-on-Maeander in the large paved area between the propylon (monumental gateway) and the temple of Artemis Leukophryene, numerous "topos" markers are inscribed on the eastern and western perimeters of the pavement, locations for groups (mainly associations) involved in processions and formal gatherings.[158] Here a compact inscription designates τόπος γυναικῶν, "The Place of Women/Wives,"[159] beneath a more expansive (partly out of picture) τό(πος) πνευστωτιόν(ου) (?).

iv) If however, the ankh-style TO is the definite article, then we might be dealing with a coded date of sorts. This articular usage occurs on an Augustan coin of Hierapolis, as TO Γ, meaning (in office) "for the third time".[160] Von

---

the logo for his commentaries. The suggestion came from his life-long friend Brooke Foss Westcott: Westcott to Lightfoot Feb 3rd 1864 "Letters to Joseph Barber Lightfoot" Dean and Chapter Library, Durham Cathedral.

155 M. Avi-Yonah, *Abbreviations in Greek Inscriptions (The Near East 200 BC – AD 1100)* (London: Oxford University Press, 1940), 105. See, for example, E. A. H. Petersen and F. von Luschan, *Reisen im südwestlichen Kleinasien II: Reisen in Lykien, Milyas und Kobyratis* (Vienna: Ministerium für Cultus und Unterricht, 1889), 29.37 (Myra); *TAM* II 816 (Arykanda). Sometimes τόπ is used as the abbreviation; see Charlotte Roueché, *Partisans and Performer at Aphrodisias* (London: Society for the Promotion of Roman Studies, 1993), 45.12,R.

156 See, for example, τόπος βαφέων "The Place of the Dyers", which may be a shop entrance paver: Şimşek, *Laodikeia*, 123, pl. 47n.

157 R. N. Frye, *et al.*, "Inscriptions from Dura-Europos," *YCIS* 14 (1955): 129–31, nr. 2 (Dura Europos, 37 CE); *SEG* 42.609 (Leukopetra, 171 CE).

158 See Kristoph Jürgens, "Pilgrimage and procession in the Panhellenic festivals: Some observations on the Hellenistic Leukophryena in Magnesia-on-the-Meander," in *Excavating Pilgrimage: Archaeological Approaches to Sacred Travel and Movement in the Ancient World* edited by T. M. Kristenden and W. Friese (London: Routledge, 2017), 87–105.

159 Compare *MAMA* 11.99 (Akmoneia). The Magnesia inscription is noted in O. Bingöl, *Magnesia on the Meander, Magnesia ad Maeandrum: the city of Artemis with "white eyebrows"* (Galatasaray: Homer Kitanevi, 2007), 87. For general discussion see Richard S. Ascough, "Carving out Public Space. τόπος Inscriptions and Early Christ Groups," in *Epigraphik und Neues Testament* edited by T. Corsten, M. Öhler and J. Verheyden (WUNT 365; Tübingen: Mohr Siebeck, 2016), 93–110.

160 *RPC* 1.2956 cf *RPC online* 6.4479 temp. (Sardis).

Aulock had rejected a dating option given that ΟΤΘ conveys a nonsensical year 379. However ΤΟ ΟΘ would mean year 79. Coins of Dionysopolis in the upper Maeander Valley, from the time of Elagabalus have ΤΟ Ο (year 70),[161] implying a counting from the year 152/3, in the reign of Antoninus Pius.[162] This only gets us so far. However, the Θ (9) might indicate the 9th Antonine emperor (on a contorted reckoning that omits some brief interlopers). The *Historia Augusta* records a priestess of Caelestis at Carthage foretelling eight Antonines.[163] Though the writer saw Elagabalus as the eighth and last, there were some short-lived emperors who might push Elagabalus into the 9th — the capstone as it were on the succession. It is difficult to have confidence in this option.

Of greater pertinence is a coin from the time of Volusian (251–253 CE) which, quite clearly adds a date into the field — ΤΟ ΡΙΑ, that is the year 111.[164] This cannot be conformed to the letters of the Elagabalus coins read as a date, except if ΤΟ ΟΘ, year 79 is accepted. The year 111 suggests 139/140 CE, for which no foundation event akin to Laodikeia's recalibration of its dating (under Caracalla) to the visit of Hadrian in 129 CE is known for Colossae. But it does demonstrate that date calculations may be a consideration for the Elagabalus coins.

For now, the most compelling option seems the third, if only because of the weight of homonoia presentation in the iconography of the three coins. The fourth also remains possible. But reserve must continue to attend these interpretations of the coin legends. What can be affirmed is that Colossae is presenting itself aesthetically as a city of Concord (and of fine artistry in its coin design!) — far from the only provincial example of such mimesis of a Roman ideal.[165] But the concord *of the gods* had a more ancient pedigree. A scholion of the fifth century neo-platonic philosopher, Hermias of Alexandria, on Plato's *Phaedra*, distilled the Platonic philosophy: "For the gods are those who shine grace on all the world and, through grace, we engage concord with the gods." (Οἱ γὰρ θεοί εἰσιν οἱ καὶ τὴν χάριν ἐπιλάμποντες παντὶ τῷ κόσμῳ, καὶ διὰ χάριτος καὶ ὁμονοίας συναπτόμεθα τοῖς θεοῖς).[166] Such appeal to antiquity was part of Colossae's overall tactic to maintain her recognized standing, an appeal that also coincided with Rome's own values — not just *concordia* but *antiquitas*.

161 *RPC online* 6.5649, 5650, 5657 temp.

162 It is speculated that this might refer to an annual festival or commemoration, perhaps celebrating the benevolence of Antoninus Pius following devastating earthquakes in 151/152 CE. See F. Imhoof-Blumer, *Kleinasiatische Münzen I* (Vienna: Alfred Hölder, 1901), 222.

163 *HA* 2.5–3.9.

164 *RPC online* 9.789A. See chapter 1.

165 See especially *I.Kition* 2009, a dedication to the goddess Homonoia along with other gods and the deified Caesar.

166 Hermias *Phaed. schol.* 3.216.

There is a sharp but mundane pointedness in the homonoia expressed in two-fold form in this last coin. This is the only instance where Colossae lays claim to the lavish beneficence (including fish!) of two river gods, the Lycus *and* the Kapros. Multiple river-gods are not unknown — Apameia even has a coin with four river-gods.[167] But the claim on the Lycus and Kapros has been, until this coin, the preserve of Laodikeia. One can understand that both Laodikeia and Colossae could claim the gifts of the Lycus given its length. But the Kapros flows within easy reach of the eastern gateway (the Syrian gate) to Laodikeia. For Colossae to mount a territorial claim with the Kapros as its western boundary seems bold, even if the minting was primarily for appreciation and use by the local population. It may be hyperbole; it may hark back to the early grievance of Colossae's loss of hegemony in the valley that accompanied the Seleucid foundation of Laodikeia in about 256/255 BCE, an hegemony that had included villages that pre-date Laodikeia (and hence were under Colossae's control), such as Kiddioukome and Babakome.[168] Certainly a constructed memory of the past shows itself at Colossae in the recycling of Homeric names, such as Tydeides, in first-second century nomenclature.[169] Herodotos and Xenophon were constantly referenced by later writers (including Josephus)[170] and though their writings hardly garnered widespread appreciation outside of literate circles, references to one's own city would have been excerpted and prized, a constant reminder of what had been. Indeed, historians of this time were sometimes honored by cities for their work on constructing the image of the city.[171]

And there is almost certainly a time when Colossae was drawn, willingly or unwillingly, into open conflict with Laodikeia. When Mithridates VI began his sweep south from his Pontus kingdom through Apameia and into the Lycus Valley, inviting heavily taxed and disgruntled Asians to revolt against the Romans, he mounted a massive siege campaign against Laodikeia and its harboring of the Roman general Quintus Oppius (88 BCE).[172] We are not told specifically of Colossae joining the rebellion but, as Josephus's detailed account of the siege of Jerusalem shows, massive resources would have been needed to sustain the besieging army. Josephus writes of the culling of wood and food up to a dis-

---

167 *RPC* 7.1.699. Usually Apameia is content with two rivers, the Maeander and Marsyas: *RPC online* 4.2.11580 temp. (time of Commodus); 8.ID20586 temp. (time of Philip I).

168 *I.Laodikeia Lykos* 1 (dated 267 BCE). See the discussion in chapter 3.

169 Tydeides (the companion of Odysseus and tamer of horses: *Od* 3.181, 4.280, *Il.* 5.1–26) occurs in the list of names honoring Korymbos, the repairer of Colossae's baths. See A. H. Cadwallader, "Honouring the Repairer of the Baths: A New Inscriptions from Kolossai," *Antichthon* 46 (2012): 167–8. On the general point, see G. H. R. Horsley, "Homer in Pisidia: Aspects of the History of Greek Education in a Remote Roman Province," *Antichthon* 34 (2000): 46–81.

170 See, for example, Josephus *C. Apion* 1.16; Diogenes Laertius 3.34; Aulus Gellius 14.3.

171 See M. Chin, "Honours for Historians: Historiography and Civic Identity in the Hellenistic and Roman Polis (Third Century BCE to Third Century CE)," MRes, Macquarie University, 2015.

172 Appian *Mith.* 24; Strabo 12.8.16.

tance of 100 *stadia* away, that is 12.5 miles (20 kilometers);[173] this is more than enough to embrace the precincts of the city of Colossae and extract its rich supplies of wood and food. Mithridates's siege objective, namely the handing over of Oppius, seems to have been achieved quicker than the objective behind the siege of Jerusalem, so that Oppius's rescue request sent to Aphrodisias was ultimately not activated.[174] However, Mithridates remained in substantial control of the Lycus Valley for some time, until the drive from Sulla gained traction for the ultimate demise of Mithridates' campaign in 83 BCE. That demise also spelled the demise of Colossae's mint, whether as punishment from Rome or simply because of the fraught economic consequences that beset Asia after Sulla's pacification.[175] Certainly, according to Christian Marek, "it seemed to the Romans that the Greeks of Asia had been perfidious almost without exception."[176] Laodikeia, with little remaining loyalist capital, frantically tried to rebuild her standing with Rome, ensuring a very public statement of her gratitude to Rome with a bilingual inscription accompanying a statue of Populus Romanus erected on the Capitoline Hill in Rome, a statement (again?) renewed with a re-cut inscription in the first century CE.[177] Oppius seems to have allowed the benefit of the doubt to Laodikeia, as there is no recriminatory language about Laodikeia's embroilment in his besiegement and capture.[178]

There is no doubt that Colossae lost political and economic control of a considerable number of villages and agricultural estates that had fuelled its importance under the Achaemenid regime.[179] Given that the Seleucid king's movement of Jews into Phrygia was designed to reinforce his hold in and from his own settlement foundations, it is likely that Colossae's recently-lost Persian credentials were remembered and the city was not a recipient of these immigrants. Colossae may even have lost territory in the promise of land granted to

173 Josephus *BJ* 6.375–6.

174 See J. Reynolds, *Aphrodisias and Rome* (London: Society for the Promotion of Roman Studies, 1982), nrs 2, 3 and commentary.

175 See L. F. Carbone, "Money and Power: The Disappearance of Autonomous Silver Issues in the Roman Province of Asia," *Omni* 8 (2014): 10–34.

176 C. Marek, *In the Land of a Thousand Gods: A History of Asia Minor in the Ancient World* (Princeton: Princeton University Press, 2016), 273.

177 *CIL* 1^2 728: [i] From the people of Laodicea near the river Lycos; a statue 'The Roman People,' which people was their salvation, because of the kind deeds which it did kindly unto them. [ii] From the populace of Laodikeia near the Lycos; a statue 'The populace of the Romans' which have become its saviour and benefactor because of their virtue and good will towards it. See A. H. Cadwallader, "The Historical Sweep of the Life of Kolossai," in *Epigraphical Evidence Illustrating Paul's Letter to the Colossians* edited by J. Verheyden, M. Öhler and T. Corsten (WUNT 411; Tübingen: Mohr Siebeck, 2018), 50–1.

178 *I.Aphrodisias and Rome* 3, l. 22.

179 See N. Sekunda, "Changing Patterns of Land-Holding in the South-Western Border Lands of Greater Phrygia in the Achaemenid and Hellenistic Periods," in *Colossae in Space and Time*, 48–76.

these interlopers.[180] Such setbacks were probably replayed in the aftermath of the Mithridatic War, perhaps even after a second, short-lived siege of Laodikeia by the Roman rebel general Labienus in 40 BCE. One surviving inscription of a letter from Octavian in response to a petition from the city of Mylasa in Caria distills the brutal consequences of Labienus' sieges — a city overwhelmed, citizens captured as prisoners of war, if not killed and burned, the city aflame with no respect for religious institutions, farms sacked and burned.[181] Colossae and other settlements, whether lured by infatuation with former glory or not, would have been siphoned into such an attack on Laodikeia.[182]

Colossae's historical nostalgia for its strategic and economic pre-eminence may well lie behind the unique self-definition in its Elagabalus coin of the two river-gods, masquerading under an avowal of a religiously-imbued, hydrological homonoia. If Francesco Guizzi is correct in his speculation on a proconsular edict of water regulations of 114/5 or 115/6 CE that Laodikeia's water supply expropriated water resources of other cities,[183] historical nostalgia held a very present, sharp edge.[184]

The continuation of antagonism between Colossae and Laodikeia

The contest over water and its control is precisely what is revealed in the popular, early Byzantine story of "St Michael of Chonai", Chonai being the successor name for Colossae. It is probably to be dated to the late fourth or early fifth century. I have written on the importance of this story at length elsewhere and I refer readers to those essays.[185] The critical point here is that the attack on the sacred spring that held the patronage of the archangel Michael is orchestrated from Laodikeia by those who are gathered to that city's cause. In my view, the language is deliberately designed caustically to echo canon 35 of the Synod of Laodikeia (the anathema against the worship of angels) by turning it back on Laodikeia. Laodikeia is now the idolatrous

180 See A. H. Cadwallader, "On the Question of Comparative Method in Historical Research: Colossae and Chonai in Larger Frame," in *First Urban Churches 5*, 130–41.

181 *SIG* 3.768.

182 See generally, C. Hersh, "The Coinage of Quintus Labienus Parthicus," *SNR* 59 (1980): 41–3.

183 F. Guizzi, "An Edict of a Proconsul of Asia on the Aqueduct of Laodikeia (114/115 CE?)," in *15. Yılında Laodikeia (2003-2018)* edited by C. Şimşek (Istanbul: Ege, 2019), 154.

184 See further chapter 3.

185 A. H. Cadwallader, "Inter-city Conflict in the Story of St Michael of Chonai," in *Religious Conflict from Early Christianity to the Rise of Islam* edited by W. Mayer and B. Neil (Arbeiten zur Kirchengeschichte 121; Tübingen: de Gruyter, 2013), 109–28; "Epiphanies and religious conflict: the contests over the hagiasma of Chonai," in *Reconceiving Religious Conflict: New Views from the Formative Centuries of Christianity* edited by C. de Wet and W. Mayer (London: Routledge, 2018), 110–35.

center, not the places venerating the archangel (among which Colossae was eminent, though not directly named in the canon).[186] The etymology of the city's name is harshly inverted in the story. Laodikeia is dubbed "the city of the lawless mob" (ὁ λαὸς τῆς ἀδικίας) as the meaning of its name.[187] The fierce battle that ensued has Colossae/Chonai drawing on the munificent protection of the archangel for its everlasting survival. One cannot but suspect that in this Christian refashioning of an earlier foundation story for the sacred site, the long-desired reversal of Laodikeia's climb above Colossae has been achieved — at least in narrative fiction.

Christ-followers within contesting cities

Here we are brought back to the brief mentions of the three cities in the Letter to the Colossians (Col 2:1, 4:13, 15–16). These cities might be neighbors geographically but it has been shown that proximity did not always (or even often) foster neighborliness. Of course, it would be desirable to have more evidence, but if the thread of argument, piecing together what we do have, has sufficient strength, then these three cities ought not be assumed to dwell concordantly with one another (one set of homonoia coins, in the case of Laodikeia and Hierapolis, notwithstanding). The early Christ-followers in and from these cities could not help but be formed in the antagonism that came from city pride, an antagonism which built on a Hellenistic origin with plenty of Roman aggregation.[188] In any case, it is hardly manifest that early Christianity was a monochromatically consensus movement.[189]

Interpreters have struggled with the circulation of letters mentioned in Col 4:16: καὶ ὅταν ἀναγνωσθῇ παρ' ὑμῖν ἡ ἐπιστολή, ποιήσατε ἵνα καὶ ἐν τῇ Λαοδικέων ἐκκλησίᾳ ἀναγνωσθῇ, καὶ τὴν ἐκ Λαοδικείας ἵνα καὶ ὑμεῖς ἀναγνῶτε "And when the letter has been read among you, ensure that it is read in the assembly of the Laodikeians, as also read that from Laodikeia." The struggle for interpreters of this verse has been to recover an impinging context that may have warranted such an instruction. Frequently, the exchange of letters is turned into a nascent canonical formulation that saw the Pauline corpus turned into

186 For the possibility that Colossae may have received an adverse pun on its name in the canon, see chapter 2.

187 *S. Mich. Chon.* 11.10 (ed. Bonnet).

188 Compare L. L. Welborn, *An End to Enmity: Paul and the "Wrongdoer" of Second Corinthians* (BZNW 185; Berlin: de Gruyter, 2011).

189 A similar situation is conceived by James Harrison for the Christ-followers in Rome, formed as many (Gentile) members were, in the Roman negativity about Jews; see J. R. Harrison, *Reading Romans with Roman Eyes* (Lanham: Lewxington, 2020), 7–9.

addresses to all churches — if to and from Laodikeia, why not to all,[190] or, on the assumption that "Colossians" is little more than a cipher, to all the churches of the Lycus,[191] or, in reality, to the Laodikeians not the (defunct) Colossians.[192] These possibilities might be theologically attractive. Indeed they have led to the re-discovery (or rather, a type of *vaticinium ex eventu* creation) of a canonical Letter to the Laodikeians in the fourth century,[193] or the reformulation in modern times of the Letter to the Ephesians as the Letter to the Laodikeians.[194] But none satisfies historically or materially.

Something has prompted this exchange. Colossians is not, as Lukas Bormann insists, a "catholic" letter, even if there is a consciousness of Christ-followers in the Lycus Valley beyond Colossae.[195] Vicky Balabanski's "circular" letter, whilst confined to a Lycus Valley reception,[196] utilizes a terminology that is usually reserved for the now-named "Letter to the Ephesians." Such a classification itself draws on the understanding of imperial and pro-consular edicts such as we will see with the Augustan "good news" calendar adjustment.[197] The consequence is that the letter's "specific references to events or situations are much less prominent,"[198] precisely because the intention is for a series of audiences not a single location. Rather, Balabanski envisages various contexts finding some expression *in* the letter, the moreso because she follows an ancient explanation noted by John Chrysostom that verse 16 does not refer to a second Pauline Letter *to* the Laodikeians but rather an earlier Letter *from* the Laodikeian church (καὶ τὴν ἐκ Λαοδικείας).[199] Theodoret argued that a second Pauline Letter would have been expressed as πρὸς not ἐκ.[200]

This is where the Hadrianic Letters to Laodikeia, Hierapolis and Tripolis, resolving their disputation over fishing rights in Lake Lycus, become important.

190 J. D. G. Dunn, *The Epistles to the Colossians and Philemon*, (NIGTC; Grand Rapids, MI: Eerdmans, 1996), 286; D. M. Hay, *Colossians* (Nashville, TN: Abingdon, 2000), 163; M. M. Thompson, *Colossians and Philemon* (Grand Rapids, MI: Eerdmans, 2005), 108; L. Bormann, *Der Brief des Paulus an die Kolosser* (ThHK 10/1; Leipzig: Evangelische Verlagsanstalt, 2012), 197–8; S. McKnight, *The Letter to the Colossians* (NICNT; Grand Rapids, MI: Eerdmans, 2018), 396.

191 J. L. Sumney, *Colossians: A Commentary* (Louisville, KY: WJKP, 2008), 278–9.

192 A. Lindemann, *Der Kolosserbrief* (ZBKNT 10; Zurich: Theologischer Verlag, 1983), 36. The notion recurs in a varied form in M.-É. Boismard, "Paul's Letter to the Laodiceans," in *The Pauline Canon* edited by S. E. Porter (Leiden: Brill, 2004), 45–57.

193 Lightfoot recognized the somewhat feeble pseudepigraphy of the Letter to the Laodikeians. He provided a thorough analysis and even a Greek reconstruction of the extant Latin: *Colossians and Philemon*, 272–98.

194 See, as one exponent, D. A. Campbell, *Framing Paul: An Epistolary Biography* (Grand Rapids, MI: Eerdmans, 2014), 309–38.

195 Bormann, *Kolosser*, 197.

196 V. Balabanski, *Colossians: An Eco-Stoic Reading* (London: T & T Clark, 2020), 11.

197 See chapter 5.

198 Balabanski, *Colossians*, 13, 111.

199 Balabanski, *Colossians*, 163. Chrysostom *Hom. Col.* 12, on 4:12–13.

200 Theodoret *Comm. Col.* 4:16. (*PG* 82.625D).

This is not a general edict for empire-wide circulation; rather letters are addressed to specific polities in regard to their specific contentions with one another. Hadrian's Letter to the Hierapolitans (the only extant record, dated 130/131 CE) makes reference to his Letter to the Laodikeians, which he expects the Hierapolitans to know about: "From the matters I have written to the Laodikeians, you will apprehend my determinations concerning the issues you have been contesting against one another."[201] The Letter to the Hierapolitans distills the resolution that concerns Laodikeia's interests and then lays out what has been granted to the Hierapolitans and the Tripolitans. The extant letter was inscribed and placed either in the median diazoma of the main theater at Hierapolis or as part of the recently-excavated monumental altar to Hadrian and the Twelve Gods.[202] Presumably, the other two cities concerned made their own arrangements for public record.

Of course, an exchange of letters or simply a consciousness of what the "other" letter contains (as in the Hadrian communication), does not demand an imperial artifact for comparison. Some associations are known to send communications of their own decisions to other associations, either for common implementation or fraternal relations or both.[203] However, given what we have outlined about the long-running tensions between the civic entities of Laodikeia and Colossae, Hadrian's further call for an expression of concord in the fishing rights inscription (l. 19) has some important implications not merely as an insight into general civic relations in the Lycus Valley, but also for the received cultural ambience carried into relationships between the *ekklêsiai* in Laodikeia and Colossae. We know of two specific churches (*ekklêsiai*) in this period — that of Philemon (Phmn 2) and that of Nympha (Col 4:15).[204] How-

---

201 ἐξ ὧν πρὸς Λαοδικεῖς ἐ- | πέστειλα μαθήσεσθε τὰ δόξαντά μοι περὶ ὧν | καταλλήλους ἠγωνίσασθε (ll. 6–8); see Ritti, *Hierapolis di Frigia IX*, 389. Epigraphical construction notations have been omitted here.

202 For the two options, see Ritti, *Storia e istituzioni*, 395–396 and F. Masino and G. Sobrà, "A monumental altar from the Hadrianic age at Hierapolis in Phrygia," in *Roma y las provincias: modelo y difusión* edited by I. Rodà (Rome: L'Erma, 2011), 169–81. For detailed examination of the inscription, see Cadwallader, "The Battle over Lake Lycus," *loc. cit.*

203 This seems especially the case with the Guild of Dionysiac Artists. Other associations seem to have established a *koinon* of common interest/endeavor; see, for example, *SEG* 59.1100 (Halaisa, 1st century BCE, for priests of Apollo).

204 I am persuaded that the better text of Col 4:15 reads τὴν κατ᾽οἶκον αὐτῆς ἐκκλησίαν (McKnight, *Colossians*, 394–5 n82) thus confirming that the feminine name Νύμφαν ought to be read rather than the masculine Νυμφᾶν. However, it should be noted that onomastic weight is entirely in favour of Νύμφη(-ν) if the name is feminine and Νυμφᾶς (-ᾶν) if masculine. Νύμφα has yet to appear in Asia as the form of a woman's name; see T. Corsten, "Mann oder Frau: Nympha oder Nymphas in Laodikeia?" in *Epigraphical Evidence*, 215–9. As yet, there is no attestation of male or female name at Laodikeia; however a Νυμφώ daughter of Ξενόστρατος (not mentioned by Corsten) does occur on a recently-discovered inscription containing a list of women's names (association/cult membership or census roll?), assigned to Laodikeia by the editors but to Hierapolis by *LGPN V.C*; see P. Özlem Aytaçlar and E. Akıncı, "A List of Female Names from Laodicea on the Lycos," *EA* 39 (2006): 113 (l. 24; late Hellenistic period). It should be acknowledged that singular names and rare spellings frequently

ever, the Letter to the Colossians, as we have seen, makes no reference to "the" or "a" church (*ekklêsia*) in Colossae, a "surprising" omission, claimed James Dunn.[205] Rather the two references to *ekklêsia* in the substance of the letter refer to a metaphysical, universal church, the body of which Christ is the head (Col 1:18, 24).[206] This alone may be a corrective to an emphasis on the *local* church in Laodikeia (either the entire group of Christ-followers that meets in Nympha's [large?] house, or one of the house-gatherings, *an ekklêsia*, that meets in Nympha's [modest?] house). Indeed, the *ekklêsia* of the Laodikeians (Col 4:16) combines the term *ekklêsia* with a city ethnic[207] — the very combination we have seen that is absent, indeed resisted, in Col 1:2.

Theodoret certainly considered that the two letters (one from the Apostle to the Colossians, one from the Laodikeians to Paul) were *not* born out of a congenial relationship. Indeed, he surmised that the Laodikeians were making some accusation against the Colossians, which "Paul" was brought in to resolve. One suspects here a combination of an imperial correction (à la Hadrian) with an echo of the Synod of Laodikeia's anathematization of Colossian malfeasance in Canon 35. Whatever the case, *some* conflict between the groups of Christ-followers is imagined.

This may well explain the references to Jewish matters in the Letter to the Colossians. The Christ-followers in Colossae received such warnings once-removed from their original setting; that is, they were something vaguely known about but not pressing. Laodikeians were more likely to be able to fill in the detail. The peculiarly un-Pauline way of referring to Jewish Christ-followers in Col 4:11 ("of the circumcision") and the categorically anti-salvation-historical prioritization of Greeks *before* Jews in Col 3:11 (unique in the Second Testament), strongly suggests that Jewish practices were not a particular concern for the Colossian Christ-followers. They lay down-river,[208] rather than in "the synagogue across the street".[209] The prime target of the Jewish references in the

---

turn up in inscriptions from the province, as in the previous mentioned list of women's names (ll. 15, 18, 20). Uniquely attested names are known at Colossae (see Cadwallader, "Honouring the Repairer of the Baths," 151 (ll. 25, 278, 34). The name Νύμφα is sometimes used as a pseudonym for Persephone (*SEG* 55.609). Occasionally, "the Nymphs" occur with a singular form (*SEG* 51.1774, 63.342; *CIL* 3.1894). Theonyms (names built on the names of gods) sometimes simply replicate a god's name rather than use a variation, so there is no *a priori* bar to the appearance of Nympha.

205 Dunn, *Colossians and Philemon*, 284.

206 This is an important qualification on Ralph Korner's "local ekklêsia" emphasis, even allowing that not all Christ-followers at the time thought the same as the writer of Colossians. See Korner, *The Origin and Meaning of Ekklêsia in the Early Jesus Movement* (Leiden Brill, 2017), 264.

207 This is recognized by Korner, *Meaning of Ekklêsia*, 185.

208 See A. H. Cadwallader, "Greeks in Colossae: shifting allegiances in the Letter to the Colossians and its context" in *Attitudes to Gentiles in Ancient Judaism and Early Christianity* edited by D. C. Sim and J. S. McLaren (London/NY: Bloomsbury, 2013), 224–41.

209 See the summation in J. C. Anderson, *Colossians: Authorship, Rhetoric, and Code* (London: T & T Clark, 2019), 63.

Letter to the Colossians was Laodikeia, and perhaps, less certainly, Hierapolis.[210] Both these cities show ample evidence of a long-established Jewish demographic.[211] Here, the "once-removed" is itself removed; the warning against entangling practices (Col 2:16–18, 20–22) makes the Jewish elements much more relevant to the second readership based in Laodikeia (and Hierapolis?), firmly placing such elements in the general sweep of religious options available in the Lycus region that the Christ-followers are to eschew.[212]

The formal exchange begins at the *ekklêsia* in Laodikeia, presumably including, even located at, the house of Nympha: Ἀσπάσθε τοὺς ἐν Λαοδικείᾳ ἀδελφοὺς καὶ Νύμφαν καὶ τὴν κατ' οἶκον αὐτῆς ἐκκλησίαν (Col 4:15). And in a move that heralds affinity, relationship and, indeed, concord, the opening of the address is greetings (ἀσπάσθε). This, of course, is familiar from thousands of letters, as also in the *chairein* of Hadrian to the Hierapolitans (l. 6). But here three elements stand out:

i) the greetings do not follow a prescribed hierarchical formula. Hadrian greeted the rulers, the council, and the citizens' assembly/people of Hierapolis (Ἱεραπολειτῶν τοῖς ἄρχουσι καὶ τῆι βουλῆι καὶ τῶι δήμωι, χαίρειν ll. 5–6), a deliberate scaling of authoritative recognition. Here the greeting is simply to the comrades, the brothers and sisters (ἀδελφοί), with Nympha singled out for special mention (Col 4:15).

ii) the naming of Nympha may indicate consciousness of the significant role she had, not just in providing a venue for the assembly of Christ-followers, but in setting the terms under which such assembly would take place. Those cult associations we know that met in individuals' houses seem to have the regulations governing the conduct of the cult set by the householder, sometimes claimed as the result of divine revelation in a dream.[213] There may then be considerable learning for Nympha from Col 2:16–23 or perhaps a vindication (as against the ἀδελφοί?) of her more liberating governance of the gathering. Perhaps if some in the Laodikeian Christ-followers had already adopted something of the more stringent requirements visible in the Apocalypse (eg Rev 2:14–16, 20 cf 3:17) then there may have been more bite in some parts of the Colossians Letter among these secondary readers/hearers.

---

210 It is significant that one Byzantine commentator, Nicetas Seides, saw the single letter as "to the Colossians and the Laodikeians." (τὴν ἐπιστολὴν τοῖς Κολασσαεῦσι καὶ Λαοδικεῦσιν): *Synopsis of the Sacred Scripture* 23.292.18–19 (ed. Simotas).

211 *I.Jud. Orientis* 2.212, 213 (Laodikeia); *I.Jud. Orientis* 2.187–209 (Hierapolis).

212 *Contrà* A. K. Petersen, "Colossian's Grounding Traditionalization of Paul," in *The Early Reception of Paul the Second Temple Jew: Text, Narrative and Reception History* edited by I. W. Oliver and G. Boccaccini (London: T & T Clark, 2019), 59–74.

213 For example, *CGRN* 191 (Philadelphia, 125–75 BCE) probably; *IG* X/2.1.225 (Thessalonike, 1st to 2nd century CE). Sometimes οἶκος/οἰκία was used in a more generic sense for a more public building or meeting house (eg *I.Jud. Orientis* 2.36).

iii) greetings to *ekklêsiai* were part of the formal procedures that Hellenistic *poleis* adopted as a means of fostering positive, congenial relationships. It was an instrument for developing concord in times of political stress, fostering concord diplomatically. Hellenistic cities frequently relied on judges from other cities to resolve civic disputes. The city of Priene, then on the Ionian coast, publically and epigraphically honored the city of Laodikeia and her judges who had helped resolve city legal cases.[214] Such honors were often set up in the judges' cities as well. But to ensure that this did not fuel any political strife, delegates were sent to read the honor to the authorities in the context of an oration. The requisite preliminary to such an address was that *greetings were to be delivered* to the *ekklêsia*, probably to be understood as the citizens of the *Dêmos* assembled for the purpose.[215] The island of Kos received just such an honoring from another city (name lost). One section of the inscription is telling:

> In order that the Koans too shall know the respect (προαίρεσις) our *Dêmos* has determined to show, it was decided to appoint two representatives (πρεσβευτές) who, upon their arrival in Kos, shall deliver the resolution (ψήφισμα) and, having come before the council (βουλή) and assembly (ἐκκλησία) and passed on the greetings (ἀσπασάμενοι) of our people (πλῆθος), shall thank the Koans for their sending (ἀποστολή) of the judge and beseech (παρακαλέσουσιν) them, who are our friends (φίλοι), to preserve their goodwill (εὔνοια) towards our polis …[216]

Substantially the same formula is set out in a first century BCE inscription on Thasos.[217] The purpose was friendship and goodwill/concord (εὔνοια/ὁμόνοια). Greetings were the necessary foundation for the delivery or performance of the text, precisely the sequence that is given in Col 4:15–16. In the Letter to the Colossians we have an escalation of the standard greetings seen in private letters, the mimetic iteration of which is found in the Pauline Letters, including here (Col 4:10–12). One second century BCE inscription from Kyme, an Aeolian city on the Mediterranean coast, records that delegates were sent so that "the city resolution should be read to every assembly" (ἀναγινώσκεσθαι δὲ τοῦτο τὸ ψάφισμα κατ᾽ἑκάσταν ἐκκλησίαν).[218] The Colossians carry a similar responsibility (ποιήσατε ἵνα … ἀναγνωσθῇ, Col 4:16).[219] This suggests that Theodoret may well have discerned the context fairly clearly in his diagnosis

214 *I.Laodikeia Lykos* 5 (200–185 BCE).
215 So Korner, *Meaning of Ekklêsia*, 263.
216 *IG* XII, 4, 1.177 = *SEG* 49.1119, ll. 9–19; translation adapted from L. Rubinstein, "Spoken Words, Written Submissions and Diplomatic Conventions: The Importance and Impact of Oral Performance in Hellenistic Inter-*polis* Relations," in *Hellenistic Oratory, Continuity and Change* edited by C. Kremmydas and K. Tempest (Oxford: Oxford University Press, 2013), 168.
217 *I.Thasos* 11a.
218 *I.Kyme* 12 = *SEG* 59.1407, ll. 14–15.
219 Compare the form ποιεῖν ἵνα … in *IG* II^3, 1.1176 = *SEG* 26.98 (Athens late 3rd century BCE).

of discontent. The delegation from Colossae may have teaching to deliver to the Laodikeians but, preeminently, it is for the restoration or cultivation of friendship, even over against what has characterized relationships between the cities and their inhabitants. The Letter from the Laodikeians in this sense is no more, but no less, than a response to the Letter to the Colossians, not an independent composition. It was expected that if the initiating letter was favorably received, that there would be an acknowledgement thereof, just as when Magnesia-on-Maeander sought recognition of its claims to asylia and for its festival of Artemis Leukophryene in the early second century — the manifold letters sent back to the initiating city frequently incorporate standardized phrasing which is sheeted home to the initial communication sent out by the city.[220] This is the motivation for the second letter that Charles Anderson struggled to discern,[221] and explains why it did not survive — it simply was (to signal an) acceptance of the content of the Letter to the Colossians, (if indeed it was accepted).[222]

Accordingly, all this delivers a textual connection for the service required of Archippos (Col 4:17): καὶ εἴπατε Ἀρχίππῳ· βλέπε τὴν διακονίαν ἣν παρέλαβες ἐν κυρίῳ, ἵνα αὐτὴν πληροῖς "And tell Archippos, attend to the ministry which you received in the Lord, that you fulfil it." The καί opening the verse indicates that the following content ought not be marooned as a "lapidary" comment.[223] Theodoret admits that some connected Archippos's service with Laodikeia.[224] It might be objected that the epigraphical illustrations given here come from Hellenistic polities, but these tracked through Roman Republican times and continued to govern the attitudes and governance of pseudo-autono-

220 See K. J. Rigsby, *Asylia: Territorial Inviolability in the Hellenistic World* (Berkeley: University of California Press, 1996), nrs 66–131.

221 C. P. Anderson, "Who wrote 'The Epistle from Laodicea'?," *JBL* 85 (1966): 436–40.

222 However, it is also possible that the suggestion about the Second Testament Letter to the Ephesians being a/the Letter to the Laodikeians is the Letter from the Laodikeians to the Colossians. In the light of the epigraphical testimony surveyed here related to diplomatic exchanges, it would explain the manifold borrowings of the Letter to the Colossians incorporated into the Letter "to the Ephesians".

223 C. R. Seitz, *Colossians* (Grand Rapids, MI: Brazos, 2014), 192; similarly, the almost forlorn resignation of Eduard Lohse, *Colossians and Philemon* (Hermenia; Philadelphia: Fortress, 1971), 175. Treated in isolation without reference to its discourse sequence, this verse has invited all manner of speculation; see McKnight, *Colossians*, 397–8. Paul Foster rightly observes that καί opening v. 17 is a connective linked to the preceding two instructions (to do with greeting and reading!) but swings the service by Archippos back to Colossae: *Colossians* (BNTC; London: Bloomsbury, 2016), 442–3. Jerry Sumney is closer however when he points to the verb πληρόω as descriptive of the memory of Paul's ministry of the word of God (Col 1:25): *Colossians*, 280 but likewise does not see the critical role of envoys in the delivery of greetings and reading of texts to an *ekklêsia*. In my view, Archippos's service (διακονία) is specific, just as, presumably, was that of Onesimos to Paul (Phmn 13).

224 Τινὲς ἔφασαν τοῦτον Λαοδικείας γεγενῆσθαι διδάσκαλον (Theodoret *Comm. Col.* 4:17, *PG* 82.629A) but, on the basis that the Letters to the Colossians and to Philemon belong to the same time-frame, Theodoret places Archippos firmly at Colossae.

> mous Greek cities under Rome. Delegations to the emperor retained similar accents on greetings, friendship, concord and return communications.[225] In any case, the rescript from Hadrian (as in many of his communications) noted that his decision stood in line with the distant past (τῶι χρόνωι l. 9) and that Concord was an ancient virtue (ὁμόνοιαν … τὴν ἀρχαίαν ταύτην, ll. 19–20). The writer of the Letter to the Colossians, the recipients and the second recipients, were all well-attuned to the protocols governing relationships, especially as they were expressed in the assembly, the *ekklêsia*. This is the communication universe that helped even small groups formulate their thinking and modes of operating. We know for example that some voluntary associations modelled their structures and office-bearers on the city polity.[226] Here there is sufficient correlation of language to conclude that the writer of Colossians has appropriated pre-existing forms for dealing with relationships between groups of Christ-followers nestled in different cities.[227]

The history that we have been able to trace from discrete pieces of evidence concerning the relation between Laodikeia and Colossae has shown that their inter-city ties were not strong, and often enough prone to distrust, disruption and disputation. Early Christ-followers were part of this environment, socialized by it, and not immune from it simply because of their new religious adherence. This has provided a context that grounds the instructions delivered at the end of the Letter to the Colossians. There is nothing canonical or canon-inducing here, regardless of what the later church and contemporary commentators have wanted to make of it confessionally. But another dimension has been materially sown, namely, the desire that friendship and concord become the hallmark of the *ekklêsia*. For this, a universal vision of *ekklêsia* was required, not a local ghetto existence (Col 1:18, 24). Colossians marks a turning point in the development of Pauline conceptions, even though seeded in the apostle's prior writings.[228] But this was not to be anchored in a temporal universality modeled on either the Roman empire or even the world-wide guild of Dionysiac artists. A cosmological pavilion was needed. To this we turn.

---

225 See *SEG* 53.659 (Maroneia, 41/2 or 46 CE).

226 See J. S. Kloppenborg and R. S. Ascough, *Greco-Roman Associations: Texts, Translations and Commentary I. Attica, Central Greece, Macedonia, Thrace* (Berlin: de Gruyter, 2011), 11.

227 For greater analysis of this perspective, see A. H. Cadwallader, "Greetings in stone: shifting the accent from papyri to epigraphy in Col 4:15–17," in *God's Grace Inscribed on the Human Heart: Festschrift for James R. Harrison* edited by P. Bolt and S. Kim (Sydney: SCD, 2022), 441–65.

228 Compare S. Grindheim who argues that the seeds are so similar to the growth as to rule out pseudepigraphy. I remain unconvinced (even though it neatly pre-empts Lincicum's conundrum already mentioned). See "A Deutero-Pauline Mystery? Ecclesiology in Colossians and Ephesians," in *Paul and Pseudepigraphy* edited by S. E. Porter and G. P. Fewster (Leiden: Brill, 2013), 173–95. No matter how advanced a fertile, creative mind might become (Grindheim's imposed educational psychology of Paul), the inversion of the order of salvation to Greeks and Jews (Col 3:11) cannot be read as authentic Pauline teaching.

Chapter Five
The Shadow of a Mountain: cosmic control

Towering above the city of Colossae was one of the highest mountains in the Taurus ranges — Mt Cadmus (Honazdağ). The play of sunrise over the ridge and the onslaught of severe weather caught on the mountaintops charged a landscape with cosmic force, the ground of Colossae's religious environment. But the hints of cosmic preoccupation find their most expressive form in a much smaller material setting — a recently-recovered, swivel signet ring. The ring is rich in cosmic symbolism and proclaims Colossae as a center of cosmogonic energy, the home of Tyche Protogeneia. The implications about the religious sensitivities of the Colossians are drawn out in detailed analysis of the ring. This generates a raft of comparative potential for the reception among the city's Christ followers of the Christological hymn at the opening of the Letter to the Colossians.

Lost and found: a Colossian intaglio

The history of Colossae is constrained by the limited array of materials from which to construct a sense of the historical movements and religious sensibilities that formed the organism of its life. So to lose any artifact that may be of assistance in the construction of its story is even more lamentable than the general loss, destruction or theft that too frequently accompanies archaeological efforts. One such item received its death certificate from Paul Meyboom in 1995.[1] His interest lay in displaying the panorama of Egyptian influence on the Italian cult of Fortuna Primigenia, especially as located in the cultic center at Praeneste/Palestrina, about 20 miles outside of Rome. It had sent him on a hunt for references to Fortuna Primigenia/Tyche Protogeneia. Among a small

1 P. G. P. Meyboom, *The Nile Mosaic of Palestrina* (Leiden: Brill, 1995), 210 n37.

array of testimony, he found a reference linked to Colossae. The source was an engraved gem that carried an abbreviated inscription that read, in retrograde form, ΤΥΧΗ ΠΡΩΤΟΓ ΚΟΛΟΣΣΑΙ. No further information was given, apart from the pronouncement of its demise.

Meyboom relied on equally succinct notes of Hans Riemann.[2] Again Riemann seemed only to be interested in the three words of inscription. His was also no more than a reiteration of a previous scholar's concentration — Joseph Demargne.[3] No mention was made of other details; the inscription had become divorced from its setting. One exception, however, is found in the assemblage of Hans Gundel, whose interest was not the inscription, left unmentioned, but an apparently disorganized zodiacal circle. Unlike Meyboom, he listed the gem as housed in Paris, but provided no photograph. Because he could make nothing of the arrangement of the zodiac signs he was skeptical about the antiquity of the gem.[4]

A decade before Meyboom, Jacqueline Champeaux had been more forthcoming in her description of the gem, having tracked the details back to what she thought was the original announcement in 1784, the fount of the reiterations since. She noted that it was a double-faced gem for a swivel-ring assemblage. Her focus was the carved bust of Tyche, her correction of the original categorization of the design as "Helios-Apollo." She dated it to "l'époque impériale" and offered a more cohesive suggestion for the interpretation, one which settled for a "syncretistic engraving".[5] Nevertheless, her silence about any further investigation suggests that, like Meyboom, she had been unable to trace the gem into the nineteenth or twentieth centuries. Understandably then, no photograph was provided.

Consequently, the only visual record available was the sketch provided by Monsignor Augustin Belley's 1784 publication (Pl. 5.1).

Plate 5.1: The sketch of the two-sided intaglio by Augustin Belley in 1784.

2 H. Riemann, "Jupiter Imperator," *MDAI* 90 (1983): 242 n42.

3 J. Demargne, "Monuments figures et inscriptions de Crète," *BCH* 24 (1900): 239.

4 H. G. Gundel, *Zodiakos. Tierkreisbilder im Altertum. Kosmische Bezüge und Jenseitsvorstellungen im antiken Alltagsleben*, (KAW 54; Mainz: von Zabern, 1992), 129, 248 § 146.

5 J. Champeaux, *Fortuna. Le culte de la Fortune à Rome et dans le monde romain. I — Fortuna dans la religion archaïque* (Rome: École Française de Rome, 1982), 120 n529. Her dating for the magazine article to 1774 requires correction.

The sketch slightly mis-represented the gem, since the retrograde incisions were righted for view, as if the intaglio (its technical name) had executed its double-sided impression. But the notice caught widespread attention. Joseph von Eckhel decided to include a brief summary of the gem's contents in his multi-volume catalogue of ancient coins — Sol, engraved with a radiate head and winged shoulders, was the patron god of the Colossians, the gemstone was "sard", that is carnelian, the bust was circled by ten signs of the zodiac and the reverse side had an owl atop a lyre.[6] A number of early writers repeated the sketch of the gem, sometimes including both sides, sometimes confined to the side containing the inscription.[7] It passed into memory as coming from the collection of the Duc d'Orléans,[8] though it had previously been part of the "cabinet" of Pierre Crozat (1661–1740).[9]

Belley became curator of the purchased gem collection and published a small pamphlet on some of the items in 1758.[10] As an "Académiciens-Pensionnaire" of the Royal Academy of France, he later delivered a lecture on the Colossae gem, which was subsequently published, along with a sketch of both faces. He suggested that the gem's purpose was a civic authorization in honor of its tutelary deities — named as Helios (from the radiate head on one side) and Athena and Apollo (from the owl and cithara on the other). This warranted both an allegorization of Helios' additional features (cornucopia = fertility; wings = rapidity of the sun's course), and an historical overview that included reference to radiate Helios on one of three Colossian coins that had been recently published by Joseph Pellerin.[11] Here we are returned to our earlier numismatic discussion.[12]

Belley reckoned that the incomplete zodiac, missing Ares and Virgo, was the position of the zodiacal constellations at the time that the city was founded

6 J. H. von Eckhel, *Doctrina numorum veterum* … (Vindobonae: J. Camesina, 8 vols, 1792–98), 3.147. *Fuisse Solem tutelarem Colossensium deum, comprobat sarda, in cuius una facie insculpta protome Solis capite radiato, et adfixis humero alis inter decem zodiaci signa, in altera facie. Noctua lyrae insistens,* … A slightly earlier citation is given by Christian Gottlob Heyne, *P. Virgilii Maronis Opera: Carmina minora*, Varietate Lectionis et Perpetua Adnotatione Illustrata Index A-E (London: T. Payne et al, 1793), 248, and François Arnaud, *Descriptions des Principales pierres gravées du Cabinet de S. A. S. Monseigneur le Duc d'Orléans, premier Prince du Sang* (Vol 1; Paris: de la Chau & le Blond, 1780), 209–12.

7 Johann Domink Fiorillo, *Parerga et ornamenta, caelo expresa ad P. Virgilii Maronis opera illustranda* (London: 1812), 14 and plate 22.

8 S. Reinach, *Pierres gravées des collection Marlborough et d'Orléans* … (Paris: Firmin-Didot, 1895), 138, pl. 125.49, 50.

9 P-J. Mariette, *Description sommaire des pierres gravées du cabinet de feu M. Crozat* (Paris: Mariette, 1741), 54 nr. 852.

10 M. l'Abbé Belley, *Remarques sur les Pierres Gravées du Cabinet de Mgr le Duc D'Orléans* (1758 [no publication details]). See also the more extensive catalogue by François Arnaud, *Description des principales pierres gravées.*

11 J. Pellerin, *Recueil de Médailles de Peuples et de Villes qui n'ont point encore été publiées* (Paris: H. L. Guerin and L. F. Delatour, 1762), Vol 2, 40 and pl. 45. Belley claims five coins were known to him.

12 See chapter 2.

(which he neglected to reveal).[13] In all the analysis, there was no explicit mention of mirror-writing (*sinistrorsum*) or inverted iconography, even though a comparison of the sketches suggests that this was the understanding of the intaglio engraving. The concentration was upon the stone with no reference to any setting for it. The type of stone was sometimes noted (carnelian, sard), but its significance omitted. The antiquarian sensibility, so distilled in the introduction to one eighteenth-century catalogue, governed the approach to description and analysis:

> … the polite Arts are, and always were, the blossoms and fruits of enlightened ages and public prosperity, and this is particularly the case of the art of engraving on hard and precious stones, which more than any other is an art of refined intellectual luxury.[14]

From this point, the trail for European research ran cold. What had escaped notice was that Catherine the Great, whose astute, aesthetic eye was only surpassed by her coffers of gold, had become aware of many of the gem collections gracing aristocratic houses. In 1783 she had commissioned the expert mold-maker, James Tassie, to make a series of impressions of engraved gems found in European cabinets.[15] An opportunity arose in November 1785 to take advantage of the acquired intelligence. The importunate heir to the duc d'Orléans collection put the entire cabinet up for auction.[16] From that moment, any new examination of the gem seems to have disappeared, though there were occasional mentions prior to the 1917 Russian Revolution, that Catherine II's vast collection displayed in her "Gem Room" included that of Philippe, duc d'Orléans.[17]

In 2001, the Hermitage at St Petersburg published a catalogue, in Russian with French summaries, for a major in-house exhibition of gems, based on the holdings purchased from the estate of the duc d'Orléans. It included a brief

13 M. l'Abbé Belley, "Observations sur une Cornaline Antique du Cabinet de Mgr le Duc D'Orléans," published first in *Histoire des Ouvrages de l'"Academie Royale des Inscriptions et Belles-Lettres* (Paris: Panckoucke, 1780), 17–27; and subsequently in *Mémoires de Littérature, tires des registres de l'Académie royale des inscriptions et Belles-Lettres* 36 (1784): 11–17.

14 R. E. Raspe, *Catalogue raisonné d'une Collection générale de Pierres gravées antiques et modernes tant en creux que Camées …* (London: Murray, 1791), ii.

15 See D. C. Kurtz, *The Reception of Classical Art in Britain: An Oxford Story of Plaster Casts from the Antique* (BAR [British Series] 308; Oxford: Archaeopress, 2000), 334.

16 *Catalogue des Pierres gravées du Cabinet de feu son altesse sérénissime Monseigneur Le Duc d'Orléans, premier Prince du Sang.* La Vente sera indiquée dans les Papiers publics. (Paris: Barrois, 1786). The gem is listed as item nr. 796 (pp. 88–89).

17 See J. Murray, *Handbook for Travellers in Russia, Poland and Finland* (London: John Murray, 1868), 98. K. Baedeker, *Russia with Teheran, Port Arthur and Peking: a handbook for travellers* (Leipzig: Karl Baedeker, 1914), 162.

note on the Colossian gem.[18] I am most grateful to Svetlana Adaxina, Zhanna Etsina and Olga Gorskaya, of the State Hermitage Museum in St Petersburg, for their assistance in retrieving the gem for scholarly research (Pl. 5.2).[19]

Face A Face B

Plate 5.2: Photograph by Dmitry Sirotkin © The State Hermitage Museum, St Petersburg, by permission.

The concentration of previous scholarship on the gem itself raises the issue of whether the setting is a secondary addition to the stone, given that the seventeenth and eighteenth century saw considerable refashioning or provision of rings,[20] though with solid not swivel mounts.[21] Two observations weigh towards authenticity. Firstly, ancient gems are rarely without settings (even though many do not survive); the bezel of the photographs appears identical to that included in Arnaud's 1780 catalogue (Pl. 5.3), which itself is consistent with those that have survived from antiquity. In this case, it is an open bezel, recommended by Pliny the Elder as the best way to expose a better specimen

18 Y. O. Kagan and O. Y. Neverov, *Le Destin d'une Collection: 500 pierres gravées du Duc d'Orléans* (St Petersburg: Musée de l'Hermitage, 2001), nr. 274/92. The inventory number was given as 2891. The reference to Belley's 1784 article was given the date of 1774 and the inscription was read as ΠΡΩΤΟΙ instead of ΠΡΩΤΟΓ, a confusion that may date back to an adaptation of the sketch made by Salomon Reinach (*supra*).

19 I want also to give my thanks to Dr. Kosta Simic who provided enthusiastic assistance in tracing the gem at The Hermitage and in guiding me to the official contacts.

20 D. Plantzos, *Hellenistic Engraved Gems* (Oxford: Clarendon, 1999), 2–3, 36.

21 For an example of an ancient stone given a modern (late eighteenth century) mount, see K. A. Piacenti and J. Boardman (eds), *Ancient and Modern Gems and Jewels in the Collection of Her Majesty the Queen* (London: Royal Collection Publications, 2008), 43 nr. 20.

of the stone.[22] At the same time, the bezel and ring are in remarkably fine condition, retaining its identification as a swivel-ring,[23] though the shank has been compressed, possibly caused by later application as a pendant.

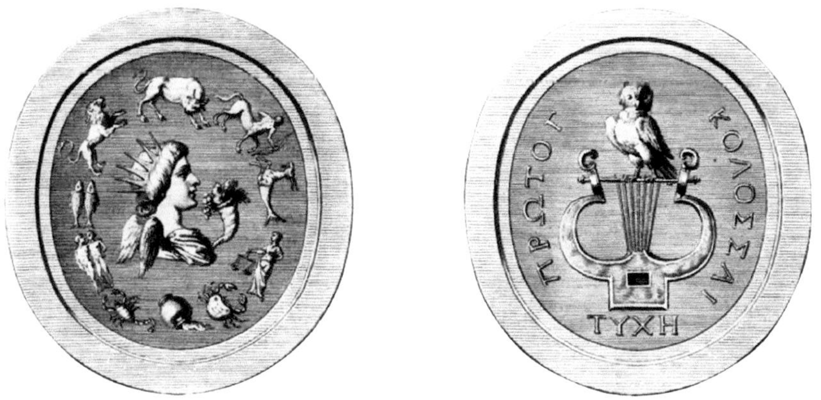

Plate 5.3: François Arnaud's 1780 sketch of the gem-in-bezel.

Gold, carnelian rings were extremely valuable.[24] Carnelian, σαρδίον, was regarded as one of the most precious stones. Theophrastus, the successor to Aristotle in Athens, wrote that even a small red stone cost forty pieces of gold.[25] A contemporary gemologist, Earle Caley, calculated that this was by far the most popular stone for use as a seal.[26] But the ancients were also convinced of a gem-stone's medicinal, even prophylactic capacity.[27] Engraved gems are mentioned as offerings a number of times in literature[28] and especially in the Delos and Athens temple inventory inscriptions (of the fourth to second centuries BCE).[29] These inventories sometimes provide further detail: a description of

22 Pliny, *NH* 37.37.116: *quam ob rem praestantiores funda cluduntur, ut sint patentes ab utraque parte nec praeter margines quicquam auro amplectente.*

23 A very similar gold swivel ring (using a rod construction) is held by the Boston Museum of Fine Arts (Boston MFA #27.734), dated to the 1st century BCE. It holds a carnelian stone portraying Sirius the dog star with the engraving signed by the artist: ΓΑΙΟΣ ΕΠΟΙΕΙ.

24 Plutarch advises one prone to angry outbursts to avoid owning seal-rings and precious stones (σφραγῖδες καὶ λίθοι πολυτελές) as their loss unleashes an intense failure of control (*Cohib. ira* [*Mor*] 461F). See the general assessment of Plantzos, *Hellenistic Engraved Gems*, 105–8.

25 Theophrastus *Lapid.* 18; see also Posidippus *Epig.* 8.

26 E. R. Caley and J. F. C. Richards, *Theophrastus on Stones* (Columbus, Ohio: Ohio State University Press, 1956), 123.

27 Pliny *NH* 37.14.54; 37.37.118, 169; Galen *Simpl.* 10.19.

28 See, for example, Pliny *NH* 37.5.11–12.

29 For an overview, see Plantzos, *Hellenistic Engraved Gems*, 12–17; see also B. Dignas, "'Inventories' or 'Offering Lists'? Assessing the Wealth of Apollo Didymaeus," *ZPE* 138 (2002): 235–44; G. Reger, "A New Inventory from Mylasa in Karia," in *Stephanèphoros: de l'Économie antique à l'Asie Mineure: Hommages à Raymond Descat* edited by K. Konuk (Bordeaux: Au-

the stone; its engraving; the god to receive the offering; the weight/value of the offering; and the person responsible for the gift. So, for example:

> [— — — — δακτύλιος χρυσοῦς σάρ]διον ἔχων, ἐφ' οὗ ἔπεστιν Ἀπόλ[λ]ων, ὅν ἀνέθηκεν τῆ[ι Λη]τοῖ, ὁ[λκὴ δραχμαὶ ·ΔΙΙ·
>
> *A gold ring having a cornelian gem on which is the image of Apollo and which [Stratonike] offered to Leto, having the weight of 12 drachmas.*[30]

In a series of inventories from Athens, an engraved carnelian (repeated listing?) is expressly mentioned as a seal.[31] At times, the deposition of a priest's seal-ring is given.[32] Sometimes the gem of the seal is mentioned and the metal of the ring in which it is set.[33]

Of particular importance for our purposes are the inscription and the two design faces. It should be noted however that these two elements ought not be separated from one another. The inscription is likely to be informed by the design of the face on which it occurs (namely, face B), significant because the inscription does not occur on the face which, as we shall see, holds the iconography of Tyche.

The inscription

The inscription on face B is in mirror lettering, ΤΥΧΗ ΠΡΩΤΟΓ ΚΟΛΟΣΣΑΙ, that is, a limited abbreviation for Τύχη Πρωτογενεία Κολοσσαίων,[34] "Tyche Protogeneia of the Colossians".

---

sonius, 2012), 145–64; J. Shaya, "The Greek Temple as Museum: The Case of the Legendary treasure of Athena," *AJA* 109.3 (2005): 423–42; A. Schachter, "Reflections on an Inscription from Tanagra," in *Boiotia in Antiquity: Selected Papers* edited by H. Beck (Cambridge: Cambridge University Press, 2016), 279–88.

30 *IG* XI 2.226 cf *I.Délos* 298, *IG* II² 1408, 1409, 1445, 1534.

31 *IG* II² 1408 (ll. 8–9) cf *IG* II² 1409, 1445, 1455 (?), 1457 (?), 1459 (?). *I.Eleusis* 149 may carry an assumption of a seal for two gold sard rings given the surrounding entries that specify seals (and on the premise that associates carnelian with signets).

32 *IG* II² 1532, 1533, 1534 (Asklepeion at Athens, 4th century BCE).

33 *IG* II² 1388.

34 Joseph Demargne suggested the second word should be expanded to Πρωτογ(ένης): Demargne, "Monuments," 239. Both forms are attested in inscriptions honouring Tyche: *I.Crete* 3.4.14 (πρωτογενής), *SIG* 3.1133 (πρωτογενεία). Both epithets were used as names, the former being more common (195 examples in *LGPN*, compared to only 5 for Πρωτογενεία). The names are not yet known at Colossae, but the male form is found at Hierapolis and Laodikeia, both dated to around 200 CE. T. Ritti, *Per la storia sociale ed economica di Hierapolis di Frigia* (Rome: Accademia Nazionale dei Lincei, 2015), 38b; J.-L. Ferrary, *Les mémoriaux de délégations du sanctuaire oraculaire de Claros* (Paris: de Boccard, 2014), 351 nr. 14, l. 22.

Plate 5.4: The inscription on face B, magnified.

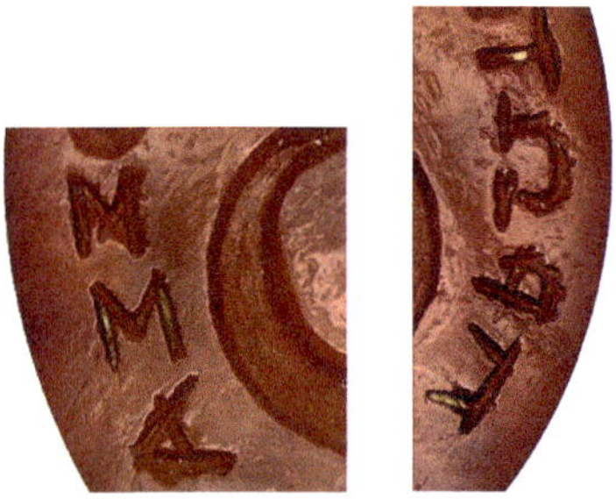

The hint of some foreign material in the letters, rather than a flaw in the stone, might corroborate the conclusion that the *sinistrorsum* writing is a seal function.[35] Each letter was cut with straight lines so that curvilinear letters were constructed with short angled strokes to create the impression of a circular form (letters O, Ω and P). The curvilinear omega with finials and the four-bar sigma occur consistently on the Hellenistic coins of Colossae. When the Colossae mint revived at the beginning of the reign of the emperor Hadrian (117 CE), the *sigmas* were lunate (the standard fashion of the time on coin legends) and remained so on the coinage throughout the period. However, inscriptions dated to the first to second century CE also manifest four-bar sigmas,[36] and perhaps suggest that the shape of the *sigmas* might be dictated at times by the tools available for cutting (let alone the skill of the artisan). The multiple short straight cuts necessary to create the curvilinear omega would support this. So it seems that doubt must attend the letter-styles as an aid to dating.

Scholarship has been preoccupied with the designation Tyche Protogenia. Earlier learneds had flatly equated the name-figure with Fortuna Primigenia, asserting a Roman derivation.[37] A comparison with Fortuna Primigenia had been made by Belley in 1780 without accenting a line of derivation. That genealogy had been intimated by Plutarch long before,[38] and seems to have become an axiomatic iteration. The assessment retains its adherents, even with some qualification.[39] Certainly, after an initial burst of recog-

---

35 The letter Λ, the second Σ, the I, of ΚΟΛΟΣΣΑΙ, the T of ΤΥΧΗ and the Π and T of ΠΡΩΤΟΓ all show signs of foreign material, though there is no knowing when the stone was used in such a fashion. There is a strong possibility that an impression was made of this gem (along with others in the d'Orléans collection) by James Tassie in 1783/4. There appear to be some traces of foreign material in Face A as well.

36 A. H. Cadwallader, "A New Inscription [=Two New Inscriptions], a Correction and a Confirmed Sighting from Colossae," *EA* 40 (2007): 110, 113.

37 "Τύχη Πρωτογένης was a Roman deity and in Italy was called Fortuna Primigenia. Her worship was closely associated with that of Jupiter. The cult spread in the East with the advance of Roman influence." Demargne, "Monuments," 239; similarly, A. J. Reinach "Inscriptions d'Itanos," *REG* 24 (1911): 411–12; P. Roussel, *Les cultes égyptiens à Délos, du IIIe au Ier siècle av. J.-C.* (Nancy: Berger-Levrault, 1916), 148.

38 Plutarch *Quaest. rom.* 289B. There are apparently scholia to the same effect: *LSJ* sv πρωτογένης.

39 Champeaux, *Fortuna*, 1.124–5.

nition in the first half of the second century BCE,[40] Fortuna Primigenia had enjoyed a massive revival in the early empire. Caligula had dedicated his newly formed XXII legion to the goddess (39 CE), which, through the next two centuries, left in the trail of its movements and stations, a series of dedications through Spain, Tunisia and Germany.[41] Tiberius's (unsuccessful) efforts to corral the oracles that emanated from her massive sanctuary at Praeneste had only served to enhance the status of the site and the reputation of Fortuna Primigenia.[42] She was laid into mosaics in houses[43] and may even have begun to influence onomastic practices.[44]

Plate 5.5a and b: Reconstruction model of the Sanctuary of Fortuna Primigenia at Palestrina/Praeneste outside of Rome. A surviving section of the right hemicycle, colonnaded stoa at the top of the entrance ramp on the third terrace, is added as a guide to the overall dimensions.

40 Livy 34.53.5 cf 29.36.8; amidst a sweep of temple dedications, Livy names the duumvir Quintus Marcius Ralla as the dedicant of a temple to Fortuna Primigenia on the Quirinal Hill, following a vow ten years previously (that is, in 204 BCE) by Publius Sempronius Sophus, consul during the Second Punic War. Some difficulties are associated with Livy's account which places a caution over certitude related to dating and personnel. Angelos Chaniotis accepts that Fortuna Primigenia was introduced into Rome in 194 BCE: "Foreign Soldiers – Native Girls? Constructing and Crossing Boundaries in Hellenistic Cities with Foreign Garrisons," in *Army and Power in the Ancient World* edited by A. Chanioties and P. Ducrey (Stuttgart: Franz Steiner, 2002), 109. However, the cult probably predates this formal recognition. One votive inscription is dated to the third century BCE (*CIL* 14.2863).

41 *AE* 1956.86 (first half of 2nd century CE); *CIL* 13.6502 (2nd century CE); *CIL* 8.15576 (163–9 CE); *CIL* 13.6728 (192 CE); *AE* 1923.36 (205 CE); *CIL* 13.6592 (232 CE). In the sanctuary itself, there have been found bullets stamped with "LEG XXII" presumably dedicated to the goddess.

42 Suetonius *Tib.* 63.

43 *AE* 1983.386 (1st century CE).

44 See, for example, *AE* 1948.67, *ARID* 1980.70–71 (nr. 5).

A demurral on the direction of influence was sounded by Stylianos Spyridakis. He was particularly taken by the importance of Tyche Protogeneia to the Ptolemaic rulers of Egypt. He noted that the inscriptions from Itanos on Crete and on Delos (from a Crete-based devotee) indicated a strong Egyptian influence. And this eventually forged access to Praeneste, as seen in a statue of Isityche, an imported Egyptian obelisk and the famous Nile mosaic installed at the Roman sanctuary (Pl. 5.6).[45]

Plate 5.6: The Nile mosaic at the Sanctuary of Fortuna Primigenia at Praeneste.

This is not to say that the cult of Tyche Protogeneia is the progenitor of Fortuna Primigenia, in spite of Plutarch's shorthand,[46] nor that Isis was a further contributor to the amalgam, as seems to have happened in the cult on Delos and at Thessalonike.[47] Indeed, the record of the offer of an Isityche statue to the temple of Fortuna Primige-

45 S. Spyridakis, "The Itanian Cult of Tyche Protogeneia," *Historia* 18.1 (1969): 42–8. One could add other items of distinct Egyptian influence, such as an intaglio featuring an Anubis figure and an Egyptian obelisk imported and dedicated by Titus Sestius Africanus some time in the 40s CE.

46 Champeaux in fact suggests that the cult of Kore Protogone may be the origin of Fortuna Primigenia: *Fortuna*, 1.125–34.

47 F. Dunand, *Le culte d'Isis en Asie Mineure: Clergé et rituel des sanctuaires isiaques* (Leiden: Brill, 3 vols, 1975) vol 3, 271; P. Martzavou, "Les cultes isiaques et les Italiens entre Délos, Thessalonique et l'Eubée," *Pallas* 84 (2010): 181–205.

nia was part of a swathe of statues that the donor, Lucius Sariolenus, contributed and, thus, is to be distinguished from the patron goddess.[48]

There is nothing in the iconography of the Colossian swivel-ring, nor in the the city's bronze issue (with multiple coin dies, possibly struck across a succession of reigns) of Sarapis and Isis that suggests any merging of Isis and Tyche. Tyche in Colossae's coinage, retains a familiar fecundity and directional symbolism, namely with the cornucopia and rudder, although we shall return to the detail in two cases below. For now, it is significant that there is nothing distinctive in Colossae's coins featuring Isis, that might mark out the city's devotion beyond its near neighbors, as the coins in Plate 5.7a and b show. In this sense, the influences noticeable at Praeneste cannot, at this stage, be paralleled at Colossae.

Plate 5.7a and b: Coins of Hierapolis (left) and Colossae (right) displaying a near-identical design, though cut by different mold-makers (19 mm, 4.51 g; 20 mm, 4.01 g respectively).[49] The obverse features the head of Sarapis wearing a modius (a grain volume-basket); the reverse has a standing Isis, wearing her distinctive head-piece, and holding a sistrum in her right hand and a situla in her left, key instruments for use in her cult.[50]

One need only recognize how important Tyche was to the cities of the east as a signal of divine patronage for the city's welfare,[51] to allow that there were mul-

48 *CIL* 14.2867. See D. Miano, *Fortuna: Deity and Concept in Archaic and Republican Italy* (Oxford: Oxford University Press, 2018), 177.

49 *RPC online* 4.2.1903 temp. (Colossae, time of Severus?); 4.2.2040 temp. (Hierapolis, time of Severus?). Laodikeia has four coins featuring the head-dress of Isis (alone) on the reverse (*RPC* 1.2903, 2905, 2909 [time of Tiberius]; 2.1278 [time of Titus]) and one similar, on its reverse, to the coin reverses shown here (*RPC online* 6.5517 temp). No coin of Laodikeia features Sarapis on the obverse; six coins feature a seated Sarapis on the reverse (*RPC online* 4.2.1485 temp., 1701 temp., 2085 temp., 2124 temp., 2125 temp., 2137 temp.). No coins with Isis in the design are found at Apameia, Aphrodisias, Attouda, Blaundos, Keretapa, Dionysopolis, Eukarpeia, Eumeneia, Tabae or Trapezopolis. One other member of the city mints providing *comparanda*, Herakleia Salbake, has one (*RPC online* 4.2.2422 temp., also with an obverse of the head of Sarapis with modius.

50 Photographs courtesy of Savoca coins.

51 See P. B. F. J. Broucke, "Tyche and the Fortune of Cities in the Greek and Roman World," *Yale University Art Gallery Bulletin* (1994): 34–49.

tiple possibilities on how Tyche might be imagined in each locale across time.[52] There is in the iconography on this double-sided intaglio a clear indication of the particularity of the Colossian conception.

Forgotten in the analysis of the inscription is the qualifier Κολοσσαίων. This provides an identifying mark, albeit with different spelling, on the civic coinage and some stone inscriptions from the city,[53] indicating not merely the location but the authority of a position, an office or institution. Once the setting for this gem is admitted, that is, a swivel seal-ring, then the ethnic implies that the ring was intended for some official function. The genitive of an individual's name is sometimes engraved into a ring for use as a private seal, such as Ἀπέλλου (*SEG* 42.1699) or Βάσσου (*SEG* 42.1700) — both gold, carnelian intaglio rings — but here both the double-sided swivel ring and the city ethnic argues that this is not a private ownership. As Robert McDowell succinctly stated, "The essential purpose of a seal is to identify the authority which it represents."[54] But here is no individual's authority.

Such city-designated seals (of differing types) are known from across the Mediterranean,[55] and appear to address different functions. A number have the name of the city combined with a mural Tyche, that is, the city goddess (*SEG* 39.1586); others are marked by the cornucopia, as in a seal impression of Tyche with an abbreviated inscription, taken as Δολιχαίων.[56] One inscribed decree conferring honors upon Menogenes son of Isidor by the koinon of the Greeks of Asia and the people's assembly and elders of Sardis (5–1 BCE) regulates that a copy of the decree is to be "sealed by the sacred seal" ἐσπραγισμένον τῇ ἱερᾷ σφραγίδι.[57] Other inscriptions simply refer to a "city seal" (ἡ δημοσία σφραγίς).[58] These do not require a ring seal but neither do they preclude it. Cicero's comment that public

52 See below on the broad range of symbols associated with Tyche in the coinage of the Eastern provinces.

53 See Cadwallader, "A New Inscription," *EA* 40 (2007): 113, nr. 3, lines 2–4; "Honouring the Repairer of the Baths: A New Inscription from Kolossai", *Antichthon* 46 (2012): 152, line 5. For the coins, see generally, *MSPhryg* 2.443–595.

54 R. H. McDowell, *Stamped and inscribed objects from Seleucia on the Tigris* (Ann Arbor: University of Michigan Press, 1935), 25.

55 See *SEG* 28.510, 45.1767, 49.1283. See generally A. Furtwängler and U. Kron, "Das Siegel der Stadt Demetrias," *MDAI(A)* 93 (1978): 137–49; R. Haensch, "Das öffentliche Siegel der griechischen Staaten — zwischen Kontrollmittel und Staatssymbol," in *Symposion 2003: Vorträge zur griecvhischen und hellenistischen Rechtsgeschichte* edited by H-A. Ruprecht (Vienna: Österreichischen Akademie der Wissenshaften, 2006), 265–89; Plantzos, *Hellenistic Engraved Gems*, 22–32.

56 M. Maaskant-Kleibrink, "Cachets de terre de Doliché (?)," *BABesch* 46 (1971): 23–63, nr. 17; A. Mastrocinque, *Les intailles magiques du département des Monnaies, Médailles et Antiques* (Paris: BnF, 2014), 161 nr. 431 Tyche as Amazon crowned by a Nike, with an inscription μετροπόλεσι Τύρος; compare an inscription requiring a sealing by the seal of the city of Kos (*SIG* 3.344, c.303 BCE).

57 *IGR* 4.1756, l. 119.

58 See for example *IG* II 204; XI.1065 cf Aristotle *Ath.* 44.1. See generally, Plantzos, *Hellenistic Engraved Gems*, 21–2; Haensch, "Das öffentliche Siegel," 265–89.

and private letters alike were sealed by an engraved ring indicates how ubiquitous the practice was.[59] A double-sided intaglio used as a seal almost certainly points to the elevated authority associated with what could be, on occasion, a double sealing,[60] a fore-runner of the pincer device that generate Byzantine lead seals.

It is clear that sacred/holy seals, that is, seals connected with a temple, are part of this category, whether the seals were a ring, as here, or a small conical engraved stone, or a metal instrument. One lacunose papyrus letter (*P.Hibeh* 1.72), famous for its mention of a priest named Manetho,[61] is pertinent to my argument.[62] The gist of the text is that the temple seal had gone missing, that is, the seal that priests used to impress the letters they had written (ἡ σφραγὶς ἧι χρῶνται οἱ [ἱ]ε̣ρ̣[ε]ῖς πρὸς τὰς γραφ[θησο]μένας ἐπιστολάς, l. 16). How valuable such a seal was is indicated by the lengths to which Petosiris, the high priest, went to recover it (the involvement of the *basilikogrammateus*, a royal scribe, and an *epistates*, an overseer, ll. 4, 8–9); by the strict control exercised over its use by priests of the temple and the inability to use any other seal (ll. 7–8); by the fear felt by those who knew where it was located in the temple store that they might be charged with theft should they bring it to the high priest (ll. 17–19); and by the specific accusations and denials of an alleged larcenist from among the temple officials (ll. 5–7, 11–12, 15). The charge was that a certain priest Chesmenis wanted to authorize some letters he was writing to Manetho. Clearly the temple seal was highly valuable, at least as to its purpose if not its content.

Unfortunately, a description of the seal is not provided but it may, if such information was not noted in the missing sections, have been assumed that the seal of a temple did not require it. The text requires that temple letters were affixed by the seal. One might reasonably suggest that the originals, if not the copies of approximately 200 temple audits that we have from Roman imperial times, contained such a seal. One inscribed decree, dated to just before 100 BCE, directed at the operations of the temple of Apollo Koropaios near Demetrias in Thessaly, actually prescribes how oracle deliveries were to be made to individuals. Before an individual was to receive the response to his/her consultation, the result, written on a tablet, was to be placed in a jar which was to be closed and receive the seal of the city governors and law-keepers and the seal from the priest. Only the following morning were the seals to be broken and the oracle delivered to the inquirer.[63] Here we see another deployment of a temple seal.

59 Cicero *Flac.* 36.

60 See A. Marsden, "Overtones of Olympus: Roman Imperial Portrait Gems, Medallions and Coins in the 3rd Century," in *Gems of Heaven: Recent Research on Engraved Gemstones in Late Antiquity, c. AD 200–600* edited by C. Entwistle and N. Adams (London: British Museum Press, 2011), 167–8.

61 G. P. Verbrugghe and J. M. Wickersham, *Berossos and Manetho, introduced and translated: Native Traditions in Ancient Mesopotamia and Egypt* (Ann Arbor: University of Michigan Press, 2001), 121.

62 The papyrus was initially published by B. P. Grenfell and A. S. Hunt, *The Hibeh Papyri, Part 1* (London: Egypt Exploration Fund, 1906), 222–5.

63 *SIG* 3.1157.

Plate 5.8: A second-century statue of a priest of the imperial cult, now in the museum at İzmir. The ring is prominent on the pointer finger of the left hand and is carved so as to suggest a stone inset.

The iconography of Tyche

The interconnection of text and iconography is critical also. In the temple inventories, a ring-seal is sometimes described by its iconography as the distinguishing feature.[64] The general interpretation for the Colossian intaglio, set in train by Belley, has been that the figure on face A, the face without the inscription, is that of Helios-Apollo.[65] The radiate crown has been pivotal to this judgment. We have seen already that Colossae, at least as far as the testimony of its coins are concerned, did not, unlike adjacent Hierapolis, combine Helios with Apollo. Jacqueline Champeaux has argued an alternative: that the figure must be Tyche. Not only is the cornucopia highly suggestive, but the inscription on Face B is instrumental in fostering the new identification. Further investigation is warranted.

The draped bust has three symbols: the cornucopia, wings and a radiate crown. Taken separately, the default association for each is Tyche, Nike (Victory) and Helios, respectively. However, none of these symbols is quarantined to particular divinities throughout the Greco-Roman world. Nike is not known on the extant coins of Colossae,[66] though she does appear in a familiar guise on a garland sarcophagus (see Pl. 12.11).

Laodikeia, from the reign of Elagabalus in the third century, produced coins with the iconography of a winged Tyche, with a mural and radiate head-piece, holding a rudder and sheaf of wheat in her right hand and a cornucopia and globe in her left — an expansive conjunction of images![67] Another Laodikeian bronze, seemingly produced by (or honoring) the association of *Neoi*, combines multiple symbols for Tyche, omitting the wings but adding a caduceus, normally associated with (winged) Hermes (Pl. 5.9).

---

64 See, for example, *I.Délos* 298 (a gold finger-ring with a sard stone on which is engraved Nike); *I.Délos* 313, 380 (… Apollo); cf the light-hearted epigram of Archias "Looking at the cows and the jasper on my hand, you will fancy that the cows breathe and the jasper puts forth grass." *Gr. Anth.* 9.750 (translation Paton).

65 Gundel, *Zodiakos*, 129, 248 nr. 146 prefers Apollo but with an option on Helios.

66 Subject to the equivocation about a single example of one coin-type that has variously been identified (hesitantly) as Nike (*BMC Phrygia* Colossae 15; *MSPhryg* 2.579) or simply "a figure" (*RPC online* 4.2.1883 temp.).

67 *RPC online* 6.5512 temp.

Plate 5.9: The rare appearance of the Synhedrion of the Neoi on coins is seen in this example from Laodikeia (25 mm, 8.21 g). It is dated to the time of Elagabalus, on the basis of the legend on the reverse affirming neokorate Laodikeia. Radiate Tyche manages to hold ears of wheat, a patera and a caduceus in her right hand, cornucopia in her left hand and has a rudder and a wheel (usually associated with Nemesis) at her feet.[68]

It demonstrates that at least at the beginning of the third century, Tyche could appear both winged and radiate. But radiate Tyche may feature earlier at Colossae: during the reign of Hadrian; one of the Tyche bronzes from Colossae appears to render the head crowned with rays. The radiate Tyche is known on other carved gems as well,[69] as also the winged variety.[70] The winged Tyche is crucial for Plutarch's first century portrayal of the translocation of Tyche from the East to Rome.[71] So, iconographically, we are firmly in the early Roman imperial period. However, one Seleucid coin from Apameia also presents a winged Tyche,[72] and an Attalid coin from Philomelion,[73] so the typology is earlier, if much more rare.

Plate 5.10a and b: At left, the reverse of a coin from neokorate Laodikeia featuring winged Tyche with a polos (that is, a symbol of the city wall/mural tower) set in a radiate headpiece (time of Elagabalus (26 mm, 9.29 g)). At right, a coin of Colossae minted by Hieronymos (24 mm, 8.30 g) during the reign of Hadrian featuring what appears to be a radiate Tyche holding a rudder and globe or patera in her right hand and a cornucopia in her left.[74]

68 *SNG Righetti* 1195 *RPC online* 6.11006 temp; photograph courtesy of Leu Numismatik.

69 One sard intaglio combines almost a complete dossier of symbols around a standing radiate Tyche: John Paul Getty Museum, 85.AN.370.73; see J. Spier, *Ancient Gems and Finger Rings of the Collection of J. Paul Getty Museum* (Malibu, CA: J. Paul Getty Museum, 1992), 137, nr. 373.

70 Reinach, *Pierres gravées*, 48, pl. 46.98.1; 51 pl. 50, 13, 1; Spier, *Ancient Gems*, 109, nr. 275.

71 Plutarch *Fort. Rom.* (*Mor.*) 317F–318A.

72 A. Houghton, C. Lorber and O. Hoover, *Seleucid Coins, Part II* (New York: ANS, 2008), nr. 2242. The two volumes of Seleucid coins form the basis for online delivery at http://numismatics.org/sco/. See also *BMC Attica* 407.

73 *SNG Copen* 644–5; *SNG von Aulock* 3916.

74 *RPC online* 6.5512 temp., 3.2312A; first photograph © Ashmolean Museum, University of Oxford, by permission; second photograph courtesy of Mark Dunning.

A comparison of various symbols connected to Tyche on provincial coins in the East reveals a wide variety of associations. Tyche can recline, be seated on a chair or rock, be placed in a temple, offer a sacrifice over an altar, have a foot on the river-god or on a globe, hold ears of corn, poppies, a patera, a globe, as well as the nigh-ubiquitous cornucopia and rudder. At Tyre, she is, as might be expected, connected with a murex shell.[75] She can be veiled, or wear a modius, kalathos, tiara, stefane or the familiar mural crown. The evidence suggests, firstly, that Tyche, like most gods of the late Hellenistic and imperial Roman period, can be accorded symbols normally associated with other gods, as a "value-adding" to the beneficence and power of the revered deity.[76] This can be as powerful a way of demonstrating the concord of the gods as the placement of one god's statue in the sanctuary of another. But the Tyche also functioned symbiotically as a reflection of civic values and promotion of the city's prosperity. One of the most powerful demonstrations of the value of Tyche to the civic leadership comes in a Colossian bronze which features the veiled head of the "Sacred *Boulê*" with the traditional display of Tyche on the reverse, that is, with rudder, cornucopia and wearing the polos, or mural headpiece signifying the city (Pl. 5.11).[77]

Plate 5.11: Colossian bronze coin featuring, on the obverse, the veiled, draped bust of the female personification of ἱερὰ βουλή, the "sacred council". The reverse features the standing Tyche with rudder, cornucopia and wearing a polos.[78]

The city Council, the *Boulê*, was the group of aristocratic elite at Colossae that not only exerted control (that is, "held the rudder") over the direction of civic policy; it was also the key instrument through which Roman authorities maintained their influence in the *poleis* of the province of Asia (and elsewhere). For a coin to be minted bearing the symbols of the *Boulê* and of Tyche is a powerful indication of the importance attached to the Tyche of Colossae as patron and promoter of civic and religious culture. The other Colossian coin type featuring the *Boulê* has, on the obverse, a standing Zeus Aetophoros.[79] These two

75 *RPC* 9.1997, 2045 (time of Trebonianus Gallus).

76 This is readily seen in magical recipes and images but is not confined there. See C. Sfameni, "Magic in Late Antiquity: The Evidence of Magical Gems," in *Religious Diversity in Late Antiquity* edited by D. M. Gwynn and S. Bangert (Leiden, Brill, 2010), 461–3.

77 *MSPhryg* 2.537–9 cf nr. 540.

78 The coin is 22 mm in diameter, and weighs 5.27 g. Photograph from a private collection, by permission.

79 *MSPhryg* 2.534–6.

types provide a strong indication of the key divine patron and benefactor of the city, at least in the second to third century CE. The veiled female figure, a somewhat standardized symbol of the city council,[80] was intended to convey the piety and matronly concern of that institution, but there was no doubt that the members of the Council exercised the ultimate government within a city,[81] a rule that attracted/claimed a religious authority. Strikingly, the *Boulê* coins of Colossae lack any identification of a sponsoring benefactor (unlike neighboring Laodikeia, for example), so it must be assumed that the *Boulê* took direct responsibility for funding their production, even if it makes it more difficult for a researcher to date the coins.[82]

The radiate and fertile Tyche of face A of the intaglio may well reflect the fecund soil, well-watered and sun-drenched lands of the upper Lycus Valley in which Colossae claimed pride of settlement. As such one can expect that future discoveries at Colossae will include votives directed to the goddess from across status-levels just as at Praeneste/Palestrina where slave, freed, and free are all attested in devotional offerings to the goddess. Voluntary associations are also found amongst the dedicants.[83]

Plate 5.12: A dedication (dated to 179 CE) to "the compassionate Fortuna Primigenia … for the safety of the Augusti, Marcus Aurelius, Lucius Aelius [Commodus — the cognomen erased, l. 6, after his *damnatio memoriae* in 192 CE]."[84] The votive was dedicated by Fortunatus, a home-born slave and also household treasurer, and the freedwoman Aurelia Restituta, probably a *contubernalis* — his de facto wife. The red-painted lettering is probably a later restoration, even though faithful to the original.

In this sense, there is a confluence between the gem and the coins, in iconography and inscription. However, the gem takes the promotion of the city several steps further. Firstly, the accent on Tyche as Proto-

80 K. Martin, *Demos • Boule • Gerousia: Personifiktaionen städtische Institutionen auf kaiserzeitlichen Münzen aus Kleinasien* (Bonn: Habelt, 2 vols, 2013), vol 1, 124.

81 Martin, *Demos • Boule • Gerousia*, vol 1, 83.

82 Von Aulock assigned the two or three coin types featuring the sacred *Boulê* to the time of Septimius Severus or later (*MSPhryg* 2.534–540, including the coin in Plate 5.11). Barclay Head tentatively assigned the coin in plate 5.11 to the time of Gallienus (*BMC Phrygia* Colossae 11). *RPC* does not include these *Boulê* coins.

83 For example, the association of fullers — *CIL* 1.1456 (130–101 BCE); the association of basket-weavers — *CIL* 1.3071 (101–71 BCE); the association of viticulturists — *ILLRP* 106d (nd).

84 *CIL* 14.2856. Another section of inscription on the left side of the altar survived the *damnatio memoriae*. There, Commodus is left unerased.

geneia in the gem's inscription adds an element unknown elsewhere in the extensively excavated sites of Laodikeia, Hierapolis and Tripolis. Such an epithet confers, fundamentally, the honor of pre-eminence both in status and in chronology. Many of the persons called *Protogenês* or *Protogeneia* seem to have been so-named solely on the basis of being first-born.[85] One early Byzantine family grave even uses πρωτογενίς to indicate the eldest brother Trophimos.[86] The more common term to indicate a first-born, apart from the given name, was πρωτότοκος, a word of critical importance in the Christological hymn in the Letter to the Colossians (Col 1:15, 18). We shall return to this below.

The ubiquitous epithet conferred on Tyche is "Good," as in the form Ἀγαθῆι Τύχηι a heading opening numerous inscriptions, including from Colossae. In this sense, it is both an appeal for the beneficence of the goddess and an affirmation that her generosity has been manifest in the matter to be related. Inevitably, it betokens an authorization of the person and his/her contribution to civic life — for example, Korymbos' repair of the baths and extension of the water infrastructure, or Kastor's victory in a boxing championship.[87] Sport and monuments have long been avenues for the demonstration of good fortune. Often enough, it can appear as little more than formulaic.[88]

Tyche and a highly-credentialed leader at Colossae

There is a much rarer affirmation of Tyche in an inscription from Colossae that ensures that we recognize that she exercised a profound influence over the Colossian religious mind-set. The honorific inscription (ostensibly for the "homeland") set up by the brother (?) of Heliodoros,[89] who supervised its installation, seems to have supported a statue of Tyche above his *cursus honorum* (a list of sixteen high offices) laid out for him. His name is lost from the damaged stone. But it is one of the most important of Colossae's inscriptions, and warrants renewed investigation.

The copy is generally held to be no longer extant. However, when originally transcribed by Ernst Renan in 1865, it was noted as being used as a paving stone between the aisle and iconostasis of the Greek church in western Honaz, hav-

85 Sometimes, elevated status (such as fame gained from painting) made more of the name; see Cengiz Işık and Christian Marek, *Das Monument des Protogenes in Kaunos* (AMS 26; Bonn: Habelt, 1997). Hence the name could be used of eminence not just chronological priority.

86 *I.Kios* 120.

87 *Antichthon* 2012.152, l. 1; *Steinepigramme* 1.02.15.01, l. 1.

88 See, for example, *I.Laodikeia Lykos* 11, 41, 42; *MAMA* 5.87, 101.

89 It should be noted that "his brother" is a reconstruction of a last line (l. 12). None of the copies (that is, of Le Bas, Weber, Anderson) provides any letter remnant to enable confidence. The addition is influenced by comparable early imperial inscriptions, for example, *CIG* 2787 (Aphrodisias), *MAMA* 8.421 (Aphrodisias), *I.Smyrna* 494.

ing been moved there from another secondary site in the fortress on the lower reaches of Honazdağ (Mount Cadmus) above the town. (The double translocation probably explains the damage to the stone.) The church, "The Church of the Nativity of the Theotokos",[90] was converted after the Greek repatriation in the 1920s into "the old cami", as the local inhabitants still refer to it. Capitals and other carved stones from the site of Colossae were also located here and remained in use in some fashion, including a Byzantine capital replete with a cross.[91] There is a possibility that the inscribed stone remains extant beneath the carpet now covering the floor of the still-operating mosque. It is worthwhile giving the inscription here, as usually presented. It is also annotated (with superscript letters) in light of previous analyses, especially interacting with Louis Robert's comments, the most recent to engage the record of the stone.

- -[a]
- - - - - - -ἀφιέρωσεν τὴ]ν[b] θεὰν Τύχην τῆι πατρίδι[c]
ὁ δεῖνα τοῦ δεῖνος][d] στρατηγήσας, ἀγορανομήσας
- - - - - - - - - - - -ήσα]ς, βουλαρχήσας, γραμματεύ-
4 σας - - - - - - - - - - - - [e] τ]αμιεύσας, ἐφηβαρχήσας, ε-
ἰρηναρχήσας,][f] νομοφυλακήσας, παραφυλάξας,
ἐπιμεληθεὶς τ]ῆς τοῦ ἐλαίου θέσεως, ἐργεπιστα-
τήσας, ἐπιμελ]ηθεὶς χωρίων δημοσίων, ἀναθεὶς θε-
8 οῖς - - - -[g]]ἀργυρᾶν, ἐκδικήσας καὶ ἐν σειτοδείᾳ πα-
ρασχὼν τὸν σεῖτ]ον[h] ἐπὶ τὸ εὐωνότερον καὶ εἰς κυριακὰς
- - - - - - - - - -][i] κ(αὶ) συνθύσας τῷ δευτέρῳ να-
11 ῷ. Ἐπιμεληθέντος τῆς ἀνα]στάσεως Ἡλιοδώρου
τοῦ ἀδελφοῦ].[j]

a The inscription is likely to have opened with Ἀγαθῆι Τύχηι on a top line with a following line giving the name (with his genealogy?) of the dedicant of the statue of Tyche and perhaps his motivation for doing so (fulfilment of a promise, recognition of a benefit or the like). Given the accent on meeting imperial obligations (ll. 4–5 *eirenarch*, ll. 9–10 delegate to neokorate festivities), the dedicant may have added φιλοσέβαστος or φιλόκαισαρ (or both) to his name.[92]

90 This is the name of the church recorded by George Lampakis in 1906. A comparison of his photographs to today's building confirms the identification: Οἱ ἑπτὰ ἀστέρες τῆς Ἀποκαλύψεως (Athens: 1909), 453–7.

91 See Cadwallader, *Fragments of Colossae*, 19, 198.

92 Compare *I.Iasos* 616 (Bargylia, 79 or 81 CE) where the dedicant, Exekestos son of Diodoros, layers up the "philos": φιλόκαισαρ, φιλόπατρις, φιλοσέβαστος (l. 10). A more modest simple φιλοσέβαστος follows immediately upon the name Gaius Iulius Epagathos from third century Ephesos, before proceeding to list further offices. If so here, this would reduce the need for Σεβαστοῖς, preferred by Robert after θεοῖς in ll. 7–8, it being understood which "gods" were being named.

b Georg Weber suggested ἀφιέρωσεν (9 letters) as the governing verb omitting the article before θεάν.[93] J. G. C. Anderson opted for the more conservative option, ἀνεθῆκεν (8 letters).

c Both Weber and Anderson, at the end of the nineteenth century, provided a cleaner reading of the first extant line. The earlier copy of Ernst Renan, as reconstructed, read θεὰν εὐχὴν Σεράπιδι,[94] whence J. B. Lightfoot interpreted the inscription as recording fulfillment of a sacred vow to Sarapis.[95]

d ὁ δεῖνα τοῦ δεῖνος (l. 2) is correctly suggested as a possible introduction to the list of offices and exemplary deeds,[96] given that the foremost office, that of the *strategos*,[97] follows. Some other extolling description might equally have been present, for example, ἀνὴρ καλὸς κἀγαθός,[98] though this expression, like the former, is usually conferred by others.

e In ll. 3–4, two further offices are to be added. Given that a *cursus honorum* usually ran from the higher offices to the lower and thence to some noteworthy performances, it is reasonable to consider the options as στεφανηφορήσας, γυμνασιαρχήσας, πανηγυριαρχήσας, ἀγωνοθετήσας. Each of these has sufficient letters to fill out the line (approximately 35 to 40 letters), and are of the requisite status to be placed among the other offices that can be made out.[99]

f Robert argued that the fracturing of the diphthong precluded the reconstruction ε-ἰρηναρχήσας. However such a break is found in another Colossian inscription, an epitaph with the name Ε-ἰρήνη,[100] and elsewhere. It would be unexpected for such a Colossian dignitary, with obvious Roman connections, not to hold the office of *eirenarch*. Moreover, other possible offices beginning with *epsilon*, such as ἐκλογιστής, an inspector of accounts, and ἐξεταστής an auditor of accounts or elections or the official entrusted with the publication of decrees, probably cannot claim the same standing here,[101] and do not cohere with the law enforcement offices with

93 Weber's communication on the inscription was reported in "Fonde" *MDAI(A)* 23 (1898): 365 nr. 6.

94 P. Le Bas, *Explication des Inscriptions Grecques et Latines recueillies en Grèce et en Asie Mineure* (Paris: Firmin Didot, 1873), 401, nr. 1693b.

95 J. B. Lightfoot, *Colossians and Philemon* (London: Macmillan, 9th ed., 1890), 13 n1.

96 See *SEG* 13.521 (Pergamon, 2nd century BCE).

97 On the shift of the title of *strategos* from a military commander to that of civic governance, see R. Bennett, *Local Elites and Local Coinage. Elite Self-Representation on the Provincial Coinage of Asia, 31 BC to AD 275* (London: RNS, 2014), 8–10.

98 See for example, *BCH* 1890.90–93, 1, l. 2 (Halicarnassus or Theangela), 3rd to 2nd century BCE); *IG* IV² 1, 63, l. 1 (Epidauros, 115/114 BCE); *I.Iasos* 98 ll. 4–5 (1st century BCE).

99 Compare, for example, T. Ritti, "La Carriera di un Cittadino do Hierapolis di Frigia: G. Memmios Eutychos," *CCG* 19 (2008): 279–80 (211–217 CE); *I.Tralleis* 73 (Eumeneia[?], 1st to early 2nd century CE) *I.Iasos* 84, 87 (175–6 and 176–7 CE, respectively), *I.Didyma* 372 (3rd century CE).

100 See A. H. Cadwallader, "Gertrude Bell's Resolution of a Disputed Inscription," *Gephyra* 20 (2020): 17, ll. 7–8 of the recovered inscription. See chapter 11.

101 See *I.Laodikeia Lykos* 2 (2nd to 3rd century CE) where there appears to be a bureau of *exetastai*. *I.Hierapolis Judeich* 32 (imperial) records the *cursus honorum* of Gaius Agelaius Apollinides running from *strategos* to *exetastes* (named last of the offices held).

which ε(ἰρηναρχήσας) is grouped, from ἐφηβαρχήσας to παραφυλάξας (ll. 4–5). εὐθηνιαρχήσας might be possible, but would incur Robert's identical objection, as well as being little known in Asia.[102]

g Robert seemed torn between naming the intended gods after θεοῖς (ll. 7–8, he suggested Σεβαστοῖς) and wanting to specify the nature of the silver offering immediately following. He preferred τράπεζαν in the sense of the presentation table for offerings to the gods.[103] This would better fit the letter space.

h The reconstruction here is problematic. The number of letters for the line as reconstructed comes to 44, considerably more than the 35 to 40 letters allowed. Presuming that the left margin is straight as the right edge appears to be, then a shorter line seems required. Robert had suggested πα-ραπωλήσας, equally at home in organizing grain distribution but the alternative suffers similarly from the issue of length — as also does another possibility παραπολῶν.[104] One possible solution is to take the *omicron* opening the surviving line 9 as an *omega* and elide the reconstruction τὸν σεῖτον. Waddington's semi-reproduction of the uncials had only a partially formed curvilinear letter-shape, allowing for *omicron* or *omega* to be formed.[105] However, a simpler solution is found in the return to Waddington's copy (from that taken by Rénan), which reveals a considerable use of ligatures,[106] most significantly for our purposes in the use of Ꝃ for καί in ll. 8, 9, 10. Only the last is signalled in the copy relied upon by Robert, giving κ(αί). This allows a simple removal of τὸν after παρασχών, an anarthrous occurrence found elsewhere,[107] and thereby satisfies with 39 letters, made the more contracted by two other ligatures.

i To give the sense of εἰς κυριακάς in l. 9, Robert made a direct comparison to a Hierapolitan honorific for G. Agelaius Apollinides where the citizen is, *inter alia*, acclaimed for his provision of services to meet imperial needs: εἰς χρίας κυριακὰς εὔχρηστον γενόμενον.[108] The papyri are more liberal in the attestation of such a formula, where χρεῖαι occurs synonymously for ὑπηρεσίαι to explicate εἰς κυριακάς;[109] hence it can simply refer to the "imperial services" of stone quarrying, for example.[110] Of particular interest is the requisition for camels from vil-

102 See however *I.Stratonikeia* 296a (Panamara, late 2nd to early 3rd century CE); compare *P.Oxy.* 3568 (273/4 CE).

103 *IG* VII 3498, ll. 2–3 (inventory for temple of Amphiaraos; Oropos, early 2nd century BCE); *SEG* 21.456 ll. 87–8 (Athens, 86–90 CE); *IGR* 3.800 (Sillyon, nd).

104 *Syll* 3.708, l. 39 (Histria, mid-1st century BCE) cf *TAM* III 62.

105 *LBW* 1693b.

106 Waddington's uncial copy reveals ligatures in l. 1 (HN) l. 2 (MH), l. 7 (HM), l. 9 (NE, TE). There is also a small *gamma* noted in l. 6, whether stylistic or a subscript correction of an omission cannot be determined.

107 *IG* X,2 2.53, ll. 2–3 (Herakleia in Macedonia, 100–150 CE); *Syll* 3.708, l. 39 (Histria, mid-1st century BCE).

108 *I.Hierapolis Judeich* 32, ll. 21–23; cf *IGR* 4.1228 (Thyateira, imperial period).

109 *BGU* 1.266 (Arsinoite, 216/7 CE, for the provision of camels for military service).

110 *P.Stras.* 9.872, l. 14 (Arsinoite, 200–225 ce); *P.Bingen* 110, l. 8 (Philoteris, 246/7 CE).

lagers at Soknopaiou Nesos (in Arsinote); the salient expression reads παρέσχον εἰς κυριακὰς χρείας "they provided for imperial service".[111] It seems then that a relatively stock expression was available. Here because of the mention of famine, χρείας is to be preferred, with some qualifier such as εὔχρηστον/ως as we find in Apollinides' provision. Waddington's uncial reproduction records an upper horizontal hasta before the contracted καί. This permits a reconstruction εἰς κυριακὰς χρείας εὐχρήστως ... granting a line of 35 letters accepting the Ꝁ as appears in Waddington's copy.[112]

j There is nothing surviving in Waddington's reproduction to admit the addition of τοῦ ἀδελφοῦ in l. 12.[113] If there was a completion of the inscription in such a line, it is just as likely that a Greek patronym was provided, viz. τοῦ N., or that of Heliodoros's office.

These critical remarks permit a generous reconstruction of the inscription as follows. It can be adjudged from the notes above that some suggestions — τράπεζαν ἀργυρᾶν and εἰς κυριακὰς χρείας εὐχρήστως for example — hold greater probability than others. Even here, the suggestions carry similar weight to those already regularly adopted from the usual reproduction of the inscription from Cagnat and Lafaye (in *IGR* 4.870).

[Ἀγαθῆι Τύχηι | N., NN. (gen.), τοῦ N. Φιλο-| σέβαστος ἀφιέρωσεν τὴ]ν θεᾶν Τύχην τῆι πατρίδι | [ὁ δεῖνα τοῦ δεῖνος] στρατηγήσας, ἀγορανομήσας | [στεφανηφορήσα]ς, βουλαρχήσας, γραμματεύ-| [σας ἀγωνοθετήσας τ]αμιεύσας, ἐφηβαρχήσας, ε-| [ἰρηναρχήσας,] νομοφυλακήσας, παραφυλάξας,| ἐπιμεληθεὶς τ]ῆς τοῦ ἐλαίου θέσεως, ἐργεπιστα-| [τῆσας, ἐπιμελ]ηθεὶς χωρίων δημοσίων, ἀναθεὶς θε-| [οῖς τράπεζαν] ἀργυρᾶν, ἐκδικήσας κ(αὶ) ἐν σειτοδείᾳ πα-| ρασχὼν σεῖτ]ον ἐπὶ τὸ εὐωνότερον κ(αὶ) εἰς κυριακὰς | [χρείας εὐχρήστως] κ(αὶ) συνθύσας τῷ δευτέρῳ να-| ῷ. Ἐπιμεληθέντος τῆς ἀνα]στάσεως Ἡλιοδώρου | [τοῦ N.].

Translation: *(For good fortune. N, son of NN, grandson of NNN, friend of the Emperor, dedicated) the (statue of) the goddess Tyche for the homeland, (the incomparable one) who was a commander, a market superintendant (the official crown-bearer), president of the Council, the city clerk, (the organizer of the games), city treasurer, director of the ephebes, keeper of the peace, public law-enforcer, warden of the interior, manager of the oil distribution, inspector of public works, overseer of the public estates, dedicator of a silver (offering table), public advocate; and in the famine, supplied grain at favorable rates and diligently met imperial obligations, and joined in the sacrifices at the second [neokorate] temple. Heliodoros, (son of N or the monument overseer), supervised the erection of the statue.*

---

111 *P.Lond.* 2.328, ll. 9–10 (163 CE).

112 The abbreviation of καί also occurs in ll. 8 and 9 of Waddington's copy.

113 The addition is influenced by comparable early imperial inscriptions, for example, *CIG* 2787 (Aphrodisias), *MAMA* 8.421 (Aphrodisias), *I.Smyrna* 494.

The state of the stone as copied means that we do not know the name of the dignitary using a dedication of a statue of Tyche to the "homeland" (τῆι πατρίδι, l. 1) to parade his own *cursus honorum*. The name of Heliodoros has no Roman citizenry marker, unlike the memorial set up for Marcus Larcius Crispinus, supervised by Tiberius Asinius Epaphroditos.[114] There is no doubt that he would have been a member of the civic elite, and hence with a symbiotic relationship of support with Rome. The absence of Roman citizenship points to the first or second century for date parameters. This can be narrowed further by two items in the text — the provision of grain for imperial needs at a time of famine and the representation of Colossae at the "second temple" celebrations. Both are regarded in the inscription as highly significant interventions by the dedicator-honorand, almost certainly tapping into the collective memory of the civic populace. Two events stand out that, given longevity of life, fall within the span of a person's service to the city — the granting of a second neokorate to the cities of Ephesos and Smyrna in 132 CE,[115] likely the former given the heavy emphasis on Artemisian iconography known at Colossae. The second event is the famine that coincided with the movement of troops through Asia Minor for confrontations with the Parthians on the eastern border in 161–166 CE.[116] There is however, no mention of the plague that came at the end of that period and which preoccupied civic leaders in the Lycus.[117] We may then be witnessing a career of, perhaps, forty years, culminating in a celebration of Colossae's prosperity that is attributed to the public service of this unknown man who claimed the patronage of the goddess of fecundity and the providential ordering of life, namely, Tyche.

There is one leader and benefactor who, shortly after this general timeframe, sponsored the minting of coins at Colossae during the co-regency of Commodus (177–80 CE), named Zosimos. The reverse iconography of the two known coins of that time gives two presentations of Artemis, one as the hunter riding in a biga (see chapter 4, Pl. 4.6), a second standing with one of her stags and holding a branch, still with her quiver slung at her shoulder. The coin legends specify his (eponymous) office of στρατηγός (cf l. 2) as well as a description which had become a titular award,[118] that is, φιλοπάτωρ.[119] Whilst this is not the same as φιλόπατρις (implied in the τῆι πατρίδι of the extant l. 1)[120] it was sometimes combined in an almost synonymous, elative formula (φιλοπάτριδας

114 *MAMA* 6.39 = *I.Mus. Denizli* 59 (1st century CE). See chapter 11.
115 See B. Burrell, *Neokoroi: Greek Cities and Roman Emperors* (Leiden: Brill, 2004), 62.
116 See D. Magie, *Roman Rule in Asia Minor* (Princeton: Princeton University Press, 2 vols, 1950), vol 1, 663.
117 See U. Huttner, *Early Christianity in the Lycus Valley* (Leiden: Brill, 2013), 266–9.
118 J. C. G. Anderson, "A Summer in Phrygia II," *JHS* 18 (1898): 90.
119 *RPC online* 4.2.1880 temp., 1881 temp.
120 φιλόπατρις is used to designate Antonius Polemo on Laodikeian bronzes from the time of Augustus (*RPC* 1.2898–2900).

καὶ φιλοπάτορας).[121] Zosimos appears in no doubt about his importance to the city, deploying the rare legend, τῶν περὶ Ζώσιμον ... Κολοσσηνῶν. In Bithynia, the coins of the Kilbianoi gave a territorial designation that they were περὶ Νείκαιαν, that is "around Nicea,"[122] clearly indicating their anchor; similar is the claim of Zosimos. In any case, the benefactor concerned bears a name held by four generations in succession, that is, Zosimos. His coins were struck during the reign of Marcus Aurelius when Commodus was co-regent (that is, 177–180 CE). It cannot be proved given our existing knowledge, but, it seems to me that the combination of *strategos* and "love of the father", may indicate that the unknown leader self-honoring in the (lost or concealed) inscription could be an ancestor of Zosimos IV, perhaps his father (or grandfather). A succession in office-holding would not be unusual.

The underscoring of Tyche as goddess (θεά) is not unique, but it is rare.[123] Other deities might similarly be inscribed as such, suggesting that the superfluity is delivering an emphasis. But the accent on Tyche as goddess removes any thought that Tyche was merely a cipher for chance luck, a shorthand, or even a convenient excuse for the vicissitudes or munificence that impact on life.[124] Here the addition that the statue of the goddess was erected for the homeland (τῆι πατρίδι) is designed to convey that Tyche was critical for the welfare of the city and its territories.[125] Given that the list of offices unfolded for the responsible benefactor makes reference to provision during a grain shortage (ll. 8–9), the impact of Tyche on the experience of Colossians was apparently much to the fore — her rudder had steered the city through the trouble that, doubtless, she had some responsibility for fulminating.[126] The fulsome list of positions held is an ample display amongst the Colossian leadership that Tyche had enabled the city (and territory) of Colossae to function with pride as an exemplary polis in the valley and in the Roman province.

---

121 *I.Sardis* 7,1.41, ll. 10–11 (Philadelphia, 1st century to early 2nd century CE).

122 *RPC* 2.1056.

123 See *IG* X,2.2.336 (Styberra, 126/127 CE); G. E. Bean and T. B. Mitford, *Journeys in Rough Cilicia 1964–68* (Vienna: ÖAW, 1970), 173, nr. 189 (Lamos, 3rd century CE); *OGIS* 479 (1st to 2nd century CE). Occasionally the common description of "great" (familiar from Acts 19:28) is added: *IG* XII 3.97 (Nisyros), *CIG* 3953d (Herakleia Salbake), an acclamation received by almost every favored god at some time. It is found on other inscribed gems in the curious formula "the Tyche of the savior gods/of Nemesis" almost in the form of the *genius/daimôn*: E. Le Blant, *750 Inscriptions de pierres gravées in édites ou peu connues* (Paris: C. Klincksieck, 1896), 80 nrs 209, 210.

124 See a convenient summary of the various ancient assessments of Tyche/Fortuna in E. Baynham, *Alexander the Great: The Unique History of Quintus Curtius* (Ann Arbor: University of Michigan Press, 1998), 104–11.

125 For a sense of the visual aesthetics of the statue, see Plutarch *Fort. Rom.* (*Mor.*) 317E–318D, Dio Chrysostom *Or.* 63.7, 64.5–7.

126 See Dio Chrysostom *Or.* 64.1–2 on the attribution of misfortune to Tyche. For a sharp criticism of Fortuna, see *Rhet. Her.* 2.23, 36 (Pacuvius).

As such it is highly likely that there was at least one temple for Tyche at Colossae, not merely as a pale replication of Rome's own preoccupation with claiming Fortuna as her own (in architecture, coinage and inscriptions attesting the favour of the goddess for the emperors and the emperor). With temple, statuary and coinage, went cultic ritual, officials and hymnody, an acclaim that could not help but visually and aurally impress upon residents of the city. Whether the Colossian Tyche Protogeneia was consulted for oracular pronouncement by prophet and/or lot (as was the case for Fortuna Primigenia at Praeneste)[127] is not known. Given the diminution (but not eradication) of Apollo in early imperial Colossae, as part of the city's reclaiming of its distinct place over and against Hierapolis and Laodikeia, it would not surprise to find such a function developing for Tyche Protogeneia. The zodiac might suggest this but other explanations of the signs are possible. Of course, a carnelian intaglio swivel-ring long held in European collections, leaves no trace of its find-spot,[128] so it is only the evidence of the ring itself, brought into dialogue with comparable material testimony, that can be suggestive of temple usage.

The erection of a statue to the goddess Tyche is therefore not only carefully chosen by the benefactor who secured returns of recognition for so doing, but it is also an index of the city's prosperity and grateful devotion in the mid-second century CE. Tyche provided the inspiration for a variety of theonyms drawing in greater or lesser measure on her favour. The name Eutyches is attested among those honoring Korymbos the repairer of the baths,[129] a limpid witness to her place in the Colossian social imagination. And, of course, there stands the famous Tychikos named in the Letter to the Colossians (Col 4:7). David Magie long ago recognized the crucial witness of this inscription as demonstrating that "Colossae was an important place in the imperial period,"[130] an observation too often overlooked by Second Testament commentators at least until recently.[131] Key to this importance, implies the inscription, was Tyche. But the Tyche of Colossae was more than the standard affirmations of her as a deity (not an abstract force or even a personification).[132] The epithet Protogeneia is similarly rare,[133] and brings dimensions that move beyond the common iconography on coins, reliefs and gems, of cornucopia, rudder and sometimes globe

127 Propertius *Eleg.* 2.32.3; Cicero *Div.* 2.86. See W. E. Klingshirn, "Inventing the *sortilegus*: lot divination and cultural identity in Italy, Rome, and the provinces," in *Religion in Republican Italy* edited by C. E. Schultz and P. B. Harvey (Cambridge: Cambridge University Press, 2006), 137–61.

128 See the circumspect comments of Andrew Goldman, "The octagonal gemstones from Gordion: observations and interpretations," *AS* 64 (2014): 163–4.

129 *Antichthon* 2012.152, l. 31.

130 D. Magie, *Roman Rule in Asia Minor* (Princeton, NJ: Princeton University Press, 1950), 986.

131 Janice Capel Anderson has named the change that has come over scholarship on the background to the Letter to the Colossians: *Colossians: Authorship, Rhetoric, and Code* (London: T & T Clark, 2019), 201.

132 These options are ancient. See, for example, Plutarch, *Quaest. Rom.* (*Mor*) 281D-E.

133 So J. Champeaux, "Primigenius, ou de l'Originaire," *Latomus* 34 (1975): 977; Miano, *Fortuna*, 175.

as her repertoire.[134] At a textual and comparative level, the affirmation is that Tyche is "first-born" of Zeus and shared with him salvific and beneficent qualities.[135] This would fit neatly with the eminence of Zeus in the Colossian pantheon. However, Tyche's beneficent attributes were frequently portrayed through her (wet?)-nursing of Zeus and Hera,[136] a paradox of daughter-mother that may have an origin in the agricultural cycle. And yet, as much as these mythological tropes can be found in literature and in material expression, there is nothing in the inscription or the iconography of the intaglio to attract such an interpretation.

Tyche, cosmic order and the zodiac

So to the second extension of interpretation. Here we look to the cosmic setting surrounding the bust of Tyche, that is, the zodiac. There is no doubt that astronomical investigation was crucial in rationalizing the establishment of the Roman empire. Augustus made considerable political mileage from the horoscope accenting the Capricornian felicity of his birth — and cities in the east were not slow to capture the goat-fish, the land-sea ruler, on their coins.[137] Manilius in many ways acted as the articulator of Augustus' divine (read astronomical) confirmation.[138] His writing will assist us in the interpretation of the zodiac face of the gem. The perimeter, zodiacal setting of the intaglio affirms that Tyche Protogeneia pervades and heads the cosmic realm. Manilius, the esteemed Augustan astronomer, saw Fortuna operating through the various influences of the twelve star-signs to cover every aspect of life.[139] This conjunction of Tyche and the zodiac is not singular. A Nabatean relief portrays poliadic Tyche surrounded by the twelve astrological symbols (though likewise not in the usual order), both upheld by a winged Atargatis.[140]

---

134 For examples of the standard iconography of Tyche/Fortuna on gems, see E. R. M. Dusinberre, *Gordion Seals and Sealings: Individuals and Society* (Philadelphia: University of Pennsylvania Museum of Archaeology and Anthropology, 2005), 86, cat. 100, fig. 110; Spier, *Ancient Gems*, 44 nr. 79, 121 nr. 315.

135 This is expressly named in a third century BCE inscribed bronze plaque from Praeneste: *Fortuna Diovo fileia Primogenia* (*CIL* 14.2863) and reiterated by Cicero *Div.* 2.85, *Leg.* 2.28. See also *Archaic Latin Inscriptions. Dedicatory Inscriptions* (LCL 359), nr. 144.

136 Cicero *Div.* 2.85.

137 See chapter 7, Pl. 7.5.

138 See S. J. Green, "*Arduum ad astra*: The poetics and politics of horoscopic failure in Manilius' *Astronomica*," in *Forgotten Stars: Rediscovering Manilius'* Astronomica edited by S. J. Green and K. Volk (Oxford: Oxford University Press, 2011), 129–38.

139 Manilius *Astron.* 3.96–158.

140 See G. Markoe, "Petra: Lost City of Stone," *Minerva* 15 (2004): 8–12, where two pieces, one from the Cincinnati Art Museum, one from the Royal Museum in Amman, Jordan, were found to belong together as one (dated 50–150 CE); see also D. G. Greenbaum, *The Daimon in Hellenistic Astrology: Origins and Influence* (Leiden: Brill, 2016), 92–5.

This is where Plutarch's rationale behind his slightly-obfuscating abbreviated equivalence of Fortuna Primigenia and Tyche Protogeneia[141] can offer a clue:

> Ἢ φυσικώτερον ἔχει λόγον τὸ πρᾶγμα καὶ φιλοσοφώτερον, ὡς τὴν τύχην πάντων οὖσαν ἀρχὴν καὶ τὴν φύσιν ἐκ τοῦ κατὰ τύχην συνισταμένην, ὅταν τισὶν ὡς ἔτυχεν ἀποκειμένοις τάξις ἐγγένηται;
>
> Or does the issue have an explanation more natural and philosophic, which assumes that Tyche is the origin of everything, and Nature acquires its solid frame by the operation of Tyche, whenever order is created in any store of matter gathered together as haphazard?[142]

Here one can detect Plutarch's reliance on accents of Middle Platonism, that matter is crucial, yet itself crucially dependent on the operations of a power beyond the material realm. In turn, that same ordered material realm bears witness in its physic or mathematical structure. Fortuna is both reliant upon the heavenly realm, inseparable from the influences of the stars and at the same time, herself, the provider of the order that governs the operations of the stars (an echo of the daughter-mother paradox). The cosmic dimension, critical to her continuous blessing, is what the circle of the star-signs, at a basic level, communicates. We shall return to this when examining Face B of the intaglio. For now it can be affirmed that we are not dealing with a horoscope. The absence of planetary signs (including sun or moon) strongly indicates this, granting that the central figure, governed by the inscription, is Tyche not Helios.[143] Consequently, Belley's speculation that here is a city foundation day (whether or not tied to Roman Fortuna's festival date of April 10/11th)[144] can be dismissed.[145] It is not unique to have signs missing from a zodiac or for the signs to be out of the familiar sequence,[146] whether for horoscopic or other purposes.

The arrangement remains problematic. However, an insight from Wolfgang Hübner is suggestive.[147] All commentators to date have taken the figure in the "mid-heaven" as Taurus, but Hübner argues that the figure is rather Ares the Ram, making Virgo and Taurus the missing signs. He further notes that the

141 Plutarch *Quaest. Rom.* (*Mor.*) 289B.

142 Plutarch *Quaest. Rom.* (*Mor.*) 289C (translation Babbitt, slightly adjusted).

143 Manilius argues that both sun and moon are crucial to the construction of a horoscope: *Astron.* 3.186–90. See especially S. Heilen and A. Mastrocinque, "A Third Horoscope-Gem, Twin of the Parisian 'Seyrig Gem,'" *MHNH* 17 (2017): 103–38.

144 Verrius Flaccus, *Fast. Praenest* (*CIL* 1^2 pp. 235, 315); Ovid *Fast.* 4.145–50. It should be noted that the official Roman calendar allotment for Fortuna did not usurp the Praenestian festival in May. See A. E. Cooley, "Beyond Rome and Latium: Roman Religion in the age of Augustus," in *Religion in Republican Italy*, 239.

145 Belley, "Observations," 13.

146 See Gundel, *Zodiakos*, 103, 116, 117, 122, 232.

147 Personal communication October 2016. I am grateful also to several other scholars whose expertise in the interpretation of ancient zodiacs has been of particular assistance — Daryn Lehoux, Cristian Tomas and Stephan Heilen.

signs at top, the now-Ares, Leo and Sagittarius are each part of the grouping assigned to the highest element, that is, fire. In Manilius' terms, they are the "allied trigonal signs".[148] The tail of the Ram accents this by its upward "flare". Manilius wrote, "the Ram heads the procession of the skies,"[149] as the leader of the zodiac (the sign of the spring solstice).[150] Indeed, elsewhere in his apportioning of the human body to the twelve signs, Ares is granted the head, "as the *princeps* over all."[151] The heaviest element, water, is traditionally assigned to Pisces, Scorpio and Cancer but in this instance is accented by Capricorn appearing as a goat-fish and by Aquarius being "reduced" to the water-vessel, its spilling contents providing the fitting symmetry to Ares' tail. This accent on the two fundamental elements of fire and water negates the need for Virgo and Taurus — both belonging to earth. The balance of Libra and Gemini, the humanoids normally connected with the element of air (along with Aquarius), are caught into the weightiness of signs belonging to or constructed for water.[152] However, that there are *seven* signs so grouped together (namely Pisces, Scorpio, Cancer, Libra, Libra, Gemini and Capricorn) will find a critical connection with the symbols on face B (on which see below). Here, the primal creativity of fire and water, given by Manilius in his survey of theories of the origin of the universe,[153] holds priority *before* any expansion into four elements (that is, adding air and earth). These two forces, just as in the arrangement on face A of the intaglio, stand over against each other, each able to bring the demise of the other but in their balanced confrontation unlocking the beneficent order of the universe.[154] With its rivers and streams, springs, snow, rainfall with light and heat pouring from above the line of the Taurus mountains, Colossae's southern boundary, no more potent astronomical demonstration of the source of the prosperity of Colossae's territory could be provided.

---

148 *sociata trigona signa*; Manilius *Astron.* 2.523–4. On fire as the highest in the heavens, see Manilius *Astron.* 1.150.

149 *Aries qua ducit Olympum*; Manilius *Astron.* 2.945 (translation of G. P. Goold). Manilius may be unique in this emphasis: see D. G. Greenbaum, "Roman Astrology," in *Astrology through History: Interpreting the Stars from Ancient Mesopotamia to the Present* edited by W. E. Burns (Santa Barbara: ABC-CLIO, 2018), 298. If so, there may be a tantalizing echo in this intaglio.

150 Manilius *Astron.* 1.263–4.

151 Manilius *Astron.* 2.456.

152 W. Hübner, "Manilius als Astrologe und Dichter," *ANRW* 2, 32, 1 (1984): 150–8. It is important to remember that "no two astrological treatises offer exactly the same classification of signs"; D. B. Martin, "Hellenistic Superstition: The Problems of Defining a Vice," in *Conventional Values of the Hellenistic Greeks* edited by P. Bilde *et al.* (Aarhus: Aarhus University Press, 1997), 144.

153 Manilius *Astron.* 1.132–6 cf Plato *Tim.* 28b, 31b–32b cf Plutarch who cites Plato to this effect *Fort. Rom.* (*Mor.*) 316E-F.

154 Cf Manilius *Astron.* 1.142–4 of the discord of the elements yet being brought into harmony from which flows lavish provision.

More pertinent however, is that the seven-signed collation for the element of water taps into one of the main explanations provided for earthquakes, namely that underground water sources have somehow lost their equilibrium and unleashed the fury of untethered power on the earth. Although the element of air was said to be the source of seismic eruption by Aristotle,[155] he allowed that there were earlier thinkers (Anaximenes of Miletus and Democritus) who targeted water as the culprit. Seneca the Younger relayed basically the same information,[156] but also admitted, citing Epicurus, that all the elements were implicated in different places at different times.[157] Water, especially underground water, was one of the mysterious if provident resources for Colossae, with springs to the south (at the St Michael shrine, now Göz Picnic Ground) and to the east (near the origins of the Ak Su, the river that runs past the höyük), with smaller streams feeding from the south, especially swollen by the spring melt of the snow-capped Taurus mountain range. The ferocity of the Lycus caused not only by the volume of water at certain times of the year but by the honey-comb pockets in the limestone river-bed, meant that the river was well-named: "the Wolf". It is little wonder that water would be the prime element for consideration as the cause of earthquakes in this setting, just as, with Tyche's benevolent face, the lavish waters fomented Colossae's fecundity.

Plate 5.13a, b and c: A montage of the Lycus River, showing, at left, the chasm of the river Lycus in 2013 coursing west through lush farmland and orchards past the acropolis at left and necropolis at the right through to the lower plain between Laodikeia and Hierapolis in the hazy distance. The line of the chasm is marked in a thin blue line. In the middle, in the autumn flow (2015), the water disappears into an underground cavern later to reappear, seemingly from underground, further along (right). In winter flow neither the ingress nor the egress of the river into carved out "dudens" are visible. The waters rush at a higher level, despite the recently-constructed channel just north syphoning much of its capacity.

155 Aristotle *Mete.* 2.7.365a.
156 Seneca *Nat.* book 6.
157 As paraphrased by Seneca *Nat.* 6.20.5.

Poseidon was often the god particularly blamed or consulted in regard to earthquakes. Of course, he is the god of the oceans but these waters were understood as running under the ground as well as visible in lakes and seas, so it is not a surprise to find Poseidon venerated in inland Asia Minor.[158] But earthquakes did not narrow attention to Poseidon; other gods were as readily sought out for protection or restoration.[159] There is no evidence, to date, of Poseidon at Colossae. His role seems likely to have been subsumed by Tyche Protogeneia. It may be that the honors for Korymbos, previously mentioned, give particular weight to the opening of the inscription — Ἀγαθῆι Τύχηι, "To Good Tyche" — as the benefactor joined the goddess in restoring order to the waters of Colossae.

At the very least then, the fecundity expressed in the cornucopia is locked into the two prime elements, fire and water, fixed in the astronomical testimony of the heavens. Tyche Protogeneia is here being placed into a realm that is interconnected with the most basic structures shaping human existence according to the ancients: the elements and the stars, or, in the language of the writer of Colossians, τὰ στοιχεῖα τοῦ κόσμου (Col 2:8, repeated in 2:20). Manilius portrays his hymnic exposition of the heavens as nothing more than cohering with what Fortuna had already implemented, reiterating and participating in her own symphonic order: "What Fortuna affirms, who would dare call that false, and contend with the casting of such a mighty lot?"[160]

The owl and the kithara

At first viewing, face B seems to introduce a novel conjunction in some tension with face A. The owl as the common symbol of Athena/Minerva and the kithara as prophetic Apollo's instrument of inspiration elicit a wealth of literary testimony. However, the encircling inscription seems to demand that Tyche Protogeneia provide the interpretation, especially in light of face A. Strikingly, the conjunction of this imagery of Minerva and Apollo is not known, to my

158 H. Güney, "Poseidon as a God of Earthquake in Roman Asia Minor," *RN* 172 (2015): 293–315; J. M. Bremmer, "The Power of Poseidon: Horses, Chaos and Brute Force," in *The World of Greek Religion and Mythology: Collected Essays II* (WUNT 433; Tübingen: Mohr Siebeck, 2019), 21–7. Poseidon is sometimes featured on coins of Phrygia, brandishing his trident: *RPC* 2.1414, 3.2637 (Doryleum); *RPC online* 4.2.1984 temp. (Eukarpeia); *RPC online* 6.5631 temp. (Bruzus).

159 See F. Graf, "Earthquakes and the Gods: Reflections on Graeco-Roman Responses to Catastrophic events," in *Myths, Martyrs and Modernity: Studies in the History of religion in Honour of Jan N. Brenner* edited by J. Dijkstra *et al.* (Leiden: Brill, 2010), 98.

160 *quod Fortuna ratum faciat, quis dicere falsum audeat et tantae suffragia vincere sortis?* Manilius *Astron.* 2.134–5, translation from K. Volk, *Manilius and His Intellectual Background* (Oxford: Oxford University Press, 2009), 66. In this sense, Fortuna is both the original (first) lot *and* the originating lot of all twelve apportionings.

knowledge, at the temple of Fortuna Primigenia at Praeneste. Indeed, Fortuna only joins them, named among a pantheon of gods on an early bronze *cista*.[161]

Athena as owl perched on a kithara is an uncommon conjunction. The clue to interpretation is to be found in the kithara itself. Colossae's Attalid coins of Apollo had two distinct dies (at least as known to date). One coin reverse had a kithara featuring three strings; another die delivered four strings.[162] There is nothing unusual in either of these.[163] What is striking in the intaglio is that, even on such a small gem, 17 mm long and 14 mm wide, the gem-cutter was careful to ensure seven strings were carved.[164] A professional musician's kithara did contain seven strings as opposed to the folk instrument of four strings.[165] The instrument was the requisite accompaniment for hymns to the gods, even gaining epigraphical attestation at Delphi.[166] However, in association with Apollo, the seven-stringed kithara took on a more esoteric significance.

Theon of Smyrna, whom we shall meet in greater detail in the next chapter, when he was exploring the significance of the hebdomad, combined two divine attestations to its crucial significance in the mathematical structure of the universe. He affirmed that the seven-stringed kithara is "the image of the divinely-orchestrated cosmos" (ἑπτάτονον κίθαριν θεομήστορος εἰκόνα κόσμου).[167] Proclus, the fifth century Neoplatonist, understood that the inspired music from the kithara not only resonated according to the beneficently-ordered universe, but actually held the immense, potentially-chaotic forces in calm process.[168] However, though Proclus and others before him credited Apollo for this beneficence,[169] the Colossian ring suggests that Apollo's kithara is part of the contribution of Tyche in her protogenic capacity.

"Athena" also was crucial in the understanding of the universe. Hers is the name given to the number seven, the "hebdomad" because, within the set of the first ten numbers (the "decad"), the hebdomad is neither created by multiplication nor does it help create any other number in that decad. Athena provided the divine image of that "seven" for she was without mother and without

161 *CIL* 14.4105 (late 4th century BCE).

162 See chapter 1, Plate 1.7, item i) and chapter 3, Plate 3.2b.

163 Compare a similar die distinction form the Megara mint: *RPC* 3.409, 411.

164 It is rare for coins to include seven strings; but see *RPC* 1.1444.

165 M. Maas and J. McI. Snyder, *Stringed Instruments of Ancient Greece* (New Haven: Yale University Press, 1989), 65.

166 *F.Delphes* III 2.192, ll. 8–9 (late 4th century BCE).

167 Theon 141.4, 8. The edition relied upon for Theon's work is that of Eduard Hiller, *Theonis Smyrnaei Philosophi Platonici Expositio Rerum Mathematicarum ad Legendum Platonem Utilium* (Leipzig: Teubner, 1878). This remains the fundamental edition for more recent commentary and emendation, such as that of F. Petrucci, *Teone di Smirne. Expositio rerum mathematicarum ad legendum Platonem itilium. Introduzione, traduzione, commento* (St. Augustin: Academia, 2012).

168 Proclus *Hymn ad Sol* 20.

169 See R.M. van den Berg, *Proclus' Hymns: Essays, Translations, Commentary* (Leiden: Brill, 2001), 168–9.

reproduction.[170] Both affirmations of such aseity were not original to Theon. He credits the third century BCE Alexander the Aetolian for the former,[171] and the Pythagoreans for the latter.[172] Similar notions are found in lengthy scholia on Hesiod where the two are brought together: "The holy hebdomad of Apollo — by her, wherefore, is brought into being his seven-stringed kithara."[173] In extended fashion, Philo of Alexandria's Sabbath-prompted speculations on the hebdomad found ample fertilizer in the developments in Middle Platonism. Significantly, Philo did not see the Sabbath as a Jewish distinctive (cf Col 2:16) but, rather, of the whole, the universe (τοῦ παντός), an all-people (πάνδημον) possession.[174] The play of connection between the hebdomad, the seven planets and the seven strings was the perfect harmony expressed in the cosmic order.

Accordingly, the assertion contained in the gem is that Colossae possessed a connection far beyond any of its neighbors. That connection was with the cosmic order that was founded by all-permeating Tyche and which, through her election, had settled on Colossae as prime testimony to her presence and activity in that universe, at least in Asia. Such a primeval claim was not singular to Colossae: the Sardians had claimed their city as πρωτόχθων,[175] and "sacred to the gods" (ἱερᾷ τῶν θεῶν).[176] So Colossae was operating squarely in the environment of competition for eminence based on antiquity. How long the cult of Tyche Protogeneia had operated in Colossae is, of course, unknown, and likely to remain so. But of greater importance is trying to understand a city that held a story promoting it to such an esteemed place in the region (and the cosmos).

A parallel of sorts is found in Pindar's fifth century (BCE) *Olympian Ode* 9. The ode is a constructed celebration of the wrestling victory in 468 BCE of Epharmostus of the city of Opous. As part of the sweep of accolades to build the honor bestowed on him, Pindar turned to the glory of the champion's home town.[177] He relates one of the well-known stories of creation, when, after an all-inundating flood, Pyrrha and Deucalion were instructed by Zeus to drop stones behind them as they walked. From them, sprang the new race of human

---

170 Theon 103.2–6.

171 Theon has two quotations that he credits to Alexander of Aetolia (139.1–10 and 140.5–141.4), but which some early and modern commentators assign rather to a near-contemporary, Alexander of Ephesos (see chapter 6). However, this particular extension of the kithara to "the image of the cosmos" is not found elsewhere for Alexander of Ephesos.

172 The Pythagorean school was also known to use the music of the lyre as the image of the music of the seven spheres (the planets: sun, moon, Mercury, Venus, Mars, Jupiter and Saturn). They extrapolated even the different musical modes from these spheres. Pliny the Elder deemed it "a refinement more entertaining than convincing" (Rackham's evocative translation of *iucunda magis quam necessaria subtilitate*!); *NH* 2.20.84.

173 ἡ ἑβδόμη ἱερὰ Ἀπόλλωνος — ἐν αὐτῇ γὰρ ἐτέχθη, διὸ καὶ ἑπτάτονος αὐτοῦ ἡ κιθάρα. See Scholia on Hesiod 768–770a, especially at 770a.5–7; see also Ion *fr.* 3.

174 Philo *Opif.* 89–128, quotation from 89.

175 *I.Sardis* 2.418, 447 (2nd to early 3rd century CE; 211–212 CE respectively).

176 *I.Sardis* 2.411 (before 212 CE).

177 Pindar *Ol.* 9.40–66.

beings. An elaborate complication of Tyche as both mother and daughter of Zeus follows.[178] In this story Tyche becomes pregnant by Zeus and enabled the city of (king) Opous to overcome the threat of demise through the king's lack of an heir. Hence Opous was called Protogeneia's city — her first-born. Pindar does not use the title of Tyche Protogeneia — his imagery is built on other mythic themes. For him, Protogeneia is probably to be understood as the daughter of Pyrrha and Deucalion (without procreation?) but the placement of the city's origins in the mythic past proclaims its ancient and exalted status.

I consider that this gem attests the same high claim mounted by and for Colossae (just as can be traced in more detail for Praeneste's own sense of its stature). In other words, to be able to sustain the worship of Tyche Protogeneia meant that a city was projecting an enormous claim to its (divinely authorized) importance. Colossae was one of very few cities in the ancient world to sustain this claim. In the Ode, the victory of the wrestler, Epharmostus, is consequently made part of this divine intervention, a confirmation of the honor due to the city. One inscription from Colossae similarly honored a victor at the games. Significantly, the accolades did not come from the usual conferring bodies — the *Boulê* (Council) or the *Dêmos* (the citizens' Assembly) — but rather the entire *patris*, "the homeland."[179]

If we were to try to assign a date to the gem, then considerations of the style of lettering, the iconography particularly of a winged Tyche, and the emphasis on the cosmic symbolism of the Athena hebdomad and seven-stringed kithara appear to be the most pertinent. Jacqueline Champeaux, reliant completely on the old sketches and descriptions of the gem, assigned a general date of the imperial period.[180] Given what I have outlined above, I think the gem can be dated to the first or second centuries of the Common Era. I find the prevalence of the winged Tyche in this period to tip the balance. Allowing that Alexander of Ephesos extended the older use of the seven-stringed kithara as a terrestrial metaphor for the music of the celestial spheres to affirm that it was the image of the cosmos, then the circulation of that imagery seems to have occurred sufficiently broadly that confusion about its origin and the composer of the cosmological hymn had already evolved by the time of Theon of Smyrna, in the first half of the second century CE.

There may be a material echo in the coinage of the Lycian League. In the time of Trajan, the league minted a coin with two touching, if not conjoined, lyres. Perched with one foot on each lyre is Athena's owl. Of particular significance is that the coin's left lyre has

178 Andrew Miller considers Pindar may have deliberately allowed multiple understandings of his use of Protogeneia; "Inventa Componere: Rhetorical Process and Poetic Composition in Pindar's Ninth Olympian Ode," *TAPA* 123 (1993): 130–2.

179 *MAMA* 6.40 cf *MAMA* 6.41; see further chapter 10.

180 Champeaux, *Fortuna* 1, 120 n529.

three strings, the right has four.[181] The twinning of the lyre might garner further esoteric astrological significance. Hyla Troxell reduces the iconography to a more mundane level, however, namely that Lycia's hemidrachmas and drachmas indicated their value simply by one or two kitharas respectively.[182] The problem is that the owl remains unexplained, even at the level of Athena's long-standing cultic presence in the region;[183] it should also be acknowledged that the iconography can fulfill both a monetary and symbolic function at the same time. The design is a variation on earlier coins minted from the reign of Augustus which consistently had twin lyres often varying in the number of strings on each lyre.[184] Regardless of the details, the parallel of owl on kithara with the Colossian intaglio point towards the first to early second centuries for such a design.

The carved carnelian intaglio from Colossae has unlocked a further crucial player in the religious make-up of the city. Moreover, it points to the contribution Tyche Protogeneia made to a city seeking to rehabilitate and restore its reputation and status within the Lycus Valley and beyond. We cannot draw unequivocal links between the stone's importance and the Pauline letters to the city's inhabitants but, as with the encounter with Helios in chapter 2, we can gain more insight into the Colossian setting for the reception of the letters into which they became players. Two particular terms in the Letter to the Colossians, when placed in dialogue with this analysis of the inscribed gemstone, yield perspectives that help to ground the letter in the material world of the city and its environs, rather than merely spar in an immaterial literary exchange. We are not looking for a reflection of Tyche in the letter but rather a response to the religious setting, for which the intaglio is a vital clue. As Peter Rose has argued, "What the text responds to is in a substantial sense, the raw material out of which it is produced."[185] More particularly, that response is frequently brought to focus by some crisis or other, whether that be a conflict at the level of ideology or some catastrophe.

The elements

I have mentioned the elements, the στοιχεία, already, accenting that the Colossians writer underscores the cosmic dimensions of their reality. The word only occurs in the phrase κατὰ/ἀπὸ τὰ στοιχεία τοῦ κόσμου (Col 2:8, 20). The gem appears to accent the two weightier elements, fire and water, in the selection

181 *SNG von Aulock* 4369; *RPC* 3.1503, 1504, 2673, 2674.
182 H. A. Troxell, *Coinage of the Lycian League* (New York: ANS, 1982), 306, 323.
183 See R. Parker, "Athena in Anatolia," *Pallas* 100 (2016): 73–90.
184 See *RPC* 1.3309 (Augustus), 2.1503 (Domitian), 3.2673 (Nerva), 3.2676 (Trajan).
185 P. Rose, *Sons of the Gods, Children of Earth: Ideology and Literary Form in Ancient Greece* (Ithaca/London: Cornell University Press, 1992), 332.

and arrangement of the zodiacal signs. But there is no question that the intaglio's iconography is flagging the cosmic realm of the stars — the elements — and the universal stability of the cosmos that holds these.[186] This is the realm and provision given by Tyche Protogeneia for the benefit of the Colossians in particular. More to the point, this is the realm that governs human beings and their environment (not least in agriculture), not necessarily in an inescapable determinism, but certainly in a conjunction of forces that impact on decisions and actions that human beings undertake.

The στοιχεία of the Tyche gem are far from elementary or earthly teaching.[187] They are part of the basic structure of the universe, τοῦ κόσμου, as here.[188] The fact that they may be a component of false and deceitful philosophy (διὰ τῆς φιλοσοφίας καὶ κενῆς ἀπάτης), impugned as human traditions (κατὰ τὴν παράδοσιν τῶν ἀνθρώπων) neither infantilizes the teaching nor colors it with the Judeo-Christian dye of Isa 29:13, Mk 7:8. The notion of received tradition was crucial to the correct observation of the universe, as Theon of Smyrna affirmed.[189] Middle Platonists developed the sense of the relation of the material to the immaterial realm on the basis that submission to the latter was crucial to correct understanding of it,[190] and a collateral means to ensure that the material realm remained well-ordered. There may be a generic battle between philosophies happening here — the Christian "non-philosophy" staking its ground amidst the religiously-imbued philosophies or philosophically-imbued religions on offer at Colossae and elsewhere, with all the demarcating rhetoric of a minority contender being deployed. In this sense, philosophy is a general reference (the indefinite τις, "anyone" of verse 8 that governs the series of descriptions is determinative, reinforced by the unspecified plural τῶν ἀνθρώπων); such an inclusive sweep is fairly common in epigraphical testimony of a "philosopher" or student of "philosophy" without further delineation.[191]

There is no conceptual need or grammatical constraint to read φιλοσοφία in the letter as specifying a definable teaching nor to use such a construct to identify a group of opponents.[192] The only syncretism, if that term can still be used, that the writer addresses is the range of religious options operating in

---

186 *Pace* T. W. Martin, *By Philosophy and Empty Deceit: Colossians as a Response to a Cynic Critique* (JSNTs 118; Sheffield: Sheffield Academic Press, 1996), 154.

187 This is the reading applied by J. L. Sumney, *Colossians: A Commentary* (Louisville/London: WJKP, 2008), 130–1, rightly rejected by Paul Foster, *Colossians* (BNTC; London: T & T Clark, 2016), 253.

188 The second κατά in verse 8 may have distributive force. See D. B. Wallace, *Greek Grammar: Beyond the Basics* (Grand Rapids, MI: Zondervan, 1996), 377.

189 Theon 14.18–19.

190 See Philo *Her.* 119.

191 See, among many examples, *IG* II^2 791, 886, 1006; *IG* VII 2519; *F.Delphes* III.1.199; *MAMA* 8.499b.

192 *Pace* C. E. Arnold, *The Colossian Syncretism: The Interface between Christianity and Folk Belief at Colossae* (Grand Rapids, MI: Baker, 1996), 186–90.

Colossae, both of a piece with other *poleis* in Asia Minor and yet also having its own particular emphases such as will enhance the position of one particular *polis* jostling for recognition among the host of others. The astonishing array of possible classifications of "the Colossian syncretism", which probably reached its unsurpassed zenith in the erudite work of Clinton Arnold, itself suggests that the whole enterprise of seeking singularity is misplaced. Syntheses, amalgamations and blends were part of the civic religious dynamism as indigenous deities found a translatability into the culturally-privileged Greek and Roman forms, at the same time bequeathing Phrygian, Egyptian and other elements into the combination.[193] But selections and distinctive accents were part of the process. For Colossae, we have come to see already that the heliotic Colossus, Artemis the hunter and Tyche Protogeneia were substantial contributors to an assertive and confident civic identity. These, I argue, must therefore become prime background for consideration in the interpretation of the Letter to the Colossians and even that to Philemon. The question of elements, στοιχεία, must proceed on that basis, if at all possible, using *comparanda* in dialogue as can be found relevant.

Foster is correct in drawing attention to the use of ἀπό to govern the second use of the phrase, τὰ στοιχεία τοῦ κόσμου, in Col 2:20.[194] The cosmic realm formed by and saturated with the character of Tyche Protogeneia is particularly revealed in the operations of the stars and the elements. It is tempting to collate the elements with the worship of/with angels (θρήσκειᾳ τῶν ἀγγέλων) of Col 2:18 in the light of the intaglio's *winged* Tyche. I am well-aware that wings do not an angel make — after all the Attalid-period Colossian coin of Zeus has a winged thunderbolt on its reverse.[195] However, the winged Tyche is clearly presumed by Plutarch in his imaginative journey of Tyche flying to Rome overlooking other aspirant empires; at Rome she removes her wings, he extemporizes, in acknowledgement of *the* empire where she will take up residence.[196] The intaglio preserves the winged cornucopia-bearer; the zodiacal star-signs, divided into the two fundamental elements, surround her, somehow as the celestial witnesses to her radiate glory; the inscribed side reinforces that perfection. This is a Tyche beyond that inspiring the Caesars and recipient of epigraphical honors in a microcosmic connection.[197] Colossae's Tyche was,

---

193 G. H. R. Horsley and J. M. Luxford, "Pagan angels in Roman Asia Minor: revisiting the epigraphic evidence," *AS* 66 (2016): 148–9.

194 Foster, *Colossians*, 297.

195 See A. H. Cadwallader, "Wealthy, widowed, astute and beneficent: Claudia Eugenetoriane and the second century revival of the Colossian mint," in *New Documents Illustrating the History of Early Christianity Volume 12: the Lycus Valley* edited by J. R. Harrison (Grand Rapids, MI: Eerdmans, 2021), forthcoming, nrs 1–5.

196 ὡς ἔοικεν ἔθηκε τὰς πτέρυγας, Plutarch *Fort. Rom.* (*Mor.*) 318A.

197 *IG* II^2 1069, 1774; *IG* V,1 1208. Plutarch seems to construe Fortune-Tyche in this fashion *Fort. Rom.* (*Mor.*) 316F–317A. A correlation can thus be drawn between the Tyche as manifest in the (good fortune of the) Caesars/Rome and that manifest in a city such as Praeneste or Colossae.

in the presentation, more ancient, more given to cosmic stability and preservation, with a witness and touchstone at the most ancient, long-standing city in the valley.

Tyche can, albeit rarely, be conferred ἄγγελος as an epithet or description. It is found in a first century scholion on Homer by the grammarian Aelius Herodianus, though here there is the further collation with δαίμων often found elsewhere in texts and inscriptions as the male partner to Good Tyche.[198] Significantly, he labelled the collation — δαίμων, ἡ τύχη καὶ ὁ θεός — a Greek contribution (καθ' Ἕλληνας).[199] In the magical papyri, rather than being an angel, Tyche communicates *through* her good-dispensing angel standing beside her.[200] The instances may be rare but then "Angelos", whilst recurring consistently in this period as an epithet given to various gods, does not seem to favor any one of them — Mên,[201] Hosios (and) Dikaios,[202] Hermes[203] even Zeus himself.[204] Female gods similarly attracted the epithet,[205] and deities with chthonic power were particularly popular in *defixiones* that sent, through their angelic capacity, underworldly harm to some victim.[206] But it is consistent with the rise of "pagan angels" in the religious landscape of the first three centuries of the common era. The presence of the gods was personalized and immanent, either by direct naming of the god as *aggelos* or by the close proximity of her/his angel.[207] Such deity-angels could also have their own prophets.[208]

Tyche Protogeneia's beneficent role as Zeus's first-born daughter and her pervasive function as the mother of Zeus and creator of the universe in general (and of specific cities in particular), fulfil many of the visual and connotive aspects associated with angels. One theonym from Colossae, Aggelikos — inscribed on a bomos-shaped epitaph — suggests that angel imagery was part of

198 See, for example, the stele to Good Daimon, Good Tyche and the seasons (*I.Byzantion* 13), apparently an agricultural votive with, probably, supplicatory intent. The conjunction of Good Tyche and Good Daimon was familiar enough in Greek culture to yield a fortuitous translation of Is 65:11 that recognized, in the Septuagint at least, the presence of Τύχη and Δαίμων as the allurements of those who forsake the Lord. See D. B. Martin, "When did Angels become Demons?" *JBL* 129 (2010): 659. Note that the evidence of inscription and Herodian shows that the conjunction is frequent enough in Greco-Roman understanding.

199 Aelius Herodianus *Part.* 19.1–2; cf Libanius *Ep.* 1512.

200 ὁ ἀγαθοφόρος ἄγγελος παρεστὼς τῇ Τύχῃ (*PGM* 4.3163–4). The designation of "Good Angel" (ἀγαθὸς ἄνγελος) is found as part of a joint votive (with Zeus Hypsistos) at Stratonikeia (*I.Stratonikeia* 1118). Horsley and Luxford take this as a distinct deity (Agathos Angelos), "Pagan Angels," 153–4.

201 Petzl, *Beichtinschriften* 3.

202 *SEG* 41.1010, 1185.

203 *I.Stratonikeia* 103 cf *IG* XII 5 235.

204 *SEG* 32.1539 (Gerasa, 2nd to 3rd century CE).

205 Arnold, *Colossian Syncretism*, 144.

206 Audollent, *Defixiones* 74, 75.

207 See N. Belayche, "Angeloi in religious practices of the imperial Roman East," *Henoch* 32 (2010): 56.

208 Malay-Petzl, *Lydia* 176 (Nisyra, Roman imperial period).

the religious thought-world of the city,[209] regardless of how intentionally-supplicative or ambitious his parents were when they named him.

The writer of the Colossians Letter argues that the death of and with Christ has secured what Middle Platonists like Theon dreamed of as the resulting reward for their dedication to the study of the elements of the cosmos. Namely, through (baptismal) unity with that death of Christ has come the vision of the invisible, the realm beyond the realm of the elements, the spheres and the stars, "having been hidden with Christ in God" (Col 3:3). It is a transposition that has removed the hold (for good or ill) of the Tyche who sometimes, even by her devotees, was experienced as fickle, ὡς ἀβέβαιον "a thing inconstant".[210]

For all that Tyche Protogeneia might have been hailed as the elector of Colossae and the one who poured out her fecundity from the fruit-bearing cornucopia, Tyche in general terms, was known to be, at times, inauspicious in her dispensing into human lives. Various authors recount the change of fortunes attending famous generals, kings and leaders, often with little explanatory data evident from a loss of virtue (often presented as key to the continued favor of Tyche).[211] Manilius perceives such power as a sign of Tyche's immense royal power, whilst acknowledging that it is manifest in capriciousness.[212] Clitarchus distilled this unease about Tyche into an especially succinct sentence "Whatever Tyche might dispense, circumstances rob these things."[213] It was not that Clitarchus was necessarily subverting Tyche's power, placing abstract "circumstances" beyond her control; rather Tyche herself was "wayward, inconstant, uncertain, fickle in her favors", as Pliny the Elder provided the peroration.[214]

The fickleness of Tyche — earthquakes

There is one particular natural phenomenon that struck at the heart of the interface between Tyche's cosmic orderliness and the consequential asserted munificence towards humanity. That fundamental demonstration of Tyche's fickle behavior was the earthquake. The earthquake brought the return to

209 See A. H. Cadwallader, "Gertrude Bell's Resolution of a Disputed Inscription," *Gephyra* 20 (2020): 17, ll. 2–3. See chapter 12.

210 See, for example, Plutarch *Fort. Rom.* (*Mor.*) 316C, 317D–E. This has particular implications for Col 2:7, as we explored in chapter 3.

211 See Horace, *Ode* 1.35.1–28; Plutarch *Fort. Rom.* (*Mor.*) 323D; Polybius 29.21.2. Hubris was sometimes charged with the departure of Tyche. Here a blurring into Nemesis can sometimes be witnessed. See Polybius 39 epilogue.

212 Manilius *Astron.* 4.93, 96–8.

213 ὅσα δίδωσι τύχη, ταῦτα περιστάσεις ἀφαιροῦνται, Clitarchus *Sent.* 121.

214 *vaga, inconstans, incerta, varia indignorumque fautrix* Pliny *NH* 2.5.22.

precosmic chaos from which Tyche was supposedly the protection,[215] the one who shaped the elements into harmonious rather than belligerent relations.[216] Earthquakes were frequently regarded as the result of the elements falling out of balance. Even Manilius allowed that they were evidence of a failure or at least a qualification on the power of the zodiac.[217] And yet she too was charged with responsibility for the down-turn in fortune.[218]

Marcus Öhler has argued that the reference in Col 2:8, 20 to τὰ στοιχεία τοῦ κόσμου brings a particular edge to a recognition that these cosmic elements can act counter to human interest — these elements were somehow indictable for the destructive force that was unleashed in an earthquake.[219] When the elements lost their harmonious relationship, one or other's chaotic capacity exploded in an effort to find restoration of that harmony. Hence, any one of the elements might be the culprit.[220] The result is a crisis of human assurance in the benevolence of the cosmos. Put simply, the elements were not to be trusted; in terms of the intaglio, the Tyche that orders the universe could not be relied upon, either because her power was limited or, more accusatory, she was capricious. Öhler takes seriously the notice of a severe earthquake in the Lycus Valley in 60 CE.[221] It is understandable that the Roman literary focus of attention should narrow to Laodikeia as dealing with the damage that the seismic upheaval dispensed. Laodikeia had already become the assize center of the Kibyran *conventus*. Cicero had used the city as one of the hubs of his proconsulship of Asia.[222] Moreover, Laodikeia had already been the beneficiary of assistance by Augustus and Tiberius for previous earthquake damage.[223] It was noteworthy to Tacitus that now the city acted independently. But other cities in the region, Hierapolis and Colossae

215 See H. Versnel, *Inconsistencies in Greek and Roman Religion Volume 2: Transition and Reversal in Myth and Ritual* (Leiden: Brill, 1993), 177.

216 Manilius calls this "a force of divine spirit, … a god" *Astron.* 1.250–1.

217 Manilius *Astron.* 4.821–39.

218 Lucretius *Rer. Nat.* 5.104–9; Seneca *Nat.* 6.1.11–12.

219 M. Öhler, "Earthquakes and the Elements of the World in the Letter to the Colossians," in *New Doc. Early Christ. 12*, forthcoming.

220 Seneca *Nat.* 6.5.1.

221 Tacitus *Ann.* 14.27.

222 Cicero *Fam.* 3.7, 15.4; *Att.* 108, 114. This is confirmed by the fact that the delegate of the Kibyran *conventus* joining in a dedication to Caligula related to a new temple in Miletus was sent from Laodikeia, Glykon son of Euarches, a Laodikeian (*I.Didyma* 148, l. 16; 37 or 41 CE).

223 Suetonius *Tib.* 8. This may have been the warrant for Strabo's singling of the city as the example of the region's susceptibility to earthquake (Strabo 12.8.16; cf Tacitus *Ann.* 2.47). See T. M. Kristensen, "Earthquakes and Late Antique Urbanism: Some Observations on the Case of the Lycus Valley," in *The Lycus Valley and Neighbourhood in Late Antiquity* edited by C. Şimşek and T. Kaçar (Istanbul: Ege, 2018), 71–8.

among them, were affected — evidence for which comes from archaeology rather than literature.[224]

Accordingly, the earthquake unleashed more than a shaking of the foundations of the earth; it unleashed the potential for a fracture of fundamental beliefs. Of course, as the literary observers recognized, the god(s) may be approached more fervently and with more self-recrimination as a mechanism of securing the god's repentance if not particular protection amidst the collapse.[225] But for others, from Thucydides to Lucretius and even, at least in part, Cicero, there might be a relinquishing of any such reliance upon her and a commitment to a human aseity in the face of life's sometimes-arduous journey — as we find with Seneca. Pliny the Younger observed in response to the Vesuvius eruption, "Many raised their hands to the gods, or they shouted that the gods were no more."[226] Both options are rejected by the author of the Colossians' Letter. Rather death, the ultimate specter of the insurrection of the elements, has already occurred in/with Christ. Moreover, that death has yielded a vision of the unseen beyond the elemental, terrestrial and celestial structure (with all its flawed instability [Col 3:2]) — here is the location and source of the integration of all things (τὰ πάντα ἐν αὐτῷ συνέστηκεν, Col 1:17).

Indeed, the sheer act of singing the Christological hymn (Col 1:12–20), more than being community-value-building or a mnemonic for instruction, might itself channel the power of the *prototokos* to hold the destructive forces at bay or at least carry the singers through the death-dealing catastrophe. When Tralles sent a delegate to inquire of the Apollonian oracle at Delphi what to do in the aftermath of a devastating earthquake, the instruction was "to erect an altar in a sacred grove to the gentle He-Who-Shakes-the-Earth (Poseidon), to sacrifice … pursuant to tradition, … and accordingly, hymn the one who comes forcefully rushing … rightly praising Poseidon and Zeus in chorus."[227] Xenophon reports that when the leader of the Spartans, Agesipolis, was at supper in the royal tent at the beginning of the campaign against the Argives, the ground was hit by a seismic disturbance. Immediately the diners lifted their voices in a paean to Poseidon; the earthquake subsided and Agesopolis took it

224 Eusebius does include these cities in the earthquake's radius of impact (*Chron.* 183.21, reiterated by Ororius 7.7.12), but he does so for reasons other than historical interest, thus shifting the date to 64 CE. The divine anger at the perversity of Nero is similarly invited by George Syncellus in his sequence of events of that time: *Chron.* 409.23–410.4. See Appendix 1.

225 In other places, as Öhler notes, this might have curried a more avid devotion to Poseidon the god of earthquakes (as well as the oceans and seas) but at Colossae as we have seen (where no trace of Poseidon has yet surfaced), Tyche is the more likely recipient. Indeed the recognition of Tyche's vehemence is made in one hymn to her, that adds, as a consequence, a fervent plea that the suppliant receive her kindness, happiness and wealth (*Orphic Hymns* 71).

226 *multi ad deos manus tollere, plures nusquam iam deos ullos aeternamque illam* Pliny *Ep.* 6.20.15; compare Dio Chrysostom *Or.* 38.20.

227 μειλιχίῃ Σεισίχθονι ἐν ἄλσεϊ βωμὸν ἐνείρας … θύεο … ἐννομίην … ὧδε, πόλις, δὲ ὑμνεῖτε δεδραγμένον εἶφι βεβῶτα … ἐν χορῷ εὖ αὀνεῖν Σεισίχθονα καὶ Δία … *I.Tralleis* 1.

as a sign of encouragement to continue the campaign. It may be then, that the Christological hymn in Colossians is designed to be a direct thwarting of the power of the elements that are set as the counterpoint to Christ (Col 2:8, 20). Indeed, not to give thanks to the Father (Col 1:12), as expressed in the hymn that follows, is potentially dangerous. Although the explanation for an earthquake shows nothing of the moralizing vengeance of later Christian writings,[228] a religious frame of interpretation is established.

A return to the elements as the ruling determinant of life, argues the writer, can be nothing other than a return to the fickleness and unreliability of Tyche, a threat of collapse so palpably demonstrated in the earthquake of 60 CE. Given the religious and cultural environment of Colossae, with its accent on the values and conceptual framework expressed in miniature in the carved intaglio, the rush (back) to Tyche would have had a potent appeal, especially if, as sometimes occurred, the abdication from belief in the controlling destiny of Tyche was itself blamed as a contributor to her wrath. The writer of the letter is only too conscious of this danger, especially when it is dressed in beguiling words and philosophical speech. The earthquake no doubt had concentrated attention for the Colossians in general and Christ-followers in particular (at least in the writer's view). From that point on, one of the marked religious alternatives in Colossae, for the fledgling groups of Christ-followers, would have been between Tyche Protogeneia and Christos Prototokos. It is to the importance of this contrasting epithet that we turn.

Christos Prototokos

The epithet πρωτότοκος, "first-born", occurs twice in Colossians (1:15, 18b) in the cosmological hymn of praise of Christ, the son. The phrases have been important for the analysis of the form and formal structure of Col 1:15–20 and division into two stanzas.[229] Here I want to concentrate on the use of πρωτότοκος in a Colossian context where πρωτογενεία carries a public, cultic and civic-endorsed privilege as the paraded Colossian epithet for Tyche.[230]

228 Tertullian *Pall.* 4.4; *Sib. Or.* 3.470–2, 7.22–3.

229 E. Norden, *Agnostos Theos: Untersuchungen zur Formengeschichte religiöser Rede* (Darmstadt: WBG, 2 vols, 1956 [1913]), vol 2, 250–4, with many subsequent imitators and modulators. See, for example, J. D. G. Dunn, *The Epistles to the Colossians and to Philemon* (NIGTC; Grand Rapids, MI: Eerdmans, 1996), 83–86 and most recently, A. Standhartinger, "Der Kolosserhymnus im Lichte epigraphischer Zeugnisse," in *Epigraphical Evidence Illustrating Paul's Letter to the Colossians* edited by J. Verheyden, M. Öhler and T. Corsten (WUNT 411; Tübingen: Mohr Siebeck, 2018), 70–6, and K. S. Kim, *The Firstborn Son in Ancient Judaism and Early Christianity* (Leiden: Brill, 2019), 176–84.

230 For further analysis of the hymn in the context of Middle Platonic cosmology, see the following chapter.

Both occurrences of πρωτότοκος in the hymn are given further predication: the first ties Christ to creation (πρωτότοκος πάσης κτίσεως), the second to the dead (πρωτότοκος ἐκ τῶν νεκρῶν). It is not a widely-used descriptor of Christ in the Second Testament, occurring but once in an authentic Pauline Letter (Rom 8:29) where it garners a sense of pre-eminence — "first-born among many sisters and brothers" (πρωτότοκον ἐν πολλοῖς ἀδελφοῖς; cf Heb 12:23). The closest parallel is Rev 1:5 where ὁ πρωτότοκος τῶν νεκρῶν invites the suggestion that we may be dealing with an Asian (not Pauline) hymnic affirmation of Christ. A number of early scribes may have thought just that, given that they dropped the ἐκ from the Colossians text.[231] The combination of "beginning/origin" with "creation" (ἡ ἀρχὴ τῆς κτίσεως τοῦ θεοῦ) in John of Patmos's Letter to Colossae's neighbor, the assembly at Laodikeia (Rev 3:14), is tantalizing in the conjunction of key words from the two syntagmemes directing the semantics of πρωτότοκος.[232]

When commentators have approached the term πρωτότοκος in the hymn, both the word and multiple other terms are tracked to Hebrew forebears, both canonical and extra-canonical. Most often, the late wisdom literature and the writings of hellenistic Judaism (especially those of Philo) are harvested to provide a multi-storeyed layering of Jewish parallels.[233] The most fulsome construction is found in the recent monograph of Kyu Seop Kim, who nonetheless argues that both the letter and the hymn are Paul's composition.[234] Almost no commentator touches the question of the reception of such a hymn (if composed by the letter author) or the relevance of the hymn (if pre-formed, in a Lycus Valley context),[235] even when Stoic and/or Middle Platonic (some-

231 𝔓⁴⁶, 2495, *א*. Conversely, some later Byzantine scribes conformed Rev 1:5 to the Colossian better reading and added ἐκ. Ulrich Huttner oscillates between Revelation borrowing from Colossians or yielding a coincidental parallel; *Early Christianity*, 120, 151. A common tradition satisfies both; Rev 3:14 may narrow the provenance of that tradition to the Lycus Valley however. See A. Standhartinger, *Studien zur Entstehungsgeschichte und Intention des Kolosserbriefs* (Leiden: Brill, 1999), 206–7.

232 See P. Pokorný, *Colossians: A Commentary* (Peabody, MA: Hendrickson, 1991), 59.

233 Lightfoot, *Colossians and Philemon*, M. M. Thompson, *Colossians & Philemon* (Grand Rapids, MI: Eerdmans, 2005), 27–35; C. R. Seitz, *Colossians* (BTCB; Grand Rapids, MI: Brazos Press, 2014), 95–6, Foster, *Colossians*, 177–82, S. McKnight, *The Letter to the Colossians* (NICNT; Grand Rapids, MI: Eerdmans, 2018), 132–67; P. Müller, *Kolosserbrief* (KEK 9/2; Göttingen: Vandenhoeck & Ruprecht, 2022), 159–64.

234 Kim, *Firstborn Son*, 178.

235 One might speculate that the Christ-followers of Laodikeia and Hierapolis, cities with a significant Jewish population, may have had a hand in its *poiesis*. Compare the general observations on the hymn as "common property of communities in Asia Minor" in E. Lohse, *Colossians and Philemon* (Hermeneia; Philadelphia: Fortress, 1971), 46. On the discussion of the hymn as pre-formed (with or without the addenda/corrigenda of the letter's author) see G. E. Cannon, *The Use of Traditional Materials in Colossians* (Macon, GA: Mercer, 1983), 19–35; R. E. DeMaris, *The Colossian Controversy: Wisdom in Dispute at Colossae* (Sheffield: JSOT Press, 1994), 136–9 where Col 2:9–15 especially is taken as commentary on the hymn.

times Cynic, just to be inclusive!) influences are traced.[236] The hymn is left to float in metaphysical space with little or no grounding in the material lives of Christ-followers in the Lycus Valley in the first century, except, anaemically, as an instructional supplement to the letter,[237] a devotional exercise in community-forming,[238] or even as a missional demonstration of the philosophical vitality of the second or third generation, Jesus movement.[239] James Dunn saw the issue: "It remains unclear what light the passage sheds on the situation at Colossae. Why should this hymn be cited and why here?" He even allowed that "an alternative religious system" might be in view.[240] But more than this is left unspoken.

The iconography and inscription of the intaglio gem at least offers a possible context within which to approach the hymn, not as an esoteric text but as a real engagement with and alternative to the religious environment of Colossae. We know generally that hymns were one of the numinous, arresting points of religious devotion. The first-century (CE) astrologer, Dorotheus of Sidon, expressed the ambition of "drawing down the stars from heaven by means of song."[241] Tyche, like numerous other gods, were recipients of such poetic accolades, sung frequently to the accompaniment of kithara and sometimes also the aulos.[242] Hymns to Tyche, some aesthetically fine, some attempting to be, are found in literature and on papyrus fragments alike.[243] Consequently the use of such high-blown, hymnic affirmations of Christ the Son of the invisible God sits comfortably in such a composing, religious culture, whether transforming prior material into Christ-devotion or repudiating certain accents to delineate the distinctiveness of Christ.[244] There is no pre-requisite that such engagement be with Jewish material, or at least that a Jewish storehouse be turned to Christian polemic within or against a Jewish syncretistic context. There may be some rem-

236 See Martin, *By Philosophy and Empty Deceit*, V. Balabanski, *Colossians: An Eco-Stoic Reading* (London: T & T Clark, 2020), 40–2, 67–76. Compare the blend given by Pokorný, *Colossians*, 63–72. Lightfoot's reliance on Philo (and "Alexandrian theology") admits that Judaism, especially in the diaspora, was not hermetically sealed from the cross-currents of philosophical thought in the first century. One does wonder whether the message has been received however with the silo-reading of the hymn according to canonical or para-Scriptural texts.

237 Seitz, *Colossians*, 91 ("Paul [*sic*] is working in the realm of … the 'rule of faith.'"). A similar earlier accent is found in M. Hengel, *Between Jesus and Paul* (London: SCM, 1983), 79–81.

238 Anderson, *Colossians*, 46.

239 Dunn, *Colossians and Philemon*, 86.

240 Dunn, *Colossians and Philemon*, 86.

241 Dorotheus Sidonius *Carm. Astrol.* 1.1–3 (translation of the Arabic version of a lost Greek original, by David Pedigree).

242 Proclus *apud* Photius *Bib.* 239.320a.18–20; Callimachus *Hymn* 4 (In Delum).312–3.

243 *Orphic Hymns* 71 (to Tyche); *TM* 63984 (Egypt, 3rd century CE). Tyche appears as an adjunct figure in two of the *Homeric Hymns* — Demeter 420 and Athena 11.5.

244 Compare just such a two-edged approach (at the conceptual level) in D. M. Hay, *Colossians* (ANTC; Nashville: Abingdon, 2000), 53–5; L. Bormann, *Der Brief des Paulus an die Kolosser* (ThHK X/1; Leipzig: Evangelische Verlagsanstalt, 2012), 77–88.

nant of such dynamics when the Letter to the Colossians was read in Laodikeia (Col 4:16; cf Hierapolis) given the demonstrable presence of Jews in that city's demography, but the dominant encounter with the hymn among the Colossian Christ-followers would be informed by a non-Jewish religious background.[245] David Hay admits that even though the hymn and the author of Colossians work from Jewish traditions, there is nothing in the hymn that requires that readers (*sic*) know that background.[246] If this is the case, then it follows that the content poured into the affirmations in the hymn and which provided a grid (perhaps, grids) for interpretation and assessment would come from a background closer to the experience and (various levels of) education of the recipients.

Firstly, it needs to be recognized at a basic level that πρωτότοκος "first-born" can carry no more significance than chronological priority in a familial line. Gynaecological observations note that women and female animals frequently experience considerable pain and difficulty giving birth for the first time.[247] Ptolemy related this chronology of birth to the position of stars and planets.[248] Sometimes an epitaph recalled that the deceased was a first-born child, πρωτοτόκον τέκνον.[249] Lk 2:7 is of a piece with this meaning. But the word does not surface in the papyri until the fourth century CE at the earliest.[250] The lexicographers simply defined the word as ἡ πρώτη τετοκυῖα/ὁ πρῶτος τεχθείς,[251] but the Suda directed the developed sense by applying the term to ἡ θεοτόκος, possibly in connection with the gospel reference.

Secondly, there is a transition to a heightened value attached to the "first-born" in religious and magical circles. One of the regulations of a *lex sacra* (or perhaps a deme decree)[252] governing the activities of an Athenian deme, the Phrearrhoi, during the Eleusinian rites, seems to have required that the sows involved in the sacrifices be first-born.[253] This may mean either that the sow was pregnant as part of the sacrifice (as Robert Simms understands it)[254] or that she had been iden-

245 See Alan H. Cadwallader, "On the Question of Comparative Method in Historical Research: Colossai and Chonai in Larger Frame," in *The First Urban Churches 5: Colossae, Hierapolis, and Laodicea* edited by J. R. Harrison and L. L. Welborn (Atlanta, GA: SBL, 2019), 130–41.

246 Hay, *Colossians*, 55.

247 Hippocrates *Diver. Caus. Mul.* 1.152; Plato *Theaet.* 151c; Aristotle *Hist. Anim.* 546a; Athenaeus *Deip.* 9.397b; *Gr. Anth.* 7.528; Dionysios of Halicarnassos *Ant. rom.* 3.14.4.

248 Ptolemy *Tetrab.* 3.119.

249 *SEG* 1.570 = *CIJud* 2.1510 (Leontopolis, 5th century BCE?); *I.Mésie sup. VI* 61 (undated); E. Bernand, *Inscriptions métriques de l'Égypte gréco-romaine* (Paris: Belles Lettres, 1969), 232 nr. 54 (Egypt, 2nd to 3rd century CE); *CIG* 9727 (Rome, 2nd to 3rd century CE, possibly Christian).

250 This observation is based on a search of the online repository at papyri.info. The earliest papyrological attestation is in fact a fragment of the Septuagint of Exodus (34:18–20).

251 Hesychius sv; Suda sv.

252 See S. M. Wijma, "The 'Others' in a lex sacra from the Attic Deme Phrearrhioi (SEG 35.113)," *ZPE* 187 (2013): 199–205.

253 *SEG* 48.138 = *CGRN* 103 (330–250 BCE).

254 R. M. Simms, "The Phrearrhian Lex Sacra: An Interpretation," *Hesperia* 67 (1998): 93.

tified as the first-born in a litter (probably bred on the sacred estates that were part of the sanctuary complex). Unfortunately the inscription was substantially damaged; the reconstruction of ὗν πρ[ωτοτόκον in line 2 must be regarded as tentative,[255] even though Simms makes a strong case in support of the reading. One piece of *comparanda* comes from a *lex sacra* at Mykonos, again governing the Demeter cult.[256] There the sow for sacrifice is specifically designated as ὗν ἐνκύμονα πρωτοτόκον. This is more than a pleonastic synonym. In the light of the genealogical and animal husbandry references given briefly above, I would suggest that it is no stock pregnant sow but rather the sow is specifically identified as pregnant *for the first time*, pregnant with her first (to be) born.

A recognition of the religious privileging of the πρωτοτόκος comes in a curse lamella from Antioch on the Orontes, dated to the third or fourth century CE. Here a grab at stories from Exodus is made part of the deluge of evil and arduous times invoked for a certain Babylas the greengrocer. The destruction of Pharaoh and the first-born of Egypt (ll. 11–12, 14–16) are specifically mentioned as the credentials of the harm-wielding Iao. The editor, Alexander Hollman, does not consider the amulet to be Jewish.[257] Origen, for example, refers to Pharoah and his forces drowning as commonly used in magical recipes.[258] However the use of the fate of the Egyptian first-born (Ex 12:29, Ps 134:8) in a curse formula is unparalleled. If the curse came from a non-Jew, it appears that Antioch's Jewish population has yielded snatches of its stories to the folk magic cartel of power formulae. It at least demonstrates a superficial knowledge of some aspects of Jewish traditions — Hollmann quarantines these as "historiolae".[259]

A third observation returns us partially to the standard observations of commentators on Col 1:15, 18b, namely that the epithet *prototokos* is honorific, designating preeminence. From the notion of Israel as God's first-born (Ex 4:22, Jer 31:9) came the extension to Christ. Such a "narrowing" was already long known within Israel; God required an offering of the first-born (of animals and sons) from among the children of Israel. The king might be declared God's first-born (Ps 89:27). Kim includes the notion of the first-born in Israel under the classification of a matrilineal connection.[260] One of the references he takes as governed by this category is Ex 13:2. Sure enough, there to be found is πρωτοτόκον as the Septuagint's translation of בכור in the Hebrew text. However, the Septuagint translator(s) went a step further, perhaps concerned that

255 Other suggestions are πρατός ("for sale"), offered by Jan-Mathieu Carbon and Saskia Peels in *CGRN* 103 or προθυόντωσαν ("let them first sacrifice"), suggested by F. Sokolowski, "On the Lex Sacra of the Deme Phrearrhioi," *GRBS* 12 (1971): 217.

256 *LSCG* 96 (c. 200 BCE).

257 A. Hollmann, "A Curse Tablet from Antioch against Babylas the Greengrocer," *ZPE* 177 (2011): 157–8.

258 Origen *Celsum* 4.34.

259 Hollmann, "Curse Tablet," 157, 161.

260 Kim, *Firstborn Son*, 167. Kim sees the patrilineal as covering inheritance (eg Gen 49:3).

πρωτοτόκος did not quite convey the meaning, at least in this particular context. The Septuagint reads:

> Ἁγίασόν μοι πᾶν πρωτότοκον πρωτογενὲς διανοῖγον πᾶσαν μήτρον ἐν τοῖς υἱοῖς Ισραηλ ἀπὸ ἀνθρώπου ἕως κτήνους

The word πρωτογενές in the text has no Hebrew base (and no mirror in the Vulgate). John Wevers called it an "appositional construction",[261] creating a twofold explanation (with διανοῖγον πᾶσαν μήτρον) of what is meant by πρωτοτόκον. It then yields the sense:

> Sanctify to me every first-born, the first offspring that breaches the womb among the children of Israel from human to beast.

Given what we have noticed already in the use of πρωτοτόκος, it might even have the sense of "the first-about-to-be-born", that is "every first-pregnancy, every first-born that breaches the womb." In this case, three different aspects of the birthing process may be in view, just as seems to be implied in the threefold sequence of offering in Ezekiel the Tragedian's poetic recapitulation of the Exodus story (some time in the second century BCE): "offering the first-born (πρωτότευκτα) of all living things as a sacrifice to God, whatever male children mothers first bring forth, those having opened their mothers' womb."[262] Here the use of πρωτότευκτα carries the sense of first-fashioned, one of the meanings of πρωτοτόκος, in the sense of bearing, rather than having borne, the first-born.[263] He does not use πρωτογενές but expands the single word of Ex 13:2, probably in the light of Ex 13:12–13, which explains that the offering of the first-born applies to the male progeny.

Philo of Alexandria, however, was keen to retain the Septuagintal text because it served his philosophical exposition. He related the -γενες of πρωτογενές to γένος, conferring the sense of an indestructible category and hence rightly assigned to the indestructible God. Strikingly he goes on to equate this γένος that opens the womb (of the mind, speech and apprehension) to the invisible, spermatic, divine–architectural *logos*.[264] No doubt the singular assisted his cause. Elsewhere, in a fragment of a comment on Exodus, he divides the two words according to gender, creating an asymmetry between the matrilineal πρωτοτόκος that yields the "daughter" and the patrilineal πρωτογενές that yields the male.[265] It may be significant that in the address to the first-born

---

261 J. W. Wevers, *Notes on the Greek Text of Exodus* (Atlanta: GA: Scholars Press, 1990), 195. Nothing more is added in D. M. Gurtner, *Exodus: A Commentary on the Greek Text of Codex Vaticanus*, (Leiden: Brill, 2013), 323, who takes πρωτογενές as no more than repeating πᾶν πρωτότοκον.

262 τὰ πρωτότευκτα ζῷα θύοντες θεῷ | ὅσ' ἂν τέκωσι παρθένοι πρώτως τέκνα | τἄρσενικὰ διανοίγοντα μήτρας μητέρων. Ezekiel Trag. *Fr.* 13.46–8 (translation Carl Holladay).

263 So *LSJ* sv πρωτοτόκος.

264 Philo, *Her.* 117–9.

265 Philo, *QE* fr.A15.

son by the wise mother in Prov 31:2, occurs the only other use of πρωτογενές in the Septuagint, again with no Hebrew base, but clearly drawing on Ex 13:2 (with its reference to "son of my womb" and "son of my vow"). It seems that Philo's gender distinction was already being fostered, at least by the time of the translator of LXX Proverbs. Consequently, in the hands of this Jewish master of Middle Platonism, no longer was the verse seen as reminder of the devastating protection of Israel in Egypt through the extermination of the Egyptian first-born. It was now another testimony to the divine ordering of the cosmos.

For the hymn composer of the Lycus Valley (presuming s/he was armed with the full arsenal of scriptural references that dot the pages of contemporary commentators on Colossians), it was at least possible that πρωτογενής, even -ές could have been used of the first-born son of God. If Philo is testimony to Hellenistic Jewish wisdom conceptions of the type frequently drawn upon for parallels to the Colossian cosmological hymn, then such a possiblity might have been considered, given that, in spite of the sole (and quite differently applied) occurrence in Rom 8:29, πρωτοτόκος could hardly be considered cemented into the color tablet of titles to be conferred on Christ in the second half of the first century. It would certainly become so in the second century and beyond, featuring frequently in Christological and Trinitarian debates.

More assuredly, when one considers the *reception* of the hymn at Colossae, πρωτοτόκος was far to be preferred to that of πρωτογενής. The Colossian religious culture had already appropriated the latter epithet. If, as argued above, Tyche was particularly relevant as a dominant figure in the Colossian panorama of deities, especially because of the recent experience of her unwelcome, seismic dispensation, then πρωτοτόκος with all its synonymity with πρωτογενής would take on a telling contrast. *Christos prototokos* was extolled as far more reliable, far more benevolent and far more powerful than Tyche Protogeneia. Of particular importance is the second predicate for πρωτοτόκος in verse 18. Death was now captured and integrated into the cosmic beneficence, something that was never found with Tyche.

In this chapter, a small artifact, recently returned to attention for understanding Colossae's religious life, has received detailed analysis because of its importance for Colossae's religious panorama. The iconography and abbreviated inscription have awakened Colossae's particular sensitivity to cosmological order. The hymn that falls early in the Letter to the Colossians therefore takes on particular significance because it too has a particular sensitivity to cosmological order, now an alternative to that engineered by Tyche Protogeneia, more to be valued because of the disturbing memories of Tyche's seismic fickleness. The hymn therefore becomes an even more important witness to the Colossian world in which it operates, indeed is sung prophylactically by the Christ-followers in the city.

Chapter Six
Cosmic Visions, Cosmic Learning

Philosophy does not feature as a flagship of fame for Colossae. Nowhere in surviving literature is Colossae known as either the residence or birthplace of a philosopher. Her literary accolades are much more mundane — baths and wool,[1] and in Byzantine times, a pilgrimage healing center.[2] The city's western neighbors, by contrast, could claim a number of philosophers or other learned intellectuals. The famous Stoic, slave-philosopher, Epictetus, hailed from Hierapolis (born c. 50 CE) and a second-third century Sophist, Antipater, made the acclaimed city his base.[3] Laodikeia boasted two significant medical theorists who were also known as philosophers of the Skeptic school, Antiochos and Theodas (late first to second century CE). On rare occasions, two cities might extol the brilliance of the same scholar, such as the rhetor and sophist, Polemo, who was elevated and memorialized at Laodikeia (his birthplace) and Smyrna (his main teaching center).[4] The mid-to-late third century Menander the Rhetor of Laodikeia, in one oration demonstrating how to praise a city's greatness, recommended, *inter alia*, the roll-call of its famous intellectuals, "its rhetors, sophists, applied-mathematicians and such other professions that depend on practical wisdom."[5] Paul McKechnie has concluded, "it is improbable that any

1 Diodorus Siculus 14.80.8, Polyaenus *Strat.* 7.16.1 (baths); Strabo 12.8.16, Pliny *NH* 21.3.5 (wool/wool color or dye).

2 There is some, limited evidence that Chonai became a center for the cultivation of literature in the tenth to twelfth century. See M. D. Lauxtermann, *The Spring of Rhythm: An Essay on the Political Verse and other Byzantine metres* (Vienna: Austrian Academy of Sciences, 1999), 99–102.

3 See T. Ritti, "Il sofista Antipatros di Hierapolis," *MGR* 13 (1988): 71–128.

4 See W. W. Reader and A. J. Chvala-Smith, *The Severed Hand and Upright Corpse: The Declamations of Marcus Antonius Polemo* (Atlanta, GA; Scholars, 1996), 7–22. Both cities claimed to have his tomb! (Philostratus *Vit. soph.* 25.543); see also *I.Smyrna* 676.

5 ῥήτορες, σοφισταί, γεωμέτραι, καὶ ὅσαι ἐπιστῆμαι προνήσεως ἤρτηνται: Menander Rhetor, *Treatise* 1.3.364, ll. 15–16. The authenticity of the treatise is disputed by some (even though the treatise is grouped in the manuscript tradition), but the point remains that a city's fame, at

such high-octane philosophers ever taught at Colossae."[6] To date, the honor-roll for Colossae is blank. It may be that some inscription commemorating a local sage, without literary legacy, will surface, as has been found in other cities,[7] perhaps even giving their "brand" or specialisation as well.[8] But, in the meantime, one might wonder what sort or level or mix of philosophy was envisaged as a potential threat to the early Christ-followers at Colossae (Col 2:8).

Such on-the-ground questions rarely trouble Second Testament commentators. The array of competitive comparisons for "the Colossian philosophy" is as broad-ranging as it is insoluble.[9] But if the Asian epigraphical testimony to philosophies is any guide, the candidates are Platonism, Stoicism, Epicureanism, Pythagoreanism, Skepticism and Eclecticism, an extensive bibliothèque of options, not all of which have been tried by Second Testament commentators. Significantly, Cynicism is not found, even if one might side-step by arguing that cynic thought had infiltrated other streams.[10] In fact, McKechnie finds that Colossae's provinciality makes modern arguments that place philosophy at Colossae within the discourse of the Greek world's "most refined level" less plausible.[11]

McKechnie was not prepared to concede that there was no interest in philosophy at Colossae: "It was lesser lights who kept the flame of Greek philosophy burning in that kind of small centre." McKechnie may be overly down-sizing the city and its involvement in the cultural currents of the wider province. It is

---

least for some, ought to include representatives of its intellectual prowess. See D. A. Russell and N. G. Wilson (eds), *Menander Rhetor* (Oxford: Oxford University Press, 1981), xxxvi–xxxix; M. Heath, *Menander: A Rhetor in Context* (Oxford: Oxford University Press, 2004), 127–31.

6 P. McKechnie, *Christianizing Asia Minor: Conversion, Communities and Social Change in the Pre-Constantinian Era* (Cambridge: Cambridge University Press, 2019), 27.

7 *BCH* 1880.405–6, 21 (Halicarnassus, nd); *I.Sinope* 198 (1st to 2nd century CE); *MAMA* 8.499b (Aphrodisias, 2nd–3rd century CE); *I.Smyrna* 725 (211/212 CE); *I.Ephesos* 616 (217/218 CE); *I.Pergamon* 3.34 (Pergamon, early 2nd century CE). Attica, as might be expected, seems to have dripped with philosophers: see *IG* II^2 1006 (ll. 20, 63, 122/121 BCE), 1028 (l. 35, 100/99 BCE), 1043 (ll. 20, 42, 38/37 BCE).

8 *I.Didyma* 285 (Philidas, an Epicurean, late 1st century BCE to 1st century CE); *I.Didyma* 310 (Ailianos, a Stoic, 3rd century CE); *I.Ephesos* 4340 (…lius Secundinus of Tralles, a Platonist (mid 2nd century); *I.Ephesos* 789 (N. of Alexandria, an Eclectic, nd); *I.Apollonia* 260 (Sopatros, a Pythagorean, "Roman period"). These are no more than a handful. For the extensive suite of ancient philosophers, see R. Goulet *et al.* (eds), *Dictionnaire des philosophes antiques* (Paris: CRNS, 6 vols, 1989–2016).

9 See U. Huttner, *Early Christianity in the Lycus Valley* (Leiden: Brill, 2013), 124.

10 T. Martin, *By Philosophy and Empty Deceit: Colossians as a Response to a Cynic Critique* (Sheffield: Sheffield Academic Press, 1996). Lucian of Samosata's claim that the decadence of cynicism had infected every city (Lucian *Fug.* 16) has the same negligible statistical weight as Philo's claims that Jews were in every city of Asia (Philo, *Leg.* 245, 281, 311 cf 214, 216; *Flacc.* 46; cf Acts 2:10). It might be argued that because cynicism had little civic approbation (cf *SEG* 49.2452), epigraphical evidence is unlikely to be voluminous. This reduces the examination to an inter-literary comparison devoid of material resonance.

11 McKechnie, *Christianizing Asia Minor*, 27.

hard to imagine Hadrian's pan-hellenic sweep including Colossae, unless there was some wider substance in its assertion of connection with Olympian Zeus. Indeed we have already noticed the astonishing claim upon a preeminence of Tyche in this location — the *protogeneia* at the center of the cosmic alignment of the stars and the elements. A small testimony to the appreciation of intellectual attainment comes from one of the known inscriptions from Colossae, an epigram.[12] The hexameters in which the lines of the inscription are cast demand a level of education for their composition, execution and cultural appreciation. These fragments hint at the educational capital in which the city invested.[13]

However, we do in fact know one of McKechnie's lesser lights, even if it dimmed before it had the chance to become luminescent, even at home. To this snatch of witness we turn, place it into a wider frame of intellectual aspiration and attainment, before returning to Colossae itself and a famous cosmological hymn located in the Letter to the Colossians.

A Colossian student in Smyrna

Sometime in the first half of the second century, possibly in the reign of Hadrian, a young man from Colossae named Diodotos was drawn to further his training at one of the hot-spots of philosophical and rhetorical education in Asia, namely, Smyrna.[14] Such movement to centers of learning was a common practice, even an expectation, for those who wanted to advance their studies and their careers. In the second century, Smyrna offered a number of key attractions. Philostratus listed one of them, Polemo. He waxed with hyperbole, "By opening his school at Smyrna he benefited the city in the following ways. … he made her appear far more populous than before, since the youth flowed into her from both continents and the islands; nor were they a dissolute and promiscuous rabble, but select and genuinely Hellenic."[15]

Colossae may not have touted a renowned school of learning, as distinct from its neighbor Laodikeia, who boasted a medical school and a school of rhetoric.[16] But whether a Colossian or a Laodikeian, intellectual development was frequently portrayed in tandem with travel to other places in pursuit of knowledge. Diodotos, bearing a theonym that drew upon the city's patron dei-

12 *Steinepigramme* 1.02.15.01.
13 We return to this inscription in chapter 10.
14 C. Laes and J. M. H. Strubbe, *Youth in the Roman Empire: The Young and the Restless Years* (Cambridge: Cambridge University Press, 2014), 76.
15 Philostratus *Vit. soph.* 25.531 (trans. Wright).
16 See Strabo 12.8.20 for the medical school at the sanctuary of Mên Karou near Laodikeia; see Huttner, *Early Christianity*, 170–77; on rhetoric, see Russell-Wilson, *Menander Rhetor*.

ty,[17] did not live to complete his training, but he had already acquired sufficient learning and shown sufficient dedication to the pursuit of knowledge to gain the epithet *philologos*. At the very least, we can be confident that Diodotos had already received foundational education at an as-yet undiscovered gymnasium in his home city.[18] The very mention of the ethnic (Κολοσηνός) underscores the polis-status that Colossae retained in the second century.[19] In Philostratus' language, Diodotos was "select and genuinely Hellenic (ἐξειλεγμένης τε καὶ καθαρῶς Ἑλλάδος)."

The only reason we know of Diodotos is that a fellow student took responsibility for erecting an epitaph (Pl. 6.1), probably at the foot of Mt Pagos (modern Kadifekale),[20] the acropolis from which the main venues of the new city (such as the theater, stadium, odeion, museion and the agora)[21] fanned out within the city walls towards the harbor. It is likely that a necropolis hugged the external wall and main road leading east to Sardis and Laodikeia.

Plate 6.1: The inscription of the epitaph for Diodotos the Colossian.[22]

17 Stephen Colvin has noted the Anatolian penchant for theophoric names: "Names in Hellenistic and Roman Lycia," in *The Greco-Roman East: Politics, Culture, Society* edited by S. Colvin (Cambridge: Cambridge University Press, 2004), 58. This would seem to be confirmed at Colossae in that, despite the few published inscriptions, names built on the name of Zeus, occur frequently. In addition to Diodotos, we have Dion (*MAMA* 6.44), along with Diodoros (a corrected reading to the *ed. prin.* following) and possibly including Theodoros, found as the name of six persons in a single inscription; see A. H. Cadwallader, "Honouring the Repairer of the Baths: A New Inscription from Kolossai," *Antichthon* 46 (2012): 151. On Zeus as the patron god of Colossae, see Cadwallader, *Fragments of Colossae: Sifting through the Traces* (Adelaide: ATF Press, 2015), 65–7.

18 There is some evidence to suggest that the baths of the Roman period are to be found to the east of the Colossae höyük, adjoining the southern bank of the Lycus river. Baths were blended with gymnasia under Roman influence, so the Colossian gymnasium is likely to be found in this area; see A. H. Cadwallader, *Fragments of Colossae*, 135–53.

19 Cf *I.Boubon* 102; see N. Sekunda, "Changing Patterns of Land-Holding in the South-Western Border Lands of Greater Phyrgia in the Achaemenid and Hellenistic Periods," in *Colossae in Space and Time: Linking to an Ancient City* edited by A. H. Cadwallader and M. Trainor (Göttingen: Vandenhoeck & Ruprecht, 2011), 71.

20 The standard edition of the inscription (held in the Louvre, Paris) is that of Georg Petzl, *Die Inschriften von Smyrna* (IGSK 23.1; Bonn: Habelt, 1982), nr. 440.

21 See Frank Sear, *Roman Theatres: An Architectural Study* (Oxford: Oxford University Press, 2006), 352–4. The old city was located to the north of modern Bayraklı.

22 Photograph courtesy of *Musée du Louvre* MND 50; MA 3301 (https://collections.louvre.fr/en/ark:/53355/cl010277026).

The epitaph was simple, a marble funerary plaque measuring 51 centimeters across and 35 centimeters high, with the four-line inscription occupying the top half of the stone. It caused a few headaches in transcription, until Louis Robert brought his forensic skill to its reconstruction:[23]

Διόδοτος Κολοσηνὸς
φιλόλογος, προοῦν-
τος τοῦ μνημείου Ἀττί-
νου τοῦ Ἀττίνου [vine-leaf]

[This grave is for] Diodotos the Colossian
a lover of learning. The grave was
set up by Attinos
the son of Attinos.

While no age is recorded on this epitaph, Robert concluded on the basis of a comparison of other epitaphs from Smyrna (and Ephesos), along with the recording of the arranger/provider of the memorial (Attinos) that Diodotos was a young, if well-credentialed, student. On some epitaphs, young men given the epithet φιλόλογος have their ages inscribed.[24] Agathokles, son of Archelaos, a Bithynian from Nicaea, has his age added, namely, 20 years at death.[25] Another, Markos Domitios Sabinos, reached only the age of 17.[26] Significantly, these ages fall below the ceiling of 25 years that their contemporary Smyrnian teacher, the middle-platonist Theon, considered the opportune time for the integration and intensification of previously distinct disciplines of learning.[27]

There is an important insight to be gained here, given that the age of 25 was the year at which, in Roman law, a person moved from the legal category of *minor* and could begin his *cursus honorum*. Since the time of Augustus, this meant he could serve as *quaestor*, having become entitled, subject to property

23 The inscription was noted at the end of the nineteenth century: A. Héron de Villefosse and E. Michon, "Erwerbungen des Louvre im Jahre 1899," *AA* 15 (1900): 156 nr. 24; A. Dain, *Inscriptions grecques du Musée du Louvre; les textes inédits* (Paris: Les Belles Lettres, 1933), 59, nr. 53, corrected by L. Robert, "Inscriptions grecques inédites au Musée du Louvre," *RArch* (1933/2): 132–3 nr. 53 *I.Smyrna* 440.

24 L. Robert *Hellenica* 13 (1965): 50; M. Dana, "Les médecins du Pont-Euxin à l'étranger: une 'Itinérance du savoir'," *Classica et Christiana* 3 (2008): 127.

25 *I.Smyrna* 439 = *IGR* 4.1446.

26 *I.Smyrna* 441 = *IGR* 4.1447.

27 Theon 2.22. Note that Theon relies here on Plato *Resp.* 7.537b but with an apparent amendment of the text from 20 years to 25 years. The variant is not noted in S. R. Slings, *Platonis Rempublicam* (Oxford: Clarendon, 2003), 291. The edition relied upon for Theon's work is that of Eduard Hiller, *Theonis Smyrnaei Philosophi Platonici Expositio Rerum Mathematicarum ad Legendum Platonem Utilium* (Leipzig: Teubner, 1878). References are to page and line numbers. A new commentary on the edition has been developed by F. M. Petrucci, *Teone di Smirne. Expositio rerum mathematicarum ad legendum Platonem utilium. Introduzione, traduzione, commentario* (Sankt Augustin: Academia Verlag, 2012), but he relies substantially, if critically, on Hiller's edition.

qualifications, to membership in the Senate. Theon provides this age *within* a quotation from Plato's *Republic*, and deftly corrects Plato's recommended age of 20 (itself the *Athenian* transition point to adult service)[28] into the Roman imperial reality of adult accountability.[29] There is little doubt that Theon's adjustment of the quotation from Plato is deliberate. Federico Petrucci, the foremost contemporary Theon scholar, whilst skipping this particular instance,[30] notes that Theon's subtle redirection of a number of quotations from Plato are deliberately designed to make Plato contemporary for his audience.[31] This eye towards the new realities of imperial legal and political life is something to which we return below. Theon certainly did not consider the advanced study of philosophy to be impractical. Rather, civic responsibilities were in view. The fact that so many φιλόλογοι were well below that Roman legal, age benchmark probably reflects the continuation of Greek legal, social and political conventions — the pluriform jurisprudential and educational systems of the empire in the second century. But in Smyrna on the western seaboard of the Mediterranean and cultivating its reputation in competitive contradistinction to Ephesos and Pergamon, Roman values were very much to the fore, even if not the only treasure-chest to display.

Pressing the *philologoi*

The ages given in these *philologos* inscriptions reflect graduation as an ephebe from the students' respective gymnasia. Given that the formal language of the epitaphs is similar, even though varying slightly with some mentioning age, and others naming the person responsible for the erection of the stone, it appears likely that, if not in close proximity to one another in the necropolis, they were in close proximity in their designation and self-presentation. None has a date (such would be unusual) but the letter styles, naming patterns, plus the fine for grave disturbance in one inscription,[32] clearly indicate the second

28 Aristotle *Pol.* 7.1329a (service in the military or political life); cf Plato *Leg.* 8.833d. See J. Bowen, *A History of Western Education: Volume 1, The Ancient World* (London: Methuen, 1972), 152.

29 *Dig.* 14.3.11.3 (Ulpian); 16.1.8.15 (Ulpian); 18.7.4 (Marcellus). See J. A. C. Thomas, *Textbook of Roman Law* (Amsterdam: North-Holland, 1976), 113, 466–8; E. Eyben, "Was the Roman 'Youth' an 'Adult' socially?" *L'antiquité classique* 50 (1981): 328–50. The age of 25 is repeatedly determinative of legal standing in Justinian's *Digest*. Little wonder that ecclesiastical positions were predicated on a similar articulation — a minimum age of 25 was prescribed for those to be made deacon.

30 Petrucci (*Teone di Smirne*, 289) notes that both Iamblichus (*Comm. Math.* 22.2–3) and Stobaeus (*Anth.* 2.31.43.1–4) quote the passage from Plato. However, they omit the opening reference to an age, perhaps as a less indictable handling of Plato's text (cf Mk 1:2–3 and Matt 3:3)!

31 Petrucci, *Teone di Smirne*, 41.

32 *I.Smyrna* 439. A fine of 500 denarii is prescribed.

century. Two points are to be noted. Firstly, students came to Smyrna from different places for their higher education.[33] One of the most famous orators of the second century, Polemo, came to Smyrna from Colossae's neighbor in the Lycus Valley, Laodikeia, to pursue his studies. This suggests that the road from the Lycus to Smyrna was well-worn by those eager to advance their education and the benefits that flowed in public life from their attainments. Polemo, after all, remained to establish his own school at Smyrna and displayed his prowess before Hadrian in 124 CE.[34] Secondly, they had already secured sufficient training as to be recognized as φιλολόγοι.

The term is imprecise.[35] However, it is not confined to an honorific for students (in spite of how Robert's specific study has been taken), even though a couple of epitaphs from another centre of learning, Ephesos, record the term in a way similar to those at Smyrna.[36] Hadrian, for example, is described as "by nature, a *philologos*",[37] an iteration, perhaps, of the description given to Alexander the Great.[38] Athenians, in general, were described as φιλόλογοι.[39] Epictetus seems to have quarantined the term for established scholars.[40] Artemidorus, the second-century dream scientist, set φιλόλογοι as equivalent in status to, but distinct from rhetors.[41] Vettius Valens, the second-century astrologer, was similar though expanding the list to include other persons of influence: kings, rulers, practical mathematicians, along with rhetors.[42] In the papyri, the term can mean a teacher or tutor.[43] It is not that there is a necessary difference between literary and epigraphical usage, since the term is found in inscriptions clearly designating an older man.[44] Indeed some inscriptions speak of νεανίας φιλόλογος,[45] whilst others acknowledge mature age with ἀνὴρ φιλόλογος.[46] What is clear, is that the status of a

33 On students dying away from home, see Laes–Strubbe, *Youth in the Roman Empire*, 77.

34 See A. R. Birley, *Hadrian: The Restless Emperor* (London/New York: Routledge, 1997), 159–61, 164–6, 170.

35 M. Kleijwegt, *Ancient Youth: the ambiguity of youth and the absence of adolescence in Greco-Roman society* (Amsterdam: J. C. Gieben, 1991), 118.

36 See *I.Ephesos* 2202, 2211; see also *TAM* IV,1 155, 232 (Nikomedia), *IGR* 3.200 (Ankara). The term seems particularly popular in Asia Minor, but is also known in the west (see, for example, *IGUR* 2.736).

37 φύσει … φιλολόγος Dio Cassius 69.3, *Epitome* S243 l. 16. Dio goes on to add that Hadrian bequeathed a variety of prose and poetic compositions in Greek and Latin.

38 Plutarch *Alex.* 8.2.

39 Diodorus Siculus 12.4.

40 Epictetus 2.4.6, 2.4.11, 3.2.13; cf Plutarch *Tu. San.* (*Mor.*) 130A, *Luc.* 42.2; Porphyry *Vit. Plot.* 20.49–50.

41 Artemidorus *Onir.* 4.18.2.

42 Vettius Valens *Anth.* 2.17.89.

43 *P.Oxy.* 2190 at ll. 7, 25. See J. Rea, "A Student's Letter to his Father: P.Oxy. XVIII.2190 Revised," *ZPE* 99 (1993): 75–88.

44 *TAM* II 919 (Rhodiapolis?), *IG* 14.908 (Fundi, 8 BCE – 8 CE).

45 *CIG* 4412b (Iotape, first century BCE?), Bean – Mitford, *Rough Cilicia II* 152, 154c.

46 *SEG* 63.1436 (Kourion, 13 CE); compare Diogenes Laertius *Vit. phil.* 5.5.

φιλόλογος was elevated, worthy of honor in its own right as well as in combination with other professions and offices.

The term is not so general as to be vacuous in application,[47] even if its spread can reach as far as arithmetic and geometry.[48] Sometimes the word can be qualified by a specialization, as for example in medicine.[49] One Ameinias, also known as Aristoboulos, is recorded as living 49 years and 6 months, and remembered as a "an accomplished and learned doctor" (ἰατρὸν τέλειον καὶ φιλόλογον).[50] One woman, Naevia Clara, is described, in Latin equivalent, as a *medica philologa* in a late first-century BCE inscription in Rome.[51] Alfredo Buonopane comments that because her husband is described as a *medicus chirurgus* ("surgical doctor") there is a likely contrast of emphasis about the nature of their respective medical learning: Clara was well-versed in theoretical medicine, being erudite in the pertinent literature on medical matters. He finds a visual representation of the quality in a funerary stele from Byzantion which portrays the deceased doctor, Mousa, daughter of Agathokles,[52] holding a scroll in her right hand, a sign of both learnedness and authority.[53]

Accordingly, the epithet φιλόλογος seems, in a school context, to be focused on the extent of one's reading and learning or at least one's commitment to scholarship, whether in a survey of disciplines or a more focused specialization. Indeed, it is sometimes found as a virtual synonym for φιλόσοφος,[54] or, at the very least, one well-read in literature as a support for philosophy. A philosopher was expected to be a *philologos* and a *philologos* might aspire to be a philosopher as one of the careers for which wide-reading was the requisite preparation.

---

47 See C. Panagopoulos, "Vocabulaire et mentalités dans les Moralia de Plutarque," *DHA* 3 (1977): 227.

48 Plutarch *Adul. am.* 52C.

49 Smyrna was famous as one of the places frequented by Galen as part of his medical training, intent, as he claimed, on attending the lectures of Albinus: Galen *Lib. Prop.* 19.16.

50 *TAM* II 147 = *IGR* 3.534 (Lydai, 1st or 2nd century CE). Evelyne Samama reads the stone as indicating an age of 19 years (ΙΘ´) rather than 49 (ΜΘ´), which brings the type close to that of the Smyrna examples of φιλόλογος; see E. Samama, *Les médecins dans le monde grec. Sources épigraphiques sur la naissance d'un corps médical* (HEMGR 31) (Geneva: Droz, 2003), 389 nr. 11 (nr. 278). Compare however *IGR* 4.1359 (Sosandra) where an alternate reconstruction reads μ[έγαν | ἰ]ατρὸν καὶ φιλ[όλο-|γ]ον (not φιλ[όσο- | φ]ον). The honorand, Menecrates son of Polyeides, has a *cursus honorum* that includes governor, *gymnasiarch*, *agonothete* — a clear indication of maturity in age; see V. Nutton, "Menecrates of Sosandra, Doctor or Vet?" *ZPE* 22 (1976): 93–6. Moreover, a young man at Smyrna named Niketes could be acclaimed on his epitaph as doctor and "hero" even though only 19 years of age at death (*I.Smyrna* 442b).

51 *AE* 2001.263.

52 Μοῦσα Ἀγαθοκλέους | ἰατρείνη (*SEG* 24.811, first century BCE).

53 A. Buonopane, "Medicae nell'occidente romano: un'indagine preliminaire", in *Donna e lavoro nella documentazione epigrafica. Atti del I Seminario sulla condizione femminile nella documentazione epigrafica* edited by A. Buonopane and F. Cenerini (Faenza: Fratelli Lega Editori, 2003), 121–2. For a brief description and photograph of the stele, see E. Pfuhl and H. Möbius, *Die Ostgriechischen Grabreliefs* (Mainz am Rhein: Philipp von Zabern, 1977), *Textband I*, 151, nr. 467 and *Tafelband 1*, pl. 77, nr. 467.

54 Plato *Resp.* 9.382e; Philodemus *P.Herc.* 1471 fr 88 column 8a (ll. 8–9).

Here we can return to Diodotos's contemporary and possible teacher at Smyrna, Theon. Theon provides a valuable demonstration of how one might qualify and operate as a φιλόλογος. At one point in his handbook on Plato's philosophy as undergirded by mathematical principles,[55] he moves from an exposition of harmony as the balance of aesthetically approved tones, appreciated through musical instruments but only formally analysed by arithmetical means, to another category, that is, the harmony of balanced proportions in numerical relationships (which is the requisite premise for his lost section on the cosmic music of the spheres).[56] To enable the transition, he provides an aside on the multiple meanings of the word λογός.[57] The semantic range is explored by reference to the works of a number of philosophers and rhetoricians (Aristotle, Demosthenes, Lysias), to common, commercial affairs (an account), to literary genres (such as fables, tales, proverbs and eulogies) and to definitions and logical structures. Thus, his sweep of human knowledge is succinctly demonstrated. Theon then provides a particular focus, giving pride of place to Plato's four-fold classification of the semantics of λογός,[58] which seems to be Theon's own distillation of and partial addition to Plato's teaching.[59] Such a narrowing of focus is extended further, with Theon announcing his intention to concentrate on λογός as "ratio", that is on the relationship between numbers (λογὸς τῆς ἀναλογίας).[60] Having fully, if briefly, demonstrated his acquisition as a φιλόλογος, he then moves into the display of detailed intellectual attainment characteristic of one who is both philosopher and teacher, with a claim on the tradition of Plato.

So valued was the epithet that it became used as a name. Indeed one Claudius Mystikos of Kibyra, perhaps in continuation of a family tradition (given his own name) dubbed his sons, Rhetorikos and Philologos — significant because they are obviously two separate entities, albeit named by a father with high aspirations, for, possibly, two different professions. There are 26 instances of the name Ῥητορικός in *LGPN* and three with the female form Ῥητορική.[61] The names Ῥητόριος, Ῥητορῖνος, and Ῥητορίων also occur, but all are relatively uncommon. Φιλόλογος is also infrequently found (39 instances

55 The *Expositio rerum mathematicarum ad legendum Platonem utilium* is in fact a later name appended to one of the manuscripts of Theon's work. It is now applied to two main manuscripts of Theonic compositions which are accepted as belonging to the one work; Petrucci, *Teone di Smirne*, 37–40. A French translation, based on the slightly amended text of Hiller, is found in J. Dupuis, *Théon de Smyrne. Exposition des connaissances mathématiques utiles pour la lecture de Platon* (Paris: Hachette, 1892); an English translation, based on Dupuis, is found in R. and D. Lawlor, *Mathematics useful for Understanding Plato by Theon of Smyrna* (San Diego: Wizards Bookshelf, 1979).

56 Theon 72.21–4. For the introductory sketch of the bipartite schema of harmony, see Theon 47.1–8; for the "music of the spheres" see Theon 12.15–19.

57 Theon 72.24–73.15.

58 The third instance is particularly striking in the echoes of its language in Col 2:8, 20, namely, ἡ τῶν τοῦ ὅλου στοιχείων ἀπόδοσις ("the explanation of the elements of the whole" Theon 73.13–14).

59 See Plato *Soph.* 263e, *Theaet.* 206d.

60 Theon 73.15, 16 *et seq*; se Petrucci, *Teone di Smirne*, 381.

61 One from the territory of Aezanis territory, 1st century CE; two from Rome, 2nd century CE. To these, should now be added IG X 2 1supp. 1425 (Thessalonike, 3rd century CE).

in *LGPN*), though one has particular interest for Pauline readers (Rom 16:15).[62] Significantly, this name occurs in Latin transcription, *Philologus*, in the west, with a number of instances from a servile context.[63] This brief survey of onomastics seems to indicate the high esteem attached to the term. However, the value attributed to φιλόσοφος is not mirrored in naming practices; only 5 instances for male names (four from early Delos, one from third century Athens)[64] and two for Φιλοσοφία, both from Caria and both late (fifth century CE).[65] Clearly the conversion of this term into a name was not favored (except on Delos in the fourth to second century BCE) whereas, although uncommon, Φιλόλογος was an acceptable name, perhaps for the bearer to "grow into".

There is a further connection frequently attested for φιλόλογος in literature and inscription alike. Attainment in education and the commitment to knowledge gained from reading, discussion and training — all part of the sweep of φιλόλογος — was valued as a crucial credential, even a necessary virtue, for public life and benefactions.[66] Some of the memorials that honour *philologoi* are actually conferred by civic bodies, the *Boulê* and/or the *Dêmos* in particular. The epitaph for Sosandros of Perta for example was set up not by his father but by the city authorities who recognized his nobility and learnedness (σεμνὸς καὶ φιλόλογος), adding that his father Iollas had performed many liturgies for his homeland.[67] The implication of the double honors is that the father had passed on the crucial values for exemplary leadership thereby conferring a stability not just within family generational succession but also the secure permanence of civic functioning. One Molês from Rhodiapolis in Lycia was described as an ἀγαθὸς φιλόλογος,[68] the description modulating that very hellenic, stereotypical description of a valued citizen as καλὸς κἀγαθός, an exemplary good man.[69] So, there was more to the term than simply a literary participant at the city gymnasium, though such a recognition can occur.[70]

62 See E. Judge, "Latin Names around a Counter-Cultural Paul," in *The Bible and the Business of Life* edited by S. Holt and G. Preece (Adelaide: ATF, 2004), 84.

63 Plutarch, *Cic.* 48.2. The slave's name matched the training given him by Cicero's brother, Quintus.

64 *I.Rhénée* 415, *IG* XI 2 161 and 162, *I.Délos* 353, 456 (Delos); *IG* II^2 2214 (Athens).

65 *I.Aphrodisias 2007* 13.309 (521–551 CE); *Suda H.* 611.

66 See J. Fischer, "Redner, Sophisten und Philosophen in Römischen Ephesos," in *Der Beitrag Kleinasiens zur Kultur- und Geistesgeschichte der griechischen-römischen Antike* edited by J. Fischer (Vienna: Österreichischen Akademia der Wissenschaften, 2014), 125–51.

67 *MAMA* 11.307 (dated 150–250 CE). See also *SEG* 39.1227, *TAM* II 147 (mentioned previously), *CIG* 4412, and, perhaps, the extensive though unfortunately fragmentary papyrus copy of an inscription honoring the grammarian and philologos (?) Apion, the renowned protagonist of Josephus: *P.Oxy.* 5202 = *SEG* 64.1883. The reconstruction of φιλόλογος is one possibility suggested by the editor of the papyrus, Amin Benaissa (p. 133).

68 *TAM* II 919 (second century CE).

69 See, for example, *IG* XII 6,1 146 (Samos, 250–200 BCE), *I.Smyrna* 585 (second to first century BCE), *IG* II 1072 (Athens 116–117 CE).

70 *I.Priene* 112 (τὸν … ἐκ φιλολογίας γραμματικόν), 113 (τῶν τε ἐκ φιλολογίας μαθημάτων) (84 or 1 BCE). It should be noted however, that, even here, the *Boulê* and *Dêmos* were named as involved in setting up the honorific display. The gymnasium was an essential component of civic, cultural infrastructure. Compare *IG* XII 9 235 (Eretria, c.100 BCE; arrangement for a Homeric *philologos*, the Athenian Dionysios son of Philôtos, to teach at the gymnasium).

The connection between familiarity with literature and civic participation is a frequent trope in standard texts. The *Ars Rhetorica*, for example, taught, "If someone is a lover of literature (φιλόλογος), praise his education by saying that well-educated people are especially deserving of command and of governing office".[71] Inscriptions, whether epitaphal or not, helped to ground such attitudes and promotion. They were part of civic display, "a conjoined individual-communal 'signal' that relayed important information to attentive citizens, nearby cities, and agents of Rome," as LuAnn Wandsnider aptly distills it.[72] Attinos, the memorialist of Diodotos, is clearly broadcasting not only his friend's Smyrnian value (φιλόλογος) but, through the benefaction of care and record of the deceased, his own εὔνοια (goodwill, loyalty) — one of the esteemed *polis*/citizenship values in antiquity. Theon himself underlines Plato's own collation of learning with utility for the polis: "wisdom is the most beautiful and greatest for the harmony of cities" (καλλίστη καὶ μεγίστη τῶν περὶ πόλεων συμφωνιῶν ἐστιν ἡ σοφία). Conversely, the threat to a city's welfare and security (οἰκοφθόρος καὶ περὶ πόλιν οὐδαμῇ σωτήριος) comes from an abject refusal to learn.[73]

Philosophy was both part of the learning of a *philologos* and often the articulation built on that learning. We need to be alert to the "practical" bent that philosophy was concerned to parade in this period, that is, the contribution that philosophical learning could make to public life. We have already seen Roman influence in Theon's recommendation of the age of 25 — the turning-point in Roman law for accountability and for holding public office. But in the east of Rome's empire, to be acknowledged as a philosopher, whilst it might mark a height of intellectual attainment, was also sometimes included as one of the accolades for a civic leader along with a recitation of the offices he had held. In this sense, φιλόσοφος could become part of the *cursus honorum* celebrated in a dedication in honor of a member of the elite of a city. At Daldis in Lydia, the city honored one of its own, Menekrates son of Polyeidos, who was recorded not only as *strategos*, *logistes*, *gymnasiarch*, *prytanis* and *agonothete* but also as a leading doctor and philosopher and "hero".[74] Significantly these last three titles/offices/professions are named before the civic offices. At Pergamon, Lucius Flavius Hermokrates was honored as philosopher and high

71 *Ars Rhet.* 274: εἰ φιλόλογος εἴη, ἐγκώμιον παιδείας, καὶ ὅτι οἱ πεπαιδευμένοι μάλιστα ἄξιοι ἀρχῆς καὶ τοιαύτης ἡγεμονίας; cf Demosthenes *Or.* 61.35–7, Lucian *Somn.* 11.

72 L. Wandsnider, "Public Buildings and Civic Benefactions in Western Rough Cilicia: insights from signaling theory," in *Rough Cilicia: New Historical and Archaeological Approaches* edited by M. C. Hoff and R. F. Townsend (Oxford: Oxbow, 2013), 176.

73 Theon 10.13–14, paraphrasing Plato *Leg.* 3.689d.

74 *TAM* V,1 650 = *IGR* 4.1359. Note that μέγαν before ἰατρόν is reconstructed from the only surviving letter, *mu*, and the assessment of the space available. Luigi Moretti has suggested rather μουλο- | ιατρός, that is, effectively, a veterinarian; see "Epigraphica" *RFIC* 103 (1975): 189–90, nr. 13. This doesn't affect the point being made here. For discussion, see V. Boudon-Millot, "Ménécratès," in *Dictionnaire des philosophes antiques*, 4.441–2.

priest of Asia.[75] Nikomedia boasted one Aurelius Demetrios as philosopher and member of the city *Boulê*.[76] A woman also might be acclaimed as a philosopher in the course of honoring her civic contributions including as *gymnasiarch*.[77]

It does not take much inquiry to recognize that Plato's philosopher-king has had its specific focus generalized into the notion of governance. This was, in fact, the alternative posed by Plato — if not philosophers as kings, than at least kings and rulers *or their sons* with "a true love of true philosophy".[78] Philosophy in such a context was a key instrument for the maintenance of political arrangements. Under Rome, hellenophilic commitment was not diminished; in fact, it was nourished,[79] but in the direction of philosophy *in service of* the new realities of governance. Little wonder that one inscription celebrates a Julius Niketes as φιλόσοφος, φιλοκαίσαρ and φιλόπατρις, "lover of wisdom, of Caesar and of homeland".[80] Even the bronze coins that kept the wheels of commerce going in the east, celebrated one or other philosopher, some of whom are portrayed holding an orb, the cosmos, in their fingers.[81] As Daryn Lehoux comments, "Governance, reason, mind, humanity and cosmos all come together under one set of relationships and responsibilities."[82] The conceptual rationale might be Greek (especially in the east) but the practical operation was Roman. It helps to explain Hadrian's backing of hymnody at the sacred contest in Smyrna (the *Hadrianeia Olympia*) established as part of a lavish foundation and expressly prescribing contributions by theologians (*theologoi*) and hymn-singers (*hymnodoi*).[83] Hymns are not neutral. They spring from historical circumstances and use contemporary literary forms. They often do little more than reinforce the power relations involved in those realities. The authority of Plato's elitist structure for the absence of *stasis* cast a long shadow into Roman Asia.[84]

We cannot be sure what path the Colossian Diodotos was pursuing as φιλόλογος at Smyrna — rhetoric, medicine, or philosophy are prime contenders. His goal was not necessarily a teaching career in the footsteps of the

75 *I.Pergamon* 3.34 (200–210 CE).

76 *SEG* 32.1255 (3rd century CE).

77 *IG* XII 5 292 (Paros, 3rd century CE) cf Magnilla a philosopher, daughter of a philosopher and wife of a philosopher (*IMT LApollon/Milet* 2365, Apollonia in Mysia, 2nd to 3rd century CE).

78 τῶν νῦν ἐν δυναστείαις ἢ βασιλείαις ὄντων ὑέσιν ἢ αὐτοῖς ἔκ τινος θείας ἐπιπνοίας ἀληθινῆς φιλοσοφίας ἀληθινὸς ἔρως ἐμπέσῃ; Plato *Resp.* 6.499b–c.

79 See G. Woolf, "Becoming Roman, Staying Greek: Culture, Identity and the Civilising Process in the Roman East," *PCPS* 40 (1994): 116–43.

80 *I.Klaudiu polis* 67.

81 *RPC* 3.1990 (the pre-socratic philosopher Anaxagoras at/from Clazomenae), 3.408 (the philosopher-mathematician Euklides at Megara); *RPC online* 4.2.1813 temp. (Lesbonax at Mytilene), 6.5278 temp. (Pythagoras at Samos), 6.5008 temp. (Heraclitos at Ephesos).

82 D. Lehoux, *What did the Romans Know? An Inquiry into Science and Worldmaking* (Chicago: University of Chicago Press, 2012), 184.

83 *I.Smyrna* 697.

84 See P. W. Rose, *Sons of the Gods, Children of Earth: Ideology and Literary Form in Ancient Greece* (Ithaca: Cornell University Press, 1992), 349–54.

famed second century masters of different schools in the museion and gymnasium of the city: Megistias, Theon, Aurelianos, Pelops, Polemo, Albinus and supplemented by international visitors such as Scopelionos, Aelius Aristides, Apollonios and Herodes Atticus. The array of names is one illustration that the second century was extremely beneficial to Smyrna's profile in the province and beyond. Diodotos was certainly captivated.

From late Hellenistic times, Smyrna had cultivated itself not only as the birth-place of Homer (one of seven such claimants!)[85] but as a (consequential) center of learning. Paul Zanker's study of the visual symbolism of Smyrnian funerary stelai reveals some distinctive features in the city's iconography, not least being the absence of the otherwise-almost-ubiquitous *klinê*-banquet scene. Rather, in this intellectual hub, communal values are to the fore: figures face the viewer drawing the voyeur into discussion; book rolls frequently appear either held or otherwise placed, sometimes with writing implements; an earnest, slightly furrowed brow sometimes supported by the fingers of a hand drawing attention to intellectual activity carves the projected identity of the deceased; some even claim civic recognition with a wreath, within which ὁ δῆμος is carved.[86] Other elements related to gender and childhood are also present but, for our purposes, it is striking that Smyrna laid a foundation exemplar for its city life in literary and educational pursuits. This may have been disrupted by the Mithridatic War of 89–85 BCE but the burgeoning of the Second Sophistic at the end of the first century CE saw Smyrna rise to prominence again as a philosophic center keen to display that standing in the fabric of the city and beyond. Epitaphs and other inscriptions that record the ethnic of a person, especially in conjunction with some title of learning, suggest Smyrna's reputation had spread considerably in this regard.[87] As Louis Robert extolled, "Smyrne, capital intellectualle de la province d'Asie, riche en livres, métropole de la rhétorique."[88]

Diodotos' attraction to Smyrna is understandable. With his education and, no doubt, considerable wealthy connections undergirding his translocation, Diodotos was seeking one of the foremost centers to fit him for advancement.

---

85 There are various stories of Homer's birth at Smyrna; see Aristotle *FHG*, Fr. 274; Ps-Skylax *Peripl.* 98.14; Plutarch *Sert.* 1.78.2. Byzantine writers replayed the Homer-Smyrna connection. For the seven cities, see *Gr. Anth.* 16.298. There is a suggestion that Homer became a focus of worship: Strabo 14.1.37.

86 P. Zanker, "The Hellenistic Grave Stelai from Smyrna: Identity and Self-image in the Polis," in *Images and Ideologies: Self-Definition in the Hellenistic World* edited by A. Bulloch *et al.* (Berkeley: University of California Press, 1993), 212–30.

87 *I.Smyrna* 372, a jurist, Menander, from Ankara, presumably young given that the grave is erected by his father cf *IGR* 4.618; *I.Smyrna* 463 a relief carver from Aizanoi; *IGR* 4.1690, a philosopher, Herodotos, from Pergamon. Compare *I.Smyrna* 331 the "friends of Agrippa", one member from Adana. Of course, Smyrna was attractive to outsiders for other pursuits — gladiators (*I.Smyrna* 309) ferrymen (*I.Smyrna* 224).

88 L. Robert, *Études anatoliennes: Recherches sur les Inscriptions grecques de l'Asie Mineure* (Paris: de Boccard, 1937), 147.

He may have been seeking the training that would fit him for public office in his Colossian homeland. His ambitions may have reached elsewhere. His death meant that only an epitaph created a memorial.

Theon of Smyrna and the critical components for higher learning

Diodotos was certainly not the only student of learning and aspirant to advanced training. When the young *philologos* felt the pull of Smyrna for his further intellectual development, he entered a celebrated pathway. But his ambition demonstrates that Colossae in general and not just the particular case of Diodotos had both the preparation for and interest in higher learning.

In the first half of the second century, there were a number of teachers that were already enhancing Smyrna's cultivated reputation. One in particular has drawn contemporary scholarly attention, to the point of linking Diodotos to a then-renowned philosopher, Theon of Smyrna.[89] Of course, we have no knowledge about Diodotos's specialist discipline, whether rhetoric, medicine or philosophy, though the term φιλόλογος probably tips slightly in the direction of the last. Claudius Mystikos's ambitiously named sons, whom we have briefly met above, seem to imply that rhetoric was to be understood as separated from the study or career of a φιλόλογος. Nevertheless, rhetoric still retained considerable importance in civic affairs, whether it be the efforts to persuade the decisions of a civic institution (such as the *Boulê*, the *Dêmos*, or the *Gerousia* and any of the *Ekklesiai*, that met formally in a city) or to spearhead a delegation to provincial gatherings (such as a koinon, or neokorate celebrations and the like).

So, I must admit that the decision to pursue a connection from Diodotos to Theon is arbitrary, albeit chronologically admissible. But the survival of Theon's handbook for his students, the *philologoi* who had gathered from across the western Mediterranean to his coastal headquarters, allows us to sift the conceptual frameworks that can be reliably entertained as having some sway in the province of Asia, including at Colossae.

Theon is thought to have been born in the latter half of the first century and flourished as a teacher at Smyrna in the first three decades of the second century.[90] We are fortunate to have a bust of Theon (Pl. 6.2), identified by an accompanying inscription. The bust was purchased by Anthoine Fouquier during his time as French consul at Smyrna (1669–1672) and shortly after-

---

89 L. L. Thompson, "ISmyrna 753: Gods and the One God," in *Reading Religions in the Ancient World: essays presented to Robert McQueen Grant* edited by R. McQ. Grant, D. E. Aune and R. D. Young (Leiden: Brill, 2007), 118.

90 F. M. Petrucci, "Théon de Smyrne," in *Dictionnaire de philosophes antiques*, 6.1019–20.

wards found its way to the Capitoline Museum in Rome (inv. 529), noted in a number of copperline engravings. A second fragmentary head (from Leptis Magna) has been tentatively identified as that of Theon,[91] suggesting that, in his time, fame accompanied his profession.

TEONE PLATONICO
Spon. Mifcell Erud antiq Sect IV p 135

Plate 6.2: Bust of the Platonic philosopher, Theon of Smyrna, with identifying inscription at its base. Engraving by Giovanni Domenico Campiglia, published 1741.

Art historical considerations date the intact bust to the time of Hadrian,[92] which coincides neatly with the date assigned to the Diodotos inscription, even though the formal linkage between the two must remain at the level of speculation. The inscription at the base of the bust is useful for again highlighting the interconnection of conventional and social values with intellectual pursuits at the time. It reads:[93]

> Θέωνα Πλατωνι- | κὸν φιλόσοφον | ὁ ἱερεὺς Θέων | τὸν πατέρα.
> *The priest Theon [set this up] for his father, Theon, the Platonist philosopher.*

Here the dutifiul son has taken responsibility for the honoring of his father, though it is uncertain whether this was an adornment for Theon's tomb or (more likely) an honorific donation to augment a stoa, garden or the famous Museion, or perhaps even the gymnasium richly endowed by Hadrian.[94] Theon is expressly identified as a Platonist, even though he has sometimes been grouped among Pythagorean philosophers.[95] The specific designation seems

91 G. M. A. Richter, *The Portraits of the Greeks* (London: Phaidon, 3 vols, 1965), vol 3, 285.

92 See Eve D'Ambra, "Kosmetai, the Second Sophistic and Portraiture in the Second Century," in *Periklean Athens and its Legacy: Problems and Perspectives* edited by J. M. Barringer and J. M. Hurwit (Austin: University of Texas Press, 2005), 210.

93 *CIG* 3198 = *IGR* 4.1449 = *I.Smyrna* 648.

94 *I.Smyrna* 697. Hadrian's benefaction specifies, *inter alia*, 98 columns for the gymnasium.

95 This does not deny Pythagorean contributions to his thought, not only on mathematics but also on the social implications of the ordered universe. John Dillon distills him as an "enthusiastic Platonist of Pythagorean tendency". J. M. Dillon, *The Middle Platonists, 80 B. C. to A. D. 220* (Ithaca, NY: Cornell University Press, 1977), 397.

to have been a recognized label of classification rather than a loose epithet; it is known in descriptions of other philosophers, as for example Ofellius Laetus renowned at Athens and nearby Ephesos.[96] Of particular note is that the filial identification underscores a civic priesthood — which office would have been purchased by the junior Theon (or his father on his behalf).

Philosophy and theology were frequent partners, as is clear in the description given to Ofellius — a Platonic philosopher in Ephesos, exalted for his theology in Athens.[97] It is this connection of interests from philosophy and the divine realm that makes what we have of Theon's teaching particularly pertinent for our inquiry into the potential background of thought at Colossae, how the Letter to the Colossians might reflect that, and how the letter negotiated an exchange with it.

Theon himself used the language of mystery cults to describe the goal and rationale for philosophical study.[98] Moreover, because the universe is ultimately constructed as perfectly harmonious according to the principles enunciated from and discernible in music, Theon turns to the order of a hexametrical composition that he credits to the third century (BCE) poet, Alexander of Aetolia.[99] His accuracy of reference has been impugned,[100] but Theon's purpose in seeking a Pythagorean poetic astronomical description was to allow him to provide a yet more accurate conception of the heavens. He adds his rationale for doing so — hymns are the only fit form in which to convey the concert of sounds

96 *I.Ephesos* 3901. There are a number of honorific dedications to philosophers in general, as already noted (eg *I.Hadrianopolis* 51, 52). The descriptor Πλατονικός indicates the specialization.

97 *IG* II^2 3816 (Ephesos; 1st century CE). See G. W. Bowersock, "Plutarch and the Sublime Hymn of Ofellius Laetus," *GBRS* 23 (1982): 275–9.

98 Theon 14.20–22. See Dillon, *Middle Platonists*, 398; K. Clinton, "The Stages of Initiation in the Eleusinian and Samothracian Mysteries," in *Greek Mysteries: The Archaeology of Ancient Greek Secret Cults* edited by M. B. Cosmopoulos (London: Routledge, 2003), 58–9; C. Hoenig, *Plato's Timaeus and the Latin Tradition* (Cambridge: Cambridge University Press, 2018), 108. Petrucci lays out the extended parallels (Theon 14.20–16.2) of the five stages of the mysteries with philosophical advancement: purification, instruction, understanding of the intelligible world, communal assistance and recognition, bliss of divine incorporation; *Teone di Smirne*, 302–3.

99 Theon 140.5–141.4. This accent on hymnic illumination of the cosmos is seen also in the roughly contemporaneous "Hymn to the Creator", known only in a Latin translation from the original Greek. Though ascribed to Plato, it is dated to the second century CE. See H. Lewy, "A Latin Hymn to the Creator ascribed to Plato," *HTR* 39 (1946): 243–58.

100 Theon gives two excerpts from Alexander of Aetolia (139:1–10 and 140:5–141:4). Two lines (139.9–10) from the first selection are credited by other early authorities to a different Alexander, namely of Ephesos (Heraclitus *Alleg.* 12.9.1–2, 1st–2nd century CE; Tzetzes, *Exeg. Hom. Il.* 601, schol. 9, 12th century CE). All twenty-six lines have thus been granted to this later Alexander: H. Lloyd-Jones and P. Parsons, *Supplementum Hellenisticum* (Berlin: de Gruyter, 1983), 10, fr. 21, though granting a discrete space between the sections to signal the derivation from Theon. The text is reproduced in similar fashion by Christophe Cusset, "Alexander of Ephesus," in *Hellenistic Poetry: A Selection* edited by D. Sider (Ann Arbor: University of Michigan Press, 2017), 56–7, 60. The probability that all come from the same source is there, but some caution is required.

(συμφώνοι) of the heavenly bodies (τὰ οὐράνια).[101] We have seen already that astronomical texts (such as the work of Manilius) were frequently cast in poetic form. For the Platonist, the poetic is not repudiated *in toto*. Rather, the reticence in turning to a hymn reflects Plato's concern that poetry be subject to the establishment of philosophical principles rather than itself be the initiating source of understanding the universe and human affairs, or, as it more often was (from Homer onwards), in the distraction that poetry engineers via the senses, to matters that distort the harmonious balance of society.[102] The only acceptable poetry, according to Plato, was to be "hymns to the gods and eulogies of good men."[103] In the hands of the Platonists, even such use of the poetic was part of a larger interpretive frame. For Plato, the realm of the heavenly bodies in harmonious arrangement was the realm of the divine, or at the very least, the *temenos* of the ultimate divine. Theon, "the Platonic philosopher", intended his handbook to lead to this realm, the heavens and beyond,[104] albeit as we have seen in the study of *philologos*, with significant reference to the connection with the requisite and mimetic patterning of this world. The hymn expressed the culminating point of the philosophical enterprise, indeed it cracked the heavens to the view of the ineffable, just as the inscribed honors for the Platonist, Ofellius Laetus, named his achievement: "Upon hearing the ethereal hymn of the theologian Laetus, I witnessed the heaven open to human contemplation."[105] Here we are in a similar realm of appreciation as the book of Revelation (see, *inter alia*, Rev 19:11). The notion of hymnody and vision of the divine realm is part of the cultural capital of the period in the province of Asia. The succession of choristers to the oracular center at Klaros is but one indication of the value attached to the praise of the gods and to the revelation of truth that the gods (in this case, Apollo) encapsulated.[106]

Training into that divine realm is the object of the surviving treatise ascribed to Theon, the Platonist philosopher of Smyrna. But the ground and structure of that education lies in a thorough familiarization with the arithmetical basis of the universe. The treatise is titled τῶν κατὰ τὸ μαθηματικὸν χρησίμων εἰς

---

101 Theon 140.1, 2. Compare the brief quotation of the "Orphic Oaths" in Theon 105.3–5.

102 Plato *Resp*. 10.608a–b; *Leg*. 2.665c.

103 ὕμνους θεοῖς καὶ ἐγκώμια τοῖς ἀγαθοῖς — Plato *Resp*. 10.607a cf *Tim*. 47b; *Sym*. 177a, 193d; *Leg*. 7.802a cf Theocritus *Idyll* 22.223. However, hymns could also be composed for weddings (in the ideal *polis* where marriages are controlled): *Resp*. 6.459e. Plato was also antagonistic towards novel developments in and mixing of musical modes: *Leg*. 7.799b. This was interpreted as corrosive not only of civic morality but also of the building of harmony in the state as replicative of the harmony of the cosmos. See S. Halliwell, "The Republic's Two Critiques of Poetry (Book II.376c–III.398b, Book X.595a–608b)," in *Platon, Politieia* edited by Otfried Höffe (Berlin: Akademia Verlag, 1997), 313–32.

104 The ὑπερουράνιος; Plato *Phaedr*. 247c; Philo *Opif*. 31.3.

105 θειολόγου Λαίτοιο μετάρσιον ὕμνον ἀκούσας | οὐρανὸν ἀνθρώποις εἶδον ἀνοιγόμενον *IG* II² 3816, ll. 1–2 (Ephesos, 1st century CE).

106 For the accent on hymnody at Klaros, see, for example, *SEG* 37.961 (126/127 CE).

τὴν Πλάτωνος ἀνάγνωσιν, that is, "Concerning ideas useful in mathematics for the reading of Plato". Certainly the work seems to have survived in Byzantine education into the second millennium,[107] even if other works by Theon passed out of transmission.[108] However, this title is but one of two titles accenting mathematics appended to two separate works or sections of works in two medieval manuscripts held in the *Biblioteca Nazionale Marciana* in Venice.[109] The nineteenth century editor, Eduard Hiller, made the connection between the two, though there is recognition, even from internal references, that the surviving portions are but substantial excerpts from a larger work. One major section, dealing with cosmic harmonies, has been lost, leaving tantalizing, brief anticipations in the extant text.[110] Nevertheless, the surviving text contains more than a narrow focus on mathematics, with significant increments into geometry (theoretical and applied — called stereometry), astronomy and music.[111] Federico Petrucci considers the unfolding development of the arguments in the handbook to be Theon's own exegesis of Plato's *Timaeus*, admittedly with an emphasis on and development of the mathematical properties of Plato's argument.[112] It demonstrates that ancient mathematics was a significantly more expansive discipline than modern preconceptions allow and one that served, at least in Platonic thought, an appreciation of the divine.

Theon's concern in his work was to provide a bridge from previous preliminary study to some of the critical emphases and developments in Platonic thought. Indeed, the work seems to build in complexity as he moved from arithmetic through to astronomy, as if relying, at least in part, on explanations already presented. He allowed that even though it would be preferable to have gained some proficiency in geometry, he anticipates that the uninitiated in mathematics would be able to gain from his work. In this sense it is a handbook — he calls it a συναγωγή, a "collation".[113] Significantly, however, he uses language familiar from mystery religions to describe progress in under-

107 See Dimiter Angelov, *The Byzantine Hellene: The Life of Emperor Theodore Laskaris and Byzantium in the Thirteenth Century* (Cambridge: Cambridge University Press, 2019), 82.

108 Theon refers to his own commentary (ἐξήγησις) on Plato's *Republic* in the course of this work (146.3–5).

109 *Marc. Gr.* 303 (14th century), *Marc. Gr.* 307 (12th century). Other, later, manuscripts of the work derive from these two.

110 A. Jones, "Translating Greek Astronomy: Theon of Smyrna on the Apparent Motions of the Planets," in *Translating Writings of Early Scholars in the ANE, Egypt, Greece and Rome: Methodological Aspects with Examples* edited by A. Imhausen and T. Pommerening (Berlin/Boston: de Gruyter, 2016), 469–73.

111 This incremental succession is specifically signaled as the intent of the work and the purpose of mathematics: Theon 1.15, 16.24–17.25, 204.24–205.4.

112 Petrucci, "Theon of Smyrna: Re-thinking Platonic Mathematics in Middle Platonism," in *Brill's Companion to the Reception of Plato* edited by H. Tarrant *et al.* (Leiden: Brill, 2018), 147.

113 Criticisms sometimes directed towards Theon's lack of originality in this work ("dilettante" opines Dillon, *Middle Platonists*, 397), seem to forget that it is an undergraduate text-book. Theon disavowed originality for the work (Theon 47.14).

standing mathematics, namely, movement from being uninitiated to that which is imperceptible to the uninitiated (ἀλλὰ ταῦτα μὲν τοῖς ἀμυήτοις μουσικῆς ἐστιν ἄδηλα).[114] There was a metaphysics to mathematics,[115] both in what it could access in understanding and perception, and in the method by which such access could be gained.[116] Numbers constitute the soul, he claimed, again relying on his reading of Plato.[117] Through the knowledge of such numbers, one might enjoy what Theon evocatively called "god-friendship" (τὸ θεοφιλές), even "likeness to god" (ὁμοίωσις θεῷ) as the crown of mathematical endeavours.[118] That is, the practical dimensions of arithmetic are but microcosmic applications of a universal ontology (most clearly demonstrated in the accent on the monad [μονάς] and the origin [ἀρχή]).

Because the work was designed as a bridging handbook, Theon gave considerable detail to basic terminology and exemplification, almost to the point of pedantry at times. He was also at pains to reference earlier writers, such as Adrastus, Eratosthenes and Alexander of Aetolia,[119] both as they applied Platonic theories and also as they explained, developed and sometimes distorted them. As to the development of Plato, he frequently relied upon Pythagorean teaching. Disputations were kept to a minimum.[120]

The larger purpose and driving assumptions of these preliminary foundations are revealed in his introduction and in numerous asides that are littered through his work. Sometimes these are grounded in explicit arithmetical demonstration, sometimes in assertions built on analogies. And sometimes, the line between the literal and the analogous was blurred, as, for example, in his piling together of examples of what he calls τετρακτύες, that is, quaternions or groups of four arithmetically bound together. Here he moved from the first four numbers as holding together the nature of all that is (τὴν τῶν ὅλων φύσιν συνέχειν)[121] to the mirroring of this four-item structure in the familiar four elements: fire, air, water and earth (what he called the fourth tetraktys); in the nature of society: human, family, village and city (the seventh tetraktys); the composition of the soul: the rational, emotional, wilful and its somatic container (the ninth tetraktys). The final group of four shows how arbitrary these groupings had become. The eleventh tetrakys defined the ages of man (and there *was* a gendered cast to

114 Theon 142.5–6. For a discussion of ἀμυήτος, see Clinton, "Stages of Initiation," 55–6.

115 Theon 10.3–4, 18.1, 47.1–5.

116 See Petrucci, "Re-thinking Platonic Mathematics," 143–55.

117 Theon 96.4–5, relying on Plato *Tim.* 34c–36b.

118 Theon 15.6, 16.1.

119 Indeed, some of the references are the only examples that survive of these ancient teachers.

120 See, for example, Theon 146.10–147.6. He allows himself an occasional modest disagreement with Plato (Theon 65.10–14), even in the context of defending and explaining Plato in the light of more recent astronomical and musical theories.

121 Theon 94.4.

his received mathematics)[122] as fourfold: infancy, adolescence, manhood (ἀνήρ) and geriatric.[123] Another "Middle Platonist,"[124] Philo of Alexandria, devised a seven-fold, rather than quaternian breakdown of the development of human beings, so, clearly such mathematical "proofs" were not immutable.[125] But what is significant is that the purest ontology of demonstration — the first quaternion — was directly related as a demonstration of the principle of quaternion to the most mundane, ephemeral example — the ageing process of human beings.[126] In this sense, the highest and the lowest (as in music) were integrally related, even when the highest was granted pre-eminence.

Philo's construction of human life pointed to a privileging of another critical number, seven, as governing humanity. Not that the hebdomad is missing from Theon's work,[127] but he imposed the revelation of the patterning of "Athenic seven"[128] on other manifestations, including the days of the week, foetal perfection in form in seven weeks, a viable birth at seven months, teeth at the seventh month, the days needed to diagnose an illness and, of particular importance for his astronomy, the full number of planets (τό τε πλῆθος τῶν πλανωμένων).[129] He approved the claim of Alexander (of Aetolia — read Ephesos) that the seven-stringed kithara is "the image of the divinely-orchestrated cosmos" (ἑπτάτονον κίθαριν θεομήστορος εἰκόνα κόσμου).[130] The Colossian intaglio previously mentioned, with Athena (the hebdomad) perched on the seven-stringed kithara, shows that such an understanding had reached the more interior regions of the Roman province of Asia.

But whether groupings of four or seven,[131] Theon operated from the presumption that the entire numerical system derived from the unity expressed in the number 1, an essence of all things in the divine monad. The "one" is what

122 Plutarch explicitly claims the Pythagoreans assign the male to odd numbers, female to even numbers. *Quaest. Rom.* 288D–E (nr. 102).

123 Theon 98.13–14.

124 The classification and exposition of Philo as a Middle Platonist are argued by Dillon, *Middle Platonists*, 139–83.

125 Philo *Opif.* 105 citing Hippocrates as his source. However, Theon's four ages is paralleled elsewhere: see Ovid *Met.* 15.199–216.

126 So, Petrucci, *Teone di Smirne*, 410.

127 Theon 103.1–104.19.

128 As mentioned in the previous chapter, Theon noted that the Pythagoreans called the hebdomad "Athena" because it was neither created (by multiplication of other numbers) nor does it create any other number in the decad (the primary sequence of numbers). Athena, similarly, was without mother nor reproductive (Theon 103.2–6).

129 Theon 104.1–13. The seven planets were the sun, moon, Mercury, Venus, Mars, Jupiter, and Saturn, with Earth, in the Platonic system, as the central fixed body. Jewish and Christian writers were often keen to demonstrate that Greek writers going back to Homer, exalted the "seven"; see, for example, Aristobulus *apud* Clement of Alexander *Strom.* 5.14.107.4–108.1, 6.16.142.4, 6.16.144.3.

130 Theon 141.4, 8.

131 Theon moves into a development of the decad from the quaternion (Theon 99.16–106.11). A similar connection of the quaternion and the decad is found in Philo *Plant.* 123–5.

activates understanding, since the one is revealed in many things.[132] Here then is the rationale for beginning with a generic education but then seeking specialization as the path to the discovery of the essential unity of all things. For it is "the one" which has the capacity, as particularly evidenced in music, to reconcile opposites and restore unity. "One is the bond that naturally shall reveal all things" (δεσμὸς γὰρ πεφυκὼς ἁπάντων εἷς ἀναφανήσεται) he wrote. And again, "Singleness is the origin of all things and has the most dominion of all ... all things are from it and it derives from nothing." (ἡ μὲν γὰρ μονὰς ἀρχὴ πάντων καὶ κυριωτάτη πασῶν ... καὶ ἐξ ἧς πάντα, αὐτὴ δὲ ἐξ οὐδενός).[133] And he proceeded to list some of the exalted things that derived therefrom. The second-century Latin, Platonist *Hymn to the Creator* similarly accented the one and the many,[134] although here the accent was on the "one" as the origin of the many; it too affirmed that numbers are the intricate bond of cosmic and mundane order.[135]

This fundamental unity must be borne in mind when contending with the manifold groupings he provides. For all the apparent arbitrariness, if not quaint impressionism, of these numeric groupings of items, the critical frame of understanding for Theon was that the mundane world is replete with testimony to the divine cosmic unity and harmony. Access to that cosmic harmony came through the study of the numeric properties of the world that is generated by that divine principle. Middle Platonism had come to understand that there was a correlation between the divine and mundane life, such that the latter was not to be dismissed but devotedly studied as the clue to the divine life and the means to break through into a vision of it.

But equally — and this is crucial to the connection between philosophy and political or civic involvement — human life, in the light of intelligible apprehension of cosmology, was to be modeled accordingly. As Theon distilled it in a decisive summation,

> The cosmos, configured by these quaternian groupings, will continue to be harmonious according to geometry, consonance and arithmetic, powerfully replete in the entire nature of number — even every macrocosm and microcosm, singular as well as complex — perfect because all things are part of it and dependent on nothing else.
>
> ὁ δὲ ἐκ τῶν τετρακτύων τούτων συστὰς κόσμος ἔσται ἡρμοσμένος κατὰ γεωμετρίαν καὶ ἁρμονίαν καὶ ἀριθμόν, δυνάμει περιειληφὼς πᾶσαν ἀριθμοῦ φύσιν πᾶν τε μέγεθος καὶ πᾶν σῶμα ἁπλοῦν τε καὶ σύνθετον, τέλειός τε, ἐπειδὴ τὰ πάντα μὲν τούτου μέρη, αὐτὸς δὲ οὐδενός.[136]

---

132 Theon 4.17–18.

133 Theon 99.24–100.1.

134 *tu solus, tu multus idem*. The composer expands this with *tu primus et idem postremus* ("you are the first and the last"). For the text, see F. Buechheler and A. Riese (eds), *Anthologia Latina* (Leipzig: G. Teubner, 1906), Part I.2, 46, nr. 490, ll. 7–8.

135 *Ibid*, ll. 30–1. See also the familiarity with some of these ideas in *Clem. Hom.* 3.33.

136 Theon 99.8–13.

Crucial here is the use of the periphrastic future perfect ἔσται ἡρμοσμένος. It seeks to convey that the unity and continuance of the world are assured but human beings need, as expression of the virtuous life in harmony with god, to understand the numeric harmony of the cosmos and model their practices on that cosmic template — the music and medicine that is the stupendous work of god that turn enemies into friends (τοῦτο μέγιστον ἔργον θεοῦ κατὰ μουσικήν τε καὶ κατὰ ἰατρικὴν τὰ ἐχθρὰ φίλα ποιεῖν).[137] The concord (ὁμόνοια) and governance (ἀριστοκρατία) that defines that realm of god cultivates the harmony of the cosmos, as well as good order in the *polis* and moderation in households (καὶ γὰρ αὕτη ἐν κόσμῳ μὲν ἁρμονία, ἐν πόλει δ' εὐνομία, ἐν οἴκοις δὲ σωφροσύνη γίνεσθαι πέφυκε.)[138] Clearly, Theon's expectation was that the understanding of cosmic realities inculcated and was designed to inculcate harmony in civic and familial life.[139] This was simply an expansion from Plato's psychogony in relation to civic polity: "There's a model equally laid out in heaven for whoever wants to perceive, and to lay a foundation for oneself based on what is perceived."[140] Resistance to this harmony, reflected in a wilful refusal to learn, is, as we have noted, the source of insecurity and disruption.

Cosmic hymn and mundane harmony

This, then, is the sort of advancement in education that a young *philologos* from Colossae might journey to Smyrna to pursue. Of course, we have no proof that Diodotos sought out Theon, though the chronological conjunction is suggestive. However, we can see in Theon's introductory course of learning a preparation for civic life that is grounded in philosophy, most particularly an understanding of the structure and ordering of the cosmos. Moreover, fragments of evidence from Colossae suggest that the city was little different from other cities in having an eye to cosmological understanding. Here philosophy and religion were inextricably intertwined. No doubt there was a keen interest in practical, mundane benefits as well, whether for agriculture or civic stability or some other concern. In more schematic sophisticated frame, this concentration facilitated the semantics of "local human phenomena within a cosmic

137 Theon 12.16–17.

138 Theon 12.19–21.

139 Theon later provides a snippet illustrative of numbers and family life. He calls the number six not only perfect (being the sum and multiplied result of the first three numbers) but also the number of marriage. Given that he calls odd numbers male and even numbers female, the multiplying effect of 2 and 3, the first even and first odd number, is to produce what replicates their own features. Hence, marriage produces offspring like (ὅμοια) their parents (Theon 102.6).

140 ἐν οὐρανῷ ἴσως παράδειγμα ἀνάκειται τῷ βουλομένῳ ὁρᾶν καὶ ὁρῶντι ἑαυτὸν κατοικίζειν. Plato *Resp*. 7.592b.

frame of reference."[141] Theon, as we have seen, made no pretense to originality in this preliminary, transitional training, though occasionally his own thinking reveals itself. However, it is precisely because his work is a handbook, sometimes compendious in its reference to previous learning, that Theon's distillation may have some relevance for understanding how cosmology and its purpose finds a place in the Letter to the Colossians. After all, Theon by his location at Smyrna and his period at the turn of the second century, provided teaching which was, in general terms, indicative of a substantial part of the ideational atmosphere of the province.

The pre-eminent cosmological concentration in the letter comes in the Christological hymn in Col 1: (12) 15–20. The passage regularly attracts detailed analyses and these can be solicited for detailed commentary on its phrases.[142] I wish to make the following points in the light of the cultural and material world of the province within which Colossae was located.

Meter and its absence in ancient hymns

The hymn chosen for extensive quotation by Theon of Smyrna was in hexameters.[143] The likelihood that the Alexander who authored it was Alexander of Ephesos not of Aetolia brings the date of the hymn's composition (the first century BCE) closer to Theon's time.[144] It demonstrates that there was a continued popularity and acceptance, even expectation, for using the hexametric form for hymns, as we see from the Homeric through to the Orphic Hymns. Epigraphical examples are similar, with hexameters often undergirding the praise of the god(s).[145] Josephus, therefore, felt compelled to claim that the song of Moses was written in hexameters.[146] Hexameters had a weight of tradition, *gravitas*

141 P. Berger, *The Sacred Canopy: Elements of a Sociological Theory of Religion* (New York: Doubleday, 1967), 35.

142 See L. Bormann, *Der Brief des Paulus an die Kolosser* (ThHK X.1; Leipzig: Evangelische Verlagsanstalt, 2012), 76–105; M. E. Gordley, *The Colossian Hymn in Context: An Exegesis in Light of Jewish and Greco-Roman Hymnic and Epistolary Conventions* (WUNT 2.228; Tübingen: Mohr Siebeck, 2011); A. Standhartinger, "Der Kolosserhymnus im Lichte epigraphischer Zeugnisse," in *Epigraphical Evidence Illustrating Paul's Letter to the Colossians* edited by J. Verheyden, M. Öhler and T. Corsten (WUNT 411; Tübingen: Mohr Siebeck, 2018), 69–91.

143 Theon 139:1–10 and 140:5–141:4.

144 The date is based on Strabo's reference to him as a recent figure (14.1.25).

145 See, for example, Malay-Petzl, *Lydia* 90; see also W. Furley and J. M. Bremer, *Greek Hymns: Selected Cult Songs from the Archaic to the Hellenistic Period* (Tübingen: Mohr Siebeck, 2 Vols, 2001), vol 1, 245. It should be noted however that other meters were deployed; see Furley and Bremer, *Greek Hymns*, vol. 1, index sv. metre.

146 Josephus *Ant.* 2.346, cf 4.303. Whether Josephus actually knew of a Greek metrical rendition (in the style, say, of Aristobulus) of the song of Moses can only be conjectured. He seems to have been acquainted with the writing of Philo the epic poet (Josephus *C. Ap.* 1.23).

and authority, no doubt anchored in the preeminent Greek poet, Homer. It should be noted that there was no template governing length.[147] The Homeric Hymns are remarkably varied in length — almost 500 lines for the *Hymn to Demeter* but the *Hymn to Asclepius* and that to the Dioskouri secure only one per cent of that figure.[148] Epigraphical examples are no less variable. A fragment of a Stoic hymn to Zeus maker of the world (as confidently deduced), found near Praeneste (the home of the famed temple to Fortuna Protogenia) contains 12 (incomplete) hexametric lines but its extant shape and the stone on which it is carved suggests that this is the substance of the composition. It is dated to the early third century CE.[149] One hymn to a Nubian deity, Mandulis-Helios, runs to 36 hexametric lines.[150] Moreover, sometimes there is evidence that the literary composition of a hymn was replicated on stone,[151] just as hymns are sometimes multiply attested in different parts of the world.[152] Wherever we find these hymns in the Greco-Roman world, the hexameter predominates though it is neither the exclusive meter nor defining of a hymn.

Analyses of the effect of this rhythmic structure have emphasized the step from the controlled organization of language that hexameters impose to the structural conservatism regulating society and demanding adherence to unchanging norms — what Bakhtin called the "closed and deaf monoglossia" of epic. Inevitably, the gods spoke in hexameters for weighty pronounce-

147 Contra G. Schille, "Rezension zu Burger Schöpfung und Versöhnung," *TLZ* 103 (1978): 276.

148 It must be admitted that the corpus known as the "Homeric Hymns" probably spans at least two centuries in its compilation. There remains some doubt as to the setting for these hymns. See W. D. Furley, "Praise and Persuasion in Greek Hymns," *JHS* 115 (1995): 29–30. At the same time, Epictetus encouraged the singing of hymns "while digging, plowing and eating" (οὐκ ἔδει καὶ σκάπτοντας καὶ ἀροῦντας καὶ ἐσθίοντας ᾄδειν τὸν ὕμνον τὸν εἰς τὸν θεόν; Epictetus 1.17.16–17); Maurice West notes that a paean was sung in a multitude of contexts and was not restricted to formal cultic settings: M. L. West, *Ancient Greek Music* (Oxford: Clarendon, 1992), 15.

149 The *editio princeps* is given by L. Moretti "Frammento di inno Tardo-Stoico sulla creazione," in *Scritti storico-epigrafici in memoria di Marcello Zambelli* edited by L. Gasperini (Rome: Centro editorial internazionale, 1978) 251–6; for updated reconstructions, see E. Magnelli, "Notes on Four Greek Verse Inscriptions," *ZPE* 160 (2007): 38–40. By comparison, a third century (BCE) hymn to Zeus creator of the world composed by Cleanthes the successor to Zeno in the Stoic school, runs to 39 hexametric lines: Cleanthes, Fr 1 (J. U. Powell, *Collectanea Alexandrina: Reliquiae minores Poetarum Graecorum Aetatis Ptolemaicae 323—146 A.C. Epicorum, Elegiacorum, Lyricorum, Ethicorum* [Oxford: Clarendon Press, 1925], 227–8 (= *SVF* 1.537). For a commentary on this hymn in relation to the Colossian affirmations of Christ, see V. Balabanski, *Colossians: An Eco-Stoic Reading* (London: T & T Clark, 2020), 40–2.

150 E. Bernand, *Inscriptions métriques de l'Égypte gréco-romaine. Recherches sur la poésie épigrammatique des Grecs en Égypte* (Besançon: Université de Franche-Comté, 1969), 591–610, nr. 168 (Talmis, 1st century CE).

151 See, on a hymn composed by the playwright Sophocles, M. Longe, "Greek hymns from performance to stone," in *Sacred Words: Orality, Literacy and Religion* edited by A. Lardinois, J. Blok and M. G. M. van der Poel (Leiden: Brill, 2011), 219–20.

152 Hence, there is nothing comparatively incongruous about asserting that the Colossian hymn had a separate existence from the letter.

ments and oracular revelations.[153] Panhellenism, whether in its Greek form or the Roman mimesis in Virgil's *Aeneid*, had as a key foundation, the hexameter.[154] Hymns under the hexametric control of language were therefore inevitably a conservative force, maintaining the order of the universe, the order of the gods and the order of human society. In a false etymology that Proclus, the fifth-century neo-platonic philosopher, constructed, "hymn" was derived from "memory" (ὕμνος ~ ὑπόμνησις) — the recalling of the deeds of gods and men for celebration, and thereby, for reinforcement.[155] Hymns were a socializing instrument, conforming of thought and constructing of community. Little wonder that the afore-mentioned Alexander of Ephesos was renowned as a political leader and historian,[156] even if Cicero poured scorn on his poetic credentials.[157] And little wonder that hexameters were regularly summoned to enhance the rendition of epitaphal memorializations or the extolling eulogies for exemplary citizens, just as we find in an epigram exalting the champion Colossian pugilist, (stage-?)named Kastor.[158]

It is not that hexameters were the only meter used for hymns (and eulogies), even if it was the dominant one. Elegaic couplets were deployed, especially (though not exclusively) in honor of Isis.[159] This poetic structure is also found in literary hymns, albeit rarely.[160] Iambics are also known, as in a hymn to Isis from Cyrene.[161] Sometimes combinations of meters are found, and sometimes the meter is an occasional entrant into the full text of a hymn. So, for example, iambics only enter the famous paeanic hymn to Hygieia, the goddess of health, at the last line: σέθεν δὲ χωρὶς οὔτις εὐδαίμων ἔφυ ("But without you no-one flourishes"). This hymn is multiply captured in inscription and literary works.[162]

153 R. Merkelbach and J. Stauber, "Die Orakel des Apollon von Klaros," *EA* 27 (1996): 3.

154 See the discussion in Rose, *Sons of the Gods*, 43–6.

155 Proclus *Chrestomathia* apud Photius *Lexic.* 320a.9–11. For the identification of Proclus's etymological speculation, see T. J. Mathiesen, *Apollo's Lyre: Greek Music and Music Theory in Antiquity and the Middle Ages* (Lincoln/London: University of Nebraska Press, 1999), 30.

156 Strabo calls him a poet, statesmen and historian (14.1.25).

157 Cicero *Att.* 42.7. Cicero's denigration of Alexander as *poeta inepta* may well reflect more on Cicero's Roman disparaging of supposed Asian Hellenistic decadence than an objective assessment.

158 *Steinepigramme* 1.02.15.01 (perhaps first or second century CE); cf *MAMA* 6.52 (Laodikeia, 3rd century CE, honorific), *I.Laodikeia Lykos* 68 (141/142 CE, oracle), *I.Mus. Denizli* 14 (Lycus Valley, provenance unknown, Hellenistic period, epitaph); 133 (Dionysopolis, 2nd century CE, epitaph). See chapter 10.

159 *SEG* 8.549, 551 (Narmouthis, 1st century BCE); see C. Faraone, "The Stanzaic Architecture of Isidorus, Hymns 2 and 4 (*SEG* 8.549 and 51 [sic])," *CQ* 62 (2012): 618–32.

160 Callimachus, *Hymn* 5 (Bath of Pallas).

161 *SEG* 9.192 (103 CE).

162 *IG* IV^2 1 132 (Epidauros; late 2nd century CE); *IG* II^2 4533 ll. 9–18 (Attica, 3rd century CE); Plutarch *Mor* 450B, 479A (excerpt); Athenaeus *Deip.* 15.701f–702b); Maximus Tyre 7.1a (excerpt). See Longe, "Greek Hymns," 220–21.

The use of iambics is particularly apt for cautionary advice to be given,[163] here the deity to be especially patronized and where to place one's real value.[164]

Meter in and of itself generates a world, especially in a cultural context where such features were a regular part of literacy and performance.[165] There is a psychagogical power in poetry that compels the direction of the content. Jeffrey Walker goes so far as to suggest that this is the element of language construction that first arrests hearing.[166] Meter performs a poetic function that not only privileges form over content; it can have its own life, forcing content into its own shape, frequently to the contortion and distortion of content and the privileging of sensuous response over connected argument or narrative.[167]

This frequently-asserted solemn aspect of poetry is precisely its dangerous capacity — the irrational or supra-rational might reflect an inspirational source; it could also be reduced to a titillation of the emotions and a corruption of the pedagogical value and ethical uplift of a text. Aristophanes might create the hymnic summons in the Thesmaphoric rites by constructing an iambic meter for the call, "Come on leap! Wheel about, tapping your feet in time."[168] But it is the "foot-tapping" that worried others — the "lascivious mode of the castenets!"[169] Dignity but also content could evaporate.[170] Aristotle compared the effect to the machinations of soothsayers (μάντες).[171] Virgil's metrical lament "I remember the numbers if only I could the words" points to the concern over content.[172]

Part of the problem was that an over-emphasis on meter compressed words into musical or rhythmical form rather than have music (and its companion, meter) serve the content.[173] Plato was particularly concerned that music and poetry should fit the truth of an object rather than merely provide pleasure. His elderly conservatism railed against the degeneracy, as he saw it, of his day — what he called the shallow showiness of θεατροκρατία, a rule by spectacle.[174] Plato credited this as the source of contempt for law and disrespect for parents, oaths, even the gods.[175]

---

163 See, A. H. Cadwallader, *Beyond the Word of a Woman: Recovering the Bodies of the Syrophoenician Women* (Adelaide: ATF Press, 2008), 86–8.

164 Hygieia is numismatically attested at Colossae (*RPC online* 4.2.1890 temp., 4.2.1902 temp. [with Asclepius]).

165 Compare Aristotle *Rhet.* 1354a; Cicero *de Or.* 3.191, 195.

166 J. Walker, *Rhetoric and Poetics in Antiquity* (Oxford: Oxford University Press, 2000), 128; similarly, J. Russo, "The Poetics of the Ancient Greek Proverb," *JFR* 20 (1983): 124.

167 A. Duranti, *Linguistic anthropology* (Cambridge: Cambridge University Press, 1997), 286.

168 ἀλλ' εἶα, πάλλ', ἀνάστρεφ' εὐρυθμῳ ποδί. Aristophanes *Thes.* 985.

169 Quintilian *Inst.* 9.4.142.

170 Quintilian *Inst.* 11.3.58–60.

171 Aristotle *Rhet.* 1407a–b.

172 *numerous memini, si verba tenerem* Virgil *Ecl.* 9.45.

173 Plato *Leg.* 3.700a–b; similarly Athenaeus *Deip.* 14.617b–f.

174 Plato *Leg.* 3.701a.

175 Plato *Leg.* 3.701b–c.

Angela Standhartinger has argued that different meters were favored by different gods (or at least by their devotees): "All goddesses and gods give preference to their own particular rhythms and their melodies."[176] This included those hymns that are classified as "prose hymns", as in the compositions of Aelius Aristides.[177] But here in Plato and in the successors who debated about music, musical accompaniment (by aulos, lyre and/or percussion) and rhythm, is laid the foundation for whether meter should be included in hymns to god/the gods at all.[178]

One first-century prose-hymn to a local deity, Mandulis (sometimes blended with Helios), was inscribed on the walls of a temple in Talmis in Nubia. It is sometimes described as a piece of graffito, but it runs to 21 lines. A Nubian-born, Roman soldier, Paccius Maximus, is credited as the composer on the basis of a number of hymns surrounding it.[179] What makes his compositions so important is that his Greek and Roman credentials are acquired, a level of assimilation that facilitated self-advancement.[180] His prowess revealed on the temple perimeter therefore is a strong indication of wider, fashionable, cultural currents in Greek hymnic composition of the first century. The other hymns on the temple structure have a metrical structure. It indicates that from Nubia to Asia, prose hymns were gaining traction as a respectable alternative to thorough-going metrical hymns … and a fitting display of the virtuosity of the composer! Hymns to Isis show a similar variety.[181]

Moreover, these hymns were on visible display and, at least from what we know in some cases, regularly performed. One first century BCE inscription from Stratonikeia details the commissioning of a certain Sosandros to compose a hymnic "approach" (πρόσοδος l. 7) and "worship" (θρησκεία l. 7 cf Col 2:18) in honor of Zeus Panamaros and Hekate.[182] We don't have the resulting creation(s),

176 Standhartinger, "Der Kolosserhymnus," 90.
177 Standhartinger, "Der Kolosserhymnus," 84.
178 See J. Quasten, *Music and Worship in Pagan and Christian Antiquity* (Washington: National Association of Pastoral Musicians, 1983), 52–3.
179 S. M. Burstein, "A Soldier and His God in Lower Nubia: The Mandulis Hymns of Paccius Maximus," *Graeco-Arabica* 7–8 (1999–2000): 45–50; see also Burstein, "Paccius Maximus: A Greek Poet in Nubia or a Nubian Greek Poet?," *CRIPEL*, 17.3 (1998): 47–51.
180 So, S. M. Burstein, "When Greek Was an African Language: The Role of Greek Culture in Ancient and Medieval Nubia," *JWH* 19 (2008): 51, 53.
181 See D. Papanikolaou, "The Aretalogy of Isis from maroneia and the Question of Hellenistic 'Asianism'," *ZPE* 168 (2009): 59–70.
182 *I.Stratonikeia* 1101 = *LSAM* 69. Angelos Chaniotis dates the hymn to the second century BCE: "Staging and Feeling the Presence of God: Emotion and Theatricality in Religious Celebrations," in *Panthée: Religious Celebrations in the Greco-Roman Empire* edited by L. Bricault and C. Bonnet (Leiden: Brill, 2013), 181. However, the reference to the Romans, to the senatorial granting of *asylia* to the temple following epiphanic manifestations and the clear tie of the city of Stratonikeia to the extramural site of the sanctuary, all point to a time after the revolt of Labienus in 39 BCE, but before the onset of formal empire. See A. H. Cadwallader, "Epiphanies and Religious Conflict: The contests over the Hagiasma of Chonai," in *Reconceiving Re-*

but the inscription records in detail the training of thirty boys from noble families (very reminiscent of Plato's instructions on education in a model city) who are to perform this thanksgiving (εὐχαριστεῖ l. 6 cf Col 1:12) to the gods *daily* before the city council. Whether visually or orally, city dwellers and sanctuary pilgrims — the Colossians among them — were "surrounded by so many hymns".[183]

The hymn in the Colossians Letter has no regulating meter.[184] It has led some to suggest that the absence of a metrical form is evidence that there is no hymn,[185] or at least considerable doubt,[186] or, alternately, that it reflects a hymnic style that is founded on Hebraic templates,[187] the very constraint from which Josephus wanted to deflect attention.[188] But as we have begun to see, prose hymns were making significant headway in the repertoire of composers and choirs.

---

ligious Conflict: New Views from the Formative Centuries of Christianity edited by C. de Wet and W. Mayer (London: Routledge, 2018), 115–6. The commissioning of the hymn by one who served as *grammateus* of the council (*Boulê*) of Stratonikeia is of-a-piece with the concerted moves of the city to tie a famous sanctuary to its interests and control.

183 Standhartinger, "Der Kolosserhymnus," 90.

184 N. T. Wright, "Poetry and Theology in Colossians 1:15–20," *NTS* 36 (1990): 450 n23.

185 R. Brucker, *"Christushymnen" oder "epideiktische Passagen"? Studien zum Stilwechsel im Neuen Testament und seiner Umwelt* (FRLANT 176; Göttingen: Vandenhoeck & Ruprecht, 1997); ibid, "'Songs,' 'Hymns,' and 'Encomia' in the New Testament?" in *Literature or Litrugy? Early Christian Hymns and Prayers in their Literary and Liturgical Context in Antiquity* edited by C. Leonhard and M. Löhr (WUNT 2.363; Tübingen: Mohr Siebeck, 2014), 1–14. Brucker argues for epideictic display and an ultra-strict definition of what constitutes a "hymn" which would actually cancel out many ancient hymns along with the Colossian offering. He fails to recognize that Plato allowed that encomia could be given hymnic form. See also Ben Edsall and J. R. Strawbridge, "The Songs we used to sing? Hymn 'traditions' and receptionin Pauline Letters," *JSNT* 37 (2015): 290–311 who argue on the basis of the citation and use of the material by later church writers that the liturgical or musical reiteration is not found. I do not find this argument convincing given that the didactic use of Scriptural material is the ubiquitous *modus operandi* of these ecclesiastical guardians. Indeed, the Letter to the Colossians itself gives warrant for this approach in how it subsequently elaborates on the material (compare Col 1:19 and 2:9 for example). The countervailing argument would be to suggest that because didactic material in the letter is found in later hymns that such material betrays a hymnic origin; See, for example *Analecta Hymnica Graeca's* canon for September, Day 1, Canon 2, Ode 4,31 in its use of Col 2:11. But that a hymn is intended to be referenced by the audience, I think is manifest in the exhortation in v. 12 (–14), on which see further below. See also, M. E. Gordley, *New Testament Christological Hymns: Exploring Texts, Contexts, and Significance* (Downers Grove, IL: IVP, 2018), 18–20, 95–6.

186 M. Hengel, *Between Jesus and Paul* (London: SCM, 1983), 78–96. Curiously, Hengel seems to follow a hermetically sealed hymnody of Christians, that owes its origins to the Hebrew psalter (albeit in translated version). He avoids the Christological hymn of Colossians, seeming to subsume it under a "word of Christ" from Col 3:16. The structure and content of the Christological hymn does not neatly fit his generic model (p. 88) deduced from fragments elsewhere in the Second Testament.

187 H. Stettler, *Der Kolosserhymnus: Untersuchungen zu Form, traditionsgeschichtlichem Hintergrund und Aussage von Kol 1, 15–20* (WUNT 2.131; Tübingen: Mohr Siebeck, 2000).

188 Matthew Gordley is kinder, suggesting that Josephus (and Philo) were merely applying a contemporary hermeneutic for the sake of their readership; see Gordley, *Colossian Hymn*, 108–9.

Given that meter is often interpreted as the means by which solemnity and elevation were given to a hymn that set it off from (some) other genres and from ordinary speech,[189] the question arises as to how prose hymns captured the aural and visual sense that "here is a hymn". Of course, the use of the term ὕμνος was a good start, precisely as Aristides deployed it in, possibly, his earliest effort "to break the barriers between prose and poetry".[190] ὕμνος can mean, simply, a song, but when the focus of the song is a god or hero, the meaning becomes clear.[191] But the array of poetic devices found in the metrical hymns was also deployed: the compilation of epithets, the deployment of rare words and superlative expressions, the production of assonance, alliteration, repetition and parallelism, the use of relatives and participles to create flow. The list could be expanded.[192]

So, for example, in the prose hymn to Mandulis previously mentioned, which is cast in terms of an incubated epiphany, the opening and peroration harness various epithets and rare words: Ἀκτινοβόλε δέσποτα, Μανδοῦλι, Τιτάν, Μακαρεῦ … σε ἔγνων, Μανδοῦλι, ἥλιον τὸν παντεπόπτην δεσπότην, ἁπάντων βασιλέα, Αἰῶνα παντοκράτορα "O Master of the spearing rays of light, Titan, radiant son of Helios … I recognized you as the sun, the all-seeing master, ruler of all, the Aion, sovereign over all …"[193] Assonance and alliteration are found in repetitions of ἐπ– and ἐν–: ἐπενόησα καὶ ἐπολυπράγμονησα "I considered deeply and took great pains" (l. 4) and ἐπεκοιμήθην καὶ ἐνθεασάμενος ἀνέγων "I slept and being granted a vision, I perceived" (l. 9). In fact, just as stylistic theorists prescribed for refined language, snatches of various meters could be worked into the text, without devolving to a consistent metrical structure.[194] Thus, the soldier Paccius Maximus worked into his prose hymn an incomplete dactylic hexameter line: σημιά σού τινα λαμπρὰ θεάμενος "I witnessed certain spectacles of your radiant power" (l. 3).[195] Even in these excerpts from the hymn, one can recognize not only stylistic similarities with the Colossian hymn but

189 M. Blanco, "The Magicians who Sang to the Gods," in *Poetic Language and Religion in Greece and Rome* edited by J. V. García and A. Ruiz (Cambridge: Cambridge Scholars, 2013), 259–60.

190 Aristides, *Or.* 45.1–14, 34 (Hymn to Sarapis); see also 37.1 (to Athena), 41.9 (to Dionysos), 43.2 (to Zeus). See G. Petridou "'One has to be so terribly religious to be an artist': Divine Inspiration and *theophilia* in Aelius Aristides' *Hieroi logoi*," *Archiv für Religiongeschichte* 20 (2018): 263 n25. However, the example of Paccius Maximus and some parts of the hymnody for Isis do not support the contention that Aristides was the inventor of prose hymns (257, 258 n4). He articulated a significant defense of what had already begun to happen. I would actually track the line of development back to Plato's nervousness about poetry in general.

191 M. Trapp, "Introduction," in *In Praise of Asclepius: Aelius Aristides, Selected Prose Hymns* (SAPERE 29; Tübingen: Mohr Siebeck, 2016), 22.

192 See Blanco, "Magicians," 259; for detailed analysis see J. Goeken, *Aelius Aristide et la rhétorique de l'hymne en prose* (RRR 15; Turnhout: Brepols, 2012), 133–88.

193 Bernand, *Inscriptions métriques*, nr 166, ll. 1–2, 17–19.

194 See Cadwallader, *Word of a Woman*, 165–7; Gordley, *Colossian Hymn*, 184–7, 196–8.

195 That is, –˘˘ –˘˘ –˘˘ ˘˘–; see Bernand, *Inscriptions métriques*, 580 n2. The Homeric influence here may be designed to assist the evocation of an epiphany.

the ready aggregation of cosmic acclamations to exalt the god. I have deliberately translated Makareus as "radiant son of Helios" (for so he was in Greek mythology) to bring out an accent in Greek hymnody where the relations of gods — whose son or daughter they were or whose illustrious progeny flowed from their supremacy — formed part of the hymn: Athena daughter of Zeus, Apollo son of Leto: Asklepios son of Apollo, Hermes son of Zeus, Artemis daughter of Leto: Isis daughter of Kronos; Eros, son of Iris and so on.[196] Inevitably, this genealogical link transmitted authority, power and characteristics.[197] This adds weight to the argument of those who see Col 1:12–14 as an introduction (whether an *epiclesis* or *proshodos*) to the hymn proper (see further below).[198]

Matthew Gordley has cracked open the Colossian hymn to metrical analysis, not in unwavering application to each line but to the use of snatches, or feet (metra), within the prose hymn. This has reinforced the division of Col 1:15–20 into two strophes,[199] using the relative pronominal opening ὅς ἐστιν εἰκὼν τοῦ (v.15) … ὅς ἐστιν ἀρχή, πρω– (v.18b) with a combination of iambics ˇ– ˇ– and spondee – –.[200] Curiously he almost defeats his purpose in arguing for a prose hymn by granting to metrical analysis an unwarranted sovereignty in ruling out certain sections as redactional insertions, that is ἐν τοῖς οὐρανοῖς καὶ ἐπὶ τῆς γῆς | τὰ ὁρατὰ καὶ τὰ ἀόρατα | εἴτε θρόνοι εἴτε κυριότητες | εἴτε ἀρχαὶ εἴτε ἐξουσίαι "in the heavens and on earth, the visible and invisible, whether thrones or kyriarchies or rulers or authorities" (Col 1:16, middle section). And yet in the parallelism, the neat balance between the pairings, there is nothing lost in the poetic cast and the contribution to the whole. Indeed, as we shall see, there may be a deliberate critique of temporal powers with their metaphysical claims, given that governing regimes and individual leaders were frequently inserted into hymns, thereby asserting either divine status for human rulers or divine backing for their rule (or both).

For now, I hope to have shown, not only that there is no objection based on metrical considerations, to the assertion of a hymn in Col 1:(12-)15–20 but that the very marks of elevated language that reinforce the poetic form of a hymn have also reinforced the cosmic dimensions that were a common feature of

196 See for example, *Homeric Hymn* 2.1 (to Hermes), Aristides *Or.* 37.2; *I.Erythrai Klazomenai* 205, l. 57; *I.Kourion* 104, l. 17.

197 See the clear exposition of transmission of power in Aristides *Or.* 42.4. The symbiotic relationship between divine genealogies and familial genealogies is clear and allowed for ready intermixture where Seleucid kings (and sometimes queens) and emperors (and sometimes empresses) were accorded divine parentage.

198 Standhartinger, "Der Kolosserhymnus," 71, 91.

199 See, for example, Bormann, *Kolosser*, 81. Almost all commentators allow two strophes. Some, like Gordley, construct an epode at the conclusion (Gordley, *Colossian Hymn*, 191), largely on the assumption that the strophes ought to contain a roughly equal number of syllables. John Barclay looks for an interlude in vv.17–18a: *Colossians and Philemon* (Sheffield: Sheffield Academic Press, 1997), 60–2.

200 Gordley, *Colossian Hymn*, 185–91.

hymns. This cosmology, with a great variety of expositions, is tied to the gods, even with its references to the various components of the realm of the universe, whether the stars of the Tyche Protogeneia ring, the mathematical proportionality and harmony of Theon, or the fullness of the creation and redemption of things seen and unseen of the Colossian hymn.[201] When Ofellios Laetus was exalted as philosopher and theologian it can be seen that what appears as two disciplines to us were, in the early imperial period, in constant exchange.

Theon's explanation of Alexander (of Aetolia/Ephesos) turning to a hymn to express cosmic realities is that only a hymn befits the musical harmony of those realities. This was no esoteric opinion shared by Alexander and Theon alone. Hymnody was the chosen form that expressed and entered into the divine realm — which was equated with the cosmic realm. This is evident in inscriptions surviving from cultic sanctuaries in Asia Minor and in texts found in the writings of Aristides and other literati. The variations in content go mainly to the degree to which scientific information — *physik* — was incorporated.[202] Indeed, Menander the third-century Laodikeian rhetorician, held that "scientific hymns" (φυσικοί) were best left to poets.[203] As Angela Standhartinger expresses it, "Hymns are the music and rhythms of the gods."[204] The ultimate fitting expression of cosmology must therefore take the form of a hymn, whatever might be the particular content, form and tone of that hymn.

Hymns and the reinforcement of mundane realities

In one of his metrical hymns at the temple in Talmis in Nubia, the soldier Paccius Maximus delivered a combined salute to the two cultural colossi of his day, Greece and Rome. He constructed a commissioning of a hymn from the god Mandulis, who descends from Olympus to overcome the barbaric tongue of the Ethiopians (θέλγων βαρβαρικὴν λέξιν ἀπ' Αἰθιόπων). Mandulis urges Maximus to soar in the sweet song of Greece (γλυκερὴν ἔσπευσεν ἐφ'Ἑλλάδα μοῦσαν ἀεῖσαι) … exulting in magnificence, the glory of the Romans (Ῥωμαίων

201 It should be noted here that the πλήρωμα of Col 1:19 makes no reference to τοῦ θεοῦ/πατρός, even though this is frequently added by translations and commentators (see Balabanski, *Colossians*, 71, as one example). Col 2:9 which adds τῆς θεότητος is almost certainly an exegetical application drawn from the hymn. Such interpretive comments as these suggest that the author of the letter interacts with the hymn as received rather than interdicts into the hymn (as Gordley has suggested). Of course, there is nothing of itself to prevent redactional or recensional rephrasing or remodeling of the hymn. This is evident in those instances where multiple copies of the same hymn exist; note especially the Isis aretalogy, known, with variations, in a number of places: *IG* X,2 1 254 (Thessalonike); *IG* XII 5 15 (Chios); *SEG* 58.583 (Kassandreia); *I.Kyme* 41.

202 See Menander Rhetor *Or.* 1.333–44 for an ancient account of types of hymns and their content.

203 Menander Rhetor *Or.* 1.336.

204 Standhartinger, "Der Kolosserhymnus," 90.

μεγέθει δόξαν ἀγαλλόμενος).[205] There was no embarrassment in the inclusion of Greece or Rome in the hymnic praise. Indeed, just as we saw in Theon's adjustment of Plato's text to accord with Roman jurisprudential realities about the age of adulthood, Maximus hymns, either under instruction (divine or not!) or by calculated devotion of the composer, uncritically and unexceptionally drew the connection between the gods and the ruling powers of the day.

The paean and hymn to Apollo and his son Asklepios that is witnessed by a number of examples from its first instance in the early fourth century BCE, gained an addition around 281 BCE. A second son of Apollo, the Seleucid king, was now included in the hymn of praise: "Give voice: a song. Praise at the libations, Seleukos, the son of dark-haired Apollo, whom the one with the golden lyre brought forth."[206] Here religion and politics are collapsed into one another; ritual involvement and leadership by rulers is extended. They become the focus of cult. We have already noted that the Seleucid queen, Laodike, was the recipient of upgraded cultic focus (often in collation with Aphrodite). This seems to be reflected at Laodikeia-on-Lycus prior to Roman control in Asia when a focus on Zeus Aetophoros usurped the earlier patronage of Aphrodite and Hermes for the city. Thus in the development of the imperial cult in Asia from the Hellenistic template, hymns to the divine emperor were cultivated, especially in a Zeus-Jupiter connection. Neokorate celebrations must have been full of these hymns!

Hadrian's cultivation of hymns at his sacred contest established at Smyrna, demonstrates how important ruling authorities viewed such compositions and their performance. Indeed, the hymn from Kourion to the deceased but deified Antinoos, the "blessed Bithynian" (μάκαρ Βειθύνιε), favorite of Hadrian, clearly shows how one of the key instruments and reinforcements of piety and religion secured a political edge reinforcing official policy and values.[207] Antinoos is drawn into being an intermediary between the gods and mortals — he is called an ἄγγελος (l. 6). Given that we have already seen the composition of a hymn at Stratonikeia described, *inter alia*, as worship (θρησκεία), in this hymn is not merely the worship of an angel but an act that had imperial backing. It therefore is no surprise to find ταπεινοφροσύνη tied to θρησκεία in the repudiated requirement in Col 2:18. The writer of Ephesians, as most subsequent Christian authors, might view such "humility" or "self-abasement" as a positive value (Eph 4:2), no doubt as was the cachet of those who may have advocated the worship of angels at Colossae. Plato too held that humiliation was the cure

205 Bernand, *Inscriptions métriques*, nr. 168, ll. 24,25, 27.

206 *I.Erythrai Klazomenai* 205, ll. 74–6 = *LSAM* 24, B. ll. 33–5. Temples to Seleukos and his son Antiochos are known, such as on Lemnos.

207 *SEG* 53.1747 (130/131 CE). Antinoos is here assimilated with Eros. In Rome his collation was with Hermes (*IGUR* 1.143). In Ephesos, he became the aesthetic model of the city hero-founder Androklos (see chapter 3). Being the king's favorite had its otherworldly benefits!

for a puffed-up mind.[208] But the writer of Colossians will have none of it (see also Col 2:23). It is a violated mindset, often politically instigated. Indeed, as Plato himself recognized, it is a mark of slavery.[209]

The Kourion example of high-flying Antinoos dates approximately sixty years after the writing of the Letter to the Colossians, but such religious-imperial amalgams were already well entrenched.[210] And hymns were a key instrument. The sheer performance of the hymn, as the fitting expression of the harmony of the cosmos, itself cultivated and reinforced that harmony in the society of those for whom the hymn was the expression of their understanding.[211] Hymnody reinforced hegemony.

The hymn in the Letter to the Colossians

At the same time, the hymn in the letter constructs an alternate universe, or at least, a universe constructed on a different basis. It recognizes how much standard hymns were used to reinforce political and philosophical control. An evocation of the political realm, of diplomacy and militarism, comes in the finale of the Colossians hymn (Col 1:20): "reconciling" (ἀποκαταλλάξαι) and "working peace" (εἰρηνοποιήσας). A number of commentators have recognized the terminology of imperial negotiations in this language.[212] But the instrument of reconciliation and peace is not the common chorus of hymns accumulating support for empire. Rather it is the very antithesis of empire, or rather, of the very instrument of torture on which violent enforcement of the empire ultimately relied.[213] The hymn affirms that in the one slain on the cross, not in the executing power, is the foundation and restoration of the harmony of the universe.

The two strophes of the hymn, unlike the descent-ascent model of the Philippians hymn (Phil 2:6–11), accent creation and redemption. But the affirmation in the cosmic pre-eminence is that thrones and kyriarchies, rulers and authorities (Col 1:16) are neither divinely endorsed by that primacy nor are they deified participants in that divine council. The hymn utilized in Colossians radically undercuts the religious reinforcement of the person and posi-

208 Plato *Lys.* 210e.

209 Plato *Pol.* 309a.

210 See, for example, Tacitus *Ann.* 14.15.

211 This is where the subtle shift from religion to magic occurs, that is, on the understanding that certain forms forge desired results; see Blanco, "The Magicians," 258–65. It also resolves the apparent tension identified by James Dunn between the harmony of the cosmos and its disruption; see Dunn, *Colossians and Philemon*, 84–5.

212 M. M. Thompson, *Colossians and Philemon* (Grand Rapids, MN: Eerdmans, 2005), 40–1; H. O. Maier, "A Sly Civility: Colossians and Empire," *JSNT* 27 (2005): 326, 329–33.

213 M. Hengel, *Crucifixion: In the ancient world and the folly of the cross* (Philadelphia: Fortress, 1977), 33–8.

tion of the emperor. Indeed, in a reprise of Col 1:16 in Col 2:15, it is those replete with the wealth and pomp of a Roman triumph who are stripped and paraded rather than those denuded and demeaned as slaves (one of the key significations of crucifixion).[214]

If, as some think, there are snatches of this hymn to be found in the book of Revelation (Rev 1:5, 3:14),[215] not only does this point to a pre-existing composition with strong ties to the Lycus Valley,[216] but it is a testimony to how the hymn could cultivate a critique of the ideological inflation of Rome. Like the Colossian hymn, Rev 1:5 ties the charged language of "first-born of the dead" (πρωτότοκος [ἐκ] τῶν νεκρῶν) to the title of "ruler over the emperors of the earth" (ὁ ἄρχων τῶν βασιλέων τῆς γῆς) in a deft collapsing of the hymnic parallelism of Col 1:16.

But there is a further element in the thanksgiving called for as the *epiclesis* (or possibly a *proshodos*, the approach to the altar) for the hymn.[217] The crucial word here seems to stand aloof from a referent, namely εὐχαριστοῦντες in Col 1:12,[218] though some tie it to the preceding participles of vv. 9–11.[219] However, vv. 12–14 provide the motivation for the hymn that follows and the rationale for thanksgiving "with joy".[220] Significantly, the Letter to the Ephesians takes up the call to sing (Eph 5:19), in a replication of Col 3:16,[221] but transforms the ἐν χάριτι … τῷ θεῷ of its *vorlage* into the introduction to the Colossian hymn in Col 1:12, that is εὐχαριστοῦντες … τῷ θεῷ καὶ πατρί (Eph 5:20).[222] Ephesians does not have the "Colossian hymn" (cf Eph 1:10) but is unequivocal about the object of hymn-singing, and the impulse for such praise — it is thanksgiving.

214 Plutarch *Caes*. 27.9–10. See Hengel, *Crucifixion*, 51–63; W. Carr, *Angels and Principalities: The Background, Meaning and Development of the Pauline Phrase hai archai kai hai exousiai* (Cambridge: Cambridge University Press, 1981), 47–86; H. O. Maier, "Reading Colossians in the Ruins: Roman Imperial Iconography, Moral Transformation, and the Construction of Christian Identity in the Lycus Valley," in *Colossae in Space and Time*, 214–6.

215 See A. Standhartinger, *Studien zur Entstehungsgeschichte und Intention des Kolosserbriefs* (Leiden: Brill, 1999), 206–7.

216 Some are content simply to note the parallels without advancing to derivation; "somewhat parallel," P. Pokorný *Colossians: A Commentary* (Peabody, MA: Hendrickson, 1991), 83; "perhaps significantly," J. G. D. Dunn, *The Epistles to the Colossians and to Philemon* (NIGTC; Grand Rapids, MI: Eerdmans, 1996), 97 cf J. L. Sumney, *Colossians* (NTL; Louisville, KY: WJKP, 2008), 72, 73.

217 There is an imaginative recall of the ritual actions involved in temple worship, made ironic because, it seems, the hymn-singing and whatever ritual attended such occasion, were held in a home (Phmn 2 cf Col 4:15).

218 Standhartinger, "Der Kolosserhymnus," 71.

219 Sumney, *Colossians*, 51–2.

220 μετὰ χαρᾶς belongs to the participle rather than being tacked on as a qualifier to the thought of verse 11.

221 For the detail of the dependence of the Letter to the Ephesians on this section in Colossians, see A. T. Lincoln, *Ephesians* (WBC 42; Waco, TX: Word, 1990), 338–9.

222 There is a disturbance in the manuscript tradition here with some manuscripts (𝔓46, D* F G among others) directing thanks to the Father (and) God. Whether this word order is driven by the Colossians references (that is, Col 1:12 and 3:16) cannot be decided.

We have seen in the Stratonikeian inscription authorizing the composition and performance of a *proshodos* and adoration, that the motivation was "thanksgiving". Another inscription records the epiphanic intervention of Zeus Panamaros to save both sanctuary and city.[223] The thanksgiving to Zeus (and Hecate) prompting the elaborate hymnic arrangements is grounded in this epiphany: εὐχαριστεῖ αἰεὶ τοῖσδε τοῖς οὕτως ἐπιφανεστάτοις θεοῖς.[224] One scholiast saw thanksgiving as a crucial part of the definition of a hymn,[225] an understanding that runs across religious traditions, as is clear from the emphases in Philo.[226] Rescue, healing, the execution of justice and the gaining of some benefit were frequently the prompts for the offering of thanks, usually in the aftermath, sometimes as a supplication.[227] The language of "Savior" and/or "benefactor" often attached to the gods who were deemed responsible and/or to the heroes who acted like those gods. At Laodikeia, for example, the city honored Hadrian as "the benefactor and savior of the universe" (τὸν εὐεργέτην καὶ σωτῆρα τοῦ κόσμου).[228]

In Col 1:12–14 three predications underscore the content of the call to give thanks, delivering a hortatory force to the participle εὐχαριστοῦντες opening in verse 12.[229] Significantly they recognize the intervention of God, named as the father:

εὐχαριστοῦντες τῷ πατρὶ
 τῷ ἱκανώσαντι ἡμᾶς εἰς τὴν μερίδα τοῦ κλήρου τῶν ἁγίων ἐν τῷ φωτί
 ὅς ἐρρύσατο ἡμᾶς ἐκ τῆς ἐξουσίας τοῦ σκότους
 καὶ μετέστησεν εἰς τὴν βασιλείαν τοῦ υἱοῦ τῆς ἀγάπης αὐτοῦ
  ἐν ᾧ ἔχομεν τὴν ἀπολύτρωσιν, τὴν ἄφεσιν τῶν ἁμαρτιῶν

Give thanks to the Father
 the one who has authorized us for an allotted share among the saints in the light
 who retrieved us from the *dominium* of darkness
 and migrated us into the reign of the Son of his love
  by whom we have secured the ransom, the release from offences.

---

223 *I.Stratonikeia* 10. See N. Belayche, "'Un dieu est né …' À Stratonicée de Carie (I Stratonikeia 10)," in *Manières de penser dans l'Antiquité méditerranéenne et orientale. Mélanges offerts à Francis Schmidt* edited by Ch. Batsch and M. Vartejanu-Joubert (JSJs 134; Leiden: Brill, 2009), 193–212.

224 *I.Stratonikeia* 1101, l. 6; of course, thanksgiving can also be the prompt for other offerings — see *I.Byzantion* 32, a dedication εὐχαριστίας χάριν (as reconstructed) by Dionysian mystery initiates (50–100 CE).

225 Scholion on Dionysos Thrax 451.6.

226 Philo *Mos.* 1.180, 2.256; *Plant.* 130; cf *Steinepigramme* 1.12.3.2.

227 See *I.Smyrna* 570.

228 F. Guizzi, "Greek and Latin Inscriptions of Laodikeia on the Lykos 2003–2018," in *15. Yılında Laodikeia (2003–2018)* edited by C. Şimşek (Istanbul: Ege, 2019), 175; cf *I.Rhod. Peraia* 607 (of Domitian, probably); *IG* XII,1.978 (Potidaion, of Trajan). There are reports that a recently recovered, as yet unpublished, epitaph from the Colossian ascribes εὐεργέτης to the deceased.

229 So Standhartinger, "Der Kolosserhymnus," 91. The imperatival use of the participle is admitted by D. B. Wallace, *Greek Grammar: Beyond the Basics* (Grand Rapids: Zondervan, 1996), 650–53. However, he severely restricts its application.

In this sense, the hymn that follows is a thanksgiving hymn to the father that relies on a creation-redemption recounting of the son through whom these predicated benefits have been achieved. Again we see the genealogical connection previously noted in many hymns. But, more importantly here, there is no thanksgiving directed towards the empire of Rome; this empire is its antithesis. Nonetheless the language of that repudiated jurisdiction is harnessed for the new affirmation.

It is not only the dominant political construction that is reconfigured on the basis of the most contemptible lynch-pin of the empire, that is, crucifixion. It is the philosophical underpinnings of that regime, the hubris that philosophy, with its religious interconnections, could deliver and preserve the harmony, the concord that was an integral part of the operations and the propaganda of empire. It was not only that Rome "will always find a means to appropriate and subsume".[230] That imposition was ardently accepted and promoted, as we have seen with Paccius Maximus and with the enthusiastic acceptance through Asia, at least among the levels of society that administered the "good news" celebrations of the Augustan presence.[231] Philosophy as we have seen was not divorced from the political fabric of Asian society under Rome; indeed, it was celebrated as an integral contributor to its practices, with some leaders acclaimed not only for the offices they held but also for their quasi-office of philosopher. Philosophy, politics and religion were interlocked in the machinery that drove society under Rome.

For the Christological hymn and for the letter writer, harmony and concord remain unassailed as virtues. It is simply that the foundation for those cosmic values was placed not in a universe factored on the (Roman) empire, but on Christ. The accent on Christ as the originator of all things (Col 1:16), the one in whom all things hold together (Col 1:17), is reminiscent of Theon's image of the "bond" uniting all things. But in Colossians, it is used as the basis of relativizing the multiplicities that exist in human relationships — of Greek and Jew and so on (Col 3:11). The rationale for the collapsing of both ethnic and status differences is given not by a vacuous, largely elitist celebration that "we are all Romans now" but by reference to a cosmological affirmation, worthy of a Middle Platonist like Theon: Christ is all things and in all things (πάντα καὶ ἐν πᾶσιν Χριστός) (Col 3:11). If Theon's mundane references within the course of his cosmological investigations are any guide,[232] it explains why, in the Letter to the Colossians, the hymn of the cosmic Christ

230 T. Whitmarsh, "Greek and Roman in Dialogue: The Pseudo-Lucianic Nero," *JHS* 119 (1999): 160, summarizing the argument of Pseudo-Lucian's *Nero or on the digging of the Isthmus*.

231 These celebrations continued at least into the second century CE and were an opportunity for the elite to provide lavish benefactions for their celebrations, gain recognition and demonstrate their commitment to the order of Rome: see Guizzi, "Greek and Latin Inscriptions," 167–68, l. 12 (Laodikeia).

232 See above the reference to Theon 12:19–21.

can be held together in the same piece of writing with the household code (Col 3:18–4:1) and with affirmations of governance (Col 2:10, 15).[233] Indeed, it is no coincidence that the wisdom that expresses itself "with psalms, hymns [and] spiritual songs" (ψαλμοῖς ὕμνοις ᾠδαῖς πνευματικαῖς Col 3:16) directed towards the *plêroma* of the universe, is the immediate preface in the writing to the *Haustafel*. It is as if, having used the fitting form to express the structure of cosmic harmony, that very harmony can now be delineated in the structure of household relationships.[234]

For all the philosophical resonances, for all the maintenance of the affirmation of harmony and stability as prime values, albeit anchored to Christ, the writer repudiated the pursuit of philosophy and (human) tradition (Col 2:8). For Theon, by contrast, all such matters were the proper concern of philosophy as initiation into the realm of truth and being, indeed into the sacred tradition (παράδοσις) of the mysteries of that realm.[235] Paul's voice in Colossians, like Theon, accented wisdom and access to the mystery (Col 1:9, 26, 28, 2:2–3, 4:3) but the ventriloquist disavowed that they can be found in the teaching of those such as Theon. Perhaps the escalation of disputation, as compared to the genteel ambience of Theon's writing, is precisely the tack needed by a minority religious group. Here we catch a glimpse of a writer, and perhaps a fledgling school, with aspirations to match, surpass and supplant the cosmologies of the city that placed so much store on the elite's ability in wealth, education and standing to make the journey, like Diodotos, to Smyrna, to purchase priesthoods in the city's temples, to sponsor the composition of exhilarating hymns.

The writer of the letter is engaged in the expanse of religious competition within Colossian (and secondarily, Laodikeian) society seeking to build an edifice that privileges Christ as the identity-marker. It is probably hyperbole to posit for the hymn and the writer a resistance to Colossian society and the wider Roman rationales of governance,[236] even though terminology from imperial language-frames and their religious undergirding is present. Indeed, the accent on wisdom was completely in accord with one of the prime values frequently acclaimed of the exemplary deceased on epitaphs — whether they be Platonists, doctors, mime artists, farmers, Jews or even a student like

233 This conjunction was proposed by Andrew Lincoln, "The Household Code and Wisdom Mode of Colossians," *JSNT* 74 (1999): 93–112. The occurrence of just such a conjunction in Theon of Smyrna was not noted.

234 Some hymns even incorporated law-giving into their contents, albeit in general terms. Thus, Isis asserts herself (as the hymn-writer constructs the first person affirmations) as the lawgiver for human activity and relationships: *I.Kyme* 41, ll. 9, 21, 30, 37 (1st century BCE).

235 Theon 14.18–19.

236 The positing of the Christological hymn as a form of "Jewish resistance hymn" was made by Matthew Gordley, *Christological Hymns*, 74–7 and embellished by Mark Medley, "Subversive song: Imagining Colossians 1:15–20 as a social protest hymn in the context of the Roman empire," *Re&E* 116 (2019): 421–35.

Diodotos.[237] One skilled mason from nearby Tripolis, went to Rome, plied his trade, founded an association and was hailed as an "Ionic sage among men" (τὸν σοφὸν ἐν ἀνδράσιν Εἰωνικὸν).[238] These "Wisdom-acclamations" had a broader compass than philosophy and could be found among those with little or no philosophical training. For Colossians, where a search for philosophical wisdom might have to take an aspirant elsewhere, the letter-writer affirmed wisdom "at home." Consequently then, the Colossian text, for all its philosophical resonances, speaks rather of a negotiation of those societal values and realities as a minority group, one that cannot but use the language and structures of the dominant groups and ideologies, indeed that may, as in the structuring of a supposedly Christian household-code on the basis of cosmic formulations, appear remarkably cohesive with the espousals of those dominant groups and ideologies. The "making a deal", "executing an exchange" (ἐξαγοραζόμενοι) with those outside (Col 4:5), necessarily meant that the language (ὁ λόγος) had to be familiar to those with whom one engaged (Col 4:6), including those with the background and education of Diodotos. The hymn, the philosophy and values that undergirded it, were therefore not idiosyncratic or radically subversive, even if distinctive features can be recognized and agonistic self-definitions were intended.

237 *I.Syringes* 1255 (Thebes, nd, Platonist), *SEG* 65.791 (Kamarina, doctors), *SEG* 43.982 (Patara, 3rd century, mime artist), *SEG* 43.911 (Caesarea, after 138 CE, farmer), *SEG* 51.1656 (Sardis, Jew), *SEG* 30.711 (Perinthos/Ephesos, 1st century CE, student).

238 *IGUR* 4.1567 (early 3rd century). Here I follow the suggestion of Heikke Solin, "Analecta Epigraphica CCXLIV–CCLI," *Arctos* 42 (2008): 232–3.

Chapter Seven
Purity, Pollution, Penalties and Power at Colossae: sacred laws and their (monetary) significance for the Colossians

The value of numismatics for insights into the life of Colossae has been explored in previous chapters. Historical reconstruction that draws on ancient coins has only relatively recently stabilized its validity.[1] Certainly the bronze coins from city mints that proliferate through Greece and Asia Minor have provided considerable insight into how these cities wanted to present themselves, at least as decided by civic elites. The most obvious communication from these coins is the avowed religiosity of civic life. It is not merely that we can rattle off the list of gods and heroes that are attested in a city through their coins. This has been a commonplace among Second Testament commentators wanting to provide a sense of the religious adherence of the inhabitants of Colossae.[2] It is a list that has increased with further discoveries of new coin types (indicated here by italics): Zeus, Athena, Apollo, Artemis, Sarapis, Isis, Asklepios, Hygieia, Leto, Helios, Mên, Demeter, Dionysos, *Silenus*, *Nemesis*, Nike (?),[3] Tyche, the river

---

1 See, M. P. Theophilos, *Numismatics and Greek Lexicography* (London: T & T Clark, 2020), 76–92.

2 See, for example, C. E. Arnold, *The Colossian Syncretism: The Interface between Christianity and Folk Religion at Colossae* (Grand Rapids, MN: Baker, 1996), 107–8. He includes Selene in his list, a coin type that should be registered as Artemis. The description appears to have been derived from Barclay Head's Catalogue of (Phrygian) Coins in the British Museum: *BMC Phrygia* Colossae 9 (Selene). Of course, this does not preclude the probability of the minor deity's presence at Colossae. The crescent on the smallest known coin minted by Claudia Eugenetoriane points towards Selene.

3 A single coin featuring a figure in a horse-drawn biga holding a wreath in the left hand and palm in the right (with Commodus on the obverse) supports the identification of Nike. The worn condition of the coin prompted both Head (*BMC Phrygia* Colossae 15 and von Aulock

gods Lycus and *Kapros*, *Herakles*. To these could be added the deified personifications of the *Boulê*, the *Dêmos* and the Senate.

We have already drilled into the expansive appearance of three deities on Colossae's coins — Helios, Artemis and Tyche. Elsewhere I have pointed to the political significance of Claudia Eugenetoriane's emphasis on Demeter on some of her coins.[4] But here it is crucial to recognize the sheer ubiquity of deities and heroes on the common commercial facilitator of exchange at Colossae. That is, commerce and the sacred cannot be separated. Coins bore the imprint of the gods; the tacit witness thereby is that the gods were supporters of this commercial reality, just as the bust of the emperor on multiple obverses was complemented by different gods on the reverse. The concord of the gods supported the concord of (imposed by) Rome, a harmony between divine and human realms.[5] The economy of Colossae was so embroiled in religion and religion in the economy that the old reminder that politics and religion could not be separated in the ancient world needs to be made even more emphatic when approaching religion and the economy.[6]

When Hadrian intervened in disputes over money-changing practices at Pergamon so as to settle the rates of exchange, he left untouched the necessity for "the so-called penny for Hermes" (τὸ εἰς τὸν Ἑρμῆ λεγόμενον). This was offered in the money-changers' offices (where market takings in bronze were converted to silver) as a cancellation of a debt incurred by an unwillingness to declare an oath of complete conformity to civic requirements in market-place exchanges.[7] As trifling as the amount probably was (the smallest coin available — perhaps a third of an assarion), every transaction at Pergamon (and probably elsewhere) was brought under the enabling oversight of the mercantile god *par excellence*, Hermes.[8] Whether or not this was simply a means to gain an extra commission is unclear, though Hadrian's willingness to leave this alone suggests that the dedication to Hermes remained sacrosanct, distinguished from the exchange commissions that money-changers were allowed to

(*MSPhryg* 2.579) to be hesitant about the attribution to Nike. *RPC online* 4.2.1883 temp. has removed any reference to Nike.

4 A. H. Cadwallader, "Wealthy, widowed, astute and beneficent: Claudia Eugenetoriane and the second century revival of the Colossian mint," in *New Documents Illustrating the History of Early Christianity vol 12: The Lycus Valley* edited by J. R. Harrison *et al.* (Grand Rapids, MN: Eerdmans, 2023), forthcoming.

5 See M. Theophilos, "Employing Numismatic Evidence in Discussions of Early Christianity in the Lycus Valley:" A Case Study from Laodicea," in *The First Urban Churches 5: Colossae, Hierapolis, and Laodicea* edited by J. R. Harrison and L. L. Welborn (Atlanta, GA: SBL, 2019), 271–4.

6 I am puzzled by the absence of any focus on the interconnection between religion and economy in some recent work; see, for example, H. D. Baker and M. Jursa (eds), *Documentary Sources in Ancient Near Eastern and Greco-Roman Economic History* (Oxford: Oxbow, 2014).

7 Oliver, *Greek Constitutions*, 84, l. 34 (129 CE?); Oliver's felicitous translation.

8 I think that the smallest coin minted by Pedia Sekounda at Eukarpeia deliberately bears Hermes on the obverse (*RPC* 3.2593) as a literal visualization of the monetary offering to be made to Hermes in the market-place. See my "Moneyed Women in Phrygia," *NC* (2023) forthcoming.

continue by Hadrian's edict. The coins were probably collected in a *thesauros* marked as the property of the god (as distinct from anyone else's).[9]

The hold of the gods on the coins meant that the near-entirety of the exchange component of trade in agriculture and goods and of loans that facilitated them was given a theological undergirding, just as the gods gained (financially and conceptually) from the ubiquity of coins.[10] Of course, the gods needed their agents — priests and other officials — to administer, organize, explain and publicize their deliberations and decisions including, most especially, how the gods were to be recognized and approached. Inevitably, the scrupulous detail of these arrangements was characterized as the maintenance of purity, a maintenance that frequently was monetized both for efficaciousness (as in payment for sacrifices) and for indebtedness (for breaches as well as loans). Money (whether as sacred offering or as payment) imbued the sacrality of ancient religion with a concomitant conferral of power to its leading controllers — the king or emperor of course, but also his underlings in cities and cults (most especially in the Roman period, the imperial cult, though antecedents can be traced).

When the Letter to the Colossians crucifies debt (Col 2:14) in the context of purity concerns (Col 2:21), a potentially massive subversion of an elaborate imperial and civic conjunction is threatened, a dire menace that helps to explain the mollification that occurs in other parts of the letter (such as Col 3:18–4:1, 4:5). To this exchange between the sacred and the economic we turn, here taking elements of the letter as our starting point but concerned throughout in recognizing the context within which these elements — of purity and debt — drew their meaningfulness.

Illustrative purity concerns in Colossae and the Letter to the Colossians

Here we might bring out a metal-detector in the hunt for bronze coins in a seemingly unlikely place. In Col 2:21, the author refers to three prohibitions — "do not grasp, do not consume, do not feel" (μὴ ἅψῃ μηδὲ γεύσῃ μηδὲ θίγῃς). These are given in what appear to be sample instances (as also Col 2:16) of what are generically introduced in the previous verse as characteristic of *cosmic* living: τί ὡς ζῶντες ἐν κόσμῳ δογματίζεσθε (Col 2:20b). I am not concerned here with whether the verb δογματίζεσθε is to be understood as a mid-

9 See I. Pafford, "Priestly Portion vs. Cult Fees — The Finances of Greek Sanctuaries," in *Cities and Priests: Cult Personnel in Asia Minor and the Aegean Islands from the Hellenistic to the Imperial Period* edited by M. Horster and A. Klöckner (Berlin: de Gruyter, 2013), 49–64.

10 See R. Boer, *The Sacred Economy of Ancient Israel* (Louisville, KY: WJKP, 2015), 144–5.

dle with active force or a passive,[11] but rather the choice of verb. Some analysis is required before we return to the question of bronze coins and their relation to cultic associations and activity.

There is a common assumption that the three instances of regulation in Col 2:21 belong to a Jewish backdrop governed by δογματίζω. This has led to a forage through the Septuagint.[12] But the returns are small. δογματίζω is used of royal decrees in three instances: Es 3:9, 1 Esd 6:34 and Dan 2:13, 15 in the OG version, with the Theodotionic version substituting the substantive δόγμα — the form we find in Col 2:14 in the plural. For the Greek translators of these First Testament texts, the fitting word-group for a royal pronouncement, a decree, was built on the stem δογμ-.[13] But the assumption of a Jewish reference, perhaps influenced by the mention of "sabbaths" in Col 2:16, has seized rather on 2 Macc 10:8 and 15:36 as connoting a religious enactment, neglecting to recognize that in both these cases, the religious enactment is a decree from the leaders of the Jews. The LXX instances of the word are few and colored by political enactment rather than religious regulation.

A government pronouncement is one of the main uses of the word especially in Roman times. In the senatorial province of Asia, of which Colossae was part, δόγμα is used to designate a decision of the Senate.[14] The word carries the sense of formal inscription and publication (cf Es 9:14 [1]). No First Testament instance of the word-group relates to such ascetic demands as illustratively unfold in Col 2:21. Certainly none refer to "characteristically Jewish concerns."[15] The incentive, then, is to look elsewhere. It is not merely, as Andrej Petrovic has argued, that the reception in hellenized Colossae would appropriate the given instances according to the conceptual framework of Greek religion.[16] The author, conversant with the aspiring Greek cultural conventions of the city of Colossae within the Roman empire, probably intended to prompt

11 For the former option, see P. Foster, *Colossians* (BNTC; London: Bloomsbury, 2016), 298; for the latter, see J. Dunn, *The Epistles to the Colossians and to Philemon* (NIGTC; Grand Rapids, MI; Eerdmans, 1996), 190.

12 See, remarkably given the examples of the use of the word in inscriptions, J. H. Moulton and G. Milligan, *The Vocabulary of the Greek Testament* (London: Hodder and Stoughton, 1952), 166 who paraphrase the verse, with a passive parsing of δογματίζω, as "Why do you allow yourselves to be overridden by Jewish enactments?".Eduard Lohse repeatedly mined Jewish texts for his exposition: *Colossians and Philemon* (Hermeneia; Philadelphia: Fortress, 1971), 123–4.

13 See also Heb 11:23 A *pc*.

14 See *IG* XII 3.173 l.C53 (Astypalaia, 105 BCE); *CIG* 3524, l. 54 (Augustan); of the *Senatus consulta* – see *MAMA* 4.143, l.C13 (Apollonia, 14–19 CE), *SEG* 32.1097, l. 20 (Aphrodisias, 222/223 CE), Oliver, *Greek Constitutions* 10 l.58 (Cyrene, 7/6 BCE). The word can be used for lower-level government decisions: *IG* XII,7 240, l. 34 (Amorgos, 207 CE); *SEG* 6.810, ll. 9–10 (Nea Paphos, Cyprus, 211 CE).

15 Dunn, *Colossians and Philemon*, 191.

16 A. Petrovic, "Do Seize, Do Eat, Do Touch — But Mind Your Thoughts: Colossians and Greek Purity Regulations," in *Epigraphical Evidence Illustrating Paul's Letter to the Colossians* edited by J. Verheyden, M. Öhler and T. Corsten (WUNT 411; Tübingen: Mohr Siebeck, 2018), 149.

such a reception. Only secondarily (perhaps with an eye towards a Laodikeian audition constituted in part by Jewish hearers), were Jewish allusions appropriated (such as Isa 29:13 for Col 2:16, perhaps via already formed gospel traditions).[17] But for the Colossian Christ-followers at least, they served merely as a convenient confirmation, already developing in the gospel traditions, of *distance* from Jewish influences (cf Tit 1:14). The arrogation now serves as authentic Christian critique of flawed and deceptive religious practices, regardless of their specific devotion (whether Greek or Jewish).

The word δόγμα, and its cognates,[18] is also used in connection with religious groups in the Greco-Roman world to refer to regulations governing acceptable ritual and moral behaviors and states or to decisions made by a particular temple board or association committee. In one lengthy list of regulations of a second-century Dionysiac association at Athens, the plural δόγματα is repeated a number of times in the inscription, with one prescribed audiential acclamation of support, "The regulations on a stele!" (ἐν στήλῃ τὰ δόγματα). Here is endorsed, after the fact of inscription, the importance given to public display of requisite behaviors,[19] whether simply for group members or, in the case of temple regulations, to approaching adherents — all enforceable by authorized officials. It is significant that the early fifth century commentator, Theodore of Mopsuestia, understood the δόγματα indicated in Col 2:20 as *leges vobis statuunt*, "laws they prominently placed for you" using terminology that indicated a formal institution for display (*statuunt*).[20] Indeed, in his paraphrase of the Latin text of Col 2:21 he used only two of the instances illustrating the δόγματα, *hoc manduca, hoc noli tangere* "eat this, do not touch" but then added *et alia quae huiusmodi sunt* "and other requirements which are much the same." His change of the eating requirement from a prohibition to an injunction and his recognition that such were but instances from a longer

---

17 See Matt 15:9, Mk 7:17. David Hay suggests that the primary reference is to the gospel story: *Colossians* (ANTC; Nashville: Abingdon, 2000), 111. This implies that access to Jewish traditions is substantially filtered through a Christian impress, such that contact with Jewish ideas is second-hand. See also Thomas Kazen, *Jesus and Purity Halakhah: Was Jesus Indifferent to Impurity?* (CBNTS 38; Winona Lake, IN: Eisenbrauns, 2010), 64. See further chapter 4.

18 Other terms can also be used, such as ψήφισμα; see *LSCG Suppl* 20, l. 8 (Athens, early 3rd century BCE); *I.Kyme* 30, l. 2 (2nd century CE). πρόγραμμα is also found: *I.Ephesos* 3418A (Metropolis, nd) cf *I.Stratonikeia* 507 (Lagina, 81 BCE). See Andrej and Ivana Petrovic, *Inner Purity and Pollution in Greek Religion, Volume 1, Early Greek Religion* (Oxford: Oxford University Press, 2016), 281–2.

19 *IG* II² 1368, ll. 16–17 (Athens 164/5 CE), cf *IG* II² 1252 + 999; Sokolowski *LSAM* 72, ll. 50–1. John Kloppenborg and Philip Harland add the bracketed words "(Inscribe)" to their translation to capture the intent. See J. S. Kloppenborg and R. S. Ascough, *Greco-Roman Associations: Texts, Translations, and Commentary I. Attica, Central Greece, Macedonia, Thrace* (Berlin: de Gruyter, 2011), 246. Inscriptions unrelated to religious observances also could prescribe stele inscription; see *I.Kyme* 19, ll. 52–3 where a stele of white stone is prescribed for the inscription and its placement in the gymnasium (honorific for Vacceus Labeo, 2 BCE – 14 CE).

20 Compare *CIL* 3.14203 (Delos, 150–51 BCE).

list, shows that he was familiar with sacred tables of regulations set up outside temples and religious meeting places.[21]

This becomes even clearer when we look at examples of sacred laws surviving on inscribed stelai,[22] and occasionally found in the papyri.[23] Some of these hark back to the classical period or earlier as well as continuing through to the third and fourth centuries CE. Whilst there are developments that occur in these laws (not least with the abrogation of religious sensibilities in Greek cities by Rome), there was also a concern to preserve and renew ancient codes. There was, at least, a fiction of aseity in the gods and the regulations governing their worship.[24] We discover that the very instances given in Col 2:21 are found in these sacred law-codes, of course with specific content following after each injunction. The letter-writer does not intend to provide particularities nor to caricature the injunctions.[25] The contemporary religious background or awareness of Colossae's Christ-followers would be only too familiar with the fuller predicates flowing on from these imperatives. Whatever religious clubs or temple precincts that accented the fit state (ἅγιος, ἁγνός, ὅσιος or other synonym) to approach Zeus, Helios, Tyche, Dionysos, Artemis or one of the other religious adherences on offer, these regulations had a formal and familial similarity.

Some inscriptions belong to elite associations. But these sacred laws are also applied to village cultic sites and to religious gatherings in homes. Even the practice of placing such regulations in more than one cultic location is known and may have some impli-

---

21 Theodore's complete Greek original is, unfortunately, lost, with 130 surviving fragments of his commentary on the Pauline Letters found only among catenae of the New Testament (marginal commentary drawn from numerous ancient writers and attached to the biblical text). Fortunately, a literal translation into Latin has survived in two versions — hence the quotations from the Latin here. An edited text was provided by Henry Swete, *Theodori episcopi Mopsuesteni In epistolas b. Pauli commentarii Vol. I* (Cambridge: Cambridge University Press, 1880), 295–6. An English translation, modified here, is found in Rowan Greer, *Theodore of Mopsuestia: The Commentaries on the Minor Epistles of Paul* (Atlanta, GA: SBL, 2010), 417. Swete's assertion (p. 296) that these represented the teaching of the false teachers is doubtful, given the interpretation adopted here. Rather, whatever false teaching might be derivative, the author, in Theodore's revealing paraphrase, offers, rather, a critique of the general religious environment from which the Christ-followers had come and in which they continued to live at Colossae.

22 The new online *Collection of Greek Ritual Norms* (cgrn.ulg.ac.be) offers a convenient and helpful gathering of inscriptions related to religious practice in the ancient world. See also Philip Harland's *Associations in the Greco-Roman World* (philipharland.com/Greco-roman-associations). A number of the examples that follow are culled from this resource. Reference should also be made to the various collections published by Francois Sokolowski and Eran Lupu.

23 See for example the Association of Zeus Hypsistos (*P.Lond.* 7.2193, [69–58 BCE]).

24 So for example, a number of codes are recognised as substantial repetitions or merely re-carved copies of more ancient inscriptions. See M. M. Miles, *The City Eleusinion* (AA 31; Princeton, NJ: American School of Classical Studies at Athens, 1998), 64–5; see also *SEG* 29.1205 (Sardis) an inscription of 426/365 BCE but re-engraved around 150 CE.

25 *Contra* J. L. Sumney, *Colossians: A Commentary* (Louisville, KY: WJKP, 2008), 162; C. R. Campbell, *Colossians and Philemon: A Handbook on the Greek Text* (Waco, TX: Baylor University Press, 2013), 46–7.

cations for the exchange of letters mentioned in Col 4:16.[26] At the outset, we need to recognize just how fundamental these sacred laws were to the fabric of society and how critical they were to the maintenance of conventional life in the polis.

One recently published inscription from Tralles, dated to the second century (CE), foregrounds the interest of civic leaders in the maintenance of the sanctity and stature of social order.[27] Considerable attention is directed towards the regulation of movements, access and behaviors. The moral alarm at wayward comportment is clear but so too is the sense that power and accepted lines of authority were being challenged. The inscription is worth giving in full, if only because of Tralles' proximity (88 miles or about five days' walk) to Colossae on the direct route east from Ephesos. I have largely followed the translation of the editors, making minor adjustments to enhance the linguistic force of the decree and adding the missing, opening lines for which they confidently provide a reconstruction on the basis of other Tralleian inscriptions.[28]

> For good fortune. The following has been decided by the council (*Boulê*) and citizens' assembly (*Dêmos*)[29] — the proposal from Anthistios (?)[30] son of …, secretary to the *Dêmos* and Moschas, son of Dionysios, secretary to the *Boulê* — since the people have always revered the prudent and decent way of life of our fathers, who fashioned the city through laws and customs that were marked by purity; and since, pervaded by shamelessness, many outlandish immaturities have been ventured, so that even those who are unable to conceal that they have labored under every unmentionable outrage do not abstain either from the sanctuaries or the gymnasiums; but, on the

26 See chapter 4.

27 H. Malay, M. Ricl and D. Amendola, "The City of Tralleis combats Immorality: Measures taken against οἱ ἐν κιναιδείᾳ βιοῦντες in a new civic decree," *EA* 51 (2018): 91–7.

28 The reconstructed Greek text (removing sigla and accepting restorations of lacunae) reads: Ἀγαθῇ τύχῃ | ἔδοξε τῇ βουλῇ καὶ | τῷ δήμῳ Ἀνθιστίου […]ητος τοῦ γραμματέως | τοῦ δήμου καὶ Μοσχᾶ Διονυσίου | τοῦ γραμματέως τῆς βουλῆς καὶ τῶν | τῆς πόλεως ἀρχόντων γνώμη | ἐπεὶ τὴν σώφρονα καὶ δικαίαν ἀγωγὴν | ὁ δῆμος ἀεὶ τετείμηκεν τῶν πατέρων | ἔν τε νόμοις καὶ ἔθεσιν καθαροῖς δια- | κεκοσμηκότων τὴν πόλιν, πολλὰ | δὲ νεώτερα δι᾽ ἀναισχυντίας τε- | τόλμηται, ὥστε μήτε τῶν ἱερῶν | μήτε τῶν γυμνασίων ἀπέχεσθαι | τοὺς οὐδὲ λαθεῖν δυναμένους | ὅτι πᾶσαν ἄρρητον ὕβριν πεπόνθασιν | ἀλλ᾽ ὡς μήτε περιραντηρίων μήτε | νόμων κειμένων εἰσβιάζονται | ὅπου μὴ καλὸν μηδὲ ὅσιον αὐτοὺς | ὁρᾶσθαι, ὁ δὲ δῆμος οὕτως ἔρρωται | πρὸς εὐκοσμίαν ὥστε καὶ τὰς ἑται- | ρούσας ἀπὸ τῶν ἐπ᾽ ἀμφοδίων ἐλάσαι | ἀεὶ τόπων ἵνα μηδὲ μέχρις οὗ τι δόξῃ | τὸ σεμνὸν ἐνοχλῆται τῆς πόλεως, | δεδόχθαι ἱερῶν καὶ γυμνασίων ἀπ- | είγεσθαι τοὺς ἐν κιναιδείᾳ βιοῦντας, εἶναι δὲ ἐπιμελὲς τοῦτο …

29 The editors wonder whether the missing opening lines included a reference to the *Gerousia*, the council of elders. Some Tralleian prescripts do refer to this body (*I.Tralleis* 66, 67, 93).

30 The name is a conjecture. Spacing (possibly 14 letters on l. 1, and 7 following on l. 2) allows for a second name (perhaps a nickname using τοῦ λεγομένου, as in Col 4:11, or τοῦ καὶ) with the patronym ending in –ητος, if the pattern of Moschas's name is determinative. The options for the father's name are considerable, from a very short Ἄρης to the longer Ἀριστωμάνης. Alternately, there may be a grandfather's name added in the formula N + genitive of patronym + τοῦ + genitive of the grandfather's name.

> contrary, as if no lustration bowls[31] or laws are in place, they force their way in to where it is neither proper nor pious for them to be seen; accordingly, given that the people, so eager for public decency that they have already begun to drive the harlots from the alley holes they frequent lest even before a decision is promulgated, the reputation of the city be besmirched, it has been resolved that those engaged in an aberrant lifestyle are to be debarred from sanctuaries and gymnasiums and that this matter is to be the responsibility of [the appropriate officials, perhaps the *nomophylakes* or, less likely, the *paraphylakes*].[32]

When the writer of the Letter to the Colossians specifically mentions examples from sacred laws and goes on to judge them as destined for oblivion (εἰς φθοράν, Col 2:22), this is no light matter in the context of Colossian society and governance. It goes to one of the key instruments by which communal, moral life was ordered and civic power was exercised. And it challenges, as explicitly castigated in the Tralleian inscription above, anciently established conventions — whether "the fathers" of line 8 were a convenient fiction or a demonstrable influence from constant reiterations of practices from antiquity. There is a hidden irony in the assertion given that Tralles, according to one late account, had been devastated by earthquake and rebuilt by Augustus (in 26 BCE).[33] Ancient convention no doubt had become Romanized to some degree but thereby infused with greater potency as the eye of Rome was a keen adjudicator of the city's reputation. We ought then to examine the content of these sacred laws more closely, attending where possible to the very instances given in the text, for, as Andrej and Ivana Petrovic note in their extensive study of Greek sacred laws, "Touching, tasting (eating) and even smelling are in the extant Greek evidence all associated with notions of purity and pollution."[34]

---

31 These lustration bowls (*periranteria*) were small and portable, sometimes placed outside the entrance to a sanctuary, sometimes inside: *I.Pergamon* 2.336, ll. 6–7 (Pergamon: Roman imperial period); *I.Didyma* 346.

32 The text breaks off after "responsibility". Enforcement of local city law continued in the early empire (see chapter 11); these civic officials are common in Asia at this time, including in the Lycus Valley: from Laodikeia (*I.Laodikeia Lykos* 44, l. 2; 82, l. 8 second half of the 2nd century and 1st–2nd century respectively) and Hierapolis (*MAMA* 4.297, about 250 CE). Tralles attests the latter (*I.Tralleis* 145, l. 7, 2nd century). Both offices are attested at second-century Colossae: *IGR* 4.870. The *paraphylakes* were usually charged with the maintenance of order in a polis's *chora* territory. These are the more likely enforcement officers (given a city decree) rather than the "bouncers" (*hippoi*) sometimes appointed for infra-sanctuary maintenance of good order (*IG* II² 1368, l. 144). I owe this delightful translation to John Kloppenborg and Philip Harland in *Greco-Roman Associations I*, 248, 253, 255.

33 Agathias *Hist.* 2.17 (6th century); earthquake destruction at Tralles that attracted Augustus's rehabilitation is mentioned by Strabo 12.8.18.

34 A. and I. Petrovic, "On Ritual Pollution by Seeing: I.Lindos II 487.1–3 and Hdt. 2.37.5," *Gephyra* 11 (2014): 29.

The application of grasping, tasting, touching

From an early second-century (CE) *eranos*-club's sacred law at Attic Liopesi, the prohibition against grasping or seizing is directed towards misappropriation of club funds: μηθεὶς κατὰ μηδένα τρόπον ἁπτέσθω "let no one in any way whatsoever touch it [the endowment]."[35] But the same prohibition, that is "do not touch/grasp", is applied at the end of the sacred law list to wood from the group's sacred grove: μὴ ἐξέστω δὲ τῶν ἐν τῷ ἄλσι ξύλων ἅπτεσθαι ("It is not lawful to touch [steal/misappropriate?] the wood in the sacred grove").[36] The prohibition may be designed to ensure proper usage of the wood for cult activities (sacrifices or heating for rituals/feasts) or may simply be protection of the club's commercial dealings with timber. Other touch might be prohibited as a means of accenting the sanctity of a site, a statue, altar or the like.[37]

A much shorter sacred law list (though containing a reference to a longer inscription, line 13?) found near a village outside Thyateira to the north-west of Colossae, succinctly orders a series of requirements to be met for someone to be pure (ἁγνεύται). They are largely focused on washings and the passage of time before a worshipper might be permitted to enter the sanctuary (of an unnamed goddess). One cause of pollution calling for purificatory expiation is garlic. Having consumed garlic (σκόρδα φαγών), a devotee is required to wait three days before entering the sanctuary; however, merely touching garlic (ἐὰν δὲ ἅψηται) necessitates a ritual bath.[38] Garlic figures in a number of sacred law inscriptions hedging the purity of religious site and practice.[39] There is considerable speculation about the rationale, ranging from some mystical or sexual association to a simple demarcation from other cultic groups where garlic was consumed (for example, the Thesmophoria). There are also prohibitions in various religious groups against consuming a range of foods — lentils and beans, pork and goat[40] — but none consistently in every cult devoted to the same god. For all the refined explanations that have explored garlic and

---

35 *SEG* 31.122, ll. 11–12 (similarly ll. 13–14), translation from Kloppenborg and Ascough, *Greco-Roman Associations I*, 236.

36 Line 45, translation adjusted from Kloppenborg and Ascough.

37 For example, *CGRN* 225, Face B, l. 79 of an altar (Larisa, 225–150 BCE); H. Malay and G. Petzl, *New Religious Texts from Lydia* (Vienna: Österreichischen Akademie der Wissenshaften, 2019), 77. (Sanctuary of Artemis Anaitis and Meis Tiamou near Maionia in Lydia, Roman imperial period).

38 Malay-Petzl, *Lydia* 1, ll. 7–8.

39 *IG* II^2 1365, ll. 10–11 + 1366, l. 3, the cult of Mên Tyrannos at Laurion in Attica, 2nd to 3rd century CE; *CGRN* 225 (Larisa, 225–150 BCE)

40 See *CGRN* 203, l. 5 (Delos, prohibition on fish); *LSCG* 139 (Lindos, prohibition on lentils, goat meat, cheese); Pausanias 1.37.4 notes the prohibition on beans in the Demeter cult.

legumes,[41] there was also the mundane concern about the effect of such food on the body's digestive system[42] — religious devotion can be seriously detered when "unpleasing odours" become part of the worship![43] Temples after all were meant to be sweet-smelling (θυώδης).[44] Other polluting items for a particular cult's purity regimen were simply rattled off with a sequence of μηδέ/μήτε phrases, doubtless enforced by exegetes who presided in gatherings.[45]

Some inscriptions, related to the Thesmophoric festivals, expressly outlaw a range of women's fashions: lavish jewelry, brightly-colored or purple clothing, cosmetics (cf 1 Pet 3:3).[46] White clothing (across all classes) seems to have been the standard (cf Rev 3:4–5, 18, 4:4).[47] Given how important Demeter seems to have been for the woman responsible for reviving Colossae's mint, Claudia Eugenetoriane, it is highly likely that there was a strong, well-patronised and beneficed cult of Demeter at Colossae. When coins featuring Demeter were viewed, her clothing would have registered as white in color despite the bronze metal.

Plate 7.1: Relief of Demeter handing grain to the hero, Triptolemos,[48] for conveying to humankind. The presentation of Demeter here captures the iconographic elements found on a number of the coin types of Claudia Eugenetoriane at Colossae.[49] The relief, now in the museum at Aphrodisias, originally formed part of the complex aesthetics of the first-century Sebasteion at the city, clearly linking the myth of the divine beneficence of agricultural prosperity with the advent of the Roman empire.

41 See the study by M. Kleijwegt, "Beans, Baths and the Barber … A Sacred Law from Thurburbo Maius," *Antiquités africaines* 30 (1994): 209–20.

42 See Petronius *Satyr.* 47.

43 Plutarch *Quaest. Rom.* 286E "the flatulent quality of the food stimulates desire(!)". Compare Martial *Ep.* 12.32 on garlic as the stinking food of the poor man.

44 Porphyry *Abst.* 2.19; *LSCG Suppl* 108, ll. 4–5 (Rhodes, 1st century CE).

45 *CGRN* 181 (Eresos, 2nd to 1st century BCE); *CGRN* 191 (Philadelphia, 125–75 BCE). See also, for the Eleusinian mysteries at Athens, J. H. Oliver and B. D. Meritt, "Greek Inscriptions," *Hesperia* 10 (1941): 65–72, nr. 31, ll. 37–8 where pollutions/offences are listed about transgressing space in initiation ceremonies of the first century BCE.

46 *CGRN* 127, ll. 3–8 (Dyme 300–200 BCE) cf *CGRN* 126, ll. 4–7 (Lykosoura, 3rd century BCE, for the cult of Despoina, one of Demeter's daughter); *CGRN* 222, A, ll. 22 (Andania, 23 CE?).

47 Elsewhere, white clothing was used as a mark of high status: *CGRN* 221, ll. 22–3 (Kos, 125–100 BCE) or specifically prescribed for initiates: *CGRN* 222 A ll. 15–16.

48 On Triptolemos, see I. K. and A. E. Raubitschek, "The Mission of Triptolemos," *Hesperia Supplements* 20 (1982): 109–17, 207–8.

49 See chapter 1.

And finally, there are the mystery cult regulations which often did not disclose the prohibitions and injunctions but simply, as in the first-century lengthy regulations at Andania (near Polichne in southern Greece), referred obliquely to another inscribed set of sacred laws (apparently available only to the initiated and those whom they were preparing): "They [the mystery cult officials — οἱ ἱεροί] also are to record publicly from what one must be pure and what one must not have in order to enter."[50]

Sometimes the prohibition against tasting/eating was directly related to the status as an uninitiated novice: ὁ δὲ τελισκόμενος μὴ γευέστω "let the one being initiated not taste it [a sacrificed bird used in the rite of initiation]. Subsequently however, but when instructed, the novice is to consume certain bread and wine."[51] Other cults might also expressly require the ingestion of some foods that other groups outlawed, a strong indication that groups were more concerned about their distinctiveness than striving for universal consistency. Theodore of Mopsuestia's shift to an injunction (*hoc manduca*) in his paraphrase of the text's prohibition of tasting/eating (Col 2:21) accurately reflects what is found in the various sacred regulations — eat this but not now or not that. Similarly, there are moments when touch *is* demanded as a response, as in the regulations of a private cult association where assent to the stipulations is signalled by touching the stele on which the inscription is carved: ἁπτέσθωσαν, ὅσοι πιστεύουσιν ἑαυτοῖς ἄνδρες τε καὶ γυναῖκες, τῆς γραφῆς ταύτης "They are to touch this writing, such men and women as assent to the stipulations."[52]

The difference between ἅπτομαι and θιγγάνω is sometimes framed in terms of intensity,[53] though we have seen already the broad semantic range of the former word in the applications it covers in the purity codes displayed in temples and religious groups. This may explain why the extant sacred laws rarely use θιγγάνω or its cognates.[54] However, this is not dismiss its use in Col 2:21. Extant inscriptions reveal how much "religion" cannot be confined to a small parcel of life but colored many aspects of society that were not necessarily directly implicated in temples or religious clubs.[55]

---

50 *SIG* 2.736, l. 37, ἀναγραψάντω δὲ καί, ἀφ' ὧν δεῖ καθαρίζειν καὶ ἃ μὴ δεῖ ἔχοντας εἰσπορεύεσθαι. Translation from M. W. Meyers (ed.), *The Ancient Mysteries: A Sourcebook* (New York: HarperCollins, 1987), 54.

51 *CGRN* 225 Face A, ll. 23–4; cf also l. 35 (of sacrificed meat). Consuming bread and wine under instruction: ll. 25–6.

52 *TAM* V,3 1539 ll. 55–7 (Philadelphia, late 2nd to early 1st century BCE).

53 See, among a number of commentators, Foster, *Colossians*, 299.

54 See however, A. Chaniotis, *Die Verträge zwischen kretischen Poleis in der hellenistischen Zeit* (Stuttgart: Steiner, 1996), nr. 54/56 testimonium b (Crete, 115 BCE).

55 Compare however, where specific instructions are given for dealing with the burial of a revered priestess, including that nothing foul was to be allowed to touch/remain on (here: ἔστω) the corpse (*CGRN* 213, l. 14 (Pedlenissos, first century BCE).

Funerary monuments, for example, were always given a sanctity both in appearance and in reverence. The prohibitions "do not open, do not touch" (μήτε ἀνοίξαι μήτε θιγείν)[56] recognize and confer the sacrality attached to the dead and their placement. The same reverential treatment could also color a stone that recorded a supplication to the gods — the inscription could end with μὴ θίγης.[57] Such sentiments are found in the famous mis-named "Nazareth Inscription" — an imperial rescript (probably from Augustus in or just after 20 BCE). In it, damage to a tomb is compared to outrage against the gods (καθάπερ περὶ θεῶν).[58]

Similarly, the manumission of slaves, especially in Greece and Asia, frequently was executed and recorded at temples where the dedication to the god(s) of the one being freed secured a divine sanctity designed to prevent any attempt to return them to incarceration. This was conveyed, in some places, by the prohibition against "laying a finger on" (ἐπιθιγγάνω).[59] A different but striking example comes from a poem on the duties of a physician where the doctor is enjoined neither to look upon or touch (or look upon in order to touch: μηδ᾽ἐσιδῆν θιγέην) a patient in any manner that contravened divine laws or the oath.[60] Presumably the prohibition was derived from (or was presented as deriving from) sacred law.[61]

The small number of inscriptions from Colossae has yet to include an example of such sacred laws. However, their prevalence across the Mediterranean world in a period covering almost a millennium suggests that this is simply an accident of restricted discovery. One can join Theodore of Mopsuestia in recognizing the three items in Col 2:21 as examples representing a vast array of purity regulations, as much present in Colossae as elsewhere in the Mediterranean world — indeed this is likely to be conveyed by the ἅ … πάντα immediately following in v.22. And we can also accept that injunctions as well as prohibitions were incorporated in such requirements.

56 *I.Anazarbos* 135, ll. 21–2 (Anazarbos in east Cilicia, 101 CE) cf *IG* XIV 319 (Thermai Himeraiai, Roman imp.) where the prohibition seems more to address the one grieving (μή με λυπήσης θιγών cf Jn 21:17 where μή μου ἅπτου is used); see also *IGLS* 4.1297 (Gabala, nd). The epitaphal prohibition from Anazarbos is reinforced by a curse on the offender's children and enjoyment of life (ll. 22–25) and possibly more — the inscription breaks off here.

57 *I.Olympia* 644 (Elis, Roman imp.), a recorded prayer for mercy to Olympian Zeus.

58 Oliver, *Greek Constitutions*, 2, l. 15. On the basis of a stable isotope analysis of the stone, the inscription is now more securely placed as directed to the inhabitants of the island of Kos, probably following the desecration of the grave of the tyrant Nikias. See K. Harper *et al*, "Establishing the provenance of the Nazareth Inscription: Using stable isotopes to resolve a historic controversy and trace ancient marble production," *JAS: Reports* 30 (2020): 1–7.

59 *IG* V 2.429 ll. 5–6 (Arkadia, nd).

60 *SEG* 28.225 (Athens, 220 CE).

61 See J. H. Oliver, "An Ancient Poem on the Duties of a Physician," *Bulletin of the History of Medicine* 7 (1939): 315–23.

From purity and pollution to penalties and power

Here we begin to return to the question of a sacralized economy, given that with so many prohibitions, one wonders at the level and nature of enforcement that might attend some infraction. Of course, the threat of divine wrath was directly expressed or assumed. The incitement of God's wrath towards attitudes and behaviors that belong to the realm of the earth (τὰ ἐπὶ τῆς γῆς) found in Col 3:5–6 would have been completely at home among most cultic teaching. One third-century (CE) text from Lindos on the island of Rhodes, reproduces earlier stipulations. It calls for purification from all that incites divine wrath (ἀπὸ παντὸς ἐναγοῦς … κεκαθαρμένους) and it is clear that moral turpitude was as much in mind as ritual pollution.[62] Impurity (ἀκαθαρσία) in the context of Col 3:5,[63] probably has both elements in mind as well, since the boundaries between cultic and moral pollution were frequently blurred. One brief inscription from Laodikeia may well show this liminal territory: a certain Epaphras recorded his consecration to Zeus and Hermes (and possibly Semele)[64] but then added an expansive word of advice (based on his own experience?), that "whoever wants to make an oath should, maintaining his purity, sacrifice an animal as an oath-offering."[65] The force of this sacrifice (not distributed for communal consumption, but devoted to the god alone) underscores the sacredness of the oath; purity seems to be attached to the sanctity of oath-keeping not (or not only) the unpolluted state in which one ought to make a sacrifice.

The Letter to the Colossians in this sense is not setting forth a novel understanding of purity, but rather participating in developments that had been unfolding for two or more centuries. Nevertheless, the advent of wrath and its expiation might be all too temporal and mundane, rather than deferred to some eschatological horizon. At the sanctuary of Apollo Lairbenos, about 43 miles to Colossae's north-west, high on a spur above the Maeander River, have been found many examples of the dumping of one or other god's wrath on some miscreant. These so-called "Confession inscriptions" relate the (usually) physical injury or disease that an individual (usually) has suffered and how it was expiated by some action, including, notably, the placement of a stele of record

62 *LSCG Suppl.* 91.4–5, following the interpretation of Andrej and Ivana Petrovic, *Inner Purity and Pollution*, 1.286.

63 Νεκρώσατε οὖν τὰ μέλη τὰ ἐπὶ τῆς γῆς, πορνείαν ἀκαθαρσίαν πάθος ἐπιθυμίαν κακήν, καὶ τὴν πλεονεξίαν, ἥτις ἐστὶν εἰδωλολατρία (Col 3:5).

64 The reconstruction of the line is debated; however, the stone itself has a number of crudely executed symbols that suggest an indigenous connection.

65 ὁ θέλων ὁρκίζειν ἁγνῶς μείνας θύσει σφάγιον ὅρκιον. *I.Laodikeia Lykos* 64 = *MAMA* 6.1 = *LSAM* 88 (1st century CE).

in the sanctuary's precincts.[66] One such fragmentary inscription yet retains the striking wording "I, N [lacuna in text] son of Klaros admit that I went unclean onto the (sanctuary's) land …".[67] Uncleanness, whether worded by this inscription's ἄναγνος or the Colossian Letter's ἀκαθαρσία (Col 3:5) was a serious business that caught the attention of the deity and warranted public warning.[68]

Often enough, the religious institution was not prepared to wait for divine wrath to unveil but took the initiative to enforce the regulations. Sometimes, this might be done by reference to local court jurisdiction,[69] although some groups, even in Athens with its long history of *polis* court involvement in religious decisions,[70] preferred to keep such adjudications in-house (*IG* II^2 1368, ll. 90–4 cf 1 Cor 6:1–7).[71] Most commonly, there were three main recourses for dealing with pollution and infractions: time, water, compensation.

The first was simply the passing of time, usually measured in days, after which a member or devotee was declared fit to join cultic activities. Offences that attracted this atoning variation on the observance of days were frequently attached to those matters that clearly differentiated gods from humans — death, reproduction, sexual intercourse, bodily fluxes.[72] Thus, the second century (CE) Dionysiac cult at Smyrna prescribed forty days' absence from the sanctuary *temenos* and shrines for exposing an infant or for contact with an abortion (ἔκτρωσις — possibly meaning miscarriage) but three days for contact with a corpse not of one's own household.[73] Other groups had sacred laws that were not so arduous in their regulation of absence — one day for intercourse with one's wife or husband; two days if with another woman or man besides one's spouse![74]

The second was to require washings or lustrations. The Tralles inscription previously noted singles out "lustration vessels" (περιραντηρίοι, along with sacred laws and sacred spaces) as ignored by those disrupting the traditional values of the city and its

66 See A. H. Cadwallader, "Bodily Display and Epigraphical Confession at the Sanctuary of Apollo Lairbenos: an examination of emotional responses," *JES* 1 (2018): 183–201 and the bibliography there cited.

67 Petzl, *Beichtinschriften* 116 = *MAMA* 4.289.

68 As is also found in the inscription of a penitent at Apollo Lairbenos: παραγέλων πᾶσι μηδὲ ἄναγον ἀναβῆτ' ἐπὶ τὸ χωρίον … "I warn everyone not to go up to the sacred precinct unclean … (Petzl, *Beichtinschriften* 110, ll. 5–7, 3rd century CE). The subsequent two lines may provide insight into what the penitent meant by "uncleanness", warning against committing perjury or engaging in sexual intercourse, at least just before approaching the god.

69 See L. B. Zuidman and P. S. Pantel, *Religion in the Ancient Greek City* translated by P. Cartledge (Cambridge: Cambridge University Press, 1992), 9–15. This concern of the city for the proper observance of religious rites is widespread.

70 See *IG* I^2 188 (Athens before 460 BCE).

71 Compare also F. Guizzi, "Novità epigrafiche da Hierapolis di Frigia." *Historika* 7 (2017): 119–30 nr. 1, l. 13 (2nd century CE).

72 Susan G. Cole, "*Gynaiki Ou Themis*: Gender Differences in the Greek *Leges Sacrae*," *Helios* 19 (1992): 107.

73 *I.Smyrna* 728 ll. 2–9; cf *CGRN* 225 B l. 26 (Larisa, 225–150 BCE).

74 *CGRN* 212, ll. 4–6 (Pergamon; after 133 BCE).

fathers. This requirement of washing could be compounded with the passage of time,[75] just as fines might also be involved. Unlike the impositions of the Dionysiac cult just mentioned, corpse contact for members of the Athena Nikephoros cult at Pergamon could be alleviated by washing on the same day as the contraction of pollution.[76] Such applications of water were often symbolic, involving perhaps sprinklings. But water-supply was safeguarded, sometimes even with the express regulatory or policing intervention by civic authorities.[77] The presence of large krater-style basins, especially near the *temenos* entrance, was crucial as a provision for members to expiate the polluting offence that may be identified or admitted.[78] All such requirements, identifications and provisions were the pragmatic particulars that enabled a cult to bolster the sense of the sacred, of the divine management of time, space and movement.

Plate 7.2: A damaged lustration basin in a storage yard at Aphrodisias. The central shield-boss is inscribed with a brief dedication, from a certain N. son of Sphêkas (?) who provided the loutron.[79] The letter shapes suggest a second century (CE) date. The longevity of the practice is indicated by the red-figure painting on a Boeotian bell-krater, dated to 450–425 BCE, held at the Louvre (CA 1341).

75 *CGRN* 214, ll. 9–10 (Miletos, 75–1 BCE).

76 *CGRN* 212, ll. 7–9.

77 The regulations from Andania mention the responsibilities of the *agoranomos* to ensure the ready access to water resources for the festival (*CGRN* 222, ll. 103–5).

78 The cult of Athena Nikephoros at Pergamon mentions the place where the *hagistêria* (another term for receptacles of water) are placed (*CGRN* 212, ll. 8–9). One such basin still graces the forecourt of St. Demetrios Church in Thessalonike. It is considerably cracked and thus communicates its water-conferring sanctity through the imagination!

79 The inscription has not, to my knowledge, been published. My photograph does not enable greater precision in identifying the donor. ἀνέθηκεν has a centuries-long testimony to its use for dedications: pottery graffiti with the formula from Mount Hymettos in Greece date back to the 8th or 7th century BCE; see M. K. Langdon, *A Sanctuary of Zeus on Mount Hermettos* (Hesperia Supp XVI; Princeton, NJ: American School of Classical Studies at Athens, 1976), 13–19.

The third expiation for purity offences involved the payment of fines. One purity regulation from Astypalaia is conveniently brief, "Whoever is not pure shall not enter the temple, otherwise he will pay a fine or else it will disturb his mind" ([ἐ]ς τὸ ἱερὸν μὴ ἐσέρπεν ὅστις μὴ ἁγνός ἐστι, ἤ τελεῖ ἤ αὐτῶι ἐν νῶι ἐσσεῖται).[80] Whilst the brevity leaves more questions unanswered than clarity might desire, it states unequivocally that the payment of money overcomes offences against purity. Of course it was easier to fine for pollution when specific physical actions of grasping, tasting and touching were in view, but fines could be imposed for singing out of turn, for failure to attend a funeral or a group meeting, for fighting or yelling abuse.[81] These penalties were often considerable. One governance of donated meeting-rooms for a synagogue in Macedonia prescribes a fine of a staggering 250,000 denarii for the attempt to introduce a novelty (τι καινοτομῆσαι) — a manifest deterrent![82] But others were clearly more modest, within reach of those far lower in the pay-grade. At Marmarina, near Larisa, where there was a second century (BCE) cult of an (unidentified) goddess, one penalty required merely a half-obol and an intact flat-bread for daring to gnaw at ritual bread prior to initiation.[83]

However, the sizable gap in amounts for financial penalties suggests a hierarchy between various temples and religious groups based on the status, wealth and location of its members. Even those groups that had slaves in their membership (probably paid for by their masters), built the traditional class hierarchy into the payments. A free person might be fined 20 drachmas for illicit interference with the water supply but a slave's penalty would be a flogging.[84] And if a slave caused some injury or damage (such as theft) and the master refused to make financial amends, the slave was to be handed over to the victim to work off the debt (εἰς ἀπεργασίαν).[85] The second-century BCE sacred constitution from a rural shrine near Thyateira neatly provides the financial value attached to flogging. Polluted entrance to the shrine incurred a fine of a silver mina, that is, about 100 drachmas. This was the judgment upon a free person. But an offending slave was to be lashed, each stroke being assessed at 3 obols (or about 6 assaria). If the slave survived the punishment, she (the word used is θεράπαινα) would have endured 600 lashes![86]

80 *IG* XII 3.183 (after 300 BCE).

81 See *IG* II^2 1368, ll. 73–90 (Athens, 164/5 CE), *IG* IX 12.670, l. 10–14 (Physkos, mid-2nd century CE).

82 *I.Jud. Orientis* 1, Mac 1, ll. 24–8 (Stobi, 2nd to 3rd century CE).

83 *CGRN* 225 A, l. 30 (225–150 BCE). One wonders at the asceticism — or perhaps curiosity — that might drive such hunger for an aspiring μύστης.

84 On the foundational differentiation of free and slave, see A. H. Cadwallader, "Complicating class in the Letter to Philemon: a prolegomenon," in *The Struggle over Class: Socioeconomic Analysis of Ancient Jewish and Christian Texts* edited by G. A. Keddie, M. Flexsenhar and S. J. Friesen (Atlanta, GA: SBL, 2021), 95–122.

85 *CGRN* 222 A ll. 76–8, 105–6 (Andania, 23 CE?). Significantly, in the instance of the temporary slave hand-over, he is called an οἰκέτης, which, though often an undifferentiated synonym of δοῦλος (used elsewhere in the inscription), seems here to indicate a house-servant or one who would perform the servile duties of an attendant. Onesimos in some subscripts to manuscripts of the Letter to Philemon is designated an οἰκέτης.

86 Malay–Petzl, *Lydia* 1, ll. 18–20.

These financial returns to a temple or religious association were supplementary to other income streams — the commercialization of "sacred lands" through leaseholds or marketing of produce; the repayments of principal and interest on loans negotiated primarily with (credentialed) devotees and members; and the benefactions that various wealthy patrons or members bestowed.[87] Both financial penalties and loan repayments were frequently expressed as monies owed to the particular deity who was the central focus of the group.[88] Thus the civic coins stamped with some deity or other were made yet more sacred by their incorporation into the fulfillment of cultic demands.[89] If the wrath of the god against a non-payment or non-performance had been diagnosed, then appeasement (ἱλάσκομαι) could come through the payment of a "ransom" (λύτρον).[90]

Perhaps most significantly of all, those high-ranking officials of the cult, especially the chief priestess or priest, derived considerable financial benefit from the position they held,[91] in addition to the public honors that attended the position.[92] Little wonder then, that even though they were expected to outlay some benefits for the sanctuary and cultic operations,[93] there was considerable competition for the purchase of priesthoods when vacancies arose.[94] One Timaios, son of Straton, surprised both the temple officials and contemporary commentators when he laid out the princely sum of seven gold and 60 bronze pieces in payment for the priesthood, "which he paid immediately" (οὓς ἔδωκε παραχρῆμα).[95]

---

87 See for example, on leaseholds and marketing *I.Beroia* 22 (7 BCE); on loans *CGRN* 195 frag. A, ll. 6–7 (Amorgos, 1st century BCE); on private munificence *IG* II² 1271, ll. 9–14 (Piraeus, 299/8 BCE). For a significant benefaction (involving buildings, statues, workshops, vineyards and slaves), see M. Ricl and E. Akıncı Öztürk, "A New Benefactor from the Upper Meander Valley (Çal Ovaşı)," *EA* 47 (2014): 16–20 (Atyochorion, 2nd century CE). See generally P. M. Nigdelis, "Voluntary Associations in Roman Thessalonikê: In Search of Identity and Support in a Cosmopolitan Society," in *From Roman to Early Christian Thessalonikê* edited by L. Nasrallah, C. Bakirtzis and S. J. Friesen (HTS 64; Cambridge, MA: Harvard University Press, 2010), 25–6.

88 This is especially so, but not confined to, texts speaking of a ransom paid to the god.

89 See generally Pafford, "Priestly Portion vs. Cult Fees" (*loc. cit.*).

90 Malay-Petzl, *Lydia* 116, ll. 7–8 (173/4 CE); cf nr. 78, ll. 4–5 (215/2 CE), 80, ll. 4–5 (Roman imperial period).

91 See, for example, *CGRN* 195 frag. B2, ll. 25–6 (Amorgos, 1st century bce).

92 See, for example, the Amorion civic honours for Aelia Ammia, who, among a set of stereotyped attributes, was hailed as high priestess of the greatest temples in Ephesos: *I.Amorium* 17 (160 CE).

93 *I.Amorium* 101 (Roman imperial period).

94 For an example of the formal sale terms for a priesthood, see *CGRN* 218 (Kos, 125–75 BCE). See generally, Beate Dignas, *The Economy of the Sacred in Hellenistic and Roman Asia Minor* (Oxford: Oxford University Press, 2002), 251–3.

95 *CGRN* 123, ll. 15–17 (Tomis, 150–50 BCE).

Bronze coinage, the record of debt and the sacred, and a Christian repudiation

The mention of τριωβελιαίαι, three obols, in the Thyateiran sacred law points to the understanding of the recognition and acceptance of bronze coins in religious life and practice. In fact, one cultic regulation from Eresos quite specifically mentions bronze coins as permitted to be carried into the sanctuary as an exception to a general prohibition, *inter alia*, on iron and bronze (probably weapons): [μη]δὲ εἰς τὸν ναῦον εἰσφέρην σίδαρον μηδὲ χάλκον πλὰν νομίσματος.[96] Even though membership of cultic groups was measured, usually, in drachmas or denarii,[97] there were ongoing costs consequent upon membership — the purchase of wine for gatherings, of items for sacrifice or of religious trinkets for sale in the markets set up for festive panegyrics, even "thanksgivings" for the birth of children (two drachmas for a son, one drachma for a daughter!).[98] Bronze coins were sometimes mentioned explicitly — seven bronze obols (χαλκῶν ἑπτ᾽ ὀβολούς) to be set aside as part of the offerings in the rites of sacrifice to Sarapis.[99] Some items were demanded and failure to make the appropriate transaction invited a fine which, on further non-payment, could result in suspension or expulsion from membership (for debt default, for example).[100] Accrued debts were sometimes inscribed for display in a group's meeting place, a naming and potential shaming incentive to repayment (cf Phmn 18–19). One inscription uses the term κοινωνία of the group to which the debt is owed — with the stele of debt record to be set up "by the altar in the temple".[101] Priests and priestesses were also to be paid for their role in ensuring that sacrifices were made decently and in good order. All these matters were commonly measured in bronze currency.[102] Even though the terminology is usually "obols" for these bronze coins, such language frequently continued on in Roman imperial times, often as a loose word for bronze coins formally measured as *assaria/assarii*.[103]

---

96 *CGRN* 181, ll. 15–17 (Eresos, 2nd to 1st century BCE).

97 50 denarii (with some variations) for membership in the Dionysiac cult in Athens in the mid-second century: *IG* II² 1368, ll. 37–8, 55; fines however were measured in "light drachmas" (probably a bronze coin value, so that 25 light drachmas amounted to just over 4 denarii).

98 *P.Mich.* 5.243, ll. 5–6 (Tebtynis, time of Tiberius).

99 *CGRN* 157, l. 21 (Priene, c. 200 BCE).

100 *IG* II² 1368, ll. 45–7.

101 *LSCG Suppl.* 20, ll. 3, 5–6 (Athens, early 3rd century BCE).

102 *CGRN* 163 (Kos, 1st century BCE).

103 K. W. Harl, *Coinage in the Roman Economy, 300 B.C. to A.D. 700* (Baltimore: Johns Hopkins University Press, 1996), 116–17; J. H. Kroll, "Hemiobols to Assaria: the Bronze Coinage of Roman Aigion," *NC* 156 (1996): 54–5.

There is one final matter to be expanded that is related to this question of debt in the context of religious practice.[104] Debt, however acquired in relation to a temple or religious association, was recorded. This was not merely the debt document (whether mortgage, contractual obligation, lease, loan or whatever) but an acknowledgement *that* the debt had been entered. The use of the term χειρόγραφον in Col 2:14 has usually been taken by Second Testament commentators as a private, hand-written note, succinctly abbreviated as an IOU,[105] not unlike Paul's brief self-insertion into the transcription of the Letter to Philemon (v.19).[106] But χειρόγραφον in Col 2:14 is interpreted as a metaphor illustrating the debt incurred by human sin.[107] Of course, as Julien Ogereau admits whilst reinforcing the traditional reading, the problems of a private document in a public context trouble interpreters, that is, legal demands (as the rendition of τοῖς δόγμασιν); to whom the debt might be owed; a nailing of the document to the cross; what is the nature of the cancellation, and so on.[108] But what is clear is that it is the χειρόγραφον that "stood over against us" (ὃ ἦν ὑπεναντίον ἡμῖν, Col 2:14a), *not*, as would be more familiar in the Pauline corpus, the (Mosaic) laws.[109]

Whatever may have been the original use and etymology of the term χειρόγραφον, it has long been recognized that such linguistic considerations are neither trans-temporally fixed nor do they necessarily operate flatly in a given context.[110] By the first and second centuries CE, Roman law had begun to note and use *chirographa*.[111] These documents may have, generally, been connected to small proprietorial amounts,[112] but they had begun to attract archival, not merely, personal record. Archival registration might simply mean the records kept by a religious group or temple, but on occasions these χειρόγραφα were kept in civic archives. Indeed, one papyrus carries a petition that a *cheirographon* be registered in the archives of the city of Alexandria.[113] In this sense, a χειρόγραφον has moved from a hand-written note (though these did

104 We shall have reason to return to the issue of sacred regulations in the context of house groups below.

105 See S. Llewelyn in *New Doc. Early Christ.* 6.18; J. Ogereau, "Χειρόγραφον in Colossians 2:14. The Contribution of Epigraphy to the Philology of the New Testament," in *Epigraphical Evidence Illustrating Colossians*, 93–121.

106 See Arzt-Grabner, *Philemon*, 240–4.

107 R. Yates, "Colossians 2,14: Metaphor of Forgiveness," *Biblica* 71 (1990): 248–59.

108 Ogereau, "Χειρόγραφον," 97–9, 121.

109 So Sumney, *Colossians*, 145. On the importance of Torah for Paul, see J. Svartvik, "'East is East and West is West:' The Concept of Torah in Paul and Mark," in *Paul and Mark: Comparative Essays, Part I: Two Authors at the Beginnings of Christianity* edited by O. Wischmeyer, D. C. Sim and I. J. Elmer (BZNW 198; Berlin: de Gruyter, 2014), 157–85.

110 See A. H. Cadwallader, "Keeping Lists or Embracing Freedom: 1 Corinthians 6:9–10 in Context," in *Five Uneasy Pieces* edited by N. McI. Wright (Adelaide: ATF Press, 2011), 47–54.

111 *Inst. Gai.* 3.134.

112 As, for example, *T.Sulpicii* 54 (a loan acknowledgement of 2000 sestertii).

113 *P.Meyer* 6 (mid-second century CE).

continue) to the technical terminology classifying a legal or quasi-legal document, *regardless of what medium held the record*. There is some suggestion that it was sometimes an additional note, a plate or an inscription added to the conclusion of a proprietorial document. This addendum formalized assent to the terms conveyed in the document; hence there was a two-step, two-document process involved.

We have seen already the regular instruction that various sacred laws, memberships and debts were to be inscribed on *stelai* which were then to be prominently placed in a temple, religious group meeting room or even in the agora or theater.[114] We ought not expect that in every instance, the inscription was neatly recorded or maintained. The famous list of officers of one of the twelve Dionysos associations known from Thessalonike (*IG* X 2 1s.1077) is notable for the great variety of stone-cutters' styles, not only in the letter shapes and sizes but in the disregard for margins.[115] We need to recognize that even on stone, we are frequently encountering "working documents", not drafts but certainly not sacrosanct in their text as, by contrast, we frequently find with epitaphs and honorific dedications.

Plate 7.3: The two-column list of officials in a Dionysos association from Thessalonike which contains names (including two which betray a Phrygian origin) and positions held. Different names and positions have been added at various times. One presumes that, eventually, if the association continued, a re-vamped update would have been necessary.

The *Lex Familiae Silvani* from Trebula Mutuesca to the north-east outside of Rome seems to have been set into a simple partition wall near a river, probably the site where members of the association met. It is known from two sections, the later one (at the left in the Pl. 7.4) dated to 60 CE.

114 See K. Harter-Uibopuu, "Epigraphische Quellen zum Archivwesen in den griechischen Poleis des ausgehenden Hellenismus und der Kaiserzeit," in *Archives and Archival Documents in Ancient Societies* edited by M. Faraguna (Trieste: Università di Trieste, 2013), 288–90 on the inscriptions from the theater in Delphi recording *cheirographa* of dedications/manumissions of slaves.

115 The most thorough study of the inscription is found in P. M. Nigdelis, Επιγραφικά Θεσσαλονίκεια (Thessalonikê: University Studio Press, vol 1, 2006), 101–28.

Plate 7.4: The *Lex Familiae Silvani*, now in the Muzeo Nazionale, Rome. Erasures of names can be seen in column 3, ll. 9, 11, 14, 15, column 4, ll. 6, 13 and column 5, ll. 3, 16, with new names written where former members' names had stood.[116]

The *lex sacra* prescribes penalties for infringement of various requirements (failure to contribute to a member's burial expenses, for example). Peter Dorcey implies that the erasures evident in the inscription were the names of deceased members. John Kloppenborg, however, considers that these had been members who had either withdrawn or been expelled.[117] The latter is more likely given that this association seems to have cultivated household memberships. Here then, in an outdoor setting, was an association's inscription that was, even so, not always "set in stone," as indicated by its erasures!

Sometimes, bronze was the medium for inscription, both of sacred law and of archival record.[118] A most significant imperial rescript from the emperor Tiberius to the city of Gytheion in Laconia lays out the sacred regulations for the imperial cult, most especially providing extensive instruction for a feast with thylemic contests. The term χειρόγραφον occurs in the text, in a context arranging the transfer of the office of *agoranomos* (whom, we have seen,

116 Compare Rev 3:5.

117 P. F. Dorcey, *The Cult of Silvanus: A Study in Roman Folk Religion* (Leiden: Brill, 1992), 86; J. S. Kloppenborg, *Christ's Associations: Connecting and Belonging in the Ancient City* (New Haven, CN: Yale University Press, 2019), 70.

118 See *SEG* 41.284 (Argos, 450 BCE and 300 BCE); *SEG* 31.315 (5th century BCE). See generally, J. H. Kroll, *Athenian Bronze Allotment Plates* (Cambridge, MA: Harvard University Press, 1972) for a sense of the ubiquity of usage.

is often given responsibility for the function of sacred festivals).[119] An inventory of equipment for the festival games connected with the imperial cult is to accompany the transfer of office. This is called a "public record" (διὰ γραφῆς δημοσίας). A related χειρόγραφον is to be given to the city (ll. 23–4). Oliver translates χειρόγραφον here as a "copy in writing".[120] This seems to deliver a redundant meaning given the prior mention of διὰ γραφῆς δημοσίας. Rather, it is likely that the χειρόγραφον has taken on the sense of an oath or declaration of acknowledgement attesting the fidelity of the requisite inventory of transfer. The same acknowledgement occurs for minor tax dues. One such document expressly opens with a reference to a copy of an acknowledgement (ἀντίγραφον χειρογράφου) deposited in some archive.[121]

This is precisely the argument developed by Kyu Seop Kim,[122] though without referring to this inscription and papyrus. This section of the imperial rescript falls within a larger set of instructions which are called, in their entirety, "sacred law" (ἱερὸς νομός, l. 37). It includes not only the reference to the χειρόγραφον but to provisions for the games — *inter alia*, paintings of the imperial family, an orchestra platform and "foot-stompers", the ones responsible for maintaining rhythms for dances and songs! It also sets down penalties for non-observance of certain sacrifices in the celebrations (ll. 30–3). But most significantly, all this sacred law is required, as part of the self-referentiality of the rescript, to be set up on a marble stele (στήλην λιθίνην, ll. 36–7), a copy of which is to be placed in the public registry (the γραμματοφυλάκια, l. 37), "in order that in a public building and in the open air where it is visible to all, the law which is in force may make apparent to all humanity the gratitude of the *Dêmos* of the Gytheates toward the rulers".[123] Here a public record, that includes references to a χειρόγραφον and to penalties, is set up for all to see and to assent to as divine law. Recordings of debts on stelai and bronze,[124] probably within temple precincts or an association's rooms, that we have previously noted, are here writ large. Tralles' sacred law gained civic recognition and defence; Gytheion attracted imperial authorization and arrangement.

119 Oliver, *Greek Constitutions*, 15, l. 24. It should also be noted that some associations adopted civic terminology for the officers of the organization. Context allows decision but sometimes the distinction is blurred.

120 Oliver, *Greek Constitutions*, p. 62.

121 *P.Col.* 8.223 (Tebtynis, 138–161 CE).

122 K. S. Kim, "The Meaning of Χειρόγραφον in Colossians 2:14 revisited," *TynBull* 68 (2017): 223–39.

123 ἵνα καὶ ἐν δημοσίωι καὶ ἐν ὑπαίθρῳ καὶ πᾶσιν ἐν φανερῷ κείμενος ὁ νόμος διηνεκῆ τὴν τοῦ δήμου τοῦ Γυθεατῶν εὐχαριστίαν εἰς τοὺς ἡγεμόνας παρέχῃ πᾶσιν ἀνθρώποις. Oliver's translation is given, slightly adjusted (*Greek Constitutions*, p. 63).

124 And probably also papyri as in *P.Lond.* 7.2193, which seems to have been a member's copy. The original editors noted that the regulations set down for this association for Zeus Hypsistos were in the same hand as the accounts on the verso side of the sheet. See C. Roberts, T. C. Skeat and A. D. Nock, "The Guild of Zeus Hypsistos," *HTR* 29 (1936): 54–5.

The expansive vista of Col 2:15 (ἐδειγμάτισεν ἐν παρρησίᾳ) is not so exaggerated by comparison to these public arraignments, even if "all humanity" of the imperial rescript has been magnified to embrace the very cosmic forces — the "principalities and powers" (αἱ ἀρχαὶ καὶ αἱ ἐξουσίαι) — appealed to in general cultic (and sometimes philosophic)[125] observance. The proclamation has now moved beyond Gytheion's "all humanity" to the whole creation/every creature under heaven (ἐν πάσῃ κτίσει τῇ ὑπὸ τὸν οὐρανόν Col 1:23). This is more than supercessionism, the supplanting of one empire by another; it renders not only empire, but the religions that such an empire has abrogated into its service, as no more than contingent aspirations, temporally confined and spatially limited, destined for oblivion — as Col 2:22 pronounces: ἅ ἐστιν πάντα εἰς φθορὰν τῇ ἀποχρήσει "All these things are designed for oblivion even in their satisfaction."[126]

Competing gospels and the religious consequences

The word used in Col 2:22 — φθορά — which I have rendered by "oblivion", may have been deliberately chosen by the author to make a pointed critique of imperial propaganda. There is no doubt from the psychopomp of Col 2:15 that imperial display, as in a triumph in Rome or an *adventus* into a provincial city, is very much in the author's mind, even with the inversion that is constructed: ἀπεκδυσάμενος τὰς ἀρχὰς καὶ τὰς ἐξουσίας ἐδειγμάρισεν ἐν παρρησίᾳ, θριαμβεύσας αὐτοὺς ἐν αὐτῷ, "having stripped the rulers and authorities, he [God] publically paraded them, leading the triumph over them by it [the cross]." One Colossian coin from the time of Commodus, contains iconography that evokes the Roman triumph — it has a figure (perhaps Nike — the coin is considerably worn) in a biga drawn by two standing horses.[127] The figure carries a wreath in the left hand and a palm branch in the right, key symbols used to portray victory and peace. The iconography has a lengthy heritage in coins of the imperial period, stretching back to the time of Tiberius.[128] It supported "a well-defined Roman cultural narrative."[129] It was particularly popular in Trajan's time; the wreath in the coin of Commodus' time is however far

125 See chapter 6.

126 This translation, I submit, accords better with the meaning of ἀπόχρησις in Greek literature (for example, Plato *Pol.* 279b, (Ps-)Plutarch *Cons. Apoll.* (*Mor.*) 119B, Galen *Const. Art.* 245K, Libanius *Or.* 13.25) and returns the focus to the observance of regulations generally rather than to the items grasped, consumed or touched. The usual translation of "perish with use" hardly matches some elements or materials that may have been required to be touched, as noted previously. See Foster, *Colossians*, 300–1.

127 *RPC online* 4.2.1883 temp.

128 *RPC* 1.610.

129 Theophilos, "Employing Numismatic Evidence," 261.

less frequent, only occurring in Colossae's minting. Nonetheless, the Roman procession, whether imperial or not, was well-implanted in the visual imagination in Colossae as it was across the province.[130] The writer of the Letter to the Colossians knew the power he was tapping into with the imagery — and the shock value of its inversion, both in the overthrow of imperial authorities and in the item paraded as symbolic of that triumph (that is, the cross, rather than a biga, wreath or palm branch).

But the contradistinction from Rome has been signaled overtly from the opening proem of the letter: … ἥν προηκούσατε ἐν τῷ λόγῳ τῆς ἀληθείας τοῦ εὐαγγελίου … ἐν παντὶ τῷ κόσμῳ "which you have already heard in the truth-filled order of the gospel … throughout the whole cosmos" (Col 1:5b–6a).[131] This is not the "good news" of a birthday or wedding narrowed in time and space to an isolated celebration.[132] Nor is it, in Christian commentary, a contrast to some supposed false-teaching among the Christ-followers at Colossae. It lays claim to a cosmic calibration (with the ἐν παντὶ τῷ κόσμῳ mirroring the ἐν τοῖς οὐρανοῖς in Col 1:5a)[133] that is arrayed by that very universality on the fulcrum of a truth-filled order (ἐν τῷ λόγῳ τῆς ἀληθείας). The three-fold repetition of prepositional phrases governed by ἐν is crucial here.

But this cosmic construction of good news was not new to inhabitants of the Roman world, especially in the east.[134]

In about 9 or 5 BCE (the date is disputed),[135] there was a concerted move to harness the core of civic and religious business for the interests of empire. That is, a new ordering of time was ardently promoted by the pro-consul of Asia, Paulus Fabius Maximus, to be the regulatory calendar across the entire province. This demanded a complete recalibration of civic and religious functions now to be launched annually from the emperor's (nominal) birthday. This was avowed as a cosmic dispensation: "the providence that orders all of human life in a divine fashion."[136] The arrangements for the calendrical organi-

---

130 Epictetus spoke of the χαρακτήρ born in the mind as on coins: *Disc.* 4.5.16.

131 The connection between Col 2.15 and Col 1.6, 23 is made by Harry O. Maier, "A Sly Civility: Colossians and Empire," *JSNT* 27 (2005): 325–6.

132 See *P.Oxy.* 3313, l. 3 (verbal form, 1st to 2nd century CE).

133 Scot McKnight rightly recognizes the cosmic dimension of this "good news" but ignores anything other than a literary (scriptural) prompt to its semantics: *The Letter to the Colossians* (Grand Rapids, MN: Eerdmans, 2018), 180. A similar literary or philological myopia is found in M. Y. McDonald, *Colossians Ephesians* (Collegeville, MN: Liturgical Press, 2008), 38, 73–4. It is exacerbated by demanding of Colossians an authentic Pauline authorship so that the sole blood-line of its usage is traced to the apostle. For a trenchant criticism of such an approach see *New Doc. Early Christ.* 5, pp. 73–4.

134 See especially, A. Standhartinger, "'… wegen der Hoffnung, die für euch im Himmel bereitliegt' (Kol 1,5)," in *Kolosser-Studien* edited by P. Müller (Göttingen: Neukirchener, 2009), 1–22.

135 B. Buxton and R. Hannah, "*OGIS* 458, the Augustan Calendar and the Succession," in *Studies in Latin Literature and Roman History XII* edited by C. Deroux (CL 287; Brussels: Latomus, 2005), 290–306.

136 ἐπειδὴ ἡ θείως διατάξασα τὸν βίον ἥμων πρόνοια *OGIS* 458II, l. 32.

zation were detailed — it seems that a dossier of edicts with addenda, ended up being promulgated. To date seven are known. Most Second Testament readers are aware of this re-calibration of the calendar to mark the start of a New Year with an annual festival celebrating the birthday of Caesar Augustus because one inscription uses the language of εὐαγγέλια, "good news", to characterize the advent of Augustus into the world (*OGIS* 458II, ll. 37, 40). This reverberates with the language used by Paul (Rom 1:1, Phmn 13, *et al*) and the Gospel of Mark (1:1, 14; 14:9), as well as being retained in the Letter to the Colossians (Col 1:5, 23). The significance of the face-off between competing gospels has been increasingly exploited by commentators.[137] In fact, as Angela Standhartinger is at pains to show, the key inscription is replete with the language and emphases found in Colossians.[138]

But the overall dossier has not gained the same attention; nor has there been much recognition that the inscription from Priene most usually cited is only one of a number of fragments (albeit the largest) that have surfaced in different cities across the province of Asia. Colossae, in fact, is somewhat encircled by find-spots — Apameia 62 miles to the east, Eumeneia 50 miles to the nor'-nor'-east and, further on the same route, to Dorylaion, 200 miles away. Swinging west towards the Mediterranean seaboard, another fragment has been found at Maionia, 70 miles away. Thence we arrive at Metropolis just north of Ephesos, where the most recent discoveries have been made, and finally to Priene, then on the coast to the south of Ephesos.[139] Significantly, one of the inscriptions in the dossier, specifically requires the assize districts' metropoleis to set up both the decree of the pro-consul Maximus and that of the koinon of Asia on white marble stelai in the precincts and temple of Roma and Augustus (*OGIS* 458II, ll. 62–7). To date, the epigraphical discoveries have come mainly from cities that are not the *conventus* centers, demonstrating how deeply pervasive the promulgation and observance were.[140]

One discovery at Colossae's adjacent city, Laodikeia, is particularly significant for our purposes, even if it has been overlooked by Second Testament commentators. The marble slab shaped as a *tabula ansata* was first published by Georg Weber in 1891.[141] Subsequent editions simply reproduced Weber's text.[142] However, in 2005, the stone was rediscovered near the Hierapolis gate.[143] It has, accordingly, been considered to have

137 S. Porter, "Paul Confronts Caesar with the Good News," in *Empire in the New Testament* edited by S. E. Porter and C. Long Westfall (Eugene, OR: Pickwick, 2011), 167–8.

138 Standhartinger, "'... wegen der Hoffnung," 17–18.

139 Heavy silting of the harbor "moved" Priene to an inland, now ruined city.

140 There is some evidence that the celebrations spilled into village environments as well; see *I.Sardis* 2.331 (settlement of the Targenoi, 37–41 CE); compare *CIL* 11.3303.

141 G. Weber, "Funde," *MDAI(A)* 16 (1891): 144–5.

142 *IGR* 4.860, *I.Laodicée Lycos nymphée* 265–77, *I.Laodikeia Lykos* 82; G. G. Fagan, *Bathing in Public in the Roman World* (Ann Arbor: University of Michigan Press, 1999), 345 nr. 331.

143 *SEG* 62.1238.

come from the north-east necropolis, where it formed part of the posthumous funerary honors adorning a heroon for Quintus Pomponius Flaccus.[144] The honors were a joint installation of "the Romans and Greeks of Asia and the Dêmos of the Laodikeians" (Οἱ ἐπὶ τῆς Ἀσίας Ῥωμαῖοι καὶ Ἕλληνες καὶ ὁ δῆμος ὁ Λαοδικέων ἐτείμησαν, ll.1–2). As common to such recognition, a *cursus honorum* is unfolded, but it is one that instead of a concentration on offices held, lists events and contributions that Flaccus bestowed for the benefit of the city.

Most significantly for our purposes, one of his noteworthy benefactions was the lavish offerings provided during the "good news" celebrations (καὶ ἐπιδίδοντα ἐν εὐανγελίοις εὐψύχως, l. 12). Francesco Guizzi unnecessarily takes the καὶ as a consequential connective with the preceding reference to his ambassadorial representation in Rome and interprets a later reference to oil provision for the city and its citizens (ll. 14–15) as having been brought from Rome for distribution during the *euaggelia* celebrations.[145] There is nothing in the inscription to suggest that these elements are connected, other than being separate examples of the leader's munificence. However it underlines how significant the good news celebrations were to both the Asian and Laodikeian elites, here following on the heels of his self-funded role as a delegate to Rome. The *euaggelia* were also a prominent focus for benefaction and self-promotion; even though the provisions and gifts Flaccus made are unspecified, one can readily identify openings for his munificence — the sacrifices, the festival banquets and the games that provided a very Roman focus for the city's life and religious calendar. These celebrations ran through the first century — the inscription is dated to the first century CE, possibly early second century. Accordingly, "good news" was drilled into the conventions and expectations of city life — as a Roman assertion over Greek practice.[146] The initiating edict from Priene instructs that all Greeks were to recognize what had hitherto been hidden, namely that Augustus' birth was the genesis of an era of life (τὸ ἀπὸ τῆς ἐκείνου γενέσεως ἄρχειν τῷ βίῳ τὸν χρόνον, ll. 48–9). Processes were to be enacted, especially through a special religious observance and the erection of inscriptions in prominent places, to make the honor and the recalibrated calendar known. As far as Rome was concerned, Paul had not brought the good news to Asia; Augustus had.

Colossae could not have avoided these good news observances. The latest discoveries at Metropolis demonstrate how widespread was the embrace of this major configuration of calendrical observance to prioritize Caesar as *the*

144 F. Guizzi, "Greek and Latin Inscriptions of Laodikeia on the Lykos 2003–2018," in *15. Yılında Laodikeia (2003–2018)* edited by C. Şimşek (Istanbul: Ege, 2019), 166–9 (late 1st or early 2nd century CE). The honorand is called a "hero" in the course of the inscription (at l. 3) and the inscription refers to τὸ μνημῆον (l. 16) a standard reference to a tomb in this region.

145 Guizzi, "Greek and Latin Inscriptions," 169.

146 The *OGIS* 458.II (Priene) inscription specifically rules that the ninth of the Kalends of October (that is the 23rd September in the modern western calendar), the birthday of Augustus, shall conform the Greek day in every city (καθ' ἑκάστην πόλιν ll. 53–4) of Asia to the Roman date. The day was to launch the New Year and the opening month was to be called "Kaisar" (ll. 50–7, 68).

divinely appointed anchor of religious and civic life.[147] A copy of the edict of the governor Paulus Fabius Maximus was set up in the courtyard of the meeting rooms of an association of *prebyteroi* (who were probably connected with the Imperial cult).[148] The editors of the new text note that it selects from the available dossier of inscriptions related to the Augustan calendar observance. The excerpts from two inscriptions, made into one, accent the blessings that Augustus brought to Asia. The editors speculate that the *presbyteroi* "recited the text of their stele as a kind of happy message on the feast days of their association."[149]

Given that there is evidence of the imperial cult in full operation at Colossae (see further below), it is inconceivable that Colossae, along with most cities on the main highways networking Asia, would or could have avoided the recalibration of time that these inscriptions attest. If the author was writing from elsewhere (indicated by the ὧδε in Col 4:9), then Ephesos is the most likely city, located between Metropolis and Priene. Ephesos's battles with Pergamon for preeminence meant that it was hardly prone to be tardy in the take-up of imperial (im)positions. The re-set of the calendar impacted the arrangements of the total *fasti* of the cities' variegated religious observances. It launched a festival of a number of days that celebrated the birthday of Augustus (deemed as September 23rd — "the ninth day before the Kalends of October")[150] with multiple sacrifices, events and feasts. But it was deliberately timed ("preordained by some divine will" claims the inscription) to coincide with the entrance of city officials into public office, following their election (*OGIS* 458I, ll. 14–15). Accordingly, religious time and civic time were conjoined ensuring that the fabric of life for inhabitants bore a pervasive imperial stamp. Inevitably, this conjunction was impressed on civic coinage. The goat-fish (Capricorn) was the zodiac sign designating this birth-date of Augustus,[151] and bronzes across the province registered it, often in combination (on the obverse) with the head of the emperor, a laurel peace branch or some other sign of fecundity, and/or the stately approval of a god. At Laodikeia, one coin from the time of Augustus, had the requisite zodiac sign, carrying a cornucopia, above the legend ΣΕΒΑΣΤΟΣ, with, on the obverse, three ears of wheat. The benefactor Sosthenes, ensured that his devotion to the Augustan gospel of prosperity was recorded in the legend (Pl. 7.5).[152]

147 B. Dreyer and H. Engelmann, "Augustus und Germanicus im ionischen Metropolis," *ZPE* 158 (2006): 173–82.

148 "Elders" are sometimes an organized sub-group of another. See *IGR* 1.562, 1122; *OGIS* II.729.

149 Dreyer and Engelmann, "Augustus und Germanicus," 182.

150 See Suetonius *Aug.* 5.1, Dio Cassius 56.30.5.

151 See T. Barton, "Augustus and Capricorn: Astrological Polyvalency and Imperial Rhetoric," *JRS* 85 (1995): 33–51.

152 *RPC* 1.2897. Photograph by courtesy of Savoca Coins. The coin was probably modeled on a coin struck by Augustus that deliberately promoted his zodiacal birth sign: see Suetonius *Aug.* 94.12 cf Manilius *Astron.* 2.507–9. On the imperial coins featuring Capricorn, see P. J. Connor,

Plate 7.5: A coin of Laodikeia (15 mm, 3.38 g) featuring on its obverse the zodiac sign of Capricorn, bearing a cornucopia, above the legend ΣΕΒΑΣΤΟΣ (Augustus) and, on the reverse, the triplet of wheat ears in a display of fecundity that is meant to be tied to the visual and epigraphical communication on the obverse.

Here we return to the term φθορά. In the inscription of the decree of the governor Maximus, the word occurs as the evocative description of the demise of the world — had not Augustus been born. The relevant lines are these:

> He [Augustus] has given to the whole world a different appearance, a world that would have wallowed in welcoming oblivion[153] had not, to the common good fortune of all, Caesar been born.
>
> ἑτέραν τε ἔδωκεν πάντι τῶι κόσμωι ὄψιν, ἥδιστα ἄν δεξαμένωι φθοράν, εἰ μὴ τὸ κοινὸν πάντων εὐτύχμα ἐπεγεννήθηι Καίσαρ.[154]

The writer of the Letter to the Colossians is patently unimpressed with such promethean claims. Maximus' decree had expressed the intent "that our proposal for honoring Augustus might endure forever" (ἵνα τὸ ἐπινοηθὲν ὑφ' ἡμῶν εἰς τὴν τειμῆν τοῦ Σεβαστοῦ μείνῃ αἰώνιον, ll. 27–8). It is likely that the experience of the latter years of Nero's rule had brought a tarnish to the golden age proclaimed by the Augustan calendar decrees. The consumption of imperial benefits had proved bilious not beneficial (cf Rev 10:10) and the sinister threat of this later oblivion (especially in the year [69 CE] of four emperors) had exposed that these imperial decrees were nothing more than the rulings and instructions of mere human beings (κατὰ τὰ ἐντάλματα καὶ διδασκαλίας τῶν ἀνθρώπων Col 2:22b). The effort to turn imperial ambition

---

"Tyrannus Hesperiae Capricornus undae," *Latomus* 44 (1985): 838. A second type minted by Sosthenes shows the head of Augustus with a standing Zeus Aetophoros on the reverse and a wreath flanked by the letters N and Ω and enclosing the letter Z, an aggregation that has defied deciphering. The editors of *RPC* tentatively date the coins to 10 BCE. However, the accent on birth and prosperity in my mind suggests a link with the inauguration of the *euaggelia* celebrations. Earlier coins with the Capricorn sign had accented domination; see Barton, "Augustus and Capricorn," 48–50.

153 This is my attempt to capture the extreme irony of the use of ἥδιστα in combination with φθορά. "With the greatest pleasure" (Sherk's translation) doesn't capture the Roman governor's construction of the abject state into which Asia had fallen in the years of civil war up to Octavian's settlement. For a translation of four of the inscriptions in the dossier, see R. K. Sherk, *Rome and the Greek East to the Death of Augustus* (Cambridge: Cambridge University Press, 1984), nr. 101.

154 *OGIS* 458 I, ll. 7–9.

into religious observance had been exposed both as limited and delimiting, constraining rather than liberating, generating indebtedness and ultimately of vacuous moral benefit (Col 2:23).

Debt, religious regulations, and cancellation in a Colossian context

Here we need to recognize that whereas commentators often draw a semantic connection between the δογματίζεσθε of Col 2:20 and the τοῖς δόγμασιν of Col 2:14, the reverse is rarely if ever considered for the significance of the tie. That is, the "oath to the regulations" (χειρόγραφον 2:14), which might be signaled, as we have seen, by touching the stele on which they are recorded, ought to be considered in the light of the examples of such regulations in 2:21 — "do not grasp, consume, touch". Accordingly, the meaning of Col 2:14 is not to be constructed on the basis of later sweeping Christian theologies of atonement and forgiveness. Rather, the delineation and separation of the Christ-followers at Colossae from their religious environment meant they were no longer bound by the sacred laws that might govern "all humanity", and which, by failure to be observant, incurred sometimes small, sometimes hefty penalties which had to be repaid if membership of and entry into a temple or religious association was to continue. Therefore, the erasure of the χειρόγραφον of Col 2:14a is not an epexegetical metaphor expanding on Col 2:13b, the forgiveness of "trespasses". It is an additional purpose and benefit of the work of Christ that impacts practically on the sometimes punitive operations of religious practice in the city.

Erasure or cancellation (ἐξαλείψας) is achieved by a quite specific act — a nailing (προσηλόω Col 2:14). This is hardly a washing or rubbing out of a private, personal inked letter! There is a subtle mixture of metaphors happening here. It is not a confused reference to the crime of a crucified victim (the *titlos* of Jn 19:19–20). Rather we find that multiple media might be nailed up for display in a variety of public and semi-public places: lead, bronze, wood, and sometimes stone. Inscribed bronze tablets are frequently found with carefully drilled nail holes indicating that they were affixed to some other support.[155] The supporting base might also be any of these materials. A first-century (BCE) honorary decree made by the priests of Apollo for a certain Nemenios was duplicated on bronze tablets, one with four nail-holes, one with three. Although the discovery location was a terraced house, the principle editors think that this was a secondary site; that originally they were nailed up for display, perhaps in

155 The evidence of a citizenship decree of Triphylioi (399–69 BCE) suggests that the nail holes were drilled before the inscription was cut (*SEG* 35.389).

separate areas of a temple.[156] Accounts of payments from sacred or public lands have been recovered at Argos, also inscribed on bronze, and nailed probably to the wall of a public building.[157] A number of bronze tablets seem to have been nailed to a wooden beam or post,[158] as also a lead tablet containing a letter fragment,[159] or another outlining a list of sacrifices.[160] A bronze fragment with nail hole seems to record the offering of an ox, probably as part of a temple archive.[161] Sometimes, the nails themselves were given additional sacrality, with a dedication or apotropaic warning.[162] One nail found at Epidauros was large enough to carry the dedication "I belong to Hera, the queen of the Epidaurians."[163] Even the most practical, mundane object might become the conveyor of religious signification. Much later, in the Roman imperial period, a fragmentary temple inventory from Pessinus mentions something that was nailed, apparently now part of the temple treasure-store.[164] At Delos, one stone tablet was nailed onto another inscribed stone. The supporting stone carried a dedication to Zeus and the Great Mother; the additional fixed stone carried the warning "Do not come after drinking or in bright-colored clothes!"[165] All these examples, reduced to a common base, demonstrate that nails were used to fix various genres of inscribed texts on different materials. But the accent throughout is display.[166]

The force of the Colossian author's imagery in using this form of display lies in the dissonance caused by nailing a χειρόγραφον … to a cross (τῷ σταυρῷ Col 2:14b). In purely functional terms the cross is acting much like a stone stele, a beam or a post, even a wall. But in the imperial Roman world of the first century, the cross was charged with far more meaning than simply a wooden support. It was the instrument of death. Behind all the Augustan imagery of peace ushering in a golden age, lay the raw power of execution. This was "the supreme penalty/punishment" (ἡ ἀνώτατος τιμωρία/κόλασις), an oblique way to refer to crucifixion which had found its way from literature into inscriptions in Asia and papyri in Egypt.[167] It was as agonizing as it was public.[168] The

156 *SEG* 59.1100 (Halaisa, Sicily).
157 *SEG* 41.284 (450 BCE and 300 BCE).
158 *SEG* 48.541 (Olympia, 525–500 BCE).
159 *SEG* 50.704 (Pantikapaion, 400–350 BCE).
160 *SEG* 54.416 (Corinth, 5th century BCE).
161 *SEG* 32.359 (Corinth).
162 *SEG* 51.2348, 56.1117.
163 τᾶς hέρας εἰμὶ τᾶς Βασιλείας τᾶς Ἐπιδαυροῖ (*SEG* 62.192, late 6th/early 5th century BCE).
164 *SEG* 46.1631, l. 3.
165 ἀπ᾽οἴνου μὴ προσιέναι μηδὲ ἐν ἀνθινοῖς (*CGRN* 173, 2nd to 1st century BCE).
166 This is not the case with *defixiones* where, frequently, a nail was used to bind together the folds of a deprecation, perhaps even as a symbol of harm. See chapter 8.
167 Philo *Flacc.* 126; *P.Lond.* 3.1171v = *Chr.Wilck.* 439, l. 11 (42 CE); *SEG* 33.1177, l. 17 (Myra in Lycia, 43 CE) cf Tacitus *Ann.* 15.44.3.
168 John Dominic Crossan rightly elicits Martin Hengel's compact work on crucifixion to capture the wretched, agonizing and humiliating dimensions of the workmanship of death engineered by Rome. See M. Hengel, *Crucifixion* (London: SCM, 1977), J. D. Crossan, *Who Killed*

Colossians composer refuses any oblique circumlocution. He baldly and boldly names the cross (Col 2:14), a mention that runs against refined Roman rhetoric and sensibilities, let alone self-deception about Roman civilization.[169] But this is not to shear crucifixion of its force, reducing it to a mere stake supporting the body of the text. Rather, it is to associate the ultimate horror of Rome's grip on the world *with the sacred laws* under which that grip was veneered into sometimes-enthusiastic acceptance. Put bluntly, Rome's gospel required crucifixion.

There were two prime associations of the cross in the ancient Roman world. It was the slave's death. When Quintus Veranius, as governor of the newly created province of Lycia (43–48 CE), threatened the ultimate punishment on a slave who allowed falsified or defaced documents into the public archives, it was precisely because this was the expected and permitted execution.[170] Roman citizens, but not necessarily citizens of other polities, were exempt from such humiliation, an ongoing reassurance that they were not slaves. A "slave's punishment" was *the* synonym of crucifixion, to the extent that the assumption attached to someone crucified was that they were a slave (or no better than one).[171] The second association was that it marked the crucified one as a "thief," usually of robbery with violence.[172] This no doubt is part of the irony crafted by the gospel writers (Mk 15:27 and parallels), but it was a connection that could gain considerable traction in the Mediterranean world because it was one of the key understandings attached to the mere mention of a cross/crucifixion.

Accordingly, the χειρόγραφον of regulations such as "do not grasp, do not consume, do not touch," with the debt penalties that attach to their breach, attracts this array of dismal associations as the letter writer constructs the argument. The regulations mean slavery and theft, the very things from which a gospel (whether of Augustus or of a Pauline author) was meant to liberate. For the writer, crucifixion — the nailing to the cross — is the fit punishment and execution of such a regimen of control. For the Christ-followers at Colossae, the Augustan gospel was (declared to be) dead. Such an inversion of expectation authorizes the subsequent image of the psychopomp leading a triumph over the exposed powers (Col 2:15).

This is a remarkable demonstration of what it might mean to be "in Christ" rather than "in Colossae" as we have raised in chapter 2. Being "in Colossae"

Jesus? Exposing the Roots of Anti-Semitism in the Gospel Story of the Death of Jesus (New York: HarperSanFrancisco, 1995), 162–3.

169 "... the very word 'cross' should be far removed not only from the person of a Roman citizen but from his thoughts, his eyes and his ears." (*et nomen ipsum cruces absit non modo a corpore civium Romanorum sed etiam a cogitatione, oculis, auribus*) Cicero *Pro Rab.* 16.

170 *SEG* 33.1177; compare a later fragmentary inscription that suggests that the threat had not stopped the abuse of records and archival deposition: Oliver, *Greek Constitutions* 186.

171 See Hengel, *Crucifixion*, 51–63.

172 *Dig.* 48.19.28.15.

meant to be subject, just like the aforementioned Gytheates, to all the demands (especially as controlled by civic and imperial authorities) that were designated "sacred law" — whether pertinent to Zeus, Helios or other city deity and to the connection of the imperial cult with one or other god or the entirety of the civic pantheon. The writer, in what was, in this regard, an agonistic letter in its original context, has set the Christ-followers into the religious panorama of Colossae as a significant alternative, mounting a massive critique of the prevailing religious conventions and regulations.

It could potentially be dangerous or at least financially detrimental, if indebted members of one religious group decided to take up membership of the Christ-cult. Even those with no interest in the Christ-followers or their beliefs, could suffer considerable disadvantage if they fell into debt to a religious institution. One debtor to the sanctuary at Leukopetra in Macedonia was compelled to relinquish a (female) slave because of her master's failure to repay.[173] This may lie in the background of the careful advice to do a timely deal — a commercially riven metaphor — with those outside the group (Col 4:5 Ἐν σοφίᾳ περιπατεῖτε πρὸς τοὺς ἔξω τὸν καιρὸν ἐξαγοραζόμενοι "Deal wisely with outsiders, transacting as opportunity permits/in a timely fashion").

The word ἐξαγοράζω is rare in inscriptions and papyri, though the simplex is common enough. It occurs in an honorific decree for a certain Agathokles of the city of Histria in Thrace where, in the context of ongoing disruptions to the city's existence, the honorand paid out a massive 600 gold pieces to ensure the city's safety and access to the produce of the surrounding territory.[174] A similar redemption payment occurs in a fragmentary inscription from Chalkis, where inhabitants who had been taken into slavery after a war were ransomed back through the financial intervention of a certain citizen.[175] The word also occurs in the Customs Law of Ephesos (62 CE) of those who had contracted to ensure the registration and payment of customs duties.[176] The middle form of the participle in Col 4:5 suggests not the exaction but the repayment of monies, whether these are to be understood as penalties or debts. Here religion and claims upon religious observance are framed in terms of indebtedness (real or potential) inextricably entwined with the political power that gave all its (calendrical and religious) authority. The cross has become a symbol of release, the place of display where the acknowledged debt has been expunged, or better, rendered of no consequence. This was no mere mind-game; this good news ostensibly removed a new adherent from the debts incurred in the course of (flawed or inadequate) devotion to other gods within the panorama of Colossae's religious offerings.

173 *I.Leukopetra* 134.
174 *I.Histriae* 15 (c. 200 BCE).
175 *SEG* 40.755 (169–7 BCE).
176 *SEG* 39.1180, ll. 29, 108.

Religious observance at Colossae

Our specific knowledge of the sacred laws operating in Colossae is limited. The coins of course bear witness to a range of gods, with accents on Helios (as we have seen), Demeter, Artemis the hunter (see chapter 4), Dionysos, Zeus, Sarapis, the river-god Lycus, just to name a handful. The onomastics of Colossae confirm the infusion of religious devotion through the society, with a significant percentage of names being "theonyms" and "heronyms", that is, names factored on gods and heroes.[177] Architectural remains that attest the religious buildings that would have dotted the landscape of the city and crop up in rural areas, either as formal sanctuaries or as devotional *realia* of villagers, are few. Georg Weber's 1891 sketch of the mound of Colossae that featured a temple wall foundation on the acropolis is as telling as it is now invisible. However, they were still present in 1894, when Émile le Camus, the French cleric, traveller and biblical commentator, noted "square walls" atop the higher of the twin mounds, which he credited to "the Acropolis."[178]

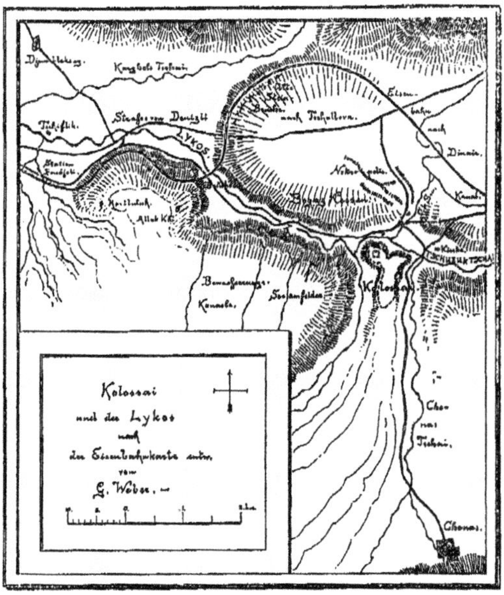

Plate 7.6a and b: The sketch-map of Colossae made by Georg Weber and published in 1891.[179] The detail shows his inclusion of a clear line of foundation stones for a temple.

177 See A. H. Cadwallader, *Fragments of Colossae: Sifting through the Traces* (Adelaide: ATF Press, 2015), 68–9, and chapter 9 herein.

178 É. Le Camus, *Voyage aux Sept Églises de l'Apocalypse* (Paris: Librairies Sanard et Derangeon, 1896), 175.

179 G. Weber, "Der unterirdische Lauf des Lykos bei Kolossai," *MDIA(A)* 16 (1891): 195.

Plate 7.7: The acropolis of the Colossae höyük as it was in 2013. The aerial view reveals not only tracks worn by tourist traffic but signs of illegal excavations. The line of wall at the entrance to the acropolis may have formed a peribolos for the temple. The outline of the temple foundations may possibly have left a trace in the photograph. We await the publication of results of a geophysical (ground penetrating radar) survey or excavation for confirmation.

On the höyük, in the depression separating the acropolis and the lower plateau of the mound, some probable remains of temple buildings are also found.

Plate 7.8a and b: Remains of a small shrine on the rise to the lower mound from the shallow depression separating the acropolis and lower plateau of the höyük at Colossae. The detail shows a section of a limestone pediment, containing a shield-boss.

Among the inscriptions, some important hints of the religious life of Colossian society are given. The first inscription registers an "association of friends", although one commentator has been loathe to admit it.[180] The inscription is a simple epitaph:[181] παροδείταις χάριν | οἱ ἑταῖροι Γλύκω- | ναν ἐτείμη- | σαν; "Greetings to passers-by; the society of friends honored Glykon" (Pl. 7.9). A more detailed examination of the epitaph is given in chapter 12.

Plate 7.9: The funerary stele set up by "the friends" to honor Glykon. The two standing figures, a female on the left and male on the right, wear distinctive clothing and head-dresses, raise their respective, covered right arms to their shoulders and hold distinct items in their left hands. The inscription is in two parts — greetings to passersby inscribed on the lintel below the pediment, and on the platform between the fluted pilasters with stylized Corinthian capitals. The inscription appears to be somewhat carelessly engraved. A four-petalled rosette (often an evocation of death) is centered in the pediment and a single-handled oionoche at top right between the acroterion and the gable of the pediment.

180 B. Eckhardt, "Romanization and Isomorphic Change in Phrygia: the case of Private Associations," *JRS* 106 (2016): 153. The prevalence of οἱ ἑταῖροι across Greece and Asia, many recorded in terse inscriptions very similar to the one at Colossae, cannot be dismissed as an "informal group of friends" as Eckhardt argues (see also http://ancientassociations.ku.dk/assoc/731). Metropolis alone records several inscriptions where οἱ ἑταῖροι are responsible for funeral arrangements, one where they are joined on the inscription with οι θιασεῖται "the association of Bacchantes/revellers" (*I.Ephesos* 3466A, 3rd to 2nd century BCE); similar alliance *OGIS* 573, Cilicia, Augustan period). Their presence in the Lycus Valley and its vicinity suggests that this was a common cultural phenomenon of the region and period (for example, *MAMA* 4.299 [Dionysopolis, 1st – 2nd century CE]; *SEG* 57.1371 [Hierapolis, late 2nd century BCE]; *I.Mus. Denizli* 99 [Hierapolis, 2nd century CE]). The expression is an ancient term and gained legal recognition in Roman law (*Dig.* 47.22.4 [Gaius, *XII Tables*, book 4] where the term ἑταιρεία is expressly used. See *MAMA* 9.86 commentary; see further chapter 12.

181 *MAMA* 6.47. The dating is disputed. Ernst Pfuhl and Hans Möbius dated it to the 3rd century CE: *Die Ostgriechischen Grabreliefs* (Mainz am Rhein: Philipp von Zabern, 2 vols 1977), 1.175 nr. 594 and pl. 94; Tullia Ritti gives the 2nd century CE (*I.Mus. Denizli* 113). Philip Harland assigns a date of 1st to 2nd century CE (http://philipharland.com/greco-roman-associations/funerary-honors-by-companions-for-glykona-i-ii-ce/). (The link reveals his earlier reading of the inscription as for a female.) After close examination of the photographs (of *MAMA* 6.47 and Ritti), I have corrected Buckler-Calder's reading of χαί(ρ)ιν. Significantly, Calder's notebook records XIIN, so some doubt attended his reading from the beginning (University of Aberdeen, Special Library, "Calder Archives" Ms 3286/3, 1933 Notebook p. 43). No squeeze was taken. The photographs (Buckler-Calder and Ritti) reveal a curvilinear "cup" attached to the first upright haste of the word. It should be noted that the first line contained a four-bar sigma and a squared epsilon whereas lunate forms for both are cut in the following lines. This may suggest a later addition.

The text is an important testimony to the presence of associations at Colossae,[182] accented by the deliberate addition of the definite article (as if there was concern that a misleading perspective would be conveyed without it).[183] But the unusual design features are of particular interest here. Even with a general acknowledgement that tombstones were sold from masons' yards already substantially carved (and so limiting selection),[184] this stele has some distinctive features, one of which — the woman's garb — is, to my knowledge, found nowhere else. Rosemary Canavan has re-focussed attention to the visual aesthetics of the relief, noting the "crinkled" appearance of the woman's *chiton* and the "arm-sling" posture of both figures, indicative of reserve and discipline.[185] Hans Pfuhl had already drawn attention to the rather elaborately sculptured *naiskos*, a small temple or shrine within which the pair is located in the relief. At one level, this merely confirms the sanctity that attached to burials that is mentioned above in regard to the prohibition "Do not touch". However, the items in the left hand of each, the suggestion of head turbans and the unusual dress of the woman add further information here. The woman is unnamed, unusual if she was the wife of Glykon as Tullia Ritti thinks. Also unusual is the absence of the funerary banquet scene that is ubiquitous and known in another stele from Colossae (*MAMA* 6.50). It raises the possibility that the honoring of Glykon was by an association of companions, a society of friends that incorporated religious functions into their gatherings.

The *hetairoi* elsewhere are occasionally mentioned in connection with cultic commitments.[186] In one association "of the Arzimneis", a clan group is specifically called ἡ ἑταιρεία. Not only does the relief on which the inscription is found contain multiple gods but it also presents a priest offering sacrifice at a small altar. One of the named members is specifically titled ἱερεύς.[187] The Dionysiac inscription from Thessalonike, pictured above (Pl. 7.3), includes ten names of women in the list of cult officials.[188] Richard Ascough thought this atypical for associations in Macedonia.[189] However, there is considerable evidence that in

182 Harland, *Greco-Roman Associations*, 168.

183 Some inscriptions do not contain the article with ἑταῖροι: see *SEG* 32.605 (Larisa, 150–200 CE); *IG* II² 4826 (Athens, 3rd – 4th century CE). Some inscriptions use οἱ ἑταῖροι with a long list of names following — probably indicating the membership behind dedications (*SEG* 44.534, Lete, 350–300 BCE). See further chapter 12.

184 So, G. Johnson, *Early-Christian Epitaphs from Anatolia* (Atlanta, GA: Scholars Press, 1995), 4.

185 R. Canavan, *Clothing the Body of Christ at Colossae* (WUNT 334; Tübingen: Mohr Siebeck, 2012), 97.

186 See for example *SEG* 56.714 (Emathia, 4th century BCE); *OGIS* 573 (Cilicia, Augustan period); *I.Prusa* 24 (1st century CE).

187 *SEG* 34.1298 (Hierapolis, 2nd – 3rd century CE); cf *SEG* 34.1299 and Ritti, *Museo Archeologico*, nr. 44 (both Hierapolis, 2nd – 3rd century CE).

188 Nigdelis, "Voluntary Associations in Roman Thessalonikê," 24 n62 and 41 nr 31.

189 R. S. Ascough, *Paul's Macedonian Associations: The Social Context of Philippians and 1 Thessalonians* (WUNT 161; Tübingen: Mohr Siebeck, 2003), 58.

Phrygia and neighboring regions, women were independently active in various groups, cultic and otherwise.[190] At Myndos, two inscriptions list women who served as priestess probably of Artemis.[191] It is likely that Claudia Eugenetoriane, the widow who revived the Colossian mint, served in the cult of Demeter. The point is that women and cultic leadership were far from occasional in Asia in the first century — indeed, as we will see, a woman named Apphia is named on an inscription from Colossae as priestess, probably of the (local) imperial cult. This is not to deny the erasure of the presence and activity of women through their minority appearance in relief and inscription.[192] However, one ought not be surprised to find a priestess involved in an association at Colossae. The worn state of the relief on the stele precludes absolute certainty of this on the basis of the stone. But this is where comparative evidence can advance and enhance the heavily-pixilated view we have from Colossian evidence alone.[193]

Two further inscriptions from Colossae involve Dionysos, though in both cases they are fragmentary and difficult to resolve. The first is an inscribed statue base:

> … τοῦ Διονύσου, διὰ Γ. Κλ. Μενάνδρου Φλαουϊανοῦ τοῦ πατρὸς, εὐεργέτου τῆς πόλεως, ἐκ τῶν ἰδίων ἀνέθηκεν.[194]

The inscription has been titled "a priest of Dionysos," which makes a judgment about the word preceding the opening, that is ἱερέα τοῦ Διονύσου.[195] The meaning would then be that a certain dedicant, whose name can be partially reconstructed from the father's name surviving in the inscription, would be offering an honor to another unknown who was a "priest of Dionysos". Thus

---

190 See P. Ö. Aytaçlar and E. Akıncı, "A List of Female Names from Laodicea on the Lycos," *EA* 36 (2006): 113–6; P. Thonemann, "The Women of Akmoneia," *JRS* 100 (2010): 163–78; T. Ritti, "Alcune figure femminili nelle iscrizioni di Hierapolis di Frigia," *MedAnt.* 16 (2013): 141–3.

191 W. R. Paton, "Inscriptions of Myndos," *BCH* 12 (1888): 277–8, nrs 1 and 2. The inscription now stands in the Archaeological Museum in Bodrum.

192 See M. Johnson-DeBaufre " 'Gazing on the Invisible': Archaeology, Historiography, and the Elusive Wo/men of 1 Thessalonians," in *From Roman to Early Christian Thessalonikê*, 73–108.

193 The use of *comparanda* is the particular contribution of Clinton Arnold's *The Colossian Syncretism*, (*loc. cit.*). My primary reserve is that he has not given enough attention to the evidence from Colossae that we do possess.

194 M. A. Clerc, "Inscriptions de la vallée du Méandre. Tralles, Nysa, Attuda, Laodicée et Colosses," *BCH* 11 (1887): 353 nr 10. The inscription is also found in G. Quandt, *De Baccho ab Alexandri Aetate in Asia Minore Culto* (Halis Saxonum: Niemeyer, 1913), 216 who offers a correction of T(iberius) for G(aius).

195 This apparently was the judgment of William Buckler and William Calder, found in their summary of additional inscriptions of Colossae in their *MAMA* volume (VI), p. 142, nr. 49*. It is perhaps possible that the wording of the inscription had ἄγαλμα τοῦ Διονύσου in which case the inscription would simply record the dedication of a statue of the god; however, the usual expression in this case is a statue *to* Dionysos: *I.Callatis* 79, l. 2 (1st century BCE).

Gaius Claudius N. set up (this honour) for NN., a priest of Dionysos, from his own resources, under the supervision of his father Gaius Claudius Menandros Flavianos, a benefactor of the city.[196]

His Roman citizenship and the name of his father point to a late first or early second century date,[197] as well as indicating the cohesive interconnection of local and Roman civic and religious interests. That the credentials of a long-standing elite family of Colossae were on display in honoring a priest of Dionysos is a mark not only of how important the Dionysiac cult was at Colossae, but also its meshing with the values and commitments of the Colossian aristocracy in its Roman connections.[198]

Even more pronounced, at neighboring Tripolis, is the dedication of an altar by a Dionysiac association (the *thiasoi*) to both the emperor (probably Hadrian) and the god Dionysos.[199] The maintenance of euergetic activity was one of the prerequisites of securing and bequeathing Roman citizenship to one's heirs in a local context. Little wonder that this is seen, also, as a crucial protection for the city. One honorific inscription made by Dionysian initiates (οἱ μύσται) at Philadelphia for a Roman citizen, also a priest of Dionysos, contains almost as a refrain πρὸ πόλεως, "for the city" and may indicate that both the initiates and the honorand acted for the city's benefit.[200]

---

196 It is remotely possible that Menandros Flavianos was also honored with the title "father of the city" but one would expect a καί between the two titles; more remote is πάτρονος καί as a correction to πατρὸς. However, this is to second-guess Clerc's transcription when the stone is no longer extant. The διά is a shortening of the phrase διὰ ἐπιμελητοῦ (see *IG* II² 3318 [132 CE]) or διὰ τροφέως (see *AJA* 9 [1905]: 306 nr. 33) and is relatively common on coins (*RPC* 2.1281–1296, Laodikeia, reign of Domitian; 2.1226–1233, Attouda, reign of Domitian; 3.2262–2265, Trapezopolis, reign of Hadrian). No coins of Colossae, to date, bear this formula of authorization.

197 So *LGPN* V.c, sv Μένανδρος.

198 This is corroborated especially by the "new" coin featuring the "Holy Senate" on the obverse and Dionysos on the reverse (see chapter 1). For other Colossian coins featuring Dionysos, see *MSPhryg* 2.469 = *RPC online* 4.2.1892 temp.; *SNG Munich*, Phrygia, 309 as corrected by Katharina Martin, *Demos•Boule•Herousia: Personifikationen stästischer Institutionen auf kaiserzeitlichen Münzen aus Kleinasien* (Bonn: Habelt, 2 vols, 2013) 2.196, nr. 4. The (Pappa-)Silenus coin minted as the lowest value coin (1/4 or 1/3 assarion) of the suite struck by Tiberius Claudius Sakerdos (time of Antoninus Pius) features one of the key players in the Dionysos myth, being the young god's carer and attendant. He had a special connection with Phrygia, supposedly being temporarily housed by King Midas for which Midas was granted the golden touch.

199 F. Guizzi and B. Yener, "An Inscribed Altar from Tripolis ad Maeandrum," in *Tripolis Araştırmaları* edited by B. Duman (Istanbul: Ege, 2017), 77. The opening of the inscription giving the name of the emperor is missing, yielding only]νι Καίσαρι.

200 Malay–Petzl, *Lydia* 206, ll. 3–6 (2nd? century CE) with commentary.

Plate 7.10: Dionysos was the patron of the arts, especially the theater. Here a relief found at Ephesos (now in the museum at İzmir) depicts a visitation from the bearded Dionysos and his entourage (mainly satyrs performing various tasks) to the Athenian actor Ikarios, reclining on the couch beneath which lie an array of theater masks. Colossae's theater likely housed or was served by an acting guild of Dionysos.[201] The theater was a key civic venue for the reinforcement of conventional social values.

The second Dionysos inscription occurs on a plain, round pedestal now cemented into the tiled courtyard of a mosque at the village of Pinarkent, west of Colossae. The pedestal is reported as having been moved from the ancient site, though the exact find-spot is unknown. The inscription is difficult to decipher because it has, in the course of being fixed into its new location, received a cement veneer over the right edge of the lettering. A second renovation in the mosque courtyard raised the level of the tiles and so "shortened" the pedestal. Erim Konakçi first published the inscription and briefly attempted a reconstruction.[202] I seek to improve the reading here, but remain cautious about the results that are offered.

201 A reference to the global (οἰκουμένη) society of Dionysian performers occurs in a fragmentary decree found at Laodikeia (*I.Laodikeia Lykos* 65A).

202 E. Konakçi and B. Duman, "Arkeolojik ve Yasılı Kanıtlar Işığında Kolossai (Kolossai in the Light of Archaeological and Historical Evidence)," in *International Symposium on the History and Culture of Denizli and its Surroundings* (Denizli: Pamukkale University, 2007), 61, 67 pl. 12d. I am grateful to Dr Konakçi for supplying me copies of all his photographs of the stone, a most useful complement to my own.

Plate 7.11a: The "Bacchus" altar from Colossae. When first seen, the limestone pedestal measured 70 centimeters high above tile flooring, 30 centimeters across the shaft and 48 centimeters at the widest point of the upper element. There is a double concave molding banding the upper element and a single concave molding at the top of the shaft. A small hollow nestles in the center at the top. The large chipped section post-dates Konakçi's discovery in 2003.

Plate 7.11b and c: A close-up of the pedestal inscription. The left photograph shows a wetted stone; the reconstructed letters for a compact supplication are highlighted (without serifs) on the right. The stone-cutter's art is simple if not crudely executed, with large rounded omegas, wide-reaching diagonals on the upsilon, lunate sigmas and epsilons and short cross-bars on the theta and eta; there is one ligature in line 3; on line 4, a small omicron is squeezed between a large gamma and omega. The use of serifs is evident but restrained. Restorations are conservative but require recognition of a rare example of an abbreviated form in line 4 — BE with what seems to be an overbar, yielding the vocative Βάκχε.[203] These letter forms and features, plus the onomastics, suggest a second century (CE) date.

---

203 Abbreviations of the alternate names for Bacchos, namely Dio(nysos) and Ia(cchos) are attested in early (6th – 5th century BCE) graffiti found at Olbia. See E. Dettori "Testi 'Orfici' dalla Magna Grecia al Mar Nero," *PP* 51 (1996): 302 nr. h = *SEG* 32.779; *SEG* 28.659–661. Latin inscriptions utilize abbreviations more frequently and so one finds B (for Baccho) as in *AE* 1976.200 (Ariminum, 31–70 CE); compare also the letter B combined with the magical cry

The fragmentary text can be reconstructed to yield a votive supplication:

Θάλλο[ς
Βακχύλ̣[ου
ἀνέδην̣
ὤ Β(άκχ)ε γόω[ν
ἑαυτ[οῦ
ἀσυλε̣[ῖ

Thallos son of Bacchylos is crying out,[204] *O Bacchus, quickly, for protection for himself.*

A more complete analysis must await another time, as also a testing of any specifically Dionysian resonances in the Letter to the Colossians itself.[205] Suffice here to accent the tie between the name of the supplicant's father and the form of the name of the god (that is, Bacchus as alternative to Dionysos), a common-enough occurrence of the name of the god and a name-sake theonym being found together. Thallos — "shoot, child" — might also carry Dionysian associations both because of Bacchus as the child of Zeus and because a significant portion of his mythological narratives is devoted to his infancy.[206] There may have been a significant inherited family devotion to the cult.[207] The language of the inscription, especially the vocative cry, the use of γοῶ and ἀσυλία are all consistent with the Dionysian cult.[208]

"Iaô" inscribed on the reverse of a third century gem: S. Michel, *Die magischen Gemmen im Britischen Museum* (London: British Museum Press, 2 vols, 2001), 1.33, nr. 51. By this time, Iao had shed its postulated origins in the Hebrew deity's name. Rings directed towards one god or other frequently carried abbreviated forms of the deity's name. See chapter 5 for an example from Colossae. Compare *col(legium) dei Sil(vani)* on a ring found at Wendens Ambtero in England, apparently a ring of membership in a religious association devoted to the Roman god Silvanus; see M. Henig, *Religion in Roman Britain* (London: Routledge, 2003), 154; see also pp. 170, 172 ΕΖΣ taken as "One Zeus, Sarapis".

204 It is possible to read γοῶ here, turning the petition into direct speech.

205 A beginning has been attempted by J. Riley "Dionysos: Myth, Cult, and Influence in Kolossai and on the Letter to the Kolossians" Hons Thesis, Flinders University, 2006.

206 There may also be a connection forged by βάκχος in its meaning as "branch", used of the ritual deployment of branches in the Dionysiac processions; see M. A. Santamaria, "The Term βάκχος and Dionysos Βάκχιος," in *Redefining Dionysos* edited by A. Bernabé *et al.* (Berlin: de Gruyter, 2013), 40. Thallos was also an epithet of Zeus — god of vegetation. See Thomas Drew-Bear, Christine M. Thomas and Melek Yıldızturan, *Phrygian Votive Steles* (Turkey: Ministry of Culture, 1999), nrs 392, 464.

207 There is a woman's name, Βάκχα from the territory of Colossae, to date unique in its attestation; see P.-E. Legrand and J. Chamonard, "Inscriptions de Phrygie," *BCH* 17 (1893): 251, nr. 27, l. B3. For commentary on this *defixio* see chapter 8.

208 See *IG* II 2948, 4694; *I.Tralleis* 3; Euripides *Bacch.* 1020; Sophocles *Ant.* 1121.

A well-functioning imperial cult is indicated in another inscription from Colossae. A certain Apphia is named in one inscription as providing an honorific dedication to Trajan (some time after 114 CE when he was declared *Optimus*=Ἄριστος). Michel Clerc provided the briefest of descriptions of the stone and its find-spot — the inscription face was broken as also the base on which it was positioned.[209] It is probably enough to suggest that Apphia had erected a statue of the emperor, important because it redirects the re-construction and interpretation of the inscription as belonging to a statue base. Clerc's minor reconstruction of the surviving two-line text yet managed to prejudice its interpretation thereafter. His rendition was Αὐτοκράτ]ορι Νερούᾳ Τραιανῷ Καίσαρι Ἀρίστῳ Σεβάστῳ | Ἀπφία Ἡρακλέου τοῦ Διὸς Κο[. . . ἱέ]ρεια. This presentation of the lettering readily invited a reconstruction of the second last word to be Κολοσσηνοῦ claiming support from the ethnic city name on Colossae's imperial-period coins, namely Κολοσσηνῶν (*IGR* 4.868) or, alternately, Κολοσσαέως.[210] Consequently, the dedication made by Apphia was in her position as priestess of Zeus. This reading is still found amongst Second Testament commentators.[211] I have also felt drawn by this reading noting that ἱέρεια at the end of the reconstructed text would normally bear some explanatory focus "of Zeus", "of Dionysos" and the like. These designations of particular cultic focus can be made antecedently or subsequently (so, for example, *SEG* 25.118, 28.848; *CIG* 2900; *SEG* 59.237).[212]

I have since become less convinced that this should be the reading, for two reasons. Firstly the original publication (by Michel Clerc) actually included a probably-ligatured letter following. It appears to be the upper, horizontal hasta of a *pi* (missing the left upright) combined with a *rho*, or, more likely, a combination of a *tau* and *rho*. It is tempting to reconstruct Τραιανοῦ here but this must remain speculative; it is not found in such a form, ἱέρεια/ἱερεύς Τραιανοῦ elsewhere. Secondly, if we avoid any efforts to reconstruct the ligature, it is possible to find parallels for a designation of someone as priestess or priest without further limitation. As we shall see in chapter 9, a certain Apphia of Eukarpeia is designated as priest (ἱέρηα) on a coin she sponsored during the

209 Clerc, "Inscriptions de la vallée du Méandre," 354, nr. 12.

210 O. Höfer, "Kolossaeus," in *Ausführliches Lexikon der griechischen und römischen Mythologie* edited by W. H Roscher (Leipzig: Teubner, Vol 2, 1894), 1274.

211 See for example, Angela Standhartinger, *Studien zur Entstehungsgeschichte und Intention des Kolosserbriefs* (Leiden: Brill, 1999), 13 n48; Lukas Bormann, *Der Brief des Paulus an die Kolosser* (THNT 10/1; Leipzig: Evangelische Verlagsanstalt, 2012), 23–4. Adam Copenhaver leaves it somewhat open but his mis-reading of Robert (see the following) has not helped: *Reconstructing the Historical Background of Paul's Rhetoric in the Letter to the Colossians* (London: T & T Clark, 2018), 176.

212 See A. H. Cadwallader, "Assessing the Potential of Archaeological Discoveries for the Interpretation of New Testament Texts: The Case of a Gladiator Fragment from Colossae and the Letter to the Colossians," in *The First Urban Churches 1: Methodological Foundations* edited by J. R. Harrison and L. L. Welborn (Atlanta, GA; SBL Press, 2015), 49.

reign of Tiberius.[213] There is no indication in the legend what particular cult is the focus of her priesthood, but the obverse of the coin contains the head of Livia, named as Σεβάστη, a title conferred in 14 CE. The implication is that Apphia was (another) imperial cult priestess, albeit with a particular focus on the wife of Augustus and mother of Tiberius. The dedication to Trajan by the Colossian Apphia functions similarly.

The great epigrapher of Anatolia, Louis Robert, recognized that the usual mode for Greek naming was to give father and grandfather, in the form of an anarthrous genitive for the father and the articular genitive for the grandfather. He suggested that a more probable reconstruction gave the name of Apphia's grandfather, namely, Διοσκορίδου or Διοσκουρίδου.[214] Robert's reconstruction is accepted by Ulrich Huttner and the editors of the *Lexicon of Greek Personal Names*.[215] Now, Apphia as priestess can only be explicated by reference to the recipient of her dedication, namely, the emperor Trajan. This makes it reasonable to understand her service as belonging to the imperial cult established at Colossae. This is the deduction made by Simon Price and I now see little reason to dispute it.[216] This allows the following reconstruction:

> Αὐτοκράτ]ορι Νερούᾳ Τραιανῷ Καίσαρι Ἀρίστῳ Σεβάστῳ | Ἀπφία Ἡρακλέου τοῦ Διοσκο[ρίδου ἱέ]ρεια Τρ[αιανοῦ.
>
> Apphia daughter of Herakles, granddaughter of Dioskorides, priestess of Trajan(?) (erected his statue) to the Emperor, Nerva Trajan Caesar Optimus Augustus.

Corroboration for the imperial cult comes from another inscription of Colossae. The key officials named in the Augustan Calendar dossier to oversee the implementation and regular observance of the decree were the "*ekdikoi*" (*OGIS* 458II, l. 64), officials who represented their city in the *koinon* of Asia in negotiations with the emperor or governor. One mid-second-century Colossian inscription honors the brother (?) of Heliodoros.[217] The list of offices and achievements justifying the honor includes his position as *ekdikos* and men-

---

213 *RPC* 1.3160.

214 L. Robert, "Les Inscriptions," in *Laodicée du Lycos: Le nymphée* edited by J. des Gagniers *et al* (Paris: de Boccard, 1969), 278–9. He gives as a parallel and as a demonstration of the threefold form, a name among a list of pilgrims from Laodikeia to the oracular temple of Apollo at Klaros: Διοσκουρίδης Εὐμένους τοῦ Εὐμένους (*SEG* 37.962).

215 U. Huttner, *Early Christianity in the Lycus Valley* (Leiden: Brill, 2013), 44 n123 cf 85; *LGPN* V.c., 122 where Robert's alternative spelling is preferred.

216 S. Price, *Rituals and Power: The Roman Imperial Cult in Asia Minor* (Cambridge: Cambridge University Press, 1984), xix, xxii, xxv.

217 The opening of the inscription in which the honorand would have been named is lost. The one responsible for supervising the installation of the stele, Heliodoros, is named at the conclusion of the inscription but the qualification that he is "brother" to the honorand is a reconstruction without evidentiary remains in the transcription given.

tions his representing the city at the celebrations of (probably) the award of the second neokorate to Ephesos.[218]

Distinguishing the Christ-followers from the religious environment of Colossae

As we have seen, the ultimate weapon of Roman executive and executionary power — the cross — becomes a disturbing counterpoint in Col 2:14 to the *lex sacra* of the imperial cult (and of other religious cults) that carved an indebtedness and dependency among the Colossian populace. The judgment that such purity and power is destined for oblivion (Col 2:22) demonstrates that at least among the Christ-followers of first-century Colossae, disillusionment at the benefits of imperial rule could be fostered and explained by a theological critique of its validity.

Colossae would have had its own emphases in how religious behaviors and practices were regulated. Perhaps the mention of "Do not touch" (μηδὲ θίγῃς) reflects a particular accent that we rarely see elsewhere in *leges sacrae*. The material evidence from Colossae points to a vibrant religious life, as diffuse and variegated as it may have been. Although the evidence is terse in its offerings, it gives us confidence to draw upon more expansive examples from across the eastern Mediterranean and Egypt in order to complement and broaden our understanding. Caution must always govern the evidence, aware that Colossae, like most Greek poleis, was interested in carving its distinct identity (religious and otherwise) amid multitudinous common elements. The author of Colossians of course understands the city's characteristics better than we, only needing to give occasional glimpses through the writing. At the same time, the prime concern is to carve a Christian identity for those who have a similar understanding of and prior formation in the religious environment of the city. That variegated environment inevitably required a richly nuanced writing that has a vista rather than one specific (Jewish or otherwise) in view.

Little wonder that over and again, the author accents the universality and cosmic authority of Christ. Nothing less could encompass the available range of offerings for religious life. "Fullness", "headship" (Col 2:9–10) offers the

218 *IGR* 4.870, ll. 8, 10–11. It also lists the presentation of a silver offering to the gods (possibly an offering-table); because the following line lists his position as *ekdikos*, this dedication may have been in the context of the imperial cult. Unfortunately, the inscription as originally copied is missing parts of the text. The inscription is no longer extant, or, at least, remains hidden beneath the carpet of the "old mosque" in Honaz, a building which was taken over from the Greek Christians at their repatriation, following the Lausanne Convention of 1923. See further, chapter 5.

language of assured and distinctive identity even as the author gathers up in multiple metaphors and allusions, snippets of the very options from which that identity has been carved even in the extraction.[219] The desire for singularity was no Christian preserve — after all, other voluntary associations were sometimes concerned to preserve the lines of their own organization against competitors. But more ironically, the shaping of the identity of Christ-followers was pursuing an ambition of distinctiveness that the Colossian *polis* was also hunting in its own regional and provincial life. Such competitiveness for the adherence of members, to the extent that bans were placed on connections with other associations, is familiar enough within the life of a *polis*. In this sense, the author was no different from the framers of such sacred regulations,[220] even if the content of the letter's teaching sought to generate an aura of uniqueness beyond any other competitor.

---

219 I am in agreement with Vicky Balabanski who thinks there is no specific "heresy" opposed in the Letter to Colossians: *Colossians, An Eco-Stoic Reading* (London: T & T Clark 2020), 112. However, I do think that the author is seeking to articulate a distinct Christian position over against the range of religious options in Colossae and beyond. The references that acknowledge a general Jewish practice (such as "Sabbaths" in Col 2:16) may indicate little more than a recognition that Jews did provide one of those options in (and perhaps from) neighboring cities such as Laodikeia and Hierapolis (cf Col 4:15–16). See Foster, *Colossians*, 280–2.

220 So, for example, temple officials of Zeus of Baradates are banned from participation in the mysteries of Sabazios, Angdistis and Ma: *SEG* 29.1205 (Sardis, 426/365 BCE but re-engraved c. 150 CE). See Philip A. Harland, *Associations, Synagogues and Congregations: Claiming a Place in Ancient Mediterranean Society* (Minneapolis: Fortress Press, 2003), 183.

Chapter Eight
Cursing Colossians

The recognition that Colossae is far more than a mound with a label on the roadside opens the gaze to further possibilities of material evidence. One inscription in particular demands attention. It came to be assigned to the city of Apameia even though its find-spot (almost certainly original) was more than four times closer to Colossae. This chapter seeks to retrieve this inscription. It was scratched onto a lead curse tablet with the form of a diptych, which was found in a grave deposit. It presents a list of names consigned to a hoped-for untimely death. A confirmation that the *katadesmos* or *defixio*, as such instances are designated, is still extant, strengthens the need to revisit it, to reconstruct its contents and to interpret its meaning by reference to its immediate and wider context. Once the sense of its place within Colossian territory is appreciated, some resonances with the Letter to the Colossians are able to be explored, not to assert direct correspondences necessarily but to appreciate a little of how the letter might be heard and appropriated in that context.

The Kaklık curse diptych

The inscription at one level underscores the separation of country from the city that we saw with Tatia's epitaph from Eleinokapria and that of Zosas from Kilaraza.[1] This inscription is a *defixio* (Greek: *katadesmos*), a curse "tablet", one of approximately 1800 known from the Far East to Britain.[2] This one comprises two pieces that were joined by a pair of small metal rings — a diptych. It was included in the collection much used by Clinton Arnold in his ground-breaking

1 See chapter 3.
2 E. Eidinow, "Binding Spells on Tablets and Papyri," in *Guide to the Study of Ancient Magic* edited by D. Frankfurter (Leiden: Brill, 2019), 353–4.

work on the contextual background for the Letter to the Colossians,[3] but it was not referenced in his monograph.[4] This may have been because the inscription, like a number of others, was assigned to another center, this time Apameia to the east of Colossae; or it may have been that its content lacked any reference to angels.[5] However, it was found at Kaklık, 50–52 miles to the west of Apameia but only 12 miles from the city of Colossae. The site is clearly part of the Lycus Valley at the eastern end, and, with no other city between Colossae and the transition to the Anatolian plateau, it is evident that this area fell within the territorial boundaries of the *polis* of Colossae. In fact, in the nineteenth century the French explorer, Alexandre Laborde, thought he had found the disappearing-reappearing river of Herodotos's Colossae, at Kaklık.[6]

The recognition that Kaklık could not (probably from Persian to Byzantine times) be assigned to Kelainai-Apameia has recently brought a change of allocation. The editors of the most recent and last volume of the *Lexicon of Greek Personal Names* have credited each of the names found on the *defixio* to the territory of Colossae. The curse tablet has received little attention, but now becomes particularly important for understanding Colossae in its *polis*-state territory.

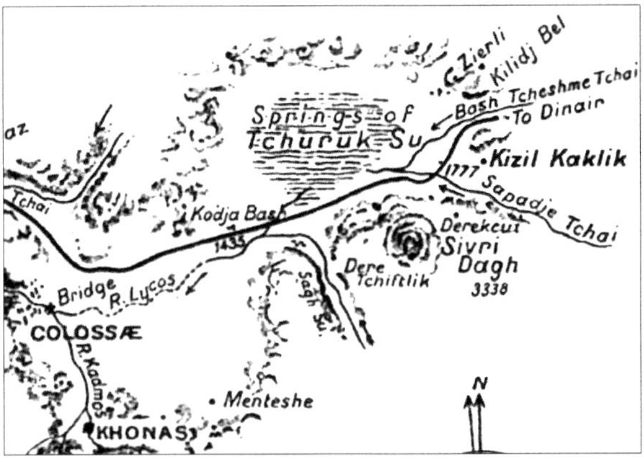

Plate 8.1: Detail of the Ottoman Railway survey map of 1897, showing Kaklık (at the upper right) in relation to Colossae (middle left).

3 A. Audollent, *Defixionum Tabellae* (Paris: A. Fontemoing, 1904), 20, nr. 14. Audollent simply classified it under "Phrygia" with a note of the find-spot.

4 C. E. Arnold, *The Colossian Syncretism: The Interface between Christianity and Folk Belief at Colossae* (Grand Rapids, MN; Baker, 1996).

5 *IGR* 4.806. This catalogue's arbitrary removal of the *defixio* to Apameia has been uncritically adopted through to the present; see L. Robert, *Noms Indigènes dans L'Asie-Mineure Gréco-Romaine* (Paris: Adrien Maisonneuve, 1963), 61 n2; S. E. Katakis, "ΦΙΛΗΜΑΤΙΟΝ ΤΕΡΕΝΤΙΑ ΧΡΗΣΤΗ ΧΑΙΡΕ: Darstellungen der Isis und mit ihrem Kult verbundener Personen auf Euböa," *MDAI(A)*s 112 (1997): 320 n4.

6 A. Laborde, *Voyage de l'Asie Mineure* (Paris: Firmin Didot, 1838), post-86. See chapter 1.

All details to do with its discovery, its design and its inscription have been dependent on the record made by Philippe-Ernest Legrand and Joseph Chamonard, published in 1893.[7] William Ramsay had apparently seen the artifact but "shrank from cleaning [it], in fear of causing damage."[8] He writes of the diptych's "inside pages" revealing the inscription given in Legrand and Chamonard's publication; this suggests he likely saw the diptych closed. Corroborating this surmise is that the corner damage to the rectangular sheets is substantially identical; that is, the broken piece on the upper left corner of the inscribed face of tablet A matches the broken piece on the upper right corner of the inscribed face of tablet B, and so on for each of the four corners (less so for the corners closest to the ring links). Given that the length of tablet A leaves more than enough space after line 12 for writing the four lines of tablet B, it seems that the initiator of the curse wanted the diptych or pinax form. This is in fact specifically named in one magical papyrus: τὰ πιττάκια … ἐγὼ γράφω.[9] This suggests there may be some significance for the magical operation of the curse in this form. Joseph Walker, the chief engineer of the Ottoman Railway, reported that it had been discovered in a grave, or strictly, a vase or pot ossuary, "near Kaklik" — a further critical piece of information for its interpretation, especially because the diptych was found among bone fragments. Those who have referred to the inscribed tablet have depended on Legrand and Chamonard.

However, the tablet was not lost. It remained in the Walker family collection until it was given to the British Museum in 1934 by daughter-in-law, Hetty Walker.[10] My impression is that the curse tablet has not been reviewed in detail since Legrand and Chamonard's meticulous restoration. This means that the original artifact can now be re-examined to test not only their readings but also other aspects that may prove important. I should stress that I have not been able to examine the diptych at first hand but have relied on the excellent online display provided by the British Museum.[11] Unfortunately only one face of each tablet is available, that which shows the obvious inscribed faces. There does appear to be some small letters in convex impression, at least between line 9 and line 10 towards the left-hand end of the names. This suggests that an investigation of both sides of each tablet is in order.

---

7 P-E. Legrand and J. Chamonard "Inscriptions de Phrygia," *BCH* 17 (1893): 250–1 nr. 27.

8 W. H. Ramsay, *The Cities and Bishoprics of Phrygia*. (Oxford: Clarendon Press, 2 vols, 1895, 1897), 1.351 nr 33.

9 *PGM* 30e.6–8 (ed. Preisendanz, Vol 2, 156).

10 The Museum record has "Mrs L. M. C. Walker". The first initial is a mistake. Charles Walker, Joseph's son (and also an engineer on the railway) married Hedwige Marie Charlotte Stengel in 1900. He died in 1935. The Museum invoice number is 1934, 1121.1.

11 See https://www.britishmuseum.org/collection/object/G_1934-1121-1.

Plate 8.2: The Kaklık diptych curse tablet.[12]

The two parts of the diptych measure 12.8 by 7 centimeters. The two lead sheets were held together by two metal rings, though one was missing at the time of decipherment. The letters, "very lightly engraved" range from 4 to 7 millimeters high. Rigorous attention to calligraphy was not a skill required of curse tablet stylists; indeed, the distortion of letters became part of the overall malicious menace of a *defixio*.[13] At the same time, the skill required to engrave on lead — the favorite *defixio* medium[14] — with any degree of scribal proficiency was considerable. The words on this diptych were written in reverse from right to left and, in the main, the letters were executed in retrograde style (that is, inverted). The letter *nu* was inconsistently retrograde (6 instances) or frontward (26 instances). *Sigmas* and *epsilons* are lunate but any curvilinear letters are awkwardly styled and vary considerably due to the difficulty of engraving the lead. There is an absence of any citizenship markers, but this probably only underscores the servility of a number of those named. However, the combination of Latin names (especially Sabina) and an epichoric name (Ammalion) suggests a mid to late second century date.

The curse tablet inscription entered two major early collections, that of Richard Wünsch and Augustus Audollent.[15] The latter provided brief snatches of interpretation.

I offer here, at right, a plain transcription of the inscription on tablet A and tablet B endeavoring to render the letter styles as accurately as possible. Adjoining a discreet text is given which offers some adjustments to that recorded by Legrand and Chamonard. The apparatus notes these differences.

12 Photograph by the late Professor Barbara F. McManus for the VRoma website by permission.

13 One curse tablet expressly states "just as these (letters) are jumbled up, so too may Proton the market-woman be jumbled up in all things" (οὕτως καὶ τὲς ἀγοραίας Πρώτο ἀναντία εἴη ἅπαντα); J. Curbera, "Seven Curse Tablets from the Collection of Richard Wünsch," *ZPE* 195 (2015): 143 (translation slightly adjusted).

14 It should be noted however that curses on wooden tablets rarely survive the ravages of time. One curse tablet suggests that lead was used because it enervated resistance: D. R. Jordan, "New Greek Curse Tablets (1985–2000)," *GBRS* 41 (2000): nr. 79.

15 Audollent, *Defixiones* 14; R. Wünsch, *Continens Defixionum* (Berlin: G. Reimer, 1897), XIII.

TabletA

Ἐγ]ὼ γράφω πάν-	I here consign all
τας τοὺς ἐμοὶ	those who worked
ἀντία ποιοῦν-	mischief against me
τας μετὰ τῶν	to
ἀώρων	untimely (deaths)[16]
Ἐπάγαθον	Epagathos
Σαβίναν	Sabina
Εὐτέρπην	Euterpes
Τερέντιον	Terentius
Ἀντίοχον	Antiochos
Τέρτιον	Tertius
Αμμαλιον	Ammalion
Ἀπολλώνιον	Apollonios,
τὸν Αμμαλιου	son of Ammalion,
τὸν Νοσσόν	called "the Chick"
Ὀνήσιμον τὸν	Onesimos the
ἀντίον ἀνι{νι}-	(prime) antagonist
ἀσ(ε)ι	to despair

Tablet B

Ῥούσων[α]	Rouson
Φιλημάτιον	Philemation
Βάκχαν	Bakcha
Χελιδόνα	Chelidon

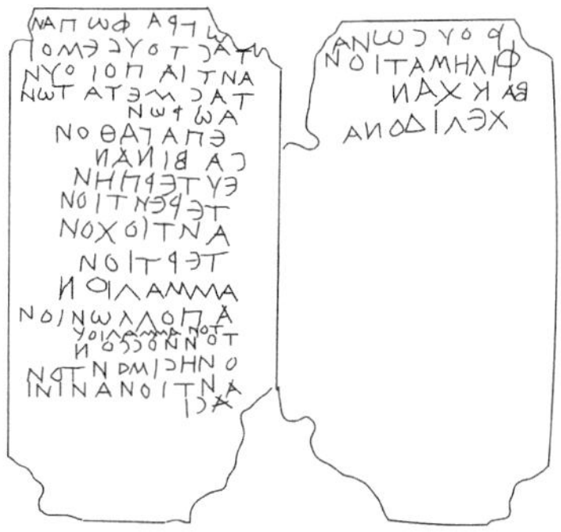

Plate 8.3: A transcription of the lead tablets reproducing the style of the engraved letters.

Tablet A

l. 1 L-C read Γράφω πά[ν. The omega is clear at the edge of the damaged right-hand corner. There are eleven letters in line 2 and ten in line 3, allowing space for the three letters of ἐγώ to open line 1. The emphasis of the pronoun is attested elsewhere.[17] Already mentioned, is the expression ἐγὼ γράφω combined with a reference to the diptych medium used for the curse. There are traces of the *nu* at the right-hand end of the line.

l. 2 L-C. read [α]. Again traces of the *alpha* are visible.

l. 3 L-C. read [ο]. The omicron is faint and small.

l. 9 The iota of Τερέντιον is clearly visible and does not require the correction of L-C.

l. 17–18 I have attempted to resolve the issue of the final word(s), which L-C. judged as not giving a satisfactory sense.

Tablet B

l. 3 The *beta* of Βάκχαν is relatively clear, though faint.

l. 4 The *omicron* may be an *omega*.

16 Cf *PGM* 4.342; Athenaeus, *Deip.* 15.694c. Photius the Lexicographer (sv) defined ἄωροι as οἱ πτὸ ὥρας ἀποθνήσκοντες, "those dying before their time." The editors of *IGR* 4.806 explain the opening as "In order that they might be with the dead, taken away violently before their time." (p. 281). I doubt whether there is any need to personify these "untimelies" as daimonic powers, as does Audollent, *Defixiones*, p. 465; compare, for the general sense of premature death, *I.Amorium* 257, 371 (left untranslated but clearly referring to a child who died too young). Rather any chthonic force that might bring about an early death is implied; in some *defixiones* seeking untimely death for a victim, the gods are explicitly named: Hades and/or Persephone, Osiris, Hermes; see Audollent, *Defixiones*, 38, 188; Jordan, "New Greek Curse Tablets," nrs 9, 23.

17 Audollent *Defixiones* 4A 1. 2.

There are thirteen names in this list. Nossos (from Neossos) I take as a nickname or soubriquet probably designed to specify the indicted person,[18] given that Apollonios (l. 13) is ubiquitous in Phrygia, let alone across the Mediterranean.[19] The specifying of his father, Ammalion (l. 14) (or the Graecized form Αμμαλιος), probably indicates the same person as in l. 12, and may have been added as part of the need for exactitude in naming the person — the letters of this line are smaller, slightly squeezed as if engraved as an afterthought. Marijana Ricl notes that "One of the most obvious and commonest reasons [for the use of second names or nicknames] is the need to distinguish between homonymous (grand)fathers and (grand)sons or simply too many homonymous members of the same community."[20] The use of the simple definite article τὸν rather than ὁ καὶ to render the "the one/also called" is rare but does occur and space was somewhat at a premium on the tablet at this point.[21] There are eight male names (Epathagos, Terentius, Tertius, Antiochos, Ammalion,[22] Apollonios, Onesimos, Rouson) and five female names (Euterpe, Sabina, Philemation, Bakcha and Chelidon) of those consigned to be slain by underworld forces. Of these names, three are Latin (Terentius, Tertius, and Sabina), nine are Greek (Epathagos, Euterpe, Antiochos, Apollonios, Onesimos, Rouson, Philemation, Bakcha and Chelidon) and one is epichoric, probably Phrygian (Ammalion/-os). Terentius and Tertius are almost certainly slave names (cf Rom 16:22), Philemation likely so and possibly Euterpe, Onesimos and Chelidon. Onesimus and Apollonios are names already attested at Colossae, provided one accepts the references in Phmn 10 and Col 4:9 (which may indicate two persons, given how ubiquitous the name was). Bakcha is unattested elsewhere. One family unit of some constituency is witnessed, that is, of the father and son, Ammalion and Apollonios; no mother seems to be mentioned, given that there are no female names immediately before or after these two. The names corroborate our dating the *defixio* to the (probably mid-) second century but they also signal a mixed community of slaves and free(d) persons.

---

18 Robert, *Noms Indigènes*, 60. On such nicknames see *SEG* 39.1176 (Ephesos, time of Tiberius); *I.Mus. Denizli* 84 (Çal plateau, 2nd century CE), 130 (Kınıklı, 2nd century CE). Significantly, Audollent does not include Nossos in his names, but rather under "Signa", that is "epithet", "nickname" (*Defixiones*, p. 447). Hence, he too finds thirteen names in the list (*Defixiones*, p. 450).

19 362 occurrences in Phrygia and another 354 in Pisidia, according to *LGPN* VC. *LGPN* has 4724 occurrences in total and this would have risen since the earlier volumes were published.

20 M. Ricl, "A New Inscription from the Cayster Valley and the Question of *Supernomina* in Hellenistic and Roman Lydia," in *Onomatologos: Studies in Greek Personal Names presented to Elaine Matthews* edited by R. W. V. Catling and F. Marchand (Oxford: Oxbow Books, 2010), 550.

21 Consequently, I am not convinced it should be included in *LGPN* VC.

22 Here, I follow Ladislav Zgusta's identification: *Kleinasiatische Personennamen* (Prague: Tschechoslowakischen Akademie, 1964), 65 nrs 57–33. *LGPN* follows a Greek standardization.

A village of Colossae near Kaklık

There has been no ancient village yet identified at Kaklık but the mention of a ceramic ossuary, probably similar to some recently discovered at the north-east necropolis at Laodikeia,[23] is indicative of a settlement. In Byzantine times, the area of the subterranean white travertine formation had conferred on the immediately surrounding area the name Graos Gala, "Crone's Curd." It was substantial enough to attract a vivid aetiological tale,[24] and to provide a temporary rural camp for the military commander, Andronikos Angelos, in battles against the invading Turks.[25] But this is twelfth century and insufficient, of its own, to warrant pre-dating a settlement by a millennium. But of particular interest is evidence of an ancient quarry in the hills to the north. Francis Arundell had referred indeterminately to some quarry he had seen in 1828,[26] which he assigned to Colossae. Celal Şimşek has claimed the Kaklık location as Colossae's quarry — at least for the limestone building blocks and *bomoi* that were still *in situ* at the date of publication.[27] More significantly, heavy floods in 2014 removed surface soils to reveal a large, unused sarcophagus, which appeared to be situated in the remains of a first-to-second century store-room.[28] The lid of the plain, unadorned sarcophagus shows the same design features as many of the *bomoi* from the northern necropolis at Colossae, namely, simple acroteria at each corner and a boss in the center of the pediment. This type of less expensive casket is familiar in a number of cities in Asia Minor.

A sarcophagus is a mark of increased Roman (and Roman mimetic) ostentation of position that developed in the first century CE when a noticeable change of preference from Roman cremation to eastern inhumation begins to be discerned.[29] This of course meant increased demand for stone and stone masonry, already exponentially expanding because of the heavy increase in urbanization across the empire. Indeed, the presence of Latin names among the targets of the *defixio* might suggest that this was a settlement either under imperial control or leased out to profiteering contractors. If so, there would

23 C. Şimşek, *Laodikeia Nekropolü (2004–2010 Yılları) (Katalog)* (Istanbul: Ege, 2011), plate 21, nrs 62–64. These ceramic pots seem to have been used as both cremated and ossuary containers. Elsewhere, such containers of remains have also yielded *defixiones*: see Jordan, "A Survey of Greek Defixiones Not Included in the Special Corpora," *GRBS* 26 (1985): 157 (Athens).

24 Michael Choniates *Or.* 2.97 (see Appendix 1).

25 Nicetas Choniates *Chron.* 195.21–3.

26 F. J. A. Arundell, *A Visit to the Seven Churches of Asia; with an Excursion into Pisidia* (London: John Rodwell, 1828), 99.

27 Şimşek, *Laodikeia*, 329.

28 This is indicated, *inter alia*, by door jams.

29 C. Thomas and C. İçten, "The *Ostothekai of Ephesos* and the Rise of Sarcophagus Inhumation: Death, Conspicuous Consumption, and Roman Freedmen," in *Akten des Symposiums des Sarkophag-Korpus 2001* edited by G. Koch (Mainz: Zabern, 2007), 343–4.

be potential conflict of laws governing disputes, that is, between the extensive Roman legal principles governing quarries,[30] and those of the city in whose territory the quarry was situated.[31]

The Lycus Valley was particularly well-endowed to add the harvesting of stone to its agricultural fecundity. Guiseppe Scardozzi has begun to map the multitude of quarries that serviced the cities and beyond, though concentrating on Hierapolis.[32] Settlements were established that were geared to the stone trade. Such villages, as they frequently morphed from work contingents, had less autonomy than Eleinokapria, being more directly under the control of either a landed estate (imperial or private), a business monopoly that had secured the commercial license from the city or a specific owner of the site. Some settlements, such as Thiounta, approximately 15 miles north-west of Hierapolis, became quite substantial places of habitation,[33] and turned local stone to urban-mimetic typologies, such as votives to gods, honors to individuals and recording of festivals and associated games.[34] Indeed, one apparent association, that of the Psapharoi, might be connected with the stone trade ("sand/gravel makers"?).[35]

Whatever the details of the quarry at Kaklık and its associated settlement, it seems clear that there was a substantial enough population to establish its own burial ground. This is crucial to the interpretation of this *defixio*, and many other *defixiones*. The depositing of the *defixio* in a grave was a fundamental contextualization of the reversal of fortunes desired for the targeted parties.[36] Here the corruption of death was close at hand ready to infect others, especially if the bones were those of someone, like Tatarin of Eleinokapria noted in chapter 3, whose death was untimely (having pre-deceased her parents).[37]

30 See B. Russell, *The Economics of the Roman Stone Trade* (Oxford: Oxford University Press, 2013), 53–61.

31 On the vexed question of the extent of Roman control of quarries, see A. M. Hirt, "Centurions, Quarries, and the Emperor," in *Ownership and Exploitation of Land and Natural Resources in the Roman World* edited by P. Erdkamp, K. Verboven and A. Zuiderhoek (Oxford: Oxford University Press, 2015), 289–314.

32 G. Scardozzi, "The Provenance of Marbles and Alabasters Used in the Monuments of Hierapolis in Phrygia (Turkey): New Information from a Systematic Review and Integration of Archaeological and Archaeometric Data," *Heritage* 2 (2019): 1–35. See generally, T. Ismaelli and G. Scardozzi (eds) *Ancient Quarries and Building Sites in Asia Minor* (Bari: Edipuglia, 2016).

33 See M. Brilli *et al.* "Petrography, geochemistry, and cathodoluminescene of ancient white marble from quarries in the southern Phrygia and northern Caria regions of Turkey: Considerations on provenance discrimination," *JAS Reports* 4 (2015): 124–42.

34 W. M. Ramsay, "Antiquities of Southern Phrygia and the Border Lands (III)," *AJA* 4 (1888): 278–9. The naming of a *Dêmos* in the first inscription points to the settlement's size, even it was not formally recognized as a *polis*.

35 Ritti, *Museo Archeologico*, 98 nr. 32.

36 Audollent, *Defixiones*, pp. CX–CXI.

37 See D. R. Jordan, "A Survey of Greek Defixiones Not Included in the Special Corpora," *GBRS* 26 (1985): 152.

Writing took on a magical/religious ambience — indicated by the opening line of the *defixio*, ἐγὼ γράφω[38] — made the more powerful by being written retrograde and reversed.[39] This invites our hazy vision of a professional, but this is not demanded[40] — indeed the use of retrograde N is inconsistent and one *sigma* is formed with two strokes much like the Hebrew letter *bet* (l. 2). The lives of the named were now (anticipated to be) doomed to reversal, not unlike Job's winding back of his life through the lengthy curse of Job 3:3–10. Writing not only fixed intent (just as nails were often driven through a written curse tablet or folded sheet as an enactment of "fixing" that intent)[41] but it gained power through reading. The ring binders (*katadesmoi*?) linking the two tablets may have had a similar symbolic force. In the grave, the hidden readers were intended to be the chthonic gods or malevolent spirits that haunted the dark realm ("nekydaimons").[42] It is likely that there was some ritualised activity involved in the preparation of the tablet, the writing of the curse, the binding of the tablets, and the transfer of the item to its sinister location.[43]

Daemons, deities and the dead

The *defixio* would not have belonged to anyone in the grave or (probably) those responsible for the interment. Their deposits, if they gave them, were amulets designed to have a protective force.[44] Rather it would have been an intrusion, a variant of the desecration that numerous epitaphs tried to guard against by warnings, penalties and, ironically, their own curses.[45] One fre-

38 Compare Audollent, *Defixiones* 47 (καταγράφω). Different initiating terms could be used; see Audollent, *Defixiones*, pp. LVIII, 474–83.

39 Audollent, *Defixiones*, pp. XLVI with fn 3 for numbered examples. For other examples of reverse writing, see Jordan, "Survey," 148 nrs 16–17; for retrograde letters, *ibid.* 155 nr. 4.

40 See J. G. Gager (ed.), *Curse Tablets and Binding Spells from the Ancient World* (Oxford: Oxford University Press, 1992), 4.

41 Horace shows his familiarity with the ritual, drawing metaphorical power from it: *Ode* 1.35. The nailing is sometimes understood as enacting the bind of death; see J. H. Mozley and G. P. Gould (trans.) *Ovid: The Art of Love and Other Poems* (LCL 232; Cambridge, MA: Harvard University Press, 1929), 366.

42 So, S. Lambert, *Inscribed Athenian Laws and Decrees in the Age of Demosthenes: Historical Essays* (Leiden: Brill, 2018), 26. Even the dead could bear chthonic power: Wünsch, *Defixiones* 100, where the deceased, named Onesimos, is asked to help fulfill the curse.

43 See L. Revell, *Roman Imperialism and Local Identities* (Cambridge: Cambridge University Press, 2009), 123–5.

44 See A. Wilburn, *Materia Magica: The Archaeology of Magic in Roman Egypt, Cyprus, and Spain* (Ann Arbor: University of Michigan Press, 2012), 48–9. One rolled metal find in a tomb from the necropolis at Laodikeia has been identified as an amulet, though its corroded state might mask a *defixio*; see Şimşek, *Laodikeia Nekropolü*, 970, nr. 1302.

45 See J. Strubbe, *APAI EΠΙΤΥΜΒΙΟΙ. Imprecations against Desecration of the Grave in the Greek Epitaphs of Asia Minor: A Catalogue* (*IGSK* 52; Bonn: Habelt, 1997).

quently cited first-century (CE) Latin inscription gives a sense of the dynamics and the accepted malevolent power involved.[46] The inscription was set up by a freedman, Lucius Cancrius Primigenius, in honor of Jupiter for saving the city council and people (*pro salute coloniae et decurionum et populi*) of the colony of Tuder in central Italy. The inscription directly states that the names of city councilors (*decurionum nomina*) had been fixed to tombs (*defixa monumentis*); the intervention of the god and exposure of the deed, had released the colony and its citizens from the dread of impending danger (*metu periculorum*). A general identification of the offending party is given, whether by accurate knowledge or as a diversion to a convenient scapegoat — no name is recorded. It was the "unspeakable villainy of a most scurrilous crime of a public slave" (*sceleratissimi servi publici infando latrocinio*).[47]

Several aspects are important for comparative purposes. Firstly, power lies in the nexus between the (distorted) written names and the place of the dead.[48] Secondly, it is assumed that there is a relationship between whoever devised the *defixio* and the intended recipients. Thirdly, it is accepted that slaves were likely to be responsible,[49] even if, as John Gager perceives, the Tuder case, by not naming the offender, probably does not have that information[50] — discovery brought dismal consequences, most especially for slaves.[51] At the same time it ought not be assumed that only slaves resorted to such measures. The deployment of curses and cursing mechanisms such as *defixiones* was widespread across society. Fourthly, the practice involved is castigated in the harshest language. Fifthly, and possibly most important of all, the curse tablet is viewed as fundamentally destabilizing the established order of society.

The attraction of *defixiones* for slaves was that they rarely had sufficient standing in society to exact justice in "acceptable" ways.[52] They are among the

46 *CIL* 11.4639 = *ILS* 3001. It is found in T. Wiedemann, *Greek and Roman Slavery* (London: Routledge, 1981), 189 nr. 210; G. Luck, *Arcana Mundi: Magic and the Occult in the Greek and Roman Worlds* (Baltimore: Johns Hopkins University Press, 1985), 90–1, nr. 14; Gager, *Curse Tablets*, 55–6, nr. 135.

47 Wiedemann, *Slavery*, 189 translates this directly as "horrid sorcery" allowing the context to dictate the intent. I have permitted *sceleratissimi* to sit as a substantive to draw out the labored horror that the text seeks to convey.

48 Compare Audollent *Defixiones* 30: "Daimons that are beneath the earth … whosoever resides here and whosoever is laid down here … take away …" Δέμονες οἳ κατὰ γῆν … οἵτινες ἐνθάδε κίσθε κὲ ἐνθάδε κάθεστε … παραλάβετε". Note this lengthy curse tablet has been considerably reconstructed but the phrasing is familiar from other curse tablets; see Jordan, "New Greek Curse Tablets," nr. 52.

49 This class of denigrated users of curse tablets was closely followed by women: see Basil *Ep*. 188.8.

50 Gager, *Curse Tablets*, 56.

51 Some individuals are known, for example, a certain Kallias of Cyprus, who cursed Krateros, his adversary; Audollent, *Defixiones* 30. These presumably relied on remaining *incognito*.

52 T. H. M. Gellar-Goad, Z. Papakonstantinou and W. Riess, "Magic in Ancient Athens: A Complete Translation of Attic Curse Tablets," in *Colloquia Attica: Neuere Forschungen zur Archaik, zum athenischen Recht und zur Magie* edited by W. Riess (Stuttgart: Franz Steiner, 2018), 266.

"subalterns", those rarely heard in acceptable (literary, even inscriptional) texts.[53] The servile status indicated by a number of the names on the Kaklık *defixio* suggests that the grievance of the writer (the *defigens*)[54] was not something that could or would be dealt with by law or a master/overseer's judgment.[55] In this sense, the antagonism (ἀντία, l. 3) of those named probably is not to be read against a juridical setting,[56] where witnesses, jurors and/or legal officials were in view,[57] even though some *defixiones* clearly manifest this intent.[58] The singling out of Onesimos as *the* opponent (ll. 16–17) probably indicates his leadership in whatever injury, loss or ill-treatment the curser had suffered. My suggested reconstruction of lines 17–18 is to read the second –νι– as a mistaken dittography. A similar mistake was made in the carving of Tatia's epitaph in line 7 — the Colossian village inscription reviewed in chapter 3 — where ΑΛ was carved in preparation for ἄλ-λω, a word-splitting that the lithographer then rejected but without erasing what had been carved. Taken as a dative, ἀνιάσει,[59] Onesimos is singled out for particularly harsh treatment — not just an untimely demise but despair as well. It may then be that the second page of the lead sheet diptych was added because of faulty memory or because new perpetrators had emerged or, as mentioned previously, because there was some occult symbolism attached to the diptych.

In the unnamed village within Colossae's orbit was a religious practice that, even when circumscribed as reprehensible, harmful magic, was nonetheless part of the gamut of devotions, ritual behavior and individual beliefs that the population of Colossae (along with other cities) held. Here there is the suggestion that class differences and differentials in levels of access to religious and legal remedies were compounded by the locality in which one was situated, that is, between city and chora. But there is also a sense that the more socially and civically acceptable means of aligning with the universe had proved inadequate to meet the existential anxieties and experience of injustice and misfortune in a person's life. Some *defixiones* were little more than an attempt to

---

53 See Z. Papakonstantinou, "Binding curses, agency and the Athenian democracy," in *Violence and Community: Law, Space and Identity in the Ancient Eastern Mediterranean World* edited by I. K. Xydopoulos, K. Vlassopoulos and E. Tounta (London: Routledge, 2017), 142–58.

54 Most curse tablets are authored/commissioned by one person; very occasionally, more than one person is involved: for example, Audollent, *Defixiones* 35, 41, 110.

55 For an example of a curse related to a court appearance, see Audollent, *Defixiones* 49, 111, 112. For a curse of another slave, see W. S. Fox, "The Johns Hopkins Tabellae Defixionum," *AJP* 33 (1912): 17–18, nr. 1, ll. 4, 19 and p. 35. For a curse tablet by a slave against a fellow slave, see *AE* 2000.795.

56 Compare the similar expression (ἐναντίοι) in Jordan "New Greek Curse Tablets," nr. 116.

57 Contra Audollent *Defixiones*, pp. XC, 471. The fourfold classification of defixiones: relationship, judicial, competition and commercial has been found to be too constraining. See Eidinow, "Binding Spells," 351–87.

58 *SEG* 42.217 Jordan "Survey," nrs 168, 173, 176.

59 The loss of the *epsilon* is a common occurrence in inscriptions of Asia Minor.

"fix" a chariot race or athletic competition.[60] But this *defixio* from Colossae's territory speaks of something deeply personal and troubling.

Defixiones and the Letter to the Colossians

Clinton Arnold has traversed the territory of *defixiones* for insights into the letter, particularly for expanding understanding into the breadth of meaning to be associated with the worship of angels (Col 2:18).[61] I do not want to repeat or critique his work. However, we can now be confident that such phenomena were very much part of Colossian territory and of the religious options open to its inhabitants — especially given that there was always a wide, liminal domain between "religion" and "magic". The material witness we have comes from the second century but the evidence of curse tablets and the recipe books that delivered rituals and language to effect remedies have an ancient pedigree, which was untrammelled by the reach of Roman law or the advent of Christianity. One canon (nr. 36) of the Synod of Laodikeia in c.365 CE, following immediately on the heels of the ban against the worship (ὀνομάζειν) of angels (nr. 35), shows that the practice of magic continued long into the fourth century. The canon prohibits priests or other members of the clergy from being magicians, enchanters, mathematicians (!)[62] or astrologers nor are they permitted to make amulets "which are chains for their own souls" (ἅτινά ἐστι δεσμωτήρια τῶν ψυχῶν αὐτῶν). Clearly the long cultural inheritance of the practice of magic in its various forms was hard to shake from the folds of the church.[63]

Consequently, there may be some benefit in reading select verses not addressed by Arnold against that background. It does not necessarily assert that *defixiones* are in the specific purview of the letter writer. But it does suggest that when these *defixiones* are factored into the context of a Colossian audience of the letter, new possibilities may be awakened as to the impact of the Christ framework that the writer formulates. The fact that from Plato to Plotinus,[64] these curse tablets and their magical content were the subject of philosophical reflection is a powerful indication that these practices were both wide-

60 Audollent *Defixiones*, 306–7 nr. 233, 323 nr. 241, 341–2 nr. 250; Jordan, "Survey," nrs 138, 140.

61 See Arnold, *Colossian Syncretism*, *infra*; Arnold has provided some supplementary essays and rejoinders; see "Sceva, Solomon, and Shamanism: The Jewish Roots of the Problem at Colossae," *JETS* 55 (2012): 7–26; "Initiation, Vision and Spiritual Power: The Hellenistic Dimensions of the Problem at Colossae," in *First Urban Churches* 5, 173–86.

62 Mathematicians (μαθηματικοί), here probably relates to astrology, just as we saw in Theon of Smyrna in chapter 6. The term, in this context, might relate to the casting of horoscopes.

63 For examples of Christian amulets, see R. Kotansky, *Greek Magical Amulets* (Opladen: Westdeutscher Verlag, 1994), 236 nr. 45, 301 nr. 53, 387 nr. 68.

64 See Plato *Resp.* 2.364c; Plotinus *Enn.* 4.4.40. Audollent provides a list of testimonia: *Defixiones*, pp. CXVIII–CXXIII, but omits Plotinus.

spread and well-known (cf Acts 19:11–20; *Dig.* 10.2.4.1). They were not part of some backwater as might be invited in a mis-interpretation of the importance of villages to a city's territory, nor an optional footnote to the myopia of the urban focus on the rise of the early Christ-followers.[65] As the great epigrapher on whom so many biblical commentators still rely, William Mitchell Ramsay, observed when focusing on Lycaonia

> ... with the rarest exceptions we find nothing whatsoever [in writings about ancient history and the early Church] with regard to the practical facts of life among the common people in that country ... The ordinary people made it possible for Churchmen to exercise their leading power, for generals to have armies to conduct to victory or defeat; and without the knowledge of their common life, a knowledge of history becomes one-sided and misleading in the highest degree.[66]

The Letter to the Colossians provides little direct description of the lives of its addressees before they became Christ-followers. I have already drawn attention to the vice-lists in Col 3:5, 8. While vice-lists are little more than rhetorical devices rather than a rap-sheet of actual misbehaviors and crimes, the recognition that these are a sweep of the world familiar to the Colossians comes in verse 7, ἐν οἷς καὶ ὑμεῖς περιπατέσατέ ποτε ὅτε ἐζῆτε ἐν τούτοις ("there was a time when you also walked among them, when you lived among these people"). The ἐν οἷς and ἐν τούτοις neatly frame the practices and the practitioners, syntactically and socially. Here again is the subtle scalpel of the writer at work to separate the Christ-followers at Colossae from being "in Colossae", just as we saw in Col 1:2. Regardless of how much the Christ-followers might identify themselves as guilty of one or more of the vices, their life "in Colossae" before becoming Christ-followers meant that the patterns of Colossian life were the atmosphere which they breathed. The vice-lists characterize those patterns in fairly sordid, if general, terms but the letter is not locked onto the constituent items of the lists. The city's ambition for advancement and prosperity combined a cultivation of Rome with a concomitant cost to those without the means, position or connections to be part of it (such as an aggrieved probable-slave at an unknown probable-quarry village near modern Kaklık). Philosophy, as a mark of preparedness for civic leadership (as we saw in chapter 6), is not something that seems to have been part of the former ways of life for the Christ-followers at Colossae except, perhaps, for the author of the letter to them (see chapter 10). Rather the criticism mounted against philosophy in Col 2:8 serves as a warning against venturing into something previously *not* a feature of their lives.

---

65 See especially T. Robinson, *Who were the First Christians? Dismantling the Urban Thesis* (Oxford: Oxford University Press, 2017) and A. H. Cadwallader et. al. (eds), *The Village in Antiquity and the Rise of Early Christianity* (London: T & T Clark 2023), forthcoming.

66 W. M. Ramsay, "A Country Town of Lycaonia. A Description of the Conditions of Christian Life under the Eastern Empire," *Journal of the Transactions of the Victoria Institute* 41 (1909): 36–7.

There is one other reference to the "when" (ποτέ) of the Christ-followers' earlier lives.[67] It is set into a long sentence that contrasts the former times with the now time of life in Christ (Col 1:20–23).[68] It is the first extrapolation from the Christological hymn of Col 1:12(15)–20.[69] A trident of descriptions pins down their prior pattern of life:

καὶ ὑμᾶς ποτε ὄντας	and you once were
ἀπηλλοτριωμένους	alienated
καὶ ἐχθροὺς τῇ διανοίᾳ	and hostile in intent
ἐν τοῖς ἔργοις τοῖς πονηροῖς	among evil deeds

The standard interpretation of this tripartite catalogue is that the writer (whether Paul or perhaps an Epaphras positioning Paul's authority) has provided a sweep of their former opposition to God and has slipped into a stock Jewish stereotype of Gentile life-style in order to do so. Scot McKnight sees ἀπηλλοτριωμένους as "alienated from God" supplying in translation what is absent in the Greek text and curiously referencing an epitaph warning against "alienating" a tomb as an authority.[70] We shall explore the significance of this grave concern below. McKnight then wrangles "evil deeds" into "a Jewish boilerplate accusation against Gentiles" asserting that from its origins in the revelation to Moses, "it became a rhetorical feature in Jewish propaganda … a stereotype for Jewish literature … the reality of Gentile behaviors seen through the lens of Torah holiness."[71] Paul Foster, who doesn't buy the package of Paul's authorship, is little different: "the Colossians were, in their former state, people opposed and hostile towards God". The author delivers "a stereotypical Jewish perspective on the ethical behaviour of Gentiles separated from God."[72] Frequently cited as part of the admission that ἀπαλλοτριόω is an extremely rare word in the Second Testament, are the only other occurrences, that is, in Eph 2:12 and 4:18 where a Jewish-style polemic against estranged Gentiles *is* evident.[73] It seems that a canonical steam-roller has

67 The importance of the two references to the Colossians' former life is laid out by L. Bormann, *Der Brief des Paulus an die Kolosser* (ThHK 10/1; Leipzig: Evangelische Verlagsanstalt, 2012), 106.

68 G. E. Cannon, *The Use of Traditional Materials in Colossians* (Macon, GA: Mercer University Press, 1983), 35.

69 H. O. Maier, "A Sly Civility: Colossians and Empire," *JSNT* 27 (2005): 330–3.

70 S. McKnight, *The Letter to the Colossians* (NICNT; Grand Rapids, MN: Eerdmans, 2018), 170 with fn 407 citing *New Doc. Early Christ.* 3, p. 62 (that is, nr. 24, a short entry on ἀπαλλοτριόω).

71 McKnight, *Colossians*, 172.

72 P. Foster, *Colossians* (BNTC; London: T & T Clark, 2016), 203.

73 So, for example, E. Lohse, *Colossians and Philemon* (Hermeneia; Philadelphia: Fortress, 1971), 63; Dunn, *Colossians and Philemon*, 106; C. R. Seitz, *Colossians* (BTCB; Grand Rapids, MN: Brazos Press, 2014), 105. On the distinctiveness of Ephesians from Colossians, see M. Immendörfer, *Ephesians and Artemis: The Cult of the Great Goddess of Ephesus as the Epistle's Context* (WUNT2.436; Tübingen: Mohr Siebeck, 2017), 308–11, 312.

flattened the meaning in Colossians into conformity to the later and derivative writing, a letter with its own distinctive, rhetorical intent.

There have been some demurrals on such an interpretation. Jerry Sumney thinks the reference to the Colossians' former state is generic and does not rely on the distinction between Jews and Gentiles. Nonetheless, he sees the opposition sketched in the three parts is to God.[74] Marianne Thompson acknowledges that there is no object (ie "God" or perhaps "Christ") to the alienation and develops a (welcome) social dimension to the notion of alienation, even recognizing the realm of international diplomacy in the timbre of the language used.[75] This is extensively developed by Harry Maier as he drives home repeated connections with the imperial ideology of *homonoia/concordia*, the desire for harmony in the political (as derivative from the cosmic) sphere.[76] This has important implications for the assessment of *defixiones*, which, as we have seen from the Tuder inscription, were deeply disturbing to city harmony at a local (as distinct from military or international) level.

There are immediate problems here with a Jewish stereotype of Gentile rebellion against God, just in the handling of the text. Christopher Seitz admits that Colossians is curiously devoid of quotations from Scripture, accenting "*because his audience does not know it*."[77] One wonders what *gravitas* would be gained, in this regard, by utilizing a Jewish stereotype (if that is what it is). Presumably a Jewish stereotype would also have by-passed the audience's recognition. If, as Foster and I think, there is no significant Jewish population at Colossae (as compared with its neighbors, Laodikeia and Hierapolis), there is not even a partial gain in adopting a view held by one (missing) part of the audience. And if Epaphras or Tychicus is in fact the author, it stretches credibility that a Gentile author writing to a Gentile audience in Gentile territory would describe them in ways that only Jews would recognize, indeed fracturing the very unity in Christ extolled later in the letter (Col 3:11). The only explanation, thin and unsatisfying at that, is the provision of a touch of Pauline verisimilitude.

But this is precisely where the problem lies. Even McKnight concedes that the grammatical construction for "evil deeds" has no parallel in the Second Testament,[78] though this might overstate the evidence — the Johannine writings are close (Jn 7:7, 1 Jn 3:12, 2 Jn 11 cf 2 Tim 4:18). The net could be cast more widely across the Judeo-Christian writings and still be relatively empty. Efforts to reward some trawling endeavors turn semblances into demonstrations (Ps 27:4, Isa 3:11, Bar 1:22 cf Ex 1:11, Prov 3:30, Jer 25:6). The singular occurrence of the adjective and noun tied together is in 1 Esdr 8.86 (τὰ

74 J. L. Sumney, *Colossians: A Commentary* (NTL; Louisville, KY: WJKP, 2008), 82–3.

75 M. M. Thompson, *Colossians and Philemon* (Grand Rapids, MN: Eerdmans, 2005), 40–1.

76 Maier, "Sly Civility," *passim*.

77 Seitz, *Colossians* 105 (italics his).

78 McKnight, *Colossians*, 172.

ἔργα ἡμῶν τὰ πονηρά), but here Jews are being castigated, not Gentiles.[79] This hardly justifies the classification of the section Col 1:21–23, and this particular phrase, as "a Jewish boilerplate characterization", nor, derivatively, a mimesis of Paul's perspective.

The conjunction of the two words, however, *is* well attested in "Gentile" texts, sometimes in the singular, sometimes the plural, and sometimes with no differentiation between πονηρός and κακός in the impugning of certain works (ἔργα).[80] Of particular significance is the occurrence of the phrase in public religious and political contexts. Demosthenes, for example, saw that the public naming of turpitude in political office was crucial to avoid earning the reputation as an accomplice "in scandalous and wicked deeds" (δεινῶν καὶ πονηρῶν ἔργων).[81] Plutarch conjured a prayer by the early Roman dictator Camillus, that opened "O greatest Jupiter, and you gods who oversee both fine and foul deeds ..." (Ζεῦ μέγιστε καὶ θεοὶ χρηστῶν ἐπίσκοποι καὶ πονηρῶν ἔργων), before he proceeded to justify a campaign against an enemy city.[82] Dionysios of Halikarnassos repeatedly portrayed "evil deeds" as the undermining of stable society.[83] No ethnic configuration colored such evil or bad deeds, though comparisons might readily be made, usually to barbarian behaviors in general.

Here we are reminded of the vehement, extended description of the impious evil that branded the use of a curse tablet at the colony of Tuder in Italy. It was not only harmful to the body politic but scurillous-in-the-extreme (*sceleratissimi*), and only able to be overcome by the intervention of the god(s). The same term (*sceleris*) occurs in an epitaph from Lambaesis in Numidia that alleges that the untimely death of a beloved wife was the result of a curse, a manifestly wicked crime.

> [six lines] ... Here lies Ennia Fructuosa, most beloved wife, of unmistakable modesty, a matron to be praised for her unusual loyalty. She took the name of wife at age 15 but was unable to live with it for more than 13 years. She did not receive the kind of death she deserved — cursed by spells, she long lay mute so that her life was rather torn from her by violence than given back to nature. Either the infernal gods or the heavenly deities will punish this wicked crime (*sceleris*) which has been perpetrated. Aelius Porculinus, her husband, a tribune in the great Third Legion, the Augusta, erected this monument.[84]

---

79 Similarly, Philo *Praem.* 142.5 of Jews who abandon God.

80 Plato *Resp.* 4.421d; Herodian *Marc.* 3.6.4; Dio Cassius 37.5.

81 Demosthenes *Or.* 19.33.8 cf 2 Jn 10–11.

82 Plutarch *Cam.* 5.7.

83 Dionysios Halicarnassus *Ant. Rom.* 2.29.15, 5.64.3.2, 10.6.3.1.

84 *Ennia hic sita est Fructuosa karissima coniunx certae pudicitiae bonoque obsequio laudanda matrona XV anno maritae nomen acce pit in quo amplius quam XIII vivere non potuit quae non ut meruit ita mortis sortem ret(t)ulit carminibus defixa iacuit per tempora muta ut eius spiritus vi extorqueretur quam naturae redderetur cuius admissi vel Manes vel di Caelestes erunt sceleris vindices Aelius haec posuit Proculinus ipse maritus legio nis tantae III Augustae*

The language that surrounds the horror at the impact of solicitation of curses is florid and uncompromising. It may explain why there was so much concern that a grave, once sealed, be left undisturbed. The familiar prohibition that we currently know from Colossae and its territory, we have come across already in Tatia's funerary inscription from Eleinokapria. It bans and penalizes (monetarily) the addition of any other corpse to the family plot. This village *bomos* epitaph echoes what has been found in inscriptions on other *bomoi* from graves in the northern necropolis of the city.[85]

But other epitaphs went further. Not only did they include the ban on disturbance of the grave by the interring of another corpse but they added a further injunction that sometimes carried with it the added potency of its own curse: "if any body lays an evil-working hand on this tomb, he will consign his children to be orphans and his home a wilderness" (εἰ δέ τις τῷ τύνβῳ τούτῳ κακοεργέα χεῖρα πρόσοισει, ὀρφανὰ λείψει τέκνα καὶ οἶον ἔρημον).[86] This evil-working hand, or hand performing evil deeds is found on a number of epitaphs.[87] Both κακός and πονηρός can occur as the description either of the hand that performs the deed or the deed itself.[88] Other Phrygian epitaphs amplified the curse: for any perpetrator, that is anyone who did badly by the grave, untimely deaths awaited his children (εἴ τις κακῶς ποιήσει τοῦτῳ μνήματι, ἄωρα τέκνα).[89] One of the most voluble of all comes from an imperial period epitaph found near Thyateira.

---

tribunus. *CIL* 8.2756 (post-212 CE); translation from R. Kraemer (ed.), *Women's Religions in the Greco-Roman World: A Sourcebook* (Oxford: Oxford University Press, 2004), 131 nr. 57.

85 See A. H. Cadwallader, "Gertrude Bell's Resolution of a Disputed Inscription," *Gephyra* 20 (2020): 1–26 and chapter 12.

86 *MAMA* 11.145 (Pentapolis, 200–250 CE). There is some suggestion that this is a Christian epitaph but this is debatable, even though Christians were as commonly involved in generating curse-tablets as others; see E. Chiricat, "The 'crypto-Christian' inscriptions of Phrygia," in *Roman Phrygia: Culture and Society* edited by P. Thonemann (Cambridge: Cambridge University Press, 2013), 198–214.

87 *MAMA* 7.147, 231; *SEG* 15.801; *ICG* 625.

88 *I.Iznik* 87; *MAMA* 7.253; *SEG* 47.1755, 53.1462.

89 C. H. E. Haspels, *The Highlands of Phrygia: Sites and Monuments* (Princeton: Princeton University Press, 2 vols, 1971), vol 1, 317 nr. 49; cf Waelkens, *Die kleinasiatischen Türsteine: typologische und epigraphische Untgersuchungen der kleinasiatischen Grabreliefs mit Scheintür* (Mainz am Rhein: Philipp von Zabern, 1986), 446 (Diokelia, 241/242 CE). For a survey of such imprecations, see L. Robert, "Malédictions funéraires grecques," *CRAI* (1978): 241–69; Strubbe, *APAI EΠΙΤΥΜΒΙΟΙ*, 289–92 *et passim*.

Plate 8.4: The long epitaph of Metrodorus carved on a slab that was probably part of a large tomb structure. It was found at Rahmiye between Thyateira and Hierokaisareia. It contains an elaborate description of potential infractions against the tomb, including the use of its materials and the interred remains for magical purposes (ll. 5–13), followed by an even longer set of curses to be rained down on the violator (ll. 13–24). It is now held in the Manisa Museum.

After the details of the people involved in the memorial structure, 20 lines roll on in fulsome detail of banned sacrilege against the tomb and the curses ready to drop on offenders. The preliminary sounding of sacrilegious acts begins with "if anyone does anything with evil intent resolving to alienate either what is in it or around it". The language of the inscription is charged with terms familiar to the Colossian text of alienation and evil (Col 1:21): δόλῳ τε πονηρῷ ποιήσει τι ἀπαλλοτριώσεως χάριν … But then the epitaph unfolds what is judged to be evil intent and alienation: damage to the architecture, invincible spell (ἀπόρου φαρμάκου), binding curse (καταδέσμου προσχώσῃ) and so on. The details of the curses aimed at any perpetrator of iniquity are even more florid and lurid, culminating with "and if there is something else fitting for curse which is not written up (here), let that be his lot as well!"[90]

In the light of the Tuder inscription, it seems clear that one of the specific infractions of the tomb's sanctity, if not the main one, was the disturbance of

90 καὶ εἴ τι κατάρας δίκαιον ἔστιν [ὃ] οὐκ ἀναγέγραπται, καὶ τοῦτο αὐτῷ γένοιτο (ll. 23–4). See H. Malay and M. Ricl "A New Imprecation against Desecrators of the Grave from Northwest Lydia," *AD* 9 (2007): 117–9 (their translation, slightly modified).

the grave and its contents in order to plant a curse tablet among the remains. It is significant that one of the means of countering such malfeasance was to replicate the curse form in the grave's inscription — a preemptive strike, as it were, but demonstrating a certain egalitarianism in access to curses and the powers that gave them effect.

Accordingly, if one was to envisage some content to pour into the expression "evil deeds" in Col 1:21, there was one key "scurrilous villainy" at the forefront of what was, doubtless, a queue of contenders similar to those in Col 3:5, 8. This evil deed, significantly, is not directly aimed at the gods or God, even though it implies a failure of the civic temples to facilitate the god(s)' resolution of an individual's concerns, and it required the intervention of an eminent deity (or deities) to overcome the severe disturbance caused. Rather, it fractured civic stability.

This evil deed had distressing social and political ramifications. Indeed, the extent of the evil was measured in terms of that disruption. Consequently, attempts to prevent the evil entered into the very wording of epitaphs. But the offence against the tomb was arraigned as manifestly an offence against god(s) — a malice and sacrilege such as listed in Col 3:8 (κακία, βλασφημία).[91] This construction of the disturbance to the concord of the gods necessarily was mirrored in the mundane realm.[92] Nowhere was that disturbance more pointedly found than in the assault upon the grave, whether by "foreign" corpse or cursing stranger. The two disturbed realms — of the gods and of the world — were inextricably intertwined.[93] The imperial Roman jurist, Ulpian (d. 228 CE), held that tomb violation was to be prosecuted as *infamia*, the most abject classification of a crime.[94]

91 See E. Akıncı Öztürk and H. Malay, "Four Funerary Curses recording the Pisidian Gods of the Acıpayam Plain," *EA* 45 (2012): 89–92.

92 This connection is explicitly named in the infamous Nazareth imperial order (Oliver, *Greek Constitutions* 2): "I order that the standard of judgement of any such [offender] against the veneration of the (dead) humans be that of an offence against the gods" (κατὰ τοῦ τοιούτου κριτήριον ἐγὼ κελεύω γενέσθαι καθάπερ περὶ θεῶν εἰς τὰς τῶν ἀνθρώπων θρησκίας). The inscription has recently been given the provenance, by stable isotope analysis, of the island of Kos and thereby should put to rest any lingering efforts to relate the command to the story of Jesus' empty tomb (cf Matt 27:62–6). See K. Harper *et al.*, "Establishing the Provenance of the Nazareth Inscription: Using stable isotopes to resolve a historic controversy and trace ancient marble production," *JASReports* 30 (2020): 1–7. The *diatagma* was likely prompted by the desecration of the grave of a local island dignitary named Nikias.

93 See *IGR* 3.571 (Oinoanda, 1st to 2nd century CE). The so-called "Eumeneian curse formula" — having to reckon with God — is but one, probably Christian, modulation on these sentiments; see P. McKechnie, *Christianizing Asia Minor: Conversion, Communities and Social Change in the Pre-Constantinian Era* (Cambridge: Cambridge University Press, 2019), 210–31.

94 *Dig.* 47.12.1. Section 12 is given over completely to the question of tomb violation. The approximate Greek equivalent is given in a sarcophagus inscription at Aphrodisias: a tomb violator is to be labeled as "impious and accursed and a tomb-breaker" (ἔστω ἀσεβὴς καὶ ἐπάρατος καὶ τυμβωρύχος, *I.Aphrodisias 2007* 13.203, l. 11). Even so, he was still to pay a fine of 2,500 denarii, no doubt to add mundane pain to the horror of the naming! The triplet characterization of the offender was stereotypical on Aphrodisian sarcophagi, but each of the items occur

But if damage to or intrusion on a tomb lacked evil intent (*dolus malus*),[95] such as in accidental breakages, the deed was less reprehensible. Many Latin epitaphs incorporated this mental frame into their injunctions: *ab hoc monument dolus malus abesto* ("let the one with malicious intent stay clear of this tomb").[96] This suggests not so much that a hostile mind leads to evil deeds but rather the malicious intent shows that the actions were evil.

The hostile mind that engineered such evil deeds (or is confirmed or compounded as hostile by the deeds done) is also ambiguous about where it may reside. There is little doubt that the initiator of the Kaklık curse tablet felt aggrieved at the hostility (in this case ἀντία) of those named. Other curse tablets explicitly target the hostile parties in language reminiscent of Col 1:21 — ἐχθροί.[97] One curse tablet, clearly aimed at gaining a favorable trial outcome, after binding (καταδεσμεύω) a number of men by name, sought to guard against any other surprise witness: "and if any other malignant (ἐχθρός) starts raging something (against me), let him be unable to testify …".[98]

Curse tablets, just like the curses on epitaphs, could be designed to prevent the efficacy of someone else's curse.[99] So the parties who resorted to curse tablets could be operating not from malice as such but out of powerlessness in the usual rhythm of ordinary life. There is a poignant fable of Aesop that captures the reality. It tells of a "twittering swallow" whose nest was built in the court-house wall "where sat the aged arbiters of law and justice". Her young were devoured by a serpent. The fable concludes with the wretched mother "mourning her babes' untimely death" (παίδων ἀώρους συμφορὰς ἐπεθρήνει) with the lament, "How strange a fate is mine that right where humanity's laws and judgments are proclaimed, here I, a swallow, have been wronged and forced to flee."[100] To be sure, slaves are in evidence seeking oracular resolution of their concerns, but these instances are few.[101] The swallow, the slave, knew how civic justice could pass them by.[102]

---

in warnings and prohibitions against disturbance of graves; see, for example, *IMT Kyz Kapu Dağ* 1825b l. 4 (ἐπάρατος), *Testament of Epicrates* (Wilhelm) ll. 78–9 (τυμβωρυχία, apparently a legally defined offence).

95 The editors of the near-Thyateiran epitaph, translate δόλῳ τε πονηρῷ by the Latin juridical test *dolo malo*.

96 *CIL* 6.9485, 30385; similarly *CIL* 8.13161; *AE* 1909.92, 1927.180; cf *BGU* 1.326 (ταύτῃ τῇ διαθήκῃ δόλος πονηρὸς ἀπέστη).

97 Jordan, "New Greek Curse Tablets," nr. 24.

98 καὶ εἴ τις ἄλλος τι μαίνεται ἐχθρὸς μὴ δυνάσσθω ἀντιλέγειν; Jordan, "New Greek Curse Tablets," nr. 40.

99 Jordan, "New Greek Curse Tablets," nr. 24; J. B. Curbera and D. R. Jordan, "A Curse Tablet from the 'Industrial District' Near the Athenian Agora," *Hesperia* 67 (1998): 215.

100 Babrius *Aesop*. 118. (trans. Perry, slightly modified).

101 See *TAM* V,1 257.

102 For an actual instance of the hierarchical inequities in the operations of justice, where the legal representative retained to prosecute a claim by Demetrius, a freedman, is completely outgunned by the advocate of Paulinus, an ex-grammateus, see *P.Mil.Vogl.* 1.25 (Arsinoe, 127 CE).

Christ the circuit-breaker

The resolution of the alienation (from society, from relationships, from the public, controlled access to the divine) to which *defixiones* remain one of the most powerful material witnesses, is the death of Christ, according to the writer of the Letter to the Colossians. This is presented in 1:22 through the overarching "now" (νυνὶ), where "in the body of his flesh through death" (ἐν τῷ σώματι τῆς σαρκὸς αὐτοῦ διὰ τοῦ θανάτου), Christ has engineered a reconciliation from the alienation that "you" had experienced. The conjunction, "body of flesh through death" is highly unusual in the Pauline corpus, found only here.[103] The two terms are occasionally found as a means of communicating the fullness of the interred corpse, that is a body made up of flesh and bones.[104] Here there is no tautology as in 1 Enoch 102:5; it may, most closely, be compared with Sir 23:17 in the sense of accenting the genus of body, given that the word σῶμα was capable of a number of different applications (just as we find in comparing Col 1:18).

Here the accent is intensely materialistic, a sharp pulling back to the mundane realm from the cosmic affirmations in the hymn of Col 1:12–20. This juxtaposition of the ethereal and the earthly is exactly what is found in the *defixiones*, where the body of flesh consumed by death is yet the place where the desire expressed in the tablet is activated. The infernal spirits and chthonic deities are somehow present with/to the body of flesh in the grave, able to be channeled similarly to bring others down to death.[105]

But the affirmation about Christ is that both entities, the ethereal/spiritual and the earthly, are *combined* in him and that, through death, Christ has conquered the jurisdiction of darkness (ἡ ἐξουσία τοῦ σκότους, Col 1:13, understood as the hostile, perhaps imperial, world *and* its graveyards). In this sense, it is not simply the cross that is understood as the instrument or agent of reconciliation, as affirmed by Col 1:20 (διὰ τοῦ αἵματος τοῦ σταυροῦ αὔτοῦ). In this first exposition of the Christological hymn (vv 21–23), the image is extended to death itself. The blood of the cross may be the execution, but death is understood as the realm drawn in to Christ's body of flesh, not only nullifying the power of the grave (such as was crucial to the operation of the *defixio*) but reconciling both *defigens* and victim to God and, potentially, to one another.

See the analysis in M. Heath, *Menander: A Rhetor in Context* (Oxford: Oxford University Press, 2004), 312–4. For slaves, even getting to court was impossible on their own initiative.

103 Dunn, *Colossians and Philemon*, 107, 108. Consequently, efforts to explain the conjunction by reference to their separate usage in the Pauline corpus misdirect the force in Colossians.

104 *SEG* 30.269 (Attica, 2nd to 3rd century) cf *SEG* 35.227 (Athens, c. 250 CE).

105 The dedications to the chthonic gods (θεοῖς καταχθονίοις = *dis manibus*) on behalf of the deceased are designed to obviate any negative disturbances, perhaps including a *defixio* deposit. For a fulsome dedication beyond the usual epitaphal Θ-K/D-M, see Malay-Petzl, *Lydia* 192.

One sequence in some curse and justice-seeking tablets that lists a string of potential inflicters of personal or property damage, illustrates how Christ has grasped adversaries for reconciliation. An Attic *defixio* held at Oxford targets "whoever bewitched me, whether woman or man, or slave or free or foreigner or citizen, or domestic or alien …" and proceeds to counter the harm with a dose of his/her own magic.[106] A number of curse tablets (seeking justice or restitution) found at Bath and Uley in Britain and Mainz in Germany, seek the assistance of one or more deities to bring down the offender (and retrieve the stolen goods): "whether man or woman, whether youth or maiden, whether slave or free"[107] The sequence of polarities, what Richard Gordon calls "illocutionary weight", bolsters the force of the argument or petition, by multiplying the elements.[108] Such embellishing replications in curse tablets are not confined to binaries of persons as here, but might, for example, proliferate the parts of the body to be attacked (cf Col 2:19).[109] Unlike the lists in the *defixiones*, Christ does not advance the destructive end that curses have in view. Curses fundamentally operate from adversarial dynamics. For the writer of Colossians, the power of Christ is manifest in the overcoming of the divisions between "Greek and Jew, circumcised and uncircumcised, barbarian, Scythian, slave, free" (Col 3:11), precisely because "all things and in all things (is) Christ" (τὰ πάντα καὶ ἐν πᾶσιν Χριστός). The formal frame of "illocutionary weight" in this verse would be readily recognized by any Colossian familiar with *defixiones*, even if the letter's specific ethnic comparisons have, to my knowledge, not been found in a curse tablet. But the fundamental contrast in intent compared to *defixiones* would be clear: it is not adversarial but reconciling.

The only binding the author advocates is that of love (Col 3:14), an extension of the clothing metaphor of Col 3:12–13,[110] and an addition to the unifying, reconciling power of love mentioned in Col 2:2 (αἱ καρδίαι συμβιβασθέντες ἐν ἀγάπῃ). Col 2:2 may have particular reference to the Christ-followers at Laodikeia. We have seen already that Archippos' special ministry is to form and strengthen the ties between those at Colossae and those in Laodikeia. In Col 3:12–14, the clothing metaphor culminates all the previous "garments" of virtues with one final tie, bond or constraint, that is, love. It is almost as if the

---

106 D. R. Jordan, "Three Curse Tablets," in *The World of Ancient Magic* edited by D. R. Jordan, H. Montgomery and E. Thomasse (Bergen: Norwegian Institute, 1999), 115–17; Papakonstantinou, "Binding Curses," 144.

107 *AE* 1992.1127 (Uley, 3rd century CE). For further examples, see R. S. O. Tomlin, "Cursing a Thief in Iberia and Britain," in *Magical Practice in the Latin west: papers from the International Conference held at the University of Zaragoza* edited by R. L. Gordon and S. F. Marco (Leiden: Brill, 2010), 248, 256.

108 See R. Gordon, "Imaginative Force and Verbal Energy in Latin Curse-Tablets," in *Litterae magicae. Studies in Honour of Roger S. O Tomlin* (Zragoza: Libros Pórtico, 2019), 111–29.

109 See, for example, *CIL* 1^2 2541.

110 See R. Canavan, *Clothing the Body of Christ at Colossae: A Visual Construction of Identity* (WUNT 334; Tübingen: Mohr Siebeck, 2012), 149–50, 156.

imagery is evoking a belt, girdle or sash, like the final, outer item of clothing mentioned in Rev 1:13b (ζώνη χρυσῆ).

The restoration of the curse tablet of Kaklık to the territory of Colossae has enabled us to see a further component in the religious panorama of the locality. Some of the language used in curses (and curse-laden epitaphs) brings a particular imaginative encounter with the language of the Letter to the Colossians. The argument is not that this is specifically what the author was addressing, nor that there was a specific syncretism to which the writer was opposed. Rather, the material evidence, always fragmented and less than desired though it may be, affords an opportunity to hear potential resonances between the letter and the Colossian context. Some of those resonances will be stronger than others, but at least in the situation of the earliest reception of the letter, those ears may well have heard echoes not only in their own lives but in the life and cultural expressions of the city and its countryside. And then, so also, those ears were to hear the expectation that they live, bound by love, apart from those patterns, even as they were to engage ("do a deal") wisely with them (Col 4:5–6).

Chapter Nine
Who's Who at Colossae: onomastics, ethnicities and status

Over 165 names are now known from the meager evidence we have from Colossae. These names enable us to discern traces of ethnicities, aspirations and status in the city. The names in the Letter to Philemon and to Colossians interweave closely with the onomastic profile we can build from the city at large and yield a snapshot of the Christ-followers at Colossae. To begin, it is important to be reminded of the limitations on the evidence that we have. It will be salutary to return to the theater at Colossae.

Theaters and spectators

The theater *cavea* in the höyük is one of the features frequently noted about Colossae. If nothing else, it points to the Hellenistic cultural infusion into the life of Colossae through the various events, gatherings and honors that the

Plate 9.1a and b: The theater cavea excavated into the mid-point of the eastern perimeter of the pre-existing mound at Colossae. Isolated remains of the theater are still visible *in situ*. To the right of the theater is evidence of illegal excavations into walled structures that were probably part of the entrance to the theater. The modern road that cuts along the edge of the höyük is visible bottom left.

theater housed. Sometimes additional information is distilled. The shape of the *cavea* is strongly suggestive of a Greek architectural plan; its excavation into a previously existing mound is corroborative of the judgment, such a construction practice being familiar at other sites, such as Laodikeia and Aphrodisias among many. At these two cities additional information (inscriptions especially) have assisted the dating and design features of the theater, as well as the range of functions that the theater served. The theater at Colossac has been substantially denuded of its surface stone and its eastern edge sliced to allow the construction of a modern road.

Traces of theater fabric dot the *cavea* and its surrounds. A slab of seating from a *cuneus* segment has been moved a short distance back from the *summa cavea*. Unfortunately there is no more than a suggestion of an inscription along the top, front edge of the seat.

Plate 9.2a and b: Remains of theater seating from Colossae. At the left is the standard bench seat that lined the *summa cavea* and most of the *ima cavea*. At right is a priority seat *(proedra)* for dignitaries and honored guests that would have been placed on the perimeter of the orchestra during Hellenistic times. In Roman times, pre-existing theaters were modified to raise the priority seating areas above the orchestra, so that more violent entertainment might be staged. There is currently no certainty that Colossae's theater was so altered.[1]

This type of inscription designated a seat reservation for some segment of patrons, an association, a civic tribe, or privileged visitors from another city, who might be granted "priority seating" in the separate front row seats (the *proedrai*), the type of which is shown in the surviving instance removed from the site and now located in Honaz (Pl. 9.2b). This suggests that Colossae's theater was originally in the Hellenistic style, such as we find at Priene on the Ionian coast. The elliptical shape of the *cavea* is reminiscent of the theater *cavea* at Tripolis on the western edge of the Lycus Valley, if slightly smaller,

---

1 See chapter 10.

that is approximately 70 meters across the *cavea* compared to that of Tripolis, of 88 meters.[2]

The theater at Colossae is substantially denuded of its stone, long ago raided for other building projects (such as the Ak Khan caravanserai just outside of Denizli). A useful comparison for the visual appearance, and a sense of its organization and use can be made with Aphrodisias. The *homonoia* coin between Aphrodisias and Colossae, dated early in the sole reign of the emperor Commodus, points to some kind of "sister-city" alliance. Here, the theater is relatively complete (Pl. 9.3), at least to the *diazoma* (walkway) separating the *ima cavea* from the *summa cavea*.

Plate 9.3: The theater at Aphrodisias, showing the eleven *cunei* of the *ima cavea*, the orchestra pit, the *proedrai* around the orchestra perimeter, a central eminent persons' seating area and the *diazoma*, and, at center left, the edge of the *proskenion*. The figure at right helps to orientate perspective on the dimensions.

Aphrodisias boasts one of the most lavishly inscribed examples of theater seating. Not only are the eleven cunei and the rows of seats contained within them numbered,[3] but various types of inscription are to be found. There are individ-

2 For a more detailed overview of the theater at Colossae, see A. H. Cadwallader, *Fragments of Colossae: Sifting through the Traces* (Adelaide: ATF Press, 2015), 74–95. The measurement of the Tripolis theater is provided by the Director of the excavations, Bahadır Duman, through kind communication September 2020.

3 C. Roueché, *Performers and Partisans at Aphrodisias in the Roman and late Roman Periods* (London: Society for the Promotion of Roman Studies, 1993), 99–100.

ual claims on seats. These are usually indicated by τόπος with the name of the individual in the genitive coming before or after "the place"; sometimes just the name in the genitive would be used. Thus in *cuneus* A (= 1), row ΚΔ (= 24) — that is two rows from the top of the *ima cavea* and on the northern extremity (just out of view at left, Pl. 9.3) — is found a seat inscribed Αἰνείου τόπος.[4] An alternate claim on a seat was by the inscription of κατέχεται, "reserved/taken". Fairly often a name was added using ὑπό "reserved by N."; less commonly the dative of the name is found, as in a faint name which can be made out on the heavily worn edge of a seat at Aphrodisias. Of special interest on this seat is an added instruction: Ἀοψοῦ! |Κατέχετ(αι) | Ὀφέλῳ "Wipe (the seat) clean! Reserved for Ofelos." (Pl. 9.4).[5]

Plate 9.4: Seating and stairs at the theater at Aphrodisias showing various inscriptions. The inscription reserving the seat for Ofelos is upper right of center, next to the stairs. (Photograph turned 180° to view inscriptions.)

Seats were also reserved for associations, for example, τόπο(ς) τῶν μακελλίτων, "the place for the butchers".[6] At the north theater at Laodikeia, an allocation is found for the Τραπεζοπολειτῶν, that is, for citizens of Trapezopolis.[7] At Aphrodisias, reservations are known in the stadium for leading visitors/delegations from a number of cities: Antioch-on-the-Maeander, Mastaura in Lydia and possibly for the Kibyrans and Milesians.[8] It seems to me likely, given the homonoia relationship between Aphrodisias and Colossae,

4 *I.Aphrodisias Performers* 46.A.24.

5 *I.Aphrodisias Performers* 46.H.19. My own investigation of the stone (see Pl. 9.4) shows a mortar line between this inscribed stone and its neighbor (also inscribed with larger letters), with the stairs bordering the other side. This suggests that there is no more text preceding any of the three lines. I agree with Charlotte Roueché's reconstruction of the first line, with only the opening alpha partly obscured (by mortar) and simply read the second person singular imperative middle form as a phonological variation (that is –οῦ rather than -ῶ). The third line is worn (from abrasion that inevitably, through use, deteriorates the seat edge) but is readable. It should be noted that Roueché limited her reproduction of inscriptions "to those which can be deciphered fairly easily" (p. 100) and admitted that the accidence "of light and position" impacted her readings (p. 83).

6 *I.Aphrodisias Performers* 46.L.13.

7 C. Şimşek and M. A. Sezgin, "Laodikeia Kuzey Tiyatrosu," *Olba* 19 (2011): 186 and fig. 20. (However, I cannot make out the inscription as indicated, in the photograph). The material is substantially repeated in a second essay by the same authors, "The West and North Theatres in Laodicea," in *Restoration and Management of Ancient Theatres in Turkey: methods, research results* edited by F. Masino, P. Mighetto and G. Sobrà (Lecce: Congedo, 2012), 122.

8 *I.Aphrodisias Performers* 45.4.O (Mastaura), 45.34.S (Antioch) cf 45.35.L (Kibyra?), 45.11.H.

that inscribed reservations would similarly have been allocated in one another's entertainment and reception venues. Theaters became the centers for staged events that could be extended to other cities (by special invitation), an expo of a city's prowess. But these seats were also ready-made canvases for other individual interests, including at a later time, those of Christians, who were apparently quite at home attending theater events. A certain Stephen simply offered a prayer: Εὐχὴ Στεφανᾶ (Pl. 9.5). Other inscriptions were more mundane — the cutting of a base for a board game, or the caricatures of gladiators and tightrope walkers, for example.

Plate 9.5: A seat with two inscriptions. The vertical inscription is the (unknown) prayer of/for Stephen. The horizontal inscription reads Νικᾷ ἡ Τύχη τῶν … "The Tyche of the (Greens/Blues) shall be victorious" — a standard cheer-squad acclamation in the factional competitions held in the theater in early-to-mid Byzantine times. But this one requires completion, perhaps by the shout of the theater-seat occupant (Stephen?): Πρασίνων "Greens", Βενέτων "Blues"!

Such vivid insights into the city's cultural life and its otherwise unknown consumers of theater events are unfortunately absent from Colossae. The visible remaining seats are anepigraphic either because of abrasive weathering or the coincidence of survival. There is little doubt that the number of names in our current list from Colossae would be more extensive if the theater had been less quarried.

The Colossian theater has a further cautionary note to offer. The theater at Aphrodisias measures 90 meters across the *cavea*, the same as the west theater at Laodikeia. These theaters are estimated to have a seating capacity of 8000 people,[9] both dwarfed by Ephesos with its massive 142 meter cavea, housing between 17,000 and 21,000 spectators.[10] This indicates that the theater at Colossae, even if constructed on a different gradient, would likely manage a smaller audience than Aphrodisias or the west theater at Laodikeia. By comparison with more intact theaters of similar size (such as at Priene), we can surmise that the seating capacity at Colossae was between 5,000 and 7,000, probably closer to the lower figure.

Some have suggested that theater capacity can be used to extrapolate a city's population, though most prefer a postulated density per hectare model

9 K. Welch, "The Stadium at Aphrodisias," *AJA* 102 (1998): 562; Şimşek-Sezgin, "West and North Theatres," 106.

10 F. Sear, *Roman Theatres: An Architectural Study* (Oxford: Oxford University Press, 2006), 334.

based on the area (size) of a city as determined by the city walls. Unfortunately, the only visible evidence of city walls at Colossae is a small length (about 30 meters) to the north of the river (that, accordingly, flowed through the city precincts). The walls, as the usual practice of cities organizing the burial of its dead, demarcated the city from the northern necropolis. Both methods for calculating population density (theaters and wall perimeters) have their limitations,[11] but at the very least, it is permissible to reckon Colossae's theater as servicing only a segment of the total population of the city proper and certainly an even smaller segment when the population is configured on the basis of the territory controlled (economically, administratively and judicially).

Plates 9.6a, b and c: A surviving section of Colossae's city wall that runs to the north of the Lycus River. Below and right are indications of how the wall blocks, and other sectioned stones (including tomb covers) have been converted to act as animal pens. These photographs were taken in 2005 and 2013 respectively, both looking south across the höyük towards Honazdağ, Mt Cadmus. By 2015, most of the blocks had gone, doubtless appropriated for other "building" projects.

This brief excursus on the theater and the city walls has provided two considerations for an estimation of Colossae's population. For our present purposes, whatever estimate is given (say, 10,000 to 15,000 people), even if bolstered by the obvious circulation of bronze coins for the city's own commercial needs, the figure can only be a guess. Suffice to say that where city walls can be rel-

11 See generally, A. Bowman and A. Wilson (eds), *Settlement, Urbanization, and Population* (Oxford: Oxford University Press, 2011), especially the essays of Andrew Wilson, Analisa Marzano and J. W. Hanson.

atively confidently drawn, as at neighboring Laodikeia, even then there is considerable disparity in the estimates of the city population. Laodikeia's city perimeter encloses 89 hectares (albeit admitting some changes to the line of the walls at different times). Jack Hanson provides the population based on different densities (from 100 people per hectare to 400 per hectare) to arrive at a population range of 8,900 to 35,600 people (for the second to third centuries CE).[12] The lower figure, in my opinion, makes a mockery of a city with two operational theaters (seating capacity 8000 and 10,000 respectively),[13] one of the largest stadia in the ancient world, four baths and five agoras.[14] Even allowing for a steady influx of travellers and visitors to a *conventus* metropolis, such monumental structures are not built merely for display. They were operational. More exuberant figures are to be found in the estimates by the director of the Laodikeian excavations and reconstructions. Celal Şimşek considers that the city population in the first two-to-three centuries of the Roman empire, was probably about 80,000 people, with 200,000 people in total if one includes the territory under Laodikeia's jurisdiction.[15]

Small returns of names

Even with considerable disparities in seating capacities and population estimates, the statistics for the known names of people who lived in city or territory attached to a city are, by comparison, remarkably miniscule. We know of 167 names of people from Colossae (mainly from the first to third century CE).[16] If we were to take the low figure for the estimated seating capacity for the Colossae theater (that is, 5,000), we have a mere 3.28 per cent of a full house, perhaps two to three rows of seats, if every one of those names attended (an imaginative compression of time and status!).

---

12 J. W. Hanson, "The Urban System of Roman Asia Minor and Wider Urban Connectivity," in *Settlement, Urbanization and Population*, 254 (Table 9.1).

13 Şimşek-Sezgin, "West and North Theatres," 106, 112. It should be noted that Turkish media reports of the reconstruction of the West theater for contemporary entertainment events put the seating capacity at 15,000 people. This either indicates an expansion of the seating capacity in the restoration, a misapplied recalculation of the northern theater capacity (from the original eighteenth century estimate by Richard Chandler), or is simply media hyperbole.

14 See A. H. Cadwallader and J. R. Harrison, "Perspectives on the Lycus Valley: An Inscriptional, Archaeological, Numismatic and Iconographic Approach," in *The First Urban Churches 5: Colossae, Hierapolis, and Laodikeia* (Atlanta, GA: SBL, 2019), 27–38 (Harrison).

15 C. Şimşek, "Urban Planning of Laodikeia on the Lykos in the Light of New Evidence," in *Landscape and History in the Lykos Valley: Laodikeia and Hierapolis in Phrygia* edited by C. Şimşek and F. D'Andria (Cambridge: Cambridge Scholars Publishing, 2016), 5. It should be recalled that Şimşek also delivered almost the entirety of the Lycus Valley to Laodikeia's territory; see chapter 3.

16 See Appendix 2 for the complete list of known names.

Colossae is not alone in offering such a small number of known people from its city and territory. Francesco Guizzi and Alister Filippini have provided an invaluable catalogue of known personnel attached to the city of Tripolis.[17] That city has received substantial excavations in the last decade and their list includes some cullings from as yet unpublished inscriptions. I have followed almost all of their readings of names, with one or two exceptions. The total number of names comes to 62, with 51 from inscriptions and 11 from coins,[18] that is, about 100 less than the unexcavated Colossae. To date in publication, Tripolis boasts no list of names such as the Colossian baths renovation honoring Korymbos or the *defixio* tablet from the city and its territory respectively. Numbers of names can be easily distorted by such lists, even though they are the equivalent of coin hoards for their evidentiary value.[19] It is a salutary reminder that the evidence of known participants in the ancient world is limited. The disturbing question of Armando Petrucci haunts analysis here: "... what proportion of the dead had a right to a "written death" ..."[20] Status and economic factors prevented many slaves, laborers, peasants and the homeless from ever being remembered; accompanying this is the oft-forgotten question of just what a city such as Colossae did with the dead who could not afford a "written death".[21]

---

17 F. Guizzi and A. Filippini, "Tripolis on the Maeander under Roman Rule (Cent. 2nd B.C. – 3rd A.D.): Epigraphy and Prosopography," in *Tripolis ad Maeandrum I: Tripolis Araştırmaları* edited by B. Duman (Istanbul: Ege, 2017), 59–73. This updates what can be scoured from *LGPN* VB.

18 Coins (sometimes including the name of the father of the sponsor): Ἀνδρόνεικος, Ἀπολλώνιος, Θεοδώρος, Θεοδώρος, Ἱερατικός, Καλλικλῆς (Καλός), Μενάνδρος, Μετρόδωρος Τρύφων, Τρύφων, Φιλόπατρις. Inscriptions: Ἄδραστος, Αἰλιανός, Αἴλιος Χαρίδημος, Ἀλέξανδρος Φρ<ο>υγίσκος, Ἀπολλώνιος, Δάμας, Ἀτταλιανός (Μ. Αὐρ.), Ἄτ]ταλος, Δημήτριος Ἄνδρων, Δημήτριος, Διομήδης (Τιβ. Κλ.), Διονύσιος, Διονυσόδωρος, Διόφαντος, Ἐθέριος, Εἰρηναῖος, Ἑορτάσιος (Αὐρ.), Ἐπαφρόδειτος (Μ. Αὐρ.), Ἐπαφρόδειτος, Ἑρμόλαος, Ζηνωνίς (Αυρ.), Ζώσιμος, Ἰουλιανός (Μ. Αὐρ.), Θεοδώρος, Ἰουλιανός, Ἰουλιανός, Κυριακός, Κῶκος, Λουκᾶς, Λούκκιος(?), Μένανδρος (Μ. Αὐρ.), Μένανδρος (Μ. Αὐρ.), Μένανδρος, Μένανδρος, Μεσσαλεῖνος (Μ. Αἴλ. Οὔλ. Ἀντ), Παιώνιος, Παπιας, Παπιας, Παπιας, Παπιας, Παπιας (Αὐρ.), Παπιας (Τι. Κλ.), Πασικράτης, Πρόκλος (Αὐρ.), Ῥούσων, Στατείλιος, Σύμμαχος (Γ. Σέξτιος), Σύμφορος (Αὐρ.), Τουενδιανός Μάγνος Χαρίδημος (Τι. Κλ.), Τύραννος, Φιλάνωρ. Not included are Μαρδόνιος, Ἀριστόμαχος, Ἀκεστορίδης, Εροιδης, all assigned by *LGPN* elsewhere, and the gladiator Χρυσόπτερος, buried at Tripolis but probably hailing from another city: see T. Ritti, "Spettacoli dell'arena in età imperiale: alcune osservazioni sulle forme e la finalità della comunicazione" in *Öffentlichkeit – Monument – Text. XIV Congressus Internationalis Epigraphiae Graecae et Latinae 27. – 31. Augusti MMXII. Akten* edited by W. Eck and P. Funke (Berlin: de Gruyter, 2014), 413.

19 R. Parker, "Introduction," in *Personal Names in Ancient Anatolia* edited by R. Parker (Oxford: British Academy, 2013), 4.

20 A. Petrucci *Writing the Dead: Death and Writing Strategies in the Western Tradition* trans. M. Sullivan (Stanford: CA: Stanford University Press, 1998), xvi. Conversely, there are the millions of epitaphs that have disappeared, even though the few hundreds of thousands give considerable evidence: see the general comments of Keith Hopkins *Death and Renewal* (Cambridge: Cambridge University Press, 1986), 204.

21 Note the insights of Hopkins, *Death and Renewal*, 209–11. Tertullian, in his own rhetorical fashion, recognized the problem of the burial of the poor: *Apol.* 39.

There is also a gender imbalance in inscriptions. The figures vary somewhat according to the region and language of the inscriptions, but generally the ratio in the naming of women lies between one woman to every seven to ten men named (that is 10–14 %).[22] The Phrygian ratio may well provide something distinctive against which to make comparisons. The editors of the *Lexicon of Greek Personal Names* note that Phrygia, Lydia, and Cilicia Pedias have female names in 21–22 % of the total names for their regions, with Bithynia not far behind (18 %). Whilst this still amply testifies to the gender asymmetry in the recording of names, these regions are considerably ahead of other places in the Greco-Roman world, where the figures can be as low as 5–10 %.[23]

We have seen already that although the number of extant provincial bronze coins is miniscule compared to projected actual circulation, the ability to gain valuable insights into city and provincial life from the surviving coins has become a critical part of historical analysis, not least in the witness to women sponsors that the coins provide.[24] Similarly, there is an incentive to investigate what the study of names — onomastics — in connection with Colossae can yield. Support comes from external and, significantly, internal comparison. The immense contribution to research made by the *Lexicon of Greek Personal Names* provides a critical check on interpretations made on the names associated with one particular city and territory. Volume VC of the *Lexicon*, recently published (2018), contains more than 15,000 instances of names from Phrygia alone, drawn from cities and more than 150 other settlements (mostly villages).[25] Colossae falls within the parameters of this compass; checks on its small number of names can be made, giving greater confidence to what might be suggested in the interpretations of those names (such as regarding theonyms and heronyms, indigenous names, Roman connections, slave names, regional concentration, and so on).

We are fortunate to have two extant name-lists, one from the city of Colossae, one from its territory (a village near Kaklık). A brief comparison of the types of names on the two lists reveals theonyms (some common), Roman names (including *nomina* or *praenomina* that are consequently suggestive of servility or servile origins), indigenous names, genealogical connections, even some singular names (that is, only attested in Colossae and its territory).

22 See L. Keppie, *Understanding Roman Inscriptions* (London: Routledge, 1991), 20; I. Kajanto, *The Latin Cognomina* (Helsinki: Societas Scientiarum Fennica, 1965), 24, 29.

23 "Introduction," *LGPN* VC, xxv, xxx.

24 For the most recent effort to compile and interpret a list of women sponsors, see my "Moneyed Women of Phrygia," *NC* (2023) forthcoming.

25 The number of cities is extracted from Thomas Drew-Bear's entry in the *Barrington Atlas*, "Map 62 Phrygia". The number of villages and other settlements is given by the editors "Introduction [*LGPN* VC]," x. Drew-Bear warns that the designation of "city" as compared with "village" is no indication of size or population (p. 957). The *LGPN* editors advise that ethnic identifiers in inscriptions are often the only knowledge we have of the existence of a settlement (p. x).

The most notable difference is that the *defixio* list contains five female names among the thirteen inscribed, whereas the honorific pedestal to Korymbos for the repair of Colossae's baths, contains only one possible female name, and that as a matronymic. The rank and status differences between the two forms of lists explains the disparity, especially if the list of donors to the Korymbos' honor is meant to replicate to some degree the ephebic lists kept at the baths-gymnasium. At the same time, those very differences give confidence that the names we do have are a fair representation of the breadth and concentrations of the naming patterns at Colossae. This will become especially important when we probe the names found in the Second Testament Letters to Philemon and the Colossians.

The contribution of onomastics

Onomastics, the study of names, has gained considerable traction as a contributor, a "precious auxiliary" says Claude Brixhe,[26] to the understanding of history and society in the ancient world. Through the study of names we can plot general movements in ethnic influences and cultural fashions, though we are often warned against making simplistic deductions about particular bearers of a name. Thus, for example, a name that can be traced to a particular ethnic origin does not, thereby, denote the ethnicity or linguistic capability of the bearer.[27] In fact, as we shall see, the period of the first two centuries of the Roman empire was a time of considerable flux where ethnicities and cultural practices were being negotiated and adjusted, as individuals and indeed, cities, were seeking to respond to the new realities in ways that maximized benefits for themselves. Christ-followers were not immune to the need and impulse to navigate these new developments. And names were one of the instruments used in path-finding.

The analyses that follow rely on the assemblage of 167 names from the extant inscriptions and coins of Colossae (see Appendix 2) but draw on considerable comparative local and regional evidence. The onomastic resource spans about three centuries, once the name Helenos (from 267 BCE) is excluded. However, even that name is consonant with the decidedly Greek impress in the catalogue (not to mention the toponym Eleinokapria, as earlier noted). The authoritative position and culture conveyed in the name of this Seleucid commander is an onomastic confirmation of the change that none-too-slowly took place in the region over the following two hundred years. The fact that no name deriving

---

26 C. Brixhe, "Anatolian Anthroponymy after Louis Robert … and Some Others," in *Personal Names in Ancient Anatolia*, 25.

27 See B. Levick, "In the Phrygian mode: a region seen from without," in *Roman Phrygia: Culture and Society* edited by P. Thonemann (Cambridge: Cambridge University Press, 2013), 47.

from an Iranian background has, as yet, been found at Colossae or in its territory, is a powerful demonstration of how readily Colossae re-fashioned its identity from being a major satrapic center to a Greek polis, with its inhabitants mirroring that adjustment in their names.

A striking example of such a movement in nomenclature comes in a simple epitaph whose provenance is, unfortunately, uncertain, though found "near Laodikeia".[28] It may join a small number of inscriptions from Laodikeia that retain Iranian names.[29] At the same time, the inscription may point, as Nicholas Sekunda noted, "to the presence of a Persian family … in the Colossae district during the Achaemenid period."[30] The inscription is dated to the late Hellenistic period and reads Νικόπολις Μιθραβωγου γυνὴ δὲ Ἀρτεμιδώρου. Χαῖρε. "(This grave is for) Nikopolis daughter of Mithraboges/os and wife of Artemidoros. Farewell". Sekunda considers that while the nobility of the Achaemenid regime would likely have been removed from the Lycus Valley after Alexander's conquest, lesser-lights would probably have remained, bequeathing their name-forms through family succession and marriage and further supplemented by the forced or enticed transpositions of people from the east under Seleucid control.[31] Here a father with a Persian name ("the favor of Mithras") gave his daughter an undeniably Greek name ("the city triumphs") and she is married to another equally Greek-named man ("gift of Artemis").

There is added significance in the naming since female names often lag behind the changes in onomastic patterns (for political or cultural reasons). Women, usually for a longer period than men, were often regarded as bearers of the memory of earlier descent at least in their names. Whether or not an actual Persian ancestry lies in the background cannot, of course, be determined. But the name is suggestive, given its rarity (compared, say, with Mithridates) and the date of the inscription. Sometimes the sheer descriptor Περσικός, "Persian" became a name that survived into the third century (see Pl. 9.7),[32] no longer an ethnic or origin identifier but a memory trace of the past. Likewise, Greek

28 H. Malay and R. Schmitt, "An Inscription recording a new Persian name: Mithrabôgês or Mithrabôgos," *EA* 5 (1985): 27–9. The names from this inscription are not found in *LGPN*. Conceivably the inscription might be accorded to Colossae but Rüdiger Schmitt broadens its provenance to the "Lydian-Phrygian border area"; see "Parthische Sprach- und Namenüberlieferung aus arsakidischer Zeit," in *Das Partherreich und seine Zeugnisse* edited by J. Wiesehöfer (Stuttgart: Franz Steiner, 1998), 180. I have not seen the stone itself, but a squeeze is retained in the collection at the British Institute in Ankara.

29 L. Robert, "Inscriptions" in *Laodicée du Lycos: Le Nymphée* edited by J. des Gagniers et al (Québec: L'université Laval, 1969), 333–4.

30 N. Sekunda, "Changing Patterns of Land-Holding in the South-Western Border Lands of Greater Phrygia in the Achaemenid and Hellenistic Periods," in *Colossae in Space and Time: Linking to an Ancient City* edited by A. H. Cadwallader and M. Trainor (NTOA 94; Göttingen: Vandenhoeck & Ruprecht, 2011), 68.

31 Sekunda, "Changing Patterns," 68.

32 *I.Mus. Denizli* 22 (provenance unknown).

gods absorbed Persian forebears often with a surviving marker in an epithet; so Artemis became in some places "Persian Artemis";[33] similarly Zeus.[34] In one case, a grave imprecation of the imperial period in Pisidia calls on the protection of "the gods of the Greeks and the Persians."[35] At the very least, it demonstrates that a (nostalgic?) memory of an Achaemenid past lingered in the region.

Plate 9.7: The inscription, a dedication of a guard post (φυλακεῖον, l. 11) by a list of donors and builders, contains at the end of line 5, the name of Persikos ("Persian") from the Lycus Valley region. It is dated to the third century largely on the basis of the regular appearance of "Aur(elius)" in the naming pattern, the citizenship marker conferred across the Roman empire by the *Constitutio Antoniniana* (212 CE). The inventory of names is typical of the region, that is, predominantly Greek, a smattering of Latin (here "Maximus") and a trace of former populations (Daos, probably of Phrygian or Thracian origin,[36] Persikos, pointing to the Persian past, and perhaps Kilibos).[37] A concern to indicate genealogical succession is also apparent.

This "Hellenizing" of Colossae has a number of strands to it that corroborate what might be seen above as an argument from silence (given that we can't source the actual Mithraboges/os inscription to the city necropolis). Curiously perhaps, there is greater evidence of the survival of Phrygian (and other ethnic) names at Colossae, again with the witness to the bearing of such names by previous generations which then yield to Greek names in the family succession. It suggests that the Achaemenid domination of the region in succession to the Phrygians, for all its remaining traces, did not eradicate the naming (and cultural identity) of the "indigenous" inhabitants. It is significant that the

33 *SEG* 31.998 (Hypaipa in Lydia, nd).

34 *SEG* 28.1186 (Nakoleia, nd).

35 *SEG* 43.692 (found near Apıcayam). See J. H. M. Strubbe, *APAI ΕΠΙΤΥΜΒΙΟΙ: Imprecations against Desecration of the Grave in Greek Epitaphs of Asia Minor. A Catalogue* (Bonn: Habelt, 1997), 94–5, nr. 127.

36 O. Masson, *Onomastica graeca selecta, volume 3* (Geneva: Droz, 2000), 241 (Phrygian); L. Robert, *Noms indigènes dans l'Asie Mineure gréco-romaine* (Amsterdam: Hakkert 1991 [1963]), 342 (Thracian). See also, P. Özlem-Aytaçlar, "An onomastic survey of the indigenous population of north-western Asia Minor," in *Onomatologos: Studies in Greek Personal Names presented to Elaine Matthews* edited by R. W. V. Catling and F. Marchand (Oxford: Oxbow, 2010), 524.

37 Κιλιβος is taken as an "indigenous" name in *LGPN*. It is difficult to decide whether it is Phrygian or Persian in origin or formation. Robert regarded the *Kil-* group both diverse and enigmatic; *Noms indigènes*, 307–8, 400 n4.

survival of indigenous names at Colossae in the early Roman imperial period is attested in village and city. It points to a survival of Phrygian sensibilities amidst the pressure and willingness to hellenize.

Apphia and the Phrygian inheritance

We have already come across a number of Phrygian names in Colossae's territory: Τατια and her daughter Ταταριν of Eleinokapria retain epichoric names, that is names belonging to a long, pre-existing substrate of the population (see chapter 3). Yet the husband-father held a Greek name (Μοσχᾶς), again a confirmation of the perception that women frequently bore the traditional, familial links longer than men, who were required to exercise their interests more in politicized, public space. At the same time, Tatia seems to have taken responsibility for burial management, a legacy perhaps of a greater participation for women in public life in Anatolia.[38] The name Tatia is often included in the group of names classified as *Lallnamen*, that is names of one or two syllables that were so frequently used as names of endearment (hypocoristic) that they lost any suggestion of ethnic association.[39] In this case however, the name of the daughter, in direct evocation of the maternal (not paternal) connection suggests that some ethnic or cultural signal is being made.

Another commonly identified *Lallname* is Apphia. Three Colossian women are known to bear the name in one spelling or another (Aphias, Apphia). One comes from a textual source, the familiar Apphia mentioned in the Letter to Philemon (verse 2) and who, from that single mention, grew in ecclesiastical stature, securing sainthood, martyrdom and calendrical recognition.[40] The second mention comes from outside Colossae. Aphias married and moved to the territory of Boubon, approximately 50 miles to the south of the Taurus range (see Pl. 9.8). However, she or her surviving husband, was concerned that her Colossian origin be memorialized on her epitaph.[41] The

---

38 Compare also another inscription from Colossae: *MAMA* 6.42 (3rd century).

39 This definition is less narrow than that of Robert Parker who sees *lallnamen* as short names "with repetitive phonemes probably deriving from baby-talk"; "Introduction," 5.

40 *Menologion of Basil.* The martyrdom of Apphia (and Philemon) is assigned to the reign of Nero, with a feast day (for Philemon, Apphia, Archippos and, sometimes, Onesimos) on the 23rd November, though the date varies among the ancient synaxaria. Some have it as 22nd November; others 21st February. See B. B. Latysev, *Menologii anonymi byzantine saeculi X quae super sunt* (Petropolis: 1911), 118–9. All are "late, Byzantine constructs," as Ulrich Huttner notes; *Early Christianity in the Lycus Valley* (Leiden: Brill, 2013), 332. See Appendix 1.

41 *I.Boubon* 102 = *CIG* 4380 k³ = *LGPN* (corr.). None of the editors have dated the inscription but the style of lettering is consistent with the first century CE (four-bar sigma, minimal serifs, variable length of cross-bars). Note that *LGPN* have mistakenly read *I.Boubon* 102 and *CIG* 4380 k³ as two inscriptions.

third Apphia was a priest, probably of the imperial cult, during the time of Trajan (98–117 CE).[42]

Plate 9.8: The Boubon epitaph for Aphias, a round pedestal style, common for Boubon and surrounding territory, but not as yet attested at Colossae for grave monuments. The inscription reads Ἑρμᾶς Ἀφιάδι | τῇ ἰδίᾳ γυναικὶ | τῇ Τρυφίωνος | θυγατρί | γένει | Κολοσσηνῇ | μνήμης ἕνεκα "Hermas (set up this epitaph) for his own wife Aphias, the daughter of Tryphion, by birth a Colossian, for the sake of her memory."[43]

We shall deal with the name and its characterization as a *Lallname* more fully below. The name is of Phrygian origin but its usage had far outgrown any ethnic tie (but not, as we shall see, its geographical spread). What is significant here is that the three Apphias are all known by association with men who bear unequivocal Greek names. The textual Apphia is positioned between Philemon (Phmn 1) and Archippos (Phmn 2), both solid Greek names (though Archippos also has significant Thracian connections). Aphias of Boubon, née Colossae, is "located" by reference to her father Tryphion (another name frequently attested at Colossae in the form Tryphon) and her husband Hermas. The priest Apphia likewise is located by genealogical succession from her father Herakleios and grandfather Dioskorides/Dioskourides. All the males embedding these women on their surviving epigraphical notice have incontestably Greek names. Significantly, among the 20 female names in the Colossian catalogue (about 12 % of the total), 8 are epichoric in origin, though all these qualify as *Lallnamen* (more than half of the total *Lallnamen* at Colossae).

In the *defixio* list from Kaklık, Αμμαλιον/-ος the father of Ἀπολλώνιος bears an epichoric, probably Phrygian name (see chapter 8). It too is constructed on a *Lallname* (from Amma),[44] but the very extension beyond "one or two syllables" suggests that the indigenous hold was strong on those who named the father. Indeed, the very definition of *Lallnamen* indicates its com-

---

42 Robert, "Inscriptions," 278–9 = *BCH* 1887.354.12 (corr.) = *IGR* 4.868. The inscription date can be narrowed to 114–17 CE; see chapters 3 and 7.

43 Photograph courtesy of Thomas Corsten and Christina Kokkinia. Text and translation from C. Kokkinia, "The Inscriptions of Boubon: A Catalogue," in *Boubon: The Inscriptions and Archaeological Remains: A Survey 2004–2006* (Athens: de Boccard, 2008), 126 (without photograph).

44 See L. Zgusta, *Kleinasiatische Personennamen* (Prague: Tschechoslowakischen Akademie, 1964), 66.

mon occurrence. One instance, as in this case, hardly qualifies. But it is again notable that the newer generation receives a ubiquitous, irreproachably Greek name, in this case Ἀπολλώνιος.

Phrygian and/to Greek

This progression from non-Greek to Greek is also noticeable in the honorific for Korymbos, the repairer of the baths at Colossae. This inscription was first noted in 2011 with the *editio princeps* published in the following year.[45] It has been commented upon a number of times since,[46] with some engagements enabling refinements to be made.

Plate 9.9: The pedestal honoring Korymbos for the repair of the baths at Colossae and the extension of the water infrastructure.

After the honorand and the rationale for the honors given him, the inscription follows with a 30-line list of those who have contributed to the acclamation with a substantial round marble pedestal and a probably-bronze sculpture (a statue or bust, now lost) fixed to the top. The list probably contained at least 97 names, perhaps more given the propensity in the list for extended genealogies (that is beyond the usual three generations of named, father and grandfather). The stone was damaged a number of times in its long life, once at least by the farmer's tractor that uncovered it, in a field close to the Colossae höyük, and, it seems, in the removal of the stone to a new location on Honazdağ. The remaining names, 66 in whole or part, sometimes contained within a genealogical succession of five generations, span the first century CE, even if an early second century dating of the inscription is preferred (see Pls. 9.10a–c). For our present purposes, the epichoric names are noteworthy, that is, Μηνογᾶς (l. 7), Μηνᾶς (l. 23), Ἀνωτ- (l. 25), Μιννίων (l. 32) Μωκεας (l. 34) and possibly Κτησᾶς (ll. 23, 25).

45 A. H. Cadwallader, "Refuting an Axiom of Scholarship on Colossae: fresh insights from new and old inscriptions" in *Colossae in Space and Time*, 171–5; "Honouring the Repairer of the Baths: A New Inscription from Kolossai," *Antichthon* 46 (2012): 150–83.

46 *New Doc. Early Christ.* 10.17, *AE* 2011.1347, *BE* 2013.407, *SEG* 61.1160, M. Reasoner, *Roman Imperial Texts: A Sourcebook* (Minneapolis: Fortress, 2013), 138–9. The inscription has begun to wend its way into introductions to commentary on the Letter to the Colossians; see P. Foster, *Colossians* (BNTC; London: Bloomsbury, 2016), 5–7.

Σκεπαρνᾶς (l. 30) is known elsewhere only in Thrace,[47] and may reflect early migration patterns.[48] The peculiar spelling in the tantalizing fragment of a name, Ανωτ- (l. 25), might, if read as Ανων-, be specifically Scythian in origin.[49]

Plate 9.10a, b and c: The marble pedestal honoring Korymbos for the repair of the Colossian baths and the extension of the water infrastructure. The three enlarged sections of the list of names show the epichoric names among a dominantly Greek selection. The section at left shows Μηνογᾶς below Τρύφων; the middle section (sprinkled with water to enhance the clarity) shows Μηνᾶς son of Κτησᾶ III, preceded on the line by a rosette (implying deceased?), below Θεόδωρος and Δημᾶς; the section at right ends the list of names with Κτησᾶς below Τυδεῖδης and Δημήτριος.

Of the epichoric names, three belong to the youngest generation, with two — Menogas and Menas — having progenitors also with epichoric names (accepting Ktesas as indigenous). Menogas in fact claims a succession of his name down four generations. Both Menogas and Menas have theophoric names, privileging the Anatolian god, Mên, who is found on Colossian coins.[50] Menogas means "born of Mên". Menas is particularly common and widespread in its occurrence. Menogas however is not. It has been claimed that it is common enough to be labeled a hypocoristic.[51] However, it needs to be noted that the particular name Menogas, unlike Menas, is not found in the Aegean, but rather seems confined to Asia Minor, especially Lydia. It is not found elsewhere in the Lycus Valley. That the family retained the name through a succession of four generations spanning the first century suggests that there is a particular association — per-

47 The form Σκέπαρνος is attested in Attica. H. W. Pleket (in *SEG* 61.1160) argued that the word indicates an occupational background. This may be its derivation, but I am not persuaded that it is not a name. A simple statement of occupation (Apollonios II son of Attalos, grandson of "the woodsman") would be singular and out of place in the list. It is accepted as a name in *LGPN*.

48 On the movement of Thracians to the south (Bithynia and beyond) during the Hellenistic period, see Özlem-Aytaçlar, "Onomastic survey," 507–8.

49 The name is, to date, impossible to complete or source given an acceptance of the surviving letters. Any reconstruction that yields an attested name requires transposition or correction of letters; the cutting is clear however. For the Scythian (or Thracian) possibilities based on reading Ανων–, see *IOSPE* 1² 685 cf *IGBulg* 1,2 206, cf *SEG* 45.1381 (Sicily).

50 *RPC* 3.2315 = *MSPhryg* 2.453, Lindgren 929A. Mên is not found on Colossae's bronzes after the time of Hadrian.

51 T. Drew-Bear, C. M. Thomas and M. Yıldızturan, *Phrygian Votive Steles* (Turkey: Ministry of Culture, 1999), 387.

haps a Phrygian remembrance — being carried in the family dynastic memory. Ktesas is rare, also not found elsewhere in the Lycus Valley or inland Asia Minor for that matter.[52] Its rare scatterings mark out the multiple usage at Colossae — the current generation's Ktesas, and the father, grandfather and great-grandfather of Menas. Ladislav Zgusta wondered whether the name was a homonym, that is, a name adopted (in this case into a Greek form) from a similar sounding one in another language, in this case either Thracian or Lycian.[53] Other epichoric names are borne by earlier generations. Mokeas, the grandfather of Demetrios, is not attested elsewhere, at least in this form. Cognate forms, Μοκας and Μωκιος again point to a Thracian or Macedonian connection,[54] even when they are attested elsewhere, such as in Egypt.[55] Μιννίων, the great, great grandfather of another Tryphon (l. 32, and visible at the right hand end in the middle of the right plate of the pedestal above), is a name fairly commonly attested in Caria, especially Rhodes,[56] but in some instances it can be a derivation from the Phrygian name Munnion.[57] Again this is the only instance of the name in the Lycus Valley and inland Asia Minor north of the Taurus range, so it is difficult to track the network. Intermarriage or migration may be the conduit.

Three particular observations are warranted.

i) Noteworthy is the sheer dominance of Greek names. The Korymbos pedestal alone contains 45 extant Greek names and originally would have contained more. Of these, 19 are theonyms (that is, names constructed on the name of a god, such as Apollo, Demeter and so on) and 11 are what might be called "heronyms", that is, names that are constructed on a demi-god, hero or illustrious leader (Herakles, Alexander, Attalos). Overall, there are 121 Greek names (here including Macedonian names such as Alexander) in the current onomastic register from Colossae out of 167, that is, about 72 %. Of these 51 are theonyms (not counting Μηνᾶς or Μηνογᾶς, names built on the Phrygian god, Mên, and, possibly, Παπιας);[58] 18 are heronyms and the remainder, 51, are names built on virtues or values, 1 probably derives from an ethnic (Μολοσσός) with another 3 unassigned. Of the four names so fragmentary that no name has been reconstructed, at least two are likely to be Greek. There are 13 *Lallnamen*

52 It is attested in Kyzikos (*SEG* 33.1056, 123–132 CE), Attica (*IG* II^2 1992, late first century BCE), Samos (*IG* XII 6 1019, graffito, 1st century BCE).

53 Zgusta, *Kleinasiatische Personennamen*, nr. 759; *Die Personennamen griechischer Städte der nördlichen Schwarzmeerküste* (Prague: Tschechoslowakische Akademie der Wissenschaften, 1955), nr. 1058.

54 *IGBulg* 4.2015a.

55 On Thracians in Egypt, see J. Bingen, *Hellenistic Egypt: Monarchy, Society, Economy, Culture* (Berkeley: University of California Press, 2007), 83–93.

56 R. Hitchman, "Carian Names and Crete," in *Onomatologos*, 46; Fabienne Marchand provides the statistics: "The Philippeis of IG VII 2433," in *Onomatologos*, 337.

57 Zgusta, *Kleinasiatische Personennamen*, 318, nr. 922–9.

58 On the god Papias/Papas, see T. Drew-Bear and C. Naour, "Divinités de Phrygie," *ANRW* II 18,3 (1990): 2019 n428.

(a significant proportion — 8 %), 7 indigenous names and 14 Latin names. Note that 11 (or 12 if the son of Menandros Flavianos is included) Greek names are cognomina to a Roman citizen formula; only three Latin cognomina carry an indication of Roman citizenship, while two *Lallnamen* are found as Roman citizens (Papias and Tatas). There are two or three persons who espouse double cognomina (Apollonios Valerius[?], Menandros Flavianos and Zosimos Philopator). The theonyms have a more restricted range than the number of gods or demigods depicted on Colossae's coins — "Angel" (in the first century seen as a divine being of itself, not just an intermediary), Zeus (under this god has been assigned the name Theodoros), Apollo, Artemis, Aphrodite, Hermes, Dionysos, Demeter, Helios and, perhaps, Tyche, to which should be added Mên and, possibly, Papias.[59]

One does not have to presume a deeply religious or traditional commitment in the naming of a child (though this can be identified in some cases),[60] to recognize how pervasive Greek culture and, indeed, a commitment to "Greekness" had become. Greek names and Greek religion, even if the interconnection was fertilized by a prior Anatolian practice,[61] were heavily intertwined. It would be myopic in the extreme for an inhabitant known by a theonym to wander through the Colossian religious landscape and not recognize that one's own name is an echo of this or that god. Indeed, a late inscription from Colossae, an early Byzantine fragment (Pl. 9.11), makes a pun on a dedicator's name (probably Theodoras, possibly Dorotheos): "for the one well-named from the divine gifts."[62] So the connections of names were there, sometimes no more than denotative but sometimes, as in this dedication, taken as connotative of the god (here the Christian one).[63]

---

59 By comparison, to repeat, the deities on Colossae's imperial-period coins are Zeus, Sarapis, Isis, Demeter, Athena, Artemis, Helios, Leto, (Silenus), (Herakles), Tyche, Asklepios, Hygieia, Nemesis, rivergods Lycus and Karpos, Mên, Apollo (only as child of Leto). Von Aulock's attribution of Zeus Nikephoros (*MSPhryg* 2.458–60) needs to be amended to Zeus Aetophoros (so *RPC online* 4.2.1889 temp.) Queen Laodike's assimilation to Aphrodite on Laodikeia's Hellenistic and Attalid coinage may explain Aphrodite's absence on Colossae's coinage.

60 So for example, the Bacchus inscription reconstructed and analyzed in chapter 3.

61 See S. Colvin, "Names in Hellenistic and Roman Lycia," in *The Greco-Roman East: Politics, Culture, Society* edited by S. Colvin (Cambridge: Cambridge University Press, 2004), 58.

62 τῷ φερονύμῳ τῶν θείων δωρημ[άτων (*MAMA* 6.49). The inscription may be tied to the church of St. Theodore, one of ten known to have existed at Colossae in the Byzantine period; see A. H. Cadwallader, "The Reverend Dr. John Luke and the Churches of Chonai," *GBRS* 48 (2008): 334–7.

63 On the distinction between denotative and connotative uses of names, see A. M. Davies, "Greek Personal Names and Linguistic Continuity," in *Greek Personal Names: Their Value as Evidence* edited by S. Hornblower and E. Matthews (Oxford: Oxford University Press, 2000), 21.

Plate 9.11: An earlier architrave has been upturned to form part of a new construction in the early Byzantine period. It was gifted, according to the punning metrical inscription, by either a Theodore or Dorotheos. Colossae is reported to have had a church of St Theodore, leaning the probable dedicator to the former name.[64]

One name stands out as a marker of Colossae's commitment to appearing Greek. That name is Τυδεΐδης. The name is extremely rare,[65] but features in Homer as the name of a loyal friend of Odysseus; he is one of the six chieftains of the Achaean League, and a master horse-whisperer.[66] The name is not found in Greece or Macedonia, though the name Tydeus is attested, even being the dedicatory name of the hoplite race at the Nemean Games.[67] It is as if the sheer authority of Homer is sufficient to attract such specific name-use becoming an emblematic display of Greek credentials, regardless of whether any actual ethnic blood-lines can be demonstrated. It helped that the two great Homeric poems held special notice of Anatolia.[68] What mattered was the display of Greek culture — and names were one of the foremost means of establishing that commitment at a first meeting, with religion providing the on-going reinforcement.

At Colossae it seems clear that it was not just a matter of class differentials. One must of course allow for the limitations in the evidence we have (coins, inscriptions) of elite and moneyed bias. The list of names honoring Korymbos would be expected, in the main, to be Greek even in this inland city, given that at this time baths and the gymnasium had generally become joint architectural structures. Gymnasia were committed to the maintenance and enhancement of Greek values. But the importance of the *defixio* tablets is that we gain an insight into those of the lower classes, slaves, metics and laborers most likely. That evidence is relatively consistent with the overall proportions of the names, apart from a slight increase proportionately in Latin names — explicable on the basis of servility. The Hellenizing project begun by the Seleucids, embraced by the Attalids and adopted by the Romans under the claim of

64 Photograph reproduced from *MAMA* 6.49 (public domain).

65 In this form, it is unparalleled; but see Τυδιδης in *I.Ephesos* 1687 and Τυτειδης *IGR* 4.1348 (Lydia). The related name Τυδεύς is more common.

66 Homer *Od.* 3.181, 4.280; *Il.* 5.1.

67 Philostratus *Gym.* 7.

68 See G. H. R. Horsley, "Homer in Pisidia: Aspects of the History of Greek Education in a Remote Roman Province," *Antichthon* 34 (2000): 48–9.

rightful inheritance, was manifestly successful at Colossae. As Greg Horsley observes, "individuals and families admired Hellenic culture for the doors it opened to a career and upward social mobility".[69] The value of Greek identity is recognized at an imperial level in Hadrian's Letter to Aphrodisias that constantly uses "Greek" as a synonym of citizenship — with direct consequences for the ability to access both local and imperial legal protections.[70] It helps to explain why the genealogical sequence almost always moves from epichoric or Phrygian hypocoristic names in past generations to Greek names in the present. Epichoric names and *Lallnamen* were part of the public memory (as in the Korymbos pedestal), even continuing to be held by women in particular, but this was because it demonstrated ancient origins suitably embedded (as often in the case of women) in proud Greek oversight.

Egypt provides an added witness to the importance of appearing Greek, even at the onset of the third century CE. One man, though bearing a solid Greek name, Eudaemon, was nonetheless identifiable as Egyptian through the name of his father (Psois) and mother (Tiathres). He sought legal certification for a name change (περὶ χρηματισμοῦ ὀνόματος l. 7) — not for himself, but for his parents. Henceforth, he was to be known as Eudaemon, son of Heron and Didyme. There is no indication that his parents authorized the change; they were possibly deceased.[71] His reason: ἵν' ὦ πεφιλανθρωπημένος (l. 17), "so that I may benefit."[72] There is no such evidence known from Colossae or the Lycus Valley, and there does seem a greater preparedness to retain, without undue concern, a notice of one's Phrygian forebears. However, it demonstrates the widespread earnest at appearing Greek, along with an anticipation that this would yield considerable benefit.[73] Nevertheless, as Ulrich Wilcken early noted, it is a warning against too quickly drawing conclusions about ethnicity from names.[74]

---

69 Horsley, "Homer in Pisidia," 74.

70 *I.Aphrodisias 2007*, 11.412, ll. 4–11. See chapter 11.

71 So U. Wilcken, "Aus der Straßburger Sammlung," in *Archiv für Papyrusforschung und verwandte Gebiete Vol. 4* edited by U. Wilcken (Leipzig: Teubner, 1908), 128–9. Wilcken notes that the name Didyme is a translation of Tiathres, and Heron probably a translation of the father's name, read as Psais.

72 *SB* 18.13175, vol. 5 (Nesyt nome, Upper Egypt delta, 194 CE). The *idiologos*, to whom the application was formally directed, was the chief financial officer in Egypt. It makes sense, for taxation purposes, that he exercised control over the registration of people's names, including name-changes, as this was the foundation of the tax system, especially the payment of tribute. Eudaemon's petition specifically mentioned that the change was without prejudice to his personal and civic assets (μηδενὸς δημοσίου ἢ ἰδιωτικοῦ καταβλαπτομένου, ll. 16–17 as reconstructed), likely a requisite reassurance to state interests, a fitting *quid pro quo* for the benefits Eudaemon hoped to gain from the authorization of the name-change. See N. Lewis, *Life in Egypt under Roman Rule* (Oxford: Clarendon Press, 1983), 32.

73 See I. F. Fikhman, *Wirtschaft und Gesellschaft im spätantiken Ägypten: kleine Schriften edited by A. Jördens* (Stuttgart: Franz Steiner, 2006), 358–60.

74 Wilcken, *Archiv für Papyrusforschung IV*, 129.

The combination of Roman citizenship with a Greek cognomen is most apparent in the names of the sponsors of Colossae's bronze coins. Even the smallest of Claudia Eugenetoriane's coins squeezes her citizenship credentials onto the face; the consistent display was almost certainly a politically deft means of ensuring her authority to mint the coins was recognized (by local citizens and imperial officials alike).[75] Another Colossian sponsor from the time of Hadrian was similarly concerned: Octavian Apollonios Val(erian?). He probably uses a double cognomen, the second only known by abbreviation but certainly a Latin name,[76] a familiar practice in citizenry formulae.[77] His citizenship dates back, seemingly, to late republican times but it is, at present, impossible to track its lineage through the Colossian elite. As late as the reign of Volusian in the mid-third century, Colossae's mint sponsors held Greek names, albeit as part of a citizenship formula.[78] Some mint sponsors, such as Hieronymos, were content with only their Greek name on the coin legends. Others such as Philopappos, as we have seen, only occasionally included the full citizenship formula.

ii) This "Greekness" is highlighted by the lack of any significant presence of Latin names on the Korymbos pedestal. Only Likinnios occurs, as the grandfather of Menandros (l. 24). The name is a Roman *gentilicium*, known in Roman citizen formulae in Asia. However, Likinnios does not have the *tria nomina* of Roman citizenship and this points to the servile origins in Menandros' family background. This was not, in itself, necessarily a matter of shame in an Asian city, as is clear from the story of the Aphrodisian leader and benefactor Zoilos — a leading slave in the imperial household who returned to Aphrodisias, on manumission, laden with imperial largesse and became one of the leading benefactors in Aphrodisian society. In smaller reflection then, the public admission of this origin at Colossae demonstrates that servility overcome (rather than servility perpetuated) was not a bar to advancement. Even so, it is clear that Likinnios did not want to perpetuate the memory of recent servility to his son (and thence to his grandson) as the fine Greek name, Menandros, became the generational succession. This would suggest that the late first/early second century inscription honoring Markos son of Markos as chief interpreter and translator of the Colossians has avoided any hint of servility,[79] even with what

75 See A. H. Cadwallader, "Wealthy, widowed, astute and beneficent: Claudia Eugenetoriane and the Second Century Revival of the Colossian mint," in *New Documents illustrating the History of Early Christianity, volume 12: The Lycus Valley* edited by J. R. Harrison *et al.* (Grand Rapids: Eerdmans, 2023), forthcoming.

76 There is a possibility that it is a second *gentilicium*, that is, Valerius (perhaps derived from his mother?).

77 See A. Chaniotis, "Second Thoughts on Second Names in Aphrodisias," in *Personal Names*, 209.

78 See chapter 1, coin xxiv).

79 *EA* 2007.112, nr. 3. This four-line (extant) inscription has attracted some debate over its meaning. See A. Chaniotis, "Epigraphic Bulletin for Greek Religion," *Kernos* 213 (2010): 285–6, nr 25 (= *SEG* 57.1382); L. Bormann, "Barbaren und Skythen im Lykostal? Epigraphischer Kommentar zu Kol 3:11," in *Epigraphical Evidence Illustrating Paul's Letter to the Colossians* edited by

in some quarters, would be seen as a *gentilicium*. The name Μᾶρκος is ubiquitous in the Mediterranean. Similarly, the name in Col 4:10 carries no servile suspicions. However, other Latin names, as we saw in the *defixio* analysed in chapter 8, do suggest servitude, that is, the names Terentius and Tertius (cf Rom 16:22). Roman control of the stone industry, either directly as imperial enterprise or contracted out by sale of rights, suggests that a settlement attached to an extraction industry was likely to display a more pronounced coloring of Latin names, as indeed other names in such a context likely bore servile associations (such as Philemation, Euterpe, Onesimos and Chelidon).

Not all Latin names (albeit transliterated into Greek) at Colossae have the stain of servitude on them. But these names are identifiably Roman citizens. Thus Crispinus ("Curly") is, formally, Marcus Larcius Crispinus. But, again, we see a movement in the background of naming, although this time it is not from epichoric to Greek but to Latin. His father also holds Roman citizenship but his name is a Phrygian *Lallname*, that is, Papias. The same inscription yields another Roman citizen, as the official who supervised the erection of a memorial monument to Crispinus. His name is recorded as T(itus or T[iberius]) Asinius Epaphroditos.[80] The citizenship formulae point to a first century conferral. The last-named displays a striking connection between the Colossian elite and the wider Roman senatorial class.

The gens name is known in a number of places in Asia, including Sardis and Alia. Its most famous name in Asia is probably G. Asinius Pollio, proconsul in 6–5 BCE. A successor of Epaphroditos at Colossae: Ti. Asinius Philopappos, perhaps a son or grandson, certainly a relative, served as *grammateus* (chief clerk) of the city and took responsibility for minting a number of bronze coins during the reign of Antoninus Pius. Significantly however he reserved his full citizenry only for coin legends that depicted the emperor on its obverse.[81] For other bronzes, he was content to give only Philopappos, along with the magistracy he held, sometimes accenting his munificence for the Colossians by the less common use of the dative ΚΟΛΟCCΗΝΟΙC.[82] Here an echo of Zoilas of Aphrodisias is in view where identity presentation, as Roman or as Greek, depended on the audience and the object in view — that is, a signal of Roman allegiance and connection on one hand and a beneficent commitment to the

J. Verheyden, M. Öhler and T. Corsten (WUNT 411; Tübingen: Mohr Siebeck, 2018), 193–6. See the critical summary in Cadwallader and Harrison, "Perspectives on the Lycus Valley," 14–17 and further discussion in chapter 11.

80 *MAMA* 6.39 = *I.Mus. Denizli* 59. Note that there is an omission of the T. in Tullia Ritti's transcription of the inscription. This is followed by *LGPN*. A squeeze of the inscription is held in the archives collection of the British Institute at Ankara (Denizli 51 = DM 23). This, and the photograph, confirm the praenomen abbreviation: see the analysis in chapter 11.

81 *MSPhryg* 2.553, 554 = *RPC online* 4.2.1874 temp.

82 *MSPhryg* 2.455–457 = *RPC online* 4.2.1888 temp.; *MSPhryg* 2.458–460 = *RPC online* 4.2.1889 temp.; *MSPhryg* 2.461–464 = *RPC online* 4.2.1890 temp.; *RPC online* 4.2.10833 temp.

city of Colossae on the other.[83] The Asinii were involved in minting in other cities as well,[84] indicating that this was perceived to be a prestigious benefaction to provide, if one had the standing and the financial ability. One Asinius, from the city of Alia to the east of Colossae (*conventus* of Apameia) also used Philopappos as a second cognomen (during the reign of Antoninus Pius),[85] which Thomas Drew-Bear interpreted as a statement of kinship.[86] But this Philopappos was not the first of the Asinii lineage to mint coins at Alia. A forebear coined bronzes during the reign of Trajan. His name is perhaps even more significant for its rare cognomen: Gaius Asinius Frugi.[87] The same cognomen is found on another Asinius minter at Sardis in the reign of Marcus Aurelius,[88] and again under Severus Alexander.[89] "Phrygian" was frequently deployed as a snide judgment by Greek and Roman writers, as a means of maintaining cultural and ethnic distinction from the intermixture of races that characterized Anatolia.[90] But within Asia, there was sufficient local pride for the toponymic and cultural association to be borne by at least some members of the Asian senatorial class.[91] The variety of onomastic forms built on Φρουγ– is not found outside Asia, with 39 of the 53 instances confined to the territory encompassed by the regions of Phrygia, Lycaonia and Pisidia. It apparently did not attract the disapprobium that some names held.[92] Colossae cannot as yet boast a senator with any certainty, unlike Tripolis at the western end of the Lycus,[93] both somewhat in the shadow of Hierapolis and Laodikeia. But it can claim those elite connections that took considerable interest in promoting its involvement with the senatorial class, as we have seen with the largest coin minted by Claudia Eugenetoriane (larger than her minting of the coin featuring the head of Hadrian).[94] Of particular interest here is that,

83 See R. R. R. Smith, *Aphrodisias I: The Monument of C. Iulius Zoilos* (Mainz: von Zabern, 1993); R. Canavan, *Clothing the Body of Christ at Colossae* (Tübingen: Mohr Siebeck, 2012), 125–7.

84 *RPC online* 4.2.1747, 1765, 1786, 8376 temp.

85 Gaius Asinius Agreus Philopappos.

86 T. Drew-Bear, "Problèmes de géographie historique en Phrygie: l'example d'Alia," *ANRW* II, 7, 2 (1980): 937.

87 *RPC* 3.2613–2614.

88 *RPC online* 4.2.2036, 9542, 9848 temp.

89 *RPC online* 6.4526–4627 temp.

90 See Levick, "In the Phrygian mode," 41–6.

91 See P. Herrmann, "Inschriften von Sardeis," *Chiron* 23 (1993): 935–7. Herrmann notes that the name Φροῦγι is also known from the Iulii senatorial family. The same ascription belongs to the Asinii (wider) family).

92 See *Dig.* 36.1.65.10 (Gaius).

93 See A. Filippini, "Tripolis on the Maeander under Roman Rule (Cent. 2nd B.C. – 3rd A.D.): History and Epigraphy," in *Tripolis ad Maeandrum I*, 52–4. The known (third century) senator representing Tripolis (and with significant Ephesian connections) was Hermolaos: *IGR* 4.1671 = *MAMA* 6.55 = *Steinepigramme* 1.02.10.01.

94 The Senate coin measures 29 mm and weighs 11.39 g. The Hadrian coin has a diameter of 24 mm and weighs 9.90 g. On the basis of the range of coins minted by Claudia Eugenetoriane and by comparison with those coins minted by her immediate successors in coin production,

unlike the other known coins of Colossae featuring the "sacred senate" (ἱερὰ σύνκλητος),[95] Eugenetoriane ensured that her name (replete with display of Roman citizenship) was included in the reverse legend (Pl. 9.12). It may indicate her own connection with senatorial families, though this needs corroboration.

Plate 9.12: The largest coin in the series minted under the sponsorship of the widow, Claudia Eugenetoriane. On the obverse is the stereotypical youthful, male head of the Senate surrounded by the legend ΙΕΡΑ CΥΝΚΛΗΤΟC. The reverse features another distinctive accent of Colossian iconography, the hunter Artemis reaching for an arrow to nock into her bow, accompanied by her hunting hound, here with a long legend that expands into the field, ΚΛ. ΕΥΓΕΝΕΤΟΡΙΑΝΗ ΚΟΛΟCCΗΝΟΙC ΑΝΕΘΗΚΕΝ, "Claudia Eugenetoriane minted this under authority for the Colossians".[96]

iii) We have encountered the "Greekness" of Colossae not only in the names and religious landscape but also in the refashioning of the ancient pedigree of the city so that a new etymology and derivation of the city toponym was promulgated. In this sense, Colossae's claim on Greek culture had an avowed historic lineage far more ancient than Laodikeia or Hierapolis could posit. Hellenic cultural capital continued to be fostered, with epichoric names and

Hieronymos and Octavian Apollonios, I have assigned the value of 3 assaria to the Senate coin and 1½ (possibly 2) assaria to the Hadrian coin. See Cadwallader, "Wealthy, widowed, astute and beneficent," forthcoming. Many "Senate coins" were struck without identifying a sponsor. This makes the dating of these coins difficult. However, where magistrates are known, this allows comparison between the size of coins bearing the head of the emperor and that of the "youthful male head" of the Senate. There does not seem to be any consistency in the size/weight differential between emperor and Senate coins. Thus, at Nakrasa, the sponsor Artemidoros ensured that Hadrian adorned the higher value coin (*RPC* 3.1808 cf 1809 for the Senate); conversely at Pionia in Mysia, the sponsor Nikomachos minted the head of Hadrian on two coins, one larger, one smaller than that for the Senate (*RPC* 3.1662 and 1663 cf 3.1665 for the Senate); at Blaundos, all Claudius Valerianos's coins featuring the emperor Marcus Aurelius (*RPC online* 4.2.1188, 1194, 2819 temp.) were smaller than that portraying the Senate (*RPC online* 4.2.9318 temp.). However, the search for influence upon Senate decision-making may be important here, as in the 18 different Laodikeian Senate coins struck, during the reign of Antoninus Pius by Publius Claudius Attalos (*RPC online* 4.2.2048 temp. etc), perhaps to gain the official decree of neokorate status from the proper conferring body, the Senate, after what appears to be a less-credentialled, local bestowal during Hadrian's pan-hellenic tour (see F. Guizzi, "Greek and Latin Inscriptions of Laodikeia on the Lykos 2003–2018," in *15. Yılında Laodikeia* edited by C. Şimşek (Istanbul: Ege, 2019), 175). Laodikeia did not celebrate its neokorate status on coins until the third century, emphatically adding δόγματι συνκλήτου, "by decree of the Senate" (*RPC online* 6.5498 temp.).

95 *MSPhryg* 2.543–544, and chapter 2, coin xxvi).

96 *RPC online* 3.2307D. Photograph by courtesy of Roma Numismatics (www.RomaNumismatics.com).

Lallnamen either being situated into a Greek embrace or consigned to the (acknowledged) past. In the names for which we have evidence, there is no Iranian instance, even though Colossae was remembered in literary testimonia as the key Achaemenid city between Apameia and Sardis. But also absent is any Jewish name or Jewish "signal" in extant inscriptions. Given that most of the surviving inscriptions are epitaphs dated to the first to third centuries and that, elsewhere, there does not appear to be any distinct "quarter" within necropoleis for the Jewish dead nor even distinctive burial practices,[97] one might have expected some survival if there was a significant Jewish population as some commentators are wont to suggest — a population of "as many as two or three thousand" claimed James Dunn.[98]

This is where references in the Letter to the Colossians actually gain some powerful resonance.[99] It could be argued that some Greek names mask a Jewish identity, though this really is special pleading from silence, more than the argument from the hushed epitaphs that I have presented. However, there is one form of this "masking/supplementing of identity" that was known in the ancient world; that is the use of homonyms. Egyptians are known to have made use of the adjustment of a name to a more recognizable and acceptable Greek phonic equivalent.[100] One slave in Rome, bearing the Greek name Phronimos, on manumission adopted a Latin homonym, Frontinus, as his cognomen.[101] Closer to Colossae, the practice has been identified at Balboura, where Pisidian and Phrygian names were overwritten with similar-sounding Greek names.[102] Jews were not immune from such a practice. Josephus notes that under the Seleucid ruler, Antiochos Epiphanes (reigned 175–164 BCE), one of the contenders for the high priesthood "changed his name" (μετωνόμασεν)

97 See C. Laforest, D. Castex and F. Blazot, "Tomb 163d in the North Necropolis of Hierapolis in Phrygia: An insight into the funerary gestures and practices of the Jewish diaspora in Asia Minor in late Antiquity and the proto-Byzantine period," in *Life and Death in Asia Minor in Hellenistic, Roman & Byzantine Times: Studies in Archaeology and Bioarchaeology*, edited by J. R. Brandt *et al.* (Oxford: Oxbow, 2017), 70–2. On the methodological difficulties of recognizing Jewish graves, see T. Ilan, "The New Jewish Inscriptions from Hierapolis and the Question of Jewish Diaspora Cemeteries," *SCI* 25 (2006): 71–86.

98 J. D. G. Dunn, *The Epistles to the Colossians and to Philemon* (NIGTC; Grand Rapids, MN: Eerdmans, 1996), 21–2.

99 See A. H. Cadwallader, "Greeks in Colossae: shifting allegiances in the Letter to the Colossians and its context," in *Attitudes to Gentiles in Ancient Judaism and Early Christianity* edited by D. C. Sim and J. S. McLaren (London/NY: Bloomsbury, 2013), 224–41.

100 *P.Berol.* 7080B. Over a century ago, this was recognized by Adolph Deissmann, *Bible Studies* (Edinburgh: T & T Clark, 1909), 315; see recently, L. Koenen, "Sale of an Egyptian Woman enslaved in an Insurrection," in *Papyri in Memory of P. J. Sijpesteijn (P. Sipj.)* edited by A. J. B. Sirks and K. A. Worp (Oakville, CT: American Society of Papyrologists, 2007), 311 (a case of an Egyptian slave likely given a Greek homonym).

101 *CIL* 6.8580, 18398 (69–100 CE), as interpreted by P. R. C. Weaver, *Familia Caesaris: A Social Study of the Emperor's Freedmen and Slaves* (Cambridge: Cambridge University Press, 1972), 143–4, n1.

102 T. J. Smith, "Votive Reliefs from Balboura and its Environs," *AS* 47 (1997): 35.

from Jesus to Jason.[103] Although Josephus is not explicit, the implication is that this was seen as an advantage under the Hellenizing regime. It also signals the antiquity of the practice.

Consequently, when the name Ἰάσων occurs in an identifiable Jewish context (usually epigraphical or associated relief), commentators have seen a homonym at play. Thus both Hierapolis and Aphrodisias witness known Jews whose Greek name, Ἰάσων "Jason", is taken as a homonym for the Hebrew name transliterated as Ἰησοῦς "Jesus".[104] The Hierapolitan instance shows the intermixture of names, Jason is identified as a Jew Ἰάσων Εἰουδέος (the inscription's spelling of Ἰουδαῖος) but in the same grave is to be buried his wife named Clementiane, a woman with a fine Latin name.[105] The person given responsibility for ensuring Jason's wishes were fulfilled is a certain Ammianos son of Hermogenes. This is a Phrygian *Lallname* albeit given the Latin ending *–ianos* (meaning "son of"),[106] with his father bearing a well-credentialed Greek name. It is uncertain whether Clementiane was a Jew.

It should not be automatically assumed that all Jews keen to use names as an assimilationist practice resorted to homonyms. The famous long list of names of Jews and god-fearers from Aphrodisias, in which the name Jason occurs, features a number of double-named Jews where the Semitic name is not phonically similar to the Greek name also adopted. These double-names are signaled by ὁ κέ/καί.[107] Usually the Jewish name is listed first, but not always. So we have Ἰακωβ ὁ κὲ Ἀπελλίων and Ἰούδας ὁ κὲ Ζώσι[μος? but also Αἰλιανὸς ὁ καὶ Σαμουηλ.[108] The phenomena are noticeable enough; it is the rationale for their use that is important. Margaret Williams argued that it was assimilationist behavior that had an eye towards social mobility and political and commercial opportunity in the context of the dominant culture.[109] It certainly indicates that at least some individuals were attempting to negotiate the manifold changes in society that rolled from Hellenistic to Roman rule. Later rabbinical disparagement of the Jewish practice of adoption of Greek names apparently did not cut

---

103 Josephus *Ant.* 12.239.

104 E. Miranda, "La communità giudaica di Hierapolis di Frigia," *EA* 31 (1999) 117, nr. 3 = *IJO* 2.190 (Hierapolis); *MAMA* 8.488, *IJO* 2.14B, l. 14 (Aphrodisias).

105 Walter Ameling curiously calls her "Olympias" in his commentary, though retaining Clementiane in his translation (*I.Jud. Orientis* 2.190 at p. 405).

106 By this time (second century CE) the *–ianos*, *-iane* ending had lost its filial function; see T. Corsten, "Names in *–ianos* in Asia Minor: A preliminary study," in *Onomatologos*, 456–63. The spread of the name can be discerned in its growing use from the second century, in Beroea; see A. B. Tataki, *Ancient Beroea: Prosopography and Society* (Paris: de Boccard, 1988), 313. He recognizes the pre-Greek origin in Asia Minor of the name (pp. 400–1).

107 For further examples, see *New Doc. Early Christ.* 1, pp. 92–3.

108 *I.Jud. Orientis* 2.14B, ll. 20, 28, 30 respectively. The date of the inscription is contested.

109 M. H. Williams, "The Use of Alternative Names by Diaspora Jews in Graeco-Roman Antiquity," *JSJ* 38 (2007): 49–50; similarly, I. M. Gafni, *Land, Center and Diaspora: Jewish Constructs in Late Antiquity* (Sheffield: Sheffield Academic Press, 1997), 49–50.

through in Asia Minor until distinction from Christians became more critical (from the fourth century).[110]

Biblical commentators have recognized the presence of homonyms in the New Testament.[111] Gerard Mussies considers the name Jason in Rom 16:21 to be the same homonym as noted previously.[112] Apart from the name Paul (the recognition of whose adoption of a homonym is indebted to Acts 13:9),[113] the clear example is that of Jesus also called Ioustos in Col 4:11:'Ἰησοῦς ὁ λεγόμενος Ἰοῦστος. Here both a homonym and double-naming are operating. However, the ὁ λεγόμενος, for which ὁ καί is often a shortened phrasing, can flag the name by which the bearer was generally known, in this case, Justus.

But Justus, for all that the name is written in Greek, is a Latin name,[114] as is Paulus. It had become ubiquitous in both languages, outperforming the strict Greek word-turned-name, Δίκαιος/Δικαιοσύνη. Δίκαιος is also the name of a god (frequently connected with a fellow/combine-deity, Ὅσιος),[115] and hence would also qualify as a theonym, a connection that the Latin does not have, being rather a virtue/value epithet.[116] It graces two other persons in the New Testament, namely Barsabbas (Acts 1:23)[117] though there is no homonymic quality in this case, nor is there any warrant, given its ubiquity, for it to be regarded as a specifically Jewish preference.[118] The second instance (Acts 18:7),

110 See H. L. Strack and P. Billerbeck, *Kommentar zum neuen Testament aus Talmud und Midrasch* (Munich: C. H. Beck, 6 vols, 1978 [1924]), vol 2, 712.

111 See R. Bauckham, *Gospel Women: Studies of the Named Women in the Gospels* (London/NY: Continuum, 2002), 182–5.

112 *New Doc. Early Christ.* 1.55 (p. 93); "Jewish Personal Names in some Non-literary Sources," in *Studies in Early Jewish Epigraphy* edited by J. W. van Henten and P. W. van der Horst (Leiden: Brill, 1994), 273. See also Josephus *Ant.* 12.239.

113 The homonym was identified at least as early as F. J. Foakes-Jackson and K. Lake, *The Acts of the Apostles* (Grand Rapids, MN: Baker, 5 vols, 1979 [1932]), vol 4, 14. It is intriguing that the writer of Acts situates this homonymic admission in the pericope of the encounter with Sergius Paulus (Acts 13:4–12). Certainly Stephen Mitchell sees it as the critical moment in the opening of the gentile mission (rather than the commissioning at Antioch Orontes). See S Mitchell and M Waelkens, *Pisidian Antioch: The Site and Its Monuments* (London: Duckworth, 1998), 12.

114 There are approximately 900 instances of the name Justus/a in the *Corpus Inscriptionum Latinarum*, according to Iiro Kajanto, *Latin Cognomina* 252.

115 See, for example, E. Erten and H. Sivas, "Eine neue Weihung aus Phrygien," *EA* 44 (2011): 185–95.

116 Jesus is called ὁ δίκαιος in Acts 7:52.

117 Codex D changes the name to the more famous Barnabas but there is no hint in Colossians that Jesus and Barnabas (Col 4:10) shared Justus as a second or substitute cognomen. See J. Read-Heimerdinger, "Barnabas in Acts: A Study of his Role in the Text of Codex Bezae" *JSNT* 72 (1998) 49–50.

118 Contra J. B. Lightfoot, *Saint Paul's Epistle to the Colossians and Philemon* (London: Macmillan, 1892), 236, followed by Dunn, *Colossians and Philemon*, 278. Sometimes no acknowledgement of Lightfoot occurs: G. J. Johnson *Early Christian Epitaphs from Anatolia* (Atlanta, GA: Scholars Press, 1995), 135; R. Kearsley *Greeks and Romans in Imperial Asia* (*IK* 59; Bonn: Habelt, 2001), 80. Even the Roberts were caught into seeing the name with a Jewish hue (*BE*

indicates a thoroughly Latinized citizen's name, Titius Justus, probably an established member of the *colonia* of Corinth. The name in male and female form (Ἰοῦστα) occurs at Hierapolis and Laodikeia without any identifiable Jewish connection.[119]

In any case, Justus in Colossians is qualified further. He is a member of a small group designated in the letter as "the only ones of the circumcision" (οἱ ὄντες ἐκ περιτομῆς οὗτοι μόνοι), that is, a reference to the collation of Barnabas, his nephew Mark, Jesus called Justus and, possibly (but not certainly) Aristarchus (Col 4:10–11).[120] Epaphras, who seems to have had a profound involvement in the spread of the gospel in the Lycus Valley (Col 1:7–8, 4:12–13), is not of this group.[121] This extra designation turns what is an unremarkable naming into something far more significant. These Jewish companions of "Paul" are now presented as in the minority. The language of distantiation is used, not dissimilar to the use of "*their* synagogue/s" in Mk 1:23, Matt 4:23. This is the only instance in the Pauline corpus where anyone is identified by reference to an ethnic or cultural distinctive. Even though the expression ἐκ περιτομῆς is found elsewhere (Gal 2:12), here in Colossians the sense is not an unqualified reference to a faction,[122] but rather a metonymy for a distinct people (cf Eph 2:11). Moreover, the way in which the Jews, those "of the circumcision" are set off from the Christ-followers addressed in the letter, generates a sense that those so named are noticeable precisely because they are a minority, removed from the ordinary experience of those in Colossae. The mark of circumcision no longer has a significant presence among those being addressed. Rather it bears a trace of memory, a mark that Roman writers used as a "metonymy for a distinct people."[123] Consequently, it can then be turned to being a metaphor that speaks of divine status, "made without hands" (Col 2:11 cf 13).

1976:798), enough to sway Thomas Drew-Bear, though the weight of contrary evidence made him hesitate: *Nouvelles Inscriptions de Phrygie* (Zutphen, Holland: Terra, 1978), 86. The identification of the "Syrophoenician" woman in the Pseudo-Clementine homilies as Justa, as one observant of the Mosaic laws, is an instance incapable of generalized application. See A. H. Cadwallader, "What's in a Name? The Tenacity of a Tradition of Interpretation [Justus/a and the Clementine Homilies]" *LTJ* 39 (2005): 218–34.

119 See *LGPN* VC svv.

120 The phrase ὁ συναιχμάλωτος μου (καί) seems to function as a separator. Dunn equates this Aristarchos with the Thessalonian named in Acts 19:29, 20:4, 27:2 (*Colossians and Philemon*, 275), a fraught suggestion given the 429 instances of the name evidenced across the Mediterranean world (*LGPN*).

121 So Huttner, *Lycus Valley*, 88.

122 Contra M. MacDonald, *Colossians and Ephesians* (Sacra Pagina 17; Collegeville: Liturgical Press, 2000), 181.

123 Cadwallader, "Greeks in Colossae", 240. See Plautus *Poen.* 1312; Horace *Sat.* 1.5.100, 9.1.65; Suetonius *Dom.* 8.12.2; Tacitus *Hist.* 5.5; Martial *Ep.* 9.94; Juvenal *Sat.* 14.100; Persius *Sat.* 5.184.

This is what makes the "race code" in Col 3:11 so striking, given the Hellenic stamp on Colossian society. As Terry Donaldson has so perceptively noted, "... religious groups cannot be understood apart from the cities in which they are embedded ..."[124] Conversely, when those cities have begun to be understood in their distinctive features, even when those features are shared with other centers in a region, resonances within a text are powerful indicators of participation in the cultural organism with all its competition and tensions. Col 3:11 has frequently been cited as simply another rendition of the baptismal formula repeated in Gal 3:28–9 and 1 Cor 12:13.[125] But it is not a reiteration; it is a departure, locally focused as it was at the outset but also an unwitting prophecy of the eventual hegemony of the gentile church.[126]

The text reads:

> ὅπου οὐκ ἔνι Ἕλλην καὶ Ἰουδαῖος, περιτομὴ καὶ ἀκροβυστία, βάρβαρος, Σκύθης, δοῦλος, ἐλεύθερος, ἀλλὰ πάντα καὶ ἐν πᾶσιν Χριστός
>
> *There is no instance here where there is Greek and Jew, circumcised and uncircumcised, barbarian, Scythian, slave, free; but Christ is all and in all.*

There is a remarkable double-play involved in this recalibration of a Pauline formula, one that is both deeply indebted to or at least cognisant of the cosmopolitan composition of Colossian society and, on the other hand, equally as deeply committed to undercut the values and aspirations that constituted its fabric. It might be argued that the change is merely another permutation encouraged by the (spare) variation in the two instances from authentic Pauline Letters, that is, with the reduction of Galatians' tripartite polarity when the Corinthians were being addressed, by the omission of "male and female".[127] More likely in my view, given what the onomastics of Colossae have revealed, is that there is a recognition by the writer that a dominant, if not proud, Greek ethos is being addressed. In this sense, Ἕλλην is not to be translated "Gentile" or even "pagan",[128] whether or not Paul himself saw any difference between

124 "Introduction," in *Religious Rivalries and the Struggle for Success in Caesarea Maritima* edited by T. L. Donaldson (Waterloo, Ontario: Wilfred Laurier University Press, 2000), 3.

125 See, for example, N. Huttunen, "Powers, Baptism and the Ethics of the Stronger: Paul among the Ancient Political Philosophers," in *Paul and the Greco-Roman Philosophical Tradition* edited by J. R. Dodson and A. W. Pitts (London: T & T Clark, 2017), 115.

126 There is a note of supercessionism added when this is turned into a generalized stage of "church development" as in D. M. Hay, *Colossians* (Nashville: Abingdon, 2000), 128. Rather, it is a mirror of the local demographic and cultural commitment.

127 Compare the expanded set of dichotomies in Clement of Alexandria *Strom.* 3.2.6.2. Curiously there is a variant carrying some weight in the Colossians text that reintroduces ἄρσεν καὶ θῆλυ (D*, F, G, 629 and a number of old Latin and Vulgate texts with Latin fathers). The reading has been argued to be original, though this view has not gained traction; see M. Grosso, "The Diversification of Colossians' Text and Women's Status in the Early Church," *TC* 16 (2011): 1–3.

128 D. Campbell, *The Deliverance of God: An Apocalyptic Re-reading of Justification in Paul* (Grand Rapids: Eerdmans, 2009), 552–4.

"Greek" and "Gentile".[129] Certainly, when Paul generates an overarching summary of the global demography he is addressing,[130] he never uses Ἰουδαῖοι καὶ ἔθνη. It is always Jew and *Greek*.

The unique "race code" of the Letter to the Colossians

This is where the opening of the Colossians formula is so striking. Never in the Pauline corpus, apart from this instance, is there a deviation from the word order of "Jew and Greek". As Michael Gese emphasizes, "Paul always places Jew before Greek."[131] This is no fixed linguistic composite, like "flesh and blood" — Heb 2:14 notwithstanding. It was a profound commitment of the "apostle to the gentiles" (Gal 2:9) that the salvific dispensation of God was to the Jew first (Rom 1:16 as the proleptic anticipation and summation of Romans 9–11). In fact, in every combination of "Jew and Greek" in Paul's authentic Letters, this is the order.[132] Paul did not have a monopoly on such a privileged sequence. His nemesis, the evangelist Matthew,[133] assumed the same hierarchy; his apologist, Luke,[134] did the same.[135]

Accordingly, it is hard to fathom those commentators who see no substantial difference between the "race codes",[136] nor, particularly, any significance in the order here.[137] Similarly, the effort to cite the Galatians and Corinthians

---

129 In favor of equivalence, W. Gutbrod, "Ἰσραήλ," *TDNT* 3.381; similarly in his constant bracketing of one as the meaning of the other, S. McKnight, *The Letter to the Colossians* (NICNT; Grand Rapids, MN: Eerdmans, 2018), 313–4; in favor of difference: C. Stanley, "'Neither Jew nor Greek': Ethnic Conflict in Graeco-Roman Society," *JSNT* 64 (1996) 101–24. The translation "Gentile" misdirects interpretation, assuming a perspective of Paul the Jew or at least a sympathizer.

130 As Lukas Bormann underscores, the summative conjunction of Jew and Greek both means "all people" and preserves a "Judeocentric perspective". L. Bormann, "Barbaren und Skythen im Lykostal? Epigraphischer Kommentar zu Kol 3:11," in *Epigraphical Evidence*, 165.

131 M. Gese, *Das Vermächtnis des Apostels: die Rezeption der paulinischen Theologie im Epheserbrief* (Tübingen: Mohr Siebeck, 1997), 113 n16.

132 Rom 1:16, 2.9,10, 3:9, 10:12; 1 Cor 1:22, 23, 24, 10:32, 12:13; Gal 3.28; cf similarly, Rom 3:29, 1 Cor 9:20–21, Gal 2:15.

133 On the disputational relationship between Paul and Matthew, see K. D. Dyer, "Paul, Matthew, Israel and the Nations," *ABR* 68 (2020): 1–15.

134 On Acts as an apology for Paul, see R. R. Dupertuis, "Socratizing Paul: The Portrait of Paul in Acts," *The Fourth R* 22 (2009): 11–18, 28.

135 Matt 10:5–6, 15:24; Acts 2:10, 13:46, 14:1, 18:4, 19:10, 17; 20.21, cf 13:5, 14:26, 16:1, 17:2, 18:6, 28:28.

136 See L. T. Johnson, *Among the Gentiles: Greco-Roman Religion and Christianity* (New Haven: Yale University Press, 2009), 357 n18.

137 M. Barth and H. Blanke, *Colossians* (AB) translated by A. B. Beck (New York: Doubleday, 1994), 415. Peter Müller assumes no difference even when arguing that close attention to the wording is critical: *Kolosserbrief* (KEK 9/2; Göttingen: Vandenhoeck & Ruprecht, 2022), 302–3; so also

sequence as showing variation to justify this as a mere inconsequence,[138] fails to feel the weight of the theological issue. One cannot slide past the confronting reversal of terms by turning the instigation of the sequence into a chiasmus that can then be argued to privilege the central elements, that is A (Greek) B (Jew) B¹ (circumcision) A¹ (uncircumcision).[139] The failure to construct a thorough-going chiastic structure across all the elements suggests that this is no more than a simple stylistic apparatus,[140] although Lukas Bormann draws the interesting distinction between an ethnic origin and a conscious decision to align with Jews by being circumcised.[141] In any case, it stretches credulity to suggest that Paul would allow a literary device to trump a theological commitment. Put simply, Paul would not have written this, nor allowed it to be written.[142] Moreover, for those commentators arguing (in spite of the absence of evidence) for a significant Jewish population at Colossae, including among the Christ-followers, this could not help to have caused affront, not least for its failure to observe Paul's own sequence. Whether or not this was part of the tensions between the Christ-followers in Colossae and those at least in Lao-

---

J. White, *Der Brief von Paulus an die Kolosser* (Witten: SCM/R. Brockhaus, 2018), 288. Morton Smith had asked the question "Is the change of order significant?": "De tuenda sanitate praecepta (Moralia 122B – 137 E)," in *Plutarch's Ethical Writings and Early Christian Literature* edited by H. D. Betz (Leiden: Brill, 1978), 50. My answer is emphatically "Yes".

138 So Foster, *Colossians*, 340; similarly Dunn, *Colossians and Philemon*, 223; A. T. Lincoln and A. J. M. Wedderburn, *The Theology of the Later Pauline Letters* (Cambridge: CUP, 1993), 10, 13. Foster is correct however, in seeing some significance in the "non-Jewish character of the recipients of the letter." The weight of evidence presented above suggests that this is more significant than Foster seems to have allowed.

139 R. McL. Wilson, *A Critical and Exegetical Commentary on Colossians and Philemon* (London: T & T Clark, 2005), 255; M. J. Harris, *Exegetical Guide to the Greek New Testament: Colossians and Philemon* (Nashville, TN: B&H Academic, 2010), 134, cf Müller, *Kolosserbrief*, 303.

140 There have been efforts to extract a chiastic structure on the second group of four elements in the code of Col 3:11. See D. A. Campbell, "Unravelling Colossians 3:11b," *NTS* 42 (1996): 120–32. The extraction is an imposition and demands a narrow perspective on Scythian in a Colossian context (as distinct from mainland Greece). See L. Bormann, "Weltbild und gruppenspezifische Raumkonfiguration des Kolosserbriefs," in *Kolosser-Studien* edited by P. Müller (Göttingen: Neukirchener, 2009), 94–6.

141 Bormann, "Barbaren und Skythen," 166. Bormann recognises that the same ability to decide also applies to "uncircumcised", precisely as found in 1 Macc 1:11–15 and 1 Cor 7:18; on epispasm and the accent on bodily integrity promoted at the gymnasium, see A. H. Cadwallader, "Paul and the Games," in *Paul in the Greco-Roman World, A Handbook, Volume 1* edited by J. P. Sampley (London: T & T Clark, 2016), 379–80.

142 Here I would bolster the assessment of non-Pauline authorship in the light of this phrasing made by Jerry Sumney, *Colossians: A Commentary* (Louisville, KY: WJKP, 2008), 205. The issue of pseudepigraphy has often been analyzed, focusing on stylistic differences, historical problems and theological distinctives, which will not be re-visited here. See especially, M. Kiley, *Colossians as Pseudepigraphy* (Sheffield: JSOT Press, 1986), O. Leppä, *The Making of Colossians: A Study on the Formation and Purpose of a Deutero-Pauline Letter* (Göttingen: Vandenhoeck & Ruprecht, 2003), B. D. Ehrman, *Forgery and Counterforgery: The Use of Literary Deceit in Early Christian Polemics* (Oxford: Oxford University Press, 2013), 171–82.

dikeia where a Jewish population is known, cannot be discerned. However, we have seen already that Archippos' special ministry seems in some measure to have been directed towards relationship building, even conflict resolution.

One of the insights that Naoíse Mac Sweeney has brought to the study of foundation stories is not only that they changed over time according to the circumstances faced by cities but that, in a region constantly situating the interaction of different ethnic groups, these stories were shaped so as to accommo date this multi-hued demography into an overall, embracing narrative. These foundation stories were far more ambiguous in their promotion of Greek culture; they were nuanced and massaged, far less committed to reinforce the old rigid dichotomies of Greek and barbarian,[143] that were real enough in the earlier experience of those who weren't Greek.[144] Indeed, βάρβαρος "barbarian" on the one hand had become democratized as a potential slur and delineating linguistic boundary laid down by any group about another group.[145] By such ubiquity it became less charged. This softening meant, on the other hand, that the term could even be used as a personal name, admittedly uncommon, but covering quite a status range. It occurs as a cognomen for a Roman citizen from Dorylaion,[146] and the first of a double cognomina in the form Βαρβαριανός ("son of Barbaros/son of the Barbarian")[147] Τειμόθεος, another Roman citizen from Baris in Pisidia.[148] Βάρβαρος seems also to have been used as a "stage-name" of a gladiator, known from a simple inscription and relief on a stele from Apollonia in Pisidia.[149] It may be significant, given Thracian migration south in the Seleucid period, that the name has a strong Thracian usage.[150] When one turns to the Latin borrowed equivalent (*Barbarus*; also attested *Barbarianus*),

143 N. M. Sweeney, *Foundation Myths and Politics in Ancient Ionia* (Cambridge: Cambridge University Press, 2013), 198–203.

144 See the lament by a non-Greek petitioner to Zenon, an official in the Ptolemaic bureaucracy "they treated me with disdain because I am a barbarian" (ἀλλὰ κατεγνώκασίμ (sic) μου ὅτι εἰμὶ βάρβαρος), *P.Cair. Zen.* 2.66 ll. 18–19, 256–255 BCE.

145 See, for example, Martial *Ep.* 11.96. Note the expansiveness of the notion of "barbarian" in a Pompeii graffito: *At quem non ceno barbarous ille mihi est* "The one with whom I do not dine, is a barbarian to me." (*CIL* 4.1880).

146 *GGA* 1897:413 nr. 68 (3rd century CE).

147 A new project of the *Lexicon of Greek Personal Names* aims to provide the etymological and semantic analysis of Greek names. The results are eagerly anticipated for the updated and expanded research opportunities begun by Friedrich Bechtel, *Die historische Personennamen des Griechischen bis zur Kaiserzeit* (Halle: Niemeyer, 1917) and supplemented by Olivier Masson, *Onomastica Graeca selecta* (Paris: Droz, 3 vols, 1990–2000).

148 Ramsay, *Phrygia* 335–6 nr. 163; the citizenship in this case is post-*Constitutio Antoniniana.* Significantly, his grandfather's name was Βάρβαρος.

149 *MAMA* 4.128 (2nd or 3rd century). The name is not included in *LGPN*. I have accepted here the interpretation of the editors, W. H. Buckler, W. M. Calder and W. K. Guthrie (p. 65); note however that Louis Robert was undecided: *Les Gladiateurs dans l'orient grec* (Amsterdam: Hakkert, 1971 [1940]), 61 n1.

150 The *LGPN* has 28 occurrences for Βάρβαρος, 11 of which come from Macedonia or Thrace. Βαρβάρα occurs once, Βαρβαριανός and Βαρβαρίων 4 times each.

the statistics become far less uncommon. The name occurs early in the reign of Augustus; it is used by Roman legionaries; a decurion can have it as a cognomen.[151] Bormann is correct in drawing attention to the difference between the singular usage in Col 3:11 rather than the plural; plurals are loaded with more stereotypical stigmatism than the singular. But he doesn't go far enough because he does not recognize that the singular could occasionally become even favorably used as a personal name.[152]

Plate 9.13a and b: Examples of the use of "barbarian" as a name. The stone on the left, now installed in the garden of the Amman Citadel, Jordan, is a small altar to Neptune Augustus set up by Cassius Barbarus (l. 4) of the Third Legion (Cyrenaica).[153] The (reproduction) stone on the right, displayed in the Museum of the Cecilia Metella Mausoleum in Rome, is an epitaph, reading "To the chthonic gods. Barbarianos (l. 3), the son of Pontianos, lies here. Amastris (on the Pontus) once reared him, but the daimon snatched the young man away."[154]

151 *CIL* 3.6588 (Alexandria, 13–12 BCE); *CIL* 8.23174 (N. Africa, nd); *AE* 1977.442 (Spain, 151–230 CE).

152 Bormann, "Barbaren und Skythen," 197; at p. 185 he claims that βάρβαρος and cognates were never used in this fashion (*Es werden zudem vom Wortfeld* βάρβαρος *keine Personennamen abgeleitet*).

153 The legion was stationed in Bosra (Jordan) in the 120s CE, lending its date to the inscribed stone. I have been unable to source the publication of the inscription.

154 *IGUR* 3.1175 = *IG* XIV 1956 (100–125 CE).

This readiness to use Βάρβαρος/*Barbarus* as a personal name is a strong indication that some of the barb of abuse was already being blunted by the time of the writer to the Colossians. We have seen from the onomastic register that non-Greek names figure often enough, albeit frequently giving way in the generational succession to obviously Greek names. But the occasional exception to this move, and the willingness to allow past non-Greek associations in the names of forebears, shows a level of acceptance of mixed ancestries, even if, through cultural commitments, a displayed "Greekness" was evident. There is no doubt that the potential for vilification remained, if the occasion arose where the dominant power or cultural authority was questioned, or where simple abuse was intended.[155] The array of various nations conquered by Rome were often portrayed as "barbarian", that is, as not Rome.[156] Indeed, in two lines of the Roman poet, Propertius, Scythian and barbarian are made implicitly synonymous.[157] At the same time, these same nations were embraced as the ἔθνη that made up the empire. In this sense, ἔθνη does not need to mean "Gentiles". It can simply refer to the nations of the world, understood as those who have come under Rome's hegemony.[158]

Strikingly, there is only one reference to ἔθνη in the Letter to the Colossians — at 1:27. It has been regularly steam-rolled into a Judeocentric perspective by being translated as "Gentiles".[159] However, there is no requirement from the context that such a perspective applies. Indeed, given what we have noted already about the change wrought by placing "Greek" first in the series in Col 3:11, the Judeocentrism can be relinquished. If the ἔθνη of 1:27 be read as "nations", then the code in Col 3:11 can be understood as an example of those nations. This turns "Scythian, barbarian" into a particular and a general example of the nations. Furthermore, the "mystery" (τὸ μυστηρίον) that is made known "among the nations" (ἐν τοῖς ἔθνεσιν) is "Christ in you" (Χριστὸς ἐν ὑμῖν). Not only is "among the nations" paralleled by "in you" (a strong indication of the cosmopolitan population at Colossae reflected in the constituency of the Christ-followers in the city) but the "Christ in you" is expanded in Col 3:11 with "Christ is all and in all" (πάντα καὶ ἐν πᾶσιν Χριστός). The "*in* you", "*in* the nations" "*in* all" pulls the two verses into mutually explicative relationship,

155 Compare the comparison of a bloated belly remedy to a crowded city by Plutarch (*Tu. san.* [*Mor.*] 134D): "It is just like someone, weighed down at the crowd of Greeks living in his city, should pile into the city Arab and Scythian migrants!"

156 So Canavan, *Clothing the Body*, 124.

157 Propertius *Eleg.* 3.16.13–14. The lines became well-known enough to turn up as a graffito at Pompeii (*CIL* 4.1950).

158 See, especially, D. C. Lopez, "Before Your Very Eyes: Roman Imperial Ideology, Gender Constructs and Paul's Inter-Nationalism," in *Mapping Gender in Ancient Religious Discourses* edited by T. Penner and C. Vander Stichele (Leiden: Brill, 2007), 115–62.

159 The commentaries are almost entirely predisposed to this understanding: see, for example, Dunn, *Colossians and Philemon*, 121–3; McKnight, *Colossians*, 197–9, Seitz, *Colossians*, 109–10. Concisely arguing for "nations" is Hay, *Colossians*, 76; for a nuanced effort to combine the two, see Foster, *Colossians*, 226–7.

with the second reference coming as a demonstrable expansion of what "in/ among the nations" means when in the mystery of Christ.

Ulrich Huttner has suggested that "the crossing of boundaries" that the relativization of ethnic, status and cultural fixities in Christ delivers "would have been glaringly at odds with the worldview of the urban majority."[160] This probably overstates the contrast. The foundation stories of inland Asia were already blurring the lines to some extent. Whatever might have been the Attic concern for Hellenic racial and cultural purity,[161] this was not, indeed could not operate in a region that had such a history of influx and exchange between different peoples. And it was recognized, even before the Roman influence became pervasive in shaping how Hellenism was to retain some influence.[162] Euripides had penned an axiom, "Greeks from barbarians finding evil ways,"[163] as much acknowledging the reality even as it was lamented. The Christian "foundation story" simply extended the impulse of the more inclusive foundation stories as part of the author's recognition of the need for the Christ-followers' involvement in the social and cultural dynamics of Colossae, dynamics that, if the names are a reliable guide, had a considerable diversity of inputs.[164] As much as the drive was to be distinctive, there was nevertheless a shared field of ideas to be appropriated. In my view, the writer (Epaphras perhaps) knew the city well,[165] even though composing with a secondary eye at least towards Laodikeia. For him, inclusiveness in Christ was far ahead of any other consideration.

The names in the letters and one in particular

Names have not been absent from New Testament commentary on Colossians and Philemon. They have figured prominently not because of any comparison with the onomasticon of Colossae and the Lycus Valley generally,[166] but because of debates over the integrity of Pauline authorship and the problems this raises

---

160 Huttner, *Lycus Valley*, 137.

161 "We are pure Greeks here [Athens] not semi-barbarians" — Plato *Menex.* 245d cf Athenaeus *Deip.* 14.624d, 632a.

162 See D. K. Buell and C. J. Hodge, "The Politics of Interpretation: The Rhetoric of Race and Ethnicity in Paul," *JBL* 123 (2004): 235–51.

163 Euripides *Tro.* 764.

164 Walter Wilson had speculated that what he calls the "roster" of Col 3:11 was a clue to the ethnic diversity of Colossae: *The hope of glory: education and exhortation in the Epistle to the Colossians* (Leiden: Brill, 1997), 83. The spread of ethnic origins of the names at least shows the cultural influences that were continuing to operate even in an avowedly helleno-centric city.

165 I think there is far more to be discerned in the letter as a player in the cultural mix of Colossae than simply an extraction from "the name of a well-known kind of colored wool"; A. Standhartinger, "A City with a Message: Colossae and Colossians," in *First Urban Churches* 5, 251.

166 A noteworthy exception is Huttner, *Lycus Valley*, 84–92.

for the provenance of the letters. Stated succinctly, the names in the greetings list in the Letter to the Colossians (Col 4:7–17) appear to be a replication of those given in the Letter to Philemon (Phmn 23–24 with additions from earlier in the letter) but the destination of the Letter to Philemon is predicated on the mention of Colossae in Col 1:2. Once Colossians is taken as deutero-Pauline (as I have argued above), the question then becomes one of how much historical worth can be given to the names in the Letter to the Colossians (that is, the problem of name-use as verisimilitude)[167] in order then to fix the destination of the Letter to Philemon.[168] Conversely, those who argue for the authenticity of both letters, have the problem of contending with the omissions of key names in the Letter to the Colossians (that is, Philemon and Apphia).[169]

I tabulate here the names in the order in which they occur in the Letter to the Colossians and the Letter to Philemon. An asterisk marks those names which are attested in other sources from Colossae; a tilde marks those names which have a cognate name attested at Colossae. Such names can be found in Appendix 2. A superscript "t" registers a theonym (including attributes, honorifics connected with god/s), an "h" indicates a heronym, a "v" marks a name built from a value/virtue, "ph" identifies a homonym, and "l" a Latin name. The column first to the right of the lists indicates whether the name or cognate[170] is found in the cities (and their territories) of the Lycus Valley. This includes those at the entrance and exit to the valley (namely, Apameia and Sanaos in the east, and Tripolis in the west) as well as those on the upper reaches of the valley. The city names are abbreviated, namely Ap for Apameia, At for Attouda, D for Dionysopolis, H for Hierapolis, L for Laodikeia, Tr for Tripolis and Tz for Trapezopolis. The last column records whether the name is found in Italy (not including Sicily), for reasons that will become apparent in the analysis that follows. The main source for these extra columns is the *Lexicon of Greek Personal Names*, Volumes III.A and V.A, C, supplemented by Ladislav Vidman's *Index cognominum* to volume VI of the *Corpus Inscriptionum Latinarum*, and Guizzi-Filippini's prosopography for Tripolis. Occasionally, some adjustments are made (Archippos, for example). I have used a four hundred year date range (1st century BCE to 3rd century CE) as the temporal parameter to avoid contamination from Christian imitation of Scriptural

167 For an inflated reification of verisimilitude to dismiss any connection between a pseudepigraphal writing and a material relationship to a "referential world", see D. Lincicum, "Mirror-Reading a Pseudepigraphal Letter," *NovT* 59 (2017): 171–93.

168 See Huttner, *Lycus Valley*, 81, 110–12.

169 V. Balabanski, "Where is Philemon? The Case for a Logical Fallacy in the Correlation of the Data in Philemon and Colossians 1.1–2; 4.7–18," *JSNT* 38 (2015): 134–5.

170 Cognates include those names where the elements are transposed, for example Θεότιμος compared with Τιμόθεος; Ἵππαρχος compared with Ἄρχιππος.

names.[171] Again an asterisk denotes the same name; a tilde denotes a cognate name. The name Ιησους in the list does not include the one designated Χριστός.[172] It should be noted that the *LGPN* for Italy accepted names written in Latin that were identified as transliterations of the Greek — outside of Rome and its close neighboring regions, including Ostia.[173] This clearly involves an increase of scholarly interference which, when it comes to the name *Ap(p)ia* is especially complicated, given that the form may be the Latin resistance to phonemic reproduction of the Greek letter *phi* (as also in the occurrence of *Affia* and cognates)[174] or may be an authentic Latin name (as in the *Via Appia*).[175] The editorial decision unfortunately has also led to the omission in the *Lexicon* of those names in Greek inscriptions from these areas. Greek homonymic transliterations — Παῦλος for *Paulus* and Ἰοῦστος for *Iustus* — further complicate the identification of the frequency of Greek names; *Paulus* and *Iustus* (similarly *Marcus*) are ubiquitous.[176] Where the occurrence of a name in Rome and its vicinity is attested (as sourced from the publications of Heikki Solin or from scouring Greek and Latin inscriptions) this is indicated by a bracketed R. A superscript "lat" confirms that the attestation is in Latin; superscript "<lat" indicates that the name in Italy is only attested in its Latin form. In many instances, the predominant language of inscription of the name is Latin (for example, *Epaphra/Epafra*, *Philemo/Filemo*, cf *Numphe/Nympe*).

Colossians	**Philemon**	**Lycus Valley**	**Italy**
Παῦλος[ph, l]	Παῦλος[ph, l]	L*	*lat (R) ~lat (R)
Τιμόθεος[t]	Τιμόθεος[t]	Ap* L* H~	*lat (R) ~lat (R)
—	Φιλήμων[~ v]	L*	*lat (R) ~lat (R)
—	Απφια[* ~]	Ap* At* D~ H*~ L*~	*<lat (R) ~lat (R)
Ἐπαφρᾶς[* ~ t]	Ἐπαφρᾶς[* ~ t]	Ap* H~ L*~ Tr~	*lat (R) ~lat (R)
Τυχικός[t]	—	At*~ H~	*lat (R) ~lat (R)
Ὀνήσιμος[* v]	Ὀνήσιμος[* v]	Ap*~ H*~ L*~	*lat (R) ~lat (R)

171 See C. Breytenbach and C. Zimmermann, *Early Christianity in Lycaonia and Adjacent Areas: From Paul to Amphilochius of Iconium* (Leiden: Brill, 2018), 60–126, 399–408. Note that the names may occur outside this temporal parameter, including before the first century BCE (especially in Magna Graecia).

172 I think the suggestion of Theodor Zahn and Ernst Amling that Ιησους ὁ λεγόμενος Ἰοῦστος is a construction based on a mistaken reading of the genitive Ιησου in Phmn 23 is far-fetched; see A. Standhartinger, "Colossians and the Pauline School," *NTS* 50 (2004): 574.

173 P. M. Fraser and E. Matthews (eds), *A Lexicon of Greek Personal Names Volume III.A* (Oxford: Clarendon Press, 1997), x. The editors have deferred to H. Solin, *Die griechischen Personennamen in Rom: Ein Namenbuch* (Berlin: de Gruyter, 3 vols, 2003[2] [1982]).

174 The editors of *LGPN* IIIA include both Apphias and Affias under Ἀπφιάς. Αφφιας (and cognates with both single and double *phi*) is well-attested in Phrygia.

175 For a more detailed analysis, see below.

176 *Lucas* (Λουκᾶς) is an uncommon Roman name.

Colossians	Philemon	Lycus Valley	Italy
Ἀρίσταρχος$^{\sim v}$	Ἀρίσταρχος$^{\sim v}$	Ap$^{\sim}$ H$^{\sim}$ L$^{\sim}$	$^{*\text{lat}}$(R) $^{\sim<\text{lat}}$(R)
Μᾶρκος$^{*\sim l}$	Μᾶρκος$^{*\sim l}$	Ap* H$^{*\sim}$ L$^{*\sim}$	$^{*\text{lat}}$(R) $^{\sim\text{lat}}$(R)
Βαρναβας^{t}	—		
(Ιησους^{t} aka) Ἰοῦστος^{vl}	—	H$^{*\sim}$ L$^{*\sim}$	$^{*\text{lat}}$(R) $^{\sim\text{lat}}$(R)
Λουκᾶς^{l}	Λουκᾶς^{l}	Ap$^{\sim}$ H$^{\sim}$ Tr$^{\sim}$	$^{*\text{lat}}$(R) $^{\sim\text{lat}}$(R)
Δημᾶς$^{*\sim v}$	Δημᾶς$^{*\sim v}$	H$^{\sim}$ Tr$^{\sim}$	$^{\sim}$(R)
Νύμφα	—	H$^{\sim}$ L$^{\sim}$	$^{\sim}$lat (R)
Ἄρχιππος^{v}	Ἄρχιππος^{v}	L* H$^{\sim}$	$^{*\sim}$lat (R)

The table provides little more than a preliminary breakdown. However, some initial points can be made:

i) There are more names given in Colossians than in Philemon.

ii) The names, even in the compression of the greetings section (Col 4:7–17), do not follow the same order of citation as in Philemon (apart from the Paul-Timothy opening).[177]

iii) There are names in Philemon not found in Colossians (Philemon, Apphia) and names in Colossians not found in Philemon (Tychicus, Barnabas, Jesus called Justus, and Nympha).

iv) A number of names found unadorned in Philemon are given a predicate expansion in Colossians, namely Aristarchus (ὁ συναιχμάλωτός μου, "my fellow prisoner"), Mark (ὁ ἀνεψιὸς Βαρναβα …, "the cousin/nephew of Barnabas concerning whom you have received instructions: if he comes to you, welcome him"), Epaphras (ὁ ἐξ ὑμῶν … "one of yourselves …") Luke (ὁ ἰατρὸς ὁ ἀγαπητός "the beloved doctor"). This would appear to mark a shift from the relatively personal Letter to Philemon, where greetings are to him (σε, Phmn 23) notwithstanding the inclusion of an address to "the *church* in your [s.] house" (Phmn 2) and the plural recipients of the final benediction (Phmn 24). The more formal Letter to the Colossians clearly has a plural address throughout, including the greetings.

v) All the names, apart from Barnabas (and Jesus), are attested directly or in related form in the Lycus Valley, although three — Philemon, Archippos and Demas — are rare.

vi) The most commonly attested names (in the east) are Apphia and Epaphras, closely followed by Onesimos.

177 This is acknowledged by Lincicum, "Mirror-reading," 186 but left unaddressed.

vii) The ubiquity of at least these names, especially Onesimos, is a caution against too readily assuming that any duplicate of the name in early Christian literature necessarily means the same person.[178]

viii) The names are predominantly Greek, apart from Apphia (a *Lallname* of Phrygian origin), Barnabas (semitic), and Paul, Mark, Justus and Luke (Latin).

ix) The names are attested in Rome and/or nearby cities such as Pompeii, Ostia and Neapolis (Naples), which is probably to be expected given the cosmopolitan hub of empire and the ubiquity of slaves (and freed) originating from elsewhere.

x) The names attested in these letters are not found in the greetings list of the Letter to the Romans (apart from Timothy: Rom 16:21, cf Paul, Rom 1:1), whereas some of the names do occur in other early texts connected with or narratively set in the east of the Roman empire, especially Asia (Tychicus in Acts 20:4, Eph 6:21, 2 Tim 4:12, Tit 3:12; Aristarchus [the Macedonian from Thessalonike] in Acts 19:29, 20:4, 27:2; Mark (Acts 12:12, 25, 15:37, 39, 2 Tim 4:11 cf 1 Pet 5:13); Barnabas (Acts from chapter 9 to 15, 1 Cor 9:6, Gal 2:1, 9, 13); Luke (2 Tim 4:11); and Onesimos (Ignatius *Eph* 1.3).

There are two matters that preoccupy Second Testament commentators — the question of whether Colossians has simply borrowed the greetings list from Philemon as part of the verisimilitude of a pseudonymous writing, and, notwithstanding the first question, the absence of Philemon and Apphia from the Letter to the Colossians.

I do not wish to become bogged down in the sometimes-interminable debates over authenticity. I make three points briefly. Firstly, pseudonymity in the ancient world was always geared towards a particular audience with both author and recipients influenced by particular circumstances, even when these particulars might be carved in broad terms. As has been the operating principle throughout this book, no writing can be divorced from a material and hence historical context either for its composition or its reception. (The two are not necessarily identical.) To argue that a supposedly "fabricated" author demands a "fabricated" problem and a "fabricated" audience, is a false requirement and aggregation. Pseudonymity had multiple forms and multiple functions — thus the stage-names (ie pseudonyms) of gladiators, already mentioned, neither erased the bearer nor fabricated the context in which it was used. Pseudonymity in this context had almost a diaphoric function — evoking, intensifying and inspiring,[179] by reference to a grand exemplar, just as with the

178 So, P. Arzt-Grabner, "Everyday Life in a Roman Town like Colossae: The Papyrological Evidence," in *First Urban Churches* 5, 212.

179 See further chapter 10.

theonyms frequently bestowed on mere human beings.[180] In literature, pseudonymity always has an artifactual base and, often, an ongoing artifactual life. Contests over pseudonymity merely confirm that material survivals not only spring from discursive interactions but continue to foster and modulate them. This, at least at the level of Second Testament literature generally, has been the clear emphasis given by the late Larry Hurtado.[181] Secondly, the lack of consistency in the number and order of names, especially in the greetings section of the letters, is actually an argument against verisimilitude,[182] unless one wants to multiply skepticism to an exaggerated degree. Thirdly, even the simple table above, points at the very least to an Asian setting, once the question of the attestation of names in and around Rome is investigated. Moreover, the concern of Paul to acknowledge communities among the Roman Christ-followers (Rom 16:3–5, 10, 11, 14, 15) starkly silhouettes the absence of any mention of Philemon, his household and the community gathering there, especially if Paul could rely on accommodation at the house (Phmn 22). Greetings were often expected in letters, so that modern commentators' disquiet over the absence of Philemon and Apphia echoes some ancient concerns,[183] and becomes relevant to the argument of a Roman provenance of Philemon, whether in terms of source composition or target audience or both.

This brings us to the second issue, namely, the absence of Philemon and Apphia in the Letter to the Colossians. Three main explanations have been mooted:

a) Ulrich Huttner has flagged the possibility that the Letter to Philemon was not well-received by Philemon and Apphia because of the leniency of treatment advocated for Onesimos (even manumission?),[184] and for the disruption to Philemon's authority in his own household by Paul usurping the paterfamilial role.[185] Philemon (and Apphia) withdrew from the assembly, which, presumably, had to meet elsewhere. Such abnegations are known in the Pauline

180 This may have implications for how "Paul" is used as such an exemplar as well as a pseudonym, especially with the shift to first person plurals (eg Col 1:28). In this sense, more than a surface reference to Timothy (Col 1:1) is meant; rather, those who stand within the template of Paul (with all his sufferings, servanthood, imprisonments and the like) are drawn under that name.

181 See L. Hurtado, *Earliest Christian Artifacts: Manuscripts and Christian Origins* (Grand Rapids, MN: Eerdmans, 2006).

182 So Balabanski, "Where is Philemon?" 135–6.

183 See *P.Giss.* 78 where Aline, the mother, wonders why her probably-teenage daughter Heraidous, did not greet her in a letter to her father: ἡ μικρά μου Ἡραιδοῦς γράφουσα τῶι πατρὶ ἐμὲ οὐκ ἀσπάζεται καὶ διά τι οὐκ οἶδα (as reconstructed).

184 I do not consider that Paul was advocating for Onesimus's manumission: see A. H. Cadwallader, "Name Punning and Social Stereotyping: reinscribing slavery in the letter to Philemon," *ABR* 61 (2013): 18–31. However, there is certainly a reconfiguration of the relationships between Paul and Philemon in regard to Onesimus; see M. Ebner, *Der Brief an Philemon* (EKKNT; Göttingen: Vandenhoeck & Ruprecht, 2017), 146.

185 U. Huttner, "The Development of Christianity in the Lycus Valley: socialization and violence," in *New Doc. Early Christ 12*, (Grand Rapids, MN: Eerdmans), forthcoming.

circle, during Paul's life and in his afterlife (Demas in 2 Tim 4:10). The difficulty here is that if ecclesiastical tradition has any historical basis — from the pilgrimage site of Philemon's house mentioned by Theodoret of Cyrrhus to the accounts of his martyrdom — then Philemon's withdrawal was not from the faith but from Pauline oversight. But this does not explain such an action for Apphia. The household is Philemon's not "theirs" (note τῇ κατ' οἶκόν *σου* ἐκκλησίᾳ, Phmn 2, compared with the joint household of Prisca and Aquila τὴν κατ' οἶκον *αὐτῶν* ἐκκλησίαν, Rom 16:5). The suggestion of some manuscripts that Onesimos was an οἰκέτης owned by Apphia only functions satisfactorily if Apphia and Philemon were married,[186] and turns Philemon into a hapless husband needing Paul's help to correct a lack of the proper exercise of authority by his wife. The ascription of "the sister" to Apphia (τῇ ἀδελφῇ) in verse 2 echoes that to Timothy (ὁ ἀδελφός) in verse 1,[187] thereby corroborating a dismissal of the ancient scribal suggestion.

b) Huttner acknowledges his speculation and allows that an alternative is that Philemon and Apphia have both died before the writing of the Letter to the Colossians. This in fact is the suggestion made by Peter Arzt-Grabner. He looks to two pairs of Egyptian papyri to garner *comparanda* for the greetings lists in Colossians and Philemon.[188] The first comparison is to demonstrate that there is no requirement that greetings name the same people when writing to the same household. Two letters, that of *BGU* 16.2618 and 2617, written two months apart in 7 BCE, the writer (or, rather, the scribe receiving dictation) a woman named Tryphas, addresses Athenodoros and adds greetings, in her own hand, at the end.[189] In the first letter, addressed to Athenodoros and also to Artemis, named as son and daughter (ll. 1–2), the letter concludes with greetings from Nardos and Neikas and all those in the household (ἀσπάζεταί σε Νάρδος καὶ Νεικᾶς καὶ οἱ ἐν οἴκωι πάντες, ll. 22–4). When Tryphas dictates the second letter (that is, *BGU* 16.2617), addressed only to "Athenodoros the son," this time Nardos, Neikas and the household are omitted, but greetings are now sent to her "lady daughters," Tryphas and Artemis (ἀσπάζου τὰς κυρίας μου θυγάτρες [for θυγατέρας] Τρυφᾶν καὶ Ἄρτεμιν, ll. 6–7). This is far from the only example. Two letters to a certain Pompeius in Arsinoe from his daughter Herennia, written probably in the same year (57 CE), again list different names in the greetings. The first (*P.Mert.* 2.63), Herennia appears to have written herself. She concludes the letter with a reference to "another letter of Syrion your son" (ἑτέραν ἐπισστολὴν [sic] Συρίωνος τοῦ υἱοῦ σου, ll. 21–3) which has a gap of two lines following on the papyrus suggesting that Syrion,

---

186 Mss L, 326, 1241.

187 So P. Arzt-Grabner, *Philemon* (PKNT 1; Göttingen: Vandenhoeck & Ruprecht, 2003), 162–3.

188 Arzt-Grabner, "Everyday Life," 214–6.

189 See R. S. Bagnall and R. Cribiore, *Women's Letters from Ancient Egypt, 300 BC – AD 800* (Ann Arbor: University of Michigan Press, 2015²), 124–5.

probably a grandson, was to write a couple of lines but procrastinated too long before the letter was sent![190] She rounds off with "We send our regards to you and Charitous [possibly Pompeius's wife] and her children. And little Pompeius sends regards to you." (ἐπισσκοπούμεθά [sic] σε καὶ Χαριτοῦν καὶ τὰ τέκνα αὐτην [for αὐτῆς] καὶ Πονπηγις [for Πομπήιος] ὠ [for ὁ] μικρὸς ἐπισσκοπῖται [sic] ἡμᾶς ll. 24–7).[191] The second letter (*SB* 6.9122), probably also written two months later, repeats the greeting from "little Pompeius" (l. 11), adding a plea for remembrance (cf Col 4:18b) and greetings "to your children and those in the household" (μὴ ἡμῶν ἐπιλάθηστε [for ἐπιλάθησηε]. ἐπισκοπούμεντά [for ἐπισκοπούμεθά] σου τὰ τέκνα καὶ ἐν τῇ οἰκίᾳ ll. 12–13). It seems that this time a scribe received Herennia's dictation (with marginal improvement in spelling!) but she appears to have added in her own hand ἔρωσ(ο) (for ἔρρωσο) at the very end along with the date.

These examples are important for the demonstration that letters to the same individual, household or group, even when written within chronological proximity, do not provide identical greetings lists.[192] Hence there is no demand that Philemon and Apphia be included in the Colossians' greetings even if one might expect a householder who hosts a gathering of Christ-followers to be acknowledged. Moreover, the relative approximation of greetings in Colossians compared with Philemon is completely coherent with the examples given here. It is precisely the lack of absolute identity, in the light of such *comparanda*, that weighs against the charge of verisimilitude, and hence provides one of a number of checks from material evidence against any thorough-going "deception" in the pseudepigraphy.[193] It certainly tells

---

190 Alternately, Syrion may have written a longer, more complete letter which accompanied this extant one. See Bagnall and Cribiore, *Women's Letters*, 128.

191 The spelling is often phonetic, with regular gemination of the sigma.

192 See also the collection of the Letters of Tasoucharion: *BGU* 2.601, 602; 3.714; *P.Giss.* 97; and those of Ammonios: *P.Ryl.* 2.230, 231; *P.Lond.* 3.893.

193 Contra Lincicum, "Mirror-reading," 183, P. La G. Du Toit, "Review of Foster, *Colossians*," *Neotestamentica* 52 (2018): 240–1. Part of the problem here is that "verisimilitude" is made synonymous with deception. Ancient philosophical discussions of the "befitting" (τὸ πρέπον) and the "persuasive" (τὸ πιθανόν) address precisely the issue of language that belongs to a character (especially, a god/the gods). See James Porter, "Content and Form in Philodemus: The History of an Evasion," in *Philodemus and Poetry: Poetic Theory and Practice in Lucretius, Philodemos and Horace* edited by D. Obbink (Oxford: Oxford University Press, 1995), 125–9. The charter of inscriptions in the agora of Magnesia-on-Maeander contains one inscription that is clearly a forgery by (an agent of) the civic authorities (*I.Magnesia* 20, a foundation story of the archaic age), but it is designed to reinforce or direct then-current understandings cultivating civic pride: see A. Chaniotis, "Empfängerformular und Urkundenfälschung: Bemerkungen zum Urkundendossier von Magnesia am Mäander," in *Urkunden und Urkundenformulare im klassichen Altertum und in den orientalischen Kulturen* edited by R. G. Khoury (Heidelberg: Universitatsverlag Winter, 1999), 51–69; N. C. Unwin, *Caria and*

against the dispatch of the Letters to Philemon and the Colossians at the same time.[194]

A further example not given by Arzt-Grabner is important for the understanding of those instances where some extra information is given by way of a predicate to a name. In numerous examples these are no more than familial designations, epexegetical and probably superfluous for the understanding of the letter recipient. Their addition is familiar to the recipient but is a way of nurturing or reaffirming family ties, though at times it may be a way of distinguishing those of the same name. Thus a second-third century Letter of Coprys and Sinthonis to their children Sarapammon and Syra has "Serenos your brother greets you and Dioskoros and Opheline and Ptolemaios and Heras" (ἀσπάζεται ὑμᾶς Σερῆνος ὁ ἀδελφὸς καὶ Ὠφελίνη καὶ Πτολεμαῖος καὶ Ἡρᾶς, *P.Oxy.* 3993, ll. 39–43).[195] An interesting contrast occurs in *BGU* 2.530, a first century Letter from Hermokrates in Arsinoites to his son Chaeras pleading that he come to help in a vineyard under threat of crop failure with a consequent loss of land from a default on tax demands. It concludes with "Your sister Helene greets you" but "your (unnamed) mother rebukes you because you did not write back to her" (ἀσπάζεταί σε ἡ ἀδελφή σου Ἑλένη καὶ ἡ μήτηρ σου μέμφεταί σε, ἐπὶ [for ἐπεὶ] μὴ ἀντέγραψας αὐτῇ ll. 32–6). Apparently the son also left his mother bearing the brunt of demands by the tax bailiffs.[196]

One of the closest parallels to the Colossian Letter's descriptors on names, comes from a woman's letter to her three children, dated second or third century CE (*BGU* 1.332).[197] Serapias's Letter ends with "Greetings from Kyrilla and the daughter of Hermias, Hermias, Hermanubis the nanny,[198] Athenais the teacher, Kyrilla, Kasia, [...] Empis — all those who are here (ἀσπάζεταί ἡμᾶς [for ὑμᾶς] Κυρίλλα, καὶ ἡ θυγάτηρ Ἑρμίας [for Ἑρμιᾶ], Ἑρμίας, Ἑρμανοῦβις ἡ τροφός, Ἀθηναΐς ἡ δέσκαλος [for διδάσκαλος],[199] Κυρίλλα, Κασία ... Ἔμπις, οἱ ἐνθάδε πάντες ll. 8–10). Here a phrase, the daughter of Hermias, substitutes for a name, five names (probably seven names — there are lacunae in the papyrus) stand alone, and two names are qualified further by a predicate of their occupation. There are a number of possible reasons for the additions to the two names and the circumlocution *sans*-name. The circumlocution suggests that the daughter is well-known to Serapias's children, Ptolemaios, Apolinaria and

Crete in Antiquity: Cultural Interaction between Anatolia and the Aegean (Cambridge: Cambridge University Press, 2017), 180. See also D. Obbink, "How to Read Poetry about Gods," in *Philodemus and Poetry*, 189–209.

194 So, Balabanski, "Where is Philemon?" 136–7.

195 See also *P.Brem.* 65, ll. 7–10 (116–120 CE)

196 See J. S. Kloppenborg, *The Tenants in the Vineyard: Ideology, Economics, and Agrarian Conflict in Jewish Palestine* (WUNT 195; Tübingen: Mohr Siebeck, 2006), 489–90.

197 See Bagnall and Cribiore, *Women's Letters*, 389–90.

198 Possibly a wet-nurse.

199 For δέσκαλος as a form of διδάσκαλος specially used of women, see R. Cribiore, *Writing, Teachers and Students in Graeco-Roman Egypt* (Atlanta, GA: Scholars Press, 1996), 22–4.

Ptolemaios the younger (cf 2 Cor 12:18 "the brother") but the additions suggest either that there were others by the same name (Hermanubis, Athenais) and therefore required distinguishing or that they were unknown altogether. The latter seems less likely given that all those named appear as members of the same household in various capacities (οἱ ἐνθάδε πάντες); indeed there appear to be two undifferentiated Kyrillas (unless a mistaken repetition) and so the predicate may well act as a reminder of their position in the household. Sometimes the position stands for the name as in *O.Krok.* 2.219 (Trajanic dating), "the praisidion greets you" (ἀσπάζεταί σε τὸ πραισίδιν, ll. 15–16), just as in the second century Paul came to be known by the circumlocution "blessed apostle".

These examples demonstrate that ancient letters occasionally provide additions to names, giving notes on family relationships (sometimes omitting the actual name of the referent) and other identifiers, such as occupation or position. Col 4:7–10 has a surfeit of identifiers but such markers are not unfamiliar from epistolary practice. It may suggest that Demas (Col 4:14), notable because without a predicate, is so well known to the Christ-followers at Colossae that no further identification is needed. Alternately, it may communicate status-differentials.[200] The analysis demonstrates that the greetings list in Colossians has little fodder for debates over pseudepigraphy.

Arzt-Grabner provides a second pair of letters, dated to the second century CE, to show that when a name is missing in the later letter, one reasonable inference is that the absentee has died. A certain Apion of Philadelphia became a Roman soldier, garrisoned at Misenum. His first letter is directed to his father, Epimachos (*BGU* 2.423). Apion informs him that his Roman name is Antonius Maximus. This becomes the only self-identification in the second letter (*BGU* 2.632, with *BL* 1.58) but he is now (possibly *de facto*) married with children, so some years have elapsed. The second letter addresses his sister Sabina but, unlike the first letter, does not mention her daughter nor is there any mention of their father. In fact, he mentions multiple letters to her, as his prime family contact for sharing about one another's welfare. Arzt-Grabner thinks the father is (long-)dead. John White also thinks that Sabina's daughter has died, given that there is no mention of her in the later letter.[201]

Accordingly, the evidence from the papyri offers three possible solutions to the differences between the names of people in the Letters to Colossians and Philemon. Firstly, letters even when written within a short time of one another, do not contain the same resumé of greetings. Secondly, on some occasions, the absence of names in the later letter is a strong indication that

200 Compare J. D. A. Weima, "Paul's Persuasive Prose: An Epistolary Analysis of the Letter to Philemon," in *Philemon in Perspective: Interpreting a Pauline Letter* edited by D. F. Tolmie (Berlin: de Gruyter, 2010), 36–7.

201 J. L. White, *Light from Ancient Letters* (Philadelphia: Fortress, 1986), 161.

death has visited.[202] Thirdly, names that have further identifying predicates may indicate status differentials, distinctions among those bearing the same name, or be a means of affirming relationships among a group of people (especially family members).

c) Vicky Balabanski has re-set the provenance of the Letter to Philemon to Rome; in fact both letters are given the authorial provenance of Rome with one travelling nearby to Philemon's house in Rome or perhaps Italy, and Colossians (following some manuscript subscripts) from Rome to Colossae.[203] With the household of Philemon and Apphia and what she calls "their house-church" relocated to the western Mediterranean, the two letters can be sent at different times and those named in the Letter to the Colossians can be located in that city. This would overcome the tyranny of distance in the movement of Onesimos from a Roman imprisonment for Paul (that is, a journey of more than 1000 miles) and potentially back again (Phlm 13–14);[204] it also would overcome the problems inherent in a supposed Ephesian imprisonment.[205] Consequently, the common tie of Archippos in the two letters (Phmn 2, Col 4:17) does not demand, in her view, a common location.[206] Crucial in her assessment is that the reference to Archippos as "our fellow soldier" (ὁ στρατιώτης ἡμῶν Phmn 2) aligns Archippos with Paul (not Philemon and Apphia) and, on the basis of Phil 2:25, where the epithet is applied to Epaphroditos, indicates someone who is delegated to specific assignments. He is mobile.[207] This is certainly of a piece with my earlier suggestion of Archippos' role in negotiating better relationships between the Christ-followers in Laodikeia and Colossae. As we shall see, his name also indicates that, on the balance of probabilities, he is not a native of Phrygia. She also argues that the expression ὅς ἐστιν ἐξ ὑμῶν (Col 4:9) indicates a geographical or ethnic origin of Onesimos not his current location (cf Col 4:12 of Epaphras), though the ἐστιν and the overall expression is problematic for such an assertion, as Arzt-Grabner notes.[208]

202 Later ecclesiastical hagiographies put death down to martyrdom, though often Archippos is included in the group execution.

203 Balabanski, "Where is Philemon?" 132, 143–4. She notes the subscripts in Codex B and A. The difficulty in claiming authority from these "two important early manuscripts" (p. 144) is that Theodoret of Cyrrhus, writing around the same time as the production of these manuscripts, appoints Philemon's house to Colossae as still a site of pilgrimage. One or both pieces of evidence are tendentious.

204 Balabanski, "Where is Philemon?" 141. An Ephesos provenance significantly overcomes the problem of distance (some 120 miles) but not, in Balabanski's view, the other difficulties.

205 Compare M. Gielen, "Paulus — Gefangener in Ephesus?" *BM Neue Folge* 131 (2006): 79–103; 133 (2007): 63–77.

206 Balabanski, "Where is Philemon?" 137.

207 Balabanski, "Where is Philemon?" 138.

208 Arzt-Grabner, "Everyday Life," 212–3.

I have already mentioned the improbability of Philemon's household in or near Rome given the complete absence of correlating names in the greetings list of Romans 16, even allowing for some few years between the Letter to the Romans and that to Philemon.[209] But this is where onomastics might be of some help. Peter Arzt-Grabner is less confident, arguing that the presence of the name Apphia in inscriptions from Colossae and, heavily, in western Asia Minor does not preclude a migration or location elsewhere (say, Rome) even though nothing is left in the material record.[210] A deeper probing of the onomastics is in order.

Apphia again: the tracking of a Phrygian *Lallname*

With the release of the final volume for Asia Minor of the *Lexicon of Greek Personal Names* (the volume that includes Colossae) it is now possible to execute a relatively thorough study of the name Apphia (with its cognate spellings), including its regional concentrations, status associations, familial relations and, sometimes, a distinctive ethnic connection. The sources for the attestation of the name are almost totally inscriptions,[211] though very occasionally other witnesses are found, such as coins.

---

209 Balabanski, "Where is Philemon?" briefly mentions the greetings of Romans 16 (p. 146) but the problems it raises for her interpretation are not addressed. She dates the Letter to Philemon to 60 CE. Robert Jewett dates the Letter to the Romans to the winter of 56–57 CE: *Romans* (Hermeneia; Minneapolis: Fortress, 2006), 21; also F. J. Matera, *Romans* (Grand Rapids, MN: Baker, 2010), 5. James Harrison puts it a year or so later, in 57–58 CE: *Reading Romans with Roman Eyes: Studies on the Social Perspective of Paul* (Lanham: Lexington, 2020), 7. Thus, a maximum four-year period has to move from none of the names in Philemon occurring in the Romans 16 list (apart from Timothy) and the aggregation of names in Philemon, with epithets such as fellow-prisoner (Epaphras v.23), fellow-workers (Mark, Aristarchus, Demas and Luke), slave-come-brother (Onesimus), fellow-soldier (Archippos), brother-and-partner (Philemon), and sister (Apphia) — a rapid rise to "fellow" status, if that time-frame be observed for a Roman provenance and Roman (or Italian) letter destination. For Philemon in particular, this three-to-four-year window has to span Philemon's conversion (Phmn 19, presumably), some catechesis, his formation of a house-church (Phmn 2), and his entry into some partnership with Paul (including, it would seem, economic underwriting) for the gospel mission (Phmn 17). All this is not completely impossible, admittedly, but the same applies to all the other names as well, if their complete absence from Romans 16 is to be explained. Such an aggregate becomes very improbable in my view, the more especially if an earlier date for Philemon is advanced, "from 54 to 58 CE" suggests Roy Jeal; see his *Exploring Philemon: Freedom, Brotherhood, and Partnership in the New Society* (Atlanta, GA: SBL Press, 2015), 30–1.

210 Arzt-Grabner, "Die Auswertung inschriftlicher Zeugnisse für die neutestamentliche Exegese: Erfahrungen, Chancen und Herausforderungen," in *Epigraphik und Neues Testament* edited by T. Corsten, M. Öhler and J. Verheyden (WUNT 365; Tübingen: Mohr Siebeck, 2016), 36–7.

211 The entry for Kolossai in *LGPN* V.C includes the attestation from church literature, such as Phmn.

Plate 9.14: A small bronze coin from Eukarpeia (13 mm, 2.11 g), featuring Livia (ΣΕΒΑΣΤΗ) on the obverse, was sponsored by Apphia the priest, who ensured her benefaction was recorded in the reverse legend.[212]

The eight volumes of *LGPN* yield 165 instances of the name Apphia and this number can already be supplemented.[213] The name was subject to a variety of orthographical forms. The editors of later volumes of the *LGPN* acknowledge that the name is subject to variant spellings but opted to record them separately.[214] This was not the case in earlier volumes.[215] The problem comes with the accenting of "indigenous" names in Greek lettering. Up to and including *LGPN* V.A diacritical marks were added. Thus Ἀπφιάς as a woman's name was distinguishable from Ἀπφιᾶς, a male name.[216] However, the accents for such names were abandoned from *LGPN* V.B, a recognition that the morphology was not Greek but Phrygian,[217] and judgments about gender had to be decided on the basis of the content of the inscription.[218] Accordingly, to round out the statistics, Απφιας occurs 69 times;[219] Αφια occurs 49 times and Αφιας 29 times.[220] Αφφια, occuring 74 times, carries its own added significance not only because it has the double aspirated sound but also because it is a form found in at least one manuscript of the Letter to Philemon (Codex D^{p*}).

The spelling drift for another woman is found in inscriptions from Hierapolis — both Απφια and Αφφια occur for the same person;[221] at Athens, a single

212 ΕΥΚΑΡΠΙΤΙΚΟΥ ΑΠΦΙΑ ΙΕΡΗΑ "Apphia the priestess for the Eukarpeian people" *RPC* 1.3160 (time of Tiberius). Photograph from a private collection by permission.

213 See *I.Amorium* 379 (Phrygia); Malay-Petzl, *Lydia* 17; T. Ritti and G. Scardozzi. "Nuove iscrizioni dai villaggi antichi del territorio di Hierapolis: Thiounta, Boyallı e 'Motala,'" in *Le attività delle champagne di scavo e restauro 2012–2015* edited by F. d'Andria, M. P. Caggia and T. Ismaelli. (Istanbul: Ege, 2022), 953–4 nr. 19.

214 *LGPN* V.A, xvi; *LGPN* V.B, xxviii.

215 Thus in *LGPN* volume 1, one Ἀφφιάς of Thasos is recorded under 'Ἀπφιάς (*IG* XII,8 850).

216 This is one of the reasons for inclusion of the accent in *LGPN* I, xiv and *LGPN* IV, x.

217 Brixhe, "Anatolian Anthroponymy," 23–4.

218 Compare the comment of Thomas Corsten that the name Apphias was mostly used for women but could also be found for men: *Die Inschriften von Kibyra vol I* (Bonn: Habelt, 2002), 147.

219 Strictly this should be adjusted to 67 times. *LGPN* III.A (which included Sicily and Magna Graecia) included as Greek names some which were written in the Latin (*CIL* 9.290, 10.2943).

220 The collation of these two names with Απφια must be qualified; it is likely that some at least are not a phonological shortening of the name but are names derived from a flowering plant (Ranunculus Ficaria), perhaps to be rendered "Buttercup"!

221 *SEG* 47.1730, 1732 and 1733 (Απφια) 47.1731 (Αφφια). This raises questions of the one responsible for the text — the stone-mason, the commissioner of the inscription, the woman herself. A similar shift in orthography occurs for one woman at Ostia *IG* XIV 929 (Αφφιας), *IG* XIV 930 (Απφιας) — see below.

curious epitaph has both Απηια and Αφφια in succession for the same woman.[222] Αφφιας occurs 35 times; Απφιον/Αφιον/Αφφιον occur 101, 37 and 43 times respectively. One might add the more obvious accommodations to the naming systems of Rome: the Latinised ending *-iana* is found in Ἀπφιανή/Ἀφφιανή 4 times and once respectively, the latter which may be a striking testimony to the tenacity of the indigenous form. Of particular interest is whether a Latin influence is to be found in the form Ἀππία (on which see below)[223] or whether it is merely a Greek transliteration of a Latin name. As Ladislav Zgusta observed in this regard, "One cannot be certain whether some of the evidence is simply a distortion of the Latin …"[224] Accordingly, excluding Ἀππία, the name in its various forms occurs 498 times — a popular name indeed.

The obvious significance is the sheer frequency of occurrence of the woman's name (ignoring the orthographical variety). Even allowing for the dominance of funerary inscriptions and extended family records, the visibility of women with this name in the epigraphic record is noteworthy.[225] The ubiquity has frequently drawn its classification among *Lallnamen*.[226] But we need to be careful that the supposed "universal" appeal of such names does not blind us to regional accents, even if the name has been loosened from its indigenous moorings.[227] (Hence, it is probably better to use the term "epichoric"). So, for example, one Αὐρηλία Απφια is expressly named a Jew, along with her husband Lucius Tatianos Diogenes.[228] But she is also a Hierapolitan citizen (and not the only Apphia with that distinction),[229] which, as we shall see, is in the heart of the region attesting most occurrences of the name.

A *Lallname* is a name that embeds a sense of endearment; it is striking that the fifth(?) century Byzantine lexicographer Hesychius takes ἀπφία as a hypocoristic word (ὑποκόρισμα) for a sister *or* brother.[230] The affective familiarity is structured around "repeated consonantal elements" with usually two syllables or two syllables dominating. It is a little misleading to reduce this to "affectionate baby names, favoured particularly for women."[231] This may be the case

222 *IG* II^2 10626a. If intentional and not dittography, it may be a recognition of the difference in pronunciation between Latin and Greek speakers. See below.

223 This was noted by Lightfoot, *Colossians and Philemon*, 306 n3.

224 "Mann kann nicht sicher sein, ob es sich in einigen Belegen nicht um eine Entstellung von lateinische …" Zgusta, *Kleinasiatische Personennamen*, 81 (see also 83).

225 Compare *LGPN* V.B for Lydia and Lycia.

226 Drew-Bear, Thomas and Yıldızturan, *Phrygian Votive Steles*, 380; Lightfoot, *Amorium*, 38.

227 Hence qualifying the frequently-cited description made by Louis Robert: "les noms indigènes sont essentiellement de ces 'Lallnamen", d'origine indigène, mais que l'on peut dire d'apparence internationale, ayant leurs semblables ou leurs parallèles en toute langue …"; *Noms indigènes*, 348; similarly Parker, "Introduction," 5. Compare C. Brixhe, "The Personal Onomastics of Roman Phrygia," in *Roman Phrygia*, 58.

228 *I.Jud. Orientis* 2.193.

229 *SEG* 47.1730.

230 Hesychius § 6899. This may be a contraction of Pollux 74.

231 *LGPN* V.B, xxix.

when the name is part of a double-naming of an individual, an Apphia Agelais or Apphia Chairemonis, though this sort of combination of the epichoric with a Greek name may reflect an awareness of the social capital to be gained by such a (Greek) addition or be a simple deference to forebears.[232] Where there is a connecting formula (such as ἡ καί N. "the one known as ...") one can see a preference operating. But Απφια or a cognate can as readily occur for the primary name as for the preferred or familiar name,[233] though Marianne Ricl points out that a mother's name can be given as the second name of a daughter — again the power of familial descent.[234] One third century double naming from Carian Olympos includes two *Lallnamen* in combination with Roman citizenship: Αὐρηλία Απφια ἡ καὶ Τατα.[235] Even allowing that this person is a beneficiary of the *Constitutio Antoniniana*, it is clear that, at least within a given locality, bearing a *Lallname* was no hindrance to prestige. Earlier attestations of Roman citizenship, with no hint of prior servility, confirm this.[236] Indeed, there are very few indications that the name Απφια is known amongst slaves or their offspring.[237] Verse epitaphs, a mark of some status, were conferred on a certain Apphias.[238] At the sanctuary of Zeus Panamara near Stratonikeia, the name regularly occurs as part of a family of priests and for a priestess herself.[239] Indeed Claude Brixhe notes that even though there is a marked adoption of Greek and then Roman names in the wake of successive colonisations, the *Lallnamen* maintain "a strong level of representation".[240] Our figures above bear this out. Overall, Apphia was a name borne proudly by members of society who had sufficient status to leave an epigraphical record: "a name for wealthy women" is the lavish judgment of Ulrich Huttner.[241] One should observe however that it was not a name unknown amongst villagers of limited if aspirational means to leave a (small) epigraphic record on discarded or off-cut stone.[242]

There is a level of ethnic stereotyping of Phrygia and Phrygian names amongst Greek and Roman *literati*. Manes especially was singled out as the

---

232 These two names come from Aphrodisias (one unpublished), in a list compiled by Angelos Chaniotis: "Second Thoughts," 221–22.

233 Αφφιον ἡ καὶ Τροφίμη (*SEG* 29.1182) Φίλα ἡ καὶ Απφιον (*TAM* V,3 1703). On the second name as a familiar name, see Horsley, "The Use of a Double Name," *New Doc. Early Christ* 1.90.

234 M. Ricl, "A New Inscription from the Cayster Valley and the Question of *Supernomina* in Hellenistic and Roman Lydia," in *Onomatologos*, 535, 549.

235 *TAM* II 1164, 2; compare Απφια Τατια in *I.Stratonikeia* 267.

236 See, for example, *I.Pergamon* 513; *MAMA* 4.304, 8.510; *TAM* V,1 301; *SEG* 49.1420.

237 *SEG* 32.1216 (a θρεπτή, likely a house-born slave, though possibly a foster-child or apprentice cf *I.Aphrodisias 2007* 14; *SEG* 31.1018, 49.1660.

238 *Gr. Anth. Suppl.* nrs 588, 623.

239 *I.Stratonikeia* 226, 227, 233 amongst a number.

240 Brixhe, "Personal Onomastics", 62.

241 Huttner, *Lycus Valley*, 85.

242 *Phrygian Votive Steles* 533, cf 215 and 349 (Αφια), 526 (Αφφια). Most of these *stelai* average only 20 centimeters in height.

stereotypical name for a Phrygian slave.[243] The name remained a marker of a Phrygian connection,[244] but, outside the vertiginous heights of political and literary rhetoric, it did not anchor nugatory markers. At lower levels of society, a Manes might be granted the honorific description of χρηστὸς ἀνήρ.[245] The ethnonym Φρυγία in classical and Hellenistic times was often enough attached to slaves in Athens.[246] However, we have seen that, within Asia, there was a counterweight where "Phrygian" as a name might be prized or at least carry no local denigratory association.

No overt demeaning attaches to the name Apphia. And yet, for all that this name can attract the designation *Lallname*, its attestation is noticeably circumscribed. The general statistics of the names given above become more revealing once they are allotted to their regions. Of the 165 instances of Απφια in the volumes of *LGPN*, 49 come from Phrygia, 41 from Caria, 31 from Lydia, 10 from Mysia, 10 from Lycia, 3 from Galatia, 2 from Pisidia, 2 from Athens, 2 from Bithynia, 1 from the Aegean, 1 from Cilicia, 1 from Aiolis, 1 from Ionia, 7 from Thrace with another 4 from its neighboring regions. Whilst the size and population of the regions differ, the clear trend is that the greatest aggregation of instances of the name are in Phrygia and its adjoining regions to the west and south (Lydia and Caria), with a rapid decline in examples in the next adjoining regions (Mysia and Lycia). Striking is the almost complete absence of the name from Ionia to the west and the provinces further east. The number of Thracian instances demonstrates a slight rise which might be explained by the historic links between Thrace and Phrygia.[247] We can affirm, then, that the *Lallname* is best attested in Phrygia and in regions of most immediate contact with Phrygia. Without going into the detail of the related spellings previously listed, this weakening ripple from the center of Phrygia-Lydia-Caria holds true.

When one turns to the West, a poverty of references replaces the wealth of evidence in Phrygia, Caria and Lydia. It is not found in the documentary papyri,[248] though the non-aspirated name is: Ἀππιανή.[249] This might indicate a Phrygian ancestry given the -ιανή effort to Romanize the name.[250] Aspirated

243 Aristophanes deploys Manes in five of his plays: *Peace, Birds, Frogs, Lysistrata, Thesmiophorazusae*.

244 Brixhe, "Anatolian Anthroponomy," 27.

245 See B. D. Meritt, "Greek Inscriptions," *Hesperia* 29 (1960): 71 nr. 131 where Manes in Athens, identified by his occupation as shearer (a necessary Phrygian occupation, adjunct to a shepherd), is commended on his epitaph. Compare (from Rhodes) *SEG* 27.467.

246 See C. Fragiadakis, *Die Attischen Sklavennamen von der spätarchaischen Epoche bis in die römische Kaiserzeit: eine historische und soziologische Untersuchung* (Athens: Mannheim, 1988), 152–3, 378.

247 Brixhe, "Personal Onomastics," 55–6.

248 Arzt-Grabner, *Philemon*, 82.

249 *P.Heid.* 3.234 (1st–2nd century CE); *SB* 20.75009 which also has her father's name, frequently found, Ἀππιανός (Theadelphia, 250–255 CE).

250 See Parker, "Introduction," 12; Corsten, "Names in -ιανός," *loc. cit.*

parallels Ἀπφιανή and Ἀπφιανός are common in Asia.[251] However, we need to allow for a Latin derivation (from *Appius*).[252]

One must accept that a person bearing the name Apphia would leave no trace in the epigraphic record,[253] but this argument from silence has little value as an argument for a Rome/Italian addressee. Nevertheless, we do have a small number of salient Greek inscriptions, all epitaphs, two from Rome, two from Ostia, with one more that is so fragmentary a decision cannot be made on the form of the name or its significance.[254] The male Ἀφφιανός occurs once.[255] While this provides some material testimony to the presence of the Phrygian name-form in Rome and its environs, proportionate to city's population it is a minuscule return. Even here, *there is no instance* of the particular spelling Απφια.[256]

The first two are simple memorials, probably first or second century. The first uses Θ(εοῖς) Κ(αταχθονίοις), the Greek imitation of *D(is) M(anibus)* with a certain Απφειν (for Απφιον) providing the epitaph for her (unnamed) son.[257] In the second, of the same date range, one Ἄπφιν (again for Ἄπφιον) provides the epitaph for her husband Ἀριστοφάνης. The Θ – Κ for D – M also heads the inscription but the husband is given the ubiquitous eastern funerary accolade of χρηστός.[258] This term rarely finds a Latin parallel and is therefore a probable indication of Asian origins of the couple. The two inscriptions do indicate however that the Phrygian name could "migrate" to the west.

The second set takes the credentials of the name-bearer one step further. The two inscriptions, dated to the early second century,[259] name the same couple but the woman's name in the first is spelt Αφφιας, in the second Απφιας,[260] with both displaying her Roman citizenry nomen, Claudia. The first occurs as part of a sarcophagus that has two panels of reliefs flanking the inscription.

---

251 See *TAM* V,1 740 for example.

252 One Ἄππιος is recorded as a foreign resident at Athens (*IG* II 10167, first century BCE – first century CE). His ethnic is given as Ῥωμαῖος, a strong indication of a Latin rather than Phrygian derivation of his name. Romans with clearly Greek names are also attested as well as one Μηνᾶς who bears Roman citizenship along with his Phrygian name (*IG* II 10160, first century CE). See M. J. Osborne and S. G. Byrne, *The Foreign Residents of Athens* (Leuven: Peeters, 1996), 266–71.

253 Arzt-Grabner, "Everyday Life," 213 and see above.

254 *IG Porto* 36 (Ἀφφια–). There are three instances that are found on recognizably Christian inscriptions (*ICUR* 9608, 12515, 15750 [Ἀφφιανός]). These are not included in the discussion here.

255 *IGUR* 2.437 = *IG* XIV 1496.

256 This is admitted by Arzt-Grabner "Auswertung inschriftlicher Zeugnisse," 37, but he is willing to put this down to the accidence of survival. My contention is that the surviving evidence from across the Mediterranean is so voluminous as to make such a future find either unlikely or of a piece with those inscriptions from Rome and its surrounds that use a varied spelling.

257 *IGUR* 2.364 = *IG* XIV 1411 (Θ – Κ | Απφειν | υἱῷ ἰδί- | ῳ ἐποί- | ησεν).

258 *IGUR* 2.365 = *IG* XIV 1412 (Θ – Κ | Απφιν | Ἀριστοφᾶ- |νει συνβίῳ | χρηστῷ μνή- | μης χάριν).

259 G. Tedeschi, *Spettacoli e trattenimenti dal IV seconol a.C. all'età tardo-antica secondo I documenti epigrafici e papiracei* (Trieste: University Press Italiane, 2017), 234.

260 *IG* XIV 929, 930. Strictly, the second was recorded as Ατφιας, rightly corrected to Απφιας.

The inscription is striking for the testimony it gives to the deceased, a certain Titus Flavius Trophimas. He had lived with the couple for a substantial part of his life, jointly involved in the business of shoe-making, but also a lover of the arts (the description of the deceased as πάνμουσος is unique).[261] They provided for his sarcophagal commemoration, probably in their own mausoleum. Significantly, their epigraphic eulogy concluded with a triplet: ὁ ἁπλοῦς, ὁ πάνμουσος, ὁ Ἐφέσιος. Given the name of the husband, Artemas, it suggests that not only Trophimos, but his life-long friend (if not also his wife) came from Ephesos.[262] It demonstrates that (occupational) travel is a further way in which names can migrate and that a shared household does not demand blood-relations for all its (free) inhabitants.[263] The second epitaph records the death of Claudia Apphias but the inscription is substantially mutilated. However its length (14 lines) and the extant mythological allusions in its text indicate substantial wealth and patronage of the arts.[264]

These may be the only extant Greek inscriptions but the exchange between Romans and Greeks especially in Rome, and also in many other places including Alexandrian Troas, Pisidian Antioch and Singidunum (Belgrade),[265] brought Latinized forms of the name Απφια and its variants. The difficulty lay in the Greek letter *phi* in the name. The first century Roman rhetorician, Quintilian, noted that there was a phonological problem with the labial aspirate for Greeks pronouncing Latin "f" and Romans pronouncing the Greek letter "*phi*." Greeks lengthened the sound of the Latin consonant. Romans shortened the Greek.[266] Latin attests at least six attempts to render the stem

261 Λ(ούκιος) Ἀτείλιος Ἀρτεμᾶς | καὶ Κλαυδία Αφφιας Τίτ(ῳ) | Φλαβίῳ Τροφιμᾶτι φίλῳ | ἀσυνκρίτῳ καὶ ἀσύλῳ | διὰ παντὸς χρόνου με- | τὰ ὑμῶν {ἡμῶν} γενομένῳ | τόπον ἐδώκαμεν τῷ | σώματι αὐτοῦ τεθῆναι | μετὰ ὑμῶν {ἡμῶν} ἵνα δι' αἰῶνος | μνήμην ἔχοι καὶ ὡς κόπων | ἰδίων ἀνάπαυσιν ὁ ἁπλοῦς, | ὁ πάνμουσος, ὁ Ἐφέσιος ἐν- | θάδε κοιμᾶται τὸν αἰώνιον ὕπ(νον) "Lucius Atilius Artemas and Claudia Aphphias (provided this for) Titus Flavius Trophimas who was always an incomparable and irreproachable friend to us, so that he might have an eternal memorial and rest from his labours. This straightforward, this highly-artistic, this Ephesian, may he lie here in eternal sleep."

262 I think their "Greek origin", offered by Marisa C. de' Spagnolis, can be narrowed (*La tomba del calzolaio: dalla necropoli monumentale romana di Nocera Superiore* [Rome: Bretschneider, 2000], 72).

263 This has implications for the question of the legal and familial ties between Philemon, Apphia and Archippos in Phmn 1–2.

264 The epitaph contains references to a story of tragic love known elsewhere in the West in Ovid (*Met* 54–166); see P. Knox, "Pyramus and Thisbe in Cyprus," *HSCP* 92 (1989): 316 n4.

265 Alexandrian Troas: *AE* 2008.1339, 1340; Pisidian Antioch: *I.Antioche Pisidie Ramsay* 199 (both *Apphia*); Singidunum: *I.Mésie sup.* 1.42 (*Apphion*).

266 Quintilian *Inst.* 1.4.14; 12.10.57. See F. Biville, "The Graeco-Romans and Graeco-Latin: A Terminological Framework for Cases of Bilingualism," in *Bilingualism in Ancient Society: Language Contact and the Written Text* edited by J. N. Adams, M. Janse and S. Swain (Oxford: Oxford University Press, 2002), 83–4.

of the name: Apph– (18 examples), Aph– (15 examples), App– (numerous),[267] Aff– (3 examples), Apf– (one example), Af– (3 examples).[268] The precise Greek name Απφια appears as *Apphia* 8 times, ranging in location from Rome (once) to Pisidian Antioch (once).[269] There is one example (date uncertain) of *Apfias*,[270] one for *Apphias*.[271]

However we have seen there was no orthographical singularity in the Greek either, even for the same woman, so we should not expect that the Latin would be any more rigorous. Indeed, the Greek forms show an occasional tendency to shorten the expiration $\pi^h = \varphi$ to the simple plosive π,[272] a possibility that might have occurred to Paul if he had in mind a house-group that comprised native Latin speakers (with or without a facility in Greek).[273] One Greek epitaph for "most sweet mother Appia" in eastern Phrygia has the dedicants bearing Greek and Phrygian names,[274] a strong indication that her name was not the (unrelated) onomastic homonym *Appia* known in the West.[275] Ladislav Zgusta thought this indicated Latin influence.[276] Walter Ameling even considered that the reverse could occur, namely Appia become Apphia.[277] Long ago, Joseph Barber Lightfoot had dismissed this as philologically improbable.[278] However, one bilingual inscription from Elaia (dated to the late first century BCE) curiously ren-

267 Because of the distinct Latin name Appius/a there are well over a hundred instances. Only a few can confidently be read as a Greek name in Latin letters.

268 G. Purnelle, *Les usages des graveurs dans la notation d'upsilon et des phonèmes aspirés: le cas des anthroponymes grecs dans les inscriptions latines de Rome* (Geneva: Droz, 1995), 147 has five variants. I have added *Afi–*.

269 *Riv. Arch. Como* 1987.35 (Comum), *I.Antioche Pisidie Ramsay*199 (Pisidian Antioch), *AE* 1979.70.32 (Rome), 2008.1339, 1340 (Alexandrian Troas), *CIL* 14.1458 (Ostia), *CIL* 10.2236 (Puteoli). Two inscriptions refer to the same woman; the final two examples included here use *Apphi* as a dative.

270 *CIL* 6.12232.

271 *ViaImp* 110 (Rome).

272 See J.-L. Ferrary *Les Mémoriaux de delegations du sanctuaire oraculaire de Claros, d'après la documentation conserve dans le Fonds Louis Robert* (2 vols; Paris: Belles-Lettres, 2015), 1.31, nr. 20.

273 Quintilian *Inst.* 12.10.57 demonstrates how important the distinction between a non-aspirate and an aspirate pronunciation was. One Roman, unversed in Greek, simply could not understand who a person was when an aspirate for the name was used; this changed when it was removed.

274 *MAMA* 7.445; see also *I.Magnesia* 117 (2nd century CE); *I.Mylasa* 920 (dated to Roman imperial period); *I.Didyma* 237I (1st century CE).

275 For example, *CIL* 3.9387, 11731; 5.6516, 7174.

276 Zgusta, *Kleinasiatische Personennamen*, 83: Die Zugehörigkeit einiger Belege zu lateinische Ἀππία (als aspirierte Nebenform) ist wahrscheinlich. "The assimilation of some evidence to the Latin Ἀππία (as aspirated subsidiary form) is likely."

277 W. Ameling, *Inscriptiones Judaicae Orientis Band II: Kleinasien* (Tübingen: Mohr Siebeck, 2004), 411: *Apphia kann eine aspirierte Form von lateinische Appia sein, kann aber auch zu der großen indigenen Namensippe …* "Apphia can be an aspirated form of the Latin Appia, but can also indicate the ubiquitous indigenous name."

278 Lightfoot, *Colossians, Philemon*, 304, 306.

ders the Latin nomen Afarius as Ἀπφάριος in the Greek.[279] Latin grammarians of the second century tried to provide rules governing the use of PH and F.[280] For a time, the learned distinction gained traction but the phonological and orthographical simplicity of P and/or F became more frequent in usage. Indeed, for the name Φιλήμων, *Filemon* and *Pilemo(n)* vied for favour,[281] although in one bilingual funerary inscription for a freedman from Laodikeia, Φιλήμων is rendered *Philemon*.[282] This Philemon in Latin was likely influenced by the regional power of the Greek *phi*, something that was lost in the West. Similar variations occurred for Sappho, Phoebe, Philadelphos and so on.[283]

This irregularity is reflected in the Greek transmission of Philemon and the Latin translations. The original hand of Codex D has Ἀφφία; minuscule 3 reads Ἀππία. The Old Latin usually reads *Appia* (so also the Vulgate) but occasionally the more refined *Apphia* (d, e); the Latin version of Theodore of Mopsuestia's commentary on the Letter to Philemon, has *Affia*.[284]

The survey of examples of the occurrence of Apphia in Greek or Latin from Rome and Italy has yielded little, no more than two examples in Latin from Rome itself, double that for Italy as a whole. Απφια as such does not occur, though the orthographical variations, Αφφια and Αφφιον have limited attestation. It is clear that the Phrygian name-group had migrated west whether for business, marriage, as slaves or for some other reason. However, there is nothing in this survey that has disrupted the sense that, for all the supposed popularity and ubiquity of a *Lallname*, the center for the name was far away from Rome, located in the region of Phrygia and its border neighbors, Caria and Lydia. Peter Arzt-Grabner is phlegmatic about the results, leaning to the sheer presence of the name in the west as demonstrating that the issue of the location of the audience for the Letter to Philemon cannot be resolved by reference to the names at the head of the letter. No clear judgment is possible, he says.[285] If the burden is raised to an absolute level of proof, he is correct, and one must always allow for the vagaries of historical survival of evidence as well as acknowledge that the onomastic testimony represents a fraction of the population. However, if one looks to the weight of occurrence of the name, even when investigating the Western examples more closely, then one must

279 *I.Asia Mixed* 3.

280 W. S. Allen, *Vox Graeca: A Guide to the Pronunciation of Classical Greek* (Cambridge: Cambridge University Press, 1968), 21.

281 *CIL* 3.14215; 6.4795, 16646, 20184, 24068; 10.532 (Filemon); *CIL* 1.949, 1555; 2.251; 6.29594; 11.4266, 7688; 13.10009,163a; M. Chelotti, R. Gaeta, V. Morizio, F. Grelle and M. Silvestrini (eds), *Le Epigrafi Romane di Canosa* (Documenti e Studi 7; Bari: Edipuglia, 1990), nr. 160 (Pilemo[n]).

282 *I.Asia Mixed* 56. Compare also Epaphroditus in *I.Asia Mixed* 13 (heavily restored).

283 See Purnelle, *Les usages des graveurs, passim.*

284 See J. T. Fitzgerald, "Theodore of Mopsuestia on Paul's Letter to Philemon," in *Philemon in Perspective*, 357.

285 P. Arzt-Grabner, "Auswertung inschriftlicher Zeugnisse," 36–37.

turn to Asia, and to Phrygia in particular. To disturb this statistical probability would require quite specific evidence. Arguments from silence can do no more than encourage careful analysis.

Arzt-Grabner in fact marks one silence that is particularly noteworthy. He does not find any example of the name Ἄρχιππος in Rome or Italy.[286] This needs minor adjustment — a single example, from Neapolis (Naples) dated to the first century BCE.[287] One does not have to tie Archippos to Philemon and Apphia as the offspring of their marriage,[288] nor even to assume that the latter two are married,[289] thus privileging *their* location as controlling that of Archippos.[290] My onomastic inquiry has yielded only one related example in the West, a certain Flavius Archippianus who set up an epitaph at Pollentia in Spain for his wife Sextia Procula.[291] All the inscribed names, with one exception, are Roman or Romanized (as in the *–ianus* ending). The Iberian example of the Romanized form of the name shows the ability of people to use Rome's empire for travel but its significance for our inquiry is minimal. The concentration of the name from Greece, through the islands into Asia clearly localizes attention to the East (234 instances). However, it should be noted that, unlike Apphia, the concentration of names is not in Phrygia-Caria-Lydia but in Greece, the Aegaean Islands and Magna Graecia (190 instances). In fact the *LGPN* only registers three instances of Archippos for Phrygia and two of these are from Christian literature, namely Phmn 2 and the story of *St Michael of Chonai*, the latter a clearly fictional text even with its occasional snapshots of historical circumstances. The third is an inscription of a Laodikeian found at the Apollo oracular sanctuary at Klaros.[292] Hence, the principle enunciated above requiring quite specific evidence to disturb statistical weight is provided, at least as evidence for an Archippos associated with Colossae.[293] This does not

286 Arzt-Grabner, "Auswertung inschriftlicher Zeugnisse," 37.

287 *IG Napoli* 101. There are earlier examples from Magna Graecia but the failure of the name to secure a hold in Italy is noteworthy.

288 Without thoroughly committing himself to the traditional tenet, Arzt-Grabner nevertheless argues that this assumption would tie him to the location of the couple. There is however nothing in the text requiring any blood or marital ties.

289 So Balabanski "Where is Philemon?" 4 n6; Ross S. Kraemer, "Apphia", in *Women in Scripture: A Dictionary of Named and Unnamed Women in the Hebrew Bible, the Apocryphal/Deuterocanonical Books, and the New Testament* edited by C. Meyers, *et al* (Grand Rapids: Eerdmans, 2003), 53.

290 Contra the drift of Nathan Leach's argument, "Epaphroditus and Archippus, Paul's Fellow Soldiers: Reexamining Paul's Rhetorical Use of συστρατιώτης," *JBL* 140 (2021): 204–5.

291 *HEp* 1999.230.

292 *I.Claros mémoriaux* 17.

293 One should allow that the shrine custodian of the story of St Michael of Chonai gains his name by reference to the New Testament text (Phmn 1, Col 4:17). However, the origin of the character is Hierapolis and the story houses considerable antagonism towards Laodikeia, hardly informed by the Christian triangulation of the three cities of the Lycus Valley in Col 4:13 nor by the ecclesiastical organization of Colossae and Hierapolis under the metropolitanate of

determine the whereabouts of the Archippos of Phmn 2 and it shows how finely balanced a case can be on the basis of individual instances. But given what we have noted above that the description of Archippos as "fellow soldier" indicates mobility and specific task, this suggests that the rarity of the name in Phrygia is actually supportive of the implication that Archippos was not a Colossian or Phrygian but has been sent there by "Paul". That he stayed, with what may be a new brief in regards to Laodikeia (Col 4:17), is perfectly explicable as fulfillment of a Pauline (com-)mission in the light of a tremor sent through the Christ-followers in the city by the deaths of Philemon and Apphia.[294]

Of some tangential significance is the name itself. The name is a compound name "the horse-controller/controlling the horse" (probably ἀρχι + ἵππος) with both parts carrying aristocratic connotations, whether actual or aspirational.[295] The parts could readily be flipped with little shift in the meaning.[296] Ἵππαρχος is common both as a name and also the title for the commander of cavalry as well as being an epithet of Poseidon. The Latin transliteration, Hipparchus, is attested ten times, including four instances in Rome.[297] Of some significance for the sense in which the elements of the name could be transposed, is the occurrence of Ἄρχιππος and Ἵππαρχος in the one family.[298] It would seem then that the Archippos of Colossians and Philemon comes from a quite different background from most of the Christ-followers at Colossae.

Onomastics has unlocked much of Colossian society. In the first century, the commitment to being and/or appearing Greek is clear. At the same time, there is an emphatic preparedness to acknowledge the Phrygian, Scythian, Thracian and other races that had contributed to the blend of the population, even when the names may have been no more than a key part of the memory trace of those

Laodikeia (Hierocles' *Synekdemos* 664.6–666.16). See A. H. Cadwallader, "'As if in a Vision of the Night …' Authorising the Healing Spring of Chonai," in *Dreams, Memory and Imagination in Byzantium* edited by B. Neil and E. Anagnostou-Laoutides (Leiden: Brill, 2018), 265–92.

294 Unlike Andrew Lincicum ("Mirror Reading", 184), my imagination has no trouble with Archippos dealing with a Pauline pseudepigraphal letter; if nothing else, the letter fostered the sense of importance of a group of Christ-followers as well as reinforcing Archippos's own position in that community. See A. Chaniotis, "Archival research, formulaic language, and ancient forgeries of legal documents," in *ΑΞΩΝ: Studies in Honor of Ronald S. Stroud* edited by A. P. Matthaios and N. Papazarkadas (Athens: Hellenic Epigraphy Society, 2015), 669–90. It exposes the limitations of twenty-first century commentators socialized into the ethics, *inter alia*, of intellectual property, who impose their assessments into a postulated first century situation.

295 L. Dubois, "Hippolytos and Lysippos: Remarks on some Compounds in Ἱππο-, -ιππος," in *Greek Personal Names*, 42.

296 Cf Dubois, "Hippolytos and Lysippos," 51.

297 *CIL* 6.6292, 6293, 19493, 28817, the last dated to the first century CE; see also *CIL* 10.2830 (Puteoli, 20 BCE to 20 CE). Hipparchianus is also found (*Epigraphica* 1959.99 [1st century CE]). The Greek form Ἵππαρχος occurs once: *SEG* 33.802 = *IG* XIV 1297 (Rome, 15/16–20 CE).

298 *IG* II^2 24, 25 (Athens, circa 393 BCE). The two names are found together (but unrelated) in *SB* 3.7169 (second century BCE).

origins. Women were the contemporary bearers of those traditions, more than men. To find the Phrygian *Lallname*, Apphia, among a host of Greek names therefore comes as no surprise. The weight of the evidence points to that situation occurring in Phrygia or its immediately neighboring regions. The western occurrences, once interrogated, do not warrant a serious caveat on this judgment. Moreover, the blend of heritage in the Colossian population, virtually all with a readiness to present as Greek, even, as far as can be discerned, in the countryside, but without the precious Attic concern for racial purity, all this meant that the "race code" of Colossians that privileged Greek but included even barbarian fell onto already lightly-tilled soil. Christ as all and in all had the capacity to embrace the cosmopolitan-and-Greek social composition of Colossae. Onomastics has provided a well-crafted lens to enable us to see something of that reality.

Chapter Ten
Christian Identity, the Gymnasium and Gladiatorial Conflict

The modern, Western esteem of athletes and soldiers has colored much interpretation of the Second Testament, the Letter to the Colossians included. Cities in the Roman province of Asia knew the athletic and military categories well, formed as they were in the Hellenic celebration of the well-honed and exemplary-mastered body. The gymnasium was the cultural center that promulgated the glories of combat, whether in athletics, in stylized military contests, in literary or musical competition. There was, as Onno van Nijf has emphasized, a "unity of athletic and cultural *paideia* as the fount of Greek cultural identity."[1] More than that, religious sensibilities and observances were the genetic code of festivals and contests,[2] to the point where the triumphant were esteemed as iterations of the divine or divine patronage. But the Roman cast of the province was marked by two notable impacts — an innovative re-shaping of the gymnasium by amalgamation with the Roman baths design and by the introduction of gladiatorial and venatorial spectacles, the performance of which took on a distinctive blend of imperial allegiance and Greek valorization. This chapter explores the gamut of bodily curation, its festive displays and cultural coding, before drilling into their remainders in the Christian identity forged in the Letter to the Colossians.

When Émile Le Camus made his railway-aided visit to the Lycus Valley in April 1894, he wondered whether he could make out the ground outline of a stadium. He was prompted to let his eye search for some such indication because he had deduced from his reading of Herodotos, Xenophon and Pliny (the Elder)

1 O. M. van Nijf, "Athletics, Andreia and the Askêsis-Culture in the Roman East," in *Andreia. Studies in Manliness and Courage in Classical Antiquity* edited by I. Sluiter and R. M. Rosen (Leiden: Brill, 2003), 283.

2 See P. A. Cartledge, "Greek religious festivals," in *Greek Religion and Society* edited by P. E. Easterling and J. V. Muir (Cambridge: Cambridge University Press, 1985), 98–127.

that Colossae was a large city and, as a large city, it would have housed a stadium and a theater.[3] If my earlier outlining of Colossae's heliotic re-branding holds, then a civic location for spectacles is rendered highly probable. Helios was one of the key gods credited with the inauguration of the games.[4] Le Camus's initial search for the theater was unrewarded. He failed to recognize the *cavea* that we briefly explored in chapter 9 until (as he flamboyantly diarizes his journey) his horse, like Balaam's ass, stopped on the edge of the eastern side "of the lower of the two mounds".[5] But "The stadium, we may have seen it on the western flank of the mound, but completely altered by the relentless labor of the farmer or the stonemason, despite all the rights and objections of archaeologists."[6] The introduction to the area in the 1960s of the motorized tractor has accelerated the re-carving of the landscape and the removal of telltale stones. However, his highly general compass directions — "on the western flank of the mound" — at least acknowledged that the city fabric was not confined to the höyük. And the areas of relatively flat ground he surveyed are long enough for the running of a *stadion*, the sprint race that ran the length of a stadium.[7] Plate 10.1 gives a photographic approximation of his view as it is today.

Plate 10.1: The western bounds of the Colossae höyük where Émile le Camus postulated the site of Colossae's stadium, which he deduced the city must have had. The aerial view faces south; to the right, whether the linear orchard in green or the elliptically-ploughed field in yellow, is the area le Camus indicated.

3 É. Le Camus, *Voyage aux Sept Églises de l'Apocalypse* (Paris: Librairies Sanard et Derangeon, 1896), 175.

4 Eumelus, fr. 22 (apud Favorinus *Cor. Or.*); Pausanias 2.1.6; Dio Chrysostom *Or.* 37.13; cf Tertullian *Spec.* 94. Games in honor of Helios were held, for example, at Stratonikeia when it was under the hegemony of Rhodes (*I.Stratonikeia* 1418, ll. 65–7 (c. 190 BCE).

5 Le Camus, *Voyage*, 175, 176. At the time, horses were hired out at the railway stations and guest houses along the Ottoman Railway line. See D. Hogarth *et al.*, *Guide to Greece, the Archipelago, Constantinople, the Coasts of Asia Minor, Crete and Cyprus* (London: Macmillan, 1908), 195.

6 Le Camus, *Voyage*, 176.

7 Unlike the modern 200 meter Olympic sprint, the *stadion* was measured according to the actual stadium in which it was run. The stadium at Laodikeia (called a *stadion amphitheatron*, *I.Laodikeia Lykos* 15, ll. 2–3, time of Titus) was one of the largest in the Roman world, measuring approximately 270 meters long, roughly the same as the stadium at Aphrodisias. See K. M. Welch, "The Stadium at Aphrodisias," *AJA* 102 (1998): 558.

Le Camus mentioned neither a gymnasium nor baths as a mark of a "large city" or as a goal of his exploration. The oft-quoted disparagement of the settlement Panopeus by the second-century travel-writer, Pausanias, left no doubt that any *polis* worth the name would boast a gymnasium: "Can one confer the title 'city' on those who have neither public buildings nor gymnasium nor theater nor agora nor water to supply a single fountain ..."[8] Hierapolis and Laodikeia could satisfy such criteria, with a generous array of building remains and/or identifying inscriptions.

Plate 10.2: The identification of the gymnasium at Hierapolis, celebrated by a minimalist reconstruction of pillars supporting the revealing inscription (ΓΥ)ΜΝΑΣΙΟΝ. Mount Cadmus (Honazdağ), in the view to the south-east (towards Colossae), towers over the urban foreground. Other white marble fragments of the inscription lie on the ground: TO MEIZON, probably to be joined to the uplifted fragment, to proclaim "the great(er) gymnasium";[9] and EK ΘΕΜΕΛΙΩ(Ν) probably indicating the provision for the building "from its foundations" made by certain benefactors.[10] Since this photograph was taken further reconstruction of pillars to support the epigraphical fragments has occurred.[11]

According to William Mitchell Ramsay, Colossae did not qualify. He based his judgment on a jaundiced reading of the inscription set up by Heliodoros in honor of someone often said to be his brother.[12] Unfortunately the "brother's" name was inscribed on a now-lost part of the inscription. We have met

8 εἴγε ὀνομάσαι τις πόλιν καὶ τούτους οἷς γε οὐκ ἀρχεῖα οὐ γυμνάσιόν ἐστιν, οὐ θέατρον οὐκ ἀγορὰν ἔχουσιν, οὐχ ὕδωρ κατερχόμενον ἐς κρήνην Pausanias 10.4.1.

9 This may imply another smaller gymnasium somewhere in the city or it may simply be an exaggerating comparative.

10 Compare *I.Ephesos* 438 (146/149 CE); *I.Prusias* 42 (76/7–77/8 CE). Part of the Hierapolitan inscription is published in *I.Hierapolis Judeich* 6.

11 See T. Ismaelli and M. Catania, "Il restauro del Ginnasio di Hierapolis," in *Hierapois di Frigia: Le Attività delle Campagne di Scavo e Restauro 2007–2011* edited by F. D'Andria, M. P. Caggia and T. Ismaelli (Istanbul: Ege, 2016), 597–608.

12 *IGR* 4.870, now amended in its reading by L. Robert, "Inscriptions," in *Laodicée du Lycos: Le Nymphée. Campagnes 1961–63* edited by J. des Gagniers *et al.* (Quebec: L'Université Laval, 1969), 269, 277–8 = *BE* 1970.584. For a new appraisal and reconstruction of this inscription, see chapter 5.

this multiply-officed dignitary in earlier chapters. Ramsay thought that the absence of the office of *gymnasiarch* from his *cursus honorum* indicated an absence of the pre-eminent, civic, educational institution at Colossae. At the same time, he opined that the inscription, listing so many offices (but needing one more!), was an indication of the shrunken size of the city, one person having to hold a full range of magistracies.[13] He ignored that the list did include the office of ἐλαιώνης,[14] that is the magistracy responsible for the supply of oil, which, primarily, was for use in the baths-gymnasium.[15] A similar long *cursus honorum* is found at Ephesos for a certain Gaius Mindius Hegoumenos, at Aphrodisias for Dionysios son of Papylos II, at Sardis for Lucius Ioulis Libonianos.[16] Smaller cities witness similar offices held by a single civic dignitary.[17] We have already seen one Menekrates who, among numerous civic offices (including *gymnasiarch*), was also acclaimed as a philosopher.[18] When Epictetus rattled off examples of offices available to a citizen (he gave Corinth as the city), he listed only four (*astynomos, ephebarch, strategos, agonothete*) but it is clear that these were merely selections from an array of possibilities.[19] (Significantly, as a clue to the template for the male body, Epictetus's illustration occurred in the course of his invective against male depilation, which, in his view, was virtually a disqualification from office.)[20] In some cities, prominent women were honored as creditably fulfilling various offices; so, for example, Cosconia Myrton held the office of *stephanophoros* in Smyrna on three separate occasions and that of *prutanis* at Kolophon and possibly Bargasa.[21] An even greater sweep of offices was held by the Histrian woman, Aba, daughter of Hekataios.[22] We are yet to find a similar inscription at Colossae, but the imperial priest Apphia daughter of Herakleios and the coin-sponsor Claudia Eugenetoriane would be prime candidates for such honors. The Roman historian, David Magie, simply recognized, on the basis of the same inscription

13 W. M. Ramsay, *The Cities and Bishoprics of Phrygia* (Oxford: Clarendon Press, 2 vols, 1895, 1897), 212.

14 *IGR* 4.870, l. 6. The line uses the more expansive rendition of ἐπιμεληθεὶς τ]ῆς τοῦ ἐλαίου θέσεως "superintending the supply of oil".

15 Ramsay claimed that "the most important duty of [the gymnasiarch] … was to arrange for the distribution of oil." *Cities and Bishoprics*, 443.

16 *SEG* 34.1093 (2nd to 3rd century CE) cf *MDAIA(A)* 1926.3–4.13 (Rhodes, 1st century BCE); *I.Ephesos* 3070; *MAMA* 8.410 (Aphrodisias, 2nd to 3rd century CE); *IGR* 4.1523 (Sardis, c. 150 CE).

17 *MAMA* 9.19 (Aizanoi, c.150 CE); *SEG* 41.1044 (Phocaea, imperial); *I.Kaunos* 140 (imperial).

18 *IGR* 4.1359 (Sosandra).

19 Epictetus 3.1.34.

20 Epictetus 3.1.1–35.

21 *I.Smyrna* 731 (83 CE), *SEG* 26.1288, 1289 (early 2nd century CE). She also was involved in the sponsorship of coinage at Smyrna (*RPC* 2.1012–1017, time of Domitian) See further, R. A. Kearsley, "Women and Public Life in Imperial Rome: Hellenistic Tradition and Augustan Ideology," *Ancient West and East* 4 (2005): 113–18.

22 *SEG* 24.1112. See R. van Bremen, *The Limits of Participation: Women and Civic Life in the Greek East in the Hellenistic and Roman Periods* (Amsterdam: J. C. Gieben, 1996), 154, 297–9.

as Ramsay reviewed, that "Colossae was an important place in the imperial period ... [showing] the usual officials."[23]

The amalgamated bath-gymnasium complex that seems to have been adopted almost universally in the Roman province of Asia, is confirmed in the city's landscape by the Korymbos honorific inscription mentioned in earlier chapters. Local knowledge of older farmers testifies to their own recognition of the distinctive hypocaust structure of Roman-style baths, lying to the east of the höyük and adjoining the Lycus River on its southern bank. Farm machinery has buried such remains but steep elevations in the topography and heavy wall-blocks set into the river-bank provide material substance to the identification, as well as an attractive invitation for future archaeological excavation.[24]

Plate 10.3: Remains of large limestone blocks probably for a walled structure that was part of the baths complex at Colossae. The base falling away from the wall is the edge of the Lycus River (here looking west), which, in the summer of 2010 and aided by a re-direction of the up-stream water flow into a newly constructed channel, enabled a surface investigation of the observations made by local farmers. The wall on the river edge lies approximately 100 metres east of the höyük.

There are additional indications that the spectacle of human achievement was as much a part of civic interaction at Colossae as in any other city, and, significantly, across a similar time-frame of the first three centuries of the Common Era. We can leave the training of the mind to the example of the *philologos*, Diodotos, whom we met in chapter 6 and perhaps allow, given the Tyche Protogeneia ring discussed in chapter 5, that astrology may have been part of the curriculum.[25] Diodotos's brief memorial presumes that Colossae provided the necessary education for its citizen population to qualify at least as ephebes. Two surviving inscriptions celebrate the harnessing of another essential feature of Greek paideia, the discipline of the body.

23 D. Magie, *Roman Rule in Asia Minor* (Princeton, NJ: Princeton University Press, 1950), 986.

24 On the baths at Colossae, see A. H. Cadwallader, *Fragments of Colossae: Sifting through the Traces* (Adelaide: ATF Press, 2015), 134–53.

25 *Syll* 3.771 (Delphi, Augustan period).

Honors for Zenon

The first has secured some limited acknowledgment amongst ancient historians and Second Testament commentators, but the interpretations have been a little contested.

Plate 10.4: Buckler and Calder's squeeze of the honorific stone for the athlete Marcus Aurelius Zenon.

The inscription reads as follows:[26]

ἡ πατρὶς
Μ(ᾶρκον) Αὐρ(ήλιον) Ζήνω-
να Διομᾶ δίς
νικήσαντα
δευτέραν τε̣-
τραετηρίδα
Νέα Ὀλύμπια
Ἀπολλωνίηα
ἀγωνοθετοῦν-
τος διὰ βίου Αὐρ̣
Τατιανοῦ Γλύ-
κ̣[ων]ο̣ς̣

The homeland (honors) Marcus Aurelius Zenon, son of Diomas, grandson of Diomas, who was victorious in the second four-yearly New Olympics Apolloneia, during the office of agonothete-for-life, Aurelius Tatianus Glykon.

The inscription was first published in a very fragmentary reading by Michal Clerc in 1887 and reported as found in "the mosque at Chonas."[27] The stone, described as a "pillar-shaped cippe" by Clerc, was still in place "in the minaret staircase" in 1933 when Buckler and Calder executed a squeeze of the "marble bomos". The squeeze still exists in the Calder Archive held by the Special

26 The reading of Buckler and Calder in *MAMA* 6.40 is followed without their punctuation and with slight adjustments based on a detailed autopsy of their squeeze.
27 *BCH* 1887.353.11.

Libraries at the University of Aberdeen.[28] My investigation of the squeeze along with Calder's notebook[29] has enabled some extra observations to be made.

i) There is no photograph. The notebook simply records the measurements and snatches of two lines of text (ll. 10–11), that there was molding above the inscription at the top and that a squeeze ("sq.") was taken.
ii) The squeeze was in fact taken with two sheets joined together with sticking plaster which explains the line of shadow mis-representing a section of molding in the published photograph of the squeeze.
iii) Some of the letters were outlined in pencil, presumably to enhance the quality for the photograph of the squeeze.
iv) A close examination of the squeeze revealed that sections of the reconstructed letters were in fact present, that is, the *epsilon* at the end of l. 5, the *rho* at the end of l. 10. Most importantly, the upper serif of the upright hasta and the upper diagonal of the distinctive *kappa* (see l. 4 — the lengthy diagonal stroke) are clearly visible in l. 11. Traces of the upper sections of some of the remaining letters, especially a final -ΟΣ can be made out. This removes doubt from Buckler and Calder's reconstruction of the cognomen of the agonothete for life, Aurelius Tatianus Glykon.[30]

The inscription has been dated to post-212 (the *Constitutio Antoniniana*) on the basis of the name of the honorand, Marcus Aurelius Zenon (ll. 2–3),[31] credited by Angela Standhartinger as a two-time champion.[32] It has been used to demonstrate that Colossae had its own *agonothete*, indeed an *agonothete* for life/in perpetuity (ll. 9–10),[33] who organized an athletic (at least) competition, the "New Olympics Apolloneia", every four years (ll. 5–8).[34] Adam Copenhaver, in spite of the reference to Apolloneia (that is, in honor of Apollo), considers that the games were likely associated with the festival obligations attached to

28 Ms 3286/10/19.

29 The notebook is included in Ms 3286/4 "Bundle of Three Notebooks." Reference to the inscription is on p. 53.

30 Buckler and Calder provided the reconstruction of the entire last line, namely [κωνος (?). The evidence of the *kappa* removes the possibility of the rare name Γλύπτος. Of the 35 variations on the "sweet" stem, Γλυκ-, listed in *LGPN*, Γλύκων is by far the most attested (544 instances), confirming that their reconstruction is correct.

31 A. Blanco-Pérez, "Nomenclature and Dating in Roman Asia Minor: (M.) Aurelius/a and the 3rd Century AD," *ZPE* 199 (2016): 288 nr. 101.

32 A. Standhartinger, *Studien zur Entstehungsgeschichte und Intention des Kolosserbriefs* (NTs 94; Leiden: Brill, 1999), 13 n50.

33 N. Sekunda,"Changing Patterns of Land-Holding in the South-Western Border Lands of Greater Phrygia in the Achaemenid and Hellenistic Periods," in *Colossae in Space and Time: Linking with an ancient city* edited by A. H. Cadwallader and M. Trainor (NTOA 94; Göttingen: Vandenhoeck & Ruprecht, 2011), 71, cf Magie, *Roman Rule*, 1523 n57.

34 L. Bormann, *Der Brief des Paulus an die Kolosser* (ThHK 10/1; Leipzig: Evangelische Verlagsanstalt, 2012), 25; U. Huttner, *Early Christianity in the Lycus Valley* (Leiden: Brill, 2013), 45.

the imperial cult.[35] My own initial reading of the inscription was influenced by a brief reference of Louis Robert which noted that Tripolis was still, in the first century BCE, able to go by the name of Apollonia.[36] I surmised that there was a nostalgic retention of the historical name (with Doric spelling: Ἀπολλωνίῃα) in some contexts (including athletic games).[37]

Many of these isolated comments need modification.

Firstly, there has come to light an inscription that attests athletic games at Tripolis.[38] They are not called the New Olympics (Apolloneia) but the Great Attaleian Olympics (ll. 9–11). The inscription records honors for a Marcus Aurelius Menander who won the boxing contest at the first festival. The games are declared to have been inaugurated at Tripolis (τὸν πρώτως παρ' ἡμεῖν ἀχθέντα ἀγῶνα, ll. 6–8) with prizes awarded by another *agonothete* for life, the locally-renowned pankratiast, Marcus Aurelius Attalianos (ll. 14–17). The Roman citizenship names of honorand and prize-giver indicate a post-212 date.[39] The name of the festival reflects the positive memory of the period of Attalid rule from Pergamon contained in the name of the prize-giver. Its commencement in the third century would likely preclude another festival in that city also using the name "Olympics"; indeed another Tripolitan festival, the Letoeia Pythia, did, tangentially, evoke its old Apollonian name.[40] The editor of the inscription, Cumhur Tanrıver, was concerned that such a name suggested isolympic status for the festival. However by this time, the name of one of the anciently esteemed games — Olympic, Nemeian, Pythian, Isthmian — had become a nigh-synonym for athletic festivals in general.[41] A number of commemorative

---

35 A. Copenhaver, *Reconstructing the Historical Background of Paul's Rhetoric in the Letter to the Colossians* (London: T & T Clark, 2018), 176.

36 *BE* 1939.508, citing *I.Milet* 1,3.74 = *SEG* 4.426 and the numismatic observations of Friedrich Imhoof-Blumer and Barclay Head.

37 A. H. Cadwallader, "Refuting an Axiom of Scholarship on Colossae: fresh insights from new and old inscriptions," in *Colossae in Space and Time*, 166; "Assessing the Potential of Archaeological Discoveries for the Interpretation of New Testament Texts: The Case of a Gladiator Fragment from Colossae and the Letter to the Colossians," in *The First Urban Churches I: Methodological Foundations* edited by J. R. Harrison and L. L. Welborn (Atlanta, GA: SBL Press, 2015), 51 n39.

38 C. Tanrıver, "Three New Inscriptions from Tripolis," *EA* 42 (2009): 83–4 nr. 2.

39 Here I follow the judgment of J.-Y. Strasser (*AE* 2009.1402) against the primary editor who dated it to the time of the emperor, Marcus Aurelius. Guizzi and Alister Filippini equivocate with late 2nd or early 3rd century: "Tripolis on the Maeander in Hellenistic and Roman Age (Cent. 3rd B.C. – 3rd A.D.): Epigraphy and Prosopography," in *Tripolis ad Maeandrum I: Tripolis Araştırmaları* edited by B. Duman (Istanbul: Ege, 2017), 69.

40 *SNG von Aulock* 3328; *BMC Lydia* 47 (time of the Severans).

41 Luigi Moretti's collection of agonistic inscriptions lists twenty different cities staging "Olympics" outside of Olympia. See *Iscrizioni Agonistische Greche* (Rome: Signorelli, 1953), 278. See the general summation of Christopher Jones, "Imaginary Athletics in Two Followers of John Chrysostom," *HSCP* 106 (2011): 327.

coins of Hierapolis celebrated its combined Pythian games[42], a mark of Apollonian reputation on a par with Delphi.[43]

Local cities readily accumulated status for their own games by appropriating such language. It reaffirmed their Greek pride in their status as *poleis* with a cultural event that marked their distinct identity when other aspects of civic life had been subsumed by Roman political transformations,[44] but paradoxically benefitting from Roman transcontinental loosening of the classical and Hellenistic strictures on such brand usage. Accordingly, the New Olympics Apolloneia of the Colossian inscription is unlikely to have been a Tripolitan offering. An inscription from Keretapa suggests they were not Colossian-sponsored either.

Secondly, Francesco Guizzi recently published the following inscription from Keretapa,[45] a city to the south of Colossae across the Taurus mountain range.[46] The damaged marble tabella contains two framed panels. In the lower panel are two standing, winged Nikes flanking a naked, bearded man with chlamys draping from his shoulders and holding an upright lance with his right hand and a small shield in his left. The Nikes are carved with their respective right and left hands close to the central figure supporting the inscription panel above his head, and each holding a victory palm in their other hand. It appears to be part of a more substantial commemorative monument. Guizzi dates the inscription to the second half of the second century. Presumably the naming formula (not the Marcus Aurelius type) and the letter shapes guided the decision. The reconstructed twelve-line inscription reads:[47]

Ὑπό[μνημα φαμιλί]- | ας μονο[μάχων] | καὶ κυνηγεσ[ίων] | Αὐρ(ηλίου) Τατιανοῦ [Γ]λύ- | κωνος Ἀσίας πανη- | γυριάρχου καὶ ἀρχιε- | ρέως πρώτου τῆς Και- | ρεταπέων πόλεως, | καὶ Αὐρηλίας Φλα- | βίας Ἀρτεμονίδος, | ἀρχιερείης, | τῆς γυναι- | κος αὐτοῦ

Commemoration of the troupe of gladiators and venators of Aurelius Tatianus Glykon, the panegyriarch and first high priest of the city of Keretapa, and of the high priestess Aurelia Flavia Artemonis, his wife.

---

42 See Plate 2.8c.

43 *RPC online* 6.5446–7 temp. (time of Elagabalus); *RPC online* 8.ID76993 (time of Philip I).

44 See, for example, *SEG* 27.841 (Ankara, imperial), *F.Delphes III* 6.143 (Delphi, after 138 CE); see S. Mitchell, "Festivals, Games and Civic Life in Roman Asia Minor," *JRS* 80 (1990): 189–90, A. Schachter, *Cults of Boiotia II: Herakles to Poseidon* (London: University of London, 1986), 30 n 1.

45 F. Guizzi, "Gladiatori," in *Museo Archeologico di Denizli-Hierapolis: Catalogo delle iscrizioni greche e latine* edited by T. Ritti (Naples: Liguori, 2008), 152–4, nr. 62 and pl. 62.

46 The exact location is still debated but it seems to bear a duplicate name, Diocaesareia. Its extant coins carry the name Keretapa alone (*RPC online* 4.2.1831 temp., 4.2.1841 temp. [time of Antoninus Pius, Commodus]) or with Diocaesareia as a second name (for example, *RPC online* 4.2.1829 temp., 4.2.1836 temp., 4.2.1838 temp. [time of Antoninus Pius, Marcus Aurelius, Commodus as Caesar]). One dedicatory inscription to Meter Kadmene probably associates the mother goddess with Mt Cadmus (*SEG* 56.1699). Ramsay considered Keretapa took the name Diocaesareia during the reign of Domitian (*Cities and Bishoprics*, 55).

47 As corrected in *SEG* 58.1537.

The arresting element of the commemoration is the name, Aurelius Tatianus Glykon. It is highly likely that the identified person is the same in both Colossian and Keretapan inscriptions. Glykon's leadership of festivals in general (*panegyriarch*) and the financial outlays involved for the gladiatorial and venatorial spectacles as an expected contribution associated with holding the high-priesthood (along with his wife) of the koinon of Asia, make it no surprise that he held the position of *agonothete* at Keretapa (here the ethnic spelled differently from that found on coin legends).[48]

The only issue would appear to be reconciling dates — a long life of civic contribution is implied, with high-ranking Olympics (that is, four-yearly) perhaps the culmination of his munificence, in this inscription only being held for the second time (and hence still very "new"). An example of long-standing endowment for games is found at Oinoanda, where a certain Julius Lucius Pilius Euarestos, sponsored a succession of games (every four, possibly five years), discreetly named the Euaresteia (!);[49] he too is named "*agonothete* for life," but it seems that this was as much for his munificence as for the longevity of his involvement over more than twenty years.[50] In any case, Pseudo-Dionysios regarded such a benefaction for the homeland as "the one most characteristically Greek (Ἑλληνικωτάτη)."[51]

There is no requirement that Glykon and his wife, Artemonis, acquired their Roman citizenship during the reign of Marcus Aurelius; the name Aurelius used as a nomen could equally have been obtained under succeeding emperors.[52] In any case, the time frame between the end of the reign of Marcus Aurelius (180 CE) and the *Constitutio Antoniniana* (212 CE) is not prohibitive of both inscriptions naming the same person. Indeed, as noted below, the Colossian *stephanophoros*, Menekles, minted local coins under successive emperors, Septimius Severus and Caracalla (a possible maximum time-frame of 24 years).

---

48 The spelling of the ethnic, Κερεταπέων is also found in the record of gifts to the imperial temple at Ephesos 88–91 CE from various Asian cities (*I.Ephesos* 2048).

49 In the particular inscription where he is named agonothete for life, the games were named the Severeia Alexandreia Euaresteia, the inscription being abbreviated by the erasure of Alexandreia, reflecting the *damnatio memoriae* of Severus Alexander (emperor 222–235 CE).

50 A. Hall and N. Milner, "Education and Athletics: Documents illustrating the festivals of Oenoanda," in *Studies in the History and Topography of Lycia and Pisidia. In Memoriam A. S.Hall* edited by D. French (Ankara: BIAA, 1994), 13–17 nrs 3–7. His benefaction is described, in inscription nr. 7, as "from his own resources, for all time" (ἐξ ἰδίων χρημάτων εἰς πάντα τὸν χρόνον, ll. 7–9). This was not mere hyperbole; a further inscription under another agonothete for life seems to have been erected after Euarestos's death but acknowledges that this sixth festival was underwritten from the gift (ἐπιτελουμένης ἀπὸ δωρεᾶς) of Julius Euarestos (18, ll. 8–9).

51 Ps-Dionysios *Ars Rhet.* 1.7.

52 See *P.Lond.* 2.348, 3.1179 (time of Septimius Severus).

The use of Aurelius as a shortened indicator of citizenship — Ramsay's "Greek incorrect fashion"[53] — after the *Constitutio Antoniniana* is also known.[54]

However, this argument is dependent on an acceptance of Blanco-Pérez's assignment of the Colossian inscription to post-212 CE and Guizzi's judgment of a second half of the second century date for the Keretapan inscription. The two inscriptions held together suggest that the date range, more likely, should be collapsed, either bringing the Zenon inscription into the second century, or, less probably, the Glykon commemoration into the third century. The Colossian inscription noting Glykon as *agonothete* for life (ll. 9–10) suggests an award of title following a significant period of financial and administrative contribution to agonistic festivals at Keretapa.[55] The four-yearly cycle of the games (ll. 5–6) is an indication of their status in the round of regional competitions and would, thereby, be precisely the sort of event favored by Glykon's benefaction.

The mention of Glykon's name in a Colossian inscription creates an eponymous grounding for the games in which a local hero, Zenon, was triumphant. It may explain why it is the *patris* that conveys the honor to the victor (l. 1). That is, Zenon's return as resplendent champion is recognized as bringing glory to the whole Colossian territory[56] — the homeland — the very identification athletes were required to register, along with their father's name, when they entered a competition.[57] It might have meant that Zenon, being so honored, was, along with a formal accolade and presentation in, say, the theater or odeion, declared eligible for tax benefits or even some sort of pension for his agonistic contribution to Colossae's standing,[58] not to mention the inscription and statue of commemoration. Pseudo-Dionysios delivers the commentary, "the fruits of his victory remain for his entire life and provide abundant resources

53 W. M. Ramsay, *Luke the Physician: and other studies in the history of religion* (London: Hodder & Stoughton, 1908), 338, 386, *cf.* L. Robert, *Noms Indigènes dans L'Asie-Mineure Gréco-Romaine* (Paris: Adrien Maisonneuve, 1963), 391, 527.

54 See *BGU* 2.655, *P.Oxy.* 1458.

55 For an indication of the enormous expense (including the responsible handling of contributions from the city's public purse) and organization incumbent on an agonothete, see the extensive inscription from Oinoanda: M. Wörrle, *Stadt und Fest in kaiserzeitlichen Kleinasien. Studien zur einer agonistischen Stiftung aus Oenoanda* (Munich: Beck, 1988).

56 So, for Oinoanda, comes the claim in the epigram on the lower section of a statue pedestal for Poplius Sthenius Fronto who "carried off for the homeland" (ἀράμενος πάτρῃ) victory in the men's division of the pankration: Hall-Milner, "Education and Athletics," 9, nr. 1, l. 18 (time of Gordion III).

57 *I.Olympia* 56, l. 20 (after 2 BCE); cf Philostratus *Gym.* 25. Sometimes, the victory lists or honor boards carried the name, father's name and the ethnic: see *IG* II^2 1138. On the reciprocity of glory between an athlete and his homeland and city, see L. Robert, "Sur des inscriptions d'Ephèse: fêtes, athletes, empereurs, épigrammes," *RevPhil* 41 (1967): 17–27.

58 See W. Slater, "The Victor's Return, and the Categories of Games," in *Epigraphical Approaches to the Post-Classical Polis: Fourth Century BC to Second Century AD* edited by P. Martzavou and N. Papazarkadas (Oxford: Oxford University Press, 2013), 139–63. For an example of an effort to secure such a reward, that also garners the support, *inter alia*, of the famous Laodikeian Olympian, Photion the boxer, see *P.Lond.* 3.1178 (Hermopolis, second half of 2nd century CE).

for living."[59] It does not mean that Colossae was without a succession of agonothetes,[60] but the eminent games mentioned in the inscription and their chief benefactor were located elsewhere.[61]

Plate 10.5: Zenon at Colossae was a minor champion compared to Aneiketos from Miletos (dated 150–175 CE), presented here in relief as a naked runner holding a victory palm and awkwardly turned in his upper body to reveal his impressive, sculpted chest. The inscription (*IG* XII 2 388) records his successes as a dolichadromos (a long-distance race in the stadium, comprising 12 to 24 lengths — up to 5000 meters) at the Asklepeion games at Pergamon (twice) and at the Tyrimneion games at Thyateira. These three victories are symbolically attested by the precious-metal ingots in the panel above — no doubt an indication of the rewards consequent upon his triumphs. Unusually, the inscription also attests that he was accepted as a competitor at the Pythian games at Delphi (κριθεὶς ἐν Δελφοῖς, ll. 6–7) and also competed at the Aktian games at Neapolis (ἀγωνισάμενος Νέαν πόλιν Ἄκτια ll. 7–8). Most athletic records are confined to successes; here the city's pride extended also to his entry into elite competitions, no doubt aided by his early demise at age 20.[62]

The compound description of the games as "New Olympics Apolloneia" (ll. 7–8) provides a new iteration of the heritage of competition from Olympos,[63] and ties them to the honoring of Apollo. As Pseudo-Dionysios affirmed, not only were such festivals gifts of the gods, but "A god always presides at any festi-

59 Παραμένουσιν τὸν βίον σύμπαντα οἱ καρποὶ οἱ ἀπὸ τῆς νίκης τὴν περιουσίαν τοῦ βίου ἄφθονον παρέχοντες Ps-Dionysios *Ars Rhet.* 288.

60 Buckler and Calder admit that the fragmentary honorific inscription for Marcus Aurelius Heraklas (*MAMA* 6.41) may contain the beginnings of his office (ἀγ[ωνοθέτην) rather than a patronymic (for example, Ἀπ[ολλωνίου). The last extant letter of l. 3 contains only one upright and a curtailed horizontal hasta. See Plate 10.5 below.

61 It should also be recognized that civic offices were not necessarily filled by local citizens. Wealthy and high-status individuals could, at times, hold offices in different cities, even at the same time. See S. Dmitriev, *City Government in Hellenistic and Roman Asia Minor* (Oxford: Oxford University Press, 2005), 159.

62 See A. Chaniotis, "Greek Festivals and Contests: definition and general characteristics," in *Festivals and Contests* edited by A. Chaniotis (ThesCRA 7; Los Angeles: Getty Publications, 2011), 27; cf. E. M. de Martino, "I vincitori dei *Sebastà* nell'anno 86 d.C." in *Munus Laetitiae: Studi miscellanei offerti a Maria Letizia Lazzarini* edited by F. Camia *et al.* (Rome: Sapienza University Press, 2018), 271.

63 Compare *MAMA* 6.76 (Attouda, 1st century BCE to 1st century CE), 80 (Attouda, probably 1st to 2nd century CE), 82 (Attouda nd).

val and gives his name to it."[64] The detailed Oinoandan inscription regulating another four-yearly musical contest, noted that its founder, Iulius Demosthenes, financed a gold crown featuring portraits of the emperor Hadrian and of the god Apollo — which needless to say, he, as founding *agonothete* (and also his successors), was authorized to wear during the course of the games and at other important civic occasions.[65] The conjunction of religious devotion, political loyalty and festive contest could not be plainer. The "Apolloneia" at Keretapa are only known from this inscription but such a designation/devotion is attested elsewhere, at Myndos, Halicarnassos and Ephesos for example.[66] We only know of many of these contests through the honors accorded to victors in their own homeland.[67] Significantly, the Doric spelling Ἀπολλωνίηα is found as the name of the games at Halicarnassos and may indicate the influence of Rhodes, a Doric stronghold, in Attalid-Roman times up to the southern reaches of the Taurus ranges. This may explain the spelling in the Colossian inscription. Our knowledge of Keretapa is limited,[68] but there is a votive altar to Apollo dated 119/120 CE that was placed among devotion to an array of deities in the city and territory.[69]

Thirdly, there has been some difficulty in fixing the meaning of δίς (l. 3). δίς has been taken as "twice-victorious",[70] but it might also indicate a succession of the name Diomas in Zenon's genealogy, that is Zenon son of Diomas, grandson of Diomas (so *LGPN*). Usually one would expect the naming pattern simply to use a numerical indicator, that is, B′.[71] However, this is not exclusively the case. There are some instances where the same person's genealogy uses B′ in one instance and δίς in another. One mint sponsor at Colossae changed his identifying legend from ΜΕΝΕΚΛΗϹ Β ϹΤΕΦΑΝΗΦΟΡΟϹ ΑΝΕΘ(ηκεν) ΚΟΛΟϹϹΗΝΩΝ for coinage under Severus (193–211) to ΜΕΝΕΚΛΗϹ DIC ϹΤΕΦΑΝΗΦΟΡΟϹ ΑΝΕΘΗΚΕΝ ΚΟΛΟϹϹΗΝΩΝ under Caracalla

64 Θεὸς μὲν γέ που πάντως πάσης ἡστινοσοῦν πανηγύρεως ἡγεμὼν καὶ ἐπώνυμος ... Ps-Dionysios *Ars Rhet.* 1–2 (translation by W. H. Race).

65 *SEG* 38.1462, III, ll. 52–3, 55–7.

66 *IG* XII 4,2 935, l. 21 (Kos, 1st century BCE); *I.Perge* 272A, ll. 3–4 (Perge, 1st century BCE); *SEG* 50.423 (Ephesos, 2nd – 1st century BCE).

67 So, Y. Kalliontzis, "La Date de la première celebration des Amphiareia Romaia d'Oropos," *REG* 129 (2016): 86; similarly, Hall and Milner, "Education and Athletics," 8.

68 See N. P. Milner, *An Epigraphical Survey in the Kibyra-Olbasa Region conducted by A. S. Hall* (RECAM III; London: British Academy, 1998), 53–8; G. H. R. Horsley, *The Greek and Latin Inscriptions in the Burdur Archaeological Museum* (RECAM V; London: British Academy, 2007), 224–5. Compare the treatment of Ramsay, *Cities and Bishoprics*, 275–80, 328–9.

69 Ramsay, *Phrygia* 307.111 = Milner-Hall, *Kibyra Olbasa* 123.2.

70 Standhartinger, *Studien*, 13 n50.

71 See, for example, *MAMA* 6.61 (Trapezopolis, 198 or 209 CE), a metrical celebration of the wrestler in Pythian games that yet used B′ after the name of the prize-gover Zeuxitheos but requiring δίς to be read or heard if the hexametric scansion was to operate, or, better, the fuller τῷ Ζευξιθέου; See R. Merkelbach, "Agonistisches Epigramm aus Trapezopolis," *ZPE* 19 (1975): 302.

(198–217), with no difference in meaning, namely, "Menekles son of Menekles, *stephanophoros*, endowed (this coinage) for the Colossians."[72] One honorific inscription set up in the second century by the popular assembly at another large Phrygian village, Thiounta, provides a list of names of worthy recipients of public recognition, including Διόδωρος Β', "Diodoros son of Diodoros" immediately followed by Μένανδρος δὶς "Menandros son of Menandros."[73]

The issue might be resolved by comparison with similar inscriptions, namely, honors for athletic prowess or perhaps for performance of some civic benefit. The word order is not consistent. The single letter B is used numerically in the memorial for Aneiketos for his double-victory at Pergamon. The more frequent usage is δίς. Thus, a certain champion, Marcus Aurelius Asklepiades, holder of the citizenships of Alexandria and Athens,[74] could be honored for twice being victor of the grand slam of the great Games (Olympic, Pythian, Nemeian and Isthmian), δὶς περιοδονείκης, but could also be acclaimed for twice winning the men's grade wrestling in the Eureklian games in Sparta, νεικήσας Εὐρύκλεια ἀνδρῶν πάλην δίς.[75] Most instances appear to place the δίς after the use of νικέω.[76] This is not universal, though the counter examples are earlier.[77] Accordingly, the more likely meaning for the Colossian inscription is the inclusion of a three-generational genealogy. The notice of three generations is frequently the norm for those of some status and are a feature of honor boards in gymnasia. Colossae's elite sometimes displayed genealogies that ran to five generations.[78] Continuity and reputation were critical bulwarks of status.[79]

So it appears in this inscription, that part of the honorifics esteemed by at least the citizenry in Colossae was generational stability, not just athletic ability. Ancient physiognomy combined the two — the successful athlete demonstrated the soundness of his ancestry.[80] The child had honored his parentage

---

72 *MSPhryg* 2.586–7, 591; see also coin xix) in chapter 1. On the language of endowment and the authorization of coinage, see P. Weiss, "The Cities and their Money," in *Coinage and Identity in the Roman Provinces* edited by C. Howgego, V. Heuchert and A. Burnett (Oxford: Oxford University Press, 2005), 61–3.

73 Ramsay, *Phrygia* 1.142–3.30.

74 Highly successful athletes were often rewarded with citizenships additional to their homeland; for an Asian example, see *MAMA* 6.58 (Tripolis, 2nd to 3rd century CE).

75 *IG* V,1 666 ll. 2, 3 (Sparta, 145–160 CE). The Antonine date of the inscription is adopted from the online database: "Connected Contests in the post-classical world" nr. 227 (connected-contests.org). A herald at the Games might similarly claim — on his epitaph (!) — a δὶς περιοδονίκης (*AAT* 1966/67.308.27, Hierapolis, 2nd century CE).

76 *SEG* 16.289 (Olympia, c. 160 BCE); *I.Tralleis* 135 (180/190 CE).

77 *SEG* 11.1239 (Olympia, after 368 BCE); *F.Delphes III* 4.202 (Delphi, 400–366 BCE); *SEG* 32.217 (Athens, c. 264 BCE).

78 *AS* 2012.152, ll. 7, 32; *MSPhryg* 2.566–578.

79 See C. P. Jones, "Ancestry and Identity in the Roman empire," in *Local Knowledges and Microidentities in the Imperial Greek World* edited by T. Whitmarsh (Cambridge: Cambridge University Press, 2010), 118–20.

80 Philostratus *Gym.* 28–9.

(cf Col 3:20). The irony is that, as far as the remains can tell us, the actual event in which Zenon was successful is omitted.[81] It may have been part of a visual display (a statue?) affixed to the top of the pedestal. More remotely, δευτέραν in line 5 might be an abbreviated reference to an age group (that is, probably, the "youth" division at the games, as distinct from the "boys" and "men").[82] This is unlikely, but it still leaves the actual event obscure. In any case, if the Keretapan "New Olympics" followed Olympic tradition, there were only two age-groups, boys and men — still technically possible with δευτέραν but passing beyond the usual terminological usage. So, unlike many athletic commemorations with their manifold citations,[83] this inscription marks the honor but not the specific discipline.

The inscription does show that, for Colossae, "how normal it was for members of the urban elites to practice athletics on local, regional and … interregional level".[84] Colossae was not shut off either within or without the Lycus Valley. Indeed, Zenon may have been successful at the Keretapa games as part of a circuit of competitions held in various cities. Athletics was a key instrument in promoting inter-regional and international connectedness; the competitors themselves with their entourage (trainers, supporters) became important agents of cultural exchange.[85] In the Roman empire, once Rome embraced the athletic ethos,[86] the games became a crucial component in the soft machinery engineering the cohesion of empire. Frequently, as in the Colossian inscriptions that carry an indebtedness to the training of the gymnasium, the primary hierarchical relationship is between an official of the games and the successful athlete. Both, usually but not exclusively, were members of the local elite, for whom the display of Greek credentials — in offices, in athleticism, in gymnasial culture, in genealogy, in hierarchy — were all part of the sedimentation of power, influence and justifying ideology.[87]

We have seen in the previous chapter that such Greekness was as much part of Colossae's aspiration as any empirical ethnicity. But other inscriptions outside of the small Colossian catalogue show how much this was a valuable

81 Compare *I.Mus. Denizli* 61.

82 See, for example, the accolades for the boxer Aurelius Philadelphos at Didyma who was, successively, twice successful in all three age divisions (κατὰ τὸ ἑξῆς πρώτην, δευτέραν, τρίτην ἡλικίαν ἑξάκις, *I.Didyma* 179, ll. 6–7, 212/230 CE).

83 See J. König, *Athletics and Literature in the Roman Empire* (Cambridge: Cambridge University Press, 2005), 124.

84 H. W. Pleket "Varia Agonistica," *EA* 26 (1998): 129.

85 Z. Papakonstantinou, "Athletics, memory and community in Hellenistic and Roman Messene," *BICS* 61 (2018): 70–1.

86 Late republican and early imperial suspicions about gymnasium practices (Cicero *Fam.* 7.1, *Tusc* 4.33.70; Plutarch *Quaest. rom.* (*Mor.*) 247D, Trajan apud Pliny *Ep.* 10.40.2) were ultimately marginalized.

87 See O. van Nijf, "Athletics, festivals and Greek identity in the Roman East," *PCPS* 45 (2000): 182–6.

instrument by which relationships with Rome were negotiated. The hint of beneficial connection with Rome is already given in this inscription with the display of Roman citizenship. Some inscriptions from other cities are quite explicit in the incorporation of Roman loyalty, affiliation and hierarchical deference. One agonistic inscription from Sardis, for example, accents the place of the city in relation to Rome, as twice keeper of the imperial cult by senatorial decrees (κατὰ τὰ δόγματα τῆς ἱερᾶς συγκλήτου ll. 8–10) and the position of the *agonothete*, Metrodoros Attalas, "as friend and ally of the Romans" (φίλη καὶ συμμάχῳ Ῥωμαίων ll. 10–11) before, finally, in the last four lines recording the essential details of the champion, that is, his name (Secundus), his father and his homeland citizenship.[88]

Colossae placed a premium on athletic prowess and generational display,[89] almost certainly locating their institutional support in the gymnasium-baths that were probably to be found east of the city acropolis, abutting the river. The cultural icon was controlled and enhanced by *ephebarchs*, and well-provided by *elaiones*, both offices of sufficiently high status to be entered in one Colossian citizen's *cursus honorum*.[90] Although this honor for Zenon can, in my view, no longer be used to attest the office of *agonothete* at Colossae, there is little doubt that the office existed as part of the provision and regulation of agonistic physical and intellectual abilities. Indeed, this may be the reconstructed office in another inscription added to the name Marcus Aurelius Heraklas, rather than the father's name: ἡ πατρὶς | Μ(ᾶρκον) Αὐρ(ήλιον) Ἡρα- | κλᾶς Ἀπ/γ[...[91] It is perhaps significant that it is the *patris*, the fatherland, that honored Heraklas, as also honored Zenon in our main focus here.

Plate 10.6: A squeeze of the fragmentary inscription recording the fatherland honoring Heraklas. The existing end of line 3 has a partial upright and horizontal hasta which might be reconstructed as a gamma (giving, perhaps, agonothete) or a pi, probably yielding a patronymic such as Apollodoros.

88 *I.Sardis* 2.411.

89 Peter Scholz confirms that the incorporation of baths into existing gymnasium structures did not diminish the more traditional accents of the institution. See his "Einführung," in *Das hellenistische Gymnasion* edited by D. Kah and P. Scholz (Berlin: de Gruyter, 2007), 24.

90 *IGR* 4.870, ll. 4, 6. Nigel Kennell holds the *ephebarch* to be "of the same status" as other magistracies, such as a *strategos* and *agoranomos*: "The Status of the Ephebarch," *Tyche* 15 (2000): 107. These offices also form part of the *cursus honorum* of the unknown honorand in this Colossian inscription. However, it should be noted that these *curriculum vitae* often scaled the offices in order of status from the greatest to the less so.

91 *MAMA* 6.41 (3rd century CE; photograph in public domain).

Certainly the *agonothete* is implied in the next inscription from Colossae to be examined. After all, the honed body and mind were a reflection of the honed civic identity. The gymnasium was the setting for citizen commitment to these values, providing a venue for general exercise, for the occasional local displays (by visitors or residents) where exhibitions or mini-competitions in what were called θέμιδες, ἐπιδείξεις and ἀποδείξεις,[92] for the Ἑρμαία where young students presented their training,[93] and for the enhancement of career paths — all of which could attract the general description as ἀγῶνες. The key aspects of such gymnasial exercise and training — the physical and the intellectual — are given a special focus in the following Colossian inscription, with a suitably aggrandizing aside to religious mythology.

Junior honors for Kastor

A second inscription celebrating athletic prowess was discovered by John Anderson in 1897 "in another field" near the ruins of the mound.[94] He bequeathed no description of the stone itself. The inscription itself remained substantially unremarked until Reinhold Merkelbach and Joseph Stauber included it in their expansive edition of metrical inscriptions.[95] They made minimal adjustments to Anderson's text, based on probabilities rather than autopsy, given that the stone was not seen again after Anderson's copy.[96] I present their text here, with one adjustment to their reconstruction sigla, here completing the last line only with the metrical scansion established by the preceding lines, but offering in the commentary two suggestions for the closing wording.

ἀγαθῇ τύχῃ
πυγμαχίης τόδ' ἄεθλον ἐγὼ Κάστωρ ἀπεδέγμην
νεικήσας σθεναραῖς παλαμ[α]ῖς ἄξυστος ἄμωμος·
οὐδὲ γὰρ ἦν θέμις ἄλλῳ ἀδελφειῷ Πολυδ[εύ]κους
χεῖρας ἀνασχ[εμ]έναι πυγμῆς χάρ⟨ι⟩ν ἀν[τι]πάλοιο·
ἀθλοθέτ[ης] δέ με παισ[⏕ | — ⏕ | — ⏑⏑ | — ⏓]

92 See, for example, *SEG* 17.619 (Pamphylia, 2nd to 3rd century CE), *SEG* 54.1197 (Magnesia-on-Maeander, 176–180 CE), *SEG* 46.1721 (Xanthos, 196 BCE), *SEG* 56.638 (Larisa, 160–150 BCE).

93 *I.Beroia* 1, ll. 45–72 (c.180 BCE); *SEG* 46.923(1) (Chersonesos, before 110 BCE).

94 J. G. C. Anderson, "A Summer in Phrygia. II" *JHS* 18 (1898): 90 nr. 26.

95 R. Merkelbach and J. Stauber, *Steinepigramme aus dem griechischen Osten* I–V (Stuttgart: Teubner/Munich: Saur, 1998–2004), nr. 1.02.15.01.

96 In line 5 they read χάριν rather than χάρμ', encouraged by Anderson's critical note that the stone appeared to read ΧΑΡΝΑΝ¯ . | ΠΟΛΟΙΟ. In line 6, they read δέ με rather than δ'ἐμὲ, which assists the scansion of the metrical line. They mistakenly shifted the opening square bracket in the last word of line 5 to cover only the iota rather than Anderson's TI.

Translation:

For good fortune.
I, Kastor, received this prize for victory in boxing,
having triumphed with fists of fury, emerging unscratched and unscathed;
nor yet has tradition ever dictated there be another brother of Polydeukes
to raise the hands as a boxing combatant;

Without the availability of any sort of reproduction of the lithograph, it is impossible to provide a date. A possible *ante quo* might be ἀντιπάλοιο in line 5. Even though the genitive morphology is categorized as an epic construction,[97] the earliest attestation of the word in this form that I have sourced outside of this inscription, is in an oracle tentatively given to the time of Hadrian.[98] It may be a word form gaining currency in the Second Sophistic, though a cognate, ἀντίπαλος, goes back at least to Pindar.[99]

Both Anderson and Merkelbach-Stauber took the extant ΠΑΙΣ of line 6 as a nominative, παῖς, considering that the *athlothetês*, the prize-giver or adjudicator, was obliquely named in the inscription, that is with a patronymic following. Their completion of the line of the metrical inscription was different. Anderson tentatively suggested "(name) κρείττον' ἔνειμε?", that is "son of N. awarded me, the better fighter"; Merkelbach-Stauber seemed to think a full name was likely ("... der Sohn des ...") with "ἀνέθηκεν" at the end implying that either the inscription itself or, if it was a statue base, the statue itself was authorized, perhaps financed, by the *athlothete*. The patronymic formula παῖς (τοῦ) N. (in genitive) is known, though it is not common,[100] and not found of any *athlothete*, even when such an official has, or is involved in, an honorific or commemorative dedication.[101] In any case, one would expect the name of the *athlothete* as well as the patronymic.[102] But then the metrical requirements would be difficult to observe given the suggested part-completions both editors have offered.

Both editors assumed the line was originally complete even though Anderson struggled to find anything "engraved after ΠΑΙΣ" — probably an indication of abrasion rather than erasure or interruption. They then took the ΠΑΙΣ as a nominative singular. However, when athletic victories are recorded, they very often give the division in which the discipline victory was achieved, that is boys (παῖδες), youths (ἀγενείοι) and/or adults (ἄνδρες).[103] Honor boards of games victors, frequently found in gymnasia,[104]

---

97 Nonnus *Dion.* 37.511, 595.

98 *IG* II/III^3 4, 1792 (Athens).

99 Pindar *Nem.* 11.26, *Ol.* 8.70 here in the context of wrestling, from which the word's expansive sense of opponent seems to have derived (πάλη), but see Pindar *Isthm.* 5.61 (boxing?).

100 See *I.Ephesos* 3207A (graffito); *I.Délos* 380, 385, 396, 424, 439, 442, 461 (c. 198–169 BCE with ἀνέθηκεν).

101 See *TAM* V,2 1021 (Thyateira, imperial period), *I.Sardis* 1.78 (imperial, fragmentary)

102 Compare *I.Laodikeia Lykos* 81, l. 7 (1st century BCE).

103 See, for example, *SEG* 59.411 (Messene, Augustan period).

104 So, for example, *SEG* 51.602 (Dephi, 2nd century CE, discovered in the xystos of the gymnasium), *TAM* III.1.199–206 (Termessos).

follow this breakdown into divisions,[105] as does an inscription from Aphrodisias listing the prizes to be awarded in the different disciplines (music included).[106] Individual honorific commemorations followed suit.[107] Some athletes curated their *cursus honorum* to detail victories from boys on to men's divisions.[108]

In local and regional games, frequently only boys and adults, that is, junior (under eighteen years)[109] and senior divisions were held, "thus reducing considerably the cost of prizes and statues."[110] Here, I have suggested that "in the boys division" (junior section) better suits the context, hence παισίν.

This entices the completion of the line to suggest an award to the winner from the *athlothete*.[111] A number of options and variations are possible.[112] My own "colobodactylic" suggestions for the last line are: ἀθλοθέτ[ης] δέ με παισ[ὶ' νικῆν γέρα τοῦτ' ἀπένειμε, "so the adjudicator, I being the victor in the junior championship, awarded me this honor", or ἀθλοθέτ[ης] δέ με παισ[ὶν πρῶτα νικῆν ἐδίκασσε, "so the adjudicator, me being preeminent in the junior championship, adjudged me victorious". Doubtless, better epic style could be achieved.

Crowns, prizes, statues, inscriptions — all are possible benefactions of the official. Sometimes the successful athlete saved the financial drain by erecting the commemoration himself, a thoroughly acceptable, even praiseworthy act, according to Pliny the Younger.[113] Whatever the inscription was attached to, it is most likely that it recorded the division in which the victory was achieved.

However much the inscription leaves many questions unanswered, it does offer considerable insight into the gymnastic culture at Colossae.

Firstly, in spite of boxing's classification as one of the extremely popular "heavy" contests, that is, wrestling, boxing and the pankration,[114] the inscription is carved with the artistic finesse of dactylic hexameters, and includes rare words or forms frequently concentrated in epic poetry (πυγμαχίης, ἄεθλον, ἀπεδέγμην in l. 2, σθεναραῖς, παλαμαῖς, ἄξυστος in l. 3, θέμις, ἀδελφειῷ in l. 4, ἀντιπάλοιο in l. 5), alliteration and assonance (ἄξυστος, ἄμωμος in l. 3, ἄλλῳ ἀδελφειῷ in l. 4). At Priene, Aelius Aemilius Zosimos not only provided

105 For example, *IG* I³ 1386 (Salamis, 450–440 BCE), *CIG* 2758 (Aphrodisias).
106 *I.Aphrodisias Performers* 52 III, IV (nd).
107 For example, *IG* XII supp. 330 (Amorgos, 2nd century BCE).
108 *SEG* 53.1355, ll. B2, C4 (Sardis, 212–217 CE) = Moretti, *I.agonistische* 84. Compare Pausanias 2.14.2–3.
109 See Pausanias 2.14.2.
110 Hall-Milner, "Education and Athletics," 29.
111 Scholia to Pindar *Ol.* 1.5.
112 I am grateful to Emeritus Professor Elizabeth Minchin for her guidance and suggestions in the assessment and reconstruction of this inscription.
113 Pliny to Cremutius Ruso *Ep.* 9.19; cf Plutarch *de Laud.* (*Mor.*). 539E–F.
114 Philostratus *Gym.* 3, 15; Milner notes that a collation of the 29 statue bases for the Euaresteia games at Oinoanda, 10 honored wrestlers, 8 pancratiasts and 5 honored boxers: Hall-Milner, "Education and Athletics," 28.

oil and ointment for the gymnasium and baths, but his provision extended to game balls and weapons and a grammatical tutor for philological study by the ephebes. The inscribed rationale was that the body become unflinching (τὸ σῶμα … ἄοκνον τυγχάνειν) and the soul progress to excellence and humane sensibility (τὰς ψυχὰς πρὸς ἀρετὴν καὶ πάθος ἀνθρώπινον προάγεσθαι).[115] The conjunction of the two aspects — of broad gymnasial education and athletic acclaim — was made by the *Ars Rhetorica*. The writer deemed that the beauty of the body should be matched with the beauty of the mind; praiseworthy deeds, the author adjudged, were rendered greater once cast in words.[116]

Metrical inscriptions added a gravity to the honor conferred. Indeed one commemoration of a boxer at Aphrodisias, Aurelius Achilles, has a double inscription, one in refined prose and one in meter.[117] The metrical inscription actually affirms its own character by the inclusion of μέτροις in its text.[118] Milner's comment probably reflects (some) modern academic attitudes but is, nevertheless, pertinent: "the character of the educated elite of these cities should probably not be seen as exclusively boorish [!], for it could combine, as we can see at Oenoanda, a taste for philosophy and poetry with exaltation of what can only be described as a heavily muscular ethos."[119] Boxing for the ancients was to be collated with dancing and singing, as the *Homeric Hymn to Apollo* espoused.[120] Here, as in other honorific, metrical inscriptions, a second exhibition was being paraded — not just the display of pugilistic skill but also of literary accomplishment, a double-facetted identity that reinforced the honorable status of the person named and the cultural values shared between that person and those involved in the stone's public performance (from commissioner to stone mason to herald to peers to general audience).[121]

---

115 *I.Priene* 112, ll. 63–4, 73–6 (84 or 1 BCE).

116 Ps-Dionysios, *Ars Rhet.* 7.2.

117 Compare Hall-Milner, "Education and Athletics," 9–11, nr. 1, also a combination of prose and meter.

118 *I.Aphrodisias Performers* 72.II.3 (3rd century CE). Here I follow the understanding of the meaning of the word given by Charlotte Roueché, who extended the tentative recognition of Christopher Jones. Merkelbach and Stauber however, took a circuitous meaning "keeping my distance" and cited Dio Chrysostom's account of the renowned boxer Melankomas who wore down his opponents by being able to hold his arms aloft (thus fending off blows?) for longer than any opponent (Dio Chrysostom *Or.* 28.7–8). See C. Roueché, *Performers and Partisans at Aphrodisias in the Roman and Late Roman Periods* (London: Society for the Promotion of Roman Studies, 1993), 204–5, C. P. Jones, "Two Inscriptions from Aphrodisias," *HSCP* 85 (1981): 121–2; Merkelbach and Stauber, *Steinepigramme* 4.20.01.02.

119 Hall-Milner, "Education and Athletics," 29.

120 *Homeric Hymn* 3.149. Whether this was a form of shadow-boxing — known and even awarded in some ancient games — is uncertain. However, according to Lucian, Kastor and Polydeukes taught dance (the Caryatic) to the Spartans: Lucian *Salt.* 10.

121 See G. Agosti, "Greek Metrical Inscriptions, Classical *Paideia* and Identity in Late Antiquity," in *Greek* Paideia *and Local Tradition in the Graeco-Roman East* edited by M-P. de Hoz, J. L. G. Alonso and L. A. G. Romero (Leuven: Peeters, 2020), 217–9.

Secondly, the evocation of literary mythology in the verses with the reference to Polydeukes draws in a vast and popular array of stories associated with the Dioscuri brothers. Not only do we have hymns to Kastor and Polydeukes (Castor and Pollux) in the *Homeric Hymns* (Hymns 17 and 33), and Theocritus (*Idyll* 22) but frequent allusions and references in other writers. The interplay between the human and divine pervades the portrait, with Polydeukes and Kastor sharing the same mother (Leda) but, in most renditions, fathered by Zeus and Leda's husband, Tyndareus respectively.[122] Even so, immortality is conferred on both, after Polydeukes refused his eternal existence offered by Zeus, unless his brother could join him.[123] Not only did the pair thus become an inspiration of friendship and love,[124] but that apotheosis was given heavenly witness in the astrological pairing of the Gemini — hence the twin's salvation of sailors (cf Acts 28:11)[125] — and the astronomical association with the morning and evening stars (cf 2 Pet 1:19, Rev 2:28) — a testimony to the myth that had them alternate, day about, in their immortal existence. They, along with Hermes and Herakles, were frequently the recipients of dedications and sacrifices in the gymnasia.[126]

The arresting element however is how such traditions can be modulated as they are harnessed to enhance the meaning of mundane existence. In the reiterations, the strong accent is on Kastor as the brilliant horseman and Polydeukes the indomitable pugilist.[127] Indeed, the exemplar of boxing is found in the detail of Polydeukes' match against the giant Amycus — which gains the entranced voyeurism of Theocritus in his 22nd *Idyll* and Apollonios of Rhodes in his *Argonautica* (Bk 2.1–163). But in this inscription, it is not Polydeukes celebrated for his prowess in boxing but his brother's namesake. As the tradition has it (θέμις, l. 4), there is no other brother who might arise to rival *this* Kastor's claim.[128] This poetic license in handling the mythology yet preserves

122 Note however an early inscription that has both as sons of Zeus: *IG* IX,1 649 (6th century BCE). This alternate tradition had a tenacious life: Dio Chrysostom *Or.* 61.11.

123 Homer *Od.* 11.299–304, Ps-Apollodorus, *Bib.* 3.2, Pindar *Pyth.* 11.61–4; cf Cicero *Leg.* 2.19.

124 Plutarch, *Frat. amor.* (*Mor.*) 478A–486D.

125 *Homeric Hymn* 33.6–9, Callimachus *Hymn* 5.24; Lucian *Nav.* 9. The Dioscuri were given the epithet "Saviors" (Plutarch *Superst.* [*Mor.*] 169B cf Diodorus Siculus 6.fr.6. They were esteemed in Rome (where a temple was erected to them in the forum; see Cicero *Verr.* 2.1.129) because their epiphany had swung a battle against the Latini (Dionysios Halicarnassus *Ant. rom.* 6.13.1–5). On the appearances of the Dioscuri, see V. J. Platt, "Double Vision: Epiphanies of the Dioscuri in Classical Antiquity," *Archiv für Religiongeschichte* 20 (2018): 229–56.

126 See for example, Rizakis *Achaïe* III.62 (Pharai, early 2nd century BCE).

127 Homer *Il.* 3.237, *Od.* 11.300, Horace *Sat.* 2.26–7; Statius *Silv.* 5.139–40; Sidonius *Poems* 2.35. *Homeric Hymn* 17.5, however, credits both as brilliant horsemen cf Stesichorus Fr. 178. Sometimes Kastor is acclaimed as a brilliant sprinter: Plutarch *Frat. Amor.* (*Mor.*) 486B. Theocritus almost stretches poetic license to breaking point by acclaiming the pair as saviors, horsemen, lyre impressarios, athletes and singers (*Idyll* 22.23–4).

128 Compare Quintus Smyrnaeus *Posthom.* 4.309–10. Although this is a fourth century text, the combination of πυγμαχιη … ἄεθλον in the same line (l. 310) is striking.

the integrity of the didymic bond, but provides a hyperbolic glorification of a lad from Colossae. Moreover, such a twist in the tradition suggests that Kastor is probably not a "stage-name" but the actual name of an athlete who found his claim to fame in boxing rather than horse-racing as mythology had delivered to the divine Kastor.

Thirdly, the inscription takes considerable pains to accent that the body remained perfectly intact; indeed the "unscratched and unscathed" (ἄξυστος ἄμωμος, l. 3) physique is presented as part of the testimony to the success of his own pugilistic skill. This is precisely the accolade bestowed on Polydeukes in *Homeric Hymn* 33 (ἀμώμητον, l. 3), from which, it would seem clear, this epigram has drawn[129] — a dramatic testimony to the power of hymns to shape conceptual and literary frames. It may even be that *Homeric Hymn* 17 with its five lines of verse has shaped the structure.

The manly paradigm was built on bodily integrity, inescapable from the gaze of spectators and trainers in the gymnasium and the games because of the requirement of nudity[130] — considered such a problem for Jews that some appear to have resorted to epispasm to reverse their circumcision (cf 1 Cor 7:18).[131] There may even have been a "body-building" competition (the *euandria* and *euexia*) where physique rather than athletic performance was prized.[132] Musculature was accentuated by the application of "manly olive oil",[133] a *sine qua non* of gymnasial education and therefore a prime target for recognized benefactions.[134] In the "heavy" contests, nudity itself might become a weapon that reduced opponents to defeat; the mere stripping by a competitor to reveal the hardened power of rippling muscles was sometimes enough to prompt other competitors to withdraw (ὃν ἀποδυσάμενον παρῃτήσαντο οἱ ἀνταγωνισταί).[135] The daunting presence of the honed body even made its way into literary homage,[136] a strong indication of the value attached to the somatic emulation of the gods in the world in which Colossae was a willing participant and competitor. It may be one of the hints contained in Kastor's lack of any further opponents.

---

129 Compare, ἀνούτατος, "never injured" in Apollonios of Rhodes *Argon.* 2.74.

130 See for example Plutarch *Tu. san.* (*Mor.*) 127E for the sense of the ubiquity of nudity at the gymnasium.

131 See A. H. Cadwallader, "Paul and the Games," in *Paul in the Greco-Roman World: A Handbook, Volume 1* edited by J. P. Sampley (London: Bloomsbury, 2016), 379–80. The involvement of Jews in the gymnasium seems to have varied across the Mediterranean: see Feldman, *Jew and Gentile in the Ancient World* (Princeton, NJ: Princeton University Press, 1993), 57–9.

132 See N. B. Crowther, "Male 'Beauty' Contests in Greece: The Euandria and Euexia," *AC* 54 (1985): 285–91.

133 ἄρσεν … ἔλαιον Callimachus *Hymn* 5.24.

134 See, for example, *SEG* 13.258 (Gytheion), *SEG* 50.1130 (Ephesos, nd), *SEG* 59.1422 (Pergamon, c.130 BCE). See A. Zuiderhoek, *The Politics of Munificence in the Roman Empire* (Cambridge: Cambridge University Press, 2009), 39, 88–92.

135 Lane, *CMRDM* 1:164, as reconstructed (Pisidian Antioch, second century CE) Moretti, *I.agonistische* 79, ll. 20–21 (Rome, c. 200 CE).

136 Dio Chrysostom, *Or.* 29.6, 11–12.

Plate 10.7: The popularity of boxing is attested in the cheap, plastic art of an oil lamp from the Santa Rosa Necropolis Museum at the Vatican. It highlights the naked, muscular athleticism of the combatants.

One might wonder how it was possible to escape the bruising and scarring of boxing when strong and fine-edged bands of leather were wound around the fists for the fight — the ancient and dangerous version of modern boxing gloves, sometimes made the more lethal by the insertion of "sharps", transforming the straps into ancient knuckle-dusters. But whatever the reality of the bruising encounter, this epigram reveals the high value attached to the sculpted form of the human body, affirmed as the ideal-type. Indeed, there was a double connection in the well-honed body. The *Ars Rhetorica*, in a slight adjustment of Homer, claimed that festival spectators "gaze upon the athlete as a god."[137] They were "godlike" (ἰσόθεοι); some ancients were even venerated as gods.[138] In an expansion of godlike bodies (θεοειδέστερα), Philostratus, in another of his physiognomic fantasies, draws a direct comparison with the form captured in statues of Heracles,[139] one of the great demi-gods of the gymnasium and the games. So the honed physique became statuesque and godlike in its pristine form, the aspiration for citizens in a gymnasium laden with statues of gods, heroes and victorious athletes — all celebrating a common form. The divinized Kastor and Polydeukes might excel the "beauty and stature" (κάλλει τε καὶ μεγέθει) of human beings,[140] but the proximate analogy was nonetheless affirmed. Thus Ps-Apollodorus asserted that it was "because of their manliness that both were called Dioscuri".[141] Jason König dubs this the "paradoxical combination of imitability and inaccessible idealization."[142] The form, as esteemed at Colossae, can, to date, be best visualized from the sculpted naked bodies of Helios or the river gods found on the city's coins.

137 *Ars Rhet.* 7.4 (7.288), citing *Od.* 8.173, but shifting the focus from a word-smith or rhetorician to an athlete. Compare, similarly, Pausanias 6.6.4, 6.11.2.

138 *Ars. Rhet.* 7.292.

139 Philostratus *Gym.* 35.

140 Dionysios of Halicarnassus *Ant. rom.* 6.13.1.

141 διὰ τὴν ἀνδρείαν ἐκλήθησαν ἀμφότεροι Διόσκουροι. Ps-Apollodorus *Bib.* 3.2.

142 König, *Athletics and Literature*, 130.

Plate 10.8a and b: The mastered body form of standing Helios on a bronze coin from the time of Antoninus Pius, and of the reclining rivergod, from the time of Hadrian.[143]

The famous scene of a boxing match on a sarcophagus from the Torlonia Collection in Rome demonstrates the application of such an idealistic typology of the human form to boxing — taut, defined musculature, unemotionally engaged in the sheer athleticism of the pugilistic punch-up.[144]

The impress of a mythological connection, the assonantial acclaim of unlacerated success (thus preserving the beauty of masculine form), the climax in public recognition for accomplishment, the celebration of a superior bestowing a reward on a junior, all combine not merely to register the honor of an athletic combatant but to reinforce, even control, fundamental values in Colossian society. The divine foundation and direction of the society runs through even the scant remains of Colossae, and is no different from other cities of Asia Minor even though the particulars may vary. Statuesque celebrations of these values adorned the colonnades, the agora and civic institutions subliminally cultivating the codes and conventions of society and, in the specific epigraphic particulars, displaying how individuals could and should conform. The emperor needless to say, epitomized such conformation of the body (regardless of the actual somatic contours he possessed).

Plate 10.9: A slightly larger-than-life statue of the emperor Trajan from the island of Samos, now housed in the Pythagorion Museum. It displays the hardened physique that extols self-mastery, discipline and emulation of the divine form that can be seen, for example, in the Helios and river-god iconography in Pl. 10.8a and b.

143 *RPC online* 4.2.11597 temp., 3.2307D. Photograph of 9a from a private collection by permission; photograph of 9b by courtesy of St. Paul Antiques.

144 See P. Veyne, "The Roman Empire," in *A History of Private Life: From Pagan Rome to Byzantium* edited by P. Veyne (Cambridge, MA: Belknap, 1987), 201.

The rewards sealed the rightness and return for the exemplary citizen, be it athlete, benefactor or officer. And with the brief almost oblique reference to the ἀθλοθέτης in the inscription, the reinforcement of the power stratification of society was displayed however seemingly innocuous, minor or theatrical the performance of the honor was. The power of Kastor is made to serve the even greater power of societal structures as his honor and reward are dependent on its recognition. The exchange however, as with any contemporary photographic opportunity of politician and athlete, is that civic structures, encapsulated in its officials, are infused with the virility, tone and skill distilled in the honorand. If the *athlothete* is taken as a synonym of *agonothete*,[145] a slide induced by metrical demands,[146] then the hierarchical structure is even more pronounced, given the status that accrued to the latter office.

Jason König has drawn attention to a seemingly divergent strain in aesthetic presentation of the boxer in Roman art — a tensive intrusion of realism onto the more classical form. Here the bodies were battered and scarred, and faces grizzled and flattened. One first century dedication to a boxer Doroclides at Thera, on the island of Santorini, actually admitted that boxers win victory by blood (ἁ νίκα πύκταισι δι᾽ αἵματος l. 3).[147] The struggle of the combat is accentuated by a description of the match as "tough" (σκληρᾶς παῖς ἀπὸ πυγμαχίας l. 5). It is a rare concession in either literature or epigraphy for the victor — Homer once admitted boxing was painful (ἀλεγεινός)[148] — but is "compensated" by a further display of his hard labor (βαρὺν ἐς πόνον l. 6) and success in the pankration. Here other features attributed to the Dioscuri are to be found that are missing from the honor for Colossae's Kastor. Valor and power are also features of ideal manliness.[149] Even though boxers frequently wore the marks of their battles, they were able to be stylistically conformed to Herculean facial and bodily beauty because of the strength and endurance that had been displayed — a mark of their inner quality if not their outer form.

Fourthly, there is an element implied in the previous comment that is not apparent in the Kastor inscription in its extant form. That element was nevertheless affirmed as a crucial component of athletic formation, whether by implication from the extolled values or sometimes expressly named. Dio Chrysostom in his eulogistic praise of the boxer Melancomas, began with his remarkable physique — "when he was stripped, nobody would look at anyone

145 At Sardis, one man held both offices simultaneously (*I.Sardis* 7,1.77, 78 [early 3rd century CE]) presumably implying a distinction between them. This is probably pronounced at Tripolis where Marcus Aurelius Attalianos is designated pre-eminent (πρῶτος) athlothete and agonothete for life (*SEG* 59.1403, ll. 11–14 (2nd century CE).

146 George Bean and T. R. Mitford offer this explanation for the occurrence of the verbal form (ἀθλοθεντοῦντος) in a metrical inscription honoring the sponsor of local games: "Sites Old and New in Rough Cilicia," *AS* 12 (1962): 203, commenting on *MAMA* 6.61.

147 *IG* XII 3 390 = *SEG* 14.521 = Moretti, *I.agonistiche* 55.

148 Homer *Il.* 23.653.

149 Diodorus Siculus fr. 6; Demosthenes *Or.* 61.30.

else." But he added that "beautiful as he was, he was even more remarkable for his self-control."[150] A lack of attention to bodily discipline therefore became no mere physical failing. As Paul Veyne put it, "... an idle character will lose its muscle tone, will "break training", so to speak, and become vulnerable to the diseases of the soul."[151]

The ideology of the gymnasium claimed that the institution was training up future leaders and also, more generally, shaping good citizens. Beauty, soundness and health were formed in its precincts through the hard work of constant and repetitive application.[152] The *literati* had a vested interest in promoting this aspect of athleticism given that cohesion of social structures was both the present and the future of their stature. Thus the writer of the *Ars Rhetorica* recommends the praise of champions not just for their victories but for "every success [that] came from their moderation, self-mastery and discipline."[153] Some writers admitted that such exemplary characteristics were not always found in prizewinners or aspirants, but the role of trainers and educators at the gymnasium was to cultivate the virtuous life as integrated into the athletic discipline.[154]

Occasionally this accent on excellence of moral fiber is epigraphically attested as part of the honors for a victor. At Aphrodisias, for example, a certain Adrastus II, is commemorated not simply for his success in the sacred games but also because he came from a leading family and had lived for excellence and distinction (ἄνδρα γένους πρώτου ζήσαντα πρὸς ἀρετὴν καὶ εὐδοξίαν ll. 7–10).[155] The matrix for such moral manliness was the gymnasium. Menas of Sestos, whom we have met already as a key benefactor inaugurating the mint of his city,[156] was also acclaimed in the long dedication from his city because, through his provision, he was "urging the young men through such love of glory towards discipline and love of hard work. From these, the lives of the young men as they strove for manliness were well directed towards excellence in character."[157] Whether or not one or other of these esteemed virtues — self-mastery, moderation, discipline, excellence, hard work and so on — completed the epigram for Kastor is of course impossible to know. But that these were the official if not always actual educational requirements at the gymnasium we can be

150 ἀποδυσαμένου δ' οὐκ ἔστιν ὅστις ἄλλον ἐθεᾶτο ... τοιοῦτος ὢν τὸ εἶδος ἔτι σωφρονέστερος ἦν. Dio Chrysostom *Or.* 28.6 (trans. Cohoon).

151 Veyne, "Roman Empire," 179.

152 Pausanias 6.3.6, 10.

153 ὅτι πάσας προῖκα καὶ ὅτι ἀπὸ σωφροσύνης, ἀπὸ ἐγκρατείας, ἀπὸ τῆς ἀσκήσεως τοιοῦτοι ἐγένοντο. Ps-Dionysios *Ars Rhet.* 7.292.

154 Philostratus *Gym.* 25.

155 *I.Aphrodisias Performers* 66 (1st–2nd century CE); see also *I.Aphrodisias Performers* 69, ll. 9–10, 72, ll. 18–21, 89, ll. 17–18.

156 See chapter 3.

157 Προτρεπόμενος δὲ διὰ τῆς τοιαύτης φιλοδοξίας πρὸς ἄσκησιν καὶ φιλοπονίαν τοὺς νέους, ἐξ ὧν αἱ τῶν νεωτέρων ψυχαὶ πρὸς ἀνδρείαν ἁμιλλώμεναι καλῶς ἄγονται τοῖς ἤθεσιν πρὸς ἀρετήν. *I.Sestos* 1 ll. 70–2.

confident.[158] Benjamin Gray suggests that the regularity of a training program was key —"habituation through repeated action" he calls it.[159] This is no more than what was recommended, supposedly, by a Pythagorean precept: "Lay hold of the life that is excellent, and constant engagement will make it pleasing."[160]

These two inscriptions from Colossae might be short and might attest minor accolades for athletic prowess. However, they provide a keyhole view into the wide gamut of influence of the gymnasium and its collateral displays, the games, on the civic mindset at Colossae. Cities such as Oinoanda and Aphrodisas show just how ubiquitous these celebrations of athletic prowess were and to what such success was connected. Accordingly, as Charlotte Roueché astutely observed, "It was … entirely natural for the Christians — from St Paul onwards — to adopt the language of contests to describe the endeavours and achievements of their own heroes and saints."[161] Such athletic and gymnasial terminology even entered later liturgical texts,[162] and Christ became the Lord *athlothete* distributing prizes,[163] the very official conferring the award to Kastor in this inscription.

Athletic imagery in the Letter to the Colossians?

It is, to channel Charlotte Roueché, entirely natural for Second Testament commentators to see athletic (and military) imagery in the Pauline corpus and beyond. Athletics and the military continue to be privileged in many societies (not just western ones). Our own cultural formation, not least in the ubiquitous celebration of the modern Olympic Games, predisposes us to perceive such imagery and metaphors in the biblical texts. Indeed, some have pushed that imagery to highlight just how indebted early Christian writers were to their environment in the shaping of the Christ figure and the Christ-followers.[164]

158 The ephebic rules that governed every gymnasium, could be quite detailed, governing everything from performance of the disciplines within the gymnasium to the appearance and behavior of students without. See for example, *I.Beroia* 1 (c.180 BCE); *SEG* 65.420 (Amphipolis, 24/23 BCE).

159 B. D. Gray, "Philosophy of Education and the Later Hellenistic *Polis*," in *Epigraphical Approaches to the Post-Classical* Polis edited by P. Martzavou and N. Papazarkadas (Oxford: Oxford University Press, 2013), 238–43.

160 ἑλοῦ βίον τὸν ἄριστον, ἡδὺν δ' αὐτὸν ἡ συνήθεια ποιήσει. Quoted by Plutarch *Exil.* (*Mor.*) 602C. It later became a proverb for Christian discipline: Metochites *Paid.* 25.52 cf *Chronica byzantina breviora* 88A.10.1.

161 Roueché, *Performers and Partisans*, 192.

162 *Analecta Hymnica Graeca*, Canon for December, Day 16, canon 26, ode 2.30.

163 Theoleptus of Philadelphia to Queen Irene, *Ep.* 3.36–7; Didymus the Blind, *C. Man.* 39.1097.15–16, Theodore Studites, *Ep.* 158.17.

164 See S. D. Moore, "The Beatific Vision as a Posing Exhibition: Revelation's Hypermasculine Deity," *JSNT* 60 (1996): 27–55, and *God's Beauty Parlor: And Other Queer Spaces in and around the Bible* (Stanford, CA: Stanford University Press, 2001); L. Huber, "Making Men in Rev 2–3:

To begin, I will cull those verses from the Letter to the Colossians that commentators have claimed point to athletic metaphors or allusions as well as verses that may be capable of such construal. There is a need for circumspection about the contextual resonance of words that are frequently found in multiple settings. Nonetheless, it is important to allow athletic imagery when this may be one of those settings, especially if there is a frequency of usage of relevant terms in athletics, gymnasia and the games and if an aggregate of instances can be found in a single text. Of course, there is always a communicative gap between an author, a text and an audience, but a term with a strength of association can not only be intended to trigger a world of association; it can also populate that world with the experiences of hearers, who will visualize connections in their receptive imagination.[165] After all, athletic imagery is not apparent in the Letter to Philemon, where, rather, it is the world of commerce that seems to have guided the choice of some of the terms, possibly because of the shared familiarity even partnership of Paul and Philemon.[166] The agora and the gymnasium were two of the key centers for public dealings and recognition in the ancient world.[167]

Certainly, the literary appropriation of such language was well-established by the time of the first century, so there is nothing singular in the epistolographer's craft to incorporate terminology that characterizes the gymnasium or athletic contest. The Cynic philosopher, Diogenes, gained considerable renown for comparing philosophy to the arduous contests of the Isthmian games — and claiming that he surpassed athletes with a greater victorious display of prowess.[168] Even Philo, sometimes understood to have benefitted from a gymnasial education,[169] compared ascent in philosophy to training for a contest.[170] Cicero

Reading the Seven Messages in the Bath-Gymnasiums of Asia Minor," in *Stones, Bones, and the Sacred: Essays on Material Culture and Ancient Religion in Honor of Dennis E. Smith* edited by A. H. Cadwallader (Atlanta, GA: SBL Press, 2016), 101–28.

165 See P. F. Esler, "Paul and the Agon: Understanding a Pauline Motif in its Cultural and Visual Context," in *Picturing the New Testament: Studies in Ancient Visual Images* edited by A. Weissenrieder, F. Wendt and P. von Gemünden (Tübingen: Mohr Siebeck, 2005), 356–84.

166 C. J. Martin, "The Rhetorical Function of Commercial Language in Paul's Letter to Philemon (Verse 18)," in *Persuasive Artistry. Studies in New Testament Rhetoric in Honor of George A. Kennedy* (Sheffield: JSOT Press, 1991), 321–37; J. M. Ogereau, *Paul's Koinonia with the Philippians* (WUNT 377; Tübingen: Mohr Siebeck, 2014), 36–7; P. Arzt-Grabner, "Everyday Life in a Roman Town like Colossae: the Papyrological Evidence," in *The First Urban Churches 5: Colossae, Hierapolis, and Laodicea* edited by J. R. Harrison and L. L. Welborn (Atlanta, GA; SBL, 2019), 229–31; A. H. H. Ip, *A Socio-Rhetorical Interpretation of the Letter to Philemon in Light of New Institutional Economics* (WUNT2.444; Tübingen: Mohr Siebeck, 2017). Note however the commercial metaphor used in Col 4:5.

167 Louis Robert called the gymnasium "un centre civique très important ... une seconde agora". "Recherches épigraphiques," *REA* 62 (1960): 298 n 3.

168 Cicero *Tusc. disp.* 2.41, Dio Chrysostom *Or.* 8.11–19, Philostratus *Vit. soph.* 8, 25.

169 J. R. Harrison, *Paul and the Ancient Celebrity Circuit: The Cross and Moral Transformation* (WUNT 430; Tübingen: Mohr Siebeck, 2019), 144.

170 *Somn.* 1.59, *Leg.* 3.48, *Migr.* 133.

could claim boxing for aspects of an orator's skill.[171] So the ubiquity of athletic contests and gymnasia across the Mediterranean not only yielded a plentiful store of metaphors for the literary realm, but, in such a utilization, there was a conscious or unconscious reinforcement of athletics and the games as a mechanism of habituation to the empire.[172] In this sense, when Paul crafts a sprint and boxing metaphor (1 Cor 9: 24–27),[173] there is a tacit acceptance of the cultural reinforcement practices of Empire,[174] even if he, like Diogenes, uses the arena as the base line for an *a fortiori* argument to highlight the surpassing worth of "an imperishable crown" (1 Cor 9:25).[175] The willing embrace of the gymnasium in 1 Tim 4:8 (again in an *a fortiori* comparison), let alone the cultivation of Christ as both *agonothete* and athlete in later Christian writings,[176] shows that whatever critique of athletics and the games may be allowed to Paul, it was not severe enough to quarantine the metaphorical resource from later Christian exploitation. Indeed, there is nothing in Paul's writings that matches the disdain of the Maccabean critique (2 Macc 4:9–19) or the second century physician Galen's preference for pigs over wrestlers as employees![177]

The potential list of verses from Colossians are 1:29, 2:1, 5, 15, 18, 23, 3:15, 4:12 and I will proceed to examine them in turn.

i) Col 1:28–2:1

> ὃν ἡμεῖς καταγγέλλομεν νουθετοῦντες πάντα ἄνθρωπον καὶ διδάσκοντες πάντα ἄνθρωπον ἐν πάσῃ σοφίᾳ, ἵνα παραστήσωμεν πάντα ἄνθρωπον τέλειον ἐν Χριστῷ εἰς ὃ καὶ κοπιῶ ἀγωνιζόμενος κατὰ τὴν ἐνέργειαν αὐτοῦ τὴν ἐνεργουμένην ἐν ἐμοὶ ἐν δυνάμει. Θέλω γὰρ ὑμᾶς εἰδέναι ἡλίκον ἀγῶνα ἔχω ὑπὲρ ὑμῶν καὶ τῶν ἐν Λαοδικείᾳ καὶ ὅσοι οὐκ ἑόρακαν τὸ πρόσωπόν μου ἐν σαρκί.

171 Cicero *Att.* 351.3.

172 See Jones, "Imaginary Athletics," 321–38.

173 For an analysis of the agonistic purpose of these metaphors, see S. Joubert, "1 Corinthians 9:24–27: An Agonistic Competition?" *Neotestamentica* 35 (2001): 57–68. Abe Malherbe thought that the double metaphor also operated in Phil 2:16; see A. J. Malherbe, *The Letters to the Thessalonians* (AB32B; New York: Doubleday, 2000), 195–6. The classic analysis is V. C. Pfitzner, *Paul and the Agon Motif: traditional athletic imagery in the Pauline literature* (Leiden: Brill, 1967); compare, more recently, M. Brändl, *Der Agon bei Paulus: Herkunft und Profil paulinischer Agonmetaphorik* (Tübingen: Mohr Siebeck, 2006), B. Heininger, "Soziale und politische Metaphorik im Kolosserbrief," in *Kolosser-Studien* edited by P. Müller (Göttingen: Neukirchener, 2009), 65–73.

174 See Z. M. Torlone, "Writing Arenas: Roman Authors and Their Games," in *A Companion to Sport and Spectacle in Greek and Roman Antiquity* edited by P. Christesen and D. G. Kyle (Oxford: Oxford University Press, 2013), 412–21.

175 See generally Cadwallader, "Paul and the Games," 376–83. On the tensions in Paul's approach to his environment in this passage, see J. R. Harrison, "Paul and the Athletic Ideal in Antiquity: A Case Study in Wrestling with Word and Image," in *Paul's World* edited by S. E. Porter (Leiden: Brill, 2008), 88–111.

176 Eusebius *Hist. eccl.* 5.1.42 (athlete); John Argyropulus to Pope Nicholas *Ep.* 140.18 (agonothete and prize-giver).

177 Galen *Parv. Pil.* 905K; compare also 909K–910K.

Him (the Christ) we proclaim, monitoring every person and teaching every person by every wise method,[178] *in order that we might present every person honed in Christ. For this I labor, fighting with his energy that he powerfully unleashes in me. I want you to know how great a contestation I have accepted on your behalf and also for those in Laodikeia — even those who have not seen my face in the flesh.*

Vic Pfitzner saw the mention of contending (ἀγωνιζόμενος) in Col 1:29 as consequential on the desire expressed in the preceding verse to present each one as perfect.[179] In this sense, there is a tie between these verses (1:28–2:1) marking them as the center of the larger section, Col 1:24–2:5. But by doing so, a context is given for the first reference to the *agôn* in Colossians — it is educational, one of the major emphases of the institution of the gymnasium. Once this context is allowed to direct the interpretation of verse 28 along educational lines, a number of integral elements can surface.

Firstly, the emphasis on proclaiming the Christ is framed in terms completely at home with the role of a *gymnasiarch*, sometimes narrowed in focus to the more specialized role of the *ephebarch*[180] — monitoring and teaching (νουθετοῦντες … καὶ διδάσκοντες).[181] The combination of verbs is known in other writers. Significantly, for Dio Chrysostom, the combination exemplified a well-performing and accountable Popular Assembly (the *Dêmos*) — that is the regulatory body of a city's citizens.[182] This hierarchical position over others is clear in other examples of the combination of these words, as when (Pseudo-)Plutarch writes of a statesman or philosopher delivering a lecture (an education setting strongly implying a lecture room or other location in the gymnasium), which is described as teaching or admonishing or discoursing on the gods, the citizenry or the rulers.[183]

Secondly, the goal of such training is maturity (τέλειον), precisely the graduation standard identified, for example, for one Agreophon of Kaunos in Caria, in his progress from boyhood to youth (ephebe) to adult. This maturity was directed into a large-hearted generosity for his homeland,[184] and service geared to repli-

178 I agree with Paul Foster (*Colossians* [BNTC; London: T & T Clark, 2016], 230) that the phrase ἐν πάσῃ σοφίᾳ refers to pedagogy rather than content. It indicates the faithful exercise of responsibility by the Christian *ephebarch/gymnasiarch*. This does not delimit the semantics of σοφία elsewhere in the letter.

179 Pfitzner, *The Agon Motif*, 109–10.

180 *CIG* 3059 (Teos, 2nd century BCE), *BCH* 1889.334.4 (southern Phrygia, 115 BCE).

181 Plato often added "punishing" (κολάζω): *Prot.* 323d, *Euthyd.* 5b, which, as is clear from the ephebic regulations which have survived, was also part of the training of boys, giving way to fines as the boys became older. I have used "monitoring" rather than admonishing here to try to capture the corrective oversight associated with the role of *ephebarch*.

182 Dio Chrysostom *Or.* 32.27.

183 (Ps-?)Plutarch *Lib. ed.* (*Mor.*) 46B–C.

184 ὧν τε αὐτὸς Ἀγρεοφῶν ἀπὸ τῆς ἐν παισὶν καὶ ἐφήβοις ἡλικίας ἀρξάμενος φιλοτείμως καὶ ἐν ἀνδράσιν τέλειον και μεγαλόψυχον ἐπλήρωσεν ἀεὶ τὴν εἰς τὴν πατρίδα διάθεσιν *I.Kaunos* 30, ll. 7–8, minimally reconstructed (2nd century CE).

cating such a model in his offices as *gymnasiarch* and *agonothete*, amongst others (ll. 8, 11). But that maturity is defined in terms of manhood (ἐν ἀνδράσιν τέλειον), not simply in terms of the final age-group for males at the gymnasium but also in his description as a most praiseworthy and noble *man* (ἀνδρὸς ἀξιολογωτάτου καὶ εὐγενεστάτου l. 2). After all, maturity — "perfection" as sometimes translated here and in the Letter to the Colossians — was defined in the gymnasium in terms of *andreia*, manliness, "honed" in body and mind. The presentation ceremony in the course of the gymnasium year not only awarded various prizes for various disciplines and achievements but also exhibited the new graduates from the ephebes.[185] This is precisely the affirmation made in the Plutarchian discourse on "Listening to Lectures" (sometimes titled "On the Education of Children"). The training of a person has, in the estimation of the writer, a special emphasis on philosophy "which alone can bestow on young men the manly and mature arraignment consistent with reason" (ἣ μόνη τὸν ἀνδρεῖον καὶ τέλειον ὡς ἀληθῶς ἐκ λόγου τοῖς νέοις περιτίθησι κόσμον).[186] *Andreia* was a lesson; so Plutarch argued.[187]

But the writer of Colossians qualifies this manly emphasis in a triplet that indicates where his focus lay, namely, "every person" (3× πάντα ἄνθρωπον).[188] Aside from a rhetorical device ("anadiplosis")[189] that delivers a literary equivalent to habituation through repetition, there is a progression from "monitoring/admonishing", to "teaching", to "presenting." It is reminiscent in structure of the succession of metaphors in Col 2:6–7 that were noted for its processional sequence of a foundation story celebration.[190] The articulation may indicate the formal stages of development in gymnasial education (from boys to ephebes to neoi) with its reflection in the larger athletic games (boys, youths, adults). There is too little expansion of the metaphors — monitoring, teaching, presenting — to be over-confident, but such stages *are* reflected in the ephebic regulations and elsewhere. At the very least, they are an illustrative piece of the education which has spawned the metaphors of the gymnasium and the games. Moreover, the Colossians writer, in entering a renegotiation of the purpose of education as Christ-formation, may have been a participant in a wider movement

---

185 *IG* II^2 1043 l. 25 (μετὰ τῶν ἐφήβων παραστήσαντος) (Athens, 38/7 BCE).

186 (Ps-?)Plutarch *Lib. ed.* (*Mor.*) 37F. James Dunn considers the "perfect man" a theme in Greek philosophy but takes eschatological fulfilment as the meaning here rather than a Christian alternative to gymnasial graduation. See *The Epistles to the Colossians and to Philemon* (NIGTC; Grand Rapids, MN: Eerdmans, 1996), 126.

187 Plutarch *Adol. poet. aud.* (*Mor.*) 31F.

188 Most commentators focus on the πάντα as a derivative of the multiple prior uses of πᾶς in Colossians 1 and so accent the universality of the author's vision — see, for example, E. Lohse, *Colossians and Philemon* (Hermeneia: Philadelphia: Fortress, 1971), 77, J. L. Sumney, *Colossians: A Commentary* (NTL; Louisville, KY: WJKP, 2008), 108. This obscures the metaphorical specifics operating in the verse, with each successive instance of πάντα ἄνθρωπον governed by its own verb.

189 *Rhet. Her.* 4.38, Quintilian *Inst.* 9.3.28.

190 See chapter 3.

in provincial society. Many other spheres of life in the first century of the new era initiated by Augustus were in the process of negotiation.[191]

Paul Foster apologizes that "the gendered language [of "every man"] is preserved to reflect the author's ancient cultural perspectives."[192] It must be admitted that ἄνθρωπος can occur in a gymnasial context, but it is rare. In Colossians, the word always indicates the generic sweep of humanity, even when it admits a context of patriarchal cultural structures (ἀνθρωπάρεσκοι, Col 3:22 cf 2:8, 22, 3:9, 23). The Letter to the Ephesians, by contrast, returns the imagery less critically to the gymnasium, even as the author appears to be reliant on Colossians as his *Vorlage*. Faith and knowledge of the Son of God are now measured in andreic not anthropic terms — εἰς ἄνδρα τέλειον — for which the template is the Christ (Eph 4:13).[193] The Letter to the Colossians is "corrected" back towards the gymnasial pinnacle by the writer to the Ephesians: manhood rather than humanity.

So, for all that we are entitled to hear and see a gymnasium font for the imagery, in Colossians at least, it is not allowed to remain unchallenged, even in Christian circles. The hefty brawn of a heliotic Colossus, encapsulated, as we have seen, in the pseudo-etymology that civic authorities crafted for the city's name, has been displaced by an anthropomorphism geared to Christ. A further qualification comes in the repetition of the participles νουθετοῦντες … διδάσκοντες in reverse order in Col 3:16. In this instance, the *ephebarch/gymnasiarch* has disappeared and the responsibility is handed to the community to provide the teaching and monitoring. It is likely that many in the group(s) of Christ-followers at Colossae had no access to the gymnasium, so gymnasial metaphors, whilst they can be assumed as pervasive within the background reservoir of local knowledge, would only be directly accessible for imaginative expansion to a few. However, the implication is that the Christ-group, in its/their teaching and monitoring/admonishing function, has become an alternative to the elite gymnasium — in content, structure and, given the virtue list of Col 3:12, purpose.

A second reference to the gymnasium comes in the next verse, again operating with a similar dialectic of utilization and critique. The agonistic effort is intensified by a polyptotonic device:[194] κατὰ τὴν ἐνέργειαν αὐτοῦ τὴν

---

191 See J. Connolly, "Like the Labors of Heracles: Andreia and Paideia in Greek Culture under Rome," in *Andreia: Studies in Manliness and Courage in Classical Antiquity* edited by R. M. Rosen and I. Sluiter (Leiden: Brill, 2003), 287–317.

192 Foster, *Colossians*, 229.

193 It seems to me that Margaret MacDonald's efforts to see the Ephesians terminology as a "general reference to persons" (*Colossians, Ephesians* [SP; Collegeville, MI: Liturgical Press, 2008], 293) forces a reading that ἀνήρ struggles to bear, especially given that ἄνθρωπος is ready at hand (cf Eph 2:15) and lay in the Ephesian writer's *Vorlage*. See A. T. Lincoln, *Ephesians* (WBC 42; Waco, TX: Word, 1990), 256. The Ephesians reference seems to concertina what John's Gospel wanted to separate (Jn 1:29–34).

194 See M. R. Leroux, "Repetition, Progression, and Persuasion in Scripture," *Neotestamentica* 29 (1995): 8–10. Other examples in Colossians are found in Col 1:11, 2:11, 19. The restrained use of such devices is in accord with the recommendations of the rhetoricians.

ἐνεργουμένην, "with his energy that he energizes." It is another literary device of repetition,[195] which, with the first example (anadiplosis) seems to reflect the honed, disciplined education of the author, almost certainly derived from the gymnasium. Of course, constant energy sacrifice is the regimen of exercise where learning develops and health is maintained. It is athletic but more generally evokes the exercising that the gymnasium supported.

But as the Hippocratic Corpus noted, such straining (κοπιᾶν) through exercise/labor (πόνος) can have different effects on the practitioner depending on how hardened the body is.[196] And here the writer has made at least two significant adjustments to the conventional gymnasial ethos. The *ephebarch/gymnasiarch* persona of verse 28 (monitoring, teaching, presenting) has given way in verse 29 to a fellow-athlete grunting through the habituation exercises of the training regimen. But even more inverting than this disturbance to hierarchy is that the energy store is not his own but that of Christ/God (the agent is ambiguous). Here, a trace of Pauline inheritance can be seen (cf 1 Cor 15:10) but in a gymnasial envisaging, a significant challenge is mounted. Deference to the god(s) of the gymnasium was a constant practice, a reminder of the unreachable image to strive towards in whatever disciplines were conducted in that setting. Sacrifices to Hermes, Herakles, the Dioscuri and other divine patrons were a regular part of the routine of membership and control of the gymnasium.[197] Hard work was to be for the benefit of the homeland;[198] it was an expectation of the gods in "their" venue.[199] But the Christian critical mimesis displaces these deities and lowers the overseeing officials to the level of participant student.

The allusion to the trial of competition in 1:29 is repeated in Col 2:1,[200] in another example of polyptonon but with a peculiar construction that hints beyond mere word play. The expression ἀγῶνα ἔχω occurs in one other place, also metaphorical, of the holding of an annual contest associated with the feast day of Aphrodite.[201] But the *agôn* is a word especially associated with Herakles and his labors, from which, according to the orator Lysias, the Olympic

195 Longinus 23.1; Quintilian *Inst.* 9.3.37.

196 (Ps-?)Hippocrates, *De diaet.* 66. This must qualify Martin Brändl's conclusion that there is no close connection between κοπιᾶν and ancient athletic imagery: *Der Agon bei Paulus*, 251–3. In any case, the word's inclusion in the agonistic setting of Col 1:28–2:1 suggests that it is quite at home in a gymnasial context.

197 See, for example, *IG* V 1 938 (Kythera, nd), Rizakis *Achaïe* III.8 (Dyme, 2nd to 1st century BCE), 62 (Pharai, early 2nd century BCE), SEG 37.508 (Antigoneia, 3rd to 2nd century BCE).

198 *SEG* 20.101 (Cestrus, imperial period).

199 Compare C. R. Seitz, *Colossians* (BTCB; Grand Rapids, MN; Baker, 2014), 111 who, in his reference to Eric Liddell (in the film, *Chariots of Fire*!) seems to shift the Christian God to a gymnasial Hermes.

200 So, amongst many, B. Witherington III, *The Letters to Philemon, the Colossians, and the Ephesians: A Socio-Rhetorical Commentary on the Captivity Epistles* (Grand Rapids, MN: Eerdmans, 2007), 148.

201 Alciphron *Ep.* 4.4.

Games sprang.[202] The writer portrays Paul engaged in a Herculean contest for the Colossians and the Laodikeians. Having moved from the *ephebarch* in 1:28 to the fellow-athlete/exerciser in 1:29, he now becomes the exemplar of agonistic endeavor (later to be replicated by Epaphras in Col 4:12, 13 — with prayer as the designated discipline).

But this athletic exemplar is flawed in terms of the usual expectations laid down in ephebic regulations, precisely because the competitor is absent. ἐν σαρκί is used in Phmn 16 as indicative of Onesimus's returned presence to Philemon, even as a brother. Here the οὐχ cancels presence. The expression (καὶ ὅσοι οὐχ ἑόρακαν) τὸ πρόσωπόν μου ἐν σαρκί is sometimes viewed as pleonastically superfluous so that some translations (for example, the RSV) omit ἐν σαρκί.[203] Consequently, the major point of the expression, in this agonistic context, is missed.

A significant part of the ephebic regulations attends to the problem of absenteeism — with beatings and fines the remedies devised to compel attendance.[204] No contest, training for a contest, or educational or physical exercise can be entered if the body is absent. The problem of not seeing Paul was an issue that

---

202 Lysias, *Or.* 33.1–2. His language is significant: ἀγῶνα … σωμάτων ἐποίησε.

203 See Dunn, *Colossians and Philemon*, 129. Few commentators address the grammatical anomaly in the verse where καὶ ὅσοι defies a translation "and on behalf of all those …". This alone precludes any sense of a universal Pauline mission (contra D. M. Hay, *Colossians* [Nashville: Abingdon, 2000], 78 among many). Lukas Bormann rightly criticizes those who demand *der kriminalistischen Raffinesse zu konstruieren* from the writer such as would support this and other tenuous theories: *Der Brief des Paulus an die Kolosser* (ThHK X/1; Leipzig: Evangelische Verlagsanstalt, 2012), 117. Rather, the expression is to be taken as referring only to those in Laodikeia and Colossae who have not encountered Paul in the flesh, that is, other than Epaphras, Onesimus, Philemon, Archippos — presumably not the majority of those in view. See M. Barth and H. Blanke, *Colossians* (AB; New York: Doubleday, 1994), 273–5. The parallels of καὶ ὅσοι as a summation of a previous, more detailed naming (Acts 4:6, Rev 18:17) are of limited assistance here precisely because there is no violation of grammatical congruence. (See J. B. Lightfoot, *Colossians and Philemon* [London: Macmillan, 1890[9]], 170.) No commentator has noted that there are some parallels to the use of (καὶ) ὅσοι … as a parenthetical nominative even though the preceding case to which the general indefinite demonstrative is linked is not in the nominative. So, for example, one defixio begins καταδέω τὸς ἐνθαῦτα ἐνγεγραμμένος καὶ ἄνδρας καὶ γυναῖκας ὅσοι ἐνθαῦτα ἐνγεγραμένοι εἰσίν πρὸς Ἑρμῆν Κάτοχον καὶ Γῆν καὶ Περσεφόνειαν … "I bond, writing hereunto, (the names) both of man and of woman and whosoever are written herein to chthonic Hermes, Gaia and Persephone …" (*SEG* 37.214A, ll. 1–3 [Athens, 400–350 BCE]). See also, *IGR* 1.944, ll. 11, 23 (Carthage, 2nd–3rd century CE), *SEG* 54.397 (Kerameikos, 400–375 BCE). For an example that is not from a *defixio*, see *SEG* 14.63, l. 10 (Attica, c.275 BCE). These examples are not exhaustive but suggest that this is a parenthetical nominative which is tied to the preceding detail and hence is not "a meaningless grammatical anomaly" (Barth-Blanke, *Colossians*, 274). On parenthetical nominatives, see A. T. Robertson, *A Grammar of the Greek New Testament in the Light of Historical Research* (Nashville, TN: Broadman, 1934), 460; D. B. Wallace, *Greek Grammar: Beyond the Basics* (Grand Rapids, MN: Zondervan, 1996), 53–4.

204 See, for example, *SEG* 65.420, l. 19 (Amphipolis, 24/23 BCE).

confronted the early church (Acts 20:25, 38). Here, as also in 2:5, the extent of the agonistic endeavor (ἡλίκον ἀγῶνα) is revealed, namely, that it is a contest that cannot be entered in the flesh, with the body — *the very antithesis of gymnasial culture*. The writer of the letter, for all the reliance on agonistic and gymnastic imagery, has configured the absence of Paul to advantage — now "in the spirit" (τῷ πνεύματι as in 2:5), he is empowered for yet greater struggles on behalf of the Christ-followers in the Lycus Valley. The accent on the male body as critical to the civic virtues and elite identity,[205] has been destabilized, just as surely as rhetoricians and philosophers, happy to use the imagery of the *agôn*, yet promoted their own disciplines as the fulfillment of its purpose. In this sense, there was a contest over the contest, and the writer of the Letter to the Colossians was one of the competitors.

ii) Col 2:5

εἰ γὰρ καὶ τῇ σαρκὶ ἄπειμι, ἀλλὰ τῷ πνεύματι σὺν ὑμῖν εἰμι, χαίρων καὶ βλέπων ὑμῶν τὴν τάξιν καὶ τὸ στερέωμα τῆς εἰς Χριστὸν πίστεως ὑμῶν.

For even if I am absent in the flesh, yet I am with you in the spirit, rejoicing at seeing[206] *your orderliness and the durability of your faith towards Christ.*[207]

It is a commonplace among Second Testament commentators to discern military metaphors incorporated here: τάξις and στερεώμα. The usual cross-references are Xenophon's *Anabasis* (1.2.18) and 1 Macc 9:14 (of a fortification) respectively.[208] There is no debate that both expressions *can* be used in a military context, but commentators are divided over how much exclusivity, and, therefore, weight of allusion are to be granted. Earlier commentators (with some later echoes) built up the army associations, even considering Paul's experience of soldiers in his imprisonment(s) as the inspiration.[209] More recent interpretations have downplayed "martial nuances".[210] Στερεώμα in particular is quite short of military examples; far more frequently it refers

205 See O. van Nijf, "Athletics, Andreia and the Askêsis-Culture in the Roman East," in *Andreia*, 284.

206 Here I follow Margaret MacDonald's argument that there is a causal connection between the two participles: *Colossians, Ephesians*, 87. Murray Harris called them a hendiadys: *Colossians and Philemon* (Nashville, TN: B&H Academic, 2010), 79.

207 It is worth noting that τῆς εἰς Χριστὸν πίστεως ὑμῶν is a unique encapsulation of Christian faith in the Second Testament, let alone the Pauline Corpus (Dunn, *Colossians and Philemon*, 135). The closest parallel is Gal 2:16, but the notion of orientation (εἰς Χριστὸν) is similar to Phmn 5. See Foster, *Colossians*, 240; Lohse, *Colossians and Philemon*, 84.

208 For the imprecise military reference of τάξις, see H. J. Mason, *Greek Terms for Roman Institutions: A Lexicon and Analysis* (Toronto: Hakkert, 1974), 163.

209 Lightfoot, *Colossians and Philemon*, 174; MacDonald, *Colossians, Ephesians*, 87. One wonders at the thrall of empire in the nineteenth century.

210 Foster, *Colossians*, 241; S. McKnight, *The Letter to the Colossians* (NICNT; Grand Rapids, MN; Eerdmans, 2018), 214.

to the firmament of the heavens,[211] though Philo specifically made a somatic comparison.[212] Greater confidence about military associations is expressed over Col 2:15. In that verse, a three-fold verbal succession is given again, this time culminating in θριαμβεύσας, a word that is almost completely restricted in its usage to a Roman triumph or a Roman victory,[213] even in its limited occurrence in inscriptions.[214] Even though the other two verbs — ἀπεκδύομαι, δειγματίζω — are also well at home in an athletic-gymnasial context, the nigh-exclusive parameters of θριαμβεύσας I now think determines the metaphorical extraction.[215]

However, in this case, given the gymnasial-athletic-games connection already found,[216] it would be blinkered to restrict the examination by excluding military associations and thereby miss a potential fecundity of meaning, whether or not we tie that meaning to authorial intent or audiential reception or simply potential contextual informant. It should be noted that athletic training was originally entangled with and preparation for military deployment. There was even one race at a number of games run in armor (the *hoplitodromos*).

There were troop recruitments and movements throughout the province;[217] we have two material witnesses to their encroaching on Colossian experience. One is the tribune cohort surrounding the pan-Hellenic tour of Hadrian (129 CE) that included Colossae in the itinerary (*IGR* 4.869). The second is a reference to provision for military requisites that the supposed brother of Heliodoros organized during the time of Antoninus Pius (*IGR* 4.870, l. 9) — always a testy imposition for locals. However, under Roman rule, in the gymnasia "military training … was an anachronism without practical consequence,"[218] even if military symbolism and military-related exercises and events continued. It is likely that the predominant, positive experience of inhabitants of Asia in the first century, was not of the army but rather of games at various levels. At the very least it reinforces Pfitzner's admission that military and athletic imag-

211 Gen 1:7–8, 20, Ps 18:2; Melito *Pasch.* 615; A. Audollent, *Defixionum Tabellae* (Paris: Fontemoing, 1904), 325–30, nr. 242, ll. 7–8, 16–17, 21–22 (Carthage, 3rd century CE, possibly influenced by Christian ideas); cf *SEG* 54.1601 (Dura Europos, 2nd to 3rd century CE).

212 Philo *Opif.* 36.

213 Plutarch traces the pomp and ceremony of a Roman triumph back to the period of the kings: *Rom.* 16. Very occasionally "triumph" is allowed for non-Roman military victories but it is clear that a Roman template is being applied. Only in later Christian writings is θρίαμβος/θριαμβεύω applied to athletic imagery.

214 See *IG* XII 4,2 951 (Kos 48–54 CE).

215 I had earlier raised the possibility of a gladiatorial context for Col 2:15 but gladiator inscriptions, with their often-athletic cast, emphasize victory (νίκη) rather than triumph (θρίαμβος); see Cadwallader, "Case of a Gladiator," 61.

216 This conjunction is not merely a heuristic device, but was recognized in the period.

217 See S. Mitchell, *Anatolia: Land, Men and Gods in Asia Minor* (Oxford: Oxford University Press, 2 vols, 1993), vol 1, 118–42.

218 A. Chaniotis, *et al.* editorial comment on *SEG* 65.420 (Amphipolis, 24/23 BCE).

ery can blur.[219] As we shall see, this blending of athlete and soldier actually had its own personification — the gladiator.

The focus for our purposes here is τάξις. In one satirical piece, Lucian of Samosata played with the arrangement of positions and competitors in athletic games, where letter-numbered lots were drawn:

> You have spoken as if all the letters are definitely written one after the other — that is, alpha first, beta second, and so on, according to the order until the number of athletes is complete from them into one group. I grant you that this is done at Olympia.[220]

Even more pertinent is a series of Letters from Hadrian to the international association of Dionysiac artists at Alexandria Troas written in late 134 CE.[221] These letters were inscribed on stone so that the contents might be publicly disseminated, a measure expressly permitted (read: encouraged) within the inscription itself in one place (συνχωρῶ δὲ ὑμεῖν, ἔνθα ἄν βούλησθε, καὶ στήλλαις ἐνγράψαι αὐτά, ὡς πᾶσιν εἴη γνώριμα, "but I permit you to inscribe them on stelai wherever you wish, so that these arrangements may be known to everyone" — ll. A55–56) and expressly commanded in another (l. B83). The πᾶσιν in this inscription would doubtless include any passer-by (such as the writers and recipients of letters that made their way into the Second Testament) let alone those organizers, athletes, musicians and the like who were directly affected by Hadrian's directives. Hadrian laid out a series of requirements regarding the organization and prosecution of awards in various contests, and, notably, in the various cities (αἱ πόλεις, l. B83 cf l. C87) in which they were held. Hence, the letters are less about the Dionysiac association as the events in which its members (and others) compete. The substantive τάξις, its cognate verb τάσσω and a number of compounds make regular appearances in the three letters — these are Hadrian's directives on the proper ordering of "sacred" and "crowned" events (ll. A6–7). The high status of these events may have meant that copies of the letters were not set up in Colossae, though the witness to the cult of Dionysos at Colossae is strong. However, some of the regulations governing the calendar of competitions and the expectations of organizers (*agonothetes*) would have been unavoidable. Indeed, local competitions are mentioned in the letters — *inter alia*, those of the Laodikeians and Hierapolitans and "any other cities from which embassies were sent" (ll. A75–6) — regarding the dates assigned for their staging.

---

219 V. C. Pfitzner, "Was St Paul a Sports Enthusiast? Realism and Rhetoric in Pauline Athletic Metaphors," in *Sports and Christianity: Historical and Contemporary Perspectives*, edited by N. J. Watson and J. Parker (London: Routledge, 2012), 90–1.

220 Σὺ μὲν γὰρ ὡς ἑξῆς πάντων γραφομένων γραμμάτων εἴρηκας, οἷον πρώτου τοῦ Α, δευτέρου δὲ τοῦ Β καὶ κατὰ τὴν τάξιν, ἄχρι ἂν ἐς ἓν αὐτῶν τελευτήσῃ ὁ ἀριθμὸς τῶν ἀθλητῶν· καὶ δίδωμί σοι Ὀλυμπίασιν οὕτω γίγνεσθαι. Lucian *Hermot.* 43.

221 *SEG* 56.1359. See, especially, C. P. Jones, "Three New Letters of the Emperor Hadrian," *ZPE* 161 (2007): 147–56, where a corrected Greek text and English translation is to be found.

The “ordering” contained in the letters touches: the allotted contributions (συντάξεις ll. A26–7) to be paid, in cash not kind, and on time; the pairings of whip-bearers to chastize an under-performing or mis-performing competitor to proceed to their disciplining task in order (τάξει l. A29); the regulating of the sources/means of administering and financing some particular aspect of the games (τάξαι πόρους l. A40); and perhaps most important of all, the (re-)arrangement of the calendar of major competitions across Asia, Greece and in Rome (Ὡς ἔδοξέ μοι τετάχθαι τοὺς ἀγῶνας l. B60). Hadrian underscored that the dates and sequence of local games had to be accommodated (τῷ καιρῷ τῆς τάξεως l. B77) to those established for the preeminent competitions. The inscription, combining three epistles, emphasizes how much “order” was attached to the games, their timing and administration and to the competitors. While it must be admitted that “order” is known in a number of contexts, it is in the athletic realm that one of the most detailed (and familiar) demonstrations occurs — in the terminology as much as in the execution. The use of such terminology by Hadrian was no invention.[222]

Such a level of disciplined regulation was not a sudden impost but rather an outgrowth of the order already expected in the training and exercise afforded at the “nursery” of such local, regional and international events — the gymnasium. In Plutarch’s accolades for the Republican Cato, he praised the discipline he retained in his old age, describing him as “like a successful athlete, he maintained his training regimen” (ὥσπερ ἀθλητὴν νικηφόρον, ἐγκαρτεροῦντα τῇ τάξει τῆς ἀσκήσεως).[223] In fact, “good order” was one of the expected and rewarded behaviors of the gymnasium.

At the Beroia “awards ceremony” (the *Hermaia*) for the ephebes and neaniskoi/neoi, prizes were given for a variety of excellences — body-building/physical conditioning (εὐεξία), hard-work (φιλοπονία) and most particularly, discipline/good behavior (εὐταξία).[224] Angelos Chaniotis has emphasized that “The cardinal virtue of ephebic education is *eutaxia*, ‘discipline’, the virtue that permits the introduction of young people to ordered life.”[225] But as John Ma perceived, the accent on that virtue is particularly critical as the means of controlling the dangers that beset liminal groups, or groups in liminal situations.[226] There is some awareness of the nature of these dangers in the Beroian gymnasiarch regulations, especially as between age groups — the youths are not to go in among the boys nor to

222 See, for example, *Syll.* 3.821D (Delphi, 90 CE).
223 Plutarch *Cato* 4.3.
224 *I.Beroia* 1, l.B47 (before 168/7 BCE).
225 A. Chaniotis, *War in the Hellenistic World: A Social and Cultural History* (Oxford: Blackwell, 2008), 51.
226 J. Ma, “‘Oversexed, Overpaid and Over Here’: A Response to Angelos Chaniotis,” in *Army and Power in the Ancient World* edited by A. Chaniotis and P. Ducrey (Stuttgart: Franz Steiner, 2002), 115.

chat them up.[227] And there are strict controls on when boys, youths or ephebes are permitted to disrobe (ἀπεγδύεσθαι, l. B.1)[228] or oil down (ἀλειφέσθω μηθείς l. B4). Undesirables (slaves, disabled, drunks and others) were barred from disrobing (μὴ ἐγδυέσθω l. B27) or any oiling down (ll. B30). There was clearly a concern that non-citizens or reprobates might exert an even greater unfavourable influence within the gymnasium than what might occur between the different age-groups of citizens.[229]

The situation of a fledgling religious group — the Christ-followers of Colossae and Laodikeia — might bring different concerns to mind (Col 2:8) but the writer similarly sees the liminality of a new formation with a fraught relationship with wider society as something requiring a "gymnasiarchal" eye. In such an imaginary construction, "Paul" appears as the *ephebarch/gymnasiarch* watching over the virtuous development of trainees. His absence (in the flesh) is not to be interpreted as a negligence of duty but, as we have seen, is intensified by the accent on "in the spirit", albeit, no doubt, identified as informed through those able to be present as his invigilators (for example, Epaphras, Archippos, perhaps Nympha). The ephebic laws recognize that those responsible for oversight receive reports as well as observe in person.[230] Indeed, those whom the gymnasiarch appoints are to be obeyed as the gymnasiarch (καθάπερ καὶ τῷ γυμνασιάρχῃ l. B8). The direct observers therefore act as extensions of the recognized authority and, in the presence of members, shape their experience of that absent authority figure.[231]

iii) Col 2:18

> μηδεὶς ὑμᾶς καταβραβευέτω …
>
> *Do not let anyone bring judgment against you …*

When Joseph Barber Lightfoot brought his forensic historical and linguistic skills to Col 2:18 he was unequivocal in asserting that here was a further athletic metaphor — "The Christian's career is the contest of the stadium".[232] The present imperative καταβραβευέτω was taken as an indication of oppositional false teachers (in the plural) who were intent on robbing the Christ-follow-

227 εἰς τοὺς παῖδας μὴ εἰσπορευέσθω τῶν νεανίσκων μηθείς, μηδὲ λαλείτω τοῖς παισίν ll. B13–14.

228 I follow the reading adopted by Louis Robert here rather than ἐπεγδύεσθαι (*BE* 1978.435). The first letter is uncertain.

229 See O. Babou, *Children in the Hellenistic World: Statues and Representation* (Oxford: Oxford University Press, 2015), 35.

230 *I.Beroia* 1, ll. B19–20, 30–31. When the gymnasiarch was a woman, this may have been a necessity.

231 On the issue of the representation(s) of Paul, see the succinct and insightful comments of Janice Capel Anderson, *Colossians: Authorship, Rhetoric, and Code* (London: T & T Clark, 2019), 25–31.

232 Lightfoot, *Colossians and Philemon*, 193.

ers at Colossae of their prize of salvation. The antagonists' method was not to deliver a false judgement to that effect — that was the injunction of Col 2:16, Μὴ οὖν τις ὑμᾶς κρινέτω a meaning, for Lightfoot, that belonged rather to a cognate, παραβαβεύειν, which carried the sense of deprivation. Rather this verse (2:18) indicated foul play, the exercise of "trickery" to upset the runner (which in Lightfoot's imagination it was, rather than a boxer!). He gave three examples of such trickery — thrusting themselves in the way, tripping up their targets or otherwise impeding them.

To establish his case, Lightfoot relied on the usage in an oration of Demosthenes, the fourth century (BCE) Athenian orator.[233] It is a singular usage in Demosthenes' corpus,[234] and in fact is not his term but the language used in a deposition supposedly from witnesses supporting his case which, along with five other such submissions, is incorporated into the oration. Lightfoot saw the usage as close to that of the author of Colossians. Paul Foster read the same passage as confirming his judgment that the meaning was "condemned".[235] However, two points need to be made:

Firstly, all the depositions in Demosthenes' *Oration 21* have been shown to be later additions, belonging probably to the late Hellenistic period. That critical assessment was made as early as 1844 and has, by and large, been accepted by classicists since.[236] This suggests that the word καταβραβεύω, itself unable to gain approval as Attic, belongs to a later invention. Significantly, the word παραβραβεύω, to which Lightfoot drew attention,[237] does occur in an honorific inscription for Aristonidas (the name is not certain) mounted by the Chrysaoric koinon in the region of Stratonikeia in Caria. It is dated to about 190 BCE and, although fragmentary, seems to indicate Aristonidas' dealings on behalf of the Stratonikeians in a dispute resolution in Rhodes. The judgment was finally won, without unfair interference or inciting partisan pressure (μὴ παραβραβευθῆναι μηδὲ καταστασιασθῆναι).[238] The earliest use of καταβραβεύω for which a date can be confidently given comes from a papyrus archive from Pathyris, a small town to the south of Thebes in Egypt. The archive includes court dealings, contracts, family ties and inheritances, and temple oaths.[239] One papyrus, dated

233 Demosthenes *Or.* 21.93.

234 The scholiast Ulpian (of unknown date, but possibly early medieval) identified the word as occurring nowhere else in Demosthenes (οὐδαμοῦ ἀλλαχοῦ εὕρηται παρὰ τῷ Δημοσθένει).

235 Foster, *Colossians*, 287, followed by A. Asano, "Colossians," in *T & T Clark Social Identity Commentary on the New Testament* edited by J. B. Tucker and A. Kuecker (London: T & T Clark, 2020), 413.

236 See E. M. Harris, "The *Against Meidias* (Dem. 21)," in *The Documents in the Attic Orators: Laws and Decrees in the Public Speeches of the Demosthenic Corpus* edited by M. Canevaro (Oxford: Oxford University Press, 2013), 209.

237 Lightfoot cited Plutarch *Vit. pud.* (*Mor.*) 535C.

238 *I.Stratonikeia* 1418 = *SEG* 53.1229, l. 54.

239 V. Wyns, "Happiness in the Kingdom of the Cleopatras: Examining Government Influence on Quality of Life in Hellenistic Egypt (332–30 BC)," *Historická Sociologie* 2 (2018): 21.

134 BCE, contains an account of court proceedings involving a dispute over land inheritance. It was briefly mentioned by Kent Yinger but dismissed as "too broken to decipher the meaning of the verb."[240] A new edition has assisted recovery.[241] The key section of a long record reads ὅθεν καταβεβραβευμένοι [...]ήρου συνεδρίου ἀξιοῦμεν,[242] "since we, those who have received a negative judgment, request of the council ..." thence to a petition for a reversal of an earlier decision. The use of the word here, in a judicial setting, clearly indicates a judgment against a person. The notion of "judgment" coheres with a minor magistrate's office, the *brabeutes*, who is sometimes to be found as an arbitrator of disputes in small towns, villages and estates.[243] In a recently discovered inscription, *brabeutai* fulfill the function of executors of a testamentary foundation.[244] When we return to the deposition added at a later date to Demosthenes' *Oration 21*, the account is about the manipulation by Meidias to gain a judgment against Strato, implementing his removal from office (and his loss of citizenship). Meidias had initially secured Strato's appointment as judge in what would be a long-running feud with Demosthenes. So confident was he that Strato would find for him, that Medias did not appear at the hearing nor submit relevant documents, such was — in the actual prosecution by Demosthenes — the hubris of the man. He had made a cataclysmic error and sought retribution against his own man, at least so the deposition runs.[245] The whole setting is judicial, even if the deposition belongs to later times.

b) The accent on an athletic backdrop for the term seems to derive from the substantive βραβεῖον and the use of the simplex βραβεύω in Col 3:15 (itself not assuredly drawn from the stadium — see below). The substantive is a common word used in the athletic and gymnasial spheres and some Christian commentators and Byzantine lexicographers were happy to exploit this connection, even when they were aware of its juridical setting.[246] But it is not the contextual determinant of the meaning of a compound to which it is related. Indeed, if we return to the ephebic regulations of Beroia, we find that adjudications in the context of games were part of an articulated structure of judicial oversight

240 K. L. Yinger, "Translating καταβραβευέτω ["Disqualify" NRSV] in Colossians 2.18," *The Bible Translator* 54 (2003): 140; see also Lohse, *Colossians and Philemon*, 117 n26.

241 K. Vandorpe and S. P. Vleeming, *The Erbstreit Papyri: A Bilingual Dossier from Pathyris of the Second Century BC* (Leuven: Peeters, 2017), 141–7.

242 *P.Erbstreit* 16. Fr. B1, ll. 57–8.

243 *SEG* 49.1622 (Nisyra, late Hellenistic period); *TAM* V,2 1316 (Hyrkanis, 2nd century CE). See W. M. Ramsay (ed.), *Studies in the History and Art of the Eastern Provinces of the Roman Empire* (Aberdeen: University of Aberdeen Press, 1906), 312.

244 F. Onur and S. Kılıç-Aslan, "New Inscriptions from Aloanda in Lycia," *Gephyra* 21 (2021): 4–25 nr. 1 (2nd century BCE); see especially 20–1.

245 See T. G. Hendren, "Meidias Tyrannos: Meidias' Tyrranical Attributes in Demosthenes 21," *ICS* 40 (2015): 32; Harris, "Against Meidias," 232.

246 Euthymius Zigabenus, *Comm. Ep. Col* 2.18, Suda *K*.486.

that sourced its "higher courts" in the civic institutions. The gymnasiarch is tasked with the responsibility of appointing various judges (βραβευταί) for the torch-race, the "long race" (ὁ μακρὸς δρόμος, l. B85, a long-distance torch-race),[247] and for "the rest of the contests" (τοῖς λοιποῖς ἀγῶσιν). But if a challenge to the decision is made, then "let it be decided according to the common laws" (εὐθυνέτω αὐτὸν κατὰ τοὺς κοινοὺς νόμους, l. B87). Again, theft is to be dealt with by the body with appropriate jurisdiction, possibly determined by the judgment of the theft as "sacrilege".[248] If a dispute arises over a fine for an alleged infraction, then the matter is referred to the appointed magistrates (l. B105). And finally, the *gymnasiarch* him/herself might be challenged about the responsible fulfillment of the office by referral to the appointed judges. Given how important the gymnasium was to a city, it comes as no surprise that the regulations were decreed (τοῦ ψηφίσματος) by the city rulers (παρὰ τῶν πολιταρχῶν τοῦ ψηφίσματος l. B110).

This constant reference to higher courts/judges indicates that the exercise of adjudication in games and gymnasia operated within a wider civic jurisprudential system. This suggests that the technical terminology said to reflect an athletic context is likely to be derivative from a legal framework, that is, a subset of a wider compass. And this is precisely what we find in Plutarch's use of παραβραβεύω mentioned above. The reference ties the (bad) judgment to a referee at the games but the context sets it into a general point about corrupt civic practices. Consequently, in the light of what follows, it is better to translate the opening of the verse as "Do not let anyone bring a judgment against you (regarding …)" and see καταβραβευέτω as an intensified modulation of the κρινέτω of verse 16 in the same section of text. Here our attention is re-directed to the question of the impact of (local) law in the territory of Colossae (see chapter 11). While I do not consider that there is a specific set of opponents at Colossae against which at least some of the text of the letter is directed, I do think that the Christ-followers' efforts to negotiate a place within Colossian society with its array of religious practices were inevitably fraught with challenges, including rights of access to gymnasium, association, or other institution (compare the use of ἐμβατεύειν in Col 2:18b).[249] It is worth recalling the particular characterization of theft from a gymnasium as "sacrilege" in the Beroian ephebic regulations. Religious practices were a key part of the regimen of the gymnasium. Enforcing expectations, religious or otherwise, was a matter of law, whether internal, procedural adjudications or wider, civic judicial oversight.

247 See *Syll.* 1.1068, l. 9 (Patmos, 3rd to 2nd century BCE), *OGIS* 339, l. 83 (Sestos, 2nd century BCE).

248 τις κλέψη τι τῶν ἐκ τοῦ γυμνασίου, ἔνοχος ἔστω ἱεροσυλίαι δίκη νικηθεὶς ἐπὶ τοῦ καθήκοντος δικαστηρίου l. B100.

249 See S. E. Porter, "Is ἀμβιτεύειν really ἐμβατεύειν (*P. Oxy.* XVII 2110.15)," *BASP* 27 (1990): 47.

iv) Col 2:23

> ἅτινά ἐστιν λόγον μὲν ἔχοντα σοφίας ἐν ἐθελοθρησκίᾳ καὶ ταπεινοφροσύνῃ καὶ ἀφειδίᾳ σώματος, οὐκ ἐν τιμῇ τινι πρὸς πλησμονήν τῆς σαρκός.
>
> *On the one hand, such matters carry a grain of wisdom; but as far as arduous devotion, cringing scrupulosity and breaking of the body are concerned, these have no value to anyone as regards the gorging of the flesh.*

Early in the third century, the Christian philosopher, Clement of Alexander, mounted a defense of marriage and brought together a range of biblical texts to support his case in repudiation of a severe ascetic practice — either celibacy (except for love of God) or abstinence in marriage. One of the examples he gave was that of athletes, who abstain from sexual intercourse, exercising restraint as part of the training of their bodies. 1 Tim 4:3 leads his scriptural rebuttal but it is pursued by an amalgam from the Letter to the Colossians presented as one text. It begins with the very opening to Col 2:18 that we have just analyzed. However, instead of proceeding with the rest of the verse, he jumps to Col 2:23 so that the proof-text now reads μηδεὶς ὑμᾶς καταβραβευέτω ἐν ἐθελοθρησκείᾳ ταπεινοφροσύνης καὶ ἀφειδίᾳ σώματος "let no-one bring a judgement against you regarding arduous devotion, cringing scrupulosity and breaking of the body."[250] Given the attention he has bestowed on the abstinence of athletes, even naming some (Astylus of Croton, Crison of Himera, and Amoebeus the lute-player), it would seem that here is an early testimony to the reading of καταβραβευέτω as an athletic metaphor. But what surprises is that the attack is not by reference to mystical visions or the worship of angels in verse 18 but ἐν ἐθελοθρησκείᾳ ταπεινοφροσύνης καὶ ἀφειδίᾳ σώματος in verse 23.

It suggests that Clement at least saw the reference to "body" as a trigger word for athletic discipline that he recommended against. Indeed, by a scriptural citation constructed by cut and paste he removed even the concession in Colossians, that such ascetic practices as outlined in the previous verses (Col 2:18, 21–2) and possibly summed up in what follows (namely ἐν ἐθελοθρησκίᾳ καὶ ταπεινοφροσύνῃ), contain a word of wisdom (ἅτινά ἐστιν λόγον μὲν ἔχοντα σοφίας). Clement certainly set the frame that has governed most Christian interpretations and translations ever since, as they refused to allow that what was being refuted might have any worth. However, the concession to bodily training is not unknown in early Christianity (see 1 Tim 4:8 cf 1 Cor 9:27). If the writer of the letter has received some education from and in the gymnasium, as his compositional register suggests, then outright rejection of that training is not the only option available to him as a Christ follower.

What is striking here is that the advice given, as also in the measured guidance dispensed by Clement, is very similar to those who prized philosophical and medical training, however much they might be alleged to promote the

---

250 Clement of Alexandria *Strom*. 3.6.51.

opposite. Aristotle argued that "the athlete's habit of body is not serviceable for bodily fitness required for a citizen." It was too extreme. Rather, moderation — balance — is called for.[251] The bodily regimen therefore requires some exercises but not those that are violent nor directed only to one form of labor (such as athletics!) nor without accommodating differences in age and gender.[252] Plutarch agreed. He not only advised a similar regimen of moderate exercise that facilitated a balance between soul and body, but he also saw the ascetic disciplines — as broaching eating and drinking as well as exercise — actually were prone to prompt a swing to the opposite end of the spectrum, that is, to over-indulgence and gorging. This first century philosopher paralleled the writer of Colossians arguing that asceticism, especially the ἀφειδία σώματος "the exhaustion of the body,"[253] was of no value for checking the indulgence of the flesh. He actually uses the Colossian Letter's negative term πλησμονή eight times in his tract, "On Keeping Healthy."[254] Asceticism *causes* it. "Most people," he argued, "fill up their bodies for the sake of emptying them and then empty them for the sake of filling them up again, thus transgressing against nature." The crucial element of a human being to be addressed was not the body so much as the soul.[255] Galen, the most influential medical writer of the period, largely concurred. He even recommended the game of small ball (played on courts in the gymnasium but also elsewhere) as the exercise that was not too arduous and yet facilitated the mind, the eye and the body.[256] His concern likewise was with disproportion; extremes at either end of the spectrum tended to reproduce its opposite.[257] It seems that the idea was a philosophical common-place. Philodemos taught that gratitude and anger are extremes of the same range. As Voula Tsouna commented, "if a person is susceptible to the one, then he will be susceptible to the other."[258] This suggests that each of the elements ἐν ἐθελοθρησκίᾳ καὶ ταπεινοφροσύνῃ καὶ ἀφειδίᾳ σώματος is to be understood as an extreme — rigorous devotion,[259] a grovelling underside of

251 See also Plato *Tim.* 88b.

252 Aristotle *Pol.* 7.1335b.

253 See also Lucian *Anach.* 24.21; Pausanias 4.8.9.

254 The small treatise has received little attention. Morton Smith made an initial reconnoiter in the *Corpus Hellenisticum Novi Testamenti* series, but made no correlations with Col 2:23. The spur to further investigation has yet to be felt. "De tuenda sanitate praecepta (Moralia 122B–137E)" in *Plutarch's Ethical Writings and Early Christian Literature* edited by H. D. Betz (Leiden: Brill, 1978), 32–50.

255 Plutarch *Tu. san.* (*Mor.*)134B, 135F.

256 See C. A. Gibson, "Encomium and Thesis in Galen's *De parvae pilae exercitio*," *GRBS* 54 (2014): 471–2.

257 Galen *Parv. pil.* 900K, 906K.

258 V. Tsouna, *The Ethics of Philodemus*, (Oxford: Oxford University Press, 2007), 230 n107.

259 ἐθελοθρησκία is likely to be a coinage of the writer (not that of the supposed opponents — *pace*, Lohse, *Colossians and Philemon*, 126). It probably means determined, rigorous, highly regulated devotion in the light of the comparison with the philosophical critique of the lack of moderation. Some commentators made direct comparisons with the worship of the old

moderation,[260] and the driving of the body beyond its limits. Implicit yet connected would be the polar opposites — either extreme was dangerous. For Plutarch, they offended against freedom and made a person unresponsive to surrounding society. It was a form of slavery.[261]

Here we see not only an alternate privileging from that of athletics in the gymnasium but in fact a contest over what is to be valued most — both finding a venue for expression in the gymnasium. We have seen how the philosopher had become a valued vocation as part of a person's civic credentials just as, for others, athletic excellence was also prized. It is also clear that ascetic disciplines that we have previously noted in the regulations of religious associations and sanctuaries also found a place in exercise regimes, especially of other groups, such as athletes, and, it would seem, some philosophies.[262] The writer to the Colossians appears very much as a participant in a contest of ideas that was being waged in the period of the Second Sophistic.

Accordingly, for all the epistle writer has warned against philosophy, again he has demonstrated if not a reliance on some of its popular teachings then

---

covenant; see Epiphanius *Pan.* 3.305.28; Euthymius Zigabenus, *Comm. Col.* 2.23; compare Dunn, *Colossians and Philemon*, 197–8. But it may mean "wanna-be worship" on a comparison with ἐθελοφιλόσοφος or ἐθελορήτωρ. Probably not envisaged is "feigning worship" by comparison with ἐθελόκωφος (*LSJ* sv and see Lightfoot, *Colossians and Philemon*, 204).

260 Σωφροσύνη was one of the prized attributes in the citizen's public face and dealings. The word was regularly recited as one of the virtues of an honorand; see *SEG* 34.1067 (1st century, Halikarnassos) as one of hundreds of epigraphical examples. ἀφροσύνη (another rare compound) might be considered the opposite extreme to ταπεινοφροσύνη, something likewise to be avoided (see *I.Klaudiu polis* 71, l. 2.22 (2nd century CE). In this sense ταπεινοφροσύνη has the sense of cringing scrupulosity as compared with complete vacuousness. This is close to the compiling of opposites we find in Philodemos *On Music*: Music, he argued, cannot replicate ethics and address various attributes: μεγαλοπρεπὲς καὶ ταπεινὸν καὶ ἀνδρῶδες καὶ ἄνανδρον καὶ κόσμιον καὶ θρασὺ "elevated and simpering, manly and unmanly, moderate and reckless" (*P.Herc.* 225 col 117.31–34). The difficulty (usually avoided!) for commentators is the return of ταπεινοφροσύνη as a positive virtue in Col 3:12, after its dismissal in 2:18 and 23. The different connections for the word in Col 2:23 (ἐθελοθρησκία … ἀφειδίᾳ σώματος) and 3:12 (σπλάγχνα οἰκτιρμοῦ, χρηστότητα, πραΰτητα, μακροθυμίαν) probably go some way to addressing the problem (so Sumney, *Colossians*, 155, 213 cf Lohse, *Colossians and Philemon*, 125–6). However, arguing that these are Judeo-Christian virtues (all except ταπεινοφροσύνη found in the LXX [but cf Ps 130(131):2]) only secures marginal increments, given that three of the five are viewed as honorific descriptions of citizens in the Greco-Roman world: οἰκτιρμός *IG* XIII 1194bis ll. 2–3 (Athens, 575–550 BCE) *IGUR* 3.1229 l. 2 (Rome nd) [more often a woman's virtue]; χρηστότης *F.Delphes III* 1.480, l. 12 (Delphi, c. 48 BCE) *IG* V 2 269, ll. 11–12 (Mantinea, 1st century CE), *SEG* 54.556, ll. 14–15 (Hypata, early 2nd century CE); πραΰτης *SEG* 57.1198, l. 28 (Maionia, 17/16 bce) *CIG* 2788, ll. 22–23 (Aphrodisias, imperial period). Μακροθυμία is rare in Greek literature and only found in Christian inscriptions and papyri. However, a synonym, μεγαλοψυχία, is ubiquitous.

261 Plutarch *Tu. san.* (*Mor.*) 135A.

262 See, for example, Plutarch *Tu. san.* (*Mor.*) 133B–C. I agree with Christopher Seitz that little is gained by trying to pin down "the actual religious practices on the ground," though many have spilt much ink attempting to do so. See Seitz, *Colossians*, 142.

at least an offering of a parallel lesson. In this sense, the difficulty of the compressed expression in Col 2:23 is overcome. Some have read "the indulgence of the flesh" *as* the ascetic disciplines; others have read the ascetic disciplines as impotent in dealing with it.[263] In light of the discussion above, the compression may be intentionally ambiguous, as warranting both.[264]

v) Col 3:15

> καὶ ἡ εἰρήνη τοῦ Χριστοῦ βραβευέτω ἐν ταῖς καρδίαις ὑμῶν …
>
> *And let the peace of Christ grant the reward in your hearts …*

This verse to some extent has been addressed indirectly by the evidence mustered for iii) above. However, commentators have frequently explored/exploited the games associations of the word βραβευέτω.[265] The sense would then be "Let the peace of Christ grant the reward in your hearts."[266] There is little dispute that the substantive βραβεῖον carries a strong games and gymnasial association (as in 1 Cor 9:24 cf Phil 3:14), and that the official (if sometimes temporary) position of βραβεύς/βραβευτής is to be found in that setting.[267] However, we have also noted that βραβευτής can be the title given to a minor adjudicator and that referees in athletic contests may well have derived the nature and standing of their position from a more general juridical context, to which they were answerable if appeals were made. Consequently, some commentators have rejected (or ignored) the games/gymnasium association.[268] Barth and Blanke find that "This verse gives no indication that there is any allusion to an athletic contest, and so we can adopt the general meaning of 'to rule' here."[269]

Whether or not the word means judge in general or to award the prize in particular, cannot be decided so easily. The key combination is with "peace". Foster notes the implicit contrast with the Roman *pax* but makes no reference to its connection with the games. But it is precisely here that we find Rome's soft-war incursion into key Asian cultural practices.[270] The role of a festival of games, as a sublimation of combat and as a celebration of peace after military battles were decided, was recognized by Lysias in his Olympic Oration. Lysias attributed the institution to Herakles, who,

263 See Foster, *Colossians*, 305–6.

264 *Pace* Dunn, *Colossians and Philemon*, 196, who cannot countenance ambiguity here.

265 Lightfoot, *Colossians and Philemon*, 221; Seitz, *Colossians*, 163.

266 Dunn accents the judgment rather than the reward with his translation "arbitrate", *Colossians and Philemon*, 211, 234.

267 See *New Doc. Early Christ.* 2.33.

268 Foster, *Colossians*, 354.

269 Barth-Blanke, *Colossians*, 425.

270 A. Blanco-Pérez, "EPINIKIA: Celebrating Roman Victory in the Eastern Provinces of the Empire," *Tyche* 33 (2018): 9–41.

> when he had defeated tyranny and truncated hubris, established a contest of bodies (ἀγῶνα σωμάτων), a pursuit of prosperity (φιλοτιμίαν πλούτου), and an exhibition of learning (γνώμης δ' ἐπίδειξιν) in the fairest part of Greece, that we might join together for all these things, spectacles for our eyes and our ears; for he decided that our gathering in this place would be a beginning of mutual friendship among the Greeks.[271]

Lysias' rhetorical conception of the connection between the games and peace is echoed in some early inscriptions.[272]

When Sulla, the late Republican Roman general, had finally put an end to Mithridates' rabid campaigns across Asia, he dragged Greek athletes to Rome in 80 BCE from across the Mediterranean to populate an Olympiad, which he removed from its home in Elis.[273] Such commemorative games multiplied as the Republic drew to a close,[274] ironically as much a testimony to ongoing friction as (repeated) self-congratulatory proclamations of peace. This connection between games and spectacles continued into the Empire. Indeed, Augustus instigated in 28/27 BCE his quadrennial Actian Games three years after his victory over Antony. These became one of the pre-eminent competitions on an elite athlete's circuit, celebrated in the *cursus honorum* of his victories.[275] These games often became known as "the great Actian Games of the Caesars",[276] and were replicated in various centers across Asia in the second century,[277] just as cities continued to celebrate the recalibration of the calendar, beginning with Augustus' "good news" birthday.[278] Games were not just a celebration of athletic prowess, they were a massive symbol of peace, Roman peace, even if they sublimated the violence by which the *pax romana* was achieved and sustained. Consequently, local priests of the imperial cult were also the benefactors for and sometimes the *agonothetai* of games at a local level.[279] The indications of the imperial cult at Colossae that we have already encountered were probably no exception to this pattern. The priest of the imperial cult, Apphia daughter

271 Lysias *Or.* 33.2–3.

272 See *SEG* 16.55 (Athens, 330/329 BCE); *SEG* 48.588II (Delphi, 289 BCE but [re-]inscribed later). See also the *Corpus Hermeticum* Fr. 24.6 (*apud* Stobaeus 1.49.45) where peace-making and the race are combined.

273 T. F. Scanlon, *Eros and Greek Athletics* (Oxford: Oxford University Press, 2002), 46.

274 See König, *Athletics and Literature*, 218–9.

275 See for example *IG* V 1 662 (Sparta, but an honorific raised by the city of Smyrna; imperial period).

276 *F.Delphes* III 1.537 (Delphi, 1sr century CE); *SEG* 37.512 (Dodona, 241/242 CE)

277 Cities holding these games frequently minted commemorative coins: *RPC* 3.501, 566 (Nikopolis, time of Hadrian); *RPC online* 6.5437, 5445 temp. (Hierapolis, time of Elagabalus); *RPC online* 7.2.ID 64215 (Neokaisareia, time of Gordian III).

278 *I.Laodikeia Lykos* 82 l. 12 (late 1st to early 2nd century CE). See chapter 3.

279 See *IG* XII 6, 2.821 (Samos, mid-1st century CE); *SEG* 49.815 (Thessalonike, 252 CE).

of Herakleios (*IGR* 4.868), would have been expected to sponsor games honoring the emperor and proclaiming the *pax romana*.

In the Letter to the Colossians, *the pax romana* is not celebrated, but the *pax Christi* is, and this suggests that the verb βραβευέτω ought not be sequestered from an agonistic association. The "one body" (ἐν ἑνὶ σώματι), later in the sentence, therefore takes on something of the very political overtone associated with the Actian and local imperial games. The identity of the Christ-followers is not configured according to the body of the emperor but the body of which Christ is the head (Col 1:18). Indeed, this reference to ἡ εἰρήνη τοῦ Χριστοῦ cannot be heard without recalling that peace-making (εἰρηνοποιήσας) was achieved by the very means by which Roman violence ostensibly ushered in its particular brand of peace — the blood of the cross (Col 1:20). This "peace-making" is the exact opposite of the method by which another "peace-maker" (εἰρηνοποιός), the Roman governor Gaius Julius Victor, imposed order on the area around Gerasa in the third century CE.[280] Subtle it may be in its crafting of an alternate conception of peace and its implicit criticism of Rome, but that is the necessity for a writer seeking to sustain a new group in the religious make-up of this Phrygian city.

These five potential examples of the influence of the gymnasium and the games have been examined in some detail. Frequently forgotten in such metaphor-detection is that athletics had no isolated existence in the ancient world, even when athletes formed their own travelling troupes or associations.[281] Athletics was part of the total gymnasial education for the formation of citizens in body, mind and character, even if there are indications of tensions between the different disciplines.[282] The high moral character of, for example, the *ephebarch* Melanion, extolled in a laudatory decree of the city of Iasos in Caria to the south of Colossae, included his "rational/ordered/gradated education in philosophy" (ἐν τοῖς κατὰ φιλοσοφίαν λόγοις ll. 15–16).[283] As we have seen, a key repudiation of the epistle's writer is of "philosophy" which can despoil a person wishing to be a Christ-follower (Col 2:8). One does not necessarily expect that the writer would be or has to be consistent in his argumentation; after all, the repudiation of philosophy is yet matched by constant references to wisdom (Col 1:9, 28, 2:3, 23, 3:16, 4:5),[284] a key ingredient of the gymnasium's values, sometimes even raised as a personifying statue — ΣΟΦΙΑ — as in

280 *SEG* 46.2061 l. 7.

281 *P.Lond.* 3.1178, ll. 2, 10–11, 18–19 (Hermopolis Magna, 194 CE). Athletes formed their own associations under the patronage of Herakles: *IGUR* 1.235, 236, 244; *I.Aphrodisias Performers* 91 cf *I.Priene* 114 (after 84 BCE). There appears also to have been a trans-national association of athletes: *I.Olympia* 436 (Olympia, 85 CE).

282 See Plutarch *Tu. san.* (*Mor.*), 133B–D. The battle between "jocks" and "geeks" is apparently ancient in origins, even if this was not the intent of a holistic gymnasial education.

283 *I.Iasos* 98 (1st century BCE).

284 This frequency is only rivaled by 1 Corinthians, with none of this authentic letter's caustic qualification of wisdom's value (eg 1 Cor 1:17–21).

the named statue placed in the facade of Celsus' library at Ephesos. And philosophical and literary influences have been frequently found in the letter. In not being uncritical of the gymnasium and the games, the writer has entered his own agonistic engagement but he is not the only such critic operating in this fashion. Athletics in the ancient world, as Onno van Nijf has reminded us, was never innocent,[285] and neither is the use of athletic imagery here.

Four particular aspects have arisen from this exploration. Firstly, it is necessary to place athletics into the total educational, civic and imperial model and method to test what ancillary connections may be present in the letter. Secondly, it is important to check whether the supposed athletic allusions are capable of another association and explanation (as, for example, with καταβραβευέτω in Col 2:18). Thirdly, there has been a recognition that the discussion about athletes (physical and musical) and gymnasia has accepted that the realm of investigation is almost totally at the level of the citizenry elite. The shifting of "teaching and admonishing" to the community of Christ-followers brought this into focus. The *paideia* of Christians at Colossae was challenging content, pedagogical method and educational setting. Fourthly, the use of such metaphors does not entail an acceptance of the context from which they are drawn even if it does indicate some (and probably with the writer, significant) familiarity.

But, there is one final aspect of the games to which we must turn that adds an important qualification to the exploration; this is where the "games" turn into "spectacles" and demand a compensatory recognition.

Enter the gladiator …

We have encountered aspects of the contests about what constituted the man trained for a role in honorable, public life. Even from the inscriptions there is no uniformity, with some accenting the philosopher and others trumpeting either athletic manliness per se or a listing of athletic triumphs that proudly exhibit the valued prowess. The polarity is satirically presented in Lucian's, *The Dream*, where the alternatives are presented as two women each vying to draw a youth into their own particular educational offering — that of τέχνη ("craft") and that of παιδεία ("learning"). The former is characterized by manliness (ἀνδρικός, ἀνδρώδης),[286] the very sculpted physique that we have noted was given as the exemplary template in the statues of Herakles and others adorning the gymnasium. The latter was adorned by the "good" (ἀγαθός, καλός), manifest in virtues,[287] and tied to the knowledge of divine and human wisdom

285 Van Nijf, "Athletics, Festivals and Greek Identity," *passim*.

286 Lucian *Somn*. 6.

287 σωφροσύνη, δικαιοσύνη, εὐσεβεία, πρᾳότης, ἐπιεικεία, σύνεσις, καρτερία.

(τά τε θεῖα τά τ' ἀνθρώπινα).[288] Occasionally, as in the honorific dedication to Aelius Aemilius Zosimos at Priene, the two sides were held together but this was an amalgam rarely achieved, even if promoted as the ideal. As Joy Connolly has demonstrated, not only were there paradoxes inherent in the concept of *andreia* as different aspects were variously accented and weighted but teachers themselves were compelled to demonstrate support for the physical whilst maintaining the expertise and leisure for knowledge-acquisition that upheld the centrality of learning as the proper formation and management of a life.[289] The tensions fragmented both sides as well, with the "heavy" contests (wrestling, boxing, pankration) esteemed over the "light" events (sprinting, archery and so on), and orators denouncing other orators for their flamboyance rather than their measured moderation. Inevitably the contest over what was most valued descended into genderized language, with claims of effeminacy dished out promiscuously. Paul himself was on the receiving end of such disparagement (2 Cor 10:10).[290]

Christ-followers in Asia were inevitably embroiled in this multi-facetted contest, one which was emblematically located in the gymnasium but which spilled into wider society. We have caught glimpses of the two main protragonists, *paideia* and *andreia*, in the surviving evidence from Colossae — of Diodotos pursuing learning as a *philologos* at Smyrna and of Zenon and Kastor committed to the athletic path to glory and honor. We know little of how Colossae dealt with the tensions, competition and arguments over what made for leadership and learning. But the presence of Claudia Eugenetoriane, albeit an elite, wealthy widow, speaks of the city's own acceptance of a level of variegated leadership not found in many other cities (but also not unique).

This is where the Letter to the Colossians becomes critically important not as a Christian text but as a participant in the social and political tensions of the age and of the region. If we allow, as has already been argued, that the letter was addressed to Christ-followers in Colossae (regardless of questions of authorship), then we have discerned a Christian contribution to wider societal debates of leadership and learning, even if the primary audience is not the society at large but members of *ekklêsiai* that are drawn from that society. They continued to be part of that society in its contests, formed by their debates even if informed by Christian responses. Indeed, the writer of the letter wants the Christ-followers to be able to answer "outsiders" (τοὺς ἔξω). This demanded an engagement between the concerns of the city (and perhaps also of the city's territory) and the refashioning of wisdom that the writer was providing (Col 4:5–6). Hence, the accent on "every person" (πάντα ἄνθρωπον Col 1:28)

---

288 Lucian *Somn.* 10.

289 Connolly, "*Andreia* and *Paideia*," 291–9.

290 See A. H. Cadwallader, "Paul speaks like a girl: when Phoebe reads Romans," in *Sexuality, Ideology and the Bible: Queer Readings from the Antipodes* edited by R. J. Myles and C. Blyth (Sheffield: Sheffield Phoenix, 2015), 69–94.

cannot be immune from conceptions of *andreia* such as that promoted in the epigram extolling Kastor's unmarked physique.

The sprinkling of σῶμα through the letter (Col 1:18, 22, 24, 2:11, 17, 19, 23, 3:15) amply demonstrates the engagement (and reconfiguration) of one of the locus-points of attention in that society. The Christ-followers were being encouraged to consider a broader, more inclusive vision of what made for education and service. And this is strikingly manifest in the communal pedagogy of Col 3:16. These are but two examples of the writer's entry into the debates of the age, not merely the debates of a sealed group battling so-called opponents from within. If nothing else it demonstrates that Colossae was not immune to the debates and contests occurring across the province and beyond.

One further element has not been listed in the "athletic potential" of the letter above. It is a marred Christ, a bloodied Christ, a slain Christ, killed by *the* instrument of Roman execution. Although very occasionally mention is made of damage to the body in honorifics for athletic prowess, this is rare and almost always compensated by reference to Herculean labor of accomplishment. But the spilling of blood and an instrument of torture unseen in the gymnasium (Col 1:20) is credited as the means of achieving the concord of heaven and earth that Rome had claimed was hers.

Here a significant contribution to these debates and contests is made, one that is not at present fed by epigraphical or literary text from Colossae. Rather, it is an artifact that bears a keyhole witness to a panoramic phenomenon introduced by the Romans and which had a destabilizing impact on the purity of elite education and training in the gymnasium. It is the gladiator.

Plate 10.10: The fragment of a gladiator frieze almost certainly removed from the site of Colossae and incorporated into a modern boundary wall at Honaz, as an atavistic gift bond between local inhabitants. The fragment has since been sequestered by the Denizli Museum at Pamukkale and lies in the depot.

Elsewhere, I have given an analysis of this two-tiered fragment that presents, probably, the narrative of a gladiatorial combat.[291] Here I simply want to underscore a few aspects as they impact on the argument here.

a) There is a gap of two hundred years between the first report of gladiator contests in Rome (in 264 BCE),[292] and those in Asia (in 69 BCE).[293] The latter

291 See Cadwallader, "Case of a Gladiator," *supra*.
292 Livy *Per.* 16; Servius *Comm. Aen.* 3.67; Valerius Maximus 2.4.7; Ausonius *Griph. tern.* 36–7.
293 Plutarch *Luc.* 23.1.

instance follows shortly after the crushing of the Mithridatic revolt and marks a common association, namely, the celebration of the (re-)assertion of Roman control, where violent combat was sublimated into the controlled architectural environment of the stadium, amphitheater or converted theater.[294] The Hellenistic period had witnessed in Asia the cultivation of combat sports tied to a military background — boxing, wrestling, the pankration.[295] So the phenomenon, even in violent extremity,[296] was not completely strange to Greek cities. But the Greek accent, as we have seen, was on aristocratic values, the heroic mastery that was an investment in status and office in the city. Rome brought a level of infrastructure, pageantry and range of weaponed combat that the Greeks had not known.

Telling in the first mention of gladiators in Asia is the accent on the sponsor, the Roman general Lucullus, with his total entertainment package that reinforced the benefits of Roman rule even as it underscored the hierarchalization that was fundamental to the Roman impress on its world. Plutarch's recounting may be colored by the ubiquity and iconic cultural status of spectacles in the first century but is insightful in its presentation of their purpose:

> Lucullus, after filling Asia to the brim with good order and peace, did not neglect the things which procure pleasure and favor, but during his stay at Ephesos won over the cities by means of processions and victory festivals and contests of athletes and gladiators. In exchange, the cities celebrated festivals which they called Luculleia, to do honor to the man, and bestowed upon him what is sweeter than honor — their genuine loyalty.[297]

Here processions, panegyrics, athletic games and gladiator spectacles are brought together in a single template at Ephesos, one which fanned out for emulation into the cities of the province and became an Ephesian main event for more than three hundred years.

---

294 See K. E. Welch, *The Roman Amphitheatre from its Origins to the Colosseum* (Cambridge: Cambridge University Press, 2007), 164–78.

295 See L. Christopoulos, "Greek Combat Sports and their Transmission to Central and East Asia," *CW* 106 (2013): 431–59.

296 The extolling of death in pursuit of glory was a surplus from the battle-field transferred to athletics, but it may also have been cross-pollinated from gladiatorial combat. For the alternative ἤ στέφος ἤ θάνατον in inscription, see G-J. te Riele "Inscriptions conserves au muse d'Olympie," *BCH* 88 (1964): 186–7 nr. 848 (Olympia, probably third century CE). Te Riele thinks the wording unique (p. 186) but compare, in literature, Pausanias 8.40.2; Philostratus *Gym.* 23; Philo *Prob.* 112–3; Plutarch *Quaest. conv.* (*Mor.*) 675C.

297 Λούκουλλος δὲ τὴν Ἀσίαν πολλῆς μὲν εὐνομίας, πολλῆς δ' εἰρήνης ἐμπεπληκώς οὐδὲ τῶν πρὸς ἡδονὴν καὶ χάριν ἠμέλησεν, ἀλλὰ πομπαῖς καὶ πανηγύρεσιν ἐπινικίοις καὶ ἀγῶσιν ἀθλητῶν καὶ μονομάχων ἐν Ἐφέσῳ καθήμενος ἐδημαγώγει τὰς πόλεις, εἰ δ' ἀμειβόμεναι Λουκούλλειά τε ἦγον ἐπὶ τιμῇ τοῦ ἀνδρός, καὶ τῆς τιμῆς ἡδίονα τὴν ἀληθινὴν εὔνοιαν αὐτῷ παρεῖχον. Translation, slightly adjusted, from M. Tröster, *Themes, Character and Politics in Plutarch's Life of Lucullus: The Construction of a Roman Aristocrat* (Stuttgart: Steiner, 2008), 38. The *Lucculleia* are not known, to my knowledge, epigraphically but Appian mentions their staging at Cyzicus (*Mith.* 76).

Plate 10.11: A gladiator frieze from Ephesos, found in the gladiator graveyard, is dated to the second or third century CE. It features, from left to right, the referee (the *summa rudis*), a *secutor* and a *retiarius*.

Within two decades of Lucullus's spectacles, we gain literary notice of gladiator contests at Laodikeia;[298] within a century (probably) we have epigraphical testimony.[299] Honor carried a prominent currency but loyalty (εὔνοια) was the ultimate objective for the personification of (militant) Rome — the general Lucullus. This connection between gladiator spectacles and loyalty to Rome became structurally enforced at a religious level with local priests of the imperial cult expected to provide festivals with gladiator contests as part of their official duties in promotion of honor for the emperor and imperial family. It is not known whether Apphia, daughter of Herakleios, the priest of the imperial cult at Colossae (*IGR* 4.868), fulfilled such munificence and devotion but it is highly likely. She may have rented a gladiator troupe for the purpose or even owned a *familia* of gladiatorial combatants.[300] As Tullia Ritti accents, the staging of these spectacles (by priests of the imperial cult) was a key factor in the integration of Roman institutions and values into the structures, rituals

298 Cicero *Att.* 117.9.

299 *I.Laodikeia Lykos* 75 = C. Mann, *"Um keinen Kranz, um das Leben kämpfen wir!" Gladiatoren im Osten des römischen Reiches und die Frage der Romanisierung* (Berlin: Antike, 2011), 263 nr. 181; *I.Aphrodisias Performers* 13. In addition to the edited collections of Mann and Roueché, two further collections of gladiator inscriptions are an essential base for research of the cultural phenomena in the East: L. Robert, *Les gladiateurs dans l'Orient grec* (Amsterdam: Hakkert, 1971 [1940]) and M. J. D. Carter, "The Presentation of Gladiatorial Spectacles in the Greek East: Roman Culture and Greek Identity," PhD thesis, McMaster University, 1999, 298–396.

300 The *Lex Italicensis* (c. 177–80 CE) indicates that gladiator (and venator) troupes were on-sold by imperial high priests to their successors (*ILS* 5163 = *CIL* 2.6278, ll. 59–61). How far this became standard practice in Asia is uncertain but the law apparently covered the empire; see M. Carter, "Gladiatorial Ranking and the 'SC de Pretiis Gladiatorum Minuendis'," *Phoenix* 57 (2003): 83–4.

and social practices of both province and cities.[301] It also reflects the mutually-beneficial cultivation by Roman authorities and local elites,[302] and enabled widespread public acclaim for the provision of the spectacles.[303] The Colossian fragment was almost certainly part of a larger complex that inscribed the details of gladiators, events and contexts and most importantly, those responsible for the beneficent provision.[304]

The extant relief fragment may have adorned the theater/stadium, been part of a gladiator barracks or designated cemetery or simply been part of Apphia's or her family's (self-?)constructed memorial. Certainly such would be parallel to the memorial for gladiators and venators set up by Aurelius Tatianus Glykon at Keretapa,[305] who is careful to name himself as the first high priest of the city in the context of honoring his troupe. Significantly, the surviving panel relief from Keretapa that is part of the inscribed stone (see above) probably evokes Glykon in the typology of the hero flanked by Nikes, but its interconnection with a commemoration of gladiators and venators has residual echoes of a shift in the perception and presentation of these combatants in Asian cultural currency compared to that in the west.

For Rome, gladiators exemplified the branding of Roman control over their own lives, with their status as *infames* and quasi- (and often actual) slaves,[306] owned and dispersed by their superiors, with a hierarchicalization mimetic of imperial status, military ranks and social structures built into their organization,[307] and with their violence restrained by the architectural and regulatory regimen within which their skills were tested.[308] This was infused with an

301 T. Ritti, "Spettacoli dell'arena in età imperiale: alcune osservazioni sulle forme e la finalità della comunicazione," in *Öffentlichkeit – Monument – Text. XIV Congressus Internationalis Epigraphiae Graecae et Latinae 27. – 31. Augusti MMXII. Akten* edited by W. Eck and P. Funke (Berlin: de Gruyter, 2014), 402. Ritti focused on the insertion of gladiator spectacles into the accepted fabric of Asian civic life but her observation bears expansion, recognizing the spectacles as a wider instrument of what has been dubbed "Romanization".

302 See E. Flaig, "Roman gladiatorial games: ritual and political consensus," in *Roman by Integration: Dimensions of Group Identity in Material Culture and Text* edited by R. Roth and J. Keller (Portsmouth, RI: Journal of Roman Archaeology, 2007), 83–92.

303 Ritti, "Spettacoli dell'arena," 406–9.

304 Compare the large nigh-complete assemblage from Hierapolis: T. Ritti and S. Yilmaz, *Gladiatori e venationes a Hierapolis di Frigia* (Rome: Accademia nazionale dei Lincei, 1998), 447–86.

305 *I. Mus. Denizli* 62 (second half of the 2nd century CE). Guizzi speculates whether it may have formed part of Glykon's funerary monument: "Gladiatori," 154.

306 See C. Edwards, "Unspeakable Professions: Public Performance and Prostitution in Ancient Rome," in *Roman Sexualities* edited by J. P. Hallett and M. B. Skinner (Princeton: Princeton University Press, 1997), 66–95.

307 For examples, see F. Aytekin, "Statonikeia'dan Provocator Stelleri," in *Stratonikeia ve Çevresi Araştırmaları* edited by B. Sögüt (Istanbul: Ege, 2015), 132–3 (with plates); see generally Carter, "Gladiatorial Ranking," *passim*.

308 The retribution with which Roman authorities came down on a "spillage" of combat from the Pompeii amphitheater into the city streets in 59 CE) shows how the spectacles were meant to express the *pax Romana* not disturb it; see Cadwallader, "Paul and the Games," 363–4, 369.

apparent acceptance of their lot as the means by which they might pursue and sometimes attain the manly performance that Rome promoted and demonstrated to its own (often contested) satisfaction. The famous gladiators' oath, their *sacramentum*, was the ultimate distillation of the ideological communication.[309] The criminals (*noxii/katadikoi*) executed, often with gruesome theatrics, at the midday intermission between gladiator and venator events were nothing other than a grim reminder of the failure to submit to Roman patterning and expectations (direct or delegated). Even if death was not the outcome of every gladiator contest — over-ruled by the entertainment value of a contest or by the sheer cost of replacement of a combatant — it was the hallmark of the spectacles and is underscored as the fitting, inevitable if regretted memory of a successful gladiatorial career.[310] Here a resonance with the center-piece of the Christ story (Col 1:20, 22) was struck even as it created a fundamental dissonance with the usual tenor of the gymnasium and the games. Death was fundamental to the Christ myth and to gladiator identity, but *not* to athletic glorification. Even more significantly, sometimes death for the gladiator came as an execution (albeit by throat-cutting rather than crucifixion).[311]

b) The imperial cult may have been the saturating religious ambience for gladiator contests but other religious devotions also embraced the gladiators. The famous Artemisian procession at Ephesos was so ordered in its route to pass the discrete gladiator cemetery, a salutary object lesson for the ephebes and others who were rewarded with Roman benefaction for their participation.[312] Nemesis, designated the *episkopos* of athletes (and, presumably, their fate in contest) in an oracle from Apollo Didymeus,[313] might sometimes join Hermes for the various games, but she became the eminent deity for gladiators. Her wheel of destiny is faintly visible resting against the herm in the Colossian fragment in Pl. 10.10. The same goddess occupied pride-of-place in gladiator venues across the Empire from Chester in the west to Aphrodisias in the east.[314]

---

309 *Uri, vinciri, verberari, ferroque necari patior* (I submit to be burned, to be bound, to be beaten and killed by an iron weapon). See G. Ville, *La gladiature en occident des origins à la mort de Domitien* (Rome: L'Erma di Bretschneider, 1981), 248–9.

310 See, for example, Mann, *Gladiatoren* 69 (Markianopolis, 2nd – early 3rd century CE), 145 (Tripolis, 2nd – 3rd century CE). Manumission was possible for gladiators but not highlighted as the goal of the career (*Dig.* 38.1.38).

311 Robert, *Gladiateurs* 180 (Halicarnassos, imperial), 343 (Hierapolis, 2nd–3rd century CE); *SEG* 58.865 (Kos, 1st century CE).

312 *I.Ephesos* 27, 104 CE. See Cadwallader, "Case of a Gladiator," 55–7. A similar high-visibility was given to some gladiator tombs at Hierapolis; see Ritti, "Spettacoli dell'arena," 418.

313 *I.Milet* I.7.205a = *SEG* 4.425 (Miletos, 2nd–3rd century CE).

314 *RIB* 3.3149 (Chester, 2nd century ce); *SEG* 56.1191 (Aphrodisias, 3rd century CE) cf *SEG* 54.1714, 58.1706, 56.1191; *I.Philippi*² 142.

Plate 10.12a and b: The Nemeseion built into a section of the Roman amphitheater at Chester. The small altar located therein, reads *Deae Nemesi/Sext(ius) Marci/anus (centurio) ex visu* "From Sextius Marcianus, centurion, for the goddess Nemesis in obedience to a vision."[315] The military connection fits the garrison town with the amphitheater's Nemeseion the obvious place for such a dedication.

Nemesis, the goddess of inevitability, of course curried devotion in a variety of contexts; as one alphabetic oracle chart affirmed, "Nemesis dispenses just deserts to human beings".[316] The twin Nemeseis of the coin of Colossae from the time of Elagabalus, which echoes the foundation mythology of Smyrna,[317] indicates that Nemesis was a featured deity in the Colossian

315 *RIB* 3.3149.

316 Ἡ Νέμεσις ἀνθρώποισι τήν δίκην νέμει. *SEG* 38.1328, l. 7 (Tymbriada in Pisidia, 2nd century CE). On the alphabetic or dice oracles, operated by the throw of an astragal, see J. R. Harrison, "The Inscriptions and Oracular Prophecy in the Eastern Mediterranean Basin: Assessing the Book of Revelation in Its Greco-Roman Revelatory Context," in *The First Urban Churches 5: Colossae, Hierapolis, and Laodikeia* edited by J. R. Harrison and L. L. Welborn (Atlanta, GA: SBL, 2019) 382–88 (allowing that these pre-set axioms were designed for use by more than the elite, who could afford a visit to an oracular sanctuary). In the nineteenth century, Georg Kaibel credited Colossae with one of these dice oracles, but had made a mistaken reading of the provenance of the discovery (from *CIG* 3956c): *Epigrammata Graeca ex lapidibus conlecta* (Berlin: Reimer, 1878), 459–50; "Inschriften aus Pisidien," *Hermes* 23 (1888): 533. Nonetheless, Colossae lies on or near the routes connecting Takina and Termessos in Pisidia where such dice oracles have been found (*TAM* III,1.34; *I.Central Pisidia* 5) with Hierapolis, which has its own selection of these divining guides: see T. Ritti, "Oracoli Alfabetici a Hierapolis di Frigia," *Miscellanea greca e romana* 14 (1989): 245–86. It is likely that Colossae accommodated similar, easily-accessible aids to conduct and decision-making.

317 *RPC online* 6.10829 temp. See the discussion in chapter 5.

religious make-up, and not confined to the arena, even if patently magnified in that context.[318]

c) For all that the influx of gladiator competition can be credited to a Roman impetus, the drift from athletes to gladiators, hinted at in Plutarch's syndetic sweep in praise of Lucullus's benefaction, is particularly evident in Asia. Plutarch even collates the contests of athletes and gladiators alike as *agones*, a term more familiar from the activities of the gymnasium. A number of writers have recognized that there is a distinctive eastern cast in the appropriation of the Roman cultural practice.[319] There is a hybridization apparent in the self-presentation of gladiators in their epitaphs and other memorials. The standard Roman presentation of gladiator-in-armor noted by a name or minimal funerary record does remain in the east.

Plate 10.13a and b: The common Roman presentation of gladiators. The worn panel (now held in the Manisa Museum) presents four gladiators; at least the first two (from left to right) appear to have stage-names: Hermes, Cyrus, Candidus and Trofonius.[320] The second memorial, from Ephesos,[321] is a pedestal memorializing Hippolytos, the name of a *thraex* gladiator (identified by the angled blade of the short sword).

318 On Nemesis, see E. Bouley, "Le culte de Nemesis et les jeux de l'amphithéâtre dans les provinces balkaniques et danubiennes," in *Spectacula I: Gladiateurs et amphithéâtres* edited by C. Domergue, C. Landes and J-M. Pailler (France: Aimgo, 1990), 241–51; M. B. Hornum, *Nemesis, the Roman State and the Games* (Leiden: Brill, 1993).

319 See the works of Carter, Mann and Ritti already cited.

320 *I.Mus. Manisa* 209.

321 *I.Ephesos* 1174, l. 4.

But there is frequently a substantial re-configuring of the western presentation to convey familiar, elevated eastern values.[322] Most particularly, there is an appropriation of key signifiers of the athletic ideal — the honed body on display in naked or semi-naked form, the inclusion of symbols of victory (the laurel wreath and/or the palm branch), and perhaps most significantly, the addition of an inscription in metrical form.[323] The muscular, trained body is revealed as heroic in curation as any athlete — indeed, the language and typology of hero is sometimes used,[324] with the beauty of the male form itself finding a presence.[325] Cavan Concannon has observed that "Greek gladiators, in their own self-presentation, sought to construct an image of themselves and their craft that was thoroughly rooted in Greek heroic and athletic traditions."[326] Of course, this meant that the armor that identified a particular type of gladiator was laid aside. In some reliefs, the hybridization is complicated by motifs that reflect the stage, where the actor's mask is removed, placed on the ground or on a pillar. Anonymity is resisted and a collation with the typology of a different discipline is encouraged. There is even a small number of reliefs where gladiators are reclined on the funerary couch,[327] the gladiator implements being no different from any other skill or occupation communicated through established symbols.[328] At Hierapolis, an exemplary husband and wife devotion is reflected in the memorial epitaph (in relief design and inscription) for the gladiator, perhaps an *essedarius*, Pardalas.[329] Pardalas is made to greet the city, in what Ritti calls "a courtly language worthy of a public figure."[330]

---

322 See C. Berns and H. A. Ekinci, "Gladiatorial games in the Greek East: a complex of reliefs from Cibyra," *AS* 65 (2015): 153–4.

323 See, for example, Robert, *Gladiateurs* 47 (Tomis, imperial); *SEG* 50.1163 (Ephesos, 2nd century CE)

324 *I.Tomis* II,2 341 (Tomis, imperial); *IGR* 3.43 (Alexandria Troas, 2nd century CE); Robert, *Gladiateurs* 41 (Tomis, 2nd–3rd century CE), 98 (Sagalassos, imperial); see Mann, *Gladiatoren*, 156–66.

325 *I.Laodikeia Lykos* 75; *IGR* 3.780 (Attaleia, imperial); Robert, *Gladiateurs*, 79 (Amisus, 2nd century CE).

326 C. W. Concannon, "'Not for an Olive Wreath, but Our Lives': Gladiators, Athletes and Early Christian Bodies," *JBL* 133.1 (2014): 203.

327 *I.Laodikeia Lykos* 81A (1st–2nd century CE).

328 Mann, *Gladiatoren* 22, pl. 1.

329 Mann, *Gladiatoren* 178 (early 3rd century CE). For a photograph of the stele, see T. Ritti, *Hierapolis di Frigia IX: Storia e Istituzioni di Hierapolis* ((Istanbul: Ege, 2017), 185, fig. 46.

330 Ritti, "Spettacoli," 416. The inscription opens with Χαῖρέ μοι Ἱεράπολι, ἄσστρον ἁπάντων. Ritti translates this as "Greetings from me, Hierapolis, star above all."

Plate 10.14a and b: The near-naked athlete-actor-gladiator Eupithanos of the first grade of gladiators ([E]ὐπιθανὸς πάλου α᾽), presented in glorified style,[331] with a mimetic adulation in a fully armored child-sized figure at his right and a hailing, muscular Eros at his left, perhaps a visual pun on his name "golden winged". The memorial is from Aphrodisias.[332] Below is an example of a gladiator presented in highly-conventional funerary banquet style at Thessalonike, with the tools of his trade (helmet atop a shield) next to three crowns, below a fawning dog and laden table. A brief, stereotypical inscription at lower left records that his wife Eutychia erected the memorial for Strobeilos, her husband (Εὐτυχία Στροβείλῳ τῷ ἀνδρὶ μνήμης χάριν).[333]

These variations communicate that there is a known, honorable human being beneath the metal and leather veneer. Moreover, the distinction between the person and the costume underscores the entertainment value of the spectacles, rivaling the more traditional thespians espoused by the gymnasium. We need to recognize that this is more than aspiration by at least some gladiators in the east. An exchange between presentation and viewer was occurring. A cultivated perception of gladiators was permitted. Gladiators were frequently received as heroes and honored with public recognition. At Tripolis, the epitaph of the gladiator Chrysopteros ("golden-winged") is written in hexameters, the figure is surrounded by twelve laurel crowns (matching the number of victories mentioned in the inscription) and he may be making an offering on an altar to his right — a hallmark of conventional piety.[334] More honorific than these signifiers of status however, is that at Hierapolis. There, Chrysopteros is rec-

---

331 See, for comparison, E. Pfuhl and H. Möbius, *Die ostgriechischen Grabreliefs* (Mainz am Rhein: Philipp von Zabern, 4 vols, 1977), plate 184–6, nrs 1226–34, 1243–4.

332 *I.Aphrodisias Performers* 22.

333 *SEG* 40.556 (c. 200 CE).

334 Mann, *Gladiatoren* 145 cf 69; a photograph of the stele is found in Pfuhl and Möbius, *Grabreliefs*, plate 184.1228. The stele is worn. Some commentators readily recognize an altar ("mit Flamme", Pfuhl-Möbius, *Grabreliefs*, 299); others are not so sure (Robert, *Gladiateurs*, 165). The stylistics are, however, very similar to reliefs that have the gladiator's right or left hand resting on a removed helmet placed on a small pedestal.

ognized by others, immortalized in a named metope inserted into the decorative elements of the frame of the central part of the great basilica of the northern agora.[335] His fame in the valley had elevated him to exemplary and public heights, leaving far behind, at least in civic appreciation, the infamy of the western Roman status of the gladiator.[336] In this sense, however much gladiator spectacles have been used as an index of Romanization of Asia, the refashioning embrace of gladiators in the East seems to have been a way by which key eastern values might yet be preserved. Certainly the ubiquity of gladiator representations in popular, consumable art-forms — lamps, graffiti, beakers and the like — points to the prevalence of common knowledge of, even esteem for, the spectacles.

However, there was one key component of status that, though a constant for athletes, is notably absent among extant gladiator inscriptions. It was a flaw remaining as an unwanted reminder, a stigma, underscoring that the gladiator (and venator) was a "spoiled identity."[337] It ensured that even the most successful and loyal gladiator never quite secured the standing that citizen-athletes held. That defect was the absence of a genealogy. Less than a handful of gladiator inscriptions, to my knowledge, contains a genealogy for a gladiator.[338] The vivid contrast is with the editors, the owners, the providers for gladiatorial contest who regularly have their genealogical reinforcement of citizenship recorded.[339]

Christ-followers and gladiators at Colossae

The fragment of a gladiator narrative panel with a herm of Nemesis does not allow us to draw unequivocal conclusions about the nature of spectacles at Colossae. Certainly the fragment does not carry the elements that allow us to recognize the hybridization of the form of the gladiator that is so much in evidence in many other Asian cities. But it is precisely because Colossae now witnesses gladiators in its own civic context and is placed in an immediate

---

335 Ritti, "Spettacoli," 412–3. For a photograph, see Ritti, *Storia e istituzioni*, 185, fig. 47.

336 "Gladiator" is one of the terms of abuse that a father might heap on a son as a signal of disinheritance: *Dig.* 28.2.3 (Ulpian).

337 The language of "spoiled identity" was coined by Erving Goffman. See his *Stigma: Notes on the Management of Spoiled Identity* (Reading: Penguin, 1968). For a summary, see A. H. Cadwallader, "Name Punning and Social Stereotyping: Re-inscribing Slavery in the Letter to Philemon," *ABR* 61 (2013): 1–8.

338 See *I.Patrai* 168 (Καλλίνικος Ἱππάρχου, identified as an *arbelas* by the relief; 2nd – 3rd century CE); *I.Laodikeia Lykos* 81A (Ἀσβολᾶς Πλατυ– … 1st–2nd century CE, combined with a funerary banquet scene). In both cases, these are likely a paternal memorial, rather than a civic citizenship marker.

339 *I.Ephesos* 721 (c. 166–7 CE); *IGR* 3.500 (Oinoanda, 115 CE), 549 (Telmessos, imperial).

and proximate location of Greek renditions of the Roman gladiatorial spectacle that we can expect to find similar examples at Colossae in the future. That is, we can anticipate that the gymnasium will have colored the gladiator at Colossae.

Consequently, the recognition of athletic imagery in the Letter to the Colossians may need to be tempered by the admission that athletic imagery was appropriated into the service of gladiators as a means of securing their place and their status in the city's life. The key correlative in the comparison is death, the confrontation with mortality that gladiators, at least in the posturing of the many panels of gladiator contests spread across the province, so encapsulated. Death for the Christ-followers may or may not have been a present threat at the time of the letter. There is little in the letter itself to suggest that. Rather death is presented as the fundamental signature of the salvation that Christ brings, a more expansive view of death than any gladiator claimed.

Although the genre of early Christian writings is not generally conducive to the relaying of genealogical information or display, it does seem that there was some early dispute over whether such marks of status and/or paternity were to retain their value. Paul himself had marginalized the importance of genealogy in Rom 1:3–4, only allowing the slightest awareness of familial succession in the greetings list (Rom 16:7, 10, 11). Pseudo-pauline writings readily endorsed a minimalist framework for Jesus (Heb 7:6, 16) and seem to have broadened the scope to others (1 Tim 1:4, Tit 3:9). There was no resiling from Jesus having a filial relationship with God (Col 1:3, 13) but the lists that we find in Matt 1:1–17 and Lk 3:23–38 have little comparison or warrant in the Pauline literature. The one pseudo-genealogical reference in Colossians, the metaphor υΐοι τῆς ἀπειθείας "sons of disobedience" (Col 3:6), is heavily disputed as to whether it is the better reading.[340] At least as far as the modicum of evidence suggests, the Christ-followers at Colossae were akin to gladiators when it came to the dearth of genealogical display.

Nonetheless, the sheer phenomena of appropriation of athletic imagery by gladiators, their families, owners/renters and games presenters shows that there was a fluidity in the use of symbols, metaphors and literary/epigraphical typologies familiar from the gymnasial realm. Early Christ-followers or at least their literate representatives therefore had exemplars to follow for such an appropriation. There was nothing novel or idiosyncratic in a writer draw-

340 Most commentators reject the addition (an assimilation to Eph 5:6): Lohse, *Colossians and Philemon*, 139 n30, McKnight, *Colossians*, 298–9, among many; a small number accept the reading: R. McL. Wilson, *Colossians and Philemon* (ICC; Edinburgh: T & T Clark, 2005), 246, 248, Dunn, *Colossians and Philemon*, 210 n4; some equivocate: B. M. Metzger, *A Textual Commentary on the Greek New Testament* (UBS, 1971[1]), 624–5; MacDonald, *Colossians, Ephesians*, 135–6.

ing on such imagery — higher literature of the time shows such a propensity.[341] A stronger case for reliance on gladiator imagery can be made for the writer of the letters to the seven churches,[342] but it does suggest that when commentators on the Letter to the Colossians discern athletic imagery, such imagery may be filtered through a gladiatorial lens.

341 Note especially the oration for the gladiators attributed to Favorinus by Philostratus (*Vit. soph.* 8), unfortunately not extant.

342 See A. H. Cadwallader, "'Bad to the Bone': Reading Revelation Rooned," *ABR* 66 (2018): 13–29.

Chapter Eleven
Slavery and its Governance at Colossae

The dearth of material evidence for slavery from the site of Colossae has prompted recourse to Roman law in an effort to understand the situation of the most famous slave in the Second Testament: Onesimos. However, the assumption that Roman law governs the Colossian organization of slavery is unfounded. Indeed, there is a dearth of material evidence for Roman jurisprudential governance of Colossian affairs as well. Both slavery and law demand a sifting for information that is often indirectly discerned as well as the gathering of comparative evidence that can deliver a probability about the legal jurisdiction(s) operating in the city and territory of Colossae. Here, recourse is made to a range of archaeological, epigraphical and literary material that takes seriously that Colossae in the first and second centuries was committed to presenting, if not developing, its Greek credentials as a means of expressing its nuanced identity and of negotiating its relationship with Rome. Multiple systems of law with varying jurisdictions are seen to operate in Colossae and throughout the East of the empire at least until the *Constitutio Antoniniani* in 212 CE. That date ought not be seen as a sudden end of the operations of local law nor even as the culmination of Romanization. The continuation of civic mints beyond that date flags the level of toleration and ongoing practice of local jurisprudential practices and jurisdictions. But the universalization of Roman citizenship to include citizens of provincial *poleis*,[1] did accelerate — "set into motion" is perhaps slightly understated[2] — the move towards the uniform application of Roman law.[3]

---

1 The edict is found, in fragmentary form, in *P.Giss.* 1.40. For recent analysis, see G. Purpura, "Il P. Giss. 40, I," *IAH* 5 (2013): 73–85.

2 G. Kantor, "Knowledge of Law in Roman Asia Minor," in *Selbstdarstellung und Kommunikation die Veröffentlichung staatlicher Urkunden auf Stein und Bronze in der römischen Welt* edited by R. Haensch (Munich: C. H. Beck, 2009), 249; Kantor restrains his language in "Greek Law under the Romans," in *The Oxford Handbook of Ancient Greek Law*, edited by E. M. Harris and M. Canevaro (Oxford: Oxford University Press, 2015), 2 (online edition).

3 For a telling, regional analysis, see M. S. Youni, "Transforming Greek practice into Roman law: manumissions in Roman Macedonia," *Legal History Review* 78 (2010): 311–40.

Multiple legal systems at Colossae

Colossae cannot boast anything like Trajan's water regulations edict displayed at Laodikeia or the Hadrianic fishing rights decision governing the layers of industry sourced from the lake between Laodikeia and Hierapolis (and Tripolis). To this point in time, the clearest statement of any regulations actually occurs in the Pauline epistle itself with the examples of cultic regulations (dubbed δόγματα) governing religious behavior (Col 2:21–2 cf 16, 18). These regulations were likely intended as an illustrative sample, doubtless evoking similar if not identical requirements inscribed and displayed in and around sanctuaries and the rooms of religious associations at Colossae. The indebtedness that might be incurred in the course of membership of or even attendance at such cults, was envisaged as one possible scenario behind Col 2:14 (see chapter 7). The moral outrage (real or paraded) at the failure to observe suchlike behavioral controls that we saw in an inscription at Tralles,[4] is a powerful indicator not only of the hierarchy of jurisdictions that might assert an interest in the actions of citizens and inhabitants (from religious settings to city *Boulê*) but that higher jurisdictions retained an overarching control, albeit exercised more through formal resolution than statute as we tend to understand the exercise of law today. These higher institutions may only occasionally intervene in the more limited jurisdiction below it, to which, by implication, such authority was delegated; but the delegation allowed a line of appeal, just as we have seen in the Beroian gymnasial regulations regarding allegations of theft.[5] Local celebrations of city foundation narratives, always carefully orchestrated by regulation, were tracked in relation to Col 1:10–12 and 2:6–7.[6] We have also raised the possibility that the "evil deeds" of Col 1:21 can productively be read against a background of sacrilege against graves committed as part of the dark ritual infusing a *defixio* with efficacious, cursing power,[7] an action that attracts full, legal retribution. At another level of authority, there is the distinctly Roman authority that governed execution by crucifixion and imperial triumphs (cf Col 1:20, 2:14–15). It is a diverse range but scarcely detailed as to specific legislation, even if, already, it can be seen that there are different jurisprudential sources for the regulation of behaviors.

If we place the Letters to the Colossians and to Philemon into a wider setting of the letters' formation and delivery, along the lines provided by Cavan Con-

---

4 H. Malay, M. Ricl and D. Amendola, "The City of Tralleis combats Immorality: Measures taken against οἱ ἐν κιναιδείᾳ βιοῦντες in a new civic decree," *EA* 51 (2018): 91–7. See chapter 3.

5 *I.Beroia* 1, l. B100. See chapter 10.

6 See chapter 3.

7 See chapter 8.

cannon's economic perspective,[8] then for every cost, custom, toll and the like, there is a law and/or regulation in the background. Onesimos is often touted/toasted as the deliverer of the letter whose main object is himself,[9] an unlikely scenario in my opinion.[10] The surveillance of law and legal authority is exponentially increased, given his slave status and the distance of the journey. If he were to travel alone over a considerable distance, an unaccompanied slave would need to have a letter of authorization, akin to a "safe conduct" pass,[11] from his master or delegate if he were to proceed unhindered and not be presumed to be a runaway. Distance, whether, in Onesimos's case, from Rome, Ephesos or Caesarea Maritima,[12] is why Patrick Reinard precludes slaves as letter-carriers (*tabellari*, βιβλιαφόροι, later ἐπιστολαφόροι, γραμματαφόροι),[13] apart from within city precincts (where the ties and eyes of the master were strongest).[14] Cicero, for example, writes of slaves fulfilling such a task within and around Rome,[15] but of professional *tabellarii* employed for longer distances, especially when fortuitous circumstances of a friend's travel arrangements were not available.[16] The potential threat and actual experience of runaways was, for him, an apparent determinant of choice.[17] Even then, Cicero was sometimes suspicious or annoyed at *tabellarii*'s behaviors (delays, spying on the contents of letters, impatience to depart, even complete failures to fulfill tasks).[18] But these were aristocratic handicaps; his wealth, rank and citizenship meant that he had more resources at his disposal across the empire than, say, an apostle confined to prison.[19] Moreover,

8 C. Concannon, "Economic Aspects of Intercity Travel among the Pauline Assemblies," in *Paul and Economics: A Handbook* edited by T. R. Blanton IV and R. Pickett (Minneapolis: Fortress, 2017), 344–5.

9 The most recent and thorough treatment is that of P. M. Head, "Onesimus the Letter-Carrier and the Initial Reception of Paul's Letter to Philemon," *JTS* 71 (2020): 628–56. Head categorizes the letter as a letter of recommendation.

10 See further below.

11 Compare *Dig.* 48.10.27.2 (Modestinus).

12 These are the usual candidates for Paul's imprisonment mentioned in Phmn 1, 9, 10, 13.

13 See A. Sarri, *Material Aspects of Letter Writing in the Graeco-Roman World: 500 BC – AD 300* (Berlin: de Gruyter, 2017), 18–24 for the development of different terms (and spellings); see also L. H. Blumell, "The Message and the Medium: Some Observations on Epistolary Communication in Late Antiquity," *JGRChJ* 10 (2014): 49–53.

14 P. Reinard, *Kommunikation und Ökonomie: Untersuchungen zu den privaten Papyrusbriefen aus dem kaiserzeitlichen Ägypten* (Rahden: Leidorf, 2016), 480.

15 Cicero *Quint.* 5.1; but cf *Amic.* 98.4.

16 Cicero *Att.* 423.1; cf *Att.* 114.4.

17 Cicero *Att.* 108.3, *Amic.* 225.2 (a slave trained as a reader — ἀναγνώστης).

18 Cicero *Att.* 280.2 (punctuality), *Quint.* 27.6 (issues of trustworthiness), *Att.* 13.1–2 (perusal of contents), *Amic.* 213.2 (impatience), *Att.* 394.1, 401.1 (failure to get through).

19 See Cicero *Quint.* 2.14 *Amic.* 212.3 (the value of contacts in another city to hunt down a runaway — in this case, a slave who had stolen some volumes from Cicero's library).

Cicero had little need to consider jurisdictional restrictions on legal or diplomatic choices for his personal concerns.[20]

But for many in Rome's provinces this was precisely the issue — a decision on what jurisdiction to exploit for the optimum result, allowing that such options might even have been available.[21] This was especially prescient to natives of provincial cities who had been awarded Roman citizenship (cf Acts 25:9–12). The simple question of what was the law (or were the laws) governing the activities mentioned in the current small crop of inscriptions, coins and non-textualized material remains at Colossae unlocks a considerable trove of potential regulations, legislation and edicts. These testify to a complexity of negotiation that has until recently been overlooked by Second Testament commentators who assume that late Republican and early Imperial Roman laws were an automatic, untrammelled and transparent imposition on the eastern provinces.[22]

It is understandable that the Roman legal presence has been the object of focus, given that from the beginning of the province of Asia's existence, the territory was placed into the context of a testamentary disposition (disputed by Attalid claimants) and given formal authorization by senatorial decree in 129 BCE. Thus the province remained senatorial in terms of its lines of authority and power relationships, even though the formal regional constituents of the province varied across its history,[23] and the realities of political change from republic to empire saw the Emperor not only direct many of the Senate's formal decisions but increasingly appear unilaterally in a decision-making role.[24] Nonetheless, in the first two centuries, reference to the Senate and to present and past senatorial decisions, underscored the formal institutional arrange-

20 See H. M. Cotton, "Private International Law or Conflicts of Laws: Reflections on Roman Provincial Jurisdiction," in *Herrschen und Verwalten. Der Alltag der römischen Administration in der Hohen Kaiserzeit*, edited by R. Haensch and J. Heinrichs (Köln: Böhlau, 2007), 243–4.

21 See H. M. Cotton, "'Diplomatics' or external aspects of the legal documents from the Judaean desert: prolegomena," in *Rabbinic Law in its Roman and Near Eastern Context* edited by C. Hezser (Tübingen: Mohr Siebeck, 2003), 49, 50.

22 See A. H. Cadwallader, "Complicating class in the Letter to Philemon: a prolegomenon," in *The Struggle over Class: Socioeconomic Analysis of Ancient Jewish and Christian Texts* edited by G. A. Keddie, M. Flexsenhar and S. J. Friesen (Atlanta, GA: SBL), 95–122.

23 For various overviews of the province, see the foundational work of D. Magie, *Roman Rule in Asia Minor* (Princeton: Princeton University Press, 2 vols, 1950); and C. Habicht, "New Evidence on the Province of Asia," *JRS* 65 (1975): 64–91; P. Trebilco, "Asia," in *The Book of Acts in its Greco-Roman Setting* edited by D. W. J. Gill and C. Gempf (Grand Rapids, MN: Eerdmans, 1994), 291–362; S. Mitchell, "The Administration of Roman Asia from 133 BC to AD 250," in *Lokale Autonomie und romischen Ordnungsmacht in den kaiserzeitlichen Provinzen vom 1. bis 3. Jahrhundert* edited by E. Müller-Luckner and W. Eck (München: R. Oldenbourg, 1999), 17–46; A. H. Cadwallader, "The Roman Province of Asia," in *The Oxford Encyclopedia of the Bible and Archaeology* edited by D. M. Master *et al* (Oxford: Oxford University Press, 2013), 303–17.

24 See P. Brunt, "The Role of the Senate in the Augustan Regime," *CQ* 34 (1984): 423–44.

ments under which the empire operated.[25] And it must be underscored that "law" was formed less by swathes of legislation as by decisions, letters and edicts, whether or not the context demonstrates that the impact and longevity was restricted to a presenting case or became of general application.[26]

Unfortunately, the Laodikeian water law from the late Trajanic period is missing a substantial amount of text, including the introduction,[27] so the process by which the regulations came about is obscure. However, the formal authority comes from a proconsular edict (διατάγμα, l. 7, with the details called a νόμος in l. 30). This was a delegated senatorial function. Of course, requisite acknowledgement of the emperor Trajan's forethought is made (l. 2) and reference is made to a ruling (διάταξις, l. 13) by Vespasian. A critical indicator ("follow the money!") of the overarching authority behind the regulations is the quite specific terminology of the office to which penalties are to be paid, namely "the fiscus of the lord Trajan Caesar" (εἰς τὸν τοῦ κυρίου Τραϊανοῦ Καίσαρος φίσκον, l. 10).

No ambiguity attends the Letter of Hadrian to the *Boulê* and *Dêmos* of the Hierapolitans making a ruling in 130 or 131 CE largely in favor of Laodikeia about fishing rights to the lake between the two cities.[28] By the beginning of the third century, even with the Senate acknowledged in official documents, the ultimate authority was the Emperor. When a dispute arose about visitors' expectations of hospitality from senators on their estates in the province, the emperor Septimius Severus and his co-regent Caracalla stepped in to reaffirm an earlier (now unknown) *senatus consultum.*[29] Werner Eck confronts the number of extant copies of the imperial letter (but not of the original senate resolution [δόγμα]) with the explanation that senators in the third century installed copies of the imperial decision at the entrance to their properties (extant in both Latin and Greek),[30] because they knew where the power of enforcement

---

25 W. Eck, "*Senatus consulta* in lateinischen Inschriften aus den Provinzen," *Quaderno Lupiensi di Storia e Diritto* 7 (2017): 38.

26 *Dig.* 1.4.1–2, Ulpian (2nd to early 3rd century).

27 F. Guizzi, "An Edict of a Proconsul of Asia on the Aqueduct of Laodikeia (114/115 CE?)," in *15. Yalındı Laodikeia (2003–2018)* edited by C. Şimşek (Istanbul: Ege, 2019), 143–64.

28 See T. Ritti, *Hierapolis di Frigia IX: Storia e istituzioni di Hierapolis* (Istanbul: Ege, 2017), 388–95; A. H. Cadwallader, "The Battle over Lake Lycus: Inter-city Conflict in the Lycus Valley," in *New Documents Illustrating the History of Early Christianity vol 12: The Lycus Valley* edited by J. R. Harrison *et al.* (Grand Rapids, MN: Eerdmans, 2023), forthcoming.

29 *CIL* 3.14203 + *IG* XII 5 132 (Paros), *TAM* V,1 607 (Adala/Satala), *AE* 1977.807 (near Pentapolis in Phrygia), *AE* 1986.640 (Antioch of Pisidia), *AE* 2016.1659 (location?); see also D. Knibbe and R. Merkelbach, "Allerhöchste Schelte (Zwei Exemplare der Sacrae Litterae aus Ephesos," *ZPE* 31 (1978): 229–32, C. P. Jones, "The *sacrae litterae* of 204: two colonial copies," *Chiron* 14 (1984): 93–9 (the Troad)

30 The surviving fragments are known mainly in discreet languages but occasionally bilingual inscriptions occur (Paros, see above; possibly Byzantion): see S. Mitchell, "EPMHNEIA. The Greek Translations of the *sacrae litterae* on Official Hospitality," in *Vir Doctus Anatolicus: Studies in Memory of Sencer Şahin* edited by B. Takmer *et al.* (Istanbul: Ege, 2016), 681–5.

lay.[31] He concluded that, at least until midway through the second century, the Senate still concerned itself with various matters related to the administration of provinces that were nominally under their control (exemplified in their formal appointment of proconsular governors). Of course the participation of the Emperor was necessary, if often implicit and *sotto voce*, but that power became more pronounced as the third century approached.[32]

Colossae clearly monitored and iterated the status quo. When Claudia Eugenetoriane revived the civic mint at the beginning of Hadrian's reign, there was an extremely delicate sensitivity to the hierarchy of authority given to the coins, conveyed through their size and related iconography.[33] Of particular note for our purposes are the coins featuring the "Sacred Senate" (Ιερὰ Σύγκλητος) and the Emperor (Ἁδριανὸς Αὐτοκράτωρ Καῖσαρ) (Pl. 11.1a and b).

Plate 11.1a: The largest coin of the series minted by Claudia Eugenetoriane features a draped youthful personification of the Sacred Senate, facing left, on the obverse. On the reverse is the hunting Artemis with leaping hound; she advances to the right with her bow in her left hand and drawing an arrow from her quiver with her right hand.[34]

Plate 11.1b: features, a youthful Hadrian facing right, draped with a paludamentum. The reverse features a standing Athena in plumed (Corinthian) helmet, facing left with an owl in her right hand; she rests her left hand on a grounded shield with a central gorgoneion(?).[35]

The larger coin measures 29 millimeters and weighs 11.39 grams; the second coin measures 24 millimeters and weighs 9.90 grams. This difference converts to the relative value assigned to the bronze coins — probably 3 assaria and 2 assaria respectively. This difference, along with the iconography, convey subtle

31 Eck, "*Senatus consulta*," 40.

32 Eck, "*Senatus consulta*," 55. This conclusion is substantially endorsed by J. Fournier, *Entre tutelle romaine et autonomie civique. L'administration judiciaire dans les provinces hellénophones de l'Empire romain (129 av. J.C. - 235 apr. J.-C.)* (Athens: École française d'Athènes, 2010), 593–6, though pushing the transition more strongly into the third century.

33 See A. H. Cadwallader, "Wealthy, widowed, astute and beneficent: Claudia Eugenetoriane and the second century revival of the Colossian mint" in *New Documents Illustrating the History of Early Christianity vol 12: The Lycus Valley* edited by J. R. Harrison *et al.* (Grand Rapids, MN: Eerdmans, 2023), forthcoming.

34 *RPC online* 3.2307D. Photograph by courtesy of Roma Numismatics.

35 *MSPhryg* 2.548 = *RPC* 3.2307 Photograph by courtesy of Numismatik Naumann. Note that the obverse inscription should now be read as ΑΥ(ΤΟΚΡΑΤΩΡ) ΚΑΙ(CAP) ΑΔΡΙΑΝΟC.

but powerful indications of the recognized hierarchy of the governance of the province. Asia was a senatorial province. Even though the power of the Senate slowly declined over the two hundred and fifty years following the Augustan revolution, the formal authority of the governing institution remained for provincial observance. Augustus was especially careful to open his *Res Gestae* with his deference to and recognition by the Senate (s.1 and see ss. 4–14, 20, 22, 34–5), regardless of what the hidden texts of political machinations actually were. When the imperial cult was formally awarded to Smyrna under the reign of Tiberius, the Senate was included with the emperor and the deified Livia as the focus of devotion.[36] That tone is reflected in Eugenetoriane's coins, just as she placed her own status, authority and religious commitments in the hierarchy of relationships far lower, only deigning to self-designate as Χήρα "widow" (Ionic spelling) in her second-lowest-value coin.[37]

Hers is the only coin of Colossae to date that registers a sponsor's name in an accompanying legend for a "Sacred Senate" coin. Other types are seen in Pl. 11.2a and b.

Plate 11.2a: A "Sacred Senate" coin of Colossae not credited to any sponsor.[38] The obverse features, on the obverse, a draped, youthful personification of the Senate, bust facing right. The legend reads ΙΕΡΑ CΥΝΚΛΗΤΟC. The reverse has Artemis, stepping forward, facing right, reaching for an arrow from her quiver with her right hand and holding a bow in her left hand. The legend reads ΚΟΛΟCCΗΝΩΝ (6.86 g).

Plate 11.2b: A second anonymous "Sacred Senate" coin of Colossae, featuring a youthful, draped personification of the Senate, bust facing right with legend ΙΕΡΑ CΥΝΚΛΗΤΟC on the obverse. The reverse features a front-standing, semi-naked Dionysos with kantharos in his right hand and a staff in his left; the legend reads simply ΚΟΛΟCCΗΝΩΝ.[39]

---

36 *RPC* 1.2469. Compare *RPC* 2.1033 with the goddess Roma and the Sacred Senate facing one another on a coin of Clazomenae, time of Vespasian. See G. Schörner, "Wie integriert man Rom in die Polis? Der Kult des Senats in Kleinasien," in *Integration in Rome and in the Roman World* edited by G. de Kleijn and S. Benoist (Leiden: Brill, 2013), 220–24.

37 *RPC online* 3.3207A.

38 *BMC Phrygia* Colossae 10 = *MSPhryg* 2.543–4. Barclay Head tentatively assigned the coin to the time of Gallienus (253–68 CE). Von Aulock removed the reserve. My autopsy of the British Museum coin raises some doubt about the legend of the reverse, namely ΚΟΛΟCCΗΝΟΙC rather than ΚΟΛΟCCΗΝΩΝ. Photograph courtesy of *Bibliothèque nationale de France*.

39 This coin has not been previously published and has not been assigned to the date of any emperor, though it is clearly second or third century, in terms of iconography and letter shape (lunate sigma): 18 mm, 4.79 g. Photograph from a private collection by permission.

These coins are considerably smaller than the "Sacred Senate" coin of Eugenetoriane, respectively weighing 6.37 grams (av.) and 4.79 grams. It suggests that the parade of deference to hierarchical authority over the province made by Eugenetoriane was not regarded as essential in the "Sacred Senate" coins that followed. Mere recognition was enough — just as we see in the lack of consistency in weight and size among the "Sacred Senate" coins minted by other cities in the province. Indeed the later Senate coins may be a tacit recognition of the increased direct involvement of Emperors in the province. Honorific inscriptions of this time tended to place the Emperor before the Senate and People of Rome.[40] But Eugenetoriane's launch demanded careful negotiation of the existing imperial realities. This might be corroborated by the choice of reverse iconography. Artemis was, of course, emblematic of Ephesos (cf Acts 19:27–8) and, though frequently represented in her richly costumed, crowned and stationary form, she was also regularly dramatized in her hunting role. Ephesos was the traditional entry point for the incoming governor of the senatorial province (from as early as 29 BCE),[41] a recognition given imperial imprimatur by Caracalla, after it was apparently challenged.[42] In Eugenetoriane's coin, the left-facing bust (not found in the other "Sacred Senate" coins of Colossae) is off-set on the reverse by the right advance of Artemis; it may well signal the west to east connection of Rome and the province. There is always a danger of over-reading the symbolics here but what is clear is the emphatic reverence (note the ἱερά) given to the Roman Senate — common though not ubiquitous in inscriptions.[43]

It is precisely this lack of due honor that may have embarrassed Laodikeia in its long-term ambition, flagged initially in 26 CE,[44] to be granted the accolade of *neokoros*, official custodian of the imperial cult. The recently published inscription (dated probably to 129 CE) from Laodikeia that has the city self-designating as *neokoros*,[45] as part of its romancing of the emperor Hadrian on his pan-Hellenic tour, may have unfolded an embarrassment from the city's obsequious hubris that required correction at a later date. The coins minted to proclaim her neokorate status — a commonly-used, self-promotional broadcast — are absent from Hadrian's time. Rather, they are deferred for nine decades

---

40 See for example *TAM* V,2 1335 = *IGR* 4.1352 (Dareioukome, nd but probably mid to late second century) where the honorific is set into the context of a temple dedicated to the "distinguished goddess, Demeter Karpophoros" (τῆι διασημοτάτηι θεᾷ Δήμητρι Καρποφόρωι, ll. 5–6); cf *I.Pessinous* 31 (time of Hadrian).

41 Dio Cassius 51.20.6–7.

42 *Dig.* 1.16.4.5 cf *I.Ephesos* 217.

43 See *I.Stratonikeia* 1101 = *LSAM* 69, l. 3 (probably shortly after 39 BCE); *I.Ephesos* 27A, l. 27 (first half 2nd century CE); *IGR* 4.1516, ll. 4–5 (Sardis, early 3rd century CE); *I.Iznik* 2.1 Add, l. 3 (Nicaea, 102–116 CE).

44 Tacitus *Ann.* 4.55–6.

45 See F. Guizzi, "Greek and Latin Inscriptions of Laodikeia on the Lykos 2003–2018," in *15. Yılında Laodikeia (2003–2018)* edited by C. Şimşek (Istanbul: Ege, 2019), 175. The inscription has previously been referenced in chapters 4 and 7.

until the reign of Caracalla-Elagabalus, almost two centuries on from its first recorded "competitive tender".

Laodikeia never claimed a neokorate for the second time; however some of the neokorate coins from the reign of Elagabalus featured two temples facing one another, each containing a cult statue. The style was repeated during the reign of Philip II (247–249 CE). Barbara Burrell has made a thorough survey of the variety of Laodikeia's neokorate coins.[46] Her conclusion is that Elagabalus simply reiterated Caracalla's restoration of neokorate status that had been initially awarded early in the reign of Commodus — subsequently retracted because of his posthumous but short-lived *damnatio memoriae*.[47] The usual words ΛΑΟΔΙΚΕΩΝ ΝΕΩΚΟΡΩΝ are ubiquitous in the coin legends at this time. But they are absent from Hadrian's time. Under Elagabalus, it is underscored that the award was by decree of the Senate, δογματι συνκλήτου,[48] that is *Senatus consultum* — the correct register for the award.[49] The inscription provides an explanation for Burrell's conundrum about this accent:

> It seems odd … that a city in Asia, that hotbed of neokoroi, with a rival neokoros like Hierapolis not far away, should be so particular to claim that it was neokoros by Senatorial decree but fail to specify that it held that honor twice over.[50]

Whether Hadrian quietly acquiesced in the honor that involved the irregularity of a failure to obtain senatorial authority for the neokorate award is of course unknown. More likely it was a syntheotic honor bestowed at the temple of Zeus during Hadrian's Olympian tour, that affirmed that Laodikeia was the metropolitical neokoros-guardian of the leading Zeus cult in the *conventus*.[51] Laodikeia's provincial ambitions however were not to be thwarted, and this local award may have been part of its larger project. Nonetheless, the city had to tread at least a little delicately; she produced an overall iconographical set that is (deliberately?) obfuscating. Not only were the two facing temples reinforced by a doubled imperial reference on some coins — ΚΟΜΟΔΟΥ ΚΕ ΑΝΤΩΝΕΙΝΟΥ ΛΑΟΔΙΚΕΩΝ ΝΕΩΚΟΡΩΝ[52] — evoking but not stating a second award. There are also coins from this time that tie a date, PH = 88, to these neokorate coins.

---

46 See B. Burrell, *Neokoroi: Greek Cities and Roman Emperors* (Leiden: Brill, 2004), 120–4.

47 See *I.Laodikeia Lykos* 45 where Louis Robert identified the erasure of νεωκόρος (replaced by φιλοσέβαστος) in ll. 4–5 and correctly tied the inscription to the time of Commodus (l. 2). See "Les Inscriptions" in *Laodicée du Lycos: Le Nymphée* edited by J. des Gagniers *et al.* (Paris: de Boccard, 1969), 281–9 followed by Thomas Corsten (commentary on *I.Laodikeia Lykos* 45) and Burrell, *Neokoroi*, 119–20.

48 *RPC online* 6.5503 temp.

49 See also the discussion in chapter 4.

50 Burrell, *Neokoroi*, 123.

51 For fuller exposition and argument, see my "The Lust for Recognition and Influence: Laodikeia and the Quest for Neokorate Status" in *Revelation, the Aegean and Material Culture* edited by A. Keddie, D. Smith and N. Leach (London: Routledge, 2023), forthcoming.

52 *RPC online* 6.5502 temp.

Plate 11.3: A coin from the time of Elagabalus, here featuring, possibly as a posthumous honor, the head of Julia Domna as Sebasta on the obverse with Laodikeia's city Tyche on the reverse. The reverse legend not only proclaims ΛΑΟΔΙΚΕΩΝ ΝΕΩΚΟΡΩΝ, but in the lower field, flanking Tyche, has † ΠΗ (with overbar), "the year 88".[53]

Burrell and Thonemann, correctly in my estimation, tie the date to Hadrian's pan-hellenic visit to Laodikeia in 129 CE.[54] Thonemann considered that that *adventus* was accorded the status of a new calendrical foundation but ties it to an invention of Caracalla that served his desire to enhance his own visit in emulation of Hadrian's famed tour.[55] The newly published inscription from Laodikeia I consider is the key to understanding the date. Guizzi was a little hesitant in dating it to 129 CE but an adjacent inscription honoring Hadrian's wife, Sabina, is most apt for the visit which saw her accompanying the emperor.[56] Year "88" thus becomes a subtle memorializing of an initial, if irregular or diminished, neokorate award. The city fostering eminence in its own mind might count three neokorates — under the reigns of Hadrian, Commodus and Caracalla-Elagabalus. But at the official level, that is, of senatorial award, it could only claim one, whatever embellishments its numismatic stylistics might use to create a muddied stereoscopic vision (cf Rev 3:17–18).

By contrast, Eugenetoriane's "Sacred Senate" coin is precise in its affirmation of loyalties to Rome — Colossae belonged to a senatorial not imperial province. At least in the first and second centuries, this was crucial to Colossae's position, even with the necessary demands (and aspirations) to gain the emperor's favor, as the inscription and coins commemorating Hadrian's visit to the city confirm.[57] And, in the iconography that her coin shared with almost all other representations of the Senate in eastern mintings, this was a youthful reality — a young man, not the aged Genius of the Senate visually displayed at Rome,[58] nor, significantly, a woman as the gender of the legend might have elicited (and which is found in representations of the local primary governing authority, the "Sacred Boulê").[59]

Hence, the question with which we began is directed to discerning where the presence of Roman regulatory authority, especially that of the Senate, might

53 *BMC Phrygia* Laodikeia 217 var. Photograph from Roma coins by permission.

54 Burrell, *Neokoroi*, 121, P. Thonemann, *The Maeander Valley: A Historical Geography from Antiquity to Byzantium* (Cambridge: Cambridge University Press, 2011), 213–4.

55 Thonemann, *Maeander Valley*, 214 n35.

56 Guizzi, "Greek and Latin Inscriptions," 175–6. Both inscriptions were found at the Eastern Byzantine Nymphaeum; however, their lithographic style indicates different stone-cutters.

57 *IGR* 4.869; *RPC* 3.2309; *RPC online* 2310A.

58 *RIC* 2.288a, c.

59 *MSPhryg* 2.537–40.

be discerned at Colossae. One might have thought that the tracking of Latin would provide a start but the few inscriptions we have from Colossae disappoint. Indeed, almost all our notice of senatorial resolutions affecting Asia come from Greek inscriptions — translations from the Latin emanating from the Senate's bureaucracy in Rome.[60] The only Latin inscription from Colossae dates to the beginning of the fourth century, notably "imposed" on the netherside of a pedestal that had registered the provision of an annual memorialization of a mother's "hero" son, recently deceased; it had been previously inscribed, authorized by the city council (the *Boulê*), barely half a century earlier.[61] At present, there are no bilingual inscriptions, such as have occasionally surfaced at Dionysopolis and Laodikeia.[62] In fact, the scarcity of Latin inscriptions is a marked feature of the Lycus Valley, as compared, say, with Ephesos. This is not an indicator of the presence or absence of Roman citizenship or Roman names generally, but our access to these is from the Greek. Nor does it preclude a similar absorption or appropriation of Roman words by Greek transliteration as, for example, occurs in the frequent use of the Latin *exemplum* (and cognates) in so-called "confession inscriptions" of the second and third centuries from the sanctuary of Apollo Lairbenos above the Maeander River at the northern extremity of the territory of Hierapolis.[63]

From Colossae, the onomastic return of Latin names, as we have seen in chapter 9, numbers 14, some of which are found in the formula of Roman citizenship (for example, Crispinus); others are an inheritance from a servile background (for example, Likinnios). Latin is clearly not the language of daily commerce, even citizenry requirements. This is no more than Werner Eck has already underscored, at the same time cautioning us about the limitations

60 Werner Eck finds fragments of only five Latin renditions of *senatus consulta* in Asia, all carved on stone not bronze, as was the practice in Rome and in western provinces: "*Senatus consulta*," 35, 37; see Polybius 3.26; Suetonius *Vesp*. 8; for an example of the senate's specific requirement, *I.Aphrodisias and Rome* 8, l. 91 (2nd to 3rd century CE).

61 *MAMA* 6.38 (Latin dedication to Constantius I, Diocletian and Maximian) on the same pedestal (reverse face) as *MAMA* 6.42 (commemoration of Aurelius Herakleon by his mother Aurelia Ammiane).

62 *I.Asia Mixed* 93, 96.

63 See Petzl, *Beichtinschriften* 106, l. 18 (as reconstructed), 111, ll. 8–9 (spelt ἐξονπλάριον), 120, l. 8, 121, l. 5; A. H. Cadwallader, "Bodily display and epigraphical confession at the Sanctuary of Apollo Lairbenos: an examination of emotional responses," *JES* 1 (2018): 184–6 nr. 1, l. 6; on the interpretation of the use of ἐξενπλάριον/ἔξενπλον in derivation from a technical Roman juristic term, see U. Huttner, "Latin Law in Greek Cities: Knowledge of Law and Latin in Imperial Asia Minor," in *Law in the Roman Provinces* edited by K. Czajkowski *et al.* (Oxford: Oxford University Press, 2020), 140–1. Confession inscriptions are found in a number of places across Asia and as far as Jerusalem, but the appropriation of this technical term to confession stelai is only attested at Apollo Lairbenos, though it is found in a Latin *defixio* from Claudia Baelo in Baetica: *AE* 1988.727, l. 5 (*exsemplaria*; late 1st to early 2nd century CE): see H. S. Versnel, "Prayers for Justice, East and West: New Finds and Publications since 1990," in *Magical Practice in the West. Papers from the International Conference Held at the University of Zaragoza* edited by R. Gordon and F. M. Simón (Leiden: Brill, 2010), 283–5.

of surviving evidence, and noting, for example, that milestones, *the* mark of authority over territory and travel, were almost exclusively in Latin.[64]

This bifurcates the question into, firstly, the presence of Roman regulatory practice at Colossae (and the province generally) and secondly, the extent to which the general population's negotiation of such regulation was an issue. There may be a third aspect, namely, the decision made by judges appointed under one jurisdiction about which jurisdiction's laws would be applied to a given case. Pliny's letters indicate that local laws were often preferred as the determinant of judgments.[65] This imperial *modus operandi* (subject to minimal disruption to imperial interests) is confirmed from non-literary sources of the first and second centuries.[66] One Letter of Hadrian to the Aphrodisians is clear about the assignment of jurisdictions:

> Having received your decree and heard from your ambassadors about the financial [cases, I concede to you that if a Greek] who is a citizen of Aphrodisias either by birth or by adoption into the citizen body [is prosecuted by a] Greek who is a citizen of Aphrodisias, the trial is to be heard under your [laws and at Aphrodisias], but if, on the contrary, a Greek [from another city (is prosecuted by a Greek Aphrodisian) the trial is to be held under] Roman law and in the province; those, however, who are [in debt to the city or stand surety for such a debt] or in short have a financial involvement with your public [treasury] are to undergo [trial in Aphrodisias].[67]

The letter cannot be provincialized; such *ad hoc* responses, whilst reflecting a general attitude, were always subject to local conditions. Nonetheless, there appears to be some survival of this methodology in the *Digest*, the massive Roman compilation ascribed to Justinian.[68] And it also seems to have operated

64 W. Eck, "The Presence, role and significance of Latin in the epigraphy and culture of the Roman Near East," in *From Hellenism to Islam: Cultural and Linguistic Change in the Roman Near East* edited by H. Cotton *et al.* (Cambridge: Cambridge University Press, 2009), 15–42 (p. 39, concerning milestones).

65 Trajan to Pliny *Ep.* 10.109, 10.113.

66 See *P.Oxy.* 237 col VIII.2–7 (186 CE); 3015 (after 117 CE); Oliver, *Greek Constitutions*, nrs 91 II, ll. 5–6 (Hadrian[?] to the Spartans, 184 II, ll. 12, 37 (Marcus Aurelius to the Athenians). It should be admitted that the constant reference of issues of local law to the senate and its proconsuls and, increasingly, to the emperor served the process of Romanization of the legal system even when the immediate response gained imperial backing for the application of local law.

67 … τῷ ψηφισ- | ματι ὑμῶν ἐντυχὼν καὶ τῶν ὑμετέρων πρεσβέων ἀκούσας περὶ τῶν χρηματικῶν δι- | κῶν, συγχωρῶ ὑμεῖν εἰ μὲν Ἕλλην, Ἀφροδεισιεὺς φύσει ἤ τῶν παρ' ὑμεῖν πολει- | τευομένων, τις ἐγκαλεῖται ὑφ' Ἕλληνος Ἀφροδεισιέως, κατὰ τοὺς ὑμετέρους | νόμους καὶ παρ' ὑμεῖν καθίστασαι τὰς δίκας· εἰ δὲ τοὐναντίον Ἕλλην πα- | ρ' ἄλλης πόλεως κατὰ Ῥωμαίων νόμους καὶ ἐν τῇ ἐπαρχίᾳ· τοὺς μέντοι χρεώστας τῆς πόλεως ἤ βεβαιωτὰς ἤ ὅλως συνβεβληκότας τῷ δημοσίῳ ὑ- | μῶν, παρ' ὑμεῖν τὴν δίκην ὑπέχειν· … *I.Aphrodisias 2007*, 11.412, ll. 4–11 (119–125 CE, reconstruction and translation by J. R. Reynolds).

68 See *Dig.* 1.3.32 prol., 1.16.7.1, 25.4.1.15.

in many *poleis* of Greek socialization as the preferred practice well into the third century, at least in some areas of legal interest (such as manumission).

For all that our limited material resources from Colossae contain no explicit set of regulations (apart from the scattered evocative samples in the Letter to the Colossians), there are some traces that at least demonstrate the pertinence of aspects of the question raised, namely of laws and their execution at Colossae. There are three types of epigraphical evidence that I wish to probe: the variety of modes by which authorization is given for the public memorialization of a deceased person; the variety of offices/institutions available for the receipt of penalties for disturbance of tombs and the implications this has for the laws governing such infractions; and the city's provision to its inhabitants of advice about the various laws and their jurisdictional reach.

Memorialization of individuals at Colossae

We are fortunate to have two surviving inscriptions from Colossae that address the honorific memorialization of deceased individuals. One is an inscription on a statue base, to be dated to the late first or early second century, accompanying the erection of a statue to honor the late Marcus Larcius Crispinus.[69] The second, a pedestal, is probably to be given a date of 212–250 CE,[70] and records permission and provision for an annual garlanding ceremony in memory of Aurelius Herakleon.[71] Here then are two sons receiving memorializing honors — one a statue, one an annual ceremony. Both arrangements come with the authorization of the local authorities but the manner of that authorization seems to follow a different process. It is worthwhile to give the full texts of the two inscriptions, which have already been mentioned previously.[72]

69 *MAMA* 6.39 = *I.Mus. Denizli* 59; the plate accompanying the latter edition clearly shows large dowel holes used to support a statue. The stone is held at the Denizli Museum at Pamukkale. A squeeze is held at the British Institute of Ankara (Denizli 51 = DM23).

70 See the observation of W. M. Ramsay, *The Cities and Bishoprics of Phrygia* (Oxford: Clarendon Press, 1897), 550 nr. 413.

71 *MAMA* 6.42. The stone, recorded as seen at a house in Honaz, is no longer known. The primary record is a squeeze held in the Calder Archives at the Special Libraries of the University of Aberdeen (Ms 3286/10/19) accompanied by his "1933 Notebook" 53 nr. 206b (Ms 3286/4 "Bundle of Three Notebooks"); see A. H. Cadwallader, "Revisiting Calder on Colossae," *AS* 56 (2006): 105, 107–8. Louis Robert implied that the pedestal provided a base ("sur une base … (la statue)") for some addition but the dimensions (height 1.020, width 0.335, depth 0.345) suggest this would be minimal: *I.Laodicée Lycos nymphée*, 328. There is no record of dowel holes.

72 For *MAMA* 6.39, see chapter 9; for *MAMA* 6.42, see above.

Memorial for Marcus Larcius Crispinus

Plate 11.4: A squeeze of the memorial inscription for Crispinus. The length of the stone defeated the size of the squeeze paper and the executor (probably Anthony Sheppard in 1975/6) completed the impression in two overlapping sections. The beginnings of the four lines of text (3 to 4 letters) are captured in the lower repetition.[73]

Ἡ βουλὴ καὶ ὁ δῆμος ἐτείμησεν Μ(ᾶρκον) Λάρ- | κιον Κρισπεῖνον ἥρωα ἐκ διατάξεως Μ(άρκου) | Λαρκίου Παπίου τοῦ πατρὸς αὐτου ἐπιμε- | ληθέντος τῆς τιμῆς Τ(ιβερίου) Ἀσινίου Ἐπαφροδείτου.

The Council and People's Assembly honored Marcus Larcius Crispinus as hero, from the deed of specifications of Marcus Larcius Papias, his father. Superintendence of the honorific display was by Tiberius Asinius Epaphroditos.

Memorial for Aurelius Herakleon

Plate 11.5: William Calder's squeeze of the memorial inscription for Herakleon.[74]

73 Photograph by permission of the Director of the British Institute of Ankara. Ligature in l. 1 (HM), l. 3 (ME) and l. 4 (HC with three-bar instead of four-bar sigma, as elsewhere). The *omicron* before the final *upsilon* is reduced in size, squeezed between the *tau* and *upsilon*. The stone-cutter appears to have been pressed for space for the last line, in order to remain within the molded border.

74 The photograph is from the plate in *MAMA* volume 6 (public domain). Ligature in l. 10 (MHH). There was no room for the final line on the squeeze (ἰδίων) for the 17 line inscription. Calder added this from his notebook entry.

Αὐρ(ήλιον)Ἡρακλέω- | να Καρπίωνος | τὸν ἥρωα, δού- | σης τῆς μη- | τρὸς αὐτοῦ Αὐ[ρ](ηλίας) | Ἀμμιανῆς | Τρύφωνος ἐ- | πὶ τῷ στεφα- | νοῦσθαι αὐ- | τὸν μη. η' ζ' ὑπ[ὸ] | τῆς κρατίστ[ης] | βουλῆς Ӿ φ' | τὴν δὲ ἀνάστ[α-] | σιν ποιησαμέ- | νου τοῦ πατρὸς | αὐτοῦ ἐκ τῶν | ἰδίων.

(This is erected) for Aurelius Herakleon, son of Karpion, as a hero. His mother Aurelia Ammiane, daughter of Tryphon, gave 500 denarii for garlanding it in the 8th month on the 7th day, by permission from the most excellent Council, and his father provided the monument at his own expense.

At first comparison, the inscriptions share a number of common elements. A parent takes the initiative in providing a memorial for a deceased child, ensuring some provision for the honor. Civic authorities are involved in the establishment. The deceased, apparently young, are called "heroes", a debasement/democratization of the language of honor that had crept into funerary dedications,[75] and would later be replicated in Christian epitaphs.[76] The generalization may have been cultivated by the sense that the heroic dead continued to exercise an influence over the living — and this could be as true of a beloved eight-year old as one who had executed heroic exploits in life.[77] Certainly, the original development of the notion of hero seems to indicate "a person whose virtue, influence and personality was so powerful in his lifetime or through the peculiar circumstances of his death that his spirit after death is regarded as a supernormal power, claiming to be reverenced and propitiated."[78] These Colossian examples of heroes are not epitaphs but memorializations for which their promoters apparently sought a wider public acknowledgement than might be afforded by a location in the necropolis;[79] the genre of installation may have

---

75 *I.Aphrodisias 2007* 2.508 (1st century CE). A deceased eight-year-old, Epitynchanon, is applauded as a "hero" in the village of Thermai Theseos in 140/141 CE (*TAM* V,1 71). See L. Robert, *Hellenica* 13, 207. The loss of status associated with the term is seen in the fourth century CE, where it can even be applied to a living benefactor (Diodorus 16.20.6). A brother and sister are both called heroes in *I.Aphrodisias 2007* 13.401 (1st to 2nd century CE).

76 *ICG* 215 (Pithoi; 300–400 CE). See C. Breytenbach and C. Zimmermann, *Early Christianity in Lycaonia and Adjacent Areas: From Paul to Amphilochius of Iconium* (Leiden: Brill, 2018), 492.

77 See C. P. Jones "A Follower of the God Glykon?" *EA* 30 (1998): 107 for this intriguing suggestion. Compare also C. C. Wenn, S. Ahrens and J. R. Brandt, "Romans, Christians, and pilgrims at Hierapolis in Phrygia: Changes in funerary practices and mental process," in *Life & Death in Asia Minor in Hellenistic, Roman and Byzantine Times: Studies in Archaeology and Bioarchaeology* edited by J. R. Brandt, *et al.* (Oxford: Oxbow, 2017), 210.

78 L. R. Farnell *Greek Hero Cults and Ideas of Immortality* (Oxford: Clarendon Press, 1921), 343. The story of "The Hero", justifying the erection of a monument with the establishment of rituals is recounted by a number of writers: see Kallimachos *Ait.* fr. 98–99, Aelian *Var. Hist.* 8.18, Pausanias 6.6.7. Compare the discussion by P. M. Fraser, *Rhodian Funerary Monuments* (Oxford: Clarendon Press, 1977), 76–81.

79 The distinction is noted by Pliny *NH* 34.9.17, and acknowledged in the *Dig.* 11.7.42 (Florentinus). It is borne out by an inscription at Kyzikos honoring the late Apollonis (*SEG* 28.953 = *New Doc. Early Christ.* 4.2; 25–50 CE). She was to be interred with her previously deceased husband in the family tomb near the great harbor (ll. 49–50) but also have a statue prominently dis-

been a means of side-stepping the widespread resistance, rarely overcome, to the incorporation of tombs within the walls of the city.[80]

However, there are also notable differences which suggest that we are dealing with more than the city's condolence honors for the early demise of a child of the elite class.[81] In the Crispinus memorialization, the city Council, the *Boulê*, and the Citizens' Assembly, the *Dêmos*, are credited as the agents conferring the honor (l. 1), whereas the Herakleon pedestal simply recognizes the authorization for the establishment of the monument by "the most excellent Council" (ll. 11–12).[82] This status articulation is underscored by the careful precision of settled (male) Roman citizenship for all parties involved in the first case, compared to the (female) newly acquired *Romanitas* (probably post-*Constitutio Antoniniani*) in the second.[83] Significantly, a member of the illustrious Asinii family takes responsibility that everything is executed faithfully.[84] Here senato-

played (ll. 64–5) and regularly crowned by those coming to register their marriage (ll. 69–70). On the importance of location for interpretation, see P. Perkins "Power, Culture and Identity in the Roman Economy," in *Experiencing Rome: Culture, Identity and Power in the Roman Empire* edited by J. Huskinson (London: Routledge, 2000), 194–5.

80 Compare the hero-sites mentioned by Thucydides 1.138.5, Herodotos 5.67, Pindar *Ol.* 1.93, Pausanias 5.13.1.

81 Compare *I.Aphrodisias 2007* 12.311 with commentary. However it should be noted that this Aphrodisian memorialization seems to be related to the boys' age-group (perhaps in a competition) connected with the gymnasium.

82 I take ὑπό in l. 11 as indicating the Council's permission. The foundational sum of 500 denarii (l. 12) is hardly sufficient for an (implied) yearly interest return to draw Colossae's elite to an annual display (again implied) of commemoration (cf κατ' ἔτος *P.Oxy.* 494, l. 24, 156–65 CE). Roman law held a presumption for annuities: *Dig.* 33.1.17 (Labeo.) Compare *CIL* 11.4815 (101–200 CE) where 250,000 sesterces was set aside for the Spoletium councillors themselves to celebrate an annual memorial banquet, that is, approximately 125 times the Colossian foundation!). The Council may have delegated the observance to a minor civic bureaucrat (cf *I.Pisidia* 119, *I.Aphrodisias 2007* 13.148 but compare *I.Aphrodisias 2007* 13.105), to some group akin to the χοαχύται — tenders of graves and memorial rituals — known in Egypt (*UPZ* 2.187 [127/126 BCE]) or to an association whose activities included funerals and memorializations (see I. Arnaoutoglou, "Hierapolis and its Professional Associations: A Comparative Analysis," in *Urban Craftsmen and Traders in the Roman World* edited by A. Wilson and M. Fohr (Oxford: Oxford University Press, 2016), 289–93. The fact that the pedestal was re-used for an imperial inscription perhaps 50 years later (*MAMA* 6.38) suggests that any implied "eternity" barely survived the mother's lifetime, at least when emperors were involved. Compare also *SEG* 63.1237 (Hierapolis; 200–250 CE) where the responsibility for adornment is given to two collegia (wool-workers and gardeners). The deferential epithet applied to the Council, κράτιστη (l. 11), is a widespread commonplace (*I.Olympia* 458, *IG* X 2 1 137, *I.Didyma* 489, *MAMA* 4.64, *P.Oxy.* 41).

83 Even so the initiative of the mother is an important consideration; see chapter 12.

84 On the Asinii connections, that can be traced back to the famous Asinius Pollio (founder of a library in Rome: Pliny *NH* 7.31.114), and proconsul of Asia in 6–5 BCE, see chapter 9. See, similarly, A. Standhartinger, "Mehr als eine Stadt in Phrygien: Das antike Kolossä und sein Brief," in *Talking God in Society: Multidisciplinary (Re)constructions of Ancient (Con)texts: Fs Peter Lampe. Volume 1: Theories and Applications* edited by Ute E. Elsen and H. E. Mader (Göttingen: Vandenhoeck & Ruprecht, 2020), 701.

rial class (or at least closely aligned to that class) is combined with equestrian class (the Larkii family connections)[85] in a διάταξις (l. 2), a technical term that can carry a weight far above the gift (δούσης, ll. 3–4) of Herakleon's mother, Ammiane, or the expense (ἐκ τῶν ἰδίων, ll. 16–17) of his father Karpion (who is not named as a newly-minted Roman citizen). For Roman law, rank was critical.[86] Both of course harness financial resources to further their initiatives.

It is certain that Herakleon's family are a local citizen family embedded in one or other of the agricultural and/or commercial pursuits that were integral to the city's economy. Crispinus's family (and probably also that of Asinius Epaphroditus) however are likely to have owned substantial estates as Roman citizens. These may have encompassed agriculture, mining and/or quarrying in the well-resourced upper Lycus Valley. Such estates were critical to the maintenance of the wealth that undergirded their rank,[87] and were pockets of territory within Colossae's borders that were directly governed by Roman legal protections and processes.[88] Consequently, the approaches to the Colossian civic authorities by these two families were backed by substantially different standings, financially and legally.

This compels a closer investigation of the procedural mechanics of the acquisition of authority to erect the statue/monument. The term διάταξις, given only in the first case, is the key. The word has a broad semantic field, connecting with the disciplined formation of the military,[89] the arrangement of topics for discursive analysis,[90] the ordering of finances in a budget,[91] and even, in later development, to express a collated law code.[92] Similarly, the word can function

85 See Thonemann, *Maeander Valley*, 218. There is one certain equestrian connected with Colossae, the procurator, Loukios Macedo: S. Demougin, "L'ordre équestre en Asie Mineure. Histoire d'une Romanization," in *L'ordre équestre. Histoire d'une aristocratie (IIe siècle av J.-C. – IIIe siècle ap J.-C.)* edited by S. Demougin, H. Devijver and M.-T. Raepsaet-Charlier (Rome: École française de Rome, 1999), 606, nr. 148. It is tenuous, however, to tie his dedication to Hadrian during the emperor's pan-Hellenic tour, found at Colossae (*IGR* 4.869), to his ethnic. It may imply some sort of patronage of the city. If so, the soft power of Rome would be felt even more by civic leaders.

86 *Dig.* 1.9.1–4.

87 O. Pelcer-Vujačić, "Roman Senators from Phrygia," in *Phrygia in Antiquity: From the Bronze Age to the Byzantine Period* edited by G. R. Tsetskhladze (Leuven: Peeters, 2019), 222–3, 232.

88 Compare *SEG* 19.765a–c (54–55 CE) a territorial dispute between the city of Sagalassos and a village on an imperial estate, the determination of which, precisely because it involved an imperial estate, passed to the procurator of the imperial province of Galatia. See, further, G. H. R. Horsley and R. Kearsley, "Another Boundary Stone between Tymbrianassos and Sagalassos in Pisidia," *ZPE* 121 (1998): 123–9.

89 Herodotos 9.6 cf Col 2:5 (τάξις).

90 Lucian *Hist. Conscr.* 24.

91 *I.Délos* 399A, 442A. See L.Migeotte, "La ΔΙΑΤΑΞΙΣ de Délos Durant l'indépendance: un budget pour la cite?" *LEC* 73 (2005): 27–38.

92 Hence, the Byzantine *Diataxis of Attaleites* (1077 CE). Josephus however uses the term to render the Mosaic constitution: Josephus *Ant.* 1.5, 11; 3.286.

as a metonymic summation for an edict,[93] a set of guidelines,[94] a testamentary disposition,[95] a deed of foundation,[96] even a temple treasury.[97] In this sense, it is sometimes used in funerary or memorialization inscriptions to indicate not merely the (monetary) provision of a tomb or monument but a course of arrangements that have been entered into by which the visible result has been executed.[98] This is particularly apparent in the *Diataxis* (sometimes translated "Testament") *of Epikrates* which contains a lengthy inscription detailing manifold arrangements (including apportionment of lands, arrangement of finances and responsibilities for cultic practices) to establish a heroized memorial for his son, Diophantos.[99] The key emphasis is the bringing of order to an array of resources: people, lands, money, archives, and so on, with a particular concentration on the *administrative process* or *regulation* by which that order was to be achieved and preserved, rather than the bureaucratic accounting of the various elements. It explains the importance of the supervision of affairs (ἐπιμεληθέντος τῆς τιμῆς, Crispinus inscription, l. 4), precisely the responsibility indicated on another Colossian honorific inscription.[100]

Given that the term διάταξις occurs in the Colossian inscription on a statue base inscription, it is likely to operate not merely as a recognized authoritative term but to signal that there was a record of the details of that διάταξις on which Tiberius Asinius Epaphroditos acted. The positioning of the Council and Citizens' Assembly into the frame of authorization suggests that the *grammateus* of the Council had a copy, probably with another deposited in the civic archives.[101] It may even be that the *diataxis* itself was inscribed (perhaps with other details of the provisioning, the positioning and installation

93 *I.Ephesos* 17, l. 14 (44 CE); *SEG* 30.568, l. 17 (Battyna, 144/5 or 192/3 CE).

94 Oliver, *Greek Constitutions*, 84 ll. 36–7 (Pergamon, 129 CE?).

95 *I.Pisidia* 46, l. 9 (Sai, before 212 CE; text slightly uncertain); *I.Pisidia* 170, l. 7–8 (Maximianoupolis? 2nd to 3rd century CE; verbal cognate); *SEG* 46.1652 (Eumeneia, imperial, possible reconstruction of text).

96 See C. P. Jones, "A Deed of Foundation from the Territory of Ephesos," *JRS* 73 (1983): 116–25.

97 *SEG* 26.121, fr. ac.00, ll. 14, 16, 20 (Athens 10/9–3/2 BCE); *SEG* 19.172 l. 18 (Athens, Hadrianic); cf *TAM* V,3 1462, ll. 8–9 (Philadelphia, 2nd century CE).

98 *SEG* 54.1314, l.3 (Hierapolis c. 200 CE, here the cognate διαταγή).

99 ὅθεν τούτων τῶν ἀφωτισμένων καὶ συνκαθωσιωμένων τῷ μνημείῳ καὶ ἥρωι Διοφάντῳ μόνην ἐμαυτῷ τὴν συνκεχωρημένην διάταξιν ἐπέτρεψα. (ll. 38–40) "here, regarding the complex and associated land for the memorial and for the hero Diophantos, I have for myself relied solely upon the terms of the consolidated diataxis." Text (Nakrason, 1st century CE) from P. Herrmann and K. Z. Ziya, *Das Testament des Epikrates und andere neue Inschriften aus dem.Museum von Manisa.* (Vienna: Böhlau, 1969), 10.

100 *IGR* 4.870, l. 11 (mid-second century CE). See also *TAM* V,3 1462, ll. 8–12 (Philadelphia, 2nd century CE; a group responsibility).

101 See *SEG* 33.679, ll. 57–65 (Paros; 175–150 BCE). On the crucial importance of archives in late Hellenistic and early Roman imperial times, see K. Harter-Uibopuu, "Epigraphische Quellen zum Archivwesen in den griechischer Poleis des ausgehenden Hellenismus und der Kaiserzeit," in *Archives and Archival Documents in Ancient Societies* edited by M. Faraguna (Triste: EUT, 2013), 273–305.

of the honor, and other associated matters such as the purchase of the site of installation),[102] just as we find in the expansive theater installation recording the details of a foundation for the temple of Artemis. The regular procession in her honor and for the wider benefit of the city was made by Gaius Vibius Salutaris at the beginning of the second century in Ephesos. Guy Rogers suggests that διάταξις was a Greek translation of the Latin *constitutio*,[103] but it is particularly striking that one bilingual panel in the series detailing the "deed(s) of gift" code-switches. The Latin adopts the Greek term (not the reverse) even though, as almost always in Latin-Greek bilingual texts in Asia, the Latin is inscribed first. The Latin reads *sicut in diataxi superiore cautum est* "just as has been laid down in the *diataxis* above"; the Greek is more emphatic, underscored by the repetition of the stem τὸ ἐν τῇ διατάξει προδιατεταγμένον "set down previously in the *diataxis*".[104]

I make no suggestion here that the Crispinus memorial in any way replicates the magnitude of Salutaris' benefactions. However, the structural pattern does carry parallels — high-ranking Roman officials approach the local civic authorities with a proposal, well-funded and well-organized. The implicit coercion combined with the advantage of city adornment brings those authorities into the picture as authenticating the Roman initiative and making it their own — the Council and *Dêmos* join the senatorial class in a combined honoring (ἐτείμησεν l. 1, τῆς τιμῆς l. 4). Roman law recognized the importance of such foundations and provisions to a city.[105] There is little doubt that such Roman laws were part of the implicit armory that the Asinii and the Larcii carried into negotiations with local civic authorities, even when those bodies retained their instruments and jurisdiction in the formal approval process. If there was any conflict of laws in this plurality of systems, there is little doubt where the *potentas* would be felt. Diane Ng captures the rationale, "The carefully considered plans by Roman elites not only to erect physical markers to themselves in the form of statues or public inscriptions but also to draw attention to such markers ..."[106] The relationships between such leaders and the city meant that the city (as a *polis*) and its leaders were confirmed in their positions (being honorers of Roman status). However, another plank was laid that con-

102 That a site, however small in area, is likely to have required a transaction is indicated by an inscription from Thiounta where a record of members of an association is listed on a stele which notes that one member, Zeuxis son of Diodorus, purchased a place for the stone (ἀγοράσας τόπον στήλης); Ramsay, *Phrygia* 1.142.30A,3 (2nd century CE).

103 G. M. Rogers, *The Sacred Identity of Ephesus* (London: Routledge repr, 1991), 24. *Constitutio* tends to imply a wide variety of imperial legislation and governs rather than constitutes deeds, foundations and the like (*Dig.* 50.12.1 [Ulpian]).

104 *I.Ephesos* 33, ll. 12–13, 21–22.

105 *Dig.* 33.2.18 (Scaevola); *Dig.* 50.12.10 (Modestinus).

106 D. Y. Ng, "The Salutaris Foundation: Monumentality through Periodic Rehearsal," in *Roman Artists, Patrons and Public Consumption: Familiar Works Reconsidered* edited by B. Longfellow and E. Perry (Ann Arbor: University of Michigan Press, 2018), 83.

firmed the inequities between imperial and local legal jurisdictions, inequities that would invite measured consideration by prospective litigants about which one to apply to, *if* they held sufficient standing.

And the issue of standing marks the jurisdictional difference for the Herakleon memorial. There is no question of sufficent standing to claim Roman authority for proceeding the request and no intent to do so. A permission is sought from "the most excellent Council"; there is no parallel to whatever influence wrought an honoring from the Council or Citizens' Assembly, apart from the standard civic responsibility to execute faithfully the terms of a trust (here provision for garlanding). Whatever supervision may have been required for its execution is left unstated. Of particular note is that, if the dating to a post-212 time is correct, then Heracleon's mother, Ammiane, continued to operate according to local processes and authorities.

A comparison of these two memorializations has only proved suggestive of the legal regulations governing the installations. These have been intimated by the use of particular terms: διάταξις and ἐπιμεληθέντος in the Crispinus inscription; δούσης and ἐκ τῶν ἰδίων in the Herakleon inscription. What is transparent is the different standings — the status, rank and wealth — of the agents involved and the consequences this is likely to have had in the different roles played by the Council (and Assembly).

Penalties for grave interference

There is another trace of the presence of Roman machinery of regulation at Colossae, though it comes from an unexpected quarter — the necropolis, one of the most local human markings of space in a Greek city. Epitaphs provide the majority of inscriptions from Colossae. Of perhaps thirty-eight inscriptions currently credited to Colossae (one is disputed),[107] twenty are funerary,[108] though two are better categorized as memorials as we have seen above. Nine of these are cut on a stone having the form of a *bomos*, with an additional fragment

107 See Appendix 4. This total includes two inscriptions (both epitaphs) identifying the deceased as "Colossian" — *I.Smyrna* 440 (2nd century CE; see chapter 6); *I.Boubon* 102 (early imperial; see chapter 9) — or "Choniates", a late Byzantine ethnonym from the territory of Smyrna. The epitaph disputed as to provenance is *MAMA* 6.43, claimed by Thomas Corsten for Laodikeia (= *I.Laodikeia Lykos* 104) on the basis of hand-notes by the nineteenth-century explorer, Adolf Wilhelm. However, some doubt remains; see A. H. Cadwallader, "Gertrude Bell's Resolution of a Disputed Inscription," *Gephyra* 20 (2020): 5–6 n26. On the basis of arguments presented previously, four inscriptions have been reassigned from Laodikeia to Colossae, two of which are epitaphs.

108 On the basis of the detailed discussion in chapter 3, *MAMA* 6.19 = *I.Laodikeia Lykos* 114, an epitaph from the village of Eleinokapria, and *I.Laodikeia Lykos* 118 = Ramsay, *Phrygia* 1.1, 77 nr. 12 have been restored to the territory of Colossae.

likely so. We have met these *bomoi* already; they are noted by an evocation of a temple in their design, with pediment, acroteria and often a central boss at the top. They are usually aniconic, though one extant stone, heavily abraded, features a couple and earlier reports note symbols of implements.[109] The iteration of a sanctified site is clear and indicates that this distinctive Phrygian style, known at Colossae and in similar (though not identical form) from a number of sites in the Lycus Valley and its surrounds, used architecture to underscore the religious significance of the location and the remains placed there, and the rites that combined both. But the *bomoi* also fulfilled a crucial function by their size and weight in holding down the slab that covered the in-ground tomb.[110]

Plate 11.6: The funerary bomos for the grave of Markos son of Roupos and of his son, Dionyseios. The stone is held at the Denizli Museum where it is captioned as from Colossae and dated to the second century. The provenance is disputed (Laodikeia?) and the date may be pushed back to the second half of the first century.[111]

Five of the ten inscribed funerary *bomoi* contain a monetary penalty for disturbance of the grave. I list here in approximate chronological sequence, the extant inscriptions of the respective epitaphs that contain a penalty:

i) Ζῶσειν (in moulding), | Μᾶρκος Ῥού- | που καὶ Διο- | νύσειος ὑὸς | αὐτοῦ ἐν ῷ̣ | κηδευθήσοṿ- | ται· εἰ δὲ τις ἕ- | τερον κηδεύσ- | ịδώσι τῷ φίσκῳ̣ | ✕ φʹ.[112] (see Pl. 11.6).

While living,[113] *Markos son of Roupos and his son Dionyseios (built this for themselves) in which they are to be interred. If anyone should bury another (in it), he must pay to the* fiskus *500 denarii.*

109 See Cadwallader, "Bell's Resolution," 5, 13–14.

110 See chapter 12. On the necropolis at Colossae generally, see A. H. Cadwallader, *Fragments of Colossae: Sifting through the Traces* (Adelaide: ATF Press, 2015), 155–75.

111 See T. Corsten, *Die Inschriften von Laodikeia am Lykos* (IGSK 49; Bonn: Habelt, 1997), 186 nr. 104.

112 G. Weber, "Inschriften aus Sued-Phrygien," *MDAI(A)* 18 (1893): 207 nr. 4 = *MAMA* 6.43 = *I.Laodikeia Lykos* 104. There is a ligature KH in l. 8. A squeeze of the inscription is held at the British Institute at Ankara (DM 192); see Cadwallader, "Revisiting Calder," 107, fig. 5. A close comparison of the squeeze, the photograph and the stone indicates traces of a *nu* at the end of l. 6 and the presence of an *iota* at the beginning of l. 9 (slight corrections to Calder and Corsten's readings).

113 For a confirmation of the status appeal of such an affirmation of preparedness for death in an epitaph, compare *I.Smyrna* 437 (Γάϊος Ἀσίνιος Νυμφόδοτος ζῶν ἑαυτῶι. Imperial); *I.Smyrna* 362 (relations of previous).

ii) τ]ὸ μνημεῖον | Διονοισίου Ἀγ- | γελικοῦ καὶ τ- | ῆς γυναικὸς | αὐτοῦ Τάτας | καὶ τῆς θυγα- | τρὸς ἡμῶν Ε- | ἰρήνης· ἐν ᾧ | ἕτερος οὐ κ- | ηδεύθῃ, ἤ δὲ | εἴ τις ἕτερον | κηδεύσῃ, δώ- | σει τῷ φίσκῳ | X α′ .[114]

(This is) the grave of Dionoisios son of Aggelikos, and of his wife Tata, and of his daughter Eirene. In it, another is not to be interred; or, if someone should bury another (in it), he will pay to the fiskus *1000 denarii.*

Plate 11.7: A photograph of the funerary bomos of Dionysios and Tata taken by Gertrude Bell in April 1907. I have computer-enhanced the photograph and numbered the lines of text.[115]

iii) Τοῦτο τὸ θέ- | μα καὶ ⟨ὁ⟩ ἐπ' αὐτῷ βωμός | ἐστιν Τατιας καὶ τοῦ ἀν- | δρὸς αὐτῆς Μοσχᾶ, ἐν ᾧ | κεκήδευται ἡμῶν | ἡ θυγάτρην Ταταριν· | οὐδενὶ δ' ἐξέσται | ἄλλῳ κηδευθῆναι | εἰ μὴ τῇ μητρὶ αὐτῆς | καὶ τῷ πατρεί. Εἰ δὲ | μετὰ τὴν ἡμετέραν | τελευτὴν ἀπ⟨ε⟩ιθή- | σει τις τῶν προγε- | γραμμένων, δώσι | τῷ χώρῳ τῷ Ἐλεινοκα- | πριτῶν X φ′ .[116] (see Pl. 7.16).

This slab and the bomos on it belongs to Tatia and her husband Moschas, in which is buried our daughter Tatarin. It is not permitted for any other person to be buried (here), except for her mother and father. And if anyone after our death should not obey (our) directives above, he will pay to the village of the Eleinokaprians 500 denarii.

iv) … φισκῷ X φ′. (fragment).[117]
… to the fiskus, *500 denarii.*

---

114 Weber, "Inschriften," 206 nr. 3 = Ramsay, *Phrygia*, 2.542.408 = G. Cousin, *Kyros le Jeune en Asie Mineure (Printemps 408–Juillet 401 avant Jésus-Christ)* (Nancy: Berger-Levrault, 1904), 431, nr. 1.2. I revised these three, independent readings recently in light of the discovery of a photograph of the *bomos* executed by Gertrude Bell; see Cadwallader, "Bell's Resolution," 17. I have dated the inscription, on the basis of letter forms and onomastics, to 50–150 CE.

115 Photograph F 210, Gertrude Bell Archive, courtesy of University of Newcastle-on-Tyne.

116 *CIG* 3954 = Ramsay, *Phrygia* 1.77.11 = *MAMA* 6.19 = *I.Laodikeia Lykos* 114 (imperial period). For the argument returning the inscription to the territory of Colossae, see chapter 3.

117 The fragment was recorded as among "recently smashed" stones in the necropolis to the north of the höyük, in William Calder's notebook (University of Aberdeen, Special Libraries, Ms 3286/4/"Bundle of Three Notebooks", 1933 Notebook, 53, no 203). It was published in Cadwallader, "Calder," 108. The size of the penalty probably points to a first or second century date.

v) Τὸ μνημεῖον Αὐρηλίου | Μάρκου Κάρπωνος καὶ | τῆ[ς] γυναικὸς αὐ- | τοῦ Αὐρηλίας Τάταδος· | ἐν ᾧ βούλομαι μηδέ-| [να] ἕτερον κηδευθ[ῆν]- | αι· εἰ δέ τις ἕτερος | κηδευθήσεται, δώσει | εἰς τὸ ταμεῖον | Ӿ φ'.[118]

This is the tomb of Aurelius Marcus Karpon and his wife Aurelia Tatas. I do not want anyone to bury another in it. If anyone shall be buried (in it, the offender) will pay to the tameion, *500 denarii.*

The number of epitaphs prescribing penalties for disturbing the tomb is small (five) and cannot be used to plot any statistical significance, such as related to the amount of the penalty. Epitaphs on *bomoi*, seen in the preceding plates, were as often without any penalty (or curse) warning against infractions against tomb, site or the buried.[119] The absence of any similar warning on funerary monuments that are identical in design does not necessarily create two classes of such tombs. It is likely that the same process for purchase of the site, commissioning of construction, ordering of monument and inscription, securing of requisite permissions and recording of the same in an archival registry would have been followed — at each step, under the governance of legal and fiscal requirements.[120]

The five epitaphs with inscribed penalties manage to contain three different agencies to which the amount is to be paid: the *fiscus*, the *tameion* and the *chora*. Here we have a transliterated Latin word, a Greek word that became a technical term for an office-building, and another Greek word that seems to have acquired an official meaning something like "village/district authority".[121] This last term indicates that we are not dealing with the same entity, at least as the other two. Further, it suggests that proximity to some body able to enforce

118 G. Weber, "Die unterirdische Lauf des Lykos bei Kolossai," *MDAI(A)* 16 (1891): 199 = *IGR* 4.871 (shortly after 212 CE, based on the confusion of the citizenry formula).

119 So *MAMA* 6.44 = A. H. Cadwallader, "One New Inscription [read: Two New Inscriptions], a Correction and a Confirmed Sighting from Colossae," *EA* 40 (2007): 111–12 nr 2 = *SEG* 57.1385; *MAMA* 6.45 (fragmentary); *CIG* 3956 = Cadwallader, "Two New Inscriptions," 114 = *SEG* 57.1383 (?, fragmentary); Cadwallader, "Two New Inscriptions," 109–11 nr. 1 = *SEG* 57.1384; Cadwallader, "One Grave, Two Women, One Man: Complicating Family Life at Colossae," in *Stones, Bones and the Sacred: Essays on Material Culture and Ancient Religion in honor of Dennis E. Smith* (Atlanta, GA: SBL, 2016), 168–71 nr. 1; Cadwallader, "One Grave," 171–5 nr. 2.

120 See *I.Milet* 6.2.613, *TAM* II 63 for elements that find expression in the funerary inscriptions.

121 Ramsay wondered whether the region had been administratively divided into choroi, a legacy of Seleucid governance: W. M. Ramsay, *Cities and Bishoprics of Phrygia* (Oxford: Clarendon, 2 vols, 1895, 1897), vol. 1, 36. On the *choros* as a formal unit of territory and administration, see also N. F. Jones, *Public Organization in ancient Greece: A Documentary Study* (Philadelphia: American Philosophical Society, 1987), 74–7, 203–4, 388. The level of responsibility falling to such *choroi* in the district can be seen in an epitaph from the village of Panoskopia, which probably lay in the high country to the south above Laodikeia or north above Hierapolis. The *choros* of the Panoskopiatans provided the grave for a certain Diogenes, celebrated as a "good hero" and extending greetings to passers-by (Ὁ χῶρος ὁ Πανοσκοπιατῶν Διογένι μνίας χάριν· ἥρως ἀγαθὸς παροδίταις χαίρειν): *SEG* 54.1362 (c. 200 CE). See also *I.Laodikeia Lykos* 118 (epitaph provided by the *choros* of the Kilarazeians; imperial).

the penalty, either directly through its own administration or through some delegated agency, is an important consideration in the governance necessary to achieve the desired protection. A village authority may be low in the hierarchy of jurisdictions, and almost certainly could be overruled or re-directed by a higher system of law or juridical decision-making,[122] but it had the advantage of local knowledge, surveillance and enforcement.

The mention of a *chora* as a clear entity suggests there is likely to be a distinction between the *fiscus* and the *tameion*. David French, as with many commentators, saw the *fiscus* as the "imperial exchequer", that is the treasury that oversaw the flow of finances administered on behalf of the emperor, and the *tameion* as governing the finances of the local city. Tullia Ritti found the instances of the latter considerably outweighed the former, at least in the region of the Lycus Valley.[123] French recognized that occasionally the terminology did not follow precise demarcations.[124] Thus a *tameion* might be qualified as the *imperial* treasury office (τὸ κυριακὸν ταμεῖον)[125] paralleling the more ubiquitous ὁ κυριακὸς (Καίσαρ) φίσκος.[126] Confusion is doubtless to be expected from local citizens early in the spread of Roman hegemony in Asian cities for whom Greek terminology was the register of familiar civic discourse; later, there is likely to have been some blending of offices as cities were increasingly Romanized, especially after the *Constitutio Antoniniani* in 212 CE.

Pertinently however, numerous epitaphs multiply the agencies to which fines were to be paid,[127] sometimes even including a payment to the one who reported the infraction. At Hierapolis, for example, disturbance of a grave attracted a fine of 500 denarii payable to the Gerousia (the Council of City Elders), 500 denarii to the *tameion* and the same amount to the one who wit-

122 We have seen exactly this in chapter 3 with the villages of Kagyetteia and Thiounta required to set up a resolution of the Hierapolitan authorities (so Thonemann, *Maeander Valley*, 194 n74) that privileged protection of vineyards from damage from wandering animals over ancient territorial (village) practice of free movement of cattle and sheep. (*MAMA* 4.297, *I. Mus. Denizli* 15, 54–5 CE).

123 T. Ritti, "*Iura sepulcrorum* a Hierapolis di Frigia quadro dell'Epigrafia sepolcrale Microasiatica: Iscrizioni edite e inedite," *Libitina e dintorni* 3 (2004): 543.

124 D. French, *Roman, Late Roman and Byzantine Inscriptions of Ankara: A Selection* (Ankara: Museum of Anatolian Civilizations, 2003), 58–60; similarly, P. Lombardi and C. Vismara, "Deux inscriptions d'Aléria (Haure-Corse)," *Gallia* 62 (2005): 287. The (in)famous Aberkios inscription refers to the *tameion* of the Romans, for example (*SEG* 30.1479, l. 21; generally dated before 216 CE).

125 *IG* X 2 1 534, l. 3 (Thessalonike, 2nd – 3rd century CE); *IG* XII 8 565, l. 4 (Thasos, nd); *TAM* IV,1 237, ll. 4–5 (Nikomedeia, nd).

126 For example *BE* 1967.546, ll.9–10, *CIG* 2827, l. 10 (Aphrodisias, imperial); *MAMA* 6.141a, l. 11 (Apollonia Salbake, imperial); *MAMA* 6.131, l. 5 (Herakleia Salbake, imperial).

127 See B. Dignas, *Economy of the Sacred in Hellenistic and Roman Asia Minor* (Oxford: Oxford University Press, 2002), 136–137, 237; see also J. H. M. Strubbe, *ΑΡΑΙ ΕΠΙΤΥΜΒΙΟΙ: Imprecations against Desecration of the Grave in Greek Epitaphs of Asia Minor. A Catalogue* (Bonn: Habelt, 1997), 364–6.

nessed and reported the offense.[128] Another fine from a Hierapolitan epitaph prescribes differing amounts: 2000 denarii to the *Boulê*, 1000 denarii to the Gerousia and 2000 denarii to the treasurer (ταμίας, probably the head of the *tameion*) with 500 denarii to be awarded to the informant.[129] At Hierapolis, associations (for example the water-mill operators) might be combined with the *tameion* as recipients of fines, though usually a lesser amount was prescribed.[130] One Jewish grave at Hierapolis similarly specified the *tameion* as the recipient of the fine, in this case for 1000 denarii, and for the informant 100 denarii,[131] — one example demonstrating that at Hierapolis, Jewish graves followed local civic conventions.[132] Sometimes, the distinction between the imperial treasury and the local *polis* bodies is explicit. Thus, at Herakleia Salbake to the south of the Taurus mountain range, one epitaph prescribed a penalty of 1000 denarii to be paid to the *fiscus* and another 1000 denarii to be paid to the *Boulê* of the Herakleians — presumably a way of explicitly demarcating civic from imperial authorities.[133]

Fines to these entities were not restricted to tomb violations. The sanctuary of Apollo Lairbenos lies high above the Maeander River on the Çal plateau north of Hierapolis. One of the key social and legal functions of these sacred centers was the manumission of slaves — a pattern of dedication to a deity that functioned to free the slave from a human master by entering, even nominally, the service of the god.[134] We will return in greater detail to this decidedly-non-Roman form of manumission below. Any attempt to return the slave to indenture was subject to quite severe financial proscription.[135] A similar array of revenue agencies is given in the inscriptions, sometimes singly, often in multiple listings. The *fiscus*, sometimes specified with the additional attributes of "belonging to the Lord(s) (Caesar)/the masters", and the "most sacred *tameion*" often occur in combination with the god (usually Apollo Lairbenos) as recip-

128 *SEG* 54.1314, l. 4; *SEG* 54.1315, l. 5 (Hierapolis, c. 200 CE).

129 *SEG* 54.1301, ll. 10–14 (nd).

130 (τῷ ἱερωτάτῳ ταμίῳ Ӿ φ' καὶ τῇ συντεχνίᾳ τῶν ὑδραλέτων τ') *AAT* 1966/67.297.7, ll. 7–8 (shortly after 212 CE); cf *I.Hierapolis Judeich* 218, ll. 6–7 (association of gardeners[?]).

131 *I.Jud. Orientis* 2.192 (150–200 CE).

132 G. J. Johnson, *Early-Christian Epitaphs from Anatolia* (Atlanta, GA: Scholars Press, 1995), 6; C. Laforest, D. Castex and F. Blazot, "Tomb 163d in the North Necropolis of Hierapolis in Phrygia: An insight into the funerary gestures and practices of the Jewish diaspora in Asia Minor in late Antiquity and the proto-Byzantine period," in *Life and Death in Asia Minor*, 78–9, 82.

133 *MAMA* 6.142, ll. 2–3 (as reconstructed).

134 M. Ricl, "Les Καταγραφαί du Sanctuaire d'Apollon Lairbenos," *Arkeologi Dergisi* 3 (1995): 167–95; "Donations of Slaves and Freeborn Children to Deities in Roman Macedonia and Phrygia. A Reconsideration," *Tyche* 16 (2001): 155–60.

135 A similar regulation could apply in cities, as at the temple of Apollo in Hierapolis itself; see F. Guizzi, "Novità epigrafiche da Hierapolis di Frigia," *Historika* 7 (2017): 119–30, nr. 1.

ient of the penalty (presumably through the medium of the sanctuary).[136] In one manumission-dedication, a triple listing occurs with the *tameion*, the god and "the polis of the Moteleians" each to receive 2500 denarii.[137]

Two main points can be derived, for our purposes, from this brief survey. Firstly, the multiplicity of agencies to which fines are to be paid, especially when such amounts vary, indicates that there is usually specific intent behind the naming of those agencies. Although none of the epitaphs from Colossae contain multiple agencies to whom the fine is to be paid, it is most likely that the naming of *tameion* or *fiscus* is deliberate. The two eminent revenue centers are not to be confused. Indeed, for all the variety and combination of agencies to which fines are prescribed to be paid, to my knowledge the *tameion* and the *fiscus* are not found together in such proscription of infraction. The closest to such a combination is an inscription from Limyra, which refers to a fine payable τῷ τοῦ φίσκου ταμείῳ. This probably refers to the strong-room office of the local branch of the Roman *fiscus*.[138]

Secondly, the frequency of multiple collection agencies and persons is a characteristic of Greek not Roman legal heritage.[139] It is striking that the *fiscus*, the imperial exchequer, however much it operated in and of itself according to Roman law, was yet drawn into the familiar operations that were part of the cultural inheritance and ongoing practice of Asian Greek cities and the villages and sanctuaries within their orbit of influence, if not territorial jurisdiction. This is not to say that there was anything approaching a common code of Greek law operating across Asia, or Greece for that matter. However, as Lene Rubinstein accents, there were significant structural and procedural similarities between the legal systems of individual Greek city-states.[140] These

---

136 *SEG* 58.1520, ll. 10–12 (172/3 CE), *SEG* 58.1521, ll. 9–10 (201/2 CE), combining a fine to the god and a fine to the *fiscus*; *SEG* 58.1527B, ll. 13–16 (223/4 CE), combining god and *tameion* (here of the city of Motella, mentioned in the inscription). For the designation of the *fiscus* as "of the masters" (τὸν δεσποτῶν φίσκον) see T. Ritti, C. Şimşek and H. Yıldız, "Dediche e Καταγράφαι dal Santuario frigio di Apollo Lairbenos," *EA* 32 (2000): 22, nr. K6, ll. 10–11 (3rd century CE, likely a time of a co-regency).

137 See E. Akıncı Öztürk and C. Tanrıver, "New Katagraphai and Dedications from the Sanctuary of Apollon Lairbenos," *EA* 41 (2008): 93–4, nr. 3. Akıncı Öztürk and Tanrıver conclude that the mention of the city of Motella — the nearest to the sanctuary — aligned control of the sanctuary to that authority (p. 94). However, the number of different cities and villages in the inscriptions from the Apollo Lairbenos sanctuary suggests rather that the city authority for receipt of a fine is likely to have been the home city (or sometimes, village) from whence hailed the recorder of the *katagraphê*.

138 *SEG* 62.1442, ll. 7–8 (imperial).

139 M. D. Hall, "Even Dogs have Erinyes: Sanctions in Athenian Practice and Thinking," in *Greek Law in its Political Setting: Justifications not Justice* edited by L. Foxhall and A. D. E. Lewis (Oxford: Clarendon, 1996), 75.

140 L. Rubinstein, "Summary Fines in Greek Inscriptions and the Question of 'Greek Law'," in *Ancient Greek Law in the 21st Century* edited by P. Perlman (Austin: University of Texas Press, 2018), 104.

carried over into the early Roman imperial period and were defended as part of local, civic pride in *polis* status.[141]

The Eleinokaprian epitaph prescibes neither of the major revenue collection agencies, that is, the *fiscus* or the *tameion*. Its reference to the village *choros* raises two particular questions: what legal governance stood behind the agency/agencies that acted as revenue collectors? What influenced the tomb owners to choose such an agency/agencies, presuming that some choice was available?

Concern about dealing with the dead attracted legal dimensions that protected against the desecration of tombs. The *Digest of Justinian*, for all that it gathers material from a wide period and ambit, is particularly heavily endowed in the section dealing with funerals and tombs (Bk 11.7, 8).[142] Greek law was little different in the amount of attention it gave to death and funerary memory,[143] often accenting in regulation the very sacrality that the architecture of the *bomos* conveyed.[144]

The reference to penalties probably indicates a legal enforcement that could be relied upon even if the formal "lawfulness" is unstated. The question however of *what* law is relied upon — Roman or local — is probably indicated by the recipients of the fine.[145] The Eleinokaprian epitaph uses the language of lawfulness (ἐξέσται, l. 7) which suggests that the *choros* held some localized legal authority.[146] The choice was significantly influenced by an assessment of the best oversight and best means of reinforcement for the sake of preserving an untainted memory. Rome, of course, meant power and, where the *fiscus* was involved, it meant the delegated authority of the procurator.[147] Its bureaucracy included an archival register wherein a record of the tomb and its provisions were to be lodged. This archive was especially directed towards any property (real or personal, that is, land or produce/possessions) in which the *fiscus* had an interest as a source of

141 Brélaz, "Understandings of Roman Law," 170.

142 On the application of Roman law dealing with the sanctity of the dead, see C. Brélaz, "Local Understandings of Roman Criminal Law and Procedure in Asia Minor," in *Law in the Roman Provinces*, 166–7.

143 See I. Arnaoutoglou, *Ancient Greek Laws: A Sourcebook* (London: Routledge, 1998), nrs 33, 78, 109, 110.

144 See Martin Dreher, "'Heliges Recht' and 'Heilege Gesetze': Law, Religion and Magic in Ancient Greece," in *Ancient Greek Law in the 21st Century*, 91.

145 Similarly, Brélaz, "Understandings of Roman Law," 167–8.

146 I differ from Cédric Brélaz on this point. He assumes that the enforcement of such fines in village communities was dependent on the civic courts: "Understandings of Roman Law," 167. If villages were capable of having their own *Boulê*/*Dêmos* and attendant officials such as a γραμματεύς, as appears in come larger settlements (for example, Thiounta: *I.Mus.Denizli* 32 [3rd century CE?], 55 [2nd century CE] then it is likely that, for that community, local enforcement was possible, however *ad hoc* that may have been. Only when disputes escalated would there be recourse to the institutions of the city center.

147 P. Weaver "*Consilium praesidis*: Advising Governors," in "*Thinking Like a Lawyer" Essays on Legal History and General History for John Crook on his Eightieth Birthday* edited by P. McKechnie (Leiden: Brill, 2002), 60–61.

revenue for the empire.[148] This could include the sale of tenancies or land as well as confiscations,[149] mortgages, and the oversight of imperial estates.[150]

One fragmentary inscription that is probably an epitaph, mentions the terms of a will as governing the erection of the funerary monument (Pl. 11.8).[151]

Plate 11.8: A 55 centimeter-thick slab containing the testamentary epitaph of Damokrates, executed in terms of its provisions, by his sons. When seen and photographed by William Calder, the fragment formed part of a wall of a house in Honaz.[152] The text, as he re-constructed it, reads, καὶ Ἀπολλ]ώνιος καὶ Ἀπολλω- | [νίδης οἱ ἀδελ]ποὶ Δαμοκράτῃ | [πατρὶ κατὰ τὴ]ν διαθήκην.[153]

The Greek phrase κατὰ τὴν διαθήκην is considered to be a translation of *ex testamento*, a formulaic expression from Roman law, apparent in bilingual inscriptions.[154] Whether this is loose mimesis or a deliberate effort to attract Roman oversight, at least potentially, cannot be decided. There is no Roman citizenship, the probable epitaph is in large Greek letters (6 to 7 centimeters) and it betrays likely Phrygian interference in the spelling of ἀδελποί (if correctly reconstructed).[155] There would have been a papyrus copy of the will registered in the city archives or possibly the registration office attached to the Roman *fiscus*.

148 See *Dig.* 50.16.17.1.

149 τὰ Ἱππάρχου χωρία τὰ ὑπὸ τοῦ φίσκου πραθέντα — Oliver, *Greek Constitutions* 92, ll. 3–5 (Hadrian's Oil Law at Athens). See F. Millar, "The Fiscus in the First Two Centuries," *JRS* 53 (1963): 30–31.

150 See D. Kehoe, "Legal Institutions and Agrarian Change in the Roman Empire," in *Documentary Sources in Ancient Near Eastern and Greco-Roman Economic History* edited by H. D. Baker and M. Jursa (Oxford: Oxbow, 2014), 141.

151 *MAMA* 6.46. Photograph now in Public Domain.

152 The detail that the stone was used in a house-wall comes from Calder's notebook: University of Aberdeen Special Libraries, Calder Archives, Ms 3286/4 "Bundle of Three Notebooks —1933 Notebook" p. 54.

153 *LGPN* V.C accept the reconstruction Ἀπολλ]ώνιος but not Ἀπολλω[νίδης.

154 See *I.Asia Mixed* 54 (Apameia, mid-1st to early 2nd century CE), 87 (Tralles, 2nd century CE), 116 (Ephesos, 80 CE). These bilingual inscriptions are all by persons with Roman citizenship, which is not apparent here.

155 See C. Brixhe, "Interactions between Greek and Phrygian under the Roman Empire," in *Bilingualism in Ancient Society: Language Contact and the Written Text* edited by J. N. Adams, M. Janse and S. Swain (Oxford: Oxford University Press, 2002), 262.

A practical consideration however, was that Roman policing and jurisprudential oversight also meant distance, and the expense of attendance at an assize,[156] even if there were local officials tinkering the cogs of the imperial machinery. Indeed, sometimes the *Boulê* and *Dêmos* were harnessed to adjudicate on financial matters that impacted the returns to the *fiscus*.[157] It also meant potential detriment to much-prized self-government.[158] Local civic authority was culturally attuned, socially integrated and more easily vigilant, responsive and notifiable. Specific delegated groups might be charged with the primary responsibility of vigilance and execution of legal warrant. One sarcophagus of a physician at Ephesos specifically mentions curating by the local Board (συνέδριον) of Physicians.[159]

Local oversight certainly appears to be the case for the Eleinokaprian grave. However, it does not answer the question of whether Tatia or her husband Moscha could have chosen otherwise, that is, whether they possessed the standing to draw the protection of the city *tameion* or the imperial *fiscus*. Hadrian's careful attention to citizenship (that is, "Greek") at Aphrodisias in distinguishing the jurisdiction of courts (see above), suggests that civic citizenship may have been required to gain the surveillance and authority of the *tameion*. However, the common reference to the *fiscus* in funerary and *katagraphai* inscriptions, may suggest that the postulated violator potentially subject to a fine was not likely to be a local; in terms of Hadrian's edict to Aphrodisias, only when an offender hailed from outside Aphrodisias's territory, was Roman law exercised — for citizens. For our epitaphal inscriptions, tomb disturbance may have been considered the action of someone with no ties or loyalty to the city; legal enforcement therefore was required from outside the city's jurisdiction by an authority whose agents were renowned for their zeal, at least in the collection of dues.[160] How this occurred, whether by summary imposition, formal judicial proceedings at an annual assize, or, if the circumstances were congenial and some authority was granted, by local courts applying Roman law, is generally opaque. The number of instances mentioning a reward for an informing witness suggests that policing was haphazard and fortuitous, whether by Roman, civic or village authority. Occasionally the grave owner and eventual occupier made explicit provision for a tomb-guard to protect the grave or an entity such as an association to maintain it.[161] This suggests that some at least had a preference for surveillance by someone close to the one(s) commissioning the tomb.

156 See G. P. Burton, "Proconsuls, Assizes and the Administration of Justice under the Empire," *JRS* 65 (1975): 99–102.

157 Oliver, *Greek Constitutions*, 92, ll. 47–50 (Hadrian's Oil Law at Athens).

158 See Magie, *Roman Rule in Asia Minor*, 639.

159 *I.Ephesos* 2304, l. 6.

160 P. A. Brunt, "The 'Fiscus' and its Development," *JRS* 56 (1966): 82–3.

161 O. M. van Nijf, *The Civic World of Professional Associations in the Roman East* (Leiden: Brill, 1997), 62.

This does not mean that there weren't certain minor officials whose duties may have extended to include surveillance of necropoleis to check against grave disturbance. One specification in a fragmentary Greek epitaph from Apollonis in Lydia includes a familiar fine of 1000 denarii but seems to imply the enforcement of the fine by a *stationarius*.[162] The Greek transliteration clearly points to a formal Roman position, possibly a guard of general description, though perhaps an outposted soldier.[163] It may point to a late second-century development. Trajan, for example, resisted the deployment of the Roman military for tasks that local enforcement had already covered, citing existing custom as his rationale.[164] Local officials such as the *paraphylax* might have been charged with similar policing as this *stationarius* by the leading magistrates — the *archons*, *strategoi*, *eirenarchoi* — the very offices already attested at Colossae in the second century.[165]

This is mentioned in a foundation inscription from Ephesian territory where a line of delegated authority passes from the *archons* to a *paraphylax* for enforcement of an infringement of the terms of the deed.[166] *Paraphylakes* appear to have been lightly armed for their tasks.[167] They are sometimes high-ranking, acting as head of a police force.[168] At other times, they appear as little more than a sentry with a specific purpose.[169] A similar range of authority seems to attach to the *ekdikoi*, known from some Hierapolitan epitaphs as being rewarded, probably for their prosecution of an offender.[170]

At Colossae, the honorific inscription established under the superintendence of one Heliodoros, lists among an array of offices, the *eirenarch*, *para-*

162 *IGR* 4.1185 (nd); see M. F. Petraccia-Lucernoni, *Gli stationarii in età imperiale* (Rome: Bretschneider, 2001), 85.

163 Stephen Mitchell calls them "gendarmes". It may be significant that the *stationarius* is frequently not named; hence, there may be an expectation that in these areas a military presence was the norm. See S. Mitchell, *Anatolia: Land, Men, and Gods in Asia Minor* (Oxford: Clarendon, 2 vols, 1993), 1.122.

164 *Perseveremus in ea consuetudine, quae isti provinciae est.* Trajan to Pliny; Pliny *Ep.* 10.20.

165 *IGR* 4.870, l. 2, 4–5 *(strategos, eirenarch)*; *RPC online* 4.2.1875 temp., 4.2.11597 temp. *(archon)*; *RPC online* 4.2.1880, 1881 temp. *(strategos)*.

166 *SEG* 33.946, ll. 4–5 (late 1st century CE).

167 *I.Ephesos* 3222 (1st/2nd century CE, with relief); *I.Prusa* 23 (mid-2nd century CE, with relief).

168 *SEG* 62.1188, 1189 (Hierapolis region, 1st century CE). Christopher Furmann thinks that a *paraphylax* frequently had charge over underlings called διωγμιταί, whilst admitting that the evidence available sees them subject to the eirenarch; see *Policing the Roman Empire: Soldiers, Administration and Public Order* (Oxford: Oxford University Press, 2011), 69.

169 Ramsay, *Phrygia* 1.143.31, l. 3 (Thiounta, 2nd century CE). Thiounta was a prosperous village and may have appointed Kasmos for an all-purpose maintenance of public order or he may have been an appointment of the brotherhood (a *phratra*) within Thiounta with a brief of duties circumscribed by the interests and benefactions of the organization. Compare *I.Perge* 234, 235 (2nd to early 3rd century CE) where the *paraphylax* has his locus of responsibility as the city acropolis.

170 See, for example, *I.Hierapolis Judeich* 111, 133; *AAT* 1966/67.316.43. On the *ekdikoi* of cities, associations and as private citizens, see S. Dmitriev, *City Government in Hellenistic and Roman Asia Minor* (Oxford: Oxford University Press, 2005), 213–6.

phylax, and *ekdikos* (along with the office of *nomophylax*) held at some time in the course of the (unfortunately anonymous) leading man's life of service in the city and its territory.[171] He also held the office of city treasurer (l. 4). There is no direct attestation linking his functions to the enforcement of the funerary penalties for grave violation but it is likely that he was involved or at least kept informed of the sanctity of the necropolis. As *eirenarch*, a first century Roman creation and annual appointment,[172] he is likely to have inherited some responsibilities on behalf of the *fiscus* as well as the *tameion*, even if his primary functions (under Roman delegation to a recognized Greek *polis*) lay in the maintenance of peace according to local law. The *tameion* marked Colossae as a functioning Greek *polis* regulating its financial affairs and economy; the *fiscus* signaled Rome's recognition of that status as well as the consequential fiduciary obligations imposed on the city. The prescribed penalties concluding the inscriptions on five funerary *bomoi* from the territory of Colossae yield a small witness to this plurality of authorities and regulations. But what is clear is that behind these simple proscriptions and penalties lay a complex of legal matters "and a deep knowledge of civil and criminal judicial procedures,"[173] precisely the purview requiring the attention of an expert or body of experts. To this we turn.

A bureaucracy for managing pluralities of (commercial and legal) interests

A third piece of evidence that is relevant to this exploration comes with an inscription from Colossae that has attracted considerable attention. In December 2005, I managed to pursue a comment from a local farmer that he had cleared a large, shaped stone from his field lying on the north side of the Ak-Su (Lycus River) by tossing it into the river. At the onset of winter, the river, fortunately, was not its roaring, wolfish beast, but had subsided. Not only were the deep, honey-comb, limestone crevices revealed (Pl. 11.9a); a one-metre high, circular pedestal had lodged horizontally in the upper level of one of the clefts,[174] held in place by mud and other debris. The limestone pedestal contained an inscription, fortunately facing upwards for an easy view (Pl. 11.9b), but sufficiently enclosed as to preclude confirmation whether there were dowel-

171 *IGR* 4.870, ll. 4–5, 8 (mid-2nd century CE). See chapter 5.

172 Dmitriev, *City Government*, 206–13. Eirenarchs were subject to direction from the provincial proconsul, as is attested for Antoninus Pius, when he was governor (134–135 CE): *Dig.* 48.3.6.1.

173 Brélaz, "Understandings of Roman Law," 168.

174 The pedestal was able to be viewed from beneath its precarious entrapment, confirming no letters were carved on the reverse of the pedestal.

Plate 11.9a: The deep fissures in the limestone floor of the Lycus riverbed.

holes in the top for the (likely) securing of a statue, bust or other addition. The spring melt returned the river to its eponymous power and the pedestal was apparently swept away. The following year's visit revealed no trace. Although the pedestal face was heavily pitted, four inscribed lines were sufficiently clear for a reasonable reconstruction to be made, although the person or institution conferring the honor probably followed in one or two lines now abraded beyond decipherment.[175]

Plate 11.9b: The (computer-righted) pedestal inscription trapped in sediment and debris of the riverbed.

Μάρκωι Μάρκου̣
Κολοσσ̣η̣ν̣ῶ̣ν̣
ἀ̣ρ̣χερμηνε̣ῖ
καὶ ἐξηγητῆ̣[ι

Translation: *[... dedicated this] to Markos son of Markos, chief interpreter and translator of the Colossians.*

When I first published the inscription, my interpretation concentrated on the use of the ἀρχ- prefix for ἀρχερμηνεύς, then only known elsewhere from a single inscription from the northern Bosphorus region,[176] and on the unique, if semantically often-indistinct, combination ἀρχερμηνεὺς καὶ ἐξεγητής. I understood the ethnic qualifier, Κολοσσηνῶν, as a strong indication that this was an official position, with the ἀρχ- prefix indicating not merely a status accrued from elevated language but a bureau head with responsibilities including the organization of staff with similar functions. Because I understood the terms as referring to translation and interpreter functions, the level of competency required for these skills suggested that we were not dealing with an annual magistracy but a bureaucratic or administrative appointment. There were two prime comparisons that informed the reading as translation and interpretation in important, mundane affairs, both oral and textual.

175 The inscription was published in 2007: "Two New Inscriptions," 112–18 (see above).
176 *CIRB* 1053 (early 3rd century CE).

The first was the lengthy history of the use of interpreters to conduct diplomatic and commercial transactions in Asia Minor.[177] Rick Strelan has, persuasively in my view, demonstrated that a wide variety of languages still circulated through Anatolia in the first and second centuries, a salutary reminder that a reliance on epigraphical testimony (overwhelmingly Greek and Latin) for the assessment of language use is fundamentally flawed, including the linguistic capacity of those who commission an inscription in one or other of the dominant languages.[178] Phrygian, Celtic, Lycian, Pisidian, Pamphylian, Solymian, Lydian, Scythian and Lycaonian (cf Acts 14:11) all attract literary notice as circulating within the Greco-Roman hegemony, inevitably requiring translation and interpreter services when linguistic exchange demanded it. Some of these languages offer small numbers of inscriptions or parts thereof; some cause phonological interference in the Greek spelling used.[179] A good example from Colossae of the latter is from the epitaph of Dion the leatherworker — spelled διφθεροπύς rather than the "correct" διφθεροποιός.[180]

William Ramsay acknowledged that early Christian commitment to the use of Greek (as in the Letter to the Colossians) "killed out the native languages of Anatolia" over time.[181] Nonetheless, one fifth-century Arian bishop, Selinas, was said to preach fluently in both Gothic and Phrygian,[182] implying that there remained substantial pockets of Christians whose native tongue warranted the use of such language from the pulpit. The 117 extant New Phrygian inscriptions (almost all epitaphs with a stereotyped Phrygian section, dated between the first and third centuries CE) demonstrate at least a commitment to pride in and partial use of Phrygian heritage, even if the lettering had become Greek in form and the finds are restricted to rural areas to the east of Colos-

177 Herodotos 1.86.4–6, 3.38.4, 3.140.3; Xenophon *Anab.* 2.5.35, 5.4.4, Arrian *Anab.* 4.3, 7 cf Hipponax fr. 27.

178 R. Strelan, "The Languages of the Lycus Valley," *in Colossae in Space and Time: Linking to an Ancient City* edited by A. H. Cadwallader and M. Trainor (Göttingen: Vandenhoeck & Ruprecht, 2011), 77–103.

179 This sought of interference, transfer and switching is noted by Strabo of the use of Carian: *Geog.* 14.2.28.

180 *MAMA* 6.44 cf ὑός for υἱος in *MAMA* 6.43. These phonologically-induced spellings are known in inscriptions across the Lycus valley; See, for example, *I.Laodikeia Lykos* 65, l. 2 (imperial), *I. Mus. Denizli* 114, ll. 1,2 (2nd century CE). See generally, C. Brixhe, "Greek and Phrygian," 246–66; P. McKechnie, *Christianizing Asia Minor: Conversion, Communities and Social Change in the Pre-Constantinian Era* (Cambridge: Cambridge University Press, 2019), 6–10.

181 Cited by A. Petrie, "Epitaphs in Phrygian Greek," in *Studies in the History and Art of the Eastern Provinces of the Roman Empire* edited by W. M. Ramsay (Aberdeen: Aberdeen University Press, 1906), 134. The tenacity of some minority languages compelled some churches to establish their own office of ἑρμηνεύς to translate the Greek scriptures into an intelligible language; see H. Gamble, *Books and Readers in the Early Church: A History of Early Christian Texts* (New Haven/London: Yale University Press, 1995), 230. Gamble relies on ancient Christian literature for this recognition. I have been unable to find a Christian honorific or funerary inscription that records the office, though other offices are readily attested epigraphically.

182 Socrates *Hist. eccl.* 5.23.

sae.[183] The fact that in the bilingual epitaphs the Greek curse is not always a translation of the Phrygian imprecation underscores the address to a Phrygian persona.[184] Indeed, Bartomeu Obrador-Cursach sees them as indicating that "Phrygian was still spoken," albeit deeply Hellenized but, importantly for our purposes, not Latinized.[185]

The second segment of *comparanda* was directed to the use of ἑρμηνεύς and ἐξηγητής in the papyri, often in dialogue with the most substantial monograph on ancient translation, that of Claudia Wiotte-Franz.[186] Here the commercial, legal and administrative aspect of the word came strongly to the fore,[187] so much so that an official involved in translation and interpretation work might become virtually a broker of deals between parties of differing linguistic or literate backgrounds.[188] Similarly, the technical intricacies of a will might require the explanatory work (ἐξηγητεύω) of an intermediary.[189] An ἐξηγητής might function as little more than a witness of a document, a signatory to an arrest warrant, or even as a spokesman,[190] somewhat akin to a πρεσβευτής. Here any sense of a translator or interpreter (the word can indicate both at times) is subsumed by the general function as an intermediary.

My conclusion was that the pedestal was likely an agora installation, probably associated with the office where these services were located. I accented the oral dimensions of the functions, such as assistance in the reading of legal documents which may or may not have included commercial exchanges. This did not preclude the textual dimensions but the emphasis was on the vibrant, fluid cosmopolitan environment which Colossae occupied, as strategically located on the cusp of the Anatolian high country and criti-

183 See B. Obrador-Cursach, "Phrygian in Contact with Greek: An Overview," in *Greek Paideia and Local Tradition in the Graeco-Roman East* edited by M-P. de Hoz, J. L. G. Alonso and L. A. G. Romero (Leuven: Peeters, 2020), 90–1.

184 Obrador-Cursach, "Phrygian in Contact," 91–5.

185 Obrador-Cursach, "Phrygian in Contact," 118.

186 C. Wiotte-Franz, *Hermeneus und Interpres: Zum Dolmetscherwesen in der Antike* (Saarbrücken: Saarbrücker Druckerei und Verlag, 2001).

187 See D. Delia, *Alexandrian Citizenship during the Roman Principate* (Atlanta, GA: Scholars Press, 1991), 79–80, 102–4 with the list of ἐξηγηταί attested from the 1st century BCE to the 3rd century CE on 152–3. An earlier attestation (2nd century BCE) to multiple ἐξηγηταί possibly at Alexandria is found in *SEG* 34.1532 which seems to relate to minor juridical concerns governing a gymnasium (ll. 16–20). Compare *SEG* 47.2142 (Thebes, 119 CE) where a petitioner at a temple, Apollonides, lists his status credentials as archon, *exegete* and *agoranomos,* all civic magistracies.

188 For example, *PSA Athen.* 21, l. 11 (Karanis, 131 CE). The translation "broker" is that of P. W. Pestman, who sees the ἑρμηνεύς as a "middleman in market trade"; *The New Papyrological Primer* (Leiden: Brill, 1990), 160. It should be noted that the woman securing a loan is described as illiterate μὴ εἰδ(υίας) γρ(άμματα) (l. 30). Compare *P.Ryl.* 2.94, l. 4 (Euhemeria in the Fayum, 14–37 CE) for which Mark Mueller translates ἐξηγητής as "advisor" (*Associations in the Greco-Roman World online* (http://philipharland.com/greco-roman-associations/letter-concerning-bail-for-five-weavers-in-a-legal-case-14-37-ce/); similarly *P.Oslo* 3.144 (Oxyrhynchos, 272–5 CE).

189 *P.Stras.* 1.41, l. 3 (Hermopolis, c. 250 CE).

190 *P.Oxy.* 56, *P.Oxy.* 4486, *P.Oxy.* 2435, respectively. In *P.Oxy* 3020 (10/9 BCE) the papyrus combines a fragmentary Letter of Augustus to the Alexandrians with one speech delivered to him (column 2 of the papyrus) by an ἐξηγητής introducing the envoys, including himself, who had presented the city's case. His task was to speak about the city itself (ii, l. 7).

cally positioned as "a point of dissemination of imperial policy," given that to the east lay the imperial province of Galatia and a number of Roman *colonia* in Pisidia. But, as Wiotte-Franz noted, this need for translation and interpretation was a common characteristic of cities in the ancient world.

A number of writers have reiterated the main elements just outlined.[191] However, a substantial caveat was delivered by Angelos Chaniotis, who argued for the inscription to be interpreted along lines that I had specifically excluded,[192] namely that the phrase ἀρχερμηνεὺς καὶ ἐξηγητής required a religious focus, related to the interpretation of oracles.[193] Chaniotis had switched the *comparanda* from Egypt to Attica where the attestation of ἐξηγητής certainly delivers a cultic functionary (sometimes equated with "priest")[194] though not exclusively so.[195] Moreover, it appears that a hierarchy among the exegetes was delivered by the term ὁ πυθόχρηστος ἐξηγητής, though such a qualifier belonged to mainland Greece, at least for its award.[196] Indeed, the use of ἐξηγητής in a ritual sense is rare outside of Greece. Only one, possibly two, from Kyzikos in Mysia, one of which records "an expositor of the great mysteries of Kore the Savior."[197] Further, Chaniotis seems to have operated from the old assumption that Colossae, in Janice Capel Anderson's evocative rendition, "more or less gave up the ghost".[198] He wrote, "it is not very likely that the translation needs of Kolossai were so substantial as to require a board of translators." This not only reduces the number of languages circulating in the Lycus Valley and its surrounding highlands. It also fails to recognize that in Egypt, far smaller settlements were endowed with translators/interpreters to meet the needs of the local population, where at least three languages (and sometimes more) were in use. Nevertheless, this alternate reading has influenced Angela Standhartinger to suggest that Markos may have been "an interpreter of the revelations of Apollo at

---

191 See Strelan, "Languages of the Lycus Valley," 91; R. Canavan, *Clothing the Body of Christ at Colossae: A Visual Construction of Identity* (Tübingen: Mohr Siebeck, 2012), 13–14; P. Foster, *Colossians* (London: Bloomsbury, 2016), 7; K. S. Kim, "The Meaning of χειρόγραφον in Colossians 2:14 revisited," *TynBull.* 68 (2017): 241 n23.

192 Cadwallader, "New Inscription," 116 n21.

193 A. Chaniotis, "Epigraphic Bulletin for Greek Religion," *Kernos* 23 (2010): 285–6 nr. 25, followed in the editorial comments to *SEG* 57.1382, *SEG* 61.1160.

194 For example, *IG* II^2 1092, ll. B29, 30. (after 131 CE). See J. H. Clinton, *Athenian Expounders of the Sacred and Ancestral Law* (Baltimore: Johns Hopkins Press, 1950); K. Clinton, "The Sacred Officials of the Eleusinian Mysteries," *TAPA* 64 (1974): 36, 89–92.

195 For example, *IG* II^2 1791 (180/1–181/2 CE).

196 *IG* II^2 1818 (after 200 CE), 3513 (end 1st century BCE), *SEG* 33.851.

197 ἐξηγητοῦ τῶν μεγάλων μυστηρίν τῆς Σωτήρας Κόρης. *IMT Kyz Kapu Dağ* 1445, ll. 11–13 (imperial). The inscription also notes that Moschas son of Stratios was priest of Kore Sotera a position apparently combined with the office of *strategos* of the city, both in addition to his office of exegete. The listing of his positions — *strategos*, priest, *exegete* — is an indication of the hierarchy of status.

198 J. C. Anderson, *Colossians: Authorship, Rhetoric, and Code* (London: T & T Clark, 2019), 21.

Hierapolis or elsewhere."[199] It is difficult to reconcile the ethnic in the inscription — Κολοσσηνῶν — with this suggestion. This would imply that oracular sanctuaries had officials ear-marked to deal with specific (citizenry) groups.

A more substantial complex of readings of the inscription has been given by Lukas Bormann and Ulrich Huttner, each taking up an undeveloped aspect of the original interpretation and providing different emphases.[200] As seen above, I had set the inscription into the cosmopolitan character of the Colossian population and its dealings. This had included brief mentions of the translation needs related to Latin speakers and texts. Both Bormann and Huttner sought to set the inscription more firmly into the context of the communication requirements between Greek and Latin.

Bormann argued, by comparison with the term ἀρχισυνάγωγος, that the title ἀρχερμηνεύς was merely honorific rather than indicating a hierarchical superior in an office of interpreters and translators.[201] In this way, he manages to sidestep Chaniotis's criticism that assumes the mooted diminutive status of Colossae. But Bormann tacitly accepts this by reducing the witness to a Phrygian presence, or at least cultural inheritance, narrowly to the name Apphia (citing *IGR* 4.868, Phmn 2), whilst allowing that there was a continued Phrygian ethnicity, identity, culture and language in the hinterland.[202] He applies this to any other "minor" language claimant (for example Carian, amongst others) and underscores this by noting that the only epigraphical witness to languages at Colossae are Greek and Latin, ignoring Rick Strelan's nuanced arguments that inscriptions (especially epitaphs) are no necessary indicator of the mother tongue of the dedicant and, further, that those at the base of society (for example hinterland Phrygians) are unlikely to have the resources to leave a witness that survives for our own academic assessment (a point underscored by Claude Brixhe).[203] Indeed, the desire to gain enforcement of the sanctity of graves and

199 A. Standhartinger, "A City with a Message: Colossae and Colossians," in *The First Urban Churches 5: Colossae, Hierapolis, and Laodicea* edited by J. R. Harrison and L. L. Welborn (Atlanta, GA: SBL, 2019), 249; similarly "Mehr al seine Stadt," 705.

200 L. Bormann, "Barbaren und Skythen im Lykostal? Epigraphischer Kommentar zu Kol 3:11," in *Epigraphical Evidence Illustrating Paul's Letter to the Colossians* edited by J. Verheyden, M. Öhler and T. Corsten (WUNT 411; Tübingen: Mohr Siebeck, 2018), 193–6; Huttner, "Latin Law," 149–51.

201 Bormann, "Barbaren und Skythen," 194. Bormann transfers the judgement of W. Bauer that ἀρχισυνάγωγος was "bloßer Titel verliehen"; *Griechisch-deutsches Wörterbuch* (Berlin: de Gruyter, 1988), 226.

202 The two supportive citations are somewhat in tension with one another in their emphases: his own *Der Brief des Paulus an der Kolosser* (Leipzig: Evangelische Verlagsanstalt, 2012), 27 and C. Brixhe, "The Personal Onomastics of Roman Phrygia," in *Roman Phrygia: Culture and Society* edited by P. Thonemann (Cambridge: Cambridge University Press, 2013), 55–69 (see especially pp 68–9). See further, A. H. Cadwallader and J. R. Harrison, "Perspectives on the Lycus Valley: An Inscriptional, Archaeological, Numismatic, and Iconographic Approach," in *First Urban Churches* 5, 15–17.

203 See C. Brixhe, "Anatolian Anthroponymy after Louis Robert ... and Some Others," in *Personal Names in Ancient Anatolia* edited by R. Parker (Oxford: The British Academy, 2013), 15–30.

manumissions as well as the recording of burials and epitaphs in city archives, previously mentioned, is likely to have delivered a powerful inducement to provide inscription and written documentation *in* the hegemonic languages.

Even so, the hinterland of Colossae is precisely the territory that the city was heavily invested in and reliant upon for its produce, as we have seen in chapter 3. The flow of agricultural produce and market activity in the city would, at the very least, have involved some difficulties in communication. Bormann seems to affirm that Markos, the chief translator and interpreter, can only have functioned in relation to the languages attested in the small number of inscriptions known to date, that is, to Greek and Latin (even though the single Latin inscription dates to the early fourth century).[204] The ethnic Κολοσσηνῶν consequently is narrowed to those speaking Greek and (or?) Latin and becomes rather a citizenship indicator. As we have seen already, citizenship (whether Colossian, Roman in Colossae, or even citizenship of the two polities) for the sake of the city's interests within the province, is likely to have demanded a facility in, if not commitment to, Greek — the language acting as an ethnic marker. In this sense, the epigraphical chest of Colossae becomes a springboard for the development of Bormann's main interpretation, namely, that Markos' prime function was to address the communication and explanation needs of Greek and Latin speakers at Colossae, especially as pertaining to the complexities of legal matters arising from what Bormann calls disputes between the rights and privileges of Colossae as a constitutional *polis* and, what he almost euphemistically dubs "foreign legal practices," presumably meaning Roman. Markos thereby becomes not only a translator, but also a lawyer and scribe.[205]

Bormann relied on more general references to ἐξηγητής, including material in Philo and Josephus, to discern a legal dimension to its semantics (including the interpretation of religious law). Ulrich Huttner, however, directly targeted the issue of the plurality and conflict of laws in the province of Asia from republican to early imperial governance. Huttner accepted that ἀρχερμηνεύς indicated that Markos headed "an entire department of ἑρμηνεῖς … institutionalised within the polis."[206] The agora and its offices, not the temples, were the expected location for these officials (perhaps connected to a *nomophylakion* or *chrematisterion*).[207] While allowing that the responsibilities and functions may have been broad-ranging, Huttner swung attention to the term ἑρμηνεύς, espe-

204 *MAMA* 6.38. Of course, it is a reasonable working hypothesis, on the basis of the catalogues from Tripolis, Hierapolis and Laodikeia, that other, earlier Latin inscriptions remain to be discovered.

205 *Als Übersetzer, Rechtsberater und Schreiber war er für die zahlreichen alltagsrechtlichen Klärungen zuständig, die sich aus dem Aufeinandertreffen des Rechts der Polis Kolossai mit fremden Rechtspraktiken ergaben.* Bormann, "Barbaren und Skythen," 196.

206 Huttner, "Latin Law," 150. So also *AE* 2007.1384.

207 Compare Seneca *Ep.* 40.6.

cially as used in the papyri, and tied it to the technical term ἑρμηνεία, that is, to the translation and explication of Roman law into Greek-speaking society.

Stephen Mitchell had placed these *hermeneia* in the third to fifth centuries CE.[208] Huttner's use of the Markos' inscription pushes at least the practice if not the formal term to the turn of the first and second centuries.[209] But the term is precisely that used of the translation of the Hebrew Scriptures into Greek.[210] The term occurs in a fragmentary senatorial (?) letter, dated 51/50 or 29 BCE and intended for the entire province of Asia, found at Miletos and Priene. Here the word is used in the context of an explanation for transmitting the instructions in Greek — it seems that the author was concerned that an accurate translation (not, I think, merely an interpretation) of his letter be conveyed to the *conventus*, their archives, and for public display "on a white stone".[211] Apparently the author was not certain that local translators would have provided the accuracy he wanted, especially given that there is a swipe at the tolerance extended to some "shameless persons" (τήν τινων … ἀναίδειαν l. 42) by the very cities being addressed about certain debts. But the exceptionality reflected in the comments indicates that the usual practice was for local functionaries to make the translation for their local audiences.

This ought not narrow the meaning simply to a regimented (or free-flowing) translated text. Hadrian himself had taken on the role of hermeneute when addressing earlier imperial decisions regarding the vexed issue of inheritance rights for soldiers' (illegitimate) children.[212] This explains why the ἑρμηνεύς might be an assistant in court proceedings.[213] Nonetheless, the formal *hermeneia* had the stamp of Augustan authority on it; Suetonius reported that the emperor Augustus was neither fluent in Greek nor would risk writing it. Accordingly, when there was a demand for a Greek response, Augustus wrote it in Latin and delivered it to be translated.[214] It was already the practice for publication of senatorial decrees and the decisions of provincial governors.[215] We have already seen how important this bilingualism was for the inscriptions detailing Salutaris' provisions for (and influence upon) the city of Ephesos. For Huttner, it required that Markos had linguistic competence in Latin, and may

---

208 Mitchell, "ΕΡΜΗΝΕΙΑ," 684.

209 See, for example, *BGU* 1.326 (Arsinoe, 189–94 CE), a Greek translation of a Roman will (ἑρμηνία διαθήκης).

210 Aristobulus fr. 3 (*apud* Eusebius *Praep. Ev.* 13.12.2); *Ep. Aristeas* 3.6, 308.3; Philo *Mos.* 2.26, 41.

211 *I.Milet* 1.2.3, l. 56 (=*I.Priene* 106).

212 φιλανθρωπότερον ἑρμηνεύω. Oliver, *Greek Constitutions* 70, ll. 19–20 (119 CE).

213 See, for example, *PSI* 13.1326, l. 4 (181–183 CE).

214 Suetonius *Aug.* 89.1. Joyce Reynolds wonders whether a curt, somewhat stunted Letter from Octavian to Stephanus, an appointee of Mark Antony based at Laodikeia shortly after the end of the revolt of Labienus (perhaps 38 BCE), is actually the Greek composition of Octavian, perhaps illustrating why he later avoided the language for his own imperial communications. See *I.Aphrodisias and Rome* 10, with comments.

215 Huttner, "Latin Law," 141.

have entailed his bureaucratic cooperation with the city archives and perhaps involvement in the translation of Latin documents into texts for display or broadcast. He even finds in the ubiquitous name Markos, a trace of a Roman background — *Marcus*, though this might indicate servile origins. However, the proud and conventionally Greek adoption of a homonymous patronymic might as easily be an indication of Greek adoption of Roman *nomina simplicia*, a signal of a measure of acculturation to the dominant power, whether or not the Roman *tria nomina* was the ambition.[216] Indeed one might add that the dedicatory dative in the inscription may reveal a trace of Latin influence as compared to the accusative of dedication familiar in Greek inscriptions.[217]

Then, Huttner turns to the second title in the inscription, ἐξηγητής. Given the limits of space, he relies on a quotation of Strabo where the author seeks to elucidate the jurisprudential operations of the Cappadocian city of Mazaka. It is worth repeating here: "the Mazakeni use the laws of Charondas and elect a *nomôde* ['singer of laws'],[218] who is for them the interpreter of their law, like the *nomikoi* for the Romans." The ἐξηγητής is here specifically aligned with the interpretation of law; yet there is a tacit acceptance of different law codes in the use of the middle present χράομαι of the Mazakeni's practice, and the use of different interpretative methods, including at least some use of song or chant, hardly applicable to Roman law.

216 See D. Rizakis, "Langue et culture ou les ambiguïtés identitaires des notables des cités grecques sous l'empire de Rome," in *Bilinguisme gréco-latin et épigraphie* edited by F. Biville, J.-C. Decourt and G. Rougemont (Lyon: Maison de l'Orient méditerranéen, 2008), 22–3. Care was needed here. The Emperor Claudius had banned the use of the Roman *gentilicium* (such as Claudius) by peregrines, that is, those not awarded Roman citizenship (Suetonius *Claud.* 25.3). The ban did not extend to praenomens, as here. However, the name Likinnios mentioned above was a *gentilicium*. It suggests that, post-Claudius, the regulation lapsed or in fact never had provincial reach.

217 This distinction cannot be pressed, but is noticeable in bilingual inscriptions; see Kearsley, *Greeks and Romans*, 152. Although there are insufficient honorific inscriptions from Colossae to mount a statistical analysis, of those available, the dative of dedication is used for honors for emperors (*IGR* 4.868, l. 1, for Trajan; *IGR* 4.869, ll. 1–6, for Hadrian); the accusative is used for honors of locals (even when Roman citizens): *MAMA* 6.39, 40, 41, 42. That this does not hold completely is patent in the Korymbos inscription (*Antichthon* 2012.152.1, l. 2, cf *MAMA* 6.44, 46). It may be unconscious, syntactic borrowing, revealing how the presence and use of Latin in the province had already exerted significant influence even among non-Latin speakers. On the varieties of exchange between Greek and Latin, see D. Langslow, "Typologies of translation techniques in Greek and Latin: Latin *elticis*: *catelticis* = Greek ἑλκτική: καθεκτική," in *Multilingualism in the Graeco-Roman Worlds* edited by A. Mullen and P. James (Cambridge: Cambridge University Press, 2012), 141–71.

218 χρῶνται δὲ οἱ Μαζακηνοὶ τοῖς Χαρώνδα νόμοις, αἱρούμενοι καὶ νομῳδόν, ὅς ἐστιν αὐτοῖς ἐξηγητὴς τῶν νόμων, καθάπερ οἱ παρὰ Ῥωμαίοις νομικοί — Strabo 12.2.9 (trans Huttner from Jones). Although Strabo equates a νομῳδός with a νομικός, the former term is likely quite specific to the laws of the 6th century (BCE) law-giver Charondas who apparently wrote his code in verse. Hermippus fr. 88 (Wehrli) wrote of them being sung at drinking parties in Athens (*apud* Athenaeus *Deip.* 14.619b). Aristotle held high praise for Charondas's accuracy if not his originality (*Pol.* 9.1274b).

A number of issues are raised by these two important analyses.
i) *The question of nominal or hierarchical title: ἀρχερμηνεύς.*
Sviatoslav Dmitriev has noted that one of the developments in the range of city officials was an increased delineation of levels. This "hierarchization" as he calls it, is manifest in the use of prefixes, the most common being *hypo*–, *proto*– and *archi*–. There was also a clear demarcation of the rank and status between various offices, not only in the order in which they might be listed in an elite person's *cursus honorum* but also in lower offices being held within the dispensation of a higher official (such as an *agonothete*).[219]

The rarity of appearance of the office of ἀρχερμηνεύς in extant texts, inscriptions and papyri ought not distract from the ubiquitous rise of *archi*-compounds among religious, military and civic office holders across the imperial Roman world, especially in Egypt and the eastern provinces.[220] In this sense, ἀρχερμηνεύς is part of a feature of civic administration and civic display/recognition in the imperial period. Dmitriev argues that it reflected "the growing sophistication of city administration in the Roman period." A number in the *archi*– group of officials were religious, though he recognizes that religious officials were integral to the administration of the city.[221] Among these, the foremost ones were ἀρχιερεύς (which could be further hierarchicalized [my term] by the addition of Ἀσίας or πατρίδος),[222] ἀρχινεωκόρος,[223] and ἀρχιπροφήτης.[224] Some of these might receive the additional honorific epithet διὰ βίου (as we have seen in chapter 10);[225] in this case, it was unlikely to reflect a hierarchical administrative elevation but rather a designation which might yield further recognition if not influence. Dmitriev also sees the prefix operating for officials within associations (here he includes ἀρχισυνάγωγος)[226] and for those who held high office in specific administrations/bureaucratic agencies below that of the governance of the city as a whole. Here we find the

219 Dmitriev, *City Government*, 228–38.

220 See H. J. Mason, *Greek Terms for Roman Institutions: a Lexicon and Analysis* (Toronto: Hakkert, 1974), 113–5.

221 Dmitriev, *City Government*, 229, 233.

222 *MAMA* 9.18, ll. 3–4 (212–260 CE), 17, l. 11 (mid-3rd century CE) respectively (both from the region of the Aezani). Emperors were sometimes titled "great(est) high priest" (ἀρχιερεὺς μέγιστος), *AE* 1969/70.593, ll. 4, 8 (Hierapolis, of Domitian, translation of *pontifex maximus*).

223 *MAMA* 9.10, l. 6 (139–61 CE)

224 *I.Alexandrie imp.* 43, l. 2 (Alexandria, imperial). It must be acknowledged that the occurrences of ἀρχιπροφήτης are from Egypt. However, Patara in Lycia laid claim not only to the title μητροπόλις but also to being ἀρχιπροφῆτις (*SEG* 44.1210, l. 12, 1st to 2nd century CE).

225 *SEG* 44.1210, ll. 3–4.

226 The ἀρχισυνάγωγος is not necessarily a Jewish office; see *TAPA* 1938.73, l. 2 (Poteidaia-Kassandreia, imperial), *I.Beroia* 371, ll. 5–6 (imperial). See generally, J. S. Kloppenborg and R. S. Ascough, *Greco-Roman Associations: Texts, Translations and Commentary, I. Attica, Central Greece, Macedonia, Thrace* (Berlin: de Gruyter, 2011), nr. 66.

ἀρχιδικαστής,[227] ἀρχισιτώνης,[228] the ἀρχιπαραφύλαξ/ἀρχιφύλακος,[229] or the ἀρχινεανίσκος.[230] Even the ἀρχιατρός is to be understood as a civic (sometimes court) position,[231] given that doctors' freedom from taxation appears to have been organized by reference to city registration and application. Indeed, cities could remove the registration of a doctor. Moreover, the number of doctors able to gain the privilege of exemption from taxation was restricted, thus, almost certainly, demanding a hierarchical ordering under a head of doctors.[232] All these are examples of a widespread phenomenon which, as a whole, seems to be a characteristic of the first two centuries of Roman imperial presence and, probably, influence.[233] But what is also clear from the analyses of these *archi*- compounds is that the prefix operates not as a mere honorific additive but as indicating the head or chief of a group that follows — "the head of a board,"[234] "the head of a government bureau,"[235] "organized under officials called …"[236] Those of lesser status equally joined the fashion. At a large weaving workshop in Alexandria the "factory manager," the ἐργαστηριάρχης, headed an establishment where many weavers worked (λινούφων πολλοὺς ἐργαζομένους ἐν τῇ ἐργασίᾳ ἔχοντα).[237]

Accordingly, the mention of ἀρχερμηνεύς in the inscription is completely in keeping with trends in titular epithets across Asia in the period, even if the word itself is rare.[238] Moreover, in almost all the cases surveyed, there is a bureau, group or office for which the *archi*- is responsible.

ii) *The search for parallels for ἀρχερμηνεύς.*

The term ἀρχερμηνεύς is extremely rare. Bormann noted, with no interpretation, a fragmentary inscription from the northern Bosphorus, also mentioned

227 *BGU* 3.888, ll. 1, 5, 6 (Arsinote, 159/60 CE)

228 *I.Side* 102, l. 4 (pre-212 CE).

229 *IGR* 4.524, ll. 8–9 (Dorylaion, 71/2 CE); *IGR* 3.474, l. 6 cf l. 16 (Balboura, 200–212 CE).

230 *IGUR* 1.160, l.B22 (Rome, mid-2nd century CE). However, some office titles with the prefix are known from Hellenistic times; see *P.Ent.* 6, ll. 4–5 (Arsinoïte nome; 221 BCE).

231 *MAMA* 9.115, l. 4 (Aezani, after 140s), with comment by Barbara Levick and Stephen Mitchell; compare Mason, *Greek Terms*, 114. See the thorough treatment of Gregory Horsley, *New Doc. Early Christ.* 2.2.

232 *Dig.* 27.1.6.2, 6.

233 A. Bülow-Jacobsen, "The Archiprophetes," in *Actes du XVe Congrès international de papyrology* edited by J. Bingen and G. Nachtergael (Brussels: Fondation Égyptolique Reine Élisaveth, 1979), 126.

234 J. H. M. Strubbe, "The Sitonia in the Cities of Asia Minor under the Principate (II)," *EA* 13 (1989): 102.

235 Bülow-Jacobsen, "The Archiprophetes," 128.

236 N. P. Milner, *An Epigraphical Survey in the Kibyra-Olbasa Region conducted by A. S Hall* (London: British Academy, 1998), 55.

237 *P.Oxy.* 2340,1 ll. 6–8 (192 CE).

238 Compare the ἀρχιτέκτων at Laodikeia: *I.Laodikeia Lykos* 58, l. 4 (imperial). Again the title reflects not only one who was the most skilled professional but also one with a sizable staff.

in the commentary in the *editio princeps*.[239] The fragment, dated by extrapolation from the Bosporan date in the text to 208 CE, reads:[240]

> Δι᾽ ἐπιμελείας Ἡρα- | κᾶ Ποντικοῦ ἀρχερ– | μηνέως Ἀλανῶν. | ἐ[ν τῷ] εφ᾽
>
> *Through the management of Herakas son of Pontikos, chief interpreter of the Alanoi, in the year 505.*

The inscription has gained little recognition from Second Testament commentators, apart from Claude Spicq who notes it in the course of an excursus on διερμηνεύω, ἑρμηνεία and ἑρμηνεύω, where the concentration is on translation.[241]

An initial investigation reveals an official with a good Greek name, who is titled chief interpreter with a specific ethnic addition that parallels the syntactical connection seen in the Colossian inscription. The Δι᾽ ἐπιμελείας (l. 1) however indicates that this chief interpreter was not the recipient of an honor. It points to the need to investigate more closely the stone in its setting.

It is in fact a building inscription that re-used a first century epitaph with farewell relief.[242] The stone was found in 1910 in the vicinity of the fortress of Phanagoria that guarded the eastern peninsula of the gateway between the Black Sea and the Azov Sea. It was a contested part of the world for which the Romans, among others perhaps, found themselves in regular need of translation services.[243] This suggests that some repair had been made to the fortress, for which the stone was a dedicatory recognition.[244] Here there is no hint of a religious connection. Rather a further inscribed element, frequently overlooked, provides a substantial clue. It is a large monogram-like figure comprising three connected elements: horns, a circle and three uprights joined by a wavy line. It is called a *tamga*, and was specific at this time for Bosporan tutelary kings,

---

239 Bormann, "Barbaren und Skythen," 194; Cadwallader, "New Inscription," 115.

240 *CIRB* 1053.

241 C. Spicq, *Notes de lexicographie néo-testamentaire: Tome I* (Göttingen: Vandenhoeck & Ruprecht, 1978), 205–10 (see 207, n5).

242 *CIRB* 1085. See N. Pavlichenko and N. Fedoseev, "A New Inscription of Herakas, Son of Pontikos, ἀρχερμηνεὺς Ἀλανῶν," *Hyperboreus* 24 (2018): 321.

243 An epitaph from a columbarium in Rome records "Aspougos, son of Biomasos, Bosporan translator for the Sarmatians (ἑρμηνεὺς Σαρματῶν Βωσποράνός)" *IGUR* 2.567 (10–37 CE). Significantly, the inscription is placed below another funerary record — of a diplomat of the Phanagorians, Hedykos (Ἥδυκος Εὐόδου πρεσβευτὴς Φαναγορειτῶν). Another inscription, an epitaph from Pantikapaion, at the head of the peninsula on the western side of the strait from Phanagoria, records Pairisalos the translator (Παιρίσαλος … ἑρμηνεύς) (*CIRB* 698, dated 2nd century CE). No ethnic is added.

244 So, M. Muratov, "The Language(s) of Images in the Arts of the Bosporan Kingdom," in *The Northern Black Sea in Antiquity: Networks, Connectivity and Cultural Interactions* edited by V. Kozlovskaya (Cambridge: Cambridge University Press, 2017), 188–9.

in this case, Sauromates II (ruled 174–210 CE).[245] This suggests that Herakas was a court official, charged with a rebuilding project that may have necessitated dealing with the Alanoi, though this is a speculative deduction. Regardless, the ethnic indicates "for (dealings with) the Alanoi," rather than "from the Alanoi".[246] Herakas's responsibility was to act as the interpreter between the Alanoi and the Greek speakers in the Bosporan kingdom. The implications for the Colossian inscription are that Markos may have been known less for his identification with the Colossians as his service *for* the Colossians. It is the same sort of tension that attaches to the usual ethnic on Colossae's coins — ΚΟΛΟϹϹΗΝΩΝ made the sharper because of the occasional use of the dative ΚΟΛΟϹϹΗΝΟΙϹ.[247]

The background history of Rome's dealings with the Alanoi, sometimes directly, sometimes through the agency of the Bosporan kings, helps to clarify the language difficulties as well as the political tensions that demanded skilled translators in the area, especially in the second century.[248] The *Historia Augusta* claimed that Antoninus Pius "many times checked the Alanoi when they were troublesome."[249]

The importance of Herakas to the building and negotiation demands in the area is borne out in a second, newly published but fragmentary dedication, dated to 204 CE. It is not known whether a *tamga* was cut in the lost section. The carefully argued reconstruction offered by Natalia Pavlichenko and Nikolaj Fedoseev, reads:

[--------]ου ε[------]
[----κα]τὰ πεσουσ[--]
[---καθιέρ]ωσεν ἐκ τῶ[ν ἰδ-]
[ίων ἀναλω]μάτων δι᾽ ἐπιμελ-
[είας Ἡρακᾶ] Ποντικοῦ ἀρχερμ-
[ηνέως Ἀλα]νῶν ἄρχοντος αὐ-
[λῆς vacat ἐν τῷ] αφ᾽, Δαεισίῳ κε᾽.

245 On *tamgas* and their significance, see Muratov, "The Language(s) of Images," 169–191; V. Kozlovskaya and S. M. Ilyashenko, "Tamgas and tamga-like signs from Tanais," in *Zeichentragende Artefakte im sakralen Raum: Zwischen Präsenz und UnSichtbarkeit* edited by W. E. Keil, S. Kiyanrad, C. Theis and L Willer (Berlin: de Gruyter, 2018) 167–98.

246 As argued by Alexander V. Podossinov, "Nomads of the Eurasian Steppe and Greeks of the Northern Black Sea Region: Encounter of Two Great Civilizations in Antiquity and Early Middle Ages," in *Competing Narratives between Nomadic People and their Sedentary Neighbours* edited by C. Hao (Szeged: University of Szeged, 2019), 244.

247 *RPC* 3.2307, *RPC online* 3.2307C, D (Claudia Eugenetoriane); *RPC online* 4.2.1888 temp., 10833 temp. (Tiberius Asinios Philopappos).

248 For a brief overview of the tensions in the region, see G. W. Bowersock and C. P. Jones, "A New Inscription from Panticapaeum," *ZPE* 156 (2006): 121–2.

249 *Alanos moilentis saepe refrenauit. HA* 5.5 (Pius).

> *[... x having reconstructed] the destroyed [buildings?] at his own expense, dedicated (them) [to some deity?] under the management of Herakas, son of Pontikos, the chief interpreter of the Alanoi, superintendent of the royal court in 201, day 25 of the month Daeisios.*[250]

Here it is clear that Herakas was a court official, one of whose functions was to provide translation skills in dealings with the Alanoi. Indeed, the editors suggest that there was "a staff of interpreters" at the Bosporan court who were "specialized in translation from the languages of neighboring barbarian tribes." Such translation needs encompassed, according to the authors, trade and diplomacy. In this sense, we are returned to my original suggestions as to the function of an ἀρχερμηνεύς. However, the context of these two finds — re-building activities in a contested frontier zone — is significantly different from a stable, long-established Greek *polis* within a Roman province.[251]

iii) *ἀρχερμηνεὺς καὶ ἐξηγητής in the Greek polis of Colossae*

Our analysis thus far has suggested that it is more probable that Markos was head of a bureau of translators and interpreters based at Colossae and that his responsibilities extended to mediating communication in one or more languages besides Greek. The primary language of discourse for the Colossians, unlike the Alanoi, was Greek, certainly in the city itself and, to a significant extent, in the country.[252] Blandly obvious as this is, it requires that Markos's interpreter skills were required with at least another language group. Bormann and Huttner have argued for Latin. I agree, especially from Huttner's analysis, and from the examination given thus far, that Latin was *one* of the languages involved, especially as regards senatorial communications and issues related to conflict of laws. This is no more than is requisite, according to the second-to-third century jurist, Ulpian, namely, that the locality determined what prime language (that is, Greek or Latin) was to be used.[253] But given Markos's heading up a bureau of translators, it is also likely that other languages were target-

250 Pavlichenko and Fedoseev, "New Inscription of Herakas," 328 (minimally adjusted in translation).

251 A third possible occurrence of the word ἀρχερμηνεύς is conjectured by Kyu Seop Kim in his reading of an Oxyrhynchos papyrus (*P.Oxy.* 1252). However, the conjecture is built on a misreading of the syntax in ll. 21–3 where τῶν ἀμφοτέρων refers to the previously mentioned two persons who are *exegetai* and the τῶν τριῶν joins them to a third person named as an *archiereus*. The τῶν βουλευτῶν that is joined to "the three" is tied to the city of Oxyrhynchos, thereby strongly indicating that the three persons are "councilors" of that city, not "senators" (of Rome) as Kim argues, reconstructing *archiereus* as *archermeneus*. See Kim, "Χειρόγραφον in Colossians 2:14," 231–2.

252 This is demonstrated in the (Greek) language of the inscriptions from Eleinokapria and Kilaraza, allowing Strelan's caution that this formal display did not necessarily transfer to domestic discourse.

253 *Dig.* 11.3.11.3.

ted, just as, in the northern Bosporus, multiple language groups (and interpreters) were present (for example, Alani and Sarmatian). Such languages are often anepigraphic.

The second-third century jurist Ulpian admitted that some legacy provisions, in law, should not only be in Latin or Greek, but in Punic, Gallic, or the language of any other people, presumably as might have had some interest in the provision.[254] At the same time, a priority was given in Roman law to Latin, to the point where, if Latin was absent from an exchange (such as a verbal agreement) involving multiple languages (such as Greek, Assyrian or some other), the Roman jurists doubted whether Roman law recognized anything binding.[255] Jurisdiction might be granted where there was a "truthful interpreter" (*per verum interpretem*). One can recognize here the importance of Markos and/or one of his officials as well as the authority granted to the interpreter in Roman law.

This might extend beyond the function of "truthful interpreter". Rome, it appears, was keenly interested in knowing the local law of the various peoples of areas under their control. In this respect, the direction of translation was not from Latin to Greek (or Punic, Gallic and so on) but from some local language into Greek (as a medium of language communication with which the provincial governor of Asia was quite familiar). In Egypt, a remarkable document, dated to the second half of the second century, is a Greek translation of demotic case law that dates back at least to the third century BCE.[256] This, the law of the land (νόμος τῆς χώρας) as the Ptolemies called it, or the law of the Egyptians (νόμος τῶν Αἰγυπτίων) as the Romans called it, was precisely what legal experts needed to know as part of the information relayed to local courts and to Roman oversight.

Of course, no such document has survived from the watery environs of Colossae and we know generally very little of Phrygian, Gallic or Celtic law, which may have retained a small legacy in Colossian territory. But the Egyptian example demonstrates the *a priori* warrant for the suggestion that Markos and his bureau may have been responsible for the documentary translation of legislation and case law from other language groups into the dominant *lingua franca*, that is, Greek. The requirement of ensuring that past decisions affecting land, property and persons be recorded takes on even greater urgency if the language in which those decisions were made has begun to fade, as Naphtali Lewis suggested of the Greek legal manual translated from the demotic in Egypt.[257] The fact that such assiduous translational cataloguing is already known from Persian practice, points to a long-standing and accepted bureaucratic service that

254 *Dig.* 32.1.11.
255 *Dig.* 45.1.1.6 (Ulpian, citing Sabinus, a jurist from the time of Tiberius).
256 *P.Oxy.* 3285. The Greek translation contains parts of a third century BCE demotic legal code, the Hermopolis Manual.
257 N. Lewis, "The Demise of the Demotic Document: When and Why," *JEA* 79 (1993): 276–81.

civic institutions relied upon. It is worth recalling how important longevity and antiquity were in law, not only to the Romans but to other ethnicities as well.[258]

If we focus on the issue of conflict of laws, that is on how Roman laws, including imperial, senatorial and proconsular communications, rubbed against the laws of the city and territory of Colossae, then the role of Markos and his office would have been closely connected with the operations of the civic courts and the execution of legal requirements. We know, for example, that Roman laws of slavery, especially of manumission, were markedly different from Greek law. The *Fragmentum Dositheanum*, a bilingual training manual for Greek jurists dated to around 200 CE, demonstrates not only that Greek and Latin laws were still operating in tandem at that time, but also that Greek jurists were feeling the need to become more adept in Roman legal requirements.[259] Of course, this only raises the possibility that something similar may have been needed at Colossae a century earlier. But we do know that the execution of law was part of the responsibilities borne by the anonymous honoree whose monument and inscribed *cursus honorum* were curated by Heliodoros in the mid-second century, probably during the time of Antoninus Pius.[260] He held the positions of *paraphylax*, *nomophylax* and *ekdikos* (ll. 5,8), all positions requiring the enforcement of different levels of laws, and, as such, demanding the expertise of one like Markos along with his staff.

Here a section enshrined in the *Digest of Justinian* makes a significant contribution. The *Digest* records the substance of an edict of Antoninus Pius for the province of Asia dealing with tax and liturgical exemptions for specially-trained individuals within a city — grammarians, doctors, teachers of rhetoric, and philosophers. Modestinus is credited with the quotations from Pius's *constitutio* but he provides explanatory comments (like a well-trained ἐξηγητής assisting a court).[261] Of crucial significance here is the division of exemptions given in Pius's edict:

> Αἱ μὲν ἐλάττους πόλεις δύναται πέντε ἰατροὺς ἀτελεῖς ἔχειν καὶ τρεῖς σοφιστὰς καὶ γραμματικοὺς τοὺς ἴσους· αἱ δὲ μείζους πόλεις ἑπτὰ τοὺς θεραπεύοντας, τέσσαρας τοὺς παιδεύοντας ἑκατέραν παιδείαν· αἱ μέγισται πόλεις δέκα ἰατροὺς καὶ ῥήτορας πέντε καὶ γραμματικοὺς τοὺς ἴσους. ὑπὲρ δὲ τοῦτον τὸν ἀριθμὸν οὐδὲ ἡ μεγίστη πόλις τὴν ἀτέλειαν παρέχει.

258 The suggestion that the document, containing the minutiae of land and building conflicts, might reflect no more than a priest's antiquarian interest is to be rejected: J. G. Manning, "Coinage as 'Code' in Ptolemaic Egypt," in *The Monetary Systems of the Greeks and Romans* edited by W. V. Harris (Oxford: Oxford University Press, 2008), 99.

259 See A. M. Honoré, "The 'Fragmentum Dositheanum'," *Revue Internationale des Droits de l'Antiquité* 12 (1965): 301–23; E. Dickey, *The Colloquia of the Hermeneumata Pseudodositheana Volume 1* (Cambridge: Cambridge University Press, 2012), 28–30.

260 *IGR* 4.870.

261 *Dig.* 27.1.6.1–10.

> *The lesser cities are permitted to have five doctors immune from public duties,*[262] *as well as three sophists, and the same number of grammarians. The cities of greater status are allowed seven medical practitioners and four exempt for each discipline of learning [viz. sophists and grammarians]. The cities enjoying the highest status may exempt ten doctors, five rhetoricians and an equal number of grammarians. Beyond this number, even the most elevated city is not granted immunity.*

Modestinus describes the communication of Antoninus as a letter (ἐπιστολή) that was written (as commonly, in Greek) to the koinon of Asia (γραφείσης μὲν τῷ κοινῷ τῆς Ἀσίας). However, although a letter (μέν), he goes on to claim that it had empire-wide application (παντὶ δὲ τῷ κόσμῳ διαφερούσης). Of course, midway through the third century, when Modestinus was making his compilation (also in Greek), this could readily be argued, and it helped his exegetical move that the letter referred (at the end of the excerpt) to a city in the singular. This appears to have driven his tripartite breakdown of cities into the capitals of provinces (the largest — seemingly now based on population rather than indicative merely of status: τῷ μεγίστῳ ἀριθμῷ), those with law courts (the second largest) and those without law courts (the remainder).[263] It was a neat breakdown and probably for Asia, accurate. That is, Ephesos gained status preeminence whence came the exemptions (which privileges partly explain the efforts to usurp that position by Pergamon and Smyrna); the *conventus* centers probably are the constituents of the middle-ranked cities, numbering 13 in the first century for the province,[264] with the largest number of cities filling the lowest rank.[265] It is likely that a copy of Antoninus Puis's letter was sent to the *conventus* (assize) centers,[266] which would then have been further copied and distributed to the cities within the administrative division.

Accordingly, Colossae is likely to have learned of the regulation of taxation exemptions for certain advanced disciplines through a letter copy that was sent from Laodikeia, given that Modestinus's defining criterion of "courts" is the Greek translation of *conventus* (ἀγορὰ δικῶν). The allocation of immunities would have remained in Colossae's hands,[267] although we have no knowledge of whether Colossae exercised this right nor the fortunate few who may have ben-

262 The translation is deliberately ambiguous. ἀτέλεια was often used synonymously with ἀλειτουργησία just as, further on in Modestinus's text, a *constitutio* of Commodus that cited a previous decision of Antoninus Pius, uses ἀτέλεια and then lists the liturgical magistracies and special offices from which they were exempt — gymnasiarch, aedile, chief priest and so on (*Dig.* 27.1.6.8). See N. Lewis, "Exemption of Physicians from Liturgy," *BASP* 2 (1965): 87.

263 *Dig.* 27.1.6.2.

264 *I.Didyma* 148 as interpreted by L. Robert, "Le Culte de Caligula à Milet et la province d'Asie," *Hellenica* 7 (1949): 206–38.

265 See Habicht, "Province of Asia," 64–91 for an indication of the large number of cities and smaller communities still within the conventus in the province.

266 See *I.Milet* I.2.3, ll. 42–50 (Miletos, 56/50 BCE).

267 See Lewis, "Exemption," 87–92 for the procedure by which cities made the allocations.

efited. On this criterion, Colossae did not have a "court", that is, a Roman assize to which a perambulatory provincial governor annually came to make decisions on important cases that were brought before him, from across the conventus division. Sometimes these were supplemented by visits from a legate of the proconsul for additional jurisprudential work.[268] At this assize gathering, the cases before this "court" were those which concerned Roman interests or at least were brought by those who might claim Roman judicial review. It did not mean that Colossae lacked courts, simply that the city did not operate as an assize center.

However, there were some individuals at Colossae, as we have seen above, who had the standing to come before the assize hearing at Laodikeia (including the key city institutions such as the *Boulê*). Such standing was grounded in citizenship, in imperial estates (where Roman law held jurisdiction), and for those whose particular interests were clearly covered by Roman law. Aelius Aristides for example, vehemently claimed that he had been granted immunity from liturgies (in his case, that of *eirenarch* and *prytanis*), precisely as detailed above.[269] His standing (he held the post of imperial orator) ensured that his case was heard at an assize, although he experienced difficulties in chasing the available assize center (and the date of hearing) where his case could be resolved. However, where the standing was lacking — as, for example, villagers with a grievance over agricultural supply, taxation or soldiers' incursions — a patron with standing (and the ability to muster and interpret critical documents) had to be found if the case was to have a chance of being admitted for a hearing.[270] Even for cities, securing a Roman patron was critical in prosecuting their interests.[271] That the practice of patronage of a settlement had a prolific life into the imperial period, demonstrates that the Roman understanding of the importance of the hierarchically superior continued to deliver practical advantages.[272] The Roman mode of manumission that required a witnessing of the formalities before a superior rank is merely a microcosmic exhibition of the character of Roman expectations.[273]

The clear implication from Pius's decision, as clarified by the jurist Modestinus, is that there was no Roman court at Colossae. Rather Colossae's courts

---

268 See Burton, "Proconsuls, Assizes," 95–6, 99.

269 Aristides *Or.* 50.78–93. This is corroborative evidence of the chronology of the decision, given in epistolary form, of Antoninus Pius.

270 See the discussion of the legal aspects of the so-called "peasants' strike" in Josephus *BJ* 2.193, 199 and *Ant.* 18.273–84 in A. H. Cadwallader, "Peasant Plucking in Mark: Conceptual and Material Issues," in *Class Struggle in the New Testament* edited by R. J. Myles (Lanham: Lexington/Fortress, 2019), 68–9. For the apparently frequent extortions of soldiers, see Mitchell, *Anatolia*, 1.228–30. See I. Sardis II. 318 f for an example of a patron (owner?) acting for the village of Thamoreita.

271 See for example, *Syll.* 3.748 (Gytheion, 71 BCE).

272 See generally C. Eilers, *Roman Patrons of Greek Cities* (Oxford: Oxford University Press, 2002).

273 *Dig.* 40.1.14 (Paulus), 40.2.7 (Gaius), 40.2.8 (Ulpian). Indeed, any effort to manumit a slave on one's own authority was null and void; see V. Arena, *Libertas and the Practice of Politics in the Late Roman Republic* (Cambridge: Cambridge University Press, 2012), 18, 27.

were predicated on the Greek "constitution", jurisdictional reach and decision-making powers that governed the city. Of course, that judicial configuration was subject to overarching Roman interests (especially regarding taxation and land), and, sometimes, Roman interference — such as the inspection of city records,[274] or the unheralded intrusion on council meetings and assemblies.[275] Markos the ἀρχερμηνεύς and ἐξηγητής, along with his staff, would have been crucial for ensuring that authoritative Roman letters and edicts along with lesser documents were understood for the legal ramifications that affected Colossian society. Thus, for example, when Heliodoros's anonymous honorand is credited with supplying grain for imperial needs (παρασχὼν τὸν σεῖτον … εἰς κυριακάς),[276] it is likely that contracts of sale and other matters were required, at least with a copy in Latin (especially if army supplies were involved). These legal documents fell outside the usual local contracts which were covered, generally, by local jurisdictions.[277] Markos' skills would have been critical for such exchanges.

When the first-century sage Apollonios of Tyana, at least according to the letters surviving in his name, sought to describe what made the distinctive culture of the citizens of a Greek *polis*, he listed their customs, laws, language and way of life.[278] Significantly, he combined this with a castigation of the desire for a Roman (citizenship) name, which, for him, meant cutting ties with ancestral connections and values. Though Apollonios' letter is directed towards "the Ionians", Markos of Colossae might well have been lashed with his acerbic tongue if he and his father had been locals (as the patronymic form might indicate).

Law was crucial to the identity of a Greek city. The pinnacle of Greek oratory, Demosthenes, was credited as holding that every law of the *polis* was "a discovery and gift of the gods, decided on by wise men, a corrector of errors both voluntary and involuntary and a common agreement of the city-state as that by which every citizen should guide his life."[279] Such a divine undergirding of law in the *polis* was inevitably strained by the gradual encroachment of Roman law, which tended to provide a rationale for law as derived from a common inheritance, "observed equally by all peoples."[280]

274 Pliny *Ep.* 10.47, 48.

275 *Dig.* 49.4.1.4.

276 *IGR* 4.870, ll. 9–10. Louis Robert translates it as "pour l'empereur"; "Les Inscriptions," 278.

277 Oliver, *Greek Constitutions*, 186, ll. 3–7 (Pisidia, 2nd century CE); *IGBulg* 4.2263, ll. 12–14 (157/8 CE).

278 ἔθη καὶ νόμοι καὶ γλῶττα καὶ βίος ἴδιος — Apollonios *Ep.* 71; see also *Ep.* 7.1. The sentiments cohere with the opening of Philostratus's *Vita* (1.2.3) and therefore are likely to reflect Apollonios's renowned (conservative) emphases.

279 πᾶς ἐστι νόμος εὕρημα μὲν καὶ δῶρον θεῶν, δόγμα δ' ἀνθρώπων φρονίμων, ἐπανόρθωμα δὲ τῶν ἑκουσίων καὶ ἀκουσίων ἁμαρτημάτων, πόλεως δὲ συνθήκη κοινή, καθ' ἣν πᾶσι προσήκει ζῆν τοῖς ἐν τῇ πόλει. *Or.* 25.16–17. There is some dispute over the authenticity of the oration but it was generally accepted as his by the ancients and has been recently endorsed by Douglas McDowell, *Demosthenes the Orator* (Oxford: Oxford University Press, 2009), 310–13.

280 *communi omnium hominum iure utuntur* (*Inst.* 1.1.1 [Gaius]).

Consequently, cities such as Colossae, in part benefitting from *not* being an assize center, clung to their own constitution, regulations, and power to make binding decisions as an expression of their identity. Laodikeia, as we have seen, had already in the late Republic hitched its identity and position to the fortunes of Rome, even as it did retain the formal institutions of a Greek *polis*. For Rome, especially in the early period of empire, this was strategically acceptable.[281] The elite — Demosthenes's "wise men" — were suitably rewarded and honored not merely for ensuring that legal processes continued to maintain the harmony of city life, but also for promoting the requisite loyalty to Rome, displayed by attendance at imperial occasions and festivities and in the facilitation of Roman legal requirements, especially in regard to taxation and estates. The balance between the exercise of Roman and local law shifted over the centuries but that there were a multiplicity of legal jurisdictions operating in Colossae and its territory, there can be no doubt.

Drawing implications: slavery and the conflict of laws

The survey above covering memorializations, penalties for grave infractions and the probable functions of a specific honored individual and his subordinates has established that Colossae continued to exercise its own legal frameworks even as it accommodated the imposition and potential of Roman legal systems. There is one particular area of interest where this multiplicity and potential conflict of laws has considerable application but which has received almost no notice in Second Testament commentary — slavery.

We know next to nothing of slavery at Colossae. Whether Colossae is to be adjudged like other *poleis* of the first two centuries as sustained by a servile third of its population (like, for example, Pergamon)[282] is impossible to judge. The closest we can venture to slaves are the hints given in the onomastic yield from inscriptions. Likinnius in the Korymbos inscription, named as the grandfather of one of the donors for the honorific monument, is significant because the name is a *gentilicium* and yields to a sound Greek name for his son and grandson (namely, Theodoros).[283] A *gentilicium* alone is usually taken as an indication of original slave status. Similarly, some of the names

281 A. Lintott, *Imperium Romanum: Politics and Administration* (London: Routledge, 1993), 129; C. Brélaz, "Maintaining Order and Exercising Justice in the Roman Provinces of Asia Minor," in *The Province Strikes Back: Imperial Dynamics in the Eastern Mediterranean* edited by B. Forsén and G. Salmeri (Helsinki: Finnish Academy, 2008), 57.

282 See W. L. Westermann, *The Slave Systems of Greek and Roman Antiquity* (Philadelphia: American Philosophical Society, 1955), 127.

283 *Antichthon* 2012.1, l. 24.

listed in the *defixio* found near Kaklık, appear to reflect servile connections (Terentius, Tertius).[284]

The poverty of witness to slaves in the material record is, of course, ubiquitous.[285] Colossae's funerary inscriptions cannot claim one of the uncommon inclusions of a slave among the family names recording those who are buried. Colossae is no different to most places in the wide-spread erasure of the engine-room of the ancient economy and household. This makes the *katagraphai* inscriptions at the sanctuary of Apollo Lairbenos so important. As yet however, there is no inscription in that catalogue that mentions Colossae as an ethnic for any named individual. This may well suggest that Colossians had another, closer sanctuary that performed the same function of dedicating a slave to a god as the means of engineering manumission — a decidedly Greek not Roman form of granting freedom to a slave. If so, I suspect that sanctuary is probably the Zeus precursor to what became the healing hagiasma under the patronage of St. Michael the Archangel,[286] now the Göz picnic ground just over two miles south of Colossae between the current towns of Emirazizli and Honaz.

The most famous Colossian slave remains the "Onesimos" named in the Letter to Philemon (v.10), now known to be not the only Onesimos from the territory of Colossae.[287] This of course only reinforces what some have underscored, namely, that the name Onesimos is so common in Asia (and Phrygia) that the Onesimos named in the Letter to the Colossians (4:9 cf Ignatius *Eph.* 1.3) is not necessarily the same person as the one named in the Letter to Philemon.[288] At the very least, this must be established on grounds other

284 See chapter 8.

285 In *LGPN* V.C for greater Phrygia, there are 122 instances of the name Onesimos, another 10 for the female form Onesime. Only 2 are listed as possibly the name of a slave. Curiously however, the listing from Col 4:9 and Phmn 10 (equated) is given as 4th century CE (!) and is not tagged as "slave".

286 See A. H. Cadwallader, "'As if in a Vision of the Night …' Authorising the Healing Spring of Chonai," in *Dreams, Memory and Imagination in Byzantium* edited by B. Neil and E. Anagnostou-Laoutides (Leiden: Brill, 2018), 265–92.

287 Another Onesimos, called "the antagonist", is scratched into side one (ll. 16–17) of the lead diptych of the *defixio* detailed in chapter 8. He, too, may have been a slave. Heikki Solin includes Onesimos in his top ten list of popular slave names: *Die stadtrömischen Sklavennamen: ein Namenbuch* (Stuttgart: Franz Steiner, 3 vols, 1996), 3.680. However, it should be recognized that free Greek men readily bore the name (see *I.Hierapolis Judeich* 126, 174, for example), whereas to Romans, the stench of servility so strongly attached to it that it is rarely found among Roman freeborn men. The slave-prostitute from Pompeii, named Onesimus (*CIL* 4.8380), is but one instance of a lack of encouragement for such naming of the freeborn, at least in Italy. The name occurs 197 times for slaves, 17 of which are feminine in morphology: *Die stadtrömischen Sklavennamen*, 2.465–8. Peter Arzt-Grabner similarly finds that Onesimos is "ein typischer Sklavenname" in the papyri: *Philemon* (PKNT 1; Göttingen: Vandenhoeck & Ruprecht, 2003), 86, and see 86–96.

288 P. Arzt-Grabner, "How to Deal with Onesimus? Paul's Solution within the Framework of Ancient Legal and Documentary Sources," in *Philemon in Perspective: Interpreting a Pauline Letter* edited by D. F. Tolmie (Berlin: de Gruyter, 2010), 141 n118; A. H. Cadwallader, "Onesi-

than onomastics.[289] It should also be recognized that Onesimos may not be the original name for this Second Testament figure; Philemon may well have given him the name Onesimos at or just after the point of sale — a common practice in master-slave practice, reinforcing the master's *dominium*.[290] Hence Onesimos was likely the virtue Philemon wanted his slave to aspire to, even if constantly bedeviled by the fundamental, nigh-irremovable essentializing of a slave as ἄχρηστος. This stereotype, not the name, is the punning ground for Paul in Phmn 11.[291]

Here I do not want to debate the standard questions related to Onesimos, subject as they are to the ambiguities of a short, often allusive (if not elusive) letter. Rather, I aim to apply the clear directions indicated above regarding the multiplicity of laws as they might inform two traditional interpretations. The first relates to Onesimos as a so-called *fugitivus*, a runaway slave,[292] and how the Greek legal heritage at Colossae might apply. The second relates to the issue of manumission, namely, how the law of Colossae might have dealt with the manumission of Onesimos, if, as some would argue, this is what Paul is advising in his Letter to Philemon. To make clear my own position at the outset: I do consider Onesimos to be a runaway, but a δραπετικός rather than a *fugitivus*, the difference in language reflecting the law which I consider to have applied, that is, Greek not Roman. Secondly, I do not consider that Paul was arguing for manumission,[293] but, if he was, I want to explore what that would

mus and the Social and Geographical World of Philemon," in *Lexham Geographic Commentary on Acts through Revelation* edited by B. J. Beitzel (Bellingham, WA: Lexham Press, 2019), 594. Most assume identity: see, for example, E. Lohse, *Colossians and Philemon* (Philadelphia: Fortress, 1971), 171; V. Balabanski, "Where is Philemon? The Case for a Logical Fallacy in the Correlation of the Data in Philemon and Colossians 1.1–2; 4.7–18," *JSNT* 38 (2015): 131–50.

289 This is admitted by Michael Gese, *Der Kolosserbrief* (Göttingen: Vandenhoeck & Ruprecht, 2020), 168. The argument for identity of the two persons on the basis that the name is not common in early Christian literature, presumes what has to be established: Foster, *Colossians*, 417.

290 *BGU* 3.887 = *CPJ* 3.490, l. 3 (Arsinote, 151 CE but written from Side in Pamphylia). Here the young Phrygian born 12 year old girl named Sambatis, sold as a slave, is renamed Athenais (κοράσιον Σαμβατίδα τὴν μετονομασθεῖσαν Ἀθηναίδα). The name Sambatis (and cognates) is rare, but known, in Phrygia (*IG* II^2 7931, Attica, 1st century BCE to 1st century CE given the ethnic Ankaran, l. 3). There is no requirement that it be a Jewish name (by connection with the Jewish Sibyl, Sambethe). The name is relatively common in Greece.

291 See A. H. Cadwallader, "Name Punning and Social Stereotyping: Re-inscribing Slavery in the Letter to Philemon," *ABR* 16 (2013): 13–15.

292 See J. G. Nordling, "Onesimus Fugitivus: A Defense of the Runaway Slave Hypothesis in Philemon," *JSNT* 41 (1991): 97–119; J. M. G. Barclay, *Colossians and Philemon* (Sheffield, Sheffield Academic Press, 1997), 98–102. On the variety of interpretations of Onesimos, with a conclusion supporting the runaway hypothesis, see L. Kreitzer, *Philemon* (Sheffield: Sheffield Phoenix Press, 2008), 38–69; for another overview but leading to historical skepticism, see R. R. Jeal, *Exploring Philemon: Freedom, Brotherhood, and Partnership in the New Society* (Atlanta, GA: SBL, 2015), 23–9. For an overview but arguing for the loan of a slave, see J. A. Harrill, *Slaves in the New Testament: Literary, Social and Moral Dimensions* (Minneapolis: Fortress, 2006), 6–16.

293 See Cadwallader, "Name Punning," 18–31.

have meant in a Greek *polis* such as Colossae. Both these major issues inextricably entail questions of law — which law(s), which jurisdiction(s) and how any conflicts might have been addressed.

Onesimos and the runaway slave hypothesis

When the runaway slave hypothesis is admitted, the operating assumption is that Roman law governs how this might be interpreted. The keenest commentary in this regard is that of Peter Arzt-Grabner.[294] Sometimes Roman law is given a non-historical blend as "Greco-Roman" law,[295] always a problematic amalgamation that ends up privileging the second element and eliminating distinctive features.

The sixth century *Digest of Justinian*, a collation that incorporated large swathes of the writings of earlier Roman jurists and selections of senatorial and imperial edicts, is riddled with both specific and tangential references to slaves. But not only is the compendium geared to the needs of a sixth century, by then a Roman empire located in the East, its focus and that of its sources presume a relatively elite audience. That is, they operate "in terms of the interests of the class to which they themselves and their clients belonged."[296] This is amply demonstrated in the third century jurist Julius Paulus, whose writings make a significant contribution to the *Digest*. When it comes to the distinction between town and country slaves (*urbanus*, *rusticus*) there is an assumption that

294 Arzt-Grabner, "How to Deal with Onesimus?" 120–35. For a critical response, which nonetheless relies on Roman law, see R. Gamhauf, "Onesimus: *fugitivus errove* – Einsichten für die Bibelexegese aus der Digestenexegese? (Rechtshistorische Anmerkungen zum Umgang mit römischen Rechtstexten in der neueren Philemon-Auslegung)" in *Constans et Perpetua Voluntas: Posta Petrovi Blahovi K 75. Narodeninám* edited by P. Mach, M. Pekarik and V. Vladár (Trnave: Trnavská Univerzita, 2014), 159–76.

295 See J. D. G. Dunn, *The Epistles to the Colossians and to Philemon* (NIGTC; Grand Rapids, Mich: 1996), 303, 304; G. Francois Wessels, "The Letter to Philemon in the Context of Slavery in Early Christianity," in *Philemon in Perspective*, 144–47 (acknowledging that legal texts, meaning, for him, Roman legal texts, do not adequately deliver an historical and social analysis of slavery); M. J. Smith, "Utility, Fraternity and Reconciliation: Ancient Slavery as a Context for the Return of Onesimus," in *Onesimus our Brother: Reading Religion, Race, and Culture in Philemon* edited by M. V. Johnson, J. A. Noel and D. K. Williams (Minneapolis: Fortress, 2012), 61–3; A. H. H. Ip, *A Socio-Rhetorical Interpretation of the Letter to Philemon in Light of the New Institutional Economics* (Tübingen: Mohr Siebeck, 2017), *passim*. Roman law is often assumed as governing Mediterranean slavery in general and hence does not need specificity, as in M. M. Thompson, *Colossians & Philemon* (Grand Rapids, MN: Eerdmans, 2005), 202–4.

296 G. E. M. de Ste Croix, *The Class Struggle in the Ancient Greek World* (London: Duckworth, 1981), 330. For a slightly extreme criticism of the use of the *Digest* for understanding the first and second centuries, see J. A. Harrill, "Using the Roman Jurists to interpret Philemon," *ZNW* 90 (1999): 135–8. For an alternate perspective, see D. Johnston, *Roman Law in Context* (Cambridge: Cambridge University Press, 2004), 24–9.

the head of the household (*paterfamilias*) owned country estates as well as town houses and apportioned his slaves accordingly.[297] He even scalpeled into the discussion the question of whether the child of a town slave sent to a rural estate to be wet-nursed counted as a country or town slave. He avoids the question of who fathered the child (a "home bred slave", *verna*) but assumes that the *paterfamilias* had patent authority to transfer the infant wherever he wishes. He even works into his general division some of the specific types of slaves that the master probably owned — hunters (*venatores*), fowlers (*aucupes*), muleteers (*muliones*), litter-bearers (*lecticarii*), cook (*cocus*), the low-ranking vanguard attendants for the litter or coach (*cursores*), and probably at least one wet-nurse (*nutrix*).[298] The excerpt provides a window into the audience and clientele of such a law-code.

Philemon's house (note κατ' οἶκόν σου, Phmn 2) suggests a multiple-slave household, given rooms for Apphia, Archippos, Philemon,[299] a guest-room (ξενία Phmn 22), rooming for slaves, a store (strong?)-room (suggested by Phmn 18) and the ability to hold (welcome, feed, arrange for) meetings of the local ἐκκλησία (or one of them). The commercial language that infiltrates the letter (vv. 13, 16, 17–19) points to the mercantile standing (and possibly partnership) of Philemon (and Paul),[300] but it is a context far removed from the standing addressed in the jurist Paul's exemplary (and stylized) world.

However, on occasion the *Digest* betrays a different world from that inhabited by its jurists, one subject to different jurisdictions and regulations. It is demonstrably a world other to that addressed by the standard operations of Roman law. Another jurist, the second century Sextus Pomponius, recounts the actual dealings with someone named Menander who had been brought to Rome as a slave, was a translator, and became a freedman.[301] In Roman law this meant citizenship.[302] The issue in law for Pomponius was whether that citizenship was to be forfeited should he return to live amongst his own people, presumably as a citizen of that polity. He appears to have argued on the basis of older Roman law that citizenship of two polities was repudiated.[303] Cicero provides us with

297 *Dig.* 32.1.99.prol. 5..

298 On the hierarchy of slaves, see *CIL* 8.12590–13186 (Carthage, various dates), a massive store of slave occupations and rankings.

299 The oft-asserted marriage of Philemon and Apphia is a fiction with no substance in the text. It is worth comparing the married couple, Prisca and Aquila, whose hospitality extended to the gathering of Christ-followers in *their* house (κατ' οἶκον αὐτῶν Rom 16:5), a suggestive if not decisive indicator.

300 C. J. Martin, "The Rhetorical Function of Commercial Language in Paul's Letter to Philemon (Verse 18)," in *Persuasive Artistry: Studies in New Testament Rhetoric in Honor of George A. Kennedy* edited by D. F. Watson (Sheffield: Sheffield Academic Press, 1991), 321–77; P. Arzt-Grabner, "Everyday Life in a Roman Town Like Colossae: The Papyrological Evidence," in *First Urban Churches 5*, 226–31.

301 *Dig.* 49.15.5.3.

302 *Dig.* 38.16.3.1 (Ulpian).

303 There is another trace of the incompatibility of dual citizenship in *Dig.* 28.5.6.2 (Ulpian).

further details. Menander was Greek by birth; his translation skills were called upon by Roman legates to support a mission in Greece.[304] Cicero was adamant that multiple citizenships, completely at home for citizens of Greek city-states, could not include Roman citizenship, but his admission that some Roman citizens were behaving as if they were citizens of such cities, without sacrifice of their Roman *civitas*, shows that the older legal scruples were softening. Dual citizenship is clearly permitted by the Letters of Octavian concerning Seleukos of Rhosos in Syria to the extent that Seleukos is granted permission to decide which jurisdiction — Roman or local — under which he is to be tried in any future court proceedings, following the award of Roman citizenship.[305]

When we turn to the operations of Greek law, we find that runaways — δραπετικοί or σωμάτα ἀποδράντα — are mentioned in inter-city treaties even into the late Republican period. These sympolitical relationships were not only designed to enhance cooperation and peaceful relationships between city-states but also to deal with practical matters that were difficult to resolve for an individual city. Lato and Olous, for example, cities on the island of Crete, negotiated a settlement (110/9 or 109/8 BCE) where slaves who had fled from their cities during recent wartime were to be returned to their respective jurisdictions (ll. 48–50). Understandably, much of the treaty is given to delineating the boundaries of the two cities, for this cartographical precision was necessary to clarify the reach of the law and policing of the respective city-states.[306] In a similar treaty between Miletos and Herakleia (around 185 BCE), the *horophylakes* had the responsibility for re-capture of slaves and secured the advantage of their re-sale if the owner(s) did not come forward to claim their property.[307] How the runaways were recognized is not mentioned.[308] Occasionally we hear of the asylum available to slaves at a sanctuary (as an acceptable means of escape from a brutal master) being restricted to the local city.[309]

These instances of course make no mention of Rome even if they occur in greater or lesser connection with the late Republic. However, Rome certainly became involved in the restoration of slaves to the city of Aphrodisias follow-

---

304 Cicero *Balb.* 28.

305 *IGLS* 3.1.718 (between 42 and 30 BCE). See also *FIRA* 1.68 (Banasa, 177 CE).

306 *I.Crete* 1.16.5; see also *IG* V 2 357, ll. 151–9 (Hellenistic treaty between Stymphalos and Demetrias).

307 *I.Milet* I.3.150. See A. Chaniotis, "The Impact of War on the Economy of Hellenistic Poleis: demand creation, short-term influences, long-term impacts," in *The Economics of Hellenistic Societies, Third to First Centuries BC* edited by Z. Archibald, J.K. Davies and V. Gabrielsen (Oxford: Oxford University Press, 2011), 139–40.

308 See P. Hunt, *Slaves, Warfare, and Ideology in the Greek Historians* (Cambridge: Cambridge University Press, 1998), 103.

309 *IG* VI 1390 = *LSCG* 65, ll. 8–10 (sanctuary at Ardania near the city of Messene; usually dated 91 BCE but 24 CE is sometimes given as an alternate date; see L. Gawlinski, *The Sacred Law of Ardania: A New Text with Commentary* [Berlin: de Gruyter, 2012], 3–11; for Hierapolis, see Guizzi, "Novità epigrafiche," 119–30, nr. 1.

ing the crushing of the revolt of the Roman renegade general, Labienus, in 39–40 BCE. It seems that, even though the orator Zeno had rallied Laodikeia to protect the Roman commander Ventidius against Labienus's Parthian forces, the defense was of limited success. It is not clear whether the slaves (and apparently some freemen) had joined Labienus's forces (a common phenomenon in war-time), only to discover that they had picked the wrong side, or whether they were looted by Labienus's soldiers. Mark Antony's legate (of sorts) in Laodikeia, named Stephanus,[310] was appointed to restore order in and from the city. The Aphrodisians sent envoys to him, recognizing his jurisdiction and Roman-backed authority, seeking the return of slaves. The envoys were given permission to wander the city of Laodikeia and identify the runaways (and "traitors").[311] Again, the boundaries of the jurisdiction of the city of Aphrodisias are acknowledged as territorially restricted. Only diplomatic representation, under the formal delegated authority of the city's *Boulê* and *Dêmos*, permitted the pursuit of runaways into another city's territory. Rome, with its overarching authority, might provide its extra-jurisdictional support but it is clear that the standing of city institutions was needed for this to occur.[312]

However, these post-war repatriations are extraordinary circumstances involving the interactions of those of significant rank. As Stephen Llewelyn has recognized, "it is difficult to contemplate that a matter between a peregrine master [the non-Roman citizen, Philemon] and his slave [Onesimos] would have been considered significant enough to be accepted within that jurisdiction."[313] The admission that slavery in Colossae and its territory primarily functioned under the city's (Greek) legal jurisdiction has a number of important consequences for the construction of Onesimos as a runaway:

i) Greek law had no equivalent of a vagrant slave, as in the Roman category of *erro*,[314] a "petty fugitive" (*pusillum fugitivum*)[315] and thereby ultimately defined as a tautology of *fugitivus*.[316] Even when slave sales in cities such as Side or elsewhere provided a warranty, based on the edict of the *Curule*

310 Stephanus is only known from two Aphrodisian inscriptions. He is not mentioned in the record at Laodikeia, possibly because he was appointed by Mark Antony.

311 *I.Aphrodisias and Rome* 11 (around 35 BCE); compare also *I.Aphrodisias and Rome* 12 for a similar offer of assistance to Ephesos.

312 Compare the *Lex Antonia de Termessibus*, col. I, l. 36 to col. II, l. 5 (c. 68 BCE).

313 *New Doc. Early Christ.* 8.3, p. 42.

314 *Contra* Arzt-Grabner, *Philemon*, 103, "How to Deal with Onesimus?", 125–35. For a more detailed address of the suggestion, see Cadwallader, "Complicating class". For the distinction, see *Dig.* 21.1.17.14 (Ulpian), 21.2.32 (Ulpian); Seneca *Contr.* 7.23; see, generally, P. Arzt-Grabner, "'Neither a Truant nor a Fugitive': Some Remarks on the Sale of Slaves in Egypt and Other Provinces," *Proceedings of the 25th International Congress of Papyrology* edited by T. Gagos (Ann Arbor: Scholarly Publishing Office, 2010), 21–32.

315 *Dig.* 21.1.17.14 (Ulpian citing Labeo).

316 *Dig.* 11.4.1.5 (Ulpian). Richard Gamhauf finds that the terminology in the legal sources is anything but uniform: "Onesimus: *fugitivus errove*," 163.

Aediles, that a slave was "neither a truant nor a fugitive" (*fugitivum erronem non esse*/μήτε ῥέμβον μήτε δραπετικόν),[317] it is more likely that this was a weak imitation of Roman legal guarantees than indicating that this was a category in Greek law.[318] There is no extant occurrence of ῥέμβος in Greek epigraphy.[319] Once Onesimos ventured alone outside Colossae's territory he was automatically a runaway, and presumed to be a thief as well.[320] He could not claim asylum at a temple altar or agora statue (likely only applicable within the city of Colossae), nor the intervention of another.[321] No amelioration by reference to intent, as was possible in Roman law, applied. Critically, both Roman and Greek law held that once a slave was a runaway (*fugitivus* or δραπετικός), this compounded stigma remained, regardless of restitution, rehabilitation, re-sale or, significantly, repentance (*paenitentia*).[322] It had become a character trait.[323] For Greeks, the assumption that slaves were so by nature, meant that governance and restraint were necessary to

317 *P.Turner* 22, l. 4 (142 CE).

318 So, G. Kantor, "Law in Roman Phrygia: rules and jurisdictions," in *Roman Phrygia*, 16. Some slave sales from the same period, do not contain any mention of the fugitive/vagrant condition; see for example *P.Oxy.* 95 ll. 19–20 (129 CE). One later sale, between soldiers, expressly excluded a warranty: *P.Oxy.* 2951, l. 23 (267 CE) — and this in a bilingual contract that expressly notes Roman law yet follows Greek legal format (that is, privileging the seller rather than the buyer in the formulary, according to the editor, G. M. Browne). The implication is that jurisdictional operations besides that of the Romans were still available for some time after the mid-third century.

319 Significantly, in the rare occurrences of ῥεμβός in the papyri, the context suggests the influence of Roman categories, not Greek. See, for example, *P.Panop. Beatty* 1.298, l.(6) 149 which mentions an οἰκέτης ῥεμβός in an army levy inventory (*annona militaris*).

320 Terence *Eun.* 776; Martial *Ep.* 11.54 *Dig.* 21.1.58.2. Compare *New Doc. Early Christ.* 8.3, p. 34. A fugitive was removing a master's property — compare *Dig.* 47.1.63. Distance of travel is also crucial in Roman law. If Onesimos journeyed to Ephesos (or even to Rome) he is most unlikely to be understood as a vagrant. The *Digest* understands a wanderer (*erro*) as one who returns to the household "at a late hour" (*Dig.* 21.1.17.14 [Ulpian citing Labeo]. Gamauf adds the component of the length of time Onesimos must have spent with Paul — time for conversion (Phmn 10) and for "service" (Phmn 11, 13) — to banish any sense of *erro*: "Onesimos: *fugitivus errove*," 170.

321 In Roman law, this amelioration of *fugitivus* did not apply if it was an attempt to find an *amicus domini* after the fact/intent, nor, likely, if that mediator was at some remove from the master; see Gamhauf, "Onesimus: *fugitivus errove*," 167, 168. Given that most Second Testament commentators have Onesimos stumbling on Paul at considerable distance (even put in prison with him — an impossibility if Onesimos was recognized as a slave), this would negate the amelioration. If theft is involved (on one interpretation of Phmn 18, albeit contested) then there is little question that the assumed intent of flight would be applied.

322 *Dig.* 21.1.17.1 cf 47.1.66; 50.16.225.

323 G. Klingennerg, *Corpus der Römischen Rechtsquellen zur antiquen Sklaverei X.6 Servus fugitivus* (Stuttgart: Franz Steiner, 2005), 1. Note *P.Hamb.* 1.72 (Philadelphia?, Egypt 2nd century CE) where slaves described as *fugitivorum servorum meorum* (l. 8) are distinguished from other slaves by the addition of *fugitivorum* and expressly excluded from manumission, even though they appear to be (now) at hand.

prevent absconding,[324] the "mechanics of carcerality" as Christopher de Wet dubs the prevention of flight.[325]

ii) Philemon's efforts to recover Onesimos are nowhere mentioned in the letter. It may indicate that the cost of publically broadcasting a reward for return and/or of hiring someone to track Onesimos down was not compensated by Onesimos's value (as a stereotyped "useless" slave, Phmn 11). It may be that Philemon wished to avoid any public questions about his ability to control his *familia*.[326] It is virtually certain that Philemon could not rely on Roman citizenship nor some Roman patron who might excite the tracking resources of Roman officials.[327]

iii) Consequently, wherever Paul was in prison — Rome, Caesarea Maritima or Ephesos — Onesimos as a runaway could not be trusted to travel alone or independently back to Philemon, either reliant on his own determination or hoping to escape the scrutiny of officials or hunters along the road.[328] Either way, Paul would have been placing an intolerable burden on "his child" (Phmn 10). The Augustan jurist, Marcus Antistius Labeo, held that sending a slave abroad to a new owner was an act of bad faith by the seller, presumably because it was not prudent to do so, the slave unlikely to reach the determined destination.[329] Indeed, Roman law prescribed careful surveillance and incarceration until a runaway be restored to her/his owner.[330] This seems also to have been the expectation in Greek law enforcement.[331] No letter (whether of recommendation or otherwise) could be entrusted to the possession of a runaway.[332] Slave letter carriers (*tabellarii*) certainly

324 See Aristotle *Pol.* 1.1254a; Philodemos *Oec.* 11.30–7.

325 C. de Wet, *Preaching Bondage: John Chrysostom and the Discourse of Slavery in Early Christianity* (Berkeley: University of California Press, 2015), 18.

326 Compare *Dig.* 39.4.13.2 (Gaius) on concerns over a disorderly (*factiosa*) *familia.*

327 *Dig.* 11.4.1.2 (Ulpian).

328 See *Dig.* 1.15.4. He may have tried to pass himself off as free (cf Cicero *Fam.* 13.77), but this presumes that he was not branded in some way as a slave (necklace, tattoo), nor subject to a warrant detailing a physical description (see, for example, *P.Par.* 10 [Memphis, 156 BCE]), and that he had the requisite language skills and register to carry it off. If Onesimos was not Greek, having been conferred a Greek name by Philemon, this cannot be assumed. If Onesimos was Greek, then the naturalist understanding that Greek equals "free" raises serious questions of Philemon (as a fellow Greek) and perhaps explains Onesimos's departure (see Plato *Resp.* 5.469c; Xenophon *Hell.* 1.6.14; Dio Chrysostom, *Or.* 15). The situation is further complicated if Philemon was by ancestry Phrygian, adopting a Greek familial persona (see chapter 9).

329 *Dig.* 19.1.13.54 (Labeo).

330 *Dig.* 11.4.1.6–8 (Ulpian). Such policing practices became more stringent under Marcus Aurelius; see S. Llewelyn, "P. Harris I 62 and the Pursuit of Fugitives," *ZPE* 118 (1997): 245.

331 *PSI* 6.570 (Philadelphia, Egypt, 252 BCE); *BGU* 8.1774 (Herakleopolis, 59/8–50/49 BCE).

332 This, to me, is the flaw in Peter Head's recent article, along with a failure to accommodate the jurisdictional limitations of Greek civic law related to slavery: "Onesimus the Letter-Carrier" *passim*. I find it curious that Head is prepared to grant Onesimos, the δραπετικός, a voice as a complement to the letter he carried on a par with Phoebe, Epaphroditus and Tychicus to whom he denies any public reading of the letter that they were meant to supplement: "Named Letter

existed but these operated precisely within circumscribed geographical bounds.[333] Some superior, in my understanding, was essential both to safeguard Onesimos and his return to Philemon, regardless of how one (re-) constructs the relationship between the master Philemon and his slave. The extant letter hardly qualifies as a "letter of safe conduct".[334]

Manumission of Onesimos?

In his treatise on *Oratory*, Cicero has one of his leading exponents, Crassus, pronounce,

> It is amazing, I might even say ridiculous, how chaotic are all legal systems other than our own. On this, I am accustomed to say many things in my daily discourses, when upholding our own jurisprudence above that of other men, especially the Greeks.[335]

It is a familiar trope of Roman self-aggrandizement over the nation and culture from which they drew so much, proclaiming themselves as the rightful inheritors, faithful preservers and sagacious improvers. But it points to one

---

Carriers among the Oxyrhynchus Papyri," *JSNT* 31 (2009): 280–2, 297. It seems to me that status differentials and flawed behaviors are crucial here. Unlike Philemon (Phmn 5, 6) Onesimos is never described in terms of trust or trustworthiness (πιστός), an attribute that elsewhere, Head sees as a key descriptor (along with sober judgment/moderation [σώφρων] and blamelessness [ἄμεμπτος]) of those who are letter carriers: "'Witnesses between You and Us': The Role of the Letter-Carriers in 1 *Clement*," in *Studies on the Text of the New Testament and early Christianity: essays in honour of Michael W. Holmes*, edited by D. Gurtner, J. Hernández and P. Foster (Leiden: Brill, 2015), 487–8. Very occasionally, one finds slaves described as faithful: Pliny *Ep.* 3.14 (*servi fideliores*, though here they may be included along with other slaves later to flee). A punning εὔχρηστος in Phmn 11 hardly commands equivalence, especially from the perspective of the master, Philemon, who as likely as not, would have agreed with the scholiast on Aristophanes, "It is not good for slaves to speak plainly to their masters, as if equal" (Schol. Aristophanes 952 cf Col 3:22). Model slaves were an invention of the owning class (for example, Tacitus *Ann.* 14.60), usually in the form of exemplary tales for the moral improvement of their possessions, that masked their fear about slaves' true intentions (Plato *Resp.* 9.578e–579b; *Gorg.* 484e; Xenophon *Hier.* 3.4.5). Model slaves held their tongue (Euripides *Phoen.* 391–2)!

333 Cicero *Att.* 372.1. See A-M. Luijendijk, "Books and Private Readers in Early Christian Oxyrhynchus: 'A Spiritual Meadow and a Garden of Delight,'" in *Books and Readers in the Premodern World: Essays in Honor of Harry Gamble* (Atlanta GA: SBL, 2018), 111–2. This point has escaped the notice of Ulrike Roth who assumes Onesimos can operate according to the bounds of empire rather than *polis*: "Paul and Slavery: Economic Perspectives," in *Paul and Economics*, 166–7.

334 P. Stuhlmacher, *Der Brief an Philemon* (Benziger: Neukirchener, 2004[4][1975]), 23.

335 *Incredibile est enim, quam sit omne ius civile praeter hoc nostrum inconditum ac paene ridiculum; de quo multa soleo in sermonibus cotidianis dicere, cum hominum nostrorum prudentiam ceteris omnibus et maxime Graecis antepono.* Cicero *Orat.* 1.197. I have deliberately translated *prudentia* as jurisprudence given the context and implication.

of the fundamental differences between Roman and Greek law, namely, that Greek law was, across the hundreds of *poleis* of Greece, Macedonia and Asia, really a collection of family resemblances found in inscriptions rather than the definitional codification of Roman precision that was as reliable in Rome as in *colonia* imposed within foreign lands. Crassus implies that Greek law remained in view as a contrast, and so it was in considerable measure, as we have seen above. But nowhere was it more apparent than in the law, or rather laws and administrative practices, governing manumission. Leigh Gibson's summation, drawing especially on the continuing influence of a foundational work on Greek manumission (that of Aristide Calderini)[336] is as critical as it is overlooked in much Second Testament scholarship: "Although Roman rule penetrated many arenas of eastern Mediterranean life, the impact of Roman law was negligible in the realm of manumissions, inscribed or otherwise, recorded in Greek."[337]

Manumission in Greek law(s) was fundamentally different from that in Roman law, in that citizenship in a Greek *polis* was never entertained as the end or result of manumission.[338] Freedom was defined other than by reference to citizenship; hence ἀπελεύθερος/ἐξελεύθερος, the Greek term often used to indicate a manumitted slave, did not fully equate with the *libertus* of Roman law. A *libertus* was understood to have joined the *civitas* of Rome;[339] an ἀπελεύθερος, when referring to Greek manumission, did not join the voting polity of a Greek city. Rather he or she secured a (non-enfranchised) free place within a city, designated by whatever term seemed most appropriate — sometimes a *paramone* (that is a free person under obligation to a former master for skilled work, usually over a designated period), sometimes, if there were sufficient numbers of freed slaves known from their geopolitical origin, simply by that classification (*romaioi, laodicenses*),[340] and sometimes, as we shall see, free yet a slave of a particular god (at the god's sanctuary).[341] The formal boundaries between citizen and non-citizen were carefully regulated.[342] Greek jurists targetted their incredulity at Roman manumission law precisely at the award

336 A. Calderini, *La Manomissione e la condizione dei liberti in Grecia* (Milan: Ulrico Hoepli, 1908).

337 E. L. Gibson, *The Jewish Manumission Inscriptions of the Bosporus Kingdom* (Tübingen: Mohr Siebeck, 1999), 33 n7.

338 Youni, "Transforming Greek practice," 313.

339 Livy *Hist.* 2.5.9; Plutarch *Publ.* 7.4–5; *Dig.* 38.16.3.1 (Ulpian). See especially *IG* IX 2 517.30–4 (Larissa, Thessaly; 217/221 BCE) for the antiquity and recognition of the practice.

340 See R. Zelnick-Abramovitz, *Not Wholly Free. The Concept of Manumission and the Status of Manumitted Slaves in the Ancient World* (Leiden/Boston: Brill, 2005).

341 This dual status is carefully delineated by Marijana Ricl as primarily related to spatial connections. That is, the person freed in connection with dedication to a god, acts as a *hierodoulos* of that god at the god's sanctuary. See Ricl, "Donations of Slaves," 158. For a recent example of the combination ἱερὸς καὶ ἐλεύθερος, see Öztürk-Tanrıver, "New Katagraphai," 102 nr. 14.

342 R. Zelnick-Abramovitz, "Freed slaves, their status and state control in Ancient Greece," *ERH* 16 (2009): 303–18.

of citizenship.[343] And, in spite of the ambiguity in Paul's phrasing, it appears that in writing to an *ekklêsia* in a city formally anchored to Roman jurisprudence, that is Corinth, his terminology around slavery and manumission (1 Cor 7:21–3), seem to presuppose Greek legal operations rather than Roman.[344]

Be that as it may, the standard administrative legal governance of manumission at Colossae would have been Greek, apart from those slaves owned by Roman citizens or at work on Roman estates in the city's territory.[345] Needless to say, the manumissions in either jurisdiction attracted a tax.[346] If Onesimos was to be manumitted, in formal Greek legal understanding he could not be of the same status as Philemon. Inequality would still mark the relationship in civic perspective, whatever meaning and value was to be attached to the Christian designation "brother" (Phmn 16). That inequality would have been mundanely underscored if Onesimos was required to fulfill *paramone* requirements for Philemon or even, by Philemon's delegation, Paul himself (Phmn 13).

Calderini divided Greek manumission practices into two basic types. The dichotomy has largely held across subsequent treatments,[347] even though some subdivisions and refinements have been proposed.[348] These two types — processes — may be described as sacral and civic. This is not to imply either process is recorded in identical terms. But one involves some sort of dedication to a god/gods and the other a hearing before city officials. However, both appear to have required some official recording in city archives. This is sometimes expressly noted, but is also implicit in the mention of the treasury to which a penalty is to be paid for infringement of the manumission (by return to slavery, or servile treatment).

---

343 G. Kantor, "Greek Law," 12–15 (online pagination).

344 In this sense, there is much to be said, albeit with modification, for the interpretation, often maligned, of Adolf Deissman, *Light from the Ancient East* translated by L. R. M. Strachan (London: Hodder & Stoughton, 1910), 332–4. For a curt dismissal of Deissman's interpretation, more interested in philosophical than material *comparanda*, and relying on the now-substantially-discredited thesis on sacral manummissions of Franz Bömer, see O. Cullmann, *1 Corinthians* translated by J. W. Leitch (Philadelphia: Fortress, 1975), 128. In the *katagraphai* inscriptions are found not only dedications of slaves to gods (as a means of manumission), but also of free persons to be "slaves" of the gods. This provides a better material comparison to Paul's supposed inversion of status in the Corinthians passage, where there is nothing of the action of a superior authority or testamentary disposition that are the two fonts of Roman manumission.

345 Slaves condemned to work in Roman-owned mines (or venatorial games) were usually deemed slaves for life/perpetuity (*servi poenae*) and prohibited from manumission; *Dig.* 30.1.44.7 (Ulpian), 31.1.76.4 (Papinian), 40.5.24.5 (Ulpian), 48.19.8.8 (Ulpian). In Roman law it was possible to prevent any manumission of a slave, by testament, sale or designated serious offence: *Dig.* 40.1.4.9 (Ulpian); 40.4.9.1 (Ulpian); 40.4.9.9 (Paul).

346 *Dig.* 31.1.8, 9, 40.5.6; *P. Oxy.* 722, ll. 17–20 (91/107 CE).

347 See D. Kamen, "Manumission, Social Rebirth and Healing Gods in Ancient Greece," in *Slaves and Religions in Graeco-Roman Antiquity and Modern Brazil* edited by S. Hodkinson and D. Geary (Newcastle-upon-Tyne: Cambridge Scholars Publishing, 2012), 176–85.

348 Zelnick-Abramovitz, *Not Wholly Free*, 69.

In the Lycus Valley and its immediate surrounds, our knowledge of Greek forms of manumission is limited to the sacral category of manumissions. There are general notices of ἀπελευθέροι that have remained connected (possibly through a *paramone* relationship) with the household of their former master,[349] and these may (but not certainly) indicate a civic manumission. It will be useful therefore to examine an example of a sacral manumission inscription from the area. The surviving inscriptions from the area are almost all from the sanctuary of Apollo Lairbenos. They are not unique — many are known from Delphi and Macedonia — but the wording on these inscriptions generally carries the distinctive terminology of *katagraphai*. I propose to highlight one of the most recently published inscriptions because of its completeness and some important features.

> Τίτος Φλάβι⟨ο⟩ς Ἀχιλ- | λεὺς καταγράφω | τὸν ἐμαυτοῦ δοῦλον | ὀνόματι Ἐπίκτη- | τον Ἡλίῳ Λαρμη- | νῷ ὃν κὲ ἐπύη- | σα ἐλεύθερον | διὰ τῶν ἐν Μο- | τελλοῖς ἀρχείω⟨ν⟩· | ἔτους τιδ′, μη(νὸς) η′, ς′, ἀ- | πιοῦσᾳ· εἴ τις δὲ ἐ- | πενκαλέσει, θή{ο}σι | προστείμου ἰς τὸν | θεὸν ἀργυρίου Χ βφ′ | κὲ ἰς τὸ ταμεῖον Χ βφ′.
>
> I, Titus Flavius Achilleus, assign to Helios Larmenos my slave named Epiktetos whom I have also registered as free in the archive office at Motella, in the year 314 (= 229/230 CE), on the 6th day from the end of the month. If anyone should countermand this action, he will pay a penalty of 2500 silver denarii to the god and also 2500 denarii to the *tameion*.[350]

The 15-line inscription was written on a square altar-shaped stone along with two other *katagraphai* records and one dedication by different dedicators, one of which is partly erased to accommodate this crudely-cut inscription. The earliest recorded date on the stone (a *katagraphe* dedication which calls the stone a *bomos*) is 257 (= 172/173 CE).[351] The dating system is that of the Sullan calendar, that is, an ordering of years from the entry in 85 BCE of the Roman general Sulla, ultimately victorious, into suppression of the revolt of Mithridates. It was a common dating convention across the province. The form of epithet to Apollo Helios, that is, Larmenos, is one of a dozen variations in the spelling of the name Lairbenos, possibly an indication of both the survival of an indigenous deity of the area (now integrated into Apollo) and the inability of Greek-speakers textually to fix the phonology of the name.

The date is especially significant when combined with the name of the person recording the sacral manumission of his slave Epictetus. The master displays Roman citizenship (ostensibly from a second-century forebear) albeit with a reputable Greek cognomen. The date is over a decade after the *Constitutio Antoniniana* was promulgated and yet he has chosen to utilize a Greek form of

349 *I.Laodikeia Lykos* 85, ll. 4–5 (3rd century CE).

350 Text (*ed. prin.*) and translation from Öztürk-Tanrıver, "New Katagraphai," 101, nr. 13, slightly amended.

351 Öztürk-Tanrıver, "New Katagraphai," 102, nr. 14. However, the undated dedicatory inscription appears to be the originating inscription (Öztürk-Tanrıver, "New Katagraphai," 100, nr. 12.

manumission. We know from an edict of the governor of Macedonia, Tertullianus Aquila,[352] that the universalisation of Roman citizenship in 212 CE became the opportunity for Roman rulers more strictly to address the question of the relationship between Roman law and the manifold juridical operations in the provinces.[353] Of course, this took time, with Greek practices sometimes struggling to catch up with the legal framework by which Roman courts made their adjudications. Here it appears that manumissions in the Lycus Valley and the adjoining hinterlands continued in Greek mode for some time. That this sacral manumission had official recognition is clear from the registration in the Motellan archives[354] and in the double fines, one of which is to "the tameion", probably the civic treasury at Motella, one of more than a dozen centers of habitation attested in inscriptions from the sanctuary.[355] Even when fines were directed to the *fiscus*, the formula indicates Greek manumission. Some of these also postdate the *Constitutio Antoniniana.*[356]

Of course, this raises serious questions for a household of Christ-followers in Colossae. If Onesimos was to be manumitted, is it conceivable that Philemon would have achieved that goal through his assignment to a god such as Apollo Lairbenos (let alone face the sullen ire of other slaves in the household contemplating the reward to a δραπετικός)? Colossae's omission from the inscriptions at Apollo Lairbenos might be attributed to the vagaries of the survival of the evidence.[357] But I think this likely indicates that Colossae had its own "manumitting" religious center (with ties to a civic registrar, including the requisite tax/recording payment),[358] closer at hand, possibly that which became the Hagiasma of St Michael, less than three miles to the south of the city center. (Again we face the chasm of little evidence.) We know from Jewish manumitting practice in Macedonia, that Jews may have been content to follow Greek practice, merely privileging "the most high god", even when a standard prohibition of interfering with

352 The edict (a κέλευσις or ἀπόφασις) is referred to in a number of manumission inscriptions from Leukopetra in Beroia: for example, *I.Leukopetra* 63, 68, 72, 76, 79, 83. Some of these are dated, for example, *I.Leukopatra* 68 (the Augustan year 249, based on the Battle of Actium = 218 CE), illustrating the relative rapidity of the adoption of the governor's directive. Nonetheless, the manumission formula retained a dedication to "the Mother of the gods".

353 For different approaches to the edict of Tertullianus Auila, see Youni *loc. cit*, Kantor, "Greek Law," 13 (online edition).

354 Archives are found in other *katagraphai* inscriptions from Apollo Lairbenos; see Ritti-Şimşek-Yıldız, "Dediche e Καταγράφαι," K21, 24, 25.

355 These centers include cities, villages and "confederations": Atyochorion, Blaundos, Dionysopolis, Er(r)iza, Hierapolis, the Hyrgaleis, [Ka?]llokepos, Kroula (possibly the second name of a person), Laodikeia, Mamakome, Masakome, Motella, Motellokepos, Mossyna, Nanylos, Tripolis. See Ritti-Şimşek-Yıldız, "Dediche e Καταγράφαι," 51–5 as updated by Akıncı Öztürk and Tanrıver. Some of these settlements await topographical identification.

356 See Akıncı Öztürk and Tanrıver, "New Katagraphai," 96–100 nrs 6–11; compare p. 102 nr. 14 (ἰς τὸν φίσκον τὸν τοῦ κυρίου Καίσαρος, the same altar as nr. 13).

357 For example, Thiounta, as yet finds no mention in the epigraphical remains from the sanctuary.

358 Cf *IG* VII 3303, 3406 (Boiotia).

the manumission secured the oversight of Zeus, Gê and Helios. More assuredly Jewish manumission procedure used the synagogue as the "place" for assignment of manumitted slaves.[359] Whether or not such a complex negotiation was within the vision of Philemon is unknown and probably would be bedevilled by apologetic concerns (cf 1 Cor 8, 10). Certainly we can be confident that his household carried no institutional recognition such as might be granted to a synagogue.

This suggests that, if manumission was to proceed, Philemon would need to make use of local civic authorities as witnesses before whom the declaration of freedom could be made (perhaps with a *paramone* condition attached), or Onesimos would need to wait for Philemon's death and hope that his will contained a posthumous conferral of manumission, rather than an assignment to an (unknown) heir or creditor. Here we have no Colossian or *comparanda* evidence at hand. However, what can be asserted with greater confidence from the analysis of traces of jurisdictions at Colossae, is that the law under which the postulated manumission of Onesimos might occur would be Greek not Roman, given that there is no evidence that Philemon had Roman citizenship and thereby could choose, if he willed, to pursue a Roman judicial remedy.[360] This jurisdictional constraint carried certain distinctive consequences with it, not least being that manumission at Colossae would assuredly underscore that Onesimos was in no way equal to Philemon in standing or status (presuming that Philemon held Colossian [Greek] citizenship and was not himself a freed man). Consequently, efforts to set manumission into an egalitarian claim for Paul's nurture of a positive relationship between Philemon and Onesimos are misplaced.

359 See Gibson, *Jewish Manumission Inscriptions*, 109–52.

360 There is a tenth century Byzantine menologion that includes a life of Onesimos (for a February 15th feast day). It calls Onesimos, "a domestic slave of Philemon, a certain Roman man" (οἰκέτης ὑπῆρξε Φιλήμονός τινος ἀνδρὸς Ῥωμαίου) and reconstructs the problem in his relationship with Philemon to be a debt which he could not repay, rather than flight. Paul attends to this issue in the letter (Phmn 19) according to the retelling. The narrative thus ameliorates any fault in the story. The bulk of the story centers on Rome and Puteoli as the setting for Onesimos's imprisonment and trial before a certain eparch named Tertylos. See Appendix 1.

Chapter Twelve
Death and Families at Colossae

We know precious little about families and family life at Colossae. Indeed, the effort to discern families and households across the region is beset with difficulties. Surviving literature almost always provides no more than narrow snapshots of elite families and generalized stereotypes. The occasional mention of peasants, agricultural laborers and slaves in this literature is usually characterized by anonymity and tendentious attitudes. Certain impressionistic deductions can be made based on the results of archaeological surveys and excavations conducted elsewhere — for example, the *insulae* recently uncovered at Laodikeia or the osteo-archaeological analysis conducted at one sealed grave at Hierapolis. In lieu of these limitations, cemeteries are increasingly being utilized as a resource for extracting information on family structures, social positions, values, and beliefs. Here, for all the poverty of material data that has become the mantra of commentary on Colossae and the famous Second Testament Letters connected with the city, we do have some promise of meaningful return on our inquiries. We are likely still to be confronted by the invisibility of peasants, laborers and slaves but here some contact can be made with those of lower status and wealth than those who populate the surviving literature, the Second Testament Letters notwithstanding. Even though the sample of information is limited, it does yield a glimpse of the range of actual family relationships, values and commitments at Colossae. This helps to provide a material check on the literary constructions of families and households found in the Letter to the Colossians and to Philemon. The engagement between material and literary sources prompts a reconsideration of the function of these constructions not only in the letters but in the engagement with wider Colossian society through the behaviors of the Christ-followers in the city.

The necropolis at Colossae

Besides the biconical höyük that today distinguishes the ancient settlement of Colossae from the plain of the Lycus Valley, there is a second feature that still carves out the place as a carefully engineered space for human habitation — the necropolis. I have previously suggested that the Lycus River was not only a key natural feature that demarcated a sense of Colossae's territory in the higher reaches of the eastern end of the valley. It was also a dominant feature in the civic mindset. Its voluminous flow, especially in spring, added its own reverberation to the city's soundscape even as it made a major contribution to the city's architectural fabric (nymphaea, temple purificatory vessels, general water supplies, baths, walkways and bridges) and industries (milling, textiles, stone-masonry, reed-receptacles, fishing, tanning).[1] I have argued that the surviving evidence of city walls to the north of the river channel, the walls of the baths directly lining the river on the south side, and indications of city buildings along the northern bank of the river point to the incorporation of the river into the architectural frame and walled confines of the city. Nonetheless, today, the river operates as the transition zone between the mound and the cemetery.

Plate 12.1a: Aerial view (2013) across the Colossae höyük to the city's northern necropolis (marked here by broken arrow-lines). The natural grabens was readily converted to a cemetery; the basin, plateau and escarpment delimiting the necropolis accommodated a variety of tomb structures.

1 These examples of the value of the river to the city's life reflect the contribution made by *comparanda* from other cities to bolster the hints given in the various sources used to reconstruct a sense of Colossae's social and economic life in the first century. For example, fish and reeds as well as the ubiquitous cornucopia are found with the river god on various Colossian coins: see *RPC* 3.2314, *RPC online* 3.2307B. Hans von Aulock even speculated whether the river god may have been holding a harpoon on the coins minted by Hieronymos during the reign of Hadrian (*MSPhryg* 2.448, 449 = *RPC* 3.2313).

Plate 12.1b: View from the höyük acropolis (2015) to the city necropolis, approximately matching the area enclosed by the dotted arrow-lines in Plate 12.1a. The stone lines across the mid-center of the photograph are the remains of farm-pens that were built substantially from wall and building foundations and grave cover slabs "quarried" from the area north of the river Lycus. The red-tiled building at top-center is a modern farm-house.

Colossae was little different from other Greek cities that planned their *necropoleis* outside the city walls in observance of the demands of purity and purification.[2] Occasionally, cities voted to incorporate a grave (usually a *heroon* or small mausoleum) of some eminent person within the confines of the walls, a mark of esteem and indebtedness that citizens bestowed on the deceased.[3] This was merely the extreme end rather than a idiosyncratic display of the inhabitants' meticulous concern over the fate of their dead and how their own reputation and values were communicated amongst the population and to those visitors who were carefully funneled into and out of the city past the monuments to previous residents. As Christine Thomas has reminded us, "graves tell us not about the dead, but about their survivors, who perform the rituals and commission the monuments: funerary activities are spectacles and displays performed by the living."[4]

2 R. Willet, *The Geography of Urbanism in Roman Asia Minor* (Sheffield: Equinox, 2020), 48, 163. For a rhetorical bombast reflecting the general attitude of convention and law, see Ps-Quintilian *Decl.* 274.9.

3 See, as one example, the heroon to Hierokles built in "Colonnade Street" at Stratonikeia (*I.Stratonikeia* 1509, 1st century BCE). See generally, H. Schörner, "The intra-urban burial inside Greek poleis in Asia Minor: The example of Termessos," in *Le Mort dans la ville Pratiques, contexts et impacts des inhumations intra-muros en Anatolie* edited by O. Henry (Istanbul: Institut français d'études anatoliennes, 2011), 223–30.

4 C. Thomas, "Placing the Dead: Funerary Practice and Social Stratification in the Early Augustan Period at Corinth and Ephesos," in *Urban Religion in Roman Corinth: Interdisciplinary Approaches* edited by D. N. Schowalter and S. J. Friesen (Cambridge, MA: Harvard University Press, 2005), 281.

The variety of tombs in the Colossian necropolis

Colossae's northern necropolis is the only known graveyard for the city, although not the only known cemetery in Colossae's territory.[5] Laodikeia, by contrast, now boasts six necropoleis assigned outside the perimeter walls.[6] Nonetheless, Colossae's necropolis sweeps around a large grabens and onto the surrounding plain, covering a vast area almost as expansive as the höyük itself.

Plate 12.2: View of a section of the north-eastern escarpment and upper rim of the basin that housed the northern necropolis of the city of Colossae. The steep sides of the graben formation rise approximately 60 feet from the floor. The limestone rock made it relatively easy to carve various types of tomb, depending on wealth and choice. The base of the grabens likely contained grave plots but later agricultural and building demands have removed surface remains.

Considerable aggregation of data has occurred for the graves of Hierapolis and Laodikeia. The two basic classifications of the excavations have been into typologies of grave design and tabulations of the finds within the graves (which sometimes yield information for assignment of a date or date range). These categories have provided an important supplement to the concentration of previous research on the inscriptions that the tombs have often supplied, and have helped restore epigraphy to the materiality of the funerary context, as much part of the display as the non-textual construction. Osteo-archaeological anal-

5 This is confirmed by the funerary bomos prescribing a penalty for grave disturbance to the village of Eleinokapria (*I.Laodikeia Lykos* 114; see chapters 3 and 9). The lead diptych *defixio* (*IGR* 4.806) was reported as found in a ceramic ossuary near Kaklık, twelve miles north-east of the city of Colossae (see chapter 8).

6 See generally, C. Şimşek, (ed.), *Laodikeia Nekropolü (2004–2010 Yılları)* (Laodikeia Çalısmaları 1) Istanbul: Ege, 2 vols, 2011).

ysis, such as has been performed on remains at Ephesos and Pergamon,[7] has only recently received substantial publication.[8]

Sven Ahrens's detailed analysis of tomb structures and social status at Hierapolis has noted the somewhat restricted range of tomb types available in the city across a period of five to six hundred years from about 200 BCE: tumuli, mausoleum-style buildings, heroons, sarcophagi, chamosoria and hyposoria.[9] Notably absent from his typology are graves that involve the use of ceramics — whether cylindrical-molded caskets, tile lined and covered graves and even discrete pots whether serving as ostotheks or as amphorae containing ashes. However, these have in fact been found in Hierapolis's northern necropolis;[10] this alone qualifies some of Ahrens's conclusions.[11] Even allowing for some doubt over his estimation of Hierapolis's population and the consequent demand for burial places,[12] and the propensity in the Laodikeian analyses towards a more minute delineation of grave-types, there remains some contrast between Hierapolis's grave types and those of the extensive range now delineated for the six necropoleis of Laodikeia, where ceramic grave containers are quite prolif-

---

7 See F. Kanz and K. Grossschmidt, "Head injuries of Roman gladiators," *Forensic Science International* 160 (2006): 207–16; J. Propstmeier, *et al.* "Diet in Roman Pergamon: Preliminary results using stable isotope (C, N, S), osteoarchaeological and historical data," in *Life and Death in Asia Minor in Hellenistic, Roman and Byzantine Times: Studies in Archaeology and Bioarchaeology* edited by J. R. Brandt *et al.* (Oxford: Oxbow, 2017), 237–49. For an overview of the contribution such analysis can offer, see S. J. Friesen, "Embodied Inequalities: Diet Reconstruction and Christian Origins," in *Stones, Bones, and the Sacred: Essays on Material Culture and Ancient Religion in Honor of Dennis E. Smith* edited by A. H. Cadwallader (Atlanta, GA: SBL Press, 2016), 9–31.

8 See T. Anderson, "Preliminary osteo-archaeological investigation in the North Necropolis," in *Hierapolis di Frigia I: Le Attività delle Campagne di Scavo e Restauro 2000–2003* edited by F. D'Andria and M. P. Caggia (Istanbul: Ege, 2007), 473–93; M. Wong, *et al.*, "Isotopic investigations of human diet and mobility at the site of Hierapolis, Turkey," in *Life and Death in Asia Minor*, 228–36.

9 S. Ahrens, "Social status and tomb monuments in Hierapolis and Roman Asia Minor," in *Life and Death in Asia Minor*, 131–48.

10 Tomb 156a; see Anderson, "Osteo-archaeological investigation," 474–5.

11 Ahrens curiously overlooks the critical section on the northern necropolis in the first volume of the *Hierapolis di Frigia* series (pp. 433–93).

12 Ahrens estimates the population of Hierapolis at 11–12,000 based on population density for 178 acres and deductions from estimations of household density per insulae. Omitted from the discussion are alternate modes of population estimations based, for example, on the number and size of theaters in a city. Hierapolis has two theaters, distinguished as the Greek theater (in the north) and the Roman theater (in the east). The Roman theater alone (completed in the time of Hadrian) is estimated to have a seating capacity of 10,050 to 12,550, that is, equal to the total population of Hierapolis as Ahrens estimates it (F. Sears, *Roman Theatres: An Architectural Study* [Oxford: Oxford University Press, 2006], 338). Even allowing for the influx of visitors at festivals and special events, and of those extra-murals who may have regularly attended, it is hard to comprehend the need for two theaters and for a Roman theater of this size for such a small city population as this, cultural commitments notwithstanding! The theater at Ephesos had a c. 20,000 seat capacity, at least a fifth of the city's estimated population.

ic.[13] No study of graves in the Lycus Valley mentions any discovery of "potter's field" burials, that is, the unmarked, multicorpse, common earth internments that virtually every city had to provide for unconnected paupers and those executed in arenas or jails.[14]

The unexcavated necropolis at Colossae still attests at surface level a variety of grave types — tumuli, cliff niche tombs, cliff chamber tombs, mausolea, ground chamber tombs, chamosoria (see Pl. 12.2).[15] To these should be added the side of a garland sarcophagus now housed at the Denizli Museum at Pamukkale but originally found at the necropolis, along with a number of inscribed funerary stelai no longer on site (either at the Denizli Museum or not extant). The stelai may have been the recording details set up outside the various types of tombs (though not for the chamosoria, for which a different stone design was provided). None of the doors of tombs with formal entrances, and few of the plug stones closing off the burial chambers, have survived, the graves long ago having been broken into and looted. Consequently, the inscribed record and relief designs likely to have been carved onto them have rendered these tombs anonymous.

Plate 12.3: A rare example of a stone tomb door on display at Tire Museum. The door shows faint evidence of crudely incised inscriptions on the upper and middle frames and panels (possibly the name ΤΡΟΦΙΜΟϹ at the top left frame).[16] This may indicate that the door contained no more than a list of the names of those deceased secured within the tomb.

13 See, for example, the fifteen types delineated for the north-east necropolis at Laodikeia: Şimşek, *Laodikeia Nekropolü*, Vol 1, 33.

14 See J. Bodel, "Dealing with the Dead: Undertakers, Executioners and Potter's Fields in Ancient Rome," in *Death and Disease in the Ancient City* edited by V. M. Hope and E. Marshall (London: Routledge, 2000), 128–35.

15 The recent initiation of formal survey and excavation at Colossae promises to remedy this, but, at the time of writing, nothing had been published.

16 Marijana Ricl's report on the inscriptions in the Tire Museum recorded three tomb doors at the museum, bearing illegible or no inscription: "Greek Inscriptions in the Museum of Tire," *DHA* 35 (2009): 189.

Flat wall stones and grave slabs that can be readily transported frequently became the quarried supply of building materials. Limestone, the stone common to all the above types apart from the marble sarcophagus, is also readily crushed and burned for the manufacture of lime, likewise crucial in the construction industry.

Plate 12.4: Examples of the types of graves visible at the necropolis at Colossae. From top left to bottom right these are: a single chamosorion (or pit tomb) carved into a leveled section of the escarpment (see Pl. 12.2, left of center);[17] a niche tomb carved into the cliff face of the escarpment with a perimeter lip possibly to be enclosed by a stone plug seal (see Pl. 12.2, left identifying arrow);[18] a gabel-roofed tomb, the chamber excavated into bedrock (see Pl. 12.2, right of center);[19] a chamber tomb with antechamber and entranceway excavated into the cliff bedrock, showing a repair to the left door-jam (see Pl. 12.2, left identifying arrow).[20]

Some of the chamber tombs visible in the necropolis that have been dug into the travertine bedrock have been shaped to present an interior *triclinium* for the housing of the deceased, though all traces of those who have been laid

17 This *chamosorion* measures approximately 0.570 wide by 1.550 long (metric). The depth has not been excavated.

18 The dimensions are approximately 1.200 m long with a depth of 0.700 m.

19 The pediment stone measures approximately 2.6 meters across the horizontal and 1.280 on the vertical to the apex.

20 The doorway to the antechamber measures approximately 1.150 m high by 0.900 wide.

to rest have disappeared. The tumuli also attest the three-sided *klinai* for the deposition of bodies. However, some of the mausoleum-style buildings, constructed using large rectangular slabs, sometimes with a rabbetted section to allow for a gable roof set over pediment ends, do not show evidence of *triclinia* arrangements. One is left to speculate how the dead were prepared for enclosure therein (such as in ostotheks, urns, pots or some other deposition).

Plate 12.5: A stone ostothek displayed at the Tire Museum, without its lid. Some ostotheks were unadorned. This small receptacle for bones has been carved with a garland draped between two rams. The inscription records the brothers whose bones were stored in the ostothek.[21] It is dated to the second century CE. Such ostotheks were usually positioned in a larger funerary monument. Given the ubiquitous looted tombs in the Colossian necropolis, it has not been confirmed whether these (or ceramic functional equivalents) were one of the preferred methods of dealing with and remembering the dead at Colossae.

Colossae was far more regularly quarried than other cities within the Lycus Valley, possibly because of the local area's continued vibrant settlement centered on Honaz.[22] Possibly also, there was a more deliberate political encouragement: Colossae-Chonai was one of the last Byzantine cities to fall into Seljuk hands;

21 Ἀνίκητος Ἕρμονος | Εὐφρόσυνος | Ἕρμονος Κρή | «η»τη. *I.Ephesos* 3325.

22 The older houses in the township of Honaz frequently contain, in buildings and fences, fragments of molded stone sourced from the old city environs of Colossae. This was already noted by Francis Arundell in 1828; see F. V. J. Arundell, *A Visit to the Seven Churches of Asia Minor with an excursion into Pisidia* (London: John Rodwell, 1828), 93; *Discoveries in Asia Minor* (London: Richard Bentley, 2 vols, 1834), vol. 1, 163.

the capture of the ancient city sanctioned provision of materials for other constructions, such as the Ak Khan (completed in 1254).[23] Here, as elsewhere and under other regimes, the stamp of the new rulers was firmly impressed on the landscape over against the most recent prior occupants, regardless of religious affiliations or sensitivities.[24] One stone bearing a fragmentary Greek inscription is set upside-down in the western wall of the caravanserai,[25] testimony to the overturning of the past.[26]

Chamosoria and their bomoi

The most numerous of the grave types visible on the surface of the necropolis at Colossae is the *chamosorion*. This is a rectangular pit dug into the bedrock limestone over which are laid two, sometimes more, slabs held in place by a large, specially carved memorial pillar.[27] When William Hamilton visited the site in 1836, he was struck by the proliferation of "paving stones" on which he walked,[28] suggesting not only that many of the graves were still intact with their stone lids but also that the predominant grave type then visible were the covered chamosoria.

---

23 The travertine blocks, occasional marble insertions, stones with reliefs and fragment of inscriptions seen in the Ak Khan caravanserai have long been deduced to have been quarried from "some antient [*sic*] ruin", as Richard Pococke wrote in 1745. See R. Pococke, *Description of the East and Some Other Countries* (London: W. Bowyer, 2 vols, 1745), vol 2, 78.

24 See A. H. Cadwallader, *Fragments of Colossae: Sifting through the Traces* (Adelaide: ATF Press, 2015), 14–16.

25 See A. H. Cadwallader, "One Grave, Two Women, One Man: Complicating Family Life at Colossae," in *Stones, Bones and the Sacred*, 164–5.

26 Compare J. Moralee, "The Stones of St Theodore: Disfiguring the Pagan Past in Christian Gerasa," *JECS* 14 (2006): 183–215.

27 The "platform" for the *bomos* is actually named as τὸ θέμα in the tombstone from the village of Eleinokapria (*I.Laodikeia Lykos* 114, ll. 1–2) which I have argued should properly be assigned to the territory of Colossae (see chapter 3). The singular is used (cf also *I.Hierapolis Judeich* 180). This might be taken as a single cover stone but I think more likely it is to be understood as the platform made by two or more slabs fitted into one another and held down in place by the *bomos*. τὸ θέμα is used at Hierapolis to designate the platform that lies under a sarcophagus (ἡ σορὸς καὶ τὸ ὑπὸ αὐτὴν θέμα *I.Hierapolis Judeich* 69; also 120, 152); one sarcophagus is described as sitting on a *bomos* over a *thema* (*I.Hierapolis Judeich* 113 cf 124). Here *bomos* is used in its general meaning of "altar," that is, its purpose, rather than to designate a specific style of construction. It is likely to refer to a heroon-style shape (cf *I.Laodikeia Lykos* 98, τὸ ἡρῷον with τὰ … θέματα in the plural, ll. 1–2).

28 "… what I had at first mistaken for pavements were the covers of sepulchers and sarcophagi cut in the rocky ground, and so close to each other, that when the covers were laid on they resembled a pavement formed of gigantic blocks; the grotesque pedestals had been placed upon them as cippi; as I found one of them still occupying its original position." W. J. Hamilton, *Researches in Asia Minor, Pontus and Armenia* (London: John Murray, 2 vols, 1842), vol. 1, 510.

Plate 12.6a and b: One chamosorion (1.950 by 0.930 m) at Colossae has survived with one of its cover slabs in place. Plate 12.6b shows a cover lid with shiplap section and a shallow revetment designed to accommodate the base of a bomos. The slab measures approximately 1.670 × 1.420 m with the revetment 1.150 × 0.950 m. The lack of an edge on the shiplap side of the lid suggests that the bomos base was to extend to cover part of the second lid as well.

The rectangular slabs were sometimes made the more secure in their position over the grave by the trimming of a shallow, edged, platform perimeter that prevented sideways movement of the lids. In addition, the slabs might be cut so as to form a shiplap joint, with the stone placed with the upper lip covering the edge of the second lid. The addition of the *bomos* thereby secured two lids through the pressure being transferred from one lid to the second. The base of the *bomos* might sometimes be accommodated securely into a revetment section on the top of the lid (Pl. 12.6b).

Chamosoria are to be found dug into the plateau that surrounds the grabens of the necropolis, sweeping from the eastern to the western rim.[29] Sometimes they occur singly (see Pl. 12.4 above). Even a small pit grave might be hollowed out of the bedrock apparently designed for (at least) one child — one is situated on the western plateau not far from a chamber tomb that was also cut into travertine rock.[30] (Whether the two are related graves is unknown.) This size of *chamosorion* would have required only one cover slab. On the east-

29 This extends the necropolis boundaries from the "northern" and "north-eastern" arc from the Colossae höyük given by Celal Şimşek, "Kolossai," *Arkeoloji ve Sanat* 107 (2002): 10.

30 The grave measures approximately 0.750 m long by 0.450 wide. See Cadwallader, *Fragments of Colossae*, 156. It is possible that the grave was intended to house a compacted body/bodies or even bones prepared elsewhere for the loss of soft material, but this seems to me less likely given the relatively standard size of other *chamosoria* on the site and the convention this would likely impose on prospective orders for graves. For these alternative explanations, see E. L. Baysal and H. Elton, "A tomb with a view: the rock cut cemetery at Alahan in Isauria, Turkey," *Adalya* 17 (2014): 186. Equini Schneider offers another alternative, whilst acknowledging the general preference for a child's tomb, namely that they might function as ostotheks for related larger graves: "Some Considerations on Elaiussa's North-Eastern Necropolis," *Olba* 7 (2003): 268–9.

ern rim of the necropolis basin are found other single *chamosoria*, but also a carefully arranged complex of *chamosoria*. Some *bomoi* are scattered on the eastern rim; many have been converted into a low stone retaining wall, by being lined up to support the addition of soil for the planting of an orchard (in 2015 wire-fenced as well, a novel agricultural development in this region of Türkiye).

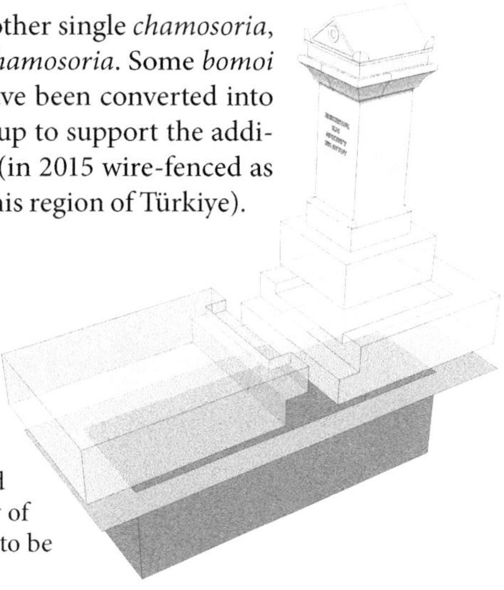

Plate 12.7: The stylized design of a chamosorion tomb at Colossae. The measurements here tend towards the larger-sized tomb. Some pits are narrower as also are the cover slabs and bomoi as dictated by the slope and consistency of the bedrock and, presumably, the amount able to be expended.[31]

The *bomos*, a (funerary) "altar", attests through its form (and sometimes self-designation as βωμός)[32] the sacredness of the dedicated site.[33] At Colossae, it is the *bomos* which makes the *chamosorion* distinctive. *Chamosoria* are known across Asia but frequently sealed with different-styled covers and, if present at all, epitaphal pillars that are different from those at Colossae.[34] Indeed, there is nothing, *a priori*, to negate the suggestion that even at Colossae, some *chamosoria* were marked by different styles of epitaphs, including stelai with tenons set into a stone base. However, the necropolis of Colossae has been noteworthy for the many *bomoi* scattered on the surface of the upper rim (though not in the basin), a characteristic feature occupying many European travel journals since Colossae began to be explored.[35]

---

31 Rendering courtesy of Daniel Cadwallader.

32 *MAMA* 6.19 = *I.Laodikeia Lykos* 114, l. 2. In chapter 3, I argue that this inscribed grave-stone should be re-assigned to the territory of Colossae.

33 See J. J. Coulton, "Pedestals as 'altars' in Roman Asia Minor," *AS* 55 (2005): 127–57.

34 See, for example, B. Köse, *Nekropolen und Grabdenkmäler von Sagalassos in Pisidien in hellenistischer und römischer Zeit* (Turnhout: Brepols, 2005), 101; N. Yılmaz, "Necropoleis and Funerary Monuments in Pisidia During the Roman Period," *Adalya* 10 (2007): 176–7; M. Şahin, "Salvage Excavations at the Necropolis of Apollonia in 2016–17: An Analysis of Grave Types," *Uluslararası Türkçe Edebiyat Kültür Eğitim Dergisi Sayı* 7 (2018): 2801–2, 2804, 2806; H. Yaman, "Death in Zeugma: A Survey of the Tombs," *Anadolu/Anatolia* 45 (2019): 129.

35 See, for example, Pococke, *Description of the East*, 75–6. The director of the newly established excavations at Colossae, Barış Yener, has reported that the surface bomoi have been moved to a central depot.

The head of the *bomos* is modeled after a temple pediment, replete with acroteria and, often, a central boss (see examples in chapter 11). The front of the shaft was usually given to the epitaphal inscription, though occasionally this was dominated by a relief.[36] The sides were also sometimes carved with a relief, such as a thunderbolt, a pine cone or other symbol connected with the gods. The entire *bomos* was probably painted, including the (red) lettering and with reliefs enhanced following a conventional color code.[37] Usually the shaft was only refined on three sides, with the fourth left unpolished, as if it was not to be in the usual line of vision, especially when placed on the *chamosoria* carefully laid out in pairs as found on the north-eastern plateau area of the necropolis. The *bomoi* at Colossae were cut as single stones, not as conjoined sections. This had a practical function of encumbering any disturbance of the grave.

Plate 12.8: A section of the necropolis where chamosoria have been neatly laid out and dug. There are at least five pairs of graves in alternating opposition with another chamosorion placed at right angles at the head of the arrangement. A number of toppled and broken bomoi are also visible.[38]

36 See A. H. Cadwallader, "Gertrude Bell's Resolution of a Disputed Inscription," *Gephyra* 20 (2020): 14.

37 See J. S. Østergaard, "Emerging Colors: Roman Sculptural Polychromy Revised," in *The Color of Life: Polychromy in Sculpture from Antiquity to the Present* edited by R. Panzanelli, E. D. Schmidt and K. D. S. Lapatin (Los Angeles: J. Paul Getty Museum and Getty Research Institute, 2008), 40–61.

38 For examples of the bomoi that would have stood here, see Plates 2.4, 3.15, 11.6, 11.7, 12.12, 12.15, 12.16.

Because the *bomos* was of a particular design and considerable weight, it had less appeal for building re-use in modern times. Consequently, many were still to be found on site prior to 2022, albeit toppled, fractured and moved. But because many of them were inscribed, they have yielded the most substantial number of inscriptions for the Colossae tally. To my knowledge, funerary stelai, whether still mounted by their tenons in a supporting base or not, are no longer visible at the necropolis. Their ease of removal has meant that the reports of this type of stone epitaphal records often note a relocation to Honaz and, sometimes, thence to a storehouse in Denizli.[39]

The tumuli

Plate 12.9: A stylized plan of a tumulus, showing the three main sections: the entrance corridor (sometimes stepped), the antechamber (where preparations and annual commemorations could take place) and the sealed burial chamber, often with a triclinium of benches for arrangement of the corpses. Depending on the topography and geology of the land, the antechamber and burial chamber might be carved from the rock or built with large stone blocks.[40]

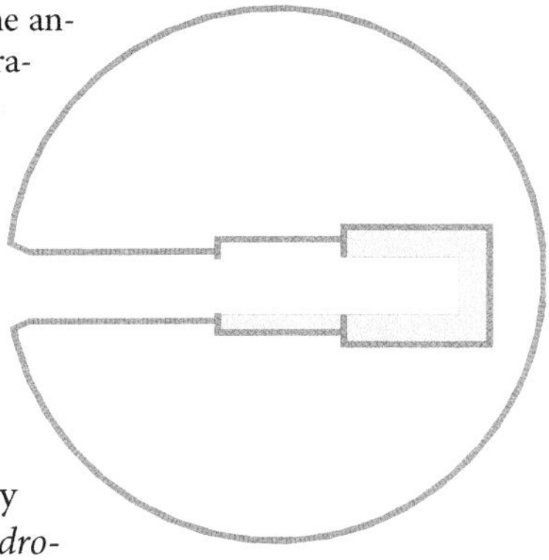

The tumuli at Colossae are elaborate tripartite burial structures which were completely covered by soil and debris apart from the entrance hallway (the *dromos* or *propylon*). They were often ringed by a stone retaining wall (the *krêpis* or *peribolos*), sometimes with a central pillar or bollard at the apex of the mound, as found on some examples at Hierapolis and elsewhere.[41] The bracing constructions of encircling walls are now only hinted at by the remains of stone blocks lining the entrance corridor, the remainder having long disappeared. This may help to explain why some of Colossae's tumuli now display little elevation in soil cover.

39 See location data given in *MAMA* 6.46, 47, 48, 49, 50. Many are now in the Denizli museum at Hierapolis. Sometimes, nonetheless, the *bomoi* were removed, though, significantly, it is only a broken section (such as a shaft) that is mentioned as incorporated into a wall (see *MAMA* 6.41 notes).

40 Rendering courtesy of Daniel Cadwallader.

41 See V. Sîrbu and M.-M. Ştefan, "Delimited Funerary Spaces – Hellenistic Tumuli with Stone Enclosures at Kallatis," *Annales d'Université Valahia Targoviste* 21 (2019): 51–76.

Plate 12.10a to d: The sequence of movement into the burial chamber of a tumulus. The entrance at the opening of the *krêpis* leads into a corridor directed to the first doorway into the antechamber and thence into the burial chamber. The remains of whitewash on the wall of the antechamber are possibly original and give a hint of the finish applied to the interior of the tomb structures.

The only systematic excavation at Colossae to date has been directed to three Hellenistic tumuli on the north-western plateau that lips back from the escarpment surrounding the expansive circular depression north of the river. This was conducted across eighteen days in May and July 1997 by Haşim Yıldız and Celal Şimşek (with Nesrin Karabay). The resulting brief studies were focused on mapping the design and dimensions of the tumuli.[42]

The interior burial chamber of each tumulus has a *triclinium* carved as part of its design, that is, a U-shaped series of conjoined benches extending from the walls of the room, where the corpses were laid. Haşim Yıldız concluded that the tumuli were each designed as a family tomb for four people.[43] However, this fails to recognize that such elaborate constructions were often intended to be a family investment, attracting generational deposition of remains,[44] just as has been found in tomb 163d (a mausoleum with a number of chambers rather than a tumulus) at Hierapolis, and the Kordon tumulus within the territory of Sardis.[45] Sometimes tumuli were re-used or re-purchased for use across longer periods,[46] though here at Colossae the small finds point to a Hellenistic time-frame.

The dating of the tumuli was secured by comparison with similar types at Hierapolis and by the small finds discovered in the course of the excavations. Unfortunately, each of the tumuli had been subject to looting in the relatively recent past. The small finds were therefore fragmentary and limited. (For example, no coins or jewellery were found.) The extant pieces were able to be identified, primarily ceramic sherds (in Tomb I–III), terracotta fusiform *unguentaria* (Tomb II, III),[47] a marble alabaster fragment (Tomb III), tile fragments and glass slag globules associated with carbonized remains of wood faggots (Tomb III). Some ceramic fragments in Tomb III were identified as (cinerary?) urns or pots with which some cremated remains were found.[48] Şimşek read the evi-

42 H. Yıldız, "Colossae Nekropolü Tümülüs Kazısı," in *IX. Müze Kurtama Kazıları Semineri* edited by H. Çakmak *et al.* (Ankara: T. C. Kültür Bakanlığı, 1999), 247–62; Şimşek, "Kolossai," 10–16.

43 Yıldız, "Colossae Nekropolü," 249.

44 Ahrens, "Social status," 134.

45 Anderson, "Osteo-archaeological investigation," 476–91; B. Aydın, "The Hellenistic Pottery and Small Finds of Kordon Tumulus at Kordon Köyü/Salihli (Manisa), 2001," *Jahreshefte des Österreichischen Archäologischen Instituts in Wien* 76 (2007): 9–10.

46 This appears to have been the case for tomb 163d, which was purchased perhaps at the beginning of the third century by a Jewish family. Even though the *klinai* benches were cleared for a new generation of corpses, the original bones were left in the tomb. See C. Laforest, D. Castex, and F. Blaizot, "Tomb 163d in the North Necropolis of Hierapolis in Phrygia: An insight into the funerary gestures and practices of the Jewish diaspora in Asia Minor in late Antiquity and the proto-Byzantine period," in *Life and Death in Asia Minor*, 69–84.

47 This is my deduction from the brief footnote in Şimşek, "Kolossai," 10 n39, describing the perfume-bottles (*unguentaria*) as "spindle-shaped" (*iğ formlu*).

48 The datum is not included in Ahrens' survey of evidence of cremation practices in Asia Minor: "'Whether by decay of fire consumed …' Cremation in Hellenistic and Roman Asia Minor," in *Death and changing rituals. Function and meaning in ancient funerary practice* edited by J. R. Brandt, M. Prusac and H. Roland (Oxford: Oxbow Books, 2015), 185–222.

dence of cremation as indicative of Roman influence, a tradition of interpretation that has long been understood as a key distinctive in burial practices between Greeks and Romans.[49] The decline of cremation has then been read as one sign that Romans in Asia and thence in Rome itself adopted the fashion of inhumation. More recent studies have questioned whether such a neat ethnic dichotomy can be sustained. Cremation and inhumation can be found in the same burial chamber apparently with no chronological succession.[50] In Asia, cremation has a long history, pre-dating the Romans and continuing in Hellenistic practice on occasion.[51] Elite Romans came to prize the elaborate sarcophagi as a status statement and advertisement of wealth and honor — one of which at some stage, graced Colossae's necropolis.

Plate 12.11: The reconstructed side of a garland sarcophagus (dated 140–160 CE) that now adorns the garden of the Denizli Museum, having found its way there, via Honaz, from the necropolis at Colossae. The extant, reconstructed side features winged erotes between a twinned mask of Melpomene, the tragic muse, and a central Medusa. The damaged remains of a lightly clothed, winged Nike adorn each of the corner edges, with two hippocampuses and birds completing the tableau.[52]

None of the items found in the tumuli have been published in diagrammatic representations or photographs, nor the dimensions given. Nor were any accession details provided for a holding depot, so that subsequent research can only draw on these generalized lists in the light of comparative data from other sites (such as Hierapolis and Laodikeia). This runs the gauntlet of the desire for dis-

49 Şimşek, "Kolossai," 16 n38. The assumption was cultivated by Roman writers themselves (Tacitus *Ann.* 16.6, Petronius *Satyr.* 111.2) and reiterated into present scholarship; see I. Morris, *Death-Ritual and Social Structure in Classical Antiquity* (Cambridge: Cambridge University Press, 1996²), 52–3.

50 See M. E. H. Walbank, "Unquiet Graves: Burial Practices of the Roman Corinthians," in *Roman Corinth*, 270–2.

51 Ahrens, "Cremation," *passim.*

52 For an analysis of this sarcophagus, see Cadwallader, *Fragments of Colossae*, 166–9.

tinctive grave practices that ancient cities sometimes exhibit, such as seems to be the case at Hierapolis, in comparison with Laodikeia.[53]

Valuing the dead at Colossae

The variety of these grave types points in part to changing fashions in the funerary industry as well as the financial constraints on burial practice. But the natural topography of the site chosen for the city cemetery also was conducive to variations in internment, some which appear to be mimetic of a Phrygian past. The time-span of at least 500 years (from c.200 BCE to c.300 CE) in the datable remains underscores the uninterrupted value that the Colossian populace placed on its dead and their proper disposal, and on the display of that value to one another. With polychromic enhancement of the funerary stones and monuments, the entrance into the city along the avenue from the Royal Highway running between Laodikeia and Apameia was orchestrated to elicit an impressed response to a proud and religious display.[54] Here was a populace marked by ritual piety and sacred remembrance with the stability, means and industry to support their commitments. Such aesthetic appreciation may even have drawn travellers into closer engagement, taking time to read some of the (probably) painted inscriptions,[55] or, if not literate, both to appreciate the use of writing as a key device in the commemoration of the dead and to hear the words ringing from the epitaphs should a herald or other necropolis official be in attendance.[56] One recently published funerary stele from the Kaystros Valley inland from Ephesos, explicitly mentions the repair of the carved relief,[57] so it is clear that visual aesthetics (not merely epigraphical content) were highly valued.

The complex constructions witness to an acceptance of the expense involved in the purchase, licensing and registering, engineering and painting of the tomb as well as the desire for the elaborate provision to be seen by others. These dis-

53 Ahrens, "Social status," 136, 144.

54 One inscription from Aphrodisias demonstrates an explicit consciousness of the passing avenue: *I.Aphrodisias 2007* 11.59, l. c8 (mid-3rd century CE); cf *I. Aphrodisias 2007* 12.107 (2nd to 3rd century CE) which places the tomb explicitly on the road (εἰς ὁδόν) between the Sebasteion and the temple *temenos* of the goddess Kore.

55 Some epitaphs explicitly recognize their readership. See for example *MAMA* 9.115, l. 1 χαῖρε ἀναγινώσκων (Aizanoi, reign of Hadrian) cf *MAMA* 5.89 (Dorylaion). The formula, whether in funerary or supplicatory contexts, became popular in Christian usage: for example *ICG* 73 = *SEG* 6.444 (Ekdaumaua, 400–550 CE); *I.Pessinous* 146 = *SEG* 31.1096 (Pessinous, 5th century CE).

56 We have seen previously the involvement of various legal and quasi-legal officials in the security and sanctity of the dead and their necropolitical place. See chapter 11.

57 γλυφὴν ἐπεσκεύακαν Ricl, *Kaystros* 60 = *SEG* 59.1386 (late Hellenistic).

plays were both mimetic of the highest ideals demonstrated by royalty (as in the tumuli) as well as relatively distinctive in its *bomoi* that seem to have enjoyed considerable popularity at Colossae,[58] but far less so at Laodikeia.[59] We have seen in the previous chapter the desire expressed by some Colossian citizens for there to be regular memorialization ceremonies attached to a designated place and context (usually a statue with suitably inscribed base erected in the agora or temple precincts).[60] Significantly, these efforts were given civic approval (by the *Boulê* and *Dêmos*), indicating that the conventions associated with the dead had *polis* sanction, indeed, reinforcement.

In general, the assumption governing the types of tombs visible at Colossae is that these are the final resting places of the elite. Certainly, in one of the few explorations of non-elite burial practice (at Gordion in rural Galatia), Andrew Goldman has catalogued a range of types vastly different from the material testimony of the Colossian necropolis. Mudbrick, wood, simple earth pits, stones with only occasional cut slabs mark a level of wealth significantly lower than indications from the tombs of Colossae, even if the commitment to dealing with death is parallel (as in the constructed tombs themselves and the small finds contained therein, though not coins or lamps which were too valuable for those on low incomes to surrender).[61]

However, are we to assume a simple jump from rural rusticity to urban elite in the differences in tomb types with consequent guestimations as to the relative amounts expended on the tombs? Christine Thomas doubts whether the cost of tombs is necessarily related to the status of the purchaser, but may have more to do with the stability of the society within which the management of the dead and their memory was conducted. An increase in expenditure may relate rather to increments in social stress.[62] Sven Ahrens, whilst admitting that sarcophagi, chamosoria, hypogea (chamber tombs) and tumuli were all expensive, suggests that those below the level of the elite by status and wealth were

---

58 Şimşek calls them "the Eumeneian type" — "Kolossai," 13. The bomos style does occur at Eumeneia (see *MAMA* 4.342, 343 [using the term βωμός, 344, 351) but in a form distinct from those of Colossae (most glaringly in the absence of a large wide base as part of the total stone). In fact, it is closer to those found at Apameia (for example, *MAMA* 6.226). The suggestion that Colossae adopted the style from Eumeneia is misplaced.

59 The two-volume monograph and catalogue on the necropoleis of Laodikeia (*Laodikeia Nekropolü* edited by Şimşek) is singularly lacking in any example of a *bomos* epitaph and functional weight for a grave. These are restricted to a small number of examples in the Denizli museum depot that had been assigned to Laodikeia. Laodikeia had a tendency to become the default provenance: see H. Malay "New Inscriptions from Phrygia (in the Denizli Museum)," *Arkeoloji Dergisi* 2 (1994): 173. Rather, it may be that Colossae was accenting its distinction from Laodikeia even here in a funerary fashion statement that Christine Thomas has called "style wars". See Thomas, "Placing the Dead," 292–9.

60 *MAMA* 6.39, 42; see chapter 11.

61 A. Goldman, "New Evidence for non-elite burial patterns in central Turkey," in *Life and Death in Asia Minor*, 149–75.

62 Thomas, "Placing the Dead," 292.

nevertheless in the market for the purchase of these graves.[63] We have little to assist us as regards Colossae — there are no inscriptions detailing the cost of construction,[64] and onomastics can only take us so far.

There are, however, two indications of occupation, one an inscription on a *bomos* designed to stabilize the covers of a chamosorion (Pl. 12.12), a second, a broken stele, the missing part probably containing the funerary inscription (Pl. 12.13). The first, an aniconic *bomos*, contains a simple inscription: Δίων Ἀππ̣ [α] | διφθερ̣ [ο]- | πύς· χ[αίρ]- | [ε]ιν. "Dion, the leatherworker, son of Appas. Greetings."[65]

Plate 12.12: The toppled and damaged bomos of Dion the leatherworker, still (in 2016) present in the Colossian necropolis. The bomos was sketched, upright and intact, in 1890 but when the inscription was recorded accurately in a squeeze in 1933, the lettering had already been damaged, though the stone was still upright.[66] A second, heavily weathered bomos lies behind.[67]

63 Ahrens, "Social status," 134–44.

64 Richard Duncan-Jones notes how few inscriptions in the Roman empire name the amount expended on the burial monument. Those that are given cover a wide range of types. See his *The Economy of the Roman Empire: Quantitative Studies* (Cambridge: Cambridge University Press, 1986^{2}), 127.

65 *MAMA* 6.44, here following the editors' reconstruction. In 2006, further letters had been lost: A. H. Cadwallader, "A New Inscription [=Two New Inscriptions], a Correction and a Confirmed Sighting from Colossae," *EA* 40 (2007): 111–12. See also *Fragments of Colossae*, 169–71 and chapter 2 herein.

66 In his notebook entry for the stone, William Calder provided full measurements of the "limestone bomos standing on platform of same block," thereby indicating that the entire bomos, even with its "platform", was, perhaps unexpectedly, a complete stone. His published measurements did not include the "platform" in the overall height. The notebook records the "platform" as 0.280 high, 0.850 width, 0.870 high. This changes the height of the *bomos* to 1.550 meters. It appears that the "platform" base was not the usual complement to the *bomoi* that he had seen (for example, at Eumeneia). University of Aberdeen, Special Libraries, Calder Archives Ms 3286/4 "Bundle of Three Notebooks", "1933 Notebook," p. 53. Certainly, rebetted bases to hold altars/*bomoi* (and also statues) are known: *RIB* 3.3270 (South Shields) with commentary.

67 The photograph has been given a highlighted rendition of the inscription on Dion's bomos.

These epitaphs may afford us some clues towards establishing who might afford these graves and perhaps some general parameters of their costs.

Dion the leatherworking specialist

The term διφθεροποιός, inscribed here with compressed orthography reflecting Phrygian influence, probably indicates the more specialized, value-added end of the leather industry, perhaps even a preparer of vellum (cf a διφθεράριος),[68] though the term is sufficiently imprecise as to cover a range of goods.[69] The usual stems for leather-workers are σκυτ– or βυρσ–.[70] Leather industries at Colossae are to be expected as a by-product associated with its renowned wool trade, the pig industry as implied in the relief on the stele already mentioned (see Pl. 12.13 below),[71] and the sacrificial demand for bulls in service of Zeus. This single inscription along with the now-anepigraphic stele pig-relief raise a host of economic, agricultural and regulatory as well as social implications for Colossae, implications that require the range of archeological inquiry into animal remains, pasture management, butchery (primary and secondary), architectural and civic organization of space, and the range of manufactured by-products and services of and for the various industries.[72]

Dion, if he weren't a member of a leather-workers association that fostered provision for funeral expenses for its constituency,[73] would have had to earn a reasonable amount to have afforded his burial place. The vast array of leather goods detailed in the extant parts of Diocletian's *Price Edict* (from sieves to beer mugs), the diversity of animal hides that were prepared for sale (from wild sheep to seal), and the gradations of quality and types of everything from belts to shoes, speaks of the enormous importance of leather in the ancient world. The Edict also indicates the high prices that sometimes could be com-

---

68 See *IG* V 1 1406 ll. 11–12 (Diocletian's *Price Edict*, 301 CE). διφθέρια in *SEG* 54.694 (Olbia; Late 6th century BCE) means documents written on leather, but the inscription is early.

69 See Plato *Crit.* 53d, Pollux 8.12, *O.Ber.* 2.144 (50–75 CE), *P.Ross. Georg.* 5.21 (200–99 CE).

70 See E. M. Harris, "Workshop, marketplace and household: the nature of technical specialization in classical Athens and its influence on economy and society" in *Money, Labour and Land: Approach to the Economies of Ancient Greece* edited by P. Cartledge, E. E. Cohen and L. Foxhall (London: Routledge, 2002), 68.

71 It should be noted however that pig leather is not found in the *Price Edict* of Diocletian. However pig products, including sandals, are specifically mentioned in prohibitions governing entry into the sanctuary of Alektrona at Ialysos (*CGRN* 90, ll. 25–7 (350–300 BCE), so their silence in the *Price Edict* is a curiosity rather than an absence from leather craft.

72 See K. Greene, *The Archaeology of the Roman Economy* (London: B. T. Batsford, 1986), 149–56.

73 See *SEG* 29.1183 (Saittai, 147/148 CE) for a leather-working association covering burial requirements.

manded.[74] The association of ἀσκοποιοί (makers of leather wine-containers) commanded three sections of the theater at Bostra in southern Syria, including an area of specially constructed seats.[75] Even tanners, critical at the more odorous production end of leather, could command a reserved section in the stadium at Aphrodisias.[76] It is sometimes overlooked that artisans and merchants were often participants in civic gatherings; occasionally they held office.[77]

All this points to how important leather-workers were to the civic (and military) economy. That they gained a wide range of technical terms indicates the high degree of specialization that they could achieve. Xenophon provides a telling insight,

> in the great cities owing to the wide demand for each particular thing, a single craft will suffice for a means of livelihood and often enough even a single department of that; there are shoe-makers who will only make sandals for men and others only for women.[78]

There is no doubt that Colossae would have met his criteria of "great city" in his time (401 BCE).[79] Regardless of what value-judgment might be placed on Colossae as a city in the first and second centuries, its *polis* standing is confirmed by multiple indicators (coins, imperial *adventus*, and so on), notwithstanding the conventus status of its neighbor Laodikeia. It may even have boasted just as significant a population as 400 years earlier, whose needs at civic and territorial levels required servicing by, *inter alia*, specialized leather products.

One wonders who took responsibility for Dion's interment and/or the actual tomb commissioning.[80] The only suggestion of family is the genealogical line — brief but, importantly, present in the mention of Dion's father Appas, the bearer of a marked Phrygian name.[81] But there is no named progeny, relatives or spouse. It may be that the *bomos* belonged amongst the group of cha-

74 For example ox-hide sandals lined with wool cost 50 denarii a pair; a leather travel-bag cost 1500 denarii. However, linen products were a step up the economic (and presumably social) scale.

75 *IGLS* 13.9158-60.

76 βυρσέων συντεχνία *I.Aphrodisias Performers* 45.12.D; compare the leather-dresser (σπατολεαστής) *SEG* 53.293 (Argos; imperial).

77 *MAMA* 3.756 a Cilician baker; *TAM* V,2 932 a Thyateiran slave-trader.

78 ἐν δὲ ταῖς μεγάλαις πόλεσι διὰ τὸ πολλοὺς ἑκάστου δεῖσθαι ἀρκεῖ καὶ μία ἑκάστῳ τέχνη είς τὸ τρέφεσθαι· πολλάκις δὲ οὐδ᾽ ὅλη μία· ἀλλ᾽ ὑποδήματα ποιεῖ ὁ μὲν ἀνδρεῖα, ὁ δὲ γυναικεῖα. Xenophon *Cyrop.* 8.2.5 (trans. Dakyns) *cf.* Plato *Symp.* 191a. Plato frequently refers to leather-workers/-making in his writings

79 Xenophon *Anab.* 1.2.6–7.

80 Another Dion is found in a fragmentary Colossian inscription on a *bomos* (*MAMA* 6.45), the father of Phoibos (?) and grandfather of Trophimos (?) but there is no way of drawing a connection.

81 L. Zgusta, *Kleinasiatische Personennamen* (Prague: Tschechoslowakische Akademie der Wissenschaften 1964), 71–3; T. Drew-Bear, C. Thomas and M. Yıldızturan, *Phrygian Votive Steles* (Turkey: Ministry of Culture, 1999), 382.

mosoria on the north-eastern section of the plateau above the basin (Pl. 12.8), so that a better idea of how to place Dion might have been conveyed there. When William Calder saw the stone in May 1933, it was upright — "standing". Its photographed position above is about 25 yards from the chamosoria complex. But this connection is no more than a possibility, probably untestable without thorough analysis of the isotopic make-up of the various stones or some fortuitously surviving small find.

Consequently, we have in the inscription on this *bomos* a witness to an artisan able to afford an identified grave, a chamosorion, with all the marks of a characteristic Colossian management of the dead and the memory thereof. That it occurs in the city necropolis strongly points to a demand for such capacity and the resultant leather goods in the city, along with sufficient standing to display the recognition in death.

The anonymous dealer in pigs large and small

The second witness to a non-elite background comes in an unfortunately-damaged stele. The shape of the stele, combined with the design of the frame and the visual presentation of the funerary banquet scene all confirm that this is a funerary marker likely to have had an inscription in the upper, lost section.[82] It is dated to around 200 CE, simply on the basis of comparative stylistics.[83] It is precisely because the funeral banquet design is so ubiquitous in funeral reliefs that we must hesitate in envisaging a family for the deceased.[84] However, the arresting footer to the scene, three pigs, is unusual for this stele type. Pigs are not common on funerary reliefs. They might contribute their heads or trotters to the banquet spread, part of the display of prosperity even in death. However, the funerary feast here is decidedly vegetarian — grapes, bread, perhaps a pomegranate and tuber of some variety. The footer containing three pigs however is more shallow than the main relief, suggesting that it may have been added after the stereotyped funerary banquet scene was carved.[85] This adds confidence to the designation of the deceased as involved in the pig industry.

82 *MAMA* 6.50; E. Pfuhl and H. Möbius, *Die Ostgriechischen Grabreliefs* (Mainz am Rhein: Philipp von Zabern, 4 vols, 1977), vol 1, 286 nr. 1165.

83 So Pfuhl-Möbius, followed by *I.Mus. Denizli* 80 and P. Thonemann, *The Maeander Valley: A Historical Geography from Antiquity to Byzantium* (Cambridge: Cambridge University Press, 2011), 184.

84 See *I.Mus. Denizli* 64–81 for a localized sample. At the same time, none of these is identical.

85 I am grateful to Steven Friesen for this observation on the stele and for discussions of the pig industry in the Roman empire.

Plate 12.13: The stele at the right,[86] unfortunately fractured probably at the cost of an identifying inscription, presents a highly conventional funerary banquet scene with the seated (female) position[87] taken by the wife holding a child with a cultivated mutual affection and the toasting husband reclining on the cushioned *klinê*. A fawning dog completes the banquet scene. Unusually, there is carved in the frame a suggestion of the deceased's occupation, with one large pig trailed by two piglets.

Considerable detail is invested in the portrayal of the pigs. There is attention to the hide, the size of legs, snouts and tails, the careful regulation of proportions, what William Calder in his notebook described as "one hog with two hoglings".[88] It suggests that the owner of the tomb had been involved in the breeding or dispersal of the animals for commercial and/or sacrificial purposes.[89] One can imagine (only) that the inscription named the deceased as a χοιρέμπορος as is found in another epitaph from Sardis,[90] or perhaps a χοιροτροφός, one focused more on the husbandry than the market (for which an agent may have been responsible).[91] There is plentiful evidence to indicate that pig-farming and sales were ubiquitous in Roman times, not least because pork was the pre-eminent meat of the Roman diet. As the Roman agricultural specialist, Varro, wrote, "Who of our people runs a farm without keeping pigs?"[92] Indeed, Cato, the esteemed Roman father of writing on agriculture, recommended the sacrifice of a pig to purify a farm — significantly offered to the god of war.[93] It is likely that there was

86 *MAMA* 6.50.

87 Lucian *Symp.* 13.

88 "1933 Notebook," 43 nr. 171.

89 Thonemann calls "him" a "swine-merchant" which may turn the meaning too far from animal husbandry (*Maeander Valley*, 184). However, it has the advantage of the presumed provenance and prominence of the funerary stele, that is, the immediate city environs. However, one ought not assume a great distance between city and pasture (cf Mk 5:14).

90 *I.Sardis* 7,1 159 (3rd century CE). See also *P.Cair. Zen.* 3.59331, l. 10 (Philadelphia? in Arsinoite nome, 248 BCE); *P.Giss.* 1.40, l. 2.18 (Apollonopolites Heptakomias, 215 CE?). Later examples in the papyri are also attested. Two χοιριδεμπόροι are mentioned in *P.Fay.* 108, l. 6 (Euhemeria, 169/170 CE). It is uncertain whether they dealt only in piglets/suckling pigs (one is mentioned in l. 16) given that diminutives are often thought to be flattening in meaning.

91 *Chr. Wilck.* 427 (187 CE).

92 *Quis enim fundum colit nostrum, quin sues habeat?* Varro *Rust.* 2.4.3.

93 Cato *Agr.* 141.

an intensification in pig husbandry in order to meet Roman consumer demand, though to what extent cannot as yet be quantified.[94] It must be remembered that pigs were a key dietary and sacrifical requirement for Greek culture as well.

Pigs figure in different contexts at Colossae. We have already seen their use in what are probably Dionysian festivities with the coin featuring the satyr Silenus on the obverse and a boar on the reverse (see chapter 3).[95] One funerary epigram at Edessa appears to extol a performing pig and is probably to be connected with phallagogic celebrations (given the relief on the stone) at a festival of Dionysos.[96] Other coins of Colossae extol the hunt for the boar in connection with Artemis.[97] These almost certainly combine Colossian pride in the hunt with the use of pigs in ritual sacrifices. Given the plentiful water and (holm-)oak forest stands around Colossae (especially on the verge of the mountains), the necessary supports for pig-farming and boar-hunting were abundantly supplied.[98]

Here a return to the iconography and its execution may be helpful. The division of the three pigs into a sow and two piglets (probably suckling pigs) is revealing. Firstly, the connection is reminiscent of a treasured portrayal in Roman design evoking a combination of an ancient foundation story (for the "city of Alba", that is, Rome) and the arrival of a golden age of prosperity under Augustus.[99] The relief of a heavily-bristled sow beneath an oak-tree feeding a plentiful array of her young is featured at the Sanctuary of Fortuna Primigenia just outside of Rome and found its way onto the coins of a number of emperors.[100] This sedentary scene gave way under Vespasian and Hadrian to greater energy with the piglets on the move following the sow.[101] There may be a measure of deliberate offensiveness towards Jews in these coins, especially with Hadri-

94 Compare C. Cummings, "Meat Consumption in Roman Britain: The Evidence from Stable Isotopes," *TRAC* (2008): 73–83.

95 *RPC online* 4.2.1890 temp.

96 *SEG* 62.417 (2nd to 3rd century CE).

97 *MSPhryg* 2.586, 587 (time of Septimus Severus; not in *RPC*); *RPC* 9.789 = *MSPhryg* 2.594, 595 (time of Trebonianus Gallus).

98 This environment coheres with the recommendations of Columella *Rust.* 9.1.1. Holm-oak charcoal residues have been found at the sanctuary of Apollo in Hierapolis, confirming that the *quercus ilex* so prevalent today in the Lycus is a reflection of availability in the first century. See G. Fiorentino, "Palaeo-vegetational Reconstructions in the Lykos Valley by Archaeobotanical Analyses at Hierapolis," in *Landscape and History in the Lykos Valley: Laodikeia and Hierapolis in Phrygia* edited by C. Şimşek and F. D'Andria (Cambridge: Cambridge Scholars Publishing, 2016), 230–33.

99 Virgil *Aen.* 8.43–8.

100 See for example *RIC* 3.629, 722, 733, 768 (Antoninus Pius), though with little discrimination over the number of offspring. Varro mentioned multiple bronze images of the scene set up in public and the holy preserved relic of the sow exhibited by the priests in Rome: *Rust.* 2.4.18–19.

101 *RIC* 2.982, 983, 986 (Vespasian); 2.2814, 2815 (Hadrian). Strictly the sow has three piglets (which distinguishes the elements from that of the stele). It may be that each of the piglets on the coins represents ten, though some of Vespasian's coins have only two piglets. The portent of the foundation story refers to the sow of Aeneas bearing thirty sucklings (compare *RIC* 3.2924, Hadrian).

an's combination of pig imagery with his renaming of Jerusalem as Aelia Capitolina — but this is hardly likely to have much effect in Asia. Rather the accent on prosperity is common to both even if our anonymous deceased was not intending a collation with Roman visual propaganda. Such stylistics were not an imperial innovation however. A sow and suckling pig also have a Greek genealogy.[102]

Secondly, the mason has deliberately chiselled marks into the hide of the three pigs. This investiture of a heavy, bristled feature to the animals is as directive to how to view the piece as it was, pragmatically, unnecessary. This, in combination with the long snouts, relatively long legs and the lack of a smooth skin, strongly indicates that the owner of the pigs worked with animals that were semi-wild, not those smooth animals who were bred in containment for the high-end demand of markets and (larger) temples. It is likely that the husbandry featured herding in forests and open grasslands only curtailed at the time of restricted gathering for fattening (on grain and especially figs) prior to delivery for sale. Here we strike the division that was familiar in the ancient world, a division that was expressed as much in artistic presentation as is now becoming evident in zooarchaeological study.[103] Indeed, there may have been a pronounced status and wealth differential in operation.

Paolo Manca and his team compared the teeth and bone fragments of domestic pigs at two locations, one at Pompeii and one at Caralis in Sardinia. They discovered that the pigs at Pompeii betrayed phenotypic features much closer to modern farmed pigs (the smooth variety) whereas those at Caralis bore greater resemblance to wild boars,[104] a difference that may reflect wealth disparities and class fashion. The latter type seem to be those indicated on the stele by the deliberate evocation of heavy bristles on the three animals in relief. The ambling gait rather than the escapist flight of the hunted seen on coins, points to a level of husbandry of these bristled animals.

Thirdly, the fact that the relief strongly evokes pigs in close proximity to their wild relatives that were one of the favored preys for hunting pastimes, does not necessarily preclude their use as sacrificial victims. Piglets at day ten were considered the most pure for sacrifice: *porci sacres*.[105] And Varro was at pains to strain an etymological connection between ὗς and θυεῖν.[106] Certainly, pigs of all ages and genders were assigned for different sacrifices, especially during the Thesmophoric festival.[107] If Varro is again to be followed, it appears that a distinction was made between animals fit for sacrifice and those handed over to be butchered.[108] The former were often heavily fattened, had consistency of coloration and soundness in frame, "very holy, pure, whole animals"

102 See *HGC* 2.21 = *SNG ANS* 1293 (Abakainon in Sicily, 410–400 BCE).

103 M. MacKinnon, "High on the Hog: Linking Zooarchaeological, literary and Artistic Data for Pig Breeds in Roman Italy," *AJA* 105 (2001): 649–73.

104 P. Manco *et al.*, "Phenotypic Features of the Domestic Pigs Bred in the Roman Settlements of Pompeii and Caralis," *Italian Journal of Anatomical Embyrology* 109 (2004): 105–14.

105 Varro *Rust.* 2.4.16.

106 Varro *Rust.* 2.4.9.

107 See K. Clinton, "Pigs in Greek Rituals," in *Greek Sacrificial Ritual, Olympian and Chthonian* edited by R. Hagg and B. Alroth (Stockholm: 2005), 167–79.

108 Varro *Rust.* 2.5.10, 11.

(εὐίερα, καθαρὰ, ὁλόκλαρα) was the requirement for sacrifice laid out in the *lex sacra* for the sanctuary at Andania.[109] But the distinction between domestic and wild is not found. It may be that the ban on pig products being taken/worn into some sanctuaries is directly related to the demand for purity in the animals and the frequent purification of sacred sites by the sacrifice of a piglet.[110]

These observations briefly underscore the ubiquity of pigs for consumption and sacrifice (and then consumption!) in the ancient Mediterranean world. Those who dealt in pigs along the chain of production and sale were therefore in considerable demand and benefitted from the capacity of sows to bare offspring twice a year.[111] Sometimes, the returns might be concentrated if the pig merchant and pig farmer were the same person, as is sometimes attested.[112] To some extent, prosperity depended on the ability to pasture the animals and on the level of demand. Varro recommended that the size of the herd be 100–150 pigs, 10 of which should be male. He allowed that some farmers kept larger ones,[113] though whether he would recognize a "legion … about two thousand" (Mk 5:9, 13) is unlikely. His optimum number might be thought to reflect his elite background and valuable holdings. But it is in fact reflected in one tax declaration in the Pharbaithite nome in Egypt where the owner reported that he owned 165 pigs.[114] So we have a reasonable probability on our side if we allow in an average year such a number for the livestock holdings of our anonymous Colossian farmer.

As we press the evidence to yield an indication of the capacity of a swine merchant/pig farmer to pay for a tomb, perhaps even a chamosorion marked, in this case, by a stele set in a heavy stone base, we need to sift for the prices that various pigs might achieve either at market or by direct supply to sanctuaries. Of course, prices vary according to location, environment and supply.[115] The default recourse is to rifle through Diocletian's *Price Edict*. This reveals quite a range of pig types and products: a suckling pig was valued at 16 dena-

109 *CGRN* 222, l. 70 (either 92 BCE or 21–23 CE).

110 Apollonios of Rhodes *Arg.* 4.704–6. See the regulations governing the sanctuary of Alektrona at Ialysos (*CGRN* 90, ll. 25–7 [350–300 BCE]). Compare the banning of pigs from the *temenos* of a temple at Talmis: *SEG* 47.2158 (248/249 CE).

111 It should be noted that in the ban (around 215 CE) on Egyptians flooding into Alexandria to avoid difficulties in the countryside, exemptions were made for pig-dealers, river-barge operators and reed-providers to the baths (χοιρέμποροι καὶ ναῦται ποτάμιοι οἵτινες κάλαμον πρὸς τὸ ὑποκαίειν τὰ βαλανεῖα *P.Giss.* 40). This is a fairly strong indication of how important these occupations were to maintaining the Roman way of life in a critical city of the empire.

112 *CIL* 9.1506 (Pesco Sannita, 2nd century CE). Compare also *CIL* 13.8351 (Colonia Claudia Ara Agrippinensium, 2nd to 3rd century CE) where the occupations of butcher and merchant are combined.

113 Varro *Rust.* 2.4.22.

114 *BGU* 1.92 (187 CE).

115 See W. Scheidel and S. J. Friesen. "The Size of the Economy and the Distribution of Income in the Roman Empire." *JRS* 99 (2009): 67.

rii per Roman *libra* with boar meat allocated the same price. Unspecified pork meat was to be sold at 12 denarii per *libra*, that is, about 329 grams, almost three-quarters of an imperial pound. This rose to 16 denari if it had been salted. The ubiquitous sausage that was bawled out by street vendors in the agoras,[116] cost 2 denarii for 1 *uncia* weight, or, by conversion, 24 denarii per *libra*. Other pork products were offered: a sow's uterus at 24 denarii; her udder at 20 denarii; a liver of a pig fed on figs, 16 denarii; pork fat or converted ointment, 12 denarii; and pig's trotters and stomach were to be 12 denarii per *libra*. By contrast, the exotica of a wild boar imported from Africa might fetch, respectively 6000 or 4000 denarii depending on whether it was adjudged first or second class.[117] There is no indication that our deceased farmer was himself responsible for value adding or butchering but these figures give us an indication of the returns that might be possible.

The *Prices Edict* of course is late for our purposes (301 CE) and manipulated by the inflation that ran rampant through the second half of the third century. However, the papyri and sanctuary regulations and inventories are of particular help here, stretching back 500 years or more from this imperial price control. One account, dated to the turn of the second century and related to the execution of a will, included the sale of a pig (χυρίδιον, piglet?) for 40 drachmae (about 35 denarii, though the two currencies tended to standardization).[118] A report of a theft in 36 CE in Euhemeria in Egypt, valued a stolen young pig (δέλφαξ) at 8 drachmae (7 denarii).[119] By contrast, a young pig (χοιροδέφακος) being purchased privately for sacrifice at a festival was allowed a maximum of 20 drachmae (17.5 denarii) for purchase.[120] Here we begin to see the difference in price between sanctuary and commercial agora. At the sale of the priesthood for Zeus Alseios on the island of Kos in the first century BCE the contract included the stipulation that the priest was to ensure that each of the *lampadarchoi* and *agonothetes* were to sacrifice annually a sow worth not less than 100 drachmae (about 88 denarii), presumably ensuring a high quality animal (and ample feasting afterwards!).

On the basis of a herd of 150 pigs of varying ages with biennial reproduction, and using the modest amount assigned to the Euhemerian theft above, it is reasonable to reckon that the annual net income of our Colossian producer would be more than 10,000 denarii if he combined the husbandry with butchering and sales. This conservative figure is based on a biennial reproduction rate of 6 to 8 piglets, turn-over sales of the breeding sows and requisite outlays (taxes, wages,

116 Aristophanes *Eq.* 180–1; Seneca *Ep.* 56.2.

117 Drawn from E. R. Graser, "A Text and Translation of the Edict of Diocletian," in *An Economic Survey of Ancient Rome Volume V: Rome and Italy of the Empire* edited by T. Frank (Baltimore: Johns Hopkins Press, 1940), 307–421.

118 *P.Oxy.* 1269, ll. 33–5 (101–125 CE).

119 *P.Ryl.* 2.140.

120 *P.Worp.* 52 (ostracon, Karanis, early 2nd century CE).

maintenance). Of course, the figure would be less if he was only the farmer or butcher or market salesman. Nonetheless, if Ahrens is right in costing a limestone sarcophagus at around 300 denarii (see below) or if the chamosorion-bomos penalties for disturbance (about 500–1000 denarii) relate to the overall costs of the grave, then the income of this deceased pig-producer would be more than adequate to pay for the costs of a funerary monument. Indeed, the marble stele may have marked a more elaborate construction, also within his financial reach.

The explorations above into the two indications of occupation in two different styles of epitaph raise the question of the commensurability between the income generated by that employment/business and the cost of the funerary monument. The white marble (probably Dokimeian) garland sarcophagus, even without any mention of occupation can with some confidence be generally assigned to "the elite,"[121] as imprecise as that classification can be.[122] Members of the elite were more likely to give a resumé of their most prestigious offices (such as high priest, *gymnasiarch*, *grammateus*, member of the *Boulê* and the like),[123] and leave skilled labor or farm management, reflected here, to those they ruled.[124] But the recently uncovered simple limestone sarcophagus from what was probably a close-to-quarry mason's storeroom near Kaklık, 12 miles from Colossae (see chapter 8), was accessible, cost-wise, to those whose status was defined by work-skills, agriculture and trade. A (very) few sarcophagi from Aphrodisias record the occupation, as distinct from office(s) held, of those buried: a sculptor (ἀγαλματογλύφος) and a painter/tinter (πιμενταρίος, in the same sarcophagus), a teacher of friends (διδασκάλος φίλων) and a steward (διοικητής, in the same sarcophagus) an ostler (κτηνείτης, an owner-drover of pack-animals), a senator's agent (συνκλητικοῦ πραγματευτής), a veteran of the Parthian legion, and possibly a builder.[125] The editors assign at least two further sarcophagi to families of middling status.[126] Most sarcophagi are more interested in naming the beneficiaries of interment and protection of the grave. Other types of grave monuments are similarly ill-inclined to record the occupation of the interred: a chief doctor, gladiator, builder, tavern-keeper,[127] matching a

---

121 R. R. R. Smith, "Sarcophagi and Roman Citizenship," in *New Research on the City and Its Monuments, vol. 4 of Aphrodisias Papers* edited by C. Ratté and R. R. R. Smith (Portsmouth, RI: Journal of Roman Archaeology, 2008), 349.

122 Scheidel and Friesen, "Size of the Economy," 63.

123 *I.Aphrodisias 2007* 12.306, 322 (both probably from mausolea).

124 See G. de Ste. Croix, *The Class Struggle in the Ancient Greek World* (London: Duckworth, 1981), 114–20. There are some exceptions nonetheless. One marble sarcophagus from Hierapolis was owned by a trader in porphyry, an extremely expensive stone; F. A. Pennachietti, "Nuove iscrizioni di Hierapolis Frigia," *Atti della Accademia delle Scienze di Torino* 101 (1967): 313 nr. 37.

125 *I.Aphrodisias 2007* 13.406, 15.345, 11.1, 12.908, 11.30, 13.111 (part of the tomb penalty to the association of builders, συντεχνία τῶν τεκτόνων) respectively.

126 *I.Aphrodisias 2007* 13.108, 13.602.

127 *I.Aphrodisias 2007* 1.184 (also 11.217, 12.522), 8.701, 1.164, 13.506 respectively.

few that mention high office.[128] It is rare to find a woman in funerary monuments given either office or occupation.[129]

This is very similar to the pattern distilled by Sven Ahrens for Hierapolis,[130] and may suggest that those registering their occupation (or that of their heirs), did so as part of the display of their successful rise through their skill and the substantial reward for their hard work (ἐκ τῶν κοινῶν κόπων, as a *pragmateutes* near Thessalonike claimed: IG X,2 1supp.1425, l. 2). They have thereby achieved a standing that most others in the necropolis have acquired through inherited accumulations. One such upwardly-mobile aspirant (the ostler, Theseus, mentioned above) declaimed in his epitaph his life lesson for posterity, "While you live, make merry, eat, drink, lay hold of luxuries; for this (tomb on display) was the end …" and, alas, the inscription meets its lacuna.[131] Nonetheless, the few occupation identifications suggest that the two extant from Colossae are not unusual in terms of their frequency of appearance. Rather it sharpens the issue of the cost of such tombs and who might afford them.

Ahrens approaches the question by attempting to plot the cost of manufacture and the wages of the artisans responsible for the product, rather than the projected wages of those who have taken the trouble to ensure that their occupations are included in the epitaphs. His resultant estimates of between 154 and 231 denarii for a simple, limestone/travertine sarcophagus at wholesale price are based on the rare inscription of price in 4th century sarcophagi from Salona. He may have depressed the price from his interest in showing that even modest quarry workers might commit to a long-term, generational investment in a burial chamber.[132] He doesn't align the proposed cost of sarcophagi to those occupations that are occasionally given in the inscriptions cut into them.

However, two contributions to the question of commensurability between occupation and a crafted grave in the Colossian necropolis can be made. Firstly, if the amount of labor needed for the excavation of a chamosorion, the construction of its covers and the sculpting of the *bomos* is proximate to that of carving out a sarcophagus, as seems reasonable to postulate, then it is clear that a leather-worker and a pig-dealer had such a grave end well within their respective financial grasp. Secondly, when one adds the purchase of the plot where the grave was to be placed, the painting of the *bomos* (at least), the prescribed inscription and the elements occasioning the funerary rites and,

---

128 *I.Aphrodisias 2007* 13.501 (priest of Zeus), 12.306 (*stephanophoros*, gymnasiarch), 12.322 (high priest, city treasurer).

129 *I.Aphrodisias 2007* 12.322 (high priestess, probably as adjunct to her husband).

130 Ahrens, "Social status."

131 ὡς ζῇς εὐφραίνου ἔσθιε πεῖνε τρύφα περιλάμβανε τοῦτο γάρ ἦν τὸ τέλος … *I.Aphrodisias 2007* 11.1, ll. 5–7 (nd; translation adjusted from Roueché and Bodard). An echo of Lk 12:19 there may be, but the sentiment was commonplace: Athenaeus *Deip* 8.336e–f.; see W. Ameling, "Φάγωμεν καὶ Πίωμεν," *ZPE* 60 (1985): 35–43; N. E. Akyürek Şahin and H. Uzunoğlu, "Neue Inschriften aus dem Museum von Eskişehir," *Gephyra* 18 (2019): 139–41.

132 Ahrens, "Social status," 133–5.

probably, the annual celebration, then the amounts given on some of Colossae's *bomoi* penalizing disturbance of the grave (namely, 500 denarii on four *bomoi,* 1000 denarii on one)[133] do approximate the projected costs of burial. Of course some stated penalties seem to have compounded the amount with exemplary damages tied to the importance of those buried therein, but at least four (and possibly the fifth) *bomoi* seem to signal a ball-park figure of the amount disbursed on dealing with the memorial and its management. This is tangentially corroborated by a common cost of burial in Italy of 2000 sestercii (that is, about 500 denarii), though types of stone and structure might be expected to vary the price. However, it is also a common allocation for burials provided by *collegia.*[134] In one rare example of the cost of a grave epigraphically recorded, Ammia, a woman from the territory of Amorion (about 155 miles north-east of Colossae, still in Phrygia), paid 550 denarii out of her own money for a tomb that was to house herself and her husband Timotheos, her children and grandchildren (unspecified).[135] The inscription, no longer extant, was described as cut on a stele of simple design but no record of the tomb which it graced was given.[136]

Community and death

The size of tumuli burial chambers, sarcophagi, cliff chambers and chamosoria is testimony to communal burials at Colossae. This is confirmed by the wording of the surviving epitaphs as well. As we shall see, the corpses and remains of the deceased were almost always set into the context of family, relatives and/or friends. Rarely do we find at Colossae the identification of a grave as intended for a single person — Dion the leatherworker (*MAMA* 6.44) is the exception rather than the rule. There is no way of knowing at present whether the small chamosorion on the north-western rim of the necropolis was intended for a single child or a number of children and whether it was intended to be included in a burial complex that included the nearby burial chamber dug into the bedrock.

Collegiality in death was flagged not only by corporate burial but by intimations of the shared banquet signaled in the *triclinium* arrangements within

133 See chapter 11.

134 Duncan-Jones, *Economy of the Roman Empire*, 80, 127. He notes that city sponsorship of funerals at Pompeii was also 2000 sesterces. He found 10 instances of costed monuments in Italy of HS 2,000. However, there were 11 instances of monuments at HS 20,000 and yet only 5 instances of those at HS 3,000. This would suggest that the contingencies of survival have affected the figures. He reckoned that the standard cost was HS 20,000.

135 *MAMA* 7.273 (2nd to 3rd century CE).

136 See C. S. Lightfoot, *Amorium Reports 5: A Catalogue of Roman and Byzantine Stone Inscriptions from Amorium and its Territory, together with Graffiti, Stamps, and Miscellanea* (Istanbul: Ege, 2017), nr. 319.

burial chambers. These were simply transferals of arrangements in houses, Mithratic clubs, taverns, association meeting rooms and sanctuary dining halls. They find their way into the reliefs on funerary stelai, with the privileged couch in the center surrounded by family, including at times, slaves and/or animals.

Plate 12.14: The funerary banquet scene is as much at home on Colossian tombstones as in many necropoleis of Asia Minor. This marble stele offers one representation of a conventional family scene, presenting husband and wife on the *klinê* fronted by a lavish spread on the small serving table, with (female) children seated at either side. A goose is lightly carved below the table.[137] The inscription has been photographically enhanced with red.[138]

The stylized frame of the stelai within which the funerary banquet scenes are set frequently cultivate the same appearance of sacrality as the *bomoi*, that is, with acroteria, triangular or arched pediment with central boss or rosette, sometimes with vertical pilasters carved into the borders at each side. These elements are designed to imitate a temple, thereby accenting the sanctity that attached to dealing with the dead. But by inserting family arrangements into the way the dead were displayed in the reliefs (and their remains arranged in larger burial chambers with *triclinia*), sacrality becomes attached to those familial arrangements, not just in static structures but in the sense that divine providence governed the succession of the family line — precisely that genealogical commitment that we have noted previously. In a sense, the genealogy — not the existing structure — *made* the family.[139] This, in part, is why so many (though not all) honorific and funerary inscriptions are concerned to name at least the father, if not grandfather as well, of the departed. Succession, especially as demonstrated in

137 *MAMA* 6.48 = *I.Mus. Denizli* 73 (2nd to 3rd century CE). I am grateful to Angela Standhartinger for precision in the identification of the bird. The shallow relief may indicate a later addition specifically commissioned as a signature of the deceased.

138 From *MAMA* 6.48 plate, public domain.

139 Compare, albeit differently constructed, the importance of ancestors in Republican Roman practice; O. Doonan, "Family Values: Ancestral Representation and Social Reproduction in Roman Houses," in *Interpretatio Rerum: Archaeological Essays on Objects and Meaning* edited by S. S. Lukesh (Providence, RI: Brown University, 1999), 77–8.

the attention bestowed on grave monuments thus indicated the bridge between the departed generation(s) and those to whom the future had been bequeathed (sometimes by formally inscribed testamentary disposition).[140] The stability of that line was testified to by those who accepted responsibility for the various elements of the burial process. Indeed, some epitaphs explicitly anticipate future generations such as wives for sons, grandchildren, great-grandchildren, all as yet unknown — presumably all able to be housed within a mausoleum.[141]

Cicero pinpointed the peculiar connection of procreation (and adoption) of children and the key aspects of death (inheritance, graves and epitaphs). The meaning of all these elements, held together, was that we think about the future.[142] Family — the propagation of the name, as Cicero would have it — was therefore inextricably bound to the sanctity — the publicly displayed and performed sanctity — of death and burial, and in Asia especially, drew on the centuries-old visual symbolism of the *klinê*. Family and the last things were interlocked. Tombs were extensions of the household, formally owned and administered as much as the household of the living, into which they fostered continuity and permanence.[143] And this was of fundamental importance to civic (and imperial) authorities, as we have seen in the memorialization inscriptions from Colossae (*MAMA* 6.39, 42).[144] This investment in the future by provision for the dead was not only inserted into wills, as we have seen already at Colossae (*MAMA* 6.46).[145] Some inscriptions explicitly state that the grave was prepared by the deceased while he/she/they still lived (ζωσεῖν, see *MAMA* 6.43).[146] Sometimes that virtue was matched by a statement about who was responsible for the final commemoration.

One recently recovered stele from just outside a large burial chamber in the north-eastern necropolis at Laodikeia, records that two children of a deceased woman, Tatas, who had been permitted to be buried there by the owner of the

140 κατὰ τὴν διαθήκην — *MAMA* 6.46, l. 3 (2nd to early 3rd century CE) cf *I.Aphrodisias 2007* 12.403, l. 3 (1st century BCE to 1st century CE).

141 *TAM* II 947, 1129 (Olympus, 3rd century CE).

142 *Quid procreatio liberorum, quid propagatio nominis, quid adoptationes filiorum, quid testamentorum diligentia, quid ipsa sepulcrorum monumenta elogia significant nisi nos future etiam cogitare? Tusc. Disp.* 1.31.

143 Compare E. P. Baughan, *Couched in Death: Klinai and Identity in Anatolia and Beyond* (Madison: University of Wisconsin Press, 2013), 152, 169.

144 See chapter 11.

145 Compare *MAMA* 6.202 = *I.Asia Mixed* 54 (Apameia, mid-1st to early 2nd century). This bilingual epitaph (*ex testamento* = κατὰ διαθήκην), one of a number, shows clearly the influence of Roman testamentary practice of incorporating provision of a burial in a will to the responsibility of heirs.

146 Sometimes however, it is clear that the surviving generation may not have imbibed Cicero's rhetorical collation. One Akmoneian extolled building the tomb for himself and his wife while he was still living but the rationale was less high-blown: "for my heirs have no care for the dead." (οἱ γὰρ κληρο(νό)μοι τῶν θνησκόντων ἀμελοῦσιν *MAMA* 6.306, ll. 6–9 [2nd to early 3rd century CE])

tomb (named Markos), completed the burial process by setting up the epitaphal stele.[147] This act was named as one of virtue, presumably to be recognized as such by those who read the inscription, a present and future cultivation of ethical behavior in the family. There is no indication that Markos was blood/marriage-related to the deceased or the children, Zosimos and Nikanor (presumably hers). Markos is simply recorded as granting his permission for the sake of memory, a stereotypical rendition in funerary inscriptions,[148] but here intensified by ensuring that the woman gathered a memory that, perhaps, she might not otherwise have enjoyed.

Funerary inscriptions, households and families

The interconnection between death, as evidenced most particularly in the variety of remains found in *necropoleis*, and family life has attracted occasional scholarly interest since Richard Saller and Brent Shaw's study of tombstones in the west of the Roman Empire.[149] The focus has been on the funerary inscriptions accompanying graves. Here the epigraphy of death is removed from the total context of the living and the dead in a tomb within a necropolis set within city precincts. There are potential rewards in pursuing what might be yielded from a concerted probe of epitaphs, subject to the caveat that the epitaphs were never intended to be removed from their context and that the resulting limited

147 Μᾶρκος συνεχώρησ- | α Ταταδι τεθῆναι ἰς | τὸν τόπον μου μό- | νην καὶ ἔδωκα στήλ- | ην μνείας ἕνεκεν· | κηδευθεῖσαν ὑπὸ τ- | ῶν τέκνων Ζωσί- | μου καὶ Νεικάνορ- | ος ἀρετῆς ἕνε- | κην {ἕνεκεν}. *SEG* 62.1245 = 65.1259. The text here is reconciled (ll. 2, 10) between the two *SEG* entries (by different editors, Thomas Corsten and H. W. Pleket respectively) in the light of the photographs in Şimşek, *Laodikeia Nekropolü*, vol 1, 44 and vol 2, 480 nr. 299. The inscription is dated to the late 3rd to 4th centuries. However, the letter style and name suggest 2nd to 3rd centuries. I consider a fourth century date unlikely. The *SEG* editors operating independently suggest that there is a syntax change in l. 6 (κηδευθεῖσαν) from the dative required by Ταταδι in l. 2, as if reading the accusative Ταταδα. However, κηδευθεῖσαν whilst often occuring in a funerary setting with the sense of "buried" may revert here to its basic meaning of "set in place", referring to στήλην in l. 4 (with which it agrees grammatically). This yields the translation, "I, Markos came to an agreement with Tatas that she alone might be buried in my tomb; and I have provided a tombstone for the sake of memory which has been set up by her children Zosimos and Nikanor for the sake of virtue."

148 It is clear from the size and arrangement of the tomb itself that it housed more than one corpse. It may be that μόνην is to be understood as an affirmation of privilege not (or not merely) a delimiting condition. Compare *MAMA* 11.280, l. 6 (Northern Lykaonia, imperial). See also James Harrison's discussion, "Perspectives on the Lycus Valley: An Inscriptional, Archaeological, Numismatic and Iconographic Approach," in *The First Urban Churches 5: Colossae, Hierapolis, and Laodicea* edited by J. R. Harrison and L. L. Welborn (Atlanta, GA: SBL, 2019), 38.

149 R. P. Saller and B. D. Shaw, "Tombstones and Roman Family Relations in the Principate: Civilians, Soldiers and Slaves," *JRS* 74 (1984): 124–56. See also, P. Garnsey and R. Saller, *The Roman Empire: Economy, Society and Culture* (London: Duckworth, 1987), 126–47.

analytical results need to be restored to the exchange with the various components of a grave monument (including the interred) and those with an interest in its erection and function. In the absence of census records that have yielded so much demographic and onomastic information for Egypt,[150] epitaphs have been raided in the hope of supplying in a limited fashion, the information more readily available in the papyri. The salutary caution is that when Sabine Heubner compared epigraphical culls from Roman Egypt with the information extracted from the papyri, the results did not match. Epigraphical collations suggested that the nuclear family (that is relationships built in the triad of husband-wife-child) accounted for 72.8 percent of Egyptian households. However, the census returns reduced this dramatically to 54.5 percent, attesting many extended family forms and multiple families in shared residence. In her assessment, "the epigraphic evidence … does not provide a reliable basis for determining family structure and household composition."[151] Again we are returned to the issue of those who could afford to leave a durable grave and epitaph and their interests in doing so. As Walter Scheidel has emphasized, "As a general rule (with the possible exception of slaves), everyone whose burial left a mark in the written record will have come from the more privileged strata of society …"[152] Nonetheless, Huebner's fatalistic conclusion has been judged as too bleak by some; after all, even with the gap in the derived percentages about family structures between epigraphy and papyrology, there is a significant overlap. The gap in knowledge is rather a warning against asserting too much and for cultivating a methodological circumspection in the handling of available material.

Previous studies that have sought to gain some insight into household and family structures in the ancient Mediterranean have relied to a significant extent on the large-scale survey conducted by Saller and Shaw, albeit driven by a need to reformulate the methodology on which they relied.[153] Key constraints on the harvesting of information are that inscriptions need to be studied and classified as a whole rather than dissected by pre-determined criteria. For example, a nuclear family cannot be identified on the basis of a named primary pair, such as father and son, when other persons are named or referred to within the same inscription.[154]

150 See R. S. Bagnall and B. W. Frier, *The Demography of Roman Egypt* (Cambridge: Cambridge University Press, 2006). The reference to three provincial censuses in a dispute arbitration by Hadrian involving Hierapolis, Tripolis and Laodikeia shows that this information was at one time available. See T. Ritti, *Hierapolis di Frigia IX: Storia e Istituzioni di Hierapolis* (Istanbul: Ege, 2017), 389–90, l. 10.

151 S. R. Huebner, "Household and Family in the Roman East and West," in *A Companion to Families in the Greek and Roman Worlds* edited by B. Rawson (Oxford: Blackwell, 2011), 84–8, quotation at p. 88.

152 W. Scheidel, *Measuring Sex, Age and Death in the Roman Empire: Explorations in ancient demography* (JRAs 21; Ann Arbor, MI: Journal of Roman Archaeology, 1996), 90.

153 See especially D. B. Martin, "The Construction of the Ancient Family: Methodological Considerations," *JRS* 86 (1996): 40–60.

154 This is the primary flaw in the Saller-Shaw investigation.

Secondly, allowance must be made for changes in fashion or convention in particular localities as to how, if at all, persons are to be named. For example, Sven Ahrens has noted that there are almost no slaves identified, let alone named (gladiators are a special case), in the high number of funerary inscriptions from Phrygian Hierapolis compared, say, with Termessos in Pisidia to the south.[155] No-one has suggested that Hierapolis was a city less undergirded by servile labor. Similarly, mention of family relationships in honorific dedications (such as briefly reviewed in chapter 6) reveals that such relationships are recorded differently (and often more narrowly), fitting the genre of the inscription.[156]

Thirdly, care must be exercised in extrapolating from the "household" of the tomb to the household of the living and thence to the assertion that household constituents as named in an inscription comprised an operating family.[157]

Fourthly, results must be circumscribed by the limitations imposed by the predicated cost of the burial monument and the, usually, urban location from which they are drawn. We have already seen something of the debate over whether to assume that sarcophagi and chamosoria (at least) are to be understood as the burial options of the wealthy, or available, given longevity in (financial and attitudinal) commitment, for purchase by those of lower socio-economic standing.[158] Noting occupations, where these are given by text, and to an extent, by relief can be a critical determinant of judgments made here.[159]

Fifthly, the gap between the ideology of literary texts (the Letter to the Colossians included) and the rhetorical purposes of epitaphs must be allowed even if the latter may be more likely to yield actual information on household (even family) structures and values. There may be interchanges but these need to be demonstrated rather than assumed. In this sense, any use of the category "nuclear family" (for either literary or epigraphical texts) is profoundly problematic.[160]

Finally, the particularity of epitaphs needs to be complemented by other insights about households (and families) that is yielded not only from other inscriptions (such as dedications) but also other material evidence (architectural, osteo-archeological, numismatic and so on). In part our analysis thus far has been directed to providing the wider context into which epitaphs must be located as well as the independent information that non-textual material can deliver.

With these constraints in mind and the cautions provided by Huebner's analysis of Roman Egypt, there have been a continued number of probings into the relationship between the epitaphs and the families that commission them. Two explorations into funerary inscriptions for their yield for the study of households and families have been chosen for their focus on localities close

155 Ahrens, "Social Status," 144.
156 Huebner, "Household and Family," 84–5.
157 Huebner, "Household and Family," 76–7, 83.
158 Huebner, "Household and Family," 82.
159 So Ahrens, "Social Status," 136–44.
160 See especially Martin, "Ancient Family," 57–8.

to Colossae. This forms a prelude to a similar analysis of Colossae's funerary (and memorialization) inscriptions simply to gain some insight into the hints of household composition at Colossae and, perhaps more significantly, into how various Colossians were prepared to present their composition.

The first exploration is that made by Peter Thonemann directed towards Roman Phrygia;[161] the second is that of Esen Öğüş who has focused on Aphrodisias.[162]

Peter Thonemann and close reading for diversity in families

Thonemann's approach to the study in Roman times of Phrygian family structures through surviving epitaphs is self-avowedly impressionistic. He fully recognizes that the evidence from epitaphs provides only an indirect access to the goal of insight into Phrygian households and families. Nonetheless, he seeks to overcome the disadvantages previously recognized in the heavyweight, demographic aggregations of epitaphs for statistical analysis as the path to households and families by more closely analyzing the detailed wording of the epitaphs and by circumscribing the study to specific localities.[163] Thus he begins by destabilizing the appearance of nuclear families in the 120 or so surviving funerary inscriptions from the city of Apameia firstly by attending to some curious phrasings found in some epitaphs where the nuclear family is broken down by allocations by gift (δώρου χάριν) to those outside the tight microcosm of husband-wife-children,[164] and where limitations are placed on children's burials in the tombs of their parents.

The first group is significant because of the resonance with the Laodikeian stele mentioned above, where, although the actual wording noted by Thonemann, δώρου χάριν, is missing, nonetheless it is clear that some sort of generous allocation has been granted, albeit for the sake of memory and virtue (μνείας/ἀρετῆς ἕνεκεν), and without any recognition of family relationship.[165] Thonemann considers the particular expression a distinctive indicator of local fashion.[166] However, Thonemann has overlooked

161 P. Thonemann, "Households and Families in Roman Phrygia," in *Roman Phrygia: Culture and Society* edited by P. Thonemann (Cambridge: Cambridge University Press, 2013), 124–42.

162 E. Öğüş, "'Til death do them part': Reconstructing Graeco-Roman family life from funerary inscriptions of Aphrodisias," in *Life and Death in Asia Minor*, 121–30. For further examinations surveying other areas in Asia, see E. Varinioğlu, "Phrygia ve Lydia'da (Kırsalda) Aile Bağları," *AST* 29/1 (2012): 91–5, Lightfoot, *Amorium Reports*, 13–18. See further, A. H. Cadwallader, "Family Life in Asia Minor" in *Ancient Literature for New Testament Studies Vol 10: Inscriptions and Papyri* edited by R. Richards and J. R. Harrison (Grand Rapids, MN: Zondervan, 2023), forthcoming.

163 Thonemann, "Households and families," 124–5, 141.

164 Thonemann cites, *inter alia*, *MAMA* 6.227, 231, 235, all of which are now included in the online *Inscriptiones Christianae Graecae* (*ICG* 965, 969, 973 respectively).

165 *SEG* 62.1245 = *SEG* 65.1259.

166 Thonemann, "Households and families," 125.

an inscription from Philippolis in Thrace which not only incorporates the terminology but accents a further aspect, critical in my mind, that is, that the motivation for such liberality is "the love of god" (ἀγάπην ἔχων παρὰ θ(εο)ῦ).[167] Both the Apameian and Philippolitan inscriptions are erected by Christians. Elsewhere, Thonemann recognizes the possibility of Christian solidarity,[168] but not here. What we may be witnessing is continuity in Christian praxis of the generosity of grave owners towards friends and other non-blood/marital relations but veneered with a Christian ideology (perhaps cultivated by widely-circulated gospel stories of the generosity of Joseph of Arimathea [Mk 15:43–6; Matt 27:57–60; Lk 23:50–4; Jn 19:38–42]).

The second group, namely the admission of deceased children to the tomb, Thonemann discovers to be circumscribed by their coming of age, in one case pointedly defined as prescribed by law (ἔννομος ἡλικία),[169] or, in the case of daughters, their marriage.[170] It is not clear whether this formal age is that of Roman law (25 years) or Greek (20 years) or some other reasonably authoritative prescription,[171] though the likelihood is the first given the post-*Constitutio Antoniniana* date implied by the Aurelian names. We have already seen the move to a Roman definition of adulthood in Theon of Smyrna's adjustment of Plato's text (see chapter 6) but here it has become a determinant of reception into a parental tomb. However, other tombs are less restrictive about admission according to their funerary inscriptions.[172] The sheer variety of conditions and permissions is an indication that households were more fluid in their memberships, something that, apparently, can be reflected in the "household of the dead" especially in "their" consciousness that the future, whilst anticipated, is not always predictable.

Thonemann is also interested in exploring possible differences between city and country practices as reflected in funerary inscriptions, concentrating on inscriptions that come from the Upper Tembris valley, a region substantially bereft of urban development. Here the distinctions become stronger. Categorization by age and gender rather than by kin relationships is more noticeable, especially as laid out in epitaphs, made the longer because of concern to list names through successive generations.[173] The self-consciousness of a multiple family kinship group by the person commissioning the epitaph seems to be reflected in the choice of the term συγγενεία which is distinguished from one's ἰδίοι, presumably on the basis of consanguinous proximity,[174] with both gaining proximity in death. Thonemann suspects that households of multiple family groups are inherently unstable, not necessarily because of interrelational friction but because of issues related

---

167 *SEG* 14.486 = *SGLIBulg* 207, ll. 3–4 (4th century CE).

168 Thonemann, "Households and families," 127 commenting on *IGR* 4.731 (Eumeneia).

169 *MAMA* 6.207 (Apameia).

170 *MAMA* 6.335 = *I.Jud. Orientis* 2.174 (Akmoneia, 2nd to 3rd century CE, a Jewish tomb). The delimiting of a daughter's right of burial to age or marriage is also found in Christian tombs (*MAMA* 11.40 [Eumeneia, 3rd century CE] cf *MAMA* 11.36A [Eumeneia, 246 CE]).

171 For example, Thonemann reckons that the marriage age for men in rural, northern Phrygia was generally below the age of 20 years. Thonemann, "Households and families," 135.

172 *MAMA* 11.40.

173 Thonemann, "Households and family," 130.

174 *Steinepigramme* 3.16.31.91 (Upper Tembris valley).

to the demarcation of property on inheritance and transitions brought by marriage.[175] He also notes how daughters/sisters-in-law (both flagged by the term usually indicating wife, namely νύμφη) secured particular recognition, suggesting that biological parentage was "treated with a certain casualness in the Phrygian peasant household"; even so, sons tended to remain tied in locale to their father (as compared to sons-in-law).[176] Age, gender and status ordered relationships in the multiple family household. Further, as distinct from many urban epitaphs, the record of these extensive family relationships was sometimes rigorously kept and displayed, so that the names and relationships might supplant all other details of a funerary inscription.[177] Thonemann crisply observes, "Phrygian peasant families were big"[178] and that size, in some epitaphs, was yet ready to accommodate the naming of slaves and *threptoi* (who might variously be young slaves or fostered children or home-bred slaves)[179] — in this sense closer to the Roman meaning of *familia*.[180]

Thonemann concluded that the presence of funerary monuments and inscriptions in both rural and urban contexts shows that they were meant to mean something, especially to those living in the wider community of city or village. At the same time, homogenization of the results in city and village (a common outcome of statistical surveys) was repudiated. At least in villages, age and gender distributions were more likely to attract notice (yet without, in the main, giving the specific ages). The precision of categories that is of such interest to Roman family law (θρεπτός, νύμφη) is not replicated in rural Phrygia, even in the third and fourth centuries whence come many of his examples. The fundamental points Thonemann wishes to make are that close reading of specific epitaphs is essential and yields the likelihood (if not the statistical demographic) that there was considerable variation in family relationships. Diversity not uniformity was not only the rule in Phrygia but between Phrygia and other parts of the Roman world. This emphasis on diversity coheres with the conclusions reached by Walter Scheidel.[181]

Esen Öğüş and the gendered hierarchy of family relationships

Like Thonemann, Öğüş pursues a narrow focus of study — in her case, the sarcophagi of Aphrodisias. She admits that no broad generalizations can therefore be drawn. However, the advantage offered by Aphrodisias is that many of the inscriptions are preserved in their original series of contexts, that is, stone, monument and, occasionally, necropolis.

175 He cites *MAMA* 10.272, an inscription that seems to combine a funerary commemoration with important elements governing testamentary inheritance. His point however is the extensive detailing of familial relationships.
176 Thonemann, "Households and family," 133.
177 Note especially *MAMA* 6.353 (Diokleia).
178 Thonemann, "Households and family," 137.
179 *SEG* 28.1154, as corrected (from a village near Eumeneia, 3rd century CE).
180 See, for example, *SEG* 49.1729 (Lydia, 59/60 or 113/114 CE).
181 Scheidel, *Measuring Sex*, 163, 165.

She too recognizes that no direct template of family relationships is to be found in epitaphs; familial obligations, so much intertwined with those relationships, are not identical to burial practices or expectations, even if some interconnection can be discerned.[182] Indeed, some of the inscriptions specify that other *unnamed* persons might be buried in the sarcophagus or the structure in which it is housed, simply by the wish or instruction of the owner (while still living), recorded elsewhere. Consequently, such details of extended family or beyond would only be discoverable by a search of the registering office (the χρεωφυλάκιον).[183] One sarcophagus inscription, which apparently originally stood within a large mausoleum, allows those named on the sarcophagus each to offer burial to two (unnamed) friends, but whether these also were to be registered is left unstated, even if implied.[184] It is clear that the wording on funerary inscriptions is potentially a segment of the extent of a family/families and beyond who may be buried therein. But this necessitates an expansive rather than narrowed understanding of family and household.

Of approximately 390 published funerary inscriptions from Aphrodisias, 153 are carved on sarcophagi, 53 of which are relatively intact, mostly dated to the second and third centuries CE. These are selected for study, along with the structures on which and in which they were placed.

Öğüş carefully places a check on the wording of the inscriptions by reference to the design and function of the sarcophagus, noting that this type of tomb was designed for multiple inhumed burials, which were carefully assigned specific places in relationship to one another in the cavity itself and, in the case of multiple sarcophagi in a large dedicated space, with the sarcophagi (and their corpses) arranged carefully in relationship to each other and to the structure where they were placed. This hierarchy of relationship is indicated not only by the wording of one sarcophagus inscription detailing placements but by stone supports projecting from the interior walls that held a (probably-) wooden platform.[185] This ἀβακεῖον (l. 5, a term peculiar to Aphrodisian burial practice but not the sarcophagus design)[186] thus separated those who had been first interred (Athenagoras and his wife Meltine) from their sons Eudamus and Athenagoras upon the latters' deaths. Significantly, the parents' two daughters (both named Meltine) are expressly conferred by the inscription a burial place in the base construction supporting the sarcophagus; that is, they are not included in the sarcophagus itself. A clear hierarchy of age and gender is thereby indicated.

Of the 53 inscribed sarcophagi she selects, the epitaphs indicate four broad categories of burials. 12 were for one person only, 14 for two people (though here the pairs

182 Öğüş, "Reconstructing Graeco-Roman family life," 121–2.

183 *I,Aphrodisias 2007* 12.917, 13.149, 13.206 cf 11.32, 12.211.

184 *I.Aphrodisias 2007* 12.1017. One non-sarcophagus inscription refers simply to a son's children who may also be buried in whatever tomb the inscription headed. No names are given: *I.Aphrodisias 2007* 11.10 (1st to 2nd century CE).

185 *I.Aphrodisias 2007* 13.203. These inscriptions are not dealt with by Öğüş but tend to support her interpretation, albeit in a more expansive manner.

186 Compare εἰσώσται, the term used for burial niches beneath the sarcophagus: *CIG* 2824, *I.Aphrodisias 2007* 2.312. Again this is a sepulchral term (and practice?) confined, it seems, to Aphrodisias.

varied considerably beyond simply husband and wife), 24 were for two parents and their children, and 3 were for more extended families, including one which expressly designated the rightful occupants as husband, wife, son, grandsons, grandfathers and uncle — a decidedly male bias,[187] only rivaled by one sarcophagus that allows the wife Meltine to be buried with the husband Polychronios therein *if* she remains faithful to him and bears a male child.[188] In another, the wife is noticeably absent from an inscription detailing those who might be interred, yet the daughter-in-law is included.[189] In others, ex-wives and illegitimate children are accorded rights of interment, but often not in the sarcophagus itself, being consigned to the platform base underneath the sarcophagus.[190]

These overall summative figures cannot replace detailed investigation of individual sarcophagus inscriptions. Öğüş points out that one sarcophagus — from its inscription designed for one corpse — was yet placed next to another sarcophagus, again for one corpse, both housed within a *hypogea* (chamber tomb) that housed two more sarcophagi (lacking inscriptions). The two inscribed sarcophagi reveal that they were first cousins.[191] Apparently wider family display (supported by financial capacity) had decided on the purchase of two sarcophagi, one incompletely carved and with a poorly executed inscription, the second, a reused sarcophagus with an erasure of an earlier inscription, and slightly defective chambers. The status of two sarcophagi apparently outweighed the placement of the cousins together. Consequently, a single grave occupant (based on the accompanying inscription) is capable of a range of interpretations which may have little to do with household structures and family arrangements. The *hypogea* suggests extended families; the sarcophagus viewed in isolation suggests, like the Dion *bomos* above, a single member household.

Öğüş gives considerable attention to the hierarchical arrangements reflected in the inscriptions especially in its gendered patterns. This is played out not only in the inscription itself but in the place in, below or aside from the sarcophagus that is accorded to certain persons.[192] Slaves and freed persons and *threptoi* are sometimes named, though rarely. When these occupy the sarcophagus it is likely that the owner was himself of servile background but had achieved sufficient wealth to stake a claim for (some) equality in death. When named in a free person's inscription, they

187 *I.Aphrodisias 2007* 12.1109 cf the non-sarcophagus inscription for a tomb that could include the owner Genethlios, his wife, children, grandchildren, *threptoi* (here probably foster-children) *and* their wives.

188 ἐὰν μείνῃ γυνὴ τοῦ Πολυχρονίου καὶ γένηται τῷ Πολυχρονίῳ ἀρρενικὸν τέκνον. *I.Aphrodisias 2007* 13.112, ll. 8–10 (shortly after 212 CE). The sarcophagus was empty when recovered so there was no way of knowing whether Meltine had fulfilled her husband's wishes.

189 Öğüş, "Reconstructing Graeco-Roman family life," 124–5, citing A. Chaniotis, "New Inscriptions from Aphrodisias (1995–2001)," *AJA* 108 (2004): 408–9, nr. 27.

190 Öğüş, "Reconstructing Graeco-Roman family life," 125–6. Sometimes however, illegitimate children are implicitly excluded by permission for burial being granted to τὰ γνήσιά μου παιδία, a specification that seems unnecessary unless meant to restrict. *I.Aphrodisias 2007* 11.43 (not mentioned by Öğüş).

191 *I.Aphrodisias 2007* 13.602, 603 (shortly after 212 CE).

192 Öğüş, "Reconstructing Graeco-Roman family life," 126–8.

are generally accorded the niches in the supporting platform below the sarcophagus. Sarcophagi (and interment therein) therefore indicated the highest rank, even if, as Ahrens argued, non-aristocrats might make the considerable financial sacrifice to purchase a sarcophagus as a family (and future family) investment. Indeed, Öğüş notes one sarcophagus was commissioned by a woman Aurelia Tate to house her second deceased husband, herself, a son, and her daughter by a previous marriage.[193] The specially designed relief below the inscribed tabella of glass-blowing indicates "a family of sub-aristocratic standing."[194]

From the survey that includes occasional detailed commentary on specific tombs, Öğüş accents the diversity of family types and sizes displayed, the range of people who could be interred together and the hierarchy, often noticeably gendered, that ordered burial arrangements, occasionally breaching the veil to demonstrate the continuity of hierarchy from affairs in life (as in the sarcophagus of Polychronios and Meltine).[195] The explicit mention of burial places below or beside the sarcophagus reinforces the hierarchy of death which, from other studies, seems to be a mirror reflection of arrangements in life. In this sense, funerary commemorations can afford some insight into family relationships and household structures and how they were organized, evoking, if not statistically ordering, certain impressions. At the same time, the preferential bias to the male was not all-consuming. 12 of the 53 sarcophagi were owned by women, with one, Neikopolis, delivering the proud boast that she was αὐτεξουσίος, that is, free to conduct her own business without a male guardian — on the basis of the Roman law of *ius liberorum*, having had three or more children.[196] This is an understandable exercise of rights conferred by Augustan law (the *Lex Iulia* and *Lex Papia Poppaea*) in a city given a privileged standing by Augustus.[197] It is striking however that she prescribes that only she was to be interred in the sarcophagus. The children (if indeed she had them!),[198] presumably were relegated to the surrounding space. Öğüş pursues neither the significant number of women-owned sarcophagi nor the attractiveness of Roman law to some women (in this case in an early third century inscription) in breaking free of the legal requirement of a *kyrios*. But it was certainly an achievement sufficiently prized for it to be named in the inscription.[199]

193 *I.Aphrodisias 2007* 13.101 (2nd to 3rd century CE).
194 Öğüş, "Reconstructing Graeco-Roman family life," 128.
195 Öğüş, "Reconstructing Graeco-Roman family life," 122, 129.
196 *I.Aphrodisias 2007* 11.413 (assigned to early 3rd century CE).
197 Oliver, *Greek Constitutions* 1.
198 The requirement of three children for free women to gain freedom from the requirement of a guardian in legal and business matters in the *Lex Iulia* and *Lex Papia Poppaea* was as much known for its flouting as its compliance. The inscription is unfortunately fragmentary between αὐτεξουσίου γε- and τέκνων (ll. 3–4). Joyce Reynolds suggested the reconstruction γεννήσει but admitted that this is not the usual phraseology. In any case this does not specify the number of children. The award of *ius (trium) liberorum* was already being granted at the beginning of the second century as an honorific privilege with no reference to the number of children actually born (Pliny *Ep.* 2.13).
199 Compare, similarly, *TAM* III,1 383, 482, 669, 705, 714 (Termessos, 3rd century CE).

Impressions of Colossian families and households

The approaches of Thonemann and Öğüş invite an investigation of the epitaphs from Colossae to catch a glimpse of the family relationships and household structures operating in Colossae. From the outset it must be admitted that the available number (16) is fewer at present than the samples that Thonemann and Öğüş investigated. Their own caution about making demographic observations from their own investigations becomes doubly true for Colossae, with evidence spread across two centuries.[200] However, even the larger sample size available to them was admitted as only capable of delivering impressions, valid as fostering further investigation but always to be circumscribed by additional evidence, should that surface. Accordingly, the gathering of observations from the Colossian funerary and memorial remains is no more than an initial surveying of the available evidence. Any conclusions are tentative precisely because they are constrained by limited material — but that is often the way with the archaeological witness which occasions the demand to construct no more than a contingent interpretation of what can be harnessed. A potential reinforcement or caveat on such interpretations is placed less by the poverty of material from one location but how it might fit with comparative data from other, but related sites, such as Amorion, the Upper Tembris valley, and Aphrodisias.

It will be helpful to draw together the available evidence here,[201] even though a number of the epitaphs and memorials have been given detailed examination elsewhere, driven by different questions — as in examples i) to ix).[202] Arguments regarding their inclusion and the readings are taken as settled for now. The style of monument is indicated by superscript ^{b} for bomos, superscript ^{s} for stele, superscript ^{m} for memorial, superscript ^{p} for plaque.

i)^{b} Τοῦτο τὸ θέ- | μα καὶ ⟨ὁ⟩ ἐπ' αὐτῷ βωμός | ἐστιν Τατιας καὶ τοῦ ἀν- | δρὸς αὐτῆς Μοσχᾶ, ἐν ᾧ | κεκήδευται ἡμῶν | ἡ θυγάτρην Ταταριν· | οὐδενὶ δ' ἐξέσται | ἄλλῳ κηδευθῆναι | εἰ μὴ τῇ μητρὶ αὐτῆς | καὶ τῷ πατρεί. Εἰ δὲ | μετὰ τὴν ἡμετέραν | τελευτὴν ἀπ⟨ε⟩ιθή- | σει τις τῶν προγε- | γραμμένων, δώσι | τῷ χώρῳ τῷ Ἐλεινοκα- | πριτῶν X̶ φ'.[203] (see Pl. 3.15).

---

200 I have previously laid out these cautions in "One Grave, Two Women," 161–6.

201 An initial collation was made in the appendix to "One Grave, Two Women," 184–7. This has been modified and expanded here on the basis of more recent consideration and examination, reflected in this book. Omitted from that list is the "very imperfect inscription" given by Arundell, *Visit,* 156 and nr. 25 which was given a minimal reconstruction — ἡ γυνὴ αὐτοῦ — in *CIG* 3955. This might possibly be expanded to Ἀρταρβίδης ἡ γυνὴ αὐτοῦ Κοκ(κ)ωνία (itself dubious syntax), but it does not allow any greater sense of the type of inscription we are facing.

202 The fragment yielding only the penalty to the *fiscus* (and no identification of the deceased) is not included here; see chapter 11.

203 *I.Laodikeia Lykos* 114 (late 2nd to early 3rd century CE; see chapter 3).

This platform and the bomos on it belongs to Tatia and her husband Moschas, in which is buried our daughter Tatarin. It is not permitted for any other person to be buried (here), except for her mother and father. And if anyone after our death should not obey (our) directives above, he will pay to the village of the Eleinokaprians 500 denarii.

ii)[s] Ζωσᾶδι Μολοσῷ ὁ χῶρος | ὁ Κιλαραζέων μνίας χάριν· | Ἐλπὶς παροδίταις χέριν.[204]

The village of Kilaraza (set up this epitaph) for Zosas, son of Molos(s)os, in his memory. Elpis offers greetings to the passers-by.

iii)[b] Ζῶσειν (in moulding), | Μᾶρκος Ῥού- | που καὶ Διο- | νύσειος ὑὸς | αὐτοῦ ἐν ᾧ | κηδευθήσοṿ | ται· εἰ δὲ τις ἕ- | τερον κηδεύσ- | ị δώσι τῷ φίσκῳ | Ӿ φ'.[205]

While living, Markos son of Roupos and his son Dionyseios (built this for themselves) in which they are to be interred. If anyone should bury another (in it), he must pay to the fiskus *500 denarii.* (see Pl. 11.6).

iv)[b] Τ]ὸ μνημεῖον | Διονοισίου Ἀγ- | γελικοῦ καὶ τ- | ῆς γυναικὸς | αὐτοῦ Τάτας | καὶ τῆς θυγα- | τρὸς ἡμῶν Ε- | ἰρήνης· ἐν ᾧ | ἕτερος οὐ κ- | ηδεύθῇ, ἤ δὲ | εἴ τις ἕτερον | κηδεύσῃ, δώ- | σει τῷ φίσκῳ | Ӿ α'.[206] (see Pl. 11.7).

(This is) the grave of Dionoisios son of Aggelikos, and of his wife Tata, and of his daughter Eirene. In it, another is not to be interred; or, if someone should bury another (in it), he will pay to the fiskus 1000 denarii.

v)[b] Τὸ μνημεῖον Αὐρηλίου | Μάρκου Κάρπωνος καὶ | τῆ[ς] γυναικὸς αὐ- | τοῦ Αὐρηλίας Τάταδος· | ἐν ᾧ βούλομαι μηδέ-| [να] ἕτερον κηδευθ[ῆν]- | αι· εἰ δέ τις ἕτερος | κηδευθήσεται, δώσει | εἰς τὸ ταμεῖον | Ӿ φ'.[207]

This is the tomb of Aurelius Marcus Karpon and his wife Aurelia Tatas. I do not want anyone to bury another in it. If anyone shall be buried (in it, the offender) will pay to the tameion, *500 denarii.*

vi)[m] Ἡ βουλὴ καὶ ὁ δῆμος ἐτείμησεν Μ(ᾶρκον) Λάρ- | κιον Κρισπεῖνον ἥρωα ἐκ διατάξεως Μ(άρκου) | Λαρκίου Παπίου τοῦ πατρὸς αὐτου ἐπιμε- | ληθέντος τῆς τιμῆς Τ(ιβερίου) Ἀσινίου Ἐπαφροδείτου (see Pl. 11.4).[208]

The Council and People's Assembly honoured Marcus Larcius Crispinus as hero, from the deed of specifications of Marcus Larcius Papias, his father. Superintendence of the honorific display was by Tiberius Asinius Epaphroditos.

---

204 *I.Laodikeia Lykos* 118 (imperial period; see chapter 3).

205 *MAMA* 6.43 = *I.Laodikeia Lykos* 104 (1st to 2nd century CE). See chapter 11.

206 Cadwallader, "Bell's Resolution," 17 (50–150 CE). See chapter 11.

207 *IGR* 4.871 (3rd century CE). See chapter 11. Note that the catalogue reference in Cadwallader, "One Grave, Two Women," 184 (*IGR* 6.871) needs correction.

208 *MAMA* 6.39 = *I.Mus. Denizli* 59 (1st century CE). See chapter 11.

vii)[m] Αὐρ(ήλιον) Ἡρακλέω- | να Καρπίωνος | τὸν ἥρωα, δού- | σης τῆς μη- | τρὸς αὐτοῦ Αὐ̣ [ρ](ηλίας) | Ἀμμιανῆς | Τρύφωνος ἐ- | πὶ τῷ στεφα- | νοῦσθαι αὐ- | τὸν μη. η' ζ' ὑπ[ὸ] | τῆς κρατίστ[ης] | βουλῆς ✗ φ' | τὴν δὲ ἀνάστ[α-] | σιν ποιησαμέ- | νου τοῦ πατρὸς | αὐτοῦ ἐκ τῶν | ἰδίων (see Pl. 11.5).[209]

(This is erected) for Aurelius Herakleon, son of Karpion, as a hero. His mother Aurelia Ammiane, daughter of Tryphon, gave 500 denarii for garlanding it in the 8th month on the 7th day, by permission from the most excellent Council, and his father provided the monument at his own expense.

viii)[p] καὶ Ἀπολλ]ώνιος καὶ Ἀπολλω- | [νίδης οἱ ἀδελ]ποὶ Δαμοκράτῃ̣ | [πατρὶ κατὰ τὴ]ν διαθήκην (see Pl. 11.8).[210]

… N. and Apollonios and Apollonides (set this up) for their father Damokrates, according to the terms of the will.

ix)[b] Δίων Ἀπ̣π̣ [α] | διφθερ̣ [ο]- | πύς· χ[αίρ]- | [ε]ιν (see Pl. 12.12).

Dion, the leatherworker, son of Appas. Greetings.[211]

x)[b] Τὸ μνημεῖον Κάρ̣ - | που καὶ Εὐθηνί̣ [ας] | τῆς γυναικὸς | αὐτοῦ καὶ Ἀρ[τε-] | μιδώρου το[ῦ] | υἱοῦ αὐτῶν· [τοῖς] | παροδίταις, | [χαί]ριν (see Pl. 2.4).[212]

(This is) the tomb of Karpos and Euthenia his wife and Artemidoros their son; greetings to the passersby.

xi)[b] Τὸ μνημεῖον Τροφ̣ [ίμου Φοί -] | βου Δίωνος καὶ Διο̣ [γενείας?] | τῆς γυνεκὸς αὐτοῦ̣ [–] | ἐ̣ν ᾧ κηδευθήσοντα[ι αὐτοί·][213]

(This is) the tomb of Trophimos son of Phoibos grandson of Dion, and of Diogeneia his wife … in which they are to be buried …

209 *MAMA* 6.42 (3rd century CE). See chapter 11.

210 *MAMA* 6.46 (1st century BCE to 1st century CE). See chapter 11.

211 *MAMA* 6.44 (2nd century CE). See above.

212 *SEG* 57.1384 = A. H. Cadwallader, "New Inscription," nr. 1 (1st century CE).

213 *MAMA* 6.45 (1st to 2nd century CE), described as "in the necropolis. Fragment of a limestone bomos lying beside its recently smashed pedestal". Some adjustments to letters have been made on a thorough analysis of the photograph: element of *phi* visible at end of l. 1; part of superscript *omicron* at end of l. 2; small omicron before upsilon at end of l. 3; remove speculative *omicron* after *upsilon* at end of l. 3, possibly able to be reconstructed as ζῶσιν (cf *SE* 2663.16 Ephesos nd). Φοῖβος as the reconstructed name rather than Buckler and Calder's Roman suggestion, Πρόβος (ll. 1–2), is much more likely (cf *I.Claros mémoriaux* 111 [150 CE]; *I.Laodikeia Lykos* 95 (2nd century CE). Also possible are Βάρβος (cf *SEG* 54.1314, Hierapolis, 3rd century CE) and Σιλβος (Ramsay, *Phrygia* 1.307.111, Pisidia, 119 CE). I have more fully reconstructed l. 4 (αὐτοί. cf *I.Iasos* 629). The inscription may have proceeded to add a reference to children or others able to be buried or simply proceeded to the standard formula prohibiting use or intrusion by others: εἰ δέ τις ἕτερον κηδεύσει δώσι τῷ φίσκῳ/ταμείῳ ✗ …

xii)[s] Συγγενικὸν νειώτερον | Τατιανῷ Β' Ἄρτου. (see Pl. 12.14).[214]
The younger relatives (arranged this) for Tatianos, son of Tatianos, grandson of Artas.

xiii)[s] Παροδείταις χα(ί)ρ(ε)ιν | οἱ ἑταῖροι Γλύκω- | ναν ἐτείμησαν (see Pl. 7.9).[215]
Greetings to the passersby. The (society of) friends (hereby) honored Glykon.

xiv)[b] [Τὸ μνημεῖον Δά(?)] τυος υ[ἱοῦ Ζ]ήνων[ος ...[216]
(This is) the tomb of Datus son of Zenon ...

xv)[b] Ἐπίκτητος | καὶ | Ἀρίστη γυ- | νὴ αὐτοῦ (see Pl. 12.16).[217]
Epictetos and his wife Ariste(are buried here).

xvi)[b] Τὸ μνημεῖον | Αὐ(ρηλίου) Μενιάνδρου | Β τοῦ Ἑρμογένου | κ(αὶ) Αὐ(ρηλίας) Ζηνωνίδος | τῆς γυναικὸς | αὐτοῦ ἐν ᾧ κη- | δευθήσειται | καὶ Ἱεικές(?) Δίου | γυνὴ Ζήνωνος (see Pl. 12.15).[218]
The tomb of Aurelius Meniandros son of Meniandros, grandson of Hermogenes; also of Aurelia Zenonis, his wife; in which grave is also to be buried Hieikis(?) daughter of Dios, wife of Zenon.

Two further epitaphs feature Colossians whose funerary inscription was located elsewhere — in Smyrna and in the area of Boubon.[219] These however are more likely to reflect the cultural influences of their respective locales and/or values of their executors.

---

214 *MAMA* 6.48 = *I.Mus. Denizli* 73 (2nd century CE). The name Βάρτου given in these two catalogues is corrected, following Robert, *BE* 1979.15. The plate for *I.Mus. Denizli* 73 reveals that the stele has had the top half broken (and presumably lost) since the photograph provided by Buckler and Calder for *MAMA* 6.48. A squeeze of the inscription (only) is found in the collection of the British Institute of Ankara (DM 39).

215 *MAMA* 6.47 = *I.Mus. Denizli* 113 (2nd century CE) — the plate accompanying the latter indicates the stele is now fractured just below the figures in relief. I had previously overlooked Buckler and Calder's note of a small tenon which confirms the stele, not a "façade" as I had described the stone in "One Grave, Two Women," 184. My close examination of the photograph indicates that the stone reads XAPIN in line 1. The squeeze held at BIA (DM 177) unfortunately only has ll. 2–3. The first line is inscribed along the lintel below the pediment carved into the stele. I have taken the name of the deceased as Γλύκων (so *LGPN* V.C sv) not Γλυκωνᾶς (otherwise unknown) as implied in Elena Miranda's translation ("Glykonas") in *I.Mus.Denizli* 113 commentary. See chapter 7, with Plate 7.9.

216 I have provided this reconstruction of the fragmentary transcription by Francis Arundell, *Visit*, 98, *Discoveries*, 169–70 on the basis that his admittedly unclear journal appears to indicate he was at the necropolis; see "Inscriptions from Colossae," 114. The name Κότυς is equally possible. No date, apart from a general 1st to 3rd century can be assigned, and this only on the basis of the presumption that we are dealing with a typical bomos from the Colossian necropolis.

217 Cadwallader, "One Grace, Two Women," 168 (1st to 2nd century CE).

218 Cadwallader, "One Grave, Two Women," 171–3 (2nd to 3rd century CE).

219 *I.Smyrna* 440; *I.Boubon* 102.

Of the sixteen instances, ten were recorded on *bomoi*, two on memorials, three on stelai and one was probably some form of plaque or base. These styles of monument can contribute to overall interpretations. Dates, in the absence of anything so inscribed, have been assigned on the basis of style of lettering and naming patterns.

Salient information for impressions of family relationships and/or household structures is distilled in the following table. Key: d. daughter, s. son, m. mother, f. father, gs. grandson, gf. grandfather, il. in-law, rel. relatives, h. husband, w. wife, c. association, a. friend(s).

Insc.	Deceased	Rel'nships	Genealogy	Provision
i C2–3	Tatarin Tatia Moschas	d. m., w. f., h.	(m., f.) — —	Tatia, m. (Moschas, f.)
ii C1–3	Zosas Elpis	s., h.(?) w.(?)	Molossos, f.	village
iii C1–2	Markos Dionyseios	f., s. s.	Roupos, f. (f.)	Markos (Dionyseios, s.)
iv 50–150	Dionoisios Tata Eirene	h., f. w., m. d.	Aggelikos, f. (f., m.)	Dionoisios, f., h.
v C3	Karpon (Aur. M.) Tatas (Aur.)	h. w.	— —	Karpon (h.)
vi C1	Crispinus (M. Lar.)	s.	Papias (M. Lar.) f.	Papias, f. Epaphroditos (T. Asin.)
vii C3	Herakleon (Aur.)	s.	Karpion, f. Ammiane (Aur.) m., d. Tryphon	Ammiane (Aur.), m. (Karpion, f.)
viii C-1-C1	Damokrates	f.	Apollonios, s., b. Apollonides, s., b.	Apollonios, (will) Apollonides, (will)
ix C2	Dion	s.	Appas, f.	Dion (c./a.?)
x C1	Karpos Euthenia Artemidoros	h., f. w., m. s.	— — (f., m.)	Karpos Euthenia
xi C1–2	Trophimos Diogeneia	h., s., gs. w.	Phoibos, f. Dion, gf.	Trophimos
xii C2	Tatianos	s., gs.	Tatianos, f. Artos, gf.	rel.

Insc.	Deceased	Rel'nships	Genealogy	Provision
xiii C2	Glykon		—	c./a.
xiv nd	Datys (?)	s.	Zenon, f.	Datys?
xv C1–2	Epictetos Ariste	h. w.	—	Epictetos, Ariste
xvi C2–3	Meniandros (Aur.) Zenonis (Aur.) Hieikis (?)	s., gs., h. w. d., w.	Meniandros, f. Hermogenes, gf. Dios, f. (Zenon, h.)	Meniandros

The table enables us to draw out some features that in some cases invite further discussion.

a) There is a notable silence. There are no slaves or freed persons named in any epitaph or memorial. With such a small number of epitaphs/memorials, this becomes an annotation inviting investigation once further funerary inscriptions are known.

b) Only two of the deceased bear Latin names. Markos had become ubiquitous and might reflect an aspiration for citizenship or at least a parade of some *Romanitas*. Crispinus is clearly a well-connected Roman citizen.[220]

c) Concern about registering one's genealogy is strong: thirteen male names are recorded as genealogical predecessors with one man named as a husband but not included in the grave. Two women, Ammiane and Hieikis(?) have their respective fathers recorded. It may be significant here that Aphias, the Colossian woman who married Hermas, a man presumably from the territory of Boubon, is yet remembered on the epitaph he set up for her memory as not only a Colossian but also the daughter of Tryphion.[221] In the case of Ammiane, the organization of the memorial for her son, Herakleon, seems to have fallen to her. Significantly, she names not only her Roman citizenship (post-*Constitutio Antoniniana*) but also her father, Tryphon. Tryphon appears as a popular name among leading men of Colossae, as indicated in the Korymbos honorific, where the leading subscriber for the honors carries that name (as also his father). The pattern contrasts markedly from her husband, Karpion, who appears without genealogy or citizenship. It may be that the almost-postscript that Karpion provided the resources for the memorial hid his posthumous disbursement

220 See chapter 11.
221 *I.Boubon* 102 = *CIG* 4380 k^3.

of funds arranged by Ammiane as heir to the estate. If so, she joins the elite woman, Claudia Eugenetoriane the mint-reviver, as one who controlled significant wealth to further her own projects. If Karpion is still alive, the initiative of Ammiane is even more notable. It may be partially paralleled by the tombstone from the village of Eleinokapria, where Tatia appears to be the one who assumes the leadership in organizing the burial place of her daughter Tatarin, even though her husband Moschas is still alive. Twice in this inscription she is named first, first by name and then as "mother". Just as Esen Öğüş found at Aphrodisias, there appear to be a number of women who take a lead role in the arrangements of funeral obligations. Here the men in the picture seem relatively inactive if not compliant. Certainly there is a sense that local authorities, the *Boulê* in the case of Ammiane, the local village in the case of Tatia, were quite accommodating of such initiative and responsibility.

Hieikis, whose inclusion on an otherwise clear funerary *bomos* becomes a little abraded at her name, rendering the spelling uncertain, receives notice of both her father, Dios, and her husband, Zenon. In her case there is no sense that she has organized the tombstone. Rather it appears that her husband has either disappeared or been killed away from Colossae. The name of her husband Zenon is a mirror of another woman named on the same stone, Zenonis. She appears without genealogy, simply identified in the more usual pattern by marital relationship to the one who appears to have organized the grave. The commonality of the names Zenon and Zenonis suggest that they were siblings, a naming pattern often found. This implies that in the aftermath of Zenon's demise or departure, the sister-in-law Hieikis joined the household and ultimately shared in the common *chamosorion* burial. Sarah Pomeroy's observation that "Care in death is consistent with care in life," is poignantly underscored here.[222] The house-

Plate 12.15: The funerary bomos, found near the line of bomoi toppled and pushed into position to enable leveling of agricultural land, records a common burial for the deceased, Meniandros, his wife Zenonis and his sister-in-law Hieikis(?). The photograph has been flipped right.

222 S. Pomeroy, *Families in Classical and Hellenistic Greece: Representations and Realities* (Oxford/New York: Oxford University Press, 1997), 120.

hold structure has been reconfigured in the light of difficult circumstances to the extent that the household tomb embeds an extended family.

Most of the twelve women named in these inscriptions (half the number of named men, outside of genealogies) are defined simply by marital ties not by genealogy. On the one hand this echoes Peter Thonemann's observation that daughter-in-laws are more frequently named in extended family epitaphs than daughters, the explanation being that their family relationship has been redefined. The concern about genealogy by three Colossian women suggests that this was not universal but might be varied, whether by necessity (perhaps to safeguard Hieikis's reputation) or other factor. In the case of Ammiane and perhaps Aphia, there is a concern to underscore their own identity as distinct from or in addition to marital ties.

d) One inscription is noteworthy for the absence of mention of a wife and mother, even though father and son — Markos and Dionyseios — jointly arrange their common burial place.[223] The absence of wife and mother proclaims a household where, for whatever reason, there is no woman/women present or, at least, no woman/women acknowledged as being present. This is made the more telling because Markos is concerned that his genealogy be recorded — son of Roupos, a spelling of the Latin that may indicate phonological difficulty in pronunciation. Again divorce, desertion or death in another place may be the explanation for the lack of a mother/wife's name. At the very least, the silence is hardly mute.

e) For all the above emphasis on genealogy, there are six cases where no genealogy is given. In one, the epitaph of Karpon and Tatas, there is concern that their Roman citizenship be recognized, almost certainly a status acquired after the promulgation of the *Constitutio*

Plate 12.16: The broken bomos recording the names of Epictetos and Ariste. The base, plinth and a substantial part of the pediment are missing. The photograph has been flipped right.

223 There is an unresolved dispute about whether to assign the provenence of this *bomos* to Colossae or Laodikeia.

Antoniniana in 212 CE. It might suggest that the new currency of citizenship had, for some, more purchasing power than the acknowledgement, through genealogy, that their Roman citizenship did not have a long pedigree (though this was no embarrassment to Meniandros). Alternately, the number of epitaphs without genealogy suggests that genealogical display was not a universal convention. Indeed one husband and wife, Epictetos and Ariste, opted for supreme simplicity, recording only their names and marriage in four neatly cut lines.

f) The premature death of Tatarin, the daughter of Tatia and Moschas at Eleinokapros, is a reminder that life expectancy in the ancient world was quite low, somewhere between 20 and 30 years as the average.[224] Early death might be indicated in the memorialization of Crispinus and Herakleon. Certainly no other relationship, such as marriage or children, is granted these two. But we see this also in the case of Dion the leatherworker, Tatianos and Glykon. Dion and Tatianos retain a genealogical link, but Tatianos' epitaph is also at pains to record that the "younger relatives" (συνγενικὸν νειώτερον) took responsibility for funeral requirements.

Peter Thonemann was struck by the term συγγενεία in its distinction from the ἰδίοι of the family. When the συγγενεία are mentioned in the same context as close family members there is an ordered sequence of connection that is frequently laid out in relation to the deceased and his proper burial. One inscription on a funerary altar from the territory of Thyateira succinctly provides the model:

> In the 283rd year [Sullan calendar = 198/199 CE] on the 7th of the month of Dystros, Apollonios and Aphianos his sons, Aphias his wife, Hermione his daughter-in-law, all his domestic slaves (set this up) for their father Apollonios; likewise the [Dionysiac] guild for their thyrsus-bearer and village leader, along with his relatives made this for a memorial. Farewell![225]

The sequence here closely follows the line of responsibility laid out in Greek and Roman law for burial.[226] The hierarchy of those to whom obligation fell was not restricted to burials. The kyriarchal government of women's legal decision-making is similar, that is running from male members of the immediate family (usually from father or grandfather to husband to son, each becoming responsible if the higher ranked is unavailable) to male relatives (such as an uncle, nephew

224 Ahrens, "Social status," 132, who notes the difficulties in gaining precision.

225 ἔτους σπγ', μη(νὸς) Δύστρου ζ'. Τ[ῷ πατρὶ Ἀπολλωνίῳ Ἀπολλώνιος καὶ Ἀφιανὸς οἱ ὑοί, Ἀπφιὰς ἡ σύμβις, Ἑρμιόνη ἡ νεὸς καὶ τὰ θρέμματα πάντα, ἡ σπεῖρα τὸν ναρθηκοφόρον κὲ πρωτοκωμήτην καὶ οἱ συνγενεῖς ἐποίησαν μνείας χάριν. Χαῖρε. *TAM* V,1 822, translation by Philip Harland, amended. See also *TAM* V,1 817, *IG* XII,7 396.

226 *Dig.* 11.7.12.4 (Ulpian).

or cousin).[227] In Greek law, relatives on whom responsibility devolved could come from the father's or mother's side.[228] There is no need to see the reference as a phatry operating as an association administering funeral arrangements.[229]

But this raises a critical question — where is Tatianos's immediate family? Grandfather and father are presumably long gone and there is no wife or children, either because Tatianos died before marriage or because marital and familial ties have been disrupted. There may be a hint of Tatianos's age in the qualification of νειώτερον added to συνγενικόν, perhaps an expression of "like to like" that had a lengthy philosophical undergirding.[230] But the younger kin were apparently old enough to be recognized as possessing the authority to handle the funerary organization, perhaps even being the beneficiaries of whatever estate Tatianos bequeathed,[231] that is, if any will was made at all.[232]

The question is sharpened by the clash between the absence of family in the inscription and the highly conventional familial scene presented in the relief of the stele (see Pl. 12.14 above). Husband and wife recline together on a couch, the former indicated by his position at right and the height differential between the figures. They are fronted by the banquet laid out on the small serving table, with (female) children seated at either side, and a goose below the table. The banquet, the familiar expression of ancient responsibility, prosperity and hospitality,[233] is set into an evocation of religious significance, a temple. In a Phrygian context the pilasters, arch and pediment had an added mimetic connection with the massive rock-tombs for ancient kings. A sacral grandeur was given to this one's death whose small stele yet lays claim to a continuing significance of his life.

Here we are confronted by the tension between the inscription and the relief, text and iconography. The inheritance of the modern period of archaeology has unwarrantedly privileged written remains (the literary bias), usually

227 M. O. Wise, *Language and literacy in Roman Judaea: A Study of the Bar Kokhba Documents* (New Haven: Yale University Press, 2015), 41.

228 S. C. Todd, *The Shape of Athenian Law* (Oxford: Clarendon Press, 1993), 207.

229 So Miranda on *I.Mus. Denizli* 73, *pace* U. Huttner, *Early Christianity in the Lycus Valley* (Leiden: Brill, 2013), 31.

230 See Homer *Od.* 17.218; Aristotle *Rhet.* 1371b, *Nic. Eth.* 1155a.

231 The presumption of the Greek laws of inheritance was that the estate would flow to the younger generation; see J. W. Jones, *Law and Legal theory of the Greeks* (Oxford: Clarendon Press, 1956), 193–4.

232 Edward Champlin's comment that "testation in Roman society was even less common than might be surmised" holds also for Greek polity. Will-making was restricted to a small group who develop an important place and recognition in law only because that group were substantial property owners. See Champlin, *Final Judgments: Duty and Emotion in Roman Wills 200 B.C. - A.D. 250* (Berkeley: University of California Press, 1991), 46, 55.

233 Paul Veyne waxed fully on the interpretation of the ubiquitous display, albeit aided by some inscribed renditions of meaning, covering everything from an apology for living a miserly life to a display of familial wealth to a general pronouncement that life is short, so live this way: see Veyne, "The Roman Empire," in *A History of Private Life I: From Pagan Rome to Byzantium* (Cambridge, MA: Belknap Press, 1978), 180, 188.

on a hierarchical gradation of scripture, classical text, inscription, papyri and "leftovers" (ostraka, graffiti etc). Where a relief co-exists with some inscriptional remains, students of the past have tended to interpret the sculptured section within the confines of the writing. John Boardman rightly uttered the complaint: "The historian who accepts archeological data only where they support a text is a phantom that still stalks the subject; as is the language man who thinks that all pictures illustrate texts."[234] Secondly, there has been an assumption that the relief is specific to the one memorialized (the particularity bias). Just as funerary texts are dominated by conventional phrases, so also funerary reliefs and monuments followed standardized formulae and symbolism. Even though a mason's yard might offer a range of offerings from which to choose, it was resolutely finite (for both economic and social reasons).[235] Some fine-tuning of features was executed and there are considerable variations even, say, in the vast collection of Pfuhl and Möbius. But the thematics are considerably restricted. The goose under the table at the very least suggests that a mark of individual requirements shows in the final presentation.

The potential clash with the wording of the inscription is that the συγγενικόν, as we have seen, is not to be identified with wife or direct children. Accordingly there is a measure of standardized representation here that communicates beyond the actual details of immediate family, none of which, father and grandfather apart, are named. The relief delivers a public display of conventionality that is more important for the purposes of memorialization than any literal incarnation of what appears in the inscription. Onno van Nijf's observation about the function of inscriptions as signaling to others that those mentioned are "bound by a morality similar to that of the polis community"[236] applies as much to the semiotics of the relief as to the writing. As we shall see in the inscription and relief for Glykon, there was available to the relatives to choose another fairly standard funerary relief, namely a standing figure, or two standing figures, fronting the "passersby" as if sending the very greetings frequently delivered in the epitaph. This suggests that there was no absence of purpose in selecting this carved stele. And that purpose was embroiled in the standard fare in funerary reliefs, a standard that was regarded as the norm in so many *poleis* in Asia. In this relief then, highlighted by the seeming dissonance with the epitaph, we catch a glimpse of the figurative family scene envisioned at Colossae by those with the means to influence artistic imagination — gender asymmetry, hierarchy (in seating), slaves invisible, animals domesticated, food plentiful and provided for all "in the family" (note the children's hands with

---

234 J. Boardman "Classical Archaeology: Whence and Whither" *Antiquity* 62 (1988): 796.

235 For examples of the impact of a limited range of tombstones, see G. J. Johnson, "Christian Business and Christian Self-Identity in Third/Fourth Century Phrygia," *VigC.* 48 (1994): 341–66.

236 O. van Nijf, *The Civic World of Professional Associations in the Roman East* (Amsterdam: J. C. Gieben, 1997), 49n98. Van Nijf is speaking in the context of funerary associations. The point has broader validity.

food in the relief). The very temple evocation in the carved frame settles such a construction within divine sanction. Tatianos and his young, dependably responsible relatives are made, by the relief, to endorse this valorized perspective, regardless of the actual structure of their own household circumstances.

g) When we turn to the epitaph and relief for Glykon a number of contentious aspects are raised (xiii above, with Pl. 7.9). Here there is no family recorded, but neither is there a family to provide visual support. In the descending order of responsibility for a person's burial, there was one final group who were granted permission to make the arrangements — friends of the deceased.

Here the first point of dispute arises, namely, whether the οἱ ἑταῖροι refers to a formal association or a loose gathering of acquaintances formed by the specific need to bury Glykon. Arguing for the former is Philip Harland.[237] Removing the inscription from a list of associations is Benedikt Eckhardt.[238] The suggestion of Buckler and Calder that it might be a Jewish association has no warrant.[239]

At a formalistic level, "the friends" could be either an established association or an informal, *ad hoc* task-driven group. For the latter, this could be comrades-in-arms in an army;[240] it was used for neighboring city-states depicting their leaders' ties, having entered into a treaty relationship.[241] These instances have a level of technicality in their use, approximating the designation found in Macedonian military units,[242] the political relationship to kings,[243] or even the attendants to the Roman emperor (the *Comites*).[244] But occasionally the word is found simply to describe the recognized friendship between persons, appearing in inscriptions to justify certain actions (such as burial) being taken. Thus two ἑταῖροι described themselves as πιστοί τε ἀλλήλοις as the warrant for a public monument which they set up as a memorial of friendship (μνημόσυνον φιλίας).[245] Indeed ἑταῖροι can be used as a synonym of φίλοι.[246]

---

237 P. A. Harland, *Greco-Roman Associations: Texts, Translations and Commentary II: North Coast of the Black Sea, Asia Minor* (Berlin: de Gruyter, 2014), 108. See also, his online site: http://philipharland.com/greco-roman-associations/funerary-honors-by-companions-for-glykona-i-ii-ce/.

238 B. Eckhardt, "Romanization and Isomorphic Change in Phrygia: the Case of Private Associations," *JRS* 106 (2016): 153. See also https://ancientassociations.ku.dk.

239 *MAMA* 6.47 comment, citing *OGIS* 573 and *MAMA* 4.299 as comparison. Only *OGIS* 573 (Elaioussa Sebaste, 27 BCE to 14 CE) can sustain a claim to be Jewish on the basis of the addition of "the Sabbatistai" as the name of the group to which "the friends" is conjoined.

240 *SEG* 49.855, l. B26 (Macedonia, 197 BCE).

241 *I.Erythrai Klazomenai* 9 (350–342 BCE).

242 Theopompos *Hist.* 217; compare G. Mendel, *Catalogue des sculptures grecques, romaines et byzantines* (Constantinople: En vent au, 1912–14), 263–264 nr. 104 (Sidon, painted inscription).

243 Curtius 3.12.16.

244 *P.Lond.* 6.1912 (Claudius).

245 *I.Rhodische Peraia* 126 (Thysannous, 3rd century BCE); cf *IG* IX 1,2 579 (Kos, 3rd century BCE), *SEG* 44.893 (Kaunos, 4th to 3rd century BCE).

246 *SEG* 32.605 (Larisa, 150–200 CE, in a funerary epigram for a gladiator).

In some of these examples, a measure of formality is present, even if a (self-) regulated voluntary association is absent. The consciousness of the formality of ἑταῖροι-friendship, with its attendant obligations, is most strongly reflected in the use of ἑταιρεία as the preeminent term in Greek law for an association. The second-century Roman jurist, Gaius, in his commentary on the Twelve Tables, recognized that this was the Greek equivalent of *collegium*. He manufactured a derivation from the great Greek law-maker Solon, whom he cites, "If the inhabitants of a city district or precinct be in association for the purpose of holding religious feasts or of dining together or to provide for their burial or to perform sacred rituals ... anything that they agree between themselves will be valid unless forbidden by public statutes."[247] The technical term continued to be found,[248] along with many other words for a formal association.[249] Even when the word was incorporated into localized prohibitions of associations,[250] it is almost certainly, in my view, in recognition of the correct term in Greek law applicable in a metropolitical Greek *polis* (Ephesos), rather than any politicized narrowing of the term to "partisanship"[251] or unauthorized gatherings.[252]

Ilias Arnaoutoglu is circumspect in claiming too formal an operation for a number of "group" words, including οἱ ἑταῖροι.[253] It seems that the term occupied a spectrum of application, although I would argue that the sheer preference for οἱ ἑταῖροι over φίλοι or the anarthrous ἑταῖροι has a long-standing lay recognition of the legal terminology in the background that undergirds the self-conscious language choice. "The friends" in a number of cases is unequivocally indicative of a ἑταιρεία, given the particular defining examples provided in the Solonic formulation. One Hellenistic inscription from Metropolis is carved into an expensive, blue marble stele beneath two wreaths. Beneath each inscription is the name of the association, one οἱ ἑταῖροι, the other οἱ θιασεῖται both above the one honored, Menophilos son of Antiochos.[254] Here two associations, possibly with membership duplicated in some cases, join to sponsor the funerary/honorific monument. H. W. Pleket adjudged the date of this stele to be about the same time as

---

247 ἐὰν δὲ δῆμος ἢ φράτορες ἢ ἱερῶν ὀργίων ἢ σύσσιτοι ἢ βωμόταφοι ἢ θιασῶται ... ὅ τι ἂν τούτων διαθῶναι πρὸς ἀλλήλους, κύριον εἶναι ἐὰν μὴ ἀπαγορεύσῃ δημόσια γράμματα. *Dig.* 47.22.4 (trans. Watson, adjusted by reference to Arnaoutoglou). Ilias Arnaoutoglou has shown that Gaius's attribution is a memory cultivation hanging a more recent development on a great name of the more distant (eight centuries!) past. The development as a legal definition belongs rather to the period of the 3rd to the 1st century BCE. See his "The Greek text of D. 47.22.4 (Gai 4 ad legem duodecim tabularum) reconsidered," *LR* 5 (2016): 87–119.

248 *LSAM* 80 = *SEG* 34.1298 (Hierapolis, 2nd to 3rd century CE).

249 See I. Arnaoutoglou, "Roman Law and *Collegia*, in Asia Minor," *Revue Internationale des droits de l'Antiquité* 48 (2002): 31–6, 39 n33.

250 *I.Ephesos* 225 (late 2nd century CE; the bakers' disturbance).

251 As seen, for example, in Appian *Bell. civ.* 3.10.75.

252 *Contra* Arnaoutoglou, "Roman Law and *Collegia*," 39–40. The proximate temporal conjunction of Gaius's commentary on ἑταιρεία with the so-called bakers' strike/riot actually reinforces Arnaoutoglou's argument against any widespread ban on associations, even as it demonstrates no suspicion of the Greek technical term in Gaius's description.

253 Arnaoutoglu "Greek text of D. 47.22.4," 92 n12, 117.

254 *I.Ephesos* 3466A = *SEG* 32.1170 (3rd to 2nd century BCE).

another similar monument from Metropolis, this time with οἱ ἑταῖροι only performing the honorifics.[255] The probability is strong, given the similar stylistics, that "the friends" is the same group, of the same associational standing and cohesion as the (Dionysian) religious group with which they were conjoined in the double-wreathed stele.

Significantly, in another inscription from Metropolis from about the same time, "the friends" become a little more expansive in the inscription. Unfortunately it is fragmentary so that the honorand's name is missing. Here "the friends honor (ἐτίμησαν) N., a good and honorable man, who lived an exemplary life." The final (substantially reconstructed) words seem to imply a funerary monument. Early in the third century CE, a group (σύνεδρος) of "the friends" (οἱ ἑταῖροι) at Termessos in Pisidia, some of whose names are listed on the monument, provided public recognition for "the honorable man and true friend" (τὸν ἄριστον καὶ ἀληθῆφίλον, ll. 6–7), nicknamed Hekebolios — probably the leader of the association. The temporal range in these inscriptions shows the tenacity of the use of οἱ ἑταῖροι in public commemorations (of death or honor).[256] The Lycus Valley amply attests its own participation in the usage.[257]

There are two elements that favor, in my view, the understanding of this stele as the responsible assemblage by a group sufficiently organized to be classed as an "association". Firstly, at a textual level, there appears to have been a deliberate effort to ensure that there be no confusion over what was to be conveyed by ἑταῖροι. The article was apparently unwittingly or ignorantly omitted by the none-too-careful lithographer. The insertion of οἱ as a superscript implies that a distinction was felt between anarthrous "friends" and the articular "the friends". The anarthrous form is known in a number of places and when it so occurs, there can be no doubt that we are dealing with a loose gathering of amicable companions.[258] This does not demand that when the article is supplied, we have an association but the pendulum of probability swings. In this case, the deliberate correction seems telling. Also of interest is the use of ἐτίμησαν rather than the ubiquitous μνείας χάριν, "for the sake of memory/in memoriam." This, as we have seen above, appears in a number of inscriptions in combination with οἱ ἑταῖροι. The combination is suggestive of the actions of a formal body, although not conclusive (and "the friends" can erect a funerary monument "for the sake of memory").[259] However, the separation of the stock funerary greeting, Παροδείταις χα(ί)ρ(ε)ιν — set into the lintel of the temple form — from the statement of honor, when both could easily have been combined on the platform below the figures might indicate a separation of functions — to which we turn.

255 *I.Ephesos* 3466B = *SEG* 32.1169; see also *SEG* 32.1185.

256 See also *I.Prusa* 24 (1st century CE).

257 See, for example, *I.Mus. Denizli* 99 (region, 2nd century CE); *MAMA* 4.299 (Dionysopolis, 1st to 2nd century CE); cf *MAMA* 9.86 (Aizanoi, 130 CE), with commentary.

258 See, for example, *SEG* 60.1288 (Attaleia, imperial).

259 So *MAMA* 4.299 (Dionysopolis, 1st to 2nd century CE).

It is the second level that is most telling given the examples of the functions of a ἑταιρεία laid out by Gaius (quoted above). Two of them resonate with this stele — the provision of burial and religious ritual. The first is indicated by the funerary farewell, reinforced by the chytra, a funerary type of oinochoe, in the right-hand corner and probably the four-petalled rosette in the center of the pediment. But it is the second that is most intriguing here. We are battling the wear of the relief, and this mildly obfuscates precision in identification, even though there is elaborate attention to the presentation of a temple. The pairing, stance and gestures of the relief need to be noticed. Again care needs to be exercised. As Sue Blundell observes "... the language of gesture is not universal, but is shaped by specific social and cultural circumstances ..."[260] The right arm raised towards the left shoulder is common to both the male and female figure and given the difference in the way the himation falls for each (with the identical arm gesture) is directly related to "clothes clutching", or more accurately to clothes control and clothes display.[261] Both figures demonstrate the capacity to gesture and yet manage their free-falling clothing at the same time, a signal of proficiency and familiarity with public manifestation. This is further confirmed by the square stance and upright faces of both. The image being conveyed is of self-assurance and proper self-management in public view.

The distinction between the two figures however is manifest in the way the himation falls (amongst other features). The woman's clothing, regardless of the identical arm position yet reveals her chiton. In combination with the himation, the initial communication is one of modesty,[262] and restricted movement unlike the man who has no long undergarment.[263] In fact his leg is partially exposed, implying a freedom of mobility denied to the former. Compare the funerary stele to Attalos at Laodikeia where the still containment of the woman contrasts with the "leaning movement" of the man, both with right arm clothes managing gestures and the woman with a folded chiton showing

260 S. Blundell, "Clutching at Clothes", in *Women's Dress in the Ancient Greek World* edited by L. Llewellyn-Jones (Swansea: Classical Press of Wales, 2002), 144.

261 See J. Bremmer, "Walking, standing and sitting in ancient Greek culture," in *A Cultural History of Gesture: from antiquity to the present day* edited by J. Bremmer and H. Roodenburg (Cambridge: Cambridge University Press, 1991), 15–35. Compare however the similar gesture of the arm (with lighter, free-flowing garments) in a restricted female context at Herculaneum, interpreted by Glenys Davies as a "disguised barrier gesture" designed to protect and simultaneously display a woman's modesty and desirability: "The Case of the Large and Small Herculaneum Women," in *Women's Dress*, 237–8.

262 *Pudicitia*, modesty, often appears thus on Roman coins. See also the imposition of dress codes on women: D. Ogden, "Controlling women's dress: gynaikonomoi," in *Women's Dress*, 203–25.

263 Compare the generalised observation of Thorstein Veblen at the turn of the twentieth century: feminine clothing "hampers the wearer at every turn and incapacitates her for all useful exertion". *The Theory of the Leisure Class* [Hammondsworth: Penguin, 1994 {1899}], 171).

under her himation.[264] Similarly here, the confirmation of the woman's modesty requires a slight lifting of the himation so that it can be seen. But now, something new and striking is manifest, a chiton which is regularly dimpled in its form, suggesting a garment far beyond the usual — likely expensive and preserved for special occasions.[265] It certainly implies that we are dealing with a priestess rather than a wife.[266]

The other elements of the relief may inform this distinctive feature. Both heads of the figures appear to be covered, the woman's by a variety of veil and the man's by a turban. Whilst the facial section is worn, this seems to be accurate, accented in part by the broaching of the lower architrave by the man's headpiece. Both figures appear to be carrying something in their left hands, unlike for example the Attalos stele just mentioned, where the left arms hang limply down the side of the figures. Here the abrasion prevents accurate identification and we are left with a range of possibilities. If we take religious praxis as the probable guide here, then one source of information lies with the iconography of the gods in Colossae's coins. Items that hang from the hand are the situla (associated with Isis),[267] the cantharus (Dionysos),[268] a patera (Hygieia),[269] a bridle (Nemesis).[270] The catalogue could be compounded from *comparanda* evidence but the abraded features on the stele defeat further precision. That items are held is fairly clear; what those items are remains speculative.

We are left with no evidence for Glykon of family relationships or household structure. For him, his memory is dependent on the "society of friends", an association committed to religious pursuits and the fulfilment of funerary obligations, in this case with no reference to family, or even genealogy. It recognizes that, in some cases, urban life was disruptive of the strength of family ties, however extended they may have been, with the concomitant result that forms of communal ties other than blood-kinship advanced — including in the groups of Christ-followers — in the Lycus Valley. The Pythagorean philosopher, Callicratidas (3rd century BCE), nonetheless saw friendship as essential to household relationships — it filled out the constituents of a fam-

264 *I.Laodikeia Lykos* 92 (2nd century CE).

265 I am grateful for discussions with Professors Celal Şimşek and Bilal Söğüt of Pamukkale University on this intriguing stele.

266 *Contra* Elena Miranda in her commentary on *I.Mus Denizli* 113 who puzzles over the absence of naming of "the wife". On women's leadership in voluntary associations, see V. A. Alikin, "Women as Leaders in the Gatherings of Early Christian Communities: A Sociohistorical Analysis," in *Stones, Bones and the Sacred*, 222–8. See also the additional comments on women in associations (including cultic activities) in chapter 7.

267 *RPC online* 4.2.1903 temp.

268 *RPC online* 4.2.1887 temp.

269 *RPC online* 4.2.1902 temp. The patera is generally associated with sacrifice, so is not particularly emblematic of Hygieia.

270 *RPC online* 6.10829 temp.

ily.[271] Here, it appears to have been the most pertinent substitute. At least in the case of "the friends", there was a preparedness to advertise — in this case in a funerary stele with what appears as a significant, meaningful relief. As more evidence comes to light from Colossae, it is likely that other associations will surface; these would have added a competitive edge to such display. As Robert Garland reminded us, "Funerary monuments were designed to impress the passer-by …"[272]

h) Some of the values undergirding burial practice at Colossae have been addressed already concentrating on what the archaeological remains suggest. Here we need to explore what values are explicit or implicit in the funerary or memorializing inscriptions. Most of the inscriptions, but not all, privilege the male. Twenty-three men are named, with a further thirteen males named in genealogies. Twelve women are named, still a significant percentage relative to inscriptions generally. However, as we have seen, the majority of inscriptions are initiated by men. This gender asymmetry is compounded by an age asymmetry. No ages are given but the language of "daughter" (in i and iv), and "son" express or implied (in iii, vi, vii and x) without reference to their marriage suggests younger children. Children are clearly valued as under the care of their father and/or mother, at least until their marriage.

However, the epitaph of Tatianos (in xii) suggests that there were some occasions when circumstances pushed the funeral responsibilities wider. In the case of Hieikis(?), where one would normally expect her husband (Zenon, in xvi) to arrange the burial, this has fallen to the brother- and sister-in-laws.

Regardless of the variegations in relationships, relationships are both important and substantially circumscribed compared with the Upper Tembris valley, for example, and in the prohibition of any unauthorized corpse joining those interred. Thonemann suggests that a lengthier aggregation of corpses named in inscription is likely to be a difference between urban and rural, but the chamosarion for Tatarin and her mother Tatia and father Moschas (see i) is a village burial and yet follows the urban model. That of Zosas and Elpis (ii) also follows a civic typology. And some mausolea at both Hierapolis and Aphrodisias also named substantial lists of extended family/families. At Colossae, communality in death is rehearsed in the inscription in

271 τὸ ἑταιρικὸν εἶδος τᾶς φιλίας, συγκαταριθματέον ἐν τᾷ συμπλαρώσει τῷ οἴκῳ. Callicratidas *Oik. eudaim. apud* Stobaeus 4.28.16. I make several references to Callicratidas, not wishing to diminish the many other philosophers often drawn upon for comparison, but because he is often overlooked and his succinct phrasing (perhaps in part due to his anthologist, John Stobaeus) captures much of the "street philosophy" behind the *Haustafel*. I am indebted to Angela Standhartinger for this felicitous encapsulation. See "The Origin and Intention of the Household Code in the Letter to the Colossians," *JSNT* 79 (2000): 122.

272 R. Garland, *The Greek Way of Death* (Ithaca, NY: Cornell University Press, 1985), 109.

almost all cases, and we have no indication of whether the single burials of Dion son of Appas (see ix) and Tatianos (see xii) were buried in a larger aggregation, similar to the twin sarcophagi, each for a single corpse, at Aphrodisias as noted by Öğüş.[273]

The sacredness of the dead and of their relationship with the living is demonstrated not only in the aesthetics of temple and altar conveyed in the design of the tombstones, but especially in the articulation of penalties for disturbance of the grave. The positive affirmation of an ongoing relationship between the dead and the living comes in the "greetings to passersby" that reaches out from the grave to the wider community via the inscription (see ii, ix, x, xiii).[274] But there are also hints at the values informing the relationships and their conduct in some of the wording. It seems that there was a value attached to preparation for one's burial (and dependants) while one was alive, either in the formal procedures necessary to secure a burial place, ritual and record — here the language of ζωσεῖν is critical (see iii) — or by provision in a will (see viii). I have suggested that the language of "honor" (ἐτείμησαν) as used to convey the actions of "the friends" for Glykon (see xiii) may be specific to the nature of that relationship (likely an association) akin to that of the honor bestowed by *Boulê* and *Dêmos* on Crispinus (see v), or by the village of Kilaraza for Zosas (ii). For family relatives the emphasis is on remembrance, which is conveyed in the designation of the *bomos* as τὸ μνημεῖον (see iv, v, x, xi, xiv?, xvi cf ii), a concretization of the motivation found elsewhere of μνείας χάριν.[275]

The role of civic institutions in the epitaphs, whether the treasuries to which penalties are to be paid or the political bodies overseeing memorializations, is a clear indication that the manner of commemoration of those who have died fell in with the values promoted by those bodies: remembrance (especially of names and the continuity of genealogical succession, sometimes of occupation); an adherence to convention; communality; family relationships (broadly defined); obedience to civic and legal regulations; the upholding of honor; the sanctified dealing with the dead including those who fell outside the usual immediacy of family ties; and perhaps above all, the monumental and inscriptional iteration of these values.

273 *I.Aphrodisias 2007* 13.602, 603.

274 On the attraction and commissioning of others in the naming of "passersby," see D. E. Lavigne, "The Authority of Archaic Greek Epigram," in *The Materiality of Text — Placement, Perception, and Presence of Inscribed Texts in Classical Antiquity* edited by A. Petrovic, I. Petrovic and E. Thomas (Leiden: Brill, 2019), 174.

275 The expression is ubiquitous in Asian epitaphs, but awaits attestation at Colossae. Compare *I.Hierapolis Judeich* 205, *I.Laodikeia Lykos* 75, 76 as nearby examples.

This survey of funerary memorials, directed towards a glimpse of at least some family relationships and household structures in the city and territory of Colossae, secures no more than that — a glimpse — and one which has relied on status and a measure of wealth for its notice. It is circumscribed by limited evidence and by the methodological difficulties of transferring results from epitaphs to actual social organization. But it is nonetheless suggestive. It certainly confirms Peter Thonemann's observation based on Akmoneia, Eumeneia, Apameia and the Upper Tembris Valley, that "restrictive 'nuclear' burial customs did not fully reflect the reality of family and other affective relations,"[276] including, I would suggest, those of non-consanguinous ties.[277] Indeed, with Dale Martin, one wonders whether "nuclear family" is a classification of much heuristic value in seeking to comprehend societal organization at Colossae and elsewhere in Asia. This in no way corrodes the importance of "family" to the Colossians (and others) in the first century but it suggests we are better advised to speak of "households" rather than infect ancient families with assumptions drawn from modern constructions.

The Colossian household code and social realities

I want here to draw out some implications from the above investigation for the contentious, so-called *Haustafel* of Col 3:18–4:1. I have no wish to rehearse the meticulous surgery to which this section of the letter has been subjected.[278] It will be helpful to lay out the basic structure of the household as the writer presents it in the letter.

276 Thonemann, "Households and Families," 127.

277 W. Scheidel, "Epigraphy and Demography: birth, marriage, family, and death," in *Epigraphy and the Historical Sciences* edited by J. K. Davies and J. J. Wilkes (Oxford: Oxford University Press, 2012), 123.

278 For various analyses that incorporate literary and, recently, some epigraphical insights, see D. Lührmann, "Neutestamentliche Haustafeln und antike Ökonomie," *NTS* 27 (1980): 83–97; P. Fiedler, "Haustafel," *RAC* 13 (1986): 1063–73; D. Balch, "Neopythagorean Moralists and the New Testament Household Codes," *ANRW* II.26.1 (1992): 380–411; Standhartinger, "Origin and Intention," 117–30; M. Y. MacDonald, "Slavery, Sexuality and House Churches: a Reassessment of Colossians 3.18–4.1 in Light of New Research on the Roman Family," *NTS* 53 (2007): 94–113; D. Hellholm, "Die Gattung Haustafel im Kolosser- und Epheserbrief: Ihre Position innerhalb der Paränese-Abschnitte und ihr Hintergrund in der spätantiken Gesellschaft," in *Kolosser-Studien* edited by P. Müller (Göttingen: Neukirchener, 2009), 102–28; H. Löhr, "The Early Christian Household Code in the Light of Epigraphic Evidence," in *Epigraphical Evidence Illustrating Paul's Letter to the Colossians* edited by J. Verheyden, M. Öhler and T. Corsten (WUNT 411; Tübingen: Mohr Siebeck, 2018), 199–214.

From the lesser	To the greater
18. Αἱ γυναῖκες, ὑποτάσσεσθε τοῖς ἀνδράσιν ὡς ἀνῆκεν ἐν κυρίῳ.	19. Οἱ ἄνδρες, ἀγαπᾶτε τὰς γυναῖκας καὶ μὴ πικραίνεσθε πρὸς αὐτάς.
20. Τὰ τέκνα, ὑπακούετε τοῖς γονεῦσιν κατὰ πάντα, τοῦτο γὰρ εὐάρεστόν ἐστιν ἐν κυρίῳ.	21. Οἱ πατέρες, μὴ ἐρεθίζετε τὰ τέκνα ὑμῶν, ἵνα μὴ ἀθυμῶσιν.
22–25. Οἱ δοῦλοι, ὑπακούετε κατὰ πάντα τοῖς κατὰ σάρκα κυρίοις, μὴ ἐν ὀφθαλμοδουλίᾳ ὡς ἀνθρωπάρεσκοι, ἀλλ᾽ ἐν ἁπλότητι καρδίας φοβούμενοι τὸν κύριον. ὃ ἐὰν ποιῆτε, ἐκ ψυχῆς ἐργάζεσθε ὡς τῷ κυρίῳ καὶ οὐκ ἀνθρώποις, εἰδότες ὅτι ἀπὸ κυρίου ἀπολήμψεσθε τὴν ἀνταπόδοσιν τῆς κληρονομίας. Τῷ κυρίῳ Χριστῷ δουλεύετε· ὁ γὰρ ἀδικῶν κομίσεται ὃ ἠδίκησεν, καὶ οὐκ ἔστιν προσωπολημψία.	4:1. Οἱ κύριοι, τὸ δίκαιον καὶ τὴν ἰσότητα τοῖς δούλοις παρέχεσθε, εἰδότες ὅτι καὶ ὑμεῖς ἔχετε κύριον ἐν οὐρανῷ.

From the outset there is a need for caution. With a literary text that mentions family relations, as in the so-called *Haustafel* of Col 3:18–4:1, there is always the danger that we consider that such households actually existed on the ground, or even that they were sufficiently proximate in configuration and, with a little prod from the pen of "Paul", could be socialized into conformity. The number of textual variants that seek to imprint the code further as a paradigmatic Christian template (not to mention the thorough-going baptism by the Ephesian epistolographer: Eph 5:22–6:9),[279] shows that the (Colossian) original did not sufficiently comply with such an agenda.[280] Here epistolary rhetoric is liable to be pushed into historical data, most notably in the unwarranted attempt to marry off Apphia to Philemon and conceive Archippos as their son (Phmn 1–2)![281] The absence of any reference to Philemon's household in the Letter

279 Assimilation of the text of Colossians to the Ephesians household code is seen in various manuscripts of Col 3:18 = Eph 5:22 (addition of ἰδιοῖς before ἀνδράσιν), Col 3:21 = Eph 6:4 (παροργίζετε for ἐρεθίζετε), Col 3:22 = Eph 6:5 (omission of κατὰ πάντα), Col 3:22 = Eph 6:6 (? Θεόν for κυρίον), Col 3:23 = Eph 6:7 (addition of δουλεύοντες after κυρίῳ), Col 3:25 = Eph 6:9 (addition of παρὰ τῷ Θεῷ after προσωπολημψία, possibly also informed by Rom 2:11).

280 v. 18 ὑμῶν after ἀνδράσιν (D*, F, G, it, sy$^{p, h**}$) and v. 19 after γυναῖκας (C2, D*, F, G, it *et al.*; or ἑαυτῶν 1175 cf ℵ, 075); v. 23 an emphatic (καὶ) πὰν ὅ (τι) for ὅ ἐάν (ℵ^{2}, D^{2}, Ψ, 104, 326 *et al.*); emphatic refinement τοῦ κυρίου ἡμῶν Ἰησοῦ Χριστοῦ, ᾧ before δουλεύετε (F, G). See also the previous note.

281 See, among a number, R. McL. Wilson, *A Critical and Exegetical Commentary on Colossians and Philemon* (London: T & T Clark, 2005), 319–20, 333–4. Roy Jeal repudiates such a construct, further proposing that the rhetoric of Philemon is not familial but fraternal; *Exploring*

to the Colossians is striking and has been taken as implying multiple "Jesus households" across the city.[282]

At the same time, we must recognize that we are asking questions of two different genres of writing. Even at a curt seventy-four words, the Colossians' pericope is a third as long again as the longest funerary inscription extant from Colossae's necropolis (see i above),[283] though the unusually heavy weighting given to slaves forces the disparity. Epitaphs and epistles make for unusual bed-fellows and are rarely found together (Egyptian papyrological linings in caskets notwithstanding!). Finally, there is the cold, hard data of life expectancy that intrudes on the easy assumption that the three pairs of relationships often existed, or existed for long.

Trevor Anderson's osteo-archaeological analysis of the skeletal remains in Tomb 163d at Hierapolis revealed that the eldest was aged no more than forty-five years and three skeletal remains, of the twenty-five that were closely examined, were aged less than three years old.[284] Life was short and fraught, even for those who could afford a sizeable mausoleum.[285] When low life-expectancy is combined with the likely median age of paternity (37–38 years in Egypt),[286] then not only are we confronting the reality of many family units that had to negotiate an absent father, but, when fathers do survive beyond the average life expectancy, it is likely because their longevity has been nourished by a steady food supply and non-menial labor. Even so, according to Walter Scheidel, "a substantial share of all children would have been fathered by men in their forties and fifties,"[287] with the implication that before reaching their majority (whether the Greek twenty-year-old or the Roman twenty-five), children in most cases would have been fatherless. The danger in the effort to interpret the *Haustafel* as indicating a real household is that it inherently privileges wealth and status: "The households structured according to this form

---

Philemon: Freedom, Brotherhood, and Partnership in the New Society (Atlanta, GA: SBL Press, 2015), 40.

282 So, M. Trainor, *Epaphras: Paul's Educator at Colossae* (Collegeville, MI: Liturgical Press, 2008), 59, 78, 79.

283 Its length is dwarfed however by material with which it is often compared, for example, the literary codes ascribed to Ps-Charondas and Ps-Zaleukos (*apud* Stobaeus *Anth*. 4.2.24, 19 respectively) or the epigraphical regulations of a Dionysian association (*TAM* V,3.1539). On this Philadelphian inscription, see S. C. Barton and G. H. R. Horsley, "A Hellenistic Cult Group and the New Testament Churches," *JAC* 24 (1981): 7–41.

284 Anderson, "Osteo-archaeologcal investigation," 473–93. Since Anderson's research was completed, it has been shown that there was a succession of ownership so that the remains reflect at least two periods of occupation. Nonetheless the age identifications remain pertinent in general identification.

285 See the touching memorialization of the premature death of a husband and father in *IG* XII,7 396.

286 Bagnall and Frier, *Demography of Roman Egypt*, 146.

287 W. Scheidel, "The demographic background," in *Growing Up Fatherless in Antiquity* edited by S. R. Hübner and D. M. Ratzan (Cambridge: Cambridge University Press, 2009), 40.

were upper-class."[288] Here we are reminded to interrogate the funerary evidence we have examined, evidence that is produced by wealth and standing, even including the Eleinokaprian epitaph. The further step of turning the *Haustafel* into a prescriptive ethical code likewise becomes a morality justifying and fostering such wealth and status.[289] It is made the more insidious by being set into a cosmic frame of thanksgiving (Col 3:17, 4:2 cf 1:12), which throws back to the Christological hymn in order to fill out the identity of "the Lord (Christ)" (Col 3:18, 20, 23, 24).[290]

The correlated elements of a family that are found in this code in the Letter to the Colossians are husband-wife, father-children, master-slave, albeit with succinct advice delivered to both constituents of each pair in an *a fortiori* structure. The template structure is a common-place and, rather than reflect the dominance of the nuclear family, is nothing more than a triadic heuristic formula.[291] Even at this skeletal level, it is clear that there is a paterfamilial assumption governing a simple, confined unit — the easy lexical slide from the κύριος (Christ, 3:[17], 18, 20, 23, 24, 4:1) to κύριοι (3:22, 4:1, masters, owners) is enough to demonstrate that authority. There is no mitigation effected by noting that the κύριοι have a "master in heaven" (κύριον ἐν οὐρανῷ) — this is no more than the relationship of free males to deities,[292] the cosmological undergirding of the household code, as we have seen formulated by Theon of Smyrna.[293]

The third century (BCE) Pythagorean exponent, Callicratidas, narrowed the confluence more tightly still. Just as the universe organized dissimilar elements by reference to one particular thing (he went on to name "god" here), so "a family is … organized in view of the best thing, namely, the father of the

---

288 J. E. Stambaugh and D. L. Balch, *The New Testament in Its Social Environment* (Philadelphia: Westminster Press, 1986), 123. I disagree, however, with their assertion that most lower-class households did not include slaves. Poverty, according to the Roman satirist, Martial, was defined by having, *inter alia*, one elderly slave: Martial *Ep.* 11.32. See generally, S. Friesen, "Poverty in Pauline Studies: Beyond the So-called New Consensus," *JSNT* 26 (2004): 341, 353–4.

289 This is the fundamental problem of, for example, Hellholm's efforts to see the *Haustafel* as both descriptive and prescriptive, "to be implemented against existing disparities in the family structure" ("Der Gattung Haustafel," 128).

290 Margaret MacDonald is correct in recognizing an independent unit in Col 3:18–4:1 (the syntactical arrangement is different from the rest of the letter) but even the loose insertion is informed by its surrounds, and, I would argue, deliberately so in terms of reference to a cosmological and societal setting. See MacDonald, *Colossians, Ephesians* (Collegeville, MI: Liturgical Press, 2008), 152–3.

291 Aristotle *Pol.* 1.1253b, Seneca *Ep.* 94.1, Dionysos of Halicarnassos *Ant. rom.* 2.25.4–26.4). For an example of repeated usage of triads, see Callicratidas, Περὶ οἴκου εὐδαιμονίας *passim*.

292 At the sanctuary of Apollo Lairbenos, near to Colossae, one thus far unpublished inscription speaks of "the Lord Larmenos"; cf *IGBulg* 1,2 370 (Anchialos, 2nd century CE). Compare also the Lord Asklepios at Scretisca (*IGBulg* 4.2018, 2nd century CE). Manumission inscriptions at sanctuaries are always controlled by the masters (sometimes free women) who are dutifully recorded as occupying the prominent, proprietorial position within the sacred transaction.

293 See chapter 5.

family."[294] There is no excavation of Pythagorean philosophy by the writer of the Letter to the Colossians; rather this is one instance of the philosophical pervasiveness of the ideas that provided an infecting cognitive atmosphere for the schema borrowed into the letter.[295] However, as much as a centripetal, paterfamilial assumption does govern most (but not all) of the epitaphs, in the Colossians household code there is a definite leaning to the Roman absorption and implementation of such philosophically defended codes.

We have already noted the suspicion that would have been cast over Philemon's credentials as a competent master by Onesimos's flight from servitude.[296] There was a recognition that, for all that such a household code might provide a model, the reality of family relations might be at considerable distance, not just in terms of structure but in terms of behavior. Athenaeus, writing at the end of the second century (CE) has one of his characters lament "men of today, who pretend to sacrifice to the gods and call together their friends and intimates, yet curse their children, quarrel with their wives and drive their slaves to tears."[297] Tyrannical perversion of the code was known also to Callicratidas to whom we have turned already. Of particular note here are the reflections of Dionysos of Halicarnassos, who, though Greek, was concerned to extol the benefits of Roman rule in regard to the household. The severity of the Roman male's control of his wife and children was deemed by him to afford a greater stability to the household than the laxity which pertained in Greek law and practice.[298] But Rome had learned all too well from slave revolts (most famously, that of Spartacus) that incentives and even-handed treatment of slaves actually helped stability and productivity.[299] Critical here is that the *a fortiori* structure of the Colossian code is completely in line with Roman sheeting home of responsibility to the *paterfamilias* for the cohesiveness of the household. In this sense, the code functions as a promotion of *Romanitas*, given that the power of the father was less about paternal authority than being the distinctive expression of Rome.[300] This concern was at the forefront of Augustus's stabilization of the

294 ἕν τι τὸ ἄριστον συντέτακται, τὸν οἰκοδεσπόταν. Callicratidas *Oik. eudaim. apud* Stobaeus 4.28.16. On Callicratidas's handling of the topos of household management, see Dorota M. Dutsch, *Pythagorean Women Philosophers: Between Belief and Suspicion* (Oxford: Oxford University Press, 2020), 145–8.

295 So J. D. G. Dunn, *The Epistles to the Colossians and to Philemon* (Grand Rapids, MN: Eerdmans, 1996), 347.

296 See chapter 11.

297 οἱ δὲ νῦν προσποιούμενοι θεοῖς θύειν καὶ συγκαλοῦντες ἐπὶ τὴν θυσίαν τοὺς φίλους καὶ τοὺς οἰκειοτάτους καταρῶνται μὲν τοῖς τέκνοις, λοιδοροῦνται δὲ ταῖς γυναιξί, κλαυθμυρίζουσιν τοὺς οἰκέτας … Athenaeus *Deip.* 8.363f–364a (trans. Gulick, slightly adjusted); see also 10.420e.

298 Dionysos of Halicarnassos *Ant. rom.* 2.25.

299 Varro *Rust.* 1.17.5–7.

300 See Gaius *Inst.* 1.55 = Justinian *Inst.* 9.2 "scarcely any other men have over their sons a power such as we have." (*nulli enim alii sunt homines qui talem in liberos habeant potestatem qualem nos habemus*).

Empire after the civil wars, and was given philosophical undergirding by one of his advisers, Arius Didymus.[301] Again, we are confronted with the difficulty of discerning the writer's purpose behind the *Haustafel*'s inclusion.

The uncomplicated heuristic structure of the household code in the letter might have warranted the classification "nuclear" (albeit strictly hierarchical), were it not for the presence of slaves, who in this letter assume an importance that precludes them being described as a mere augmentation of a more fundamental organization.[302] Hermut Löhr rightly points out that the structural constraint ill-fitted the realities of most families in the early communities of Christ-followers and was soon to require in Christian reflection a loosening or broadening to include older and younger men and women, older and younger widows and grandchildren (1 Tim 5:1–16; Tit 2:2–6).[303] But there were no embellishing differentiations of slaves (such as the recognition of the hierarchicalization of slaves we have noted in the previous chapter). Slaves remained an amorphous engine-room of labor. He is also correct, I think, to shift comparative analysis from the search for shared vocabulary in the household codes, to that of structural elements and the praxis of general virtues operating within those elements.[304] There is a danger in lexicographical minutiae of surreptitiously immunizing Christian formulations from the world in which they emerged by adopting a methodology that will *a priori* guarantee the desired hermetic seal (even if broadened to include a filter of Hellenistic Judaism).[305]

Here the comparisons with literary and epigraphical evidence have yielded similarities in the tripartite breakdowns and the *a fortiori* patterns of address. Further, the cosmological undergirding and the correlation with the proper functioning of society (note Col 4:5–6 following on the heels of the *Haustafel*) are standard rationales attached to the schema. As Callicratidas succinctly put it, "A household and a city are a reflection (of each other) according to the pattern of the polity of the cosmos."[306] However, it is precisely such stylized similarities that urge caution in transferring the structure to actual households. In any case, as we have seen briefly with Callicratidas' exploration of the topos of

---

301 Arius Didymus *apud* Stobaeus 2.7.26.

302 Varying the attempt to salvage something of the "nuclear" by Hermut Löhr, "Early Christian Household Codes," 205. On the importance of slavery in the Colossians' household code, see J. E. Crouch, *The Origins and Intention of the Colossian Haustafel* (Göttingen: Vandenhoeck & Ruprecht, 1972), J. A. Glancy, *Slavery in Early Christianity* (Oxford: Oxford University Press, 2002), 149–50. The bedeviling issue is whether the code addresses specific issues among the Christ-followers or not.

303 Löhr, "Early Christian Household Codes," 205.

304 Löhr, "Early Chrisitan Household Codes," 201–7.

305 So M. Barth and H. Blanke, *Colossians* (New York: Doubleday, 1994), 473–4; Hellholm "Der Gattung Haustafel," 127.

306 Μίμαμα δ' οἶκος καὶ πόλις καττὰν ἀναλογίαν τᾶς τῷ κόσμῳ διοικήσεως. Callicratidas *Oik. eudaim. apud* Stobaeus 4.28.16.

the household, the boundaries of "family" were extended to included relatives and friends. These were all included in the οἶκος.

This raises the intra-textual difficulty: no relationship of actual persons in the Letter to the Colossians or to Philemon falls into the ordered structure of the household laid out in the passage.[307] Indeed, if the named household at Laodikeia is headed by Nympha (not Nymphas),[308] there is a household at odds with the authority structures of the household code itself, yet quite able to be called οἶκος-ἐκκλησία (Col 4:15).[309] The functioning of Nympha's house appears closer to the leadership model displayed by Tatia in the Colossian village of Eleinokapria (see i) and c) above) and by Ammiane who sought a memorial for her son Herakleon (see vii) and c) above), although it must be admitted that husbands are not absent from the memories managed in these two records. Nonetheless, the epitaph where the father-husband and grave-provider, Karpon, has his own express, personal instructions inscribed — βούλομαι (see v) above) — better fits the privileging of the ἀνήρ in the household code of the Letter to the Colossians. The absence of uniformity in initiative and arrangements in the few epitaphs from Colossae that we have, shows however that there was no inflexible pattern on/in the ground. Even at this point, there may be some cause to demur on whether the Christian *Haustafeln* were designed to address "the general social structure of the communities" receiving the apostolic epistles,[310] or whether there were other purposes afoot.

The relationships that are mentioned in the two Second Testament Letters do find proximate echoes in Colossae's remembered dead, but not in line with the household code. Tatianos, whose burial is organized by his younger relatives (see xii) and f) above) more closely reflects the relationship between Mark and Barnabas (Col 4:10), especially given the later hagiographical tradition that had Mark perform the burial obligations for Barnabas (on the island of Cyprus).[311] The relational term used for the Mark-Barnabas connection, namely ἀνεψιός, usually taken as "nephew", often occurs as a synonym of συγγενής.[312] The important relationships in the letters, accented in the language of ἀδελφός (Phmn 1, 20, Col 1:1, 4:7, 9, 15) and even capable of including a slave (Phmn 16) cohere more closely with Glykon's "society of friends" (see xiii) and g) above) than the family, household envisaged in Col 3:18–4:1. The closest we come to the paterfamilial form listed in the Letter to the Colossians (where the father

307 So, Standhartinger, "Origin and Intention," 125.

308 See chapter 4.

309 See M. Y. MacDonald, "Can Nympha Rule This House? The Role of Domesticity in Colossians," in *Rhetoric and Reality in Early Christianities* edited by W. Braun (Waterloo, ON: Wilfred Laurier University Press, 2005), 99–120.

310 Löhr at this point ("Early Christian Household Codes," 201) makes an assumption that has yet to be demonstrated.

311 *Acts of Barnabas* 24.

312 *IGR* 4.617, ll. 8–9 (Temenouthyrai, 247–249 CE), *I.Perge* 317, ll. 13–14 (3rd century CE), *I.Arykanda* 50, col 2, l. 4 (138 CE).

controls the marital, paternal and servile relationships) is in one metaphor Paul uses of his own relationship with Onesimos — that is where Onesimos is called τέκνον, child, to the πατήρ, the father Paul (Phmn 10). But there is no mention of mother or wife even in metaphorical terms. Here we have trodden on the grave of Markos and Dionyseios (see iii) above) where wife and mother are glaringly absent.

The most notable contrast between the glimpse of family relationships and household structures provided by Colossae's epitaphs and the Pauline Letter's own apparent vision, is that the invisible slaves of funerary remembrance are made highly prominent in the written text. The absence in the letters of any genealogical notation (apart from that of Jesus to God the father: Col 1:3, 12–13, 3:17) is countermanded in the epitaphs and memorials by its high visibility. So the epitaphs (and other epigraphic genres) favor inscribing genealogical relationships far above those of slaves. Conversely, slaves dominate both Second Testament Letters. This double-edged contrast presents a conundrum. Some, from James Crouch to Ulrich Huttner, have sought to provide an intertextual explanation. They explain the *Haustafel* emphasis as arising from slave-owners' concerns about the supposed lifting of slave status in the Letter to Philemon. The figure personifying this elevation is Onesimos, not only because he is named "brother" in the Letter to Philemon, but because, on one interpretation, he is the same person as the Onesimos of Colossians (Col 4:9). In that letter, Onesimos seems to be exercising considerable influence within the group of Christ-followers,[313] thereby imaging a different role for slaves in the household of Christ-followers from the household of general social and familial operations, exactly the sort of inversion that drew the satirical barbs if not the ire of Romans.[314] The tension within the letter itself is that the embrace of Christ includes slave and free (δοῦλος ἐλεύθερος, Col 3:11) but, according to the *Haustafel*, this "justice and equity" (τὸ δίκαιον καὶ τὴν ἰσότητα, Col 4:1) did not promote manumission. Such "inherited testamentary disposition" (ἡ ἀνταπόδοσις τῆς κληρονομίας Col 3:24)[315] was deferred to another age. The slave is accorded membership of the Christ-followers and recognition in the household, but not freedom or authority.

Whatever tensions might be seen in that intertextual combination are even more problematic for women, since they are elided from the list of embrace in Col 3:11 but specified for (marital) subjection in the *Haustafel* (Col 3:18). Peter Thonemann had seen in Akmoneia, the demise of a measure of women's

313 Huttner, *Christianity in the Lycus Valley*, 145.

314 See Martial *Ep.* 11.70 cf *Ep.* 2.18.

315 The notion of ἀνταπόδοσις as reward rather than retribution (Ps 69:9, Isa 34:8 *et al*) fits more securely in a Greek background (*IG* I³ 66, *CIG* 3088). The legal arrangements implied by the use of κληρονομία clearly recognize that a will (or even a treaty) is in operation (see *I.Labrandos* 47, *I.Ephesos* 3009), something only a κυρίος could execute. So, an image from mundane jurisprudence is used to imagine a future, heavenly release.

autonomy that had been expressed through a formal body, perhaps an association, of "Greek and Roman women." A correction had occurred to a mistaken, parochial apprehension about the elevation of Livia in Rome — against distant perceptions, there was to be no general application derived therefrom.[316] There may here be a Colossian counterpart to this diminution as well, now only inferred through the Second Testament Letter in the missing piece of the "race code" in Col 3:11.

These correlations between epistles and epitaphs are of course somewhat manufactured, extracting snatches from two different genres of material. But they serve an important purpose of demonstrating that the recipients and hearers of the Letters to Philemon and to the Colossians knew a variety of family relationships and household structures, many of which would have provided an ill-fit with the household code of Colossians, *if that were the intent.* And this continues to abut the highly contested issue of the purpose(s) of the household code in Colossians.

We have seen already the trigonometric correlation and mutual reinforcement of cosmos, household and state. In the ancient, conventional mind-set informed and impressed by philosophical reflection, these three facets could not be separated. Accordingly, if the writer to the Colossians saw fit to portray the Christ in high-blown cosmological terms (Col 1:12–20), whatever may have been the privileging of Christ above other cosmic claimants for influence over the lives of human beings, then, almost inevitably, the implication for the standardized human household *had* to be stated. Andrew Lincoln is correct, in my view, in tying the two pericopae together.[317] However, this is not to isolate the teaching of the letter from so-called speculative, esoteric wisdom. After all, such an accusation could easily be fired at Theon of Smyrna, even in his handbook teachings. Rather such cosmic wisdom was expected to influence and have implications for the harmony of human relationships in both the household and its extension, the (*polis*) state. In this sense, if the writer had omitted such a paraenetic complement, the cosmology of the Christ-hymn would have been assailable as deficient and fracturing of the cosmic harmony that must include this mundane reality. The sheer departure in syntax and lexicography in much of the *Haustafel* from that pertaining in the rest of the letter suggests that the writer was well-aware of the necessity to say something about the household but adopted a pre-baked, popular source that then received some "in the Lord" icing on the cake, and a Christian extension of the gnomic maxim of verse 25: "for the rule-breaker will reap the returns for the infraction …".[318]

316 P. Thonemann, "The Women of Akmoneia," *JRS* 100 (2010): 178.

317 A. T. Lincoln, "The Household Code and Wisdom mode of Colossians," *JSNT* 74 (1999): 93–112.

318 On the distinctiveness of the code in language and syntax form the rest of the letter, see Standhartinger, "Origin and Intention," 123; on the standard proverbial form at the beginning of verse 25, see P. Foster, *Colossians* (London: Bloomsbury, 2016), 392–3.

Disruption of the conventional household was precisely the charge leveled against Christ-followers by Celsus at the end of the second century.[319] The "inverted household codes" of Mark and Matthew (Mk 10:1–31, Matt 19:1–29)[320] show not only that Celsus may have had some justification in his vehement denunciation but that an alternative to the paraenetic template of the Letter to the Colossians was possible. One Asian hagiography, the *Life of St Thecla*, demonstrates that a counter-household praxis remained alive in the region, ironically grounded in the imitation of Paul.[321] Thecla's determined choice for a celibate, short hair, cross-dressing, itinerant ministry is portrayed as a deliberate undermining of the conventions of the household. The grief at her decision is given precisely the tripartite embellishment that we see upheld in this Pauline Letter — Thamyris, her betrothed "that he had lost his wife"; Theocleia, her widowed mother, "that she had lost her child"; and the slave-maids "that they had lost their mistress", all summed up as a "great compounding of grief in the household."[322]

The writer to the Colossians, for all that a competitive positioning of the Christ-followers' distinctive identity in the Colossian environment is a major concern, has made a fateful decision. The adoption of the code, even with its Christian embellishment, yet is a measure of accommodation to the surrounding society, one with decided leanings in its ruling class and dominant ideology to an imitation of *Romanitas*. Indeed, the Colossians' form of the code engages in its own mystification of the pragmatic purpose of a well-functioning household, namely, the assurance, if not the increase, of prosperity. David Balch overlooked the Markan/Matthean critique of wealth in the evangelists' dismantling of the household code when he thought that the Second Testament had omitted discussion of this aspect.[323] This makes the silence in Colossians extremely important for discussion. Here the accent on slave performance is critical, for slave labor was the fuel of household wealth.[324] A number of permutations of the household code substitute a general mention of property for the

---

319 *apud* Origen *Cels*. 3.44.

320 The classification was formulated by Warren Carter (for Matthew): *Households and Discipleship: A Study of Matthew 19–20* (Sheffield: Sheffield Academic Press, 1994), 216. It has garnered considerable support. See W. D. Davies and D. C. Allison, *Matthew 19–28* (London: T & T Clark, 1997), 1–2.

321 An ivory relief of St Thecla, in standing orant position, has been uncovered at Laodikeia (Temple A, later refashioned as a Byzantine church) and has been dated to the late 5th – early 6th century. See C. Şimşek and B. Yener, "An Ivory Relief of Saint Thecla," *Adalya* 13 (2010): 321–34.

322 Καὶ οἱ μὲν ἔκλαιον δεινῶς, Θάμυρις μὲν γυναικὸς ἀστοχῶν, Θεοκλεία δὲ τέκνον, αἱ δὲ παιδίσκαι κυρίας· πολλὴ οὖν σύγχυσις ἦν ἐν τῷ οἴκῳ πένθους. *AThecla* 10.6–8.

323 D. Balch, "Household Codes," in *Greco-Roman Literature and the New Testament* edited by D. E. Aune (Atlanta, GA: Scholars Press, 1988), 45.

324 I develop this aspect at length in "The Struggle for Paul in the Context of Empire: Mark as a Deutero-Pauline Text," in *Paul and Mark in Comparison: Authors at the Beginning of Christianity* edited by D. C. Sim and O. Wischmeyer (Berlin/New York: de Gruyter, 2014), 557–87.

explicit address of slaves.[325] After all, slaves were property (note Rev 18:12–17 where slaves [σώματα] are included within an exhibition of merchants' goods). Augustus's adviser, Arius Didymus, retained slaves in his code and simply made a quaternity of elements by adding prosperity; the role of a household leader was to manage "the arts of fatherhood, marriage, being a master and money-making."[326] The wealth and status of Colossae's extant funerary remains, if not the actual familial relationships, are here, in the letter, given an ideological support and economic mechanism. That is, slaves are missing from the funerary epigraphical record to date, but they were the ones who made possible that record.

The interconnection between the household and the surrounding society which is so much part of the microcosm (house) to macrocosm (state) of commonplace philosophical thought finds an echo in the Letter to the Colossians within a few verses of the conclusion to the *Haustafel*. Col 4:5 calls for pursuing a path of wisdom among or in regard to those outside the Christ-followers (Ἐν σοφίᾳ περιπατεῖτε πρὸς τοὺς ἔξω). Commentators frequently give this a missionary stance as if corporatizing "Paul's" own desire for evangelistic opportunity (Col 4: 2–4).[327] Indeed, the movement from the *Haustafel* to mission is seen as abrupt, marking a departure into a new line of thought.[328] However, the language of driving a commercial agreement given the opportune moment (τὸν καιρὸν ἐξαγοραζόμενοι) is telling, allowing the concern for a prosperous co-existence in Colossian society to emerge. It is used of the negotiation of the contract for tax-collection in the famous *Lex Portorii Asiae*, the Customs Law of Asia.[329] Here the gnomic wisdom of the household code provides the conventional storehouse necessary for gracious, seasoned speech (Col 4:6), an answer to perhaps-suspicious onlookers perturbed at what Christ-followers might mean to the fundamental rubrics of wider society and the state. And with "Paul" providing both the code and the apologetic exemplar (in Col 4:2–4), there can be no impugning of its novel inclusion in a letter. The writer to the Colossians has made a decision that the Christian message needed to be presented in terms of the best conceptual basis for the strengthening of the household values that were held dear and promoted, especially by those holding power and influence, in the Greco-Roman world. In this sense, the presence of the *Haustafel* in the letter (especially if the letter escapes to those outside, at least orally, as Col 4:6 encourages) is a reassurance that the Christians

325 Horace *Ode* 3.6.

326 Ταύτης δὲ τὸ μὲν εἶναι πατρικόν, τὸ δὲ γαμικόν, τὸ δὲ δεσποτικόν, τὸ δὲ χρηματιστικόν. Arius Didymus *apud* Stobaeus 2.7.26 (trans. Balch); compare also Philodemos *Vit.* 9.38.5–9, 17–19.

327 S. McKnight, *The Letter to the Colossians* (Grand Rapids, MN: Eerdmans, 2018), 367–80.

328 So McKnight, *Colossians*, 367–8.

329 *SEG* 39.1180, ll. 124, 125–6 (Ephesos, 62 CE). See also *SEG* 24.1095, ll. 29–30 (Histria, late 3rd to early 2nd century BCE) where a certain Agathocles is honored for, *inter alia*, his fit negotiations (κατὰ τρόπον ἐξαγοράζειν) regarding farms and harvests crucial for the livelihood of the city.

are not the manic subversives that some have alleged. Conflict with surrounding values and divine conceptions has been discerned in the letter as we have seen. But these may be little more than the necessary strategy to strengthen the boundaries of the identity of Colossian Christ-followers especially as they negotiate their way in the city and its territory. And, of course, as they armed themselves with this piece of wisdom for the household, it came to be imbibed as a personal, not just presented as a public, code. But this, in my understanding, was a consequence of, not a motivation for, the code's original incorporation into the letter.[330]

The visit to the Colossian necropolis has yielded a small harvest. But the funerary evidence has allowed us to explore not only the values imbuing the mechanics of dealing with death, but have found a hint of the commercial realities required to fund the display of adherence to those values. Moreover, Colossae has been found to give corroborative evidence for analyses that have concentrated on more voluminous returns elsewhere both archaeological and epigraphical. Here "family" has been found to be both singularly valued and multiply constructed. This has enabled a detailed interaction with both the household code in the Letter to the Colossians and the various relationship ties that are found in the two Second Testament Letters associated with the city.

330 Here I am in substantial agreement with Standhartinger, "Origin and Intention," 126–30, though she does not explore the significance of Col 4:5–6 following so closely on the inserted code.

Afterword

Colossae's life remains substantially hidden from us. The same is true of all ancient sites where the rhythms of human interactions can only ever be reconstructed with a contribution from our own contemporary imagination. However, as the material life of an ancient site is increasingly revealed and as new questions and methodologies drive our inquiry even into pre-existing artifacts and their contexts, the control on that imaginative reconstruction gives a growing measure of confidence that there is a proximity between the interpretation and the reality. This study has shown that when the existing materiality of Colossae is taken seriously, new understandings can be made that diminish the heavy demand on a small aggregation of literary sources that has previously been the operating epistemology. Of course, an increase in the amount of material evidence in the future will enhance the understanding of its life and history, sometimes strengthening the insights presented here, sometimes correcting or modulating them. But whatever emerging understanding occurs will yet remain a controlled, imaginative reconstruction.

The fundamental commitment of this study, that is to insights and understanding that can be ascertained from the material remains and context of a site, has necessitated as wide a trawling as possible to ensure that the current store of evidence is complete, or as complete as possible. At the raw level of data collection, the store of material has been increased in the course of this study — in the coin-types, inscriptions and artifacts that can be legitimately claimed as Colossae's or fed into the dynamism of its history. But these sources have also been subjected to detailed examination to yield new patterns and insights, sometimes new readings and reconstructions, whether that be Colossae's heliotic self-positioning as a distinctive mark of its civic presentation in the Lycus Valley and the wider region, its creative exchanges in gymnasial culture, or the diversity of its households and family structures.

One of the repetitions dogging the study has been the limitations on our understanding, sometimes yielding an admission of ignorance, sometimes leaving us astride alternate possibilities. The use of comparative material has forced itself into the study as a critical contributor to the analyses. However, an essential control on accessing *comparanda* has been the actual evidence from Colossae itself. This has guided the search for relevant material from elsewhere but has also been subjected to the issue of Colossae's own distinctive life. Even where that has remained elusive, it is submitted that the methodological control of resisting the assumption of monochromicity but rather being alert to diversity in the city and its region is to be preferred.

Walter Scheidel's early demographic research, even with limited comparative research, concluded that "significant regional variation" was increasingly revealed as the norm rather than the exception, and he anticipated that the focus of historical research must shift to detailed studies.[1] More recent analyses have reinforced these understandings, even as methodologies have been refined and new questions have been asked of the (increasing volume of) evidence. Such diversity has been traced within Colossae's own corporate life, whether it be in burial practices, in onomastics, in jurisprudence, in underlying ethnic backgrounds and other concentrations. How Colossae sought to manage this cosmopolitan assortment of ingredients has only been able to be glimpsed — in snippets of official foundation narratives, in the promotion of encompassing religious affirmations (such as in Tyche Protogeneia) and, disruptively, in the reaction visible in a curse tablet where a segment of Colossae's population felt anything but included in its confident espousal of communal integration.

This distinctive self-portrayal has been tracked in its growing confidence especially in and beyond the second century CE, whence derives most of the numismatic and epigraphical sources for our examination. But the tap-roots of this display stretch back centuries, not least to the constant, abrasive rub against proximate, equally competitive cities. Colossae appears to have been continually concerned to carve its own identity distinct from Laodikeia, even as it was vigilant to protect its territorial and cultural boundaries as much as a smaller city was able. At the same time, whether in the pursuit of athletic glory in regional competitions or the desire for educational advancement at external centers of learning, Colossae was far from isolationist in its provincial stance. Indeed, the re-establishment of its civic mint speaks of a growing strength in its own economic position and a willingness to proclaim, promote and protect its contribution to the region's economic and religious vibrancy.

The constant interface with these expressions of Colossae's material life has come from the major literary works associated with the city, the Letters to the Colossians and Philemon of the Second Testament. The fundamental positioning of this interface has been the operational principle that these writings are significant threads in the overall weave of that life. The working hypothesis (as against alternative suggestions as to a Roman provenance and against an ultra-skeptical, and, I would argue, ahistorical loosening of any material

1 W. Scheidel, *Measuring Sex, Age and Death in the Roman Empire: Exploration sin ancient demography* (Ann Arbor, MI: Journal of Roman Archaeology, 1996), 195.

mooring on the basis of an over-reading of pseudonymity) has established at the very least an envisaged Phrygian audience for the letters. But whereas snatches of the specifics of Colossae's life in these letters must be conservatively restricted (themselves subject to the limitations of existing material evidence), the accent on tailoring a Colossian reception to the construction of existing material evidence has yielded a considerable store of new interpretations of those texts. Here, fledgling groups of Christ-followers have become one of the competitors for meaningful existence in Colossae's life and, secondarily, in that of Laodikeia. Significant new readings of parts of the Letter to the Colossians and to Philemon have been proposed, some of which offer resolutions to problems (such as connections between metaphors or the role of Archippos) that have perturbed Second Testament commentators.

In this sense, written texts have become subject to material culture, not the reverse. This has continued the radical awakening to new perspectives begun 350 years ago as Christian texts were restored to the material grounding that had given them life. As such these texts have been allowed to return to being players in the material environment rather than esoteric writings locked into some immaterial ghetto. This cannot replace one gold standard (the "text") with another (the "realia"). Rather, it has been my hope as much as my endeavor to allow them to be restored to a common resource, as participants in a measure of integrated exchange. Of course as the one engineering this encounter, I am fully aware that my own historically-bound assumptions, even when consciously acknowledged, will have left their fingerprints on the materials, the environment and texts that have been included in these pages. Later forensic inquiries, examinations and assessments will construct new appreciations. That is to be welcomed, even as they will remain materialistically and imaginatively bound. This work then is a station as much as it is, hopefully, a contribution on the journey towards a greater elucidation of an ancient city, its territory and relationships, and the various actors in its succession of lives.

Appendix 1
Ancient Testimonia for Colossae

The list of testimonia concludes with a selection of Byzantine testimonia. The Byzantine entries are primarily for Chonai.[2] However evidence giving both toponyms — Colossae and Chonai — is substantially complete, including one sixteenth century Greek witness that reiterates the memory of their collation. Where Chonai occurs alone, the texts have been selected on the basis of details pertinent to the site. A number of Byzantine texts mentioning Chonai are substantial repetitions of the story of the miracle of Michael the archangel, in most cases called the Archistrategos, commander of the heavenly hosts. The story has not been given, apart from one summary from the Menologion of Basil. Similarly, the Encomium by Michael Choniates for Nicetas metropolitan bishop of Chonai (*Oration* 2) has received only partial selections.[3] However where the identification of the site of the miracle is given in various forms, these are included. Two entries are included which do not mention Colossae or Chonai directly, one from Tacitus, one from Michael Choniates, because of how important they have been to the history of research into the city and of interpretation of the Letters to the Colossians and Philemon. These might have been expanded to include Josephus and Philo on Jews in Asia but a decision had to be made on compelling applicability.[4] The selections are listed in

---

2 For further detail on Byzantine Chonai, see K. Belke and N. Mersich, *Tabula Imperii Byzantini Bd 7: Phrygien und Pisidien* (Vienna: Österreichische Akademie der Wissenschaften, 1990), sv. Chonai, Kolossai, Hierapolis, Laodikeia, Lykos.

3 See further P. Magdalino, *The Empire of Manuel I Komnenos, 1143–1180* (Cambridge: Cambridge University Press, 2002), 130–2.

4 On the issue of how relevant the generalized statements of Josephus and Philo are to Colossae, see A. H. Cadwallader, "On the Question of Comparative Method in Historical Research: Colossae and Chonai in Larger Frame," in *The First Urban Churches 5: Colossae, Hierapolis, and Laodicea* edited by J. R. Harrison and L. L. Welborn (Atlanta, GA: SBL, 2019), 105–51.

approximate chronological order. (Some Byzantine texts are notoriously difficult to date, such as the *Life of Nicholas of Myra*.) In general, commentaries on the Letters to Colossians and Philemon have not been accessed, apart from Theodoret of Cyrrhus since he adds snippets of information of historical significance. Many minuscule manuscripts of these letters contain prologues but these are frequently standardized in their summaries, including the notation that Colossae was a city of Phrygia. The translations are my own but where others exist they have been consulted as far as possible. The editions from which the texts are drawn are given by reference to the editor(s) and may be pursued, along with translators, in the general bibliography.

i) Herodotos *History* 7.30 (ed. Wilson).

Ἄναυα δὲ καλεομένην Φρυγῶν πόλιν παραμειβόμενος καὶ λίμνην ἐκ τῆς ἅλες γίνονται, ἀπίκετο ἐς Κολοσσὰς πόλιν μεγάλην Φρυγίης· ἐν τῇ Λύκος ποταμὸς ἐς χάσμα γῆς ἐσβάλλων ἀφανίζεται, ἔπειτα διὰ σταδίων ὡς πέντε μάλιστά κῃ ἀναφαινόμενος ἐκδιδοσῖ καὶ οὗτος ἐς τὸν Μαίανδρον. ἐκ δὲ Κολοσσέων ὁ στρατὸς ὁρμώμενος ἐπὶ τοὺς οὔρους τῶν Φρυγῶν καὶ Λυδῶν ἀπίκετο ἐς Κύδραρα πόλιν …

Passing by the Phrygian city called Anaua, and the lake from which salt is obtained, he [Xerxes] came into Colossae, a great city in Phrygia; there the river Lycus empties into a chasm in the land and disappears, until it reappears about five stadia away; this river then issues into the Maeander. From Colossae, the army held its course for the borders of Phrygia and Lydia and came to the city of Kydrara.

ii) Xenophon *Anabasis* 1.2.5–7 (ed. Marchant).

Κῦρος δὲ ἔχων οὓς εἴρηκα ὡρμᾶτο ἀπὸ Σάρδεων· καὶ ἐξελαύνει διὰ τῆς Λυδίας σταθμοὺς τρεῖς παρασάγγαρ εἴκοσε καὶ δύο ἐπὶ τὸν Μαίανδρον ποταμόν. τούτον τὸ εὖρος δύο πλέθρα. Γέφυρα δὲ ἐπῆν ἐζευγμένη πλοίοις ἑπτὰ. τοῦτον διαβὰς ἐξελαύνει διὰ Φρυγίας σταθμὸν ἕνα παρασάγγας ὀκτὼ εἰς Κολοσσάς, πόλιν οἰκουμένην εὐδαίμονα καὶ μεγάλην. ἐνταῦθα ἔμεινεν ἡμέρας ἑπτά· καὶ ἧκε Μένων ὁ Θετταλὸς ὁπλίτας ἔχων χιλίους καὶ πελταστὰς πεντακοσίους, Δόλοπας καὶ Αἰνιᾶνας καὶ Ὀλυνθίους. ἐντεῦθεν ἐξελαύνει σταθμοὺς τρεῖς παρασάγγας εἴκοσιν εἰς Κελαινάς, τῆς Φρυγίας πόλιν οἰκουμένην, μεγάλην καὶ εὐδαίμονα

Cyrus was now advancing from Sardis leading the troops about which I have previously spoken; and he marched through Lydia three stations [three days' journey], a distance of twenty-two parasangs [c. 72.5 miles/52.3 kilometers], to the Maeander river. The width of this river was two plethora [c. 32 yards/29 meters], and there was a bridge over it made of seven boats. After crossing this river, he pressed on through Phrygia one day's journey, a distance of eight parasangs [c. 26 miles/41 kilometers], to Colossae, a settled city, prosperous and large. He remained there seven days. Menon the Thessalian came with a thousand hoplites and five hundred peltasts, comprising Dolopians, Aenianians, and Olynthians. Then Cyrus marched on another three stations, twenty parasangs [c. 66 miles/106 kilometers] in length, to Celaenae, a settled city of Phrygia, large and prosperous.

iii) Diodorus Siculus 14.80.7–8 (ed. Fischer).

καταστήσας οὖν Τιθραύστην ἡγεμόνα, τούτῳ μὲν παρήγγειλε συλλαμβάνειν Τισσαφέρνην, πρὶς δὲ τὰς πόλεις καὶ τοὺς σατράπας ἔπεμψεν ἐπιστολὰς ὅπως πάντες τούτῳ ποιῶσι τὸ προσταττόμενον. ὁ δὲ Τιθραύστης παραγενόμενος εἰς Κολοσσὰς τῆς Φρυγίας συνέλαβε τὸν Τισσαφέρνην διά τινος Ἀριαίου σατράπου λουίμενον, καὶ τὴν κεφαλὴν ἀποκόψας ἀπέστειλε πρὸς τὸν βασιλέα·

Artaxerxes appointed Tithraustes commander, giving him, on the one hand, orders to arrest Tissaphernes and, on the other, sending letters to the cities and the satraps that all should perform whatever Tithraustes commanded. For his part, Tithraustes, on arriving at Colossae in Phrygia, through the agency of Ariaeus, a satrap, arrested Tissaphernes while he was in the bath, cut off his head, and sent it to the King.

iv) (?) Flavius Arrian *History of Alexander's Successors* 25,235v, ll. 4–11 (eds. Roos and Wirth).

δὲ Κλεοπάτρα μαθοῦσα τοῦ τε Ἀντιγόνου τὴν ὁρμὴν καὶ τὴν ἐνέδραν τὴν ἐπὶ Εὐμένει παρεσκευασμένην ἡ μὲν φράζει πρὸς Εὐμένη τὰ ἐξηγ̣γ̣ε̣λ̣μ̣ ἐ̣ν̣α̣, ὁ δὲ ἀμφὶ δείλην ξυναγαγὼν τοὺς ξ̣υ̣νηκολουθηκ̣ό̣τ. α̣ς̣ α̣ὐτῷ ψιλοὺς καὶ ἱππέας παραγγέλλει μήτε σάλπιγγα μήτε ἄλλο τι τῶν περιφανῶν σημείων προσμείναντας ὡς τάχιστα πρὸς πορείαν ἐσκευασμένους παρεῖναι. καὶ ἦν μὲν αὐτῷ ἡ φανερὰ ὁδὸς ὡς ἐπ' ἀνίσχοντα ἥλιον ἐ̣π̣ὶ̣ Κ̣ο̣λ̣ο̣[σσάς] …[5]

And when Cleopatra [of Macedon, Alexander the Great's sister] learned of Antigonos's treacherous intent [in the aftermath of Alexander's death] fomented against Eumenes, she revealed the plans to Eumenes. Accordingly, throughout the afternoon he gathered to him dispossessed supporters and cavalrymen and ordered that there be neither trumpet/clarion call nor any other splendid signal. They remained for a brief period making preparations for the journey that lay before them. For him, the road was plain — unfolding to the east towards Colossae.

v) Polyaenus *Stratagems* 7.16.1 (ed. Melber and Woelfflin).

Ἀριαῖος ἀναγνοὺς τὴν ἐπιστολὴν ἐν Κολοσσαῖς τῆς Φρυγίας καλεῖ Τισσαφέρνην ὡς ὁμοῦ βουλεύσασθαι δέον τά τε ἄλλα καὶ περὶ τῶν Ἑλλήνων. ὁδὲ μηδὲν ὑπιδόμενος τὸ μὲν στρατόπεδον κατέλιπεν ἐν Σαρδεσιν, αὐτὸς δὲ μετὰ τριακοσίων λογάδων Ἀρκάδων καὶ Μιλησίων ἀφικόμενος ἐν Ἀριαίου κατέλυεν· ἤδη δὲ περὶ λουτρὸν

5 Note that the manuscript from which this transcription has been published is considerably abraided at the end of line 11. Felix Jacoby provided ὁ δὲ κολο all letters with underdots and did not offer a suggested completion of the word beginning with κολο …: F. Jacoby, *Die Fragmente der griechischen Historiker* (Leiden: Brill, 1954–69 [1923–58]), 156F, frag. 10, l. 71. Gerhard Wirth's reconstruction ("*supplevi*") is consistent with the immediate context in the text but considerable doubt must remain for the reading of the only known manuscript of this part of Photius's ninth century excerpts of Arrian's history (the *Myriobiblos*).

ἔχων τὸν ἀκινάκην ἀπέθετο. Ἀριαῖος μετὰ τῶν θεραπευτήρων συναρπάσας αὐτὸν, καθείρξας εἰς ἁρμάμαξαν κατερραμμένην ἄγειν Τιθραύστῃ παρέδωκεν. ὁ δὲ μέχρι μὲν Κελαινῶν ἐγκατερραμμένον ἤγαγεν, ἐνταῦθα δὲ ἀποτεμὼν αὐτοῦ τὴν κεφαλὴν ἀνεκόμισε βασιλεῖ.

As soon as Ariaios, who then resided in Colossae, a city of Phrygia, had read the letter, he summonsed Tissaphernes, as though desiring a conference with him on important affairs, and particularly on matters concerning the Greeks. Tissaphernes did not suspect anything, and so left his forces at Sardis. He hurried to Ariaios attended by a company of 300 Arcadians and Milesians. Having completed his journey, he laid aside his short sword and settled into a bath. Ariaios, with his aides, grappled with him, bundled him into a covered carriage, and conveyed him to Tithraustes, who transferred him to Celaenae. There he beheaded him and transported the trophy to the king.

vi) Strabo *Geography* 12.8.13 (ed. Meineke).

ἐν ᾗ ἐστὶν ἥ τε Παρώρειος λεγομένη Φρυγία καὶ ἡ πρὸς Πισιδίαν καὶ τὰ περὶ Ἀμόριον καὶ Εὐμένειαν καὶ Σύνναδα, εἶτα Ἀπάμεια ἡ Κιβωτὸς λεγομένη καὶ Λαοδίκεια, αἵπερ εἰσὶ μέγισται τῶν κατὰ τὴν Φρυγίαν πόλεων· περίκειται δὲ ταύταις πολίσματα καί........... Ἀφροδισιάς, Κολοσσαί, Θεμισώνιον, Σαναός, Μητρόπολις, Ἀπολλωνίας·

In it [Phrygia Epictetus] are Phrygia "Paroreia" [bordering the mountain range] as it is called, and the part of Phrygia that is adjacent to Pisidia, and the parts round Amorium and Eumeneia and Synnada, and then Apameia Cibotus, as it is called, and Laodikeia — these two are the largest of the Phrygian cities. In the neighborhood of these are situated other cities, and. . .[lacuna], Aphrodisias, Colossae, Themisonion, Sanaos, Metropolis, and Apollonias.

vii) Strabo *Geography* 12.8.16 (ed. Meineke).

φέρει δ' ὁ περὶ τὴν Λαοδίκειαν τόπος προβάτων ἀρετὰς οὐκ εἰς μαλακότητα μόνον τῶν ἐρίων, ᾗ καὶ τῶν Μιλησίων διαφέρει, ἀλλὰ καὶ εἰς τὴν κοραξὴν χρόαν, ὥστε καὶ προσοδεύονται λαμπρῶς ἀπ' αὐτῶν· ὥσπερ καὶ οἱ Κολοσσηνοὶ ἀπὸ τοῦ ὁμωνύμου χρώματος πλησίον οἰκοῦντες.

The surrounding territory of Laodikeia supports sheep that are excellent not only for the very fine softness of the wool, surpassing even that of Milesian wool but also for its raven-black color. As a result, the Laodikeians profit immensely from them; so also do the Colossians, the neighboring settlement, whose name attaches to the color.

viii) Pliny *Natural History* 5.41.145 (ed. Mayhoff).

oppida ibi celeberrima praeter iam dicta Ancyra, Andria, Celaenae, Colossae, Carina Cotyaion, Ceraine, Conium, Midaium.

The most famous towns [of Phrygia], besides those already named [Cibyra, Laodikeia],[6] are Ancyra, Andria, Celaenae, Colossae, Carina, Cotyaion, Ceraine, Conium and Midaium.

ix) Pliny *Natural History* 31.20.29 (ed. Mayhoff).

in Colossis flumen est quo lateres coniecti lapidei extrahuntur.

At Colossae there is a river, and bricks when immersed into it are of stone when extracted.

x) Pliny *Natural History* 21.27.51 (ed. Mayhoff).

flos eius colossinus in coronas admittitur.

Its flower [of the cyclamen] is Colossian purple and is added to garlands.[7]

xi) Tacitus *Annals* 14.27.1 (ed. Koestermann).

Eodem anno ex inlustribus Asiae urbibus Laodicea tremor terrae prolapse, nullo a nobis remedio, propriis opibus revaluit.

In the same year [as Nero appointed Tigranes VI as titular king of Armenia], Laodicea, among the illustrious cities of Asia, was devastated by an earthquake. But the city restored its position from its own resources, without aid from ourselves.

---

6 Pliny *NH* 5.29.105. The naming of Cibyra as Phrygian is misleading. It was originally the conventus metropolis and this has swayed Pliny to the Roman administrative imposition that paid little regard to historical regional shapings.

7 There must remain some opacity about this reference in Pliny the Elder. Pliny mentions the color of types of cyclamen flower in two places, here as "Colossian" and in another place, simply as "purple flowers." (*floribus purpureis, NH* 25.67.114). This has driven the periphrasis "Colossian purple" by W. H. S. Jones (in LCL). The adjective occurs nowhere else, so it is difficult to decide whether it had entered the chromatic lexicon or not. If it had, then it suggests that Strabo's "raven black" and Pliny's "*colossinus*" may coincide. Andrea Armstrong seems to separate the two colors, arguing that "Colossae gave its name to a particular purple dye." This brings greater certainty than the texts can bear. See A. L. Armstrong, "Roman Phrygia: Cities and their Coinage," unpublished PhD Thesis, University of London, 1998, 5–6, 47; similarly, F. F. Bruce *The Epistles to the Colossians, to Philemon, and to the Ephesians* (Grand Rapids, MN: Eerdmans, 1984), 8. Ralph Martin and Carl Toney, by contrast, combine them: *New Testament Foundations: An Introduction for Students* (Eugene, OR: Cascade, 2018), 443.

xii) Eusebius *Chronicon* 210 (=Orosios 7.7.12) (PL 27.453).
[210th Olympiad]

In Asia tres urbes terraemotu conciderunt, Laodicia, Hierapolis, Colossae.

In Asia, three cities were ruined in an earthquake: Laodikeia, Hierapolis and Colossae.

xiii) Theodoret *Commentary on Colossians* 2:18 (PG 82.613B).

Ἔμεινε δὲ τοῦτο τὸ πάθος ἐν τῇ Φρυγίᾳ καὶ Πισιδίᾳ μέχρι πολλοῦ. Οὗ δὴ χάριν καὶ συνελθοῦσα σύνοδος ἐν Λαοδικείᾳ τῆς Φρυγίας, νόμῳ κεκώλυκε τὸ τοῖς ἀγγέλοις προσεύχεσθαι· καὶ μέχρι δὲ τοῦ νῦν εὐκτήρια τοῦ ἁγίου Μιχαὴλ παρ' ἐκείνοις καὶ τοῖς ὁμόροις ἐκείνων ἔστιν ἰδεῖν.

But this distortion [the worship of angels] prevailed in Phrygia and Pisidia for a long time. On account of this a synod came together at Laodikeia of Phrygia and circumscribed by law any offering of prayers to angels. Even now, a shrine of holy Michael can be seen by them lying at their borders.

xiv) Theodoret *Commentary on Colossians* 3:17 (PG 620D–621A).

Καὶ τῷ Θεῷ δὲ καὶ Πατρὶ τὴν εὐχαριστίαν δι' αὐτοῦ, φησὶν, ἀναπέμπετε, μὴ διὰ τῶν ἀγγέλων. Τούτῳ ἑπομένη τῷ νόμῳ καὶ ἡ ἐν Λαοδικείᾳ σύνοδος, καὶ τὸ παλαιὸν ἐκεῖνο πάθος θεραπεῦσαι βουλομένη, ἐνομοθέτησε μὴ εὔχεσθαι ἀγγέλοις, μηδὲ καταλιμπάνειν τὸν Κύριον ἡμῶν Ἰησοῦν Χριστόν.

And offering up thanksgiving to God and to the Father "through him" as he says, not through the angels. The synod in Laodikeia pursued this by a law; and, wanting to rectify that ancient distortion, it legislated against prayer to angels, and not to abandon our Lord Jesus Christ.

xv) Theodoret *Commentary on Philemon* prologue (PG 82.871A).

Τῶν πεπιστευκότων ὁ Φιλήμων ἐτύγχανεν· ὧν πόλιν δὲ εἶχε τὰς Κολασσάς. Καὶ ἡ οἰκία δὲ αὐτοῦ μέχρι τοῦ παρόντος μεμένηκε. Τούτου οἰκέτης Ὀνήσιμος τοὔνομα …

Philemon happened to be among those who believed. They were from the city of Colassae. And his house has remained standing to the present time. Here there was a domestic slave named Onesimos …

xvi) Hierocles *Synekdemos* 664.6–666.6 (… 668.16) (ed. Honigmann).

Φρυγία Πακατιανή: Λαοδίκεια, Ἱεράπολις, Μόσσυνα, Ἄττουδα, Τραπεζούπολις, Κολοσσαί, Κερέταπα, Θεμισώνιον, Οὐαλεντία, Σαναός, Κονιούπολις [… 39 named cities in all]

Phrygia Pacatiane: Laodikeia, Hierapolis, Mossyna, Attouda, Trapezopolis, Colossae, Keretapa, Themisonion, Valentia, Sanaos, Konioupolis …

vii) *The Life of Nicholas of Myra* 15.1–18 (ed. Anrich).

Καὶ τότε κελεύει ὁ ἅγιος τοῦ θεοῦ ἀπελθεῖν πρὸς τὸ εὐκτήριον τοῦ ἀρχιστρατήγου Μιχαὴλ ἐν ταῖς Χώναις, τοῦ προσκυνεῖν. καὶ παραλαβὼν τὸν ἀρχιδιάκονα αὐτοῦ, ἐπορεύθη αὐτῷ ἅμα. καὶ ποιήσας ὁδοιπορίαν ἡμερῶν δύο, καὶ φθάσας ἐπὶ τὸν ποταμόν, καὶ γενομένης πλημμύρας τῶν ὑδάτων, ἦν ἡ ῥύσις τοῦ ποταμοῦ σφόδρα. καὶ εἰσελθόντων ὁδοιπόρων πολλῶν, καὶ ἰδόντες τὴν ῥύσιν τῶν ὑδάτων καὶ μὴ δυνηθέντες περᾶσαι, ἐκαθέζοντο παρὰ τὰς ὄχθας τοῦ ποταμοῦ καὶ ἐξέδεχον τὴν τοῦ ὕδατος ἐλάττωσιν. καὶ φθάσας ὁ ἅγιος ἐπὶ τὸν ποταμόν, καὶ ἰδὼν τὴν ῥύσιν τῶν ὑδάτων καὶ πλῆθος τῶν ὁδοιπόρων παρὰ τὴν ὄχθαν τοῦ ποταμοῦ, σταθεὶς προσηύξατο ἐπὶ ὥραν ἱκανήν. καὶ σφραγίσας τὸ ὕδωρ καὶ κρατήσας τὴν ῥάβδον αὐτοῦ, ἔδωκεν ἐπὶ τὸ ὕδωρ <πληγάς>· καὶ τὸ ὑποκάτω τὸ ὕδωρ ἐπορεύετο σφόδρα· τὸ δὲ ἄνωθεν ὕδωρ ἔστη ὑψούμενον ἐπὶ πῆχες δέκα. καὶ περάσαντες οἱ ὁδοιπόροι μετὰ τοῦ ἁγίου Νικολάου, καὶ ἐκτείνας τὴν χεῖρα, πάλιν ἐρράπισεν τὸ ὕδωρ μετὰ τῆς βακτηρίας αὐτοῦ καὶ εἶπεν· 'Πορεύου εἰς εἰρήνην ἐπὶ τὸν τόπον σου,' καὶ ἀπέλυσεν αὐτό. καὶ ἐβάδισεν τὴν ὁδὸν αὐτοῦ. καὶ ἀπελθὼν ἐν τῷ εὐκτηρίῳ τοῦ ἀρχιστρατήγου καὶ προσκυνήσας καὶ τὰς εὐχὰς αὐτοῦ ἀποδώσας τῷ θεῷ, ὑπέστρεψεν ἐν τῇ Λυκίᾳ, καὶ ἐπανεπαύσατο ἐν τῇ πόλει αὐτοῦ.

Then the holy man of God decided to go on to the shrine of the Archistrategos Michael in Chonai, in order to worship there. So, taking his archdeacon, he went with him. And he made the journey in two days. When he reached the river, there was a flood of water. The rush of the river was very swift. Many travellers had arrived and seeing the flow of waters, they were unable to cross. So they sat down beside the banks of the river and waited for the water to subside. But the holy man anticipated the river, seeing the rush of waters and the crowd of travellers on the bank of the river, so he stood praying at that very hour. And making the sign of the cross over the water and grasping his staff, he delivered a blow on the water and it immediately went down. But again, the water rose up a full ten cubits in height. And the travellers rallied to be with holy Nicholas. And he, extending his hand, again struck the water with his staff, and said, "Go in peace to your appointed place." And he dismissed it. Then he proceeded on his way. He continued on to the shrine of the Archistrategos, prostrated himself and offered up his prayer to God. Then he returned to Lycia and took rest in his city.

xviii) Second Ecumenical Council of Nicaea (787 CE) (ed. Lamberz).

212.190 Θεοδόσιος ὁ ὁσιώτατος ἐπίσκοπος Χωνῶν ἐξεφώνησεν ὁμοίως.
Theodosios[8] the most holy bishop of Chonai decided similarly by acclamation.

---

8 It is thought that Theodosios and Dositheos are the same person, with the names being either two versions of the same "God's gift" or two different readings of the original minuted notes. Frequently letters of a word can be written above others (especially in cursive script). Copyists may then have made different choices about how to reconstruct the name; given the hundreds of bishops in attendance, there is no expectation that a minor clerk would know all the bishops and their dioceses.

516.266 Δοσίθεος ἐπίσκοπος Χωνῶν ἤτοι Κολασσαέων ὁμοίως.
Dositheos, bishop of Chonai, also known as Colossae, similarly [assent to the declarations condemning iconoclasts].

812.263 Δοσιθέου ἐπισκόπου Χωνῶν ἤτοι Κολασσαέων
[Assent] from Dositheos bishop of Chonai, also known as Colossae.

848.241 Δοσίθεος ἀνάξιος ἐπίσκοπος Χωνῶν ὁμοίως.
Dositheos "unworthy" bishop of Chonai, similarly.

xix) Theodore the Studite *Epistle* 63 (ed. Fatouros).

Ἐπεὶ γὰρ δεῖ οἰκονομίᾳ κεχρῆσθαι ἐν τοῖς ἀναγκαίοις. Ὀπηνίκα συνωψίσθημεν τῷ Χωνῶν αἱρεσιάρχῃ (ἐκεῖ γὰρ πρῶτον ἀπήχθημεν ὑπὸ τῶν ἀπὸ Ἀνατολικῶν ἀράντων ἡμᾶς) καὶ γόνυ ἐκλίναμεν, συγγονυκλιτήσαντος κἀκείνου. Κὰι ἠσπασάμεθα αὐτὸν. ...

For the stewardship needs to be exposed in these important matters, as when we were granted an interview with the leader of the heretics in Chonai [capital of the Thakesion theme?] (for there we departed from those who had taken us from the Anatolikon theme) and we bowed the knee, kneeling together there, and greeted him. ...

xx) George Syncellus, *Chronicon* 409.23–410.4 (=Eusebius in part) (ed. Mosshammer).

Κόσμου ἔτη εφνγ'
ῆς θείας σαρκώσεως ἔτη νγ'
Νέρων ἀνεῖλε τὴν ἑαυτοῦ μητέρα Ἀγριππίναν καὶ τὴν τοῦ πατρὸς ἀδελφήν. Ἐν Ῥώμῃ σεισμὸς μέγας ἐγένετο. Νέρων ἐπὶ Ῥώμης κιθαρίζων ἐνίκησε. Κατὰ τῆς Νέρωνος τραπέζης κεραυνὸς ἔπεσεν. Ἐμπρησμοὶ γεγόνασι πολλοὶ ἐν Ῥώμῃ, πόλεις τε τῆς Ἀσίας κατέπεσον τρεῖς, Λαοδίκεια, Ἱεράπολις καὶ Κολοσσαί.

Year 5553 after the creation of the world
Year 53 after the divine incarnation
Nero killed his own mother Agrippina and his father's sister. In Rome there was a great earthquake. Nero won the kithara competition at Rome. A thunderbolt struck the sacred altar of Nero. There was a great conflagration in Rome, and three cities of Asia collapsed: Laodikeia, Hierapolis and Kolossai.

xxi) Nicetas David, *Life of the Patriarch Ignatius* 27.7–9 (ed. Smithies).

Ἀποστέλλει τοίνυν Θεόφιλον ἐπίσκοπον τοῦ Ἀμορίου καὶ
Σαμουὴλ ἐπίσκοπον ἄχρις ἐκείνου τῶν Χωνῶν ὑπὸ Λαοδίκειαν
τυγχάνοντα ἀρχιεπίσκοπον τετιμηκώς·

Therefore he [Photius] sent Theophilos bishop of Amorion and also Samuel, until then bishop of Chonai under the jurisdiction of Laodikeia but, as it happened, elevated to be archbishop.

xxii) *Notitia Episcopatuum* 13.col 1.750–1 (ed. Darrouzès). [one of seventeen, sometimes duplicated, references, that trace not only attendance and absence, but also the hierarchy of ecclesiastical position from bishopric to metropolitanate]

ταῖς Χώναις Φρυγίας θρόνος ὑποκείμενος οὐκ ἔστι.

The curial chair for Chonai in Phrygia is not adjudged lower.

xxiii) Constantine Porphyrogenitos *On the Themes* 1.3 (ed. Bekker).

δωδεκάτη Κολοσσαὶ αἱ νῦν λεγόμεναι Χῶναι, οὗ ἐστι ναὸς διαβόητος τοῦ ἀρχαγγέλου Μιχαήλ.

Colossae, the place now called Chonai, where there is a famous shrine of the archangel Michael.

xxiv) Alexander of Nicaea *Epistle* 7 (ed. Darrouzès).

Προκοπίῳ μητροπολίτῃ Χωνῶν

To Procopios Metropolitan of Chonai

xxv) *The Life of the Holy Apostle Titus* 6.1–10 (ed. Halkin).

Ἀναχωρησάντων δὲ τῶν ἀποστόλων ἐκ τῆς Κρήτης ἦλθον εἰς τὴν Ἀσίαν· καὶ ἐν Ἐφέσῳ διδάσκοντος Παύλου, πολὺ πλῆθος ἐπίστευσεν ἐπὶ τὸν κύριον· ἐν ᾗ καὶ ἐθηριομάχησεν ὁ Παῦλος λέοντι παραβληθείς. Μετὰ ταῦτα συνὼν ἀεὶ τῷ μακαρίῳ Παύλῳ καὶ συμπαραμείνας αὐτῷ μέχρι τῆς ὑπὸ Νέρωνος τελειώσεως αὐτοῦ ὑπέστρεψεν ἐν Ἑλλάδι σὺν Τιμοθέῳ καὶ Λουκᾷ· καὶ ὁ μὲν Λουκᾶς ἐκεῖσε ἐναπέμεινε, Τιμόθεος δὲ καὶ Τίτος ἀπῆλθον ἐν Κολασσαῖς πόλιν τῆς Φρυγίας τὴν νῦν Χώνας λεγομένην. Αὖθις δὲ Τιμοθέου ἐν Ἐφέσῳ παραμείναντος, Τίτος τὴν Κρήτην κατέλαβεν.
And the apostles departed from Crete and went into Asia. In Ephesos, Paul was teaching and a great many believed in the Lord. There Paul fought with wild animals, even thrown to a lion. After these things being joined with the blessed Paul eternally and staying with him until his end under Nero, Titus returned to Greece with Timothy and Luke. Luke meanwhile was content to stay there, but went on to Kolossai, a city of Phrygia, now called Chonai. Afterwards while Timothy remained in Ephesos, Titus returned to Crete.

xxvi) Anonymous Greek Menologion 21, Feb 21st (ed. Latysev).

Μαρτυριον τοῦ ἁγίου ἀποστολου Ἀρχιππου, Φιλημονος καὶ Ἀπφίας.
… εἷς ἐκείνων καὶ ὁ θαυμαστὸς ἐγνωρίζετο καὶ σοφώτατος Ἄρχιππος, μεθ' ὃν καὶ Φιλήμων ὁ τὰ πάντα καλὸς καὶ ἡ καλλίστη τῶν γυναικῶν Ἀπφία· καὶ γὰρ οὐδὲ γυναιξὶν ἀποκέκλειστο τὰ τῆς ἀποστολῆς, ἀλλ' οὐδ' αὐτὸ πάντως τὸ τοῦ μαρτυρίου στάδιον· … ὥστε τοὺς εὑρισκομένους χριστιανοὺς μετὰ πολλὰς τὰς τιμωρίας τῇ τελευταίᾳ τοῦ θανάτου καθυπούργεσθαι ψήφῳ συλλαμβάνονται παρὰ τῶν εἰδωλολατρῶν ἐν τῇ πόλει Κολασαέων (μία δὲ αὕτη τῆς Φρυγίας τυγχάνει),

Θεῷ τοὺς ὕμνους ἀναφέροντες κατ' αὐτὴν δὴ τὴν καθολικὴν ἐκκλησίαν, καὶ ἄγονται πρὸς τὸ βῆμα τοῦ δυσσεβοῦς Ἀνδροκλέους· ...

The Martyrdom of the holy apostles Archippos, Philemon and Apphia. ... one of whom [fellow-workers with Paul in the proclamation of the gospel through virtually the whole world] was the renowned wonderful and most wise Archippos, with whom also is to be counted Philemon, a man fine in every way, and Apphia most illustrious of women — for the affairs pertaining to apostleship are not circumscribed for women, including, above all, the arena of martyrdom itself ... they were subjected to the final sentence of death having been revealed as Christians after many trials. They were arrested, as they were offering hymns to God according to the rubric of the universal church, by the idolaters in the city of Colasians (a city which is in Phrygia), and taken before the judgment seat of the wicked Androkles ...

xxvii) The *Menologion of Basil II*, Sept 6th [Cod. Vat. Gr. 1613, facsimile edition 2005].

Μηνὶ τῷ αὐτῷ ς' ἡ ἀνάμνησις τοῦ ἐν Χώναις θαύματος τοῦ μεγάλου ἀρχιστρατηγου τοῦ Θεοῦ
Ἐν τῇ καλουμένῃ ἤν μὲν τῶν Χωνῶν πόλει· πρότερον δὲ Κωλασσαέων ὑπῆρχε ἀνὴρ τίς ὄνομα Ἄρχιππος. εὐλαβὴς καὶ φοβούμενος τὸν θεόν· οὗτος προσκαθεζόμενος ἐν τῷ ϋδατι τῷ διὰ τῆς ἐπισκέψεως τοῦ μεγάλου Ἀρχιστρατηγοῦ ἀναβρύοντι καὶ διὰ τὰ γενόμενα διὰ τοῦ ὕδατος θαύματα· πολλοὺς τῶν ἀπίστων ἐπιστρέφων καὶ βαπτίζων. ἐκίνησε πρὸς φθόνον τοὺς Ἕλληνας μὴ φέροντας βλέπειν τὰ παράδοξα θαύματα· βρύχοντες οὖν τοὺς ὀδόντας κατὰ τοὺ σεπτοῦ ἁγιάσματος καὶ τοῦ ὁσίου Ἀρχίππου· συναχθέντες ἄπειρα πλήθη· καὶ δήσαντες δύο μεγάλους ποτάμους· καὶ μίξαντες ἀμφοτέρους ἀπέλυσαν εὐθέως τοῦ καταστρέψαι τὸν ναὸν καὶ τὸ ἁγίασμα καὶ τὸν Ἀρχίππον· ὡς δὲ ἤκουσεν ὁ Ἄρχιππος τοῦ βρυγμοῦ τῶν ὑδάτων, παρεκάλεσε τὸν Ἀρχιστράτηγον βοηθῆσαι. Καὶ εὐθεως φανεὶς ἔκρουσε τὴν πέτραν μετὰ τῆς ῥάβδου ἧς κατεῖχε· καὶ ἐχώνευσε τὰ ὕδατα ἐν αὐτῇ· καὶ ἐκλήθη ὁ τόπος ἐκ τότε Χῶναι.

The 6th of this month [September]. The memorialization of the miracle at Chonai by the mighty Archistrategos of God
Once in the city called Chonai, which was previously called Côlassae, there was a man whose name was Archippos, a pious and God-fearing man. He became custodian for the spring that gushed forth there that had been brought by the visitation of the mighty Archistrategos [commander of the heavenly hosts, Michael], and because of the miracles that were associated with the water. Many unbelievers were converted and baptized. This incited many Greeks to envy, they refusing to accept the marvelous miracles. They ground their teeth against the sacred spring and the holy man Archippos. A huge multitude amassed. They dammed up two great rivers, merging them into a massive barrage which they instantly unleashed in order to crush the sanctuary, the spring and Archippos. When Archippos heard the roar of waters, he cried out for the Archistrategos to help. Immediately, he appeared and split the bedrock with the scepter he held. And he funneled the waters into the chasm. From that time on, the place was called Chonai ["Funnels"].

xxviii) The *Menologion of Basil II*, Nov 23rd [Cod. Vat. Gr. 1613, facsimile edition 2005].

Ἄθλησις τῶν ἁγίων Μαρτύρων Ἀρχίππου μαθητοῦ Παύλου τοῦ Ἀποστόλου καὶ Φιλήμονος τοῦ στρατιώτου.
Οὗτοι ὑπῆρχον ἐπὶ Νέρωνος τοῦ βασιλέως. Μαθηταὶ δὲ γεγονότες τοῦ ἁγίου Παύλου, ἐμαρτύρησαν ἐν Χώναις πόλει τῆς Φρυγίας, ἥτις ἐστί πλησίον Λαοδικείας. Ἑορτῆς γὰρ ἀγομένης μυσαρᾷ Ἀρτέμιδι, ἐν τῷ ταύτης ναῷ, τῷ ἐν Χώναις, παρὰ τῶν πεπλανημένων Ἑλλήνων, οὗτοι οἱ ἅγιοι τὴν δοξολογίαν ἀνέπεμπον τῷ Θεῷ ἐν τῇ ἁγιωτάτῃ ἐκκλησίᾳ, μετὰ τῶν Χριστιανῶν. Εἶτα ἐπιθέμενοι αὐτοῖς οἱ εἰδωλολάτραι, τῶν μὲν λοιπῶν φυγόντων, μόνου δὲ Ἀρχίππου καὶ Φιλήμονος, καὶ Ἀπφίας ὑπομεινάντων, κρατήσαντες αὐτοὺς, ἤγαγον πρὸς Ἀνδροκλέα τὸν σιτοφύλακα Ἐφέσου. Τύπτεται οὖν παρ' αὐτοῦ ὁ Ἄρχιππος. Καὶ μὴ πεισθεὶς θῦσαι τοῖς εἰδώλοις, εἰς βόθρον ἐμβάλλεται, καὶ χώννυται μέχρι τοῦ ὀμφάλου. Καὶ ὑπὸ παίδων σχολιτῶν γραφείοις κατακεντηθεῖς ὅλον τὸ σῶμα πρότερον, ὕστερον ἐλιθοβολήθη. Εἶτα ἐστιν ὁ ἅγιος Φιλήμων μετὰ ξύλων τυφθεὶς ἀνηλεῶς τελειοῦται.

The tribulation of the holy martyrs, Archippos the disciple of Paul the apostle and Philemon the soldier.
All this took place when Nero was emperor. These having become disciples of Saint Paul, began to bear witness in Chonai, a city of Phrygia, which neighbors Laodikeia. When a feast was scheduled by the deceived Greeks for foul Artemis at her temple in Chonai, these holy men joined with the Christians in offering up praise to God in the most sacred church. Then the idolaters railed against them. When the rest took flight, and only Archippos and Philemon and Apphia remained, the antagonists seized them and hauled them before Androkles, the Sitophylax [Superintendent of grain supply] of Ephesos. Archippos was assaulted by him. And further, when he refused to sacrifice to idols, he was hurled into a ditch where he sank up to his middle. And his whole body was punctured by young students with their styluses, before then being pelted with stones. Finally, he was beaten mercilessly with clubs until he died.

xxix) *Analecta Hymnica Graeca* 8.18 (Synaxarium for Nov. 8th) (ed. Kominis and Schirò) [similar story summary to *Synaxarium Ecclesiae Constantinopoleos* for Sept. 6th, ed. Delehaye].

Ἑορτὴν ἐπιτελοῦμεν τοῦ ἀρχιστρατήγου Μιχαήλ, ἀνάμνησιν ποιούμενοι τοῦ θαύματος τοῦ δι' αὐτοῦ γενομένου ἐν Κολασσαῖς τῆς Φρυγίας, ταῖς μετὰ τοῦτο ἐπικληθείσαις Χώναις …

We celebrate the feast of the Archistrategos Michael, remembering the miracle he worked at Colassae of Phrygia, which, thereafter, was called Chonai. …

xxx) Michael Attaliates *History* 19.3 (ed. Kaldellis and Krallis) (see also John Scylitzes *Chronicles continuation* 140.10–22, ed. Tsolakes).

Οὔπω δὲ τὰ τῆς φήμης παρήκμασε καὶ αὖθις ἑτέρα ἐπῆλθε τοὺς Τούρκους ἀπαγγέλλουσα τὴν ἐν Χώναις πολιτείαν καὶ αὐτὸν τὸν περιβόητον ἐν θαύμασι καὶ ἀναθήμασι τοῦ Ἀρχιστρατήγου ναὸν καταλαβεῖν ἐν μαχαίρᾳ καὶ φόνου μὲν ἅπαντα τὰ ἐκεῖσε πληρῶσαι καὶ λύθρου, πολλὰς δὲ ὕβρεις τῷ ἱερῷ ἐμπαροινηθῆναι. Καὶ τὸ δὴ σχετλιώτερον μὴ τὰς τοῦ χάσματος σήραγγας ἐν ᾧπερ οἱ παραρρέοντες ποταμοὶ ἐκεῖσε χωνευόμενοι διὰ τῆς τοῦ Ἀρχιστρατήγου παλαιᾶς ἐπιδημίας καὶ θεοσημίας ὡς διὰ πρανοῦς ἀστατοῦν τὸ ῥεῦμα καὶ λίαν εὐδρομοῦν ἔχουσι, τοὺς καταφυγόντας διατηρῆσαι καὶ ὑπαλύξαι τὸν κίνδυνον μελετῆσαι, ἀλλ' ὅπερ οὐ γέγονέ ποτε, πλημμυρῆσαι τὸ ὕδωρ καὶ οἷον ἀναρροιβδῆσαι καὶ ἀνερεύξασθαι καὶ πάντας ἄρδην τοὺς καταπεφευγότας κατακλῦσαι καὶ διὰ ξηρὰς ὑποβρυχίους ὑποποιήσασθαι.

These things had not yet outworn their urgency when another calamity hit, prompting a further report: the Turks [sent by Alp Arslan] seized the citizenry in Chonai and the church of the Archistrategos itself, famed for its miracle and its dedication. They were put to the sword; everything was awash with the defilement of spilled blood and many through their arrogance became drunk in their desecration of the church. And most heartless of all, the rivers flowing past were not funneled away into the hollows of the chasm as once happened through the visitation and miracle of the Archistrategos. The waters there form a treacherous and turbulent torrent. Those who fled were seeking to escape in order to preserve themselves from the imminent threat. Never before had it occurred but the waters turned into a thundering deluge, heaving against them, in the inundation utterly overwhelming those who had fled for safety to dry ground.

xxxi) John Zonaras *Epitome of History* 695.4–7 (ed. Büttner-Wobst).

ἡ δὲ περὶ τούτων ἀγγελία τὸν αὐτοκράτορα διετάραξε, καὶ ἔτι φήμη τις γενομένη ὡς ἡ ἐν Χώναις πολιτεία καὶ τὸ ἐκεῖ τοῦ ἀρχιστρατήγου περίπυστον τέμενος τοῖς βαρβάροις παρείληπται.

The message concerning these things [the advance of the Turks] perplexed the emperor [Manuel Comnenos], and besides, a certain report arrived that the municipality of Chonai, where lies the celebrated sanctuary of the Archistrategos, was taken by the barbarians.

xxxii) Nilos Doxapatres *Notitia patriarchatuum* 29.35–30.2, 30.9–10, 31.1–2, 32.5–6, 32.36 (ed. Finck).

Εἰσὶν οὖν αἱ ἀναγεγραμμέναι ἐπαρχίαι καὶ μητροπόλεις αἱ ὑποκείμεναι τῷ Κωνσταντινουπόλεως αὗται αἱ ἐν τῇ ἀνατολῇ καὶ τῇ δύσει καὶ τοῖς λοιποῖς μέρεσιν …
ς'. αἱ Σάρδεις τῆς Ἀσίας, ἔχουσα ἐπισκοπὰς κε' …
κβ'. ἡ Λαοδίκεια τῆς Φρυγίας Καπατιανῆς, ἔχουσα ἐπισκοπὰς κς' …
μα'. ἡ Ἱεράπολις Φρυγίας Καπατιανῆς, ἔχουσα ἐπισκοπὰς θ' …
νθ'. αἱ Χῶναι Φρυγίας …

Accordingly, these are the metropolitical dioceses subject to Constantinople, those in the east and the west and in other parts …
6. Sardis in Asia, having 25 bishops …
22. Laodikeia in Phrygia Capatiane [=Pacatiane] having 26 bishops …
41. Hierapolis in Phrygia Capatiane, having 9 bishops …
59. Chonai in Phrygia …

xxxiii) Prochiron *Auctum* 40.50 (ed. Zepos).

Θεσπίζομεν οὖν ἐκείνας εἶναι τῶν ἡμερῶν ἀπράκτους, ἃς ἐν τῇ παρούσῃ διατάξει ῥητῶς ἀπαριθμησόμεθα. … ἡ ς' τοῦ σεπτεμβρίου μηνός, ὅτι ἐν αὐτῇ τὸ ἐν χώναις τοῦ ἀρχιστρατήγου μιχαὴλ θαῦμα τερατουργεῖται.

We declare those days to be holidays, which we have reckoned as belonging in the present order. … the 6th of the month of September, because on this day the miracle of the Archistrategos Michael was worked in Chonai.

xxxiv) Theodore Prodromos *Monostiches* for Sept 6th (ed. Acconcia Longo).

Τὸ ἐν Χώναις τοῦ ἀρχαγγέλου Μιχαὴλ θαῦμα.
Χώναις Μιχαὴλ ὑδάτων χώνη ξένη.

The miracle of the archangel Michael in Chonai —
An astonishing fount of Michael's waters at Chonai.

xxxv) Nicolaus Catascepenus *Life of St Cyril Phileotes* (ed. Sargologos).

Ἄλλοτε δὲ πάλιν ἐπεθύμησεν ὁ ὅσιος ἀπελθεῖν ἐν Χώναις καὶ προσκυνῆσαι τὸ γεγονὸς θαῦμα παρὰ τοῦ ἀρχιστρατήγου Μιχαήλ. Συνέβη δὲ αὐτῷ ἐν πανδοχείῳ τινὶ καταλῦσαι· καὶ ὁ πανδοχεὺς ἦν ληστής. Ἤρξατο οὖν πειράζειν αὐτὸν καὶ λέγειν· Σύ, τίς εἶ; Καὶ πόθεν ἔρχῃ; Οἱ γὰρ ὀφθαλμοί σου κλέπτου εἰσὶ καὶ ʻἡ λαλιά σου δῆλόν σε ποιεῖ.' Τὸ δὲ μαλάκιόν σου τί κέκτηται ἔνδον; Ὁ δὲ ἀποκριθεὶς εἶπεν· ʻἼνα τί ἡ ἐλευθερία μου κρίνεται ὑπὸ ἑτέρας συνειδήσεως;' Ἐγὼ διὰ τῆς τοῦ Χριστοῦ μου χάριτος κλέπτης οὐκ εἰμι· ἄνθρωπος δὲ ὢν ἁμαρτωλὸς ἀπέρχομαι ἐν Χώναις προσκυνήσων τὸν ἀρχιστράτηγόν μου Μιχαήλ. …

Another time the holy man [Cyril] desired to go to Chonai, in order to venerate [the icon of] the miracle performed by the Archistrategos Michael. It happened that he went to stay at a certain inn. But the inn-keeper was a rogue. He began to tempt him saying, "Who are you? And where do you come from? For your eyes are those of a thief and your speech gives you away [Matt 26:73]. What things are secreted in your pouch?" He replied, saying, "Why is my freedom being judged by another's scruples [1 Cor 10:29]. Through the grace of Christ, I am no thief. But being a frail sinner I ventured to Chonai that I might venerate my Archistrategos Michael. …

xxxvi) Michael Choniates *Oration* 2.39 (ed. Lampros).

Ἐγκωμιον εἰς τὸν μακάριον μητροπολίτην Χωνῶν κύριον Νικήταν.
Κολασσαὶ πόλις ἐστὶ Φρυγίας· παρὰ τοσοῦτον οὐ γείτων ἡ πόλις Μαιάνδρῳ τῷ ποταμῷ παρ' ὅσον ἀπῴκισται πρὸς ἕω, ἕνα που σταθμὸν διέχουσα. Οἶδε τὴν πόλιν

καὶ Ξενοφῶν καὶ Ἡρόδοτος οἱ καλοὶ, εὐδαίμονά τε καὶ μεγάλην ἱστοροῦντες ἐξυμνοῦσι τῷ λόγῳ, κοσμεῖ δὲ καὶ ὁ σοφώτατος Παῦλος οἷς πλεῖστα τῶν παρ' αὐτῷ ἀπορρήτων ὅσα τοῦ τρίτου κατήγαγεν οὐρανοῦ δι' ἐπιστολιμαίων τετέλεκε καὶ μίαν τῶν τετειχισμένων ἀποστολικοῖς γράμμασιν εἴργαστο· πολιουχεῖ δὲ Μιχαὴλ ὁ ἀΰλων οὐσιῶν ἡγεμὼν ἐξ οὗ δῆτα ὑβριστῶν ποταμῶν ἐκαινοτόμησεν ἐκεῖ που κατάποσιν καὶ ταῖς πάλαι Κολασσαῖς οἰκειότερον τῇ περιπτώσει τῆς μεγαλουργίας δέδωκεν ὄνομα.

Encomium for Nicetas, the blessed lord metropolitan of Chonai.
Colossae is a city of Phrygia. The city has no neighbor dwelling near it, right up to the Maeander river, whence there is one station [Kydrara]. The noble Xenophon and Herodotos knew the city as very prosperous and presented it as great, extolling it in their works. The most sagacious Paul adorned it with the greatest of ineffable accolades which he brought down with him from the third heaven, and delivered through letters. He composed one writing for the fortification for those engaged in the apostolic mission. And Michael the immaterial one, being the commander of the heavenly beings, indeed protected it from the violence of the rivers and established there a subterranean reservoir. By the intervention of this mighty miracle he conferred on old Kolossae a literal name [Chonai].

xxxvii) Michael Choniates *Oration* 2.88 (ed. Lampros).

ἐκεῖνος καὶ τοὺς Ἰουδαίους οὕτω τι ἐβδελύξατο, ὡς μηδὲ τὴν αὐτοῦ παροικεῖν ἐφεῖναί ποτε. Ἠκροᾶτο γὰρ Παύλου βοῶντος· "βλέπετε τοὺς κακοὺς κύνας, τοὺς κακοὺς ἐργάτας." [Phil 3:2]

For this reason, he [Nicetas] detested the Jews so much so that, from that time, he refused to allow them to dwell there. He heeded the bellowing of Paul "Beware the foul dogs, the workers of evil."

xxxviii) Michael Choniates *Oration* 2.95 (ed. Lampros).

Πανήγυριν περὶ τὸν ἐκεῖ που νεὼν τὰ ἐν αὐτῷ συνίστησι θαύματα καὶ πανήγυριν πολυάνθρωπον· πάνυ μέντοι πολυάνθρωπον. Ἕλκει γὰρ, οὐ μέγα εἰπεῖν, τὰς περιοικίδας ἁπάσας πόλεις, ἀλλ' ἔτι γε δὴ καὶ τοὺς ἐξ ὑπερορίων Λυδούς τε καὶ Ἴωνας καὶ Κᾶρας καὶ Παμφύλους καὶ Λυκίους, πρὸς δὲ καὶ βαρβάρους Ἰκονιεῖς ἕνεκά γε τοῦ ἀποδοῦναι καὶ πρίασθαι.

There a festival occurred for the sanctuary wherein miracles had been performed. It was a panegyric of many people, indeed, truly of many people. It attracted, without saying how many, all the surrounding cities, but even moreso, from outside the region, Lydians and Ionians and Carians and Pamphylians and Lycians, as far as to the barbarians of Iconium in order to buy and sell. [then to retelling the story of Michael of Chonai]

xxxix) Michael Choniates *Oration* 2.97 (ed. Lampros).

Ἐπὶ τούτοις τῶν θαυμάζεσθαι ἀξίων καὶ ἡ περὶ τὰς πηγὰς τῶν ποταμῶν λευκὴ ψάμαθος, οὐ φύσει χρώματος ἔχουσα οὕτως· ἀλλ' ἦν τι γύναιον ἀσεβὲς, ποιμενικὸν, πολύθρεμμον, θυμῷ καὶ αὐτὸ ῥέον κατὰ τοῦ ἱεροῦ, ὃ γάλακτος ἀρύεται πᾶσαν πηγὴν καὶ ἀμέλγει πᾶσαν μὲν αἶγα, πᾶσαν δὲ βοῦν, εἶτα ὁμοῦ τοὺς γαυλοὺς ἐκκενοῖ καὶ γαλαξίαν ποταμὸν σχεδιάζει καὶ συμβάλλει τοῖν δυοῖν τοῦτον τρίτον καὶ αὔξεται τὸ ῥεῖθρον Λύκου καὶ Κάπρου, τραφὲν λεαίνης ταύτης πολλῷ γάλακτι. Καὶ ἵνα μὴ τὸ ῥεῦμα τοῦ χρόνου τὸ πεπραγμένον ἀποκλύσῃ μνήμης ἀνθρώπων κέχρωσται γαλακτώδει ψαμάθῳ ἡ προχοὴ καὶ κηρύσσει τὸ τέρας ἐπικληθεῖσα Γάλα Γραός.

Added to these matters eliciting astonishment, is the white surface around the sources of the rivers. It is not this color by nature. But there was a certain weasely woman, a shepherd of many flocks, by temperament irascibly antagonistic to the church. Sucking out every source of milk, this lioness's runt drained every goat and every cow, and then, emptying all her vats at once, she orchestrated a galactic cascade, a third flow which joined and amplified the two, the Lycus and Kapros, bloating their stream with the volume of milk. And so that the course of time might not expunge the affair from human recall, the well-spring of the river remains dyed with a milky surface, and the wonder is heralded through what it has been called: Gala Graos, crone's curd.

xl) Nicetas Choniates *Chronicon* 178.14–18 (ed. van Dieten).

ἀπάρας οὖν τῆς βασιλίδος τῶν πόλεων, Φρυγίαν τε καὶ Λαοδίκειαν διελθὼν ἀφιμνεῖται ἐς Χώνας, πόλιν εὐδαίμονα καὶ μεγάλην, πάλαι τὰς Κολασσάς, τὴν ἐμοῦ τοῦ συγγραφέως πατρίδα. καὶ τὸν ἀρχαγγελικὸν ναὸν εἰσιών, μεγέθει μέγιστον καὶ κάλλει κάλλιστον ὄντα καὶ θαυμασίας χειρὸς ἅπαντα ἔργον …

Therefore he [the emperor Manuel, in 1176] departed from the royal city [Constantinople] and travelled through the cities of Phrygia, including Laodikeia, and came to Chonai, a prosperous and great city, of old known as Colossae — my, the author's, homeland. And he went into the archangelic church, a vast structure most beautiful in its appearance, a work of wondrous human skill …

xli) Nicetas Choniates *Chronicon* 195.21–196.4 (ed. van Dieten).

τὰς δυνάμεις τοίνυν ἀναλαβὼν Ἀνδρόνικος πρῶτα μὲν εἰς τὸ τῆς Γραὸς παρεμβάλλει Γάλα, ἔπειτα δ' ἐκεῖσε τὰ ὑποζύγια καὶ τὴν ἄλλην ἀποσκευὴν καταθέμενος ἄνεισιν ἐς νέωτα πρὸς τὸν Χάρακα κούφως ὡπλισμένην ἔχων τὴν στρατιάν. οὐ γενναῖον δέ τι δράσας οὐδ' ἄξιον τοῦ τοσούτου στρατεύματος, ὃ τηνικαῦτα ἐπήγετο, ἀλλὰ συμμετρήσας τὸ ἔργον βοσκημάτων ἁρπαγαῖς καὶ ποιμνίταις ὀλίγοις Τούρκοις περιδεὴς ἐκεῖθεν ἀπονοστεῖ. ἐπιφανέντων γὰρ ἐκ τῶν ὄπισθεν νυκτὸς βαρβάρων τινῶν καὶ βοησάντων, μὴ ἀναμείνας ἢ τὸ πλῆθος τῶν ἐπιόντων κατεξετάσαι ἢ τοὺς ὑπ' αὐτὸν εἰς μάχην καταστησάμενος ἀνεὶς τὸν ὑπεκφέροντα ἵππον καὶ χερσὶ καὶ ποσὶ καὶ φωνῇ πρὸς τὸ φέρεσθαι ὀξέως διήγειρεν, οὐ τὴν εἰς τὸ στρατήγιον φέρουσαν ὁδεύων, ἀλλ' εὐθὺ τῆς τῶν Χωνῶν ὁρμώμενος πόλεως. ἰδὼν δὲ τὸν ἵππον καὶ πορρωτέρω χωρεῖν ἔχοντα οὐδ' ἐκεῖσε τὸν δρόμον ἵστησιν, ἀλλ' ἐς τὴν ἐν Φρυγίᾳ Λαοδίκειαν ὅλον συντείνει τὸ πρόθυμον.

Andronikos [a commander appointed by the emperor Manuel] having mustered his troops, first stationed them at Graos Gala ["Crone's Curd" northeast of Colossae]. There he quartered his pack animals and other supplies before next venturing towards Charax [a little to the north] with a force only lightly armed. He did not accomplish anything noble, nothing worthy of such a cohort furbished in such a way. The only outcome was the confiscation of cattle and capture of a few Turkish shepherds before, in trepidation, he retreated to his base. Afterwards, when some of the barbarians bobbed up bellowing in the night, he did not wait around to discern the size of those who were approaching nor were they engaged in battle by him. Rather, he abandoned the scene and spurred away on his horse, riding hand and foot, shouting to rouse it to streak swiftly away, not beating a path to the camp but retreating directly for the city of Chonai. But when he perceived that the horse was capable of further flight, he did not halt there but strained feverishly onwards to Phrygian Laodikeia.

xlii) Nicetas Choniates *Chronicon* 197.8–11 (ed. van Dieten).

Τότε καὶ ἐμὸς συγγενής, τῷ κλήρῳ μὲν τῆς πόλεως κατειλεγμένος Χωνῶν, λευίτης τὴν τάξιν, λήματος δ' ἀνδρείου πλήρης, συνανελθὼν τῷ λοιπῷ στρατεύματι ἐς τὸν Χάρακα μετὰ σκευῆς πολεμικῆς καὶ σκυλεύσας, εἴ τι που ἐφεῦρεν ἡ χεὶρ ἐν τοῖς τῶν Τούρκων σκηνώμασιν, …

Then one of my kinsman, a member in the levitical [diaconal] order of the clergy of the city of Chonai, a man full of courageous spirit, went out armed for war with the remaining forces to Charax intent on looting whatever he could from the Turkish camps. …

xliii) Nicetas Choniates *Chronicon* 219.3–12 (ed. van Dieten).

Ἀλλὰ γὰρ οὐχ ὑπερβήσομαί τι καὶ ἄλλο τῶν ἀξίων εἰρῆσθαι, τοῦ ἱστορεῖν ἐνταῦθα γενόμενος. ἦν τις εὐνοῦχος ἀρχιερατικῶς προεδρεύων τῆς τῶν Χωνῶν πόλεως, Νικήτας τοὔνομα, πάσης ἀρετῆς καταγώγιον, οὕτω δὴ προφητικὸς καὶ προβλέπων τὰ ἔμπροσθεν, ὡς τοῖς μεγίστοις τῶν ὁρώντων ἐγκρίνεσθαι καὶ εἰς θαῦμα κεῖσθαι παρ' οἷς ὁ ἀνὴρ ἐγνώριστο, εἴπερ ἡ καθ' ἡμᾶς γενεὰ πονηρὰ οὖσα καὶ μοιχαλὶς τοιοῦτον ηὐτύχησεν ἀγαθόν. ἀμέλει καὶ τοῦ βασιλέως τούτου ἐξ Ἀρμενίας παριόντος τὰς Χώνας ἀρτιστεφοῦς καὶ τῆς πατρῴας διαδόχου ἀρχῆς καὶ τὸν ἀρχαγγελικὸν ναὸν εἰσελθόντος καὶ χειρὶ τοῦ ἀρχιερέως τούτου εὐλογηθέντος,

But while we are relating affairs worthy of note, I must not overlook another matter. There was a certain eunuch who presided in high-priestly fashion in the city of Chonai. His name was Nicetas and he was the epitome of every virtue. As such he was endowed with prophetic insight such as to forsee the things to come with such acuity to be judged among the greatest seers, reckoned as a marvel by those whom the man encountered. A wicked and adulterous generation is a judgment applicable to us [cf Matt 12:39, 16:4, Mk 8:38], so it was fortuitous that there such a good man was present. At any rate, when this emperor [Manuel] came from Armenia to Chonai, having been newly appointed as successor to his father's rule and having entered the Church of the Archangel, he was blessed by the hand of this high-priest [hyperbolic synonym for "archbishop"].

xliv) Gregory II *Life of Lazarus* 7 (ed. Delehaye).

Πορευόμενος δὲ εὗρέ τινας ἐκ τῆς τῶν Καππαδοκῶν χώρας ὁρμωμένους καὶ πρὸς τὸν τοῦ ἀρχαγγέλου ναὸν καὶ αὐτοὺς ἀπιόντας· ... Ὡς γὰρ ἡ νὺξ κατέλαβε, στὰς ἐν μιᾷ γωνίᾳ τοῦ νάρθηκος καὶ τὰς εὐχὰς αὐτοῦ τῷ Κυρίῳ ἀναπέμψας, εἶθ' οὕτως ἐπὶ τοῦ τόπου κατεκλίθη πρὸς τὸ ὑπνῶσαι·

Going on his way [to Chonai] Lazaros found some people originating from Cappadocia who were also heading toward the church of the Archangel. He joined their ranks and went on with them.
... when night fell, Lazaros stood in one corner of the narthex of the church of the Archangel and addressed his prayers to the Lord and then lay down to sleep in the same place.

xlv) Manuel Philes *Carmen* 44 (ed. Miller).

Εἰς τὴν πρὸς Κολασαεῖς τούτου ἐπιστολήν.
Χαλκοῦν κολοσσὸν ὁ χρυσοῦς Παῦλος νικᾷ (1)
Ἀρθεὶς ὑπὲρ γῆν οὐρανοῦ μέχρι τρίτου.
Καὶ θραῦε γοργῶς τῶν λόγων τῇ σφενδόνῃ,
Βαλὼν τὸν ἀκρόγωνον ἐν μέσῳ λίθον.

For his (Paul's) epistle to the Colassians
The golden Paul conquered the bronze Colossos,
Having been taken from earth to the third heaven.
And he shatters the monstrous by the sling-shot of his words,
Setting the foundation stone in their midst.

xlvi) Manuel Philes Carmen 226 (ed. Miller).

Εἰς ἀνάγνωσιν αὐθωρὸν τοῦ ἐν ταῖς Χώναις θαύματος.
Ὕδωρ τὸ πῦρ ἄπειρον εἰς Χώνην χέον,
Πῦρ γὰρ ὁ Δαβὶδ μαρτυρεῖ τοὺς ἀγγέλους,
Ὡς πνεῦμα καὶ φῶς εἰς θεοῦ λειτουργίαν,
Τὴν συρφετώδη τοῦ Σατὰν ὕλην φλέγει,
Εἰπεῖν δὲ ταυτὸν τοὺς ἀκανθώδεις πόνους,
Οὓς χερσομανήσασα καρδία τρέφει·
Τὰ ῥεῖθρα λοιπὸν τοῦ προκειμένου λόγου,
Ὡς ἀπὸ Χωνῶν τῶν ἀκουστικῶν πόρων,
Εἰς τοὺς μυχοὺς δέχεσθε τοὺς ἀποκρύφους,
Ὡς ἂν ὁ νοῦς ἄσειστος ἐντεῦθεν μένοι
Μὴ παρασυρεὶς τῶν παθῶν τῇ προσχύσει.

To accompany the reading of the miracle at Chonai.
The fire poured the flood into the funnel
For David attests that fire is the angels [Ps 104:4 Hbs1:7]
Just as spirit and light are the ministry of God.
So the refuse of Satan prepared a tinderbox.
And the thorn-filled toilers muttered as one,
Those whom a frenzied, wasting heart curried.

Moreover, the deluge according to the prescribed word
Diverting as from the renowned Chonai
"Be ushered into the hidden depths, the innermost recesses."
Henceforth may your resolve remain unshaken,
Not swept away by the flood of passions.

xlvii) Codex Neapol. II.C.33,[9] fol 104v for Sept. 6th.

Θαῦμα γενόμενος ἐν ταῖς Χώναις ἐν Κολασσαῖς τῆς Φρυγίας παρὰ τοῦ ἀρχαγγέλου Μιχαήλ. …

The miracle that was performed in Chonai in Colassae of Phrygia by the archangel Michael. …

xlviii) Damascene the Studite *Oration* 18.752–5, 796–8 (ed. Deledemou).

Ἄλλο δὲ θαῦμα ἀκούσατε, εὐλογημένοι Χριστιανοί, θαυμαστὸν καὶ παράδοξον περὶ τοῦ Ἀρχιστρατήγου Μιχαήλ. Κάστρον εἶναι εἰς τὴν Φρυγίαν, ὁποῦ ὀνομάζεται Χῶναι· ἐκεῖ ἦτον ἁγίασμα τοῦ Ἀρχιστρατήγου Μιχαήλ, ὁποῦ τὸ ἐπρωτοεῦρεν ὁ Θεολόγος Ἰωάννης· … Αὐτὸ τὸ θαῦμα ὠνομάσθη ὁ τόπος Χῶναι, ἀμὴ πρῶτα ὠνομάζετο Κολασσαί.

Listen to another wonderful, indeed astounding miracle, blessed Christians, concerning the Archistrategos Michael, There was a garrison in Phrygia called Chonai. At that place there was a hagiasma of the Archistrategos Michael, first discovered by John the Theologian. … The place was named Chonai because of this miracle, though at first it was called Colassae.

9 Citation of the codex in H. Delehaye, "Catalogus Codicum Hagiographicorum Graecorum: Bibliothecae Nationalis Neapolitanae." Microfilm copy at Dumbarton Oaks, Washington DC.

Appendix 2
A Concordance of the coin types in von Aulock's Catalogue and Roman Provincial Coinage online

The coins are listed according to their numbered sequence in volume 2 of Hans von Aulock's *Münzen und Stadte Phrygiens* (Tübingen: Ernst Wasmuth, 2 vols, 1980, 1987), abbreviated as *MSPhryg*. The list is only interrupted when *Roman Provincial Coinage online*, abbreviated as *RPC online*, provides coins not found in von Aulock's catalogue. The "t" following an *RPC online* number indicates a temporary listing, that is, still subject to a final decision. Some *RPC online* numbers have letters following the number. This has been a pragmatic decision of the editors to use the printed publication as the basis of online numbering. When new types sponsored by a particular benefactor have emerged since that publication (usually *Roman Provincial Coinage* volume III), this attracts a distinct letter added to the number. Where coins are listed in only one catalogue this is simply indicated by a dash in the column where the type is omitted. The final column gives page numbers where the coins receive some analysis.

In two instances, *RPC online* has amalgamated coins identified as two distinct types by von Aulock (496–505 and 506; 518–519 and 520–533).[10] *RPC*

10 I am inclined to agree with von Aulock's separation as distinct types in both cases. As to the second, the coin features on the obverse, the head of Sarapis wearing a kalathos with no legend; on the reverse the standing figure of Isis holding a raised sistrum in her right hand and a carrying a situla in her left. The key distinction in the types is in the arrangement of the legend ΚΟΛΟCCΗΝΩΝ. The majority of cases (*MSPhryg* 2.520–533) arrange the ten letters of the ethnic evenly to the right and left of the figure, thus ΚΟΛΟC | CΗΝΩΝ beginning in the upper right position on the flan. The minority of coins arrange the letters differently with seven letters at the right of Isis and three at her left, thus ΚΟΛΟCCΗ | ΝΩΝ. In fact, two examples of this iconography and legend, unknown to both von Aulock and *RPC online*, has the legend ΚΟΛΟC | CΗΝΩΝ beginning in the lower left position and moving in a clockwise direction around the perimeter of the flan (Pecunem online auction 38, lot 537, 6th December, 2015; Savoca Blue Auction 111, lot 1146, 29th August 2021) and adding a crescent to the shoulders of Isis. Given that *RPC online* accords different types to Hieronymos's radiate

online has correctly omitted *MSPhryg* 2.545 following its identification as a re-tooled forgery.[11] It is, accordingly, omitted from this concordance. Both von Aulock 493 and *RPC online* 4.2.1897 temp., #8 have subsumed a differently arranged legend (ANEΘHKEN in field) under those coins with the reverse legend completely in the perimeter. The coin is now known from two examples,[12] and should probably be given a separate entry. A similar type, that is with *Dêmos* on the obverse and Helios riding in a quadriga on the reverse, has only the ethnic in the reverse legend. However, both von Aulock and *RPC online*, combine as one type, examples that have ΚΟΛΟCCΗΝΩΝ around the perimeter of the reverse (*MSPhryg* 2.496, *RPC online* 4.2.1899 temp., specimen #14 — different coins)[13] and entangled in the legs of the horses drawing the quadriga. Again, the quite distinct layout of the legend invites classification as a separate type.

For each coin type, the number of examples follows the entry for the respective catalogue (totalling 148 for *MSPhryg* and 211 for *RPC online*, 228 examples in total). The number of extra examples for each coin type as known to me is given in brackets in the final column (total of 79 extra specimens). The total number of coin types for von Aulock is 55, for *RPC online* 59 (as at August 2022). *RPC online* omit some of von Aulock's entries and von Aulock was unaware of some coin types now included in *RPC online*. In all there are 71 coin types combined from these two catalogues. A further 11 types await entry into *RPC online*, giving a total of 82 types. These can be found in chapter 1. Because *RPC online* is regularly updated, and new coin types have regularly appeared in the coin world over the last two decades, there may be some minor adjustments to be made to this concordance (compiled in isolation in mid-2021, revised in August 2022).

Helios and rivergod mintings, simply on the basis that in one type the head of Helios faces right (*RPC online* 3.2313) and in another type faces left (*RPC online* 2313A), then in this case, a re-arrangement of the position of the letters of the ethnic warrants acknowledgement of distinct types, with a third type, and possibly a fourth, in the series now also to be admitted. As to the second collation, the series is marked by the ethnic identifier on both sides of the coin: ΔΗΜΟϹ ΚΟΛΟCCΗΝΩΝ on the obverse, ΚΟΛΟCCΗΝΩΝ on the reverse. One coin however lacks the ethnic (or any legend) on the reverse which was sufficient warrant for von Aulock to allocate a distinct type. Given that a second example has surfaced that also is without a legend on the reverse (Praefectus coins 21st December, 2019), von Aulock's decision should be followed.

11 See A. Burnett, M. Amandry and P. Ripollès, *Roman Provincial Coinage: Supplement 1* (London: British Museum/Paris: Bibliothèque nationale de France, 1998), 35, no. 2891; M. Amandry and A. Burnett, *Roman Provincial Coinage, Volume III: Nerva, Trajan and Hadrian (AD 96–138), Part I: Catalogue* (London: British Museum/Paris: Bibliothèque nationale de France, 2015), 286.

12 Lydia Numismatics Online Auction 7, lot 462, 9th May 2021 (31.1 mm, 15 g.).

13 The editors of *RPC online* for this coin suggest that this specimen is a cast. The authenticity of the type is not disputed. See, for a further example, Obolos Web Auction 24, lot 884, 21st August 2022.

MSPhryg 2	Examples	*RPC online*	Examples	Total known examples	Pages
447	1	3.2316	1	-	80
448–450	3	3.2313	3	+1	67
—	—	3.2313A	1	-	67, 114, 572, 664–5
451	1	3.2314	1	-	572
452	1	3.2317	3	-	114
453	1	3.2315	1	-	402
454	1	4.2.1887t	1	-	268
455–457	3	4.2.1888t	4	-	198, 408, 549
458–460	3	4.2.1889t	3	+1	404, 408
461–464	4	4.2.1890t	7	+5	408, 594
465–468	4	4.2.1891t	5	-	116
469	1	4.2.1892t	1	+1	354
470	1	4.2.1893t	2	+1	—
471–482	12	4.2.1894t	14	+6	80
483	1	4.2.1895t	3	+3	67
484–486	3	4.2.1896t	6	+1	68, 112–15
487–493	7	4.2.1897t	9	+2	115, 211
494–495	2	4.2.1898t	3	-	107, 198
496–505	10			+11	665
506	1	4.2.1899t	19	-	115, 211
507–512	6	4.2.1900t	8	+3	198
513–514	2	4.2.1901t	4	+1	200
515–517	3	4.2.1902t	7	+3	304, 627
518–519	2			+8 (Afyon)	—
520–533	14	4.2.1903t	22 (5+17)	+9	79, 241, 627
534–536	3	—	—	-	246, 247
537–539	3	—	—	+2	81, 516
540	1	—	—	-	—
541–542	2	—	—	-	—
543–544	2	—	—	+3	87, 410, 513
546	1	3.2308	1	-	—
547	1	3.2309	2	-	203, 516
548	1	3.2307	2	+1	512, 549
—	—	3.2307A	2	-	66
—	—	3.2307B	1	-	66, 572
—	—	3.2307C	1	-	66, 549
—	—	3.2307D	1	-	66, 410, 468, 512, 549

MSPhryg 2	Examples	*RPC online*	Examples	Total known examples	Pages
—	—	3.2307E	1	-	66
—	—	3.2307F	2	-	66
549	1	3.2310	4	-	—
—	—	3.2310A	2	-	67, 203, 516
550	1	3.2311	2	-	107
551–552	2	3.2312	2	-	—
—	—	3.2312A	1	-	67, 245
553–554	2	4.2.1874t	2	-	408
555–558	4	4.2.1875t	4	+2	536
559–562	4	4.2.1876t	5	+3	—
563	1	4.2.1877t	2	+1	—
564	1	4.2.1878t	1	-	108
565	1	4.2.1879t	1	-	—
566–574	9	4.2.1880t	14	+1	200, 205, 253–4, 536
575–577	3	4.2.1881t	5	+2	253, 536
578	1	4.2.1882t	2	+1	107
579	1	4.2.1883t	1	-	244, 318, 339
580	1	4.2.1884t	1	-	—
581–584	4	4.2.1885t	6	+2	—
585	1	4.2.1886t	1	+1	—
—	—	4.2.2446t	2	-	67, 208–11
—	—	4.2.10833t	1	-	408, 549
—	—	4.2.11597t	1	+1	67, 468, 536
—	—	4.2.11890t	2	-	67, 154
586–587	2	—	—	+1	154, 458, 594
588	1	—	—	+1	—
589	1	—	—	-	—
590	1	—	—	-	—
591	1	—	—	-	—
592–593	2	6.5521t	2	-	113, 212–4
—	—	6.10900t	2	-	68, 113, 152, 215–9
—	—	6.10829t	1	+1?	68, 113, 214–5, 500, 627
594–595	2	9.789	2	-	154, 214, 594
		9.789A	1	-	68, 113, 218

Appendix 3
List of names from Colossae

The following list of names of inhabitants of Colossae (understood as the city and the territory the city controlled) has been culled from coins, inscriptions and texts. The commencement date is 267 BCE, having taken the inscription *I.Laodikeia Lykos* 1, as indirect testimony to the Seleucid commander, Helenos, governing from Colossae (see chapter 3). The cut-off date (c. 300 CE) is the last inscription to provide names, that is, *MAMA* 6.38, even though the names there included the emperor Constantius I and probably Diocletian and Maximian (the text is fragmentary), are omitted in the list, given that the inscription is in Latin and Colossae was not their base. Byzantine-period names (of bishops, exarchs and others including Theodore/Dorotheos in *MAMA* 6.49) are not included, even though hagiographies built on key names in the Epistles to Philemon and Colossians (Philemon, Apphia, Archippos, Onesimos) are to be found. There are some further exclusions from the list. Emperors are excluded: Trajan to the co-regents Constantius I, Diocletian and Maximian; the co-regents are the last named emperors in the currently known inscriptions and coins. Lucius Makedo (*IGR* 4.869) is part of Hadrian's entourage in 129 CE. There are some names in the New Testament texts (Epistle to the Colossians, Philemon) where it is clear that the identified person does not hail from Colossae: Paul, Timothy, Archippos, Jesus known as Iustos, Mark, Barnabas, Tychikos, Luke, Demas, Aristarchos; only Archippos might be disputed as not from Colossae. A second Archippos, the custodian of the hagiasma of the Archangel Michael of Chonai, is named in the popular story. The naming is probably fictional (a deliberate, "faithful servant" evocation of Col 4:17). In any case, the story places his origins in Hierapolis. I have presented the argument in chapter nine herein. Aurelius Tatianos Glykon (*MAMA* 6.40) has been excluded from the list of names because it is highly likely that he came from Keretapa; see chapter ten. Some epitaphs have misleadingly been provenanced to Colossae or its territory (*PM* nrs 236, 1607, 1634, 1920, 1973, 2005); they belong rather to Attouda or Trapezopolis (*LGPN* sometimes simply "Phrygia (S.W.)". The names they bear (Ζώσιμος, Βάσσος husband of Μαρκία, Ἀπελλᾶς, Ζεῦξις father of Ζεῦξις,

Μέγας son of Μέγας grandson of Μηνόφιλος, Μάξιμος) have accordingly not been included. Francis Arundell in 1828 published what he described as a "very imperfect inscription." It was republished as *CIG* 3955 which deciphered ἡ γυνὴ αὐτοῦ from the letters Arundell recorded. A further examination of Arundell's transcription does allow two names to be deciphered with little adjustment to Arundell's record, namely, Ἀρταρβίδης and Κοκ(κ)ωνία. The first is rare, only attested elsewhere in *I.Eleusis* 86. The second is not attested but the stem Κοκκ– (probably from κόκκος "seed, berry" or κόκκυ/κόκκυξ "cuckoo") has seventeen derived names according to *LGPN* (occasionally dropping the gemination) The problem however is that even though these two names appear quite possible, the inscription becomes even more difficult to render once these are applied. Caution has urged me to hold these names from the list that follows, resigned to Arundell's "very imperfect" transcription. Others may be able to propose a more persuasive conjectural reconstruction.

The names are given in their familial relationships, where known. Sometimes the genealogies are extensive and lead to multiple repetitions of the same name as it is passed on down the generations (sometimes as many as four in succession). To avoid over-complication, it has been assumed that the genealogy indicates a continuous family presence in Colossae. There is no evidence in the existing legends, epigraphical and literary texts to suggest otherwise. Conversely, the origins of Diodotos and Aphias, even though their evidence indicates a move elsewhere (temporary or otherwise), that is, to Smyrna and Boubon respectively, has required their inclusion under Colossae (so *LGPN*). Where an indigenous name is confidently recognized, no diacritical marks are added, following the later practice of *LGPN* (hence, for example, Απφια, Αφιας).

An abbreviations key for the source(s) of the evidence follows the list, for facility of reference. Family relationships are restricted to genealogical lines and direct marriage: f. father, m. mother, s. son, d. daughter, gs. grandson, ggs. great grandson, gggs. great, great grandson, gf. grandfather, ggs. great grandfather, gggs great, great grandfather, h. husband, w. wife. Where a name is incomplete but indicated by other means (for example, τοῦ …), this is indicated by N. in the secondary genealogy (and once as the prime name) or, if available, by the beginning letter. Fragments of names are included even when a reconstruction is uncertain or resistant to completion. Occasionally, some decision as to the interpretation of the text has been made. For example, Τατιανός Β' Ἄρτου is read rather than Τατιανός Βάρτου largely on the basis of a (single!) occurrence of the name. Brief notes are added to explain certain decisions.

Name and relations	**Source**	**Notes**
Ἀγγελικός f. Διονύσιος	*Gephyra* 2020:1–26, *Kyros* 431.1.2, *AM* 1893: 206–7, *CBP* 542.408, *CCPI* 528, 613	Correction *CBP* 542.408, *LGPN* (city)
Ἀκρί[σιος (?) f. N gf. N	*SEG* 61.1160, *NewDocs* 10.17, *LGPN*, *CCPI* 401–6	Name completion *apud LGPN*
Ἀλέξανδρος s. Ἡρακλείδου gs. N.	*SEG* 61.1160, *NewDocs* 10.17, *CCPI* 401–6	
Αμμαλιον f. Ἀπολλώνιος	*BCH* 1893.250.27, *IGR* 4.806, Audollent 14, *CBP* 351.83, Wuensch XIII, *CCPI* 363–8	
Ἀμμιανή, Αὐρ. d. Τρύφων h. Καρπίων m. Ἡρακλέων, Αὐρ.	*MAMA* 6.42, *CCPI* 520–3	
Ἀντιμήδης f. Ζώσιμος gf. Εὐτύχης	*SEG* 61.1160, *NewDocs* 10.17, *CCPI* 401–6	
Ἀντίοχος	*BCH* 1893.250.27, *IGR* 4.806, Audollent 14, *CBP* 351.83, Wuensch XIII, *CCPI* 363–8	
Ἀνωτ[... f. Ἡρακλέων gf. Ἡρακλέων	*SEG* 61.1160, *NewDocs* 10.17, *CCPI* 401–6	
Ἀπολλω[νίδης b. Ἀπολλ]ώνιος s. Δαμοκράτης	*MAMA* 6.46, *CCPI* 534, 614	*LGPN* omit Calder's reconstruction
Ἀπολλώνιος s. Αμμαλιον	*BCH* 1893.250.27, *IGR* 4.806, Audollent 14, *CBP* 351.83, Wuensch XIII, *CCPI* 363–8	Ἀπολλώνιος is called Νοσσός, "the Chick"
Ἀπολλ]ώνιος b. Ἀπολλω[νίδης s. Δαμοκράτης	*MAMA* 6.46, *CCPI* 534, 614	*LGPN* accept Calder's reconstruction
Ἀπολλώνιος Οὐα[λέριος (?), Ὀκτ.	*MSPhryg* 2.447, *RPC* 3.2310A, 2311–2, 2316–7, *CCPI* 67, 407	Abbreviated Οὐα has options.
Ἀπολλώνιος s. Ἀπολλώνιος gs. Ζώσιμος ggs. Διοκράτης	*MSPhryg* 2.487–95, 578, *RPC* 4.2.1882t, 1897t, 1898t, *CCPI* 67, 198	
Ἀπολλώνιος f. Ἀπολλώνιος s. Ζώσιμος gs. Διοκράτης	*MSPhryg* 2.487–95, 578, *RPC* 4.2.1882t, 1897t, 1898t, *CCPI* 67, 198	
Ἀπολλώνιος f. Δῆμας	*SEG* 61.1160, *NewDocs* 10.17, *CCPI* 401–6	
Ἀπολλώνιος s. Ἀπολλώνιος gs. Ἄτταλος ggs. Σκεπαρνᾶς	*SEG* 61.1160, *NewDocs* 10.17, *CCPI* 401–6	

Name and relations	Source	Notes
Ἀπολλώνιος s. Ἄτταλος gs. Σκεπαρνᾶς f. Ἀπολλώνιος	*SEG* 61.1160, *NewDocs* 10.17, *CCPI* 401–6	
Ἀπολλώνιος s. Μωκεας f. Δημήτριος	*SEG* 61.1160, *NewDocs* 10.17, *CCPI* 401–6	
Ἀπ[- (?) f. Ἡρακλᾶς, Μ. Αὐρ.	*MAMA* 6.41, *AS* 2006:105, *CCPI* 460–1	Patronymic may be an office (agonothete).
Απ̣πας f. Δίων	*MAMA* 6.44, *SEG* 57.1385, *CCPI* 590–2, 614	
Απφια	Phmn 2, *CCPI* 432–43	Correction *LGPN*
Απφια d. Ἡράκλειος gd. Διοσκουρίδης	*BCH* 1887:354.12, *IGR* 4.868, *I.Laodicée Lycos nymphée* 278–9, *CCPI* 358–60	
Ἀρίστη w. Ἐπίκτητος	*Smith Fs* 168, *CCPI* 615, 619	
Ἀρτεμίδωρος f. Κάρπος	*SEG* 57.1384, *CCPI* 92, 614	
Ἄρτος f. Τατιανός gf. Τατιανός	*MAMA* 6.48, *I.Mus. Denizli* 73, *PM* 1974, *BE* 1979.15, *CCPI* 601, 615, 619–23	Correction (likely) *MAMA* 6.48, *I.Mus. Denizli* 73, *PM* 1974
Ἄτταλος s. Τρυφωνιάνος	*SEG* 61.1160, *NewDocs* 10.17, *CCPI* 401–6	
Ἄτταλος s. Σκεπαρνᾶς f. Ἀπολλώνιος gf. Ἀπολλώνιος	*SEG* 61.1160, *NewDocs* 10.17, *CCPI* 401–6	
Αφιας d. Τρύφιων h. Ἑρμᾶς	*I.Boubon* 102, *CIG* 4380 k³, *CCPI* 400	Correction S-F 2.289, *CIG* 4380 k³, *LGPN*
Βάκχα	*BCH* 1893.250.27, *IGR* 4.806, Audollent 14, *CBP* 351.83, Wuensch XIII, *CCPI* 363–8	
Βακχύλος f. Θάλλος	*CCPI* 355–7	
Γλύκων	*MAMA* 6.47, *I.Mus. Denizli* 113, PM 594, *CCPI* 623–8	
Δ.[… f. Διόδωρος gf. Διόδωρος ggf. Διόδωρος	*SEG* 61.1160, *NewDocs* 10.17, *CCPI* 401–6	Given the succession of Διόδωρος, a similar name likely eg Διόδοτος
Δαμοκράτης f. Ἀπολλ]ώνιος f. Ἀπολλω[νίδης	*MAMA* 6.46, *CCPI* 534, 614	
Δάτυς (?) f. Ζ]ήνων	Arundell 98, *EA* 2007: 114, 3.1, *CCPI* 615	Reconstruction
Δῆμας s. Ἀπολλώνιος	*SEG* 61.1160, *NewDocs* 10.17, *CCPI* 401–6	

Name and relations	Source	Notes
Δημήτριος s. Δημήτριος gs. Θεόδωρος f. Θεόδωρος	*SEG* 61.1160, *NewDocs* 10.17, *CCPI* 401–6	
Δημήτριος s. Θεόδωρος f. Δημήτριος gf. Θεόδωρος	*SEG* 61.1160, *NewDocs* 10.17, *CCPI* 401–6	
Δημήτριος s.]νεια f. Θεόδωρος gf. Θεόδωρος	*SEG* 61.1160, *NewDocs* 10.17, *CCPI* 401–6	Further name/ethnic/? after Δημητρίου —> Αἰνείας? (but space for 5–6 letters)
Δημήτριος s. Ἀπολλώνιος gs. Μωκεας	*SEG* 61.1160, *NewDocs* 10.17, *CCPI* 401–6	
Δι[ογενεία (?) w. Τρόφ[ιμος	*MAMA* 6.45, *CCPI* 614	Fragmentary
Διόδοτος	*I.Smyrna* 440, *CCPI* 281–92	
Διόδωρος f. Τρύφων gf. Τρύφων	*SEG* 61.1160, *NewDocs* 10.17, *CCPI* 401–6	
Διόδωρος s. Διόδωρος gs. Διόδωρος ggs. Δ[...	*SEG* 61.1160, *NewDocs* 10.17, *CCPI* 401–6	Correction *SEG* 61.1160 (l. 8)
Διόδωρος s. Διόδωρος gs. Δ[... f. Διόδωρος	*SEG* 61.1160, *NewDocs* 10.17, *CCPI* 401–6	Correction *SEG* 61.1160 (l. 8)
Διόδωρος s. Δ[... f. Διόδωρος gf. Διόδωρος	*SEG* 61.1160, *NewDocs* 10.17, *CCPI* 401–6	Correction *SEG* 61.1160 (l. 8)
Διοκράτης f. Ζώσιμος gf. Ἀπολλώνιος ggf. Ἀπολλώνιος	*MSPhryg* 2.487–95, 578, *RPC online* 4.2.1882t, 1897t, 1898t, *CCPI* 67, 198	
Διομᾶς s. Διομᾶς f. Ζήνων, Μ. Αὐρ.	*BCH* 1887.353.11, *MAMA* 6.40, *CCPI* 450–61	Genealogical succession rather than multiple games' victory
Διομᾶς f. Διομᾶς gf. Ζήνων, Μ. Αὐρ.	*BCH* 1887.353.11, *MAMA* 6.40, *CCPI* 450–61	Genealogical succession rather than multiple games' victory
Διονύσιος s. Ἀγγελικός h. Τατα f. Εἰρήνη	*Gephyra* 2020:1–26, *Kyros* 431.1.2, *AM* 1893: 206–7, *CBP* 542.408, *CCPI* 528, 613	Spelling: –νοίσιος Correction *LGPN* (city)
Διονύσιος s. Μᾶρκος gs. Ῥοῦφος	*MAMA* 6.43, *I.Laodikeia Lykos* 104, *I.Mus. Denizli* 167, *CCPI* 517, 619	Spelling –σειος, Ῥοῦπος Disputed provenance (Colossae/Laodikeia)
Δῖος f. Ἱεικίς(?)	*Smith Fs* 171–3, *CCPI* 618–9	

Name and relations	Source	Notes
Διοσκουρίδης f. Ἡράκλειος gf. Απφια	*BCH* 1887:354.12, *IGR* 4.868, *I.Laodicée Lycos nymphée* 278–9, *CCPI* 358–60	Correction *BCH* 1887:354.12, *IGR* 4.868
Δίων f. Φοῖ]βος (?) gf. Τρό[φιμος	*MAMA* 6.45, *CCPI* 614	Fragmentary; Πρόβος possible, but less likely
Δίων s. Αππας	*MAMA* 6.44, *SEG* 57.1385, *CCPI* 590–2	
Εἰρήνη d. Διονύσιος + Τατα	*Gephyra* 2020:1–26, *Kyros* 431.1.2, *AM* 1893: 206–7, *CBP* 542.408, *CCPI* 528, 613	Correction *AM* 1893: 206–7, *CBP* 542.408, *LGPN* (city)
Ἐκλέγων	*MSPhryg* 2.564, *RPC* 4.2.1878t	Correction *MSPhryg* 2.564, *RPC* 4.2.1878t
Ἕλενος	*I.Laodikeia Lykos* 1, *CCPI* 136–43	Seleucid regional commander at Colossae; reassign *I.Laodikeia Lykos* 1
Ἐλπίς w.(?) Ζωσᾶς	*I.Laodikeia Lykos* 118, *CBP* 77.12, *CCPI* 167–9	Reassign *I.Laodikeia Lykos* 118 to Colossae
Ἐπάγαθος	*BCH* 1893.250.27, *IGR* 4.806, Audollent 14, *CBP* 351.83, Wuensch XIII, *CCPI* 363–8	
Ἐπαφρᾶς	Col 1:7, 4:12	
Ἐπαφρᾶς f. Μαρκιανός, Αὐ.	*MSPhryg* 2.594–5, *RPC* 9.789, *CCPI* 68	Correction *MSPhryg* 2.594–5
Ἐπαφρόδιτος, Τ. Ἀσίνιος	*MAMA* 6.39, *I.Mus. Denizli* 59, *CCPI* 408, 519–26	Correction *I.Mus. Denizli* 59, *LGPN*
Ἐπίκτητος h. Ἀρίστη	*Smith Fs* 168, *CCPI* 615, 619	
Ἑρμογένης f. Μενιάνδρος gf. Μενιάνδρος, Αὐ.	*Smith Fs* 171–3, *CCPI* 615, 618–9	
Εὐγενετοριανή, Κλ.	*MSPhryg* 2.548, *RPC online* 3.2307, 2307A–E, *CCPI* 65, 205, 407–10, 512–4	
Εὐθηνία w. Κάρπος	*SEG* 57.1384, *CCPI* 92, 613	
Εὐτέρπη	*BCH* 1893.250.27, *IGR* 4.806, Audollent 14, *CBP* 351.83, Wuensch XIII, *CCPI* 363–8	
Εὐτύχης s. Ζώσιμος gs. Ἀντιμήδης	*SEG* 61.1160, *NewDocs* 10.17, *CCPI* 401–6	
Ζήνων, Μ. Αὐρ. s. Διομᾶς gs. Διομᾶς	*BCH* 1887.353.11, *MAMA* 6.40, *CCPI* 450–61	
Ζ]ήνων f. Δάτυς(?)	Arundell 98, *EA* 2007:114, 3.1	Reconstruction
Ζήνων h. Ἰεικίς(?)	*Smith Fs* 171–3, *CCPI* 615, 618–9	

Name and relations	Source	Notes
Ζηνωνίς, Αὐ. w. Μενιάνδρος, Αὐ.	*Smith Fs* 171–3, *CCPI* 615, 618–9	
Ζωσᾶς s. Μολοσ(σ)ός	*I.Laodikeia Lykos* 118, *CBP* 77.12, *CCPI* 167–9	Reassign *I.Laodikeia Lykos* 118 to Colossae
Ζώσιμος Φιλοπάτωρ s. Ζώσιμος gs. Ζώσιμος ggs. Ζώσιμος	*MSPhryg* 2.566–77, *RPC online* 4.2.1880–1t, *CCPI* 200, 205, 253–4, 256	
Ζώσιμος f. Ζώσιμος Φιλοπάτωρ s. Ζώσιμος gs. Ζώσιμος	*MSPhryg* 2.566–77, *RPC online* 4.2.1880–1t, *CCPI* 200, 205, 253–4, 256	
Ζώσιμος f. Ζώσιμος gf. Ζώσιμος Φιλοπάτωρ s. Ζώσιμος	*MSPhryg* 2.566–77, *RPC online* 4.2.1880–1t, *CCPI* 200, 205, 253–4, 256	
Ζώσιμος f. Ζώσιμος gf. Ζώσιμος ggf. Ζώσιμος Φιλοπάτωρ	*MSPhryg* 2.566–77, *RPC online* 4.2.1880–1t, *CCPI* 200, 205, 253–4, 256	
Ζώσιμος f. Ἀπολλώνιος gf. Ἀπολλώνιος s. Διοκράτης	*MSPhryg* 2.487–95, 578, *RPC online* 4.2.1882t, 1897t, 1898t, *CCPI* 67, 198	
Ζώσιμος s. Ἀντιδήμης f. Εὐτύχης	*SEG* 61.1160, *NewDocs* 10.17, *CCPI* 401–6	
Ζώσιμος f. Τυδείδης	*SEG* 61.1160, *NewDocs* 10.17, *CCPI* 401–6	
Ζωσίμων f. N.	*SEG* 61.1160, *NewDocs* 10.17, *CCPI* 401–6	
Ἡλιόδωρος	*IGR* 4.870, *I.Laodicée Lycos nymphée* 269, 277–9, *CCPI* 248–56	
Ἡρακλᾶς, M. Αὐρ. s. Ἀπ[- (?)	*MAMA* 6.41, *AS* 2006:105, *CCPI* 456, 460	With patronymic or office (agonothete)?
Ἡρακλείδης s. Ἡρακλέων f. Ἡρακλέων	*SEG* 61.1160, *NewDocs* 10.17, *CCPI* 401–6	
Ἡρακλείδης s. N. f. Ἀλέξανδρος	*SEG* 61.1160, *NewDocs* 10.17, *CCPI* 401–6	
Ἡρακλείδης s. Ἰουλις f. Κτησᾶς	*SEG* 61.1160, *NewDocs* 10.17, *CCPI* 401–6	Spelling –λίδης
Ἡράκλειος s. Διοσκουρίδης f. Απφια	*BCH* 1887:354.12, *IGR* 4.868, *I.Laodicée Lycos nymphée* 278–9	

Name and relations	Source	Notes
Ἡρακλέων, Αὐρ. s. Καρπίων + Ἀμμιανή gs. Τρύφων	*MAMA* 6.42	
Ἡρακλέων s. Ἡρακλέων gs. Ἀνωτ[...	*SEG* 61.1160, *NewDocs* 10.17, *CCPI* 401–6	
Ἡρακλέων s. Ἀνωτ[... f. Ἡρακλέων	*SEG* 61.1160, *NewDocs* 10.17, *CCPI* 401–6	
Ἡρακλέων s. Ἡρακλείδης gs. Ἡρακλέων	*SEG* 61.1160, *NewDocs* 10.17, *CCPI* 401–6	
Ἡρακλέων f. Ἡρακλείδης gf. Ἡρακλέων	*SEG* 61.1160, *NewDocs* 10.17, *CCPI* 401–6	Probable reconstruction
Θάλλος s. Βακχύλος	*CCPI* 355–7	
Θεόδωρος s. Δημήτριος gs. Δημήτριος ggs. Θεόδωρος	*SEG* 61.1160, *NewDocs* 10.17, *CCPI* 401–6	
Θεόδωρος f. Δημήτριος gf. Δημήτριος ggf. Θεόδωρος	*SEG* 61.1160, *NewDocs* 10.17, *CCPI* 401–6	
Θεόδωρος s. Θεόδωρος gs. Λικιννίος	*SEG* 61.1160, *NewDocs* 10.17, *CCPI* 401–6	
Θεόδωρος s. Λικιννίος f. Θεόδωρος	*SEG* 61.1160, *NewDocs* 10.17, *CCPI* 401–6	
Θεόδωρος s. Θεόδωρος gs. Δημήτριος	*SEG* 61.1160, *NewDocs* 10.17, *CCPI* 401–6	
Θεόδωρος s. Δημήτριος f. Θεόδωρος	*SEG* 61.1160, *NewDocs* 10.17, *CCPI* 401–6	
Ἰεικίς (?) d. Δῖος h. Ζήνων	*Smith Fs* 171–3, *CCPI* 615, 618–9	Ἰεικίς(?) possible sister-in-law of Ζηνωνίς
Ἱερώνυμος	*MSPhryg* 2.448–51, 453, 546–7, *RPC* 3.2308–10, 2312A, 2313–5, 2313A, *CCPI* 67	
Ἰουλις m/f. Ἡρακλείδης gm/gf. Κτησᾶς	*SEG* 61.1160, *NewDocs* 10.17, *CCPI* 401–6	Ἰουλις may be grandmother/-father
Καρπίων h. Ἀμμιανή, Αὐρ. f. Ἡρακλέων, Αὐρ.	*MAMA* 6.42, *CCPI* 520–3	

Name and relations	Source	Notes
Κάρπος s. Ἀρτεμίδωρος h. Εὐθηνία	*SEG* 57.1384, *CCPI* 92, 614	
Κάρπων, Αὐρήλιος Μᾶρκος h. Τατας, Αὐρηλία	*IGR* 4.871, *CCPI* 92, 529, 613	
Κάστωρ	*JHS* 1898:90.26; *SGO* 1.02.15.01, *CCPI* 461–71	
Κόρυμβος	*SEG* 61.1160, *NewDocs* 10.17, *CCPI* 401–6	
Κρισπῖνος, Μ. Λάρκιος s. Παπιας, Μ. Λάρκιος	*MAMA* 6.39, *I.Mus. Denizli* 59, *CCPI* 408, 519–26	Spelling -εῖνος
Κτῆσας s. Κτῆσας gs. Κτῆσας ggs. N. f. Μηνᾶς	*SEG* 61.1160, *NewDocs* 10.17, *CCPI* 401–6	
Κτῆσας s. Κτῆσας gs. N. f. Κτῆσας gf. Μηνᾶς	*SEG* 61.1160, *NewDocs* 10.17, *CCPI* 401–6	
Κτῆσας s. N. f. Κτῆσας gf. Κτῆσας ggf. Μηνᾶς	*SEG* 61.1160, *NewDocs* 10.17, *CCPI* 401–6	
Κτῆσας s. Ἡρακλείδης gs. Ἰουλις	*SEG* 61.1160, *NewDocs* 10.17, *CCPI* 401–6	
Κτησικλῆς, Π. Αἴλ.	*MSPhryg* 2.484–6, 580, *RPC* 4.2.1879t, 1884t, 1896t	
Λικιννίος f. Θεόδωρος gf. Θεόδωρος	*SEG* 61.1160, *NewDocs* 10.17, *CCPI* 401–6	
Μᾶρκος f. Μᾶρκος	*SEG* 57.1382, *CCPI* 537–56	
Μᾶρκος s. Μᾶρκος	*SEG* 57.1382, *CCPI* 537–56	
Μᾶρκος s. Ῥοῦφος f. Διονύσιος	*MAMA* 6.43, *I.Laodikeia Lykos* 104, *I.Mus. Denizli* 167, *CCPI* 517, 619	Spelling -πος, -σειος Disputed provenance (Colossae/ Laodikeia)
Μαρκιανός, Αὐ. f. Ἐπαφρᾶς	*MSPhryg* 2.594–5, *RPC* 9.789, *CCPI* 205, 214	Correction *MSPhryg* 2.594–5
Μένανδρος Φλαουϊανός, Γ. Κλ. f. Γ. Κλ. N.	*BCH* 1887:353.10, Quandt 216.	Correction Quandt 216
Μένανδρος s. Μένανδρος gs. Μιννίων f. Τρύφων	*SEG* 61.1160, *NewDocs* 10.17, *CCPI* 401–6	

Name and relations	Source	Notes
Μένανδρος s. Μιννίων f. Μένανδρος gf. Τρύφων	*SEG* 61.1160, *NewDocs* 10.17, *CCPI* 401–6	
Μενεκλῆς s. Μενεκλῆς	*MSPhryg* 2.586–7, 591, *CCPI* 454, 458 nr xviii)	
Μενεκλῆς f. Μενεκλῆς	*MSPhryg* 2.586–7, 591, *CCPI* 68	
Μενιάνδρος, Αὐ. s. Μενιάνδρος gs. Ἑρμογένης h. Ζηνωνίς	*Smith Fs* 171–3, *CCPI* 615, 618–9	Correction *LGPN* (spelling: Μένανδρος)
Μενιάνδρος s. Ἑρμογένης f. Μενιάνδρος, Αὐ.	*Smith Fs* 171–3, *CCPI* 615, 618–9	Correction *LGPN* (spelling: Μένανδρος)
Μηνᾶς s. Κτῆσας gs. Κτῆσας ggs. Κτῆσας gggs. N.	*SEG* 61.1160, *NewDocs* 10.17, *CCPI* 401–6	
Μηνογᾶς s. Μηνογᾶς gs. Μηνογᾶς ggs. Μηνογᾶς gggs. N[...	*SEG* 61.1160, *NewDocs* 10.17, *CCPI* 401–6	
Μηνογᾶς s. Μηνογᾶς gs. Μηνογᾶς ggs. N[... f. Μηνογᾶς	*SEG* 61.1160, *NewDocs* 10.17, *CCPI* 401–6	
Μηνογᾶς s. Μηνογᾶς gs. N[... f. Μηνογᾶς gf. Μηνογᾶς	*SEG* 61.1160, *NewDocs* 10.17, *CCPI* 401–6	
Μηνογᾶς s. N[... f. Μηνογᾶς gf. Μηνογᾶς ggf. Μηνογᾶς	*SEG* 61.1160, *NewDocs* 10.17, *CCPI* 401–6	
Μιννίων f. Μένανδρος gf. Μένανδρος ggf. Τρύφων	*SEG* 61.1160, *NewDocs* 10.17, *CCPI* 401–6	
Μολοσ(σ)ός f. Ζωσᾶς	*I.Laodikeia Lykos* 118, *CBP* 77.12, *CCPI* 167–9	Reassign *I.Laodikeia Lykos* 118 to Colossae
Μοσχᾶς h. Τατια f. Ταταριν	*CIG* 3954, *LBW* 1693a, *CBP* 77.11, *MAMA* 6.19, *I.Laodikeia Lykos* 114, *I.Mus. Denizli* 178, *CCPI* 162–7	Correction *CIG* 3954, *CBP* 77.11, *MAMA* 6.19, *I.Laodikeia Lykos* 114, *I.Mus. Denizli* 178, *LGPN* (reassign territory)
Μωκεας f. Ἀπολλώνιος gf. Δημήτριος	*SEG* 61.1160, *NewDocs* 10.17, *CCPI* 401–6	

Name and relations	Source	Notes
N., Γ. Κλ. s. Μένανδρος Φλαουϊανός, Γ. Κλ.	*BCH* 1887:353.10, Quandt 216, *CCPI* 353–4	Correction Quandt 216
Νίγρος s. Νίγρος gs. Νίγρος	*MSPhryg* 2.588–90	
Νίγρος f. Νίγρος s. Νίγρος	*MSPhryg* 2.588–90	
Νίγρος f. Νίγρος gf. Νίγρος	*MSPhryg* 2.588–90	
Ὀνήσιμος	*BCH* 1893.250.27, *IGR* 4.806, Audollent 14, *CBP* 351.83, Wuensch XIII, *CCPI* 363–8	
Ὀνήσιμος	Phmn 10	May be the same person as in Col 4:9
Ὀνήσιμος	Col 4:9	May be the same person as in Phmn 10
Παπιας, Μ. Λάρκιος f. Κρισπῖνος, Μ. Λάρκιος	*MAMA* 6.39, *I.Mus. Denizli* 59, *CCPI* 408, 519–26	
Πρίσκος, Κλ.	FN 993, *CCPI* 67, 208–10	Spelling –είσκος Homonoia coin with Aphrodisias
Ῥοῦφος f. Μᾶρκος gf. Διονύσιος	*MAMA* 6.43, *I.Laodikeia Lykos* 104, *I.Mus. Denizli* 167, *CCPI* 517, 619	Spelling –πος Disputed provenance (Colossae/ Laodikeia)
Ῥούσων	*BCH* 1893.250.27, *IGR* 4.806, Audollent 14, *CBP* 351.83, Wuensch XIII, *CCPI* 363–8	
Σαβῖνα	*BCH* 1893.250.27, *IGR* 4.806, Audollent 14, *CBP* 351.83, Wuensch XIII, *CCPI* 363–8	
Σακέρδως, Τι. Κλ.	*MSPhryg* 2.470–83, 555–63, *RPC online* 4.2.1875–7t, 1893–5, 4.2.11597t, *CCPI* 67	
Τατα w. Διονύσιος m. Εἰρήνη	*Gephyra* 2020:1–26, *Kyros* 431.1.2, *AM* 1893: 206–7, *CBP* 542.408, *CCPI* 528, 613	Correction *CBP* 542.408, *LGPN* (city)
Ταταριν d. Τατια + Μοσχᾶς	*CIG* 3954, *LBW* 1693a, *CBP* 77.11, *MAMA* 6.19, *I.Laodikeia Lykos* 114, *I.Mus. Denizli* 178, *CCPI* 162–7	Correction *CIG* 3954, *CBP* 77.11, *MAMA* 6.19, *I.Laodikeia Lykos* 114, *I.Mus. Denizli* 178, *LGPN* (reassign territory)
Τατας, Αὐρηλία w. Κάρπων, Αὐρήλιος Μᾶρκος	*IGR* 4.871, *CCPI* 92, 529, 613	
Τατια w. Μοσχᾶς m. Ταταριν	*CIG* 3954, *LBW* 1693a, *CBP* 77.11, *MAMA* 6.19, *I.Laodikeia Lykos* 114, *I.Mus. Denizli* 178, *CCPI* 162–7	Correction *CIG* 3954, *CBP* 77.11, *MAMA* 6.19, *I.Laodikeia Lykos* 114, *I.Mus. Denizli* 178, *LGPN* (reassign territory)

Name and relations	Source	Notes
Τατιανός s. Τατιανός gs. Ἄρτος	*MAMA* 6.48, *I.Mus. Denizli* 73, PM 1974, *BE* 1979.15, *CCPI* 601, 615, 619–23	Correction (likely) *MAMA* 6.48, *I.Mus Denizli* 73, *PM* 1974
Τατιανός f. Τατιανός s. Ἄρτος	*MAMA* 6.48, *I.Mus. Denizli* 73, PM 1974, *BE* 1979.15, *CCPI* 601, 615, 619–23	Correction (likely) *MAMA* 6.48, *I.Mus. Denizli* 73, *PM* 1974
Τερέντιος	*BCH* 1893.250.27, *IGR* 4.806, Audollent 14, *CBP* 351.83, Wuensch XIII, *CCPI* 363–8	Correction *BCH* 1893.250.27, *IGR* 4.806, Audollent 14, *CBP* 351.83, Wuensch XIII
Τέρτιος	*BCH* 1893.250.27, *IGR* 4.806, Audollent 14, *CBP* 351.83, Wuensch XIII, *CCPI* 363–8	
Τρόφ[ιμος s. Φοῖ]βος (?) gs. Δίων h. Δι[ογενεία (?)	*MAMA* 6.45, *CCPI* 614	Fragmentary; photograph shows base of vertical hasta of φ
Τρύφιων f. Αφιας	*I.Boubon* 102, *CIG* 4380 k[3], *CCPI* 144, 400	Correction SF 2.289, *CIG* 4380 k[3], *LGPN*
Τρύφων s. Τρύφων gs. Διόδωρος	*SEG* 61.1160, *NewDocs* 10.17, *CCPI* 401–6	
Τρύφων s. Διόδωρος f. Τρύφων	*SEG* 61.1160, *NewDocs* 10.17, *CCPI* 401–6	
Τρύφων f. Ἀμμιανή, Αὐρ. gf. Ἡρακλέων, Αὐρ.	*MAMA* 6.42, *CCPI* 520–3	
Τρύφων s. Μένανδρος gs. Μένανδρος ggs. Μιννίων	*SEG* 61.1160, *NewDocs* 10.17, *CCPI* 401–6	
Τρυφωνᾶς s. N. f. NN.	*SEG* 61.1160, *NewDocs* 10.17, *CCPI* 401–6	
Τρυφωνιάνος f. Ἄτταλος	*SEG* 61.1160 (alt. Τρυφωνίων), *NewDocs* 10.17, *CCPI* 401–6	Spelling -ιώνος?
Τυδείδης s. Ζώσιμος	*SEG* 61.1160, *NewDocs* 10.17, *CCPI* 401–6	
Φιλημάτιον	*BCH* 1893.250.27, *IGR* 4.806, Audollent 14, *CBP* 351.83, Wuensch XIII, *CCPI* 363–8	
Φιλόπαππος, Τι. Ἀσίνιος	*MSPhryg* 2.455–69, 553–4 *RPC online* 4.1874t, 1888–92t, 10833t, *CCPI* 116, 408–9	
Φοῖ]βος (?) s. Δίων f. Τρό[φιμος	*MAMA* 6.45, *CCPI* 614	Fragmentary; Calder's Latin name (Πρό]βος unlikely. Βάρβος or Σιλβος also possible
Χελιδών	*BCH* 1893.250.27, *IGR* 4.806, Audollent 14, *CBP* 351.83, Wuensch XIII, *CCPI* 363–8	

Key to Abbreviations

Arundell	F. V. J. Arundell, *A Visit to the Seven Churches of Asia Minor* (London: John Rodwell, 1828).
Audollent	A. Audollent, *Defixionum Tabellae* (Paris: A. Fontemoing, 1904).
BCH	*Bulletin de Correspondance Hellénique*
BE	*Bulletin épigraphiques*
CBP	W. M. Ramsay, *Cities and Bishoprics of Phrygia* (Oxford: Clarendon, 2 vols, 1895, 1897).
CIG	Boeckh, *Corpus inscriptionum Graecarum* (Berlin: 1828–1877).
CCPI	This book.
FN	P. R. Franke and M. K. Nollé, *Die Homonoia-Münzen Kleinasiens I. Katalog* (Saarbrücken Verlag, 1997).
Gephyra	A. H. Cadwallader, "Gertrude Bell's Resolution of a Disputed Inscription" *Gephyra* (2020):1–26.
I.Boubon	Chr. Kokkinia (ed.), *Boubon. The Inscriptions and Archaeological Remains. A Survey 2004–2006* (Athens: 2008).
I.Mus. Denizli	T. Ritti (ed.), *Museo Archeologico di Denizli-Hierapolis. Catalogo delle iscrizioni greche e latine. Distretto di Denizli* (Naples: 2008).
IGR	G. Lafaye, *Inscriptiones Graecae ad res Romanas pertinentes* (Paris: 1927).
I.Laodikeia Lykos	T. Corsten, *Die Inschriften von Laodikeia am Lykos*, I (IGSK 49; Bonn 1997).
JHS	*Journal of Hellenic Studies*
Kyros	G. Cousin, *Kyros le Jeune en Asie Mineure (Printemps 408–Juillet 401 avant Jésus-Christ)*, (Nancy: 1904).
I.Laodicée Lycos mymphée	L. Robert, "Inscriptions" in J. des Gagniers *et al.*, *Laodicée du Lycos. Le nymphée. Campagnes 1961–1963* (Paris: 1969).
LBW	P. LeBas and W. H. Waddington, *Voyage archéologique en Grèce et en Asie Mineure, fait par ordre du gouvernement français pendant les années 1843 et 1844* III. *Inscriptions grecques et latines* (Paris: 1870).
LGPN	J-S. Balzat, R. W. V. Catling, É. Chiricat and T. Corsten (eds), *Lexicon of Greek Personal Names Volume V.C, Inland Asia Minor* (Oxford: Clarendon, 2018).
MAMA	W. H. Buckler and W. M. Calder, *Monumenta Asiae Minoris Antiqua Vol VI, Monuments and Documents from Phrygia and Caria* (Manchester: Manchester University Press, 1939).

MSPhryg	H. von Aulock, *Münzen und Städte Phrygiens 2* (Tübingen: Ernst Wasmuth, 1987).
NewDocs	*New Documents Illustrating Early Christianity* edited by S. R. Llewelyn and J. R. Harrison (Grand Rapids, MN: Eerdmans, 2012).
PM	E. Pfuhl, H. Möbius, *Die ostgriechischen Grabreliefs*, I–II (Mainz am Rhein: Philipp von Zabern, 1977–1979).
Quandt	G. Quandt, *De Baccho ab Alexandri Aetate in Asia Minore Culto* (Halis Saxonum: Niemeyer, 1913.
RPC and *online*	*Roman Provincial Coinage* (Volume 3 and online).
SEG	*Supplementum Epigraphicum Graecum* (Leiden 1923–).
SF	T. A. B. Spratt and E. Forbes, *Travels in Lycia, Milyas and the Cibyratis in Company with the late Rev. E. T. Daniell* (London: John van Voorst, 2 vols, 1847).
Smith Fs	*Stones, Bones and the Sacred: Essays on Material Culture and Ancient Religion in Honor of Dennis E. Smith* edited by A. H. Cadwallader (Atlanta, GA: SBL Press, 2016.
Wuensch	R. Wünsch, *Continens Defixionum* (Berlin: G. Reimer, 1897).

Appendix 4
Concordance of Colossian inscriptions

The following concordance does not follow the usual model, because the inscriptions critically analyzed and often reconstructed in the course of the book occur as part of larger interests rather than seeking only to provide an epigraphic catalogue. Consequently, the references in the list that are given in abbreviated form demand a bibliographic key below. (Note that an asterisk after the *MAMA* number indicates inclusion in a supplementary list to the main inscriptions. No transcriptions are given for these in *MAMA*.) Where detailed treatments of an inscription are given in this book, the page references are added in the last column. The fragmentary Greek inscriptions incorporated into the walls of the Ak Khan caravanserai are not included even though the presumption of quarrying raids upon Colossae is relatively strong.

	Title for inscription	**References**	**Analysis**
1	Tyche Protogeneia of the Kolossians (intaglio)	Belley 1780:17–27 = Belley 1784:11–14 = Kagan-Neverov 2001:274/92	231–48
2	Epitaph for Trophimos and Diogeneia	*MAMA* 6.45	614
3	Epitaph for Dion the leatherworker	*MAMA* 6.44 = *EA* 40.112.2 = *SEG* 57.1385	590–2
4	Epitaph of Datys (?) son of Zenon	*CIG* 3956 = Arundell *Discoveries* 170 = Arundell *Visit* 98 = *MAMA* 6.51 = *EA* 40.114 = *SEG* 57.1383	615
5	Epitaph for Damokrates by will	*MAMA* 6.46	534
6	Honor for Heraklas	*MAMA* 6.41 = *AS* 2006.105	456, 460
7	Epitaph(?) for Atarbides and Kokonia(?)	*CIG* 3955 = Arundell *Visit* 156.25 = *MAMA* 6.53*	612, 669
8	Athletic honor for Zenon	*BCH* 11.353.11 = *MAMA* 6.40 = Magie 1523n57	450–61
9	Epitaph for Tatianos	*MAMA* 6.48 = *PfMb* 2.1974 = *BE* 1979.15 = *SEG* 29.1391 = *I.Mus. Denizli* 73 = Huttner *Early Christianity* 31	601, 615, 619–23

	Title for inscription	References	Analysis
10	Dedication to the Emperor Hadrian	*IGR* 4.869 = *JHS* 18.90.25 = *MAMA* 6.47* = Magie 1479n28 = Pflaum *Les Carrières* I.262.109	480, 523
11	Kastor the pugilist	*JHS* 18.90.26 = *MAMA* 6.50* = *Steinepigramme* 1.02.15.01	461–71
12	Offering at St Theodore's (?) Church	*MAMA* 6.49 = *GRBS* 48.334	404–5
13	Epitaph of Karpon	*MDAI(A)* 16.199 = *IGR* 4.871 = *MAMA* 6.52*	92, 529, 614
14	Memorial for Herakleon	*MAMA* 6.42 = *I.Laodicée Lycos nymphée* 328	520–3
15	Dedication to Constantius I, Diocletian, Maximian	*MAMA* 6.38 = Foss *History* 2.483	517
16	Honor for a boularch	*LBW* 1693b = *IGR* 4.870 = Ramsay *Phrygia* 212 = *MAMA* 6.48* = *I.Laodicée Lycos nymphée* 269, 277–8 = *BE* 1970.584 = Magie 986n22	248–56
17	Funerary fine to the *fiskos*	*AS* 56.108	528
18	Epitaph for Dionoisios and his family	*MDAI(A)* 18.206.3 = Ramsay *Phrygia* 542.408 = Cousin *Kyros* 431.1.2 = *Gephyra* 2020:1–26	528, 613
19	Dedication to Trajan	*BCH* 11.354.12 = *IGR* 4.868 = *MAMA* 6.46* = *I.Laodicée Lycos nymphée* 278	358–60
20	Priest of Dionysos	*BCH* 11.353.10 = Quandt 216 = *MAMA* 6.49*	353–4
21	Epitaph for Markos	*MDAI(A)* 18.207.4 = *MAMA* 6.43= *I.Laodikeia Lykos* 104 = *CQ* 12.162 (disputed provenance)	526–7, 613
22	Honor for Markos, chief translator of Colossae	*EA* 40.114.3 = *EBGR* 2007.25 = *SEG* 57.1382 = Bormann 2018.193–6 = Huttner *Law* 149–51	537–56
23	Epitaph for Glykon	*MAMA* 6.47 = *BE* 1939.392 = *PfMb* 1.594 = *I.Mus. Denizli* 113	623–8
24	Epitaph for Karpos and family	*EA* 40.109.1 = *SEG* 57.1384	92, 614
25	Memorial for Crispinus	*MAMA* 6.39 = *I.Mus. Denizli* 59	408, 519–26
26	Epitaph for Aphias	Spratt & Forbes 2.289 = *LBW*1220 = *CIG* 3.4380k^3 = *BCH* 107.552n9 = *RECAM* 3.4.11 (p. 5) = *I.Boubon* 102	144, 400
27	Epitaph for Diodotos, philologos	*I.Smyrna* 440 = *AA* 1900.156.24 = Dain *Inscr* 53 = Robert *OMS* 3.1587.53	281–92
28	Altar for Bacchus	Konakçi-Duman *Denizli Sempozyumu* I.61.8	355–7
29	Honor for Korymbos for repair of the baths	*Antichthon* 2012 = *NDIEC* 10.17 = *AE* 2011.1347 = *BE* 2013.407 = *SEG* 61.1160 = *SEG* 62.1235 = Reasoner *Roman Imperial Texts* 138–9	401–6
30	Epitaph for Epictetus and Ariste	Cadwallader 2016:168	615, 619
31	Epitaph for Menian-dros, Zenonis and Hieikis(?)	Cadwallader 2016:171	615, 618–9
32	Fragment	Le Camus 1896:176	—

	Title for inscription	References	Analysis
33	Honors for Achaios, Banabelos and Lachares	*I.Laodikeia Lykos* 1 = *Chiron* 5.59–87 (reassigned to Colossae)	136–43
34	Epitaph for Tatia, Moschas and Tatarin	*I.Laodikeia Lykos* 114 = Arundel *Visit* 157.26 = *CIG* 3954 = Ramsay *Phrygia* 1.77.11 = *MAMA* 6.19 (reassigned to Colossae)	162–7
35	Epitaph for Zosas and Elpis	*I.Laodikeia Lykos* 118 = Ramsay, *Phrygia* 1.77.12 (reassigned to Colossae)	167–9
36?	Dedication to the most high god	*I.Laodikeia Lykos* 61 = Mitchell, "Theos Hypsistos" 142.217 = Ramsay, *Phrygia* 1.78.14 (re-assigned to Colossae)	169
37	Curse diptych	Audollent *Defixiones* 14 = *IGR* 4.806 (reassigned to Colossae territory)	363–8
38?	The sinner Choniates, builder/benefactor of church near Smyrna	Kourouniotis 4 = Bouras 547	—

Bibliographic key:

Arundell *Discoveries* F. V. J. Arundell *Discoveries in Asia Minor.* London: Richard Bentley, 2 vols, 1834.

Arundell *Visit* F. V. J. Arundell *A Visit to the Seven Churches of Asia Minor with an excursion into Pisidia.* London: John Rodwell, 1828.

Antichthon *Antichthon* (followed by year).

AS *Anatolian Studies* (followed by year number).

Audollent *Defixiones* A. Audollent, *Defixionum Tabellae.* Paris: Fontemoing, 1904.

BCH *Bulletin de Correspondance hellénique* (followed by volume number).

BE *Bulletin épigraphique* (in *Revue des études grecques*).

Belley M. A. Belley, "Observations sur une Cornaline Antique du Cabinet de Mgr le Duc D'Orléans." Pages 17–27 in *Histoire des Ouvrages de l'"Academie Royale des Inscriptions et Belles-Lettres.* Paris: Panckoucke, 1780.
Mémoires de Littérature, tires des registres de l'Académie royale des inscriptions et Belles-Lettres 36 (1784): 11–17.

Bormann L. Bormann, "Barbaren und Skythen im Lykostal? Epigraphischer Kommentar zu Kol 3:11." Pages 161–98 in *Epigraphical Evidence Illustrating Paul's Letter to the Colossians* edited by J. Verheyden, M Öhler and T. Corsten. Tübingen: Mohr Siebeck, 2018.

Cadwallader A. H. Cadwallader, "One Grave, Two Women, One Man: Complicating Family Life at Colossae." Pages 157–94 in

	Stones, Bones, and the Sacred: Essays on Material Culture and Ancient Religion in Honor of Dennis E. Smith edited by A. H. Cadwallader. Atlanta, GA: SBL Press, 2016.
Chiron	*Chiron* (followed by volume number).
CIG	*Corpus Inscriptionum Graecarum.*
Cousin *Kyros*	G. Cousin, *Kyros le Jeune en Asie Mineure (Printemps 408–Juillet 401 avant Jésus-Christ).* Nancy: Berger-Levrault, 1904.
CQ	*Classical Quarterly.*
Dain *Inscr*	A. Dain, A. *Inscriptions grecques du Musée du Louvre; les textes inédits.* Paris: Les Belles Lettres, 1933.
EA	*Epigraphica Anatolica* (followed by volume number).
EBGR	*Epigraphical Bulletin of Greek Religion (Kernos)* (followed by year).
Foss *History*	C. Foss, *History and Archaeology of Byzantine Asia Minor.* Aldershot: Variorum, 1990.
GRBS	*Journal for Greek, Roman and Byzantine Studies* (followed by volume number).
Huttner *Early Christianity*	U. Huttner, *Early Christianity in the Lycus Valley.* Leiden: Brill, 2013.
Huttner *Law*	U. Huttner, "Latin Law in Greek Cities: Knowledge of Law and Latin in Imperial Asia Minor." Pages 137–56 in *Law in the Roman Provinces* edited by K. Czajkowski *et al.* Oxford: Oxford University Press, 2020.
I.Boubon	C. Kokkinia, "The Inscriptions of Boubon: A Catalogue." Pages 27–126 in *Boubon: The Inscriptions and Archaeological Remains: A Survey 2004–2006.* Athens: de Boccard, 2008.
IGR	*Inscriptiones graecae ad res romanas pertinentes.*
I.Laodicée Lycos nymphé	L. Robert, "Les Inscriptions." Pages 247–389 in J. des Gagniers *et al.*, *Laodicée du Lycos. Le nymphée. Campagnes 1961–1963.* Paris: de Boccard, 1969.
I.Laodikeia Lykos	T. Corsten, *Die Inschriften von Laodikeia am Lykos.* Bonn: Habelt, 1997.
I.Mus. Denizli	T. Ritti *et al.* (eds), *Museo Archeologico di Denizli-Hierapolis. Catalogo delle iscrizioni greche e latine. Distretto di Denizli.* Napoli: Liguori, 2008.
I.Smyrna	G. Petzl, *Die Inschriften von Smyrna,* I–II 1/2. Bonn: Habelt, 1982–1990.
JHS	*Journal of Hellenic Studies* (followed by volume number).
Kagan-Neverov	Y. O. Kagan and O. Y. Neverov, *Le Destin d'une Collection: 500 pierres gravées du Duc d'Orléans.* St Petersburg: Musée de l'Hermitage, 2001.
Konakçi-Duman *Denizli Sempozyumu*	E. Konakçi and B. Duman, "Arkeolojik ve Yasılı Kanıtlar Işığında Kolossai (Kolossai in the Light of Archaeological and Historical Evidence)." Pages 57–67 in

Uluslararası Denizli ve Çevresi Tarih ve Kültür Semposyumu Bildiriler (*International Symposium on the History and Culture of Denizli and its Surroundings*) edited by A. Özçelik *et al.* Denizli: Pamukkale University, 2 vols, 2007.

Kourouniotis — K. Kourouniotis, "Τὸ ἔργον τῆς ἑλληνικῆς Ἀρχαιολογικῆς Ὑπηρεσίας ἐν Μικρᾷ Ἀσίᾳ," ΑΔ 7 (1921–22): Παράρτημα, 1–6.

LBW — P. Le Bas, *Explication des Inscriptions Grecques et Latines recueillies en Grèce et en Asie Mineure.* Paris: Firmin Didot, 1873.

Le Camus — É. Le Camus, *Voyage aux Sept Églises de l'Apocalypse.* Paris: Librairies Sanard et Derangeon, 1896.

Magie — D. Magie, *Roman Rule in Asia Minor.* Princeton: Princeton University Press, 2 vols, 1950.

MAMA — W. H. Buckler and W. M. Calder, *Monumenta Asiae Minoris Antiqua Vol. VI: Monuments and Documents from Phrygia and Caria.* Manchester: Manchester University Press, 1939.

MDAI(A) — *Mitteilungen des Deutschen Archaeologischen Instituts, Athenische Abteilung* (followed by volume number).

Mitchell "Theos Hypsistos" — S. Mitchell, "The Cult of Theos Hypsistos." Pages 81–148 in *Pagan Monotheism in Late Antiquity* edited by P. Athanassiadi and M. Frede. Oxford: Clarendon, 1999.

NDIEC — *New Documents Illustrating Early Christianity* (followed by volume number).

Pflaum *Les Carrières* — H.-G. Pflaum, *Les c arrières procuratoriennes équestres sous le Haut-Empire romain.* Paris, P. Geuthner, 1960–1.

PfMb — P. Pfuhl, P. and H. Möbius, *Die Ostgriechischen Grabreliefs.* Mainz am Rhein: Philipp von Zabern, 4 vols, 1977.

Quandt — G. Quandt, *De Baccho ab Alexandri Aetate in Asia Minore Culto.* Halis Saxonum: Niemeyer, 1913.

Ramsay *Phrygia* — W. M. Ramsay, *The Cities and Bishoprics of Phrygia.* Oxford: Clarendon Press, 2 vols, 1895, 1897.

Reasoner *Roman Imperial Texts* — M. Reasoner, *Roman Imperial Texts: A Sourcebook.* Minneapolis: Fortress, 2013.

RECAM — *Regional Epigraphic Catalogues of Asia Minor* (followed by volume number).

Robert *OMS* — L. Robert, *Opera minora selecta: Epigraphie et antiquités grecques.* Amsterdam: Hakkert, 7 vols 1969–1990.

SEG — *Supplementum Epigraphicum Graecum* (followed by volume and entry number).

Spratt & Forbes — T. A. B. Spratt, T. A. B. and E. Forbes. *Travels in Lycia, Milyas and the Cibyratis in Company with the late Rev. E. T. Daniell.* London: John van Voorst, 2 vols, 1847.

Steinepigramme — R. Merkelbach and J. Stauber, *Steinepigramme aus dem griechischen Osten* I–V. Stuttgart: Teubner/Munich: Saur, 1998–2004.

Map of Asia Minor and the Mediterranean

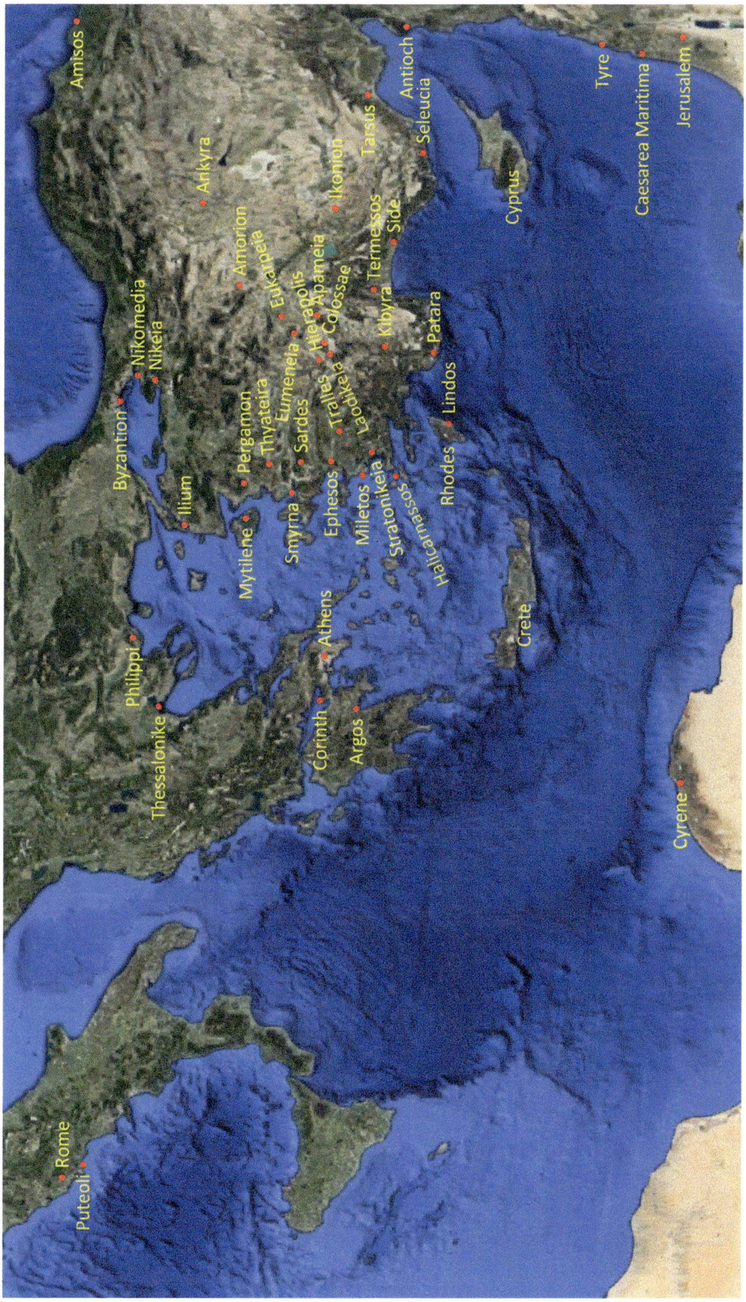

Map of the Lycus Valley and environs

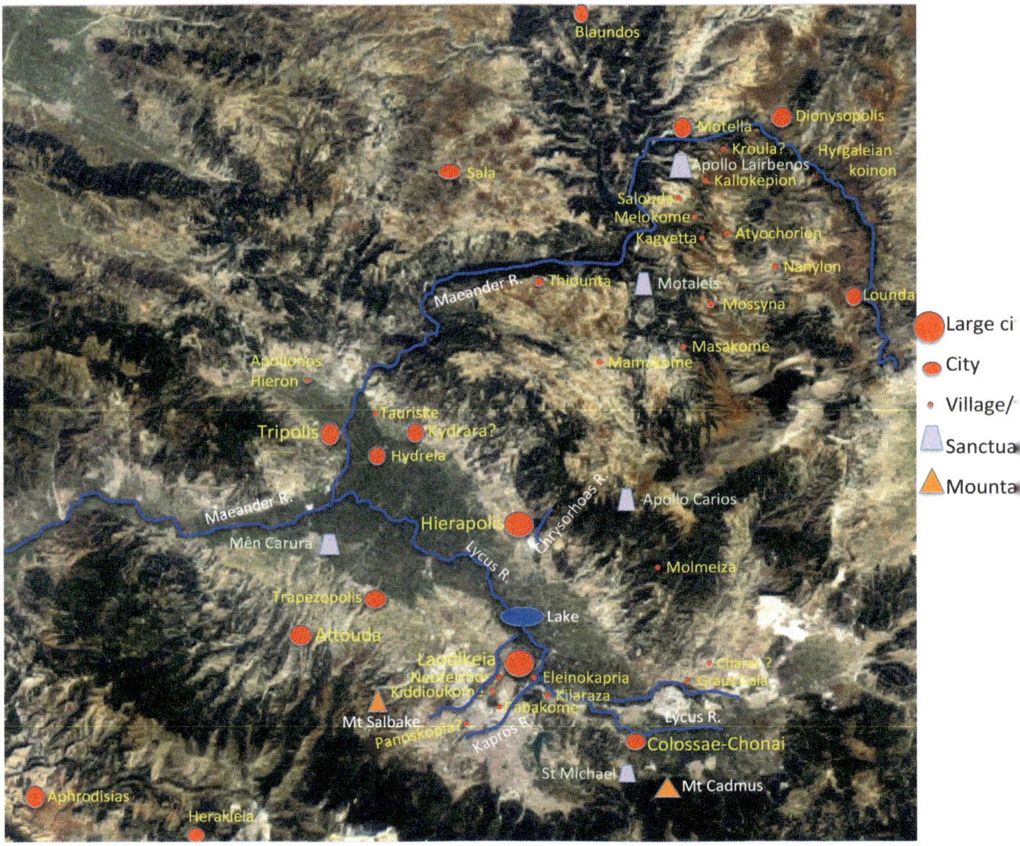

Bibliography

Acconcia Longo, A. *Il calendario giambico in monostici di Teodoro Prodromo*. Rome: Istituto di Studi Bizantini e Neoellenici, Università di Roma, 1983.

Adler, A. *Suidae lexicon*. Leipzig: Teubner, 4 vols, 1928–1935.

Adler, W. and P. Tuffin. *The chronography of George Synkellos: a Byzantine chronicle of universal history from the creation*. Oxford: Oxford University Press, 2002.

Agosti, G. "Greek Metrical Inscriptions, Classical *Paideia* and Identity in Late Antiquity." Pages 217–31 in *Greek* Paideia *and Local Tradition in the Graeco-Roman East* edited by M-P. de Hoz, J. L. G. Alonso and L. A. G. Romero. Leuven: Peeters, 2020.

Ahrens, S. "'Whether by decay or fire consumed …' Cremation in Hellenistic and Roman Asia Minor." Pages 185–222 in *Death and changing rituals. Function and meaning in ancient funerary practice* edited by J. R. Brandt, M. Prusac and H. Roland. Oxford: Oxbow Books, 2015.

— "Social status and tomb monuments in Hierapolis and Roman Asia Minor." Pages 131–48 in *Life and Death in Asia Minor in Hellenistic, Roman and Byzantine Times: Studies in Archaeology and Bioarchaeology* edited by J. R. Brandt *et al.* Oxford: Oxbow, 2017.

Ainsworth, W. F. *Travels in the Track of the Ten Thousand Greeks …* London: John W. Parker, 1844.

Akıncı Öztürk, E. and H. Malay. "Four Funerary Curses recording the Pisidian Gods of the Acıpayam Plain." *EA* 45 (2012): 89–92.

Akıncı Öztürk, E. and C. Tanrıver. "New Katagraphai and Dedications from the Sanctuary of Apollon Lairbenos." *EA* 41 (2008): 91–111.

Akyürek Şahin, N. E. and H. Uzunoğlu. "Neue Inschriften aus dem Museum von Eskişehir." *Gephyra* 18 (2019): 139–41.

Alexander, R. L. "The Storm-God at 'Ain Dara." Pages 11–19 in *Recent Developments in Hittite Archaeology and History: Papers in Honor of Hans Gustav Güterbock* edited by K. A. Yener and H. A. Hoffner. Winona Lake, IN: Eisenbraun, 2002.

Alikin, V. A. "Women as Leaders in the Gatherings of Early Christian Communities: A Sociohistorical Analysis." Pages 221–40 in *Stones, Bones, and the Sacred: Essays on Material Culture and Ancient Religion in Honor of Dennis E. Smith* edited by A. H. Cadwallader. Atlanta, GA: SBL Press, 2016.

Allen, R. E. *The Attalid Kingdom: A Constitutional History.* Oxford: Oxford University Press, 1983.

Allen, W. S. *Vox Graeca: A Guide to the Pronunciation of Classical Greek.* Cambridge: Cambridge University Press, 1968.

Altunel, E. and F. D'Andria. "Pamukkale Travertines: A Natural and Cultural Monument in the World Heritage List." Pages 219–29 in *Landscapes and Landforms of Turkey*, edited by C. Kuzucuoğlu, A. Çiner, and N. Kazankı. Switzerland: Springer, 2019.

Amandry, M. and A. Burnett. *Roman Provincial Coinage, Volume III: Nerva, Trajan and Hadrian (AD 96–138), Part I: Catalogue.* London: British Museum/Paris: Bibliothèque nationale de France, 2015.

Ameling, W. "Φάγωμεν καὶ Πίωμεν." *ZPE* 60 (1985): 35–43.

— *Inscriptiones Judaicae Orientis Band II: Kleinasien.* Tübingen: Mohr Siebeck, 2004.

Anderson, J. C. *Colossians: Authorship, Rhetoric, and Code.* London: T & T Clark, 2019.

Anderson, J. G. C. "Summer in Phrygia. I." *JHS* 17 (1897): 396–424.

— "A Summer in Phrygia. II." *JHS* 18 (1898): 81–128, 340–4.

Anderson, C. P. "Who wrote 'The Epistle from Laodicea'?," *JBL* 85 (1966): 436–40.

Anderson, R. C. (ed.). *The Journals of Sir Thomas Allin.* London: Navy Records Society, 2 vols, 1939–40.

Anderson, S. *An English Consul in Turkey: Paul Rycaut at Smyrna 1667–1668.* Oxford: Clarendon Press, 1989.

Anderson, T. "Preliminary osteo-archaeological investigation in the North Necropolis." Pages 473–93 in *Hierapolis di Frigia I: Le Attività delle Campagne di Scavo e Restauro 2000–2003* edited by F. D'Andria and M. P. Caggia. Istanbul: Ege, 2007.

Angelov, D. *The Byzantine Hellene: The Life of Emperor Theodore Laskaris and Byzantium in the Thirteenth Century.* Cambridge: Cambridge University Press, 2019.

Anrich, G. *Hagios Nikolaos. Der Heilige Nikolaos in der griechischen Kirche.* Berlin: Teubner, 1913.

Arena, V. *Libertas and the Practice of Politics in the Late Roman Republic.* Cambridge: Cambridge University Press, 2012.

Armstrong, A. L. "Roman Phrygia: Cities and their Coinage." Unpublished PhD Thesis, University of London, 1998.

Arnaoutoglou, I. *Ancient Greek Laws: A Sourcebook.* London: Routledge, 1998.

— "Roman Law and *Collegia*, in Asia Minor." *Revue Internationale des droits de l'Antiquité* 48 (2002): 27–44.

— "The Greek text of D. 47.22.4 (Gai 4 ad legem duodecim tabularum) reconsidered." *LR* 5 (2016): 87–119.

— "Hierapolis and its Professional Associations: A Comparative Analysis." Pages 278–300 in *Urban Craftsmen and Traders in the Roman World* edited by A. Wilson and M. Fohr. Oxford: Oxford University Press, 2016.

Arnaud, F. *Descriptions des Principales pierres gravées du Cabinet de S. A. S. Monseigneur le Duc d'Orléans, premier Prince du Sang.* Vol 1; Paris: de la Chau & le Blond, 1780.

Arnhold, M., H. O. Maier, and J. Rüpke (eds.). *Seeing the God: Image, Space, Performance and Vision in the Religion of the Roman Empire.* Tübingen: Mohr Siebeck, 2018.

Arnold, C. E. *The Colossian Syncretism: The Interface between Christianity and Folk Belief at Colossae.* Grand Rapids, MN: Baker, 1996.

— "Sceva, Solomon, and Shamanism: The Jewish Roots of the Problem at Colossae." *JETS* 55 (2012): 7–26.

— "Initiation, Vision and Spiritual Power: The Hellenistic Dimensions of the Problem at Colossae." Pages 173–86 in *The First Urban Churches 5: Colossae, Hierapolis, and Laodicea* edited by J. R. Harrison and L. L. Welborn. Atlanta, GA: SBL Press, 2019.

Arundell, F. V. J. *A Visit to the Seven Churches of Asia Minor with an excursion into Pisidia.* London: John Rodwell, 1828.

— *Discoveries in Asia Minor.* London: Richard Bentley, 2 vols, 1834.

Arzt-Grabner, P. *Philemon.* Göttingen: Vandenhoeck & Ruprecht, 2003.

— "How to Deal with Onesimus? Paul's Solution within the Framework of Ancient Legal and Documentary Sources." Pages 113–42 in *Philemon in Perspective: Interpreting a Pauline Letter* edited by D. F. Tolmie. Berlin: de Gruyter, 2010.

— "'Neither a Truant nor a Fugitive': Some Remarks on the Sale of Slaves in Egypt and Other Provinces." Pages 21–32 in *Proceedings of the 25th International Congress of Papyrology* edited by T. Gagos. Ann Arbor: Scholarly Publishing Office, 2010.

— "Die Auswertung inschriftlicher Zeugnisses für die neutestamentliche Exegese: Erfahrungen, Chancen und Herausforderungen." Pages 27–44 in *Epigraphik und Neues Testament* edited by T. Corsten, M. Öhler and J. Verheyden. Tübingen: Mohr Siebeck, 2016.

— "Everyday Life in a Roman Town Like Colossae: The Papyrological Evidence." Pages 187–238 in *The First Urban Churches 5: Colossae, Hierapolis, and Laodicea* edited by J. R. Harrison and L. L. Welborn. Atlanta, GA: SBL Press, 2019.

Arzt-Grabner, P. *et al, 1. Korinther.* Göttingen: Vandenhoeck & Ruprecht, 2006.

Asano, A. "Colossians." Pages 407–19 in *T & T Clark Social Identity Commentary on the New Testament* edited by J. B. Tucker and A. Kuecker. London: T & T Clark, 2020.

Ascough, R. S. *Paul's Macedonian Associations: The Social Context of Philippians and 1 Thessalonians.* Tübingen: Mohr Siebeck, 2003.

— "Carving out Public Space. τόπος Inscriptions and Early Christ Groups." Pages 93–110 in *Epigraphik und Neues Testament* edited by T. Corsten, M. Öhler and J. Verheyden. Tübingen: Mohr Siebeck, 2016.

Ashton, R. "Rhodian Coinage and the Colossus." *RN* (ser. 6) 30 (1988): 75–90.

— "Rhodian Coinage in the Early Imperial Period," in *Recent Turkish Coin Hoards and Numismatic Studies* edited by C. S. Lightfoot (Oxford: Oxbow, 1991), 71–90.

Ashton, R. and G. Reger. "The Pseudo-Rhodian Drachms of Mylasa Revisited." Pages 125–50 in *Agoranomia: Studies in Money and Exchange presented to John H. Kroll* edited by P. G. van Alfen. New York: American Numismatic Society, 2006.

Audollent, A. *Defixionum Tabellae.* Paris: Fontemoing, 1904.

Aulock, H. von. *Münzen und Stadte Phrygiens.* Tübingen: Ernst Wasmuth, 2 vols, 1980, 1987.

Aus, R. D. *Two Puzzling Baptisms: First Corinthians 10:1–5 and 15:29: Studies in their Judaic Background.* Lanham: Hamilton, 2017.

Avi-Yonah, M. *Abbreviations in Greek Inscriptions (The Near East 200 BC – AD 1100).* London: Oxford University Press, 1940.

Aydın, B. "The Hellenistic Pottery and Small Finds of Kordon Tumulus at Kordon Köyü/ Salihli (Manisa), 2001." *Jahreshefte des Österreichischen Archäologischen Instituts in Wien* 76 (2007): 7–63. Bagnall, R. S. and B. W. Frier. *The Demography of Roman Egypt*. Cambridge: Cambridge University Press, 2nd ed., 2006.

Aytaçlar, P. Ö and E. Akıncı. "A List of Female Names from Laodicea on the Lycos." *EA* 36 (2006): 113–6.

Aytekin, F. "Statonikeia'dan Provocator Stelleri." Pages 125–36 in *Stratonikeia ve Çevresi Araştırmaları* edited by B. Sögüt. Istanbul: Ege, 2015.

Babelon, E. *Inventaire Sommaire de la Collection Waddington acquise par l'État en 1897*. Paris: Rollin & Feuardent, 1898.

Babington, C. "On Two unedited Autonomous Coins of Colossae in Phrygia." *NC* (ns) 3 (1863): 1–7.

Babou, O. *Children in the Hellenistic World: Statues and Representation*. Oxford: Oxford University Press, 2015.

Badoud, N. "Les colosses de Rhodes." *CRAI* (2011): 111–52.

Baedeker, K. *Russia with Teheran, Port Arthur and Peking: a handbook for travellers*. Leipzig: Karl Baedeker, 1914.

Bagnall, R. S. and R. Cribiore. *Women's Letters from Ancient Egypt, 300 BC – AD 800*. Ann Arbor: University of Michigan Press, 2nd ed., 2015.

Bagwanath, E. *Motivation and Narrative in Herodotus*. Oxford: Oxford University Press, 2008.

Baker, H. D. and M. Jursa (eds.). *Documentary Sources in Ancient Near Eastern and Greco-Roman Economic History*. Oxford: Oxbow, 2014.

Balabanski, V. "Where is Philemon? The Case for a Logical Fallacy in the Correlation of the Data in Philemon and Colossians 1.1–2; 4.7–18." *JSNT* 38 (2015): 131–50.

— *Colossians: An Eco-Stoic Reading*. London: T & T Clark, 2020.

Balch, D. "Household Codes." Pages 25–50 in *Greco-Roman Literature and the New Testament* edited by D. E. Aune. Atlanta, GA: Scholars Press, 1988.

— "Neopythagorean Moralists and the New Testament Household Codes." *ANRW* II.26.1 (1992): 380–411.

Baldi, D. *Etymologicum Symeonis (Γ—Ε)*. Turnhout: Brepols, 2013.

Baldwin, A. "Symbolism on Greek Coins." *AJN* 49 (1915): 89–194.

Banks, E. J. "Colossae." Pages 2.676 in *The International Standard Bible Encyclopaedia* edited by James Orr *et al.* Grand Rapids, MI: Eerdmans, 5 vols, 1939.

Barclay, J. *Colossians and Philemon*. Sheffield: Sheffield Academic Press, 1997.

Barth, M. and H. Blanke. *Colossians*. New York: Doubleday, 1994.

Barton, S. C. and G. H. R. Horsley. "A Hellenistic Cult Group and the New Testament Churches." *JAC* 24 (1981): 7–41.

Barton, T. "Augustus and Capricorn: Astrological Polyvalency and Imperial Rhetoric." *JRS* 85 (1995): 33–51.

Bauckham, R. *Gospel Women: Studies of the Named Women in the Gospels*. London/ NY: Continuum, 2002.

Bauer, W. *Griechisch-deutsches Wörterbuch*. Berlin: de Gruyter, 1988.

Baughan, E. P. *Couched in Death: Klinai and Identity in Anatolia and Beyond*. Madison: University of Wisconsin Press, 2013.

Baynham, E. *Alexander the Great: The Unique History of Quintus Curtius* (Ann Arbor: University of Michigan Press, 1998.

Baysal, E. L. and H. Elton. "A tomb with a view: the rock cut cemetery at Alahan in Isauria, Turkey." *Adalya* 17 (2014): 181–208.

Bean, G. E. and T. R. Mitford. "Sites Old and New in Rough Cilicia." *AS* 12 (1962): 185–217.

— *Journeys in Rough Cilicia 1964–68* (Vienna: Osterreichische Akademie der Wissenschaften, 1970.

Bechtel, F. *Die historische Personennamen des Griechischen bis zur Kaiserzeit.* Halle: Niemeyer, 1917.

Beckman, G. "Hittite Chronology." *Akkadica* 119–20 (2000): 19–32.

Bekker, I. *Ioelis chronographia compendiaria.* Bonn: Weber, 1836.

— *Georgius Cedrenus Ioannis Scylitzae ope.* Bonn: Weber, 2 vols, 1838–1839.

— *De thematibus et De administrando imperio.* Bonn: Weber, 1840.

Belayche, N. "'Un dieu est né …' À Stratonicée de Carie (I Stratonikeia 10)." Pages 193–212 in *Manières de penser dans l'Antiquité méditerranéenne et orientale. Mélanges offerts à Francis Schmidt* edited by Ch. Batsch and M. Vartejanu-Joubert. Leiden: Brill, 2009.

— "Angeloi in religious practices of the imperial Roman East." *Henoch* 32 (2010): 44–65.

Belley, M. A. l'Abbé. *Remarques sur les Pierres Gravées du Cabinet de Mgr le Duc D'Orléans.* 1758.

— "Observations sur une Cornaline Antique du Cabinet de Mgr le Duc D'Orléans." Pages 17–27 in *Histoire des Ouvrages de l''Academie Royale des Inscriptions et Belles-Lettres.* Paris: Panckoucke, 1780; also in *Mémoires de Littérature, tires des registres de l'Académie royale des inscriptions et Belles-Lettres* 36 (1784): 11–17.

Belke, K. and N. Mersich. *Tabula Imperii Byzantini Bd 7: Phrygien und Pisidien.* Vienna: Österreichische Akademie der Wissenschaften, 1990.

Bennett, C. "Thomas Smith." Pages 58–67 in *Christian-Muslim Relations: A Bibliographical History Volume 13, Western Europe (1700–1800)* edited by D. Thomas and J. Chesworth *et al.* Leiden: Brill, 2019.

Bennett, R. *Local Elites and Local Coinage. Elite Self-Representation on the Provincial Coinage of Asia, 31 BC to AD 275.* London: RNS, 2014.

Berg, R. M. van den. *Proclus' Hymns: Essays, Translations, Commentary.* Leiden: Brill, 2001.

Berger, P. *The Sacred Canopy: Elements of a Sociological Theory of Religion.* New York: Doubleday, 1967.

Bernand, E. *Inscriptions métriques de l'Égypte gréco-romaine. Recherches sur la poésie épigrammatique des Grecs en Égypte.* Besançon: Université de Franche-Comté, 1969.

Berns, C. and H. A. Ekinci. "Gladiatorial games in the Greek East: a complex of reliefs from Cibyra." *AS* 65 (2015): 143–79.

Bertholdt, L. *Historische-Kritische Einleitung in Schriften des Alten und Neuen Testaments.* Erlangen: Palmschen, 6 vols, 1812–1819.

Billerbeck, M. *Stephani Byzantii Ethnika (Volumen I: Α-Γ).* Berlin: De Gruyter, 2006.

Billò, C. "Manuele Crisolora, Confronto tra l'Antica e la Nuova Roma." *Medioevo Greco* "0" (2000): 6–26.

Bingen, J. *Hellenistic Egypt: Monarchy, Society, Economy, Culture.* Berkeley: University of California Press, 2007.

Bingöl, O. *Magnesia on the Meander,Magnesia ad Maeandrum: the city of Artemis with "white eyebrows"*. Galatasaray: Homer Kitanevi, 2007.

Birley, A. R. *Hadrian: The Restless Emperor.* London/New York: Routledge, 1997.

Biville, F. "The Graeco-Romans and Graeco-Latin: A Terminological Framework for Cases of Bilingualism." Pages 77–102 in *Bilingualism in Ancient Society: Language Contact and the Written Text* edited by J. N. Adams, M. Janse and S. Swain Oxford: Oxford University Press, 2002.

Blanco, M. "The Magicians who Sang to the Gods." Pages 258–65 in *Poetic Language and Religion in Greece and Rome* edited by J. V. García and A. Ruiz (Cambridge: Cambridge Scholars, 2013.

Blanco-Pérez, A. "Nomenclature and Dating in Roman Asia Minor: (M.) Aurelius/a and the 3rd Century AD." *ZPE* 199 (2016): 271–93.

— "EPINIKIA: Celebrating Roman Victory in the Eastern Provinces of the Empire." *Tyche* 33 (2018): 9–41.

Blass, F. *Grammar of New Testament Greek* trans. H StJ. Thackeray; London: Macmillan, 2nd ed., 1911.

Blois, L. de. *The Policy of the Emperor Gallienus.* Leiden: Brill, 1976.

Blumell, L. H. "The Message and the Medium: Some Observations on Epistolary Communication in Late Antiquity." *JGRChJ* 10 (2014): 24–67.

Blundell, S. "Clutching at Clothes." Pages 143–69 in *Women's Dress in the Ancient Greek World* edited by L. Llewellyn-Jones. Swansea: Classical Press of Wales, 2002.

Bodel, J. "Dealing with the Dead: Undertakers, Executioners and Potter's Fields in Ancient Rome." Pages 128–35 in *Death and Disease in the Ancient City* edited by V. M. Hope and E. Marshall. London: Routledge, 2000.

Boeckh, A. *Corpus Inscriptionum Graecarum.* Berlin: G. Reimer, 4 vols, 1828–1877.

Boer, R. *The Sacred Economy of Ancient Israel.* Louisville, KY: WJKP, 2015.

Bogensperger, I. "Purple and its Various Kinds in Documentary Papyri." Pages 235–49 in *Textile Terminologies from the Orient to the Mediterranean and Europe, 1000 BC to 1000 AD* edited by S. Gaspa, C. Michel and M.-L. Nosch. Lincoln, NE: Zea, 2017.

Boismard, M.-É. "Paul's Letter to the Laodiceans." Pages 45–57 in *The Pauline Canon* edited by S. E. Porter. Leiden: Brill, 2004.

Bonnet, M. *Narratio de Miraculo a Michele Archangelo Chonis Patrato.* Paris: Librairie Hachette, 1890.

Bormann, L. "Weltbild und gruppenspezifische Raumkonfiguration des Kolosserbriefs." Pages 83–102 in *Kolosser-Studien* edited by P. Müller. Göttingen: Neukirchener, 2009.

— *Der Brief des Paulus an der Kolosser.* Leipzig: Evangelische Verlagsanstalt, 2012.

— "Barbaren und Skythen im Lykostal? Epigraphischer Kommentar zu Kol 3:11." Pages 161–98 in *Epigraphical Evidence Illustrating Paul's Letter to the Colossians* edited by J. Verheyden, M Öhler and T. Corsten. Tübingen: Mohr Siebeck, 2018.

— "Early Christians in the Lycus Valley." Pages 211–29 in *Early Christian Encounters with Town and Countryside: Essays on the Urban and Rural Worlds of Early Christianity* edited by M. Tiwald and J. K. Zangenberg. Göttingen: Vandenhoeck & Ruprecht, 2021.

Borrell, H. P. "Unedited Autonomous and imperial Greek Coins." *NC* 8 (1845–6): 2–35.

Boudon-Millot, V. “Ménécratès.” Vol 4, pages 441–2 in *Dictionnaire des philosophes antiques* edited by Goulet, R. *et al.* Paris: CRNS, 6 vols, 1989–2016.
Bouley, E. “Le culte de Nemesis et les jeux de l'amphithéâtre dans les provinces balkaniques et danubiennes.” Pages 241–51 in *Spectacula I: Gladiateurs et amphithéâtres* edited by C. Domergue, C. Landes and J-M. Pailler. France: Aimgo, 1990.
Bouras, C. “Master Craftsmen, Craftsmen, and Building Activities in Byzantium.” Pages 539–54 in *The Economic History of Byzantium: from the Seventh through the Fifteenth Century* edited by A. E. Laiou. Washington DC: Harvard University Press, 2002.
Bowen, J. *A History of Western Education: Volume 1, The Ancient World.* London: Methuen, 1972.
Bowersock, G. W. “Plutarch and the Sublime Hymn of Ofellius Laetus.” *GBRS* 23 (1982): 275–9.
Bowersock, G. W. and C. P. Jones. “A New Inscription from Panticapaeum.” *ZPE* 156 (2006): 117–28.
Bowman, A. and A. Wilson (eds). *Settlement, Urbanization, and Population.* Oxford: Oxford University Press, 2011.
Brändl, M. *Der Agon bei Paulus: Herkunft und Profil paulinischer Agonmetaphorik.* Tübingen: Mohr Siebeck, 2006.
Brélaz, C. “Maintaining Order and Exercising Justice in the Roman Provinces of Asia Minor.” Pages 45–64 in *The Province Strikes Back: Imperial Dynamics in the Eastern Mediterranean* edited by B. Forsén and G. Salmeri. Helsinki: Finnish Academy, 2008.
— “Local Understandings of Roman Criminal Law and Procedure in Asia Minor.” Pages 157–84 in *Law in the Roman Provinces* edited by K. Czajkowski *et al.* Oxford: Oxford University Press, 2020.
Bremen, R. van. *The Limits of Participation: Women and Civic Life in the Greek East in the Hellenistic and Roman Periods.* Amsterdam: J. C. Gieben, 1996.
Bremmer, J. M. “Walking, standing and sitting in ancient Greek culture.” Pages 15–35 in *A Cultural History of Gesture: from antiquity to the present day* edited by J. Bremmer and H. Roodenburg. Cambridge: Cambridge University Press, 1991.
— “The Power of Poseidon: Horses, Chaos and Brute Force.” Pages 21–7 in *The World of Greek Religion and Mythology: Collected Essays II* (WUNT 433; Tübingen: Mohr Siebeck, 2019.
Brennan, M. G. (ed.). *The Travel Diary of Robert Bargrave, Levant merchant 1637–1656.* London: Hakluyt Society, 1999.
Bresson, A. “Drachmes rhodiennes et imitations.” *REA* 98 (1996): 65–77.
Breytenbach, C. and C. Zimmermann. *Early Christianity in Lycaonia and Adjacent Areas: From Paul to Amphilochius of Iconium.* Leiden: Brill, 2018.
(British Museum). *The Codex Alexandrinus (Royal MS. 1 D v–viii) in Reduced Photographic Facsimile.* London: British Museum, 1909.
Brixhe, C. “La langue comme critère d'acculturation: l'exemple du Grec d'un district phrygien.” *Hethitica* 8 (1987): 45–80.
— *Essai sur le grec anatolien au début de notre ère.* Nancy: Presses universitaires, 1987.
— “Interactions between Greek and Phrygian under the Roman Empire.” Pages 246–66

in *Bilingualism in Ancient Society: Language Contact and the Written Text* edited by J. N. Adams, M. Janse and S. Swain. Oxford: Oxford University Press, 2002.

— "Linguistic Diversity in Asia Minor during the Empire: *Koine* and Non-Greek Languages." Pages 228–52 in *A Companion to the Ancient Greek Language* edited by E. J. Bakker. Oxford: Blackwell, 2010.

— "The Personal Onomastics of Roman Phrygia." Pages 55–69 in *Roman Phrygia: Culture and Society* edited by P. Thonemann. Cambridge: Cambridge University Press, 2013.

— "Anatolian Anthroponymy after Louis Robert … and Some Others." Pages 15–30 in *Personal Names in Ancient Anatolia* edited by R. Parker. Oxford: The British Academy, 2013.

Broucke, P. B. F. J. "Tyche and the Fortune of Cities in the Greek and Roman World." *Yale University Art Gallery Bulletin* (1994): 34–49.

Bruce, F. F. *The Epistles to the Colossians, to Philemon, and to the Ephesians.* Grand Rapids, MI; Eerdmans, 1984.

Brucker, R. *"Christushymnen" oder "epideiktische Passagen"? Studien zum Stilwechsel im Neuen Testament und seiner Umwelt.* Göttingen: Vandenhoeck & Ruprecht, 1997.

— "'Songs,' 'Hymns,' and 'Encomia' in the New Testament?" Pages 1–14 in *Literature or Litrugy? Early Christian Hymns and Prayers in their Literary and Liturgical Context in Antiquity* edited by C. Leonhard and M. Löhr. Tübingen: Mohr Siebeck, 2014.

Brunt, P. A. "The 'Fiscus' and its Development." *JRS* 56 (1966): 75–91.

— "The Role of the Senate in the Augustan Regime." *CQ* 34 (1984): 423–44.

Bruun, P. "Coins and the Roman Imperial Government." Pages 19–40 in *Roman Coins and Public Life under the Empire* edited by G. M. Paul and M. Ierardi. Ann Arbor: University of Michigan Press, 1999.

Buckler, W. H. and W. M. Calder. *Monumenta Asiae Minoris Antiqua Vol. VI: Monuments and Documents from Phrygia and Caria.* Manchester: Manchester University Press, 1939.

Buechheler, F. and A. Riese (eds). *Anthologia Latina.* Leipzig: G. Tuebner, 1906.

Buell, D. K. and C. J. Hodge. "The Politics of Interpretation: The Rhetoric of Race and Ethnicity in Paul." *JBL* 123 (2004): 235–51.

Bülow-Jacobsen, A. "The Archiprophetes." Pages 124–31 in *Actes du XVe Congrès international de papyrology* edited by J. Bingen and G. Nachtergael. Brussels: Fondation Égyptolique Reine Élisaveth, 1979.

Buonopane, A. "Medicae nell'occidente romano: un'indagine preliminaire." Pages 113–30 in *Donna e lavoro nella documentazione epigrafica. Atti del I Seminario sulla condizione femminile nella documentazione epigrafica* edited by A. Buonopane and F. Cenerini. Faenza: Fratelli Lega Editori, 2003.

Burke, T. *De infantia Jesu evangelium Thomae Graece.* Turnhout: Brepols, 2010.

Burnett, A. *Coinage in the Roman World.* London: Spink, 1987.

Burnett, A., M. Amandry and P. Ripollès. *Roman Provincial Coinage: Supplement 1.* London: British Museum/Paris: Bibliothèque nationale de France, 1998.

Burnett, D. C. *Studying the New Testament through Inscriptions: An Introduction.* Peabody, MA: Hendrickson Academic, 2019.

Burrell, B. *Neokoroi: Greek Cities and Roman Emperors.* Leiden: Brill, 2004.
Burstein, S. M. "Paccius Maximus: A Greek Poet in Nubia or a Nubian Greek Poet?" *CRIPEL* 17.3 (1998): 47–51.
— "A Soldier and His God in Lower Nubia: The Mandulis Hymns of Paccius Maximus." *Graeco-Arabica* 7–8 (1999–2000): 45–50.
— "When Greek Was an African Language: The Role of Greek Culture in Ancient and Medieval Nubia." *JWH* 19 (2008): 41–61.
Burton, G. P. "Proconsuls, Assizes and the Administration of Justice under the Empire." *JRS* 65 (1975): 92–106.
— "The Resolution of Territorial Disputes in the Provinces of the Roman Empire." *Chiron* 30 (2000): 195–215.
Büttner-Wobst, T. *Ioannis Zonarae epitomae historiarum libri xviii.* Bonn: Weber, 1897.
Buxton, B. and R. Hannah. "*OGIS* 458, the Augustan Calendar and the Succession." Pages 290–306 in *Studies in Latin Literature and Roman History XII* edited by C. Deroux. Brussels: Latomus, 2005.
Cadwallader, A. H. "Revisiting Calder on Colossae." *AS* 56 (2006): 103–11.
— "In Go(l)d we trust: Literary and Economic Currency Exchange in the Debate over Caesar's Coin (Mark 12:13–17)." *BibInterp* 14 (2006): 486–507.
— "A New Inscription [=Two New Inscriptions], a Correction and a Confirmed Sighting from Colossae." *EA* 40 (2007): 109–18.
— *Beyond the Word of a Woman: Recovering the Bodies of the Syrophoenician Women.* Adelaide: ATF Press, 2008.
— "Refuting an Axiom of Scholarship on Colossae: fresh insights from new and old inscriptions." Pages 151–79 in *Colossae in Space and Time: Linking to an Ancient City* edited by A. H. Cadwallader and M. Trainor. Göttingen: Vandenhoeck & Ruprecht, 2011.
— "A Stratigraphy of an ancient city through its key story: the archistrategos of Chonai." Pages 282–95 in *Colossae in Space and Time: Linking to an Ancient City* edited by A. H. Cadwallader and M. Trainor. Göttingen: Vandenhoeck & Ruprecht, 2011.
— "The Story of the Archistrategos, St Michael of Chonai." Pages 323–30 in *Colossae in Space and Time: Linking to an Ancient City* edited by A. H. Cadwallader and M. Trainor. Göttingen: Vandenhoeck & Ruprecht, 2011.
— "Keeping Lists or Embracing Freedom: 1 Corinthians 6:9–10 in Context." Pages 47–67 in *Five Uneasy Pieces* edited by N. McI. Wright. Adelaide: ATF Press, 2011.
— "Honouring the Repairer of the Baths: A New Inscription from Kolossai." *Antichthon* 46 (2012): 150–83.
— "St Michael of Chonai and the Tenacity of Paganism." Pages 37–59 in *Intercultural Transmission throughout the Medieval Mediterranean: 100–1600 CE* edited by D. Kim and S. Hathaway. London/NY: Continuum, 2012.
— "The Roman Province of Asia." Pages 303–17 in *The Oxford Encyclopedia of the Bible and Archaeology* edited by D. M. Master *et al.* Oxford: Oxford University Press, 2013.
— "Name Punning and Social Stereotyping: Re-inscribing Slavery in the Letter to Philemon." *ABR* 16 (2013): 18–31.

— "Inter-city Conflict in the Story of St Michael of Chonai." Pages 109–28 in *Religious Conflict from Early Christianity to the Rise of Islam* edited by W. Mayer and B. Neil. Tübingen: de Gruyter, 2013.

— "Greeks in Colossae: shifting allegiances in the Letter to the Colossians and its context." Pages 224–41 in *Attitudes to Gentiles in Ancient Judaism and Early Christianity* edited by D. C. Sim and J. S. McLaren. London/NY: Bloomsbury, 2013.

— "The Struggle for Paul in the Context of Empire: Mark as a Deutero-Pauline Text." Pages 557–87 in *Paul and Mark in Comparison: Authors at the Beginning of Christianity* edited by D. C. Sim and O. Wischmeyer. Berlin/New York: de Gruyter, 2014.

— *Fragments of Colossae: Sifting through the Traces.* Adelaide: ATF Press, 2015.

— "Assessing the Potential of Archaeological Discoveries for the Interpretation of New Testament Texts: The Case of a Gladiator Fragment from Colossae and the Letter to the Colossians." Pages 41–66 in *The First Urban Churches I: Methodological Foundations* edited by J. R. Harrison and L. L. Welborn. Atlanta, GA: SBL Press, 2015.

— "Paul speaks like a girl: when Phoebe reads Romans." Pages 69–94 in *Sexuality, Ideology and the Bible: Queer Readings from the Antipodes* edited by R. J. Myles and C. Blyth. Sheffield: Sheffield Phoenix, 2015.

— "One Grave, Two Women, One Man: Complicating Family Life at Colossae." Pages 157–94 in *Stones, Bones, and the Sacred: Essays on Material Culture and Ancient Religion in Honor of Dennis E. Smith* edited by A. H. Cadwallader. Atlanta, GA: SBL Press, 2016.

— "Paul and the Games." Pages 365–92 in *Paul in the Greco-Roman World: A Handbook, Volume 1* edited by J. P. Sampley. London: Bloomsbury, 2016.

— "Bodily display and epigraphical confession at the Sanctuary of Apollo Lairbenos: an examination of emotional responses." *JES* 1 (2018): 183–201.

— "'As if in a Vision of the Night …' Authorising the Healing Spring of Chonai." Pages 265–92 in *Dreams, Memory and Imagination in Byzantium* edited by B. Neil and E. Anagnostou-Laoutides. Leiden: Brill, 2018.

— "Epiphanies and religious conflict: the contests over the hagiasma of Chonai." Pages 110–35 in *Reconceiving Religious Conflict: New Views from the Formative Centuries of Christianity* edited by C. de Wet and W. Mayer. London: Routledge, 2018.

— "The Historical Sweep of the Life of Kolossai." Pages 25–67 in *Epigraphical Evidence Illustrating Paul's Letter to the Colossians* edited by J. Verheyden, M Öhler and T. Corsten. Tübingen: Mohr Siebeck, 2018.

— "'Bad to the Bone': Reading Revelation Rooned." *ABR* 66 (2018): 13–29.

— "Peasant Plucking in Mark: Conceptual and Material Issues." Pages 67–87 in *Class Struggle in the New Testament* edited by R. J. Myles. Lanham: Lexington/Fortress, 2019.

— "On the Question of Comparative Method in Historical Research: Colossae and Chonai in Larger Frame." Pages 105–51 in *The First Urban Churches 5: Colossae, Hierapolis, and Laodicea* edited by J. R. Harrison and L. L. Welborn. Atlanta, GA: SBL, 2019.

— "Onesimus and the Social and Geographical World of Philemon." Pages 569–82 in *Lexham Geographic Commentary on Acts through Revelation* edited by B. J. Beitzel. Bellingham, WA: Lexham Press, 2019.

— "Gertrude Bell's Resolution of a Disputed Inscription." *Gephyra* 20 (2020): 1–26.
— "Sometimes one word makes a world of difference: rethinking the origins of Mark's Gospel." Pages 233–64 in *The Impact of Jesus of Nazareth: Historical, Theological and Pastoral Perspectives* edited by J. R. Harrison and P. Bolt. Sydney: SCD Press, 2020.
— "Complicating Class in the Letter to Philemon: A Prolegomenon." Pages 95–122 in *The Struggle over Class: Socioeconomic Analysis of Ancient Jewish and Christian Texts* edited by G. A. Keddie, M. Flexsenhar and S. J. Friesen. Atlanta, GA: SBL Press, 2021.
— "The Devil as an Agent of Diplomacy: variations in the transmission of the story of St Michael of Chonai." in *Dealing with Difference: Patterns of Response to Religious Rivalry in Late Antiquity* edited by G. Dunn and C. Shepardson. Göttingen: Mohr Siebeck, 2021.
— "Greetings in stone: shifting the accent from papyri to epigraphy in Col 4:15–17." Pages 441–65 in *God's Grace Inscribed on the Human Heart: Festschrift for James R. Harrison* edited by P. Bolt and S. Kim. Sydney: SCD, 2022.
— "Family Life in Asia Minor." in *Ancient Literature for New Testament Studies Vol 10: Inscriptions, Graffiti and Documentary Papyri* edited by R. Richards and J. R.Harrison. Grand Rapids, MN: Zondervan, 2023, forthcoming.
— "Value-adding a slave, or, how much is an Onesimus worth?" forthcoming 2023.
— "Wealthy, widowed, astute and beneficent: Claudia Eugenetoriane and the second century revival of the Colossian mint." In *New Documents Illustrating the History of Early Christianity vol 12: The Lycus Valley* edited by J. R. Harrison *et al.* Grand Rapids, MN: Eerdmans, 2024, forthcoming.
— "The Battle over Lake Lycus: Inter-city Conflict in the Lycus Valley." In *New Documents Illustrating the History of Early Christianity vol 12: The Lycus Valley* edited by J. R. Harrison *et al.* Grand Rapids, MN: Eerdmans, 2024, forthcoming.
— "The Lust for Recognition and Influence: Laodikeia and the Quest for Neokorate Status." Forthcoming in *Revelation, the Aegean and Material Culture* edited by A. Keddie, D. Smith and N. Leach. London: Routledge, 2023.
— "Methodological Issues in the Study of Ancient Villages." Forthcoming in *The Village in Antiquity and the Rise of Early Christianity* edited by A. H. Cadwallader *et al.* London: T & T Clark, 2023.
— "Village Life in the Lycus Valley." Forthcoming in *The Village in Antiquity and the Rise of Early Christianity* edited by A. H. Cadwallader *et al.* London: T & T Clark, 2023.
— "Moneyed Women in Phrygia." *NC* (2023).
Cadwallader, A. H. and M. Trainor. "Colossae in Space and Time: Overcoming Dislocation, Dismemberment and Anachronicity." Pages 1–47 in *Colossae in Space and Time: Linking to an Ancient City* edited by A. H. Cadwallader and M. Trainor. Göttingen: Vandenhoek and Ruprecht, 2011.
Cadwallader, A. H. and J. R. Harrison. "Perspectives on the Lycus Valley: An Inscriptional, Archaeological, Numismatic, and Iconographic Approach." Pages 3–70 in *The First Urban Churches 5: Colossae, Hierapolis, and Laodicea* edited by J. R. Harrison and L. L. Welborn. Atlanta, GA: SBL Press, 2019.
Calderini, A. *La Manomissione e la condizione dei liberti in Grecia.* Milan: Ulrico Hoepli, 1908.

Caley, E. R. and J. F. C. Richards. *Theophrastus on Stones.* Columbus, Ohio: Ohio State University Press, 1956.

Calixtus, A. *In epistolam Sancti apostoli Pauli ad Colossenses.* Braunschweig: A. Duncker, 1654.

Callataÿ, F. de. "Calculating Ancient Coin Production: Seeking a Balance." *NC* 155 (1995): 289–312.

Calmet, A. *Dictionnaire historique, critique, chronologoque, geographique et litteral de la Bible*. Geneva: Marc-Michel Bousquet, 2nd ed., 1730 (1722).

Campbell, B. *The Writings of the Roman Land Surveyors.* London: Society for the Promotion of Roman Studies, 2000.

Campbell, C. R. *Colossians and Philemon: A Handbook on the Greek Text.* Waco, TX: Baylor University Press, 2013.

Campbell, D. A. *The Deliverance of God: An Apocalyptic Re-reading of Justification in Paul.* Grand Rapids: Eerdmans, 2009.

— *Framing Paul: An Epistolary Biography.* Grand Rapids, MI: Eerdmans, 2014.

Campbell, J. B. *Rivers and the Power of Ancient Rome.* Chapel Hill: University of North Carolina Press, 2012.

Campanelli, S. "Family Cult Foundations in the Hellenistic Age: Family and Sacred Space in a Private Religious Context." Pages 131–202 in *Understanding Material Text Culture: A Multidisciplinary View* edited by M. Hilgert. Berlin: de Gruyter, 2016.

Canavan, R. *Clothing the Body of Christ at Colossae: A Visual Construction of Identity.* Tübingen: Mohr Siebeck, 2012.

— "A Woman, a Coin and the Prosperity of Colossae." *ABR* 67 (2019): 1–16.

Cannon, G. E. *The Use of Traditional Materials in Colossians.* Macon, GA: Mercer University Press, 1983.

Carbone, L. F. "Money and Power: The Disappearance of Autonomous Silver Issues in the Roman Province of Asia." *Omni* 8 (2014): 10–34.

Carr, W. *Angels and Principalities: The Background, Meaning and Development of the Pauline Phrase hai archai kai hai exousiai.* Cambridge: Cambridge University Press, 1981.

Carter, M. J. D. "The Presentation of Gladiatorial Spectacles in the Greek East: Roman Culture and Greek Identity." PhD thesis, McMaster University, 1999.

— "Gladiatorial Ranking and the 'SC de Pretiis Gladiatorum Minuendis'." *Phoenix* 57 (2003): 83–114.

Carter, W. *Households and Discipleship: A Study of Matthew 19–20.* Sheffield: Sheffield Academic Press, 1994.

Cartledge, P. A. "Greek religious festivals." Pages 98–127 in *Greek Religion and Society* edited by P. E. Easterling and J. V. Muir. Cambridge: Cambridge University Press, 1985.

Casey, P. J. *Understanding Ancient Coins: an Introduction for Archaeologists and Historians.* London: Batsford, 1986.

Catling, R. W. V. "Sparta's Friends at Ephesos: the Onomastic Evidence." Pages 195–237 in *Onomatologos: Studies in Greek personal Names presented to Elaine Matthews* edited by R. W. V. Catling and F. Marchand. Oxford: Oxbow, 2010.

Champeaux, J. "Primigenius, ou de l'Originaire." *Latomus* 34 (1975): 909–85.

— *Fortuna. Le culte de la Fortune à Rome et dans le monde romain. I — Fortuna dans la religion archaïque.* Rome: École Française de Rome, 1982.

Champlin, E. *Final Judgments: Duty and Emotion in Roman Wills 200 B.C. - A.D. 250.* Berkeley: University of California Press, 1991.

Chandler, R. *Travels in Asia Minor and Greece or An Account of a Tour made at the Expense of the Society of Dilettanti.* London: J. Booker, 1775.

Chaniotis, A. *Die Verträge zwischen kretischen Poleis in der hellenistischen Zeit.* Stuttgart: Steiner, 1996.

— "Empfängerformular und Urkundenfälschung: Bemerkungen zum Urkundendossier von Magnesia am Mäander." Pages 51–69 in *Urkunden und Urkundenformulare im klassichen Altertum und in den orientalischen Kulturen* edited by R. G. Khoury. Heidelberg: Universitätsverlag C. Winter, 1999.

— "Foreign Soldiers - Native Girls? Constructing and Crossing Boundaries in Hellenistic Cities with Foreign Garrisons." Pages 99–113 in *Army and Power in the Ancient World* edited by A. Chanioties and P. Ducrey. Stuttgart: Franz Steiner, 2002.

— "New Inscriptions from Aphrodisias (1995–2001)." *AJA* 108 (2004): 377–416.

— *War in the Hellenistic World: A Social and Cultural History.* Oxford: Blackwell, 2008.

— "Epigraphic Bulletin for Greek Religion." *Kernos* 23 (2010): 241–302.

—"The Impact of War on the Economy of Hellenistic Poleis: demand creation, short-term influences, long-term impacts." Pages 122–41 in *The Economics of Hellenistic Societies, Third to First Centuries BC* edited by Z. Archibald, J. K. Davies and V. Gabrielsen. Oxford: Oxford University Press, 2011.

— "Greek Festivals and Contests: definition and general characteristics." Pages 4–42 in *Festivals and Contests* edited by A. Chaniotis. Los Angeles: Getty Publications, 2011.

— "Second Thoughts on Second Names in Aphrodisias." Pages 207–29 in *Personal Names in Ancient Anatolia* edited by R. Parker. Oxford: British Academy, 2013.

— "Staging and Feeling the Presence of God: Emotion and Theatricality in Religious Celebrations." Pages 169–89 in *Panthée: Religious Celebrations in the Greco-Roman Empire* edited by L. Bricault and C. Bonnet. Leiden: Brill, 2013.

— "Archival research, formulaic language, and ancient forgeries of legal documents." Pages 669–90 in *ΑΞΩΝ: Studies in Honor of Ronald S. Stroud* edited by A. P. Matthaios and N. Papazarkadas. Athens: Hellenic Epigraphy Society, 2015.

Charles, A. *A Classical Dictionary, containing an account of the principal proper names mentioned in Ancient Authors.* New York: Harper, 1841.

Chelotti, M., R. Gaeta, V. Morizio, F. Grelle and M. Silvestrini (eds). *Le Epigrafi Romane di Canosa.* Documenti e Studi 7; Bari: Ediplugia, 1990.

Chia, G. F. "Creating Sacred Landscapes in Roman Phrygia: the cases of Laodicea on the Lycus and Aizanoi." Pages 209–18 in *Sacred Landscapes in Antiquity: Creation, Manipulation, Transformation* edited by R. Häussler and G. F. Chiai Oxford: Oxbow, 2020.

Chin, M. "Honours for Historians: Historiography and Civic Identity in the Hellenistic and Roman Polis (Third Century BCE to Third Century CE)." MRes (unpub.), Macquarie University 2015.

Chiricat, E. "The 'crypto-Christian' inscriptions of Phrygia." Pages 198–214 in *Roman Phrygia: Culture and Society* edited by P. Thonemann. Cambridge: Cambridge University Press, 2013.

Chishull, E. *Sermon preached before the honourable company of merchants trading to the Levant-seas at St Hellen's, January 16 being Sunday 1697/8*. London: S. Manship, 1698.

Christmas, H. *The Shores and Islands of the Mediterranean, including a visit to the Seven Churches of Asia*. London: R. Bentley, 3 vols, 1851.

Christol, M. and T. Drew-Bear. "Un senateur de Xanthos." *Journal des Savants* 3 (1991): 195–226.

Christopoulos, L. "Greek Combat Sports and their Transmission to Central and East Asia." *CW* 106 (2013): 431–59.

Chrysos, E. "El Reinardo de Basilio II: El Marco Histórico." Pages 3–8 in *El 'Menologio de Basilio II': Città de estudios con ocasión de la edición facsimil* edited by F. D'Aiuto. Vatican: Biblioteca Apostolica Vaticana, 2008.

Clerc, M. A. "Inscriptions de la vallée du Méandre. Tralles, Nysa, Attuda, Laodicée et Colosses." *BCH* 11 (1887): 346–54.

Clinton, J. H. *Athenian Expounders of the Sacred and Ancestral Law*. Baltimore: Johns Hopkins Press, 1950.

Clinton, K. "The Sacred Officials of the Eleusinian Mysteries." *TAPA* 64 (1974): 1–143.

— "The Stages of Initiation in the Eleusinian and Samothracian Mysteries." Pages 50–78 in *Greek Mysteries: The Archaeology of Ancient Greek Secret Cults* edited by M. B. Cosmopoulos. London: Routledge, 2003.

— "Pigs in Greek Rituals." Pages 167–79 in *Greek Sacrificial Ritual, Olympian and Chthonian* edited by R. Hagg and B. Alroth. Stockholm: Swedish Institute in Athens, 2005.

Cohen, G. M. *The Seleucid Colonies: Studies in Founding, Administration and Organization*. Vienna: Franz Steiner, 1978.

Cohn, L. *De Heraclide Milesio grammatico*. Berlin: Calvary, 1884.

Cole, S. G. "*Gynaiki Ou Themis*: Gender Differences in the Greek *Leges Sacrae*." *Helios* 19 (1992): 104–22.

Colvin, S. "Names in Hellenistic and Roman Lycia." Pages 44–84 in *The Greco-Roman East: Politics, Culture, Society* edited by S. Colvin. Cambridge: Cambridge University Press, 2004.

Concannon, C. "'Not for an Olive Wreath, but Our Lives': Gladiators, Athletes and Early Christian Bodies." *JBL* 133.1 (2014): 193–214.

— "Economic Aspects of Intercity Travel among the Pauline Assemblies." Pages 333–60 in *Paul and Economics: A Handbook* edited by T. R. Blanton IV and R. Pickett. Minneapolis: Fortress, 2017.

Conder, J. *The Modern Traveller: A Description, Geographical, Historical and Topographical, of the Various Countries of the Globe*. London. James Duncan, 2 vols, 1824.

Connolly, J. "Like the Labors of Heracles: Andreia and Paideia in Greek Culture under Rome." Pages 287–317 in *Andreia: Studies in Manliness and Courage in Classical Antiquity* edited by R. M. Rosen and I. Sluiter. Leiden: Brill, 2003.

Connor, P. J. "Tyrannus Hesperiae Capricornus undae." *Latomus* 44 (1985): 836–40.

Cook, S. A. "A Lydian-Aramaic Bilingual II." *JHS* 37 (1917): 219–31.

Cooley, A. E. "Beyond Rome and Latium: Roman Religion in the Age of Augustus." Pages 228–52 in *Religion in Republican Italy* edited by C. E. Schultz and P. B. Harvey. Cambridge: Cambridge University Press, 2006.

— *Res Gestae Divi Augusti*. Cambridge: Cambridge University Press, 2009.

Copenhaver, A. *Reconstructing the Historical Background of Paul's Rhetoric in the Letter to the Colossians*. London: T & T Clark, 2018.

Corancez, L. A. O. de. *Itineraire d'une partie peu connu de l'Asie Mineure*. Paris: 1816.

Cornelius, F. *Geschichte der Hethiter: Mit besonderer Berücksichtigung der geographischen Verhältnisse und der Rechtsgeschichte*. Darmstadt: Wissenschaftliche Buchgesellschaft, 1973.

Corsten, T. *Die Inschriften von Laodikeia am Lykos*. Bonn: Habelt, 1997.

— *Die Inschriften von Kibyra vol I*. Bonn: Habelt, 2002.

— "The Foundation of Laodikeia on the Lykos: An Example of Hellenistic City Foundations in Asia Minor." Pages 131–6 in *Regionalism in Hellenistic and Roman Asia Minor* edited by H. Elton and G. Reger. Bordeaux: Ausonius, 2007.

— "Names in *-ianos* in Asia Minor: A preliminary study." Pages 456–63 *Onomatologos: Studies in Greek Personal Names presented to Elaine Matthews* edited by R. W. V. Catling and F. Marchand. Oxford: Oxbow, 2010.

— "Mann oder Frau: Nympha oder Nymphas in Laodikeia?" Pages 215–9 in *Epigraphical Evidence Illustrating Paul's Letter to the Colossians* edited by J. Verheyden, M. Öhler and T. Corsten. Tübingen: Mohr Siebeck, 2018.

Cosby, M. R. *Apostle on the Edge: An Inductive Approach to Paul*. Louisville, KY: Westminster John Knox Press, 2009.

Cotton, H. M. "'Diplomatics' or external aspects of the legal documents from the Judaean desert: prolegomena." Pages 49–61 in *Rabbinic Law in its Roman and Near Eastern Context* edited by C. Hezser. Tübingen: Mohr Siebeck, 2003.

— "Private International Law or Conflicts of Laws: Reflections on Roman Provincial Jurisdiction." Pages 235–55 in *Herrschen und Verwalten. Der Alltag der römischen Administration in der Hohen Kaiserzeit*, edited by R. Haensch and J. Heinrichs. Köln: Böhlau, 2007.

Coulton, J. J. "Pedestals as 'altars' in Roman Asia Minor." *AS* 55 (2005): 127–57.

Cousin, G. *Kyros le Jeune en Asie Mineure (Printemps 408–Juillet 401 avant Jésus-Christ)*. Nancy: Berger-Levrault, 1904.

Cramer, J. A. *A Geographical and Historical Description of Asia Minor*. Oxford: Oxford University Press, 2 vols, 1832.

Cribiore, R. *Writing, Teachers and Students in Graeco-Roman Egypt*. Atlanta, GA: Scholars Press, 1996.

Crossan, J. D. *Who Killed Jesus? Exposing the Roots of Anti-Semitism in the Gospel Story of the Death of Jesus*. New York: HarperSanFrancisco, 1995.

Crouch, J. E. *The Origins and Intention of the Colossian Haustafel*. Göttingen: Vandenhoeck & Ruprecht, 1972.

Crowther, N. B. "Male 'Beauty' Contests in Greece: The Euandria and Euexia." *AC* 54 (1985): 285–91.

Cullmann, O. *1 Corinthians* translated by J. W. Leitch. Philadelphia: Fortress, 1975.

Cummings, C. "Meat Consumption in Roman Britain: The Evidence from Stable Isotopes." *TRAC* (2008): 73–83.

Cunnally, J. *Images of the Illustrious: The Numismatic Presence in the Renaissance*. Princeton: Princeton University Press, 1999.

Curbera, J. B. "Simple Names in Ionia." Pages 107–43 in *Personal Names in Ancient Anatolia* edited by R. Parker. Oxford: Oxford University Press, 2013.

— "Seven Curse Tablets from the Collection of Richard Wünsch." *ZPE* 195 (2015): 143–56.

Curbera, J. B. and D. R. Jordan. "A Curse Tablet from the 'Industrial District' Near the Athenian Agora." *Hesperia* 67 (1998): 215–18.

Cusset, C. "Alexander of Ephesus." Pages 56–64 in *Hellenistic Poetry: A Selection* edited by D. Sider. Ann Arbor: University of Michigan Press, 2017.

de Boor, C. *Georgii monachi chronicon*. 2 vols, Leipzig: Teubner, 1904.

de Ste. Croix, G. *The Class Struggle in the Ancient Greek World*. London: Duckworth, 1981.

Dain, A. *Inscriptions grecques du Musée du Louvre; les textes inédits*. Paris: Les Belles Lettres, 1933.

Dana, M. "Les médecins du Pont-Euxin à l'étranger: une 'Itinérance du savoir'." *Classica et Christiana* 3 (2008): 109–30.

D'Ambra, E. "Kosmetai, the Second Sophistic and Portraiture in the Second Century." Pages 201–16 in *Periklean Athens and its Legacy: Problems and Perspectives* edited by J. M. Barringer and J. M. Hurwit. Austin: University of Texas Press, 2005.

D'Andria, F. "Saints and Pilgrims in the Lykos Valley (Asia Minor)." *Deltion* 38 (2017): 35–56.

Darrouzès, J. *Notitiae Episcopatuum Ecclesiae Constantinopolitanae*. Paris: Institut français d'études byzantines, 1981.

Davenant, J. *Expositio Epistolae D. Pauli ad Colossenses*. Geneva: Samuel Chouët, 9th ed., 1655 (1625).

Davies, A. M. "The Linguistic Evidence: Is there any?" Pages 93–123 in *The End of the Early Bronze Age in the Aegean* edited by G. Cadogan. Leiden: Brill, 1986.

Davies, G. "The Case of the Large and Small Herculaneum Women." Pages 227–42 in *Women's Dress in the Ancient Greek World* edited by L. Llewellyn-Jones. Swansea: Classical Press of Wales, 2002.

Davies, J. K. "Rhodes Forward: Meditations on the Progress of a Discipline." Pages 265–74 in *Greek History and Epigraphy: Essays in honour of P. J. Rhodes* edited by L. Mitchell and L. Rubinstein. Swansea: Classical Press of Wales, 2009.

Davies, W. D. and D. C. Allison. *Matthew 19–28*. London: T & T Clark, 1997.

Debord, P. "Questions stratonicéennes." Pages 157–72 in *Les cités d'Asie Mineure occidentale au IIe siècle a.C.* edited by A. Bresson and R. Descat. Bordeaux: Ausonius, 2001.

Deissman, A. *Bible Studies*. Edinburgh: T & T Clark, 1909.

— *Light from the Ancient East* translated by L. R. M. Strachan. London: Hodder & Stoughton, 1910.

Deledemou, E. *Θησαυρὸς Δαμασκηνοῦ τοῦ ὑποδιακόνου καὶ Στουδίτου*. New York: Atlantis Greek Book Co., 1943.

Delehaye, H. *Synaxarium ecclesiae Constantinopolitanae (e codice Sirmondiano nunc Berolinensi)*. Brussels: Society of Bollandists, 1985 [1902].

— "Catalogus Codicum Hagiographicorum Graecorum: Bibliothecae Nationalis Neapolitanae." *AB* 21 (1902): 381–400.

— *Synaxarium ecclesiae Constantinopolitanae (e codice Sirmondiano nunc Berolinensi)*. Brussels: Society of Bollandists, 1985 [1902].

— *Acta Sanctorum (Novembris), Tomus III*. Brussels: Society of Bollandists, 1965 [1910], 588–606.

Delia, D. *Alexandrian Citizenship during the Roman Principate*. Atlanta, GA: Scholars Press, 1991.

Demargne, J. "Monuments figures et inscriptions de Crète." *BCH* 24 (1900): 222–46.

DeMaris, R. E. *The Colossian Controversy: Wisdom in Dispute at Colossae*. Sheffield: JSOT Press, 1994.

Demougin, S. "L'ordre équestre en Asie Mineure. Histoire d'une Romanization." Pages 579–612 in *L'ordre équestre. Histoire d'une aristocratie (IIe siècle av J.-C. - IIIe siècle ap J.-C.)* edited by S. Demougin, H. Devijver and M.-T. Raepsaet-Charlier. Rome: École française de Rome, 1999.

DesRosiers, N. P. and L. C. Vuong (eds.). *Religious Competition in the Greco-Roman World*. Atlanta, GA: SBL, 2016.

Dettori, E. "Testi 'Orfici' dalla Magna Grecia al Mar Nero." *PP* 51 (1996): 292–310.

Dickey, E. *The Colloquia of the Hermeneumata Pseudodositheana Volume 1*. Cambridge: Cambridge University Press, 2012.

Dickie, M. W. "What is a *Kolossos* and How Were *Kolossoi* Made in the Hellenistic Period?" *GRBS* 37 (1996): 237–57.

Dieten, J. van. *Nicetae Choniatae historia, pars prior*. Berlin: de Gruyter, 1975.

Dignas, B. *Economy of the Sacred in Hellenistic and Roman Asia Minor*. Oxford: Oxford University Press, 2002.

— "'Inventories' or 'Offering Lists'? Assessing the Wealth of Apollo Didymaeus." *ZPE* 138 (2002): 235–44.

Dillon, J. M. *The Middle Platonists, 80 B.C. to A.D. 220*. Ithaca, NY: Cornell University Press, 1977.

Dmitriev, S. *City Government in Hellenistic and Roman Asia Minor*. Oxford: Oxford University Press, 2005.

Donaldson, T. (ed). *Religious Rivalries and the Struggle for Success in Caesarea Maritima*. Waterloo, Ontario: Wilfred Laurier University Press, 2000.

Doonan, O. "Family Values: Ancestral Representation and Social Reproduction in Roman Houses." Pages 73–84 in *Interpretatio Rerum: Archaeological Essays on Objects and Meaning* edited by S. S. Lukesh. Providence, RI: Brown University, 1999.

Dorcey, P. F. *The Cult of Silvanus: A Study in Roman Folk Religion*. Leiden: Brill, 1992.

Dougherty, C. *The Poetics of Colonization: From City to Text in Archaic Greece*. Oxford: Oxford University Press, 1993.

Dreher, M. "'Heliges Recht' and 'Heilege Gesetze': Law, Religion and Magic in Ancient Greece." Pages 85–103 in *Ancient Greek Law in the 21st Century* edited by P. Perlman. Austin: University of Texas Press, 2018.

Drew-Bear, T. C. *Nouvelles Inscriptions de Phrygie.* Zutphen, Holland: Terra, 1978.

— "Problèmes de géographie historique en Phrygie: l'example d'Alia." *ANRW* II, 7, 2 (1980): 932–52.

— "Map 62 Phrygia." Pages 957–75 in *Barrington Atlas of the Greek and Roman World: Map-by-Map Directory* edited by R. J. A. Talbert. Princeton, NJ: Princeton University Press, 2 vols 2000.

Drew-Bear, T. C. and C. Naour. "Divinités de Phrygie." *ANRW* II 18,3 (1990): 1907–2044.

Drew-Bear, T., C. Thomas and M. Yıldızturan. *Phrygian Votive Steles.* Turkey: Ministry of Culture, 1999.

Drexhage, H.-J. *Preise, Mieten/Pachten, Kosten und Löhne im Römischen Ägypten bis zum Regierungsantritt Diokletians.* St Katherinen: Scripta Mercaturae, 1991.

Dreyer, B. and H. Engelmann. "Augustus und Germanicus im ionischen Metropolis." *ZPE* 158 (2006): 173–82.

Dubois, L. "Hippolytos and Lysippos: Remarks on some Compounds in Ἱππο-, -ιππος." Pages 41–52 *Greek Personal Names: Their Value as Evidence* edited by S. Hornblower and E. Matthews. Oxford: Oxford University Press, 2000.

Ducat, J. "Fonctions de la statue dans la Grèce archaïque: Kouros et Kolossos." *BCH* 101 (1976): 246–51.

Duggan, T. M. P. "On early antiquarians in Asia Minor to the start of the 19th century." *Gephyra* 17 (2019): 115–67.

Duman, B. "Tripolis'in Yeri, Önemi ve Kısa Tarihi/Location, Importance and Short History of Tripolis." Pages 1–16 in *Tripolis Araştırmaları* edited by B. Duman. Istanbul: Ege, 2017.

— "Location, Importance and Short History of Tripolis." Pages 17–22 in *Tripolis Araştırmaları* edited by B. Duman. Istanbul: Ege, 2017.

Duman, B. and E. Konakçı. "The Silent Witness of the Mound of Colossae: Pottery Remains." Pages 247–81 in *Colossae in Space and Time: Linking to an Ancient City* edited by A. H. Cadwallader and M. Trainor. Göttingen: Vandenhoek and Ruprecht, 2011.

Dunand, F. *Le culte d'Isis en Asie Mineure: Clergé et rituel des sanctuaires isiaques.* Leiden: Brill, 3 vols, 1975.

Duncan-Jones, R. *The Economy of the Roman Empire: Quantitative Studies.* Cambridge: Cambridge University Press, 2nd ed., 1986.

Dunn, J. D. G. *The Epistles to the Colossians and to Philemon.* Grand Rapids, MN: Eerdmans, 1996.

Dupertuis, R. R. "Socratizing Paul: The Portrait of Paul in Acts." *The Fourth R* 22 (2009): 11–18, 28.

Dupuis, J. *Théon de Smyrne. Exposition des connaissances mathématiques utiles pour la lecture de Platon.* Paris: Hachette, 1892.

Duranti, A. *Linguistic anthropology.* Cambridge: Cambridge University Press, 1997.

Düşen, O. *et al.* "Laodikeia Antik Kenti'nin Floristik Yapısı." Pages 369–86 in *10. Yalındı Laodikeia (2003-2013 Yılları)* edited by C. Şimşek. Istanbul: Ege, 2014.

Dusinberre, E. R. M. *Gordion Seals and Sealings: Individuals and Society.* Philadelphia: University of Pennsylvania Museum of Archaeology and Anthropology, 2005.

Dutsch, D. M. *Pythagorean Women Philosophers: Between Belief and Suspicion*. Oxford: Oxford University Press, 2020.

Eadie, J. *A Biblical Cyclopaedia*. London: Charles Griffin, 20th ed., 1878.

Ebner, M. *Der Brief an Philemon*. Göttingen: Vandenhoeck & Ruprecht, 2017.

Ebojo, E. B. "A Scribe and his Manuscript: An Investigation into the Scribal Habits of Papyrus 46 (P. Chester Beatty II – P. Mich. Inv. 6238)." PhD (unpub), University of Birmingham, 2014.

Eck, W. "The Presence, role and significance of Latin in the epigraphy and culture of the Roman Near East." Pages 15–42 in *From Hellenism to Islam: Cultural and Linguistic Change in the Roman Near East* edited by H. Cotton *et al.* Cambridge: Cambridge University Press, 2009.

— "*Senatus consulta* in lateinischen Inschriften aus den Provinzen." *Quaderno Lupiensi di Storia e Diritto* 7 (2017): 31–55.

Eckhardt, B. "Romanization and Isomorphic Change in Phrygia: the Case of Private Associations." *JRS* 106 (2016): 147–71.

Eckhel, J. H. von. *Doctrina numorum veterum …* Vindobonae: J. Camesina, 8 vols, 1792–98.

Edsall, B. and J. R. Strawbridge. "The Songs we used to sing? Hymn 'traditions' and receptionin Pauline letters." *JSNT* 37 (2015): 290–311.

Edwards, C. "Unspeakable Professions: Public Performance and Prostitution in Ancient Rome." Pages 66–95 in *Roman Sexualities* edited by J. P. Hallett and M. B. Skinner. Princeton: Princeton University Press, 1997.

Ehrman, B. *Forgery and Counterforgery: The Use of Literary Deceit in Early Christian Polemics*. Oxford: Oxford University Press, 2013.

Eidinow, E. "Binding Spells on Tablets and Papyri." Pages 351–87 in *Guide to the Study of Ancient Magic* edited by D. Frankfurter. Leiden: Brill, 2019.

Eilers, C. *Roman Patrons of Greek Cities*. Oxford: Oxford University Press, 2002.

Elderkin, G. W. "A Christian Stele from Cappadocia." *AJA* 41 (1937): 97–9.

Elsner, J. "Describing self in the language of Other: Pseudo(?) Lucian at the temple of Hierapolis." Pages 123–53 in *Being Greek under Rome: Cultural Identity, the Second Sophistic, and the Development of Empire* edited by S. Goldhill. Cambridge: Cambridge University Press, 2001.

Elton, H. "Military Supply on the South Coast of Anatolia in the 3rd century AD." Pages 289–304 in *Patterns in the Economy of Roman Asia Minor* edited by S. Mitchell and C. Katsari. Swansea: Classical Press of Wales, 2005.

Erten, E. and H. Sivas. "Eine neue Weihung aus Phrygien." *EA* 44 (2011): 185–95.

Esler, P. F. "Paul and the Agon: Understanding a Pauline Motif in its Cultural and Visual Context." Pages 356–84 in *Picturing the New Testament: Studies in Ancient Visual Images* edited by A. Weissenrieder, F. Wendt and P. von Gemünden. Tübingen: Mohr Siebeck, 2005.

Eyben, E. "Was the Roman 'Youth' an 'Adult' socially?" *L'antiquité classique* 50 (1981): 328–50.

Fagan, G. G. *Bathing in Public in the Roman World*. Ann Arbor: University of Michigan Press, 1999.

Faraone, C. "The Stanzaic Architecture of Isidorus, Hymns 2 and 4 (*SEG* 8.549 and 51 [sic])." *CQ* 62 (2012): 618–32.

Farnell, L. R. *Greek Hero Cults and Ideas of Immortality.* Oxford: Clarendon Press, 1921.

Farrar, J. *A Biblical and Theological Dictionary.* London: John Mason, 1852.

Fatouros, G. *Theodori Studitae Epistulae.* Berlin/New York: de Gruyter, 2 vols, 1992.

Fellows, C. *A Journal Written During an Excursion in Asia Minor.* London: John Murray, 1838.

Ferrary, J.-L. *Les Mémoriaux de delegations du sanctuaire oraculaire de Claros, d'après la documentation conserve dans le Fonds Louis Robert.* Paris: Belles-Lettres, 2 vols, 2015.

Fiedler, P. "Haustafel." *RAC* 13 (1986): 1063–73.

Fikhman, I. F. *Wirtschaft und Gesellschaft im spätantiken Ägypten: kleine Schriften edited by A. Jördens.* Stuttgart: Franz Steiner, 2006.

Finck, F. N. *Des Nilos Doxopatres Τάξις τῶν πατριαρχικῶν θρόνων (armenisch und griechisch).* Marburg: N. G. Elwerfs Verlag, 1902.

Finnegan, R. (ed.) *Letters from Abroad: the Grand Tour Correspondence of Richard Pococke and Jeremiah Milles.* Piltown: Pococke Press, vol 3, 2019.

Fiorentino, G. "Palaeo-vegetational Reconstructions in the Lykos Valley by Archaeobotanical Analyses at Hierapolis." Pages 219–37 in *Landscape and History in the Lykos Valley: Laodikeia and Hierapolis in Phrygia* edited by C. Şimşek and F. D'Andria. Cambridge: Cambridge Scholars Publishing, 2016.

Fiorillo, J. D. *Parerga et ornamenta, caelo expresa ad P. Virgilii Maronis opera illustranda.* London: 1812.

Fischer, J. "Redner, Sophisten und Philosophen in Römischen Ephesos." Pages 125–51 in *Der Beitrag Kleinasiens zur Kultur- und Geistesgeschichte der griechischen--römischen Antike* edited by J. Fischer. Vienna: Österreichischen Akademia der Wissenschaften, 2014.

Fischer, K. T. and F. Vogel. *Diodori bibliotheca historica.* Leipzig: Teubner, 5 vols, 3rd edition, 1964 [1888–1906].

Fitzgerald, J. T. "Theodore of Mopsuestia on Paul's Letter to Philemon." Pages 333–63 in *Philemon in Perspective: Interpreting a Pauline Letter* edited by D. F. Tolmie. Berlin/New York: de Gruyter, 2010.

Flaig, E. "Roman gladiatorial games: ritual and political consensus." Pages 83–92 in *Roman by Integration: Dimensions of Group Identity in Material Culture and Text* edited by R. Roth and J. Keller. Portsmouth, RI: Journal of Roman Archaeology, 2007.

Fleming, W. *A Gazetteer of the Old and New Testaments: to which is added the Natural History of the Bible.* Edinburgh: Edinburgh Printing and Publishing, 2 vols, 1838.

Foakes-Jackson, F. J. and K. Lake. *The Acts of the Apostles.* Grand Rapids, MN: Baker, 5 vols, 1979 (1932).

Follet, S. "Lettres d'Hadrien aux Épicuriens d'Athènes." *REG* 107 (1994): 158–71.

Foss, C. *History and Archaeology of Byzantine Asia Minor.* Aldershot: Variorum, 1990.

Foster, P. *Colossians.* London: Bloomsbury, 2016.

Fournier, P. *Entre tutelle romaine et autonomie civique. L'administration judiciaire dans les provinces hellénophones de l'Empire romain (129 av. J. C. - 235 apr. J.-C.).* Athens: École française d'Athènes, 2010.

Fox, W. S. "The Johns Hopkins Tabellae Defixionum." *AJP* 33 (1912): 1–9, 11–68.
Fragiadakis, C. *Die Attischen Sklavennamen von der spätarchaischen Epoche bis in die römische Kaiserzeit: eine historische und soziologische Untersuchung.* Athens: Mannheim, 1988.
Franke, P. R. and M. K. Nollé. *Die Homonoia-Münzen Kleinasiens under der thraksichen Randgebeite: I Katalog.* Saarbrücken: Saarbrücker Verlag, 1997.
Fraser, P. M. *Rhodian Funerary Monuments.* Oxford: Clarendon Press, 1977.
— *Greek Ethnic Terminology.* Oxford: Oxford University Press, 2009.
French, D. *Roman, Late Roman and Byzantine Inscriptions of Ankara: A Selection.* Ankara: Museum of Anatolian Civilizations, 2003.
Freu, J. "Les débuts du nouvel Empire Hittite et les origins de l'expansion Mycénienne. A propos d'une nouvelle datation des textes des rois Tuthaliya et Arnuwanda." *Annales de la Faculté des Lettres et Sciences humaines de Nice* 35 (1979): 7–37.
Friesen, S. J. "Poverty in Pauline Studies: Beyond the So-called New Consensus." *JSNT* 26 (2004): 323–61.
— "Embodied Inequalities: Diet Reconstruction and Christian Origins." Pages 9–31 in *Stones, Bones, and the Sacred: Essays on Material Culture and Ancient Religion in Honor of Dennis E. Smith* edited by A. H. Cadwallader. Atlanta, GA: SBL Press, 2016.
Frye, R. N. *et al.* "Inscriptions from Dura-Europos." *YCIS* 14 (1955): 127–213.
Furley, W. D. "Praise and Persuasion in Greek Hymns." *JHS* 115 (1995): 29–46.
Furley, W. and J. M. Bremmer. *Greek Hymns: Selected Cult Songs from the Archaic to the Hellenistic Period.* Tübingen: Mohr Siebeck, 2 Vols, 2001.
Furmann, C. *Policing the Roman Empire: Soldiers, Administration and Public Order.* Oxford: Oxford University Press, 2011.
Furtwängler, A. and U. Kron. "Das Siegel der Stadt Demetrias." *MDAI(A)* 93 (1978): 137–49.
Gafni, I. M. *Land, Center and Diaspora: Jewish Constructs in Late Antiquity.* Sheffield: Sheffield Academic Press, 1997.
Gager, J. G. (ed.) *Curse Tablets and Binding Spells from the Ancient World.* Oxford: Oxford University Press, 1992.
Gaisford, T. *Etymologicum magnum.* Oxford: Oxford University Press, 1848.
Gamhauf, R. "Onesimus: *fugitivus errove* –Einsichten für die Bibelexegese aus der Digestenexegese? (Rechtshistorische Anmerkungen zum Umgang mit römischen Rechtstexten in der neueren Philemon-Auslegung)." Pages 159–76 in *Constans et Perpetua Voluntas: Posta Petrovi Blahovi K 75. Narodeninám* edited by P. Mach, M. Pekarik and V. Vladár. Trnave: Trnavská Univerzita, 2014.
Ganes, A. *The Web of Empire: English Cosmopolitans in an Age of Expansion, 1560–1660.* Oxford: Oxford University Press, 2008.
Garland, R. *The Greek Way of Death.* Ithaca, NY: Cornell University Press, 1985.
Garnsey, P. and R. Saller. *The Roman Empire: Economy, Society and Culture.* London: Duckworth, 1987.
Gawlinski, L. *The Sacred Law of Ardania: A New Text with Commentary.* Berlin: de Gruyter, 2012.
Gellar-Goad, T. H. M., Z. Papakonstantinou and W. Riess. "Magic in Ancient Athens: A Complete Translation of Attic Curse Tablets." Pages 261–76 in *Colloquia Attica:*

Neuere Forschungen zur Archaik, zum athenischen Recht und zur Magie edited by W. Riess. Stuttgart: Franz Steiner, 2018.
Gellner, E. *Plough, Sword and Book: The Structure of Human History.* Chicago: University of Chicago Press, 1988.
Gese, M. *Der Kolosserbrief.* Göttingen: Vandenhoeck & Ruprecht, 2020.
Giacchero, M. *Edictum Diocletiani et collegarum de pretiis rerum venalium in integrum fere restitutum e Latinis Graecisque fragmentis.* Genoa: Istituto di storia antica e scienze ausiliarie, 2 vols, 1974.
Gibson, C. A. "Encomium and Thesis in Galen's *De parvae pilae exercitio.*" *GRBS* 54 (2014): 462–73.
Gibson, E. L. *The Jewish Manumission Inscriptions of the Bosporus Kingdom.* Tübingen: Mohr Siebeck, 1999.
Gielen, M. "Paulus — Gefangener in Ephesus?" *BM Neue Folge* 131 (2006): 79–103; 133 (2007): 63–77.
Glaisyer, N. *The Culture of Commerce in England 1660–1720.* Suffolk: Boydell, 2006.
Glancy, J. A. *Slavery in Early Christianity.* Oxford: Oxford University Press, 2002.
Glare, P. "The Temple of Jupiter Capitolinus at Arsinoe and the Imperial Cult." Pages 550–4 in *Proceedings of the 20th International Congress of Papyrologists, Copenhagen, 23–29 August, 1992* edited by A. Bülow-Jacobsen. Copenhagen: Museum Tusculan Press, 1994.
Goeken, J. *Aelius Aristide et la rhétorique de l'hymne en prose.* Turnhout: Brepols, 2012.
Goffmann, E. *Stigma: Notes on the Management of Spoiled Identity.* Reading: Penguin, 1968.
Goldman, A. "New Evidence for non-elite burial patterns in central Turkey." Pages 149–75 in *Life and Death in Asia Minor in Hellenistic, Roman and Byzantine Times: Studies in Archaeology and Bioarchaeology* edited by J. R. Brandt *et al.* Oxford: Oxbow, 2017.
— "The octagonal gemstones from Gordion: observations and interpretations." *AS* 64 (2014): 163–97.
Golomb, B. and Y. Kedar. "Ancient Agriculture in the Galilee Mountains." *IEJ* 21 (1971): 136–40.
Gordley, M. E. *The Colossian Hymn in Context: An Exegesis in Light of Jewish and Greco-Roman Hymnic and Epistolary Conventions.* Tübingen: Mohr Siebeck, 2011.
— *New Testament Christological Hymns: Exploring Texts, Contexts, and Significance* (Downers Grove, IL: IVP, 2018.
Gordon, R. "Imaginative Force and Verbal Energy in Latin Curse-Tablets." Pages 111–29 in *Litterae magicae. Studies in Honour of Roger S. O Tomlin.* Zragoza: Libros Pórtico, 2019.
Goulet, R. *et al.* (eds). *Dictionnaire des philosophes antiques.* Paris: CRNS, 6 vols, 1989–2016.
Graf, F. "Earthquakes and the Gods: Reflections on Graeco-Roman Responses to Catastrophic events." Pages 95–113 in *Myths, Martyrs and Modernity: Studies in the History of religion in Honour of Jan N. Brenner* edited by J. Dijkstra et al. Leiden: Brill, 2010.
Graser, E. R. "A Text and Translation of the Edict of Diocletian." Pages 307–421 in *An Economic Survey of Ancient Rome Volume V: Rome and Italy of the Empire* edited by T. Frank. Baltimore: Johns Hopkins Press, 1940.

Gray, B. D. "Philosophy of Education and the Later Hellenistic *Polis*." Pages 233–53 in *Epigraphical Approaches to the Post-Classical* Polis edited by P. Martzavou and N. Papazarkadas. Oxford: Oxford University Press, 2013.

Green, S. J. "*Arduum ad astra*: The poetics and politics of horoscopic failure in Manilius' *Astronomica*." Pages 129–38 in *Forgotten Stars: Rediscovering Manilius'* Astronomica edited by S. J. Green and K. Volk. Oxford: Oxford Univesrity Press, 2011.

Greenbaum, D. G. *The Daimon in Hellenistic Astrology: Origins and Influence*. Leiden: Brill, 2016.

— "Roman Astrology." Pages 294–301 in *Astrology through History: Interpreting the Stars from Ancient Mesopotamia to the Present* edited by W. E. Burns. Santa Barbara: ABC-CLIO, 2018.

Greene, K. *The Archaeology of the Roman Economy*. London: B. T. Batsford, 1986.

Greenewalt, C. H. "Croesus of Sardis and the Lydian Kingdom." Pages 1173–83 in *Civilizations of the Ancient Near East* edited by J. M. Sasson *et al.* New York: Scribner, 2 vols, 1995.

Greenfield, R. P. H. *The Life of Lazaros of Mt Galesion: An Eleventh-Century Pillar Saint*. Washington DC: Dumbarton Oaks Library, 2000.

Greenhalgh, M. *From the Romans to the Railways: The Fate of Antiquities in Asia Minor*. Leiden: Brill, 2013.

Greer, R. *Theodore of Mopsuestia: The Commentaries on the Minor Epistles of Paul*. Atlanta, GA: SBL, 2010.

Grenfell, B. P. and A. S. Hunt. *The Hibeh Papyri, Part 1*. London: Egypt Exploration Fund, 1906.

Grindheim, S. "A Deutero-Pauline Mystery? Ecclesiology in Colossians and Ephesians." Pages 173–95 in *Paul and Pseudepigraphy* edited by S. E. Porter and G. P. Fewster. Leiden: Brill, 2013.

Grosso, M. "The Diversification of Colossians' Text and Women's Status in the Early Church." *TC* 16 (2011): 1–5.

Guizzi, F. "Gladiatori." Pages 152–4 in *Museo Archeologico di Denizli-Hierapolis: Catalogo delle iscrizioni greche e latine* edited by T. Ritti. Naples: Liguori, 2008.

— "Iscrizioni ellenistiche." Pages 38–66 *Museo Archeologico di Denizli-Hierapolis: Catalogo delle iscrizioni greche e latine* edited by T. Ritti. Naples: Liguori, 2008.

— "Novità epigrafiche da Hierapolis di Frigia." *Historika* 7 (2017): 119–41.

— "An Edict of a Proconsul of Asia on the Aqueduct of Laodikeia (114/115 CE?)." Pages 143–64 in *15. Yalındı Laodikeia (2003–2018)* edited by C. Şimşek. Istanbul: Ege, 2019.

— "Greek and Latin Inscriptions of Laodikeia on the Lykos 2003–2018." Pages 165–80 in *15. Yılında Laodikeia (2003–2018)* edited by C. Şimşek (Istanbul: Ege, 2019.

Guizzi, F. and E. Miranda. "*Iura sepulcrorum* nel Museo di Denizli a Pamukkale (Hierapolis di Frigia)." *Libitina e dintorni* 3 (2004): 635–52.

Guizzi, F. and A. Filippini. "Tripolis on the Maeander in Hellenistic and Roman Age (Cent. 3rd B.C. - 3rd A.D.): Epigraphy and Prosopography." Pages 59–73 in *Tripolis ad Maeandrum I: Tripolis Araştırmaları* edited by B. Duman. Istanbul: Ege, 2017.

Guizzi, F. And B. Yener. "An Inscribed Altar from Tripolis ad Maeandrum." Pages 75–9 in *Tripolis Araştırmaları* edited by B. Duman. Istanbul: Ege, 2017.

Gundel, H. G. *Zodiakos. Tierkreisbilder im Altertum. Kosmische Bezüge und Jenseitsvorstellungen im antiken Alltagsleben*. Mainz: von Zabern, 1992.

Güney, H. "Poseidon as a God of Earthquake in Roman Asia Minor." *RN* 172 (2015): 293–315.

Gurtner, D. M. *Exodus: A Commentary on the Greek Text of Codex Vaticanus*. Leiden: Brill, 2013.

Gutbrod, W. "Ἰσραήλ." *TDNT* 3.369–91.

Haas, O. *Die phrygischen Sprachdenkmäler*. Sofia: Académie bulgare des sciences, 1966.

Habicht, C. "New Evidence on the Province of Asia." *JRS* 65 (1975): 64–91.

Haensch, R. "Das öffentliche Siegel der griechischen Staaten — zwischen Kontrollmittel und Staatssymbol." Pages 265–89 in *Symposion 2003: Vorträge zur griecvhischen und hellenistischen Rechtsgeschichte* edited by H-A. Ruprecht. Vienna: Österreichischen Akademie der Wissenshaften, 2006.

Halfmann, H. *Itinera principium: Geschichte und Typologie der Kaiserreisen im Römischen Reich*. Stuttgart: Franz Steiner, 1986.

Halkin, F. "La légende crétoise de Saint Tite." *Anal.Boll.* 24 (1905): 241–56.

Hall, A. and N. Milner. "Education and Athletics: Documents illustrating the festivals of Oenoanda." Pages 7–47 in *Studies in the History and Topography of Lycia and Pisidia. In Memoriam A.S.Hall* edited by D. French. Ankara: BIAA, 1994.

Hall, M. D. "Even Dogs have Erinyes: Sanctions in Athenian Practice and Thinking." Pages 73–89 in *Greek Law in its Political Setting: Justifications not Justice* edited by L. Foxhall and A. D. E. Lewis. Oxford: Clarendon, 1996.

Halliwell, S. "The Republic's Two Critiques of Poetry (Book II.376c–III.398b, Book X.595a–608b)." Pages 313–32 in *Platon, Politieia* edited by Otfried Höffe. Berlin: Akademia Verlag, 1997.

Hamilton, W. J. "Extracts from Notes made on a Journey in Asia Minor in 1836." *JRGS* 7 (1837): 34–61.

— *Researches in Asia Minor, Pontus and Armenia*. London: John Murray, 2 vols, 1842.

Hanges, J. C. *Paul, Founder of Churches: A Study in Light of the Evidence of the Role of "Founder-Figures" in the Hellenistic-Roman Period*. Tübingen: Mohr Siebeck, 2012.

Hanson, J. W. "The Urban System of Roman Asia Minor and Wider Urban Connectivity." Pages 229–75 in *Settlement, Urbanization and Population* edited by A. Bowman and A. Wilson. Oxford: Oxford University Press, 2011.

Harl, K. W. *Coinage in the Roman Economy, 300 B.C. to A.D. 700*. Baltimore: Johns Hopkins University Press, 1996.

Harland, P. A. *Associations, Synagogues and Congregations: Claiming a Place in Ancient Mediterranean Society*. Minneapolis: Fortress Press, 2003.

— *Greco-Roman Associations: Texts, Translations and Commentary II: North Coast of the Black Sea, Asia Minor*. Berlin: de Gruyter, 2014.

Harper, K. *et al.* "Establishing the Provenance of the Nazareth Inscription: Using stable isotopes to resolve a historic controversy and trace ancient marble production." *JASReports* 30 (2020): 1–7.

Harrill, J. A. "Using the Roman Jurists to interpret Philemon." *ZNW* 90 (1999): 135–8.

Harris, E. M. "Workshop, marketplace and household: the nature of technical specialization in classical Athens and its influence on economy and society." Pages 67–99 in *Money, Labour and Land: Approach to the Economies of Ancient Greece* edited by P. Cartledge, E. E. Cohen and L. Foxhall. London: Routledge, 2002.
— "The *Against Meidias* (Dem. 21)." Pages 209–36 in *The Documents in the Attic Orators: Laws and Decrees in the Public Speeches of the Demosthenic Corpus* edited by M. Canevaro. Oxford: Oxford University Press, 2013.
Harris, M. J. *Colossians and Philemon.* Nashville, TN: B&H Academic, 2010.
Harrison, J. R. "Paul and the Athletic Ideal in Antiquity: A Case Study in Wrestling with Word and Image." Pages 88–111 in *Paul's World* edited by S. E. Porter. Leiden: Brill, 2008.
— *Paul and the Ancient Celebrity Circuit: The Cross and Moral Transformation.* Tübingen: Mohr Siebeck, 2019.
— "The Inscriptions and Oracular Prophecy in the Eastern Mediterranean Basin: Assessing the Book of Revelation in Its Greco-Roman Revelatory Context." Pages 363–415 in *The First Urban Churches 5: Colossae, Hierapolis, and Laodikeia* edited by J. R. Harrison and L. L. Welborn. Atlanta, GA: SBL Press, 2019.
Harter-Uibopuu, K. "Epigraphische Quellen zum Archivwesen in den griechischer Poleis des ausgehenden Hellenismus und der Kaiserzeit." Pages 273–305 in *Archives and Archival Documents in Ancient Societies* edited by M. Faraguna. Triste: EUT, 2013.
Hartley, J. *Researches in Greece and the Levant.* London: Seeley, 1833.
Haspels, C. H. E. *The Highlands of Phrygia: Sites and Monuments.* Princeton: Princeton University Press, 2 vols, 1971.
Hasselquist, F. *Voyages and travels in the Levant: in the years 1749, 50, 51, 52. Containing observations in natural history etc, particularly on the Holy Land and the natural history of the Scriptures.* London: L. Davis and C. Reymers, 1766.
Hawkins, S. "Greek and the Languages of Asia Minor." Pages 213–27 in *A Companion to the Ancient Greek Language* edited by E. J. Bakker. Oxford: Blackwell, 2010.
Hay, D. M. *Colossians.* Nashville: Abingdon, 2000.
Head, B. V. M. *A Catalogue of the Greek Coins in the British Museum: Catalogue of the Greek Coins of Phrygia.* London: British Museum, 1906.
Head, P. M. "Named Letter Carriers among the Oxyrhynchus Papyri." *JSNT* 31 (2009): 279–99.
— "'Witnesses between You and Us': The Role of the Letter-Carriers in 1 *Clement*." Pages 477–93 in *Studies on the Text of the New Testament and early Christianity: essays in honour of Michael W. Holmes*, edited by D. Gurtner, J. Hernández and P. Foster. Leiden: Brill, 2015.
— "Onesimus the Letter-Carrier and the Initial Reception of Paul's Letter to Philemon." *JTS* 71 (2020): 628–56.
Heath, M. *Menander: A Rhetor in Context.* Oxford: Oxford University Press, 2004.
Héfélé, C.-J. *A History of the Councils of the Church* translated by W. R. Clark and H. N. Oxenham. Edinburgh: T & T Clark, 1876.
Heilen, S. and A. Mastrocinque. "A Third Horoscope-Gem, Twin of the Parisian 'Seyrig Gem.'" *MHNH* 17 (2017): 103–38.

Heininger, B. "Soziale und politische Metaphorik im Kolosserbrief." Pages 65–73 in *Kolosser-Studien* edited by P. Müller. Göttingen: Neukirchener, 2009.

Hellholm, D. "Die Gattung Haustafel im Kolosser- und Epheserbrief: Ihre Position innerhalb der Paränese-Abschnitte und ihr Hintergrund in der spätantiken Gesellschaft." Pages 102–28 in *Kolosser-Studien* edited by P. Müller. Göttingen: Neukirchener, 2009.

Hemer, C. J. *The Letters to the Seven Churches of Asia in their Local Setting.* Sheffield JSOT Press, 1986.

Hendren, T. G. "Meidias Tyrannos: Meidias' Tyrranical Attributes in Demosthenes 21." *ICS* 40 (2015): 21–43.

Hengel, M. *Crucifixion: In the ancient world and the folly of the cross.* Philadelphia: Fortress, 1977.

— *Between Jesus and Paul.* London: SCM, 1983.

Henig, M. *Religion in Roman Britain.* London: Routledge, 2003.

Héron de Villefosse, A. and E. Michon. "Erwerbungen des Louvre im Jahre 1899." *AA* 15 (1900): 155–59.

Herrmann, P. "Inschriften von Sardeis," *Chiron* 23 (1993): 233–66.

Herrmann, P. and K. Z. Ziya. *Das* Testament *des Epikrates und andere neue Inschriften aus dem.Museum von Manisa.* Vienna: Böhlau, 1969.

Hersh, C. "The Coinage of Quintus Labienus Parthicus." *SNR* 59 (1980): 41–51.

Heubeck, A. "Zu einigen kleinasiatischen Ortsnamen." *Glotta* 63 (1985): 115–36.

Heyne, C. G. *P. Virgilii Maronis Opera: Carmina minora,* Varietate Lectionis et Perpetua Adnotatione Illustrata Index A-E London: T. Payne *et al.*, 1793.

Hiller, E. *Theonis Smyrnaei Philosophi Platonici Expositio Rerum Mathematicarum ad Legendum Platonem Utilium.* Leipzig: Teubner, 1878.

Hirt, A. M. "Centurions, Quarries, and the Emperor." Pages 289–314 in *Ownership and Exploitation of Land and Natural Resources in the Roman World* edited by P. Erdkamp, K. Verboven and A. Zuiderhoek. Oxford: Oxford University Press, 2015.

Hitchman, R. "Carian Names and Crete." Pages 45–64 in *Onomatologos: Studies in Greek Personal Names presented to Elaine Matthews* edited by R. W. V. Catling and F. Marchand. Oxford: Oxbow, 2010.

Hoenig, C. *Plato's Timaeus and the Latin Tradition.* Cambridge: Cambridge University Press, 2018.

Hoffmann, S. F. W. *Griechenland und Die Griechen im Althethum.* Leipzig: Vol. 6, 1841.

Hoffner, H. A. *Laws of the Hittites: A Critical Edition.* Leiden: Brill, 1997.

Hogarth, D. *et al. Guide to Greece, the Archipelago, Constantinople, the Coasts of Asia Minor, Crete and Cyprus.* London: Macmillan, 1908.

Hollmann, A. "A Curse Tablet from Antioch against Babylas the Greengrocer." *ZPE* 177 (2011): 157–65.

Honigmann, E. *Le Synekdemos g'Hierocles et l'opuscule geographique de Georges de Chypre.* Brussels: L'institut de Philogie et d'Histoier Orientales et Slaves, 1939.

Honoré, A. M. "The 'Fragmentum Dositheanum'." *Revue Internationale des Droits de l'Antiquité* 12 (1965): 301–23.

Hopkins, K. *Death and Renewal.* Cambridge: Cambridge University Press, 1986.
Horne, T. H. *An Introduction to the Critical Study and Knowledge of the Holy Scriptures Volume 4.* The Strand: T. Cadell, 6th ed., 1828.
— *Landscape Illustrations of the Bible, consisting of views of the most remarkable places mentioned in the Old and New Testaments from original sketches taken on the spot.* London: John Murray, 2 vols 1836.
Hornum, M. B. *Nemesis, the Roman State and the Games.* Leiden: Brill, 1993.
Horsley, G. H. R. "Homer in Pisidia: Aspects of the History of Greek Education in a Remote Roman Province." *Antichthon* 34 (2000): 46–81.
— *The Greek and Latin Inscriptions in the Burdur Archaeological Museum.* London: British Academy, 2007.
Horsley, G. H. R. and R. Kearsley. "Another Boundary Stone between Tymbrianassos and Sagalassos in Pisidia." *ZPE* 121 (1998): 123–9.
Horsley, G. H. R. and J. M. Luxford. "Pagan angels in Roman Asia Minor: revisiting the epigraphic evidence." *AS* 66 (2016): 141–83.
Houghton, A., C. Lorber and O. Hoover. *Seleucid Coins, Part II.* New York: ANS, 2008.
Howgego, C. *Greek Imperial Countermarks: Studies in the Provincial Coinage of the Roman Empire.* London: Royal Numismatic Society, 1985.
— "Why did Ancient States Strike Coins?" *NC* 150 (1990): 1–25.
— "Coinage and Identity in the Roman Provinces." Pages 1–17 in *Coinage and Identity in the Roman Provinces* edited by C Howgego, V. Heuchert and A. Burnett. Oxford: Oxford University Press, 2005.
Huber, L. "Making Men in Rev 2–3: Reading the Seven Messages in the Bath-Gymnasiums of Asia Minor." Pages 101–28 in *Stones, Bones, and the Sacred: Essays on Material Culture and Ancient Religion in Honor of Dennis E. Smith* edited by A. H. Cadwallader. Atlanta, GA: SBL Press, 2016.
Huebner, S. R. "Household and Family in the Roman East and West." Pages 73–91 in *A Companion to Families in the Greek and Roman Worlds* edited by B. Rawson. Oxford: Blackwell, 2011.
Hübner, W. "*Manilius als Astrologe und Dichter.*" ANRW 2, 32, 1 (1984): 126–320.
Hull, M. F. *Baptism on account of the Dead (1 Cor 15:29): An Act of Faith in the Resurrection.* Leiden: Brill, 2005.
Hunt, P. *Slaves, Warfare, and Ideology in the Greek Historians.* Cambridge: Cambridge University Press, 1998.
Hurtado, L. *Earliest Christian Artifacts: Manuscripts and Christian Origins.* Grand Rapids, MN: Eerdmans, 2006.
Huttner, U. "Wolf und Eber: die Flüsse von Laodikeia in Phrygien." Pages 93–109 in *Internationales Kolloquium zur kaiserseitlichen Münzprägung Kleinasiens* edited by J. Nollé, B. Overbeck and P. Weiss. Nomismata 1; Milan: Ennerre, 1997.
— *Early Christianity in the Lycus Valley.* Leiden: Brill, 2013.
—"*Colossians, Hierapolitan Coins* — and the Young Bearers of Hope." Pages 73–9 in *The First Urban Churches 5: Colossae, Hierapolis, and Laodicea* edited by J. R. Harrison and L. L. Welborn. Atlanta, GA: SBL, 2019.

— "Latin Law in Greek Cities: Knowledge of Law and Latin in Imperial Asia Minor." Pages 137–56 in *Law in the Roman Provinces* edited by K. Czajkowski *et al.* Oxford: Oxford University Press, 2020.

— "The Development of Christianity in the Lycus Valley: socialization and violence." Forthcoming in *New Documents Illustrating the History of Early Christianity vol 12: The Lycus Valley* edited by J. R. Harrison *et al.* Grand Rapids, MN: Eerdmans, 2023.

Huttunen, N. I. "Powers, Baptism and the Ethics of the Stronger: Paul among the Ancient Political Philosophers." Pages 101–16 in *Paul and the Greco-Roman Philosophical Tradition* edited by J. R. Dodson and A. W. Pitts. London: T & T Clark, 2017.

Ilan, T. "The New Jewish Inscriptions from Hierapolis and the Question of Jewish Diaspora Cemeteries." *SCI* 25 (2006): 71–86.

Imhoof-Blumer, F. "Fluss- und Meergötter auf griechischen und römischen Münzen (Personifikationen der Gewässer)." *RN* 23 (1924): 173–421.

Immendörfer, M. *Ephesians and Artemis: The Cult of the Great Goddess of Ephesus as the Epistle's Context.* Tübingen: Mohr Siebeck, 2017.

Ip, A. H. H. *A Socio-Rhetorical Interpretation of the Letter to Philemon in Light of the New Institutional Economics.* Tübingen: Mohr Siebeck, 2017.

Irby, C. and J. Mangles. *Travels in Egypt and Nubia, Syria and Asia Minor during the years 1817 and 1818.* London: T. White, 1823.

Işık, C. and C. Marek. *Das Monument des Protogenes in Kaunos.* Bonn: Habelt, 1997.

Ismaelli, T. and M. Catania. "Il restauro del Ginnasio di Hierapolis." Pages 597–608 in *Hierapois di Frigia: Le Attività delle Campagne di Scavo e Restauro 2007–2011* edited by F. D'Andria, M. P. Caggia and T. Ismaelli. Istanbul: Ege, 2016.

Ismaelli T. and G. Scardozzi (eds.) *Ancient Quarries and Building Sites in Asia Minor: Research on Hierapolis in Phrygia and other cities in south-western Anatolia: archaeology, archaeometry, conservation.* Bari: Edipuglia, 2016.

Jeal, R. *Exploring Philemon: Freedom, Brotherhood, and Partnership in the New Society.* Atlanta, GA: SBL Press, 2015.

Jewett, R. *Romans.* Hermeneia; Minneapolis: Fortress, 2006.

Joannou, P. P. (ed.) *Discipline générale antique (IIe–IXe s.)*, I.2, *Les canons des synodes particuliers (IVe–IXe s.).* Rome–Grottaferrata: Tipografia Italo-Orientale "S. Nilo", 1962.

Johnson, G. J. "Christian Business and Christian Self-Identity in Third/Fourth Century Phrygia." *VigC.* 48 (1994): 341–66.

— *Early-Christian Epitaphs from Anatolia.* Atlanta, GA: Scholars Press, 1995.

Johnson, L. *Worship in the Early Church: An Anthology of Historical Sources.* Collegeville, MN: Liturgical Press, 4 vols, 2009.

Johnson, L. T. *Among the Gentiles: Greco-Roman Religion and Christianity.* New Haven: Yale University Press, 2009.

Johnson-DeBaufre, M. "'Gazing on the Invisible': Archaeology, Historiography, and the Elusive Wo/men of 1 Thessalonians." Pages 73–108 in *From Roman to Early Christian Thessalonikê* edited by L. Nasrallah, C. Bakirtzis and S. J. Friesen. Cambridge, MA: Harvard University Press, 2010.

Johnston, A. "Caracalla or Elagabalus? A Case of Unnecessarily Mistaken Identity." *ANS* 27 (1982): 97–147.

— "Hierapolis Revisited." *NC* 144 (1984): 52–80.

Johnston, D. *Roman Law in Context.* Cambridge: Cambridge University Press, 2004.

Jones, A. "Translating Greek Astronomy: Theon of Smyrna on the Apparent Motions of the Planets." Pages 465–505 in *Translating Writings of Early Scholars in the ANE, Egypt, Greece and Rome: Methodological Aspects with Examples* edited by A. Imhausen and T. Pommerening. Berlin/Boston: de Gruyter, 2016.

Jones, A. H. M. "The Inscriptions." Pages 43–5 in *Preliminary Report upon the Excavations carried out in the Hippodrome of Constantinople in 1927* edited by S. Casson. London: British Academy, 1928.

— "A Deed of Foundation from the Territory of Ephesos." *JRS* 73 (1983): 116–25.

Jones, C. P. "Two Inscriptions from Aphrodisias." *HSCP* 85 (1981): 107–29.

— "A Deed of Foundation from the Territory of Ephesos." *JRS* 73 (1983): 116–25.

— "The *sacrae litterae* of 204: two colonial copies." *Chiron* 14 (1984): 93–9.

— "A Follower of the God Glykon?" *EA* 30 (1998): 107–9.

— "Three New Letters of the Emperor Hadrian." *ZPE* 161 (2007): 147–56.

— "Ancestry and Identity in the Roman empire." Pages 111–24 in *Local Knowledges and Microidentities in the Imperial Greek World* edited by T. Whitmarsh. Cambridge: Cambridge University Press, 2010.

— "Imaginary Athletics in Two Followers of John Chrysostom." *HSCP* 106 (2011): 321–38.

Jones, J. W. *Law and Legal theory of the Greeks.* Oxford: Clarendon Press, 1956.

Jones, N. F. *Public Organization in ancient Greece: A Documentary Study.* Philadelphia: American Philosophical Society, 1987.

Jones, T. B. "A Numismatic Riddle: The So-Called Greek Imperials." *PAPS* 107 (1963): 308–47.

Jonge, C. C. de and J. M. van Ophuijsen. "Greek Philosophers on Language." Pages 485–98 in *A Companion to the Ancient Greek Language* edited by E. J. Bakker. Oxford: Blackwell, 2010.

Jordan, D. R. "A Survey of Greek Defixiones Not Included in the Special Corpora." *GRBS* 26 (1985): 151–97.

— "Three Curse Tablets." Pages 116–34 in *The World of Ancient Magic* edited by D. R. Jordan, H. Montgomery and E. Thomasse. Bergen: Norwegian Institute, 1999.

— "New Greek Curse Tablets (1985–2000)." *GBRS* 41 (2000): 5–46.

Joubert, S. "1 Corinthians 9:24–27: An Agonistic Competition?" *Neotestamentica* 35 (2001): 57–68.

Judge, E. "Latin Names around a Counter-Cultural Paul." Pages 68–84 in *The Bible and the Business of Life* edited by S. Holt and G. Preece. Adelaide: ATF, 2004.

Jürgens, K. "Pilgrimage and procession in the Panhellenic festivals: Some observations on the Hellenistic Leukophryena in Magnesia-on-the-Meander." Pages 87–105 in *Excavating Pilgrimage: Archaeological Approaches to Sacred Travel and Movement in the Ancient World* edited by T. M. Kristenden and W. Friese. London: Routledge, 2017.

Kagan, Y. O. and O. Y. Neverov. *Le Destin d'une Collection: 500 pierres gravées du Duc d'Orléans.* St Petersburg: Musée de l'Hermitage, 2001.

Kaibel, G. *Epigrammata Graeca ex lapidibus conlecta.* Berlin: Reimer, 1878.

— "Inschriften aus Pisidien." *Hermes* 23 (1888): 532–45.

Kajanto, I. *The Latin Cognomina.* Helsinki: Societas Scientiarum Fennica, 1965.

Kaldellis, A. and D. Krallis. *The History: Michael Attaleiates.* Cambridge, MA: Harvard University Press, 2012.

Kalliontzis, Y. "La Date de la première celebration des Amphiareia Romaia d'Oropos." *REG* 129 (2016): 85–105.

Kamen, D. "Manumission, Social Rebirth and Healing Gods in Ancient Greece." Pages 174–94 in *Slaves and Religions in Graeco-Roman Antiquity and Modern Brazil* edited by S. Hodkinson and D. Geary. Newcastle-upon-Tyne: Cambridge Scholars Publishing, 2012.

Kampmann, U. *Die Homonoia-Verbindungen der Stadt Pergamon, oder, Der Versuch einer kleinasiatischen Stadt unter römischer Herrschaft eigenständige Politik zu betreiben.* Saarbrücken: Saarbrücker Druckerei, 1996.

— "*Homonoia* Politics in Asia Minor: The Example of Pergamon." Pages 373–93 in *Pergamon: Citadel of the Gods: Archaeological Record, Literary Description, and Religious Development* edited by H. Koester. Harrisburg, PA: Trinity Press International, 1998.

Kantor, G. "Knowledge of Law in Roman Asia Minor." Pages 249–65 in *Selbstdarstellung und Kommunikation die Veröffentlichung staatlicher Urkunden auf Stein und Bronze in der römischen Welt* edited by R. Haensch. Munich: C. H. Beck, 2009.

— "Law in Roman Phrygia: rules and jurisdictions." Pages 143–67 in *Roman Phrygia: Culture and Society* edited by P. Thonemann. Cambridge: Cambridge University Press, 2013.

— "Greek Law under the Romans." in *The Oxford Handbook of Ancient Greek Law,* ed. E. M. Harris and M. Canevaro (Oxford: Oxford University Press, 2015. online.

Kanz, F. and K. Grossschmidt. "Head injuries of Roman gladiators." *Forensic Science International* 160 (2006): 207–16.

Katakis, S. E. "ΦΙΛΗΜΑΤΙΟΝ ΤΕΡΕΝΤΙΑ ΧΡΗΣΤΗ ΧΑΙΡΕ: Darstellungen der Isis und mit ihrem Kult verbundener Personen auf Euböa." *MDAI(A)*s 112 (1997): 317–34.

Katsari, C. "Opramoas and the importation of bronze coins into Roman Lycia." *EA* 35 (2003): 141–5.

— *The Roman Monetary System: The Eastern Provinces from the First to the Third Century AD.* Cambridge: Cambridge University Press, 2011.

Kazen, T. *Jesus and Purity Halakhah: Was Jesus Indifferent to Impurity?* Winona Lake, IN: Eisenbrauns, 2010.

Kearsley, R. A. *Greeks and Romans in Imperial Asia.* Bonn: Habelt, 2001.

Kehoe, D. "Legal Institutions and Agrarian Change in the Roman Empire." Pages 139–53 in *Documentary Sources in Ancient Near Eastern and Greco-Roman Economic History* edited by H. D. Baker and M. Jursa. Oxford: Oxbow, 2014.

Kemezis, A. M. "Greek Ethnicity and the Second Sophistic." Pages 390–404 in *A Companion to Ethnicity in the Ancient Mediterranean* edited by J. McInerney. Malden, MA: Wiley, 2014.

Kenyon, F. *The Chester Beatty Biblical Papyri: Descriptions and Texts of Twelve Manuscripts on Papyrus of the Greek Bible Fasciculus III, Part 2.* London: Emery Walker, 1937.

Keppie, L. *Understanding Roman Inscriptions.* London: Routledge, 1991.

Kerschbaum, S. "Die Apollines von Hierapolis in Phrygien." *JNG* 64 (2014): 15–42.

Kienast, D. "Die Homonoiaverträge in der römischen Kaiserzeit." *JNG* 14 (1964): 51–64.

Kiley, M. *Colossians as Pseudepigraphy.* Sheffield: JSOT Press, 1986.

Kim, K. S. "The Meaning of χειρόγραφον in Colossians 2:14 revisited." *TynBull.* 68 (2017): 223–39.

— *The Firstborn Son in Ancient Judaism and Early Christianity.* Leiden: Brill, 2019.

Kirbihler, F. "Les émissions de monnaies d'homonoia et les crises alimentaires en asie sous marc-aurèle." *REA* 108 (2006): 613–40.

Kleijwegt, M. *Ancient Youth: the ambiguity of youth and the absence of adolescence in Greco-Roman society.* Amsterdam: J. C. Gieben, 1991.

— "Beans, Baths and the Barber … A Sacred Law from Thurburbo Maius." *Antiquités africaines* 30 (1994): 209–20.

Klingennerg, G. *Corpus der Römischen Rechtsquellen zur antiquen Sklaverei X.6 Servus fugitivus.* Stuttgart: Franz Steiner, 2005.

Kloppenborg, J. S. *The Tenants in the Vineyard: Ideology, Economics, and Agrarian Conflict in Jewish Palestine.* Tübingen: Mohr Siebeck, 2006.

— *Christ's Associations: Connecting and Belonging in the Ancient City.* New Haven, CN: Yale University Press, 2019.

Kloppenborg, J. S. and R. S. Ascough. *Greco-Roman Associations: Texts, Translations and Commentary, I. Attica, Central Greece, Macedonia, Thrace.* Berlin: de Gruyter, 2011.

Knibbe, D. and R. Merkelbach. "Allerhöchste Schelte (Zwei Exemplare der Sacrae Litterae aus Ephesos)." *ZPE* 31 (1978): 229–32.

Knox, P. E. "Pyramus and Thisbe in Cyprus." *HSCP* 92 (1989): 315–28.

Koenen, L. "Sale of an Egyptian Woman enslaved in an Insurrection." Pages 915–6 in *Papyri in Memory of P. J. Sijpesteijn (P. Sipj.)* edited by A. J. B. Sirks and K. A. Worp. Oakville, CT: American Society of Papyrologists, 2007.

Koester, H. "Epilogue: Current Issues in New Testament Scholarship." Pages 467–76 in *The Future of Early Christianity: Essays in Honor of Helmut Koester* edited by B. A. Pearson. Minneapolis: Fortress Press, 1991.

Koestermann, E. *Cornelius Tacitus I: Annales.* Leipzig, Teubner, 1960.

Kokkinia, C. *Die Opramoas-Inschrift von Rhodiapolis. Euergetismus und soziale Elite in Lykien.* Bonn: Habelt, 2000.

— "The Inscriptions of Boubon: A Catalogue." Pages 27–126 in *Boubon: The Inscriptions and Archaeological Remains: A Survey 2004–2006.* Athens: de Boccard, 2008.

Kokkinia, C. (ed.) *Boubon: The Inscription and Archaeological Remains, A Survey 2004–2006.* Athens: de Boccard, 2008.

Kolb, F. "Zur Geschichte der Stadt Hierapolis in Phrygien: Die Phyleninschriften im Theater." *ZPE* 15 (1975): 255–70.

Kolb, F. (ed.) *Chora und Polis.* München: Oldenbourg, 2004.

Kominis, A. and G. Schirò. *Analecta hymnica graeca e codicibus eruta Italiae inferioris, 3. Canones Novembris.* Rome: Istituto di Studi Bizantini e Neoellenici, Università di Roma, 1972.

Konakçi, E. "Prehistorik Tripolis: Akkaya (Yenice) ve Hamambükü Höyük." Pages 23–46 in *Tripolis Araştırmaları* edited by B. Duman. Istanbul: Ege, 2017.

Konakçi, E. and B. Duman. "Arkeolojik ve Yasılı Kanıtlar Işığında Kolossai (Kolossai in the Light of Archaeological and Historical Evidence)." Pages 57–67 in *Uluslararası Denizli ve Çevresi Tarih ve Kültür Semposyumu Bildiriler* (*International Symposium on the History and Culture of Denizli and its Surroundings*) edited by A. Özçelik *et al.* Denizli: Pamukkale University, 2 vols, 2007.

König, J. *Athletics and Literature in the Roman Empire.* Cambridge: Cambridge University Press, 2005.

Korner, R. *The Origin and Meaning of Ekklêsia in the Early Jesus Movement.* Leiden Brill, 2017.

Köse, B. *Nekropolen und Grabdenkmäler von Sagalassos in Pisidien in hellenistischer und römischer Zeit.* Turnhout: Brepols, 2005.

Kotansky, R. *Greek Magical Amulets.* Opladen: Westdeutscher Verlag, 1994.

Kotrosits, M. *The Lives of Objects: Material Culture, Experience and the Real in the History of Early Christianity.* Chicago: University of Chicago Press, 2020.

Kourouniotis, K. "Τὸ ἔργον τῆς ἑλληνικῆς Ἀρχαιολογικῆς Ὑπηρεσίας ἐν Μικρᾷ Ἀσίᾳ." ΑΔ 7 (1921–22): Παράρτημα, 1–6.

Kovacs, F. L. *Ancient Bronze Coins of Asia Minor and the Levant from the Lindgren Collection* [vol. 1]. San Francisco: Chrysopylon Publications, 1985.

Kozlovskaya, V. and S. M. Ilyashenko. "Tamgas and tamga-like signs from Tanais." Pages 167–98 in *Zeichentragende Artefakte im sakralen Raum: Zwischen Präsenz und UnSichtbarkeit* edited by W. E. Keil, S. Kiyanrad, C. Theis and L Willer. Berlin: de Gruyter, 2018.

Kraemer, R. S. (ed.) *Women's Religions in the Greco-Roman World: A Sourcebook.* Oxford: Oxford University Press, 2004.

Kraemer, R. S. "Apphia." Page 53 in *Women in Scripture: A Dictionary of Named and Unnamed Women in the Hebrew Bible, the Apocryphal/Deuterocanonical Books, and the New Testament* edited by C. Meyers, *et al.* Grand Rapids: Eerdmans, 2003.

Krentz, P. and E. L. Wheeler (eds). *Polyaenus Stratagems of War.* Chicago, IL: Ares, 2 vols, 1994.

Kristensen, T. M. "Earthquakes and Late Antique Urbanism: Some Observations on the Case of the Lycus Valley." Pages 71–8 in *The Lycus Valley and Neighbourhood in Late Antiquity* edited by C. Şimşek and T. Kaçar. Istanbul: Ege, 2018.

Kroll, J. H. *Athenian Bronze Allotment Plates.* Cambridge, MA: Harvard University Press, 1972.

— "Hemiobols to Assaria: the Bronze Coinage of Roman Aigion." *NC* 156 (1996): 49–78.

Kubínska, J. *Les monuments funéraires dans les inscriptions Grecques de l'Asie Mineure.* Warsaw: PWN, 1968.

Kurek-Chomycz, D. and R. Beringer. "The Corinthian ΚΑΙΝΑΙ ΚΤΙΣΕΙΣ? Second Corinthians 5:17 and the Roman Refoundation of Corinth." Pages 195–220 in *Stones, Bones and the Sacred: Essays on Material Culture and Ancient Religion in Honor of Dennis E. Smith* edited by A. H. Cadwallader. Atlanta, GA: SBL, 2016.

Kurtz, D. C. *The Reception of Classical Art in Britain: An Oxford Story of Plaster Casts from the Antique.* Oxford: Archaeopress, 2000.

Labarre, G. and M.-Th. Le Dinahet. “Les Metiers du textile en Asie Mineure: de l’époque hellénistique à l’époque imperial.” Pages 2.49–116 in *Aspects de l’artisanat du textile dans le monde méditerranéen (Égypte, Grèce, monde romain)*. Lyon: Université Lumière, 2 vols, 1996.

Laborde, A. *Extrait d’un rapport fait à l’Académie royale des Inscriptions et Belles-Lettres* Paris: L’Institut Royal de France, 1828.

— *Voyage de l’Asie Mineure*. Paris: Firmin Didot, 1838.

Labuff, J. *Polis Expansion and Elite Power in Hellenistic Karia*. Lanham, MD: Lexington, 2016.

Laes, C. and J. M. H. Strubbe. *Youth in the Roman Empire: The Young and the Restless Years*. Cambridge: Cambridge University Press, 2014.

Laforest, C., D. Castex, and F. Blaizot. “Tomb 163d in the North Necropolis of Hierapolis in Phrygia: An insight into the funerary gestures and practices of the Jewish diaspora in Asia Minor in late Antiquity and the proto-Byzantine period.” Pages 69–84 in *Life and Death in Asia Minor in Hellenistic, Roman and Byzantine Times: Studies in Archaeology and Bioarchaeology* edited by J. R. Brandt *et al.* Oxford: Oxbow, 2017.

Lambert, S. *Inscribed Athenian Laws and Decrees in the Age of Demosthenes: Historical Essays*. Leiden: Brill, 2018.

Lamberz, E. *Acta conciliorum oecumenicorum, Series secunda, volumen tertium: Concilium universale Nicaenum secundum, Pars 1–3*. Berlin/Boston: de Gruyter, 2008–2016.

Lampakis, G. *Οί ἑπτὰ ἀστέρες τῆς Ἀποκαλύψεως*. Athens: 1909/Thessalonike, 1995.

Lampros, S. P. *Μιχαὴλ Ἀκομινάτου τοῦ χωνιάτου τὰ σωζόμενα*. Athens: 1879–1880; Groningen: Bouma’s Boekhuis, 1968.

Lane, C. S. “Archegetes, Oikistes, and New-oikistes: the Cults of Founders in Greek Southern Italy and Sicily.” Ph.D thesis, University of British Columbia, 2009.

Langdon, M. K. *A Sanctuary of Zeus on Mount Hermettos*. Princeton, NJ: American School of Classical Studies at Athens, 1976.

Langslow, D. “Typologies of translation techniques in Greek and Latin: Latin *elticis*: *catelticis* = Greek ἑλκτική: καθεκτική.” Pages 141–71 in *Multilingualism in the Graeco-Roman Worlds* edited by A. Mullen and P. James. Cambridge: Cambridge University Press, 2012.

Lapatin, K. “Grylloi.” Pages 88–98 in *Gems of Heaven: Recent Research on Engraved Gemstones in Late Antiquity, c. AD 200–600* edited by C. Entwistle and N. Adams. London: British Museum, 2011.

Latte, K. *Hesychii Alexandrini lexicon*. Copenhagen: Munksgaard, 2 vols, 1953, 1966.

Latyšev, B. B. *Menologii anonymi byzantine saeculi X quae super sunt*. Petropolis: 1911.

Lauffer, S. *Diokletians Preisedikt*. Berlin: de Gruyter, 1971.

Lauxtermann, M. D. *The Spring of Rhythm: An Essay on the Political Verse and other Byzantine metres*. Vienna: Austrian Academy of Sciences, 1999.

Lavigne, D. E. “The Authority of Archaic Greek Epigram.” Pages 169–86 in *The Materiality of Text — Placement, Perception, and Presence of Inscribed Texts in Classical Antiquity* edited by A. Petrovic, I. Petrovic and E. Thomas. Leiden: Brill, 2019.

Lawlor, R. and D. *Mathematics useful for Understanding Plato by Theon of Smyrna*. San Diego: Wizards Bookshelf, 1979.

Le Bas, P. *Explication des Inscriptions Grecques et Latines recueillies en Grèce et en Asie Mineure.* Paris: Firmin Didot, 1873.

Le Blant, E. *750 Inscriptions de pierres gravées in édites ou peu connues.* Paris: C. Klincksieck, 1896.

Le Camus, É. *Voyage aux Sept Églises de l'Apocalypse.* Paris: Librairies Sanard et Derangeon, 1896.

Leach, N. "Epaphroditus and Archippus. Paul's Fellow Soldiers: Reexamining Paul's Rhetorical Use of συστρατιώτης." *JBL* 140 (2021): 187–206.

Leake, W. M. *Journal of a Tour in Asia Minor with Comparative Remarks on the Ancient and Modern Geography of that Country Accompanied by a Map.* London: 1824.

Legrand, P.-E. and J. Chamonard. "Inscriptions de Phrygia." *BCH* 17 (1893): 241–93.

Lehoux, D. *What did the Romans Know? An Inquiry into Science and Worldmaking.* Chicago: University of Chicago Press, 2012.

Lentz, A. *Grammatici Graeci.* Leipzig: Teubner, vol 3.2, 1870.

Leppä, O. *The Making of Colossians: A Study on the Formation and Purpose of a Deutero-Pauline Letter.* Göttingen: Vandenhoeck & Ruprecht, 2003.

Leroux, M. R. "Repetition, Progression, and Persuasion in Scripture." *Neotestamentica* 29 (1995): 1–25.

Leschhorn, W. *Antike Ären. Zeitrechnung, Politik, und Geschichte im Schwarzmeerraum und in Kleinasien nördlich des Tauros* Stuttgart: Steiner, 1993.

Leschhorn, W. and P. R. Franke. *Lexikon der Aufschriften auf griechischen Münzen Band I.* Vienna, OAW, 2009.

Levick, B. "In the Phrygian mode: a region seen from without." Pages 41–54 in *Roman Phrygia: Culture and Society* edited by P. Thonemann. Cambridge: Cambridge University Press, 2013.

Lewis, N. "Exemption of Physicians from Liturgy." *BASP* 2 (1965): 87–92.

— *Life in Egypt under Roman Rule.* Oxford: Clarendon Press, 1983.

— "The Demise of the Demotic Document: When and Why." *JEA* 79 (1993): 276–81.

Lewis, N. and R. Meyer. *Roman Civilisation: The Empire (Selected Readings).* New York: Columbia University Press, 2 vols, 1990.

Lewy, H. "A Latin Hymn to the Creator ascribed to Plato." *HTR* 39 (1946): 243–58.

LiDonnici, L. R. *The Epidaurian Miracle Inscriptions: Text, Translation and Commentary.* Atlanta, GA: Scholars, 1995.

Lightfoot, C. S. *Amorium Reports 5: A Catalogue of Roman and Byzantine Stone Inscriptions from Amorium and its Territory, together with Graffiti, Stamps and Miscellanea.* Istanbul: Ege, 2017.

Lightfoot, J. B. *Colossians and Philemon.* London: Macmillan, 9th ed., 1890.

Ligorio, O. and A. Lubotsky. "Languages of Fragmentary Attestation: Phrygian." Pages 1816–31 in *Handbook of Comparative and Historical Indo-European Linguistics* edited by J. Klein, B. Joseph and M. Fritz. HSK 41.3; Boston: de Gruyter Mouton, 2017.

Lincicum, D. "Mirror-Reading a Pseudepigraphal Letter." *NovT* 59 (2017): 171–93.

Lincoln, A. T. *Ephesians.* Waco, TX: Word, 1990.

— "The Household Code and Wisdom mode of Colossians." *JSNT* 74 (1999): 93–112.

Lincoln, A. T. and A. J. M. Wedderburn. *The Theology of the Later Pauline Letters.* Cambridge: Cambridge University Press, 1993.

Lindemann, A. "Die Gemeinde von 'Kolossä': Erwägungen zum 'Sitz im Leben' eines pseudopaulinischen Briefes." *WuD* 16 (1981): 111–34.
— *Der Kolosserbrief.* Zurich: Theologischer Verlag, 1983.
Lindgren, H. C. and F. L. Kovacs. *Ancient Bronze Coins of Asia Minor and the Levant from the Lindgren Collection* [vol. 1]. San Francisco: Chrysopylon Publications, 1985.
Lintott, A. *Imperium Romanum: Politics and Administration.* London: Routledge, 1993.
Lisdonk, M. L. van Poll-van de. *VI–9 Ordinis sexti tomus nonus: Annotationes in novum testamentum (pars quinta).* Leiden: Brill, 2009.
Livingstone, J. N. "Urbanization in the Roman East and the Inter-Religious Struggle for Success." Pages 211–41 in *Religious Rivalries and the Struggle for Success in Sardis and Smyrna* edited by R. S. Ascough (Waterloo, Ont: Wilfred Laurier University Press, 2005.
Llewellyn, S. "P. Harris I 62 and the Pursuit of Fugitives." *ZPE* 118 (1997): 245–50.
Lloyd-Jones, H. and P. Parsons. *Supplementum Hellenisticum.* Berlin: de Gruyter, 1983.
Lobur, J. A. *Consensus and Concordia and the Formation of Roman Imperial Ideology.* London/NY: Routledge, 2008.
Löhr, H. "The Early Christian Household Code in the Light of Epigraphic Evidence." Pages 199–214 in *Epigraphical Evidence Illustrating Paul's Letter to the Colossians* edited by J. Verheyden, M Öhler and T. Corsten. Tübingen: Mohr Siebeck, 2018.
Lohse, E. *Colossians and Philemon.* Philadelphia: Fortress, 1971.
Lombardi, P. and C. Vismara. "Deux inscriptions d'Aléria (Haure-Corse)." *Gallia* 62 (2005): 279–92.
Longe, M. "Greek hymns from performance to stone." Pages 217–34 in *Sacred Words: Orality, Literacy and Religion* edited by A. Lardinois, J. Blok and M. G. M. van der Poel (Leiden: Brill, 2011), 219–20.
Lopez, D. C. "Before Your Very Eyes: Roman Imperial Ideology, Gender Constructs and Paul's Inter-Nationalism." Pages 115–62 in *Mapping Gender in Ancient Religious Discourses* edited by T. Penner and C. Vander Stichele. Leiden: Brill, 2007.
Lorber, C. C. and P. Iossif. "The Cult of Helios in the Seleucid East." *Topoi* 16.1 (2009): 19–42.
Luck, G. *Arcana Mundi: Magic and the Occult in the Greek and Roman Worlds.* Baltimore: Johns Hopkins University Press, 1985.
Lucke, B., M. Schmidt, Z. Al-Saad and R. Bäumler. "Water Systems of the Decapolis (Northern Jordan) and their Relation to the Landscape During the Hellenistic and Roman Periods." Pages 223–34 in *L'Eau comme patrimoine: De la Méditerranée à l'Amérique du Nord* edited by E. Hermon. Quebec: PUL, 2008.
Lührmann, D. "Neutestamentliche Haustafeln und antike Ökonomie." *NTS* 27 (1980): 83–97.
Luijendijk, A.-M. "Books and Private Readers in Early Christian Oxyrhynchus: 'A Spiritual Meadow and a Garden of Delight.'" Pages 101–35 in *Books and Readers in the Premodern World: Essays in Honor of Harry Gamble.* Atlanta GA: SBL Press, 2018.
Luke, J. *Sermon Preached before the Right Worshipfull Company of the Levant Merchants at St Olav's Hart-Street, Thursday Dec 15, 1664.* London: R. Daniell, 1698.
Lupu, E. *Greek Sacred Law: A Collection of New Documents.* Leiden: Brill, 2nd ed. 2009.

Ma, J. "Oversexed, Overpaid and Over Here': A Response to Angelos Chaniotis." Pages 115–22 in *Army and Power in the Ancient World* edited by A. Chaniotis and P. Ducrey. Stuttgart: Franz Steiner, 2002.

MacDonald, D. J. "The *Homonoia* of Colossae and Aphrodisias." *JNG* 33 (1983): 25–27.

— *The Coinage of Aphrodisias.* London: Royal Numismatic Society, 1992.

MacDonald, M. Y. "Can Nympha Rule This House? The Role of Domesticity in Colossians." Pages 99–120 in *Rhetoric and Reality in Early Christianities* edited by W. Braun. Waterloo, ON: Wilfred Laurier University Press, 2005.

— "Slavery, Sexuality and House Churches: a Reassessment of Colossians 3.18–4.1 in Light of New Research on the Roman Family." *NTS* 53 (2007): 94–113.

— *Colossians, Ephesians.* Collegeville, MI: Liturgical Press, 2008.

MacKinnon, M. "High on the Hog: Linking Zooarchaeological, literary and Artistic Data for Pig Breeds in Roman Italy." *AJA* 105 (2001): 649–73.

MacMillan & Co. *Guide to Greece, the Archipelago, Constantinople, the Coasts of Asia Minor, Crete and Cyprus.* London: Macmillan, 1908.

McCartney, E. S. "Canting Puns on Ancient Monuments." *AJA* 23.1 (1919): 59–64.

McDowell, D. *Demosthenes the Orator.* Oxford: Oxford University Press, 2009.

McDowell, R. H. *Stamped and inscribed objects from Seleucia on the Tigris.* Ann Arbor: University of Michigan Press, 1935.

McKechnie, P. *Christianizing Asia Minor: Conversion, Communities and Social Change in the Pre-Constantinian Era.* Cambridge: Cambridge University Press, 2019.

McKnight, S. *The Letter to the Colossians.* Grand Rapids, MN: Eerdmans, 2018.

Maas, M. and J. McI. Snyder, *Stringed Instruments of Ancient Greece.* New Haven: Yale University Press, 1989.

Maaskant-Kleibrink, M. "Cachets de terre de Doliché (?)." *BABesch* 46 (1971): 23–63.

Magdalino, P. *The Empire of Manuel I Komnenos, 1143–1180.* Cambridge: Cambridge University Press, 2002.

Magie, D. *Roman Rule in Asia Minor.* Princeton: Princeton University Press, 2 vols, 1950.

Magnelli, E. "Notes on Four Greek Verse Inscriptions." *ZPE* 160 (2007): 38–40.

Magoulias, H. J. *O City of Byzantium, Annals of Niketas Choniates.* Detroit: Wayne State University Press, 1984.

Maier, H. O. "A Sly Civility: Colossians and Empire." *JSNT* 27 (2005): 323–49.

— "Reading Colossians in the Ruins: Roman Imperial Iconography, Moral Transformation, and the Construction of Christian Identity in the Lycus Valley." Pages 212–31 in *Colossae in Space and Time: Linking to an Ancient City* edited by A. H. Cadwallader and M. Trainor. Göttingen: Vandenhoeck & Ruprecht, 2011.

Malay, H. "New Inscriptions from Phrygia (in the Denizli Museum)." *Arkeoloji Dergisi* 2 (1994): 173–83.

Malay, H. and R. Schmitt. "An Inscription recording a new Persian name: Mithrabôgês or Mithrabôgos." *EA* 5 (1985): 27–9.

Malay, H. and M. Ricl. "A New Imprecation against Desecrators of the Grave from Northwest Lydia." *AD* 9 (2007): 117–121.

Malay, H. and G. Petzl. *New Religious Texts from Lydia.* Vienna: ÖAW, 2017.

Malay, H., M. Ricl and D. Amendola. "The City of Tralleis combats Immorality: Measures taken against οἱ ἐν κιναιδείᾳ βιοῦντες in a new civic decree." *EA* 51 (2018): 91–7.

Malherbe, A. J. *The Letters to the Thessalonians.* New York: Doubleday, 2000.

Manco, P. *et al.* "Phenotypic Features of the Domestic Pigs Bred in the Roman Settlements of Pompeii and Caralis." *Italian Journal of Anatomical Embyrology* 109 (2004): 105–14.

Mann, C. *"Um keinen Kranz, um das Leben kämpfen wir!" Gladiatoren im Osten des römischen Reiches und die Frage der Romanisierung.* Berlin: Antike, 2011.

Manning, J. G. "Coinage as 'Code' in Ptolemaic Egypt." Pages 84–112 in *The Monetary Systems of the Greeks and Romans* edited by W. V. Harris. Oxford: Oxford University Press, 2008.

Marchand, F. "The Philippeis of IG VII 2433." Pages 332–43 in *Onomatologos: Studies in Greek Personal Names presented to Elaine Matthews* edited by R. W. V. Catling and F. Marchand. Oxford: Oxbow, 2010.

Marchant, E. C. *Xenophontis opera Omnia.* Oxford: Clarendon Press, 1961 [1904].

Marek, C. *In the Land of a Thousand Gods: A History of Asia Minor in the Ancient World.* Princeton, NJ: Princeton University Press, 2016.

Markoe, G. "Petra: Lost City of Stone." *Minerva* 15 (2004): 8–12.

Mariette, P.-J. *Description sommaire des pierres gravées du cabinet de feu M. Crozat.* Paris: Mariette, 1741.

Marsden, A. "Overtones of Olympus: Roman Imperial Portrait Gems, Medallions and Coins in the 3rd Century." Pages 163–78 in *Gems of Heaven: Recent Research on Engraved Gemstones in Late Antiquity, c. AD 200–600* edited by C. Entwistle and N. Adams London: British Museum Press, 2011.

Martin, C. J. "The Rhetorical Function of Commercial Language in Paul's Letter to Philemon (Verse 18)." Pages 321–77 in *Persuasive Artistry: Studies in New Testament Rhetoric in Honor of George A. Kennedy* edited by D. F. Watson. Sheffield: Sheffield Academic Press, 1991.

Martin, D. B. "The Construction of the Ancient Family: Methodological Considerations." *JRS* 86 (1996): 40–60.

— "Hellenistic Superstition: The Problems of Defining a Vice." Pages 136–61 in *Conventional Values of the Hellenistic Greeks* edited by P. Bilde *et al.* Aarhus: Aarhus University Press, 1997.

Martin, D. *By Philosophy and Empty Deceit: Colossians as a Response to a Cynic Critique.* Sheffield: Sheffield Academic Press, 1996.

Martin, K. *Demos • Boule • Gerousia: Personifiktaionen städtische Institutionen auf kaiserzeitlichen Münzen aus Kleinasien.* Bonn: Habelt, 2 vols, 2013.

Martin, R. and C. Toney. *New Testament Foundations: An Introduction for Students.* Eugene, OR: Cascade, 2018.

Martin, T. W. *By Philosophy and Empty Deceit: Colossians as a Response to a Cynic Critique.* Sheffield: Sheffield Academic Press, 1996.

Martino, E. M. de. "I vincitori dei *Sebastà* nell'anno 86 d.C." Pages 267–86 in *Munus Laetitiae: Studi miscellanei offerti a Maria Letizia Lazzarini* edited by F. Camia *et al.* Rome: Sapienza University Press, 2018.

Martzavou, P. "Les cultes isiaques et les Italiens entre Délos, Thessalonique et l'Eubée." *Pallas* 84 (2010): 181–205.

Masino, F. and G. Sobrà. "A monumental altar from the Hadrianic age at Hierapolis in Phrygia." Pages 169–81 in *Roma y las provincias: modelo y difusión* edited by I. Rodà. Rome: L'Erma, 2011.

Mason, H. J. *Greek Terms for Roman Institutions: a Lexicon and Analysis*. Toronto: Hakkert, 1974.

Masson, O. *Onomastica graeca selecta*. Geneva: Droz, 3 vols, 1990–2000.

Mastrocinque, A. *Les intailles magiques du département des Monnaies, Médailles et Antiques*. Paris: BnF, 2014.

Matar, N. "Britons and Muslims in the early modern period: from prejudice to (a theory of) toleration." Pages 7–26 in *Anti-Muslim Prejudice in the West, Past and Present: an introduction* edited by M. Malik. Oxford: Routledge, 2010.

Matera, F. J. *Romans*. Grand Rapids, MN: Baker, 2010.

Matessi, A. "The Making of Hittite Imperial Landscapes: Territoriality and Balance of Power in South-Central Anatolia during the Late Bronze Age." *JANEH* 3.2 (2016): 117–62.

Mathiesen, T. J. *Apollo's Lyre: Greek Music and Music Theory in Antiquity and the Middle Ages*. Lincoln/London: University of Nebraska Press, 1999.

Mayhoff, K. F. T. *Naturalis Historia*. Leipzig: Teubner, 4 vols, 1897–1909.

Meadows, A. "The Spread of Coins in the Hellenistic World." Pages 169–94 in *Explaining Monetary and Financial Innovation: A Historical Analysis* edited by P. Bernholz and R. Vaubel. Cham: Springer, 2014.

Medley, M. "Subversive song: Imagining Colossians 1:15–20 as a social protest hymn in the context of the Roman empire." *R&E* 116 (2019): 421–35.

Meineke, A. *Stephani Byzantii ethnicorum quae supersunt*. Berlin: Reimer, 1849.

— *Strabonis geographica*. Leipzig: Teubner, 3 vols, 1877.

Melber, M. and E. Woelfflin, *Polyaeni strategematon libri viii*. Leipzig: Teubner, 1887.

Meletios of Ioannina, *Γεωγραφία παλαιὰ καὶ νέα* [*Ancient and New Geography*]. Venice: 1728; new edition in 4 vols, 1807.

Mellaart, J. "Preliminary Report on Pre-Classical Remains in Southern Turkey." *AS* 4 (1954): 175–240.

Mellink, M. "Anatolia." Pages 211–33 in *The Cambridge Ancient History: IV, Persia, Greece and the Western Mediterranean c. 525–479 B.C.* edited by J. Boardman, *et al.* Cambridge: Cambridge University Press, 1988.

Mendel, G. *Catalogue des sculptures grecques, romaines et byzantines*. Constantinople: En vent au, 1912–14.

Merkelbach, R. "Agonistisches Epigramm aus Trapezopolis." *ZPE* 19 (1975): 301–2.

Merkelbach, R. and J. Stauber. "Die Orakel des Apollon von Klaros." *EA* 27 (1996): 1–54.

— *Steinepigramme aus dem griechischen Osten* I–V. Stuttgart: Teubner/Munich: Saur, 1998–2004.

Meritt, B. D. "Greek Inscriptions." *Hesperia* 29 (1960): 77–160.

Mészáros, T. "Two Critical Notes on the Ancient Biographical Tradition of Thucydides." Pages 55–68 in *Investigatio Fontium. Griechische und lateinische Quellen mit Erläuterungen* edited by H. László. Budapest: Eötvös-József, 2014.

Metcalfe, W. E. *The Cistophori of Hadrian*. New York: American Numismatic Society, 1980.

Metzger, B. M. *A Textual Commentary on the Greek New Testament* Stuttgart: UBS, 1st ed., 1971.
Meyboom, P. G. P. *The Nile Mosaic of Palestrina.* Leiden: Brill, 1995.
Meyers, M. W. (ed.) *The Ancient Mysteries: A Sourcebook.* New York: HarperCollins, 1987.
Miano, D. *Fortuna: Deity and Concept in Archaic and Republican Italy.* Oxford: Oxford University Press, 2018.
Michel, S. *Die magischen Gemmen im Britischen Museum.* London: British Museum Press, 2 vols, 2001.
Michels, C."Unlike any Other: The Attalid Kingdom after Apameia." Pages 333–52 in *Rome and the Seleukid East* edited by A. Coşkun and D. Engels. Brussels: Latomus, 2019.
Mielke, D. "Key Sites of the Hittite Empire." Pages 1031–54 in *The Oxford Handbook of Ancient Anatolia* edited by G. McMahon and S. Steadman. Oxford: Oxford University Press, 2011.
— "Hittite Cities: Looking for a Concept." Pages 153–94 in *Insights into Hittite History and Archaeology* edited by H. Genz and D. P. Mielke. Leuven: Peeters, 2011.
— "Hittite Settlement Policy." Pages 13–27 in *Places and Spaces in Hittite Anatolia I: Hatti and the East* edited by M. Alparslan. Istanbul: Türk Eskiçağ Bilimleri Enstitüsü, 2017.
Migeotte, L. "La ΔΙΑΤΑΞΙΣ de Délos Durant l'indépendance: un budget pour la cite?" *LEC* 73 (2005): 27–38.
Miles, M. M. *The City Eleusinion.* Princeton, NJ: American School of Classical Studies at Athens, 1998.
Millar, F. "The Fiscus in the First Two Centuries." *JRS* 53 (1963): 29–42.
Miller, A. "Inventa Componere: Rhetorical Process and Poetic Composition in Pindar's Ninth Olympian Ode." *TAPA* 123 (1993): 109–47.
Miller, E. (ed.) *Manuelis Philae carmina ex codicibus Escurialensis, Florentinis, Parisinis et Vaticanis.* Paris: Imperial Printers,1855–1857.
Miller, K. M. "Apollo Lairbenos." *Numen* 32 (1985): 46–70.
Milner, N. P. *An Epigraphical Survey in the Kibyra-Olbasa Region conducted by A. S Hall.* London: British Academy, 1998.
Minns, E. H. "Parchments of the Parthian Period from Avromanin Kurdistan." *JHS* 35 (1915): 22–65.
Mionnet, T. E. *Description de médailles antiques, Grecques et Romaines …* Paris: vol 4, 1809.
Miranda, E. "La communità giudaica di Hierapolis di Frigia." *EA* 31 (1999): 109–56.
Mitchell, L. and L. Rubinstein (eds.). *Greek History and Epigraphy: Essays in honour of P. J. Rhodes.* Swansea: Classical Press of Wales, 2009.
Mitchell, S. "Festivals, Games and Civic Life in Roman Asia Minor." *JRS* 80 (1990): 183–93.
— *Anatolia: Land, Men, and Gods in Asia Minor.* Oxford: Clarendon, 2 vols, 1993.
— "The Administration of Roman Asia from 133 BC to AD 250." Pages 17–46 in *Lokale Autonomie und romischen Ordnungsmacht in den kaiserzeitlichen Provinzen vom 1. bis 3. Jahrhundert* edited by E. Müller-Luckner and W. Eck. München: R. Oldenbourg, 1999.

— “The Cult of Theos Hypsistos.” Pages 81–148 in *Pagan Monotheism in Late Antiquity* edited by P. Athanassiadi and M. Frede. Oxford: Clarendon, 1999.
— “Further Thoughts on the Cult of Theos Hypsistos.” Pages 167–208 in *One God: Pagan monotheism in the Roman Empire* edited by S. Mitchell and P. van Nuffelen. Cambridge: Cambridge University Press, 2010.
— “EPMHNEIA. The Greek Translations of the *sacrae litterae* on Official Hospitality.” Pages 681–5 in *Vir Doctus Anatolicus: Studies in Memory of Sencer Şahin* edited by B. Takmer *et al.* Istanbul: Ege, 2016.
Mitchell, S. and M. Waelkens. *Pisidian Antioch: The Site and Its Monuments.* London: Duckworth, 1998.
Moga, I. *Religious Excitement in Ancient Anatolia: Cult and Devotional Forms for Solar and Lunar Gods.* Leuven: Peeters, 2019.
Moore, S. D. “The Beatific Vision as a Posing Exhibition: Revelation’s Hypermasculine Deity.” *JSNT* 60 (1996): 27–55.
— *God’s Beauty Parlor: And Other Queer Spaces in and around the Bible.* Stanford, CA: Stanford University Press, 2001.
Moralee, J. “The Stones of St Theodore: Disfiguring the Pagan Past in Christian Gerasa.” *JECS* 14 (2006): 183–215.
Moretti, L. *Iscrizioni Agonistische Greche.* Rome: Signorelli, 1953.
— “Epigraphica 11.” *RFIC* 103 (1975): 182–90.
— “Frammento di inno Tardo-Stoico sulla creazione.” Pages 251–6 in *Scritti storico-epigrafici in memoria di Marcello Zambelli* edited by L. Gasperini. Rome: Centro editorial internazionale, 1978.
— “Epigraphica 18: A proposito di Apollonia al Meandro.” *RFIC* 107 (1979): 295–300.
Morris, I. *Death-Ritual and Social Structure in Classical Antiquity.* Cambridge: Cambridge University Press, 2nd ed., 1996.
Mosshammer, A. A. *Georgius Syncellus. Ecloga chronographica.* Leipzig: Teubner, 1984.
Moulton, J. H. and W. F. Howard. *A Grammar of New Testament Greek Vol. II Accidence and Word Formation.* Edinburgh: T & T Clark, 1939.
Moulton, J. H. and G. Milligan. *The Vocabulary of the Greek Testament.* London: Hodder & Stoughton, 1952.
Mozley, J. H. and G. P. Gould (trans.) *Ovid: The Art of Love and Other Poems.* Cambridge, MA: Harvard University Press, 1929.
Müller, K. *Fragmenta historicorum Graecorum.* Paris: Didot, 4 vols, 1841–1870.
Müller, P. *Kolosserbrief.* KEK 9/2; Göttingen: Vandenhoeck & Ruprecht, 2022.
Müller-Karpe, A. “Planning a Sacred Landscape: Examples from Sarissa and Ḫattusa.” Pages 83–92 in *Sacred Landscapes of Luwians and Hittites: Proceedings of the International Conference* edited by A. D’Agostino, V. Orsi and G. Torri. Florence: Firenze University Press, 2015.
Muratov, M. “The Language(s) of Images in the Arts of the Bosporan Kingdom.” Pages 169–91 in *The Northern Black Sea in Antiquity: Networks, Connectivity and Cultural Interactions* edited by V. Kozlovskaya. Cambridge: Cambridge University Press, 2017.
Murray, J. *Handbook for Travellers in Russia, Poland and Finland.* London: John Murray, 1868.

Mussies, G. "Jewish Personal Names in some Non-literary Sources." Pages 242–76 in *Studies in Early Jewish Epigraphy* edited by J. W. van Henten and P. W. van der Horst. Leiden: Brill, 1994.

Nasrallah, L. S. *Archaeology and the Letters of Paul.* Oxford: Oxford University Press, 2019.

Ng, D. Y. "The Salutaris Foundation: Monumentality through Periodic Rehearsal." Pages 63–87 in *Roman Artists, Patrons and Public Consumption: Familiar Works Reconsidered* edited by B. Longfellow and E. Perry. Ann Arbor: University of Michigan Press, 2018.

Nigdelis, P. M. *Επιγραφικά Θεσσαλονίκεια.* Thessalonikê: University Studio Press, vol 1, 2006.

— "Voluntary Associations in Roman Thessalonikê: In Search of Identity and Support in a Cosmopolitan Society." Pages 13–47 in *From Roman to Early Christian Thessalonikê* edited by L. Nasrallah, C. Bakirtzis and S. J. Friesen. Cambridge, MA: Harvard University Press, 2010.

Nijf, O. van. *The Civic World of Professional Associations in the Roman East.* Amsterdam: J. C. Gieben, 1997.

— "Athletics, festivals and Greek identity in the Roman East." *PCPS* 45 (2000): 176–200.

— "Athletics, Andreia and the Askêsis-Culture in the Roman East." Pages 263–86 in *Andreia. Studies in Manliness and Courage in Classical Antiquity* edited by I. Sluiter and R. M. Rosen. Leiden: Brill, 2003.

Nollé, J. "Vielerorts war Bethlehem — Göttergeburten im kaiserzeitlichen Kleinasien." *AW* 34.6 (2003), 635–43.

Norden, E. *Agnostos Theos: Untersuchungen zur Formengeschichte religiöser Rede.* Darmstadt: WBG, 2 vols, 1956 (1913).

Nutton, V. "Menecrates of Sosandra, Doctor or Vet?" *ZPE* 22 (1976): 93–6.

O'Brien, P. *Colossians and Philemon.* WBC; Waco, TX: Word, 1982.

Obbink, D. "How to Read Poetry about Gods." Pages 189–209 in *Philodemus and Poetry: Poetic Theory and Practice in Lucretius, Philodemos and Horace* edited by D. Obbink. Oxford: Oxford University Press, 1995.

Obrador-Cursach, B. "Phrygian in Contact with Greek: An Overview." Pages 89–121 in *Greek Paideia and Local Tradition in the Graeco-Roman East* edited by M-P. de Hoz, J. L. G. Alonso and L. A. G. Romero. Leuven: Peeters, 2020.

Ogden, D. "Controlling women's dress: gynaikonomoi." Pages 203–25 in *Women's Dress in the Ancient Greek World* edited by L. Llewellyn-Jones. Swansea: Classical Press of Wales, 2002.

Ogereau, J. M. "Χειρόγραφον in Colossians 2:14. The Contribution of Epigraphy to the Philology of the New Testament." Pages 93–121 in *Epigraphical Evidence Illustrating Paul's Letter to the Colossians* edited by J. Verheyden, M. Öhler and T. Corsten. Tübingen: Mohr Siebeck, 2018.

— *Paul's Koinonia with the Philippians.* Tübingen: Mohr Siebeck, 2014.

Öğüş, E. "'Til death do them part': Reconstructing Graeco-Roman family life from funerary inscriptions of Aphrodisias." Pages 121–30 in *Life and Death in Asia Minor in Hellenistic, Roman and Byzantine Times: Studies in Archaeology and Bioarchaeology* edited by J. R. Brandt *et al.* Oxford: Oxbow, 2017.

Öhler, M. "Graeco-Roman Associations, Judean Synagogues and Early Christianity in Bithynia-Pontus." Pages 62–88 in *Authority and Identity in Emerging Christianities in Asia Minor and Greece* edited by C. Breytenbach and J. Ogereau. Leiden: Brill, 2018.

— "Earthquakes and the Elements of the World in the Letter to the Colossians." in *New Documents Illustrating the History of Early Christianity vol 12: The Lycus Valley* edited by J. R. Harrison *et al.* Grand Rapids, MN: Eerdmans, 2024, forthcoming.

Oliver, J. H. "An Ancient Poem on the Duties of a Physician." *Bulletin of the History of Medicine* 7 (1939): 315–23.

— *Greek Constitutions of Early Roman Emperors from Inscriptions and Papyri*. Philadelphia: American Philosophical Society, 1989.

Oliver, J. H. and B. D. Meritt. "Greek Inscriptions." *Hesperia* 10 (1941): 65–90.

Önal, M. "Deities and Cultures Meet on the Seal Impressions in Zeugma." *Bollettino di Archeologia* (Special Volume) online (2010): 25–53.

Onur, F and S. Kılıç-Aslan. "New Inscriptions from Aloanda in Lycia." *Gephyra* 21 (2021): 1–45.

Osborne, M. J. and S. G. Byrne. *The Foreign Residents of Athens*. Leuven: Peeters, 1996.

Østergaard, J. S. "Emerging Colors: Roman Sculptural Polychromy Revised." Pages 40–61 in *The Color of Life: Polychromy in Sculpture from Antiquity to the Present* edited by R. Panzanelli, E. D. Schmidt and K. D. S. Lapatin. Los Angeles: J. Paul Getty Museum and Getty Research Institute, 2008.

Özlem-Aytaçlar, P. "An onomastic survey of the indigenous population of north-western Asia Minor." Pages 506–29 in *Onomatologos: Studies in Greek Personal Names presented to Elaine Matthews* edited by R. W. V. Catling and F. Marchand. Oxford: Oxbow, 2010.

Özlem-Aytaçlar, P. and E. Akıncı. "A List of Female Names from Laodicea on the Lycos." *EA* 39 (2006): 113–6.

Pafford, I. "Priestly Portion vs. Cult Fees — The Finances of Greek Sanctuaries." Pages 49–64 in *Cities and Priests: Cult Personnel in Asia Minor and the Aegean Islands from the Hellenistic to the Imperial Period* edited by M. Horster and A. Klöckner. Berlin: de Gruyter, 2013.

Panagopoulos, C. "Vocabulaire et mentalités dans les Moralia de Plutarque." *DHA* 3 (1977): 197–235.

Papakonstantinou, Z. "Binding curses, agency and the Athenian democracy." Pages 142–58 in *Violence and Community: Law, Space and Identity in the Ancient Eastern Mediterranean World* edited by I. K. Xydopoulos, K. Vlassopoulos and E. Tounta. London: Routledge, 2017.

— "Athletics, memory and community in Hellenistic and Roman Messene." *BICS* 61 (2018): 64–78.

Papanikolaou, D. "The Aretalogy of Isis from maroneia and the Question of Hellenistic 'Asianism'." *ZPE* 168 (2009): 59–70.

Parker, R. "Athena in Anatolia." *Pallas* 100 (2016): 73–90.

— *Greek Gods Abroad: Names, Natures and Transformations*. Berkeley: University of California Press, 2017.

Parker, R. (ed.) *Personal Names in Ancient Anatolia*. Oxford: British Academy, 2013.

Paton, W. R. "Inscriptions of Myndos." *BCH* 12 (1888): 277–83.

Pavlichenko, N. and N. Fedoseev. "A New Inscription of Herakas, Son of Pontikos, ἀρχερμηνεὺς Ἀλανῶν." *Hyperboreus* 24 (2018): 315–36.

Peckham, R. S. *National Histories, Natural States: Nationalism and the Politics of Place in Greece*. London: I. B. Tauris, 2001.

Peers, G. *Subtle Bodies: Representing Angels in Byzantium*. Berkeley: University of California Press, 2001.

Pelcer-Vujačić, O. "Roman Senators from Phrygia." Pages 221–34 in *Phrygia in Antiquity: From the Bronze Age to the Byzantine Period* edited by G. R. Tsetskhladze. Leuven: Peeters, 2019.

Pellerin, J. *Recueil de Médailles de Peuples et de Villes qui n'ont point encore été publiées*. Paris: H. L. Guerin and L. F. Delatour, 1762.

Pennachietti, F. A. "Nuove iscrizioni di Hierapolis Frigia." *Atti della Accademia delle Scienze di Torino* 101 (1967): 286–328.

Perkins, P. "Power, Culture and Identity in the Roman Economy." Pages 183–212 in *Experiencing Rome: Culture, Identity and Power in the Roman Empire* edited by J. Huskinson. London: Routledge, 2000.

Pernin, I. *Les baux ruraux en Grèce ancienne: corpus épigraphique et etude*. Lyon: Maison de l'Orient et de la Méditerranée, 2014.

Perry, B. (1965) *Babrius and Phaedrus Fables*. Cambridge MA: Harvard University Press.

Perry, C. *A View of the Levant particularly of Syria, Egypt and Greece, In which their Antiquities, Government, Politics, Maxims, Manners and Customs (with many other Circumstances and Contingencies) are attempted to be Described and Treated on*. London: T. Woodward, C. Davis & J. Shuckburgh, 1743.

Pertusi, A. *Costantino Porfirogenito de Thematibus*. Vatican: Biblioteca Apostolica Vaticana, 1952.

Pestman, P. W. *The New Papyrological Primer*. Leiden: Brill, 1990.

Petersen, A. K. "Colossian's Grounding Trditionalization of Paul." Pages 59–74 in *The Early Reception of Paul the Second Temple Jew: Text, Narrative and Reception History* edited by I. W. Oliver and G. Boccaccini. London: T & T Clark, 2019.

Petersen, E. A. H. and F. von Luschan. *Reisen im südwestlichen Kleinasien II: Reisen in Lykien, Milyas und Kobyratis*. Vienna: Ministerium für Cultus und Unterricht, 1889.

Petraccia-Lucernoni, M. F. *Gli stationarii in età imperial*. Rome: Bretschneider, 2001.

Petridou, D. "'One has to be so terribly religious to be an artist': Divine Inspiration and *theophilia* in Aelius Aristides' *Hieroi logoi*." *Archiv für Religiongeschichte* 20 (2018): 257–71.

Petrie, A. "Epitaphs in Phrygian Greek." Pages 119–36 in *Studies in the History and Art of the Eastern Provinces of the Roman Empire* edited by W. M. Ramsay. Aberdeen: Aberdeen University Press, 1906.

Petrovic, A. "Do Seize, Do Eat, Do Touch — But Mind Your Thoughts: Colossians and Greek Purity Regulations." Pages 147–60 in *Epigraphical Evidence Illustrating Paul's*

Letter to the Colossians edited by J. Verheyden, M. Öhler and T. Corsten. Tübingen: Mohr Siebeck, 2018.

— "The Materiality of Text: An Introduction." Pages 1–25 in *The Materiality of Text — Placement, Perception, and Presence of Inscribed Texts in Classical Antiquity* edited by A. Petrovic, I. Petrovic and E. Thomas. Leiden: Brill, 2019.

Petrovic, A. and I. "On Ritual Pollution by Seeing: I.Lindos II 487.1–3 and Hdt. 2.37.5." *Gephyra* 11 (2014): 29–35.

— *Inner Purity and Pollution in Greek Religion, Volume 1, Early Greek Religion.* Oxford: Oxford University Press, 2016.

Petrucci, A. *Writing the Dead: Death and Writing Strategies in the Western Tradition* trans. M. Sullivan. Stanford: CA: Stanford University Press, 1998.

Petrucci, F. M. *Teone di Smirne. Expositio rerum mathematicarum ad legendum Platonem utilium. Introduzione, traduzione, commentario.* Sankt Augustin: Academia Verlag, 2012.

— "Théon de Smyrne." Pages 6.1019–20 in *Dictionnaire des philosophes antiques* edited by Goulet, R. *et al.* Paris: CRNS, 6 vols, 1989–2016.

— "Theon of Smyrna: Re-thinking Platonic Mathematics in Middle Platonism." Pages 143–55 in *Brill's Companion to the Reception of Plato* edited by H. Tarrant *et al.* Leiden: Brill, 2018.

Pettis, J. B. "Seeing the God in the Greco-Roman World." Pages 21–45 in *Seeing the God: Ways of Envisioning the Divine in Ancient Mediterranean Religion* edited by J. B. Pettis. Piscataway, NJ: Gorgias, 2013.

Petzl, G. and E. Schwertheim. *Hadrian und die dionysischen Künstler: drei in Alexandria Troas neugefundene Briefe des kaisers an die Künster-Vereinigung.* Bonn: Habelt, 2006.

Pfitzner, V. C. *Paul and the Agon Motif: traditional athletic imagery in the Pauline literature.* Leiden: Brill, 1967.

— "Was St Paul a Sports Enthusiast? Realism and Rhetoric in Pauline Athletic Metaphors." Pages 89–111 in *Sports and Christianity: Historical and Contemporary Perspectives*, edited by N. J. Watson and J. Parker. London: Routledge, 2012.

Pflaum, H.-G. *Les c arrières procuratoriennes équestres sous le Haut-Empire romain.* Paris, P. Geuthner, 1960–1.

Pfuhl, P. and H. Möbius. *Die Ostgriechischen Grabreliefs.* Mainz am Rhein: Philipp von Zabern, 4 vols, 1977.

Philipson, A. *Reisen und Forschungen im westlichen Kleinasien IV: Das östliche Lydien und südwestliche Phrygien.* Gotha: Perthes, 1914.

Piacenti, K. A. and J. Boardman (eds). *Ancient and Modern Gems and Jewels in the Collection of Her Majesty the Queen.* London: Royal Collection Publications, 2008.

Plantzos, D. *Hellenistic Engraved Gems.* Oxford: Clarendon, 1999.

Platt, V. "Double Vision: Epiphanies of the Dioscuri in Classical Antiquity." *Archiv für Religiongeschichte* 20 (2018): 229–56.

Pleket, H. W. "Varia Agonistica." *EA* 26 (1998): 117–28.

Pococke, R. *Description of the East and Some Other Countries.* London: W. Bowyer, 2 vols, 1745.

— *Inscriptionum antiquarum Graec. Et Latin liber: Accedit, numismatum Ptolemaeorum, imperatorun, Augustarum, et Caesarum, in Ægypto cusorum, e scriniis Britannicis, catalogus*. London: 1752.

Podossinov, A. V. "Nomads of the Eurasian Steppe and Greeks of the Northern Black Sea Region: Encounter of Two Great Civilizations in Antiquity and Early Middle Ages." Pages 237–51 in *Competing Narratives between Nomadic People and their Sedentary Neighbours* edited by C. Hao. Szeged: University of Szeged, 2019.

Pokorný, P. *Colossians: A Commentary*. Peabody, MA: Hendricksen, 1991.

Pollard, L. "'Every stone tells a story': the uses of classical texts by seventeenth-century English visitors to Greece and Asia Minor." *Classical Receptions Journal* 4 (2012): 48–65.

Pomeroy, S. *Families in Classical and Hellenistic Greece: Representations and Realities*. Oxford/New York: Oxford University Press, 1997.

Porter, J. I. "Content and Form in Philodemus: The History of an Evasion." Pages 97–147 in *Philodemus and Poetry: Poetic Theory and Practice in Lucretius, Philodemos and Horace* edited by D. Obbink. Oxford: Oxford University Press, 1995.

Porter, S. E. "Is ἀμβιτεύειν really ἐμβατεύειν (*P. Oxy*. XVII 2110.15)," *BASP* 27 (1990): 45–7.

— "Paul Confronts Caesar with the Good News." Pages 164–96 in *Empire in the New Testament* edited by S. E. Porter and C. Long Westfall. Eugene, OR: Pickwick, 2011.

Powell, J. U. *Collectanea Alexandrina*: Reliquiae minores Poetarum Graecorum Aetatis Ptolemaicae 323—146 A. C. Epicorum, Elegiacorum, Lyricorum, Ethicorum. Oxford: Clarendon Press, 1925.

Preisendanz, K. *Papyri Graecae Magicae: die griechischen Zauberpapyri*. Leipzig: Teubner, 2 vols, 1928, 1932.

Price, S. *Rituals and Power: The Roman Imperial Cult in Asia Minor*. Cambridge: Cambridge University Press, 1984.

Propstmeier, J., *et al*. "Diet in Roman Pergamon: Preliminary results using stable isotope (C, N, S), osteoarchaeological and historical data." Pages 237–49 in *Life and Death in Asia Minor in Hellenistic, Roman and Byzantine Times: Studies in Archaeology and Bioarchaeology* edited by J. R. Brandt *et al*. Oxford: Oxbow, 2017.

Purnelle, G. *Les usages des graveurs dans la notation d'upsilon et des phonèmes aspirés: le cas des anthroponymes grecs dans les inscriptions latines de Rome*. Geneva: Droz, 1995.

Purpura, G. "Il P. Giss. 40, I." *IAH* 5 (2013): 73–85.

Quandt, G. *De Baccho ab Alexandri Aetate in Asia Minore Culto*. Halis Saxonum: Niemeyer, 1913.

Quasten, J. *Music and Worship in Pagan and Christian Antiquity*. Washington: National Association of Pastoral Musicians, 1983.

Ramsay, W. M. "Antiquities of Southern Phrygia and the Border Lands (I)." *AJA* 3 (1887): 344–68.

— *The Cities and Bishoprics of Phrygia*. Oxford: Clarendon Press, 2 vols, 1895, 1897.

— *Studies in the History and Art of the Eastern Provinces of the Roman Empire*. Aberdeen: University of Aberdeen Press, 1906.

— *Luke the Physician: and other studies in the history of religion*. London: Hodder & Stoughton, 1908.

— "A Country Town of Lycaonia. A Description of the Conditions of Christian Life under the Eastern Empire." *Journal of the Transactions of the Victoria Institute* 41 (1909): 36–46.

Ramsay, W. M. (ed.) *Studies in the History and Art of the Eastern Provinces of the Roman Empire*. Aberdeen: University of Aberdeen Press, 1906.

Raspe, R. E. *Catalogue raisonné d'une Collection générale de Pierres gravées antiques et modernes tant en creux que Camées* … London: Murray, 1791.

Raubitschek, I. K. and A. E. "The Mission of Triptolemos." *Hesperia Supplements* 20 (1982): 109–17, 207–8.

Rea, J. "A Student's Letter to his Father: P.Oxy. XVIII.2190 Revised." *ZPE* 99 (1993): 75–88.

Reader, W. W. and A. J. Chvala-Smith. *The Severed Hand and Upright Corpse: The Declamations of Marcus Antonius Polemo*. Atlanta, GA; Scholars, 1996.

Reasoner, M. *Roman Imperial Texts: A Sourcebook*. Minneapolis: Fortress, 2013.

Reger, G. "A New Inventory from Mylasa in Karia." Pages 145–64 in *Stephanèphoros: de l'Économie antique à l'Asie Mineure: Hommages à Raymond Descat* edited by K. Konuk. Bordeaux: Ausonius, 2012.

Reicke, B. "The Historical Setting of Colossians." *RevExp* 70 (1973): 429–38.

Reinach, A. J. "Inscriptions d'Itanos." *REG* 24 (1911): 377–425.

Reinach, S. *Pierres gravées des collection Marlborough et d'Orléans* … Paris: Firmin-Didot, 1895.

Reinard, P. *Kommunikation und Ökonomie: Untersuchungen zu den privaten Papyrusbriefen aus dem kaiserzeitlichen Ägypten*. Rahden: Leidorf, 2016.

Renan, E. *Histoire des origins du Christianisme*. Paris: Michel Lèvy Frères, 6 vols, 1863–79.

Revell, L. *Roman Imperialism and Local Identities*. Cambridge: Cambridge University Press, 2009.

Reynolds, J. R. *Aphrodisias and Rome*. London: Society for the Promotion of Roman Studies, 1982.

Richter, G. M. A. *The Portraits of the Greeks*. London: Phaidon, 3 vols, 1965.

Ricl, M. "Les Καταγραφαί du Sanctuaire d'Apollon Lairbenos." *Arkeologi Dergisi* 3 (1995): 167–95.

— "Donations of Slaves and Freeborn Children to Deities in Roman Macedonia and Phrygia. A Reconsideration." *Tyche* 16 (2001): 155–60.

— "Greek Inscriptions in the Museum of Tire." *DHA* 35 (2009): 186–89.

— "A New Inscription from the Cayster Valley and the Question of *Supernomina* in Hellenistic and Roman Lydia." Pages 530–51 in *Onomatologos: Studies in Greek Personal Names presented to Elaine Matthews* edited by R. W. V. Catling and F. Marchand. Oxford: Oxbow, 2010.

— *New Inscriptions from the Kaystros River (Küçük Menderes) Valley*. Belgrade: Novi Sad, 2020.

Ricl, M. and E. Akıncı Öztürk. "A New Benefactor from the Upper Meander Valley (Çal Ovaşı)." *EA* 47 (2014): 16–20.

Riele, G.-J. te. "Inscriptions conserves au muse d'Olympie." *BCH* 88 (1964): 169–95.

Riemann, H. "Jupiter Imperator." *MDAI(A)* 90 (1983): 233–55.

Rigsby, K. J. *Asylia: Territorial Inviolability in the Hellenistic World.* Berkeley: University of California Press, 1996.

Riley, J. "Dionysos: Myth, Cult, and Influence in Kolossai and on the Letter to the Kolossians." Hons Thesis (unpub), Flinders University, 2006.

Ritti, T. "Il sofista Antipatros di Hierapolis." *MGR* 13 (1988): 71–128.

— "Oracoli Alfabetici a Hierapolis di Frigia." *Miscellanea greca e romana* 14 (1989): 245–86.

— "Iura sepulcrorum a Hierapolis di Frigia. Proprietà, trasmissione, uso e tutela dei sepolcri nelle iscrizioni edite e inedited della dittà. Rassegna dei formulary e confronti." *Libitina e dintorni* 3 (2004): 455–634.

— "La Carriera di un Cittadino do Hierapolis di Frigia: G. Memmios Eutychos." *CCG* 19 (2008): 279–308.

— "Alcune figure femminili nelle Iscrizioni di Hierapolis di Frigia." *Med.Ant.* 16 (2013): 139–80.

— "Spettacoli dell'arena in età imperiale: alcune osservazioni sulle forme e la finalità della comunicazione." Pages 401–29 in *Öffentlichkeit – Monument – Text. XIV Congressus Internationalis Epigraphiae Graecae et Latinae 27. – 31. Augusti MMXII. Akten* edited by W. Eck and P. Funke. Berlin: de Gruyter, 2014.

— *Per la storia sociale ed economica di Hierapolis di Frigia.* Rome: Accademia Nazionale dei Lincei, 2015.

— *Hierapolis di Frigia IX: Storia e Istituzioni di Hierapolis.* Istanbul: Ege, 2017.

Ritti, T. and G. Scardozzi. "Nuove iscrizioni dai villaggi antichi del territorio di Hierapolis: Thiounta, Boyallı e 'Motala.'" Pages 921–83 in *Le attività delle champagne di scavo e restauro 2012–2015* edited by F. d'Andria, M. P. Caggia and T. Ismaelli. Istanbul: Ege, 2022.

Ritti, T. and S. Yilmaz. *Gladiatori e venationes a Hierapolis di Frigia.* Rome: Accademia nazionale dei Lincei, 1998.

Ritti, T., C. Şimşek and H. Yıldız. "Dediche e Καταγράφαι dal Santuario frigio di Apollo Lairbenos." *EA* 32 (2000): 1–88.

Ritti, T., E. Miranda and F. Guizzi. "La ricerca epigrafica: risultati dell'ultimo quadrennio e prospettive future." Pages 583–618 in *Hierapolis di Frigia I: Le attività delle campagne di scavo e restauro 2000–2003*, edited by F. D'Andria and M. Piera Caggia (Istanbul: Ege, 2007),

Rizakis, A. D. "Langue et culture ou les ambiguïtés identitaires des notables des cités grecques sous l'empire de Rome." Pages 17–34 in *Bilinguisme gréco-latin et épigraphie* edited by F. Biville, J.-C. Decourt and G. Rougemont. Lyon: Maison de l'Orient méditerranéen, 2008.

— "Town and Country in Early Imperial Greece." *Pharos* 20 (2014): 241–67.

Robert, L. "Inscriptions grecques inédites au Musée du Louvre." *RArch* (1933/2): 121–47.

— *Études anatoliennes: Recherches sur les Inscriptions grecques de l'Asie Mineure.* Paris: de Boccard, 1937.

— "Le Culte de Caligula à Milet et la province d'Asie." *Hellenica* 7 (1949): 206–38.

— "Recherches épigraphiques." *REA* 62 (1960): 276–361.

— *Noms Indigènes dans L'Asie-Mineure Gréco-Romaine.* Paris: Adrien Maisonneuve, 1963.
— "Pierres errantes, muséographie et onomastique." *Berytus* 16 (1966): 5–40.
— "Sur des inscriptions d'Ephèse: fêtes, athletes, empereurs, épigrammes." *RevPhil* 41 (1967): 17–27.
— "Les Inscriptions." Pages 247–389 in *Laodicée du Lycos: Le Nymphée* edited by J. des Gagniers *et al.* Paris: de Boccard, 1969.
— *Les gladiateurs dans l'Orient grec.* Amsterdam: Hakkert, 1971 (1940).
— "Malédictions funéraires grecques." *CRAI* (1978): 241–69.
— "Documents d'Asie Mineure XXIII–XXVIII." *BCH* 107 (1983): 497–599.
Robert, L. and J. *La Carie: Histoire et géographie historique avec le recueil des inscriptions antiques. Le Plateau de Tabai et ses environs II.* Paris: Adrien-Maisonneuve, 1954.
Roberto, U. *Ioannis Antiocheni Fragmenta ex Historia chronica.* Berlin: de Gruyter, 2012.
Roberts, C., T. C. Skeat and A. D. Nock. "The Gild of Zeus Hypsistos." *HTR* 29 (1936): 49–78.
Robertson, A. T. *A Grammar of the Greek New Testament in the Light of Historical Research.* Nashville, TN: Broadman, 1934.
Robinson, T. *Who were the First Christians? Dismantling the Urban Thesis.* Oxford: Oxford University Press, 2017.
Rogers, G. M. *The Sacred Identity of Ephesus: Foundation Legends of a Roman City.* London: Routledge repr, 1991.
Rojas, F. *The Pasts of Roman Anatolia: Interpreters, Traces, Horizons.* Cambridge: Cambridge University Press, 2019.
Rojas, F. and V. Sergueenkova. "Traces of Tarhuntas: Greek, Roman, and Byzantine Interaction with Hittite Monuments." *JMA* 27.2 (2014): 135–60.
Rookhuizen, J. Z. van. *Herodotus and the Topography of Xerxes' Invasion: Place and Memory in Greece.* Berlin: de Gruyter, 2019.
Roos, A. G. and G. Wirth. *Flavii Arriani quae exstant Omnia: Alexandri Anabasin cum excerptis Photii.* Leipzig: Teubner, vol 2, 1968.
Roosevelt, C. H. "The Inhabited Landscapes of Lydia." Pages 145–64 in *Spear-won Land: Sardis from the King's Peace to the Peace of Apamea* edited by A. M. Berlin and P. J. Kosmin. Madison, WN: University of Wisconsin Press, 2019.
Rose, P. W. *Sons of the Gods, Children of Earth: Ideology and Literary Form in Ancient Greece.* Ithaca: Cornell University Press, 1992.
Roth, U. "Paul and Slavery: Economic Perspectives." Pages 155–82 in *Paul and Economics: A Handbook* edited by T. R. Blanton IV and R. Pockett. Minneapolis, MN: Fortress, 2017.
Roueché, C. *Performers and Partisans at Aphrodisias in the Roman and Late Roman Periods.* London: Society for the Promotion of Roman Studies, 1993.
Rougé, J. "Un negotiator Laudecenarius à Lyon." *ZPE* 27 (1977): 263–9.
Roussel, P. *Les cultes égyptiens à Délos, du IIIe au Ier siècle av. J.-C.* Nancy: Berger-Levrault, 1916.
Rubinstein, L. "Spoken Words, Written Submissions and Diplomatic Conventions: The Importance and Impact of Oral Performance in Hellenistic Inter-*polis* Relations." Pages 164–99 in *Hellenistic Oratory, Continuity and Change* edited by C. Kremmydas and K. Tempest. Oxford: Oxford University Press, 2013.

— "Summary Fines in Greek Inscriptions and the Question of 'Greek Law'." Pages 104–43 in *Ancient Greek Law in the 21st Century* edited by P. Perlman. Austin: University of Texas Press, 2018.

Russell, B. *The Economics of the Roman Stone Trade.* Oxford: Oxford University Press, 2013.

Russell, D. A. and N. G. Wilson (eds). *Menander Rhetor.* Oxford: Oxford University Press, 1981.

Russo, J. "The Poetics of the Ancient Greek Proverb." *JFR* 20 (1983): 121–30.

Rycaut, P. *The Present State of the Greek and Armenian Churches, anno Christi 1678.* London: John Starkey, 1679.

Sagona, A. and P. Zimansky. *Ancient Turkey.* London/New York: Routledge, 2009.

Şahin, M. "Salvage Excavations at the Necropolis of Apollonia in 2016–17: An Analysis of Grave Types." *Uluslararası Türkçe Edebiyat Kültür Eğitim Dergisi Sayı* 7 (2018): 2788–812.

Saller R. P. and B. D. Shaw. "Tombstones and Roman Family Relations in the Principate: Civilians, Soldiers and Slaves." *JRS* 74 (1984): 124–56.

Samama, E. *Les médecins dans le monde grec. Sources épigraphiques sur la naissance d'un corps medical.* Geneva: Droz, 2003.

Sancisi-Weerdenburg, H. "The Fifth Oriental Monarchy and Hellenocentrism." Pages 117–31 in *Achaemenid History II: The Greek Sources* edited by A. Kuhrt and H. Sancisi-Weerdenburg. Leiden: Netherlands Institute for the Near East, 1987.

Sandbach, F. H. *Plutarchi moralia.* Leipzig: Teubner, vol 7, 1967.

Santamaria, M. A. "The Term βάκχος and Dionysos Βάκχιος." Pages 38–57 in *Redefining Dionysos* edited by A. Bernabé *et al.* Berlin: de Gruyter, 2013.

Santangelo, F. *Sulla, the Elites and the Empire: A Study of Roman Policies in Italy and the Greek East.* Leiden/Boston: Brill, 2007.

Sargologos, É. *La Vie de Saint Cyrille le Philéote moine byzantin (†1110).* Brussels: Society of Bollandists, 1964.

Sarri, A. *Material Aspects of Letter Writing in the Graeco-Roman World: 500 BC – AD 300.* Berlin: de Gruyter, 2017.

Sauer, V. "Urban Space: The Evidence of Coins." Pages 109–24 in *Space, Place and Identity in Northern Anatolia* edited by T. Bekker-Nielsen. Stuttgart: Franz Steiner, 2014.

Scanlon, T. F. *Eros and Greek Athletics.* Oxford: Oxford University Press, 2002.

Scardozzi, G. "Remote sensing and archaeological survey in the Hierapolis of Phrygia territory, Turkey." Pages 674904–1–12 in *Remote Sensing for Environmental Monitoring, GIS Applications, and Geology VII*, edited by M. Ehlers and U. Michel. SPIE Proceedings 6749; Washington: SPIE, 2007.

— "The Provenance of Marbles and Alabasters Used in the Monuments of Hierapolis in Phrygia (Turkey): New Information from a Systematic Review and Integration of Archaeological and Archaeometric Data." *Heritage* 2 (2019): 1–35.

— *The Territory of Hierapolis in Phrygia.* Istanbul: Ege, 2020.

Schachter, A. *Cults of Boiotia II: Herakles to Poseidon.* London: University of London, 1986.

— "Reflections on an Inscription from Tanagra." Pages 279–88 in *Boiotia in Antiquity: Selected Papers* edited by H. Beck. Cambridge: Cambridge University Press, 2016.

Scheidel, W. *Measuring Sex, Age and Death in the Roman Empire: Explorations in ancient demography.* Ann Arbor, MI: Journal of Roman Archaeology, 1996.

— "Real Slave Prices and the Relative Cost of Slave Labor in the Greco-Roman World." *AncSoc* 35 (2005): 1–17.

— "The demographic background." Pages 31–40 in *Growing Up Fatherless in Antiquity* edited by S. R. Hübner and D. M. Ratzan. Cambridge: Cambridge University Press, 2009.

— "Epigraphy and Demography: birth, marriage, family, and death." Pages 101–29 in *Epigraphy and the Historical Sciences* edited by J. K. Davies and J. J. Wilkes. Oxford: Oxford University Press, 2012.

— "Slavery." Pages 89–113 in *The Cambridge Companion to the Roman Economy* edited by W. Scheidel. Cambridge: Cambridge University Press, 2012.

Scheidel, W. and S. J. Friesen. "The Size of the Economy and the Distribution of Income in the Roman Empire." *JRS* 99 (2009): 61–91.

Sheppard, A. R. R. "R.E.C.A.M. Notes and Studies No. 6: Jews, Christians and Heretics in Acmonia and Eumeneia." *AS* 29 (1979): 169–80.

Scherer, A. "Paphlagonische Namenstudien." Pages 377–86 in *Studien zur Sprachwissenschaft und Kulturkunde, Gedenkschrift für W. Brandenstein* edited by M. Mayrhofer. Innsbruck: Amoe, 1968.

Schille, G. "Rezension zu Burger Schöpfung und Versöhnung." *TLZ* 103 (1978): 274–7.

Schmitt, R. "Parthische Sprach- und Namenüberlieferung aus arsakidischer Zeit." Pages 95–146 in *Das Partherreich und seine Zeugnisse* edited by J. Wiesehöfer. Stuttgart: Franz Steiner, 1998.

Schmitz, L. *A Manual of Ancient Geography: with Map Showing the Retreat of the 10,000 Greeks under Xenophon.* Philadelphia: Blanchard and Lea, 1857.

Schneider, E. "Some Considerations on Elaiussa's North-Eastern Necropolis." *Olba* 7 (2003): 251–61.

Schneider, R. *Grammatici Graeci*, Leipzig: Teubner, vol 2, 1878.

Scholz, P. "Einführung." Pages 11–24 in *Das hellenistische Gymnasion* edited by D. Kah and P. Scholz. Berlin: de Gruyter, 2007.

Schörner, G. "Wie integriert man Rom in die Polis? Der Kult des Senats in Kleinasien." Pages 217–42 in *Integration in Rome and in the Roman World* edited by G. de Kleijn and S. Benoist. Leiden: Brill, 2013.

Schörner, H. "The intra-urban burial inside Greek poleis in Asia Minor: The example of Termessos." Pages 223–30 in *Le Mort dans la ville Pratiques, contexts et impacts des inhumations intra-muros en Anatolie* edited by O. Henry. Istanbul: Institut français d'études anatoliennes, 2011.

Schuler, C. *Ländliche Siedlungen und Gemeinden im hellenistischen und römischen Kleinasien.* München: C. H. Beck, 1996.

Sears, F. *Roman Theatres: An Architectural Study.* Oxford: Oxford University Press, 2006.

Seitz, C. R. *Colossians.* Grand Rapids, MN; Baker, 2014.

Sekunda, N. "Changing Patterns of Land-Holding in the South-Western Border Lands of Greater Phrygia in the Achaemenid and Hellenistic Periods." Pages 48–76 in *Colossae in Space and Time: Linking with an ancient city* edited by A. H. Cadwallader and M. Trainor. Göttingen: Vandenhoeck & Ruprecht, 2011.

Sfameni, C. "Magic in Late Antiquity: The Evidence of Magical Gems." Pages 435–76 in *Religious Diversity in Late Antiquity.* Edited by D. M. Gwynn and S. Bangert. Leiden, Brill, 2010.

Shaya, J. "The Greek Temple as Museum: The Case of the Legendary treasure of Athena." *AJA* 109.3 (2005): 423–42.

Sherk, R. K. *Rome and the Greek East to the Death of Augustus.* Cambridge: Cambridge University Press, 1984.

Sherwin-White, A. N. "Roman Involvement in Anatolia, 167–88 B.C." *JRS* 67 (1977): 62–75.

Silver, M. "At the Base of Rome's *Peculium* Economy." *Fundamina* 22 (2016): 67–93.

Silwa, J. *Egyptian Scarabs and Magical Gems from the Collection of Constantine Schmidt-Ciazynski.* Cracow: Jagiellonian University Press, 1989.

Simms, R. M. "The Phrearrhian Lex Sacra: An Interpretation." *Hesperia* 67 (1998): 91–107.

Simotas, P. N. *Νικήτα Σεΐδου Σύνοψις τῆς Ἁγίας Γραφῆς.* Thessalonica: Patriarchal Institute for Patristic Studies, 1984.

Şimşek, C. "Kolossai." *Arkeoloji ve Sanat* 107 (2002): 3–16.

— *Laodikeia (Laodikeia ad Lycum).* Istanbul: Ege, 2007.

— "Lykos Vadisi Içinde yer Alan Laodikeia (Laodikeia in the Lycos Valley)." Pages 33–69 on *10. Yılında Laodikeia (2003–2013 Yılları)* edited by C. Şimşek. Istanbul: Ege, 2014.

— "Laodikeia 'da Tekstil ve Üretim Atölyeleri(Textile and Manufacturing Ateliers at Laodikeia)." *Home Textile* 86 (2015): 138–44.

— "Urban Planning of Laodikeia on the Lykos in the Light of New Evidence." Pages 1–46 in *Landscape and History in the Lykos Valley: Laodikeia and Hierapolis in Phrygia* edited by C. Şimşek and F. D'Andria. Cambridge: Cambridge Scholars Publishing, 2016.

Şimşek, C. (ed.) *Laodikeia Nekropolü (2004–2010 Yılları)* (Laodikeia Çalısmaları 1). Istanbul: Ege, 2 vols, 2011.

Şimşek, C. and B. Yener. "An Ivory Relief of Saint Thecla." *Adalya* 13 (2010): 321–34.

Şimşek, C. and M. A. Sezgin. "Laodikeia Kuzey Tiyatrosu." *Olba* 19 (2011): 173–201.

— "The West and North Theatres in Laodicea." Pages 103–28 in *Restoration and Management of Ancient Theatres in Turkey: methods, research, results,* edited by F. Masino, P. Mighetto and G. Sobrà. Lecce: Congedo, 2012.

Şimşek, C. and B. Yılmaz Kolancı. "Laodikeia, Mimari Bloklarında yer Alan Balık Kabartmaları aları Üzerine Gözlemler (Observations on Fish Reliefs on Laodikeia Architectural Blocks)." Pages 273–86 in *15. Yılında Laodikeia (2003–2018)* (Laodikeia Çalısmaları 5) edited by C. Şimşek. Istanbul: Ege, 2019.

Şimşek, C., H. Baysal and M. Ohunak. "Korucuk Kurtama Kazısında Açiğa Cıkartılan Mezarlar (The Tombs unearthed in the Korucuk Rescue Excavation)." Pages 229–81 in *10. Yılında Laodikeia (2003–2013 Yılları,* edited by C. Şimşek. Istanbul: Ege, 2014.

Sîrbu V. and M.-M. Ştefan. "Delimited Funerary Spaces – Hellenistic Tumuli with Stone Enclosures at Kallatis." *Annales d'Université Valahia Targoviste* 21 (2019): 51–76.

Slater, T. B. "Translating Ἅγιος in Col 1,2 and Eph 1,1." *Biblica* 87 (2006): 52–4.

Slater, W. "The Victor's Return, and the Categories of Games." Pages 139–63 in *Epigraphical Approaches to the Post-Classical Polis: Fourth Century BC to Second Century AD* edited by P. Martzavou and N. Papazarkadas. Oxford: Oxford University Press, 2013.
Smith, H. I. *The Course of Ancient Geography.* New York: D. Appleton, 1861.
Smith, J. Z. *Map is not Territory: Studies in the History of Religions.* Chicago: University of Chicago Press, 1978.
Smith, M. "De tuenda sanitate praecepta (Moralia 122B – 137 E)." Pages 32–50 in *Plutarch's Ethical Writings and Early Christian Literature* edited by H. D. Betz. Leiden: Brill, 1978.
Smith, M. J. "Utility, Fraternity and Reconciliation: Ancient Slavery as a Context for the Return of Onesimus." Pages 47–58 in *Onesimus our Brother: Reading Religion, Race, and Culture in Philemon* edited by M. V. Johnson, J. A. Noel and D. K. Williams. Minneapolis: Fortress, 2012.
Smith, R. R. R. *Aphrodisias I: The Monument of C. Iulius Zoilos.* Mainz: von Zabern, 1993.
— "Sarcophagi and Roman Citizenship." Pages 347–95 in *New Research on the City and Its Monuments, vol. 4 of Aphrodisias Papers* edited by C. Ratté and R. R. R. Smith. Portsmouth, RI: Journal of Roman Archaeology, 2008.
Smith, T. *Epistolae duae, quarum altera de moribus ac institutis Turcarum agit, altera septem Asiae ecclesiarum notitiam continent.* Oxford: H. Hall, 1672.
— *Remarks upon the Manners, Religion and Government of the Turks together with a Survey of the Seven Churches of Asia, as They Now Lye in Their Ruines.* London: Moses Pitt, 1678.
— *Admodum reverend & doctissimi viri, D. Roberti Huntingtoni, S. theologiae doctoris et episcopi rapotensis, epistolae.* London: 1704.
— "The Life and Travels of the Right Rev. and Learned Dr. Robert Huntington." *Gentleman's Magazine* 95 (1825): 11–12.
Smith, T. J. "Votive Reliefs from Balboura and its Environs." *AS* 47 (1997): 3–49.
Smithies, A. *The Life of Patriarch Ignatius.* Washington, D. C.: Dumbarton Oaks, 2013.
Sokolowski, F. *Lois sacrées de l'Asie Mineure.* Paris: de Boccard, 1955.
— *Lois sacrées des cites grecques: Supplément.* Paris: de Boccard, 1962.
— "On the Lex Sacra of the Deme Phrearrhioi." *GRBS* 12 (1971): 217–20.
Solin, H. *Die stadtrömischen Sklavennamen: ein Namenbuch.* Stuttgart: Franz Steiner, 3 vols, 1996.
— "Analecta Epigraphica CCXLIV–CCLI." *Arctos* 42 (2008): 215–46.
Somerville, W. F. *The Churches in Asia: Extracts from the Home Letters of Rev. A. N. Somerville DD from the Region of the Seven Churches.* Paisley: J & R Parlane, 1885.
Spagnolis, M. C. de'. *La tomba del calzolaio: dalla necropoli monumentale romana di Nocera Superiore.* Rome: Bretschneider, 2000.
Speed, J. *A Prospect of the Most Famous Parts of the World.* London: George Humble, 1626/7.
Spicq, C. *Notes de lexicographie néo-testamentaire: Tome I.* Göttingen: Vandenhoeck & Ruprecht, 1978.
Spier, J. *Ancient Gems and Finger Rings of the Collection of J. Paul Getty Museum.* Malibu, CA: J. Paul Getty Museum, 1992.

Spon, J. and G. Wheler. *Voyage d'Italie, de Dalmatie, de Grece, et du Levant.* Lyon: Antoine Cellier, 1678.

Spratt, T. A. B. and E. Forbes. *Travels in Lycia, Milyas and the Cibyratis in Company with the late Rev. E. T. Daniell.* London: John van Voorst, 2 vols, 1847.

Spyridakis, S. "The Itanian Cult of Tyche Protogeneia." *Historia* 18.1 (1969): 42–8.

Stambaugh, J. E. and D. L. Balch. *The New Testament in Its Social Environment.* Philadelphia: Westminster Press, 1986.

Standhartinger, A. *Studien zur Entstehungsgeschichte und Intention des Kolosserbriefs.* Leiden: Brill, 1999.

— "The Origin and Intention of the Household Code in the Letter to the Colossians." *JSNT* 79 (2000): 117–30.

— "Colossians and the Pauline School." *NTS* 50 (2004): 572–93.

— "'... wegen der Hoffnung, die für euch im Himmel bereitliegt' (Kol 1,5)." Pages 1–22 in *Kolosser-Studien* edited by P. Müller. Göttingen: Neukirchener, 2009.

— "Der Kolosserhymnus im Lichte epigraphischer Zeugnisse." Pages 69–91 in *Epigraphical Evidence Illustrating Paul's Letter to the Colossians* edited by J. Verheyden, M. Öhler and T. Corsten. Tübingen: Mohr Siebeck, 2018.

— "A City with a Message: Colossae and Colossians." Pages 239–56 in *The First Urban Churches 5: Colossae, Hierapolis, and Laodicea* edited by J. R. Harrison and L. L. Welborn. Atlanta, GA: SBL Press, 2019.

— "Mehr als eine Stadt in Phrygien: Das antike Kolossä und sein Brief." Pages 697–711 in *Talking God in Society: Multidisciplinary (Re)constructions of Ancient (Con)texts: Fs Peter Lampe. Volume 1: Theories and Applications* edited by Ute E. Elsen and H. E. Mader. Göttingen: Vandenhoeck & Ruprecht, 2020.

Stanley, C. "'Neither Jew nor Greek': Ethnic Conflict in Graeco-Roman Society." *JSNT* 64 (1996) 101–24.

Steigerwald, G. "Die Purpursortenim Preisedikt Diokletians vom Jahre 301." *ByzF* 15 (1990): 219–76.

Sterrett, J. R. S. *An Epigraphical Journey in Asia Minor during the Summer of 1884.* Boston: Damrell & Upham, 1888.

Stettler, H. *Der Kolosserhymnus: Untersuchungen zu Form, traditionsgeschichtlichem Hintergrund und Aussage von Kol 1, 15–20.* Tübingen: Mohr Siebeck, 2000.

Story-Maskelyne, M. H. *The Marlborough Gems: Being a Collection of Works in Cameo and Intaglio ...* London: 1870.

Strack, H. L. and P. Billerbeck. *Kommentar zum neuen Testament aus Talmud und Midrasch.* Munich: C. H. Beck, 6 vols, 1978 (1924).

Strelan, R. "The Languages of the Lycus Valley." Pages 77–103 in *Colossae in Space and Time: Linking to an Ancient City* edited by A. H. Cadwallader and M. Trainor. Göttingen: Vandenhoeck & Ruprecht, 2011.

Strootman, R. "Kings against Celts: Deliverance from Barbarians as a Theme in Hellenistic Royal Propaganda." Pages 101–41 in *The Manipulative Mode: Political Propaganda in Antiquity: A Collection of Case Studies* edited by K. A. E. Enenkel and I. L. Pfeijffer. Leiden: Brill, 2005.

Strubbe, J. H. M. "Curses against Violation of the Grave in Jewish Epitaphs of Asia Minor." Pages 70–128 in *Studies in Early Jewish Epigraphy* edited by J. W. van Henten and P. W. van der Horst. Leiden: Brill, 1994.

— *ΑΡΑΙ ΕΠΙΤΥΜΒΙΟΙ: Imprecations against Desecration of the Grave in Greek Epitaphs of Asia Minor. A Catalogue.* Bonn: Habelt, 1997.

Stuhlmacher, P. *Der Brief an Philemon.* Benziger: Neukirchener, 4th ed., 2004 (1975).

Stumpf, G. R. *Numismatische Studien zur Chronologie der römischen Statthalter in Kleinasien (122 v. Chr. - 163 n. Chr.).* Saarbrücken: Saarbrücken Druckerei und Verlag, 1991.

Sumney, J. L. *Colossians: A Commentary.* Louisville, KY: WJKP, 2008.

Sutherland, C. H. V. "The Intelligibility of Roman Imperial Coin Types." *JRS* 49 (1959) 46–55.

Svartvik, J. "'East is East and West is West:' The Concept of Torah in Paul and Mark." Pages 157–85 in *Paul and Mark: Comparative Essays, Part I: Two Authors at the Beginnings of Christianity* edited by O. Wischmeyer, D. C. Sim and I. J. Elmer. Berlin: de Gruyter, 2014.

Sweeney, N. M. *Foundation Myths and Politics in Ancient Ionia.* Cambridge: Cambridge University Press, 2013.

Swete, H. *Theodori episcopi Mopsuesteni In epistolas b. Pauli commentarii Vol. I.* Cambridge: Cambridge University Press, 1880.

Taeuber, H. H. Graffiti und Inschriften." Pages 233–57 in *Hanghaus 2 in Ephesos: Die Wohneinheit 7* edited by E. Rathmayr. Vienna: Österreichische Akademia der Wissenschaften, 2016.

Taft, R. F. *The Christian East, its institutions and its thought.* Rome: Pontificio Istituto orientale, 1996.

Talbert, R. J. A. (ed.) *Barrington Atlas of the Greek and Roman World: Map-by-Map Directory.* Princeton, NJ: Princeton University Press, 2 vols, 2000.

Tanrıver, C. "Three New Inscriptions from Tripolis." *EA* 42 (2009): 81–6.

Tartaglia, L. *Theodorus II Ducas Lascaris Opuscula Rhetorica.* Munich/Leipzig: K. G. Saur, 2000.

Tataki, A. B. *Ancient Beroea: Prosopography and Society.* Paris: de Boccard, 1988.

Taylor, N. H. "Baptism for the dead (1 Cor 15:29)?" *Neotestamentica* 36 (2002): 111–20.

Tedeschi, G. *Spettacoli e trattenimenti dal IV seconol a.C. all'età tardo-antica secondo I documenti epigrafici e papiracei.* Trieste: University Press Italiane, 2017.

Tekin, O. and A. Yacı. *SNG: Turkey 11, The Çetin Erdem Collection.* Istanbul: TEBE, 2019.

Texier, C. and R. Popplewell Pullan. *The Principal Ruins of Asia Minor Illustrated and Described.* London: Day & Son, 1865.

Theophilos, M. P. "Employing Numismatic Evidence in Discussions of Early Christianity in the Lycus Valley: A Case Study from Laodicea." Pages 257–92 in *The First Urban Churches 5: Colossae, Hierapolis, and Laodicea* edited by J. R. Harrison and L. L. Welborn. Atlanta, GA: SBL Press, 2019.

— *Numismatics and Greek Lexicography.* London: T & T Clark, 2020.

Thomas, C. "The 'Mountain Mother': The Other Anatolian Goddess at Ephesos." Pages 249–62 in *Les cultes Locaux dans les mondes grec et romain: actes du colloque, de Lyon 7–8 Juin 2001.* Lyon/Paris: Université Lumière-Lyon, 2004.

— "Placing the Dead: Funerary Practice and Social Stratification in the Early Augustan Period at Corinth and Ephesos." Pages 281–304 in *Urban Religion in Roman Corinth: Interdisciplinary Approaches* edited by D. N. Schowalter and S. J. Friesen. Cambridge, MA: Harvard University Press, 2005.

Thomas, C. and C. İçten. "The *Ostothekai of Ephesos* and the Rise of Sarcophagus Inhumation: Death, Conspicuous Consumption, and Roman Freedmen." Pages 335–44 in *Akten des Symposiums des Sarkophag-Korpus 2001* edited by G. Koch. Mainz: Zabern, 2007.

Thomas, J. A. C. *Textbook of Roman Law.* Amsterdam: North-Holland, 1976.

Thompson, L. L. "ISmyrna 753: Gods and the One God." Pages 101–22 in *Reading Religions in the Ancient World: essays presented to Robert McQueen Grant* edited by R. McQ. Grant, D. E. Aune and R. D. Young. Leiden: Brill, 2007.

Thompson, M. M. *Colossians & Philemon.* Grand Rapids, MN: Eerdmans, 2005.

Thonemann, P. "Hellenistic Inscriptions from Lydia." *EA* 36 (2003): 95–108.

— "The Women of Akmoneia." *JRS* 100 (2010): 163–78.

— *The Maeander Valley: A Historical Geography from Antiquity to Byzantium.* Cambridge: Cambridge University Press, 2011.

— "Households and Families in Roman Phrygia." Pages 124–42 in *Roman Phrygia: Culture and Society* edited by P. Thonemann. Cambridge: Cambridge University Press, 2013.

— "The Attalid State, 188–133 BC." Pages 1–48 in *Attalid Asia Minor: Money, International Relations, and the State* edited by P. Thonemann. Oxford: Oxford University Press, 2013.

— "Alexander, Priene, and Naulochon." Pages 23–36 in *Epigraphical Approaches to the Post-Classical Polis — Fourth Century BC to Second Century AD* edited by P. Martzavou and N. Papazarkadas. Oxford: Oxford University Press, 2013.

— *The Hellenistic World: Using Coins as Sources.* Cambridge: Cambridge University Press, 2015.

Thurn, I. *Ioannis Malalae chronographia.* Berlin - New York: De Gruyter, 2000.

Till, W. *An Essay on the Roman Denarius and English Silver Penny …* London: Longman, Brown, Green and Longmans, 1838.

Tittmann, J. A. H. *Iohannis Zonarae lexicon ex tribus codicibus manuscriptis.* Leipzig: Crusius, 2 vols, 1808.

Todd, S. C. *The Shape of Athenian Law.* Oxford: Clarendon Press, 1993.

Tomlin, R. S. O. "Cursing a Thief in Iberia and Britain." Pages 245–73 in *Magical Practice in the Latin west: papers from the International Conference held at the University of Zaragoza* edited by R. L. Gordon and S. F. Marco. Leiden: Brill, 2010.

Torlone, Z. M. "Writing Arenas: Roman Authors and Their Games." Pages 412–21 in *A Companion to Sport and Spectacle in Greek and Roman Antiquity* edited by P. Christesen and D. G. Kyle. Oxford: Oxford University Press, 2013.

Tournefort, P. de. *Relation d'un Voyage du Levant.* Paris: L'imprimerie Royale, 2 vols, 1717.

Trainor, M. *Epaphras: Paul's Educator at Colossae.* Collegeville, MI: Liturgical Press, 2008.

— "Rome's Market Economy in the Lycus Valley: Soundings from Laodicea and Colossae." Pages 293–324 in *The First Urban Churches 5: Colossae, Hierapolis, and Laodicea* edited by J. R. Harrison and L. L. Welborn. Atlanta, GA: SBL Press, 2019.

Trapp, M. *In Praise of Asclepius: Aelius Aristides, Selected Prose Hymns*. Tübingen: Mohr Siebeck, 2016.

Travaglini, A. and V. G. Camilleri. *Hierapolis di Frigia: Le Monete, Campagne di Scavo 1957–2004*. Istanbul: Ege, 2010.

Trebilco, P. "Asia." Pages 291–362 in *The Book of Acts in its Greco-Roman Setting* edited by D. W. J. Gill and C. Gempf. Grand Rapids, MN: Eerdmans, 1994.

Tröster, M. *Themes, Character and Politics in Plutarch's Life of Lucullus: The Construction of a Roman Aristocrat*. Stuttgart: Steiner, 2008.

Troxell, H. A. *Coinage of the Lycian League*. New York: ANS, 1982.

Tsolakes, E. T. *Ἡ συνέχεια τῆς χρονογραφίας τοῦ Ἰωάννου Σκυλίτση*. Thessalonike: 1968.

Tsouna, V. *The Ethics of Philodemus*. Oxford: Oxford University Press, 2007.

Tuplin, C. "Xenophon and the Garrisons of the Achaemenid Empire." *Archäologische Mitteilungen aus Iran* 20 (1987): 167–245.

Ünal, M. A. "Yüzyılda Honaz Kazâsı." Pages 1.104–10 in *Uluslararası Denizli ve Çevresi Tarih ve Kültür Semposyumu Bildiriler* (*International Symposium on the History and Culture of Denizli and its Surroundings*) edited by A. Özçelik *et al.* Denizli: Pamukkale University, 2 vols, 2007.

Unwin, N. C. *Caria and Crete in Antiquity: Cultural Interaction between Anatolia and the Aegean*. Cambridge: Cambridge University Press, 2017.

Valente, S. "From Plato to the Byzantine Etymologica: The etymologies of 'ἥρωες' in the *Etymologicum Gudianum*." Pages 79–91 in *Studies in Greek Lexicography* edited by G. K. Giannakis *et al.* Berlin: de Gruyter, 2019.

Vandorpe, K. and S. P. Vleeming. *The Erbstreit Papyri: A Bilingual Dossier from Pathyris of the Second Century BC*. Leuven: Peeters, 2017.

Varinioğlu, E. "Phrygia ve Lydia'da (Kırsalda) Aile Bağları." *AST* 29/1 (2012): 91–5.

Veblen, T. *The Theory of the Leisure Class*. Hammondsworth: Penguin, 1994 (1899).

Verbrugghe, G. P. and J. M. Wickersham. *Berossos and Manetho, introduced and translated: Native Traditions in Ancient Mesopotamia and Egypt*. Ann Arbor: University of Michigan Press, 2001.

Verheyden, J., M. Öhler and T. Corsten (eds). *Epigraphical Evidence Illustrating Paul's Letter to the Colossians*. Tübingen: Mohr Siebeck, 2018.

Vermeule, C. C. *Roman Imperial Art in Greece and Asia Minor*. Cambridge, MA: Belknap Press, 1968.

Vernant, J. P. *Myth and Thought among the Greeks* translated by J. Lloyd and J. Fort. London: Routledge, 1983.

Versnel, H. S. *Inconsistencies in Greek and Roman Religion Volume 2: Transition and Reversal in Myth and Ritual*. Leiden: Brill, 1993.

— "Prayers for Justice, East and West: New Finds and Publications since 1990." Pages 275–354 in *Magical Practice in the West. Papers from the International Conference Held at the University of Zaragoza* edited by R. Gordon and F. M. Simón. Leiden: Brill, 2010.

Veyne, P. "The Roman Empire." Pages 5–405 in *A History of Private Life I: From Pagan Rome to Byzantium*. Cambridge, MA: Belknap Press, 1978.

Ville, G. *La gladiature en occident des origins à la mort de Domitien*. Rome: L'Erma di Bretschneider, 1981.

Volk, K. *Manilius and His Intellectual Background*. Oxford: Oxford University Press, 2009.

Waelkens, M. *Die kleinasiatischen Türsteine: typologische und epigraphische Untgersuchungen der kleinasiatischen Grabreliefs mit Scheintür*. Mainz em Rhein: Philipp von Zabern, 1986.

Walbank, M. E. H. "Aspects of Corinthian Coinage in the Late 1st and early 2nd Centuries A.C." Pages 337–49 in *Corinth: The Centenary 1896–1996* edited by C. K. Williams II and N. Bookidis. Princeton: American School of Classical Studies at Athens, 2003.

— "Unquiet Graves: Burial Practices of the Roman Corinthians." Pages 249–80 in *Urban Religion in Roman Corinth: Interdisciplinary Approaches* edited by D. N. Schowalter and S. J. Friesen. Cambridge, MA: Harvard University Press, 2005.

Walker, J. *Rhetoric and Poetics in Antiquity*. Oxford: Oxford University Press, 2000.

Wallace, D. B. *Greek Grammar: Beyond the Basics*. Grand Rapids, MN: Zondervan, 1996.

Walser, A. V. *Bauern und Zinsnehmer: Politik, Recht und Wirtschaft im frühhellenistichen Ephesos*. Munich: CH Beck, 2008.

Walsh, B. and S. C. Keesmart, *Colossians Remixed: Subverting the Empire*. Downers Grove, IL: IVP, 2004.

Walsh, R. *Account of the Levant Company; with some notices of the benefits conferred upon society by its officers, in promoting the cause of humanity, literature and the fine arts*. London: J. and A. Arch, 1825.

Wandsnider, L. "Public Buildings and Civic Benefactions in Western Rough Cilicia: insights from signaling theory." Pages 176–88 in *Rough Cilicia: New Historical and Archaeological Approaches* edited by M. C. Hoff and R. F. Townsend. Oxford: Oxbow, 2013.

Weaver, C. D. *In the Levant*. Boston: Houghton, Mifflin and Co, 1894.

Weaver, P. *Familia Caesaris: A Social Study of the Emperor's Freedmen and Slaves*. Cambridge: Cambridge University Press, 1972.

— "*Consilium praesidis*: Advising Governors." Pages 43–62 in "*Thinking Like a Lawyer*" *Essays on Legal History and General History for John Crook on his Eightieth Birthday* edited by P. McKechnie. Leiden: Brill, 2002.

Weber, G. "Funde." *MDAI(A)* 16 (1891): 144–5.

— "Die unterirdische Lauf des Lykos bei Kolossai." *MDAI*(*A*) 16 (1891): 194–9.

— "Inschriften aus Sued-Phrygien." *MDAI*(*A*) 18 (1893): 206–7.

— "Die Flüsse von Laodicea: Lykos, Kadmos, Kapros, Eleinos und Asopos." *MDAI(A)* 23 (1898): 178–95.

Weima, J. D. A. "Paul's Persuasive Prose: An Epistolary Analysis of the Letter to Philemon." Pages 29–60 in *Philemon in Perspective: Interpreting a Pauline Letter* edited by D. F. Tolmie. Berlin: de Gruyter, 2010.

Weiss, P. "The Cities and their Money." Pages 57–68 in *Coinage and Identity in the Roman Provinces* edited by C. Howgego, V. Heuchert and A. Burnett. Oxford: Oxford University Press, 2005.

Welborn, L. L. *An End to Enmity: Paul and the "Wrongdoer" of Second Corinthians.* Berlin: de Gruyter, 2011.
Welch, K. M. "The Stadium at Aphrodisias." *AJA* 102 (1998): 547–69.
— *The Roman Amphitheatre from its Origins to the Colosseum.* Cambridge: Cambridge University Press, 2007.
Wells, E. *Sacred Geography or A Companion to the Holy Bible being a Geographical and Historical Account of Places mentioned in the Holy Scriptures …* Charlestown: Samuel Etheridge, 1817.
Wenn, C. C., S. Ahrens and J. R. Brandt. "Romans, Christians, and pilgrims at Hierapolis in Phrygia: Changes in funerary practices and mental process." Pages 196–216 in *Life & Death in Asia Minor in Hellenistic, Roman and Byzantine Times: Studies in Archaeology and Bioarchaeology* edited by J. R. Brandt, *et al.* Oxford: Oxbow, 2017.
Wessels, D. F. "The Letter to Philemon in the Context of Slavery in Early Christianity." Pages 143–68 in *Philemon in Perspective: Interpreting a Pauline Letter* edited by D. F. Tolmie. Berlin: de Gruyter, 2010.
West, M. L. *Ancient Greek Music.* Oxford: Clarendon, 1992.
Westcott, B. F. and F. J. A. Hort. *The New Testament in the Original Greek: Introduction, Appendix.* London: Macmillan, 1881.
Westermann, W. L. *The Slave Systems of Greek and Roman Antiquity.* Philadelphia: American Philosophical Society, 1955.
Wet, C. de. *Preaching Bondage: John Chrysostom and the Discourse of Slavery in Early Christianity.* Berkeley: University of California Press, 2015.
Wevers, J. W. *Notes on the Greek Text of Exodus.* Atlanta: GA: Scholars Press, 1990.
Wheler, G. *A Journey to Greece.* London: 1682.
White, J. L. *Light from Ancient Letters.* Philadelphia: Fortress, 1986.
White, J. R. "'Baptized on Account of the Dead': The Meaning of 1 Corinthians 15:29 in its Context." *JBL* 116 (1997): 487–99.
White, J. *Der Brief von Paulus an die Kolosser.* Witten: SCM/R. Brockhaus, 2018.
Whitmarsh, T. "Greek and Roman in Dialogue: The Pseudo-Lucianic Nero." *JHS* 119 (1999): 142–60.
Wiedemann, T. *Greek and Roman Slavery.* London: Routledge, 1981.
Wijma, S. M. "The 'Others' in a lex sacra from the Attic Deme Phrearrhioi (SEG 35.113)." *ZPE* 187 (2013): 199–205.
Wilburn, A. *Materia Magica: The Archaeology of Magic in Roman Egypt, Cyprus, and Spain.* Ann Arbor: University of Michigan Press, 2012.
Wilcken, U. "Aus der Straßburger Sammlung." Pages 115–47 in *Archiv für Papyrusforschung und verwandte Gebiete Vol. 4* edited by U. Wilcken. Leipzig: Teubner, 1908.
Willet, R. *The Geography of Urbanism in Roman Asia Minor.* Sheffield: Equinox, 2020.
Williams, J. *Two Essays on the Geography of Ancient Asia: intended partly to illustrate the campaigns of Alexander and the Anabasis of Xenophon.* London: John Murray, 1829.
Williams, M. H. "The Use of Alternative Names by Diaspora Jews in Graeco-Roman Antiquity." *JSJ* 38 (2007): 307–27.
Williams, S. *Diocletian and the Roman Recovery.* London: Routledge, 2000 (1985).
Wilson, N. G. *Photius: The Bibliotheca.* Bristol: Bristol Classical Press, 1994.

— *Herodoti Historiae*. Oxford: Oxford University Press, 2 vols, 2015.

Wilson, R. McL. *A Critical and Exegetical Commentary on Colossians and Philemon*. London: T & T Clark, 2005.

Wilson, W. T. *The hope of glory: education and exhortation in the Epistle to the Colossians*. Leiden: Brill, 1997.

Winer, G. B. *A Treatise on the Grammar of New Testament Greek*. Trans. W. F. Moulton; Edinburgh: T & T Clark, 1870.

Wiotte-Franz, C. *Hermeneus und Interpres: Zum Dolmetscherwesen in der Antike*. Saarbrücken: Saarbrücker Druckerei und Verlag, 2001.

Wise, M. O. *Language and literacy in Roman Judaea: A Study of the Bar Kokhba Documents*. New Haven: Yale University Press, 2015.

Witherington III, B. *The Letters to Philemon, the Colossians, and the Ephesians: A Socio-Rhetorical Commentary on the Captivity Epistles*. Grand Rapids, MN: Eerdmans, 2007.

— "The Case of the Imprisonment that did not happen: Paul at Ephesus." *JETS* 60 (2017): 525–32.

Wittman, W. *Travels in Turkey, Asia Minor, Syria and across the desert into Egypt during the years 1799, 1800 and 1801 in company with the Turkish army and the British MM mission to which are annexed observations on the plaque and on the diseases prevalent in Turkey and a meteorological journal*. London: 1803.

Wong, M. *et al.* "Isotopic investigations of human diet and mobility at the site of Hierapolis, Turkey." Pages 228–36 in *Life and Death in Asia Minor in Hellenistic, Roman and Byzantine Times: Studies in Archaeology and Bioarchaeology* edited by J. R. Brandt *et al.* Oxford: Oxbow, 2017.

Wood, J. T. *Discoveries at Ephesus: including the Site and Remains of the Great Temple of Diana*. Boston: Osgood, 1877.

Woodhouse, R. "An Overview of Research on Phrygian from the Nineteenth Century to the Present." *Studia Linguistica* 126 (2009): 167–88.

Woolf, G. "Becoming Roman, Staying Greek: Culture, Identity and the Civilising Process in the Roman East." *PCPS* 40 (1994): 116–43.

Wordsworth, C. *New Testament of our Lord and Saviour Jesus Christ, Volume II, St Paul's Epistles*. London: Rivingtons, 1870 (1859).

Wörrle, M. *Stadt und Fest in kaiserzeitlichen Kleinasien. Studien zur einer agonistischen Stiftung aus Oenoanda*. Munich: Beck, 1988.

Woudhuizen, F. C. "Phrygian & Greek." *Talanta* 40–41 (2008–2009): 183–91.

— *The Luwians of Western Anatolia: Their Neighbours and Predecessors* (Oxford: Archaeopress, 2018.

Wright, N. T. "Poetry and Theology in Colossians 1:15–20." *NTS* 36 (1990): 444–68.

— *Judas and the Gospel of Jesus*. Grand Rapids, MN: Baker, 2006.

Wünsch, R. *Continens Defixionum*. Berlin: G. Reimer, 1897.

Wyns, V. "Happiness in the Kingdom of the Cleopatras: Examining Government Influence on Quality of Life in Hellenistic Egypt (332–30 BC)." *Historická Sociologie* 2 (2018): 9–26.

Ximinez, S. *Asia Minor in Ruins* translated by A. Chambers. London: Hutchinson, 1925.

Yaman, H. "Death in Zeugma: A Survey of the Tombs." *Anadolu/Anatolia* 45 (2019): 125–68.

Yates, R. "Colossians 2,14: Metaphor of Forgiveness." *Biblica* 71 (1990): 248–59.

Yener, K. A. "Excavations in Hittite Heartlands: Recent Investigations in Late Bronze Age Anatolia." Pages 1–10 in *Recent Developments in Hittite Archaeology and History: Papers in Honor of Hans Gustav Güterbock* edited by K. A. Yener and H. A. Hoffner. Winona Lake, IN: Eisenbraun, 2002.

Yıldız, H. "Colossae Nekropolü Tümülüs Kazısı." Pages 247–62 in *IX. Müze Kurtama Kazıları Semineri* edited by H. Çakmak *et al.* Ankara: T. C. Kültür Bakanlığı, 1999.

Yılmaz, N. "Necropoleis and Funerary Monuments in Pisidia During the Roman Period." *Adalya* 10 (2007): 155–204.

Yinger, K. L. "Translating καταβραβεθέτω ["Disqualify" NRSV] in Colossians 2.18." *The Bible Translator* 54 (2003): 138–45.

Youni, M. S. "Transforming Greek practice into Roman law: manumissions in Roman Macedonia." *Legal History Review* 78 (2010): 311–40.

Zajac, B. "Who, why and when? Pseudo-autonomous coins of Bithynia and Pontus dated to the beginning of the second century AD." Pages 75–91 in *Pecunia Omnes Vincit: Coin as a Medium of Exchange throughout Centuries* edited by B. Zając, P. Koczwara and S. Jellonek. Kraków: Jagiellonian University, 2018.

Zangger, E. *The Luwian Civilization: The Missing Link in the Aegean Bronze Age.* Istanbul: Ege, 2016.

Zanker, P. "The Hellenistic Grave Stelai from Smyrna: Identity and Self-image in the Polis." Pages 212–30 in *Images and Ideologies: Self-Definition in the Hellenistic World* edited by A. Bulloch *et al.* Berkeley: University of California Press, 1993.

Zelnick-Abramovitz, R. *Not Wholly Free. The Concept of Manumission and the Status of Manumitted Slaves in the Ancient World.* Leiden/Boston: Brill, 2005.

— "Freed slaves, their status and state control in Ancient Greece." *ERH* 16 (2009): 303–18.

Zepos, P. *Prochiron Auctum* Athens: Fexis, 1931.

Zgusta, L. *Die Personennamen griechischer Städte der nördlichen Schwarzmeerküste.* Prague: Tschechoslowakische Akademie der Wissenschaften, 1955.

— *Kleinasiatische Personennamen.* Prague: Tschechoslowakische Akademie der Wissenschaften, 1964.

Zimmermann, M. *Untersuchungen zur historischen Landeskunde Zentrallykiens.* Bonn: Habelt, 1992.

Zoroğlu, C. "Tripolis'ten Kolossal Zırhlı Heykel Ayağı." Pages 83–90 in *Tripolis Araştırmaları* edited by B. Duman. Istanbul: Ege, 2017.

Zuiderhoek, A. *The Politics of Munificence in the Roman Empire: Citizens, Elites and Benefactors in Asia Minor.* Cambridge: Cambridge University Press, 2009.

Zuidman, L. B. and P. S. Pantel. *Religion in the Ancient Greek City* translated by P. Cartledge. Cambridge: Cambridge University Press, 1992.

Index of Ancient, Early Christian and Byzantine Literature

Index of Inscriptions and Papyri

Inscriptiones graecae ad res romanas pertinentes

Index of Coins

Index of Modern Authors

Index of Place Names, Ancient and Modern

Index of Subjects

Index of Key Greek and Latin Words

Greek

Latin